TOM BINGHAM AND THE TRANSFORMATION
OF THE LAW

C000080794

A Liber Amicorum

Editors

MADS ANDENAS   DUNCAN FAIRGRIEVE

Tom Bingham and the Transformation of the Law

A Liber Amicorum

Editors
MADS ANDENAS
and
DUNCAN FAIRGRIEVE

Editorial advisory committee
Professor Sir Basil Markesinis, Professor Ewan McKendrick
and
Sir Bernard Rix

OXFORD
UNIVERSITY PRESS

OXFORD
UNIVERSITY PRESS

Great Clarendon Street, Oxford OX2 6DP

Oxford University Press is a department of the University of Oxford.
It furthers the University's objective of excellence in research, scholarship,
and education by publishing worldwide in

Oxford New York

Auckland Cape Town Dar es Salaam Hong Kong Karachi
Kuala Lumpur Madrid Melbourne Mexico City Nairobi
New Delhi Shanghai Taipei Toronto

With offices in

Argentina Austria Brazil Chile Czech Republic France Greece
Guatemala Hungary Italy Japan Poland Portugal Singapore
South Korea Switzerland Thailand Turkey Ukraine Vietnam

Oxford is a registered trade mark of Oxford University Press
in the UK and in certain other countries

Published in the United States
by Oxford University Press Inc., New York

British Library Cataloguing in Publication Data

Data available

Library of Congress Cataloging in Publication Data

Tom Bingham and the Transformation of the Law : *A Liber Amicorum* / Editors Mads
Andenas and Duncan Fairgrieve; editorial advisory committee Professor Sir Basil
Markesinis, Professor Ewan McKendrick and Sir Bernard Rix.
   p. cm.
   Includes index.
   ISBN 978-0-19-956618-1
   1. Bingham, T. H. (Thomas Henry), 1933- 2. Judges—England—Biography.
3. Law—England. 4. International and municipal law—Great Britain.
I. Andenas, Mads Tønnesson, 1957- II. Fairgrieve, Duncan. III. Markesinis,
Basil. IV. McKendrick, Ewan. V. Rix, Bernard Anthony, Sir, 1944-
   KD632.B56.T66 2009
   347.42'014092—dc22
   [B]   2009005315

Typeset by Newgen Imaging Systems (P) Ltd., Chennai, India
Printed in Great Britain
on acid-free paper by
CPI Antony Rowe, Chippenham, Wiltshire

ISBN 978-0-19-956618-1

ISBN 978-0-19-969334-4 (pbk.)

1 3 5 7 9 10 8 6 4 2

Table of Contents

II THE INDEPENDENCE AND ORGANIZATION OF COURTS

III EUROPEAN AND INTERNATIONAL LAW IN NATIONAL COURTS

Editors' Preface

This *Liber Amicorum* is published in recognition of Lord Bingham's many contributions to the law and the academic world.

Lord Bingham is the great lawyer of his generation. He was an outstanding barrister and gained early promotion to the Bench. He will be remembered for his lucid and learned judgments that have fashioned the development of the common law in the United Kingdom and influenced legal developments far beyond. As a judge he has upheld the rule of law in the face of challenges unprecedented since the last war.

Lord Bingham is the first judge to have held in succession the two highest judicial offices in England and Wales, as Master of the Rolls and Lord Chief Justice, followed by the highest judicial office in the United Kingdom, as Senior Law Lord. Outside his judicial work, he has made extraordinary contributions to academic life, the legal community and society in general. He also has made important scholarly contributions in a wide field, covering international law, commercial law and constitutional law.

It is not unrealistic to speak about a transformation of the law taking place in the last twenty years. Both the role of law and the rule of law have changed in a fundamental manner; this follows from developments in human rights, in the independence of courts and judges, and in the relationship between the common law and European law. The impact of international law, the development of a new commercial law, the reform of principles of procedure and changes in court organization are further features of this transformation of the law.

Due both to the central positions he has held, and to his personal authority, Lord Bingham has had an influence on legal developments in a wider field than other judges in modern times. The courts he has presided over have become effective constitutional and administrative courts while continuing to develop commercial and civil law in times of rapid change.

Lord Bingham's scholarly writing has been influential. In the early 1990s he wrote in favour of UK incorporation of the European Human Rights Convention, and advocated the use of comparative law in the courts. He later argued for a UK supreme court, and for developing the principle of judicial independence. His analysis of the judgments on detention during the first and second world wars showed convincingly that they could not be upheld.

Putting theory into practice, as a judge, Lord Bingham has first paved the way for, and then given effect to, the legislative incorporation of the ECHR. His recent writing on the rule of law has attracted international attention. He has also developed the use of comparative law sources. He has given judgments seeking to strengthen judicial independence.

There have been other seminars, conferences and books published on the occasion of Lord Bingham's retirement as Senior Law Lord at 75. Many of the contributors to this book have also been involved in other initiatives. But this book is called *Liber Amicorum* precisely because it is written by friends of Lord Bingham, in the United Kingdom, Europe, the Commonwealth, and the wider common law world. It offers many of us the opportunity to write in his honour, and is not limited to a specific topic or category of contributors.

The purpose has been to celebrate Lord Bingham, and we hope the book will give him pleasure. The two editors have received much assistance and encouragement in completing this project from the many contributors and the publishers, including three anonymous referees. Thanks go in particular to the three members of the editorial advisory committee: Professor Sir Basil Markesinis, Oxford's Pro-Vice-Chancellor for Research Professor Ewan McKendrick, and Sir Bernard Rix.

Mads Andenas and *Duncan Fairgrieve*
July 2008.

Table of Contributors

This list of contributors is in alphabetical order.

The Right Honourable Lord Justice Aikens (Sir Richard Aikens) is a member of the Court of Appeal of England and Wales.

Professor Guido Alpa is a Professor at the University of Rome *La Sapienza*, and the President of the Italian Bar Council.

Professor Mads Andenas is a Professor at the University of Oslo and the University of Leicester.

The Right Honourable Lady Justice Arden DBE (Dame Mary Arden) is a member of the Court of Appeal of England and Wales.

Professor John Bell QC is a Professor at the University of Cambridge.

The Honorable Justice Stephen Breyer is a Justice of the Supreme Court of the United States.

Professor Andrew Burrows QC is the Norton Rose Professor of Commercial Law at the University of Oxford.

Conseiller Guy Canivet is Premier président honoraire de la Cour de cassation and Member of the Conseil constitutionnel, France.

The Right Honourable Sir Anthony Clarke is the Master of the Rolls (President of the Civil Division of the Court of Appeal), the Royal Courts of Justice, London.

Richard Clayton QC is a barrister at 39 Essex Street, London and an Associate Fellow at the Centre for Public Law, Cambridge.

The Right Honourable Lord Justice Lawrence Collins (Sir Lawrence Collins) is a member of the Court of Appeal of England and Wales.

The Right Honourable Lord Cooke of Thorndon (Robin Brunskill Cooke) (9 May 1926–30 August 2006), served as President of the New Zealand Court of Appeal and as a Lord of Appeal in the House of Lords.

Jean-Paul Costa is Conseiller d'Etat honoraire and President of the European Court of Human Rights, Strasbourg.

Professor Paul Craig QC is a Professor at the University of Oxford.

The Honourable Mr Justice Cranston (Sir Ross Cranston) is a member of the High Court of England and Wales.

Professor J H Dalhuisen is a Professor at King's College, University of London.

Conseiller Olivier Dutheillet de Lamothe is a member of Conseil constitutionnel, France.

The Right Honourable Dame Sian Elias is the Chief Justice of New Zealand.

Roger Errera is Conseiller d'Etat honoraire and Visiting Professor at the Central European University, Budapest.

Duncan Fairgrieve is a Fellow at the British Institute of International and Comparative Law, London and Maître de Conférences, Sciences Po, Paris.

Steven Gee QC is a barrister at Stone Chambers, Gray's Inn, London.

Professor Baron Walter Van Gerven is a Professor at the University of Leuven, and a former Advocate General to the Court of Justice of the European Communities, Luxembourg.

The Honourable Chief Justice Anthony Murray Gleeson is the former Chief Justice of the High Court of Australia.

Professor Sir Roy Goode QC is a Professor of the University of Oxford.

Blinne Ní Ghrálaigh is a barrister at Matrix Chambers, Gray's Inn, London.

Elizabeth-Anne Gumbel QC is a barrister at One Crown Office Row, Temple, London.

The Right Honourable Baroness Hale of Richmond is a Lord of Appeal in Ordinary, and from October 2009 a Justice of the Supreme Court of the United Kingdom.

Her Excellency Dame Rosalyn Higgins QC is the President of the International Court of Justice, The Hague.

The Honourable Justice David Ipp is Judge of Appeal, the New South Wales Court of Appeal, Australia.

The Right Honourable Professor Sir Francis Jacobs QC is a Professor of Law and Jean Monnet Professor at King's College London; Advocate General, Court of Justice of the European Communities, 1988–2006.

Professor Jeffrey Jowell QC is Professor of Law at University College, London, and a practising barrister at Blackstone Chambers, London.

The Right Honourable Lord Justice Keene (Sir David Keene) is a member of the Court of Appeal of England and Wales.

The Honourable Justice Michael Kirby is a former Justice of the High Court of Australia.

Professor Vaughan Lowe QC is Chichele Professor of Public International Law and Fellow of All Souls College, Oxford University.

Professor Sir Basil Markesinis QC has held chairs at the universities of London and Oxford, and presently at the University of Texas.

Professor Robert McCorquodale is the Director of the British Institute of International and Comparative Law and Professor of International Law and Human Rights at the University of Nottingham.

The Right Honourable Beverley McLachlin PC is the Chief Justice of Canada.

Professor Horatia Muir Watt is a Professor at University of Paris I, Panthéon-Sorbonne.

The Right Honourable Lord Justice Mummery (Sir John Mummery) is a member of the Court of Appeal of England and Wales.

Professor Dawn Oliver QC is Emeritus Professor of Constitutional Law at University College, University of London.

The Right Honourable Lord Phillips of Worth Matravers is the Senior Law Lord and appointed as the first President of the new Supreme Court of the United Kingdom from October 2009.

The Right Honourable Lord Justice Rix (Sir Bernard Rix) is a member of the Court of Appeal of England and Wales.

The Honourable Mr Justice Sales (Sir Philip Sales) is a member of the High Court of England and Wales and was formerly First Treasury Counsel, Common Law.

Professor Philippe Sands QC is a Professor at University College, University of London.

Jean-Marc Sauvé is the *Vice-Président* of the Conseil d'Etat, France.

The Right Honourable Sir Konrad Schiemann is a Judge at the European Court of Justice and former Lord Justice.

The Right Honourable Lord Justice Sedley (Sir Stephen Sedley) is a member of the Court of Appeal of England and Wales.

Professor Brian Simpson QC is a Professor of Law at the University of Michigan.

Vassilios Skouris is the President of the Court of Justice to the European Communities, Luxembourg.

Professor Anne-Marie Slaughter is the Dean of the Woodrow Wilson School of Public and International Affairs at Princeton University.

John Sorabji is a Barrister and Legal Secretary to the Master of the Rolls.

Professor Jane Stapleton is Ernest E. Smith Professor at the University of Texas, Austin, a Research Professor at the Australian National University in Canberra, Statutory Visiting Professor of Law at Oxford University, and Visiting Commonwealth Fellow of the British Institute of International and Comparative Law, London.

Bernard Stirn is the *Président de Section du Contentieux*, Conseil d'Etat, Paris.

Patrick Titiun is a French magistrate and the Head of Cabinet of the President of the European Court of Human Rights, Strasbourg.

Professor Gillian Triggs is the Dean of the School of Law at the University of Sydney.

Hugh Tomlinson QC is a barrister at Matrix Chambers, Gray's Inn, London.

Professor Colin Warbrick is the Barber Professor of Jurisprudence at the University of Birmingham.

Professor Vincenzo Zeno-Zencovich is a Professor at University of Roma Tre.

Table of Cases

Table of Statutory Instruments

Table of Statutes

Table of Treaties and Conventions

Introductory Tribute: Lord Bingham of Cornhill

Nicholas Phillips

When I wrote the Introductory Tribute for the first edition of this book it seemed that Lord Bingham was about to embark on providing the material for a further substantial chapter of his biography. He had reached the statutory retirement age and had relinquished the office of Senior Law Lord when still at the height of his powers. His energy was undiminished. He had accepted a host of speaking engagements. He was lending his enthusiastic support to the establishment of the Rule of Law Centre that was to bear his name. We all anticipated that he would in many ways be building on the foundations of the rule of law in the 21st Century that he had laid by a series of remarkable judgments during the eight years that he presided in the Lords. Tragically, it was not to be, and this Liber Amicorum now stands as a memorial to a remarkable jurist and a man of great humanity.

One of the most memorable of many memorable addresses that I have heard given by Tom Bingham was his tribute to Lord Denning in Westminster Abbey on 17 June 1999. What an occasion and, as always, Tom rose to it. As I listened to him reciting, in a fair imitation of the Denning accent, 'It was bluebell time in Kent', I reflected on the contrast between the two Toms, the two great legal figures of my lifetime in the law.

No one of my vintage could have heard Tom Denning's advocacy at the Bar and it did not live on in reputation. Tom Bingham was, however, one of the three outstanding advocates of his generation. Each had his own style. Bob MacCrindle, silver tongued, gave the impression that his only concern was to prevent the court from making a terrible mistake. Bob Alexander always appeared personally to be persuaded of the merits of his client's case and not prepared to leave a point until he had talked the court into sharing his viewpoint. Tom's approach was to present a series of propositions, each one honed with precision and supported by authority, the effect of each item of which would be summarized in a pellucid précis. This advocacy, firmly delivered but with a tactful deference, was devastatingly effective.

Bob MacCrindle and Bob Alexander both declined the bench, considering that the restrictions of a judicial life would rob it of its savour. In this I believe that they were mistaken, and it certainly could not be said of Tom Bingham's judicial career. The 'tap on the shoulder' from the Lord Chancellor, Lord Hailsham, came when he was only 46. On 14 April 1980 Bingham J was appointed to the Queen's Bench Division and assigned to the Commercial Court, then the seedbed of most of the jurisprudence by which the House of Lords developed the principles of the common law. Clients of Mr Bingham QC, not least the Republic of Cuba,[1] deprived of the counsel who had led them to success in the Court of Appeal, found themselves robbed of the fruits of victory in the House of Lords.

Six years in the Queen's Bench Division saw Bingham J promoted to Bingham LJ. Perhaps the most exacting of his duties before his appointment as Master of the Rolls in 1992 was chairing the Inquiry into the supervision of BCCI. Clarke J and the Court of Appeal were influenced by his conclusions in holding that the action by creditors against the Bank of England based on the tort of misfeasance in public office should be struck out on the ground that it had no reasonable prospect of success. Alas the House of Lords held that it was not legitimate to have regard to his report and reversed the strike out decision, leading to the most expensive piece of hopeless litigation that the Commercial Court has ever seen.

Following in Lord Denning's shoes as Master of the Rolls might have seemed a prestigious zenith of Tom Bingham's legal career, but on Lord Taylor's untimely retirement from office in 1996, Lord Mackay, the Lord Chancellor, selected him as the new Lord Chief Justice. This was not an appointment that was received with universal enthusiasm, but doubts were quickly stilled when Lord Bingham showed himself as much a master of the criminal jurisdiction as he had been of the civil. Then came a further move in 2000 to the newly created post of Senior Lord of Appeal in Ordinary.

One quality of Lord Denning that has always been manifest in Tom Bingham is courtesy. He will not remember, but I do, the time that we first met. I had just moved from Admiralty to common law chambers and was instructed as his junior in a competition case, an area where I had no feel for either the law or the procedure. We had a consultation, at the end of which he turned to me and said 'right, we will need the usual summons and affidavit in support'. My dismay must have been apparent to him for, after the solicitors had gone, he said quietly 'don't worry, I'll draft the documents'. That kindness was typical of the courtesy that Tom Bingham has always shown to counsel, and indeed to his colleagues, on the Bench. He is the epitome of the motto of Winchester College, of which for ten years he was a Fellow.

Lord Denning enjoyed advocacy and dialogue with counsel, always kindly, although sometimes the advocate would find that he had been led along a path only to be confronted by a brick wall at the end of it. Tom Bingham presided more quietly, occasionally placing the tips of his fingers together as he formulated a question which went to the heart of the case and then sometimes indicating

---

[1] *I Congreso* [1983] AC 244.

his reaction to the response by a quizzically raised eyebrow, before noting it carefully.

Lord Denning's approach to precedent was to set it. He had a wide knowledge of the common law that he sometimes used eclectically to support the result that he considered accorded with the ends of justice. Tom Bingham has a more conventional regard for precedent, which is part and parcel of his respect for the rule of law. As a judge his influence, both in court and out of it, has done more than that of any other person in these uncertain times to buttress the rule of law as he so clearly defined it in the sixth Sir David Williams Lecture. Out of court he lent his support to the incorporation of the European Convention on Human Rights. In court he has scrupulously applied it, as required by the Human Rights Act 1998.

Notably he presided over the seven-man Committee that wrested from the Home Secretary the setting of the minimum tariffs to be served by those sentenced to life imprisonment.[2] In a lecture on 'Personal Freedom' he had suggested that freedom from executive detention was arguably the most fundamental right of all. It was not that personal belief, but the requirement of the Act, that led him and his colleagues[3] to quash the Derogation Order and rule incompatible with the Convention the legislation that permitted detention without trial of a person suspected of being an international terrorist. It was, however, no doubt his personal belief in the importance of the separation of powers that led him to decline an invitation from the Home Secretary, Charles Clarke to meet for a general discussion about the problems of terrorism, a stance which the latter neither understood nor forgave.

Throughout the 16 years that he was first Master of the Rolls, then Lord Chief Justice, and finally Senior Law Lord, Tom Bingham's leadership inspired loyalty and inspiration. Somehow he found the time to write, to lecture, to be High Steward of Oxford University, and to chair or preside over many and varied bodies—not least the Hay Festival. Many honoured him, including Her Majesty with the Order of a Knighthood of the Garter, the first time that this has ever been conferred on a serving judge. He had always been a firm supporter of the establishment of the Supreme Court and, but for the delays inherent in preparing the building, would and should have been its first President. Throughout my time in the law Tom Bingham has set an example that I have sought, inadequately, to follow. He will remain an inspiration to me and to many.

---

[2] *R v Anderson* [2002] UKHL 57; [2003] 1 AC 837.
[3] *A v Secretary of State for the Home Department* [2005] 2 AC 58.

A Biographical Sketch: The Early Years

Ross Cranston

Legal biography is a neglected form of scholarly writing in Britain. There are legal biographies but few match the detail and scholarship of comparable North American efforts.[1] With important judges and legal academics often all that is available in Britain are the helpful, yet necessarily brief, accounts in the *Oxford Dictionary of National Biography*. It is sometimes said that judges lead uninteresting, possibly boring, lives, which cannot be of any interest to the outside world. Given the increased prominence of law and judicial decisions in the media, even if the premise be true the conclusion is no longer supportable, at least as regards our most senior judges.

What follows is a biographical sketch of one of the greatest of English judges. It offers some explanation of why Thomas Henry Bingham rose to such heights. It also casts light on modern English social history, or at least that part lived out by a boy born in the 1930s of professional middle class parents. It is, however, a sketch. It began with an interview with Lord Bingham for the Legal Biography Project, based at the Law Department of the London School of Economics.[2] Lord Bingham then provided a short account himself, much of which is reflected in this essay. There then followed interviews with friends and colleagues and some archival research. But there has been no access to personal papers. Moreover, the story ends some 25 years ago, on the cusp of Lord Bingham's rise to formal legal prominence.

Early Years

Thomas Henry Bingham was born in London on 13 October 1933, his parents' second child. At the time of his birth Bingham's father, also Thomas Henry, was medical officer of health for Reigate, Surrey. Dr TH Bingham had been born and brought up in Belfast and retained an Ulster accent throughout his life. His father, Bingham's grandfather, also Thomas Henry, had been a solicitor's managing clerk. On Bingham's birth in 1933 the tradition of using the same names,

---

[1] E.g., G Gunter, *Learned Hand. The Man and the Judge* (Camb, Mass, Harvard UP, 1995); A Kaufman, *Cardozo* (Camb, Mass, Harvard UP, 2000).

[2] Available at <http://lse.ac.uk/>A Life In Law.

Thomas Henry, was almost broken. Bingham's mother suggested that 'O'Neill', his paternal grandmother's maiden name, should be added, but the suggestion provoked the grandfather into sending Bingham's parents the only telegram he was ever known to send: 'Omit O'Neill'.

Bingham's father was born in 1901. He had left elementary school at 14, and became a pupil-teacher, a form of apprenticeship for aspiring teachers. He was not attracted by teaching, for which he was temperamentally ill-suited, and wanted to become a doctor. To do this he had to matriculate, which meant learning Latin from scratch. He entered medical school at Queen's University, Belfast. By the first decades of the 20th century Belfast had grown to become the eighth city of the United Kingdom, with important linen, tobacco, engineering, and ship-building industries. There were many 'self-made men in the self-made city'. Queen's University medical school, reflecting the society where it was located, was pragmatic and clinically oriented. 'Ulster's doctors were never Oxbridge or Pall Mall gentlemen, younger sons of noble or patrician families... there was no great social or cultural gulf between themselves and those they treated'.[3]

Graduating with an MD and Diploma in Public Health in July 1926,[4] Dr TH Bingham spent a period in practice in the Welsh Valleys, and moved on to Swansea, where he met his wife, Bingham's mother. He there devoted himself to public health, becoming a medical officer of health in Reigate at a very young age. From its creation in the mid-19th century, until its abolition in the 1970s, the office of medical officer of health was an important one. The historical background was the great advance in the 19th century in public health and sanitary reform. Medical officers of health first appeared in the 1840s, and the Public Health Act 1872 made it compulsory for local authorities to appoint them. Initially their duties covered infectious diseases, water supply, sewerage, nuisance removal, fever hospitals, regulation of markets and offensive trades. By 1930 they were senior local government officers and their responsibilities had extended to the public health aspects of housing, maternity and child welfare clinics, tuberculosis and venereal disease clinics, school health services, and the administration of local hospitals.[5]

Bingham's mother, Catherine Watterson, was also a doctor. Although Manx by parentage, she was born in Bishop in the High Sierra country of California. Her father, Mark Watterson, had a ranch on which, according to family tradition, he

---

[3] Peter Froggatt, 'The Distinctiveness of Belfast Medicine and its Medical School' (1985) 54 *Ulster Medical Journal* 89, 105. See also TW Moody & JC Beckett, *Queen's, Belfast 1845–1949* (Faber & Faber, London, 1959) v 1, 426, v 2, 483.

[4] Earlier, in July 1923, he had graduated with his primary degrees (MB, BCh, BAO) with a pass.

[5] C Eastwood, *The Life and Death of the Medical Officer of Health* (Braunton, Devon, Merlin Books, 1992); A Engineer, 'The Society of Medical Officers of Health. Its History and Archive' (2001) 45 *Medical History* 97, 102.

had reared the first herd of Hereford cattle west of the Rockies. He had migrated to California in pioneering days. On one occasion, returning to the ranch after a week-long visit to Los Angeles to buy farm equipment, by horseback across the Mojave Desert, he found that his wife, whom he had not known to be ill, was dead and buried. On a visit to the Isle of Man after 18 years as a widower, he married a childhood sweetheart. They returned to California together and had four daughters, of whom Catherine was the youngest. He fell ill and in 1904, when Catherine was aged two, the family returned to the Isle of Man where he died. His widow brought up the four girls. Catherine went to Huyton College, a girls' boarding school outside Liverpool, and qualified in medicine and dentistry at University College in London.[6] Women doctors were not unusual by this time but tended to be excluded from medicine's highest reaches. She met Bingham's father when they were both working in Swansea. After marriage Bingham's mother spent her career as a dentist and dental anaesthetist.

Bingham and his elder sister enjoyed a conventional middle class upbringing. Aged seven, he began as a weekly boarder at a boys' preparatory school, The Hawthorns, a short distance away from Reigate at Gatton Point, between Redhill and Merstham. Founded in the 1920s by the Bull family, it seems unexceptional yet typical of the boys' preparatory schools dotting southern England to cater for the demands of the commercial and professional middle classes.[7] Bingham recalls that it was humane, decent and well-run, somewhat unexciting, with the teaching on the whole good. It was 'a palpably Christian school but without being oppressively so'.[8] The younger teachers were by then away in the services. When Bingham arrived in September 1941 the Battle of Britain had been won but German bombing of the country was still a regular feature. The previous year, in September 1940, a bomb had landed, relatively harmlessly, in the school grounds, an experience greatly cherished by the pupils. The boarders all slept in the quite extensive cellars. No doubt this gave some security against enemy bombs, although Bingham adds it also gave security against the matron, whose footsteps on the wooden stairs down to the cellar were very audible. He recalls one recycled colonial veteran umpiring a boys' game of cricket in 1944, when the engine of a doodlebug overhead cut out, a sign it was to fall. The youthful cricketers paused, looking a little anxiously at the sky, but were rallied by the umpire, waving his shooting stick and crying 'Play on, boys'. Bingham became captain of Scott house and head boy.

---

[6] See E Moberly Bell, *Storming the Citadel: The Rise of the Woman Doctor* (London, Constable, 1953), 171; C Blake, *The Charge of the Parasols: Women's Entry to the Medical Profession* (The Women's Press, London, 1990) 164.

[7] See J Ryder and H Silver, *Modern English Society. History and Structure 1850–1970* (Methuen, London, 1970) 92–3.

[8] Timothy R Johns, *75 Years at the Hawthorns. The Hawthorns School 1926–2001* (Gresham Books, Oxford, 2001) 5.

Sedbergh School

In September 1947 Bingham began at Sedbergh School. The school was chosen because many of the brothers of his mother's contemporaries at Huyton College had been there and she liked the sound of it. One of William Wordsworth's sons had been a student there. It was at Sedbergh School that Bingham refined many of the qualities still evident today, especially hard work and self-discipline. It was also where he began to display his exceptional qualities and leadership.

Sedburgh School is set in a beautiful part of Cumbria, the Howgill Fells on the western side of the Yorkshire Dales, just to the east of Kendal. It was founded as a Chantry School in 1525 by the Provost of Eton and re-endowed as a grammar school in 1551. The school's fortunes fluctuated over the centuries but as with other public schools in the 19th century Sedburgh's prestige grew and its buildings expanded. One notable headmaster was Frederick Heppenstall in the 1870s, another Henry George Hart, who from 1880 was responsible for the creation of the prefectorial system, the inaugural Wilson Run, and the confirmation of the school motto as *Dura Virum Nutrix* ('Stern Nurse of Men'). Toughness was part of the Victorian ethos of public schools, to forge boys into imperial leaders, but Sedbergh seemed determined to live up to the school motto. Boys of all ages wore shorts and open-necked shirts all the year round, except on Sundays; cold baths and showers were compulsory; rules were rules; and sporting prowess, particularly on the rugby field, was highly prized. Even the most unathletic spent much time, whatever the weather, particularly if it was very bad, running over the surrounding fells. Fell running culminated in the annual Wilson Run, an extremely testing ten-mile cross-country race which involves negotiating rivers and streams and climbing walls. It is still considered an achievement to complete the race in a reasonable time.

On arrival Bingham was placed in Winder House. He began quietly. In 1949 he appeared in the house play 'Laburnum Grove', written in 1933 by JB Priestley. A reviewer noted that Bingham, Vickerman, and Shaw naturally had their limitations in the female parts but did well enough to sustain the illusion that they were the characters they were playing, 'Bingham indeed having moments of conviction as the banana-eater's wife'.[9] By 1950 his intellectual accomplishments were becoming evident: that year he was awarded the Weech History Prize, the Heppenstall Essay Prize, and the Sterling Verse Prize for his poems 'Since Sinai' and 'Pageantry'. 'Since Sinai' expresses a familiar theme, God revealed through the beauty and force of nature. 'Pageantry' concluded with the thought that it enabled us to see 'the promise of an age that is to be'.[10] The following year he won the Rankin Shakespeare Prize. He participated in the school debating society.

---

[9] *The Sedberghian*, December 1949, 126.
[10] Sedbergh School Archives.

In later years he became an editor of the *Sedberghian*, the school magazine, and librarian.

Bingham left with an enduring sense of gratitude to Sedbergh for the intellectual awakening which he enjoyed under the tutelage of some notably inspiring teachers. Prominent among these was Andrew Morgan who was fresh from Oxford, after wartime service in submarines, and senior history master. Bingham says he never forgot, or ever quite recovered from, the excitement of Morgan's teaching of the puritan revolution in England. Among those Morgan taught were two future historians of great distinction, Colin Matthew and Robert Rhodes James.[11] Teaching English literature was the Revd Bill Long (as he later became), a modest and rather saintly man, whose own degree was in French and whose teaching of English literature was to some extent enhanced by its being a shared learning experience. Long remembers Bingham as a quiet, modest, friendly boy, not needing to draw attention to himself, highly gifted, and a pleasure to teach. Michael Thorneley, later the headmaster of Sedbergh, taught English and also remembers Bingham sitting quietly and unobtrusively at the back of the class. Bingham remembers Thorneley as a gifted teacher of Shakespeare: particularly unforgettable was his rendering of Othello, large tracts of which generations of his pupils could effortlessly recite years later.

Physically lean, Bingham was never keen on rugby. However, he enjoyed fell running and with his self-discipline ran more miles than many of the other boys. He completed the Wilson Run twice, with an honourable 12th place on one occasion, despite the fact that he had run most of the course with an acute internal disorder and had to be taken to the sanatorium immediately the race finished.[12] With his physical strength he also walked far and wide on the surrounding fells. In the late 1940s and the early 1950s the area was largely devoid of traffic and tourists.[13] The boys were free to roam and some, like Bingham, covered considerable distances. He developed a love for walking and the countryside, which continued throughout his life, although landscapes after this were judged according to their similarity with this, in his view, matchless area.

Bingham's Sterling Verse Prize, 'Since Sinai', had finished with the lines:

> Thou canst not see her valleys green,
> The star-aspiring hills between,
> Thou canst not with these wonders seen
> Declare there is no God.[14]

---

[11] Matthew became Professor of Modern History at Oxford in 1992, and editor of the Oxford Dictionary of National Biography; Rhodes James was a notable biographer, historian of late 19th and early 20th century Britain, and for a time MP for Cambridge.

[12] David Sutcliffe (Winder House 1948–1953), 'Bingham', Sedbergh School archives.

[13] See N Nicholson, *Cumberland and Westmorland*, The County Book Series (Robert Hale, London, 1949).

[14] Sedbergh School archives.

No doubt there was much of Bingham's love of the surrounding countryside in the poem but he was, and still is, religious. At one point, at the end of his time at Sedbergh, he considered ordination. That acutely religious phase may have been triggered by the influence of Father Horner, of the Community of the Resurrection of Mirfield, an Anglican college in Yorkshire. The Revd (later Canon) Peter Newell, then the classical upper sixth form master and a chaplain at Sedbergh, but also with pastoral responsibilities in the school, took Bingham to stay with the Rt Rev Roger Wilson, then Bishop of Wakefield.[15] One of Bingham's contemporaries at Sedbergh, David Sutcliffe, recalls Bingham telling him that the first thing the Bishop did was to offer him a glass of sherry, a gesture of hospitality which in Sutcliffe's view may have weakened Bingham's confidence in the purity of the religious vocation.[16] In any event, Bingham was saved from holy orders for the law, although not without further twists and turns in the story.

By now Bingham had a place at Oxford. Winning an open scholarship at Oxford or Cambridge was the pinnacle of school academic achievement. Boys stayed on for a year or more after the Higher Certificate, the predecessor of A levels, to prepare themselves. In March 1951 he travelled to Oxford in his attempt. His first choice as a college was Balliol which, on Bingham's account, was because of alliteration, his housemaster, a Cambridge graduate, having said: 'Bingham of b...b...Balliol, I think'. Many years later, when a candidate for Chancellor of the university, Bingham recounted the interview at Balliol.

I applied for a scholarship. My first impression was awe. It seemed like a holy city. I vividly remember being interviewed by Christopher Hill. I had a passion for Cromwell and, to this day, I kick myself that when I was asked whom he most resembled in modern times, I froze. The answer, of course, was Lenin. I got a scholarship but it wasn't a very good one.[17]

Given Hill's own passion for Cromwell—he sat in his Balliol room beneath a portrait of the man—and his favourable portrayal of Lenin in a little book on the subject, it was perhaps an opportunity missed.[18] Bingham returned to Sedbergh just in time to compete in the Wilson Run. Minutes before the race began he received a telegram from Christopher Hill, congratulating him on the award of the Deakin, a Balliol history scholarship.

To try to improve the Balliol scholarship Bingham remained at the school for an additional year. An attempt in December 1951 failed. He kept working. In February 1952 he gave a lecture to the school 'Forum', a once a term event

[15] Newell later became headmaster of Bradford Grammar School and the King's School, Canterbury. Wilson was translated to Chichester.
[16] David Sutcliffe (Winder House 1948–1953), 'Bingham', Sedbergh School archives.
[17] 'Legal men put their cases for Oxford post. Alice Thompson talks to Lord Bingham of Cornhill', *Daily Telegraph*, 1 March 2003.
[18] Robin Briggs, 'Hill, (John Edward) Christopher (1912–2003)', *Oxford Dictionary of National Biography*, online edn, Oxford University Press, Jan 2007; online edn, Jan 2009 [http://www.oxforddnb.com/view/article/89437, accessed 8 Feb 2009]; C. Hill, *Lenin and the Russian Revolution* (English Universities Press, London 1947).

where a student presented a paper they had researched and answered questions. The subject was 'British Socialism', especially topical since the previous October the Labour Party had been defeated after six years in office. The paper outlined the history of socialist thought from its earliest philosophical origins until the creation of the Labour Party. The school magazine described it as 'always scholarly and often humorous... concluding with a few provocative comments on the history of the Party in this century'.[19] His own leanings at the time were strongly Bevanite. Despite his dislike for rugby he seems to have played a part in Winder House winning the Rugby House Cup in the winter of 1952, his 'hard tackling and well organized defence being particularly noticeable'.[20]

Bingham's qualities of leadership had been recognized by his appointment as Head of Winder House in 1951–1952 and in his final year at school he was also a school prefect. But he was not necessarily identified as one who would travel so far. It seemed to some that the headmaster, JH Bruce Lockhart, thought Giles Shaw would prove to be the star of the early 1950s. Shaw became president of the Union at Cambridge and eventually entered the House of Commons. After a period as a middle ranking minister he fell out of favour with the then Prime Minister, Mrs Thatcher, and served out his time, as many a senior backbencher does, in the rather mundane task of chairing committees. If in fact Bruce Lockhart had that view, he would not be the first mistakenly to back the witty and clever extrovert at the expense of the one less flamboyant but as intelligent and more determined.

The Army

Before taking up his place at Oxford Bingham spent two years in National Service. After World War II all physically able men of 18 years faced conscription until the system was abolished in 1960. Many enjoyed their National Service and the experiences, travelling abroad to places they would never otherwise visit. Many developed the skills they had or discovered new talents. Many found too much of the two years a waste of time or bridled at what they perceived to be the petty tyranny and incompetence of the organization. For Bingham the experience was wholly positive: he adored life in the services and seriously contemplated life as a full-time soldier.

Partly because of his father's background, and partly because its battalion was then fighting in Korea, Bingham joined the Royal Ulster Rifles, with their regimental depot in Ballymena, County Antrim. Perhaps typically he spent the three months awaiting call-up studying, in some detail, the military campaigns of the Second World War. It was a body of knowledge hardly valued in recruits

[19] *The Sedberghian*, March 1952, 18.
[20] Ibid, 25.

at St Patrick's Barracks, Ballymena, which was something of a culture shock. (Bingham recalls an interview with a recruiting sergeant who asked if he was a good scholar. Bingham, recalling his failure to win a major scholarship, answered 'Not really'. 'Well,' said the sergeant, 'Can you read and write?') Within a fortnight, however, Bingham was identified as officer material. This was not in the least surprising. He had been an under officer in the Combined Cadet Force (CCF) at Sedbergh and had a place at Oxford. Moreover, there was a relative absence of local talent since the political situation in Northern Ireland meant national service did not extend there. Thus he was despatched to Winchester, where those seeking commission in the four rifle regiments were then trained. It was here at a football match he first met Maurice Keen, who was to be a friend in the Ulster Rifles, at Balliol, and later in life. Bingham's recollection of Winchester was that standards were high, and they were intelligently applied. Several platoons were composed almost entirely of Oxbridge entrants, plus the odd graduate, which made for congenial company.

The next step in officer training was at Eaton Hall Officer Cadet School, outside Chester. Here Bingham excelled. Eaton Hall has been home to the Grosvenor family, headed by the Duke of Westminster, since the 15th century. In both the First and Second World Wars it was a hospital, from 1943 to 1946 the home of HMS Britannia Royal Naval College, Dartmouth, whose base had been bombed, and then from 1946 until the end of National Service in 1960 one of the two places used for training national service and short service officer cadets. Eaton Hall was mainly for infantry training, Mons Barracks in Aldershot for officer cadets of the Royal Armoured Corps and Royal Artillery. The Royal Military Academy, Sandhurst, continued as the place for future officers in the regular army. The course at Eaton Hall was short and intense, given that its graduates would typically remain in the army for only two years and that it was Sandhurst which was designed to produce the future field officers and generals. The course was tough. Over four months there were lectures and tactical exercises without troops.[21] As a member of the cross-country running team Bingham was excused attendance at early morning parades, until he became a senior under-officer and was required to command them. The bonus, however, was a private room in the stable block, with a fire lit every evening by an old man. Second Lieutenant Bingham was commissioned in the Royal Ulster Rifles on 27 February 1953, receiving the award of merit from a colonel in the regiment for graduating as top of his intake.

As a commissioned officer Bingham had the respect of those in the Ulster Rifles he commanded. His father's background helped him to establish the necessary rapport. If necessary he could mimic the Ulster accent. His first real task was to

---

[21] K Taylor and B Stewart, *Call to Arms. Officer Cadet Training at Eaton Hall 1943–1958* (Meigle, Galashiels, 2006) 42–3, 110, 218. cf the publisher Christopher Hurst's more jaundiced view: *The View from King Street. An Essay in Autobiography* (Hurst & Co, London, 1997) 121–5.

take a draft of 70 men to join the battalion, now in the New Territories of Hong Kong, having completed its Korean duty. This involved a 24-day voyage by sea through the Mediterranean to Port Said, Aden, Colombo, Singapore, and Hong Kong. In Bingham's recollection the training regime aboard the troopship was not strenuous: a little map reading, regimental history, and shooting at balloons trailed over the stern of the ship during the morning; leisure to read *War and Peace, Anna Karenina*, and *Crime and Punishment* on the sun-deck during the afternoon; Red Sea order for dinner in the evening. There was then five months in Hong Kong, at Queen's Hill Camp at Fanling. The camp was hardly hospitable, perched on the side of a bare, sun-baked hillside. Finally the battalion marched overnight along the railway line, and through the tunnel, to Kowloon, surprising the residents at dawn with a noisy performance of the Irish pipes and drums, before embarking for the long and leisurely voyage home.

At this point Second Lieutenant Bingham's life could have taken a quite different turn, as it could have at the earlier point with entry to the church. Bingham could have become a professional soldier. He was stationed at Colchester and there were only a few months before his National Service ended. His new Company Commander there was HEN 'Bala' Bredin, by all accounts an extraordinary professional soldier[22] (the nickname 'Bala' derived from the name of one of the Aga Khan's race horses whom Bredin recommended to friends as always out in front). In 1965 Bredin became a Major-General, but in 1954 he had returned from a period with the Eastern Arab Corps and Sudan Defence Force, having suffered a loss of rank on the contraction of the army when the war ended. Before the war, when serving as a subaltern with the Royal Ulster Rifles in Palestine, he had won his first military cross in an ambush on the Tulkarn-Nablus road, and his second a month later in a similar clash. Distinguished Service Orders then followed during the war in 1944 and 1945 and again in 1956. So tall, handsome, friendly, unassuming on the one hand, brave, a born leader, and much decorated on the other: who could fail to be impressed? Bingham clearly was—one of the most attractive and inspiring people he had ever met and one of only two people he has ever met he would literally die for.[23] And Bingham impressed Bredin, for he very nearly persuaded him to adopt 'the proud profession of arms', as Bredin described it. After much thought there were two factors which dissuaded Bingham from doing so, at least immediately. One was the disadvantage he would be at in not having been to Sandhurst, the second was the attraction of Oxford. So he decided to go to Oxford, obtain a degree, and re-enter the army. Once he was at Oxford, however, the ambition faded, although he remained in the territorial army, with the London Irish Rifles, until 1959.

---

[22] See *The Times*, Obituary, 9 March 2005; M. Marin, 'Warrior in the Line of Duty', *Daily Telegraph*, 2 March 1991.
[23] LSE Interview.

Oxford

Like many before and since, Bingham was captivated by Oxford, in particular his college, Balliol College. He quotes Hilaire Belloc:

> Balliol made me, Balliol fed me,
> Whatever I had she gave me again.[24]

Bingham has maintained the connection throughout his life. In 1986 he became Balliol's Visitor, a position he still occupies today. Balliol enjoys the ancient and, among the old colleges, unique privilege of electing their own Visitor, an office concerned, among other things, with adjudicating in student disputes with the college. By all accounts Bingham has been a great success in this role, generous with his time, unfailingly supportive, and a source of wise and valued advice. The university conferred an honorary DCL on him in 1994 and in 2002 he became its High Steward, a largely ceremonial office. The following year he tried, unsuccessfully, to be elected as Chancellor of the University, losing to the former Tory MP, Governor of Hong Kong and European Commissioner, Christopher Patten.

Bingham arrived at Balliol in Michaelmas 1954 to read PPE (Politics, Philosophy, and Economics). AB Rodger, one of the history fellows, had written to JP Corbett, the PPE tutor two years previously: 'I think he has the wits to get quite a respectable Second in PPE'.[25] After two terms of PPE, however, Bingham found that symbolic logic and economics were not to his taste and he reverted to history. At the time Balliol's historians were especially formidable, Richard Southern (a notable medieval historian and later, as Sir Richard Southern, president of St John's College), Christopher Hill, who had interviewed him in 1952 (well known for his work on 17th century England, as a Marxist, and later Master of Balliol), AB Rodger, and John Prest. Their range as historians meant that the whole history syllabus could be covered within Balliol. Relations between the teachers and the taught were close and informal. Bingham's change to history, a school favourite, proved, in retrospect, a wise decision.

During Bingham's time at Oxford Balliol as a college was well placed academically, although non-academic achievements, sporting prowess in particular, were still highly valued.[26] Despite admissions through scholarship examination, and the consequent presence of grammar school boys, members of the College were predominantly from the more privileged sectors of society and there was still a degree of class consciousness.[27] Bingham recalls the students as on the whole gifted and lively, the College succeeding in blending a high degree of seriousness and idealism with a high level of levity and wit. The latter were especially

---

[24] *Verses*, 1910.
[25] Dated 7 April 1952, Balliol College Archives.
[26] John Jones, *Balliol College. A History* (2nd rev edn, OUP, Oxford, 2005), 285.
[27] Ibid, 289n.

evident in a Balliol society Bingham joined, the Arnold and Brackenbury society. Amongst other things it organized debates, considering mock serious topics. Otherwise Bingham's time at Oxford was heavily academic: he did not row, play other sport, or participate at the Oxford Union.

At the end of his first year Bingham was one of eight Balliol students awarded a Coolidge Pathfinder award. William Coolidge was a benefactor of the College and funded students so they could explore the United States during the long vacation. Bingham began his tour on 23 July 1955 and completed it on 21 September.[28] Beginning on the East Coast, he travelled, via Pittsburg and Detroit, to Portland on the west coast. From there he travelled down to Los Angeles, across to New Orleans, and then back to New York and Boston. At various points he met his American cousins and, in Oklahoma, his aunt. He visited the site of his grandfather's ranch, which by then had reverted to desert with the appropriation of water being used for irrigation by the City of Los Angeles. He met a Native American employed by his grandfather before the turn of the century. The journey was accomplished by train, Greyhound and Trailways buses, car, and hitchhiking. Amongst other things he was impressed by the confidence of the American young, had heated discussions of extreme right-wing Republican views, and was struck by parts of the landscape, including Mount Hood in the Rockies and the Grand Canyon ('a thousand times worth the effort to get there'). In some places he visited courts and commented on United States legal procedure and a prolonged dispute,' at times almost vituperative', in the Federal District Court in San Francisco between the judge and one of the attorneys. In the Hall of Justice in San Francisco, dealing with petty crime, he found the atmosphere squalid, the procedure uninteresting, but the session significant sociologically: '[O]ut of perhaps forty defendants there are not more than seven or eight, at the most, who are not Negro or Oriental. Surely, this cannot be a coincidence'. In Memphis he briefly attended an all-black Baptist Convention—it 'raises interesting questions of segregation'—and a number of civil war sites (the site of the dramatic days preceding Lee's surrender in 1865 'has an enormous fascination', and two or three 'most absorbing hours' at the Gettysburg battlefield).

Bingham had a group of close friends at Balliol, whom he saw most days, friends who kept in touch long after they had left Oxford. These included Maurice Keen, Robert Oakeshott,[29] John Keegan,[30] and David Hancock.[31] Bingham was also close friends with Peter Brooke.[32] Keen became a fellow of Balliol, a notable

---

[28] Students had to produce an account of their travels and, meticulous as ever, Bingham produced a detailed account typed by Coolidge's legendary secretary: Balliol College Archives.

[29] Author of *The Case for Workers Co-ops* (Routledge and Kegan Paul, London, 1978).

[30] Later Sir John Keegan, the military historian and defence editor of the *Daily Telegraph*.

[31] Later Sir David Hancock, Permanent Secretary at the Department of Education and Science.

[32] Brooke was the son of Henry Brooke MP, then a minister in the Conservative Government. Peter Brooke himself became an MP, chairman of the Conservative Party and Secretary of State for Northern Ireland, and Culture Secretary before elevation to the House of Lords as Lord Brooke of Sutton Mandeville.

medieval historian and an FBA. He had been with Bingham in the Royal Ulster Rifles, and, when Oxford students, they went on summer camp together as members of the territorial army. In the following long vacation there was a bicycle tour with Keen of Romanesque churches in Provence. Oakeshott's father, former headmaster at Winchester College, and by then Rector of Lincoln College, furnished a hand-written list with notes. Peter Brooke recommended a vineyard, also visited with profit, Bingham insisting on a thorough sampling of its wares. The holiday ended with a few days in the chalet Balliol owned at Chamonix. Bingham ascended Mont Blanc, it seems in one of the fastest times then achieved by an amateur. He recalled one aspect of that climb many years later:

I'm not a colossally serious climber but one has always loved the mountains, and one can become rather competitive. I remember once climbing Mont Blanc. We discovered some climbers who had been lying in a crevasse for several days. We had to decide whether to help them or go the top and retrieve them on the way down. We did the latter. I suppose I can be ruthless.[33]

In his final year Bingham was elected President of Balliol JCR (junior common room), succeeding his friend Peter Brooke. Apart from his attempt to become Chancellor of the university almost half a century later this was Bingham's only attempt at elected office. He did not stand on a party political ticket, although at that time this was common. The other candidate was an American Rhodes scholar, Paul Sarbanes, later a senator from Maryland and well known for legislation he promoted following the Enron scandal, the Sarbanes-Oxley Act. Bingham won by one vote. It was the time of Suez and the Hungarian uprising. Robert Oakeshott and other Oxford students had arranged to travel to Hungary to take medical and other supplies to the Hungarians, now resisting the Russian invasion.[34] Oakeshott told the story to a newspaper. The agreement had been not to inform the College authorities until after their departure. The proctors became involved. Bingham sent the students, without authority, a fraternal message of support. There was disquiet in the JCR and he faced a vote of censure. Bingham handled the meeting with skilful efficiency. There were sensible measures proposed for money raised to be sanctioned by the JCR and vetted by the College authorities. In fact a significant amount was collected. Bingham escaped censure and served as a popular JCR president.

Partly as a result of his Coolidge Pathfinder Bingham had chosen 'Slavery and Secession 1850–1862' as his special subject; it was also an attraction that the sources were all in English and not, as with most of the alternatives, Latin, French, or Italian. Early in his final year he won the Gibbs Prize for Modern History, by

---

[33] Alice Thompson, op. cit.
[34] See also M Korda, *Journey to a Revolution* (Harper Collins, New York, 2006) 111ff; M Czigany, 'Treated as other Students? 1956 Hungarian Refugee Students at Imperial College, London', Conference: British-Hungarian Relations Since 1848, School of Slavonic and East European Studies, University College London, 16–17 April 2004.

examination ('When would you begin a history of Parliament', 'Should children love their parents?'). It was a university-wide prize, won in Bingham's view against the odds and an encouragement for finals. In the result he obtained a first. It was rumoured that the three best firsts that year were obtained by Balliol candidates, of whom Bingham was one. The Master of Balliol, the British constitutional historian Sir David Keir, wrote to Bingham:

I am very glad you got your First; a year ago I would have been very doubtful, but you made enormous strides in your last year and richly deserve it. Here in Balliol we are very much in your debt, both by doing so well in scholarship and by taking the part that you did in its general life. If only all undergraduates would put as much into the place as you did, the sky would be the limit![35]

On the basis of his degree results Bingham was awarded the Eldon Law Scholarship in 1957, given to a member of the University of Oxford intending to read for the bar.

It was a disappointment but not a surprise when he was not elected to a Prize Fellowship at All Souls College shortly after. All Souls fellows by examination have been said to be the cleverest people in the country, although that reflects a particular definition of cleverness and is no necessary indication of later success. Perhaps the outcome is not surprising. A clear favourite in his year was Jeremy Lever, who had a first in jurisprudence and had been president of the Oxford Union.[36] The other was Jeremy Wolfenden, whose friends at Eton and Oxford hailed him as the cleverest boy in England.[37] Ultimately both were chosen. On Bingham's own account it may not have been wise to prepare for so exacting an exam by working in a concreting gang laying the runway for the new airport at Gatwick, near his parents' home. Bingham was later grateful to Pope John Paul who, disembarking from his aircraft on arrival at the airport in 1982, knelt and kissed the ground.

The Bar

Bingham's contemporaries at Oxford thought on graduation that he would want the outside world rather than the life of an academic historian. At one point, contacts through the London Irish Rifles suggested a career in industry with, say, ICI. But his mother suggested the bar. It had some attractions. He had seen United States legal practice through the Coolidge Pathfinder visit; in the army he had enjoyed appearing as a defence officer in a court martial; and he was taken

---

[35] Balliol College Archives.

[36] Later Sir Jeremy Lever KCMG QC, a notable expert in competition and European law.

[37] Sebastian Faulks, *The Fatal Englishman. Three Short Lives* (Vintage, London, 1997), 236, 252, 257. After Oxford Wolfenden became a journalist with the *Telegraph*, was recruited by the intelligence services and drank himself to death at the age of 31.

by the legal aspects of the constitutional documents he had studied. So towards the end of his second year at Oxford, on 30 May 1956, he was admitted to Gray's Inn. Like with so many before and since, the choice of an Inn was fortuitous: the wife of the then Under-Treasurer of Gray's Inn[38] was a dental patient of one of his mother's friends, so Gray's it was. Bingham began dining in hall, a compulsory part of admission to the bar, involving at least 36 dinners over 12 terms. Bingham found the experience tiresome and uneducative; as we shall see he was able to escape eating his full quota.

It was, and is still, possible to be called as a barrister without a law degree. In the late 1950s and for some time after, it was not necessary to attend any recognized establishment in preparation for the bar exams. The bar exams themselves were narrowly technical, with an emphasis on memory, and to the exclusion of subjects such as administrative law and taxation law. Agitation in the 1930s, and again in the 1950s, to reform this met with a brick wall.[39] Most English barristers sat the examination after attending a crammer, the best known being Gibson & Weldon, a private profit sharing partnership. Gibson & Weldon had provided the service since 1876 although they cavilled at being called crammers, preferring the description good, well-organized teaching.[40] The good, well-organized teaching is described by Bingham:

It was a scandal of course because you could do it very quickly if you worked hard enough and it was completely uneducational. And I recall an occasion when one of the pupils in a class looking at a handout, said 'I don't understand'. And the lecturer said 'It doesn't matter if you understand it or not, just learn it by heart'. And that was the technique. If you learnt everything by heart they told you and then retold it in answer to the right question you passed the Bar exams.[41]

There was a respite in Hilary Term 1958 when Bingham acted as marshal (unpaid assistant) to Mr Justice Finnemore as he travelled the Northern Eastern Circuit. Finnemore, an Oxford graduate himself, regularly had students from Oxford to act as his marshal.[42] Going on circuit was, and still is, part and parcel of the lives of most Queen's Bench judges; judges travel to major centres through England and Wales, trying heavy crime and some civil work, residing in fine houses, the judicial lodgings. The circuit began in Newcastle—with coal fires in the bedrooms in the lodgings in January—via Durham, York, and Leeds to Sheffield at Easter. Finnemore had been a High Court judge since 1947, a county court judge before

---

[38] Oswald (Oz) Terry, a graduate chartered accountant, and legend of the Inn, said to be largely responsible for its post-war recovery following the considerable destruction wrought by German bombing.

[39] B Abel-Smith and R Stevens, *Lawyers and the Courts* (Cambridge, Mass, Harvard UP, 1967), 183–5, 358–9.

[40] RH Kersley, *Gibson's 1871–1962. A Chapter in Legal Education* (Law Notes Lending Library Ltd, London 1973) 2.

[41] LSE Interview.

[42] Information from Sir Peter Gibson, formerly of the Court of Appeal.

that. A bachelor, he was an outwardly austere, teetotal, non-smoking Baptist.[43] In fact Bingham found him a rewarding companion, a wise, broadminded, and compassionate judge, and a great friend of the young. Bingham regarded this exposure, day by day, to the flow of court business, criminal and civil, garnished by the judge's out-of-court comments, as immensely educative.

Having passed his Part I exams, Bingham sat his Part II exams in Hilary Term 1959. The examination comprised papers divided into five sections: common law, equity, procedure, evidence and company law, and then two of four subjects (practical conveyancing, divorce, conflict of laws, and public international law).[44] Disciplined hard work reaped dividends when he was placed first in the examination with a certificate of honour. That meant lunch with the partners of Gibson & Weldon at the Charing Cross Hotel. At Gray's Inn he was awarded the Society's prize for a first-class pass in the Bar finals, the Arden Scholarship, and a Stuart Cunningham Masaskic KC scholarship.[45] He had previously applied to Gray's Inn for a term's dispensation of dining, subject to his passing the bar exam, and on 22 January 1959, in the light of his results, the benchers of the Inn unanimously relieved him of the obligation to eat any more dinners.[46]

Pupillage, a form of apprenticeship for barristers, had just become compulsory: although not yet a rule, from 1958 barristers had to give an undertaking to their Inn, on being called, that they would not practise at the English bar without a 12-month pupillage.[47] Bingham served his pupillage, and after 12 months became a tenant at a set of barristers' chambers now known as Fountain Court in the Temple. It is one of the leading sets of commercial chambers. At the time it was at 2 Crown Office Row in the Temple. By the standards of the day it was reasonably large, despite having fewer than a dozen barristers. Its reputation was growing.[48] Until his appointment as a High Court judge in 1957 the head of chambers had been Melford Stevenson QC, a larger than life character who attracted notoriety as a judge in criminal cases.[49] When Bingham arrived the head of chambers was Leslie Scarman QC, who had fairly recently taken silk and was shortly after to begin his distinguished career as a judge, chairman of the Law Commission, and public figure.[50]

---

[43] He was President of the Baptist Union of Great Britain, 1966–67, and involved in the Boys' Brigade.

[44] *Council of Legal Education, Calendar 1959–60* Consolidated Regulations r.21.

[45] Honourable Society of Gray's Inn, *Graya*, No 51, 1960, 50.

[46] Gray's Inn Archives.

[47] B Abel-Smith & R Stevens, op cit. 359.

[48] Of those there when Bingham joined AS Orr and DRM Henry became Lord Justices of Appeal, J R Phillips and PE Webster, High Court judges, and WAB Forbes a Law Commissioner.

[49] Roskill, 'Stevenson, Sir (Aubrey) Melford Steed (1902–1987)', *Oxford Dictionary of National Biography*, online edn, Oxford University Press, 2004 [http://www.oxforddnb.com/view/article/40101, accessed 8 Feb 2009].

[50] Stephen Sedley, 'Scarman, Leslie George, Baron Scarman (1911–2004)', *Oxford Dictionary of National Biography*, online edn, Oxford University Press, Jan 2008 [http://www.oxforddnb.com/view/article/94622, accessed 8 Feb 2009].

2 Crown Office Row was referred to by some as a Balliol annex and it was Denis Henry, who had left Balliol a few years before, who introduced Bingham to the chambers. Henry supplemented his income by teaching law at Trinity College, Oxford, at the weekend. Encountering Bingham, and learning his intentions, Henry suggested he should do a pupillage in his chambers with Alan Orr, then common law junior to the Inland Revenue, who had been Henry's pupil-master. Bingham accepted the suggestion, but it turned out that Orr already had a pupil, so Bingham was allocated to Owen Stable instead. As was the practice, he duly paid his pupillage fee of one hundred guineas to Stable and began his pupillage in January 1959. Shortly thereafter, with a generosity almost unheard of at the time, Stable paid Bingham a weekly banker's order, an arrangement which he continued for years on the understanding that if Bingham had any spare time he would make it available to him. Son of a prominent High Court judge, Stable had a varied and high quality junior practice. Bingham regarded him as being far from a pedantic or pedagogic pupil-master. He recounts Winston Churchill's anecdote, that having Philip Sassoon MP as a parliamentary private secretary was like hitching a restaurant car onto the train. The same, he says, could be said of Stable as pupil-master: Bingham spent a hardworking but very convivial year with him, many days culminating in dinner at the Cock in Fleet Street or, on more relaxed occasions, Boodle's. There was then no restriction on pupils accepting instructions if any solicitor gave them, and a number of briefs came Bingham's way, particularly after Easter when Scarman told him he would be kept on as a tenant in the chambers. In January 1960 his name was painted up on the board as a tenant.

The senior members of 2 Crown Office Row had more or less specialized practices; the younger members learned their trade in county, magistrates', and coroners' courts, with some undefended divorces and ill-paid jury trials thrown in. Bingham recalls the early years:

At the bottom of chambers in those days we were completely unspecialised. We would do really virtually anything. A lot of it was extremely menial and an awful lot of it was extremely ill paid. So that one would rush round the magistrates' courts and if they were in Central London defend drivers who were accused of careless driving for which you were paid £2.3s.6d I think. But if it was a little bit further out of London you were paid £3.5s.6d. If you conducted a jury trial at London Sessions or the Old Bailey I think it was about £4 or something like that. So this work was not greatly sought after, with the result that there was a certain amount of it about which we were all very pleased to do.[51]

Success at the bar in the early years depended importantly on the clerk and the amount of work attracted to chambers by the more experienced barristers, some of which might come the way of the more junior tenants.[52] The directing genius of the chambers was the clerk, Cyril Batchelor, who quickly identified Bingham as a capable and safe pair of hands. Bingham continued to work with his former pupil-master, Stable, both on paper work and litigation. That continued to an

[51] LSE Interview.
[52] Richard L Abel, *The Legal Profession England and Wales* (Basil Blackwell, Oxford, 1988) 61.

extent after Stable took silk in 1963. Some of the litigation was commercial in nature. Thus they appeared together in the Restrictive Practices Court on behalf of the paper industries trade associations. The issue was whether the implementation of the recommendations of a report of the Economic Development Committee for the Paper and Board Industry would be in breach of undertakings given to the Court.[53] Not all appearances with Stable were commercial. On one occasion they unsuccessfully visited the Court of Criminal Appeal on behalf of a defendant convicted of uttering a forged receipt for the purchase of two motor cars.[54] On another occasion they appeared before the former Solicitor-General, then President of the Probate, Divorce and Admiralty Division, Sir Jocelyn Simon, contending that a divorce should not be made final because of non-disclosure of a material fact before the trial judge.[55]

As well as a busy advisory practice, Bingham was appearing in reported cases within a relatively short period, instructed in some instances by prominent solicitors. In an early reported case he was instructed by the leading firm, Slaughter and May, to apologize on behalf of the English subsidiary of an American trading stamp company.[56] *Eastern Holdings Establishment of Vaduz v Singer & Friedlander Ltd*[57] was a more substantial appearance for Slaughter and May in the Chancery Division. In *PA Thomas & Co v Mould*[58] he was instructed by another City law firm, Freshfields, acting for a company specializing in tax minimization schemes. While a junior, he was also led by a number of distinguished Queen's Counsel. Instructed again by Slaughter and May he appeared in *Shulton (Great Britain) Ltd v Slough BC*[59] with the former Attorney-General, Sir John Hobson QC, before the Divisional Court (Diplock LJ, Ashworth, and Paul JJ). The brief was on behalf of a manufacturer convicted, by the justices, of applying a false trade description to their products. Michael Kerr QC, later a leading commercial judge, led Bingham in a case which went to the House of Lords, still quoted in the contract books on issues such as estoppel and variation.[60] Morris Finer, later a High Court judge and the chairman of the Committee on One Parent Families (1974), led him in a case where they represented some newspaper companies. The newspapers had been charged with offences under the Betting, Gaming and Lotteries Act 1963 for running spot-the-ball competitions, where readers marked the position of the football on a photograph. The newspapers were unsuccessful before the lower courts in their contention that spot-the-ball competitions were a game of skill, not chance. Bingham recalls that in unsuccessfully seeking leave before the House of Lords Finer drew an analogy between a spot-the-ball competition and

---

[53] *British Paper and Board Makers Association's Agreement and British Waste Paper Association's Agreement (No 2)* [1966] 1 WLR 1476; [1966] 3 All ER 836.
[54] *R v Harris* [1996] 1 QB 184.
[55] *Rudman v Rudman and Lee (Queen's Proctor Showing Cause)* [1964] 2 All ER 102.
[56] *J Sainsbury Ltd v The Sperry & Hutchinson Co Ltd*, The Times, 4 June 1965.
[57] [1967] 1 WLR 1017.
[58] [1968] 2 QB 913.
[59] [1967] 2 QB 471.
[60] *Woodhouse AC Israel Cocoa Ltd SA v Nigerian Produce Marketing Co* [1972] AC 741.

chess. Viscount Dilhorne, the former Attorney-General, Reginald Manningham-Buller, said that he thought Finer did not know much about chess. Bingham's comment is: 'I think there was nobody there who wouldn't have backed Morris against the Viscount Dilhorne in a game of chess.'[61]

So relatively early on Bingham was in the appeal courts. In 1964 he appeared before Pearson and Diplock LJJ in the Court of Appeal on behalf of a mother in an adoption case.[62] Appearances before that court, as sole counsel, brought him to the notice, importantly, of the Master of the Rolls, Lord Denning. *Allen v Sir Alfred McAlpine & Sons Ltd*[63] involved a number of appeals, where solicitors had been guilty of delay. In Bingham's appeal the Southwark Group Hospital Management Committee, whom he represented, were responsible for delay, as was the plaintiff nurse's solicitors: the Court of Appeal allowed the action to proceed. But his appearance for the Law Society before that court (Lord Denning MR, Diplock, and Salmon JJ) was more successful in what was, for a time, an important case on legal professional privilege.[64] In 1968 the Attorney-General, Sir Elwyn Jones QC, appointed Bingham to succeed Gordon Slynn (later Lord Slynn) as standing junior counsel to the Ministry of Labour, later the Ministry of Employment and Productivity. Bingham consequently appeared in several cases in the Divisional Court and Court of Appeal in litigation involving selective employment tax, a form of tax which the Labour Government had introduced in 1966 to tax 'non-productive' employment and encourage capital investment.[65] In one of these selective employment tax cases he was led in the House of Lords by the future Lord Chancellor, James Mackay.[66]

In 1972 Bingham applied for silk on the advice of his clerk, Cyril Batchelor, who enlisted the powerful support of the former head of chambers, Melford Stevenson. When Melford Stevenson spoke to the Lord Chief Justice, Lord Parker, he was told that he did not support any individual candidate but would remember the name. Bingham achieved the coveted bottom place on this list, the most junior of the barristers that year to be made Queen's Counsel. In silk Bingham did a good deal of work for the government and as time went on his practice assumed a more commercial and maritime hue. The government work included an appearance in the Court of Appeal on a Sunday evening, led by Sir Geoffrey Howe QC, the Solicitor-General, in *ASLEF (No 2)*[67] on 14 May 1972. Then, with a Labour Government in power, he appeared in the House of Lords on a Saturday morning, 31 July 1976, in the vacation in the *Tameside* schools

---

[61] LSE Interview.

[62] *In re C (L) (An infant)* [1965] 2 QB 449.

[63] [1968] 2 QB 229.   [64] *Parry-Jones v The Law Society* [1969] 1 Ch 1.

[65] *Cotton Controllers (Liverpool) Ltd v Secretary of State for Employment and Productivity* [1969] 2 Lloyd's Rep 323; *Fisher-Bendix Ltd v Secretary of State for Employment and Productivity* [1970] 1 WLR 856; *Secretary of State for Employment and Productivity v Clarke Chapman & Co* [1971] 1 WLR 1094.

[66] *Lord Advocate v Babcock & Wilcox (Operations) Ltd* [1972] 1 WLR 488.

[67] *Secretary of State for Employment v Associated Society of Locomotive Engineers and Firemen (No 2)* [1972] 2 QB 455. The case involved working to rule.

case. That was politically charged litigation over comprehensive schooling. Harry Woolf, Bingham's successor as Lord Chief Justice, but then Treasury devil, had won the case at first instance. It was lost comprehensively in the House of Lords.[68] Less politically fraught government work included appearing for the Pay Board, where companies were seeking declarations that pay awards for their employees did not fall foul of the counter-inflation legislation;[69] for the Science Research Council in a complaint involving racial discrimination;[70] and for the Secretary of State for Employment, in a dispute over whether employers were entitled to a full rebate for a redundancy payment made to an employee.[71]

But there was other litigation as well, as when Bingham appeared for the National Society for the Prevention of Cruelty to Children.[72] Bingham has a friendly recollection of the case.

The story was that somebody reported to the NSPCC that a young child had been the subject of abuse. So they sent an inspector round who interviewed the mother and had a look at the child and found nothing to substantiate this allegation at all. It so happened that the father was a merchant banker and his wife was a woman of irreproachable behaviour towards the children. They were terrifically upset by the fact that this accusation had been anonymously made and were determined to find out who had made it. Thus they brought an action, the sole object of which was to discover who had given this information to the NSPCC. The NSPCC's position was that if they were going to start revealing the names of people who had given them information people simply would not give information. And albeit sometimes the information might turn out to be false, on other occasions it was true and thank goodness people did alert them to the fact that dreadful things were going on. So it was a case about which the NSPCC certainly felt very strongly. And I think we won in front of the Master and in front of the judge and then we lost by 2–1 in the Court of Appeal. My old head of chambers [Leslie Scarman] found against me but Tom Denning dissented in our favour. And it was very unpromising because we were relying on what was still called in those days Crown Privilege. Therefore they said you're not the Crown. How can a charitable organisation arrogate to itself all the privileges that had previously been reserved to the Crown. And we said we were a public body discharging a public function in large measure dependent on public funds, apart from charitable contributions, and the same rules ought to apply. However in the House of Lords I'm happy to say we did succeed, I think 5–0. And my abiding memory, when my former head of chambers saw me and I was rather expecting him to congratulate me on having reversed the Court of Appeal, he said 'You must have been very disappointed to have won on the narrower of the two grounds'. He was not the most gracious loser.

Acting for the *Daily Mail*, he was unable to persuade the Court of Appeal that, in the light of the voluminous documentation, trial by jury was inappropriate

[68] *Secretary of State for Education and Science v Tameside MBC* [1977] AC 1014.
[69] *British Leyland UK Ltd v The Pay Board* [1974] IRLR 60; *Racal Communications Ltd v The Pay Board* [1974] 1 WLR 1149. On the other side in both cases was one AA Irvine, a future Lord Chancellor.
[70] *Science Research Council v Nasse* [1980] AC 1028.
[71] *Secretary of State for Employment v Globe Elastic Thread Co Ltd* [1980] AC 506.
[72] *D v National Society for the Prevention of Cruelty to Children* [1978] AC 171.

in a libel action against *The Times*.[73] In *Birkett v James*[74] he was instructed by Freshfields on behalf of a person being sued by someone dismissed from an executive position in a large group of companies he owned and controlled. Bingham also did a considerable amount of work for the Medical Defence Union.

On the commercial side there was litigation both domestic and international. Of the former, *Moorgate Mercantile Credit Co Ltd v Twitchings*[75] arose in the context of a hire purchase agreement and is still an important authority on estoppel. Among cases with an international flavour Bingham represented the United States giant, the Westinghouse Electric Corporation. It was satellite litigation in England relating to an action in which Westinghouse was involved in the United States concerning, *inter alia*, an international uranium cartel. In at least two cases Bingham represented foreign states.[76] He unsuccessfully represented the Republic of the Philippines in an appeal to the Privy Council from Hong Kong.[77] The issue was whether the Philippines had the benefit of sovereign immunity in relation to a merchant ship it owned, engaged in ordinary trade. The *Playa Larga* was another sovereign immunity case, where Bingham was defending Cuba. He was successful before Robert Goff J at first instance, and a two judge Court of Appeal having failed to agree, the plaintiff's appeals were dismissed.[78] However, Cuba lost before the House of Lords, although by this time Bingham was on the bench and it was represented by others.[79]

Not all of Bingham's time at the bar was advisory work or litigation. During 1974 and 1975, Bingham acted as counsel to a public enquiry conducted by Roger Parker QC into a devastating explosion at a chemical plant near Flixborough, in Lincolnshire. His junior was Michael Howard, later an MP and Leader of the Opposition. Twenty-eight workers were killed and nearly 90 others, workers and persons off-site, were injured. The enquiry was charged with establishing the cause and circumstances of the disaster.[80] In 1977–1978, on the appointment of David Owen MP, then the Foreign Secretary, Bingham led an inquiry into the supply of oil to Rhodesia, as it then was, during the United Nations sanctions.[81] His report, thought to reflect adversely on Harold Wilson's Government, prompted journalistic allusions to 'Oilgate'.[82] Following the change of government in 1979

[73] *Rothermere v Times Newspapers Ltd* [1973] 1 WLR 448; [1973] 1 All ER 1013.

[74] [1978] AC 297.   [75] [1977] AC 890.

[76] *Rio Tinto Zinc Corporation v Westinghouse Electric Corporation* [1978] AC 547.

[77] *The Philippine Admiral* [1977] AC 373. The case was argued over ten days in the Privy Council.

[78] [1978] QB 500; [1980] 1 Lloyd's Rep 23 respectively. In this case Bingham appeared against another leader of the bar, Robert (later Lord) Alexander QC.

[79] [1983] 1 AC 244.

[80] Health and Safety Executive, *The Flixborough Disaster: Report of the Court of Inquiry* (London, Her Majesty's Statutory Office, 1975. For a critique: J Cox, 'Flixborough Revisited', *Chemical Engineer (London)*, April 2005.

[81] *Report on the Supply of Petroleum and Petroleum Products to Rhodesia* (Her Majesty's Stationery Office, London, 1978).

[82] See M Bailey, *Oilgate. The Sanctions Scandal* (Sevenoaks, Coronet 1979); A Philips, *The Bingham Report, A Social Audit Special Report*, (London, 1978).

there was some talk of a further inquiry into the role of the former government. But the new Lord Chancellor, Lord Hailsham of St Marylebone, observed: 'Bingham is enough; perhaps too much.'

In April 1980 Bingham was appointed by Hailsham to be a judge of the Queen's Bench Division. Although he was only 46 at the time, a remarkable young age for such an appointment, it was in no way surprising. Simply put, Bingham was at the top of his profession.

What impelled me to become a judge? It used to be quite unusual to say no. There were always well known cases of individuals who for some reason or another had said to the Lord Chancellor, thank you very much for asking me but I'd sooner stay in practice. But there weren't all that many. And I think most people, despite the loss of income regarded it as a sort of natural culmination of a career at the Bar. People do it with varying degrees of enthusiasm, but there are some people who feel like heavyweight boxers who just can't bear to go back into the ring. And I think that can happen to advocates. And in particular I think as you get more senior the cases get longer, which makes them more burdensome and in a sense more worrying, particularly if they are going wrong. And I found I liked my clients less as time went on and they got richer. I got on very well with criminals in earlier days.[83]

A great deal of Bingham's time as a puisne judge was spent in the Commercial Court. Elevation to the Court of Appeal followed in 1986: Bingham preferred the collegiality and exchange of views characteristic of a composite court. In 1991 he was appointed by the Chancellor of the Exchequer and the Governor of the Bank of England to conduct another enquiry, this time into the Bank of England's supervision of the Bank of Credit and Commerce International, which had recently failed. This exacting assignment took him away from the Court of Appeal but he produced a massive report within a year. His report was critical of the Bank of England in a number of serious respects, but acquitted the Bank and its officers of any dishonest or knowing breach of the law.[84] On completion of the report Bingham was made Master of the Rolls. Appointment as Lord Chief Justice and senior law lord followed in 1996 and 2000 respectively.

Conclusion

This is not an exploration of Lord Bingham's judicial philosophy. Nor is it an essay in psychobiography. And it covers only part of his life. However, it does offer some explanation of how Thomas Henry Bingham has been in a category of his own. Cleverness by itself is only part of the story. First, it is evident how at an early age Bingham developed the talents of hard work, determination, and

---

[83] LSE Interview.
[84] *Inquiry into the Supervision of the Bank of Credit and Commerce International*, House of Commons Paper, Session 1992–93; 198. Had Bingham's judgment been accepted it would have avoided 14 years of fruitless litigation by the liquidators of BCCI.

self-discipline which were to stand him in good stead for the rest of his life. David Sutcliffe, a Winder House contemporary at Sedbergh writes, recalls:

I recall his use of time. He was, quite simply, never idle. This was not just a matter of completing set tasks. Classroom work, even the preparation for the sixth form essays and the Balliol scholarship examinations, was just a springboard and a point of departure for additional reading. I imagine he still has those large notebooks he filled with summaries, analyses and reflections. He turned to them at weekends, on half-holidays, and whenever he was otherwise unoccupied. Nor was it a matter of simply filling every hour of the working day. The day was not long enough, so he trained himself, after the House was quiet and all (including his fellow prefects) were in bed, to rise quietly and put in another hour or two (or more), not on impulse, not in response to a deadline crisis, but systematically, night after night, in pursuit of long term knowledge and excellence. He has what we might now look on as a Victorian attitude towards the number of hours required daily, weekly and annually, to achieve success in worthwhile endeavours. Even the most cursory study of Gladstone's life tells the same story. I think Tom's first commandment would be nothing of note is accomplished without very long hours of very hard work.[85]

Secondly, there was his capacity to deal with disappointments—the Oxford Scholarship, the All Souls Prize Fellowship—and to persevere in the face of them. When he returned to Sedbergh School as Lord Chief Justice, for the Speech Day and Prizegiving in 1998, he told the story of Curzon, who in 1923 had broken down into uncontrollable tears when told he would not be Prime Minister. What this really went to show, said Bingham, was that Curzon had never had the experience of being passed over as Captain of the Colts C2 rugby team at 15. If he had, he would have known that no disappointment could ever prove quite so mortifying again, and he could have laughed off the loss of number 10 Downing Street with some ease. Thirdly, this account throws some light on how important posts and leadership came Bingham's way, not because he necessarily sought them but because whatever he did he did well. Perhaps the best example was his appointment as Lord Chief Justice, not covered here but controversial at the time. When appointed Bingham's obvious competence, even in criminal law where he had comparatively little experience, quickly dispelled doubts. What may not be immediately obvious from this account, but for the historical record needs to be mentioned, are other Bingham qualities—integrity, judgment, courtesy, kindliness, and humour. But the story of these is for another day.[86]

---

[85] Sedbergh School Archives.

[86] I am grateful to the assistance of a considerable number of people in writing this: at Sedbergh School, the present Headmaster, CH Hirst, a former headmaster, Michael Thorneley, one of Bingham's teachers, Revd EPE Long, a Bingham contemporary, David Sutcliffe, and the archivist Katy Iliffe; at Balliol College: the Master, Andrew Graham, the Fellow Archivist, Dr John Jones, Dr Maurice Keen FBA, John Prest and DR Harris; at Gray's Inn, the Treasurer, Anthony Faith, the librarian Theresa Thom; at Lincoln's Inn, the librarian Guy Holborn; at Fountain Court, Conrad Dehn QC, Peter Scott QC, and Sir Henry Brooke. I am also grateful to the Lord Chief Justice, Lord Phillips of Worth Matravers.

I

THE RULE OF LAW AND THE ROLE OF LAW

1

On Liberty and the European Convention on Human Rights

Mary Arden

Introduction

A *Liber Amicorum* is an opportunity to celebrate the work of a great judge, Lord Bingham. I propose in this short essay to bring together some thoughts about the unique contribution of Lord Bingham to the development of human rights in this country. I shall focus on one very small part of Lord Bingham's work but on a part that I regard as of great importance to all who value the law in this jurisdiction. From there, I go on to draw some parallels between human rights jurisprudence and the philosophy of John Stuart Mill, as expressed in his famous essay, *On Liberty*. My object is to show that, as one would expect, one of the foundations of human rights jurisprudence is philosophical thinking on the nature of freedom in society.

Time to Incorporate

It is well known that, although lawyers from the United Kingdom played a major part in the drafting of the Convention, Parliament did not incorporate it into English domestic law until it passed the Human Rights Act in 1998. However, there was an important turning point some five years previously when Lord Bingham, then Sir Thomas Bingham MR, threw his considerable intellectual weight behind incorporation into domestic law in a lecture which argued in vigorous terms that the Convention should be incorporated.

The lecture was entitled 'The European Convention on Human Rights: time to incorporate'.[1] In this lecture, Lord Bingham emphasized the centrality to both democracy and the judicial function of protecting the individual against the state. Under traditional constitutional theory, Parliament protected the rights of

---

[1] (1993) 109 LQR pp 390–400.

the citizen. However, there had been important changes in the way the constitutional arrangements worked. For example, the power of the executive had grown considerably. This had led to the increase in judicial review. However, the doctrine of Parliamentary sovereignty left the protection of individual rights in an unsatisfactory position. Lord Bingham suggested that:

[A] government intent on implementing a programme may overlook the human rights aspects of its policies, and that, if a government of more sinister intent were to gain power, we should be defenceless. There would not, certainly, be much the judges could do about it.

Lord Bingham added:

So anyone who sees Parliament as a reliable guardian of human rights in practice is, I suggest, guilty of wishful thinking.

He referred to the 'increasingly heterogenous nature of our society and the increasingly assertive stance of minorities'. He referred to the 'general lessening of deference to authority, a growing unwillingness to accept the say-so of the teacher, a local government officer or the man from the ministry.'

Lord Bingham predicted a growing number of cases in which prevailing practice, perhaps of very long standing, will be said to infringe the human rights of some smaller group or some individual. He concluded: 'As it stands, courts are not well-fitted to mediate in these situations.' From this standpoint, Lord Bingham went on to declare that the Convention offered a clear improvement on the then position. He drew on the work in this field of Anthony Lester QC (now Lord Lester of Herne Hill).[2]

Lord Bingham observed that incorporation of the Convention was 'at first blush...a simple and obvious way' of protecting the rights of minorities. He cogently observed that, whenever the United Kingdom was found to have acted in violation of Convention rights, the government had taken steps to cure the default and pay compensation.

Lord Bingham reviewed the arguments both for and against incorporation. He may have seen some force in the argument that incorporation could politicize the judiciary and lead to the decisions of the court trumping the power of Parliament because he proceeded on the basis that incorporation would not give the judges power to strike down legislation but rather that it would enable them to interpret legislation in accordance with the Convention, in accordance with the express will of Parliament as a result of having incorporated the Convention. Foreshadowing his later contribution to the debate on Parliamentary sovereignty, Lord Bingham expressed the view that 'in the scarcely imagined case of an express abrogation or derogation by Parliament, the judges would give effect to that provision also'.

---

[2] It is not possible within the scope of this article to pay tribute to the monumental work of Lord Lester in this field, but for many years he actively promoted the idea of incorporation.

It was Lord Bingham's view that, while the Convention could not be entrenched, in practical terms it was inconceivable that a government would want to derogate from Convention obligations. He noted the argument that judges could become the subject of damaging controversy when deciding Convention issues but observed that there was no evidence that this had occurred elsewhere. Lord Bingham considered, but strongly disavowed, the suggestion that it was not appropriate for judges to decide questions about the relations between an individual and society. It was illogical to allow these decisions to be taken by the Strasbourg court, but not in the first instance by judges of the United Kingdom. Moreover, judges were already involved in scrutinizing the decisions of ministers through the process of judicial review. The common law had not always provided the degree of protection conferred by the Convention. Although the Convention had been drafted in the 1950s, the argument that the Convention was in some way dated was ill founded, because of the evolutive nature of Convention jurisprudence. He noted that the Court of Justice recognized principles of Convention jurisprudence, and in that way the United Kingdom became bound to apply the Convention to Community law. Lord Bingham noted that incorporation had the support of Lord Slynn of Hadley, an eminent one-time Advocate–General and later a judge of the Court of Justice and member of the Appellate Committee of the House of Lords.

The final paragraph of the lecture was written in those magisterial tones which we now so strongly associate with the judgments of Lord Bingham:

> I end on a downbeat note. It would be naïve to suppose that incorporation of the Convention would usher in the new Jerusalem. As on the morrow of a general election, however glamorous the promises of the campaign, the world would not at once feel very different. But the change would over time stifle the insidious and damaging belief that it is necessary to go abroad to obtain justice. It would restore this country to its former place as an international standard bearer of liberty and justice. It would help to reinvigorate the faith, which our eighteenth and nineteenth century forbears would not for an instant have doubted, that these were fields in which Britain was the world's teacher, not its pupil. And it would enable the judges more effectively to honour their ancient and sacred undertaking to do right to all manner of people after the laws and usages of this realm, without fear or favour, affection or ill will.

The use of the word 'downbeat' in the first sentence of this passage is perhaps a little Delphic, but as I read it Lord Bingham was drawing an allusion with the first beat of a grand overture, rather than using the word in its colloquial sense suggesting a pessimistic tone. The 'forbears' to whom he referred may have included the great English philosophers such as John Locke and John Stuart Mill, as well as eminent judges.

A most impressive feature of the lecture is, however, the marshalling of cogent arguments so that they became in legal terms unanswerable. Furthermore, the support for the Convention from such a senior and well-respected member of the judiciary was highly influential and changed the thinking of many lawyers in this country. A whole generation of lawyers, whose first studies in the law would probably not have included human rights and some of whom might then have confused the European Court of Human Rights with the Court of Justice sitting in Luxembourg, began to take an interest in the issue. It was characteristic of Lord Bingham to speak in forthright terms on an issue of high constitutional importance. Its importance in that context cannot be overstated. The fact that he threw his powerful intellectual weight behind it must surely have been one of the factors that led to the incorporation into domestic law of the Convention by the Human Rights Act 1998. The Act was not brought into force immediately so that judges and others had time to become adjusted to the implications of the Act. In 2000, Lord Bingham, who had been appointed Lord Chief Justice in 1996, retired from that office and became the senior Lord of Appeal in Ordinary just four months before the Human Rights Act 1998 came into force.

Building a Human Rights Jurisprudence

In the eight years since he became senior Law Lord, Lord Bingham has been instrumental in making the Convention part of the waft and weave of English law. All his speeches repay careful study, but I would make a brief reference to two decisions which bear on the theme of this essay. The first is *R(Pretty) v Director of Public Prosecutions* [2002] 1 AC 800. In this case, the appellant suffered from a progressive and degenerative terminal illness. She wanted to control the timing and manner of her death but she could not do so without the assistance of her husband because of her illness. She requested an assurance from the Director of Public Prosecutions that her husband would not be prosecuted for the offence of assisting her to commit suicide contrary to section 2 of the Suicide Act 1961. She claimed that she had a right under the Convention to commit suicide with assistance. The Director of Public Prosecutions refused to give her any undertaking. The appellant relied on Articles 2, 3, 8, 9, and 14 of the Convention. Article 8 guarantees respect for a person's private life. Mrs Pretty's case under Article 8 was that this article gave her a right to self-determination and that there had to be serious reasons to justify interference with an intimate part of her private life. However, on that particular issue Lord Bingham held:

Article 8 is expressed in terms directed to protection of personal autonomy while individuals were living their lives, and there is nothing to suggest that the article has reference to the choice to live no longer.[3]

The other members of the House agreed with Lord Bingham. The case subsequently went to the European Court of Human Rights, which took the unusual step of setting out the whole of Lord Bingham's judgment in its judgment. On

---

[3] At [23].

the specific issue of Article 8, it was not prepared to hold that there was no interference with her private life for the purpose of article 8. However, it held that the interference was within the state's margin of appreciation, and justified because of the risk of abuse of the claimed right, which meant that the ban on assisted suicide was not disproportionate. It found that there was no violation of any article of the Convention.

The second case to which I would briefly refer is *A v Secretary of State for the Home Department* [2005] 2 AC 68, known as the *Belmarsh* case. This concerned the right to liberty of persons who were suspected terrorists who had been detained indefinitely under certificates issued by the Home Secretary under section 23 of the Anti-terrorism, Crime and Security Act 2001. The House quashed an order derogating from the Convention on the grounds that the requirements for derogation had not been fulfilled. The House also held that section 23 of the 2001 Act was incompatible with the Convention. I have considered this landmark case in depth elsewhere.[4] For present purposes, I draw attention to the powerful statement of the importance of the right to personal freedom in Lord Bingham's speech:

36 In urging the fundamental importance of the right to personal freedom, as the sixth step in their proportionality argument, the appellants were able to draw on the long libertarian tradition of English law, dating back to chapter 39 of Magna Carta 1215, given effect in the ancient remedy of habeas corpus, declared in the Petition of Right 1628, upheld in a series of landmark decisions down the centuries and embodied in the substance and procedure of the law to our own day. Recent statements, not in themselves remarkable, may be found in *In re S-C (Mental Patient: Habeas Corpus)*[1996] QB 599, 603 and *In re Wasfi Suleman Mahmod* [1995] Imm AR 311, 314. In its treatment of article 5 of the European Convention, the European Court also has recognised the prime importance of personal freedom. In *Kurt v Turkey* (1998) 27 EHRR 373, para 122, it referred to 'the fundamental importance of the guarantees contained in article 5 for securing the right of individuals in a democracy to be free from arbitrary detention at the hands of the authorities' and to the need to interpret narrowly any exception to 'a most basic guarantee of individual freedom'. In *Garcia Alva v Germany* (2001) 37 EHRR 335, para 39, it referred to 'the dramatic impact of deprivation of liberty on the fundamental rights of the person concerned'. The authors of the 'Siracusa Principles', although acknowledging that the protection against arbitrary detention (article 9 of the ICCPR) might be limited if strictly required by the exigencies of an emergency situation (article 4), were none the less of the opinion that some rights could never be denied in any conceivable emergency and, in particular (para 70 (b)), 'no person shall be detained for an indefinite period of time, whether detained pending judicial investigation or trial or detained without charge...

This is a timeless reminder of the fundamental nature of the right to liberty of the person.

---

[4] 'Human Rights in an Age of Terrorism' (2005) 121 LQR 604.

John Stuart Mill—a Little About the Man and his Place in History

Mill lived from 1806 to 1873. From a very early age, he was educated by his father to be a utilitarian after the philosopher, Jeremy Bentham. The details of his extraordinary education can be found in Mill's autobiography.[5] But Mill used his intense early education to go beyond the utilitarian thinking on which his father had brought him up. In his early 20s, he went through a personal crisis which he describes in his autobiography. He overcame that crisis and went on to revise utilitarian philosophy. His theory focused on the importance of the individuality and autonomy of individual members of society. He wrote several works, of which *On Liberty* is probably the best known.

Mill wrote *On Liberty* in 1859 in memory of Harriet Taylor, his long time confidante, who, after her first husband's death, became his wife. She died in 1858. In 1865, Mill became a Member of Parliament. He campaigned unsuccessfully for women to be given the vote in Parliamentary elections. However, in his time as an MP, a bill giving women the right to vote in municipal elections passed through the House of Commons unopposed in June 1869. Mill helped to bring about the passing of The Married Women's Property Act 1870, which gave women the right to hold property in their own name after matrimony. It has been said that, by the beginning of the 20th century, Mill had come to displace Locke as the guardian of liberty.[6] I do not, of course, suggest that Mill was the only philosopher who has had any influence on the Convention but he may well have been one of the philosophers who had the greatest influence on it.

On Liberty—The Basic Themes

Much had been written about Mill's short but powerful essay, *On Liberty*. In his recent biography of Mill,[7] Richard Reeves wrote that:

Few will doubt the status of *On Liberty* as a masterpiece; as a panegyric for individual liberty and the nobility of a self-governed life it remains unsurpassed.[8]

Mill's work had an immense effect on Victorian thought and continues to have a great influence today. Reeves describes *On Liberty* as an intellectual hand grenade rolled into the reading rooms of all the best clubs.[9]

---

[5] JS Mill, *Autobiography* (1873).
[6] AW Brian Simpson, *Human Rights and the End of Empire: Britain and the Genesis of the European Convention* (Oxford) 22.
[7] Richard Reeves, *John Stuart Mill Victorian Firebrand* (Atlantic Books, 2007).
[8] Ibid, p 263.
[9] P 296.

There are two particular arguments in *On Liberty* that are of interest in relation to the Convention. They are intertwined with each other. The first argument is known as the harm principle. Mill wrote that the object of the essay was to assert this principle as one which should govern all control exerted by society over an individual whether by controlling him physically or by 'the moral coercion of public opinion'. He famously wrote that:

That principle is, that the sole end for which mankind are warranted, individually or collectively, in interfering with the liberty of action of any of their number, is self-protection. That the only purpose for which power can be rightfully exercised over any member of the civilised community, against his will, is to prevent harm to others. His own good, either physical or moral, is not a sufficient warrant.

An individual was entitled to act without restriction unless his conduct concerned others:

To justify [compulsion], the conduct from which it is desired to deter him, must be calculated to produce evil to someone else. The only part of the conduct of any one, for which he is amenable to society, is that which concerns others. In the part which merely concerns himself, his independence is, of right, absolute. Over himself, over his own body and mind, the individual is sovereign.

Another argument which Mill develops in his essay is that each individual has a right to liberty of self-development. Again this is subject to the rights of others. He says in *On Liberty*:

It is not by wearing down into uniformity all that is individual in themselves, but by cultivating it and calling it forth, within the limits imposed by the rights and interests of others, that human beings become a noble and beautiful object of contemplation; and as the works partake the character of those who do them, by the same process human life also becomes rich, diversified and animating, furnishing more abundant aliment to high thoughts and elevating feelings, and strengthening the tie which binds every individual to the race, by making the race infinitely better worth belonging to. In proportion to the development of his individuality, each person becomes more valuable to himself, and is therefore capable of being more valuable to others. There is a greater fullness of life about his own existence, and when there is more life in the units there is more in the mass which is composed of them... it is only the cultivation of individuality which produces, or can produce, well developed human beings...

The more that individuals developed themselves the more they and society would benefit.

In drawing a line between liberty of self-development and harm to others, Mill was talking about what might be called today the individual's need for private space or privacy, as opposed to the public space that the state or other members of society can enter. Both arguments share an underlying belief that people should be allowed to act in accordance with their own beliefs. This is not simply liberty in a political sense of freedom from state interference but liberty in a much wider, personal sense.

Liberty should be allowed to individuals as far as possible. That is not to say that there are no limits on the right of an individual to cause harm to himself. Mill recognized, for example, that a man should not be free to sell himself into slavery: 'The principle of freedom cannot require that the person be free not to be free.'

Liberty in this wider sense used by Mill is an essential element of a plural society which enjoys freedom under the law. Liberty in this sense is consistent with, for example, diversity of religious practices, and it facilitates and mandates toleration of them. This is important because religious and cultural differences often pose challenges for societies which, like that of the United Kingdom, are increasingly heterogeneous. This point was one of the points which Lord Bingham noted in his lecture. But toleration of difference comes to an end if it leads to violence or other harm. Moreover, as Passayat J of the Supreme Court of India said, a religion which teaches violence 'strikes at the very root of an orderly society'.[10]

There are many questions that Mill's arguments leave unanswered or that are not worked out. For instance, many aspects of the concept of 'harm' are unclear. Does it, for example, include harm of which the victim of it is unaware? One might be tempted to answer that question in the negative, but the question whether harm takes place may well depend on the type of harm. It is thus possible to envisage examples of harm where knowledge of it is irrelevant to an invasion of another's rights (such as the inclusion of erroneous information about an individual in his personnel file, thus adversely affecting his promotion prospects in his employment). There can be differences of view as to what constitutes harm. Smoking in public places is now illegal, but there were those who argued that smoking caused no harm to others because of the heavy taxes which smokers pay on the purchase of cigarettes, which are said to outweigh the cost to the National Health Service of illnesses caused by smoking.

So far as the right to liberty of self-development is concerned, this is open to objection that individuals cannot simply live in isolation from others. As John Donne wrote, no man is an island entire of itself.[11] In the modern world, governments often claim the right to regulate the conduct of individual, which only harms themselves. Moreover, the right to liberty of self-development assumes that that is what most individuals want and what will bring them greatest satisfaction. That is not always the case, and Mill's argument has been described as elitist. Although Mill was a campaigner for women's rights and many other causes, he does not enter into the problems that arise from the fact that some individuals are unable to exercise their right of liberty of self-development for lack of resources. Mill does not argue that resources should be redistributed so that everyone is able effectively to exercise their right of liberty to self-development: without resources, liberty, like justice, may be said to be open to everyone like the Ritz Hotel.[12] The right to liberty of self-development might mean that a person

---

[10] *Zahira Habibulla H Sheik v Gujurat* (The Best Bakery case) 2004 (4) SCC 158.

[11] J Donne, *Devotions*.

[12] Meaning the reverse, namely that it is effectively not so open because of the high costs of litigation and the costs-shifting rule.

should not, for instance, have the right to medical help if he chose to harm himself. Some people are in a weak position, and some are in a strong position: if the weak are to be protected the state must sometimes interfere with the freedom of action of the strong. A person who suffers from an addiction may need help to throw off his addiction: it is not clear whether he should be treated like the person who agrees to sell himself into slavery. These are some of the issues that *On Liberty* does not address or resolve.

In the 20th century, Isaiah Berlin went on to draw a distinction between negative liberty and positive liberty.[13] Negative liberty is freedom from interference, such as freedom to ride a bicycle without a helmet. Berlin regarded positive liberty as freedom to achieve one's potential. Berlin argued that democracy must confer both sorts of liberty on its citizens. The arguments are advanced in this essay are important. There are similarities between this analysis and the arguments in *On Liberty*.

The Convention and *On Liberty*

Interestingly, the word 'liberty' is only used in the Convention in one place, namely Article 5, which guarantees the right to liberty and security of person.[14]

---

[13] Isaiah Berlin, *Two Concepts of Liberty* republished in *Liberty* (edited by Henry Hardy) (Oxford, 2002).

[14] Art 5 provides: (1) Everyone has the right to liberty and security of person. No one shall be deprived of his liberty save in the following cases and in accordance with a procedure prescribed by law:

(a) the lawful detention of a person after conviction by a competent court;
(b) the lawful arrest or detention of a person for non-compliance with the lawful order of a court or in order to secure the fulfilment of any obligation prescribed by law;
(c) the lawful arrest or detention of a person effected for the purpose of bringing him before the competent legal authority on reasonable suspicion of having committed an offence or when it is reasonably considered necessary to prevent his committing an offence or fleeing after having done so;
(d) the detention of a minor by lawful order for the purpose of educational supervision or his lawful detention for the purpose of bringing him before the competent legal authority;
(e) the lawful detention of persons for the prevention of the spreading of infectious diseases, of persons of unsound mind, alcoholics or drug addicts or vagrants;
(f) the lawful arrest or detention of a person to prevent his effecting an unauthorized entry into the country or of a person against whom action is being taken with a view to deportation or extradition.

(2) Everyone who is arrested shall be informed promptly, in a language which he understands, of the reasons for his arrest and of any charge against him.

(3) Everyone arrested or detained in accordance with the provisions of paragraph 1(c) of this Article shall be brought promptly before a judge or other officer authorized by law to exercise judicial power and shall be entitled to trial within a reasonable time or to release pending trial. Release may be conditioned by guarantees to appear for trial.

(4) Everyone who is deprived of his liberty by arrest or detention shall be entitled to take proceedings by which the lawfulness of his detention shall be decided speedily by a court and his release ordered if the detention is not lawful.

(5) Everyone who has been the victim of arrest or detention in contravention of the provisions of this Article shall have an enforceable right to compensation.

Lawyers tend to think of liberty in terms of physical liberty and that is the sense in which the word 'liberty' is used in the European Convention on Human Rights. The word 'freedom' is the word used by the Convention to denote liberty in the wide sense used by Mill. Thus, for example, the fourth preamble to the Convention states that the signatories reaffirm 'their profound belief in those fundamental freedoms which are the foundation of justice and peace in the world and best maintained on the one hand by an effective political democracy and on the other by a common understanding and observance of human rights on which they depend'. Article 1 states that the parties to the Convention agree to secure within their jurisdiction the rights and freedoms defined in the Convention. Article 9 guarantees the right to freedom of thought, conscience, and religion. Article 10 guarantees the right to freedom of expression and Article 11 guarantees the right to freedom of peaceful assembly and to freedom of association with others. Article 17 states that Convention rights do not imply the right to engage in any activity aimed at the destruction of the rights and freedoms set out in the Convention. Thus the Convention uses the word 'freedom' as freedom from control by others and the state. This is the sense in which Mill has principally used the term 'liberty' in his essay.

Mill stressed the importance of the individual. This idea is consistent with the Convention, which confers a series of rights on each individual member of society being a person who is entitled to rights. The individual, and not the state, assumes the centre stage.

Mill tells us that the core idea in *On Liberty* is what has become known as the harm principle. He describes a very generalized right of liberty, which is always subject to a limitation if harm is caused to third parties. There is a direct parallel here with the Convention. Although the Convention does not create a general right of liberty, it creates a number of separate rights. Some of them are what are known as 'qualified' rights, such as the right to freedom of expression in Article 10:

(1) Everyone has the right to freedom of expression. This right shall include freedom to hold opinions and to receive and impart information and ideas without interference by public authority and regardless of frontiers. This Article shall not prevent States from requiring the licensing of broadcasting, television or cinema enterprises.

(2) The exercise of these freedoms, since it carries with it duties and responsibilities, may be subject to such formalities, conditions, restrictions or penalties as are prescribed by law and are necessary in a democratic society, in the interests of national security, territorial integrity or public safety, for the prevention of disorder or crime, for the protection of health or morals, for the protection of the reputation or rights of others, for preventing the disclosure of information received in confidence, or for maintaining the authority and impartiality of the judiciary.

Qualified rights are designed to give the individual the maximum private space in which to exercise his freedom but his freedom ends when the limitation is applicable. As can be seen from Article 10(2), this can broadly be described as the point at which harm to others begins. So, instead of creating a general right of liberty, the Convention may be said to create a number of specific rights of liberty, which, like Mill's concept of liberty, are subject to limitation where harm to others occurs. Mill's concept of harm is a very general concept. The Convention concretizes harm in terms of the types of harm specified in the limitations on Convention rights, for example in Article 10(2).

Not all rights are qualified rights. For instance, Article 3 guarantees the right not to be subjected to inhuman or degrading treatment. This right is not subject to any qualification. Under the Convention, this right is of such importance that a violation cannot be justified. Thus a violation cannot, for instance, be justified on the grounds that it is necessary for the purpose of preventing crime, which may cause harm to others.

The parallels between *On Liberty* and the Convention do not end there. The right to liberty of self-development appears to finds its reflection in the jurisprudence of the Strasbourg court under Article 8. This, too, is a qualified right. It provides:

(1) Everyone has the right to respect for his private and family life, his home and his correspondence.
(2) There shall be no interference by a public authority with the exercise of this right except such as is in accordance with the law and is necessary in a democratic society in the interests of national security, public safety or the economic well-being of the country, for the prevention of disorder or crime, for the protection of health or morals, or for the protection of the rights and freedoms of others.

The concept of respect for private life is a wide one. One of the leading cases is *Bensaid v United Kingdom*.[15] In this case the Strasbourg court emphasized the width of this concept and did so in language redolent of Mill's right to liberty of self-development:

47. Private life is a broad term not susceptible to exhaustive definition. The Court has already held that elements such as gender identification, name and sexual orientation and sexual life are important elements of the personal sphere protected by Art 8 (see e.g. the *B v France* judgment of 25 March 1992, Series A No. 232-C, para 63; the *Burghartz v Switzerland* judgment of 22 February 1994, Series A No. 280-B, para 24; the *Dudgeon v the United Kingdom* judgment of 22 October 1991, Series A No. 45, para 41, and the *Laskey, Jaggard and Brown v the United Kingdom* judgment of 19 February 1997, *Reports* 1997-1, para 36). Mental health must also be regarded as a crucial part of private life associated with the aspect of moral integrity. Article 8 protects a right to identity and personal development, and the right to establish and develop relationships with other human beings and the outside world (see e.g., *Burghartz v Switzerland*, Comm. Report, *op cit*, para 47; *Friedl v Austria*, Series A No. 305-B, Comm Report, para 45). The preservation of mental stability is in that context an indispensable precondition to effective enjoyment of the right to respect for private life.

---

[15] [2001] ECHR 44599/98.

In *R(Razgar) v Secretary of State for the Home Department* [2004] 2 AC 368, Lord Walker rightly warned that the language of the last two sentences of this paragraph is imprecise and and must be treated with caution. He said:

This language is wide and imprecise and it must in my opinion be treated with some caution. There is no general human right to good physical and mental health any more than there is a human right to expect (rather than to pursue) happiness.[16]

Nonetheless, the parallel between the Convention jurisprudence, with its reference to the protection of a right to personal development, and the right to liberty of self-development expressed in *On Liberty*, is striking.

As I have already indicated, Mill did not deal with a number of issues to which his idea of liberty gave rise. Mill never had to tackle the question of proportionality. But he would no doubt have approved of the idea of proportionality in the sense of requiring a minimum interference with human rights. Mill did not have to deal with the conflicts that arise in cases under Article 1 of the first protocol to the Convention between the right of individual members of society to property and the right of the state to take away the property for the good of the community. Here the state has a large margin of appreciation, and the level of protection guaranteed by the Convention for the individual is comparatively low.[17]

Conclusions

For all its imprecision and imperfections Mill's essay *On Liberty* has within it a fundamental truth about the importance of the individual and the value of human life in its fullest sense, which is also at the heart of the Convention. I would not say that Mill was the only philosopher whose thinking reflects Convention values. I would not say that his thinking always reflects Convention values. It is sufficient for the purposes of this essay that he is one such philosopher and that some parallels can be found between his work and Convention jurisprudence. This may not seem a wholly surprising conclusion, but it is one which enables the reader to see the Convention, its structure, jurisprudence and achievement in a new and different light and from a different perspective.

Mill's *On Liberty* does not, of course, provide anything approaching a comprehensive insight into the Convention. Nor could it do so, as it is not itself a hard-edged analysis of liberty. However, Mill's work underscores the role of the Convention as an instrument of a liberal society.

A half-forgotten statue of John Stuart Mill, with his finely-chiselled face looking to the horizon, stands in Temple Place, just outside the Middle Temple on the edge of legal London. Lord Bingham must often have walked past it on his way to and from the Temple. Perhaps Mill's writing provided some inspiration for his

---

[16] [34].   [17] See, e.g., *James v United Kingdom* [1986] ECHR 8793/79.

work. We shall remember Lord Bingham for many achievements, not least that of being the senior Law Lord when the Human Rights Act 1998 was brought into force. He was also very much in favour of the institution of a Supreme Court of the United Kingdom, which will open after his retirement. The institution of the new Supreme Court will be another major development in the justice system of this country that owes much to Lord Bingham.

Indeed, the brief survey of Mill's work in this essay suggests that the new justices of the Supreme Court could do worse than to ask for the statue of John Stuart Mill to be moved to Parliament Square outside the new Supreme Court building. It would remind the justices, and those who visit the new Supreme Court as litigants or otherwise, of the meaning of liberty in its fullest sense, and the importance of the concept of liberty to a society which places value on the individual and his or her self-realization.

2

Variations sur la politique jurisprudentielle: Les juges ont-ils une âme?

Guy Canivet

'La logique juridique se présente comme une argumentation qui dépend de la manière dont les juges conçoivent leur missions et de l'idée qu'ils se font du droit et de son fonctionnement dans la société'.[1]

Par cette phrase, Chaïm Perelman conclut son livre *Logique juridique, Nouvelle rhétorique*. Assurément, il y a, comme il le dit, une relation entre le raisonnement juridique, c'est à dire entre la détermination logique du jugement, et la nature de la mission du juge.[2] Selon ce que peut en comprendre un esprit civiliste, en *Common Law* ce lien se réalise par la règle du stare decisis, la logique du raisonnement par analogie ou différenciation est liée à la mission du juge d'inscrire ses jugements dans une continuité historique.[3] En droit civil, selon une culture différente, la décision du juge se situe dans une ligne jurisprudentielle, qui comme en *Common Law*, prend naissance dans l'histoire, mais s'inscrit dans une perspective d'ordre géométrique; outre la reconnaissance des droits des individus, la mission du juge est le maintien d'une cohérence logique d'ensemble du système de droit. Inspirée de l'idée de justice, la décision individuelle s'inscrit dans un courant jurisprudentiel cohérent dans ses évolutions, tant à l'égard du passé que du contexte. Il y a donc une intention dans la réalisation du droit par le juge civiliste, une volonté orientée selon une ligne de construction continue et harmonieuse de l'ordre juridique, en d'autres termes, «une politique jurisprudentielle».

Pourtant, le terme «politique jurisprudentielle» n'est pas référencé dans la doctrine juridique française. On ne le trouve pas dans l'index des ouvrages qui traitent de la jurisprudence. A première vue, ce n'est pas un concept opératoire de la pensée juridique ni même, semble-t-il, un angle d'observation du phénomène de l'activité juridictionnelle.[4] Dans la partie traitant de la jurisprudence de son

---

[1] Chaïm Perelman, *Logique juridique, nouvelle rhétorique*, 2ème édition, Dalloz, 1990.
[2] *La logique judiciaire*, 5ème colloque des instituts d'études judiciaires, PUF, 1969.
[3] Antoine J. Bullier, *La Common Law*, Dalloz, Coll. Connaissance du droit, 2002.
[4] Evelyne Serverin, *De la jurisprudence en droit privé: théorie d'une pratique*, Presses Universitaires de Lyon, 1985; «Juridiction et jurisprudence, deux aspects des activités de justice», *Droit et Société*,

Introduction au droit civil, Jean Carbonnier – dont les travaux sont cependant inspirés par la sociologie du droit – l'ignore lui aussi.[5] Il s'en approche toutefois par deux termes voisins et mieux répertoriés, celui de «politique judiciaire» et celui de «politique législative à l'égard de la jurisprudence». S'il y a évidemment des relations étroites entre la politique jurisprudentielle et ces deux autres concepts, ils ne se recouvrent toutefois pas. Le premier comprend l'ensemble des politiques gouvernant l'organisation et le fonctionnement des juridictions, dépassant par conséquent largement la fonction du jugement, même s'il y a un indéniable lien entre la gestion administrative des contentieux et la politique jurisprudentielle, tandis que le second, examine la relation du législateur avec la jurisprudence et non les fins visées par le juge lorsqu'il applique et interprète la règle de droit.

Toutefois, une recherche informatique à partir de la locution «politique juris-prudentielle» révèle une grande fréquence et une large variété d'emplois du terme, en même temps que le caractère approximatif, intuitif, souvent ambigu du sens qui lui est donné. Les exemples découverts au hasard de cette polysémie vont de «la politique jurisprudentielle» élaborée par la Cour européenne des droits de l'homme pour réguler le flux des recours dont elle est envahie[6] à la «politique jurisprudentielle» du Conseil d'Etat dans l'application des lois portant sur le statut des juifs entre 1940 et 1944.[7]

Il est donc nécessaire de définir méthodiquement l'objet «politique juris-prudentielle», par ses composantes. S'agissant de la jurisprudence,[8] il n'est pas utile ici d'entrer dans l'interminable et vaine discussion sur sa nature: source du droit ou simple autorité. Il suffit de retenir le plus petit dénominateur commun de toutes les définitions qu'en donne la doctrine et que l'on retrouve, par exem-ple, dans la littérature de Gérard Cornu, qui, classant la jurisprudence dans les autorités pour éviter de l'ériger en source du droit, la définit comme *«l'habitude prise par les tribunaux d'appliquer une règle de droit d'une certaine façon, c'est à dire la façon répétitive de juger dans tel ou tel sens».*[9] *«Elle se constitue comme telle»*, dit-il *«par l'accumulation de décisions individuelles»*, un enchaînement de déci-sions spécifiques à chaque espèce, mais constantes dans l'application du même corps de règles. Selon cette conception minimaliste, la jurisprudence s'établit

25, 1993, p 339 et suiv., V° Jurisprudence in *Dictionnaire de la justice*, sous la direction de Loïc Cadièt, Presses Universitaires de France (PUF), 2004.

[5] Jean Carbonnier, Droit civil: Introduction, 27ème édition, Thémis, 2002, p 279 et suiv.

[6] Rapport présenté à l'Assemblée générale des 12–13 décembre 2003, *Quelle réforme pour la Cour européenne des droits de l'homme ?* Disponible sur: <http://archives.cnb.avocat.fr/PDF/2003-12-13_Martin.pdf>.

[7] Philippe Fabre, «L'identité légale des Juifs sous Vichy: La contribution des juges», *Labyrinthe*, mis en ligne le 28 mars 2005. Disponible sur: <http://www.revuelabyrinthe.org/document501.html>.

[8] Frédéric Zenati, *La jurisprudence*, Dalloz, 1991; Maryse Deguergue, V° Jurisprudence in *Dictionnaire de la Culture juridique*, sous la direction de Denis Alland et Stéphane Rials; Christian Chêne, Jean Carbonnier et la querelle de la source ou de l'autorité: permanence d'un vieux débat, disponible sur: <http://www.courdecassation.fr/IMG/File/3-intervention_chene.pdf>.

[9] Gérard Cornu, *Introduction au droit*, 13ème édition, Montchrestien, 2007, p 227.

par la répétition de jugements distincts mais similaires qui finissent par former une série, une suite, une tendance. Elle s'attache donc aux points de droit constamment jugés de la même manière. En cela elle suggère par habitude, autorité ou conviction le sens des jugements à venir. On comprend alors que la fonction juridictionnelle est source de la formation de la jurisprudence. L'activité de juger est primaire, principale, primordiale, tandis que la jurisprudence en est le dérivé, l'accessoire, le sous-produit, l'externalité.

Toute la question est de savoir si cette production de décisions judiciaires neutres, impartiales, objectives, solutionnant des litiges particuliers, appliquant ou interprétant la règle de droit sur un même sujet peut, par répétition, se construire au fil du temps selon une ligne logique, dans une direction déterminée, suivant une tendance voulue, à des fins choisies. Y aurait-il une volonté, une intentionnalité, une «âme» de la jurisprudence? Peut-il y avoir dans la réitération de l'acte de juger une ligne d'action, une inspiration, une direction tendue vers des objectifs choisis? Autrement dit, le juge peut-il donner à son exercice juridictionnel une dimension prospective, en marge de la meilleure solution juridique apportée à chacune des composantes de la suite des jugements? La succession de ces décisions individuelles peut-elle être rationnellement anticipée? Cette construction peut-elle être voulue, décidée, préméditée, peut-elle répondre à un programme? Peut-il y avoir de la part du juge, dans la création de la jurisprudence, une intention tournée vers la réalisation d'un intérêt général, vers une fin dépassant les solutions individuelles? Peut-il, en définitive, y avoir une «politique» dans la construction raisonnée de la jurisprudence?

Se posant la question à propos de la Cour constitutionnelle italienne dont il fut le président, Gustavo Zagrebelsky y apporte une réponse nuancée en introduisant une distinction subtile mais essentielle:[10]

'D'aucuns diront que dans ses décisions, la Cour constitutionnelle exprime des orientations, et les qualifieront alors tranquillement de politiques jurisprudentielles. On peut admettre cette expression, mais certainement pas dans le sens de la politique d'un gouvernement ou d'une majorité parlementaire. Chaque cause est un cas particulier. Pour chacune des décisions de la Cour constitutionnelle, il n'existe ni une majorité préconstituée ni l'élaboration d'orientations programmatiques générales qu'il faudrait poursuivre. Un programme qui s'interposerait entre chaque décision et la Constitution serait nécessairement inconstitutionnel et contraire au devoir de fidélité à la Constitution en général, devoir qui exclut tout lien constitué par des accords contingents dérivant d'un programme de parti. Si l'on peut parler de politique jurisprudentielle, c'est seulement dans un sens rétrospectif. C'est à dire comme bilan a posteriori d'une œuvre qui se prête à être mise en cohérence, à la manière d'un paramètre d'interprétation, même si elle n'obéit pas à des desseins prémédités'.

On comprend aisément le refus de principe d'une orientation partisane de la jurisprudence constitutionnelle. Ce rejet est à replacer dans la situation spécifique

---

[10] Gustavo Zagrebelsky, «Existe-t-il une politique jurisprudentielle de la Cour constitutionnelle italienne?», *Cahiers du Conseil constitutionnel*, n° 20, 2006, Dalloz, p 132 et suiv.

d'une juridiction chargée de faire respecter des équilibres institutionnels et qui entend naturellement se démarquer d'une assemblée politique. Il ne peut y avoir d'orientation politique programmée dans l'interprétation juridictionnelle de la Constitution. Néanmoins Gustavo Zagrebelsky ajoute:

'L'absence d'orientation préconstituée ne signifie pas, cependant, discontinuité de la jurisprudence. Il existe en vérité, une continuité, mais il s'agit d'une continuité sur un plan plus élevé, celui de la Constitution [...] Lorsqu'une question est portée à [l]'examen [de la Cour constitutionnelle], c'est pour confirmer la continuité de la valeur de la Constitution. On ne peut jamais repartir à zéro. S'il n'en était pas ainsi, la décision apparaîtrait, ou plus exactement serait le produit de la pure volonté du moment et non de la raison juridique enracinée dans les textes juridictionnels et élaborée au fil des années par la jurisprudence'.

Ces observations sont le préalable d'un exposé sur les moyens par lesquels la Cour constitutionnelle suit, corrige, reconsidère ou renverse les lignes directrices de sa propre jurisprudence. Une politique jurisprudentielle est une orientation construite de la jurisprudence, selon une trajectoire trouvant son origine, son ancrage dans les précédents et se prolongeant par un examen critique effectué à l'occasion de chacune des espèces qui se succèderont dans le futur. L'orientation «supérieure» de la politique jurisprudentielle est donc la continuité du droit dans son application à des situations inédites. La logique de continuité n'est pas nécessairement linéaire, elle tolère des infléchissements plus ou moins sensibles et même des revirements.

C'est précisément à partir de l'idée de continuité dans l'interprétation du droit, qu'en 2003, le Professeur Nicolas Molfessis avait risqué un argumentaire visant à expliquer la nécessité, pour la Cour de cassation, d'opérer des choix interprétatif dans les divers domaines du contentieux afin de satisfaire le besoin de sécurité juridique.[11] Construite sur les impératifs d'accessibilité du droit, la politique jurisprudentielle suppose une lisibilité et une prévisibilité des solutions juridiques successives qui doivent s'inscrire dans une perspective délibérée, discernable et quelquefois même explicite. Cette réflexion et les réactions auxquelles elle a donné lieu ont montré que, si l'élaboration d'une politique jurisprudentielle procédurale, c'est à dire une directive de la pratique du jugement n'était guère contestée, plus délicate et plus discutée était la justification d'une ligne doctrinale dans l'interprétation continue de la règle de fond. La réponse sur la légitimité d'une politique jurisprudentielle ne serait donc pas absolue mais relative, elle serait conditionnée par les domaines, procéduraux ou matériels, méthodologiques ou idéologiques, dans lesquelles elle se déploie. En définitive, toute la question est de savoir dans quels cas et jusqu'à quel point une juridiction du modèle de la Cour de cassation française peut, à partir de l'ensemble des interprétations du droit

---

[11] Nicolas Molfessis, Conférence intitulée '*La politique jurisprudentielle*' donnée à la Cour de cassation le 10 décembre 2003, <http://www.courdecassation.fr/formation_br_4/2003_2035/presentation_br_politique_jurisprudentielle_8313.html>.

qu'elle énonce, façonner délibérément l'ordre juridique. En opérant de tels choix, en affirmant plus ou moins une volonté créatrice de règles générales, la Cour de cassation adopte nécessairement une posture à l'égard des autres producteurs de normes, législateur, pouvoir réglementaire ou autres ordres juridictionnels internes et internationaux. Elle agit dans et sur un contexte institutionnel pour assumer l'idée qu'elle se fait de sa propre mission.[12]

Il est alors nécessaire d'examiner l'environnement dans lequel se déploie une possible doctrine d'action du juge par la jurisprudence. S'agissant de la Cour de cassation française, on rappellera d'abord qu'elle œuvre dans un système de séparation des pouvoirs qui lui interdit d'empiéter sur la fonction législative et impose la suprématie de la loi.[13] On observera ensuite qu'elle n'est qu'un élément d'un ensemble juridictionnel divisé. Placée au sommet de l'ordre judiciaire national, elle partage la fonction de juger avec deux autres ordres de juridictions, un ordre constitutionnel investi du monopole du contrôle de la constitutionnalité des lois et un ordre administratif, désormais achevé et complet, né de l'interdiction faite au juge judiciaire de s'immiscer dans le fonctionnement de l'administration.[14] Cet ordre administratif s'est vu reconnaître par le Conseil constitutionnel un statut d'indépendance et une compétence propre pour l'annulation et la réformation des décisions prises par l'autorité publique dans l'exercice de prérogatives de puissance publique.[15]

La Cour de cassation est en outre située à l'articulation entre un ordre juridique interne et deux ordres européens. Souveraines dans l'ordre interne, ses décisions sont, dans l'ordre communautaire, subordonnées à l'interprétation des traités donné par la Cour de justice des communautés européennes[16] et, dans celui de la Convention européenne des droits de l'homme, soumises au contrôle a posteriori de la Cour européenne, en ce qui concerne la conformité de ses arrêts aux garanties de la Convention européenne.[17]

Dans un tel cadre, l'élaboration d'une politique jurisprudentielle, destinée à permettre à la Cour de cassation de remplir sa mission, est expressément comprise dans la méthode de réalisation pratique du droit, comme elle est de la nature de

[12] Guy Canivet, *Vision prospective de la Cour de cassation*, Conférence à l'Académie des sciences morales et politiques, texte disponible sur: <http://www.asmp.fr/travaux/communications/2006/canivet.htm>.
[13] Michel Troper, *La Séparation des pouvoirs et l'histoire constitutionnelle de la France*, 2ème édition, Librairie générale de droit et de jurisprudence (LGDJ), 1980; Thierry S. Renoux, V° Séparation des pouvoirs, in *Dictionnaire de la justice*, sous la direction de Loïc Cadiet, PUF, 2004.
[14] Serge Gunchard, *Institutions judiciaires*, 9ème édition, Dalloz, 2007.
[15] Conseil constitutionnel, décisions n° 71-44 du 16 juillet 1971, n°80-119-DC du 22 juillet 1980 et n° 86-224-DC du 23 janvier 1987; Jean-Louis Debré, Jean-Louis Debré, discours intitulée «*Justice et séparation des pouvoirs en droit constitutionnel français*» prononcée *lors de la deuxième conférence régionale du monde arabe à DOHA, au Qatar, les 27 et 28 avril 2008.*
[16] Joël Rideau, *Droit institutionnel de l'Union et des Communautés européennes*, 5ème édition, LGDJ, 2006, p. 881 et suiv.
[17] Jean-François Renucci, *Traité de droit européen des droits de l'homme*, LGDJ, 2007, p 715 et suiv.

sa fonction de gardienne de la cohérence de l'ordre juridique général national et de son articulation avec l'ordre supranational. Fixant, à cette occasion, les règles de bonne exécution de leurs tâches par les juridictions, autrement dit les normes du «bien juger», elle est un instrument de gouvernance de la justice. La politique jurisprudentielle est donc tout à la fois une méthode de réalisation du droit et un instrument de gouvernance de la justice. Comprises au sens rhétorique, ces propositions ne prétendent pas définir des règles de conduites; elles ne sont que des énoncés éphémères, vrais ou faux, destinés à poursuivre un raisonnement qui ne s'épuise évidemment pas dans cette modeste variation, dédiée à Lord Bingham of Cornhill, l'un des grands architectes du système de *Common Law* et rénovateur de l'organisation judiciaire du Royaume Uni.

La politique jurisprudentielle comme méthode de réalisation du droit

Parmi les différentes missions d'une Cour de cassation, la régulation de la méthode de réalisation pratique du droit est le domaine dans lequel la légitimité d'une politique jurisprudentielle est le moins discutable, tandis que, tout autant dans la nature de sa mission de gardien de la cohérence de l'ordre juridique, sa fonction d'interprète est davantage controversée.

La politique jurisprudentielle d'unification du droit

Historiquement la Cour de cassation, créée dès le début de l'époque révolutionnaire, en 1790, sous la dénomination de Tribunal de cassation, a été spécifiquement instituée pour assurer l'interprétation uniforme de la règle de droit votée par le corps législatif.[18] Une seule loi pour l'ensemble du territoire national **est** uniformément interprétée sous le contrôle d'une juridiction unique. *«Il y a, pour toute la République, une cour de cassation»* reprend à la suite des textes révolutionnaires l'article L. 411-1 du Code de l'organisation judiciaire. Elle statue sur des pourvois formés contre les décisions des juridictions judiciaires de dernier ressort,[19] en général les cours d'appel. Ces pourvois compris comme des recours extraordinaires visant, selon l'expression légale consacrée, à faire *«censurer la non conformité du jugement attaqué aux règles de droit».*[20]

Pour assurer cette police unificatrice de la loi, la Cour de cassation, qui ne juge pas les affaires[21] et abandonne les questions de fait aux juges du fond, dispose de

---

[18] F. Zénati, La nature de la Cour de cassation, *Bulletin d'information de la Cour de cassation*, 15 avril 2003, pp 3–10.
[19] Art L 411-2 du Code de l'organisation judiciaire.
[20] Art 604 du Code de procédure civile.
[21] Art L 411-2, alinéa 2 du Code de l'organisation judiciaire.

règles de procédure et de principes d'organisation appropriés.[22] La pratique plus ou moins rationnelle, systématique, efficiente, stratégique de mise en œuvre de ces moyens de régulation est le premier stade de l'élaboration de sa politique jurisprudentielle. Dans la variété des instruments qui déterminent l'interprétation et la portée que la Cour de cassation donne de ses propres règles de fonctionnement, se distinguent, d'une part, les règles du pourvoi en cassation, d'autre part, la technique du contrôle normatif exercé sur les jugements qui lui sont soumis.[23]

La politique unificatrice de la procédure de cassation

L'obligation primordiale de la fonction unificatrice de la Cour de cassation est évidemment la cohérence interne de ses propres décisions. Le gardien doit se garder lui-même. L'unité allait de soi lorsque les formations de la Cour de cassation étaient limitées à une chambre civile et une chambre criminelle, composées d'un nombre restreint de juges. Elle est devenue problématique avec la prolifération des juges et des formations de jugement successivement créées pour faire face à l'augmentation des recours, soit par la multiplication des chambres civiles, de une à cinq,[24] soit par leur division en sections, puis en formations restreintes à trois juges.[25] Le phénomène est connu: la multiplication des juges et des formations de jugement engendre un risque d'interprétations différentes de la loi. La nécessité de régler ces divergences internes a été prise en compte par le législateur puisqu'une procédure et une formation particulières de la Cour, la Chambre mixte, réunissant des magistrats de plusieurs chambres, ont été spécialement instituées pour traiter les questions *«ayant reçu ou étant susceptibles de recevoir devant les chambres des solutions divergentes».*[26]

Pour répondre à cet impératif de sécurité dans l'interprétation du droit, Il a fallu se doter d'instruments d'observation de la production jurisprudentielle interne et de traitements curatifs et préventifs de possibles incohérences interprétatives. Détection par le service de documentation et d'études[27] en collaboration avec le corps d'avocat institué auprès de la Cour, règlements informels par des réunions de travail entre présidents de chambre, renvois en chambre mixte,[28] enfin détection préventive des occurrences de contradiction dans le contentieux en cours sont les diverses démarches de cette politique d'harmonisation de la jurisprudence.

---

[22] Arts 604 et suiv. et 973 et suiv. du Code de procédure civile; Art 567 et suiv. du Code de procédure pénale; Art. L. 411–1 et suiv. et R 121-1 et suiv. du Code de l'organisation judiciaire.

[23] Jacques Boré, *La cassation en matière civile*, 4ème édition, Dalloz, 2008; Jacques et Louis Boré, *la cassation en matière pénale*, Dalloz, 2004; Jean Buffet (dir.), *Droit et pratique de la cassation en matière civile*, 2ème éd., Litec, 2003; Marie-Noëlle Jobard-Bachellier, La technique de cassation: *Pourvois et arrêts en matière civile*, Dalloz, 2006.

[24] Art L 421-1, R 121-3 du Code de l'organisation judiciaire.

[25] Art L 431-1 du Code de l'organisation judiciaire.

[26] Art L 431-5 du Code de l'organisation judiciaire.

[27] Art R 131-16 du Code de l'organisation judiciaire.

[28] Art L 431-5 du Code de l'organisation judiciaire.

La mission unificatrice de la Cour de cassation comprend aussi l'objectif d'assurer le respect des interprétations qu'elle donne par les juridictions du fond.[29] Là encore des mécanismes ont été spécialement institués par la loi, notamment le renvoi en une formation solennelle réunissant les présidents et membres aînés de toutes les chambres de la Cour: l'assemblée plénière,[30] qui a pour fonction de régler les solutions divergentes entre les juges du fond et la cour de cassation. Le recours à cette procédure est destiné, soit à imposer l'autorité de la doctrine de la Cour de cassation après un premier arrêt dans une affaire, suivi d'une rébellion de la Cour de renvoi, soit de régler définitivement une question sur laquelle est constaté un rejet par certaines juridictions du fond de la solution interprétative donnée par la Cour. On transite ainsi du particulier au général, de la solution individuelle et de l'autorité juridique spécifique à l'arrêt de la cour, à la solution collective par recours à une directive d'interprétative ayant l'autorité générale qui s'attache à la règle énoncée par la formation la plus solennelle de la Cour.[31] Par sa composition, l'assemblée plénière représente, en effet, l'unité et l'autorité de la Cour.[32]

Selon le Code de l'organisation judiciaire, le recours à cette formation solennelle peut être décidé d'emblée en cas de solutions divergentes entre les juges du fond.[33] On gravit ici un échelon dans la police jurisprudentielle. Par cette disposition, la Cour de cassation est investie d'une mission générale de maintenance de l'ordre juridique qu'elle ne peut évidemment régler que par sa propre jurisprudence. Ce sont ici les instruments de détection qui sont indispensables. Pour discerner les courants d'interprétations divergentes de la loi au sein des juridictions du fond, encore faut-il avoir une vision exhaustive de leur production. Il a donc été nécessaire de créer une base complète de la jurisprudence des cours d'appel,[34] en attendant la réalisation d'un programme plus ample de collecte et d'exploitation de l'ensemble des jugements rendus dans l'ordre judiciaire au premier et second degré de juridiction. C'est l'exploitation systématique de cette base qui permet à la Cour de cassation de vérifier, non pas au gré des espèces remarquables et spécialement signalées par la doctrine, mais dans la masse des jugements, méthodiquement organisée, classée et répertoriée, comment la loi est interprétée. Elle peut ainsi choisir méthodiquement ses terrains d'intervention interprétative par la sélection des recours. Pour agir sur l'ensemble de la production judiciaire, il faut se donner les moyens de distinguer, dans les affaires en cours, celles qui permettent d'apporter des solutions aux questions controversées.

Ces opérations de sélection des affaires pertinentes pour la régulation interprétative requièrent, elles aussi, des instruments dont la Cour de cassation s'est

[29] Art 621 du Code de procédure pénale.
[30] Art L 431-6 du Code de l'organisation judiciaire.
[31] Art L 431-4 alinéa 2 du Code de l'organisation judiciaire.
[32] Guy Canivet, L'autorité du jugement, *De L'autorité*, Colloque de rentrée du Collège de France, 18 et 19 octobre 2007 *Lettre du Collège de France*, n° 21, disponible sur: <http://www.college-de-france.fr/media/ins_let/UPL55996_J21COLRENTREE.pdf>.
[33] Arts L 431- et L 431-7 du Code l'organisation judiciaire.
[34] Art R 131-16 du Code de l'organisation judiciaire.

dotée. L'importance des procédures et des formations de jugement est graduée en fonction de la nature et de la complexité des affaires à traiter: formations de base à trois juges, section d'une chambre comprenant en général 7 juges, sections réunies de la chambre, ou assemblée plénière. Des procédures d'urgence permettant, en outre, de juger les affaires qui nécessitent une intervention immédiate de la Cour régulatrice?[35] Récemment a été institué un système général de tri qui offre la possibilité de rejeter sans motifs, par une décision de «non admission»[36] équivalente à un rejet, les pourvois qui ne posent pas de question sérieuse. Au fil du temps toute une logistique judiciaire, constituée de tamis successifs, a été conçue et mise en place dans le cadre d'un programme méthodique de traitement sélectif et rationnel des affaires.[37]

Au rang de ces moyens figure la possibilité pour la Cour de cassation, lorsqu'elle veut imposer sa solution sans discussion possible aux juridictions du fond, de casser sans renvoi lorsque le motif de cassation n'implique pas qu'il soit à nouveau statué au fond ou lorsqu'elle dispose de tous les éléments de fait lui permettant de mettre fin au litige.[38] En ce cas son interprétation du droit est d'emblée indiscutable. Une observation statistique des arrêts de cassation sans renvoi montre que les chambres ont des pratiques bien différentes dans l'utilisation de cette faculté, selon la conception plus ou mois rigoureuse qu'elles ont de la mission de la Cour et de la souveraineté du pouvoir du juge du fond dans la détermination des faits de l'espèce.

En définitive, à la faveur de réformes successives, la Cour de cassation peut utiliser des moyens l'autorisant, comme le font les cours suprêmes de *Common Law*, à concentrer son activité sur les affaires importantes afin de traiter les questions juridiques problématiques de manière approfondie selon un agenda qu'elle décide. La notion «de question de principe», qui requiert une attention particulière et la mise en œuvre de moyens d'étude plus importants, résulte de la loi. Le Code de l'organisation judiciaire indique, qu'à l'initiative du premier président, des chambres ou du parquet général, les affaires posant une question de principe peuvent être traitées directement par l'assemblée plénière.[39] Ces autorités étant libre dans leur appréciation de la «question de principe», on mesure la part de choix qui leur est concédée pour distinguer le cas dans lesquels il convient d'aborder des difficultés d'interprétation ou d'adaptation de la loi estimées prioritaires et à quel moment il convient de le faire.

Une telle initiative peut venir des juridictions de base qui, grâce à une procédure d'avis[40] sont habilitées à saisir la Cour de cassation, en cours d'instance et par renvoi préjudiciel, des difficultés d'interprétation nouvellement révélées. L'avis de

---

[35] Art 1009 du Code de procédure civile.
[36] Art L 431-1 du Code de l'organisation judiciaire.
[37] Jean-François Weber, *La Cour de cassation*, La Documentation française, 2006.
[38] Art L 411-3 du Code de l'organisation judiciaire.
[39] Art L 431-6 du Code de l'organisation judiciaire
[40] Art R 151-1 du Code de l'organisation judiciaire; Art 1031-1 et suiv. du Code de procédure civile; Art 706-64 à 706-70 du Code de procédure pénale.

la Cour sur le sens de la disposition ambiguë est décidé par une formation spéciale réunissant les présidents de toutes les chambres, sous la présidence du premier président. Il leur est donné dans un délai bref. Ces juridictions sont ensuite en mesure de résoudre le litige selon une interprétation vérifiée, en quelque sorte «labellisée» de la loi. Publiée au Journal officiel, l'interprétation de la Cour de cassation s'impose alors naturellement pour la solution de tous les litiges semblables.

Dans son ensemble, cet appareil rend possible la mise en place d'efficaces politiques jurisprudentielles d'interprétation des nouvelles lois.[41] Avant de laisser se développer un contentieux important et étalé dans le temps sur les difficultés d'interprétation de lois récemment promulguées, la Cour de cassation est en mesure, en relation avec l'ensemble des juridictions du fond, de détecter et de traiter sans délais, par des moyens documentaires ou juridictionels appropriés, , les difficultés d'application du texte qui se révèlent dès les premiers procès engagés. Un tel système a été mis en place dès la promulgation de la Loi de sauvegarde des entreprises du 26 juillet 2005[42], grâce auquel ont pu être interprétées très vite et très tôt les règles et notions nouvelles contenues dans cette loi qui réforme en profondeur le traitement des entreprises en difficulté.

Au delà de la cohérence interne du droit se pose la question de l'intégration des droits supranationaux dans le droit national. A défaut de pouvoir se faire spontanément, cette intégration doit être stimulée par une politique volontaire qui passe par la formation des juges au droit européen et l'observation systématique de la jurisprudence des cours supranationales.[43] A cette fin a été institué au sein de la Cour de cassation un service de veille de la jurisprudence européenne qui, examinant au jour le jour les arrêts rendus par les cours de Luxembourg et de Strasbourg, établit et diffuse des notes sur l'impact de ces jurisprudences sur le droit national.

La jurisprudence d'une cour nationale comme la Cour de cassation doit enfin se positionner dans l'ordre mondial et se construire en contemplation de la jurisprudence des grandes cours sur les questions universelles.[44] L'ouverture sur le droit comparé se réalise par la mise à disposition des juges de systèmes informatiques de recherche dans la jurisprudence des ces cours et par la réalisation d'études comparatives confiées à des laboratoires universitaires spécialisés en droit comparé dans les affaires qui le justifient. Tel fut le cas pour la préparation des décisions à rendre en matière de «*wrongful life*»,[45] de statut de fœtus[46] ou de commerce

---

[41] Guy Canivet, L'organisation interne de la Cour de cassation favorise-t-elle l'élaboration de sa jurisprudence?, in *La Cour de cassation et l'élaboration du droit*, Economica, 2004, p 3 et surtout p. 10 et suiv.

[42] <http://www.courdecassation.fr/jurisprudence_publications_documentation_2/actualite_jurisprudence_21/Chambre_comme>.

[43] Cette observation systématique est assurée au sein de la Cour de cassation par l'Observatoire du droit européen, créé en 2002 et dont les publications sont disponibles au: <http://www.courdecassation.fr/jurisprudence_publications_documentation_2/du_droit_2185/>

[44] Guy Canivet, Mads Andenas et Duncan Fairgrieve, *Comparative Law before the Courts*, British Institute of International and Comparative law, 2004.

[45] Cour de cassation, Assemblée plénière, 17 novembre 2000, Bulletin 2000, Assemblée plénière, n° 9, p 15 et 13 juillet 2001, Bulletin 2001 Assemblée plénièreP. n° 10 p 21.

[46] Cour de cassation, Assemblée plénière, 29 juin 2001, Bulletin criminel 2001, n° 165, p 546.

international.[47] Sur ces grandes questions la loi nationale est interprétée en connaissance de ou en référence aux solutions élaborées dans d'autres systèmes.[48]

La politique d'unification de la méthode du jugement

Si, par le travail d'interprétation de la loi, la Cour de cassation a incontestablement une fonction normative, elle est en revanche privée du pouvoir de trancher les litiges. Désormais contenue dans l'article L. 411–2, alinéa 2, du Code de l'organisation judiciaire cette restriction de pouvoir lui interdit en effet, sauf disposition législative contraire, de «connaître du fond des affaires». La technique du contrôle de cassation impose donc une distinction du droit et du fait[49] qui s'applique différemment selon les cas d'ouverture plus ou moins normatif du pourvoi en cassation.[50] D'un côté se trouve la notion de «violation de la loi», destinée à régler les pures questions d'interprétation, de l'autre, les notions de «manque de base légale» et de «défaut de motifs», qui visent à contrôler les qualifications des faits et la logique du raisonnement judiciaire. Ce rapport dialectique entre règle de droit et données de fait pose en définitive la question du contrôle de la Cour de cassation sur les qualifications des notions juridiques opératoires principales ou intermédiaires[51]: notion de faute (dans le droit de la responsabilité), de dol, de violence, d'erreur (dans le droit des contrats), de motif sérieux du licenciement (dans le droit du travail) ou encore d'entreprise (dans le droit économique).

Pendant longtemps la question de l'intensité du contrôle sur ces qualifications s'est posée en termes d'encombrement de la Cour de cassation. L'élargissement du champ de l'examen était à éviter pour ne pas provoquer une augmentation du nombre des recours en l'état d'une juridiction déjà surchargée. Cette question étant désormais résolue,[52] le débat prend tout son sens au regard des choix de politique jurisprudentielle. Jusqu'à quel point la Cour entend-elle guider l'application de la loi par les juges du fond?[53] A cet égard, deux conceptions s'affrontent. La première entend réduire la Cour de cassation à un rôle purement normatif: dès lors que le jugement énonce exactement la loi, peu importe l'application plus ou

---

[47] Cour de cassation, Chambre mixte, 22 avril 2005, Bulletin 2005 Mixt. n° 3 p 9.

[48] Sir Basil Markesinis, *Le droit étranger devant le juge américain et le juge français*, conférence à l'Académie des sciences morales et politiques, Paris, 13 mars 2006, disponible sur: <http://www.asmp.fr/travaux/communications/2006/markesinis.htm>.

[49] Yves Chartier, *La Cour de cassation*, 2ème édition, coll. Connaissance du droit, Dalloz, 2001, p 63.

[50] Art 605 du Code de procédure civile.

[51] Alain Bénabent, *Violation de la loi ou manque de base légale?*, Cycle Droit et technique de cassation 2004–2005 <http://www.courdecassation.fr/formation_br_4/2005_2033/br_violation_8105.html>.

[52] Cour de cassation, rapport annuel de 2007, activité de la Cour, disponible sur: <http://www.courdecassation.fr/jurisprudence_publications_documentation_2/publications_cour_26/em_rapport_annuel_em_36/rapport_2007_2640/>.

[53] Guy Canivet, *Vision prospective de la Cour de cassation*, Conférence à l'Académie des sciences morales et politiques, Paris, 13 novembre 2006, disponible sur: <http://www.courdecassation.fr/jurisprudence_publications_documentation_2/autres_publications_discours_2039/discours_2202/2006_2203/sciences_morales_9619.html>.

moins exacte qu'il en fait à la situation d'espèce soumise à jugement. Selon la seconde , il appartient à la Cour d'exercer une «police du jugement», c'est à dire de vérifier, au-delà de la bonne lecture de la loi, l'application qui en est faite, dans la logique de raisonnement qu'elle impose.[54] Ce contrôle peut aller jusqu'à l'exacte compréhension des pièces ou des éléments de preuve, c'est à dire de «la dénaturation», ce que l'on nomme autrement «l'erreur manifeste d'appréciation» dans le contentieux administratif. Cette différence de conception a des conséquences pratiques non seulement en termes d'unification et d'interprétation de la loi, mais aussi en termes de pertinence de son application à des situations de fait identiques. A une époque où les contrats sont tous plus ou moins normalisés et donnent lieu à des situations contentieuses identiquement répétées, est-il acceptable que la même clause d'un contrat de société, de concession commerciale, de distribution ou de travail, soit diversement appliquée selon la juridiction à laquelle on s'adresse surtout si ce sont les mêmes contractants qui sont en cause ?

On se rend compte que le besoin de sécurité juridique, donc de normalisation, va jusqu'à l'unité des solutions. Cela est particulièrement sensible dans la mise en œuvre du droit de la responsabilité pour la détermination et les éléments d'évaluation du préjudice.[55] Il n'est plus accepté, aussi bien par ceux qui sont victimes de dommages que par ceux qui les réparent, que la nomenclature des préjudices soit aléatoire et que le montant des sommes allouées,[56] soit, dans de larges proportions, différemment apprécié au gré des juridictions. En 1983, le professeur Basil Markesinis avait déjà publié une étude comparative entre droit allemand, anglais et français, montrant l'importance des politiques jurisprudentielles dans la réparation du préjudice économique en terme d'efficacité réparatrice et préventive du droit de la responsabilité.[57] En France, aujourd'hui, se pose donc la question de la normalisation non seulement des postes du dommage corporel mais aussi de l'édition d'une échelle d'évaluation des différentes catégories de préjudice. Estimant qu'il s'agit d'une question de pur fait, la Cour de cassation s'est jusqu'ici abstenue de s'engager dans cette voie. Sa politique jurisprudentielle se borne à la vérification – d'ailleurs distante – du caractère intégral de la réparation?[58]

---

[54] *Rendre compte de la qualité de la justice*, Colloque franco-britannique 14–15 novembre 2003, organisé par le British Institute of International and Comparative Law, l'Institut des hautes études sur la justice, la Société de législation comparée et l'U.M.R de droit comparé de Paris, avec le soutien de l'association Sorbonne-Oxford, , <http://www.courdecassation.fr/ jurisprudence_publications_documentation_2/bulletin_information_cour_cassation_27/ bulletins_information_2003_1615/no_586_1719/>.

[55] Rapport du groupe de travail chargé d'élaborer une nomenclature des préjudices corporels, Groupe de travail dirigé par Jean-Pierre Dinthilac, disponible sur: <http://lesrapports.ladocumentationfrancaise.fr/BRP/064000217/0000.pdf>.

[56] Cour de Cassation, Cycle Risques, assurances, responsabilités 2006–2007 <http://www. courdecassation.fr/jurisprudence_publications_documentation_2/autres_publications_ discours_2039/discours_2202/2006_2203/sciences_morales_9619.html>.

[57] Basil S. Markesinis, «La politique jurisprudentielle et la réparan du préjudice économique en Angleterre: une approche comparative», *Revue internationale de droit comparé*, vol 35 n° 1 , 1983, pp 31–50.

[58] Cour de cassation, chambre civile 2ème, 20 octobre 2005, N° 04-13633, publié au bulletin.

S'agissant d'harmoniser la méthode juridictionnelle dans un domaine essentiel du droit de la responsabilité dont l'application a des conséquences économiques et sociales considérables, son rôle ne serait-il pas d'établir une méthode uniforme d'évaluation des préjudices et d'en contrôler la mise en œuvre?

En droit criminel, une question identique se pose relativement aux principes de détermination du quantum des peines. En cette matière, la chambre criminelle se refuse, elle aussi, à tout contrôle des critères de détermination de la sanction, de sa proportionnalité et de son montant. Elle se borne à vérifier que la peine prononcée se situe dans les limites fixées par la loi?[59] Il en résulte, ici aussi, une large variété d'appréciation des juges, un même fait étant, dans d'importantes proportions, différemment sanctionné selon la juridiction qui se prononce. On sait que dans les systèmes anglais et américain cette question, prise très au sérieux, est réglée par la jurisprudence qui conduit à l'élaboration de lignes directrices de calcul des peines à l'intention des juges.[60] Un tel programme jurisprudentiel ne serait-il pas de la mission de la chambre criminelle de la Cour de cassation? On sait en tout cas que le vide de méthode que laisse son abstention a récemment provoqué l'intervention du législateur qui, à défaut de politique jurisprudentielle, a imposé aux juges.des directives de fixation des peines minimum.[61]

Par l'interprétation du droit matériel

Les politiques jurisprudentielles d'interprétation des lois de fond posent des questions d'une autre nature. Si ces politiques sont inévitables autant qu'indispensables, elles ne peuvent être ni dogmatiques ni intangibles afin de pouvoir s'accorder avec les principes essentiels de la méthode du jugement.

Des politiques inhérentes à la production de la jurisprudence

Les politiques d'interprétation de la loi sont inévitables parce qu'elles sont de la nature de la jurisprudence.[62] Dès lors qu'elle s'inscrit dans la continuité de décisions successives, la jurisprudence suit nécessairement une ligne de force. Ces orientations, déduites des décisions déjà rendues dont elles constituent la cohérence, gouvernent les jugements à venir. Il en est d'abord ainsi parce que les arrêts de la Cour de cassation sont rendus par les mêmes juges. A la Cour, les affaires sont réparties entre les chambres en fonction des matières et les juges sont spécialisés dans des catégories spécifiques de contentieux. Cette spécialisation

---

[59] Cour de cassation, chambre criminelle, 1 avril 2008, N° 07–82787, publié au bulletin.

[60] Au Royaume-Uni ces directives sont élaborées par le Sentencing Guidelines Council dont le site internet est accessible au: <http://www.sentencing-guidelines.gov.uk/> Aux Etats-unis elles sont élaborées par la United States Sentencing Commission et sont disponibles sur <http://www.ussc.gov/guidelin.htm>.

[61] Loi n°2007-1198 du 10 août 2007 renforçant la lutte contre la récidive des majeurs et des mineurs parue au Journal Officiel n°185 du 11 août 2007.

[62] Guy Canivet et Nicolas Molfessis, «La politique jurisprudentielle», in *Mélanges en l'honneur de Jacques Boré la création du droit jurisprudentiel*, Dalloz, 2007, p 79 et suiv.

et la répétition des affaires engendrent une doctrine d'interprétation construite et suivie par un groupe restreint de juges; cette doctrine détermine les solutions futures qu'ils décideront sur les mêmes questions. Au fil des décisions successives, les options se ferment; les interprétations se précisent et s'emboîtent logiquement au point de constituer un système. Ainsi s'élaborent des politiques jurisprudentielles dans chacun des compartiments du droit. Dans chaque matière – droit de la responsabilité, des contrats ou des entreprises en difficulté – on discerne parfaitement, dans la suite des arrêts rendus, les orientations éthiques, économiques ou sociales. Comme le montre la pratique du rapport annuel de la Cour, cette recherche d'unité conceptuelle peut prendre un sens très général. Cependant et depuis quelques années, la Cour y propose aussi un examen raisonné de sa jurisprudence sur un thème déterminé. Un chapitre du rapport pour l'année de 2007[63] est ainsi consacré à l'examen de la santé dans la jurisprudence de la Cour de cassation tandis que le rapport de l'année 2005 s'est penché sur l'innovation technologique.[64] Est donc recherchée, sur ces grandes questions de société, par le bilan qui en est fait, une unité d'ensemble de la jurisprudence, une mise en cohérence à la fois conceptuelle, intellectuelle et philosophique des arrêts rendus dans les divers compartiments du droit pénal, civil, commercial ou social.

Il en va en effet de la jurisprudence comme en tout autre domaine : la politique qui la guide ne procède pas du hasard. Elle implique un choix. Dans cette manière de gouverner et de décider que postule une «politique», il faut en effet une opinion préalable, non seulement un accord sur la décision à prendre mais aussi sur une insertion de cette décision dans un mouvement d'ensemble qui la justifie, la guide, l'explique et la prolonge.[65] Vouloir soumettre le contrat de cession d'actions ou de parts sociales aux garanties de la vente de choses mobilières impose une construction attentive et continue qui se réalise de manière volontaire et cohérente au cours de plusieurs années[66]; insérer le droit des sûretés dans le droit des entreprises en difficultés impose la même démarche patiente et attentive.[67] Ces choix ne sont pas seulement juridiques, ils sont de nature diverse. Ainsi en va-t-il des jurisprudences qui tendent, par exemple, à arrêter la pratique des mères porteuses,[68] à faciliter l'indemnisation des victimes d'accidents de la circulation[69] ou à encadrer le pouvoir du chef d'entreprise sur la vie privée des salariés.[70] Toutes ces illustrations montrent que, derrière les choix juridiques,

[63] Cour de cassation, *rapport annuel 2007*, "La santé dans la jurisprudence de la cour de cassation", La Documentation française, disponible sur: <http://www.courdecassation.fr/jurisprudence_publications_documentation_2/publications_cour_26/em_rapport_annuel_em_36/rapport_2007_2640/>.

[64] Cour de cassation, *rapport annuel 2005*, La Documentation française, disponible sur: <http://www.courdecassation.fr/publications_cour_26/rapport_annuel_36/rapport_2005_582/>.

[65] Guy Canivet et Nicolas Molfessis, «La politique jurisprudentielle», op. cit.

[66] Cour de cassation, chambre commerciale, 23 octobre 2007, N° 06-13979, publié au bulletin.

[67] Cour de cassation, chambre commerciale, 9 mai 2007, N°06-12111, publié au bulletin.

[68] Cour de cassation, Assemblée Plénière, 31 mai 1991, Bulletin 1991 A.P. n° 4 p 5.

[69] Arrêt Desmares, Cour de cassation, 2e Chambre civile, 21 juillet 1982, Bulletin des arrêts Cour de cassation Chambre civile 2 N. 111.

[70] Cour de cassation, chambre mixte, 18 mai 2007, N° 05-40803, publié au bulletin Cassation.

s'impose une pensée plus ou moins structurée – on devrait dire une doctrine – qui commande la décision. De cette ligne générale on déduira être en présence d'une politique du juge libérale ou sociale, progressiste ou conservatrice, nationaliste ou internationaliste, audacieuse ou timorée, répressive ou non, etc. Les appréciations pourraient être multipliées; elles sont mises en lumière par les commentaires des professeurs qui ne s'y trompent guère. Deux aspects spécifiques permettent de mieux montrer les conséquences de ce choix.

Sur le fond, tout d'abord, on observera que les options du juge procèdent nécessairement d'une confrontation entre l'appréciation portée sur la situation sociale constituant l'arrière-fond de sa décision et son désir d'agir sur cette situation. Ainsi, si toute politique jurisprudentielle engage l'avenir, le choix qui la détermine résulte par hypothèse de l'évaluation d'une situation présente, sur laquelle la décision entend influer. C'est la prise de conscience du risque industriel qui a inspiré la jurisprudence sur les accidents du travail.[71] C'est la volonté d'agir sur les risques liés au développement de la circulation automobile qui a systématisé la responsabilité du fait des choses.[72] C'est la considération de l'évolution des formes de rééducation sociale en milieux ouvert des malades mentaux, des mineurs en rééducation ou des délinquants qui a poussé la Cour de cassation à élaborer un principe général de responsabilité du fait d'autrui à la charge de ceux qui les organisent.[73] Un tel constat n'est pas négligeable: il implique en particulier que les juges soient en mesure d'évaluer les situations sur lesquelles ils entendent agir.

La question est alors de savoir jusqu'à quel point une cour, conçue sur le modèle de la Cour de cassation française, peut, en fonction des moyens intellectuels et d'instruction dont elle dispose, s'informer exactement sur le contexte de réception de ses décisions. D'aucuns estiment que ce n'est ni de son aptitude ni de sa fonction. A leurs yeux, seul le législateur est légitimé à apprécier l'intérêt général d'une norme dans le champ économique et social et dispose des moyens appropriés pour agir: le débat parlementaire et la loi votée par les représentants de la nation. Mais si elle ne le fait pas, la Cour se prive des éléments de prise en compte des intérêts directement concernés par la solution jurisprudentielle à décider, à partir de situations contentieuses étroites qui lui sont soumises. Juger qu'un contrat de placement financier cessible à une personne déterminée est un contrat d'épargne ou d'assurance dépasse évidemment largement le litige privé successoral dans lequel la question est posée,[74] admettre que la responsabilité du transporteur de courrier rapide peut ou non être sanctionnée par une indemnisation forfaitaire a évidemment des conséquences sur la compétitivité des entreprises nationales soumises à ce régime.[75] Le juge peut-il ou doit-il évaluer l'impact de ses

---

[71] Philippe Malinvaud, *Droit des obligations*, 10e édition, LITEC, 2007, p 369 et suiv.
[72] Philippe Malinvaud, *ibid.* p 460 et suiv.
[73] Philippe Malinvaud, *ibid.* p 440 et suiv.
[74] Cour de cassation, chambre mixte, 23 novembre 2004, N° 01-13592, Bulletin 2004 Mixte n° 4 p 9.
[75] Cour de cassation, chambre mixte, 22 avril 2005, 2 arrêts Bulletin civil ch. mixte n° 3 et 4.

décisions? Peut-il avoir une approche «conséquentialiste» des solutions jurisprudentielle? C'est de manière interrogative, sinon polémique, qu'ont été reçues et
commentées les initiatives prises par la Cour de cassation qui, en marge des règles
de procédure, consistent à recevoir et parfois à initier des mémoires de groupes
d'intérêts concernés par la jurisprudence. Ces pratiques font ainsi entrer ces éléments de nature économique et sociale dans le débat, à l'instar de la pratique des
briefs d'amicus curiae dans les cours de *Common Law.*[76] C'est de manière tout
aussi dubitative qu'a été appréciée, il y a quelques années, l'expérience d'audition
en séance publique d'une autorité morale sur une grande question éthique en
débat.[77]

Le phénomène d'orientation de la production du juge se renforce par
l'interaction entre la doctrine et la jurisprudence: les arrêts sont commentés par
les professeurs, approuvés par certains, critiqués par d'autres, ce qui les situent
dans une tendance doctrinale qui en constitue la trame intellectuelle. Ainsi se
déterminent par rapport à des écoles de pensée des chaînes de jurisprudences
dans tous les domaines du droit. Solidarisme contractuel contre autonomie de
la volonté, conception contractuelle ou institutionnelle de l'entreprise, spécificité
du contrat de travail, ces orientations s'identifient, se classent et se précisent; elles
guident l'activité d'interprétation.[78]

Inhérente à l'activité jurisprudentielle ces constructions logiques sont indispensables à la prévisibilité de la jurisprudence comme à l'autorité des décisions.
S'il en est ainsi, c'est parce que toute politique jurisprudentielle a vocation à relier
entre elles les décisions passées et les décisions futures. Elle assure donc la prévisibilité du droit, la cohérence et la constance de l'enchaînement des solutions, elle
légitime la décision par son encrage chronologique et renforce le crédit du juge.
Elle est une aspiration à l'unité et à la rationalité puisqu'elle prétend mettre en
ordre rangé des décisions individuelles censées tendre vers un même but général,
sans pour autant s'imposer comme une directive rigide. C'est précisément cet
ordre logique qui convainc que la décision n'est pas le fruit d'un arbitraire du juge
ou d'un caprice du moment mais qu'elle est fondée sur la raison juridique enracinée dans les textes jurisprudentiels anciens.

Pour vérifier l'existence d'un tel besoin de continuité, il suffirait de s'attarder
sur les contre-exemples qui ne manquent pas, toutes ces hypothèses d'absence

---

[76] Extraits l'Amicus Curiae Brief de Robert Badinter à l'intention des juges d'Omar Khadr, Le
Philosophe dans la Cité.

[77] Yves Laurin, «La consultation par la Cour de cassation de "'personnes qualifiées'" et la notion
"'d'amicus curiae'»", *Semaine juridique,* édition générale, n° 38, 2001, pp 1709–1710; Au sujet de:
Ass. Plén. 29 juin 2001, Ass. Plén., n° 8, p 17 Dominique Fenouillet «Les données acquises de la
science et l'expérience générale des mères» au soutien de «la vie distincte de l'enfant in utero matris
dès avant la naissance»; Un avis de Jean Carbonnier sur le statut pénal de l'enfant à naître, *L'Année
sociologique* 2007-2 vol 57, pp 473–518.

[78] Guy Canivet, La Cour de cassation et la doctrine, Effets d'optique, in *Propos sur les obligations
et quelques autres thèmes fondamentaux du droit: Mélanges offerts à Jean-Luc Aubert,* Dalloz, 2005,
p 373 et suiv.

de politique jurisprudentielle, qui ne sont jamais que les manifestations de jurisprudences sans lien entre elles, arrêts qui ne s'assemblent pas et restent sans fil directeur et sans pensée commune. La doctrine ne manque d'ailleurs pas de dénoncer de telles situations comme un manquement de la Cour à sa mission régulatrice. L'une des plus notables illustrations peut être trouvée dans la succession de décisions portant sur l'abus de fonction du préposé, dans le contexte de la responsabilité du commettant[79] ou sur les «aller- retour» de la jurisprudence sur la responsabilité des clubs sportifs pour les dommages corporels subis par les joueurs à l'occasion de compétitions.[80]

En contrepartie de ces orientations lisibleset pour être acceptable, la politique jurisprudentielle ne peut être ni intangible ni dogmatique. La règle créée par le juge doit pouvoir évoluer sous l'influence des évaluations critiques auxquelles elle est naturellement soumise. Si elle s'inscrit dans une continuité, celle-ci doit pouvoir être remise en cause à chaque nouvelle application à la faveur du débat contradictoire. Elle peut d'abord être contestée du point de vue de l'orientation générale adoptée, ensuite sous l'angle de sa conformité par rapport au texte, à l'ordre juridique dans son ensemble, à l'esprit et à la finalité de la loi, à son adaptation aux réalités économiques et sociales. La jurisprudence peut encore être discutée au regard de la cohérence des arrêts rendus avec une ligne logique dont ils se seraient éloignés. Elle peut enfin être mise en cause dans son aptitude à produire une solution juste et adaptée à la situation contentieuse. Ces discussions peuvent alors provoquer des infléchissements, des réorientations ou des revirements de la jurisprudence. Semblables variations sont dans la nature de la jurisprudence. Elles en constituent le principe de continuité souple et évolutive. Elles montrent qu'une interprétation de la loi donnée par le juge peut se corriger en fonction de l'évolution du contexte économique est social et s'adapter aux situations individuelles. Par sa souplesse d'évolution et son absence de permanence formelle, la jurisprudence se distingue de la loi. C'est sa fluidité qui la justifie par rapport à la permanence de la règle écrite. C'est cette souplesse qui permet de passer du droit à la justice, de l'interprétation uniforme, de la généralité de la loi, à la satisfaction de l'impératif individuel d'équité. On en vient alors à la politique jurisprudentielle comme mode de gouvernance de la justice.

La politique jurisprudentielle comme mode de gouvernance de la justice

Les orientations normatives choisies par les juridictions supérieures les situent nécessairement dans leur environnement institutionnel, elles influent sur

---

[79] Philippe Malinvaud, op. cit., p 430 et suiv.
[80] Cour de cassation 2e chambre civile, 13 janvier 2005 Bulletin 2005 II n° 10 p 10; 21 octobre 2004, Bulletin 2004, II, n° 477, p 404; 2 mars 2000, Bulletin 2000, II, n° 26, p 18.

l'organisation générale du système juridictionnel comme sur la qualité de la justice rendue par les juridictions subordonnées. Par les principes qu'elles établissent,
ces politiques jurisprudentielles assurent le bon fonctionnement du système judiciaire. D'un côté, les choix de jurisprudence que font ces grandes cours les placent
en effet en harmonie ou en conflit non seulement avec le législateur mais aussi
avec les autres ordres de juridictions dès lors qu'elles bousculent ou contrarient
leurs propres pouvoirs . D'un autre côté, la politique jurisprudentielle mise en
œuvre par ces cours supérieures influe sur la qualité de la justice rendue dans
l'ordre juridictionnel qu'elles gouvernent.

La politique jurisprudentielle comme moyen d'articulation des ordres juridiques

En premier lieu, lorsque la Cour de cassation exerce sa fonction jurisprudentielle, elle se positionne à l'égard du pouvoir législatif, posture respectueuse si
les interprétations données sont conformes au texte et à l'esprit de la loi, posture
de conflit, si la règle de jurisprudence prend des distance avec la loi au point de
modifier l'ordre juridique voulu par le législateur. Ces débats sur le thème du
«gouvernement des juges» sont connus, on n'y insistera pas.[81]

On s'attachera davantage à examiner les rapports réciproques qu'entretiennent
les ordres juridictionnels à travers leurs jurisprudences respectives. C'est en effet
par leurs arrêts que les Cours nationales se situent dans l'ordre international et
qu'elles règlent leurs relations réciproques dans l'ordre interne.

La politique jurisprudentielle d'intégration de l'ordre international dans l'ordre interne

Il est remarquable que c'est par la jurisprudence que se sont réglés les rapports
entre les ordres juridiques européens et les ordres juridiques internes. C'est d'abord
par des arrêts devenus emblématiques[82] que la Cour de justice des communautés
européennes a décidé de l'applicabilité directe et de la primauté du droit communautaire dans les ordres juridiques des Etats membres, en miroir, c'est par la jurisprudence que la Cour de cassation[83] puis plus tardivement le Conseil d'Etat[84]
ont, en France, admis le double effet du droit communautaire.[85] C'est également
par sa propre jurisprudence que la Cour européenne des droits de l'homme a

---

[81] Guy Canivet, «Activisme judiciaire et prudence interprétative», *Archives de philosophie du droit*, n° 50, Sirey, 2006, p 9.
[82] CJCE, Costa/Enel, 15 juillet 1964, aff. 6/64, Rec., p 1141; Simmenthal, 9 mars 1978, aff. 106/77, p 629.
[83] Cour de cassation, Chambre mixte, 24 mai 1975, Société des cafés Jacques Vabre, D 1975, p 497.
[84] Conseil d'Etat, 20 octobre 1989, Nicolo, Rec. Lebon, p 190.
[85] Joël Rideau, *Droit institutionnel de l'Union et des Communautés européennes*, 5ème édition, LGDJ, 2006.

imposé l'autorité de ses décisions dans les ordres juridiques des états signataires,[86] comme c'est réciproquement, par leurs propres décisions que les juridictions nationales admettent – entièrement, partiellement ou pas du tout – l'application directe et la primauté de la Convention européenne sur le droit national. C'est encore par leurs jurisprudences, délibérément coopératives, que la Cour de justice des communautés européennes et la Cour européenne des droits de l'homme règlent les rapports entre l'ordre communautaire et celui de la Convention.[87] C'est au moyen de sa politique jurisprudentielle que le Conseil constitutionnel français a, à partir de 1975, refusé de contrôler la conformité des lois aux traités internationaux et renvoyé aux juges ordinaires un tel contrôle.[88] C'est par ses décisions que comme ses homologues, et comme l'ont fait le Conseil d'Etat et la Cour de cassation, le Conseil constitutionnel a affirmé, dans l'ordre interne, la supériorité de la Constitution sur les ordres juridiques européens. C'est au moyen d'une jurisprudence conjuguée du Conseil constitutionnel et du Conseil d'Etat que s'est réglée la question du contrôle de la conformité au droit communautaire et à la Constitution des lois de transposition des directives communautaires.[89]

A travers leur jurisprudence ces juridictions prennent des orientations monistes ou dualistes, souverainistes ou internationalistes, nationalistes ou européennes, respectueuses, réservées ou encore hostiles à l'égard du droit international. L'analyse de la jurisprudence récente de la Cour suprême des Etats-Unis à l'égard des traités internationaux et des décisions de la Cour internationale de justice est une parfaite illustration de ces orientations politiques. Ainsi, par la jurisprudence s'organise un ordre juridique original à l'échelle de l'Europe, ordre juridique qualifié de «pluralisme ordonné» par Mireille Delmas Marty.

Un des exemples les plus aboutis de l'organisation par la jurisprudence des relations entre les ordres juridiques est un arrêt rendu le 10 avril dernier par le Conseil d'Etat français.[90] Pour statuer sur la légalité d'un décret du 26 juin 2006 sur le blanchiment des capitaux, le Conseil d'Etat s'est prononcé sur la conformité à la Convention européenne des droits de l'homme et aux principes généraux du droit communautaire de la directive du 4 décembre 2001 et de la loi de transposition de cette directive du 11 février 2004. Le Conseil d'Etat s'est reconnu le pouvoir de rechercher si cette directive communautaire était compatible avec les droits fondamentaux garantis par la Convention européenne des droits de l'homme. Sa décision est l'aboutissement d'un mouvement jurisprudentiel qui a été engagé par

---

[86] CEDH, 18 décembre 1986, Johnston et a. c/Irlande, Série A n° 112, *Cahiers de droit européen*, 1988, p 464.

[87] Jean-François Renucci, *Traité de droit européen des droits de l'homme*, LGDJ, 2007, p 956 et suiv.

[88] Conseil constitutionnel, 15 janvier 1975 – Décision n° 74-54 DC, Loi relative à l'interruption volontaire de la grossesse, Journal officiel du 16 janvier 1975, p 671.

[89] Joël Rideau, *Droit institutionnel de l'Union et des Communautés européennes*, 5ème édition, LGDJ, 2006.

[90] Conseil d'Etat, N°s 296845,296907, 10 avril 2008, Conseil national des barreaux et autres, disponible sur: <http://www.conseil-etat.fr/ce/jurispd/index_ac_ld0807.shtml>.

le Conseil constitutionnel et le Conseil d'Etat et qui s'est appuyé sur l'analyse des solutions apportées depuis plusieurs années par d'autres juridictions européennes concernant la légalité interne et communautaire des textes de transpositions des directives communautaires.

La politique jurisprudentielle de répartition des compétences entre les ordres internes

Les mêmes observations peuvent être faites dans l'ordre interne. Relevons d'abord les jurisprudences par lesquelles aussi bien le conseil d'Etat[91] que la Cour de cassation[92] se sont abstenus de procéder au contrôle de constitutionalité de la loi. Le contraste de tels choix avec ceux, inverses, opérés par la Cour suprême des Etats-Unis révèle[93] évidemment la nature politique et l'importance systémique de ces orientations qui règlent en France les relations entre le juge ordinaire et le juge constitutionnel en même temps qu'ils ferment la question du contrôle[94] concret, a posteriori et diffus de la constitutionnalité des lois.

Toujours dans l'ordre interne, c'est par la jurisprudence du tribunal des conflits, précisément institué pour faire respecter le principe de répartition des pouvoirs qu'a été progressivement construite la compétence protégée du Conseil d'Etat[95] et c'est la jurisprudence du Conseil constitutionnel qui a donné valeur constitutionnelle à cette compétence réservée.[96] C'est enfin la politique jurisprudentielle du Conseil constitutionnel qui a réduit à la seule protection contre la détention arbitraire la fonction de sauvegarde des libertés assignée par la Constitution à l'autorité judiciaire.[97]

L'examen de ces jurisprudences montre que par le moyen de leurs propres décisions toutes ces juridictions développent des stratégies de conflits, d'articulation, de coopération ou de dialogue – entre ordres européen et ordre national, et, dans l'espace national, entre ordres judiciaire et administratif. De multiples autres exemples pourraient être donnés de stratégies déployées par les juridictions au moyen de leur propre jurisprudence. On a ainsi parlé, dans l'Italie deses années 60, d'une guerre des juges entre la Cour suprême de cassation et la Cour constitutionnelle nouvellement créée, à propos de l'autorité des décisions de cette dernière

---

[91] Conseil d'Etat, 6 novembre 1936, Recueil Lebon, p 966; Dominique Turpin, *Contentieux constitutionnel*, PUF, 1994, pp 27 et 260.

[92] Cour de cassation, chambre criminelle, 11 avril 1833, Dalloz 1833, I, 227; Dominique Turpin, op. cit. pp 26 et 272.

[93] Marbury v. Madison, arrêt 5 U.S. 137, 24 février 1803; Elisabeth Zoller, *Droit constitutionnel*, PUF, 1998, p 101 et suiv.

[94] Jean-Jacques Pardini, *Réalisme et contrôle des lois en Italie*, Les cahiers du Conseil constitutionnel, n° 22, 2007, Etudes et doctrines, p 160.

[95] René Chapus, *Droit administratif général*, 15ème édition, Tome I, Montchrestien, p 989 et suiv.

[96] Décision n°s 86–224 DC du 23 janvier 1987, cons 15, 89–261 DC du 28 septembre 1989, cons 19 et 2001-451 DC du 27 novembre 2001, cons 42.

[97] Art 66 de la Constitution; Thierry S. Renoux et Michel de Villiers, *Code constitutionnel*, LITEC, Edition 2005, p 576 et suiv.

à l'égard des juridictions judiciaires. L'observation de ce phénomène donne un sens particulier à l'avertissement de Aharon Barak, ancien président de la Cour suprême d'Israël:

'Une autre condition que je considère essentielle par rapport au magistrat c'est la confiance du public dans le respect de la déontologie judiciaire; la confiance accordée au juges quant au fait qu'ils n'ont pas d'intérêt dans le contentieux et qu'ils ne luttent pas pour leur propre pouvoir mais pour la protection de la Constitution et de la démocratie'.[98]

La politique jurisprudentielle comme moyen de promotion des bonnes pratiques juridictionnelles

En exerçant par sa jurisprudence la police du jugement, la Cour de cassation procède à un contrôle de qualité de la justice rendue par les juridictions placées sous son contrôle. Elle veille à ce que, dans leur activité juridictionnelle, celles-ci respectent les garanties fondamentales de bonne justice: accès au juge, garantie de la défense, principe du procès équitables, principes directeurs de la justice civile et de la justice pénale. Ainsi, la jurisprudence trace les contours d'une éthique judiciaire qui s'impose à l'ensemble des juridictions.[99]

Le contrôle de la discipline du jugement comprend aussi la vérification du raisonnement judiciaire: exactitude des opérations de qualification, de la logique de l'argumentation, de l'existence ainsi que de la suffisance de la motivation. Ce sont en définitive les règles de la rhétorique judiciaire telle que l'a définie Chaïm Perelman, qui sont consacrées par la jurisprudence. Le niveau d'exigence qui résulte de l'ensemble de ces décisions détermine la qualité de la justice.

Abordant l'interprétation des règles de procédure civiles et pénales, on déduit des orientations jurisprudentielles décidées par les chambres civiles et criminelle une idée d'ensemble du procès, une conception particulières de la régularité et du niveau d'exigence dans l'administration des preuves, une certaine conception de l'expertise et du rôle des auxiliaires de justice. En définitive la jurisprudence fonde une certaine tradition processuelle qui identifie et situe la justice française dans l'ordre international.

À cette fin, la Cour de cassation édicte, au gré de ses décisions, des normes de qualité de la justice dont elle vérifie l'application dans les affaires soumises à son examen. Elle remplit à cet égard une triple fonction, normative, de police et pédagogique. Son rôle est tout à la fois prescriptif par les normes qu'elle crée, correctif

---

[98] Aharon BARAK, "«A Judge on Judging: The Role of a Supreme Court in a Democracy»", *The Harvard Law Review*, novembre 2002, vol 116, n°1 (pour la version résumée et traduite en français de cet article: RFDC, 2006, n°66).

[99] Guy Canivet, Conférence à l'Académie des sciences morales et politiques, 13 novembre 2006, *Vision prospective de la Cour de cassation*, disponible sur: <http://www.courdecassation.fr/jurisprudence_publications_documentation_2/autres_publications_discours_2039/discours_2202/2006_2203/sciences_morales_9619.html>.

par les cassations qu'elle prononce, préventif en ce qu'elle entend éviter la réitération de ces irrégularités et enfin explicatif par la diffusion qu'elle donne à ses arrêts. On comprend que la politique jurisprudentielle débouche sur une action de communication sur la jurisprudence. C'est alors une autre forme d'action qui s'engage, complémentaire mais séparée de l'activité de juger.

La question s'est posée de la rationalisation de ce contrôle de qualité. Ainsi la Cour a édicté et diffusé des lignes directrices d'application des principes et règles de procédure par les juges.[100] Cette démarche est indicative d'un changement du mode d'action de la Cour sur la justice. On passe ici du prononcé de l'élaboration d'une jurisprudence à une action directement prescriptive à l'égard des juges par la diffusion de référentiels de bonnes pratiques judiciaires. Ces procédés sont communément admis dans les systèmes de *Common Law* et ont été repris par la Commission des communautés européennes.

On peut estimer que le sens ici donné au concept de politique jurisprudentielle est large, peut être trop vaste, mais il permet de montrer tous les objectifs que peut poursuivre une juridiction suprême au moyen de sa jurisprudence, au-delà de la mission primaire de trancher les litiges, unifier l'application de la loi, assurer la cohérence de l'ordre juridique, mettre le droit national en conformité avec des ordres internationaux, affirmer son pouvoir, assurer la gouvernance du système de justice, ou encore s'opposer, coopérer ou dialoguer avec les autres ordres juridictions.

Ceux qui contestent la jurisprudence seront sans doute effrayés de comprendre, qu'au-delà de la fonction jurisprudentielle mais à partir de celle-ci, les juridictions expriment des intentions générales qui influent non seulement sur l'ordre juridique mais aussi sur la répartition des pouvoirs. Si l'utilisation par les juridictions suprêmes de leur jurisprudence à des fins stratégiques n'est pas objectivement contestable – c'est un fait – elle n'est pas pour autant sans limites. Comme tout autre puissance, le pouvoir du juge de créer la jurisprudence doit s'imposer des restrictions fondées sur des principes de sagesse: la raison, la loyauté, l'équilibre, le dialogue et l'éthique. On touche ici à la mission universelle du juge. S'il y a une transcendance dans la morale du jugement, alors les juges ont une âme.

---

[100] Bulletins d'information de la Cour de cassation 1995–2007, disponible sur: <http://www.courdecassation.fr/jurisprudence_publications_documentation_2/bulletin_information_cour_cassation_27/>.

3

The Rule of Law and Our Changing Constitution[1]

Anthony Clarke and John Sorabji

The Constitutional Reform Act 2005

The Constitutional Reform Act 2005 (the 2005 Act) received the Royal Assent on 24 March 2005. The Act did many things. Among them, it reformed the office of Lord Chancellor, removing both the Lord Chancellor's judicial role and his (or her) role as Speaker of the House of Lords. It created an independent Judicial Appointments Commission, which is now responsible for the selection, through open competition, of individuals for judicial appointments in England and Wales. It provided for the introduction of the formal legal, as opposed to constitutional, separation of the judicial and legislative functions of the House of Lords.[2] Thus, when the Supreme Court finally opens its doors in 2009, the United Kingdom's final court of appeal will no longer sit in the House of Lords. Taken together, these three reforms in the opening years of the 21st century will have so changed the UK's constitutional framework that Montesquieu and Locke would be satisfied that it gives proper expression in its constitutional arrangements to the doctrine of the separation of powers.[3]

The 2005 Act does more than give effect to a number of significant constitutional reforms. It also contains for the first time in UK legal history a provision in an Act of Parliament that refers to the rule of law.[4] It does so in the following terms in section 1:

The rule of law

1. This Act does not adversely affect—

---

[1] The authors would like to express their thanks for being afforded the great privilege to contribute to this book.

[2] Maitland, *The Constitutional History of England*, (Cambridge, 1920) at 473.

[3] Locke, *Two Treatise of Government* (1690), (Cambridge, 1994) (Locke (1994)) at 326; Montesquieu, *De L'Esprit des Lois* (1748), (Cambridge, 1989), Book XI, 6.

[4] The commitment has since then been repeated in s 1(1)(b) of the Legal Services Act 2007.

(a) the existing constitutional principle of the rule of law, or

(b) the Lord Chancellor's existing constitutional role in relation to that principle.[5]

The section perhaps invites the question how an Act, the purpose of which is to further the independence of the judiciary, could adversely affect the rule of law. It is certainly not intuitively obvious how it could do so by rendering the Lord Chancellor a member of the executive in circumstances in which he was previously a member of the executive (in the Cabinet), the legislature (as Speaker of the House of Lords) and the judiciary (as its head). It is difficult to see how removing this constitutional anomaly, as Bagehot put it, could adversely affect the rule of law or for that matter the Lord Chancellor's constitutional role regarding it.[6] The answer may lie in there being a difference between the rule of law *per se* and, as the Act puts it, the existing constitutional principle of the rule of law. Perhaps the answer is simply this; that the then existing (that is pre-2005) constitutional principle of the rule of law was of a more limited nature than the principle as it now stands post-2005. It may one day be necessary for the courts to grapple with the true meaning of the rule of law in section 1 of the 2005 Act and how that meaning is different from the existing (or previous) position.

Section 1 of the 2005 Act thus raises a fundamental question, which (like many fundamental questions of the day) has recently been raised by Lord Bingham. He put it this way:

… the Act does not define the existing constitutional principle of the rule of law, or the Lord Chancellor's existing constitutional role in relation to it.

The meaning of this existing constitutional principle may no doubt have been thought to be too clear and well-understood to call for statutory definition, and it is true that the rule of law has been routinely invoked by judges in their judgments. But they have not explained what they meant by the expression and well-respected authors have thrown doubt on its meaning…

It is perhaps more likely that the authors of the 2005 Act recognised the extreme difficulty of formulating a succinct and accurate definition suitable for inclusion in a statute, and preferred to leave the task of definition to the courts if and when occasion arose.[7]

Discretion is after all the better part of valour.[8] The problem is that it does not assist us to find an answer to the question what content is to be given to the existing constitutional principle. Nor does it assist us in discerning what role constitutional principles play in our constitution? Do constitutional principles differ from constitutional law or laws, whether statutory or common law ones? Do they differ from constitutional conventions? Are they prior to, and perhaps unalterable by, law? The 2005 Act would perhaps suggest not. Questions about the scope and

---

[5] S 1 of the Constitutional Reform Act 2005.

[6] Bagehot, *The English Constitution*, (Cambridge, 2001) at VI; ss 2, 3, 17, 18 of the Constitutional Reform Act 2005.

[7] Lord Bingham, *The Rule of Law*, 6th David Williams Annual Lecture, Centre for Public Law, Cambridge University (2006) (Bingham (2006)) at 2.

[8] Shakespeare, Henry IV, Pt 1, Act 5, Scene IV.

meaning of constitutional principles are important. They are important because, as Lord Bingham again pointed out, the reference to the rule of law in the 2005 Act has far reaching consequences. He said:

... the statutory affirmation of the rule of law as an existing constitutional principle and of the Lord Chancellor's existing role in relation to it does have an important consequence: that the judges, in their role as journeymen judgment-makers, are not free to dismiss the rule of law as meaningless verbiage, the jurisprudential equivalent of motherhood and apple pie, even if they were inclined to do so. They would be bound to construe a statute so that it did not infringe an existing constitutional principle, if it were reasonably possible to do so. And the Lord Chancellor's conduct in relation to that principle would no doubt be susceptible, in principle, to judicial review.[9]

It is not sufficient then to refer to the rule of law as a constitutional principle and, like Justice Potter Stewart of the US Supreme Court, conclude that we know it when we see it, even if we cannot at the present time either define it or give it content.[10] Nor can we, in the fashion of a latter day (early) Wittgenstein, adopt a knowing yet inscrutable expression and, in response to a query as to what is meant by the constitutional principle of the rule of law, respond with 'What we cannot speak about we must pass over in silence'.[11]

Lord Bingham does not duck the question. He identifies eight sub-rules which he understands to provide the content of the constitutional principle of the rule of law as we know it in the UK today.[12] The sub-rules are: one, that the law must be accessible, intelligible, clear, and predictable; two, that it is by the application of law and not through the exercise of discretion that questions of legal rights should be resolved; three, that law should apply to all equally, except where differential treatment can be justified objectively; four, that the adequate protection of fundamental human rights must be guaranteed by law; five, that effective and accessible means must be provided to enable the proper and timely determination of genuine disputes, i.e., there must be effective access to justice; six, that government ministers and public officers must exercise power reasonably, in good faith and for the purpose for which the power was provided by law; seven, that adjudicative processes must be fair and be seen to be fair i.e., that justice must be carried out in the open by independent and impartial courts which decide cases on their legal and factual merits having given the parties adequate opportunity effectively to participate in the proceedings—as Bentham put it, there must be rectitude of decision;[13] and finally, that the state ought to comply with its international legal obligations.

[9] Bingham (2006) at 4.

[10] *Jacobellis v Ohio* 378 U.S. 184 (1964) at 197. Justice Potter Stewart's comments arose in, as is well known, a markedly different context than the present, viz., pornography.

[11] Wittgenstein, *Tractatus Logico-Philosophicus*, (Routledge, 1974) at 74. It is sometimes translated as 'Whereof one cannot speak, thereof one must be silent.'

[12] Bingham (2006) *passim*.

[13] Bentham, *The Works of Jeremy Bentham*, (ed. Bowring) (1843) (William Tait, Edinburgh), Vol. 6 *Rationale of Judicial Evidence* at 212–213.

Each of the eight sub-rules, which encompass both formal and substantive aspects of the rule of law, are worthy of detailed discussion in their own right.[14] Sub-rule six, however, is expressed to form the core of what it means to talk of the rule of law. Lord Bingham expresses it this way:

[The] sixth sub-rule expresses what many would, with reason, regard as the core of the rule of law principle. It is that ministers and public officers at all levels must exercise the powers conferred on them reasonably, in good faith, for the purpose for which the powers were conferred and without exceeding the limits of such powers. This sub-rule reflects the well-established and familiar grounds of judicial review. It is indeed fundamental. For although the citizens of a democracy empower their representative institutions to make laws which, duly made, bind all to whom they apply, and it falls to the executive, the government of the day, to carry those laws into effect, nothing ordinarily authorises the executive to act otherwise than in strict accordance with those laws. (I say 'ordinarily' to acknowledge the survival of a shrinking body of unreviewable prerogative powers). The historic role of the courts has of course been to check excesses of executive power, a role greatly expanded in recent years due to the increased complexity of government and the greater willingness of the public to challenge governmental (in the broadest sense) decisions. Even under our constitution the separation of powers is crucial in guaranteeing the integrity of the courts' performance of this role.[15]

This sub-rule, or at least one application of it, has been the focus of considerable recent discussion in the context of the constitutional reforms in the 2005 Act. The traditional approach to holding state power to account has been via judicial review; viz., the assessment of whether or not the state is in some way exceeding the powers conferred by law. The ambit of this power does, of course, vary in different countries. In the UK the courts' traditional role, consistently with sub-rule six, as well as sub-rules three and seven, has been to ensure that state bodies act according to law. At its heart this form of judicial review asks a simple question: has a state body or a public official acted lawfully under authority given by primary or secondary legislation. It is, as Carnap would have put it, an internal question: one to be decided within the framework of laws.[16]

Marbury v Madison, **Marshall, Hamilton, and the Rule of Law**

There is however a more significant question, which has traditionally featured in other jurisdictions, but not in the UK. It is the type of question that Carnap

---

[14] Craig, *The Rule of Law*, in *Relations between the executive, the judiciary and Parliament*, (Report of 6th Session of the House of Lords' Select Committee on the Constitution 2006–2007, HMSO) at 102–104, discusses this distinction in the context of Bingham's treatment of the rule of law in Bingham (2006).

[15] Bingham (2006) at 23.

[16] Carnap (1956), *Empiricism, Semantics and Ontology*. Carnap might have made the point that a true external question would question the entire framework of law rather than whether a law was itself valid; its validity presupposes a valid framework.

referred to as an external question. It is a question that challenges the status of a law itself rather than the purported exercise of power consistently with a law or laws. It is the type of question that, since its landmark decision in *Marbury v Madison* (*Marbury*), the US Supreme Court has been required to resolve on numerous occasions.[17] *Marbury* established that the Supreme Court had the power under the US Constitution to review the legality of US laws and to render void those which it found to be, as Chief Justice Marshall put it, 'repugnant to the constitution'.[18]

The *Marbury* decision is predicated upon the understanding that there exists in the United States 'limited sovereignty'. There is no doctrine of parliamentary, or legislative, supremacy in the US. On the contrary the US Congress, its legislative body, has a limited legal competence. Its limits are set by the Constitution which, as the supreme law in the US, provides the framework within which all three branches of government can act lawfully.[19] Chief Justice Marshall expressed his view thus:

...all those who have framed written constitutions contemplate them as forming the fundamental and paramount law of the nation, and consequently the theory of every such government must be, that an act of the legislature repugnant to the constitution is void.

This theory is essentially attached to a written constitution, and is consequently to be considered by this court as one of the fundamental principles of our society. It is not therefore to be lost sight of in the further consideration of this subject.

If an act of the legislature, repugnant to the constitution, is void, does it, notwithstanding its invalidity, bind the courts and oblige them to give it effect? Or, in other words, though it be not law, does it constitute a rule as operative as if it was a law? This would be to overthrow in fact what was established in theory; and would seem, at first view, an absurdity too gross to be insisted on. It shall, however, receive a more attentive consideration.

It is emphatically the province and duty of the judicial department to say what the law is. Those who apply the rule to particular cases, must of necessity expound and interpret that rule. If two laws conflict with each other, the courts must decide on the operation of each. So if a law be in opposition to the constitution: if both the law and the constitution apply to a particular case, so that the court must either decide that case conformably to the law, disregarding the constitution; or conformably to the constitution, disregarding the law: the court must determine which of these conflicting rules governs the case. This is of the very essence of judicial duty.

If then the courts are to regard the constitution; and the constitution is superior to any ordinary act of the legislature; the constitution, and not such ordinary act, must govern the case to which they both apply.

---

[17] 5 US 137 (1803).

[18] 5 US 137 (1803) at 180.

[19] Art VI (2) of the US Constitution: 'This Constitution, and the Laws of the United States which shall be made in Pursuance thereof; and all Treaties made, or which shall be made, under the Authority of the United States, shall be the supreme Law of the Land...'

Those then who controvert the principle that the constitution is to be considered, in court, as a paramount law, are reduced to the necessity of maintaining that courts must close their eyes on the constitution, and see only the law.

This doctrine would subvert the very foundation of all written constitutions.[20]

Chief Justice Marshall's judgment was not *sui generis*. Its roots can be traced back most immediately to Alexander Hamilton. In Federalist Paper No 78 he outlined what is today known as constitutionalism. This is the idea, which has recently been described by Sir Francis Jacobs as:

...found in those systems which accept judicial review of legislation, that the constitution—or equivalent constitutional principles—is the fundamental law which entitles the courts to set aside even the laws enacted by democratic legislatures.[21]

Hamilton notes a written, or 'limited', constitution is one which places limits upon legislative power. It does so by specifying, for instance, certain actions which it cannot take or certain laws which it cannot enact. This has a consequence. By setting out the legislative body's powers—its vires—the constitution is master and the legislature is servant. The legislature, and for that matter the executive and the judiciary, are simply bodies which act under delegated authority and, like any agent, cannot lawfully exceed the terms of their agency. He put it this way:

There is no position which depends on clearer principles, than that every act of a delegated authority, contrary to the tenor of the commission under which it is exercised, is void. No legislative act, therefore contrary the Constitution, can be valid. To deny this, would be affirm, that the deputy is greater than the principal; that the servant is above his master; that the representatives of the people are superior to the people themselves; that men acting by virtue of powers, may do not only what their powers do not authorize, but what they forbid.

Hamilton makes three points of fundamental importance here. The first is the one already adverted to: that legislative power is limited by the powers granted to it by the Constitution. The second is that the Constitution, as the document which sets out the powers granted, is superior to the legislative power, not because it is the supreme source of legitimacy within the state, but because it is the expression of the powers granted to the instruments of government by the sovereign body in the state. The third is that the people are the sovereign body in the state; a point which equally finds expression in the statement that the US Constitution was ordained and established by the people of the United States.[22]

---

[20] 5 US 137 (1803) at 177–178.

[21] Jacobs, *The Sovereignty of Law: The European Way*, (Cambridge University Press, 2006) at 6.

[22] As the Preamble to the US Constitution states famously 'We the people of the United States, in order to form a more perfect union, establish justice, insure domestic tranquility, provide for the common defense, promote the general welfare, and secure the blessings of liberty to ourselves and our posterity, do ordain and establish this Constitution for the United States of America.'

Hamilton thus establishes a three-way relationship between the people, the Constitution, and the legislature. The sovereign power in the state resides in the people. The Constitution is the document in which the sovereign power sets out how the state is to be governed. The Constitution is the supreme law in the state because it is in effect the only law made by the sovereign body in that state. The Constitution's legal and political legitimacy stems from it being the expression of the sovereign will. It gains its legitimacy because it is the true sovereign's instrument. Finally, the Constitution establishes by whom the sovereign power is to be exercised on the sovereign's behalf and establishes the limits upon the exercise of that power. It thus sets out the delegated powers through which the legislature can lawfully act.

These ideas were not of course new. Locke had previously developed them in his Second Treatise of Government. He described the sovereignty of the people and the delegation of its authority to the legislative body in this way:

> ...in a Constituted Commonwealth, standing upon its own Basis, and acting accordingly to its own Nature, that is, acting for the preservation of the Community, there can be but one Supream Power, which is the Legislative, to which all the rest are and must be subordinate, yet the Legislative being only a Fiduciary Power to act for certain ends, there remains still in the People a Supream Power to remove or alter the Legislative, when they find the Legislative act contrary to the trust reposed in them.[23]

The legislative body may be the supreme power whilst it subsists, but at all points it simply exercises that power, which is delegated on trust to it, for the true sovereign: the people. Equally, Locke developed the idea that would find expression in the US Constitution's preamble that the grant of fiduciary power to the legislative is a voluntary act by the sovereign body which defines the extent of the power so granted. He put it this way:

> The power of the Legislative being derived from the People by a positive voluntary Grant and Institution, can be no other, than what that positive Grant conveyed...[24]

This three-way relationship gives rise to two questions: first, what is to happen where the legislature acts beyond the scope of its delegated authority; and secondly, as Locke put it, '...Who shall be Judge whether the... Legislative act contrary to their Trust?'[25] There are a number of possible answers to these questions but perhaps the most satisfactory are those given by Chief Justice Marshall in *Marbury*. To answer the second question first, it is to give the US Supreme Court the power to judge whether the US Congress, the legislature, has overstepped the bounds of its delegated authority. It is to give the courts the power to mediate between the people and their delegate. If the delegate is found to have overstepped the bounds of its authority, in answer to the first question, it is to give the

[23] Locke (1994) at 366–377.
[24] Locke (1994) at 363.
[25] Locke (1994) at 427.

court the power to render any such acts void.[26] Hamilton elaborated this power in his discussion of the three-way relationship between people, Constitution, and the legislative body. He put it this way:

If it be said that the legislative body are themselves the constitutional judges of their own powers, and that the construction they put upon them is conclusive upon the other departments, it may be answered, that this cannot be the natural presumption, where it is not to be collected from any particular provisions in the Constitution. It is not otherwise to be supposed, that the Constitution could intend to enable the representatives of the people to substitute their WILL to that of their constituents. It is far more rational to suppose, that the courts were designed to be an intermediate body between the people and the legislature, in order, among other things, to keep the latter within the limits assigned to their authority. The interpretation of the laws is the proper and peculiar province of the courts. A constitution is, in fact, and must be regarded by the judges, as a fundamental law. It therefore belongs to them to ascertain its meaning, as well as the meaning of any particular act proceeding from the legislative body. If there should happen to be an irreconcilable variance between the two, that which has the superior obligation and validity ought, of course, to be preferred; or, in other words, the Constitution ought to be preferred to the statute, the intention of the people to the intention of their agents.

Nor does this conclusion by any means suppose a superiority of the judicial to the legislative power. It only supposes that the power of the people is superior to both; and that where the will of the legislature, declared in its statutes, stands in opposition to that of the people, declared in the Constitution, the judges ought to be governed by the latter rather than the former. They ought to regulate their decisions by the fundamental laws, rather than by those which are not fundamental.

For Hamilton one of the functions of courts of justice, if not the most important function, is thus to ensure that the will of the people is not subverted by the legislature. It is for the court to ensure that the people remain master and the legislature remains servant and that the legislature does not act as if it were the true sovereign body in the nation. They do so by ensuring that the legislature acts consistently with the powers granted to it by the people in the fundamental law, the Constitution. In this way Hamilton set out the basis on which Chief Justice Marshall would justify the US Supreme Court's innovation in *Marbury*.

Parliamentary Sovereignty and the UK Constitution

Taken together Locke, Hamilton, and Chief Justice Marshall develop a theory which understands the courts as the arbiter between the people and the legislative body. The courts do so by interpreting the nature and extent of the powers granted to the legislative body by the people as set out in the state's fundamental

---

[26] As an answer this is a significant advance on Locke's answer to these questions: armed insurrection by the people and the dissolution of the constitutional settlement: Locke (1994) at 427–428; Goldsworthy, *The Sovereignty of Parliament* (Oxford 1999) (Goldsworthy (1999)) at 232.

law, its Constitution. This theory of limited legal sovereignty stands in stark contrast to the notion of sovereignty which has historically been accepted as governing the UK's constitutional arrangements, viz. that the sovereignty of Parliament is unlimited. We note in passing that Hamilton would perhaps have disagreed with this view. He appears to have taken the view that the UK's constitution was one which incorporated a theory of limited sovereignty. Discussing the nature and status of Bills of Rights in Federalist Paper No 84 he expressed the view that the UK did indeed have a written constitution on a par with the US Constitution, then in draft. He put it this way:

The truth is, after all the declamations we have heard, that the Constitution is itself, in every rational sense, and to every useful purpose, A BILL OF RIGHTS. The several bills of rights in Great Britain [by which he referred to the Magna Carta, the Petition of Right and the Declaration of Right] form its Constitution...

It can thus be seen that in Hamilton's view a number of documents set out the UK's written (albeit uncodified in the US-sense) constitution. As a necessary corollary to this, given his views as to the nature of written constitutions, the UK Parliament would, like the US Congress operate within the bounds of limited legal sovereignty. Just as in the US, the UK's written constitution would set the limits of Parliamentary power, limits which the courts would of necessity have to protect. This carries with it two obvious consequences. First, on this view the UK Parliament was not the sovereign body within the state, but the true sovereign's delegate. It is to be assumed that he would have viewed the British people to be the true sovereign in the nation. Secondly, the House of Lords in its judicial capacity could with complete legitimacy have struck down Acts of Parliament if they were *ultra vires* the UK's constitution.

This Hamiltonian view runs contrary to the established understanding of the UK's constitutional arrangements. While the UK or, perhaps it is better to say England as one of the constituent parts of the UK, has in its history briefly experimented with the idea of sovereignty limited by a constitutional document in the US-sense of the term, the documents Hamilton referred to are not properly understood as having that status.[27] They do not have that status because they do not place limits on what Parliament can lawfully do. As de Smith and Brazier put it, ultimate authority in the UK lies with Parliament and not with the documents which go to make up its uncodified constitution.[28] This is the traditional picture of the UK's constitutional settlement. It is a picture which sees Parliament, properly the Queen-in-Parliament, as the true sovereign. This view was expressed

[27] The Instrument of Government, which took effect on 15 December 1653, following the conclusion of the civil war was England's first codified, written constitution. It was a short-lived document, which was replaced in 1657 by the 'Humble Petition and Advice'. That too was short-lived, lasting no longer than Oliver and Richard Cromwells' Protectorates. Charles II's restoration in 1660 did more than simply restore the monarchy, it reintroduced our uncodified (i.e., unwritten) constitution.

[28] De Smith and Brazier, *Constitutional and Administrative Law*, (8th edn, Penguin, 1998) at 77.

by James Madison, who was *inter alios* a co-author of the Federalist Papers with Hamilton. As Madison put it, in contrast with Hamilton:

Even in Great Britain, where the principles of political and civil liberty have been most discussed, and where we hear most of the rights of the Constitution, it is maintained that the authority of the Parliament is transcendent and uncontrollable, as well with regard to the Constitution, as the ordinary objects of legislative provision. They have accordingly, in several instances, actually changed, by legislative acts, some of the most fundamental articles of the government...An attention to these dangerous practices has produced a very natural alarm in the votaries of free government, of which frequency of elections is the corner-stone; and has led them to seek for some security to liberty, against the danger to which it is exposed. Where no Constitution, paramount to the government, either existed or could be obtained, no constitutional security, similar to that established in the United States, was to be attempted... [29]

Madison's critical view of the 'transcendent and uncontrollable' authority of the UK Parliament was classically, and uncritically, developed by Dicey who described it in this way:

The principle of Parliamentary sovereignty means neither nor less than this, namely, that Parliament thus defined has, under the English constitution, the right to make or unmake any law whatever; and, further, that no person or body is recognised by the Law of England as having a right to override or set aside the legislation of Parliament. [30]

He added that from a 'legal point of view Parliament is neither the agent of the electors nor in any sense a trustee for its constituents. It is legally the sovereign legislative power in the state...'. [31] In this lies the rejection of the Hamiltonian view that the UK Parliament is a delegate of the people: that true sovereignty lies elsewhere than in Parliament itself. Lord Bingham made the same point, in slightly different terms, in *R (Jackson) v Her Majesty's Attorney-General (Jackson)*: 'The bedrock of the British constitution is...the supremacy of the Crown in Parliament. [32]

One consequence of Dicey's view is that Parliament can lawfully alter or repeal any *soi-disant* constitutional law or statute and no body in the state can lawfully challenge such Acts. It can do so without any reference to what for Hamilton was the true sovereign body within the state: namely the people. Parliament can do so because it is the true sovereign. It has done so on numerous occasions; Magna Carta, the Petition of Right, and the Acts of Union, which are also sometimes referred to as basic constitutional texts, do not stand today as they did when they were initially assented to or enacted. This is a point Dicey himself acknowledged

[29] Madison, Federalist Paper No 53.
[30] Dicey, *An Introduction to the Study of the Law of the Constitution* (1885), (10th edn, Macmillan Press, 1959) (Dicey (1959)) at 39–40.
[31] Dicey (1959) at 47–48.
[32] [2005] UKHL 56; [2006] 1 AC 262 at [9]; also see Bingham, *A Written Constitution* (2004) (Judicial Studies Board Annual Lecture) (Bingham (2004)).

by reference to the provision in the 1706 Act of Union with Scotland, which provided that professors at Scottish universities had to make a confession of faith, but which was repealed by nothing more than an ordinary Act of Parliament.[33]

As Lord Bingham, amongst others, has recently pointed out, this concept of parliamentary sovereignty poses a potential if not actual problem for the rule of law.[34] It is a problem which is succinctly encapsulated by the 2005 Act's reference to the fact that it does not adversely affect the existing constitutional principle of the rule of law. This is of considerable potential importance because it suggests that the Act *could have* affected the existing principle of the rule of law and that it could therefore do so in the future. In other words, section 1 of the 2005 Act sets out an implicit acknowledgment of the doctrine of parliamentary sovereignty. It implies, as parliamentary sovereignty requires, that if it so wished Parliament could properly enact laws which might in some way attenuate or abridge the rule of law. It might, for instance, lawfully enact an abridgment of the right to a fair trial, contrary to Bingham's fifth sub-rule; a right which the courts have on more than one occasion held to be a constitutional right.[35] Equally, it could consistently with parliamentary sovereignty abolish judicial review, contrary to Bingham's sixth sub-rule.

Parliament could act in this way because, consistently with parliamentary sovereignty, there is no limit on what it can lawfully do. As Stephen J noted as long ago as 1884 in *Bradlaugh v Gossett*: 'There is no legal remedy...for oppressive legislation...'[36] There is no legal remedy, even if the legislation is so abhorrent that it violates the current constitutional principle of the rule of law.[37] There is no legal remedy because an important consequence of parliamentary sovereignty is that there is no basis upon which the courts can superintend Parliament; there is no sovereign other than Parliament and there is no constitutional document which defines the limits within which Parliament can lawfully act. All the courts can do on this model is interpret and apply the laws made by Parliament.

As Willes J stated in *Lee v Bude & Torrington Junction Railway Co*:

Are we [the courts] to act as regents over what is done by parliament with the consent of the Queen, lords, and commons? I deny that any such authority exists. If an Act of

---

[33] Dicey (1959) at 65.

[34] Bingham *The Rule of Law and the Sovereignty of Parliament*, (2007 Commemoration Oration, King's College, London University) (31 October 2007); Bogdanor, *The Sovereignty of Parliament or the Rule of Law*, (2006 Magna Carta Lecture) (15 June 2006).

[35] *Bremer Vulcan Schiffbau und Maschinenfabrik v South India Shipping Corp Ltd* [1981] AC 909 per Lord Diplock at 979; *Attorney General v Times Newspapers Ltd* [1974] AC 273 at 307.

[36] (1884) 12 QBD 271 at 285.

[37] Bingham (2006) at 18: 'A state which savagely repressed or persecuted sections of its people could not in my view be regarded as observing the rule of law, even if the transport of the persecuted minority to the concentration camp or the compulsory exposure of female children on the mountainside were the subject of detailed laws duly enacted and scrupulously observed. So to hold would, I think, be to strip the existing constitutional principle affirmed by section 1 of the 2005 Act of much of its virtue and infringe the fundamental compact which, as I shall suggest at the end, underpins the rule of law.'

Parliament has been obtained improperly, it is for the legislature to correct it by repealing it: but so long as it exists as law, the Courts are bound to obey it. The proceedings here are judicial, not autocratic, which they would be if we could make laws instead of administering them.[38]

Lord Mustill expressed the same view in *R v Secretary of State for the Home Department, ex p Fire Brigades Union*:

It is a feature of the peculiarly British conception of the separation of powers that Parliament, the executive and the courts have each their distinct and largely exclusive domain. Parliament has a legally unchallengeable right to make whatever laws it thinks fit. The executive carries on the administration of the country in accordance with the powers conferred on it by law. The courts interpret the laws, and see that they are obeyed.[39]

This idea is expressed most succinctly, however, by Lord Simon of Glaisdale in *British Railways Board v Pickin*, when he said, 'the courts in this country have no power to declare enacted law to be invalid'.[40]

Jackson v The Attorney-General and the Common Law

The possibility that Parliament could enact legislation which is repugnant to the rule of law is something which is difficult to reconcile with the UK being a liberal democracy existing in the early years of the 21st century. However, it is a concern which has led some to postulate that the UK Constitution is now one which ought properly to be understood as incorporating a doctrine of limited sovereignty on a par with the US model. Mullen has suggested that there is a fear on the part of some members of the UK's judiciary that '... Parliament and governments cannot be trusted in all circumstances to refrain from passing legislation inconsistent with fundamental rights, the rule of law or democracy'.[41] The most prominent judicial statements which favour this view were expressed in the speeches of Lord Steyn, Lord Hope, and Baroness Hale in *Jackson*. As is now well known, the decision in *Jackson* decided the question as to whether the enactment of the Parliament Act 1949 was a valid use of the procedure laid down in the Parliament Act 1911. The case arose out of the enactment of the Hunting Act 2004 using the procedure laid down in the 1949 Act. The 2004 Act banned hunting wild animals except in limited circumstances.

Lord Steyn expressed his concerns by reference to an argument advanced by the Attorney-General that the Parliament Act 1949 could be used to 'alter the

---

[38] (1871) LR 6 CP 576; *Edinburgh & Dalkeith Railway Co v Wauchope* (1842) 8 Cl & Fin 710 at 725; *DPP of Jamaica v Mollison* [2003] UKPC 6; [2003] 2 AC 411 per Lord Bingham at [13].
[39] [1995] 2 AC 513 at 597.
[40] [1974] AC 765 at 798.
[41] Mullen, 'Reflections on *Jackson v Attorney General*: questioning sovereignty', Legal Studies, Vol 27 (2007) 1 at 15.

composition of the House of Lords', the logic of which was that it could be used to abolish the House of Lords. Lord Steyn said this:

... strict legalism suggests that the Attorney General may be right. But I am deeply troubled about assenting to the validity of such an exorbitant assertion of government power in our bi-cameral system. It may be that such an issue would test the relative merits of strict legalism and constitutional legal principle in the courts at the most fundamental level.

But the implications are much wider. If the Attorney General is right the 1949 Act could also be used to introduce oppressive and wholly undemocratic legislation. For example, it could theoretically be used to abolish judicial review of flagrant abuse of power by a government or even the role of the ordinary courts in standing between the executive and citizens. This is where we may have to come back to the point about the supremacy of Parliament. We do not in the United Kingdom have an uncontrolled constitution as the Attorney General implausibly asserts. In the European context the second Factortame decision made that clear: [1991] 1 AC 603. The settlement contained in the Scotland Act 1998 also point to a divided sovereignty. Moreover, the European Convention on Human Rights as incorporated into our law by the Human Rights Act, 1998, created a new legal order. One must not assimilate the ECHR with multilateral treaties of the traditional type. Instead it is a legal order in which the United Kingdom assumes obligations to protect fundamental rights, not in relation to other states, but towards all individuals within its jurisdiction. The classic account given by Dicey of the doctrine of the supremacy of Parliament, pure and absolute as it was, can now be seen to be out of place in the modern United Kingdom. Nevertheless, the supremacy of Parliament is still the general principle of our constitution. It is a construct of the common law. The judges created this principle. If that is so, it is not unthinkable that circumstances could arise where the courts may have to qualify a principle established on a different hypothesis of constitutionalism. In exceptional circumstances involving an attempt to abolish judicial review or the ordinary role of the courts, the Appellate Committee of the House of Lords or a new Supreme Court may have to consider whether this is a constitutional fundamental which even a sovereign Parliament acting at the behest of a complaisant House of Commons cannot abolish. It is not necessary to explore the ramifications of this question in this opinion. No such issues arise on the present appeal.[42]

Lord Hope expressed similar views. He put them this way:

I start where my learned friend Lord Steyn has just ended. Our constitution is dominated by the sovereignty of Parliament. But Parliamentary sovereignty is no longer, if it ever was, absolute. It is not uncontrolled in the sense referred to by Lord Birkenhead LC in McCawley v The King [1920] AC 691, 720. It is no longer right to say that its freedom to legislate admits of no qualification whatever. Step by step, gradually but surely, the English principle of the absolute legislative sovereignty of Parliament which Dicey derived from Coke and Blackstone is being qualified.

...

Nor should we overlook the fact that one of the guiding principles that were identified by Dicey at p 35 was the universal rule or supremacy throughout the constitution

---

[42] [2005] UKHL 56; [2006] 1 AC 262 at [101]–[102].

of ordinary law. Owen Dixon, 'The Law and Constitution' (1935) 51 LQR 590, 596 was making the same point when he said that it is of the essence of supremacy of the law that the courts shall disregard as unauthorised and void the acts of any organ of government, whether legislative or administrative, which exceed the limits of the power that organ derives from the law. In its modern form, now reinforced by the European Convention on Human Rights and the enactment by Parliament of the Human Rights Act 1998, this principle protects the individual from arbitrary government. The rule of law enforced by the courts is the ultimate controlling factor on which our constitution is based. The fact that your Lordships have been willing to hear this appeal and to give judgment upon it is another indication that the courts have a part to play in defining the limits of Parliament's legislative sovereignty.[43]

Baroness Hale said:

... The question of the legislative competence of the United Kingdom Parliament is quite distinct from the question of the composition of Parliament for this purpose. The concept of Parliamentary sovereignty which has been fundamental to the constitution of England and Wales since the 17th century (I appreciate that Scotland may have taken a different view) means that Parliament can do anything. The courts will, of course, decline to hold that Parliament has interfered with fundamental rights unless it has made its intentions crystal clear. The courts will treat with particular suspicion (and might even reject) any attempt to subvert the rule of law by removing governmental action affecting the rights of the individual from all judicial scrutiny. Parliament has also, for the time being at least, limited its own powers by the European Communities Act 1972 and, in a different way, by the Human Rights Act 1998. It is possible that other qualifications may emerge in due course. In general, however, the constraints upon what Parliament can do are political and diplomatic rather than constitutional.[44]

It is worth noting, as Mullen does in his detailed examination of the constitutional implications of the *Jackson* decision, that Lord Bingham and Lord Carswell affirmed the Diceyan account of Parliamentary sovereignty; the other four members of the Lords' constitution expressed no view either way.[45]

Between them Lord Steyn, Lord Hope, and Baroness Hale canvass a number of traditional arguments as to why the UK constitution ought not properly to be viewed as one which incorporates Diceyan parliamentary sovereignty. Between them they suggest that the Act of Union 1707, the European Communities Act 1972, the Scotland Act 1998, and the incorporation of the European Convention on Human Rights 1950 by the Human Rights Act 1998 in various ways limit parliamentary sovereignty. However, the difficulties with reliance on these various provisions in order to establish that the UK constitution is not one which incorporates Diceyan parliamentary sovereignty are well known. As noted above,

---

[43] [2005] UKHL 56; [2006] 1 AC 262 at [104].
[44] [2005] UKHL 56; [2006] 1 AC 262 at [159].
[45] [2005] UKHL 56; [2006] 1 AC 262 per Lord Bingham at [9] & per Lord Carswell at [168]; Mullen, 'Reflections on *Jackson v Attorney General*: questioning sovereignty', Legal Studies, Vol 27 (2007) 1 at 14–15.

various provisions of the Acts of Union have been repealed by ordinary Acts of Parliament. Although the European Communities Act 1972 is said by some to have ceded part of the UK's sovereignty to what was then the European Economic Community, it has never been explained how a sovereign state could have ceded its sovereignty to what was then a free trade union.[46] As to the Scotland Act and the Human Rights Act, the former merely delegates certain aspects of the UK Parliament's sovereignty to the Scottish Parliament, and the latter expressly limits the European Convention's effect by limiting judicial room for manoeuvre to making declarations of incompatibility and thus expressly precludes any notion that it could be used as the basis for US-style judicial review of Acts of Parliament; so it is difficult to see how they limit parliamentary sovereignty.

In any event they are all Acts of Parliament, which, like any other Act of Parliament, can be repealed at any time. If any of them divides or limits parliamentary sovereignty, it does so only to the extent that Parliament has chosen to do so for the present time. Any limit on sovereignty is, as we see it, no more than a temporary limit which may mask the continued existence of Diceyan parliamentary sovereignty but does not replace it for all time with a more limited form of sovereignty.[47] As we see it, none of these Acts provides any real assistance for the argument in favour of limited legal sovereignty.

The reason why these, and indeed any Act of Parliament, could not limit parliamentary sovereignty can be seen by comparing the UK constitutional settlement on the one hand and the US constitutional settlement on the other. As discussed earlier, the US settlement, on the Hamiltonian view, contains three parties: the People as sovereign, the Constitution, and Congress. The sovereign delegates its unlimited legal authority into the hands of Congress but the nature of the delegation is limited by the terms of the Constitution, which is the vehicle through which the sovereign's delegation is affected. This is not to say that the terms of the delegation are necessarily static. The delegation of sovereignty in the US Constitution provides Congress with the necessary authority to change the terms of the delegation and thereby, if the appropriate formalities are satisfied, extend the limits of its authority.[48] The UK settlement contains only two

---

[46] As Goldsworthy (1999) at 15, amongst others, has pointed out the European Communities Act 1972 simply provides a procedural rule which the courts are required to give effect unless and until Parliament enacts the UK's withdrawal from the European Union. That the UK Parliament retains the power to lawfully repeal the 1972 Act demonstrates its continued substantive supremacy and that despite *Ex p Factortame* [1991] 1 AC 603 parliamentary sovereignty remains substantively untrammelled.

[47] See Mullen (2007) at 7–13 for a discussion of these traditional arguments for limited sovereignty.

[48] Art V of the US Constitution provides the constitutional amendment power through which the legislature can amend the terms of its delegated authority. Ultimate authority here resides, however, in the People, who through the vehicles of various state legislatures are required to ratify the proposed amendment. The People's ultimate political sovereignty is also maintained through this Article as it also provides for them, again through the state legislatures, to convoke a constitutional convention through which they can amend the terms of the Constitution.

parties: the sovereign, i.e., the Queen-in-Parliament, and the constitution. By contrast with Congress in the US, the Queen-in-Parliament does not exercise sovereignty as the delegate of the people. Its powers are not constrained by the terms of any delegation. It exercises sovereignty in the same way as the people in the US would have exercised sovereignty absent the framing of its Constitution in Philadelphia on the 17 September 1787 (as ratified on 21 June 1788). Its sovereignty is legally unlimited because it exercises it as principal and not as agent. Acts of Parliament, ordinary or constitutional, common law principles, constitutional or otherwise, which delineate the nature of the sovereign power are different in kind from the Articles of the US Constitution.[49] The latter define delegated powers, whereas the former amount to statements as to how Parliament chooses procedurally to fetter its unlimited legal sovereignty at any particular time. They are temporary self-denying ordinances rather than permanent substantive limitations. As with any self-denying ordinance, since they exist by virtue of a power which is being denied, the ordinance may be lifted at any time. It is not therefore surprising that the UK Constitution can be amended at any time by ordinary Act of Parliament, that is by an exercise of the sovereign's unlimited substantive legal authority. Put in Hartian terms, in the US the ultimate rule of recognition recognizes that ultimate legal sovereignty, which resides in the people, is delegated to Congress (as the legislative body) via the Constitution, which places substantive limits on it, whereas in the UK the ultimate rule of recognition recognizes that ultimate legal sovereignty inherently resides in Parliament and in so doing involves no delegation from another body.[50]

This has a consequence for the UK courts. The rationale behind the existence of the judicial review power over legislative acts which *Marbury* established in the US for the Supreme Court is that there is a need to ensure, in the absence of Lockean insurrection, that the terms of the sovereign's delegation are not exceeded. The UK courts have no such role because there is no delegation of sovereign legal authority to Parliament from another separate body for the courts to police. The UK courts cannot review Parliament's laws because there is nothing against which they can review them. Reviewing the exercise of parliamentary sovereignty in the UK would be as pointless an exercise, to borrow a phrase from (the later) Wittgenstein, as comparing two copies of the same edition of the morning newspaper with each other to check whether what they report on page one actually happened.[51] Each Act of Parliament is an exercise of Parliament's unlimited legal authority, which if it contradicts a previous constitutional principle does so but in doing so overrides it. This unfettered and unlimited sovereignty may seem absurd or irrational to some commentators, such as Allan, but it is the defining feature of the UK constitution; just as it is for the US Constitution given the

---

[49] See *Thoburn v Sunderland City Council* [2003] QB 151, where a statute, in that case the European Communities Act 1972, was ascribed the status of a constitutional statute.

[50] Hart, *The Concept of Law* (Oxford 1961).

[51] Wittgenstein, *Philosophical Investigations* (Blackwell 1953) at § 265.

nature of the sovereign authority which resided in the People who delegated their authority to the US Legislative body—Congress.[52]

Lord Steyn has an answer to this. In *Jackson* he adverted to what is known as common law constitutionalism as placing a limit on parliamentary sovereignty. Common law constitutionalism is the view, as Goldsworthy has recently summarized it, that:

> Britain's 'unwritten' constitution consists of common law principles, and therefore Parliament's authority to enact statutes derives from the common law. As Trevor Allan puts it, 'the common law is prior to legislative supremacy, which it defines and regulates'.[53]

Lord Steyn showed his commitment to this when he stated in *Jackson* that while:

> …the supremacy of Parliament is still the general principle of our constitution, it is a construct of the common law. The judges created this principle. If that is so, it is not unthinkable that circumstances could arise where the courts may have to qualify a principle established on a different hypothesis of constitutionalism.[54]

He was not the first to express this view in this way. Brazier in *Constitutional Reform: Reshaping the British Political System* described common law constitutionalism in remarkably similar terms:

> It is for the judges … to say what they will recognize as valid and binding legislation. They invented the doctrine of parliamentary sovereignty; they have the power to curb their own invention.[55]

Brazier's view can be questioned on its own terms: it is one thing to invent a doctrine, it is quite another to have or retain the power to curb that invention. Even if he is correct that the judiciary created parliamentary sovereignty, it is another thing to suggest that they retain the power to revoke that doctrine by, for instance, stating that their previous view as to the common law's effect was wrong.

Steyn, Brazier, and Allan are not alone, however, in advocating common law constitutionalism. Both Lord Woolf and Sir John Laws have adverted to the idea that parliamentary sovereignty is limited by aspects of the UK's unwritten (i.e., common law) constitution, and that it is the role of the courts to ensure, if necessary, that those limits are not overstepped.[56] Common law constitutionalism thus sees the UK's unwritten constitution playing the same role as the US Constitution,

[52] Allan, *The Common Law as Constitution: Fundamental Rights and First Principles*, in Saunders (ed), *Courts of Final Jurisdiction: the Mason Court in Australia* (Federation Press 1996) at 156.

[53] Goldsworthy, *The Myth of the Common Law Constitution*, in Edlin (ed), *Common Law Theory* (Cambridge 2007) (Goldsworthy (2007))at 204.

[54] [2005] UKHL 56; [2006] 1 AC 262 at [102].

[55] (2nd edn Oxford 1998) at 155.

[56] Woolf, 'Droit Public—English Style', Public Law (1995) 57; Laws, 'Law and Democracy', Public Law (1995) 72.

even though it is not a constitution which defines delegated authority as does the US Constitution. It is a theory which posits the existence of no sovereign in the sense in which one is present in the US or, on the traditional Diceyan conception of parliamentary sovereignty, in the UK.

Protecting the Rule of Law—The Future?

Common law constitutionalism appears capable, therefore, of providing quietus to fears that the rule of law may be overridden in the future by a 'sovereign Parliament acting at the behest of a complaisant House of Commons'. It does so because, so the argument would go, the rule of law forms part of the UK's common law constitution, which in turn limits the extent of parliamentary sovereignty. As parliamentary sovereignty is so limited, the courts have the same role to play as they do in the US: they ensure that Parliament does not act outwith the ambit of its lawful authority. The courts are not, contrary to Wade's view, sovereign in this respect; they are simply the arbiters of the lawful exercise of parliamentary power according to the terms set for its lawful exercise by the unwritten constitution.[57]

There are, however, a number of fundamental problems with common law constitutionalism, which call into question reliance on it as the guardian of fundamental aspects of our constitutional framework. Those problems are developed in detail by Goldsworthy in *The Sovereignty of Parliament* and his more recent contribution to the debate in *The Myth of the Common Law Constitution*.[58] The most telling argument he deploys is one which rests on an historical analysis of the development of parliamentary sovereignty in England and then the UK. That analysis cogently undermines any suggestion that it is a constitutional *parvenu*, which first and improperly appeared in the mid-18th century. He demonstrates persuasively that it is a doctrine which has formed part of our constitutional framework since at least the mid-16th century and that parliamentary sovereignty was not a product of the common law. For Goldsworthy, all points towards to there never having been a

golden age of constitutionalism, in which the judiciary enforced limits to the authority of Parliament imposed by the common law or natural law.[59]

If Goldsworthy is right in this, Lord Steyn's suggestion that the judiciary, if faced with an Act of Parliament which purported to enact laws inconsistent with, or which adversely affected, the existing principle of the rule of law, could rely on the common law and reframe the terms of the constitution, is fatally flawed. It is fatally flawed because it rests on a false premise; namely that the judiciary through

---

[57] Wade, *Constitutional Fundamentals*, (Stevens 1989, revised edition) at 33.
[58] Goldsworthy (1999) and (2007).
[59] Goldsworthy (1999) at 235.

interpreting the common law themselves gave rise to parliamentary sovereignty. Goldsworthy demonstrates that the first limb of the argument, that the judiciary created parliamentary sovereignty, is a false premise and therefore the argument's conclusion, that the judiciary can exercise the same creative power in order to refashion it, cannot arise.

There is much to be said for Goldsworthy's view. It does, however, leave the rule of law in the limbo, some would say jeopardy, in which section 1 of the 2005 Act and parliamentary sovereignty places it. In one sense this is perhaps not as bad a thing as it might initially appear to be. Common law constitutionalism calls for the judiciary to enter into a conflict with Parliament. As Wade would have it, it requires the judiciary effectively to declare themselves sovereign in this respect. In a democracy, where the House of Commons is elected by universal suffrage, a unilateral declaration by the (unelected) judiciary that they are a sovereign power in the state, at least in the restricted sense set by the common law constitutionalists, is a step, which is at best inconsistent with modern notions of where political sovereignty resides in the UK. At worst, it would lead to a constitutional crisis which the UK has not known since 1688.

While it is true that legal and political sovereignty do not need to reside in the same bodies within a state, it is another thing to suggest that the courts, which have until now had no political role in the UK, should now seek to exercise a degree of political sovereignty, such as any attempt to redefine Parliament's legal sovereignty would necessarily involve. It is a suggestion upon which the courts should at the very least hesitate to act. It is perhaps a suggestion which is as inconsistent with the rule of law as the abolition of judicial review or the right to fair trial would be. It is inconsistent with it because it fails to recognize (as the 2005 Act does) the doctrine of the separation of powers. It would involve the court having some form of political sovereignty, albeit perhaps indirectly as the common law's interpreter, whereas political sovereignty is the proper province of Parliament elected by the citizens of the UK. As Bentham rightly noted in 1790, the judiciary should have 'no share in legislative power'.[60] They should certainly not seek to take upon themselves political—legislative—power in the 21st century.

Is there however a way to protect the rule of law? The US model is an obvious example of how a polity can protect the rule of law through the delegation of legal sovereignty from the people via the Constitution to the US Congress. The UK is currently undergoing the single most sustained period of constitutional reform since the 19th century. It might even be said, given the possibility of further reform of the House of Lords, of further possible changes to the Union with Scotland, of further possible changes to the UK's relationship with the European

---

[60] Bentham, *The Works of Jeremy Bentham*, (ed Bowring) (William Tait, Edinburgh 1843), Vol 4 at 310. Montesquieu (1989), Book XI, 6: 'Again, there is no liberty, if the judiciary power be not separated from the legislative and executive. Were it joined with the legislative, the life and liberty of the subject would be exposed to arbitrary control; for the judge would be then the legislator. Were it joined to the executive power, the judge might behave with violence and oppression.'

Union, and the UK Government's 2007 consultation on the Governance of Britain, that the UK is entering a period of constitutional reform the nature of which it has not seen since the Glorious Revolution of 1688.[61]

The 2007 consultation raises the suggestion as to whether the UK may have reached the point where a written constitution is a possible development. Such a step could refashion the UK's constitutional settlement, and perhaps represents the best method whereby the rule of law could be safeguarded. It might perhaps do so through the introduction of a written constitution, which, as in the US, gives expression to limited sovereignty. It might thereby provide a proper and lawful basis upon which the courts could review the legitimacy of legislative acts. It could, or perhaps should, however, only do so if the UK Parliament, as part of the process of incorporation of the new written constitution, delegated its authority to a new legislative body whose powers, like those of the US Congress, would be limited by the terms of its delegation.

Such a process might see the UK Parliament ensure that its political and legal sovereignty is transferred to a new sovereign body—the electorate—and in so doing dissolve itself in the fashion that the English and Scottish Parliaments did in 1707 at the birth of the United Kingdom. The written constitution could then, as it does in the US, embody a transfer of legal and political sovereignty from the electorate as sovereign to the new, now legally limited Parliament (as Queen-in-Parliament). Such a step would no doubt amount to something which Professor King submits rightly the UK has not so far had:

a defining 'constitutional moment' analogous to the Philadelphia convention of 1787 or the debates that led to Germany's Basic Law in 1949...[62]

Such a development would, however, be no more than another step in the UK's organic evolution, which has been ongoing since 1066. Most importantly, such a development would, as it properly ought to, stem from political action by Parliament and not the arrogation of power by the judiciary to themselves. It might well be thought, given his extra-judicial writing, that development at the instigation of Parliament through the democratic process rather than by the judiciary is something of which Lord Bingham may well approve.[63]

In his lecture entitled *A Written Constitution* Lord Bingham himself discussed the pros and cons of a written constitution, saying that he had moved from being strongly opposed to one to a condition of agnosticism.[64] He identified seven basic, but very important, rules with which a codified constitution should comply:

(1) its adoption should be subject to popular endorsement;

(2) it should eschew undue detail;

---

[61] *The Governance of Britain* (HMSO: CM 7170) (2007) at 62–63.
[62] King, *Does the United Kingdom still have a constitution?* (Sweet & Maxwell 2001) at 39.
[63] This is also a point with which Goldsworthy would agree, see Goldsworthy (1999) at 279.
[64] Bingham (2004) *passim*.

(3) it should set out the fundamental principles;

(4) all its provisions should be justiciable;

(5) subject to the constraints of parliamentary supremacy, some degree of entrenchment would be necessary;

(6) it should be neutral and not be allowed to hamper growth, prevent diversity, or restrict scope for new ideas; and

(7) it should not make provision for a constitutional court.

Those are all matters for discussion in the future, especially perhaps the last, now that we are to have a new Supreme Court in 2009. We very much hope that Lord Bingham will develop his ideas on all the questions which we have tried to touch upon above (and many others) with the same sagacity and spare prose as he has in his judgments, speeches, and writings over very many years.

4

Lord Bingham and the Human Rights Act 1998: The Search for Democratic Legitimacy During the 'War on Terror'

Richard Clayton and Hugh Tomlinson

Introduction

In March 1993, Lord Bingham added his voice to those calling for the incorporation of the European Convention on Human Rights into domestic law. He concluded his Denning Lecture on what he described as a 'downbeat note':

> It would be naive to suppose that incorporation of the Convention would usher in a new Jerusalem. As on the morrow of a general election, however glamorous the promises of the campaign, the world will not at once feel very different. But the change would over time stifle the insidious and damaging belief that it is necessary to go abroad to obtain justice. It would restore our country to its former place as an international standard-bearer of liberty and justice. It would help to reinvigorate the faith, which our eighteenth and nineteenth century forbears would not for an instant have doubted, that these were fields in which Britain was the world's teacher, not its pupil. And it would enable the judges more effectively to honour their ancient and sacred undertaking to do right to all manner of people after the laws and usages of their realm, without fear or favour, affection or ill will.[1]

This characteristic combination of caution, history, and vision gives an important insight into the approach taken by Lord Bingham to human rights issues over the last decade and a half of his judicial career.

Lord Bingham was by no means the only senior judicial figure to support incorporation. One of the most noticeable features of the Bill of Rights debate during this period was that senior British judges explicitly participated in the process. Lord Scarman had been a powerful advocate of a bill of rights in the 1970s.[2] In the 1990s Lord Browne-Wilkinson suggested a bill of rights should be

---

[1] T Bingham, 'The European Convention on Human Rights: Time to Incorporate' in *The Business of Judging: Selected Essays and Speeches* (Oxford University Press, 2000), 140.
[2] Sir Leslie Scarman, *English Law–The New Dimension* (Stevens, 1974).

formulated as a rule of construction[3] and Lord Woolf favoured a form of incorp-oration which did not threaten parliamentary sovereignty.[4] By the mid 1990s the momentum in favour of a Bill of Rights had become irresistible[5] and in September 1993 the Labour Party published *A New Agenda for Change: Labour's Proposals for Constitutional Reform* arguing for a Human Rights Bill which would incorporate the European Convention. Such a bill was introduced within five months of the Labour Government being elected in 1997 and the Human Rights Act ('HRA') was given royal assent on 9 November 1998.

The HRA did not come into force until 2 October 2000. On 6 June of that year Lord Bingham became the Senior Law Lord. In his eight years in post the HRA has become central to the work of the Judicial Committee. Lord Bingham has presided in nearly 200 cases in which the HRA has been considered by the House, often giving the leading speech and only on rare occasions finding him-self in the minority.[6]

These decisions of the House of Lords in HRA cases have ranged over the whole area of English private and public law, and even a brief survey of Lord Bingham's contributions to the development of this case law is beyond the scope of this paper. We want to deal with one specific area, that of the political legitim-acy of the HRA itself.

The political background is well known. Over those eight years, the HRA has often been the subject of acute political controversy. The government's initial enthusiasm for its enactment cooled appreciably with the terrorist attacks in New York and London; as the Prime Minister, Tony Blair, put it in 2005 'the rules of the game are changing'.[7] Mr Blair himself challenged the value of the Convention

---

[3] Lord Browne-Wilkinson 'The Infiltration of a Bill of Rights' [1992] PL 397; See also Lord Browne-Wilkinson, 'The Impact on Judicial Reasoning' in B Markesinis (ed), *The Impact of the Human Rights Bill on English Law* (Clarendon Press, 1998).

[4] Lord Woolf 'Droit Public—English Style' [1995] PL 57.

[5] For the background to the debate, see e.g., A Lester, *A Bill of Rights for England* (Charter 88, 1991); F Mount, *The Recovery of the Constitution* (Charter 88, 1992); A Lester, *The Crisis Facing Human Rights in Europe; Does the British Government Really Care?* (Charter 88, 1993); F Klug, *Reinventing the Community: The Rights and Responsibilities Debate* (Charter 88, 1996); Liberty *A People's Charter—Liberty's Bill of Rights* (1993); (and see also, F Klug and J Wadham, 'The 'demo-cratic entrenchment' of a Bill of Rights: Liberty's Proposals' [1993] PL 579); The Institute for Public Policy Research *A British Bill of Rights* (1993).

[6] On most of those occasions, he has favoured a more expansive approach to the HRA: see *R (Roberts) v Parole Board* [2005] 2 AC 738 (dissenting on the issue as to whether the appointment of a special advocate satisfied Art 5(4) fairness requirements); *Qazi v LB Harrow* [2004] 1 AC 983 and *Kay v Lambeth* [2006] 2 AC 465 (dissenting on the issue of whether Art 8 could be taken into account in possession actions); *YL v Birmingham City Council* [2008] AC 95 (favouring a broader concept of 'functional public authority' under s 6 of the HRA); but see *R (Al-Skeini) v Secretary of State for Defence* [2008] AC 153 (Lord Bingham dissenting on the issue as to whether the HRA applied to persons in the custody of British troops in Iraq). It is also noteworthy that the first HRA case to reach the House of Lords, *R v Director of Public Prosecutions, ex p Kebilene* [2000] 2 AC 326, was a successful appeal against a decision of a Divisional Court presided over by Lord Bingham CJ.

[7] PM's Press Conference 5 August 2005 <http://www.pm.gov.uk/output/Page8041.asp>.

and the HRA: focusing attention on the problems involved in deporting terrorists under Article 3 regardless of the danger they face in their home countries.[8] Despite the 2006 attempt by the Department of Constitutional Affairs to
rehabilitate the HRA,[9] many in the Labour Government have remained deeply
sceptical about its benefits. Similar attitudes are common in the Conservative
opposition which is now committed to replacing the HRA which is said to have
'undermined the Government's ability to deal with crime and terrorism' with a
British Bill of Rights, the nature and content of which are, as yet, undefined.

In this troubled political climate steering a course which maintains the values
of the Convention but avoids the charge of excessive judicial activism was not
straightforward. In a series of important decisions, Lord Bingham piloted the
way in this difficult exercise in navigation. Central to his approach, we suggest,
has been an attempt to establish the democratic legitimacy of the HRA whilst,
at the same time, giving practical effect to its values in the most important areas
where they are under threat.

In this paper we will concentrate on two topics: first, the way in which the
House of Lords has dealt with Strasbourg case law as a means of emphasizing
democratic legitimacy; and secondly, its approach to the vital but politically controversial subject of terrorism. In both areas Lord Bingham has taken the lead and
has, in general, carried his colleagues with him. We will argue that the cautious
conservatism of the approach in the first area has assisted the House of Lords in
taking a more forthright approach in the second.

The HRA and the Strasbourg Case Law

The most fundamental way in which the House of Lords has sought to preserve
the democratic legitimacy of the HRA is in its approach to Strasbourg case law.
If, the argument goes, the judges are simply applying the Convention case law
then they are implementing the will of Parliament as found in the HRA and are
not forging new rights without democratic accountability. This approach, developed by Lord Bingham, has found wide acceptance among his colleagues. It is,
however, not without difficulties.

The starting point for consideration of this issue is section 2(1) of the HRA
which requires a court to 'take account' of any relevant Strasbourg judgments
or decisions. The approach under the HRA is therefore very different from section 3(1) of the European Communities Act 1972.[10] In the first instance the

---

[8] BBC News, 17 May 2006.
[9] Department for Constitutional Affairs, *Review of the Implementation of the Human Rights Act*,
July 2006, <http://www.dca.gov.uk/peoples-rights/human-rights/pdf/full_review.pdf>.
[10] S 3(1) of the European Community Act states: 'For the purpose of all legal proceedings
any question as to the effect of any of the Treaties or as to the validity, meaning or effect of any
Community instrument, shall be treated as a question of law (and, if not referred to the European

House of Lords took a literal approach to section 2. In *R (Alconbury Developments Ltd) v Environment Secretary* Lord Slynn said that in the absence of some special circumstances the court should follow any clear and constant jurisprudence of the European Court of Human Rights.[11]

However, in *R (Ullah) v Secretary of State for the Home Department*,[12] in a case which established the potentially radical point that a person resisting removal from the United Kingdom might, in exceptional circumstances, rely on 'qualified Convention rights' to challenge the decision to remove him, Lord Bingham took a rather different approach to the effect of Strasbourg cases, stating that:

a national court subject to a duty such as that imposed by section 2 should not without strong reason dilute or weaken the effect of the Strasbourg case law...It is of course open to member states to provide for rights more generous than those guaranteed by the Convention, but such provision should not be the product of interpretation of the Convention by national courts, since the meaning of the Convention should be uniform throughout the states party to it. The duty of national courts is to keep pace with the Strasbourg jurisprudence as it evolves over time: no more, but certainly no less.

Lord Bingham explained the rationale for this approach in *R (SB) v Denbigh High School*:[13] saying that the purpose of the HRA was not to enlarge the rights or remedies of those in the UK whose Convention rights have been violated, but to enable Convention rights and remedies to be asserted and enforced by the domestic courts—and not only by recourse to Strasbourg, focusing on the principle of 'bringing rights back home'.[14] The approach has been approved and followed in a number of subsequent cases.[15]

The principle that the English courts should focus on Strasbourg case law has important ramifications in relation to the issue of democratic legitimacy. It places strict limits on 'judicial activism'. Thus, for example, it enabled the House of Lords in *R (Countryside Alliance) v Attorney-General*[16] to say that, whatever their individual views, the Strasbourg case law did not permit the claims of those who engaged in fox-hunting to be brought within the scope of Article 8. Although the

Court, be treated for determination as such in accordance with the principles laid down by and by any relevant decision [of the European Court of Justice or any court attached thereto]).'

[11] [2003] 2 AC 295 para 26; see also *R (Anderson) v Secretary of State for the Home Department* [2003] 1 AC 837, para 18.

[12] [2004] 2 AC 323 para 20.

[13] [2007] 1 AC 100, para 29.

[14] A principle he held to be firmly established by *Aston Cantlow v Wallbank* [2004] 1 AC 546, paras 6–7, 44 ; *R (Greenfield) v Secretary of State for the Home Department* [2005] 1 WLR 673, paras 18–19; and *R (Quark Fishing Ltd) v Secretary of State for Foreign and Commonwealth Affairs* [2006] 1 AC 529, paras 25, 33, 34, 88, and 92.

[15] See, e.g., *R (S) v Chief Constable of South Yorkshire Police* [2004] 1 WLR 2196 para 27 (Lord Steyn); *R (Quark Fishing) v Secretary of State for Foreign and Commonwealth Affairs* [2006] 1 AC 529, para 34; *R (Animal Defenders International) v Secretary of State for Culture Media and Sport* [2008] 2 WLR 781 , para 37; *R (Al-Skeini) v Ministry of Defence* [2008] 1 AC 153, para 106 (Lord Brown).

[16] [2008] 1 AC 719.

House also dealt, somewhat unconvincingly, with the 'justification' issue in the alternative, the *Ullah* principle helped to divert a potentially explosive political conflict with the House of Commons.

Nevertheless, despite its political attractions, the *Ullah* principle is not without its difficulties. On the clear words of section 2(1) it plainly does not mean that English courts must *only* look at Strasbourg,[17] still less does it oblige the English courts to apply those cases strictly as precedent,[18] unlike the position under European Community law. Although the White Paper issued prior to the enactment of the HRA provides some support for asserting that the purpose of enacting the HRA was to bring rights home,[19] it certainly does not seek to define the government's objectives in such a specific or restrictive way. Furthermore, when the HRA was being enacted, clear statements[20] were made by the Home Secretary in the House of Commons[21] and by the Lord Chancellor in the House of Lords[22] that the courts must be free to develop human rights jurisprudence and to move out in new directions.

It seems unfortunate for the English courts to have sought democratic legitimacy by means a self-denying ordinance which has the effect of severely restricting their ability to be 'an international standard-bearer of liberty and justice' as envisaged by Lord Bingham in 1993.[23]

A number of commentators have drawn attention to the difficulties deriving from the *Ullah* doctrine.[24] These have been acknowledged by Baroness Hale in her 2008 'Justice' Lecture.[25] The legal and practical difficulties inherent to the doctrine have troubled the House of Lords in subsequent cases.[26] In *R (Animal*

[17] Thus, Laws LJ expressed the view in *Begum v Tower Hamlets London Borough Council* [2002] 1 WLR 2491 para 17 that 'the courts task under the HRA... is not simply to add on the Strasbourg learning to the corpus of English law, as if it were a compulsory adjunct taken from an alien source, but to develop a municipal law of human rights by the incremental method of the common law, case by case, taking account of the Strasbourg jurisprudence, as the HRA enjoins us to do'; and see to similar effect, his remarks in *R (Pro-life Alliance) v BBC* [2004] 1 AC 185 para 33.

[18] cf *Huang v Secretary of State for the Home Department* [2007] 2 AC 167, para 18 per Lord Bingham 'the case law of the Strasbourg court is not strictly binding'; and see *R (Animal Defenders International) v Secretary of State for Culture Media and Sport* [2008] 2 WLR 781 paras 44–45 (Lord Scott drawing attention to the possibility of the domestic courts and the Court of Human Rights reaching conflicting interpretations of the Convention, and see also Lord Bingham's response at para 37).

[19] See *Rights Brought Home: The Human Rights Bill* Cm 3782 para 1.18.

[20] *In re G (Adoption: Unmarried Couple* [2008] 3 WLR 76 para 119 per Baroness Hale.

[21] Hansard (HC Debates), 16 February 1998, col 768.

[22] Hansard (HL Debates), 18 November 1997, cols 514–515.

[23] See, n 1 above.

[24] See e.g., J Lewis, 'The European Ceiling on Human Rights' [2007] PL 720; R Masterman, 'Aspiration or foundation? The status of Strasbourg jurisprudence and "Convention rights" in domestic law' in H Fenwick, G Phillipson, and R Masterman, *Judicial Reasoning under the UK Human Rights Act* (Cambridge University Press, 2007).

[25] Baroness Hale, 'Law Lords at the Margin: Who defines Convention rights?' 15 October 2008.

[26] See also *In re G (Adoption: Unmarried Couple)* n 20 above.

Defenders International) v Secretary of State for Culture[27] the claimant was prevented from placing an advertisement about the threat to the survival of primates
on the ground that this would breach the ban on political advertising contained
in section 321(2) of the Communications Act 2003. The claimant alleged that
Article 10 had been breached, relying strongly on a decision of the Court of
Human Rights, *VgT Verein v Switzerland*.[28] In fact, when the 2003 Act had been
passed, the Secretary of State felt unable to make a statement of compatibility
under section 19(1)(a) of the HRA; instead, she made a statement under section
19(1)(b) that, although unable to make a statement under section 19(1)(a), the
government wished the House of Commons to proceed with the Bill. The government's position was that it believed and had been advised that the ban on political
advertising in what became sections 319 and 321 was compatible with Article 10,
but because of the Court's decision in *VgT* it could not be sure.[29] Nevertheless,
in *Animal Defenders* the House of Lords declined to follow *VgT* and held that the
ban did not violate Article 10. However, their treatment of the *Ullah* principle
was not entirely persuasive.

The principle that the English courts must apply the Convention strictly in line
with Strasbourg case law is not the approach of other signatories to the Convention
such as France or Germany.[30] Furthermore, the focus on Strasbourg case law
could distract the English courts from benefiting from the views expressed in
cases from other jurisdictions when wrestling with universal human rights problems—unlike the South African Constitutional Court which has shaped its decisions by reference to the wisdom to be derived from other jurisdictions. Finally
and most importantly, the concentration on Strasbourg decisions has prevented
the English courts from developing indigenous human rights jurisprudence.

There are a number of factors to be borne in mind in identifying the proper
perspective approach to be applied to Strasbourg cases.[31] The Court of Human
Rights does not develop its principles and reasoning in the more discursive analytical style of the common law tradition. In fact, Convention principles are often
extended—even if the reasoning for doing so is sometimes exiguous.[32] A number
of the Strasbourg cases do not, on analysis, withstand close scrutiny; and the

---

[27] [2008] 2 WLR 781.   [28] (2001) 34 EHRR 159.   [29] Ibid, para 13.
[30] See e.g., E Orucu (ed), *Judicial Comparativism in Human Rights Cases* (United Kingdom
National Committee of Comparative Law, 2003).
[31] See e.g., R Masterman, 'Aspiration or foundation? The status of Strasbourg jurisprudence
and "Convention rights" in domestic law' in H Fenwick, G Phillipson, and R Masterman, *Judicial
Reasoning under the UK Human Rights Act* (Cambridge University Press, 2007).
[32] E.g., the principle from *Z v Finland* (1997) 25 EHRR 371 para 103 that Art 8 interferences
with confidential medical information must be subject to important limitations and accompanied
by effective and adequate safeguards against abuse has been applied in the rather different contexts
of the broadcast of a CCTV film showing the claimant's suicide attempt (*Peck v United Kingdom*
(2003) 36 EHRR 719, para 78) and to the release of telephone taps into the public domain concerning the well known Italian politician (*Craxi v Italy (No 2)* (2003) (2004) 38 EHRR 47, para
74)—although the Court has not provide detailed reasoning for that extension.

nature and style of the reasoning in many Strasbourg decisions gives rise to acute difficulties of interpretation.[33]

All these arguments suggest that the price to be paid for 'democratic legitimacy' by the adoption of the *Ullah* principle may be too high. Although, during the first eight turbulent years of the HRA, the course steered by Lord Bingham has been a wise one, we suggest that the time may shortly come when a change of direction is required, with English judges having the confidence to move to a new phase in the development of a domestic rights jurisprudence.

Terrorism and Democracy

Nevertheless, the *Ullah* principle—with its acknowledgment of strict limits on judicial activism—has served an important purpose in the early years of the HRA. When faced with the accusation of unaccountable judicial activism, the judges have had the ready answer that they are simply doing the will of the elected Parliament, following Strasbourg, and 'bringing rights home'.

As already mentioned, the most fundamental challenge to the HRA has come from politicians demanding vigorous judicial prosecution of the war on terror. The Home Secretary, Mr Charles Clarke, famously complained that the Law Lords had refused to meet him to discuss 'issues of principle' arising in terrorism cases.[34] In a magazine interview he said:

I have been frustrated at the inability to have general conversations of principle with the law lords…because of their sense of propriety. I do find that frustrating. I have never met any of them. I think there is a view that it's not appropriate to meet in terms of their integrity. I'm not sure I agree…and I regret that. I think some dialogue between the senior judiciary and the executive would be beneficial, and finding a channel is quite important.[35]

This complaint was roundly dismissed by Lord Bingham who in a 2005 lecture said that ministers did not always understand the reality of the independence of the judiciary. He warned that judges were 'bound to take no notice' of a prime minister who ordered them 'to do something' that was inconsistent with the rule of law. He said that 'The ultimate treason for any judge is to uphold as lawful that which is unlawful'.[36] More recently, Lord Bingham rejected Mr Blair's assertion that as a result of terrorism, 'the rules of the game have changed'.[37]

The conflict between the perceived demands of the 'war on terror' and the HRA arose in perhaps its sharpest form in the seminal Belmarsh case, *A v The*

---

[33] See e.g., *N v Secretary of State for the Home Department* [2005] 2 AC 296.

[34] Report of the Select Committee of the House of Lords, *Relations between the executive, the judiciary and Parliament*, Evide, p 26.

[35] Interview, *New Statesman*, 26 September 2005.

[36] Speech to Law Society, 14 September 2005.

[37] Interview, BBC Law in Action, 15 July 2007.

Secretary of State for the Home Department.[38] A panel of nine Law Lords was convened to examine the proportionality of the control order regime for terrorist
suspects under section 23 of the Anti-Terrorism Crime and Security Act 2001.
Lord Bingham delivered the leading speech. He rejected the government's argument that the court should not conduct a proportionality review because this
was a matter for the democratic institutions and not the courts. In rejecting this
distinction he said:

It is of course true that the judges in this country are not elected and are not answerable
to Parliament. It is also of course true...that Parliament, the executive and the courts
have different functions. But the function of independent judges charged to interpret
and apply the law is universally recognised as a cardinal feature of the modern democratic state, a cornerstone of the rule of law itself. The Attorney General is fully entitled
to insist on the proper limits of judicial authority, but he is wrong to stigmatise judicial
decision-making as in some way undemocratic... The [HRA] gives the courts a very specific, wholly democratic, mandate. As Professor Jowell has put it 'The courts are charged
by Parliament with delineating the boundaries of a rights-based democracy'[39]

He went on to hold, with the support of seven of his colleagues, that the detention
of suspected terrorists which was confined to detaining non-nationals was a disproportionate response, not strictly required by the exigencies of the situation for
derogating from the Convention under Article 15, and was also discriminatory
in breach of Article 14 of the Convention. The approach of the House of Lords in
the Belmarsh case makes it a decision of the first magnitude, bearing comparison
with *Anisminic*,[40] *Ridge v Baldwin*,[41] and *Conway v Rimmer*.[42]

The case against the Belmarsh detainees returned to the House of Lords in *A
v Secretary of State for the Home Department (No 2)*[43] where the complaint was
that the Secretary of State sought the ability to rely on evidence of a third party
obtained through his torture in a foreign state. This time the issue was considered by a seven-member Judicial Committee. Led by Lord Bingham the House
unanimously held that evidence obtained by torture could not be relied on in any
circumstances. Lord Bingham observed:[44]

It trivialises the issue before the House to treat it as an argument about the law of evidence. The issue is one of constitutional principle, whether evidence obtained by tortur-
ing another human being may lawfully be admitted against a party to proceedings in a
British court, irrespective of where, or by whom, or on whose authority the torture was
inflicted. To that question I would give a very clear negative answer.

It should be noted, however, that Lord Bingham found himself in a minority
on the crucial practical issue of the burden of proof in cases where it was alleged
that evidence had been obtained by torture. In contrast to the majority of his

---

38   [2005] 2 AC 68.   39   Ibid, para 42.   40   [1969] 2 AC 147.
41   [1964] AC 40.   42   [1968] AC 910.   43   [2006] 2 AC 221.
44   Ibid, para 51.

colleagues, he took the view that evidence should be excluded if there was a real risk that evidence may have been obtained by torture.[45]

The first Belmarsh decision led to a recasting of the control order regime for those suspected of terrorist activities. In due course, this came before the House of Lords again in a series of linked cases. In *Secretary of State v JJ*,[46] the House of Lords addressed the question as to whether the obligations imposed by the non-derogating control orders considered cumulatively infringed Article 5. The terms of the control orders confined the individual to a one-bedroom flat for 18 hours every day, required visitors to be approved in advance, and prevented the individual from leaving a defined urban area. The majority, led by Lord Bingham, held that the control orders constituted a deprivation of liberty for the purposes of Article 5. Consistent with the Strasbourg case law,[47] the Court considered the cumulative effect of the control order obligations on the individual's Article 5 right to liberty.

In *Secretary of State for the Home Department v MB*[48] an application for a control order was made without notice to MB and was supported by an open and a closed statement. The open statement asserted that MB was an Islamic extremist who was involved in terrorist-related activities but no details were given of those assertions and it was clear that the justification for making the order lay in the closed material. The Court of Appeal had held that the 'special advocate' procedure provided sufficient protection for the Article 6 rights of the controlee.[49] In the House of Lords, only Lord Hoffmann agreed with this approach. The majority were of the view that, although the right to a fair trial required that a person be informed of the case against him and be permitted to respond to it, the right was not absolute and might be limited in the interests of national security; but that only such measures restricting the individual's rights as were strictly necessary were permissible. Any difficulties MB suffered in making his case were to be sufficiently counterbalanced by the procedures employed by the judicial authorities; and the court's task was to ascertain whether, looking at the process as a whole, a procedure had been used which involved significant injustice to the controlled person. The House of Lords accepted that the statutory provisions by which material might be withheld from the controlled person might be mitigated by procedural means, including the appointment of special advocates; but took the view that since there could be cases where the core, irreducible minimum of procedural protection would not be met, the Prevention of Terrorism Act and CPR Part 76 had to be read down under section 3 of the Human Rights Act 1998 so as to take effect only where it was consistent with fairness for them to do so.

---

[45] Ibid, para 56 (Lord Nicholls and Lord Hoffmann agreed with Lord Bingham), the majority were of the view that the burden was on the party challenging the evidence to show that, on a balance of probabilities, it was obtained by torture.

[46] [2008] 1 AC 385.   [47] See *Guzzardi v Italy* (1981) 3 EHRR 333.

[48] [2008] 1 AC 440.   [49] [2007] QB 415.

Three of the four Lord Law Lords making up the majority[50] favoured remitting the case to the first instance court for reconsideration. However, Lord Bingham was of the view that the concept of fairness 'imports a core, irreducible minimum of procedural protection' involving disclosure to the controllee of the thrust of the case against him.[51]

In these cases the House of Lords has resolutely refused to bow to political pressure and or criticism and has upheld the Convention rights of unpopular terrorist suspects. The democratic legitimacy identified by Lord Bingham in the first Belmarsh case has both explicitly and implicitly buttressed the approach which has been taken.

Conclusion

When the HRA came into effect, Lord Bingham observed that its implementation 'has assumed something of the character of a religious event: an event eagerly-sought and long-awaited but arousing feelings of apprehension as well as expectation, the uncertainty that accompanies any new and testing experience'.[52] Over the past eight years he has sought to temper the fervour of the zealots whilst reinvigorating domestic traditions of rights-based jurisprudence. The maintenance of the democratic legitimacy of the HRA has been a key feature in this approach.

After eight years, the HRA has become an established feature of the legal landscape. It has penetrated every aspect of private and public law. If the New Jerusalem remains unbuilt, the modest foundations of a domestic Bill of Rights are still intact. English law has absorbed 'rights discourse' without cataclysmic upheaval. Although some sacred jurisprudential cows have been culled[53] many human rights principles appear reassuringly familiar to common lawyers. The 'war on terror' has been met head on and the HRA has survived the encounter.

The success in preserving and maintaining Convention values during such a turbulent period reflects the careful stewardship of Lord Bingham. His cautious conservation of democratic legitimacy through the *Ullah* principle has provided vital support for the HRA over this period. The consistent approach in his opinions has been to graft long-established common law principles onto the firmer constitutional bedrock created by the Convention, developing a creative and

---

[50] Baroness Hale, Lord Carswell, and Lord Brown.

[51] Ibid, paras 41 and 43; the issue continues to divide judicial opinion with a majority of the Court of Appeal rejecting the approach of Lord Bingham and overturning the views of first instance judges on the issue, *Secretary of State for the Home Department v AF, AM and AN* [2008] EWCA Civ 1148. The case is due to be reconsidered by the House of Lords.

[52] Lord Bingham 'Foreword', in R Clayton and H Tomlinson, *The Law of Human Rights* (Oxford University Press, 2000).

[53] The metaphor is Lord Slynn's, see *R v Lambert* [2002] 2 AC 545, para 6.

delicate synthesis of domestic legal principle and Convention rights, a perspective Lord Bingham described in January 2000 as 'recognising the important values which infuse the Act, but also recognising the strengths of our own native trad-ition, idiosyncratic though some of them doubtless are'.[54] As a result of the enact-ment of the HRA, rights jurisprudence has taken firm root in the legal landscape. Lord Bingham's contribution to that process has been vital and irreplaceable.

[54] Lord Bingham 'Foreword', in R Clayton and H Tomlinson, *The Law of Human Rights* (n 52 above).

5

Substance and Procedure in Judicial Review

Paul Craig

1. Introduction

It is a great pleasure to contribute to this volume of essays in honour of Lord Bingham. There is no doubt of his status as one of the very best judges of this generation. His judgments have always been elegant, analytical, clear, and succinct. They have provided a model of legal reasoning at its best. This chapter cannot do justice to the many important judgments that Lord Bingham has given in the field of public law, whether under the Human Rights Act 1998, or in terms of general judicial review.

His contribution to the jurisprudence under the Human Rights Act (HRA) is exemplified by his judgment in *A v Secretary of State for the Home Department*,[1] in which he disagreed with the submissions made by the Attorney–General and made clear the role of the courts in delineating the boundaries of a rights-based democracy. Lord Bingham's contribution to the human rights case law was apparent once again in his dissent in the *YL* case,[2] concerning the meaning of public authority for the purpose of the HRA, where his view is to be preferred to that of the majority. Many other examples could be given.[3]

The present chapter will, however, focus primarily on judicial review outside the Human Rights Act 1998. It seeks to explore, with the aid of Lord Bingham's judgments, the interrelationship between a number of important topics within judicial review that are distinct, albeit connected, both pragmatically and conceptually. These are the test for substantive review, the provision of reasons, the evidentiary foundation for those reasons, disclosure and access to evidence, and case-management within judicial review. The nature of the connection can be briefly stated here and will be developed in more detail in the subsequent discussion.

---

[1] [2005] 2 AC 68, para 42.

[2] *YL v Birmingham City Council* [2007] 3 WLR 112.

[3] See, e.g., *R (on the application of Countryside Alliance) v Attorney General* [2007] 3 WLR 922; *Huang v Secretary of State for the Home Department* [2007] 2 AC 167; *R (on the application of Begum) v Denbigh High School Governors* [2007] 1 AC 100.

It will be for the courts to decide on the appropriate criteria for substantive review, whether this is cast in terms of rationality or proportionality. It will be for the courts to imbue these abstract concepts with more concrete meaning, which specifies with greater exactitude the intensity of judicial scrutiny. There are perennial debates about how intensive this scrutiny should be, and whether it should be framed in terms of rationality or proportionality.

The courts will also decide on the provision of reasons. There are a number of advantages to be secured by insisting upon reasons for decisions.[4] They can assist the courts in performing their supervisory function. Substantive review based on relevancy, propriety of purpose, or proportionality is easier to apply if the public authority's reasons are evident. An obligation to provide reasons will often help to ensure that the decision has been thought through by the public body. The provision of reasons can help to ensure that other objectives of administrative law are not frustrated. If, for example, we decide to grant consultation rights in certain areas, then a duty to furnish reasons will make it more difficult for the decision-maker merely to go through the motions of hearing interested parties without actually taking their views into account. Finally, it is arbitrary to have one's status redefined without an adequate explanation of the reasons for the action. The provision of reasons can, by way of contrast, increase public confidence in the administrative process and enhance its legitimacy. A duty to provide reasons can, therefore, help to attain both the instrumental and non-instrumental objectives that underlie process rights.

It will also be for the courts to decide whether, and if so how far, to consider the evidentiary foundation for the reasons proffered by the administration. This is more uncertain terrain. It was until recently difficult to distil clear principles as to when the courts would inquire into such matters, in part at least because of the close link between judicial scrutiny of evidence and the general issue as to the reviewability of fact in judicial review proceedings. More recent jurisprudence has gone some way to clarifying this issue,[5] although a number of difficulties still remain.[6] This should not however serve to mask the significance of evidentiary review within the overall scheme of judicial review, and the connection between substantive review, the provision of reasons and review of the evidence. Thus in the same way that substantive review, whether cast in terms of rationality or

---

[4] M Akehurst, 'Statements of Reasons for Judicial and Administrative Decisions' (1970) 33 MLR 154; G Flick, 'Administrative Adjudications and the Duty to Give Reasons—A Search for Criteria' [1978] PL 16; D Galligan, 'Judicial Review and the Textbook Writers' (1982) 2 OJLS 257; G Richardson, 'The Duty to Give Reasons: Potential and Practice' [1986] PL 437; P Craig, 'The Common Law, Reasons and Administrative Justice' [1994] CLJ 282; Sir Patrick Neil, 'The Duty to Give Reasons: The Openness of Decision-Making', in C Forsyth and I Hare (eds), *The Golden Metwand and the Crooked Cord* (Oxford University Press, 1998), 161–184.

[5] *E v Secretary of State for the Home Department* [2004] QB 1044; *R (Iran) v Secretary of State for the Home Department* [2005] EWCA Civ 982.

[6] T Jones, 'Mistake of Fact in Administrative Law' [1990] PL 507; M Kent, 'Widening the Scope of Review for Error of Fact' [1999] JR 239; P Craig, 'Judicial Review, Appeal and Factual Error' [2004] PL 788; P Craig, *Administrative Law* (Sweet & Maxwell, 6th edn, 2008), Ch 15.

proportionality, will be enhanced by the obligation to provide reasons, the force of the latter obligation will in turn be furthered by the extent to which the courts are willing to consider the evidentiary foundation for those reasons. The extent to which courts take this step will however be influenced by prudential considerations in terms of not overburdening the courts and the process of judicial review, and by more normative consideration relating to the perceived role of court and primary decision-maker concerning matters of fact and evidence.

There is also a proximate connection between review of fact and evidence on the one hand and disclosure on the other, insofar as the latter is concerned with the ability of the claimant to gain access to evidentiary material relied on by the public authority when it made its decision. The courts have traditionally been reluctant to order discovery, now disclosure, in proceedings for judicial review, in part because of the burdens that this could place on the public body, and in part because those proceedings often involved issues of law in relation to which it was felt that discovery was not necessary for resolving the case. The judicial approach, however, was criticized as being too restrictive, and recent case law has revealed some shift in judicial thinking on this matter.

Problems of case management and the length of judicial review proceedings have been a prominent consideration in shaping the public law remedial procedure and the judicial interpretation thereof, including the provisions concerning disclosure. The chapter concludes by considering the impact of the Tribunals, Courts and Enforcement Act 2007, which contains important innovations by empowering the new Upper Tribunal to exercise powers of judicial review in certain types of case.

2. *Smith* and Rationality Review

The interconnection between substantive review, the provision of reasons, and the review of evidence can be exemplified by some prominent cases in which Lord Bingham was involved. It played a part, as will be seen, in the classic exchange between the domestic courts and Strasbourg concerning homosexuals serving in the military.

The facts in the *Smith* case are well known.[7] In 1994 the Ministry of Defence reaffirmed its policy that homosexuality was incompatible with service in the armed forces and personnel known to be homosexual or engaging in homosexual activity would be administratively discharged. The policy was considered by both Houses of Parliament and by select committees of the House of Commons in 1986 and 1991. It was consistent with advice received from senior members of the services, but was in contradistinction to that recently adopted in respect of NATO and Commonwealth forces where similar bans had been removed. The

---

[7] *R v Ministry of Defence, ex p Smith* [1996] QB 517.

applicants were serving members of the armed forces who had been administratively discharged between November 1994 and January 1995 because of their homosexual orientation. They argued, *inter alia*, that this policy was irrational and constituted breach of Article 8 ECHR. The applicants accepted that membership of the armed forces involved curtailment of freedoms enjoyed by others in civilian employments, and recognized that the exigencies of service life could justify restrictions on homosexual activity and manifestations of homosexual orientation. They challenged, however, the blanket, non-discretionary, nature of the existing policy. The claim failed in the Divisional Court and the Court of Appeal, but the case nonetheless developed the law relating to substantive rationality review.

Sir Thomas Bingham MR gave the leading judgment in the Court of Appeal, and noted the changed perceptions of homosexuality. He considered the reports of the select committees on the matter, and observed that they did not appear to have considered whether the objectives of the existing policy could be met by a less absolute rule, notwithstanding the fact that since 1991 neither homosexual orientation, nor private homosexual activity, precluded appointment to posts in the home civil service, the diplomatic service, or to the judiciary, and notwithstanding the fact that very few NATO countries barred homosexuals from their armed forces.

In terms of the law concerning rationality review, Sir Thomas Bingham MR adopted the formulation proposed by David Pannick:

The court may not interfere with the exercise of an administrative discretion on substantive grounds save where the court is satisfied that the decision is unreasonable in the sense that it is beyond the range of responses open to a reasonable decision-maker. But in judging whether the decision-maker has exceeded this margin of appreciation the human rights context is important. The more substantial the interference with human rights, the more the court will require by way of justification before it is satisfied that the decision is reasonable in the sense outlined above.[8]

This heightened rationality review was justified by previous House of Lords' authority in *Bugdaycay*[9] and *Brind*,[10] where various of the judgments had endorsed, explicitly or implicitly, more intensive rationality scrutiny in cases concerned with Convention rights. Sir Thomas Bingham was also cognizant of the need for the UK courts to meet the requirements of Article 13 ECHR, that there should be a national remedy to enforce the substance of the Convention rights and freedoms, coupled with the fact that the Strasbourg Court attached considerable weight to the power of the English courts to review administrative decisions by way of judicial review.[11] He nonetheless cautioned that the court should

---

[8] Ibid, 554.
[9] *R v Home Secretary, ex p Bugdaycay* [1987] AC 514.
[10] *R v Home Secretary, ex p Brind* [1991] 1 AC 696.
[11] *Smith*, n 7, 556.

not be thrust into the position of the primary decision-maker: it was not the constitutional role of the court to regulate conditions in the armed forces, nor did the courts have the expertise to do so.

The rationale for the army's policy concerning homosexuality was then analyzed in the light of the rationality test adumbrated above. Sir Thomas Bingham MR took seriously the critique of the challenged policy advanced by counsel for the applicants, who vigorously challenged the idea that morale and unit effectiveness would suffer if the policy were to be changed, or that it could place in jeopardy young or under-age members of the services. He nonetheless concluded that the army policy could not be deemed legally irrational at the time that the applicants were discharged, more especially because it was supported by both Houses of Parliament, there was no evidence before the ministry which plainly invalidated that advice, and because changes elsewhere had been adopted too recently for their effect to be evaluated. The threshold of irrationality was, said Sir Thomas Bingham MR, a high one and was not crossed in this case.

The endorsement of more searching rationality scrutiny in *Smith* was a welcome development. The 'green light' given by the House of Lords in *Bugdaycay* and *Brind* to more intensive rationality review had been developed in cases such as *Leech*,[12] where the court considered the validity of a rule that allowed a prison governor to read letters from prisoners and stop those which were inordinately long or objectionable, and held that the more fundamental the right which had been interfered with, the more difficult was it to imply any such rule-making power in the primary legislation. The judgment in *Smith*[13] was in the same vein and this mode of reasoning was developed by lower courts prior to the enactment of the Human Rights Act 1998.[14] Thus in *McQuillan*[15] the applicant challenged the legality of an exclusion order prohibiting him from entering Great Britain on the ground that he was or had been involved in acts of terrorism. He maintained that he was no longer a member of a terrorist organization and that his life was in danger if he continued to live in Northern Ireland. The Home Secretary was not persuaded and refused to revoke the exclusion order. Sedley J recognized that freedom of movement, subject only to the general law, was a fundamental value of the common law.[16] The power given to the Home Secretary to restrict this freedom, not by modifying the general law, but by depriving certain persons of the full extent of this right, was a draconian measure, which could be justified only by a grave emergency. It was for this reason that the courts would scrutinize

---

[12] *R v Secretary of State for the Home Department, ex p Leech* [1994] QB 198.

[13] *Smith*, n 7.

[14] See, e.g., *R v Broadcasting Complaints Commission, ex p Granada Television Ltd* [1995] COD 207; *R v Secretary of State for the Home Department, ex p Norney* (1995) 7 Admin LR 861; *R v Secretary of State for the Home Department, ex p Moon* [1996] Imm AR 477; *R v Secretary of State for Social Security, ex p Joint Council for the Welfare of Immigrants* [1997] 1 WLR 275; *R v Chief Constable for the North Wales Police Area Authority, ex p AB and DC* [1997] 3 WLR 724.

[15] *R v Secretary of State for the Home Department, ex p McQuillan* [1995] 4 All ER 400.

[16] [1995] 4 All ER 400, 421–422.

the minister's reasoning closely and 'draw the boundaries of rationality tightly around his judgment'.[17] This was equally true in relation to the right to life. This too was recognized and protected by the common law and 'attracted the most anxious scrutiny by the courts of administrative decision-making'.[18]

3. *Murray* and the Provision of Reasons

In the *Smith* case there was no live issue concerning the giving of reasons for the challenged policy, since the relevant officials furnished the reasons underlying the absolute ban on homosexuals in the armed forces. The issue, as we have seen, was as to the cogency of these reasons and the judicial role in assessing them, an issue to which we shall return below.

Lord Bingham has, however, supported the provision of reasons. The general position in UK law is that there is no general duty to provide reasons, but this proposition can be displaced by an obligation to provide reasons, whether derived from statute,[19] inference from the right of appeal,[20] EU law,[21] Convention jurisprudence,[22] or from common law conceptions of fairness or natural justice.[23]

The development of the duty to give reasons based directly on common law conceptions of fairness and natural justice was especially interesting and promising. Thus in *Cunningham*[24] Lord Donaldson MR re-affirmed previous orthodoxy by making it clear that there was no general duty to provide reasons, but nonetheless imposed such a duty on the Civil Service Appeal Board (CSAB), which had given the applicant far less compensation for unfair dismissal than he would have received under the normal employment protection legislation. The duty was imposed because the CSAB was held to be a judicial body performing functions analogous to those of an industrial tribunal. The latter would have to provide reasons, and fairness demanded that so too should the CSAB. The same approach was evident in later cases. Thus, in *Wilson*,[25] Taylor LJ based his decision that the applicant should be entitled to know the reasons why the Parole Board was not recommending him for release, on the general ground of natural justice. This method is also apparent in *Doody*.[26] Lord Mustill noted the recent tendency to greater transparency and openness in the making of administrative decisions, and gave an alternative rationale for his judgment to that considered above. His Lordship stated that the statutory scheme should be operated as fairly

---

[17] Ibid, 422.   [18] Ibid, 422D.
[19] Tribunal and Inquiries Act 1992, s 10.
[20] *Minister of National Revenue v Wrights' Canadian Ropes Ltd* [1947] AC 109, 123.
[21] Case 222/86, *Unectef v Heylens* [1987] ECR 4097, para 15.
[22] *Stefan v General Medical Council* [2000] HRLR 1.
[23] *R v Civil Service Appeal Board, ex p Cunningham* [1991] 4 All ER 310.
[24] *R v Civil Service Appeal Board, ex p Cunningham* [1991] 4 All ER 310.
[25] *R v Parole Board, ex p Wilson* [1992] 1 QB 740.
[26] *R v Secretary of State for the Home Department, ex p Doody* [1994] AC 531.

as possible in the circumstances, and that one should ask whether the refusal to give reasons was fair. On the facts of the case he thought not, since the prisoner had a real interest in understanding how long might be the term of imprisonment and why this particular period was imposed.

Lord Bingham, as Chief Justice, added his own authority to such developments in *Murray*,[27] in which he distilled certain principles concerning the duty to give reasons from earlier decisions. His Lordship stated that there was at present no general duty to give reasons, and that the public interest might outweigh the advantages of giving reasons in a particular case. He held that certain factors militated against the giving of reasons: it could place an undue burden on the decision-maker; demand the articulation of inexpressible value judgments; and offer an invitation to the captious to comb the reasons for grounds of challenge.

Lord Bingham recognized however that there was a perceptible trend towards greater transparency in decision-making. He acknowledged that there were significant factors in favour of giving reasons: it could concentrate the mind of the decision-maker; demonstrate to the recipient that this was so; show that the issues had been properly addressed; and alert the individual to possible justiciable flaws in the process. Where a body had power to affect individuals a court would therefore readily imply procedural safeguards in addition to any stipulated in the relevant statute if they were necessary to ensure the attainment of fairness. If a just decision could not be given without the provision of reasons then they should be given, and so too where the decision appeared to be aberrant. In deciding whether reasons should have been given, the court would take into account the absence of any right of appeal, and the role reasons can play in detecting the kind of error which would entitle the court to intervene by way of review. The fact that a tribunal was carrying out a judicial function was a consideration in favour of the giving of reasons, particularly where personal liberty was concerned.

4. *Smith and Grady*, Review, Reasons, and Evidence

The applicants who had lost on the facts in *Smith* took their case to Strasbourg where the European Court of Human Rights found in their favour. The decision was, as is well known, the catalyst for proportionality as the standard of review adopted under the Human Rights Act 1998. The reasoning of the Strasbourg Court in *Smith and Grady*[28] is worth revisiting, since it reveals the interconnection between the test for substantive review, the provision of reasons, and the evidentiary foundation for those reasons.

The applicants relied on Articles 3 and 8 ECHR and contended that they had no effective remedy, contrary to Article 13 ECHR. The Strasbourg Court

---

[27] *R v Ministry of Defence, ex p Murray* [1998] COD 134.
[28] *Smith and Grady v UK* [2000] 29 EHRR 493.

found that there had been a violation of Article 8 ECHR, that there had been no violation of Article 3 ECHR, and that there had been a violation of Article 13 ECHR.

In relation to the Article 8 claim, the Court held that Article 8 still applied when a person joined the armed forces and that the investigations by the military police into the applicants' sexuality constituted breach of Article 8(1) that required justification under Article 8(2). The Court accepted that the policy was designed to ensure the operational effectiveness of the armed forces and that, therefore, the resulting interferences could be said to pursue the legitimate aims of 'the interests of national security' and 'the prevention of disorder'. It then considered whether the interference was necessary in a democratic society, with the consequential requirements that it answered a pressing social need and was proportionate to the legitimate aim pursued. It was for the national authorities to make the initial assessment of necessity, and it had a margin of appreciation in this respect, although the final evaluation was for the Strasbourg Court.

The Strasbourg Court accepted that operational effectiveness of the armed forces was a valid objective and then considered the evidence proffered by armed forces as to the alleged impact of homosexuals. The UK Government had relied on the report of the Homosexuality Policy Assessment Team (HPAT), but the Strasbourg Court was unwilling to accord it significant weight for a number of reasons: it questioned the independence of the assessment contained in the report given that it was produced by the Ministry of Defence; only a very small proportion of the armed forces' personnel participated in the assessment; the methods of assessment were not anonymous; many of the questions in the attitude survey suggested answers in support of the existing policy; and many of the views reported were founded solely on the negative attitudes of heterosexual personnel towards those of homosexual orientation.[29] The Strasbourg Court emphasized, moreover, the lack of concrete evidence to substantiate the alleged damage to morale and fighting power that any change in the policy would entail,[30] and felt that any behavioural problems could be dealt with by appropriate disciplinary rules and conduct codes.

The Strasbourg Court was moreover willing to place real weight on the evidence from other countries. The UK Government had argued that no worthwhile lessons could be gleaned from recent legal changes in those foreign armed forces that now admitted homosexuals. The Court noted that the European countries operating a blanket legal ban on homosexuals in their armed forces were now in a small minority, and that, although recent, the Court could not overlook the widespread changing views of contracting states on this issue. It was therefore incumbent on the UK Government to proffer particularly convincing and weighty reasons to justify their policy, and the Court concluded that it was unable to do so.

---

[29] Ibid, paras 95–96.   [30] Ibid, para 99.

The Strasbourg Court's reasoning with respect to the Article 13 claim was formally distinct from that concerning Article 8 considered above, but there were nonetheless connections between the two. The Court acknowledged that Article 13 did not demand a particular form of remedy. However since, at that time, the Convention had not been incorporated into domestic law issues concerning Article 8, pressing social need and the like could not be fully addressed by UK courts, which were limited to consideration of the rationality of the contested policy. The Strasbourg Court considered the rationality test set out by the Court of Appeal, with heightened rationality review for cases concerned with human rights, but concluded that this test was still too difficult for applicants to satisfy, such that it effectively excluded any consideration by the domestic courts of the question whether the interference with the applicants' rights answered a pressing social need or was proportionate to the national security and public order aims pursued.[31]

There is no doubt that the difference of view as between the Strasbourg Court and the UK courts in *Smith* was affected by the fact that the Convention was not at that time incorporated into UK law, with the consequence that Convention rights were relevant simply by way of background to the determination of rationality.[32] This meant that the UK courts could not engage in detailed analysis of Article 8 through examination of necessity, pressing social need, proportionality, and the like. The need to secure compliance with Convention jurisprudence in terms of the criteria for substantive judicial review was of course the reason for adoption of proportionality as the test for review under the Human Rights Act 1998.[33]

The decisions of the UK courts and the Strasbourg Court nonetheless exemplify the interrelationship between substantive review and review of the evidentiary foundations of the reasons proffered by the public authority. There is in a very real sense a symbiotic relationship between these two aspects of judicial review.

On the one hand, more intensive substantive review cast in terms of proportionality review will often generate, directly or indirectly, the imperative for more scrutiny of the reasons and the evidentiary foundations for those reasons than is the case where the test for review is less intensive, *and* the evidence thus gleaned will facilitate application of the test for substantive review, giving the court more to bite on and thus rendering it more secure in its determination as to whether the decision really was proportionate. This is readily apparent from the Strasbourg Court's decision in *Smith and Grady* where it viewed the evidence to support the reasons proffered by the UK government for its policy with some considerable scepticism. This clearly affected its overall conclusion as to whether the UK Government really had demonstrated a pressing social need, which was

---

[31] Ibid, paras 135–138.   [32] *Smith*, n 7, 558.
[33] *R (on the application of Daly) v Secretary of State for the Home Department* [2001] 2 AC 532.

proportionate, for the contested policy concerning homosexuality in the armed forces. We shall see this connection at work once again when we consider the relationship between substantive review, proportionality, and discovery in the following section.

On the other hand, where substantive review is less intensive there will be less motivation to scrutinize closely the evidentiary foundations for the reasons given, in part because of the very fact that the applicant has to surmount a relatively high hurdle in order to persuade the court to annul the relevant decision. Thus if one takes the literal *Wednesbury* formula, to the effect that the decision will be annulled only if the public authority makes a decision that no reasonable public authority would have made, there was little if any judicial incentive to consider the factual basis of the decision, both because the law relating to the provision of reasons was yet to develop, and because even if the reasons were apparent there was little incentive to consider the evidence underlying the reasons since the decision would only be overturned in extreme circumstances and thus the fact that the applicant could show some shortcomings in the evidence would be to no avail. It follows also that as rationality review becomes more intensive, the demand for more searching review of the reasons and evidence to support them grows. This is readily apparent from the heightened rationality review in *Smith*. In hindsight it is not surprising that the more searching rationality scrutiny led the court to consider more closely than hitherto the arguments adduced by counsel for the applicants, which were, in effect, questioning the evidentiary foundations for the MOD's policy. It is clear that the Court of Appeal sympathized with these arguments, although at the end of the day it did not feel able to quash the challenged policy on the criterion for review that it had articulated.

5. *Tweed*, Disclosure and Access to Evidence

The discussion thus far has been concerned with the connection between substantive review, the provision of reasons, and the judicial assessment of the evidentiary foundation for those reasons. Access to the available documents is however the fourth link in this chain, since the evidence may simply be unknown to the applicants unless they can obtain it by way of discovery, or disclosure as it is now known, thereby precluding any form of judicial assessment of the cogency of the evidence.

A brief word concerning the history relating to discovery and judicial review is in order here. Prior to 1977 grant of leave to cross-examine under the prerogative orders was very rare. This was one of the main reasons why people preferred to use the declaration or the injunction, since unless one could cross-examine it might be impossible to prove the alleged error. The new Order 53 procedure made provision for discovery and cross-examination. There were, however, early indications that the ability to cross-examine should be used sparingly, and that the ordinary trial procedure was preferable for complex factual questions.[34] Later judicial[35] and extra-judicial[36] statements appeared to confirm the reluctance to allow discovery and cross-examination within section 31, because of the delays and extra costs generated by such concessions to the individual. This led to a restrictive judicial interpretation, whereby the courts held that, unless there was some prima facie case for suggesting that the evidence relied upon by the deciding authority was in some respects incorrect or inadequate, it was improper to allow disclosure of documents, the only purpose of which would be to act as a challenge to the accuracy of the affidavit evidence.

This was somewhat paradoxical. A principal reason for making the new procedure prima facie exclusive in *O'Reilly v Mackman*[37] was that the reforms removed defects in the previous law, including the inability to cross-examine and seek discovery. This was the justification for confining the individual to section 31 of the Supreme Court Act 1981, with its protections for the public body. If, however, the individual applicant was rarely allowed to use these procedural aids, the applicant might be unable to prove the invalidity alleged, more especially so in relation to emerging doctrines such as proportionality.

The difficulties posed by the restrictive interpretation of the rules on discovery were remarked on by practitioners and academics alike. Thus Gordon noted that 'the restrictive rules that have bedevilled discovery in recent years only permit access to documentation where such is necessary to undermine an apparent lack of candour in the affidavits lodged'.[38] The Law Commission's 1994 Report[39] recorded that two-thirds of those who responded to the consultation paper favoured the introduction of a more liberal regime of discovery, and concluded that the requirements of the accepted rule were unduly restrictive. It was moreover clear from the empirical work done by Le Sueur and Sunkin that the most common reason for refusing permission was that the claimant could not, without discovery, establish the factual foundation for the case so as to convince the judge that the claim was arguable.[40]

---

[34] *R v Inland Revenue Commissioners, ex p Rossminster Ltd* [1980] AC 952, 1027.

[35] *Air Canada v Secretary of State for Trade (No 2)* [1983] 2 AC 394; *Lonrho plc v Tebbit* [1992] 4 All ER 280; *R v Inland Revenue Commissioners, ex p Taylor* [1989] 1 All ER 906; *R v Secretary of State for the Environment, ex p Doncaster Borough Council* [1990] COD 441; *R v Secretary of State for the Home Department, ex p BH* [1990] COD 445; *R v Secretary of State for the Environment, ex p Islington London Borough* [1992] COD 67; *R v Secretary of State for Education, ex p J* [1993] COD 146; *R v Secretary of State for Transport, ex p APH Road Safety Ltd* [1993] COD 150; *R v Secretary of State for Health, ex p London Borough of Hackney* [1994] COD 432; *R v Arts Council of England, ex p Women's Playhouse Trust* [1998] COD 175.

[36] Lord Woolf [1986] PL 220, 229, 231.   [37] [1983] 2 AC 237.

[38] R Gordon, 'The Law Commission and Judicial Review: Managing the Tension between Case Management and Public Interest Challenges' [1995] PL 11, 16; O Sanders, 'Disclosure of Documents in Claims for Judicial Review' [2006] JR 194.

[39] *Administrative Law: Judicial Review and Statutory Appeals* (Law Com No 226 1994; HC 669), para 7.8.

[40] A le Sueur and M Sunkin, 'Applications for Judicial Review: The Requirement of Leave' [1992] PL 102.

Disclosure is now governed by the relevant CPR rules. CPR 31 deals with disclosure and inspection of documents. A party discloses a document by stating that the document exists or has existed.[41] A party to whom a document has been disclosed has, subject to certain exceptions, a right to inspect it.[42] An order to give disclosure is, unless the court otherwise directs, an order to give standard disclosure.[43] It is open to the court to dispense with or limit standard disclosure.[44] Where a court does make such an order then it requires a party to disclose the documents on which it relies, and the documents which adversely affect its own, or another party's, case, or support another party's case, and such documents which it is required to disclose by a relevant practice direction.[45] A party is under an obligation to make a reasonable search for such documents.[46] The court is also empowered to make an order for specific disclosure or specific inspection, requiring the party to disclose those documents specified in the order.[47]

There is little doubt that these rules give the court ample powers through which to require the public body to provide the information needed for the applicant to sustain its case. It is, however, open to the court to dispense with or limit standard disclosure, and the court also has discretion in relation to requests for more specific disclosure. Much will, therefore, depend upon how the courts use the powers at their disposal.

The House of Lords' decision in *Tweed* is important in this respect.[48] The claimant challenged a determination of the Parades Commission for Northern Ireland permitting, on conditions, a proposed procession by a local Orange lodge to take place in a predominately Catholic town on Easter Day 2004. The claimant asserted that the conditions were unlawful since they constituted a disproportionate interference with his rights protected by Articles 9, 10, and 11 ECHR. The chairman of the commission swore an affidavit summarizing the effect of specific documents, including police reports, an internal memorandum of the commission, and two situation reports, which were material to the determination. The claimant sought specific disclosure of the documents under the relevant civil procedure rules for Northern Ireland, which used the same principles as those applicable under the Civil Procedure Rules 1998. The judge concluded that disclosure of the documents was necessary for fairly disposing of the proportionality issues and made the order sought, but this was reversed by the Court of Appeal in Northern Ireland.

The House of Lords allowed the appeal. Their Lordships held that since a challenge to an administrative decision by way of judicial review raised predominately legal issues, disclosure would not ordinarily be necessary for fairly disposing of the matters in issue. However, their Lordships held that it was no longer the

[41] CPR 31.2.   [42] Ibid, 31.3.   [43] Ibid, 31.5(1).
[44] Ibid, 31.5(2).   [45] Ibid, 31.6.   [46] Ibid, 31.7(1).
[47] Ibid, 31.12.
[48] *Tweed v Parades Commission for Northern Ireland* [2007] 1 AC 650.

rule that disclosure would only be ordered where the decision-maker's affidavit could be shown to be materially inaccurate or misleading. The courts should now adopt a more flexible, less prescriptive approach and judge the need for disclosure on the facts of the individual case.[49]

Their Lordships held, moreover, that disclosure would be more necessary in judicial review cases raising issues of proportionality. The disclosure of documents referred to in affidavits would not, however, always take place where proportionality was in issue. The proportionality issue formed part of the context in which the court had to consider whether it was necessary for fairly disposing of the case to order the disclosure of such documents. It did not give rise automatically to the need for the disclosure of all the documents. Whether disclosure should be ordered would depend on a balancing of several factors, of which proportionality was only one, albeit one of some significance. In cases involving issues of proportionality, disclosure should be carefully limited to the issues which required it in the interests of justice.

The instant case was concerned with the proportionality of a decision restricting a protected Convention right and would call for careful factual assessment in the context of the relevant margin of appreciation, and this should be taken into account by the court when considering disclosure. This was more especially so since summaries, however faithfully compiled, might not give the full flavour of the original documents. The court when making the difficult assessment about disclosure should have access so far as possible to the original documents before the Commission, and therefore disclosure should be ordered to the judge who would consider whether and in what form disclosure should be made in the substantive proceedings.

Lord Bingham's judgment in *Tweed* encapsulated the difficulties concerning the law relating to discovery/disclosure. He stated that 'disclosure of documents in civil litigation has been recognized throughout the common law world as a valuable means of eliciting the truth and thus of enabling courts to base their decisions on a sure foundation of fact', but noted that disclosure could be 'costly, time-consuming, oppressive and unnecessary'.[50] Judicial review applications often raised issues of law where the facts were taken as given, or relevant only to show how the issue arises, and hence disclosure of documents was not regarded as necessary.

Lord Bingham nonetheless acknowledged that facts were significant in some judicial review cases, hence the rules relating to disclosure of specific documents. Such applications were, moreover, 'likely to increase in frequency, since human rights decisions under the Convention tend to be very fact-specific and any judgment on the proportionality of a public authority's interference with a protected Convention right is likely to call for a careful and accurate evaluation of the facts'.[51] Disclosure in such cases, however, should not be regarded as automatic;

---

[49] Ibid, paras 3, 32, 56.   [50] Ibid, para 2.   [51] Ibid, para 3.

the test was whether disclosure appeared to be necessary in order to resolve the matter fairly and justly.

His Lordship took the view that where a public authority relied on a document as significant to its decision, it was normally good practice to exhibit it as the primary evidence, since any summary could distort the original. However, where the authority chose to summarize the effect of a document it was, said Lord Bingham, not necessary for 'the applicant, seeking sight of the document, to suggest some inaccuracy or incompleteness in the summary, usually an impossible task without sight of the document'.[52] There could, however, be reasons concerning confidentiality, or the volume of the material in question as to why the document should not be exhibited, and hence it was for the judge to whom application for disclosure was made to rule on whether, and to what extent, disclosure should be made.

Lord Bingham then applied these principles to the instant case. The applicant's challenge was based on the proportionality of the Parades Commission's interference with his claimed Convention rights. The Commission's deponent had summarized five documents which the applicant wished to see, and had resisted disclosure because this would breach the assurance of confidentiality given to the Commission's informants. Lord Bingham felt that in such circumstances the five documents should be disclosed by the Commission to the judge alone, who would then assess whether the documents contained information given in confidence by informants.[53]

If not, he is likely to order disclosure to Mr Tweed, since there will be no reason not to do so. If they do appear to disclose such information, he must consider whether the documents add anything of value to the summaries in the evidence. If not, that will be the end of the matter. If he judges that they do add something of value to the summaries, he will move on to consider the submissions of the parties on redaction and, if raised, public interest immunity.

Lord Bingham's reasoning was echoed by the other principal judgments in the case. Thus Lord Carswell held that 'it would now be desirable to substitute for the rules hitherto applied a more flexible and less prescriptive principle, which judges the need for disclosure in accordance with the requirements of the particular case, taking into account the facts and circumstances'.[54] He held that this would not arise in most applications for judicial review, since they raised legal issues which did not call for disclosure of documents. The need for disclosure was greater, however, when the case involved proportionality, and that 'in order to assess the difficult issues of proportionality in this case the court should have access as far as possible to the original documents from which the commission received information and advice'.[55]

Lord Brown also highlighted the challenge posed by proportionality cases since they entailed more intensive review and closer factual analysis of the justification

---

[52] Ibid, para 4. [53] Ibid, para 5. [54] Ibid, para 38. [55] Ibid, para 39.

for the restrictions imposed than would be undertaken on ordinary judicial review challenges, while emphasizing that even in such cases judicial review was still a very different process from the litigation in which disclosure orders were ordinarily made.[56] He agreed with Lord Bingham and Lord Carswell 'that the time has come to do away with the rule that there must be a demonstrable contradiction or inconsistency or incompleteness in the respondent's affidavits before disclosure will be ordered', and that instead there should be a more flexible and less prescriptive principle, whereby the judge could decide upon the need for disclosure depending on the facts of the case.[57]

6. The Tribunals, Courts and Enforcement Act 2007, Judicial Review and Case Management

The discussion thus far has been concerned with developments in judicial review made by the courts in relation to important topics that are distinct, albeit linked both practically and conceptually. It is clear, however, that case management has cast its shadow over some of these issues, more particularly those relating to disclosure and the more general law relating to remedies. The desire not to overburden the courts and to facilitate the expeditious discharge of cases has impacted on the very shape of the public law procedure, including the requirement of permission and the extent to which disclosure and cross-examination would be allowed in such proceedings. The Tribunals, Courts and Enforcement Act (TCE) 2007 is therefore of the first importance, not only because of the wide-ranging reforms that it has made in the tribunal system, but also because of its impact on judicial review and case management.

The TCE 2007 built on the the Leggatt Report, *Tribunals for Users—One System, One Service*.[58] The government's response to the Leggatt recommendation for a single tribunal system was to create two new, generic tribunals, the First-tier Tribunal and the Upper Tribunal, into which existing tribunal jurisdictions could be transferred. Thus the TCE 2007, section 3, provides for the creation of a First-tier Tribunal and an Upper Tribunal, each consisting of judges and other members, and presided over by the Senior President of Tribunals. It is intended that the Upper Tribunal will primarily, but not exclusively, be an appellate tribunal from the First-tier Tribunal. The intent is that not only existing, but new tribunal jurisdictions will be fitted into this framework, such that in the future, when Parliament creates a new appeal right or jurisdiction, it will not have to create a new tribunal to administer it. The Upper Tribunal is a superior court of record, like the High Court and the Employment Appeal Tribunal. The TCE

---

[56] Ibid, para 54.   [57] Ibid, para 56.
[58] Report of the Review of Tribunals by Sir Andrew Leggatt: *Tribunals for Users—One System, One Service*, 16 August 2001, <http://www.tribunals-review.org.uk>.

2007 makes detailed provision for the appointment of judges and other members of the First-tier Tribunal and Upper Tribunal.[59] The Act also provides for the establishment of 'chambers' within the two tribunals so that the many jurisdictions that will be transferred into the tribunals can be grouped together appropriately. Each chamber will be headed by a Chamber President.[60]

The TCE 2007 contains an interesting and novel array of mechanisms for checking decisions made by the First-tier Tribunal and the Upper Tribunal. The speedy and efficient discharge of tribunal business is central to the TCE 2007. This serves to explain the powers contained in sections 9 and 10 of the TCE 2007 to allow the First-tier Tribunal and the Upper Tribunal to review their own decisions. In addition, a party to a case generally has a right of appeal on a point of law from the First-tier Tribunal to the Upper Tribunal.[61] The right of appeal is subject to permission being given, by either the First-tier Tribunal or the Upper Tribunal. The TCE 2007, section 13 provides for a right of appeal to the relevant appellate court[62] on any point of law arising from a decision made by the Upper Tribunal, other than an excluded decision.[63]

The TCE 2007 is innovatory in that it has vested judicial review powers in the Upper Tribunal. The TCE 2007, section 15(1) empowers the Upper Tribunal to grant mandatory, prohibiting and quashing orders, and a declaration and an injunction, in the circumstances described below. The Upper Tribunal can also grant restitution or monetary relief, if satisfied that the High Court would have done so.[64] The relief granted by the Upper Tribunal has the same effect as that granted by the High Court on an application for judicial review, and is enforceable in the same way. The Upper Tribunal must apply the principles of judicial review developed by the High Court. Applications under section 15 are subject to the same hurdles as they would be if judicial review were sought before the High Court. Thus, permission is required, the applicant must have a sufficient interest in the matter to which the application relates, and there are provisions concerning undue delay.[65]

The circumstances in which the Upper Tribunal can exercise powers of judicial review are set out in TCE 2007, section 18, which specifies four conditions. The first condition[66] is that the application does not seek anything other than the relief that the Upper Tribunal is able to grant, a monetary award under section 15(1) and interest and costs under section 16(6). The second condition[67] is that the application does not call into question anything done by the Crown Court, the rationale being that it would be anomalous for a tribunal, a superior court of record, to have supervisory powers over another superior court of record. The third condition[68] is that the application falls within a class specified for the purposes of section 18(6), in a direction given in accordance with the Constitutional

---

[59] TCE 2007, ss 4–5, Schs 2–3.   [60] Ibid, s 7, Sched 4.   [61] Ibid, s 11.
[62] Ibid, s 13(12).   [63] Ibid, s 13(8).   [64] Ibid, s 16(6).
[65] Ibid, s 16.   [66] Ibid, s 18(4).   [67] Ibid, s 18(5).
[68] Ibid, s 18(6).

Reform Act 2005.[69] The direction is made by or on behalf of the Lord Chief Justice with the concurrence of the Lord Chancellor. The final condition[70] relates to the status of the judge presiding at the hearing of the application.

If these conditions are not met the judicial review application is transferred to the High Court.[71] If all four conditions are met then an application for judicial review made to the High Court must be transferred to the Upper Tribunal.[72] If all conditions are met apart from the third, the High Court may nonetheless decide to transfer the case to the Upper Tribunal if it appears just and convenient to do so. Thus even if the case does not fall with a class of case designated for the Upper Tribunal by a direction, the High Court has a discretion to transfer it to the Upper Tribunal, subject to the caveat that this does not apply to matters concerning immigration and nationality.

If the Upper Tribunal makes a quashing order it can in addition remit the matter to the court, tribunal, or authority that made the decision, with a direction to reconsider the matter and reach a decision in accordance with the findings of the Upper Tribunal. It can alternatively substitute its own decision for the decision in question, provided that the decision was made by a court or tribunal, the decision was quashed for error of law, and without the error, there would have been only one decision that the court or tribunal could have reached.[73]

The TCE 2007 is the most important piece of legislation ever enacted dealing with tribunals and introduces some real 'system' into the pre-existing institutional structure that had not existed hitherto. It is also novel for the provisions concerning judicial review, which vest such powers in the Upper Tribunal subject to the conditions set out above. The Act will pose novel challenges for the Upper Tribunal and the ordinary courts in relation to judicial review. The divide between appeal and judicial review exercised by the Upper Tribunal may well prove difficult to maintain, and we will all have to become accustomed to reading decisions from the Upper Tribunal in judicial review cases. The TCE 2007 should, however, have a beneficial impact on case management by relieving the High Court of some of its case load burdens and that is to be welcomed. It remains to be seen whether this has consequential implications for the way in which the remedial regime is applied by the High Court, whether this be in relation to the grant of permission to seek judicial review, the availability of disclosure, cross-examination and the like.

---

[69] Constitutional Reform Act 2005, Sch 2, Pt 1.
[70] TCE 2007, s 18(8).
[71] Ibid, s 18(3), (9).
[72] Ibid, s 19, inserting a new s 31(A) into the Supreme Court Act 1981.
[73] Ibid, s 17.

6

Scandals, Political Accountability and the Rule of Law. Counting Heads?

Walter Van Gerven

On 16 November 2006, Lord Bingham delivered the sixth annual Sir David Williams lecture hosted by the Centre for Public Law at the University of Cambridge. The subject was the rule of law.[1] In this essay I will discuss concepts like rule of law, political accountability, and ministerial responsibility showing how they also emerge in European Union (EU) law with a similar but not identical content. I will start with relating some political scandals and the way in which they were dealt with in the jurisdictions concerned, not just to draw attention—as scandals always do—but to display the differences between institutional mentalities and constitutional traditions in the EU member states. In so far as space permits my presentation will be 'comparative' in honour of Lord Bingham's outstanding contribution to comparative law in his judgments and other writings, and also to thank him for his willingness to serve as a member of the steering committee of the 'Ius commune series casebooks on the common law of Europe' from the moment of its start in 1994.

Political Accountability for Scandals

Scandals—particularly political scandals—have rightfully been labelled 'potential reputation and "trust depleters" in a field where vibrant democratic government depends on social trust'.[2] Political scandals not dealt with in the correct way will harm both democracy and the rule of law, whilst a democracy's forceful reaction to high-level political scandals will display its willingness to maintain

---

[1] <http://www.cpl.law.cam.ac.uk/past_activities/the_rt_hon_lord_bingham_the_rule_of_law.php>.
[2] John B Thompson, *Political Scandal: Power and Visibility in the Media Age* (Cambridge: Polity Press, 2000) 252.

trust in the political system. However, there are many ways to deal with political scandals depending on the tradition, the mentality, and the legal system
of a given country. As a general rule, at least in a parliamentary regime, political *accountability* towards Parliament of high officials, cabinet members, or
civil servants for whom they are politically responsible, is in theory the strongest weapon as it forces the official to resign, and not infrequently to leave public
life entirely. But it may be too strong in the case of a cabinet minister forced to
resign not for misbehaviour or mismanagement of his own but on the part of
civil servants. Moreover, the allegiance of a parliamentary majority to the ruling political party or parties may be such that Parliament does not withdraw
its confidence. Thus it has been observed, that in the Netherlands in the period
1945 to 1996, out of a total of 42 ministers and Secretaries of State who resigned,
only 10 resigned because a majority in Parliament or one of the governing parties
had made known its lack of confidence in the policy of the minister concerned.[3]
However, political accountability of high officials will not only be put in practice
through political means—often by voluntary resignation, albeit frequently at the
request of the head of government or of a political party—but also through other
means as mentioned below.

Open government and free access to public documents are no doubt crucial in avoiding wrongful behaviour by high officials. Within the EU, Sweden
is a champion of open government. The country already had its first constitutional statute on the freedom of the press in 1766, during the period of
the Enlightenment, including a constitutional right for citizens to access and
to copy official documents.[4] Today the Freedom of the Press Act of 1949 and
the Freedom of Expression Act of 1991 form part of the Swedish Constitution.
The former protects freedom of expression and of information in the printed
media, the latter protects most other mass media, e.g., radio and TV.[5] As a rule
the public authority concerned is not allowed to ask for the identity of the person who makes the request for access, or to ask for the purpose of the request.
Moreover, public officials, among others, are free to supply information about
the contents of official documents (as opposed to supplying the actual documents) to the press, referred to as the *freedom of the informant*, which includes
secret documents. Furthermore, a person involved in the production or publication of printed matter shall not disclose the identity of a person having provided

---

[3] Mark Bovens, *The Quest for Responsibility: Accountability and Citizenship in Complex Organizations* (Cambridge, Cambridge University Press, 1998) 88.
[4] U Bernitz, 'Sweden and the European Union: on Sweden's implementation and application of European Law', (2001) Common Market Law Review, 903–934, 916. The author mentions how this historically unique development came about as a result of the victory in 1765 of one of two factions in Parliament, the Caps, over the other faction, the Hats, which had been in power for a long time and were accused by the Caps of secrecy, corruption, misuse of power, and administrative mismanagement. The Caps therefore introduced the 1766 Freedom of the Press Act in order to stop censorship and open up freedom of the press and administrative transparency: Ibid, in n 42.
[5] Ibid, at 916.

information for publication.[6] To be sure, no causal link can be proven to exist between open government and the prevention of scandals, but it will be difficult to deny that there is no such link at all.

Criminal prosecution is another means to combat political misbehaviour or mismanagement. This is the way that was chosen when France was confronted with a blood contamination scandal in the mid-1980s. Approximately 1200 hae-mophiliacs were infected with HIV following blood transfusions, of whom 250 died. Immense public commotion ensued and all legal avenues were used to placate the victims. Mr Fabius, a former prime minister, and two other ministers were indicted, and a special court, the Cour de Justice de la République, was set up to try them in accordance with common criminal procedures. Several doctors were sentenced to prison by a criminal court in Paris. A special fund was created to indemnify victims for pecuniary and non-pecuniary damages. In 1999 the former prime minister and one of the two ministers were acquitted; the other, the Secretary of Health, was found guilty, but not punished. The recourse, in this complex and delicate case, to criminal law was criticized by many for being an inadmissible change in emphasis from political to penal responsibility. It finally led to the unwritten rule which requires ministers to step down when they are at risk of becoming involved in criminal proceedings.[7]

Compared to the French approach of using criminal law as an instrument to combat political misbehaviour or mismanagement, the UK and Ireland play it 'softly' by using the device of 'ad hoc' tribunals of inquiry in view of exposing and judging the bad behaviour of cabinet ministers and other high officials. And indeed, at least viewed from the outside, it appears to be an effective way to interrogate not only cabinet ministers who might have a tendency to 'pass the buck' but also civil servants. It is also a flexible (but expensive) instrument, as it is for the chairman, usually a senior judge, to decide how to conduct the inquiry, which witnesses to hear and which documents to investigate, and how long the inquiry will take. A famous example in the UK was the inquiry in the 1990s concerning the involvement of the Thatcher and Major governments in exports of arms and defence-related goods to Iraq and Iran which took place in the 1980s. In the end, none of the three ministers involved was politically sanctioned: two of them were no longer in office when the report was released and the third one was not forced to resign because resignation was considered to be 'constitutionally unnecessary and politically undesirable' by the Major Government. However, the affair led in 1994 to the creation of a Committee on Standards in Public Life which was asked to stem the tide of corruption by recommending codes of conduct for ministers, civil servants, and independent agencies. A more recent and less complex example

---

[6] On all this and many other matters, see further Österdahl, 'Openness and secrecy', 23 *European Law Review*, 1998, 336, at 339 ff. For recent developments, see Thomas Bull, 'Changing Principles of Freedom of Speech in Sweden?' 8 *European Public Law*, 2002, 333–347.

[7] See further W Van Gerven, *The European Union. A Polity of State and Peoples* (Stanford University Press, Stanford and Hart Publishing, Oxford, 2005) at 72–73.

was the Hutton inquiry into the suicide of Dr Kelly, the British expert who had allegedly said to a journalist that the Blair administration was responsible for consciously misleading the public on the issue of weapons of mass destruction in Iraq. Not only did the prime minister's head of communication, Mr Campbell, and other civil servants appear before the tribunal, but Prime Minister Blair himself appeared as well. Mr Campbell resigned in the aftermath and Mr Blair took political responsibility, however without admitting personal fault.[8]

Germany is another example of a country which, like France, makes use of legal instruments, this time of constitutional law. In the Federal Republic ministerial accountability at the federal level is regulated in Article 64 of the Basic law which provides that ministers shall be appointed and dismissed by the federal president at the proposal of the federal chancellor, who is himself elected by the Bundestag upon the proposal of the president and who must be dismissed by the president when a vote of no confidence in the chancellor is cast by a majority in the Bundestag (Articles 63 (1) and 67 (1)). In Germany political scandals have arisen, as in many other countries, in connection with illegal funding of political parties which came known after Chancellor Kohl's mandate expired. If the scandal had arisen earlier he would certainly have been made to resign and take the blame for his political party's wrongdoing, as happened in 1974 when Chancellor Willy Brandt took full responsibility for the espionage activities of his personal secretary, Günter Guillaume. Illegal funding is a matter which over the years has been the object of much case law from the constitutional court, first deciding in 1958 that it is not unconstitutional for the state to make funds available to allow political parties to finance their election campaign. However, in 1966 it changed position, holding that it is not for the state to contribute to the formation of the people's political will, but for the people to determine state politics. Later on, the court changed its position again, now recognizing that many civil organizations are funded by the state and that private funding of political parties may have the same, or even a greater, adverse effect on the formation of the people's will as state funding—provided that state funding remains within appropriate limits. This is an illustration, out of many, of the politically important role that the constitutional court plays—and therefore the rule of law—both with respect to fundamental citizen rights in relation to the state, and to other citizens.[9]

Rule of Law and *Rechtsstaat*

The role which constitutional law and the German constitution play in such deeply intricate political matters shows how incrusted the principle of *Rechtsstaat* is in the German legal order. Rule of law and *Rechtsstaat* are used in Article 6(1) EU Treaty as synonyms—not fully justified as we will see. In the English version

---

[8] Ibid, at 73–75.   [9] Ibid, 75–77.

the paragraph reads: 'The Union is founded on the principles of liberty, democracy, respect for human rights and fundamental freedoms, and the rule of law, principles which are common to the Member States.' As far as I know (far enough, I hope), in the UK the principle of *rule of law* has never been linked to the idea of state, but rather has been seen as one of the three overarching principles of British constitutionalism, together with the doctrines of separation of power and legislative supremacy[10]—the third meaning, in Dicey's words, that Parliament has 'the right to make or unmake any law whatsoever'; and the second meaning that the three types (legislative, executive, and judicial) of political power should be separated from each other so that no one person or institution should exercise more than one type of power.[11] The first type (rule of law) is the most difficult to define: in simple terms the doctrine requires that the subject is entitled to be ruled according to law, and that the law should be predictable.[12] The rule was first propounded in 1885 by Dicey, and, as noted by Lord Bingham in his aforementioned lecture, had 'attracted considerable controversy over the years which had elapsed since then'.[13] Nevertheless, reference was made to the doctrine in section 1 of the Constitutional Reform Act 2005 which provides that 'the Act does not adversely affect 'the existing constitutional principle of law' or 'the Lord Chancellor's existing constitutional role in relation to that principle'. However, this inclusion in the Reform Act does not prevent Lord Bingham stating that:

the meaning of this existing constitutional principle may no doubt have been thought to be too clear and well-understood to call for statutory definition, and it is true that the rule of law has been routinely invoked by judges in their judgments. But they have not explained what they meant by the expression, and well-respected authors have thrown doubt on its meaning and value.

Whence Lord Bingham's attempt in his lecture to define the concept and break it down into eight sub-rules. First the definition: 'The core of the existing principle is that all persons and authorities within the state, whether public or private, should be bound by and entitled to the benefit of laws publicly and prospectively promulgated and publicly administered in the courts.'[14] Then the eight sub-rules:

(i) the law must be accessible and so far as possible intelligible, clear, and predictable;

(ii) questions of legal right and liability should ordinarily be resolved by application of the law and not the exercise of discretion;

(iii) the laws of the land should apply equally to all, save to the extent that objective differences justify differentiation;

---

[10] Ian McLeod, *Legal Method* (3rd edn, Basington, Macmillan, 1999) 58.
[11] Ibid, 64–65.   [12] Ibid, at 66.
[13] Lord Bingham, n 1 above, p 1–2.
[14] N 1 above, first full paragraph preceding n 13 of the lecture.

(iv) the law must afford adequate protection of fundamental human rights;

(v)   means must be provided for resolving, without prohibitive cost or inordin-
      ate delay, bona fide civil disputes which the parties themselves are unable
      to resolve;

(vi) ministers and public officers at all levels must exercise the powers conferred
      on them reasonably, in good faith, for the purpose for which the powers
      were conferred and without exceeding the limits of such powers;

(vii) adjudicative procedures provided by the state should be fair;

(viii) the rule of law requires compliance by the state with its obligations in inter-
      national law, the law whether deriving from treaty or international custom
      and practice governs the conduct of nations.

The German concept of *Rechtsstaat* finds its origin in the *Vernunftstheorie* (theory
of rationality) which vests the legitimacy of the *state* in natural law, and in the
'enlightened absolutism' of the late-18th-century Prussian state of King Frederick
the Great (1712–1786). Under these theories of rational man and freedom, it is
for the state, seen as a liberal state submitted to individual rights and freedoms
of its citizens, to support those citizens in the pursuit of personal liberty and self-
development. This focus on human dignity and a liberal state at the service of its
citizens explains the emphasis laid, with the enactment on 23 May 1949 of the
Basic law, on the dignity of men, and the duty for all public authority 'to respect
and protect it', in its very first article. The Basic law then starts out with a list of
basic rights which 'shall bind the legislature, the executive and the judiciary as
directly enforceable law' (Article 1 (3)), and establishes a framework for a federal state that, according to Article 20 (1), shall be 'democratic and social'—thus
linking the principle of *Rechtsstaat* to the principle of *Socialstaat*. It further states
that 'the legislature shall be bound by the constitutional order, the executive and
the judiciary by law and justice' (Article 20 (3)). The Basic law recognizes some
principles as being of a higher order than the Basic law itself by prohibiting in
Article 79(3) the amendment of Articles 1 and 20 as well as the federal structure
of the state. To underline how untouchable these provisions are, Article 20 (4)
grants all citizens 'the right to resist anybody attempting to do away with this
constitutional order, should no other remedy be possible'.[15]

     In addition to all of this, the principle of *Rechtsstaat* also encompasses a large
number of principles relating to diverse subjects such as separation of powers,
submission of all public authority to law, the requirement of a legal basis for all
administrative action, judicial protection, state liability, legal certainty, basic
principles of criminal law and procedure, and the principle of proportionality.[16]
Interestingly enough, these principles bear more resemblance to the sub-rules

---

[15] On the foregoing, see further W Van Gerven, n 7 above, at 107–109.
[16] For a full description, see H Maurer, *Staatsrecht* I, (3rd edn, Verlag CH Beck, Munich 2003)
215–238.

formulated by Lord Bingham than the articles of the German constitution itself: for indeed, like these sub-rules, they come closer to the British concept of the rule of law seen as a 'principle of institutional morality' that guides 'all forms of law-making and law-enforcement. In particular it suggests that legal certainty and procedural protections...are fundamental requirements of good governance.'[17] By contrast, the provisions of the German Basic Law itself purport to organize the state structure, in itself and in its relationship with the citizens and, more-over, focuses directly on human dignity, human rights, and social welfare—but that does not belong to the substantive content of the British rule of law; as Lord Bingham points out, not even adequate protection of fundamental human rights would 'be universally accepted as embraced within the rule of law'.[18]

Head-Counting in the EU

Turning to EU law, I start with a famous excerpt from Lord Bingham's judgment in *Fairchild*:[19]

Development in the law in this country cannot of course depend on a head-count of decisions and codes adopted in other countries around the world, often against a background of different rules and traditions. The law must be developed coherently, in accordance with principle, so as to serve, evenhandedly, the ends of justice. If, however, a decision is given in this country which offends one's basic sense of justice, and if consideration of international sources suggests that a different and more acceptable decision would be given in most other jurisdictions, whatever their legal tradition, this must prompt anxious review of the decision in question.

The excerpt is not about EU law but about English law and concerns the use of comparative law in considering a change in English law on a point deemed

[17] J Jowell, 'The Rule of Law Today', in *The Changing Constitution*, (3rd edn (D Oliver, O Jowell, and J Jowell, eds), Clarendon Press, Oxford, 1994) 57.

[18] Lord Bingham, n 1 above, text accompanying n 32 ff, who himself does not accept that proposition—a proposition which makes Professor Raz even say that 'a non-democratic legal system, based on the denial of human rights, on extensive poverty, on racial segregation, sexual inequalities, and racial persecution may, in principle, conform to the requirements of the rule of law better than any of the legal systems of the more enlightened Western democracies' (as quoted by Lord Bingham). Which reminds me of a passage written by the president of Israel's Supreme Court, Aharon Barak: 'A friend once told me that during World War II, several Jews were in prison in Germany as a result of sentences received before the war broke out. The Gestapo did not harm those Jews because the law mandated that they are not be exterminated in the death camps before finishing their prison sentences, and this rule of law had to be maintained. But when the prisoners finished serving their sentences, the Gestapo was waiting for them at the gate. The prisoners were taken to the death camps and murdered. The formal rule of law was observed': *The Judge in a Democracy* (Princeton University Press, 2006) at 54.

[19] The HL judgment of 20 June 2002 in *Fairchild v Glenhaven* concerns three joined cases. The point of law referred to in the excerpt relates to the issue of double or multiple causation in an asbestos case.

to be regulated in other legal systems in a more satisfactory and coherent way. Comparative law has persuasive force, in some jurisdictions more than in others. Arguments of comparative law may persuade judges, as in *Fairchild*, to bring about a change in their own law when they are convinced that a solution applied in another system would lead to better, more acceptable results. In the context of European Union law, comparative law arguments drawn from member state laws have not only persuasive force but also creative force in that rules which member states have in common will in certain instances explicitly, and sometimes impliedly, be considered to be part of EC/EU law. The most explicit example is found in Article 288 (2) EC Treaty which reads: 'In the case of non-contractual liability, the Community shall, in accordance with the general principles common to the laws of the Member States, make good any damage caused by its institutions or by its servants in the performance of their duties.' It is thus for the European Court of Justice (ECJ) in last instance, to give substantive content to tort liability rules for breaches of Community law by Community institutions or organs, and, by analogy (as proclaimed in the ECJ's Francovich judgment), by member state institutions and organs.[20] Another example of judicial 'law finding' in EU law is Article 6 EU Treaty quoted above in connection with rule of law and *Rechtsstaat*, where these and other principles are called to be 'principles which are common to the Member States'. It is up to the member state and European judiciaries, in last instance the ECJ, to give substance to these common principles when their content is disputed—a task which will not be easy, given the fact that these principles will not be as common as may be assumed, and like our discussion of the principles rule of law and *Rechtsstaat* will have displayed. To be sure, 'common' does not mean 'identical', certainly not now in a Union of 27 member states. And indeed, within the EU, principles and solutions that are 'common to the legal systems of the Member States' are not ready-made but come about as a result of a long process of cross-fertilization within and among Community and member state institutions, legislative, judicial, administrative, and educational, and in a context of understanding, cooperation, and convergence.[21]

As in the member states, also in the EU political scandals have helped to shape political accountability, in this case on behalf of Members of the European Commission—to be compared with cabinet ministers at the national level. According to Article 201 EC Treaty, the European Parliament can vote a motion of censure with special quorum and voting majorities against the Commission

---

[20] See my contribution on 'The emergence of a common European law in the area of tort law: the EU contribution' in *Tort Liability of Public Authorities in Comparative Perspective* (D Fairgrieve, M Andenas, J Bell, eds), BIICL, 2002, 125–147: also in the same book T Tridimas, 'Liability for Breach of Community Law: Growing up and Mellowing down?' 149–181.

[21] See further my contribution n 20 above, at 138–144. See also my contribution 'About Rules and Principles, Codification and Legislation, Harmonization and Convergence, and Education in the area of Contract Law', in *Continuity and Change in EU Law, Essays in Honour of Sir Francis Jacobs*, (A Arnull, P Eeckhout and T Tridimas, eds) (Oxford University Press, 2008) 400–414, at 406 ff.

who then 'shall resign as a body'. After all these years the procedure has not yet been applied in full but came very close to that back in 1999 when allegations of mismanagement and nepotism were raised against some Members of the Commission, particularly Mrs Cresson, then under the presidency of Mr Santer. The motion of censure would have been voted if the two major political parliaments had not disagreed as to whether the whole Commission should resign or whether only Mrs Cresson should be forced to resign. In the absence of a qualified majority the European Parliament finally decided to install a committee of five, called independent experts, three in auditing and two in law. The committee examined the allegations and interviewed several of the Commissioners, apart from the president, mainly those allegedly involved. When the report was submitted to the Parliament in the afternoon of 15 March 1999, the Commission decided the same night to resign as a body of its own initiative (and stay on as a caretaker Commission until the appointment of a new Commission under Mr Prodi).[22] After the Commission's resignation the same committee was asked to analyze the Commission's 'current practice and proposals for tackling mismanagement, irregularities and fraud.' The second report, 286 pages long, and formulating more than 90 recommendations, was submitted on 10 September 1999.[23] The last chapter, Chapter 7, of the report dealt with the subject of integrity, responsibility, and accountability in European political and administrative life.

Needless to say that, in their two reports, the members of the committee drew to a large extent on the (auditing and legal) heritage of the member states. That was particularly true for the introduction of the first report for which the committee members had to rely on their own knowledge and wisdom in order to describe and analyze the status and independence of the committee, the scope of its inquiries, the nature of reprehensible acts to be examined, the standards of proper behaviour to be applied, and the kind of responsibility to be used as a benchmark. Regarding these points much inspiration was found in the 'Seven principles of public life' as set out in the first report on Standards in Public life of the UK (then Nolan) Committee. Actually, the creation of the committee may itself have been modelled after the British 'ad hoc' tribunals of inquiry (see above)—strangely enough, because the European Parliament could have found a more specific and more solid legal basis in Article 193 EC Treaty. That Article allows the European Parliament, 'at the request of quarter of its Members, to set up a temporary Committee of Inquiry to investigate...alleged contraventions or maladministration in the implementation of Community law...'. As a matter of fact, not only the conduct of EU institutions, but even that of national authorities in implementing Community law may be the subject of such

---

[22] For a full account, see W van Gerven, 'Managing the European Union: For better or for worse?' in *The Clifford Chance Millenium Lectures. The coming together of the common law and the civil law* (BS Markesinis, ed) (Hart Publishing, Oxford, 2000) 91–104.

[23] For a discussion of the role of the committee and an important part of its recommendations, see P Craig, *EU Administrative Law* (Oxford University Press, 2006) 1–30.

an inquiry by the European Parliament.[24] In preparing the second report the committee of independent experts was bound to draw even more inspiration from the member states' constitutional laws and traditions. That was particularly true for Chapter 7 when it came to lay down a code of conduct for Members of the Commission, their cabinets, and their administration, to describe their political, individual, and collective, responsibility for own conduct and for that of 'their' civil servants, and to address issues such as enforcement of ethical responsibility, whistle-blowing, and outsourcing.

As with the principle of political accountability, also with regard to the principle of rule of law or *Rechtsstaat*, member state laws have served as a model for the introduction or rather transplantation of the principle in EU law, at least with regard to the Union's first pillar, the European Community. Although Article 6 EU Treaty refers to both concepts explicitly, in the English and German versions of the treaty respectively (see above), no definition was supplied in the text, leaving it to the European and national institutions, legislators, and courts to give substantive and procedural content to the principle. This has been done over the years, mainly in case law of the ECJ. Characteristic of this evolution has been the emphasis on two basic features: submission of all public authority, including the legislature proper, to judicial review through efficient remedies; and the obligation of public authorities to provide legal certainty and to act only when there is a legal basis for it in the EC/EU treaties. I have described these features at length on another occasion and have then added some other characteristics relating to good governance, more particularly, the duty of officials to behave with integrity and efficiency and in accordance with due process requirements, to respect human rights in the performance of all their tasks, and to pursue equality and social justice in the performance of their duties.[25] This enumeration may show that 'commonality' at the European level does not preclude the European principle of rule of law from going further than the principle as it is applied in some member states, particularly the UK where review of legislative action, respect for human rights, and pursuit of social justice are not universally accepted to be components of the rule of law.

'Ministerial' Status of EU Commissioners

One specific application of the rule of law by way of judicial review regarding the behaviour of EU officials is the ECJ judgment of 11 July 2006 in *Commission v Cresson*[26]—a late sequel of the Santer Commission's resignation in 1999 described

---

[24] K Lenaerts and P Van Nuffel, (R Bray, ed), *Constitutional Law of the European Union* (2nd edn, Thomson, London, 2005) at 397–399.

[25] N 7 above, 109. For discussion of these themes, see 110–157 and 158–212.

[26] C 432/04, [2006] ECR I-6387.

above. The judgment gives me the opportunity to briefly discuss, at the end of this essay, the constitutional status of Commission Members, to be compared with cabinet ministers in the member states—a subject that is not often discussed.

According to paragraph (1) of Article 213 EC, in order to be lawfully appointed Commissioners, persons must be: 'nationals of Member States'; 'be chosen on the grounds of their general competence'; and possess 'independence beyond doubt'. In its first and second sub-paragraphs, Article 213(2) EC clarifies the latter by stating that they 'shall, in the general interest of the Community, be completely independent in the performance of their duties'—'in (which) performance...they shall neither seek nor take any instructions from any government or from any other body. They shall refrain from any action incompatible with their duties. Each Member State undertakes to respect this principle and not to seek influence (them) in the performance of their tasks'. In its third subparagraph, it goes on to state that Commissioners 'may not, during the term of office, engage in any other occupation, whether gainful or not. When entering upon their duties they shall give a solemn undertaking that, both during and after their term of office, they will respect the obligations arising there from and in particular the duty to behave with integrity and discretion as regards the acceptance, after they have ceased to hold office, of certain appointments or benefits'.

In its *Cresson* judgment, the (full) Court had the occasion to clarify the expression 'duties or obligations arising from their office' in the third sub-paragraph of Article 213(2) EC. The Court stated:

Those obligations include, in particular, the duties of integrity and discretion...of the member of the Commission... [It] is important, as the Advocate General stated in point 74 of his Opinion, that the Members of the Commission observe the highest standards of conduct. That concept therefore falls to be understood as extending...to all of the duties which arise from the office of Member of the Commission, which include the obligation laid down in the first subparagraph of Article 213 (2) EC to be completely independent and to act in the general interest of the Community...It is therefore the duty of Members of the Commission to ensure that the general interest of the Community takes precedence at all times, not only over national interests, but also over personal interests. (paragraphs 69–71).

In the case of Mrs Cresson, the Court opined that she had given precedence to her personal interests by being personally involved in the appointment of a close friend as a personal adviser in her cabinet, in circumvention of standing rules, which the Court regarded as a breach of a certain degree of gravity of the obligations arising from her office as Commissioner. However—and rather controversially[27]—the Court considered this finding, of itself, as an appropriate penalty without there being a need, as asked by the Commission, to be deprived of her right to a pension (paragraphs 150–1 and below).

---

[27] Advocate-General A Geelhoed had proposed to deprive the former Commissioner of her pension right up to 50%: see paras 124–126 at [2006] ECR I-6424.

This brings us to the issue of sanctions which Articles 213(2) and 216 EC Treaty impose on Members of the Commission who have breached their duties. According to the last sentence of the third sub-paragraph of Article 213 EC, the Court of Justice may, in the event of any breach of obligations by a Commissioner, on application by the Council or the Commission, 'rule that the Member concerned be, according to the circumstances, either compulsory retired in accordance with Article 216 or deprived of his right to a pension or other benefits in its stead'. Article 216 EC reads: 'If any Member of the Commission no longer fulfils the conditions required for the performance of his duties or if he has been guilty of serious misconduct, the Court of Justice may, on application by the Council or the Commission, compulsory retire him.' In the *Cresson* judgment, both articles were invoked before the Court (Article 213(2) in paragraphs 61 and 64 ff, Article 216 in paragraphs 60 and 62 of the judgment) but only the first was relevant in Mrs Cresson's case because her office had already expired at the time of the judgment. After having stated that, for the application of the article, 'a breach of a certain degree of gravity is concerned' (paragraph 72),[28] the Court observed that—where the penalty of compulsory retirement in Article 213(2) 'will apply only where a breach has arisen, and continues, during the term of office of the Member of the Commission in question'—by contrast, the latter 'may be deprived of the right to a pension … whether the breach occurs during or after his term of office' (paragraph 73). Furthermore: 'As there is no provision as to the extent of the deprivation of the right to a pension … it is open to the Court to order deprivation in whole or in part thereof, depending on the degree of gravity of the breach' (Ibid).[29] As already mentioned, in its judgment the Court did not find it appropriate to impose a penalty in the form of a deprivation of her right to pension, since 'having regard to the circumstances of the case, the finding of breach constitutes, of itself, an appropriate penalty' (paragraph 150).

From a viewpoint of equality under the rule of law, it is important to note, as Mrs Cresson observed before the Court (paragraph 86) and as the Court acknowledged in its judgment (paragraph 111), that, in Mrs Cresson's words, 'an official of the European Communities benefits from considerably more extensive safeguards than those provided for Members of the Commission, both at the stage of the administrative procedure and in proceedings before the Court'. The latter is particularly true in that 'an official may challenge a decision of the Appointing

[28] The Court explains: 'While the members of the Commission are…under an obligation to conduct themselves in a manner which is beyond reproach, it does not, however follow that the slightest deviation from those standards falls to be censured under Article 213(2) EC.' (para 72, first sentence). Compare with Art 216 EC, where, in a similar vein, 'serious misconduct' is required.

[29] That does not prevent the Commission and the Court from being bound to apply general principles, thus, for instance, as regards the timely initiation of proceedings under Art 213(2) EC. In para 90 of the *Cresson* judgment the Court acknowledges that the Commission 'must not indefinitely delay the exercise of its powers, in order to comply with the fundamental requirement of legal certainty' (follow references to the Court's case law).

Authority before the Court of First Instance...and then bring an appeal before the Court of Justice' (both quotations in paragraph 86) whereas a Commissioner lacks 'any opportunity to challenge the decision of the Court of Justice which, according to Mrs Cresson constitutes a breach of fundamental rights' (Ibid). The Court did not accept this argument though relying on Article 2(2) of Protocol No 7 to the ECHR which provides in an exception to the requirement of two levels of jurisdiction, 'where the person concerned was tried in the first instance by the highest court or tribunal' (paragraph 112). The argument is interesting in that it illustrates the difference between the legal status of Commissioners compared with that of civil servants: Commissioners are not subjected to staff regulations—as they are not servants but holders of public office (and in that capacity representing their institution)—for better or for worse. *For worse*, that is, as mentioned by Mrs Cresson, for not enjoying the same procedural safeguards; *for better*, that is, for example, for not being subjected to the application of Article 288(4) EC which provides in personal liability of Community servants in regress claims; regress may occur when the Commission or other EU institution has been ordered to pay compensation to third parties for breaches of Community law committed by 'its servants in the performance of their duties' (Article 288(2) and (3) EC). According to Article 288(4) EC, those regress claims brought by the Commission are to be decided by the Community court 'in accordance with the provisions laid down in the servant's staff regulations or conditions of employment'.[30] On the other hand, both Members of the Commission and EU civil servants (present or former) of Community institutions may be sued before a national court by third persons, external or internal to EU institutions,[31] in which case national law applies, albeit only insofar as the Member's or servant's immunity does not come into play.[32]

Let me, on a final point, return briefly to the duty of independence of Commissioners. As stated in Article 213(1) and (2) EC (see above), the independence of Commissioners must be beyond doubt. This means that, in the performance of their duties, they shall neither seek nor take instructions from any government or from any other body. Moreover, they may not, during their

---

[30] That does not mean that, in such an instance, the Commission, or other institution, such as Parliament, could not exercise a regress claim against a Commissioner (or member of that other institution), who has committed a wrongful act or omission resulting in his institution being liable in compensation on the basis of Art 288(2) EC towards a third person who has sustained damage by it. However, not then on the basis of staff regulations but on the basis of 'general principles common to the laws of the Member States' (thus Art 288(2)) which may hold principals liable for acts of their agents. To my knowledge that issue has not been decided yet by a Community court.

[31] See *Cresson* judgment (n 26 above), para 35, where it is mentioned that the Commission claimed damages against Mrs Cresson in criminal proceedings brought before the Belgian courts following a complaint by a Member of Parliament.

[32] See Protocol on the privileges and immunities of the European Communities which provides in Art 12, sub (a) that 'officials and other servants of the Community [shall]...be immune from legal proceedings in respect of acts performed by them in their official capacity'.

term of office, engage in any other occupation, whether gainful or not. In these provisions, the terms 'from any other body' and 'not engage in any other occupation, whether gainful or not' give rise to difficult questions as to whether and in how far Commissioners may take instructions from political parties and/or engage in political activities in their state of origin, or elsewhere. As mentioned above, Commissioners are not servants but holders of public office and, moreover, are part of the Community's main policy-formulating and law-initiating body. A delicate question that arises in regard of independence is in how far Commissioners are permitted to represent views advocated by the political party of which they are, or perceived to be (mainly because of their affiliation with that party 'in their national past'), if not an active, then at least a passive member. In my opinion, the answer is somewhere in the middle. On the one hand it is clear that Commissioners, who carry out an essentially political function, may not be prevented from having a political view and expressing it in an independent and responsible way—that is, not in an unnecessarily controversial or partisan manner.[33] In other words, in expressing their views, Commissioners must check and weigh these against, and in light of, opposing reasonable views. For all these views to be heard in Commission deliberations, it is therefore acceptable and even desirable that, in the appointment of 'their' Commissioners, member states seek to agree on a balanced representation of European political tendencies within the Commission.[34] On the other hand, it should be equally clear that Commissioners may not seek instructions, not even occasionally, from a political party, whether national or European, on how to vote in the Commission on an issue that is politically controversial. Taking instructions from a political party is, in my view, clearly in conflict with the neutrality that the function of Commissioner requires.

What about being an active member in such a political party[35] and, more specifically, taking part in a national or European election campaign on behalf of such a party? Insofar as these activities constitute an 'occupation, gainful or not, outside the Commission' in the sense of Article 213(2) EC—which in my opinion is to be understood as 'taking up working time'—such activities are not allowed under the wording of the Treaty itself, and therefore cannot be permitted. But even if they are not 'occupational', for example because they are carried

---

[33] According to the Commission, members of the Commission are politicians carrying out a political function, who, while honouring the obligations imposed by their function, remain free to express their personal opinions quite independently and on their own responsibility: thus in answers to written questions particularly the answer of 7 February 2000 to questions E-2459/99, E- 2600/99, and E-2628/99, [2000] OJ C255E/139 (taken from K Lenaerts and P Van Nuffel (R Bray, ed), *Constitutional Law of the European Union*, n 24 above, p 435, n 247.

[34] As has happened in the past: see PJG Kapteyn and VerLoren van Themaat, ed and rev by LW Gormley, *Introduction to the Law of the European Communities* (3rd edn, Kluwer Law International, 1998) at 195, n 90.

[35] In some member states (the UK) civil servants in policy grades may not even be passive members of a political party: Kapteyn and VerLoren van Themaat (n 34 above), at p 200, n 112.

out during vacation periods, or leave of absence, I would think that such active engagement is not in conformity with the wording of the Treaty: being an active member of a political party, or campaigning for that party, implies in my view that the person concerned accepts the party line, and therefore implicitly accepts instructions from the party, at least ceases to be neutral, that is *im*partial.[36] That would, obviously, be different if it were decided, sooner or later, that, as a body, the Commission be transformed into a parliamentarian government.[37] In this respect, it would be interesting to see or know how the institutional structure of the EU would or should then evolve if that transformation were to go hand in hand with the situation after the Lisbon Treaty, when approved, which would have turned the European Council into an institution and the office of president into a semi-stable presidency. Would that mean that the EU would be transformed into a semi-presidential (and therefore also semi-parliamentary) system, French style? That would not necessarily have to be the case: even member states with a universally elected head of state and a parliamentary elected head of government, like Ireland, do not, unlike France, have to evolve into a semi-presidential system with a president/head of state who shares real (not just ceremonial, representative, or moral authority) powers with a prime minister or chancellor/head of government. As in France, such a system leads to conflict situations in times of 'cohabitation', that is, when each of the two heads (of state and government) has been elected by a different people's or parliamentary majority. That would not be a happy situation in a Union which needs strong leadership, that is, in my view, a strong Commission with a strong multi-party parliamentary supported president. I would think that to be a more acceptable solution than a solution modelled after an example, the French, that came about in a very peculiar situation.[38] To quote Lord Bingham again, as a final tribute here and now: 'if consideration of international sources suggests that a different and more acceptable solution would be given in most other jurisdictions'[39]— then the different solution should be preferred.

---

[36] I know that my opinion is in conflict with the provisions of the code of conduct for Commissioners, dated 20 August 2004, as prepared by the Secretariat-General, Directorate B. I find my interpretation more in line with the text and the spirit of the Treaty, and with the terms 'independence beyond doubt' in Art 213(1) EC.

[37] On this W Van Gerven, n 7 above, at 309–374.

[38] The French semi-presidential system, with a universally elected president and a parliamentary-approved prime minister, is a system which has been shaped in its (then) final form in 1962 after General De Gaulle became president in 1958 following the Algerian insurrection, and in accordance with his wishes. See L Favoreu et al, *Droit constitutionnel*, (4th edn, Dalloz, Paris, 2001) pp 476 ff, and 558.

[39] Quotation accompanying n 19 above.

7

The Value of Clarity

Murray Gleeson

The report of the argument in *Midland Silicones Ltd v Scruttons Ltd*[1] records that Mr Ashton Roskill QC, urging the House of Lords not to depart from settled law concerning privity of contract, said: 'It is more important that the law should be clear than that it should be clever.' Those who make contracts, he submitted, are entitled to have them applied according to established legal principle. An emphasis on the importance which English commercial law places upon certainty and predictability has been a theme of a number of important judgments, and extra-judicial writings, of Lord Bingham of Cornhill. It appeared recently, for example, in *Golden Strait Corpn v Nippon Yusen Kubishika Kaisha*.[2] It is an honour, and a pleasure, to participate in this tribute to Lord Bingham's contribution to the law. The Australian judiciary is deeply indebted to him for the guidance to be obtained from his judgments. My present purpose is to offer some reflections, from an Australian perspective, upon the theme mentioned above, and to relate it to some recent decisions of the High Court of Australia.

There is always a tension between the need for reasonable certainty, which is one aspect of the concept of justice, and the requirements of fairness, flexibility, and appropriate attention to the circumstances of individual cases. In discussions of the interest of certainty, a contrast sometimes is made between 'rules' and 'principles'.[3] Which of the two better promotes certainty may depend upon the context. The minimum age of voting is best dealt with by drawing a bright line, even though some people below the line are more mature than some above it. In other areas, attempts to draw bright lines result in confusion, because the subject matter does not lend itself to simple and clear distinctions. If there is a mismatch between the complexity of a problem and the apparent simplicity of a law designed to cover it, the result is likely to be a proliferation of rules, each developed in further response to a demonstration of the incompleteness of an earlier

---

[1] [1962] AC 446 (HL) 459.
[2] [2007] 2 WLR 691 (HL) 704.
[3] See, e.g., John Braithwaite, 'Rules and Principles: A Theory of Legal Certainty' (2002) 27 Australian Journal of Legal Philosophy 47.

response. Common law and statute provide many examples. Principles, also, may at the one time solve some problems and create others. The principle according to which the common law of tort identifies a duty of care, in its development over time, may illustrate the point.

Nobody supposes that there is any area of the law in which certainty is to be pursued at all costs. Yet its value is generally acknowledged, and in some areas is given special emphasis. Legal unpredictability itself may be a form of injustice. The rule of law implies that citizens may know, with reasonable assurance, their rights and obligations, and that the outcome of litigation will depend as little as reasonably possible upon the chance factor of the identity of the judge assigned to hear the case. In commerce, legal uncertainty creates risk. Profit is a reward for taking risk, and, as a rule, the greater the risk involved in a transaction the greater will be the return needed to induce a party to enter into it. An example is what is sometimes called 'sovereign risk'. This is why governments, even in places that do not accept, or accept fully, the values inherent in the concept of the rule of law as understood in a liberal democracy recognize that, without a credible, equitable, and predictable law and dispute resolution system, investment and trade either will be impossible or will involve exorbitant cost. Where risk exists, somebody will have to pay for it.

Identifying a legal context as commercial, and, therefore, as one in which certainty is of particular importance, may not always be easy. Some legal problems arise in a setting that is unmistakably commercial. The issues may be such that parties need to know, quickly and surely, where they stand. Both, or all, parties may be commercial people with ready access to legal advice, and capable of looking after their own interests so long as they know their rights and potential liabilities. In *The Scaptrade*,[4] the need to know whether a shipowner is entitled to withdraw a ship from the service of a time charterer was regarded as a powerful reason for rejecting a jurisdiction to grant relief against forfeiture. In the Court of Appeal,[5] Robert Goff LJ referred to the importance of each party knowing its legal position because of the possible need to take, without delay, action that may be irrevocable and that may have far-reaching consequences. This was accepted in the House of Lords as a practical reason of legal policy for declining to recognize the equitable jurisdiction invoked by the charterers.[6] What Lord Diplock described as other 'juristic difficulties' in the way of such recognition were, perhaps, less obvious.[7] The Court of Appeal, in *Lauritzencool AB v Lady Navigation*

---

[4] *Scandinavian Trading Tanker Co AB v Flota Petrolera Ecuatoriana* [1983] 2 AC 694 (HL) (*The Scaptrade*).

[5] [1983] 1 QB 529 (CA) 540.

[6] *The Scaptrade* (n 4) 703.

[7] For an Australian view on the subject, see W M C Gummow, 'Forfeiture and Certainty: The High Court and the House of Lords' in P Finn (ed), *Essays in Equity* (Law Book Company, Sydney 1985) 30.

Inc,[8] upholding a grant of injunctive relief to restrain conduct inconsistent with a time charter, questioned the generality of some of what Lord Diplock said in *The Scaptrade*, pointing out that it did not reflect the reasoning of Robert Goff LJ in that case, or the reported arguments of counsel.[9] From one point of view, to recognize that some aspects of the juristic basis of the decision in *The Scaptrade* may have been inconclusive is at the same time to acknowledge the importance, in the outcome, of the practical considerations that were stressed by both the Court of Appeal and the House of Lords.

Reservations about the relevance of equitable principles to the enforcement of commercial contracts need to take account of a well known form of contract, which often has a strongly commercial aspect, but which historically has been a subject of equitable relief: a contract relating to an interest in land, whether it be a sale of land, a mortgage, or a lease. In Australian litigation, it has not been unusual for equitable principles concerning penalties, relief against forfeiture, specific performance, and injunctions to arise for consideration in this context. The differences between these various kinds of real estate contract are not always clear-cut. A leading High Court case on relief against forfeiture and unconscionability, *Stern v McArthur*,[10] concerned a long-term contract for the sale of land which was characterized by some members of the court as essentially an agreement by which the vendor undertook to finance the purchase upon the security of the land. In Australia, contracts for the sale of land often involve vendor finance, and, even where there is no such element, at least one of the parties to a contract (and, often, both) may be buying or selling as part of a business. As Lord Hoffmann said in *Union Eagle Ltd v Golden Achievement Ltd*,[11] it is impossible to draw a broad distinction between commercial cases and transactions relating to land, which are traditionally the subject of equitable rules—land (in that case, a flat in Hong Kong) can be an article of commerce.

There is an historical curiosity that might be not entirely unrelated to a degree of Australian reluctance to draw a bright line excluding equity from commercial cases. It was not until 1970 that the Judicature Act system was adopted in New South Wales, which is by far the most litigious State in Australia. A number of our most prominent judges developed as lawyers in that tradition. Furthermore, as a rule, in New South Wales commercial work went to the Equity bar rather than the common law bar. Most common law barristers concerned themselves mainly with the law of tort. Commercial law and Equity were in the same professional hands. The two were not regarded as antithetical. Equity was not regarded as unresponsive to the needs and reasonable expectations of business people.

The difficulty of isolating commercial contracts is increased by legislative intervention. Such legislation is expressed in broad terms of normative prescription.

---

[8] [2005] 1 WLR 3686 (CA).   [9] Ibid, 3639.
[10] (1988) 165 CLR 489.   [11] [1997] AC 514 (PC) 519.

Two Australian examples, which now feature in much commercial litigation, appear in a Commonwealth Act that rests primarily upon the Commonwealth Parliament's constitutional power to make laws with respect to trading and financial corporations. It has an extended operation in reliance on other heads of power, but the trade and commerce of at least one of the parties to a transaction is the element that primarily attracts the federal legislative power. Part IVA of the Trade Practices Act 1974 (Cth) deals with 'unconscionable conduct'. It includes section 51AA, which provides that a corporation must not, in trade or commerce, 'engage in conduct that is unconscionable within the meaning of the unwritten law'. Sections 51AB and 51AC, which apply to more restricted forms of trade and commerce, prohibit unconscionable conduct by reference to a relatively detailed statutory exposition of that concept. Where they apply, section 51AA does not. Part V of the Act, which deals with 'unfair practices', includes section 52, which provides that a corporation shall not, in trade or commerce, engage in conduct that is misleading or deceptive or is likely to mislead or deceive. The reference in section 51AA to the unwritten law is a reference to the general principles of equity. Section 52 covers conduct that is innocently misleading as well as deliberately deceptive. Part VI of the Act provides remedies for contraventions of Part IVA and Part V. They include damages and injunctions. Australian States have enacted legislation, unrestricted by the need for reliance on specific heads of legislative power, but subject to the paramountcy of Commonwealth law in cases of inconsistency, which mirrors the Commonwealth legislation. For present purposes, it is convenient to concentrate on the Federal law.

The High Court considered section 51AA, and the concept of unconscionability, in *Australian Competition and Consumer Commission v CG Berbatis Holdings Pty Ltd*,[12] a case concerning the enforceability of a term imposed by a lessor as a condition of agreeing to a renewal of a lease of business premises.[13] The context was plainly commercial, a factor reflected in the Court's decision that good conscience did not require the lessor, in circumstances where there was no exploitation of any special disability or disadvantage, to do other than pursue its own legitimate business interests. Reference was made to the parliamentary history of section 51AA. In the Second Reading speech, the Minister said:

Unconscionability is a well understood equitable doctrine, the meaning of which has been discussed by the High Court in recent times. It involves a party who suffers from some special disability or is placed in some special situation of disadvantage and an 'unconscionable' taking advantage of that disability or disadvantage by another. The doctrine does not apply simply because one party has made a poor bargain. In the vast majority of commercial transactions neither party would be likely to be in a position of special disability or special disadvantage, and no question of unconscionable conduct would arise.

[12] (2003) 214 CLR 51.
[13] Another recent example of examination by the High Court of unconscionability, but in a non-commercial context, is *Bridgewater v Leahy* (1998) 194 CLR 457.

Nevertheless, unconscionable conduct can occur in commercial transaction, and there is no reason why the Trade Practices Act should not recognise this.[14]

It was pointed out in *Berbatis* that, in its colloquial meaning, 'unconscionable' may be no more than an emphatic method of expressing personal disapproval of someone's behaviour. If so, it is legally irrelevant. Commercial conduct does not require judicial approval in order to be legally effective. The legal meaning of the term, however, is more precise.[15] It is used to describe various established grounds of equitable intervention in transactions which offend equity and good conscience. Forms of disadvantage or disability, exploitation of which is unconscientious, have been held to include infirmity of body or mind, illiteracy, or emotional dependence. Unconscionability does not include mere inequality of bargaining power, or subjection to adverse market conditions. The possibility that commercial transactions can give rise to situations where certain forms of behaviour, although consistent with contractual rights, would be unconscientious, cannot be overlooked. For an Australian court, section 51AA is there; it is frequently invoked by commercial litigants; and the general principles of common law and equity cannot be developed in a manner that disregards the statutory prescription. Australia is not alone in having legislation which applies, to commercial dealings, broadly stated normative standards of this kind.[16]

Recent decisions of the High Court have stressed the need, in applying the legislation, and 'the unwritten law', in a commercial and contractual setting, to avoid loose and unprincipled application of equitable concepts. An example may be seen in an area where the Privy Council (on appeal from Hong Kong) and the High Court have reached similar practical conclusions on an important question concerning contracts for the sale of land.

Union Eagle Ltd v Golden Achievement Ltd,[17] decided in 1997, concerned a contract for the sale of real estate, in which time for payment of the price was of the essence. The purchaser was ten minutes late in tendering the purchase price. The vendor terminated the contract. The purchaser sued for specific performance, claiming what is described in the report of the argument as 'relief against forfeiture by extending the time for completion'.[18] (To that claim, an Australian court would ask: forfeiture of what? Plainly it was not only the forfeiture of the deposit that was in issue, but if what was said to have been forfeited was an equitable interest in the real estate, then that raised the same question as whether the purchaser was entitled to specific performance.) The purchaser argued that it was

[14] Australia, House of Representatives, *Parliamentary Debates* (Hansard), 3 November 1992, 2408.

[15] *Berbatis* (n 12) 63.

[16] See, e.g., the United States models discussed in Liam Brown, 'The Impact of Section 51AC of the Trade Practices Act 1974 (Cth) on Commercial Certainty' (2004) 28 Melbourne University Law Review 589.

[17] *Union Eagle* (n 11).

[18] Ibid, 516.

unconscionable for the vendor to exercise its right to terminate the contract.[19] (To that, an Australian court would ask: why? There may be an answer to such a question, but if it exists it must be found in some conduct or circumstance which binds the vendor's conscience, and not merely in the fact that the contract contained strict provisions as to time.) The Privy Council, applying *The Scaptrade* and *Steedman v Drinkle*,[20] held that, there being no question of relief against any penalty, or of unjust enrichment, or of the vendor's conduct having contributed to the breach, or of the transaction being in substance in mortgage, the principle to be applied was 'that in cases of rescission of an ordinary contract of sale of land for failure to comply with an essential condition as to time, equity will not intervene'.[21]

The purchaser argued that the Australian High Court decisions of *Legione v Hateley*[22] and *Stern v McArthur*[23] had recognized an equitable jurisdiction to grant relief in a case where it was unconscientious of a vendor to exercise a legal right to terminate a contract for the sale of land for breach of an essential condition by a purchaser. So they did, but they did not hold that such jurisdiction would be exercised in ordinary cases where none of the qualifications mentioned by the Privy Council applied, and where no more was involved than the application of strict contractual provisions as to time. The question of the extent to which those authorities relaxed the effect of *Steedman v Drinkle* arose in two cases that were heard together by the High Court in 2003: *Tanwar Enterprises Pty Ltd v Cauchi*[24] and *Romanos v Pentagold Investments Pty Ltd*.[25] It is sufficient to examine the former.

Tanwar concerned three contracts, in the standard form used in New South Wales, for the sale of development land for a total price of $4.5 million. Time was made of the essence, in circumstances of previous extension of the completion date and contractual variation. The purchasers were relying on finance to come from Singapore. On the day fixed for settlement the purchasers' solicitors found that, because of checks on international transfers of funds being conducted by the Singapore authorities, the purchase price would not be available until the following day. The vendors terminated the contracts and refused to settle when the purchase money was tendered next day. The purchasers sued for specific performance. (There had already been part payment of the purchase price in addition to the deposit, and it was common ground that, if the action for specific performance failed, this amount would be refunded to the purchasers by way of relief against forfeiture. Relief against that particular forfeiture was not in issue.)[26] They claimed it was unconscientious of the vendors to exercise their right to rescind. They failed because they were unable to explain why that was so.

[19] Ibid.	[20] [1916] 1 AC 275.	[21] *Union Eagle* (n 11) 523.
[22] (1983) 152 CLR 406.	[23] (1988) 165 CLR 489.	[24] (2003) 217 CLR 315.
[25] (2003) 217 CLR 367.	[26] *Tanwar* (n 24) 321.

The plurality judgment, noting significant differences in the reasoning of the Justices who decided *Legione v Hately* and *Stern v McArthur*, rejected, as circular, reliance by the purchasers upon their equitable interest in the land as the subject of a forfeiture in respect of which equity would grant relief. The interest of a purchaser under an uncompleted contract for the sale of real estate is commensurate with the right to obtain specific performance of the contract. Where a vendor has terminated pursuant to a contractual right, the availability of specific performance is the very issue. If the reliance by the vendors upon their contractual right to terminate were unconscientious, then equity would intervene; if it were not, it did not advance the case of the purchasers to claim that an equitable interest in the land had been forfeited. Upon analysis, both *Legione* and *Stern* were cases where questions of relief against forfeiture turned upon particular features of the contracts. The general principle that governed the outcome of *Tanwar* was that the equitable jurisdiction to relieve against unconscientious exercise of legal rights was not an authority:

... to reshape contractual relations into a form the court thinks more reasonable or fair where subsequent events have rendered one side's situation more favourable.[27]

At least where accident and mistake are not involved, it will be necessary to point to some conduct of the vendor as having in a significant respect caused or contributed to the breach of the essential time stipulation.[28] There was no such conduct on the part of the vendor. As to accident and mistake, they were not relevantly involved. There was no mistake. The concept of 'accident' does not cover:

... situations where the event which has come to pass is one for which an express exculpatory provision might have been made, but was not sought or was not agreed to, and where to relieve against its consequences after it has occurred would deprive the other party to the contract of an essential right.[29]

It is difficult to see that, in the case of what the Privy Council described as an 'ordinary' contract for the sale of land, and in the absence of circumstances falling within the qualifications mentioned by the Privy Council, there is much practical difference between the approaches of the Privy Council and the High Court to the question of the availability of specific performance to a purchaser who has failed to complete on time, where time is of the essence. In Australia, there is no categorical rejection of the possible relevance of unconscionability, but the qualifications expressed in the Privy Council's rejection make it less categorical than might otherwise appear. In the light of statutory provisions such as section 51AA of the Trade Practices Act, as well as earlier authority, it is not open to 'the unwritten law' in Australia to deny that conscience and commerce know each other. The important matter is that conscience does not roam at large,

---

[27] Ibid, 328, citing (1988) 165 CLR 489, H 503.
[28] Ibid, 335.   [29] Ibid, 337.

re-shaping contractual relations and denying parties rights for which they have contracted simply on the ground that such rights are, in their nature, strict. Conscience, properly formed and adequately informed, discriminates between good and evil. It is a strong thing to conclude that an exercise of legal rights requires intervention to relieve a person's conscience.

In the second case, *Romanos*, the purchasers were a day late in paying the required deposit, and the vendors terminated. The plurality judgment said that:

...the decision in *Tanwar* indicates that equity does not intervene in such a case to reshape contractual relations in a form the court thinks more reasonable or fair where subsequent events have rendered the situation of one side more favourable than that of the other side

and that:

...one asks in the present case whether the conduct of the vendors caused or contributed to a circumstance rendering it unconscientious for them to insist upon their legal rights to terminate the contracts.[30]

The exercise of contractual rights in a commercial setting occurs against the background of a market. If the market is rising, it may be in the interests of the vendor (or supplier), and against the interests of the purchaser (or consumer), to terminate. If the market is falling, the vendor (or supplier) may prefer not to terminate, especially if the other party appears willing and able to effect substantial performance. A breach of an essential term by a purchaser may present a vendor with a choice. The exercise of a rational choice, based on the vendor's self-interest as affected by market conditions, ordinarily is not against good conscience. Contracts are entered into by parties in pursuit of their own interests and in the light of their individual appreciation of the present, and likely future, state of the market. If, after a contract is made, the market rises, then, provided the purchaser abides by the terms of the contract, that will normally be to the advantage of the purchaser. If the purchaser, by failing to comply with an essential term, gives the vendor an opportunity to terminate, the advantage switches to the vendor. On the face of things, it is no more unconscientious of a vendor to take that advantage than it is for a purchaser to hold a vendor to a sale at a price below market value at the time of completion.

Furthermore, the reason why a purchaser is unable to comply with an essential term is usually of no concern to the vendor. If a purchaser fails to make an essential payment by a stipulated time, the reason for that is likely to be beyond the knowledge or control of the vendor. It is in cases where the vendor has in some way become implicated, for example, by representing that delay will be tolerated, that it may be against conscience to exercise a right to terminate. The vendor may have become implicated because of an uncertainty about the market and about the value of keeping the contract on foot. Whatever the reason, the conduct of a vendor could give rise to an impediment to the exercise of a power of termination. Such an impediment is least likely to exist where the vendor remains detached from any difficulties of the purchaser, and offers no relaxation of contractual rights. This makes it difficult to appeal to some supervening standard of reasonableness, by reference to which a court may declare that it is against conscience to insist that a contract be implemented according to its terms. Other things being equal, equity is less likely to intervene where a vendor takes a consistently strict line, perhaps in one sense 'unreasonably', and more likely to intervene where a vendor has encouraged relaxation of standards, even though conduct of the latter kind may exhibit a form of reasonableness.

The High Court of Australia has repeatedly reaffirmed the principle of objectivity by which the rights and liabilities of the parties to a contract are determined.[31] That principle is of particular importance in relation to commercial contracts, where documents often are intended to be relied upon, and provide security or title to, third parties who may have no access to any information, external to the document, as to what went on between the original parties. The legal relations of the parties to a contract are primarily determined, not by their individual subjective beliefs and understandings, but by what each party by words and conduct would have led a reasonable person on the position of the other party to believe. The meaning of a contractual document is determined by what a reasonable person would have understood them to mean. A commercial contract is to be given a businesslike interpretation. This requires attention to the language used by the parties, the commercial circumstances which the document addresses, and the objects which it is intended to secure.[32]

In a 2004 decision, *Toll (FGCT) Pty Ltd v Alphapharm Pty Ltd*,[33] the High Court rejected the proposition that in order to rely on an exclusion clause in a signed contract, which the person signing had not read, it was necessary to show that due notice of the clause had been given. The Court held that where a person signed a document which was intended to create legal relations and knew that it contained contractual terms, and there was no suggested vitiating element, such as misrepresentation, duress, or mistake, and no claim for equitable on statutory relief, that person was bound by those terms and it was immaterial that the person had not read the document. In such circumstances, the other party did not have to show that due notice had been given of the terms. The Court applied *L'Estrange v F Graucob Limited*.[34] The reasons considered in some detail the significance of a signature on a legal document, noting that such a signature represents to a reasonable reader of the document that the person who signs either has read and approved the contents of the document or is willing to take the chance

---

[31] See, e.g., *Pacific Carriers Ltd v BNP Paribas* (2004) 218 CLR 451.

[32] *McCann v Switzerland Insurance* (2000) 203 CLR 579, 589; *Lake v Simmons* [1927] AC 487 (HL) 509.

[33] (2004) 219 CLR 165.

[34] [1934] 2 KB 394 (KB).

of being bound by those contents. The representation is even stronger where (as in *Toll*) the signature appears below a written request to read the document before signing it. The Court distinguished cases where there is an issue about whether a particular document forms part of a contract, or whether there has been some material misrepresentation as to the nature or effect of the document. The joint reasons stated:

The importance which, for a very long time, the common law has assigned to the act of signing is not limited to contractual documents ... The passage [from an earlier High Court decision] quoted above is preceded by a general statement that, where a man signs a document knowing that it is a legal document relating to an interest in property, he is in general bound by the act of signature. Legal instruments of various kinds take their efficacy from signature or execution. Such instruments are often signed by people who have not read and understood all their terms, but who are nevertheless committed to those terms by the act of signature or execution. It is that commitment which enables third parties to assume the legal efficacy of the instrument. To undermine that assumption would cause serious mischief.[35]

While a consideration of the position of a third party relying on a document is of importance in many commercial transactions, such transactions often occur in circumstances where the parties themselves may have no means, apart from the document, of knowing what attention the other party has given to its terms. In *Toll*, for example, the carrier relying on the exemption clause could not have known that its customer had signed the contractual document in question without bothering to read it.

The existence of legislation such as is found in Parts IVA and V of the Trade Practices Act means that courts should not feel tempted to bend the general law in order to seek to achieve what may appear to be a just outcome in a particular case.[36] Such legislation, by providing a safety net in certain kinds of case, leaves the parties to commercial contracts free to apportion risks as they see fit. As noted above, risk is related to price or cost. A commonly understood allocation of risk, upon which the parties to a contract can rely with reasonable confidence, promotes the efficiency and fairness of the market. To undermine such confidence, and to disturb the assumptions upon which participants in the market act, produces serious mischief.

In another 2004 decision, *Equuscorp Pty Ltd v Glengallan Investments Pty Ltd*,[37] the High Court rejected an attempt by parties to a complex series of written agreements, entered into for tax avoidance purposes, to escape the consequences of those agreements by relying on anterior oral agreements and by characterizing the documents as shams because they were implemented by a series of book

---

[35] *Toll* (n 33) 182.
[36] *Photo Production Ltd v Securicor Transport Ltd* [1980] AC 827 (HL) 843; *Esso Australia Resources Ltd v Commissioner of Taxation* (1999) 201 CLR 49, 62.
[37] (2004) 218 CLR 471.

entries rather than by payments of 'real money'. There was no allegation of misrepresentation or mistake, and no claim for rectification. The joint reasons for judgment stressed the need for the law to uphold obligations undertaken in written agreements, and pointed out that the parol evidence rule, the limited operation of the defence of non est factum, and the equitable remedy of rectification, all proceed from the premise that a party executing a written agreement is bound by it.[38] The transactions were artificial and contrived, but they were not a 'sham', which refers to steps which take the form of a legally effective transaction but which the parties intend should not have the apparent, or any, legal consequences.[39] No such intention was shown. The parties entered into complicated and somewhat artificial agreements for fiscal purposes, and they were bound by them according to their terms.

In 2008, in *International Air Transport Association v Ansett Australia Holdings Limited*,[40] the High Court construed the agreement on which the IATA Clearing House system was based so as to give effect to its commercial history and purpose, and applied it according to its terms so as to give effect to the evident intention of the parties. The relevant provisions had been included for a known purpose, they were consistent with commercial practicality, and they were applied literally. The Court's general understanding of background and purpose was supplemented by specific information as to the genesis of the transaction and that history formed part of the context in which the contract took its meaning. It confirmed that the language of the contract meant exactly what it said.

A general disposition to start from the premise that contracting parties mean what they have agreed in writing, and that they should be bound to it, is not formalism or literalism. It accords with the reasonable expectations of honest people. It promotes the fair and efficient operation of the markets in which they transact business. The general law and statute provide means of intervention where justice requires it, but the qualifications to the general principle that contracts are binding according to their terms are meant to reinforce the principle by relieving, where necessary, against its unjust application; they are not meant to undermine it.

To return to *Midland Silicones Ltd v Scruttons Ltd*, the later history of that dispute suggests that cleverness and clarity are not always in opposition. The history was recounted by the House of Lords in *Homburg Houtimport BV v Agrosin Private Ltd*.[41] The initial attempt to circumvent the principle of privity of contract failed. The next step was to redraft the commercial document to include a clause to extend to servants, agents, and independent contractors of the carrier defences and immunities available to the courier and to use the law of agency to make that effective. The effectiveness of this technique was upheld in *The Eurymedon*[42] and

[38] Ibid, 483. [39] Ibid, 486.
[40] [2008] HCA 3. [41] [2004] 1 AC 715 (HL).
[42] *New Zealand Shipping Co Ltd v A M Satterthwaite & Co Ltd* [1975] AC 154 (PC) (*The Eurymedon*).

The New York Star.[43] The contractual provision was described by Lord Bingham as 'a deft and commercially-inspired response to technical English rules of contract, particularly those governing privity and consideration'.[44] In *The Eurymedon*,[45] Lord Wilberforce said:

The carrier [in an American case] contracted, in an exemption clause, as agent for, inter alios, all stevedores and other independent contractors, and although it is no doubt true that the law in the United States is more liberal than ours as regards third party contracts, their Lordships see no reason why the law of the Commonwealth should be more restrictive and technical as regards agency contracts. Commercial considerations should have the same force on both sides of the Pacific.

In the opinion of their Lordships, to give the appellant the benefit of the exemption and limitations contained in the bill of lading is to give effect to the clear intentions of a commercial document, and can be given within existing principles. They see no reason to strain the law or the facts in order to defeat these intentions.

Straining the law or the facts to defeat the clearly expressed intentions of the parties to a commercial contract is not consistent with sound legal policy.

---

[43] *Port Jackson Stevedoring Pty Ltd v Salmond & Spraggon (Australia) Pty Ltd* [1981] 1 WLR 138 (PC) (*The New York Star*).
[44] *Homburg Houtimport* (n 41) 744.
[45] *The Eurymedon* (n 42) 169.

8

Duty of Care and Public Authority Liability

Elizabeth-Anne Gumbel

Lord Bingham has made an important contribution to altering the boundaries that limit claims for breach of duty by public authorities. This has stemmed from his instinctive need to examine the fairness of the situation on a factual case-by-case basis, rather than to apply a narrow legalistic approach. In essence Lord Bingham's approach has been not to unnecessarily confine the situations where a duty of care exists, but to stress the difficulties for a claimant in proving breach of duty. The emphasis has been placed upon allowing cases to proceed and ultimately succeed, even in unusual circumstances, as long as there is a rigorous examination of fault.

At the heart of the litigation in tort involving public authorities are issues of public policy. Whilst there have been attempts by judges to depart from the analysis of tort cases in terms of 'public policy', for example by using the concept of 'distributive justice',[1] fundamentally public policy is a determining factor. Public policy considerations have of course increasingly included human rights issues. As Lady Justice Arden described in the case of *Jain v Trent Strategic Health Authority*.[2]

... the Human Rights Act 1998 has also had a perceptible impact in this field. As a result of the Act giving further protection in domestic law to Convention rights, the courts are now more conscious that the denial of a duty of care may result in the denial of Convention rights. The effect has been to encourage courts to identify more specific policy factors and to consider the interests of the individual affected by the decision-making by the public authority.

The question of how widely the boundaries of duty of care should be drawn where there are novel claims in tort has therefore been driven by developments in Strasbourg and the development of domestic human rights jurisprudence, as well as by domestic public policy.

---

[1] See, e.g., the speech of Lord Hoffmann in *Frost v Chief Constable of South Yorkshire Police* [1999] 2 AC 455 and the speech of Lord Steyn in *McFarlane v Tayside Health Board* [2000] 2 AC 59.

[2] *Jain v Trent Strategic Health Authority* [2007] EWCA Civ 1186 at para 64.

Lord Bingham's analysis of the issues can be seen through his judgments in the Court of Appeal in *Caparo Plc v Dickman*[3] to the House of Lords in *D v East Berkshire Community Health NHS Trust*.[4] In general, the approach has been to broaden the scope of duty of care whilst seeking to ensure that on a case-by-case basis the facts justify a finding of fault and an award of damages.

Lord Bingham's application of the public policy issues in tort claims is encapsulated in the following passage in his dissenting judgment in the Court of Appeal in *X v Bedfordshire County Council*:

...It would require very potent considerations of public policy, which do not in my view exist here, to override the rule of public policy which has first claim on the loyalty of the law that wrongs should be remedied.[5]

This approach was adopted by Lord Browne-Wilkinson in the House of Lords as being the proper approach, although ultimately he came to the opposite conclusion to Bingham MR (as he then was) as to whether a duty existed on the facts of the *X v Bedfordshire CC* cases.[6]

Further, in *X v Bedfordshire CC*, Lord Bingham recognized the significance of examining the beneficial consequences that the imposition of a duty of care might have. He stated:

I cannot accept as a general proposition, that the imposition of a duty of care makes no contribution to the maintenance of high standards. The common belief that the imposition of such a duty may lead to overkill is not easily reconciled with the suggestion that it has no effect.[7]

And

One argument on public policy was addressed to us which seemed to have more relevance to the local authority than to the health authority and the psychiatrist. If a duty of care were imposed on the local authority and claims such as the child's permitted to continue, the already overstretched resources of local authorities, human and financial, would be diverted from the valuable purpose of looking after children and wasted on the sterile processes of litigation.[8]

In respect of this argument Lord Bingham concluded:

Save in clear cases, it is not for the Courts to decide how public money will be wasted on litigation against the hope that the possibility of suit may contribute towards the maintenance of the highest standards.[9]

[3] *Caparo Plc v Dickman* [1989] 1 QB 653.
[4] *D v East Berkshire Community Health NHS Trust* [2005] 2 AC 373.
[5] *X v Bedfordshire County Council* [1995] 2 AC 633 at 663D.
[6] *X v Bedfordshire County Council* [1995] 2 AC 633 at 749G.
[7] *X v Bedfordshire County Council* [1995] 2 AC 633 at 662G.
[8] *X v Bedfordshire County Council* [1995] 2 AC 633 at 667E–F.
[9] *X v Bedfordshire County Council* [1995] 2 AC 633 at 667G.

In looking at the question of the imposition of a duty of care, the *Caparo* test remains pre-eminent notwithstanding Lord Justice Brooke's description of the need to look at the 'battery of tests that the House of Lords has taught us to use';[10] that is: the 'purpose' test;[11] the 'assumption of responsibility' test;[12] 'the distributive justice' test;[13] and the 'three-pronged' test in *Caparo*.[14]

The *Caparo* test, therefore, remains the benchmark test. It is important to recognize that fairness was the overriding issue identified by Lord Bingham (then Lord Justice Bingham) in the Court of Appeal in *Caparo*:

> The third requirement to be met before a duty of care will be held to be owed by A to B is that a Court should find it just and reasonable to impose such a duty... The requirement cannot, perhaps be better put than it was by Weintraub C.J. in Goldberg v Housing Authority of the City of Newark (1962) 186A 2d 291, 293:
>
> 'Whether a duty exists is ultimately a question of fairness. The inquiry involves a weighing of the relationship of the parties, the nature of the risk, and the public interest in the proposed solution'.[15]

When considering the application of the third requirement to the facts in *Caparo*, Lord Bingham emphasized that the shareholders claims would be difficult to establish, and that the test in *Bolam v Friern Hospital Management Committee*[16] would apply as it does to professionals in any context. Lord Bingham described how the principles in *Bolam* afforded special protection to auditors, and would make it difficult for shareholders to establish a failure to exercise ordinary skill and care. He concluded: 'Most shareholders will not do so'. He pointed out that damage would also need to be proved, that is the error had a real and palpable effect. He stated: 'Not many claims by shareholders will I think, fulfil these stringent requirements'. He concluded, however, that:

> If a shareholder can prove these things, I think it is just and reasonable that he should obtain redress. I am not persuaded any compelling consideration of policy should deny him. It may be that to begin with auditors will be put to the expense of defending some bad claims, but the problems facing plaintiffs will be quickly appreciated and the liability for costs is likely to be an effective deterrent. I simply do not think that a decision in principle in favour of the plaintiffs will lead to an uncontrollable inrush of claims.

The approach of finding that a duty exists, but emphasizing the difficulties for a claimant in proving the breach was adopted again by Lord Bingham in *D v East*

---

[10] See *McLoughlin v Groves (A Firm)* [2002] PIQR 223 at 229 and *Parkinson v St James NHS Trust* [2001] 3 WLR 376.

[11] *Banque Bruxelles Lambert SA v Eagle Star Insurance Company Limited* [1997] AC 191, 211G.

[12] *Hedley Byne & Co Ltd v Heller & Partners Ltd* [1964] and *Henderson v Merrett Syndicates Limited* [1995] 2 AC 145, 180G–181F.

[13] *Frost v Chief Constable of South Yorkshire Police* [1999] 2 AC 455 at 503H–504C.

[14] *Caparo Industries Plc v Dickinson* [1990] 2 AC 605, 617H–618A.

[15] *Caparo Industries Plc v Dickinson* [1989] 1 QB 653 at 688.

[16] [1957] 1 WLR 582.

Berkshire Health Authority.[17] The position is summarized by Lord Bingham as follows:

The courts below have concluded that in such a situation no duty of care can be owed by the doctor or the social worker to the parent, that accordingly no claim may lie and that these claims brought by the parents must be dismissed with no evidence called and no detailed examination of the facts. In the second appeal there is also a claim by the child, but that has been treated differently. I understand that a majority of my noble and learned friends agree with this conclusion, for which there is considerable authority in the United Kingdom and abroad. But the law in this area has evolved very markedly over the last decade. What appeared to be hard-edged rules precluding the possibility of any claim by parent or child have been eroded or restricted. *And a series of decisions of the European Court of Human Rights has shown that application of an exclusionary rule in this sensitive area may lead to serious breaches of Convention rights for which domestic law affords no remedy and for which, at any rate arguably, the law of tort should afford a remedy if facts of sufficient gravity are shown.*

I would not, for my part, strike out these claims but would allow them to go to trial. A judgment can then be made on the liability of the respective defendants on facts which have been full explored.[18] (emphasis added)

There followed an illuminating review by Lord Bingham of how the position of public authority liability had changed in the ten years between *X v Bedfordshire CC* case and the *D v East Berkshire Community Health NHS Trust* case. The review focused in particular on the cases concerning the potential liability of public authorities for the actions of their employees where allegations of child abuse had arisen. He described the position as follows:

There are, broadly speaking, three theoretical answers which may be given to the question whether doctors and social workers (to whom I shall refer compendiously as 'healthcare professionals') owe any common law duty of care other than to their employer, and if so what, in a case of potential child abuse. The first is that they owe no such duty. The second is that they may on appropriate facts owe a duty to the child, but owe no duty to the parent. The third is that they may on appropriate facts owe a limited duty to the parent as well as the child. The appellants contend that this third answer is the correct one. The respondents, by not challenging the continuance of the child's claim against the health authority and the local authority in the second appeal, effectively contend for the second answer. The first answer was that given by a majority of the Court of Appeal and a unanimous House of Lords in X (Minors) v Bedfordshire County Council and M (A Minor) v Newham London Borough Council [1995] 2 AC 633. In para 83 of its judgment under appeal the Court of Appeal boldly, and in the view of some commentators impermissibly (see Wright: '"Immunity" no more: Child abuse cases and public authority liability in negligence after D v East Berkshire Community Health NHS Trust' (2004) 20 PN 58, 63), held that that decision of the House, in its relation to claims by children, could not survive the Human Rights Act 1998, and before the House no party sought to maintain

[17] *D v East Berkshire Community Health NHS Trust* [2005] 2 AC 373.
[18] *D v East Berkshire Community Health NHS Trust* [2005] 2 AC 373 at 382F.

the full breadth of the decision. But much of the reasoning supporting the decision is relied on, and it has been followed in other jurisdictions. It is where examination of the authorities must begin.

In X v Bedfordshire itself, five child claimants complained that they had been the victims of maltreatment and neglect which had been brought to the notice of the defendant council but on which, for a long time, the council had failed to act. The facts, only assumed when the strike-out application was heard in this country but established or accepted when the claimants took their complaint to Strasbourg, were very strong. An experienced and highly respected child psychiatrist described the children's experiences as 'to put it bluntly, "horrific"' and added that it was the worst case of neglect and emotional abuse that she had seen in her professional career: Z v United Kingdom (2001) 34 EHRR 97, para 40. It was accepted in Strasbourg that the neglect and abuse suffered by the four child applicants reached the threshold of inhuman and degrading treatment (para 74) and a violation of article 3 of the European Convention was found, arising from the failure of the system to protect the child applicants from serious, long-term neglect and abuse (paras 74–75). The Court awarded compensation amounting to £320,000, a substantial figure by Strasbourg standards. Yet the local authority's failure to intervene, which had permitted the abuse and neglect to continue, was held by the Court of Appeal and the House of Lords to afford the children no tortious remedy in negligence against the local authority in English law.

In a further detailed analysis Lord Bingham explained the history of the cases since *X v Bedfordshire CC* starting with *Barrett v Enfield London Borough Council*:[19]

In that case, the claimant, who had spent his childhood in foster care, claimed damages against a local authority for decisions made and not made during that period. The judge's decision to strike out the claim had been upheld by the Court of Appeal but was unanimously reversed by the House. There are four points worthy of note for present purposes. First, it was accepted that a claim may lie against a local authority arising from child-care decisions in certain circumstances: see pp 557, 573, 575, 587–590. Secondly, the general undesirability of striking out claims arising in uncertain and developing areas of the law without full exploration of the facts was emphasised: pp 557–558, 575. This was a point made in X v Bedfordshire at pp 740–741 and is a point strongly echoed in later cases such as Waters v Commissioner of Metropolitan Police [2000] 1 WLR 1607, 1613; W v Essex County Council [2001] 2 AC 592, 598; Phelps v Hillingdon London Borough Council [2001] 2 AC 619, 659–660; and L (A Child) and another v Reading Borough Council and another [2001] EWCA Civ 346, [2001] 1 WLR 1575, 1587. Thirdly, the notion of an exclusionary rule conferring immunity on particular classes of defendant was rejected: pp 559, 570, 575. This rejection has been echoed with approval in later cases such as Kent v Griffiths [2001] QB 36, para 38; S v Gloucestershire County Council, above, p 338; and E and Others v United Kingdom (2002) 36 EHRR 519. Fourthly, it was not considered that the policy factors which had weighed with the House in X v Bedfordshire and M v Newham had the same weight where complaints related to acts and omissions after a child had been taken into care: [2001] 2 AC 550, 568, 575. The argument that imposition

---

[19] *Barrett v Enfield London Borough Council* [2001] 2 AC 550, 558–560.

of a duty might lead to defensiveness and excessive caution was discounted, the remedies available to the claimant were not thought to be as efficacious as recognition of a common law duty of care and it was not accepted that imposition of a duty made no contribution to the maintenance of high standards: pp 568, 575. There was nothing to displace the general rule, recognised in X v Bedfordshire and M v Newham at pp 663 and 749, that the public policy consideration which had first claim on the loyalty of the law was that wrongs should be remedied: p 588.

In S v Gloucestershire County Council [2001] Fam 313 the plaintiff claimed damages in negligence against a local authority for abuse suffered by him during a placement with foster parents. The Court of Appeal allowed the plaintiff's appeal against the striking out of his action while upholding the decision to strike out another action which was also the subject of appeal.

The claim in W v Essex County Council [2001] 2 AC 592 was made not only by children (or those who had been children when they suffered abuse) but also by parents. The parents had fostered a child on an assurance that he was not a known sexual abuser when, to the knowledge of the local authority, he was, and during his placement with the parents he sexually abused their children. Hooper J struck out the parents' claims but not those of the children: [1997] 2 FLR 535. The Court of Appeal (Stuart-Smith, Judge and Mantell LJJ) unanimously upheld the judge's decision striking out the parents' claim and by a majority (Stuart-Smith LJ dissenting) upheld his decision on the children's claim, which was accordingly allowed to proceed: [1999] Fam 90. The House unanimously allowed the parents' appeal. It could not be said that the claim that there was a duty of care owed to the parents and a breach of that duty by the local authority was unarguable and it was inappropriate to strike out without investigation of the full facts known to, and the factors influencing the decision of, the local authority: p 598. In A and B v Essex County Council [2002] EWHC 2707 (QB), [2003] 1 FLR 615 a claim by adoptive parents for damages against a local authority came to trial on liability before Buckley J and succeeded. An appeal against his decision was dismissed, although on somewhat different grounds: A and another v Essex County Council [2003] EWCA Civ 1848, [2004] 1 WLR 1881.

Phelps v Hillingdon London Borough Council [2001] 2 AC 619 was one of four appeals heard together by an enlarged committee of the House. In each case the plaintiff complained of allegedly negligent decisions concerning his or her education made by the defendant local authorities. The procedural histories of the four cases were different, but in three of them the Court of Appeal had struck out the plaintiff's claim and in only one had it been allowed to proceed. The House unanimously dismissed the local authority's appeal in that last case but allowed the plaintiff's appeal in the other three. It was held to be clear in principle that a teacher or educational psychologist could in principle owe a duty of care to a child as well as an employing authority: pp 654, 665, 667, 670, 676. Valid claims in negligence were not to be excluded because claims which were without foundation or exaggerated might be made: pp 655, 665, 676. There was no reason to exclude the claims on grounds of public policy alone: pp 665, 672, 677. As my noble and learned friend Lord Nicholls of Birkenhead perceptively observed, 'Never' is an unattractive absolute in this context': p 667.

The plaintiffs in L (A Child) and another v Reading Borough Council and another [2001] 1 WLR 1575 were a daughter and her father. The proceedings arose out of a fabricated complaint made by the mother of the child to a local authority and police authority that he had sexually abused the child. The authorities had erroneously accepted the complaint as true, and the plaintiffs claimed damages for negligence against both authorities. The local authority did not apply to strike out either claim, but the police authority applied to strike out both claims against it. Goldring J struck out the father's claim against the police but allowed the child's negligence claim to proceed. The Court of Appeal allowed the father's appeal, holding that it was inappropriate to strike out on the basis of assumed facts: p 1587.

In the light of all this authority, coupled with *Z v United Kingdom* and *TP and KM v United Kingdom*, above, it could not now be plausibly argued that a common law duty of care may not be owed by a publicly-employed healthcare professional to a child with whom the professional is dealing. In *E and others v United Kingdom* (2002) 36 EHRR 519, a case in which four children complained of a local authority's failure to protect them from abuse by their stepfather, the European Court noted (in para 114 of its judgment):

'The Government submitted that it was not correct to assert that this House of Lords decision [in X v Bedfordshire, M v Newham, et al] prevented all claims in negligence against local authorities in the exercise of their child protection duties, and argued that it could not be regarded as beyond doubt that these applicants would have failed as, in the case of these applicants, the social services arguably were negligent in the way they approached operational, as well as policy, matters.'

Thus the respondents' reaction to the claims of the child RK in the second appeal is in no way surprising. But nor is it without significance. For in X v Bedfordshire itself the only claim was by the children, and in M v Newham the parent's claims were a very secondary issue: see my definition of the question at p 651, Peter Gibson LJ's reference to the 'primary question' at p 676 and Staughton LJ's omission of any express reference to the parent save when holding, at p 676, that money would not be an appropriate remedy. In the House, the parent's entitlement was not separately addressed. Thus the policy considerations on which the decision of the House rested were primarily directed to justifying the exclusion of a class of claim which, it is accepted, can no longer be excluded on application of a simple exclusionary rule. That conclusion makes it necessary to examine those considerations to ascertain how much force they retain if they no longer automatically exclude claims by children.

This summary by Lord Bingham vividly describes the progress and developments in the law in the period of almost exactly a decade. The position can be contrasted with the state of the law of tort when on 3 July 1993 Lord Bingham, then Master of the Rolls, chaired a conference at All Souls, Oxford entitled: 'The Frontiers of Liability: The Condition of the Law of Tort'.

Dr Jane Stapleton, speaking at that conference, described how in 1993:

The principal current concern with the condition of tort law, centering on the law of negligence, relates to the retreat by appellate courts from broad principle to timid pragmatism. McGee is overtaken by Wilsher, McLoughlin by Alcock, Hedley Byrne by Caparo and most famously Anns by Murphy. Dealing with this complaint requires, however, the same agenda for future action as does the concern with the potentially vast new liabilities generated by broad principles: an explicit focus on those policy concerns which militate against the protection by tort of everyone who has been injured by the carelessness of the defendant.

And

Current criticism of the state of tort law can be resolved into two forms: that which makes a political line and boils down simply to a complaint about the House of Lord's conservative vision for the overall reach of tort protection: and that which concerns the process by which decisions are taken.

In respect of the process by which decisions are taken Dr Stapleton commented:

Just as, in Lord Goff's words 'piecemeal legislation may exercise a distorting effect on the law' so too can the ad hockery implicit in the Caparo 'pocket' approach to new cases.

Dr Stapleton suggested that:

The way forward lies in a more careful, separate consideration of the counterveiling factors which militate against the imposition of tort', that is 'The 'pockets' analysis should be replaced with an analysis based on an agenda of counterveiling factors to the imposition of tort liability which have been explicitly construed from policy concerns.

The statement of Lord Bingham in *X v Bedfordshire CC* that: 'It would require very potent considerations of public policy, to override the rule of public policy which has first claim on the loyalty of the law that wrongs should be remedied',[20] chimes with this academic aspiration for the law of tort. The development of the law of tort described by Lord Bingham in *D v East Berkshire Community Health NHS Trust*[21] has also in many respects fulfilled this aspiration. This trend can also be seen through the unwillingness of courts to allow strike out applications in respect of claims brought on a novel basis. The cases of *Swinney v Chief Constable of Northumbria Police Force*,[22] *Barrett v Enfield London Borough Council*,[23] *W v Essex County Council*,[24] *L (A Child) and another v Reading Borough Council and another*,[25] *S v Gloucestershire County Council*,[26] *Kent v London Ambulance Service*,[27] *Thames Trains v Health & Safety Executive*,[28] and *Phelps v Hillingdon London Borough Council*[29] were all strike out applications that ultimately failed.

To this list of cases must be added the case of *Smith v Chief Constable of Sussex*[30] in which the House of Lords Committee chaired by Lord Bingham is considering an appeal from the Court of Appeal who refused to strike out a claim against the police. The decisions in this case and the case of *Chief Constable of Hertfordshire Police v Van Colle*[31] are awaited with interest. Against the backdrop

---

[20] *X v Bedfordshire County Council* [1995] 2 AC 633 at 663D.
[21] *D v East Berkshire Community Health NHS Trust* [2005] 2 AC 373.
[22] [1997] QB 464.
[23] [2001] 2 AC 550, 558–560.
[24] [2001] 2 AC 592.
[25] [2001] 1 WLR 1575.
[26] [2001] Fam 313.
[27] [1999] Lloyds Rep Med 58.
[28] [2003] EWCA Civ 720.
[29] [2001] 2 AC 619.
[30] [2008] EWCA Civ 39.
[31] [2007] 1 WLR 1821.

of *Osman v United Kingdom*[32] and *Hill v Chief Constable of West Yorkshire*[33] there is now active consideration as to whether the boundaries of the law of tort in the sphere of public bodies should extend to police investigation. The issue for Lord Bingham, once more, will be whether a line should be drawn at the duty stage or whether fairness requires a public authority should be entitled to defend its conduct but only after assessment of the facts and of fault at trial.[34]

---

[32] (1999) 1 FLR 193 ECHR.   [33] [1989] AC 53.

[34] In the event Lord Bingham gave a dissenting opinion in the case of Smith setting out a liability principle which would have allowed the Smith case to proceed. The rest of the committee allowed the police appeal. It remains to be seen whether this dissenting opinion is a pointer to future change.

9

What Decisions Should Judges Not Take?

Jeffrey Jowell

Judicial review, as has often been noted, has advanced greatly in recent years. But its progress is uncertain on the crunch question: to what extent can or should judges decide the substance of official decisions? As some of the cases cited below show, Lord Bingham has made a significant contribution to this issue, among so many others.

The question is more complex these days, now that our judges have been granted, or have assumed, the authority to decide upon the compatibility of legislation—both in relation to European Union Law and Convention rights under the Human Rights Act 1998. Perhaps judges have always had to pronounce upon difficult issues, but few could be as complex as the matters currently passing through the courts, particularly those involving the assessment of risk—in relation to matters such as international terrorism or the regulation of new medicines, or chemical sprays with uncertain effects.

For many years judges and scholars would recite the incantation that judicial review (as opposed to appeal) permits judges to interfere with the 'procedure' (sometimes called 'process') by which a decision was reached, but that they have absolutely no authority to interfere with the 'merits' of the decision. Yet time and again they would interfere with decisions on the ground that they involved excessive penalties or oppressive planning conditions. They justified this interference on the ground that the decisions were not merely unreasonable but, to employ another incantation, were 'so unreasonable that no reasonable decision-maker could make them'. For some reason this formulation, associated with the small Midlands market town of Wednesbury,[1] worked its magic spin and endorsed the impression that judges had not fallen into the forbidden embrace of merits review.

There are two arguments in favour of the courts forsaking the substance of a decision. The first is an argument from constitutional theory—the notion of separation of powers as a cornerstone of representative democracy. The second is based upon the practical limits of the adversarial process. Both those arguments

---

[1] *Associated Provincial Picture Houses Ltd v Wednesbury Corporation* [1948] 1 KB 223.

must be seen in the context of the fact that our judges (and this is not true in all systems) are appointed and not elected, and drawn not from the ranks of administrators (as, for example, are many judges in the conseil d'etat) but from senior legal practitioners. This independence from the political or managerial may well be a strength, but it also has its limits.

Turning first to the argument from constitutional principle. Under our system, the notion of representative government, together with the separation of powers, limits the authority of the courts to make decisions of 'policy'. Policy is a matter for the elected representatives to decide, for it is they who are invested with the authority to make utilitarian calculations of social, economic, or political preference.[2] Courts should not decide the siting of an airport, or whether this country should renew its nuclear power capacity or its nuclear warheads. Levels and rates of tax are, similarly, the domain of government's elected branches. Why so? Because these decisions, based as they are upon estimates of the greatest good, are, in our democratic system, rightfully taken by the greatest number. The expression of the majority is appropriate for deciding those issues and is checked by the opportunity of the electorate to reject a decision-maker who does not faithfully reflect its wishes.

The second argument for judicial restraint is not one from constitutional but from institutional capacity. It asserts that there are limits to the adversarial decision-making process ideally to decide certain questions. Certain matters are not 'amenable' to the judicial process. Of course courts could in theory decide anything—such as whether the judge in a village produce show rightly favoured one set of matching marrows over another. They could surely even find plausible criteria to justify why an apple should not have won the prize for best fruit over an orange or pear. But the question is often not whether the judge lacks capacity to decide the matter, but whether another body is better equipped to make that decision—a matter of *relative* institutional capacity. If so, a further question is whether the courts should therefore abdicate their authority to decide the matter, or merely accord a degree of weight to the primary decision-maker's judgment. And the last question is, what degree of weight?

Take, for example, the decision as to whether a new development, say a shiny high building, enhances or unacceptably detracts from the architectural heritage and character of an area. This is not exactly a 'policy' decision in itself, although it may contain elements of policy (for example, whether to sacrifice heritage in favour of economic development and the affordable housing that the development promises). But shorn of that policy element, do elected representatives have more expertise than a particular bench of judges on the question of heritage and architectural standards? It may be that the bench of the moment happens to be

[2] See *Lord Hoffmann in R (Pro Life Alliance) v BBC* [2003] UKHL 23 at [76]; *R (Alconbury) v Secretary of State for the Environment, Transport and the Regions* [2001] UKHL 23 at [76]. See also Ronald Dworkin's distinction between policy and principle in *Taking Rights Seriously* (1977) 82–87.

composed of amateur architectural experts, confident in their ability to assess the aesthetic context of the building. But we need to consider, too, the institutional context of the decision-making process: the elected representatives who made the decision were fully advised by the professional expertise of their planning officers. The institutional expertise built in to the primary decision therefore counsels judicial deference, irrespective of how greatly the development offends the judges' sensibilities.

But what if the politicians in this case had rejected the advice of their officers? Could that tempt the judges to intervene? It is here that we encounter another aspect of a decision such as this. Are there any *objective criteria* by which the decision to overrule the planning committee be justified? Or is this essentially a matter of individual preference? If the latter, it is said, judges have no right to impose their personal preference over that of the primary decision-maker. Since both decisions are inherently subjective, there can be no objective justification for so doing.

Where the Secretary of State had the power to decide whether the expenditure of local authorities had been 'excessive', and to penalize them if it had been, the House of Lords held that the decision was not suited to judicial determination because of the absence of 'objective criteria' by which to determine the extent of excessive expenditure.[3] After 9/11, the government sought to derogate from ECHR Article 5 on the ground specified in Article 15 that there was a 'public emergency threatening the life of the Nation'. The majority of the House of Lords held, through Lord Bingham, that the assessment of the government on that issue raised a 'pre-eminently political question' on the ground that it would involve a 'prediction of what people around the world would do'. The deference here was not based on the fact the matter was 'political', in the sense that it lay constitutionally with the executive rather than the court, but on the fact that the issue admitted of 'no objective challenge'.[4]

So there are two aspects of institutional capacity that lead to judicial deference. The first relates to expertise and on that subject there are many examples of the courts in effect disqualifying themselves from entering on the issue before them. For example, refusing to enter into the merits of the official ranking of the research standards of university departments.[5] The second has to do with the lack of objective criteria by which to judge a matter.

Here we must place a gloss on the notion of expertise. It involves not only the knowledge that comes from a particular training and experience, but also the capacity to carry out an assessment of risk. National security provides such an example. The courts seem to have eschewed their previous habit of automatically deferring to the executive on national security matters on the ground of lack of constitutional competence (because the executive are responsible for those

---

[3] *Secretary of State for the Environment, ex p Hammersmith and Fulham LBC* [1991] 1 AC 521 at 593, 597.
[4] *A v Secretary of State* [2004] UKHL 56.
[5] *R v Higher Education Funding Council ex p Institute of Dental Surgery* [1994] 1 WLR 242.

decisions to Parliament, which is in turn accountable to the electorate). However, there is force in the argument that the executive, with its direct access to the intelligence services with their access to a network of informers, possesses superior institutional capacity to assess the risk of the dangers involved. We have seen that Lord Bingham in the *Belmarsh Prison* case deferred to the executive on the question of whether the emergency threatened the 'life of the nation' on the ground that that assessment was based on a 'prediction of what people around the world would do'.[6]

Perhaps public administration always involved aspects of risk-assessment. But the cases that came to court at the time of the great growth of administrative law from the mid-1960s to the 1990s did not reflect that preoccupation. They dealt mainly with licensing matters, perhaps some immigration, and, at the most complex, matters of town and country planning and the interpretation of statutory powers. These days risk-assessment features to a significantly greater extent, for example, in decisions about the possibility of toxicity in chemicals, the standards needed to manage a problem before its adverse effects become obvious. Planning for uncertainty arises in respect of the potential dangers of crop spraying, nano-technology, or genetically modified crops. Decisions as to whether or not to control, regulate, or ban such activities or substances have in common with those on national security the fact that they are made in conditions of uncertainty and that they require the evaluation of risk. Do the courts really have the expertise, the knowledge, the capacity to assess evidence in the face of these kinds of uncertainties?

In addition to the institutional limits of courts considered above, it is often said that the adversarial process in our courts disables them from resolving certain problems because of the inherent character of those problems in themselves. The 'polycentric problem' is identified in this regard as being 'non-justiciable'. Most 'allocative decisions', that is, decisions involving the distribution of limited resources, fall into this category. A common example is a budget which allocates sums to different areas (housing, health, sport, education, and so on). If the budget as a whole were challenged on the ground that more should go on education and health rather than sport, and if the courts upheld that challenge, the whole budget would have to be recalibrated. Apart from the judges here entering into policy issues, they also set up a chain reaction, requiring a rearrangement and readjustment of other decisions with which the original has interacting points of influence. The polycentric problem has been compared to a spider's web:

A pull on one strand will distribute tensions throughout the web as a whole. Doubling the original pull will, in all likelihood, not simply double each of the resulting tensions but rather create a different complicated pattern [especially] if the double pull caused one or more of the weaker strands to snap.[7]

---

[6] N 4 above. Compare Lord Hoffmann in that case, who held that the notion of life of the nation was based on more than physical harm but included the values of liberty.

[7] L Fuller, 'The Forms and Limits of Adjudication' (1978–79) 92 Harv L Rev 353.

Lord Bingham recognized the polycentricity inherent in a decision about whether a hospital should provide expensive treatment to a child with a rare form of cancer and who was not expected, even with the treatment, to live very long after the treatment. He said:

difficult and agonizing judgments have to be made as to how a limited budget is best allocated to the maximum advantage of the maximum number of patients. This is not a judgment which the court can make.[8]

The polycentricity involved in that case arose out of the fact that, if the treatment were ordered to be provided by the court, a set of compensating adjustments would have to be made to the hospital budget. Further agonizing choices would need to be made between kidney dialysis and heart by-passes, and so on.

There have been a number of cases where the courts have refused to be drawn into allocative decisions between competing policy considerations for this reason, such as where the House of Lords refused to interfere in a decision of a chief constable to deploy his resources in a way which gave partial protection (on certain days of the week only) to exporters at risk of disruption of their trade from animal rights protestors. It was recognized that if the chief constable were to deploy all the resources necessary to protect the exporters throughout the week, then he would have to remove protection from other parts of the county, and engage in a complex pattern of reallocation elsewhere. That kind of allocative decision was not for the courts to make.[9]

Another reason for the fact that polycentric decisions are held to be non-justiciable is that the subsequent reallocation of resources in consequence of the court's judgment will often involve interests who were not represented in the litigation before the court (unlike Parliament, where a variety of interests are represented, or can be consulted more easily than court procedures allow).

The above arguments in favour of judicial deference are valid insofar as they identify areas of decision-making and types of decision where the courts ought to exercise restraint. But they are by no means conclusive.

First, we should note that the Human Rights Act has the specific effect of requiring all decisions of all branches of government to conform with Convention rights (subject to Parliament's ability to ignore a declaration of incompatibility with Convention rights). When adjudicating on the issue of an interference with Convention rights, therefore, the courts need not defer to the executive on the ground of their responsibility to Parliament, nor need the courts defer to Parliament on the ground that it is elected.[10] The courts possess full authority now to guard the invasion of those rights that now formally ground our

---

[8] *R v Cambridge DHA, ex p B (No 1)* [1995] WLR 898, at 906.

[9] *R v Chief Constable of Sussex*, ex parte ITF [1999] 2 AC 418.

[10] See Lord Steyn, 'Deference: A Tangled Story' [2005] PL 346, Jeffrey Jowell, 'Judicial Deference and Human Rights: A Question of Competence', in Craig and Rawlings (eds), *Law and Administration in Europe: Essays in Honour of Carol Harlow* (2005) 67; Jowell, 'Judicial Deference: Servility, Civility or Institutional Capacity?' [2003] PL 592.

constitutional democracy and which even the popular will is expected not to override.

Even a polycentric decision does not connote total judicial servility. The courts are not entirely disabled from scrutiny of the allocative decision. They must always consider whether lawful and relevant considerations have been taken into account by the decision-maker. If hospital treatment is refused for irrelevant reasons (for example, because of the child's race) of course the decision could be invalidated. The fact that compensating readjustments to the hospital's budget would need to be made would be no reason for lack of judicial intervention. Sorry, but the hospital planners just have to go back to the drawing board. There have in fact been many cases where budgetary decisions have been challenged by the courts. The matter depends upon the relevant statute and context[11] and whether the statute provides a mere power to the decision-maker to act in his discretion, a duty, or a mere 'target duty'.[12]

We noted that one of the reasons why it is said that a polycentric decision is not ideally amenable to judicial review is that the reallocation of resources would involve parties who may not be represented in the proceedings before the court. The legislature is said to be a more suitable forum for these decisions. Yet in *Huang*,[13] Lord Bingham probed this issue more deeply. He considered a case in which the court had not wished to intervene in an allocative decision where the issue related to housing policy[14] and where the result represented a 'considered democratic compromise', and where all parties were represented in the parliamentary debate. However, such a case was very different from the situation in *Huang*, which involved immigration policy, where the voice of immigrants was not directly heard in the decision-making process. In such a case the courts have less reason to be diffident about interfering, irrespective of their ideal capacity, or lack of capacity, to decide.[15]

Even in relation to decisions involving high national policy, courts are able, and indeed obliged, to insist that all decisions conform to the scope of the decision-maker's relevant power or duty; to constitutional principles such as the rule of law or equality (unless the statute speaks clearly to the contrary), and have been arrived at by the common law standards of procedural fairness. A recent challenge to a government review which reversed the 'high policy' against nuclear power was struck down by the Administrative Court on the ground that the review was

---

[11] *Compare R v Gloucestershire CC ex p Barry* [1997] AC 206 (the authority entitled to take limited resources into account in the decision whether to fulfil 'needs') with *R v Sussex CC ex p Tandy* [1998] AC 714 (the authority could not take limited resources into account when considering whether it could provide 'reasonable education').

[12] For a fuller discussion see Woolf, Jowell and Le Sueur, *de Smith's Judicial Review* (6th edn, 2007), paras 9/5-064 *et seq*, 5-128 *et seq*.

[13] *Huang v Secretary of State for the Home Department* [2007] UKHL 11.

[14] As in *Kay v Lambeth LBC* [2006] UKHL 10.

[15] For a powerful critique of the notion of polycentricity as excusing judicial review see Jeff King, 'The Pervasiveness of Polycentricity' [2008] Pub L 101.

so deficient in content and form that its process was 'manifestly unfair'.[16] And in a case involving national housing policy (a matter which is pre-eminently a question for the elected branch of government), Lord Nicholls said:

Parliament has to hold a fair balance between the competing interests of tenants and landlords, taking into account broad issues of social and economic policy. But, even in such a field, where the alleged violation comprises differential treatment based upon ground such as race or sex or sexual orientation the courts will scrutinise with intensity any reasons said to constitute justification.[17]

In the realm of risk-assessment, too, the courts need not throw up their hands in the face of the uncertainty or defer automatically to public officials trained in the area involved. The judges may not be able to provide the substantive answers to the questions, but they can assist greatly by establishing the *relevant standard* by which the issue needs to be resolved (such as proportionality, the precautionary principle, and so on). In *Belmarsh Prison*,[18] although the Lords were not willing to second-guess the government's assessment of whether the 'life of the nation' was imperilled, they nevertheless held that the measures that were introduced, namely, indefinite detention for foreigners, were disproportionate and failed to meet the test under Article 15 of the Convention of measures justified by the 'exigencies of the situation'.

The late and great South African scholar Etienne Mureinik identified a fundamental shift in our democratic culture from what he called a 'culture of authority' to a 'culture of justification'.[19] This new culture does not by any means require the courts to ignore their constitutional or institutional limitations. Due weight must be given to the constitutional status of an elected body, as well as the superior institutional capacity of elected representatives to pronounce upon matters of public interest in areas such as housing, taxation, and so on. Allocative decisions should not lightly be interfered with. Expertise should always be respected.

On the other hand, the culture of justification does not permit our courts to renounce their responsibility to challenge decisions that are devoid of logic, based upon mistake of fact, or otherwise not properly justified. Judges always possess the capacity to probe the evidence and assess whether the reasons and motives for decisions rationally relate to their aims. These tasks are central to judicial expertise, do not require undue deference or political approval for their legitimacy, and are indeed what judges do best.

Irrespective of ideal competence, there is therefore much work for judges to do, short of the dreaded 'merits review'. Yet how else do we explain the number of cases where judges have invalidated the excessive penalty or the oppressive planning condition?

---

[16]　*R (Greenpeace Ltd) v Secretary of State for Trade and Industry* [2007] EWHC 311 Admin.

[17]　*Ghaidan v Godin-Mendoza* [2004] 2 AC 557 at [19].

[18]　Note 14, above.

[19]　Etienne Mureinik, 'A Bridge Too Far: Introducing the Interim Bill of Rights' (1944) 10 S African J of Human Rights 31.

There is a view that holds meaningless the distinction between the substance of a decision and its merits.[20] And indeed perhaps such a label is not clear. What is clear is that the double-unreasonableness *Wednesbury* formulation no longer works its mystique. It has been redefined into a decision 'within the range of reasonable responses'.[21] There are a number of decisions for which such a test is appropriate and where the burden of proof should continue to fall on the claimant for reasons set out above. However, one class of decision, presently falling under the ground of the 'unreasonable' decision,[22] would in my view more appropriately be tested by the standard of 'proportionality'. I refer to the oppressive or unduly onerous decision, which has a 'profoundly intrusive effect' on a person's rights, freedoms or significant interests.[23] The reason for this can be simply stated: it is fundamental to our constitutional system that individuals possess freedoms and liberties unless they are lawfully limited or curtailed. Unlike the notion of reasonableness, proportionality underscores the notion that the conferment of power does not necessarily sanction the infliction of unnecessary hardship. However, it provides more than a mere moral incantation. It also provides a structured method of deciding whether its strictures have been properly observed. It places the burden of proof on the decision-maker and requires a series of justifications on his part. First, the decision-maker must have considered the imposition of less intrusive and onerous measures. If these are not possible, the decision-maker must demonstrate that the measure is not merely desirable but also necessary in the kind of constitutional democracy, based on freedom, equality, and human dignity, in which we are fortunate to live.

As has been amply demonstrated in the context of the Human Rights Act and European Union law, our courts are well able to wield proportionality as a legitimate tool of judicial decision-making without crossing forbidden borders. Its application to a limited area of domestic administrative decision-making will be more effective than unreasonableness, however defined, in explaining and legitimizing what decisions judges may properly make.

[20] A Barak, *Judicial Discretion* (2006).

[21] Dyson LJ in *R (ABCIFER) v Secretary of State for Defence* [2003] EWCA Civ 473, [2003] QB 1397.

[22] See de Smith, n 11 above, Ch 11, where different categories of unreasonable decision are set out.

[23] A phrase used by Lord Hoffmann in R *(Bancoult) v Secretary of State for Foreign and Commonwealth Affairs* [2008] UKHL 61, at [53].

10

The Rule of Law Internationally: Lord Bingham and the British Institute of International and Comparative Law

*Robert McCorquodale**

[T]he rule of law requires compliance by the state with its obligations in international law, the law which whether deriving from treaty or international custom and practice governs the conduct of nations. I do not think this proposition is contentious.[1]

Lord Bingham's words quoted above highlight two areas of the law where he has made a distinctive and positive contribution as the Senior Law Lord since 2000. One area is in the significant impacts he has made to the legal system, and to the public awareness of it, in regard to his clarification of the rule of law and his affirmation that it is at the core of the administration of justice. The other area has been his strong confirmation that compliance with international law forms part of the rule of law.

It is in regard to his latter contribution that is the focus of this paper. Whilst other contributors have dealt with issues such as the impact of international law in national law and the international rule of law, this paper aims to provide a small insight into how Lord Bingham has assisted in the application of the rule of law in the international community through his active role with the British Institute of International and Comparative Law.

British Institute of International and Comparative Law

The British Institute of International and Comparative Law (BIICL) was founded in 1958. It was created by the merger of the Society of Comparative Legislation (founded in 1894) and the Grotius Society (founded in 1915 and named after the

* I am very grateful for the time and interest that Lord Bingham has given to the Institute and for the interview he gave me in June 2008 for the purposes of this paper.
[1] Lord Bingham, 'The Rule of Law', 66 *Cambridge Law Journal* (2007) 67 at 81–82.

16th-century Dutch jurist Hugo Grotius, regarded by many as one of the parents of modern international law). This merger created an independent research body, unaffiliated to any university, which is committed to the understanding, development, and practical application of international law (both public and private) and comparative law, including aspects of European law.

The Institute is a unique body in the United Kingdom and one of very few in the world. It brings together scholars and practitioners, serving as an invaluable focal point and network for both its members and others who participate in its work. Its membership comprises lawyers from the academic community, from legal practice (including judges, solicitors, and barristers), and from government and non-governmental organizations, as well as non-lawyers who are interested in the many aspects of international and comparative law. It engages with all these members, and especially with the public, through its various high quality research projects, in its seminars, conferences, and other events, and by its publications (including its widely respected journal, the *International and Comparative Law Quarterly*, and the *Bulletin of International Legal Developments*). The breadth of areas of law dealt with by the Institute continues to grow, not least because international and comparative law issues are not limited to government matters or litigation but are now an integral part of many transactional activities in the legal field. Indeed, throughout its history a hallmark of the Institute has been a strong link between the Institute and leading academics and practitioners, including senior judges.

In fact the creation of the Institute was largely driven by the powerful energy of Lord (Tom) Denning, one of the most influential and well-known judges of the 20th century. He became the Institute's first Chairman of its Council of Management (as the Board of Trustees was then known), and then its first President. The second President of the Institute was Lord (Robert) Goff, who, prior to being President, was the Chairman of the Council of Management and senior law lord. The current President of the Institute is Lord (Tom) Bingham, who had become the Chairman of the Board of Trustees in November 2001, not long after he was appointed Senior Law Lord.

The Rule of Law

When Tom Bingham joined BIICL he was joining an organization that was committed to the same principle that he had made his own focus: the rule of law. In fact, as he has recently noted: 'Over the last 50 years, the Institute has been promoting the rule of law through all its activities. The same core principle will continue to inspire and inform the work of the Institute in the years ahead.'[2]

---

[2] Lord Bingham, 'Introduction', *British Institute of International and Comparative Law brochure* (2008), p 1.

The rule of law is frequently referred to in national and international documents and decisions.[3] Yet the level of agreement as to its importance has largely been due to the vagueness as to its meaning, with it being criticized as being no more than 'ruling-class chatter'.[4] Yet it is important to make its meaning clear, as it affects all decision-makers and, as Bingham has commented: 'the judges, in their role as journeymen judgment-makers, are not free to dismiss the rule of law as meaningless verbiage, the jurisprudential equivalent of motherhood and apple pie, even if they were inclined to do so'.[5]

There are a variety of definitions of the rule of law. In the common law tradition, there is great reliance on Dicey's three principles of the rule of law: the absolute supremacy of law as opposed to the influence of arbitrary power; equality before the law in the sense of the equal subjection of all to the law; and the law must be defined and enforced by the courts.[6] The civil law tradition tends to focus on the idea of a law-based state, constrained by a constitution and protecting the citizen.[7] Legal rules have also existed for centuries outside Europe.[8]

Bingham has clarified the meaning of the rule of law within the national legal system. He considers that the 'core of the existing principle [of the rule of law] is...that all persons and authorities within the state, whether public or private, should be bound by and entitled to the benefit of laws publicly and prospectively promulgated and publicly administered in the courts'.[9] He then identifies eight sub-rules.[10] These are:

(1) the law must be accessible and, so far as possible, be intelligible, clear, and predictable;

(2) questions of legal right and liability should ordinarily be resolved by application of the law and not by the exercise of discretion;

(3) the law applies equally to all, except to the extent that objective differences justify differentiation;

(4) the law must afford adequate protection of fundamental human rights;

---

[3] See, e.g., The Constitutional Reform Act (UK) 2005, where it is provided that the Act must not adversely affect the 'existing constitutional principle of the rule of law' (s 1), and the United Nations World Summit 2005 where states reaffirmed their commitment to 'an international order based on the rule of law' (General Assembly Resolution 60/1 (2005) para 134).

[4] J Shklar, 'Political Theory and the Rule of Law', in A Hutchinson and P Monahan (eds), *The Rule of Law: Ideal or Ideology* (1987) p 1. See also the contributions to the discussions at the World Justice Forum, created by the American Bar Association, held in July 2008.

[5] Op. cit., n 1, p 69.

[6] AV Dicey, *An Introduction to the Study of the Law of the Constitution* (1885) Part II.

[7] See, e.g., H Kelsen, *Pure Theory of Law* (2nd edn, 1967) and J Chevallier, *L'État de Droit* (3rd edn, 1999).

[8] See, e.g., the Code of Hammurabi (dated about 1700 BCE) and other ancient Assyrian documents: F Kern, *Kingship and Law in the Middle Ages: Studies by Fritz Kern* (trans S Chrimes, 1956), and Yongpin Liu, *Origins of Chinese Law* (1998).

[9] Op. cit., n 1, p 69.

[10] Op. cit., n 1, 69–84.

(5) means must be provided for resolving, without prohibitive cost or inordinate delay, bona fide civil disputes which the parties themselves are unable to resolve;

(6) ministers and public officers at all levels must exercise the powers conferred on them reasonably, in good faith, for the purpose for which the powers were conferred and without exceeding the limits of such powers;

(7) judicial and other adjudicative procedures must be fair and independent; and

(8) there must be compliance by the state with its international law obligations.

This definition is powerful and persuasive. It also sets the rule of law within a contemporary national system (and that system does not have to be a capitalist, liberal democracy)[11] and, as a consequence, distinguishes the rule of law from rule by law and rule by power. However, it is not clear how these national principles of the rule of law can apply internationally.

The Rule of Law Internationally

The rule of law has been asserted in different contexts within the international community. It is found in human rights, where the rule of law is 'an essential factor in the protection of human rights'[12] and as part of the economic development agenda, where, for example, the World Bank has considered that the practical application of the rule of law means 'the extent to which agents have confidence in and abide by the rules of society, and in particular the quality of contract enforcement, the police, and the courts, as well as the likelihood of crime and violence'.[13] Many United Nations (UN) peacekeeping operations have included the restoration or establishment of the rule of law as part of their aims, in the context of the overall purpose of enhancing peace and security.[14] The (then) UN Secretary-General, Kofi Annan stated that:

[The rule of law is] a concept at the very heart of the [UN] Organization's mission. It refers to the principle of governance to which all persons, institutions and entities, public and private, including the State itself, are accountable to laws that are publicly promulgated, equally enforced and independently adjudicated, and which are consistent with

---

[11] See B Tamanaha, *On the Rule of Law* (2004), p 37. Note that Bingham argues that 'the rule of law does depend on an unspoken but fundamental bargain between the individual and the state, the governed and the governor, by which both sacrifice a measure of freedom and power which they would otherwise enjoy', op. cit., n 1, p 84.

[12] See, e.g., the Vienna Declaration and Programme of Action on Human Rights 1993, UN Doc A/Conf 157/24, para 69, and various General Assembly resolutions, such as Resolutions 55/99 (2000) and 57/221 (2002).

[13] World Bank, *A Decade of Measuring the Quality of Governance* (2006), p 3.

[14] See, e.g., Security Council resolution 152 (2004) (concerning Haiti) and Security Council resolution 1756 (2007) (concerning the Democratic Republic of Congo).

international human rights norms and standards. It requires, as well, measures to ensure adherence to the principles of supremacy of law, equality before the law, accountability to the law, fairness in the application of the law, separation of powers, participation in decision-making, legal certainty, avoidance of arbitrariness, and procedural and legal transparency.[15]

What is seen in these statements and documents is an idea of the rule of law in the international community that largely mirrors that of Bingham's national rule of law principles. The main elements are (following the pattern of the Bingham principles):

(1) the law must be publicly promulgated and legally certain;
(2) all decisions are subject to the law;
(3) all persons and institutions, including the state, are equally accountable to the law;
(4) the law must be consistent with international human rights law;
(5) the law must be equally enforced;
(6) there is accountability to the law;
(7) laws must be independently adjudicated, with avoidance of arbitrariness and with transparency; and
(8) states should comply with their international legal obligations (whilst this is not stated above it is constantly and consistently reiterated within the UN system and in customary international law)[16].

What can be seen from this position is that there is a general acceptance in the international community, through their ratification of treaties and adherence to international statements and resolutions, of the importance of the rule of law.

The Rule of Law in the International Legal System

While it can be seen that the Bingham principles of the rule of law for the national legal system can be applied internationally, it does not necessarily mean that these principles are applied, or are able to be applied, in the international legal system. It still needs to be shown that it is possible to apply the rule of law to the states (and other participants) in the international legal system, as against applying it to all states within their national legal systems.

Most studies have tended to indicate that the rule of law cannot be applied to the international legal system, as that system has not yet developed sufficiently to have the necessary frameworks and institutions to allow the rule of law to

---

[15] Report of the Secretary-General on the Rule of Law and Transitional Justice in Conflict and Post-Conflict Societies, UN Doc S/2004/616 (2004), para 6.
[16] See, e.g., the Vienna Convention on the Law of Treaties 1969.

operate in any meaningful way.[17] Indeed, there is a question as to what such an 'international rule of law' means, as it could mean an international legal system that deals directly with individuals without national legal system mediation, or it could mean the primacy of international law over national law. However, it is most often understood as 'the application of the rule of law principles to relations between States and other subjects of international law'.[18]

The following is a (necessarily brief) attempt to apply the international Bingham rule of law principles to the participants in the international legal system:

(1) The law must be publicly promulgated and legally certain.

With the increasing use of treaties as the means to create and develop international law, and the use of Security Council and General Assembly resolutions, especially post-Cold War, international law is now generally publicly promulgated and accessible to states and others. This is in contrast to the development of international law through customary means, which was not as open or accessible for many states.[19] There remain questions about the clarity of the law, especially where, in order to reach agreement, many terms in an international document may be deliberately opaque. This issue does apply equally at national levels.

(2) All decisions are subject to the law.

The proliferation of international courts, tribunals, and other judicial and arbitral bodies in the past few decades has been extraordinary. These now enable the possibility of resolution of a wide-range of disputes, from financial to criminal, and between states and non-state actors, through international legal recourse. Some international law disputes are also resolved through national legal processes. However, all of this is still piecemeal, with many areas of international law, such as international environmental law, having no or few means to have decisions subjected to law. Indeed, in the international system, this principle is difficult to apply directly. There are an array of decisions that seem to be beyond the law, especially within the UN system where the Permanent Members of the Security Council can appear to be executive, legislator, and judiciary.[20] Yet there remains the possibility of review of decisions by the Security Council, as has been stated by members of the International Court of Justice:

---

[17] See, e.g., Austrian Government, *The UN Security Council and the Rule of Law*, (New York University School of Law, available at <http://www.bmeia.gv.at/newyorkov>, last checked 13 July 2008) and R Higgins, 'The Rule of Law: Some Sceptical Thoughts' Grotius Lecture, BIICL, 2007 (copy with the author).

[18] S Chesterman, 'An International Rule of Law?', 56 *American Journal of Comparative Law* (2008).

[19] See A Angie, *Imperialism, Sovereignty and the Making of International Law* (2005).

[20] See M Koskenniemi, 'The Police in the Temple: Order, Justice and the United Nations', 6 *European Journal of International Law* (1995) 325.

This is not to say that the Security Council can act free of all legal controls but only that the Court's power of judicial review is limited. That the Court has some power of this kind can hardly be doubted... But the Court, as the principal judicial organ of the United Nations, is entitled, indeed bound, to ensure the rule of law within the United Nations system and, in cases properly brought before it, to insist on adherence by all United Nations organs to the rules governing their operation.[21]

This issue is also found in national legal systems, where national courts may be reluctant to review decisions of the executive. In fact, decisions of some international bodies are subject to review, such as decisions within the European Union system. The major difficulty is the lack of a coherent and effective international system to ensure effective compliance with international law.

(3) All persons and institutions, including the state, are equally accountable to the law.

The UN Charter claims that it is based on 'the principle of the sovereign equality of all its Members'.[22] Yet the Charter itself sets up an unequal power relationship between the five Permanent Members of the Security Council and all other states, which means, in effect, that international law (insofar as it can be made by the Security Council) can be applied differently to different states, especially when dealing with matters of international peace and security. As clarified by Bingham, the issue is the extent to which that inequality is based on objective differences. It is hard to justify these differences—which are essentially based on economic, military, or historical power—as being objective. However, in most national legal systems there has been unequal applications of the law during times of threats to national security (as Bingham himself notes)[23], so perhaps this principle is always at some risk in those situations. It is also the case that generally non-state actors have international law applied to them differently from states, even in international criminal law areas, though sometimes economically powerful corporations can ensure that international law is applied to states.[24]

(4) The law must be consistent with international human rights law.

International human rights law applies to all states. All states are parties to at least one major global human rights treaty and so accept that there are legal obligations that arise from human rights. Indeed, all states accept that 'human rights are a legitimate concern of the international community,'[25] and so how they treat anyone within their jurisdiction is not solely a matter for

---

[21] *Genocide Convention Case (Bosnia and Herzegovina v Yugoslavia (Serbia and Montenegro))* ICJ Rep 1993, Lauterpacht (Separate Opinion), para 99.
[22] UN Charter, Art 2.1.
[23] Op. cit., n 1, p 74–75.
[24] E.g., the application of the World Trade Organization rules.
[25] Op. cit., n 12, para 4.

them. Whilst the reality is that states continue to violate human rights, their actions are violations of international law and not outside the law. Whilst there is now a considerable body of international human rights supervisory mechanisms, these are often weak in terms of ensuring compliance by states with their obligations. In addition, non-state actors are largely not subject to international human rights law and so their responsibility is dependent on the application of the rule of law within national legal systems.

(5) The law must be equally enforced.

This principle is more frequently found in the international legal system than is often expected. A number of areas of international law, from airline journeys to postal systems, operate effectively on all states, and economic and other pressures usually ensure this. Other areas operate unequally between states and non-state actors, and between states, mainly due to the current approach to the structure of the international legal system[26] and the lack of a fully effective dispute settlement system. As noted above, this unequal enforcement between states is often when there is a crisis or threat to international peace and security, even though all legal systems have problems at these times.[27] Yet even the economically and militarily powerful states can be pushed towards compliance with international law, as is slowly happening with the United States in relation to their actions in Guantanamo Bay.[28]

(6) There is accountability to the law.

There are international legal limits placed on the actions of states, for which there is some accountability in the international legal system. An example of this is in the rules concerning states' international legal responsibilities, as shown in the International Law Commission's Articles on State Responsibility.[29] While these rules on state responsibility are rightly criticized as being a law developed by states in which states determine their own obligations for certain public acts in relation to other states,[30] nevertheless, they do limit the ability of a state to act without any accountability. Even if there is no appropriate or available dispute settlement mechanism, states and non-state actors (such as in international criminal law) are still accountable in international law. Pressure on states to act responsibly and with accountability is

---

[26] For a critique of the current international legal system see R McCorquodale, 'An Inclusive International Legal System', 17 *Leiden Journal of International Law* (2004) 477.

[27] See H Charlesworth, 'International Law: A Discipline of Crisis' 65 *Modern Law Review* (2002) 377.

[28] See, generally, M Byers and G Nolte, *United States Hegemony and the Foundations of International Law* (2003).

[29] International Law Commission, Articles on Responsibility of States for Internationally Wrongful Acts, Report of the International Law Commission Report, 53rd session, A/56/10, August 2001.

[30] See the strong critique by P Allott, 'State Responsibility and the Unmaking of International Law' (1988) 29 *Harvard International Law Journal* 1.

growing, especially in relation to international financial institutions focus in good governance as a key principle for providing funding to states.

(7) Laws must be independently adjudicated, with avoidance of arbitrariness and with transparency.

While it is generally the position that international judicial and arbitral procedures are reasonably fair (though many UN and other international organization's administrative procedures are not),[31] it is not always the case that the members of these bodies are chosen through fair means or free from bias, so as to give an assurance of independence. Transparency is improving, especially in relation to international arbitration decisions but many non-state actors would consider that their access to international dispute procedures is very limited.

(8) Compliance by the state with its international law obligations.

Article 2.2 of the UN Charter provides that: '[a]ll Members, in order to ensure to all of them the rights and benefits resulting from membership, shall fulfil in good faith the obligations assumed by them in accordance with the present Charter.' As noted above, this principle is constantly and consistently reiterated within the UN system and in customary international law.

This brief summary of the application of the Bingham rule of law principles into the international legal system has shown that it is possible to apply them but that there are also many areas where the international legal system falls short. Yet, national legal systems also often fall short of these requirements. Indeed, Bingham uses an example from the United Kingdom in 1956 (when the United Kingdom government decided to make an armed intervention in Egypt in order to control the Suez Canal) to show how limited law can be in some circumstances. He demonstrates how the Prime Minister refused to ask for full legal advice as it was 'a political affair' and that the Attorney-General, Sir Reginald Manningham-Buller (who became an early supporter of BIICL), said that 'I support and have supported the Government's actions though I cannot do so on legal grounds'.[32]

It is the fact that national legal systems fall short of the rule of law, despite its clear importance, that has led to the determination by the UN to apply the rule of law internationally. It is also one reason why it will remain difficult to apply the rule of law to the international legal system.

Conclusions

The rule of law remains an important aspect of all national legal systems and would enable a better international legal system. The interaction between the two

---

[31] E.g., the Counter-Terrorism Committee established by the UN Security Council under resolution 1373 (2001).

[32] Op. cit., n 1, p 83–84.

systems and between national legal systems enables the rule of law to be applied more effectively. Indeed, the rule of law is vital for many reasons, including: for the creation and good functioning of international and national institutions, including those that administer the law; for effective cooperation in trade, investment, and financial activities (where supremacy of law, fairness in the application of the law, and accountability to the law are essential); for the establishment and protection of civil society, good governance, and human rights; for ensuring respected guidelines for societies in conflict and post-conflict; for supporting capacity-building (especially of institutions, the judiciary, law reform, and infrastructure); and for the assurance of a just order determined and enforced by law rather than by other means, which distinguishes it from rule by law and rule by power. Above all, it is clear that the rule of law is a key requirement to enable peace and justice for all people, organizations, and governments within international and national societies. All of these reasons also justify the need for institutions such as BIICL, which seek to apply an effective and informed international and comparative approach to the rule of law.

The Institute is therefore a natural place for Bingham to lead, as he brings to bear his own strong vision of the rule of law and his interest in engaging with other legal systems. Through his role in the British Institute of International and Comparative Law, Tom Bingham encourages and strengthens its role in the promotion of the rule of law in international affairs. For the rule of law requires many to support it, not just senior judges, who are 'not, as we are sometimes seen, mere custodians of a body of arid prescriptive rules but are, with others, the guardians of an all but sacred flame which animates and enlightens the society in which we live'.[33]

---

[33] Op. cit., n 1, p 85.

11

The United Kingdom Constitution in Transition: from where to where?

Dawn Oliver

Introduction

In this paper I shall discuss four constitutional transitions that have been taking place in the UK. They are transitions from a political towards a principled constitution, from government to governance, from quasi-subjecthood to quasi-citizenship, and from unionism to separatism. I shall try to make sense of them. I do not propose to discuss all the transitions that are taking place at present. I shall not, for instance, say much about the government's *Governance of Britain* Green Paper (July 2007) and the *Constitutional Renewal* White Paper and draft Constitutional Renewal Bill that were published after Easter 2008,[1] or about our relationship with Europe. I am trying to focus on the UK, and given the UK, on broad themes.

Transition 1—Towards a Principled Constitution

A starting point here is Griffith's seminal lecture on 'The Political Constitution' which was published in the Modern Law Review in 1979.[2] That year was, it so happens, a turning point for many aspects of the UK's constitution. With the election of a Conservative government after the Winter of Discontent of 1978–79 the post-war consensus about the role of the state came to an end,[3] the corporate bias[4] that had typified politics for some decades was dismantled. Nationalized industries were privatized,[5] public administration was influenced by public

---

[1] Cm 7342—I and II.
[2] 42 MLR 1–21.
[3] See S Beer, *Britain Against Itself,* 1982; R Rose *The Problem of Party Government,* 1976.
[4] See K Middlemas, *Politics in Industrial Society,* 1979.
[5] See C Veljanowski, *Selling the State,* 1987.

choice theory,[6] new public management, governance, and other new trends.[7] The centralized nature of politics stimulated growth in pressure for devolution in Scotland and Wales.

To return to 1979, Griffith considered that it was appropriate that our system should be run by politicians and not by judges. In particular, the rights to which individuals were entitled should be determined by Parliament and not, under a Bill of Rights, by the courts. Ultimately the British constitution was the outcome of political conflicts. Our system was not, therefore, based on stable principles. It was not appropriate for judges to determine the outcomes of political conflicts, because they are not politically accountable. The constitution was 'what happens'. If nothing happened, then that too was constitutional.

Whether Griffith's denial of a normative content to the constitution was accurate at the time I doubt. I believe there was quite a lot of political morality—and immorality—about, and that when politically immoral things happened everyone thought they were wrong: but the responses would have been purely political—or at least not judicial. Be that as it may, over the last nearly 30 years our constitutional actors—even politicians—have become much more concerned about 'what ought to happen' than they were when Griffith delivered his lecture. (I refer here to the development of principles to do with the operation of the system rather than substantive principles—save in relation to human rights, which span both system and substance.)[8] There remain, of course, many areas in which politics dominates.

This new principled content can be found both in hard law, and in much soft law. Taking the hard law first, the Human Rights Act 1998 is an obvious example of the introduction of principles into our constitutional arrangements. Griffith would have disapproved—his lecture was largely targeted at the campaign for a bill of rights that was being conducted at the time by Lord Hailsham, Lord Chancellor in waiting, in particular in his Dimbleby lecture *Elective Dictatorship* of 1976,[9] and by others. But under the Human Rights Act the courts are not entitled to disapply an Act of Parliament for incompatibility with Convention rights. All they can do is make a declaration of incompatibility under section 4. Thus parliamentary supremacy is maintained. Griffith must be relieved. We shall return to this issue of parliamentary supremacy shortly.

Other recent legislation introduces further principles into our constitution. The Freedom of Information Act (FOI), requiring access to a lot of information, binds ministers, and local authorities and a very large number of other

[6] J P W B McAuslan, 'Public law and public choice' 51 *Modern Law Review* 681 (1988).

[7] See R A W Rhodes, *Understanding Governance: Policy Networks, Governance, Reflexivity and Accountability*, 1997.

[8] The development of substantive common law constitutional principles has been very significant, and Lord Bingham has contributed enormously to it. This is, however, beyond the scope of this paper.

[9] See also Hailsham, *The Dilemma of Democracy*, 1978; Sir Leslie Scarman, *English Law. The New Dimension*, 1974.

'public' authorities. Griffith was greatly in favour of openness. He was just against judges—and judges do not have much of a role under the FOI regime. The Act takes the place of the earlier ministerial monopoly over the provision of access to most official information.

Next, the Constitutional Reform Act 2005: it establishes a separation of powers between the judiciary and the other branches of government, it formalizes judicial appointments, and it seeks to protect the rule of law[10] and judicial independence as constitutional principles.[11] Thus a lot more of our constitution is principle-based, and law-based, than it was when Griffith wrote about 'The political constitution'. But not all of the principled legal basis gives rise to increases in judicial power. In fact many of these provisions emphasize the participation of bodies other than judges in giving effect to constitutional principles. For instance, the statement of compatibility provision in the Human Rights Act, section 19 places responsibility for the human rights compliance of bills on ministers and the Cabinet itself; the Information Commissioner's and Information Tribunal's roles in relation to Freedom of Information keep most issues out of the courts; and the Constitutional Reform Act itself does not depend upon judicial review for its effectiveness. Griffith would, presumably, approve of this approach.

The principles of judicial review are another large source of hard law, which elaborates principles of a constitutional kind. Even when Griffith delivered his lecture these principles were quite developed, and bound ministers and local authorities. I doubt if Griffith would have wanted to abolish those principles— who would abolish principles of natural justice and legality, for instance? His point might have been that the principles should be laid down in statute, not developed in the incremental way of the common law. Be that as it may, it is clear that judicial review principles and their reach have developed enormously even since 1979. This is not the place to list or analyze the changes, but a few examples will illustrate the fact of extensive development.

- Ministers may be subject to interim injunctions.[12]

- Royal prerogative powers will be judicially reviewable unless they are not justiciable.[13]

- Legitimate expectations of a procedural or substantive kind may be protected by the courts, thus requiring decision makers to be reliable, trustworthy, and honest.[14]

---

[10] On the meaning of 'the rule of law' see Lord Bingham's seminal lecture 'The rule of law' 66 *Cambridge Law Journal* 67–85 (2007).

[11] The White Paper Cm 7342 proposes to remove the participation of the Lord Chancellor in appointments below the High Court, and to end the Prime Minister's participation in all appointments: paras 114–115.

[12] *M v Home Office* [1994] 1 AC 377.

[13] *Council for Civil Service Unions v Minister for the Civil Service* [1985] AC 374.

[14] *R v North and East Devon Health Authority, ex p Coughlan* [2000] 2 WLR 622.

- Reasons should normally be given for decisions, or if not, then the gist of a decision-maker's concerns should be communicated to the object of the decision in advance so that he may respond.[15]
- There are fundamental common law constitutional principles such as rights of access to justice,[16] a rule against retroactive adverse decision-making,[17] no change of a person's legal entitlements without notification,[18] which can only be displaced by very clear words in a statute.
- Constitutional statutes can only be amended by express or very clear words.[19]

All of these are instances of the elaboration of principles of a pretty deep constitutional kind: they represent acceptance first, of the need for legal protection of the dignity and autonomy of individuals, and secondly of duties on the part of public bodies to be reliable, altruistic, and trustworthy, and to cooperate with the courts.

The replacement of unregulated—whether formally or informally—freedom of political decision-making with principles that govern decision-making by politicians extends significantly into the soft law areas of the constitution too. Obiter dicta presumably count as soft law: there are hints in some judicial observations that we are in a process of transition from parliamentary sovereignty to constitutional supremacy, and that the rule of law rather than parliamentary sovereignty may emerge as the controlling constitutional principle[20] in the UK.

Here we should pause to consider the implications of the drift away from acceptance of parliamentary supremacy which these dicta and observations appear to signify. In my view parliamentary supremacy never was a principled principle—or if it once was it no longer is. It is certainly not a democratic principle. It is an example of the continued importance of the political constitution. We have all, I think, moved away from the view that a majority can claim to be acting in a principled way when it enacts laws that discriminate against a majority (e.g., women) or a minority (e.g., Catholics). Northern Ireland taught us a lesson there. It is hard to see how a doctrine can be regarded as a 'principle' if it permits and legitimates unprincipled activity. And anyway, given that a parliamentary majority does not nowadays represent anything like a majority of the population, its claim to authority cannot rest on the assumption that it gives effect to the public will. So the doctrine of parliamentary supremacy rests not on a (democratic) principle, but on a number of pragmatic claims. First, that the country needs to have arrangements in place that enable government to be carried on with a degree of consent

---

[15] *R v Civil Service Appeal Board, ex p Cunningham* [1992] ICR 816; *R v Ministry of Defence, ex p Murray* [1998] COD 134; *R v Secretary of State for the Home Department, ex p Fayed* [1996] Imm AR.

[16] *R v Lord Chancellor, ex p Witham* [1998] QB 575.

[17] *R v Home Secretary, ex p Pierson* [1998] AC 539.

[18] *R v Anufrieva v Southwark Borough Council* [2004] 2 QB 1124.

[19] *Thoburn v Sunderland City Council* [2002] 3 WLR 247.

[20] See per Lord Hope in *Jackson and others v Her Majesty's Attorney General* [2005] UKHL 56.

or acquiescence on the part of the population. The role of Parliament is to hold government to account for, and sometimes to veto, its decisions and legislative proposals. Secondly, that the electorate should have the opportunity to remove a government. And thirdly, that if the judges were to set aside a provision in an Act on the ground that it was undemocratic or contrary to the rule of law, the resulting conflict with the executive might be one that the judges could not win.

Let us imagine the following. Parliament has recently passed an Act authorizing the indefinite detention without trial of suspected foreign terrorists. A minister has ordered detention under this provision. The court finds this to be contrary to fundamental common law principles and orders the release of the suspect. The minister refuses, his point being that the judges have created a new common law rule which, he would say, is undemocratic etc. He orders the prison governor to refuse to release the suspect. The court declares the minister and the prison governor to be in contempt, and the minister ignores the declaration for the reasons above. Or the court orders the committal of the minister to prison for contempt of court in refusing to obey the court order. Such a confrontation would generate such turmoil, not only among politicians but also among the public, the press and so on, that the courts would doubtless emerge having lost authority. And that would be bad for the rule of law itself. In such a scenario the press and the public would not be on the side of the suspected terrorist; it would be against the judges and in favour of the government.

Lord Bingham and his fellows were faced with an assertion that it would be legitimate for the courts to refuse to give effect to a statutory provision in the *Jackson* case.[21] The substance of the case, the outlawing of hunting with dogs, was not itself of constitutional importance. But the fact that the Act had been passed under the Parliament Acts clearly was constitutionally significant. In the Court of Appeal some judges had indicated that there might be situations in which it would be legitimate for a court to disapply a statutory provision on constitutional grounds. In the House of Lords it was not necessary to resolve this issue. However, a number of the Law Lords indicated that the court might reconsider the position that the courts will not disapply a statutory provision. Lord Steyn indicated that 'The supremacy of Parliament is a construct of the common law and it is not unthinkable that the courts may qualify the principle on the basis that there are constitutional fundamentals which even a sovereign Parliament cannot abolish'. Lord Hope and Lord Carswell both noted that the courts and Parliament take care to avoid conflict. Lord Bingham, very wisely in my view, avoided commenting on whether the courts would ever feel justified in disapplying a provision. (European law is exceptional here.)

The doctrine of the legislative supremacy of Parliament is in effect a pragmatic solution to the problem of what might without it be possibly unresolvable, non-negotiable conflicts not only between the executive and Parliament, but also

---

[21] *Jackson and others v Her Majesty's Attorney General* [2005] UKHL 56.

between the executive, Parliament, and the courts. It takes Griffith's insight that much of our constitution is the outcome of conflicts between the courts and the executive further: this particular tenet is prophylactic, being about ways of avoiding conflicts and their possible negative outcomes for the authority of the courts and the rule of law.

The relationship between the executive and the courts in the UK, lacking as it does a written constitution, depends upon reciprocity, trust, cooperation. This is part of our culture. If those collapse then the very constitutional system itself might collapse into conflict, self-advancing competition, ostracism of the courts by ministers, and mistrust. These would not just affect relations between the executive and the courts, but also relations between parties, and between the two Houses of Parliament and other institutions. In my view, therefore, it could well be wrong for the courts to disapply an Act, however much it is contrary to some of the sub-principles of the rule of law and other constitutional principles. The duties of judges are not limited to upholding individuals' rights. They include ensuring the practical working of constitutional arrangements, which in turn facilitate the rule of law. The courts could develop other ways than disapplication of a statutory provision to signal their concerns about the implications of such Acts, for instance by common law 'advisory declarations' of incompatibility with constitutional principles. There are in other words respectable consequentialist reasons for judges to hold back from creating new common law principles enabling them to give judgments against the executive in a nuclear option situation. So in my view a 'principle' that the rule of law is *the* controlling principle[22] (my italics) and entitles courts to disapply statutory provisions would come up against the typical, pragmatic, and wise English response: that is all very well in principle, but what about the practice? The practice of judicial disapplication of statutory provisions in our unwritten constitution and constitutional culture would not work.[23]

To return to the transition from politics towards principle, there has been a proliferation of soft law sources for principles in the last decade and more. They include the—in my view very significant—Seven Principles of Public Life that were elaborated by the Committee on Standards in Public Life in its First Report in 1995.[24] These set out some of the most fundamental principles of the constitution, without observance of which democracy, the rule of law, and rights protection could not operate effectively. They can only operate in an uncorrupt system. These requirements of selflessness, leadership, integrity, openness, objectivity, accountability, and honesty have been adopted as principles in the *Ministerial Code*,[25] and by the two Houses of Parliament and in local authority standing

[22] Pace Lord Hope in *Jackson*.
[23] The primacy of European is a different matter because of the external pressures on government and parliament to respect European law.
[24] Cm 2850.
[25] Cabinet Office, July 2007.

orders. They are reflected in some judicial review principles;[26] but the important point about them is that they are supposed to be internalized by those in public life and to become part of the culture. Non-legal methods can be just as effective as, or more so than, legal methods for upholding principles. Politicians and others found to be in breach of the Seven Principles are likely to find themselves ostracized by those they are in contact with, to find that others will not cooperate with them, that they are mistrusted, that colleagues will not negotiate with them. They lose authority and credibility.

The proliferation of principle in soft law is further illustrated by the growth in importance of principle-based scrutiny of legislation in both Houses, through the Joint Committee on Human Rights, the Constitution Committee, and the Delegated Powers and Regulatory Reform Committee of the House of Lords, and the Justice (formerly Constitutional Affairs) and Public Administration Select Committees of the House of Commons. Their reports articulate standards of a constitutional kind, and the Committees advise Parliament as to whether bills and draft bills comply with these standards. But they are very soft—these committees do not seek to prevent Parliament passing measures that breach these principles. Their activities mean only that this is not likely to be done inadvertently.[27]

In sum, there has been a transition from a largely political towards a largely principled constitution in the last 30 years. Generally this has been very positive. However, there are aspects of the system where the interests of politicians prevail excessively over those of individuals and of the general population. While we have far more articulated 'constitutional' principles than existed when Griffith wrote 'The political constitution', we also have, increasingly, two divergent cultures: the principled culture and the political one—the latter worryingly ignorant of the importance of the principled constitution. This can be seen in instances where ministers and MPs have departed from the precepts and principles of the principled constitution, for instance criticizing judges, misrepresenting and objecting to disclosure of their own claims for reimbursement of expenses and so on.

Transition 2—From Government to Governance

'Governance' is currently a fashionable buzz word.[28] The sense in which I use the term here is as a process by which policies are delivered through networks of relationships between public bodies, and between public and private bodies. These involve cooperation and reciprocity between the partners, and mutual trust. This

---

[26] E.g., *Porter v Magill* [2001] UKHL 67 (selflessness, integrity); *Derbyshire County Council v Times Newspapers* [1993] AC 534 (selflessness).

[27] On the desirability of developing checklists and standards see D Oliver, 'Improving the scrutiny of bills: The case for standards and checklists' [2006] *Public Law* 219.

[28] See J Newman, *Modernising Governance. New Labour, Policy and Society*, 2001; R A W Rhodes, above.

is a departure from the pre-1980s model which involved direct top-down delivery of policies, including services, by central and local government employing public employees.

The transition to governance has taken a number of forms. In the 1980s and into the 1990s many formerly publicly owned industries, including public service ones such as the utilities, were privatized.[29] The continuing public service obligations formed part of, in effect, a contract between government and the now privately owned utility, and were subject to regulation by statutory regulators rather than, as hitherto, by ministers. Privatizations constitute, then, transitions from political ownership and control of industry to private ownership controlled by professional regulators: a reduction in the scope of the political constitution.[30] Some elements of the public service ethos that ministers were supposed to display in their control of state industries have been transferred to the privatized bodies. This is an interesting trend. It does not necessarily imply that privatized bodies are exercising public functions. Rather it shows an extension of civic responsibility and duties of public service into the private sector.

Next in time, in the mid-1980s a process of agencification of public services remaining under government ownership and control took place:[31] the Next Steps programme. Function-based chunks of government departments, though remaining within the civil service and the department, were 'hived off' into agencies headed by Chief Executives. They are governed by a framework document that is negotiated between the Chief Executive and the department. The Chief Executives are normally the Accounting Officers for their agencies. The Chief Executive is responsible to the minister and to auditing bodies, and to some extent to Parliament, for the operation of the agency. This has proved a very durable change, and one which is being emulated in many other countries.

More recently a process of 'networking' has been taking place, consisting of partnerships between public bodies and private companies and other organizations, many of them working in the charitable or voluntary sector.[32]

These processes of transition have, again, important constitutional implications. They involve the depoliticization of activities in various ways—shifts from political to professional decision-making and from ministerial responsibility to Parliament to agency accountability to a whole range of 'accountees'—auditors, regulators, courts in judicial review cases, tribunals, ombudsmen, and so on. They blur the public–private divide and require new bases for the imposition of public service and human rights obligations on private network partners. They create anomalies between those dealing directly with public bodies and those receiving services from private 'agents' of the state.

---

[29] See C Veljanowski, above.

[30] See T Prosser in Jowell and Oliver, eds, *The Changing Constitution*, 6th edn, 2007.

[31] See D Oliver and G Drewry, *Public Service Reforms. Issues of Accountability and Public Law*, 1996.

[32] Newman, above; and see I Harden, *The Contracting State*, 1992.

Transition 3—From Quasi-Subject to Quasi-Citizen

Our third transition takes us back to the political constitution, particularly in the relationships of the state to individuals and society generally. It has been a commonplace to claim that in Britain individuals are 'subjects'[33] rather than citizens.[34] The implication of subjecthood is that individuals are in a compact with government in which we owe the government allegiance—loyalty—in exchange for which we get protection. This is a form of social contract, though a pretty minimalist one. Interestingly it mirrors outdated conceptions of the relationships between wives and their husbands, and between children and their parents. These attitudes reflected Hobbesian fears of social collapse if people were not subject to authority and control. Those familial relationships are now largely emancipated. Husbands and wives are equal partners, expected to make cooperative joint decisions and to negotiate their ways out of disagreements; and where parental authority survives, over immature children, it must be exercised for the benefit of children and not of the parents.

But what of the relationship between the individual and the state? Is that also emancipated? Are we subject to extensive unilateral authority exercised by the state? Is state authority exercisable and exercised for the benefit of the individuals who are subject to it, or for the benefit of powerful sections within society—for instance the parties, or government, businesses, or trade unions and their members? Are we citizens now, or still subjects?

For over a century it has actually been something of a simplification or caricature of the position of individuals in Britain to regard us as subjects.[35] Individuals have enjoyed considerable freedom of speech and association under the common law—freedoms without which individuals cannot have influence in political decision-making. A system of social and economic rights has been in place since the end of the Second World War. Universal suffrage has long been in place. Elections have been fairly conducted and the ballot has—until recently—been secret. Election results have—again until recently—accurately recorded the numbers of votes honestly cast for each candidate. I shall say no more here about what to me is the deeply worrying corruption of our electoral arrangements that has begun to take place.

But civil and political rights are not all that citizenship is about. Citizenship is a very slippery concept, but I suggest that one of its elements is equal membership of a cohesive population that is served altruistically, selflessly, by its governmental institutions. Does this exist in the UK? Do we feel that we are one people and that we are all served by our politicians?

---

[33] See A Dummett and A Nicol, *Subjects, Citizens, Aliens and Others*, 1990.
[34] See D Heater, *Citizenship: The Civic Idea in World History, Politics and Education*, 1990.
[35] See the still seminal work TH Marshall, *Citizenship and Social Class*, 1950.

We expect politicians to act altruistically and in the public's interests—not in the interests of their families or themselves, their party or supporters; but the papers repeatedly report that they do not do so; and the opposition parties are constantly telling us that ministers are untrustworthy. We expect politicians to be responsive to us; but commonly they are responsive only to some of us, notably the supporters of their party and others who might be persuaded to vote for them next time. The prime minister exercises the right to decide on an election date in the interests of his government and party, not in the interests of the public. This is not an altruistic, selfless decision. If the right to determine the election date is transferred to Parliament as the *Governance* Green Paper of July 2007 contemplates, the same will be true: the Prime Minister will mobilize his front and back benchers to approve of his decision to call an election. The only way to stop this particular bit of self-interested partisanship in government is to introduce fixed term Parliaments, so that the constitution is neutral between parties and interests in these matters. But that will not happen because governments are not interested in constitutional neutrality or, in cricketing terms, in level playing fields. Indeed it is striking that during the debates about whether there should be an election in the autumn of 2007, no-one accused the prime minister of unconstitutional partisanship. He was accused by the Conservatives of cowardice when he did not call an election. The Conservatives do not see the implications for the duties of altruism—selflessness—and constitutional neutrality either—because they look forward to enjoying this power too in due course.

Next is the question of the aspects of individuals' existence that are served by government. These have changed enormously over the last 30 years or more. In the post-Second World War period until the 1980s the Labour party was virtually owned by its affiliated trade unions. Business and middle class interests had great influence in the Conservative party, though it was not institutionalized in the ways it was in Labour. Governments in the 1960s and 1970s took to negotiating policy with trade unions and business. This process had serious implications for the relationships between individuals and the state and society. In 1979, a year of massive transitions, Middlemas produced his oeuvre *Politics in Industrial Society*, in which he focused on the *corporate bias* which the influence of powerful trade unions and business gave rise to in government.

The point about all this is that *producers*—both workers and owners of businesses—had the greatest influence in politics. Production and productivity were the aspects of individuals' existence that concerned politicians. This was reflected in the ways in which the party divides operated. And the many people who fitted into no productive category or who did not regard that aspect of their existence as the most significant, were left out in the cold—and literally so in the Winter of Discontent of 1978–79.

The Conservative government under Mrs Thatcher that was elected in 1979 put an end to that corporate bias. The trades unions were disempowered in various ways, including the growth in unemployment among those who would have joined them, and by privatization, legislation banning secondary picketing, requiring ballots before strikes and so on.

At the same time many individual working class people were empowered, notably through the right to buy granted to council tenants in the 1980s; and to some small extent through encouragement to purchase shares in the privatized industries. This changed their psychology and identity—they came to regard themselves as middle class rather than working class. This brought substantial electoral pay-offs for the Conservative party. The focus on the role and power of individuals in relation to the state shifted away from their productive to their property-owning lives, and the opportunities for self-determination that property brought to them. Of course, for the growing band of the unemployed who were neither producers nor property owners, that shift was unimportant.

In the early 1990s the *Citizen's Charter*[36] initiative was introduced, alongside the introduction of choice in public services, e.g., as to schools. This approach morphed into *Service First* in 1998. The provision of many services for which public bodies were responsible was contracted out under the competitive tendering regime—an aspect of the shift towards governance. And individual users of these services were given soft law rights to complain, to choose, and even to exit. Individuals, no longer so important to politicians in their roles as producers, could become instead property owners and consumers.

In the latter part of the 1990s further transitions affecting citizenship took place under New Labour, notably the explicit statutory protection of civil and political rights under the Human Rights Act 1998 and rights of access to information under the Freedom of Information Act. Under these Acts ordinary unorganized individuals have acquired additional layers in their identities, as rights-bearing individuals. Here the two transitions, towards a principled constitution and the development of the relationship between the individual and the state, converge for a while.

There are strong concessions to citizenship and against individualism in the Human Rights Act and the European Convention on Human Rights much of which it brings home. While the rights under this Act reinforce the opportunities of individuals to participate in the political process, via freedom of expression and association in particular, they explicitly recognize that it can be legitimate to restrict those rights in the public interest. This is part of what citizenship is about—recognition that we live in a society (which, recall, Mrs Thatcher denied) and there has to be give and take, reciprocity, both in consideration of other individuals and for the general or greater good.

This transition from quasi-subject-producer to quasi-citizen-consumer-and-rights-bearing individual with tinges of community obligation does not, however, add up to citizenship in any strong sense—especially in England. In England we are not equal members of the groups—the populations of England, and of the

---

[36] Cm 1599, 1991.

UK—which the government is supposed to serve. Our influence in the inputs into and outcome of elections is very limited. And it is clearly perceived by the electorate to be limited—what else can we deduce from falling electoral turn out?

The current position on citizenship in the UK is very asymmetrical. In the devolved areas of the UK, voters' influence on politics and politicians has been increased by proportional representation (PR) and by the very fact of devolution, which enables local needs to be met by local solutions, articulated by and with their citizens. These needs may embrace social and economic entitlements, access to culture, environmental protection, and so on. Politicians in those areas need to be in a more direct reciprocal relationship with their voters, less mediated by parties, than politicians in England; the parties therefore have to negotiate their ways out of disagreements. Politicians in the devolved areas are under greater pressure to act in the interests of the population and not in their own or those of their parties than politicians in England.

There is no PR or preferential voting—which I would prefer—in England (except for the Greater London Assembly). To give him due credit, Tony Blair operated an informal proportional system for appointments to the House of Lords. Consequently in that House minor parties have greater influence than in the House of Commons. And anyway mercifully party is less important in that House. The independent members are in a position to articulate the views and interests of, roughly, unorganized individuals—including women and minority ethnics, the disabled, and so on, rather well. And interests in culture, the environment, the economy, and so on are also given voices in that chamber. Not so in the House of Commons. There voters for small parties' candidates have disproportionately low chances that the candidates they vote for will achieve seats. The first past the post system means that only voters in marginal seats can, realistically, affect election results. This is incompatible with the notion of equal citizenship.

The *Governance* Green Paper promised review of the operation of voting systems. Actually it was a review of the evidence then available about voting systems, and it did not seek to review that evidence against any particular criteria, such as citizenship ones. It did not review the current operation of the first past the post system. Nor does it investigate current concerns about postal voting. But it states the government's firm belief that 'the current voting system for UK general elections works well, and…any future change would require the consent of the British people in a referendum'. Voting systems, it says 'must not become a focus of partisan action but need to endure for many years'. One cannot help wondering whether it is in order for a voting system to be retained for partisan reasons, such as its benefits to the two main parties.

There is no provision in our constitutional arrangements for the needs of the population of England to be reflected in policies for England. England and its citizens are neither seen nor heard to any effect in UK politics. If they do exist they have no voice or opportunities for their own and their country's interests to be promoted. Here they are at great disadvantage compared with their cousins in the other countries that make up the UK. The duty of the government of the UK is to look after the interests of the UK. If there is a conflict between the interests of England and of the UK, the government should, constitutionally, promote the interests of England only if they are also in the interests of the UK. By contrast it is entirely proper for the devolved bodies to seek to promote the interests of their own populations even to the detriment of the rest of the UK.

It is difficult to resist the conclusion that politicians in Whitehall and Westminster do not want to have to deal with real citizens, whether of England or of the UK. They might, of course, have valid non-partisan reasons for this, though I doubt it. And yet from time to time they use the language of citizenship. In reality they prefer obedient quasi-subjects, consumers who complain, or who will blame the market rather than politics when things go wrong for them. They prefer people preoccupied with their rights, who do not look beyond them to the bigger picture and politics. PR was granted to the devolved bodies as a way of inhibiting them from being too radical without taking the public with them. But politicians at Westminster do not want to operate within such limits themselves. What is left of the political constitution in England and Westminster is owned by elected politicians and parties, not by citizens. The parties and politicians would like to keep it that way.

Citizenship is not of course an all-or-nothing institution. It can be all or quite a lot. It should not be nothing or only a little bit. It is hypocritical of governments to claim to want to promote citizenship and turnout in elections and so on, and at the same time to refuse to open up the opportunities for voters to have a real influence over politics.

And yet it is beginning to dawn on some MPs that their own individual legitimacy is suffering partly because of the fact that few of them won their seats on 50 per cent plus one of the votes cast in their constituencies. So in March 2008 the possibility of a shift to the Alternative Vote for elections to the Commons began to be mooted. Voters would mark their first and second preferences on the ballot paper, and if their first choice did not achieve enough votes, it would be discarded and the second vote used instead. This system would ensure in most constituencies that each MP received 50 per cent plus one of the votes cast. It would thus enhance legitimacy. (It would not have much effect on the proportionality of the representation of parties, but the main object of an electoral system should be to be fair to the voters rather than to the parties.)

Last in this section of my presentation, let us look briefly at the question of shared national identity, often a sign of real citizenship in a country. This is about what goes on in people's heads—psychology. How we think about ourselves and about other people. The Government is right to be concerned about this: it is important for all members and sections of the population to feel that they and other members of society belong, and that they and others are served, altruistically and selflessly, by governmental bodies. Without this sense—which would form part of the psychology of individuals—conflicts will develop between groups and sections in society, important values such as trust, cooperation, and reciprocity will be undermined, and the legitimacy of the system will be called in question.

In a homogeneous society the existence of a shared sense of national identity can be taken for granted. But the population of the UK is not homogeneous. The heterogeneity of the population is enriching for our society, culture, and economy. But it does mean that care has to be taken to ensure that groups within society do not feel detached. There can of course be sub-groups within an overarching group. But if they are citizens they acknowledge that the interests of the wider or general population may trump those of other groups.

National identities do exist in Scotland and Wales, strengthened perhaps by a desire to differentiate themselves from the English. No one has yet been able to articulate a printable, accurate sense of English or British identity. In fact it would in my view be more productive to articulate aspirational identities—what about tolerant, civilized, and democratic?

Part of the problem is that the political process at Westminster makes it difficult for senses of British or English identity to develop. The political parties and their members, especially Labour and the Conservatives, are in fierce competition with one another within and outside Parliament. They are frequently playing tit for tat: if you accuse one of us of cheating on election expenditure or use of parliamentary allowances, we shall accuse one of you of doing so too. If you accuse us of neglecting the public interest, we shall do the same to you. I cannot help thinking that this behaviour discourages the growth of a sense of shared national identity or of belonging, among other things, to the national grouping. That is not easy when each political party constantly reminds us of the differences between them and their opponents, and attaches negative stereotypes to those differences, rather than focusing on what they, and we, all have in common. An electoral system that enabled coalitions and pacts to form—i.e., that produced wider, more representative groupings with which voters could identify, that encouraged consensus, cooperation between parties, reciprocity rather than competition and conflict—might encourage the growth of a sense of shared identity and thus a psychological sense of citizenship.

Transition 4—From Unionism to Separatism?

The fourth transition I want to discuss, briefly, is from unionism to separatism, both in the attitudes of parties and people, and in constitutional developments. The passage of the devolution legislation of 1998 was a milestone in this process, but its origins are much older. Nationalist parties are in government in Scotland and Wales, and British and Irish nationalists are sharing power in Northern Ireland. At present there is a spirit of cooperation and reciprocity between parties in the devolved bodies, and between the UK and the devolved bodies. Northern Ireland is free to leave the UK as and when its people wish to do so.

However, it is not inconceivable that this spirit of cooperation and reciprocity could come to an end with the election of sharply opposed parties to government in the UK and the devolved bodies. And that might stimulate pressure for independence from the UK in devolved areas—or (almost unthinkable) in England.

While before the UK joined the European Communities separation would have meant that Scotland and Wales would have been tiny, vulnerable countries surrounded by much larger ones, if they separated now they would be protected by their membership—assuming it existed—of the European Union. Separation is a less scary prospect than it used to be.

I foresee a growing wish in Scotland for independence. And a growth of support for union with Ireland in Northern Ireland. And I foresee such moves being welcomed in many quarters in England—for the simple reason that England would benefit from such changes. England is neglected in our current arrangements, and people will come to realize that. Without Scotland the interests of the UK generally would be closer to those of England. Independence for Wales is less likely, but if it came about I see no reason why England or the rest of the UK should object. Such changes would get rid of the West Lothian question, and the tensions that will be generated as and when different parties with opposing ideologies are in power at Westminster and in the devolved bodies.

My own sense is that if England, or England and Wales, were a separate country, then a sense of shared identity would flourish and regional initiatives could be taken to deal with regional problems to a greater degree than at present. And we could continue to be friends with our 'exes'.

Reflections

So where are we heading in our transitions?

We have moved pretty firmly away from a largely political constitution to one where principles are articulated and are supposed to govern much political activity. But we are nowhere near politicians being willing to give up the right to act in ways which are incompatible with constitutional principles if that is what they want to do. A two culture system is evolving.

The move to principle has depoliticized many functions previously performed by or under the control of politicians. And so has the shift from government to governance. Between them they have resulted in the professionalization of much of public administration and the development of regulation, networks, and webs of accountability. Some of this misfires from time to time, creating perverse incentives in the delivery of public services, and bureaucratization. Dealing with this will be an important project for any government.

We are moving away from quasi-subjecthood, through individualism—but barely towards even quasi-citizenship. We are not heading towards equal opportunities to influence politics or the emergence of a sense of common or shared British or English national identity.

Lastly, we are going to have to get used to the idea of separatism—the self-hiving off of Scotland and Northern Ireland and possibly Wales from the rest of the state currently called UK. That would resolve many problems of a constitutional kind for England and would help the development of English identity if, in a single nation country that would be England, the political parties were able to adopt less confrontational and more cooperative attitudes to one another. This is, however, unlikely to happen unless the electoral system is changed to increase the opportunities for voters to be represented by a person they have voted for.

Reciprocity, altruism, cooperation, and trust, qualities identified in evolutionary psychology and other sciences as innate aspects of human nature,[37] all affect the behaviour of our politicians, and our citizens. It should be obvious that democracy, human rights, and government by consent cannot survive without those qualities being strong and positive in our culture, and associated with the good of the population. In that sense they are foundational. My fear is that the importance of these qualities may not be sufficiently understood and appreciated by those with power to influence the operation of the constitution. If they are not valued we are in danger of their being replaced or infected with their opposites or negatives in UK politics—selfishness, lack of trust, untrustworthiness, non-negotiable conflict between groups and institutions, tit for tat, and defection. All of these would undermine our governmental arrangements and damage any development of the sense of being one people—on which also our democracy and sense of citizenship depend. Thus shifts away from political partisanship towards a principled approach to the political process, away from treating individuals as consumers and lobby fodder towards treating them—and developing them—as mature citizens and members of one people, would be the right outcomes of these transitions.

---

[37] See for instance M Ridley, *The Origins of Virtue*, 1996; L Workman and W Reader, *Evolutionary Psychology*, 2006; L Barrett, R Dunbar and J Lycett, *Human Evolutionary Psychology*, 2002; DM Buss, *Evolutionary Psychology. The New Science of the Mind*, 2008; DM Buss, ed, *The Handbook of Evolutionary Psychology*, 2005; J Cartwright, *Evolution and Human Behaviour. Darwinian Perspectives on Human Nature*, 2008.

12

The General and the Particular: Parliament and the Courts under the Scheme of the European Convention on Human Rights

*Philip Sales**

In his famous work, *An Introduction to the Study of the Law of the Constitution*, Dicey identified the two pillars of the English constitution as the sovereignty of Parliament and the rule of law. Lord Bingham has written a penetrating assessment of Dicey's analysis,[1] and has made his own important contributions both in his judicial[2] and extra-judicial writing.[3] The two pillars are aspects of a more general concern, that public power should be properly deployed.[4] In this essay I examine the relationship between these two pillars of the constitution through the prism of the law relating to the European Convention on Human Rights (ECHR).

The Statute of the Council of Europe, which preceded the ECHR, made reference in its preamble to 'individual freedom, political liberty and the rule of law, principles which form the basis of all genuine democracy' and by Article 3 required that member states should 'accept the principles of the rule of law and of the enjoyment by all persons within its jurisdiction of human rights and fundamental freedoms...'. The preamble to the ECHR identifies the twin pillars of the European public order which it establishes as 'an effective political democracy' and 'a common understanding and observance of...human rights', and makes reference to the 'common heritage of political traditions, ideals, freedom and the rule of law'. It thus appears to echo to some degree the conceptual structure which Dicey had set out in relation to England, albeit it generalizes from it and strengthens it by reference to positive human rights. This echo is probably

---

* The author is grateful for the legal reserach and analytical ideas suggested by M Laupa Crommeli.

[1] Lord Bingham, 'Dicey revisited' [2002] *Public Law* 39.

[2] E.g., his speeches in *Secretary of State for the Home Department v A* [2005] 2 AC 68 and *R (Jackson) v Attorney General* [2006] 1 AC 262.

[3] E.g., Lord Bingham, 'The Rule of Law' [2007] CLJ 67.

[4] A formulation which, of course, begs the important questions about who should have what power, and how it should be exercised.

not accidental, given the prominent role of British lawyers in the drafting of the Statute and the ECHR.[5]

Dicey resolved the potential tensions and conflicts between the sovereignty of Parliament and the concept of the rule of law by, in effect, suppressing any significant substantive (as opposed to formal) content for the rule of law in that regard.[6] In his scheme, Parliamentary sovereignty allows the legislature to override what might otherwise be the requirements of the rule of law. But the ECHR lays down positive rights for individuals which do limit what contracting states are able to do, including through legislative action. Articles 5 and 6 of the ECHR guarantee access in certain cases to the courts, and stringent requirements have been established by the European Court of Human Rights (ECtHR) regarding their constitution and the safeguards of their independence and impartiality. In addition, the ECtHR has developed through interpretation of the express terms of the ECHR what amounts to a substantive set of doctrines which may be grouped under the heading of 'the rule of law', and which operate as further implied constraints upon the legislatures and other authorities of contracting states. In light of the abuses which the ECHR was introduced to counter and its hybrid background of continental and common law legal systems,[7] it was inevitable that the ECtHR would engage with and constrain to some degree the freedom of the legislatures of the contracting states in making law, by imposing standards reflecting a more substantive conception of the rule of law. Further, the nature of the ECHR as an international treaty and of the ECtHR as an international court has allowed it to impose standards from a perspective outside, and not limited by, the domestic constitutional order of any contracting state.

It is obvious that, in adopting a more substantive concept of the rule of law, the ECtHR has had to operate in the context of a more acute tension between that concept and the idea of democracy, which Dicey had in large measure removed from his scheme. A substantive version of the rule of law and the techniques and doctrines developed by the ECtHR to accommodate this tension are now being reflected back into domestic law under the Human Rights Act 1998 (HRA). The domestic courts now have to confront this tension for themselves. This process may be seen as an example of the continuing interplay between domestic and European constitutional ideas traced by JWF Allison.[8]

The tension between ideas related to the rule of law and those related to democratic ways of ordering public decision-taking is not simple. It operates at different

---

[5] AWB Simpson, *Human Rights and the End of Empire: Britain and the Genesis of the European Convention* (2001), pp 33–41 and chs 12–14.

[6] JWF Allison, *The English Historical Constitution: Continuity, Change and European Effects* (2007), chs 7–8; PP Craig, 'Dicey: unitary self-correcting democracy and public law' (1990) 106 LQR 105; PP Craig, 'Formal and substantive conceptions of the rule of law: an analytical framework' [1997] *Public Law* 467.

[7] AWB Simpson, *Human Rights and the End of Empire*, pp 713–714.

[8] JWF Allison, *A Continental Distinction in the Common Law: A Historical and Comparative Perspective on English Public Law* (1996, rev pbk edn, 2000) and *The English Historical Constitution*.

levels, and also reflects ambiguities and tensions within each set of ideas itself. Since antiquity, one conception of the rule of law has been expressed by way of a contrast with the rule of men.[9] On this formulation, the idea is put in terms of a requirement for decisions on the basis of generally applicable, socially endorsed rules in particular cases, rather than leaving them to be determined by the potentially arbitrary or capricious decision of an individual applying their own idea of what should be done. This approach to the rule of law suggests an important role for the legislature, as a body well equipped to lay down general rules and capable of providing social endorsement through the legitimacy conferred by the democratic process. It also suggests that individual decision-makers deciding particular cases, be they judges or other state officials, should be constrained and limited in the discretion they may exercise in deciding how to determine the outcome of those cases. This is the impulse under which doctrines of equity came to be settled in the form of determinate rules over time, to preclude judgment according to the length of the Lord Chancellor's foot.[10]

A powerful substantive conception of the rule of law has been derived from the European idea of the *Rechtsstaat*. Under this conception, particularly associated by English jurists with the work of FA Hayek, 'government in all its actions is bound by rules fixed and announced beforehand—rules which make it possible to foresee with fair certainty how the authority will use its coercive powers in given circumstances, and to plan one's individual affairs on the basis of this knowledge'.[11] Under this formulation, again, there may be scope for an extensive role for the legislature in laying down general rules in advance, and for seeking to limit excessive discretion (and the unpredictability it brings with it) for judges and other state officials who decide particular cases.

At the same time, both these approaches suggest substantive constraints which ought to exist upon the legislature, precluding, for example, retrospective legislation or legislation which confers discretionary powers with insufficient safeguards

---

[9] For discussion of the approach of Plato and Aristotle, and the adaptation of their ideas in medieval and early modern English thinking about the law, see JGA Pocock, *The Machiavellian Moment: Florentine Political Thought and the Atlantic Republican Tradition* (2nd edn, 2003), pp 9–30; also Martin Loughlin, *Sword & Scales: An Examination of the Relationship Between Law & Politics* (2000), ch 5.

[10] cf Richard A Posner, *How Judges Think* (2008) pp 89, 355; also see the Foreword by Lord Bingham to Supperstone, Goudie and Walker, *Judicial Review* (3rd edn, 2005): 'It is, after all, important to remember, as Lord Hailsham of St Marylebone pointed out in his 1983 Hamlyn Lectures, that Thomas Fuller's great injunction—"Be you never so high, the law is above you"—applies to judges no less than ministers.'

[11] FA Hayek, *The Road to Serfdom* (1944), discussed in JWF Allison, *The English Historical Constitution*, pp 197–205. cf Lon Fuller, *The Morality of Law* (rev edn 1969). It has been observed that although the ideal of the *Rechtsstaat* promotes some of the interests favoured by liberals favouring a pluralistic society, it is also compatible with forms of politics which would not be compatible with liberalism; and that 'to attempt in a thoroughgoing and comprehensive way to oppose a discretionary power which is to some extent unpredictable is not a coherent project, because such discretionary power is of the essence of politics': Raymond Geuss, *History and Illusion in Politics* (2001), pp 106–108.

against their unpredictable or capricious exercise. Other approaches to the notion of the rule of law tend to emphasize more strongly a conflict between substantive value judgments arrived at through democratic decision-making procedures and those arrived at in the name of fundamental human or constitutional rights through judicial determination by judges immune from the democratic process (and immune from the tyranny of the majority which is associated with democracy), suggesting that judicial decisions should prevail in some cases over those made by the legislature.[12]

The approach adopted by Hayek tends to be associated with his preference for a particular form of non-paternalistic, laissez-faire state, and is contested by those who favour a more interventionist, regulatory, and paternalist form of the state.[13] If the state is to be interventionist and provide targeted forms of assistance, it requires administrative processes which tend to emphasize the importance of the individual decision and the scope for individual assessment by state officials who have fuller relevant information available to them about particular cases when deciding what to do than the legislature could possibly have when legislating in advance. The approach adopted by those concerned to provide protection against the potential tyranny of the majority is contested by those who emphasize the superior legitimacy—in terms of ideas of self-government and equal rights of participation—of decision-making through democratic processes and by political compromise, and who emphasize the counter-majoritarian difficulties and questionable legitimacy associated with judicial decision-making on issues of ultimate values within a state.[14] Standard forms of representative democracy may be subjected to criticism that they are not sufficiently participatory,[15] but it is difficult to see an expanded power of substantive decision-making by unelected courts following court procedures as an obvious answer to this criti-

---

[12] TRS Allan, *Law, Liberty and Justice: The Legal Foundations of British Constitutionalism* (1993); *Constitutional Justice: A Liberal Theory of the Rule of Law* (2001); Ronald Dworkin, *Law's Empire* (1986); Sir John Laws, 'Is the High Court the guardian of fundamental constitutional rights?' [1993] *Public Law* 59; 'Law and democracy' [1995] *Public Law* 72.

[13] cf JWF Allison, *The English Historical Constitution*, p 200. Hayek was writing very much against the trend of thought of his own time: see Tony Judt, *Postwar: a History of Europe since 1945* (2005) pp 67 ff.

[14] JAG Griffith, 'The Political Constitution' (1979) 42 MLR 1; AM Bickel, *The Least Dangerous Branch: The Supreme Court at the Bar of Politics* (2nd edn, 1986); Benjamin Barber, *The Conquest of Politics: Liberal Philosophy in Democratic Times* (1988); Jennifer Nedelsky, *Private Property and the Limits of American Constitutionalism: The Madisonian Framework and its Legacy* (1990); Robert H. Bork, *The Tempting of America: the Political Seduction of the Law* (1991); Jeremy Waldron, *Law and Disagreement* (1999); Jeffrey Goldsworthy, *The Sovereignty of Parliament: History and Philosophy* (1999); cf Gunnar Beck, 'Human Rights Adjudication under the ECHR between Value Pluralism and Essential Contestability' [2008] EHRLR 214. For a thoughtful discussion of the inherent tensions between the different conceptual elements comprising the model of the democratic liberal state committed to a doctrine of human rights, see Geuss, *History and Illusion in Politics*, esp ch 3.

[15] Benjamin Barber, *Strong Democracy* (1984); Paul Hirst, *Representative Democracy and its Limits* (1990).

cism.[16] The greater the substantive content given to interests claimed to be human or constitutional rights, the more it is pointed out that those rights are in conflict with other important ideas of pluralism and tolerance within a society subject to neutral rules, where negotiation and compromise through the political process provide what may be a more acceptable and legitimate method of achieving a framework for communal living.[17] This may also be seen as providing a quite distinct underpinning for a conception of the rule of law, based on the respect due to the legal products of such processes and the political obligation associated with that respect.[18] Apart from the theoretical debates, the historical contingencies out of which rule of law thinking and the ECHR itself have developed, and a sense that these are to a degree fragile and by no means necessary features of the public order even in Europe,[19] give pause for thought about how far the claims for judicial (as distinct from political) resolution of profound conflicts within society can or should be pressed.

These are large issues, discussed in a very extensive literature, and cannot be debated further in this essay. The point to be noted, however, is that legal concepts and legal doctrine emerge from the interplay of these underlying political and philosophical ideas which are in conflict and are subject to shifting perceptions of their relative force and weight over time. Legal theory aims to provide an island of stability and determinacy resting on top of this shifting ground; but because of the shifting nature of the ideas which underlie it, the stability can only be relative, and legal theory is inevitably subject to greater or lesser degrees of change over time.

Of course, the ECHR imposes many explicit constraints upon what states may do, and hence upon what their legislatures may do. The focus of this essay, however, is the judicial development of legal doctrine by the ECtHR going beyond

---

[16] Although the emphasis on the extent and quality of consultation upon and consideration of measures in cases such as *Hirst v UK (No 2)* (2004) 38 EHRR 40, *Hatton v UK* (2003) 37 EHRR 28, *Draon v France* (2006) 42 EHRR 40, and *Evans v UK* (2008) 46 EHRR 34 may reflect this factor to some degree; they also reflect a shift by the ECtHR to focusing more on procedural values in circumstances where the substantive outcome in a particular context is politically controversial and the court is accordingly reticent about substituting its assessment for that of the national authorities.

[17] John Gray, *Two Faces of Liberalism* (2000); Richard Bellamy, *Liberalism and Pluralism: Towards a Politics of Compromise* (1999); Cass R Sunstein, *Legal Reasoning and Political Conflict* (1996), esp ch 2; Bork, *The Tempting of America*, esp at pp 65, 81, and 352–353, quoting Edmund Burke ('All government, indeed every human benefit and enjoyment, every virtue, and every prudent act, is founded on compromise and barter...'); see also John Dunn, *The Cunning of Unreason: Making Sense of Politics* (2000), and John Dunn, 'Political Obligation' in David Held (ed), *Political Theory Today* (1991), esp at pp 29, 34, and 46–47.

[18] J Waldron, *Law and Disagreement*, at pp 101–102 ('...[The circumstances of politics] are essential for understanding many of the distinctively political virtues, such as civility, the toleration of dissent, the practice of loyal opposition, and—not least—the rule of law').

[19] See e.g., Judt, *Postwar*; AW B Simpson, *Human Rights and the End of Empire*; R Geuss, *History and Illusion in Politics*; Raymond Aron, *Plaidoyer pour l'Europe decadent* (1977, translated as *In Defense of Decadent Europe*, 1979); James Sheehan, *The Monopoly of Violence: Why Europeans Hate Going to War* (2007).

the bare text of the Convention itself to give substantive content to notions gathered together under the general idea of the rule of law, and which addresses the tension of that idea with the general idea of democracy. I will examine below the following areas of legal doctrine developed by the ECtHR: the concept of 'law' in the ECHR; the rule of law requirements imposed by Article 6 ECHR; the constraints upon the form of legislation imposed by the requirement of proportionality under various Articles of the ECHR; the constraints upon the form of legislation imposed by the developing law of indirect discrimination under Article 14 ECHR; and the margin of appreciation.

(a) The Concept of 'Law' in the ECHR

In its seminal judgment in *Sunday Times v UK*,[20] the ECtHR interpreted the concept of 'law', as used in the requirement in Article 10(2) that interferences with freedom of expression should be 'prescribed by law', as involving three elements: a basis in domestic law, together with the substantive requirements that the law in question should be accessible to the individual affected, and that its application and effects should be reasonably foreseeable. This interpretation of 'law' and 'lawful' as these terms are used in the ECHR has now been generalized and the rule of law has been described as inherent in all the Articles of the Convention.[21] In some cases, the ECtHR appears to identify a fourth requirement, that the legal regime in question should provide sufficient protection against arbitrariness[22] or that it is 'compatible with the rule of law';[23] and in some contexts this appears to import a need for the availability of independent review of decisions which are taken.[24]

However, the ECtHR also recognizes the legitimacy of using generally worded legal provisions, even though they are less precise and their effects may be less foreseeable, where it is appropriate for there to be legal regulation across a range of cases calling for individualized assessment at the point of application of the law, or where it is important to avoid excessive rigidity and to allow the application of the law to keep pace with changing circumstances.[25] The degree of precision required depends upon the content of the instrument, the field it is designed to

[20] (1979) 2 EHRR 245.

[21] See e.g., *Malone v UK* (1985) 7 EHRR 14 (Art 8); *SW v UK* (1996) 21 EHRR 23, at [35]; *Ukraine-Tyumen v Ukraine* ECHR judgment of 22 Nov 2007, [49].

[22] See e.g., *Grande Oriente v Italy* (2002) 34 EHRR 22; *Maestri v Italy* (2004) 39 EHRR 38; *Hasan and Chaush v Bulgaria* (2002) 34 EHRR 55, at [84].

[23] See e.g., *Kopp v Switzerland* (1999) 27 EHRR 91; *Weber v Germany* (2008) 46 EHRR SE5, with the ECtHR giving at [95] a fairly full prescription for the content required of domestic legislation in the area of secret surveillance; and *Association for European Integration and Human Rights v Bulgaria*, judgment of 28 June 2007, at [76].

[24] See e.g., *Al Nashif v Bulgaria* (2003) 36 EHRR 37; *HL v UK* (2005) 40 EHRR 35.

[25] E.g., *SW v UK* (1996) 21 EHRR 23; *Kuijper v Netherlands* (2005) 41 EHRR SE16.

cover, and the number and status of those to whom it is addressed.[26] The extent to which the law is required to be foreseeable in its effects may be reduced in certain contexts, such as those involving secret surveillance for security purposes (but that may be balanced by stricter requirements for other safeguards).[27] Where the relevant law provides for a high degree of discretion exercisable by state officials, that may be acceptable if balanced by the availability of judicial review of what they do, as a safeguard against arbitrariness.[28]

(b) The Rule of Law and Article 6

Article 6 sets out the principal procedural obligation in relation to access to justice through the court system, and as such is a central protection for the rule of law under the ECHR. The case law under it is extensive. Three aspects may be highlighted here.

First, Article 6 (and the similar provision in Article 5(4)) has been taken to import very strict standards of impartiality and independence from the executive, in terms both of subjective independence and of giving a full objective appearance of such independence.[29]

Secondly, Article 6 has been interpreted as importing a right to have access to the courts for resolution of disputes covered by it.[30] In addition to express rights to legal assistance under Article 6(3) in criminal proceedings, the ECtHR has implied what amounts to a right to legal aid in certain civil cases (where the dispute is unusually complex or there are procedural rules requiring representation by lawyers).[31] At the same time, however, the ECtHR has confirmed the entitlement of states to seek to control the costs associated with legal aid through application of merits and means tests.[32]

Thirdly, Article 6 (and other Articles) impose an obligation on state authorities to respect the court process and to implement judgments delivered by the courts. The rule of law is said to be inherent in all the Articles of the Convention, and to entail a duty on the part of public authorities to comply with judicial orders or decisions against them.[33] The principle of the rule of law in this context

---

[26] E.g., *Vereinigung Demokratischer Soldaten v Austria* (1994) 20 EHRR 56; *Amihalachiaie v Moldova* (2005) 40 EHRR 35.

[27] E.g., *Malone v UK* (1985) 7 EHRR 14, at [67].

[28] E.g., *Bronda v Italy* (2001) 33 EHRR 4; *Landvreugd v Netherlands* (2003) 36 EHRR 56.

[29] For a review of the authorities, see e.g., *Starrs and Ruxton v Procurator Fiscal* (2000) HRLR 191 (the temporary sheriffs case); *R (Brooke) v Parole Board* [2008] EWCA Civ 29.

[30] *Golder v UK* (1975) 1 EHRR 524; *Ashingdane v UK* (1985) 7 EHRR 528; *Omar v France* (2000) 29 EHRR 210.

[31] E.g., *Airey v Ireland* (1979) 2 EHRR 305; *Steel and Morris v UK* (2005) 41 EHRR 22.

[32] E.g., *Del Sol v France* (2002) 35 EHRR 38; *Steel and Morris v UK* (2005) 41 EHRR 22.

[33] E.g., *Iatridis v Greece* (1999) 30 EHRR 97, [58] (a case under Art 1 of Protocol 1, rather than Art 6); *Ion Rosca v Moldova*, ECtHR, judgment of 22 March 2005; *Salov v Italy* (2007) 45 EHRR 51. For the general obligation on contracting states to ensure the implementation of judicial deci-

also carries with it strict constraints against legislation which affects the judicial determination of a dispute involving the state or private parties, which is permissible only on compelling grounds of the public interest.[34]

(c) Proportionality and the Form of Legislation

A significant number of Articles in the ECHR and its protocols import the requirement that interferences with the rights they contain should be proportionate to some legitimate public interest which the interfering measure pursues.[35] The general approach is to require proportionality of interference in the particular case itself.[36] This tends to undermine the possibility of formulation by a legislature of simple, clear rules covering a range of different cases and providing for the same result in all of them, as opposed to setting up a scheme for detailed assessment of individual cases on their individual facts, by judges or other state officials. Whilst it reinforces the rule of law in the particular sense that it tends to confer practical decision-making power upon judges, this approach also has a tendency to run counter to other aspects of rule of law thinking. These include the idea that individual cases should be determined by abstract and general laws, without excessive recourse to the individual discretion of the decision-maker; the idea that laws should be declared as precisely as possible in advance so that citizens can plan their affairs in knowledge of how they will be applied; and the idea that cases should be determined directly by rules promulgated by the body with authority to lay down the law for all (the legislature).[37] In that respect, the doctrine of proportionality is in tension to some degree with the value given foreseeability in the case law on the 'prescribed by law' test.[38]

sions between private parties without undue delay, arising by implication from the concept of the rule of law inherent in Art 6, see e.g., *GL v Italy* (2002) 34 EHRR 41 at [33]; *Melnic v Moldova* (2008) 47 EHRR 31, [38] (Art 6 must be interpreted in light of the Preamble of the ECHR which 'declares the rule of law to be part of the common heritage of the Contracting States').

[34] E.g., *Scordino v Italy* (2007) 45 EHRR 7; *Lizarraga v Spain* (2007) 45 EHRR 45; *Arnolin v France*, ECtHR, judgment of 9 January 2007.

[35] A requirement of proportionality is inherent in the 'necessary in a democratic society' rubric in Arts 8(2), 9(2), 10(2), and 11(2). It is also implied into aspects of the rights in other Arts such as Arts 6 and 14, and Arts 1 and 3 of the First Protocol.

[36] See e.g., *Campbell v UK* (1992) 15 EHRR 137; *Tinnelly and McElduff v UK* (1998) 27 EHRR 249; *Papachelas v Greece* (2000) 30 EHRR 923; *Shofman v Russia* (2007) 44 EHRR 35.

[37] See Frederic Schauer, *Playing by the Rules: A Philosophical Examination of Rule-Based Decision-Making in Law and Life* (1991), esp chs 5–8; Sunstein, *Legal Reasoning and Political Conflict*, esp chs 4–7; Kathleen M Sullivan, 'Foreword: The Justices of Rules and Standards' (1992) 106 Harv LR 24; Posner, *How Judges Think*, pp 176 ff.

[38] See Philip Sales and Ben Hooper, 'Proportionality and the Form of Law' (2003) 119 LQR 426 for discussion of the circumstances in which bright line rules, rather than discretionary and standards-based provisions, will be compliant with the ECHR. The connection with ideas associated with the rule of law is clear: cf Schauer, *Playing by the Rules*, p 140 ('Since following a rule may produce a suboptimal decision in some particular case, the question of the comparative value of

The Strasbourg and domestic case law has shown a growing acceptance of the legitimacy of clear, bright line rules in certain contexts. Such rules operate by reference to broad categories of case, and to the general justifications which may exist for the rules taking the category as a whole, without detailed adjustment to take account of the particular circumstances of individual cases within those categories. The circumstances in which bright line rules are accepted as compatible with the ECHR, rather than castigated as blanket rules which fall foul of the proportionality requirement in the individual case, depend upon the width of the margin of appreciation accorded to the state in the particular context and the identification of legitimate objectives in Convention terms which are best promoted by a bright line approach.[39] The application of general bright line rules laid down by the legislature which make sure that a particular goal is met, even if the absence of exceptions means that the rules will sometimes catch cases which do not fall on their own particular facts within the mischief of the rule, also affects the balance of decision-making power between legislature and the courts. The legislature is in a position to lay down general, bright line rules dealing with broad categories of case; but often it will be impossible for it to legislate in the required level of detail if a fine-grained approach is required by the proportionality requirement, and important choices may then in practice have to be left to the evaluation of courts hearing the particular cases before them.[40]

On this topic, in paragraph [29] of his speech in *R (Pretty) v DPP* Lord Bingham quoted Dr Johnson: 'Laws are not made for particular cases but for men in general'. 'To permit a law to be modified at discretion is to leave the community without law. It is to withdraw the direction of that public wisdom by which the deficiencies of private understanding are to be supplied.'[41] Lord Bingham returned to this theme at paragraph [33] of his speech in *R (Animal Defenders International) v Secretary of State for Culture, Media and Sport*:[42]

... legislation cannot be framed so as to address particular cases. It must lay down general rules... A general rule means that a line must be drawn, and it is for Parliament to decide where. The drawing of a line inevitably means that hard cases will arise falling on the

rule-based reliance is the question of the extent to which a decision-making environment is willing to tolerate suboptimal results in order that those affected by the decisions in that environment will be able to plan certain aspects of their lives').

[39] Sales and Hooper, 'Proportionality and the Form of Law', pp 441ff; and see e.g., *James v UK* (1986) 8 EHRR 123, [46], [68]; *Mellacher v Austria* (1990) 12 EHRR 391; *Pretty v UK* (2002) 35 EHRR 1, [72] (following in this respect the approach set out in Lord Bingham's speech in *R (Pretty) v DPP* [2001] 1 AC 800 at [29]); *Zdanoka v Latvia* (2007) 54 EHRR 17, [112], [125]; *Wilson v First County Trust Ltd (No 2)* [2004] 1 AC 816, [68]–[78] (Lord Nicholls); *R (Wilson) v Wychavon DC* [2007] QB 801; *R (Carson and Reynolds) v Secretary of State for Work and Pensions* [2006] 1 AC 173, [36]–[41], [45], [86]–[91].

[40] cf Schauer, *Playing by the Rules*, pp 158–162.

[41] Boswell, *Life of Johnson*, Oxford Standard Authors (3rd edn, 1970) at pp 735, 496. See also Jeremy Waldron, *The Dignity of Legislation* (1999).

[42] [2008] 2 WLR 781, HL.

wrong side of it, but that should not be held to invalidate the rule if, judged in the round, it is beneficial.

In the Strasbourg jurisprudence, it is instructive to compare the majority and minority judgments in *Slivenko v Latvia*[43] concerning general rules governing expulsion of ethnic Russians from Latvia, with the majority holding that a fine-grained legal regime was required for compatibility with Article 8 because of the potentially weighty interests of some (but not all) individuals who were to be subject to the regime. In relation to the operation of the tax and welfare benefits regimes, the ECtHR accepts that legal rules may be framed by reference to general categories of case, rather than required to provide for fine-grained differentiation between individual cases on their particular facts.[44] In *Sahin v Turkey*[45] a strict rule prohibiting the wearing of an Islamic headscarf in educational institutions was upheld as compatible with the ECHR.

Evans v UK[46] is another recent case in which the Grand Chamber has accepted the validity of a bright line approach established by the legislature, this time in relation to regulation of IVF treatment, in which a balance between the interests of the prospective mother and prospective father was necessary, and the regime laid down a clear requirement of consent from both parties. In the absence of clear rules in this area, it would be difficult for individuals to know their rights prior to giving their consent to IVF treatment, there would be scope for much more extensive and acrimonious argument about what should happen in any particular case, and there would be greater scope for arbitrary differences in outcomes based on the invidious choices to be made in similar cases.

(d) Indirect Discrimination

Article 14 ECHR sets out a prohibition on discrimination in the enjoyment of the rights and freedoms in the ECHR, where the differential treatment cannot be justified. The main body of case law concerns cases of direct discrimination. However, in recent years the ECtHR has moved to accept that Article 14 also impliedly contains a prohibition against indirect discrimination.[47] This is

---

[43] ECtHR [GC], judgment of 9 October 2003.

[44] See e.g., *Burden v UK* (2007) 44 EHRR 51, [60] (tax); *Stec v UK*, ECtHR [GC], decision of 12 April 2006, [51]–[52] (welfare benefits); *White and Runkee v UK*, ECtHR, judgment of 10 May 2007, [39] (welfare benefits, following the approach of the House of Lords in *R (Hooper) v Secretary of State for Work and Pensions* [2005] 1 WLR 1681). The general rule approach can be justified under Art 14 as well, even if direct sex discrimination is involved in the way the rule is formulated.

[45] (2005) 41 EHRR 8.

[46] (2008) 46 EHRR 34.

[47] *Thlimmenos v Greece* (2001) 31 EHRR 15, [44]; *Jordan v UK* (2001) 37 EHRR 52, [154]; *McShane v UK* (2002 35 EHRR 23, [135]; *Pretty v UK* (2002) 35 EHRR 23, [88]–[90]; *Hoogendijk v Netherlands* (2005) 40 EHRR SE22, at 206–207; *DH v Czech Republic* (2008) 47 EHRR 3 [GC] (discussed in Gemma Hobcraft, 'Roma Children and Education in the Czech Republic: *DH v Czech Republic*: Opening the Door to Indirect Discrimination Findings in Strasbourg?' [2008] EHRLR 245). For domestic authority see *Gallagher (Valuation Officer) v Church of Jesus Christ of*

unsurprising, in view of the widespread application of the concept of indirect discrimination in the laws of European states and in the law of the European Union. It is a development which is also in line with the general disposition under the ECHR, by reference to the proportionality requirement as discussed above, to subject general rules to scrutiny to ensure that they do not create effects in particular cases which are incompatible with Convention values. A complaint of indirect discrimination is a complaint that a rule or measure of general application creates disproportionately prejudicial effects for a particular group to which it applies, such that their situation ought properly to have been addressed by a more fine-grained and particularized system of rules or measures. The essence of a claim of indirect discrimination is that the same rule or measure is applied to different groups which ought to be treated differently.[48]

However, having recognized the coherence within the scheme of the ECHR of implying a concept of indirect discrimination into Article 14, difficulties in the application of Article 14 in this way will have to be faced. Unlike those forms of indirect discrimination that derive from statute or EU legislation,[49] Article 14 contains no precise definition of the concept of indirect discrimination, nor does it even set out exhaustively the grounds upon which such discrimination might be unlawful.[50] So, potentially, a claim of indirect discrimination contrary to Article 14 could be brought in a very wide variety of contexts and on a very wide variety of bases, by reference to a wide variety of groups said to be prejudiced by the application of the general rule defined by claimants in their own interests (so as to produce the required disproportionate impact upon the particular group so defined). Similarly, as the test for the applicability of Article 14 is not an infringement of another Convention right but merely that the case falls 'within the ambit of' another Convention right, the range of schemes, policies, and decisions which may, at least in principle, be the subject of an indirect discrimination complaint is potentially vast. If the recognition that Article 14 covers indirect discrimination is not to create an unmanageable burden on the courts and public authorities, and if values associated with the rule of law are not to be unduly disrupted and undermined, it seems that mechanisms will need to be found to keep this form of discrimination within careful limits.

It seems likely that the ECtHR will adapt the analysis for direct discrimination claims under Article 14 (are the comparators in an analogous situation? Is there objective justification for the difference in their treatment?) so as to ask the equivalent questions in an indirect discrimination claim: (1) is a general rule or measure being applied to two or more relevant groups which are *not* on the

Latter-day Saints [2008] UKHL 56 and *R (Esfandiari) v Secretary of State for Work and Pensions* [2006] EWCA Civ 282.

[48] *R (Carson and Reynolds) v Secretary of State for Work and Pensions* [2006] 1 AC 173, [14] (Lord Hoffmann).

[49] E.g., under the Sex Discrimination Act 1975, the Race Relations Act 1976, and Directives 2000/43/EC and 2000/78/EC.

[50] Because of the words 'or other status' at the end of Art 14.

face of it in a relevantly analogous position?[51] (2) Was the similarity in treatment objectively justifiable in the sense that it had a legitimate aim and bore a reasonable relationship of proportionality to that aim?[52]

It seems logical that courts should apply the disproportionately prejudicial effect test in the context of the Convention right that is said to be engaged for Article 14 purposes. Thus, if the complaint is of a breach of Article 14 read together with Article 8, then the courts should consider whether the claimant's group has suffered a disproportionately prejudicial effect that is referable to their enjoyment of the Article 8 right to respect for their 'private and family life', 'home', or 'correspondence'. Presumably, the test of disproportionately prejudicial effect will be taken to import some threshold requirement relating to just how different the impact on the two comparator groups has to be before it is satisfied.[53] This may be an important control mechanism.

Perhaps most important will be the approach to be adopted to the margin of appreciation in consideration of objective justification in indirect discrimination cases. When dealing with direct discrimination under particular 'suspect' categories (such as sex or race), the margin of appreciation for the purposes of application of Article 14 tends to be narrow.[54] But when one is dealing with indirect discrimination, which is not an effect which the rule is directed at achieving, it is submitted that a more generous approach to the margin of appreciation and to the weight which may properly be attached to other legitimate objectives the state may be seeking to pursue by such a rule is appropriate. The underlying rationale for the Convention prohibition against discrimination is to ensure that individuals are accorded equal respect.[55] Where the legislature has promulgated a rule which treats everyone the same way regardless of their sex, race, etc, it has on the face of the rule sought to accord equal respect to all. Moreover, where the legislature has acted to protect the Convention rights of everyone to equal treatment, it is entitled to a wide margin of appreciation where it has to balance the claims of

---

[51] It is only if the same rule or measure is applied to groups which are not in an analogous position that the State should be called upon to justify its decision to treat them in the same way—if on proper analysis the two groups are in the same position in the relevant respect, then it would seem that there is no warrant for requiring the State to produce any further justification for applying the same rule or measure to both groups. See *Hoogendijk v Netherlands* at 206–207: '...persons whose situations are significantly different must be treated differently...An issue will arise under Article 14...when states without an objective and reasonable justification fail to treat differently persons whose situations are significantly different...'.

[52] See e.g., *Thlimmenos v Greece* at [44]; *Hoogendijk v Netherlands* at 206–208.

[53] See e.g., *Hoogendijk v Netherlands* at 207: 'Although statistics in themselves are not automatically sufficient for disclosing a practice which could be classified as discriminatory under Article 14...the applicant is able to show...the existence of a *prima facie* indication that a specific rule—although formulated in a neutral manner—in fact affects *a clearly higher percentage* of women than men...' (emphasis added).

[54] Although other factors might also be applicable to widen it: see e.g., *Stec v UK*, ECtHR [GC], decision of 12 April 2006, [51]–[52].

[55] *R (Carson and Reynolds) v Secretary of State for Work and Pensions* [2006] 1 AC 173, [14]–[17] (Lord Hoffmann).

some groups to equal treatment and of others to differential treatment,[56] where there is no clear criterion given by the ECHR of which value judgment should prevail.[57] In addition, it may be said that the concept of the fair balance between the personal rights of individuals and the general interest of the community which underlies the whole of the Convention[58] supports this approach. This is because, having regard to the range of potential indirect discrimination claims which could in theory be brought in respect of any general rule under Article 14, the state authorities will not at the point of promulgating the rule be distinctly on notice of all or any potential indirectly discriminatory effects it might have, but rather will legitimately be focusing on other public interest reasons for adopting the rule. It would seem unfair and unduly disruptive to apply the stricter standards appropriate for cases of direct discrimination on the face of a rule or set of rules (where the state authorities are on notice when they promulgate the rules that distinctions are being drawn which they should, in principle, be willing and able to explain and justify) to cases of indirect discrimination, where that is not the case.

The Strasbourg case law already contains some indicators that, in the context of indirect discrimination claims, the threat to the Convention values inherent in Article 14 is less acute, and may therefore be capable of being more readily justified. *Chapman v UK*[59] should be analyzed as a case of indirect discrimination. In that case, neutral planning laws prohibiting development in the Green Belt were applied to prevent a gypsy establishing a mobile home on land which she had bought within the Green Belt, where there was evidence of generally inadequate provision of caravan sites which could accommodate the gypsy way of life. Her complaints under Article 8 and Article 14 were dismissed. The ECtHR emphasized the complexity and sensitivity of the issues involved in policies balancing the interests of the general population and of a minority with conflicting requirements,[60] pointed to the substantial problems which might arise under Article 14 if gypsies were given preferential treatment to accommodate their special position,[61] and emphasized that the law was not aimed against them as

---

[56] Both claims being potentially capable of being supported under Art 14, since the first set of groups may have a claim that rules should not be adopted which create benefits for others which are not accorded to them (direct discrimination, potentially contrary to Art 14), while the second set of groups may have a claim that rules should be adopted which do treat them differently and, on the face of it, preferentially (to avoid what might otherwise be indirect discrimination, again potentially contrary to Art 14).

[57] cf *Chassagnou v France* (1999) 29 EHRR 615, [112]–[113]; *Evans v UK* (2008) 46 EHRR 34, [77]; *Dickson v UK*, ECtHR [GC], judgment of 14 December 2007, [78]; *Hoogendijk v Netherlands* at 207 (indirectly discriminatory rule introduced to remove a former discriminatory exclusion of women from a benefits scheme, but keeping the cost of that change within reasonable limits): *R v Shayler* [2003] 1 AC 247, [80] (Lord Hope). See also the restrained approach adopted by the ECtHR to review under Art 9 in *Vergos v Greece* (2005) 41 EHRR 41, at [41], in relation to a law that was *prima facie* neutral in its application.

[58] *Brown v Stott* [2003] 1 AC 681, 704.   [59] (2001) 33 EHRR 18.

[60] [94].   [61] [95].

a group.[62] A wide margin of appreciation was held to be appropriate, and the application of the neutral rules in her case was held to be compatible with the ECHR.

Also in *Chapman*, the special respect which the ECtHR accepted in that case should be accorded to gypsies was said to be an aspect of a positive obligation which could be found in Article 8.[63] A claim of indirect discrimination may be regarded as a claim that the state owes a positive obligation under the ECHR (to recast its rules and measures to make special provision for the affected group). There is often a wider margin of appreciation in relation to action taken in respect of an area where a positive obligation is claimed than in other areas under the ECHR, in particular by comparison with direct interferences with Convention rights.[64]

The case law on the circumstances in which legislation which affects the outcome of court cases is compatible with the ECHR also affords an analogy. As explained above,[65] the requirements of the rule of law inherent in Article 6 generally prohibit legislation introduced to influence the judicial determination of a dispute. However, if a general law is introduced pursuing a legitimate public interest objective, which is not directed to influencing litigation but which affects the outcome of litigation as an incidental effect, the rule of law requirement will not be infringed.[66] The nature of the complaint in this sort of case resembles a complaint of indirect discrimination,[67] and the ECtHR's approach suggests that justification for a neutral rule with an incidental, disproportionate impact upon a particular person or group may more readily be made out.

(e) The Margin of Appreciation and Respect for the Legislature's Judgment

The main doctrine by which the ECtHR moderates the impact of the proportionality requirement as a factor capable of undermining the judgment of the legislature in the formulation of legal rules is the margin of appreciation. Strictly, this is a doctrine extended by the ECtHR as an international court to the authorities in a state, as distinct from the legislature in particular. However, in light of the importance of democracy as a pillar of the ECHR system, particular respect is shown for the judgments of and laws laid down by a democratic legislature. The issue is one of the separation of powers. The doctrine of the margin of appreciation operates in relation to those questions more apt in a democratic society

---

[62] [97].

[63] [96].   [64] E.g., *Goodwin v UK* (2002) 35 EHRR 18, [72].

[65] See text at n 34.

[66] E.g., *Forrer-Niedenthal v Germany*, ECtHR, judgment of 20 February 2003, [60]–[64]; *Lizarraga v Spain* (2007) 45 EHRR 45.

[67] In substance, the person whose legal case is affected is maintaining that he suffers a different and more prejudicial effect than members of the general population affected by the rule.

for decision by the legislature, distinguishing them from those appropriate for decision by courts which are independent of the political process. Leading factors which tend to increase the width of the margin of appreciation include the sensitivity and complexity of the area governed by legislation,[68] whether it relates to matters of social and economic policy,[69] whether it is an area of general policy in relation to which opinions may reasonably differ in a democracy,[70] whether the legal approach calls for a balancing of interests and rights (including, in particular, Convention rights),[71] and the absence of a clear common approach across Members of the Council of Europe.[72]

There are two features of the developing case law which call for comment in the light of the relationship between Dicey's two pillars of the constitution. First, the domestic courts have in practice adopted the margin of appreciation into the domestic law under the Human Rights Act 1998 (HRA). This occurred through a dual process. In the early domestic case law in relation to the Act, the courts recognized that domestic law should operate with a similar doctrine so as to preserve to a similar degree the authority of Parliament to lay down law without it being declared incompatible with Convention rights by the courts. The domestic doctrine was called the discretionary area of judgment, to distinguish it from the international doctrine of the margin of appreciation.[73] However, it is unclear whether and to what extent it differs in substance from the margin of appreciation. Whatever the difference may have been, it appears now to have been overtaken and submerged to a considerable extent by the development of a second principle of interpretation under the HRA, based on the definition of 'Convention rights' in section 1(1) and the definition of the 'Convention' in section 21(1) as the ECHR 'as it has effect for the time being in relation to the United Kingdom'. The House of Lords has in several cases appeared to affirm what may be called the mirror principle, namely that the interpretation and application of Convention rights under the HRA should replicate their interpretation and application by the ECtHR under the ECHR.[74] The adoption of that principle would suggest that the margin of appreciation or something very close to it should be applied directly by domestic courts.[75] Since the practical reality is that, where the domestic

---

[68] E.g., *Odievre v France* (2004) 38 EHRR 43, [47]–[49].

[69] E.g., *James v UK* (1986) 8 EHRR 123, [46].

[70] E.g., *Hatton v UK* (2003) 37 EHRR 611, [97]; *Draon v France* (2006) 42 EHRR 40.

[71] E.g., *Odievre v France*; *Evans v UK* (2008) 46 EHRR 34, [77].

[72] E.g., *Rasmussen v Denmark* (1984) 7 EHRR 371, [40]–[41]; *Odievre v France*; *Evans v UK*.

[73] *R v DPP, ex p Kebiline* [2000] 2 AC 326, 380–381 (Lord Hope).

[74] *R (Ullah) v Special Adjudicator* [2004] 2 AC 323, [20] (Lord Bingham); *R (Quark Fishing Ltd) v Secretary of State for Foreign and Commonwealth Affairs* [2006] 1 AC 529; *R (Al Skeini) v Secretary of State for Defence* [2007] 3 WLR 33, HL; *R (Countryside Alliance) v AG* [2007] 3 WLR 922, HL; *R (Al Jeddah) v Secretary of State for Defence* [2008] 2 WLR 31, HL.

[75] It is submitted that this remains the case despite the recent decision of the House of Lords in *In re G (Adoption: Unmarried Couple)* [2008] 3 WLR 76. That decision suggests that in some cases in interpreting Convention rights in the HRA the domestic courts might adopt a different approach from that of the ECtHR, and decline to afford as wide a margin of appreciation to the

courts issue a declaration of incompatibility of statutory provisions in respect of Convention rights, legislation is introduced to remedy the defect so identified,[76] the doctrine of the margin of appreciation is now therefore at the centre of the domestic constitutional relationship between Parliament and the courts.

The second feature of the Strasbourg case law which has potentially major implications for the relationship between the courts and Parliament is the way in which the ECtHR has been prepared in recent cases to examine the quality of consideration of contentious issues by Parliament itself. Even in an area in which a wide margin of appreciation may ordinarily be expected to apply, it may be qualified and reduced if the ECtHR is not satisfied that Parliament has given an issue governed by legislation extended consideration.[77] This approach appears to

legislature as the ECtHR affords to the United Kingdom as a contracting state. Strictly, it seems that this part of the decision is *obiter*. It is unfortunate that the Committee in that case did not refer to the full range of previous decisions of the House bearing on this question, and it is respectfully submitted that there continues to be some doubt whether this approach is correct as a matter of interpretation of the HRA. Be that as it may, even if it is correct, it seems likely that the divergence from the Strasbourg margin of appreciation will arise only in a narrow class of case, perhaps where there is a compelling case of irrational discrimination, and that the sorts of factors which weigh with the ECtHR in deciding the width of the margin of appreciation afforded to the state will also be strongly indicative of the margin of appreciation to be afforded to the legislature.

[76] And see the discussion whether a declaration of incompatibility constitutes a remedy which ought to be exhausted before recourse to the ECtHR in *Burden v UK*, ECtHR [GC], judgment of 28 April 2008.

[77] *Hirst v UK (No 2)* (2004) 38 EHRR 40, [79]; *Dickson v UK*, ECtHR [GC], judgment of 14 December 2007, [79]. It is not altogether clear from *Hirst (No 2)* how significant the absence of recent debate in Parliament on prisoner voting rights actually was for the decision. The essence of the reasoning of the majority in holding that a law framed as a complete ban against prisoners voting involved a violation of Art 3 of Protocol No 1 is at [68]–[71] and [82], and is in the usual form of a disproportionality analysis: the law in question was a blanket restriction, 'a general, automatic and indiscriminate restriction on a vitally important Convention right'. The absence of debate in Parliament was not a critical element—it seems that such a similar provision in the law of any other contracting state would be found to be incompatible, whatever the quality of debate in the legislature: see [82]–[84] (esp [84], 'the Court must confine itself to determining whether the restriction affecting all convicted prisoners in custody exceeds *any* acceptable margin of appreciation…' [emphasis supplied]). Judge Caflisch in his concurring opinion emphasized that the result turned on the margin of appreciation applicable to all European states ([O-I2]–[O-I3]), without making reference to the quality or otherwise of the debate in the legislature. There was a powerful Joint Dissenting Opinion by Judges Wildhaber, Costa, Lorenzen, Kovler, and Jebens, who would have held that the measure fell within the general margin of appreciation available to all contracting states (it is important to note that this is the real area of dispute in relation to the outcome of the case) and who also went out of their way to disapprove the reference to the quality of the consideration in the legislature in para [79] of the judgment, because 'it is not for the Court to prescribe the way in which national legislatures carry out their legislative functions. It must be assumed that [the legislation in question] reflects political, social and cultural values in the United Kingdom' ([O-III7]); and a further concurring opinion by Judges Tulkens and Zagrebelsky, who agreed with the decision, but wished in particular to associate themselves with the dissenting opinion in relation to reference to the quality of debate in Parliament ([O-II7]: '…we note that the discussion about proportionality has led the Court to evaluate not only the law and its consequences, but also the parliamentary debate. This is an area in which two sources of legitimacy meet, the Court on the one hand and the national Parliament on the other. This is a difficult and slippery terrain for the Court in view of the nature of its role, especially when it itself accepts that a wide margin of appreciation must be given to the Contracting States'.

conflict with a central constitutional doctrine in domestic law, that proceedings in Parliament may not be criticized or called in question by the courts—which is itself an important protection for the sovereignty of Parliament.[78] It also calls in question the nature of parliamentary practice, since Parliament is a multi-member decision-making body whose decisions on points of substance are set out in the text of legislation which is adopted (which may simply represent what may be arrived at by a process of negotiation and compromise between representatives with very different views—the stuff of politics—rather than a pure and principled collective view), and is not necessarily revealed by a scrutiny of its debates. The same general practices are common to legislatures across Europe.

It may be argued that this recent aspect of the ECtHR's case law pays insufficient attention to the nature of the legislative process. Parliament is not a court, nor a public body required to give reasons for its decisions. It seems inappropriate for the courts to seek to hold the legislature to account in relation to the legislative process by reference to the standards and norms of non-political, non-negotiated judicial decision-making (determined by a narrowly structured and carefully delimited reasoning process). Parliament is a large multi-member body, whose members may have a number of different reasons for choosing to vote in favour of a provision of legislation. They may mention their reasons in debate, or they may not. Others who vote may accept the reasons offered in debate, or they may not but still decide to vote in a particular way for their own specific unannounced reasons. Parliament as a collective entity does not give reasons for choosing to adopt legislation, and no-one has any responsibility to do so on its behalf.[79] The collective will and intent of Parliament is given primarily by the text of the provision which is carried into law on the basis of voting on that text. The purposes of Parliament as a collective entity can be assessed only very broadly by reference to the general background to legislation and by identification of a mischief in White Papers and other reports, rather than by picking through debates in Parliament.[80]

---

[78] Art IX of the Bill of Rights; *Prebble v Television New Zealand Ltd* [1995] 1 AC 321, 332; *Hamilton v Al Fayed* [2001] 1 AC 395, 402F–403F; *Wilson v First County Trust Ltd (No 2)* [2004] 1 AC 816, [61]–[67] (Lord Nicholls), [115]–[118] (Lord Hope), [140]–[143] (Lord Hobhouse), [173] (Lord Scott), [178] (Lord Rodger); *R (Williamson) v Secretary of State for Education and Employment* [2005] 2 AC 246 at [51] (Lord Nicholls); *International Transport Roth GmbH v Secretary of State for the Home Department* [2003] QB 728 at [113]–[114] (Laws LJ).

[79] See e.g., *Wilson v First County Trust Ltd (No 2)* at [143]; cf *International Transport Roth* at [95]. See also Waldron, *Law and Disagreement*, ch 6, esp at pp 142–146. It would be unduly onerous and unrealistic to expect those preparing and debating legislation to do so in refined ECHR terms: compare *Davis v Johnson* [1979] AC 264, 350. A good deal by way of background assumptions about the appropriate form of the law and its financial implications, e.g., will simply be taken as read without being on the face of Hansard.

[80] The thoroughness of reports prepared outside Parliament, but to inform the debates in Parliament, was a factor relevant to the width of the margin of appreciation in *Evans v UK* (2008) 46 EHRR 34.

The approach of the ECtHR in this regard is also in tension with the decision of the House of Lords in *R (SB) v Denbigh High School*,[81] in which it rejected the ruling of the Court of Appeal that a school's decision to ban the wearing of the jilbab should be struck down because the school had not followed a set decision-making process stipulated by the court to address in terms issues involving Convention rights.[82]

However, there is a certain attraction in the idea that, if respect is to be accorded to the judgment made by a body other than the court (in this case, Parliament), it should be demonstrated that the body has given serious consideration to the issue in question. The domestic rules preventing the courts from criticizing or questioning proceedings in Parliament require, in effect, that a presumption be made that proper consideration has been given to legislation. In light of the ECtHR's recent case law, the acceptability of that presumption for the purposes of analysis under the ECHR appears in doubt. This may then emerge as an issue in which a clash between the approach of the ECtHR and the requirements of Article IX of the Bill of Rights and firmly established domestic constitutional principle arises. Should the common law doctrine[83] requiring non-review of proceedings in Parliament then be overridden by section 6(1) of the HRA, which imposes a duty on the court as a public authority to act compatibly with Convention rights, subject to section 6(2)?[84] Should the interpretation of Article IX of the Bill of Rights be altered by application of section 3 of the HRA? Or is this an area in which the HRA should itself be interpreted as subject to fundamental domestic constitutional principles,[85] even though that creates a divergence in practice between the domestic courts and the ECtHR?[86] This is not a comfortable choice.

---

[81] [2007] 1 AC 100.

[82] See [26]–[31] per Lord Bingham (esp. at [29], '... the focus at Strasbourg is not and has never been on whether a challenged decision or action is the product of a defective decision-making process, but on whether, in the case under consideration, the applicant's Convention rights have been violated...', and [31], '... what matters in any case is the practical outcome, not the quality of the decision-making process that led to it.') and [66]–[68] per Lord Hoffmann (esp. [68], '... article 9 [the Convention right at issue in that case] is concerned with substance, not procedure. It confers no right to have a decision made in any particular way. What matters is the result... The fact that the decision-maker is allowed an area of judgment in imposing requirements which may have the effect of restricting the right does not entitle a court to say that a justifiable and proportionate restriction should be struck down because the decision-maker did not approach the question in the structured way in which a judge might have done...').

[83] See *Prebble v Television New Zealand Ltd* [1995] 1 AC 321; *Hamilton v Al Fayed* [2001] 1 AC 395.

[84] cf *Doherty v Birmingham City Council* [2008] 3 WLR 636, HL.

[85] cf *Thoburn v Sunderland City Council* [2003] QB 151.

[86] cf *R (Alconbury Developments Ltd) v Secretary of State for the Environment, Transport and the Regions* [2004] 1 AC 295 at [76] (Lord Hoffmann: '... if I thought that... [decisions of the ECtHR] compelled a conclusion fundamentally at odds with the distribution of powers under the British constitution, I would have considerable doubt as to whether they should be followed'). The courts have not thus far been willing to confront this choice: see *R (Wilson) v Wychavon DC* [2007] QB 801, [32]–[36], [38], [107].

In conclusion, a far more substantive conception of the rule of law, in its various aspects, than English law has hitherto recognized has now entered our constitutional law. It is derived from the case law of the ECtHR, as received through the medium of the Human Rights Act 1998. However, in addition, the HRA itself preserves the principle of the sovereignty of Parliament in its drafting. That principle remains the bedrock of the English constitution. The domestic courts in future will have to address directly a tension between Dicey's two pillars of the rule of law and the sovereignty of Parliament, which he sought to suppress and avoid in his intellectual scheme. It seems likely that at the forefront of the mechanisms which will have to be developed to cope with this tension will be the margin of appreciation, an increasingly refined and articulated conception of the separation of powers, and a considered theory about the form of legislative provisions (in terms of the divide between general and particular approaches to legal regulation) which may be appropriate in the multitude of different situations which Parliament has to address.

13

The Long Sleep

Stephen Sedley

Among Tom Bingham's numerous achievements has been his piloting of public law between the shoals of political deference and the reefs of judicial supremacism. He has been equally firm in the judicial protection of fundamental values and due process and in his insistence on rendering to Parliament what is Parliament's and to the executive what is the executive's.

What has given the separation of powers a new importance is the resurgence, in and since the last quarter of the 20th century, of a system of public law which, when Tom Bingham was called to the Bar, was all but defunct. What follow are no more than notes towards one segment of the still unwritten history of the public law of England and Wales: the period when, after its great Victorian flowering, it all but died. Why did it go to sleep like a lamb? Why did it wake like a lion?

I

'If ministerial responsibility were more than the mere shadow of a name, the matter would be less important; but as it is,' Lord Justice Farwell thundered,[1] 'the courts are the only defence of the liberty of the subject against departmental aggression.'

The experience of the late-Victorian generation to which Sir George Farwell belonged had been of a state which was becoming increasingly managed and corporatized, invading area after area of previously unregulated economic and social activity with commissions, boards and inspectorates, with regulations, certificates, and orders. Dicey, magnificently wrong about this as about much else, regarded it as an unhappy aberration from a natural state of laissez-faire. He could not discern, even in retrospect, what both Adam Smith and Bentham had discerned in prospect: that a strong state was a necessary evil if a vigorous industrial and mercantile economy was not to collapse under the weight of its own by-products—crime, disease and injury, pollution, poverty, mass migration—or

---

[1] *Dyson v Attorney-General* [1911] KB 410.

for want of needed infrastructures—literacy, technical skills, public health, sewerage, housing, canals, railways, water, gas, and electricity.

It was this perception which underlay the seminal Report on the Organization of the Permanent Civil Service presented to Parliament in 1854 by Sir Stafford Northcote, Secretary to the Board of Trade, and the assistant secretary to the Treasury, Sir Charles Trevelyan. They realized, as ministers and legislators within a decade or two also came to realize, that the civil service was becoming (in a recent Home Secretary's phrase) unfit for purpose. 'Admission into the Civil Service,' they wrote, 'is indeed eagerly sought after, but it is for the unambitious, the indolent or incapable that it is chiefly desired.'

The reforms which the Northcote-Trevelyan report eventually brought about not only made the United Kingdom's civil service a model for much of the rest of the world and contributed materially to the country's continuing status on the world stage: they alerted its judiciary to the risk of over-government and to the possibility that principles of fair dealing would be swallowed up in the processes of regulation and management.

In this there was, no doubt, a strong element of the same political conservatism as moved Dicey. But where Dicey was able to assert, counterfactually, that in Britain we had no *droit administratif* and that the same law applied to the prime minister and the policeman (an odd choice, given the legal position of the latter) as applied to the citizen,[2] the judges who were his contemporaries showed a subtler understanding of what was going on. As Hobbes' Leviathan rose from the deep, their classic mode of operation was to fasten on the administrative processes by which the state intervened in economic activity. They had developed, in truth, a body of administrative law, using inherited tools—the prerogative writs—to regulate relations between the individual and the newly corporeal state. While Dicey was right to say that the common law was no respecter of persons and would hold ministers personally accountable for civil wrongs committed in office, he seems to have been blind to the fact that the great majority of wrongs committed by government and officialdom are not civil wrongs, because the relationship between government and the citizen is governed neither by contract nor by tort law. What the courts had brought into being by the end of the 19th century was a power, on the motion of a properly interested individual, to call public administration to account by other means for exceeding or abusing its powers.

The notion that *droit adminisitratif* was not law because the tribunals that administered it were part of the administration owed rather more to xenophobia than to reality. The reality was that western Europe's civil law systems, like the courts of common law, had by the end of the 19th century established independent adjudicative control of acts of public administration.[3] In this country Parliament, sympathetic (if not symbiotic) with the landowners who populated

---

[2] Dicey, *The Law of the Constitution*, (5th edn, Macmillan, London, 1897) 185.
[3] The 30 or so leading cases decided by the French Conseil d'État between 1873 and 1914, summarized in Long et al, *Les grands arrêts de la jurisprudence administrative* (16th edn, Dalloz, Paris, 2007), constitute a solid jurisprudence of public law.

the benches of local justices which were still responsible for much local administration, repeatedly sought to shield their decisions from over-exacting judicial review by enacting no-certiorari clauses. The court of Queen's Bench repeatedly held these to be ineffectual if the lower tribunal had acted without jurisdiction. But their determination to preserve jurisdictional legality was in the 20th century to sink beneath the waves until the House of Lords rescued and revived it in *Anisminic*,[4] just as it was not until the House's decision in *Ridge v Baldwin*[5] that the full force was restored of Byles J's memorable assertion in *Cooper v Wandsworth Board of Works*[6] that, where legislative provision fell short, procedural fairness would be supplied by the justice of the common law. By the turn of the 19th century, pretty well all the principles that law students are now taught to ascribe to the *Wednesbury* case were established, and more besides.[7]

It is true that the courts of Victorian England and Wales, while willing on occasion to call ministers to account, were not in the habit of taking on central government. Their targets were principally local justices and what would today be called quangos. Maitland[8] in his 1887–8 lectures noted that about half the currently reported Queen's Bench cases concerned what he identified as administrative law—'local rating, the powers of local boards, the granting of licences for various trades and professions, the Public Health Acts, the Education Acts, and so forth'. As to central government, there seems to have developed among the judges towards the end of the 19th century a sense that the divinity which hedged a king (and with which Disraeli had taken much trouble to surround Queen Victoria) also embraced the monarch's ministers,[9] a sense which was not finally dispelled until the decision of the House of Lords in *M v Home Office*[10] brought us back to the constitutional position established in the 18th century.[11] But while it was held that mandamus would not lie against ministers of the Crown or their servants, it was not doubted that prohibition and certiorari would lie against them.[12] Both the analytical and the remedial tools, although their names have changed, have remained essentially the same.

II

The history of the Home Office[13] illustrates what the judges who developed this jurisprudence were responding to. The Home Secretary's entire establishment in 1848 consisted of 22 officials, who placed all correspondence before him for his

---

[4] [1969] 2 AC 147. [5] [1964] AC 40.
[6] (1863) 14 CB (NS) 180. [7] See e.g., *Kruse v Johnson* [1898] 2 QB 91.
[8] *The Constitutional History of England* (1908), 505.
[9] See *Raleigh v Goschen* [1898] 1 ch 73. [10] [1994] 1 AC 377.
[11] *R v Lords Commissioners of the Treasury* (1872) LR 7 QB 387, per Cockburn CJ.
[12] *R v Local Government Board* (1882) 10 QBD 309 (prohibition); *R v Woodhouse* [1906] 2 KB 501 (certiorari).
[13] Those familiar with Jill Pellew's study *The Home Office 1848–1914: from clerks to bureaucrats* (Heinemann Educational Books, London, 1982) will recognize my debt to it in what follows.

decision. Within a year of the presentation of the Northcote-Trevelyan report, and partly in response to public concern at some of the ineptitude displayed in the Crimean War, the Civil Service Commission was set up with the object of vetting the fitness of candidates by examination, albeit their nominations continued to come principally through patronage.

Competitive entry took a typically long and tortured time to arrive. Robert Lowe, Gladstone's chancellor, raised the issue in 1869. It was doggedly opposed by Henry Bruce, the Home Secretary, supported by Sir James Stephen (later Stephen J), who contended that the 'self-reliance, self-possession, promptitude, address, resource, hopefulness and courage' which in his view characterized the best Oxbridge graduates were qualities 'ill-suited... to one who is entombed for life as clerk in a public office in Downing Street'. The argument about the relative merits of brains (success in examinations) and character (public-school virtue and breeding, perceived by both its proponents and its critics as antithetical to brains) continued to retard the professionalization of the civil service until after the turn of the century, when brains finally superseded character in the latter's last bastion, the Foreign Office.

It was not until Gladstone in 1873 replaced Bruce with Lowe as Home Secretary that entry to all established posts became by examination only, and not until 1880 that the first candidate so appointed took up his post. He was CE Troup, with behind him a Scottish parish school education, a first from Aberdeen in philosophy, and an Oxford BA, who entered as a junior clerk and ended as permanent secretary. The day of the meritocrat had come. But Bruce had had a point when he argued that the examination filter introduced by Grey had been all the 'security against dunces' that a routine-based department needed; and it is likely that Sir James Fitzjames Stephen was not alone among the judges in fearing that a new generation of public administrators, now a self-assured intellectual elite, would become enamoured of power and a threat both to the political judgment of their ministers and to the entitlement of citizens to be left alone by the state. This, for sure, was what Lord Justice Farwell found himself denouncing on the eve of the Great War.

By 1870 the Home Office establishment was still only 33 men, many of them under-employed, playing cricket in the corridors and betting on how many vehicles would go by in the next ten minutes. But over the next four decades the volume of incoming and outgoing papers steadily increased, and with it the size of the establishment. More important, the semi-autonomous bodies for which the Home Secretary had ultimate responsibility were growing in number and in authority. Disraeli's government of 1874–1880 carried through a major programme of social regulation. In 1879 alone legislation introduced provision for habitual drunkards, industrial schools, shipping casualties and salmon fisheries, all of them requiring central administration in one form or another. By 1914 there were inspectorates of factories, mines, explosives, prisons, police, reformatory and industrial schools, aliens, anatomy, animal welfare and inebriate retreats, all of them answerable to the Home Office and most of them staffed by inspectors (a surprising proportion of them women) of an intellectual calibre to match that of the Oxbridge elite now running the central department. To take a single instance, it was the East London factory inspector who in 1898 first established the link between asbestos manufacture and lung fibrosis. These specialized bodies were not simply a further administrative burden. They afforded an expertise which the generalists at the centre, however brilliant, lacked, and which gave the latter's advice a content and an edge which it could not otherwise have had.

By the 1880s senior officials had begun to complain that they were having to take work home with them. But more was at issue than workload. The volume of work meant that an increasing number of decisions was having to be taken by officials without reference upwards, a creeping delegation of power which was not challenged until, in the *Carltona* case,[14] it was simultaneously recognized and sanctified. And as early as 1881 Gladstone's Home Secretary, Sir William Harcourt, noting the beginnings of a phenomenon which Lord Hewart was to describe half a century later as the new despotism, remarked with irritation on 'Acts of Parliament that are passed now not defining exactly what is to be done, but leaving a great deal of the detail to be worked out afterwards by the Secretary of State'.

But what began as an uncovenanted burden of work for the old establishment was to become for the new meritocracy a consummation of power devoutly to be wished. It was also a consummation increasingly readily achieved by civil servants who themselves serviced the committees which proposed new measures, drafted legislation containing large delegated powers, and occasionally minuted decisions that bills they found inconvenient should be blocked.

By the outbreak of the Great War the civil service was not only staffed but run by a well-educated, well-paid, socially and intellectually confident mandarin class, secure in a lifetime's service with the prospect, all being well, of an eventual place in the honours list. If they felt themselves to be more capable of running the country than most of their transient political masters, and if the judges who had been at university with them and now sat in neighbouring armchairs at the Athenaeum had begun to feel the same about them, it would be entirely unsurprising.

The mutual confidence had begun to show. In 1915 *Arlidge v Local Government Board* reached the House of Lords,[15] who refused to introduce the now accepted principles of a fair hearing into the new machinery of statutory inquiries. Like their more defensible decision, three years earlier, to abstain from intervention in the Board of Education's arbitral functions in the dispute between local authorities and voluntary schools about the level of teachers' pay,[16] the decision suggested a developing judicial confidence in the capacity of government and its agencies to cope without a judge peering over their shoulder.

---

[14] [1943] 2 All ER 560.   [15] [1915] AC 120.
[16] *Board of Education v Rice* [1911] AC 179.

III

There is much evidence of the corresponding administrative confidence with which the mandarins of the civil service manipulated the balance of power in the state that emerged from the ruins of the Great War. There is also substantial evidence that the judiciary were fully conscious of Whitehall's creeping coup d'état and not at all happy about it. The puzzle is why, being both aware of it and alarmed by it, the judges did so little in their adjudications to resist it.

The closed world which the future Sir Humphrey Appleby must have entered in these years, with his double first from Bailey College, Oxford,[17] was a world in which the heads of the civil service had become accustomed to almost unquestioned power. The exigencies of war and the sense of patriotic necessity which it engendered must have made cavilling at government through the courts seem disloyal. Certainly the King's Bench reports for the period of the war record little in the way of decisions on individual rights beyond holdings that the Crown in wartime had an unfettered power to expropriate without compensation,[18] to intern naturalized British citizens without trial,[19] and to deport aliens at will to their country of origin.[20]

In the course of the war, as such cases illustrate, large and draconic powers had been handed, without any serious judicial oversight, to the executive; and huge tranches of judgment and discretion had been delegated to civil servants by ministers as a practical necessity. But, beyond this, Parliament, at the bidding of the departments themselves, began giving ministers power not only to implement its legislation but to amend it if it proved expedient to do so. Here at last was real departmental power.

One of the most remarkable publications of the inter-war years, given its authorship, was Lord Hewart's *The New Despotism*. Hewart, a Liberal politician, had served three years as attorney-general when, in 1922, the attorney's right of pre-emption enabled him to claim the post of Lord Chief Justice. Seven years into the job, he felt it appropriate to publish a diatribe (Hewart's first job had been as a journalist and leader-writer) against a mode of government—legislation by delegation—in which, as a Member of Parliament since 1913, he had participated without known protest.

Hewart's illustrations do not entirely bear out his thesis. The early examples he gives, from the 1880s, are no more than instances of subordinate rule-making powers created by statute.[21] What is striking—perhaps more striking than

---

[17] The college of which, as aficionados will recall, he was to become Master on his retirement from the civil service, having got rid of an obstructive college dean by advising the prime minister to appoint him to a vacant bishopric.

[18] *In the matter of a Petition of Right* [1915] 3 KB 649.   [19] *R v Halliday* [1917] AC 260.

[20] *R v Home Secretary, ex p Duke of Château Thierry* [1917] 1 KB 922.

[21] Albeit the Local Government Act 1888 contained power to modify any legislation for the purpose of bringing the Act itself into effect.

Hewart appreciated—is that it is in the years from 1918 onwards that the acts of Parliament which he cites begin to contain Henry VIII clauses giving ministers power to amend primary legislation.[22] The new despotism, while its origins lay in an earlier period, was perhaps newer than Hewart was ready to recognize.

The arrogance which had by now come to characterize the upper echelons of the civil service has become legendary. Peter Hennessy[23] records a second secretary in the wartime Ministry of Supply who felt able to refer to his two ministers—Duncan Sandys and Harold Macmillan, as it happened—as 'our two parliamentary liabilities'.[24] Historians of the civil service are pretty unanimous in fixing the end of the Great War as the beginning of a Treasury-led drive for power without accountability in Whitehall. Hennessy, though entirely alive to this, considers nevertheless that it was in the inter-war years that the British civil service 'matured and came of age'. And Hewart, although he characterized it more belligerently, was describing the same process.

IV

Why then did the judges do little or nothing to impede or reverse this Machiavellian transfer of power? To be sure, the law reports from the time of the First World War to the 1960s contain public law decisions, some of them significant. But their tone and culture are acquiescent and abstentionist.[25] The case which hit a judicial nerve was the Poplar councillors' doomed challenge to the district auditor's surcharge for having resolved to pay a living wage to workers whom they could have got for near-starvation wages, and to pay women the same as men.[26] By reading reasonableness into the powers of the local authority, the courts made adherence to the market a canon of law. Lord Atkinson's fulmination against the pursuit, on the rates, of 'eccentric principles of socialistic philanthropy and feminist ambition' has come to symbolize a political nadir in the judicial function.

It was also widely recognized, or at least believed, that judicial control—as evidenced, for example, in the 1897 workmen's compensation scheme—meant the introduction of endless technicality. The Edwardian systems of social insurance

---

[22] The Trade Boards Act 1918, the Animals (Anaesthetics) Act 1919, the Gas Regulation Act 1920, the London Traffic Act 1924.

[23] *Whitehall* (Secker & Warburg, London, 1989).

[24] As late as 1978 Brian Sedgemore MP, himself a former principal in Whitehall, almost secured a majority on the Commons expenditure committee for a draft report which included: 'The Home Office, the graveyard of free thinking since the days of Lord Sidmouth . . . is stuffed with reactionaries ruthlessly pursuing their own reactionary policies . . . The Vichy mentality which undoubtedly exists in some parts of our Foreign Office establishment does not . . . reflect the views of Her Majesty's ministers.'

[25] E.g., *R v Electricity Commissioners* [1924] 1 KB 171, which was largely responsible for introducing the long-lived error that only judicial, not administrative, decisions were governed by the principles of fairness.

[26] *Roberts v Hopwood* [1925] AC 578.

against sickness, unemployment and old age were consequently given their own tribunals, a step which the judges may have viewed with relief rather than frustration but which again sent them a hands-off message. And the now politically influential labour movement, whose experience of the judiciary had been almost uniformly negative, had no inclination to turn to the courts for the redress of wrongs and no desire to see the judges interfering with anything.

From time to time the courts reasserted their role. In 1931, reacting against a particular phenomenon which had angered Hewart—the immunization of delegated legislation against challenge by deeming it to be part of the empowering statute—the Law Lords held that such provisions could not stifle *vires* challenges.[27] But the larger tally of the pre- and post-war years is, in Sir William Wade's phrase, a dreary catalogue of abdication and error, including denial of a fair hearing before cancellation of a licence on which a livelihood depended,[28] literal reading of privative clauses,[29] immunity from production at the will of the Crown,[30] and an unreviewable discretion where the formula 'if the minister is satisfied' was employed.[31]

The *Wednesbury* case,[32] which belongs in this depressing catalogue of abdication, is another example of failure to apply an elementary rule of public law to an errant authority. A sabbatarian majority which had gained power on Wednesbury council had used its cinema licensing powers, designed to ensure public safety, to ban children from going to the pictures on a Sunday. A more obvious pursuit of a collateral purpose—a textbook *ultra vires* act—is hard to imagine. But what has made the decision ironic is that, before declining to intervene, Lord Greene had set out a tally of grounds for intervention (omitting, among others, the one material to the case) which for an unhelpfully long time became the Bar's catechism.

What many have found particularly surprising is that even in the post-war years a conservative judiciary continued to acquiesce in acts of government which offended not only against public law principles[33] but, almost certainly, against their own convictions. In many ways such abstention did them credit. Professor Zines recalls Sir Raymond Evershed MR speaking in the early 1950s:

It was believed by many when the Attlee government was elected in 1945 that, based on past performance, the courts of England would emasculate any social welfare or other collectivist legislation... He was pleased to say that that had not happened. The judges had not sabotaged the social welfare state.[34]

[27] *R v Minister of Health, ex p Yaffe* [1931] AC 494; cf *Institute of Patent Agents v Lockwood* [1894] AC 347.
[28] *Nakkuda Ali v Jayaratne* [1951] AC 66.
[29] *Smith v East Elloe RDC* [1956] AC 736.
[30] *Duncan v Cammel, Laird and Co* [1942] AC 624.
[31] *Liversidge v Anderson* [1942] AC 206.
[32] *Associated Provincial Picture Houses v Wednesbury Corporation* [1948] 1 KB 223.
[33] Most remarkably, *Franklin v Minister of Housing and Local Government* [1948] AC 87.
[34] Leslie Zines, *Constitutional Change in the Commonwealth* (Cambridge University Press, Cambridge 1991), 36–7.

The criticism, however, was they had not done much else either. It is not possible, with the best will in the world, to look on this period of dormant public law as an exemplar of the rule of law in a democracy.

My own best guess at the reason would be that the judges' sense, in a time of unstable governments and inexperienced ministers, that the central administration of the state was in safe hands, with values and virtues close to the judges' own, disinclined them to intervene even in misgovernment.

V

What then brought about the revival of public law in the last decades of the 20th century? There is always, of course, the Rumsfeldian explanation: stuff happens. But Sir William Wade was never in any doubt that, despite the carry-over of judicial abstentionism into the first two post-war decades, the silent imperative was that no government should again be ceded such unchallenged command of public administration as the Attlee government was allowed. Given that reversing legal policy is like turning a tanker round, this may not be as odd as it sounds; and it has the muted but unmistakable support of what Lord Diplock took the opportunity to say at a time when a recrudescent public law was beginning to flower, using the issue of standing as a window on a much larger issue:

The rules as to 'standing' for the purpose of applying for prerogative orders, like most of English public law, are not to be found in any statute. They were made by judges, by judges they can be changed; and so they have been over the years to meet the need to preserve the integrity of the rule of law despite changes in the social structure, methods of government and the extent to which the activities of private citizens are controlled by governmental authorities, that have been taking place continuously, sometimes slowly, sometimes swiftly, since the rules were originally propounded. Those changes have been particularly rapid since World War II. Any judicial statements on matters of public law if made before 1950 are likely to be a misleading guide to what the law is today.[35]

What is new is the ability and readiness of public law today to call ministers to account on what would once have been regarded as matters of pure administration or—at the other end of the scale—matters of high policy. It calls in turn for a heightened sensitivity on the part of the courts to the separation of powers. But this is not the place for an account of modern public law. Let me instead give one illustration of how far we have now come from the night of the long sleep. The latter part of the story is well known but the early part, I believe, is so far untold.

In the mid-1960s, when Mauritius was due to be accorded full independence, the leader of its largest party, Sir Seewoosagur Ramgoolam, came to London to see the Colonial Secretary, Anthony Greenwood, about the terms of the independence constitution. To his surprise he was received at the Colonial Office not

---

[35] *R v IRC, ex p National Federation of the Self-Employed* [1982] AC 617, 639–40.

by Greenwood but by a senior official, who took him into a room, closed the door and said:

Look, old chap, you have a problem and we have a problem. Our problem is that the Americans want the population of the Chagos Islands removed, and we need somewhere to put them. Your problem is that you don't yet know what system of government you're going to get.

Now, you have a choice. You can be sensible and take the Chagos Islanders, and we'll give you some money to help. In that case you can have a first-past-the post electoral system and you'll be prime minister for ever. Or you can be difficult and refuse to take them, in which case we'll give you proportional representation, and nobody will ever be able to form a stable government. It's a matter entirely for you.

Thirty years after the deportation of the Chagos islanders to Mauritius the Colonial Office files, incautiously unweeded, were placed in the Public Record Office. The resultant litigation[36] is significant for more than one reason. Instead of retrenching behind a plea of high policy formation, the government put all its cards on the table. The judgment of the Divisional Court contains in consequence an informed and severe account of departmental duplicity, culminating in the striking down of the ordinance by which the islanders had been exiled. The government told Parliament that it would accept the court's decision.

The story of the Chagos islanders is not yet over,[37] but the history I have recounted illustrates the sea-change in the judicial control of public administration which occurred between the 1960s and the 1990s. Departmental memoranda with captions like 'Maintaining the fiction' can no longer be written in the confident belief that only their addressees will ever see them. Civil servants who methodically keep their ministers in the dark are, if not a dead, a dying breed. Both ministers and civil servants know—or should know—that it is necessary, or at least prudent, to act within the law. And the courts for their part know—or should know—that it is not their job to run the country: only to ensure, so far as they can, that it is lawfully run.

*

Some years ago I attended an appellate lawyers' congress in Chicago, where Lord Cooke of Thorndon gave an after-dinner talk on the many jurisdictions of which he was or had been a judge. Someone asked him to name the members of the appellate court on which he would most like to sit.

'It wouldn't be right to tell you their names, though I've thought about who they would be' he said, 'But I can tell you that Tom Bingham would be in the chair.'

---

[36] *R v Secretary of State for Foreign and Commonwealth Affairs, ex p Bancoult* [2001] QB 1067 (Laws LJ and Gibbs J).

[37] See now, however, the adverse 3–2 decision of the House of Lords ([2008] UKHL 61), despite Tom Bingham's superb dissenting opinion.

14

The Reflections of a Craftsman

Brian Simpson

In the history of the common law judicial decisions have, from the earliest times, played a central role. So when Chaucer, in the Prologue to the Canterbury Tales, set out to provide a picture of a leading common lawyer of his time he equipped him with just one kind of hardware—a set of law reports:

In bookes had he cas and doomes alle,
That from the time of King Willyam had yfalle.

His common lawyer, thought by some to have been based on a real individual, Sergeant Pinchbec, was a member of the order of serjeants, whose members, some holding the office of justice, and thus possessing adjudicative power, formed the intellectual centre of the system. But over the centuries very few judges, or similarly eminent common lawyers, have made any attempt to give a connected account of what they conceive to be their role, or how they go about the job of adjudication, or that of arguing cases, or of giving considered legal opinions. In the main they do the job, but avoid philosophizing about it, just as artists who belong to a craft tradition leave the theory of art to the critics.

It all reminds me of an incident in Oxford many years ago, when my college, Lincoln, was bequeathed a considerable sum of money by one Paul Shuffrey, to be used, at least in part, to endow lectures, or whatever, on the history of art and its relation in western European culture to the Christian tradition. Some of us, out of line with the normal traditions of Oxford colleges, thought that the money should indeed be spent as the donor had wished. The proposal which secured support was to organize in Oxford an exhibition of the works of Henry Moore, to be accompanied by lectures by the artist on his work; quite what this had to do with the Christian tradition I can no longer recall, but it may be that its lack of connection appealed to my colleagues as reflecting at least some disdain for the wishes of the benefactor. As to the exhibition Henry Moore was entirely agreeable, but he declined to cooperate over the lectures, explaining that if his mission had been to talk about art he would not have dedicated so much of his life to the demanding and difficult task of working as a sculptor. That was what he did—create art, rather than talk about it. So Sir Kenneth Clark was engaged to give the lectures, and Henry Moore sat beside him, occasionally nodding his head or shaking it, but otherwise taking virtually no part in the proceedings. So it is with common law judges. Hence we have to construct our vision of their role and mode of operation from what they do, rather than what they say about what they do.

And this is, in the main, how we have to proceed even in the case of Lord Bingham, a legal craftsman if ever there was one, whose work as a judge is celebrated in this collection, as, in my very humble opinion, it well deserves to be. But in 1990 he delivered a lecture in Oxford on 'The Discretion of the Judge'.[1] Some years later, in 1997, in a collection of essays published in honour of Lord Cooke of Thorndon, he contributed a piece on 'The Judge as Lawmaker: An English Perspective'.[2] And in 2005 he delivered the Maccabean Lecture in Jurisprudence at the Cardiff Law School on the subject: 'The Judges: Active or Passive?' By these and indeed other writings Lord Bingham joined the ranks of the very small number of common law judges who have published their reflections on the judicial role, a minute percentage, surely a very small fraction of 1 per cent, of those who have held judicial office over the 900 or more years during which the common law system has existed. In England they include Sir William Fortescue (circa 1385–1477/79), Sir Edward Coke (1552–1634), Sir Francis Bacon (1561–1626), Sir Mathew Hale (1609–1676), and Sir William Blackstone (1723–1780), though his views were formed before he became a judge in 1770. They include some notable Americans: Benjamin Cardozo,[3] the eccentric Jerome Frank, writing whilst in thrall to the psychoanalysts,[4] and more recently Judge Richard Posner,[5] whose literary output, reinforced by his musings on the Posner-Becker blog on this or that, puts the rest of us to shame, though a shame somewhat alleviated by a slightly smug feeling that there are perhaps some merits and not merely excuses for writers in the injunction *festina lente.* In addition to the Americans, who have the misfortune to live in a world in which disagreements over the judicial function are exacerbated by the decline in the standards of collegiality and even civility in their Supreme Court, there have been a number of Australians, including Sir Owen Dixon[6] and Dyson Heydon,[7] and contributions from elsewhere in the common law world, notably from SP

---

[1] [1990] Denning Law Journal 27, reprinted in *The Business of Judging. Selected Essays and Speeches* (Oxford, 2000).

[2] P Rishworth (ed), *The Struggle for Simplicity in the Law: Essays for Lord Cooke of Thorndon* (Wellington, 1997) at 3–12, reprinted in *The Business of Judging.*

[3] BN Cardozo, *The Nature of the Judicial Process* (Yale, 1921).

[4] J Frank, *Law and the Modern Mind* (London, 1949 but first published in the USA in 1930).

[5] RA Posner, *How Judges Think* (Harvard, 2008) and of his other writings especially *Law, Pragmatism and Democracy* (Harvard, 2003).

[6] See his speech delivered in 1952, 85 CLR xi at xiv, and his article 'Concerning Judicial Method' in 29 ALJ (1956) at 468. See also M Kirby, *Judicial Activism. Authority, Principle and Policy in the Judicial Method* (London, 2004).

[7] D Heydon, 'Judicial Activism and the Death of the Rule of Law' *Quadrant,* January–February 2003 at 9.

Sathe, in *Judicial Activism in India*.[8] There is also of course a very considerable academic literature, much of it coming from the USA, which I do not attempt to list here or in the main consider. Its bulk reflects an understandable unease as to the health of the rule of law in a country whose vast legal system lacks the professional cohesion which is more easy to maintain in a smaller legal world, and one in which the conduct of the judiciary ranges from the admirable through the very respectable to the bizarre.

In the first of these pieces, which I shall only briefly mention here, Lord Bingham is concerned with situations in which its judges are said, in the professional world which they inhabit, to enjoy a discretion in coming to a decision. After pointing out that the concept of judicial discretion has been variously used, he offers his own working definition:

... an issue falls within a judge's discretion if, being governed by no rule of law, its resolution depends on the individual judge's assessment (within such boundaries as have been laid down) of what is fair and just to do in the particular case.[9]

Essentially the concept as he uses it is rooted in the professional legal culture in which he has worked as lawyer and judge. In conformity with this approach in the discussion which follows Lord Bingham takes the position that when a judge gives a ruling on the law he is not exercising a discretion in the sense in which he uses the concept, whilst making it quite clear that he appreciates that some theoretical writers (starting I think with HLA Hart) have applied the concept to this aspect of the judicial role.[10] But, as he puts it, in this lecture he '...side-stepped a very high level philosophical debate...'[11] Hart in his *The Concept of Law* explained the existence of a discretionary aspect of the judicial role in part by reference to what he presented as an aspect of language; he thought of the law as comprising rules in a textual form, and since words in texts have a penumbra in which meaning is uncertain, judges applying such rules must exercise some element of free choice.[12] Though having some plausibility in relation to statute law this theory makes little sense in relation to the common law, which has no authentic text. Lord Bingham does not discuss it. The general drift of Hart's theory tends to explain uncertainty in part also from human inability to foresee the future. He tended to play down the fact that often the root of the problem is not the scope of a given rule, but controversy over what that rule is.

In his 1997 essay on the judge as lawmaker Lord Bingham reviews four schools of thought on the role of judges as lawmakers. Briefly the first is that they have no

[8] Oxford, 2002.   [9] At 36.
[10] See at p 39 where a note cites to writing by HLA Hart, R Dworkin, N MacCormick, and A Barak. Hart's own final views are in the Postscript to the second edition of *The Concept of Law* (Oxford, 1994) at 272–6 where he responds to criticisms by Ronald Dworkin.
[11] At 38.
[12] In *The Concept of Law* this idea is explained by reference to what is called the open texture of language and by using the metaphor of the core and the penumbra. See e.g., 123 and n 4 on 278 and n to 278 on 297.

such role, since it is their job to say what the law is, not to create it. The second is that they do have such a role but should so far as possible pretend that they do not, since otherwise their decisions might lack popular legitimacy. The third is that they do have such a role, whether we like it or not, and the important questions are how they in fact exercise this role, and how they ought to do so. The fourth is that they do have such a role, basically because they enjoy free choice and the power to issue binding rulings, and they should enthusiastically exercise their lawmaking role whenever the call of justice requires this. Lord Bingham locates his own position as belonging to the third school, and, as he says, surely correctly, this is that of most English professional lawyers, or at least of those few who have ever worried their heads about the matter. His essay, in addition to investigating some of the difficulties which arise over the other schools of thought, briefly discusses some of the limitations loosely established in professional culture which either do or ought to restrain judges in their role as lawmakers.

In his 2005 Maccabean Lecture, the second such lecture to be concerned with the judicial role,[13] he addressed the charge which had recently been levelled against the British judiciary by that less than notable jurist, but experienced minister and politician, Michael Howard, of a peculiarly pernicious form of that ill defined vice, 'judicial activism'. For Michael Howard, who for a while presided over the most unhappy of British government departments, the Home Office, had accused the judges of 'aggressive judicial activism', to be distinguished presumably from mere activism, whatever that is. Since the Home Office is in charge of what might be called the mechanisms of domestic repression its activities, be they right or wrong, tend to involve it in embarrassing litigation in the courts, and this has long been the case. There was a time back in the last century when the functions of the department were thought to be twofold: the protection of civil liberty and the preservation of public order.[14] What it conceives its functions to be today is not known, but the protection of civil liberty has, since the passage of the Human Rights Act in 1998, somewhat passed to the judiciary, and it is this which is part of the explanation of the uneasy relationship with the judges. Michael Howard's accusation was an example of this uneasy relationship. In this lecture Lord Bingham further developed the idea that if those who condemn judicial activism as a vice imagine that it is possible for judges to conform perfectly to what he calls, in this lecture, the traditionalist conception of their role, they are seriously misguided. For according to this conception they are merely 'to declare what the common law is, and by implication always has been', but judges, whether they like it or not, do have to make choices between competing contentions arising in litigation, and in doing so they make new law, and always have done. But at the same time Lord Bingham does not reject the traditionalist view entirely; instead he sees merit in the underlying idea which is that it is the role of judges to base their

[13] See Lord Mackay of Clashfern, 'Can Judges Change the Law?', Proceedings of the British Academy (1987) Vol LXXIII, 285–308.

[14] So stated by the then Permanent Under-Secretary, FA Newsam in the preface to *The Home Office* (London, 1954).

decisions on the existing law and not, to put it crudely, on law which they make up as they go along. So the important question in his view is that of establishing 'the elusive boundary between legitimate judicial development of the law on the one hand and impermissible judicial legislation on the other'.[15]

His suggestion is that under established professional conventions judges have to give reasons for their decisions. If the obligation to give reasons is honestly discharged, in the sense that the judge gives what really were his reasons, then it will in principle be possible to say whether the decision has been motivated by proper or improper considerations. So long as it is motivated by proper reasons then it will be possible to disagree as to whether the decision was, as lawyers say, 'correct' or 'incorrect', but the manner in which the decision has been reached will be a legitimate exercise of the judicial role. To put this in another way, the judge will then have acted as judge, and not as legislator. Lord Bingham, as I understand him, is not here seeking to offer some simple rule for defining the elusive boundary, but merely suggesting a way of looking at the matter which makes sense of the intuition of most English lawyers that there is a boundary, even if we may legitimately disagree in particular cases whether it has been crossed or not. Most of the categories in terms of which we understand the world possess elusive boundaries, and are none the worse for that. In explaining this approach Lord Bingham contrasts decisions which are 'legally motivated' as being justified 'on principle, or authority, or the particular facts' in which the judge is exercising his 'legal expertise', with decisions 'motivated not by legal but by extraneous considerations, as by the prejudice or predilection of the judge, or, worse, by any personal agenda of the judge, whether conservative, liberal, feminist, libertarian or whatever'.[16] Insofar as the intuition of professional lawyers is that there is a boundary it must, I think, be determined by professional opinion, and if so then it is bound to be imprecise, and if a particular decision is generally accepted as a legitimate exercise of the judicial function then this will depend at least in part upon the persuasive craftsmanship of the judicial opinion.

One problem with Lord Bingham's argument turns on the requirement that the judge's opinion must be *honest*, in the sense that it sets out what really were the motives for the decision. Thus one possibility, which he does not address, is that of a judge ruling for one side for some improper reason (an extreme example would be after taking a bribe) but coming up, using his legal expertise, with well argued legal justifications. A less problematic case would be where a judge comes to a conclusion, as must not infrequently happen, based on his general sense of what the right decision is, and then tries to construct a respectable and convincing legal justification for the decision.[17] Perhaps in such a case the requirement of

---

[15] See p 21; this way of putting the issue is derived from Lord Goff.

[16] At pp 21–22.

[17] The decision of the *House of Lords in AG v Blake* (27 June 2000) could be thought to be such a case; the majority who favoured preventing the former spy George Blake (described in the leading opinion, incorrectly, as a self-confessed traitor), and clearly conceived to be a villain, from collecting royalties on his book seem to have been somewhat in difficulties in constructing a justification,

honesty would be satisfied if the judge genuinely believed that the legal justifications for the decision were sound ones. There are more radical problems, or so it has been argued. There exists a mass of literature, mainly American, which reflects the idea, perhaps ultimately derived at least in part from Freud, that we simply cannot trust the self-reporting of motivations. So even if a judge honestly believes that he is deciding the case in a particular way because he thinks he is bound to do so because of an earlier decision of an appellate court, he may in reality have been motivated by the attractiveness of the counsel who argued the case on that side, or because of some unhappy incident in his childhood, or something nasty in the woodshed. Richard Posner, himself a very experienced federal judge, in his *How Judges Think*, explores this literature and sets out no less than nine possible models of how judges, it has been argued, 'really' decide cases: the attitudinal; the strategic; the sociological; the psychological; the economic; the organizational; the pragmatic; the phenomenological; and finally what he calls the legalistic.[18] These theories purport to be descriptive of what judges actually do; they are not offered as recipes for what they ought to do, though some of the literature, for example on the economic theory, can be found which confuses description with prescription. All, he thinks, are 'overstated or incomplete' but all have some merit.[19] The legalistic model remains, he argues, 'the judiciary's "official" theory of judicial behavior', especially in relation to the US Supreme Court, which, being a 'political court', as he argues provocatively, at least when it is deciding constitutional cases, is especially in need of what he calls 'protective coloration'.[20] It cannot appear naked and unashamed, given the way it behaves, without there being something of a political crisis. He explains:

Legalism, considered as a positive theory of judicial behavior (it is more commonly a normative theory)[21], hypothesizes that judicial decisions are determined by 'the law' conceived of as a body of pre-existing rules found stated in canonical legal materials.[22]

---

and in the end the Lords by a majority conjured up a principle of contract law to explain their decision. The case was in the event determined without their Lordships apparently being aware that the relationship between Blake and the Crown at the relevant time was non-contractual under well established legal principle. Quite how this point was missed is beyond me.

[18] See ch 1, 'Nine Theories of Judicial Behavior'.   [19] See 19.

[20] His argument on the nature of the court is presented in ch 10. Briefly he relies in part on the supposed nature of the issues of constitutional law which the court has to determine; being political issues they cannot 'by definition be referred to a neutral expert for resolution' (see 272) In part he relies on the fact that the US Constitution, meaning the documentary text, provides such inadequate guidance that it is impossible for the justices to act judicially in interpreting it (see 272). In part he relies on the claim that the issues which the Supreme Court Justices decide are often issues on which there is no public consensus; hence he argues a decision one way or the other is political (see 277). In part he relies on the fact that the Court appears to adopt an inconsistent attitude to *stare decisis*. This list does not claim to be comprehensive. He explains the continued support of legalism by Supreme Court Justices in psychological terms; to acknowledge the essentially arbitrary, personal, subjective, and political nature would open up a 'psychologically unsettling gap between their official job description and their actual job' (see 289). Posner does not address the question whether, if what he says is correct, the Supreme Court can be thought of as a court of law at all, nor does he engage in any comparative study of other countries' supreme and constitutional courts.

[21] I.e., a theory as to how they ought to decide cases.   [22] See in particular at 41.

The other theories have in common the fact that they claim to identify the reality of what courts and judges do which differs from the picture which perfectly honest and respectable judges and lawyers would themselves paint of their work.[23]

Such theories do not really address the consequences which would follow if the theory in question was taken both literally and seriously. Thus suppose it to be the case that judges are *really* self interested utility maximizers, utility including 'money income, leisure, power, prestige, reputation, self respect, the intrinsic pleasure (challenge, stimulation) of the work …', and we all frankly recognized this as a complete explanatory theory, it would seem to be impossible to make much sense of the forms of argument and justification which are currently commonplace in the courts. 'What's in it for us?' would be the matter counsel would need to concentrate upon in arguing a case. They also seem to downplay the fact that the social significance of human behaviour is liable to be distorted unless we accept the description which the actors themselves give of their actions. When two lovers kiss in the moonlight we would miss something important if we said that what they were *really* doing was transmitting oral bacteria, even though it may be true that this is indeed what they are doing. So at best, as Posner himself argues, such theories only serve to illuminate some aspects of judicial behaviour. And they belong to bodies of thought which are distinct from legal thought.

Posner's legalistic theory, stated in its most simplistic form, is not something which I should expect many professional lawyers on this side of the Atlantic to accept, if any at all, and certainly not Lord Bingham. Perversely it may be true, as Posner argues, that its last true home may be in the jurisprudence of that most aberrational of all the supreme or constitutional courts of the Western world, the Supreme Court of the United States. The notion that legal decisions are *determined* by the law, meaning roughly the applicable corpus of specifically legal materials such as reported cases, involves the mistaken assumption that the relationship between general propositions and the 'facts' of cases is that of logical entailment, an absurd idea.

I wish in the remainder of this essay to make some suggestions, necessarily briefly, about some of the other issues to which Lord Bingham's writings on the judicial role have focused our attention.

The first is this. Underlying both much of what Lord Bingham has written on the subject, and much of what others have written, is what amounts to a conundrum. It was identified many years ago by Sir Henry Maine in his discussion of legal fictions as a mechanism of legal change:

With respect to that great portion of our legal system which is enshrined in cases and recorded in law reports, we habitually employ a double language and entertain, as it would appear, a double and inconsistent set of ideas. When a group of facts come before an English Court for adjudication, the whole course of the discussion between the judge

---

[23] Posner does not really address whether the legalistic pretension of Supreme Court Justices are sincere or not, but he seems to think them sincere if misguided. Or perhaps he is just being polite. I myself just cannot tell.

and the advocate assumes that no question is, or can be, raised which will call for the application of any principles but old ones, or any distinctions but such as have long been allowed. It is taken absolutely for granted that there is somewhere a rule of known law which will cover the facts of the dispute now litigated, and that, if such a rule be not discovered, it is only that the necessary patience, knowledge, or acumen is not forthcoming to detect it. Yet the moment the judgement has been rendered and reported, we slide unconsciously or unavowedly into a new language and a new train of thought. We now admit that the new decision *has* modified the law.[24]

This phenomenon is to be found everywhere when what is thought to be the appropriate standard of conduct—whether it concerns adjudication, social entertaining, the burial of the dead or whatever—is at least in part thought to be derived from past practice, and the common law itself evolved out of the practice of the Royal courts.

It may be useful to mention another context in which something like Maine's double talk is familiar. Some years ago I wanted to use the word 'inruption' in a book to be published by the Oxford University Press. Their copy editor objected; there was, she pointed out in an email, no such word. Why not? Because it was not in the Oxford Dictionary, which, recording how words have been used, moves, in defiance of the ghost of Hume, from is to ought. By *describing* how words have been and are used, it *prescribes* how they ought in the future to be used. Hence it serves an adjudicative function in the game of Scrabble. I replied to the query by pointing out that the word was properly formed from latin roots, *in* and *rumpere* (as the copy editor conceded) and, once it appeared in my book, would at once exist as an English word; there was therefore no occasion to alter my text. Once in print 'inruption' could then be recorded in the Oxford dictionaries, and, as if by magic, become correct English, even if it was incorrect at the moment at which the copy reached the printer. I won, but not because my argument was accepted; it turned out that we had both failed to check all the versions of the Oxford Dictionary; it did appear in one of them, somebody else having got there first. So there was in reality nothing to argue about.[25] I was sad that I had thus not achieved the feat of adding a new word to the language, something I had always wanted to do. But insofar as we did argue we were locked in a dispute which seems to me to closely resemble the disagreement between those who conceive of courts as institutions which apply the law and those who conceive of them as making law. What is involved is two different ways of talking about exactly the same phenomenon. When you conform to a social practice you also sustain that practice. If people stop conforming it ceases to be a social practice. If people conform but engage in variations then there will come a time when the old practice has gone and a new practice has come into existence. And the precise definition of the practice may at all times be problematic and disputable. In my world you

[24] HS Maine, *Ancient Law* (Everyman Library edition 1972) at 18–19.
[25] See my *Leading Cases in the Common Law* at 211.

take a bottle of wine to friends who ask you out to dinner. But must it be of good quality? French? Or will Chilean do? Will a box of chocolates be a legitimate substitute? Or flowers? May one return the bottle they brought last time? Can the practice be encapsulated in a rule? And if we do formulate a rule it will have to go something like this:

In English middle class circles it is proper when asked to a friend's home for dinner to take a reasonably good bottle of wine or some acceptable substitute such as a bunch of flowers or a box of chocolates unless they are teetotallers.

This provides guidance, but we still have to decide what to bring on this particular occasion. And whether to wrap it, or, if white, chill it.

Why is it that in relation to the law we employ the two ways of talking which Maine identified? This is a puzzling question, but the explanation has to lie in the existence of conventions of legal argument, which express the ideal of the rule of laws and not of men, and this ties in with Lord Bingham's discussion of the place of reasons in judicial decision taking. The anonymous author of the very first attempt to give a coherent account of the nascent Royal common law, 'Glanvill',[26] was somewhat concerned by the fact that the English laws were not written,[27] but after dealing with this problem he went on to explain that the subject matter of his book was going to be:

... some general rules frequently observed in court which it does not seem to me to be presumptuous to put into writing, but rather very useful for most people and highly necessary to aid the memory.[28]

In saying this Glanvill expressed the view that the essence of the Royal common law was to be sought in the practice of the Royal court, and the understanding that this practice was not simply arbitrary, but was related in some way to the general rules which he set out to expound.

If we move forward some two centuries we find ourselves in a legal world which is in many ways not very dissimilar to what exists today. We have an elaborately organized lay legal profession in which the court-speaking lawyers of the principal Royal civil court, the Court of Common Pleas, have become a guild which monopolizes practice in that Court, and from whom the lay Justices of the

---

[26] Ranulf de Glanvill (c 1130–1190) held the office of Justiciar for Henry II from 1180–1189), and the *Treatise* (c 1187) was written by an official who probably acted either as a justice or as a clerk in the *Curia Regis* under him. Edition by GDG Hall, *The Treatise on the Laws and Customs of the Realm of England Commonly Called Glanvill* (1963).

[27] Glanvill noted the fact that some laws had been 'promulgated about problems settled in council on the advice of the magnates and with the supporting authority of the prince', and one might have supposed that these would count for him as '*lex scripta*', but he did not do so, presumably because such laws were not then embodied in authoritative texts. In any event important members of the council would have not been literate.

[28] I 1–2. The Latin text as in Hall's edition reads: *Verum sunt quedam in curia generalia et frequentius usitata, que scripto commendare non mihi uidetur presumptuosum, sed plerisque perutile et ad iuuandum memoriam admodum necessarium.*

Common Pleas and the King's Bench are selected. We have a complex procedural system under which issues which fall to be determined in litigation are conceived to be either issues of fact, which are with some exceptions judged by lay jurors, and issues of law, both substantive and procedural, which are for the justices to decide, but only (at least in the cases we know much about) after argumentative disputation between the court lawyers and the justices. It is in this world that we first meet with a discussion of the nature of the judicial role.

In 1345 the justices, sitting in the Court of Common Pleas in Westminster Hall, had an argument about the judicial role. Counsel, one Thorpe had raised the subject of how the justices should discharge their function under the rule of law; he argued for respecting tradition. Unless judges did as other judges had done in the past nobody would know what the law was. This provoked Justice Hillary, who seems to have been some sort of early American realist, to explain to him that 'Law is the will of the Justices' *(volunte des justices)*. This seems to have rather shocked another member of the court, the Chief Justice, Stonore, who responded, using very emphatic language, by saying 'Certainly not. Law is reason' *(Nanyl, ley est resoun)*.[29] The argument, which was inconclusive has, one way or the other, been going on ever since. Arguably there is no fundamental conflict involved. Hillary is making the point that the justices possess free will, much as today we say that the judges always have a choice. Stonore is making a normative point that their choices should be exercised rationally. And Thorpe was making a slightly different normative point, which was that judicial decisions should be consistent, and consistency here has to mean consistent with what has been the practice in the past. Much of the elaborate theorizing on the nature of judicial decision juggles with these three points of view.

The convention whereby judges are expected to give reasons publicly for their decisions only seems to emerge in the 17th century,[30] but the idea that legal decisions ought to be consistent with the past, as Thorpe argued, and rational, as Stonore claimed, long preceded this, and underlay the elaborate processes of legal argument recorded in the year books and early reports, which would make no sense otherwise. Both ideas are inherently problematic. So far as the first is concerned the theory was developed (and it is assumed that the process of legal decision was rational) that consistency with the past was to be sought in the consistent application of the legal doctrine which was thought to underlay and explain the past practice of the courts. Various versions of this type of theory can be found from the 15th century onwards,[31] and Lord Bingham quotes an example from

---

[29] Yearbook 19 Edw III No 3 at 377 and following.

[30] In the 16 century and earlier the judges argued publicly *before* coming to a decision, but there was no regular practice of giving an explanation *after* they had privately decided the case. For discussion of this see my *Leading Cases in the Common Law* at 33–4.

[31] I have written about this in 'The Rise and Fall of the Legal Treatise. Legal Principles and the Forms of Legal Literature' in *Legal Theory and Legal History. Essays on the Common Law* (London, 1987) at 273–320, reprinted from U Chicago LR 48 (1981) 265.

the 19th, where Baron Parke said:

Our common law system consists in the applying to new combinations of circumstances those rules of law which we derive from legal principles and judicial precedents; and for the sake of attaining uniformity, consistency and certainty, we must apply those rules, where they are not plainly unreasonable and inconvenient, to all cases which arise; and we are not at liberty to reject them, and to abandon all analogy to them, in those to which they have yet been judicially applied, because the rules are not as convenient and reasonable as we ourselves could have devised.[32]

It will be seen that in this version the law comprises rules derived from precedents and legal principles, which are thus on a higher plain, and that these rules may be departed from or I suppose rejected (or perhaps limited by exceptions) in particular cases if they are *plainly* inconvenient or unreasonable. The idea that rationality can be used to limit respect for consistency with the past, or tradition, is also to be found in Blackstone and other writers.[33]

So far as the concept of rationality is concerned there are a number of difficulties. To act rationally is to act for a good reason, but the reason may not be a conclusive reason, and what counts as a good reason is always contingent. The fact that cyanide kills you is an excellent reason for not swallowing it, but not if you are Heinrich Himmler and have just been captured. In addition what counts as a good reason in legal argument and justification is determined by the conventions accepted in the legal community, itself an ill defined entity, and these conventions may be to a greater or less degree vague, varied, disputed, and changeable. These conventions certainly rule out certain sorts of reason, and legitimate others, but there is a considerable grey area, and sometimes dramatic changes, as when the House of Lords announced that it was no longer absolutely bound to follow its earlier decisions. Hence identifying good reasons in legal discourse is perhaps more a craft than a science. In the common law world legal justification is argumentative and rhetorical, and arguments are there to persuade; persuasion is a craft, and although rhetoric may have principles they are of a very general nature. Further to this in the practical world of legal decision good reasons do not have to be conclusive reasons, and conclusive reasons for most practical decisions do not exist. And what are accepted as being good reasons for acting in a particular way (for example consider good reasons for choosing a restaurant, such a price, quality of food, type of cuisine, location, availability of a table) may point to different results in particular circumstances.

As if all this was not enough the common law system has never operated on the basis that there was a settled and closed list of the sorts of reasons which could count as good reasons, or as lawyers put it serve as authorities. One well known legal theory, that of the late HLA Hart, claimed that there exists a rule or rules

---

[32] *Mirehouse v Rennell* (1833) 1 Cl & F 527, 6 ER 1015 at 1023.
[33] W Blackstone, *Commentaries on the Laws of England* (Oxford, 1765–9) Vol I at 69.

of recognition,[34] but this would only be the case if legal convention embodied the notion that rationality could be reduced to rule, and nobody has ever come close to arguing that this can be or has been done. Hart himself never so much as devoted a paragraph of his book to telling us what the rule or rules of recognition of the common law were or are. So far as consistency with tradition is concerned immense efforts have been devoted to attempting to formulate precise rules of precedent, but those who have made the attempt have run into much the same difficulties.

Lord Bingham has argued that so long as a judge honestly sets out, in his opinion, the reasons for decision, and these are reasons which show that the decision was 'legally motivated', and not motivated by 'extraneous considerations' then the judge is:

… doing what a judge is employed to do, applying his legal expertise to the resolution of the problem raised by the particular case. If his colleagues, or professional or academic opinion, consider that he has erred, that is a ground for questioning the correctness of the decision but it is not a ground for the propriety of his reaching it at all.

I take it that a 'legally motivated' is a legal decision which can be plausibly justified by reasoning which is acceptable within the professional culture in which the judge operates, even if a different decision could also be plausibly justified. Many legal decisions do not excite the attention of ministers and government departments, or parliamentarians, or the media or the public generally, so that acceptability outside the upper reaches of the profession is often not in issue. But sometimes they do, just as wisdom and judgement are qualities which a good judge will employ in order to set for himself what he takes to be the boundaries of the proper role of the judiciary, which will ultimately involve a view as to what is in some very loose sense acceptable. What seems to me to be involved here is necessarily a political decision, or if you like a constitutional decision in a broad sense. Getting it right is an art and not a science.

I began this essay with recalling the lectures given many years ago in Oxford on the work of Henry Moore, and made the point that in the main he took little active part in the lecture series delivered by Sir Kenneth Clark. I do, however, recall two of his interventions, which particularly struck me at the time. One was in response to a question about the holes in some of his sculptures. Why? With eyes sparkling he explained that he found it such fun then, working from both sides, he made them meet in the middle. The second arose in connection with a sculptural group fashioned in white marble that had been exhibited in a church in the Durham coal field; a female form was involved, and the miners would pat appropriate (or if you like inappropriate) areas with their coal dusty hands. In the course of time a rich black patina had developed—ought it not to be cleaned off?

---

[34] Though he conceded the rule or rules might themselves be open-textured. This metaphor is radically different from that of the core and the penumbra.

Henry Moore's response that was how the people enjoyed his work so be it; he was proud and pleased with their interaction with his sculpture. All this was a voice of a craftsman who delighted both in the exercise of his craft, and in its appreciation by the people—all the people, not just arty people.

Lord Bingham concluded his Maccabean Lecture[35] by quoting the late Peter Birks:

Authority in interpretation of the law naturally derives from learning combined with good judgment and discretion in its employment.

and Lord Devlin:

The first quality of a good judge is good judgement.

Lord Bingham has been an advocate in favour of a restrained and disciplined exercise of the lawmaking power of the higher judiciary; judgment and discretion pervade both. In his extra-judicial writings he has given us an insight into the world of a consummate legal craftsman, who, rather like Henry Moore in the world of the artistic craftsman, takes both pride and pleasure in doing a fine job, and takes particular concern to follow the injunction embodied in the first article of the European Convention which is to ensure to everyone, not just some people, within the jurisdiction, the fundamental rights and freedoms which are the basis for a decent society under the rule of law.

[35] At 23.

II

THE INDEPENDENCE AND ORGANIZATION OF COURTS

1

A Supreme Judicial Leader

Brenda Hale

The Supreme Court for the United Kingdom will, we hope, open its doors on 1 October 2009. It will have a fine judicial leader in Lord Phillips of Worth Matravers. But many of us cannot stifle our regret that Lord Bingham is not to be its first President. The Supreme Court is very much his baby. He may not have been the first to moot the idea, but it would scarcely have got off the ground without his enthusiastic support. And without his wise approach to the whole business of Supreme Court judging, the politicians might well have taken fright at where the whole idea might lead. No throwing the baby out with the bathwater from him. His intriguing mix of innovation and prudence means that the Supreme Court may be his most important and long-lasting legacy.

The Idea of a Supreme Court

Labour came to power in 1997 with a programme of constitutional reform, much of it drawing on the work of the Institute for Public Policy Research (IPPR) and later the Constitution Unit at University College London. IPPR had published a draft of a written Constitution for the United Kingdom in 1991, with a fully fledged Supreme Court like those in any other country with a written Constitution. This would have had an original jurisdiction to adjudicate upon cases brought by the governments of Scotland, Wales, Northern Ireland, or the English regions challenging the validity of Acts of Parliament or brought by the UK Government challenging the validity of Acts of the Assemblies. It would also have had an appellate jurisdiction just like that of the current House of Lords, but with an absolute right of appeal against any decision of a lower court holding an Act of Parliament wholly or partly void.[1] Labour's programme was more

---

[1] IPPR Constitution Paper No 4, *The Constitution of the United Kingdom*, 1991, cl 98 and Commentary, pp 88–90. The Liberal Democrats' Federal Green Paper No 13, *We the People… Towards a Written Constitution*, 1990, para 9.1, had also proposed a Supreme Court with power to strike down unconstitutional legislation.

modest but it included three measures which inevitably fuelled the debate about a Supreme Court.

The Human Rights Act 1998 introduced domestic remedies to enforce the rights guaranteed by the European Convention on Human Rights. All the courts have power to do this. The idea that they might have to refer cases to a separate constitutional court was rejected in the preceding white paper.[2] Questions were immediately asked about whether the role of the Lord Chancellor as judge and head of the judiciary was compatible with the Article 6 right to a fair trial before an independent and impartial tribunal.[3] Some even extended the question to the role of the Lords of Appeal in Ordinary as members of the body which makes the laws as well as the body which interprets and applies them. Lord Bingham wisely declined to express a view on this when he appeared before the Joint Committee on Human Rights in March 2001, because he thought it bound to become litigious at some point.[4] Fortunately, no one took the point when the Law Lords came to rule on whether or not the Hunting Act 2004 was a valid Act of Parliament. If they had, what could have been the answer? How could we be qualified to decide upon the meaning and effect of the Parliament Acts 1911 and 1949, which were passed to curtail the legislative powers of the House of Lords, of which we were all members?[5]

Then came the devolution of legislative and executive power to the Scots[6] and Welsh nations[7] and the promise of home rule restored to Northern Ireland.[8] Any federal state requires a court to adjudicate upon whether the devolved institutions have exceeded the powers which the federal Parliament has given them (if not *vice versa*). The obvious candidate was the top court for the whole United Kingdom. But that court was a committee of the Upper House of that federal Parliament. If there were ever to be a full-blown battle between two Parliaments, it would be wrong for members of one of them to be adjudicating that dispute. Lord Lester and Lord Goodhart tabled an amendment to the Scotland Bill to create a new constitutional court.[9] But by then it had already been decided that the devolution job would go, not to the House of Lords, but to the Judicial Committee of the Privy Council, thus not only creating two top courts for the United Kingdom but also glossing over the real problem, because the same judges sit in both places.

Last but not least came reform of the House of Lords. Realizing that if everything had to be done at once, nothing would be done at all, the government's first step was to remove most of the hereditary peers.[10] But what to do next? Any

---

[2] *Rights Brought Home: The Human Rights Bill*, 1997, Cm 3782, para 2.4.

[3] Reinforced by the decision of the European Court of Human Rights in *McGonnell v United Kingdom* (2000) 30 EHRR 289.

[4] Joint Committee on Human Rights, Minutes of Evidence, 26 March 2001, Q 103.

[5] *Jackson v Attorney General* [2005] UKHL 56, [2006] 1 AC 262.

[6] Scotland Act 1998.   [7] Government of Wales Act 1998.

[8] Northern Ireland Act 1998.

[9] Moved by Lord Steel of Aikwood at Report stage because Lord Lester was unavoidably detained and arrived late: see Hansard (HL), 28 October 1998, cols 1963 *et seq.*

[10] House of Lords Act 1999.

move towards an elected Upper House would have to decide what to do about the Bishops and the Law Lords. The Royal Commission on the Reform of the House of Lords saw 'no reason why the second chamber should not continue to exercise the judicial functions of the present House of Lords'.[11] As Lord Bingham tactfully commented:

This was no doubt a reasonable conclusion for the Commission, considering the shape of a reformed chamber, to reach. But it does not address a more fundamental question, whether it is desirable that the House of Lords or a reformed second chamber should exercise judicial functions at all.[12]

The Royal Commission did recommend that the Law Lords should clarify the principles they intended to observe 'when participating in debates and votes in the second chamber and considering their eligibility to sit on related cases'.[13] They responded with a statement read to the House by Lord Bingham soon after he became senior Law Lord:[14]

As full members of the House of Lords, the Lords of Appeal in Ordinary have a right to participate in the business of the House. However, mindful of their judicial role, they consider themselves bound by two general principles when deciding whether to participate in a particular matter or to vote: first, the Lords of Appeal in Ordinary do not think it appropriate to engage in matters where there is a strong element of party political controversy; and secondly the Lords of Appeal in Ordinary bear in mind that they might render themselves ineligible to sit judicially if they were to express an opinion on a matter which might later be relevant to an appeal in the House.

The Lords of Appeal in Ordinary will continue to be guided by these broad principles. They stress that it is impossible to frame rules which cover every eventuality. In the end it must be for the judgment of each individual Lord of Appeal to decide how to conduct himself in any particular situation.

This statement may have been drafted by his predecessor, Lord Browne-Wilkinson, but there is no doubt that Lord Bingham thoroughly agreed with it. As Lord Chief Justice he did from time to time contribute to debates on matters of concern to the Judiciary. As senior Law Lord, he has not done so. There has also been a marked decrease in the contributions from other Law Lords. Their self denying ordinance has also formed an important part of the argument about whether they should be there at all.

The UCL Constitution Unit produced a series of papers discussing the future of the Law Lords and various models for reform.[15] Lord Bingham declared his

---

[11] *A House for the Future*, Cm 4534, 2000, paras 9.1 to 9.5.

[12] JUSTICE Annual Lecture, 'The Evolving Constitution', 4 October 2001.

[13] *A House for the Future*, paras 9.9–9.10 and Recommendation 59.

[14] Hansard (HL), 22 June 2000, cols 419–420.

[15] R Cornes, *Reforming the Lords: the Role of the Law Lords*, Constitution Unit, 1999; A le Sueur and R Cornes, *What do Top Courts Do?*, Constitution Unit, 2000; A Le Sueur and R Cornes, *The Future of the United Kingdom's Highest Courts*, Constitution Unit, 2001; A le Sueur, *What is the future for the Judicial Committee of the Privy Council?*, Constitution Unit, 2001.

support for change in 2001,[16] a view which impressed the House of Commons
Public Administration Committee.[17] He went on to discuss the idea in more
detail in the Constitution Unit Spring lecture in May 2002.[18] Lord Steyn[19]
and Lord Phillips of Worth Matravers, then Master of the Rolls,[20] had also
expressed their support, as did JUSTICE.[21] All in all, it is not surprising that the
Government should have thought that establishing a Supreme Court to take over
the role of the Law Lords would be relatively uncontroversial when the famous
package of constitutional reforms was announced on 12 June 2003.

The case for reform advanced by Lord Bingham was simple. The institutional
structure should reflect the practical reality. The Law Lords are a court and should
be seen to be such. The public and people from overseas should not be misled into
thinking that we are also legislators. We 'do not belong in a House to whose
business we can make no more than a slight contribution'.[22] Furthermore, we
get in the way. There is not enough room for the Parliamentarians to do their job
properly. They may well be sorry to lose the Law Lords as people. The debate on
the constitutional reforms in February 2004 certainly gave every impression that
that was so.[23] But they will not be sorry to get their hands on the offices which the
Law Lords and the judicial office now occupy. Yet there are not enough rooms for
each of the 12 Law Lords to have his or her own office. We share four secretaries
and four research assistants because there is no room for any more. The House
authorities must understandably give priority to the needs of the legislators over
those of the judges.

Of course, there were arguments the other way. Lord Bingham was in a minority among the then serving Law Lords. There was (and still is) a strong element
of 'if it ain't broke, don't fix it'. The Lord Chancellor had already said that he
would not sit 'in any case concerning legislation in the passage of which he had
been directly involved nor in any case where the interests of the executive were
directly engaged'.[24] There are all sorts of advantages in staying in Parliament, and
not just the richness of the surroundings and the cheapness of the catering. The
Law Lords are not dependent on a government department for their resources
but on Parliament which has a direct line to the consolidated fund. Would it
really enhance our independence if our finances had to come from a departmental budget rather than from Parliament?

[16] *Loc cit* n 10.
[17] *The Second Chamber: Continuing the Reform*, 2001–02, HC 494.
[18] *A New Supreme Court for the United Kingdom*, Constitution Unit, 2002.
[19] 'The case for a Supreme Court' (2002) 118 LQR 382.
[20] Interviews in *The Times*, 22 May 2001, and *Independent*, 18 June 2002.
[21] R Smith and R Brander, *A Supreme Court for the United Kingdom*, JUSTICE Policy Paper,
November 2002.
[22] Bingham 2002, p 8.
[23] Hansard (HL), 12 February 2004, cols 1211–1240, 1253–1322, esp Lord Elton at col 1239,
Lord Borrie at col 1262, Lord Norton of Louth at col 1268, and the resounding 'hear hear!' which
greeted Lord Woolf's gratitude that he was still able to take part in the debate, at col 1290. Lord
Bingham, Lord Steyn, and Lord Phillips did not take part.
[24] Hansard (HL), 23 February 2000, col WA 33.

This is now water under the bridge. The argument is over. The search for a suitable building in which to house the new court is also over. Lord Bingham was not much of an enthusiast for the former Middlesex Guildhall. Like other barristers of his generation, he had unhappy memories of appearing there in criminal cases a long time ago. Would it be possible to rid the building of the ghosts of its past as a criminal court? Would it be possible to turn those gloomy courtrooms, built to impress and oppress, replete with docks, jury boxes, witness boxes, and a judge's bench sitting 'halfway up the wall', into bright but dignified spaces in which to debate serious questions of law between judges and lawyers on the same level? At its best, said Lord Bingham, the atmosphere in the House of Lords' hearings is something like a post-graduate seminar.[25] Nor would it be right for the Supreme Court to be sitting in the 'attic of a museum' to the memory of Middlesex.[26]

But the situation of the building could not be better. It sits on the west side of Parliament Square, opposite the Houses of Parliament to the east and between the Treasury to the north and Westminster Abbey to the south. It is exactly the right size to house the Supreme Court and the Judicial Committee of the Privy Council, which will move from its purpose-built premises in Downing Street to share the building. Two of the old courtrooms will be transformed into courts modelled on the committee rooms in the House of Lords, but keeping their old panelling and some of the best of the old carvings. A new double-height courtroom will be created where there were two rather makeshift Crown courts before. The other grand old courtroom will be transformed into a triple height library at the centre of the building, symbolizing how the centuries of development of the 'law in books' are at the centre of the judges' task in interpreting, applying, and developing the law. The facilities for lawyers, litigants, and visitors will be much better than they were before. Those of us who have been working hard to create the best possible working environment for the new Court hope that, even if Edwardian gothic romanticism is not to everyone's architectural taste, the finished product will be something of which Lord Bingham can be proud.

Some of us believe that achieving physical as well as functional separation between the House of Lords and the Supreme Court is worth doing for its own sake. But is it enough? Does it not raise the whole question of what a Supreme Court is for? In his Constitution Unit lecture, Lord Bingham discussed the various models which had been put forward for debate.[27]

One was to combine the appellate committee of the House of Lords with the Judicial Committee of the Privy Council in a single institution. They are, after all, largely staffed by the same judges, although their administration is completely separate. But this would require legislation, and sometimes a constitutional

---

[25] House of Commons Select Committee on Constitutional Affairs, Minutes of Evidence, 11 December 2003, Q 453, Lord Bingham. If so, it is perhaps not clear who is the teacher and who are the taught.

[26] House of Commons Select Committee on Constitutional Affairs, Minutes of Evidence, 25 May 2004, Q 106, Lord Bingham.

[27] A Le Sueur and R Cornes, 2001.

amendment, in all the Commonwealth countries which have kept the right of appeal to the Privy Council. They are unlikely to want their final appeals heard by the Supreme Court of the United Kingdom, the very country from which they have achieved their independence.

Another model was to set up a Constitutional Court along continental lines, separate from the ordinary courts of the land, in order to decide questions of constitutional importance. But this would require us to have a much clearer idea of what was, and was not, a constitutional question than is possible in a country without a written constitution. Lord Bingham has since moved from a position of strong opposition to a codified constitution 'towards agnosticism'.[28]

A third idea was to set up a court on similar lines to the European Court of Justice, to which questions of United Kingdom law could be referred by the courts of each of the three jurisdictions which make up the United Kingdom. This is a neat way of preserving the integrity of the legal systems of each member state in the European Union while achieving some consistency in their interpretation and application of Community Law. But this too would be alien to the common law tradition, in which questions of law are decided in the course of deciding real cases. There is already a school of thought which thinks the House of Lords too far removed from the realities of life. A Supreme Court which could decide abstract questions of law put to it, without having to decide the outcome for the parties to the case, would be even more remote from reality.

Not surprisingly, therefore, Lord Bingham did not warm to any of these alternative ideas. His preference was for the minimalist option:

a supreme court severed from the legislature, established as a court in its own right, re-named and appropriately re-housed, properly equipped and resourced and affording facilities for litigants, judges and staff such as, in most countries in the world, are taken for granted.[29]

Otherwise, it would be business very much as usual. And that is what the Constitutional Reform Act 2005 gives us. No doubt we have Lord Bingham, among others, to thank for the guarantees which it contains of the Court's financial autonomy and independence.[30] The only change is that devolution cases will now come to the Supreme Court rather than to the Judicial Committee of the Privy Council.

But other people have argued that things are not as simple as that. Devolution cases will bring with them a new constitutional role for the new Supreme Court. This is to add to the constitutional roles the Law Lords (along with other courts) already have: protecting the individual from abuses of power by the executive, ensuring that United Kingdom legislation complies with the requirements of

---

[28] Lord Bingham, *A Written Constitution?* Judicial Studies Board Annual Lecture, 2004, p 22.
[29] Bingham, 2002, p 9.
[30] See, e.g., his evidence to the House of Commons' Select Committee on Constitutional Affairs, 25 May 2004.

European Community law, recognizing and enforcing the rights of individuals under the European Convention on Human Rights. Those roles may become more obvious to all, not only to lawyers and Parliamentarians, once the highest court is visibly separate from the legislature. It has been suggested that

institutional separation could result in the Supreme Court becoming a political institution in its own right, in the sense of being subject to increased use and lobbying by pressure and interest groups, many of which believe they are more likely to achieve their ends through the court than through elected representatives.[31]

More than this, it may

ultimately, affect the basis on which our constitution operates... in the long term, it is possible to see parliamentary sovereignty being replaced as the defining principle of the constitution by a more robust version of the separation of powers and a system of checks and balances which recognises the devolved institutions, as well as the Supreme Court, as having a checking function on central government.[32]

Indeed, it has been argued that

the debate about the Supreme Court has been a shadow debate, purporting to be about the independence of the judiciary, but vitiated by its reliance on a superficial and formalistic conception of judicial independence and by confusion over the true motive for reform: the desire to move the United Kingdom incrementally towards a constitutionally limited political order.[33]

It is difficult to believe that any such idea was in the minds of the politicians and civil servants who were responsible for the Consultation Paper which followed the announcement of the new Supreme Court on 12 June 2003.[34] Nor does it chime with the approach which Lord Bingham himself has taken to constitutional adjudication. Few judges have done more to uphold the essential liberties of the subject while reassuring the politicians that their Parliamentary sovereignty is undiminished. His distinctive intellectual stance is marked by respect for the recent decisions of the elected legislature, for the international obligations the United Kingdom has undertaken, and for the long-standing common law principles of personal freedom and fair trials, which he thinks are enhanced rather than undermined by the European Convention.[35]

---

[31] D Woodhouse, 'The constitutional and political implications of a United Kingdom Supreme Court' (2004) 24 Legal Studies 134, 144, referring to D Robertson, 'The House of Lords as a Political and Constitutional Court. Lessons from the Pinochet Case' in D Woodhouse (ed), *The Pinochet case: a Legal and Constitutional Analysis*, (Hart Publishing, Oxford, 2000), and C Harlow, 'Public Law and Popular Justice' (2002) 65 MLR 1.

[32] Ibid, pp 152, 153.

[33] J Webber, 'Supreme Courts, independence and democratic agency' (2004) 24 Legal Studies 55, 71.

[34] Department for Constitutional Affairs, *Constitutional Reform: A Supreme Court for the United Kingdom*, CP 11/03, July 2003.

[35] See, e.g., Joint Committee on Human Rights, Minutes of Evidence, 26 March 2001, esp QQ 127 and 134, Lord Bingham.

This is well-illustrated in the three cases which have come before the House of Lords to challenge the Hunting Act 2004. The first had nothing to do with human rights or European community law. In *R (Jackson) v Attorney-General*,[36] the Act was said to be invalid because it had been passed without the consent of the House of Lords, under the procedures laid down in the Parliament Act 1911 as amended by the Parliament Act 1949 which had also been passed without the consent of the House of Lords. All nine Law Lords had no difficulty in rejecting the argument that the 1911 Act procedure could not be used to amend that procedure. Nor was there any problem with rejecting the views expressed in the Court of Appeal, that the procedure might not be used to effect fundamental constitutional change.[37] Lord Bingham thought that completely unhistorical, given that the whole object of the 1911 Act was to enable Parliament to legislate for home rule for Ireland and the disestablishment of the Church in Wales.[38] But the other Law Lords thought that there was at least one limitation on what could be done under the 1911 and 1949 Acts: neither directly nor indirectly could they be used to prolong the life of a Parliament beyond five years.[39] Lord Bingham disagreed.[40] Still less did he associate himself with any of the wider *obiter dicta* on the possible limits of Parliament's power to legislate to subvert the rule of law itself.[41]

The next two cases were heard together. In *R (Countryside Alliance) v Attorney General*,[42] the claim was that the Act was an unjustified and discriminatory interference with the right to respect for private and family life under Article 8 of the European Convention on Human Rights; with the right to freedom of assembly and association under Article 11; and with the peaceful enjoyment of property under Article 1 of the First Protocol. There was no doubt that Article 1 of the First Protocol was engaged and a possibility that Article 11 was also engaged. But Lord Bingham had no difficulty in finding the interference justified. He had done some research on the history of legislation to prevent cruelty to animals. The British had led the world. These attempts began in 1800 with a Bill to ban bull-baiting. This was rejected but in 1822 an Act was passed to prevent the cruel and improper treatment of cattle, horses, and sheep. The Society for the Prevention of Cruelty to Animals was founded in 1824 and became the Royal Society in 1840. Numerous statutes followed. 'The familiar suggestion that the British mind more about their animals than their children does not lack a certain foundation of fact.'[43] The arguments against such legislation were always the same: that it was

---

[36] [2005] UKHL 56, [2006] 1 AC 262.
[37] [2005] EWCA Civ 126, [2005] QB 579.
[38] [2005] UKHL 56, [2006] 1 AC 262, para 31.
[39] Lord Nicholls, para 59; Lord Steyn, para 79; Lord Hope, paras 118, 122; Baroness Hale, paras 163, 164; Lord Carswell, para 175; Lord Brown, para 194.
[40] Para 32.
[41] Lord Steyn, para 102; Lord Hope, paras 104, 107, 120; Baroness Hale, para 159.
[42] [2007] UKHL 52, [2007] 3 WLR 922.
[43] Ibid, para 37.

an unwarranted interference with the freedom to do as one pleases with one's time and property; and that it was selective or inconsistent. But just because one does not do something else that may also be justified does not mean that the things one does do cannot be justified. Above all:[44]

Here we are dealing with a law which is very recent and must (unless and until reversed) be taken to reflect the conscience of a majority of the nation. The degree of respect to be shown to the considered judgment of a democratic assembly will vary according to the subject matter and the circumstances. But the present case seems to me pre-eminently one in which respect should be shown to what the House of Commons decided. The democratic process is liable to be subverted if, on a question of moral and political judgment, opponents of the Act achieve through the courts what they could not achieve in Parliament.

For the same reasons, in *R (Derwin) v Attorney General*,[45] he held that, if (which was not clear) the ban did engage the right to free movement of goods and the freedom to provide services under Articles 28 and 49 of the EC Treaty, it was justified. The question did not have to be referred to the European Court of Justice in Luxembourg.

Thus the recent and carefully considered expression of the will of the people justified putting limits to what might otherwise have been fundamental rights. To similar effect were his judgments upholding the recently re-enacted ban on political advertising[46] and the ban on corporal punishment in all schools.[47] It is interesting to speculate upon whether he would have thought it proper for the House to impose its own view of the Convention compatibility of 1980s legislation in Northern Ireland which restricts the right to apply to adopt jointly to married couples.[48] Would he have taken the view that, as this might well lie within the margin of appreciation which Strasbourg would allow to member states, it was open to the United Kingdom courts rather than to the competent United Kingdom legislature[49] to decide whether the continued discrimination against unmarried couples could be justified?

Lord Bingham has certainly been cautious about determining the content of the Convention rights. Thus 'judicial recognition and assertion of the human rights defined in the Convention is not a substitute for the processes of democratic government but a complement to them'.[50] If rights are to be implied into the express words of the Convention, the process 'is one to be carried out with

---

[44] Ibid, para 45.   [45] [2007] UKHL 52, [2007] 3 WLR 922.

[46] *R (Animal Defenders International) v Secretary of State for Culture, Media and Sport* [2008] UKHL 15, [2008] 2 WLR 781.

[47] *R (Williamson) v Secretary of State for Education and Employment* [2005] UKHL 15, [2005] 2 AC 246.

[48] *Re P and Others (Northern Ireland)* [2008] UKHL 38, [2008] 3 WLR 76. Is this, perhaps, a case in which the constitution of the committee might have influenced the result?

[49] In this case, the Northern Ireland Assembly.

[50] *Brown v Stott (Procurator Fiscal, Dunfermline)* [2003] 1 AC 681, 703 (decided on 5 December 2000, before the introduction of neutral citation numbers).

caution, if the risk is to be averted that the contracting parties may, by judicial interpretation, become bound by obligations which they did not expressly accept and might not have been willing to accept'.[51] While decisions of the European Court of Human Rights are not strictly binding, we should follow any 'clear and constant jurisprudence' of the court:

This reflects the fact that the European Convention is an international instrument, the correct interpretation of which can be authoritatively expounded only by the ECtHR ... It is of course open to member states to provide for rights more generous than those guaranteed by the Convention, but such provision should not be the product of interpretation of the Convention by national courts, since the meaning of the Convention should be uniform throughout the states party to it. The duty of national courts is to keep pace with the Strasbourg jurisprudence as it develops over time, no more, but certainly no less.[52]

Once again we have an approach which is redolent of democratic sensitivity. Parliament has given us the task of enforcing the Convention rights. But the rights concerned are primarily those defined by Strasbourg. This does not, of course, mean that Lord Bingham is not prepared to hold that what Parliament has done is contrary to the Convention. In the famous *Belmarsh* case,[53] he led the way in holding that the power to detain foreign suspected terrorists without trial contravened the Convention. But this was because Parliament, by enacting the 1998 Act, had 'given the courts a very specific, wholly democratic mandate':

I do not in particular accept the distinction which [the attorney general] drew between democratic institutions and the courts. It is of course true that the judges in this country are not elected and are not answerable to Parliament. It is also of course true...that Parliament, the executive and the courts have different functions. But the function of independent judges charged to interpret and apply the law is universally recognised as a cardinal feature of the modern democratic state, a cornerstone of the rule of law itself. The Attorney General is fully entitled to insist on the proper limits of judicial authority, but he is wrong to stigmatise judicial decision-making as in some way undemocratic.[54]

This was not a decision lightly reached. It was strongly influenced by the traditional role of the courts in protecting liberty. It was also strongly influenced by the traditional concept of equality before the law. In the words of Hersch Lauterpacht, 'The claim to equality before the law is in a substantial sense the most fundamental of the rights of man'.[55] Wherever possible, Lord Bingham appeals, not only to the modern notion of universal human rights, but also to the more ancient respect of the common law for freedom and fair trials. A notable example is the second *Belmarsh* case,[56] on the admissibility of evidence which may have

[51] Ibid.
[52] *R (Ullah) v Special Adjudicator* [2004] UKHL 26, [2004] 2 AC 323, para 20.
[53] *A v Secretary of State for the Home Department* [2004] UKHL 56, [2005] 2 AC 68.
[54] Ibid, para 42.
[55] Ibid, para 46; quoting H Lauterpacht, *An International Bill of the Rights of Man*, 1945, p 115.
[56] *A v Secretary of State for the Home Department (No 2)* [2005] UKHL 71, [2006] 2 AC 221.

been obtained by torture, where it came as no surprise that Lord Bingham held that fairness required that the government prove that the evidence was admissible rather than the other way about. Nor did it come as any surprise that, in the control order cases, he would favour a broad application of the concept of deprivation of liberty[57] and a procedure which would keep non-disclosure of the evidence to a minimum and refuse the application if there could not be a fair trial.[58]

Lord Bingham himself would deny that he brings a consistent philosophy to the business of judging. He would hate to be thought of, as so many judges are, as a claimants' judge or defendants' judge, a prosecution-minded judge, or a judge who stands up for the women and children. In his Maccabaean lecture on Jurisprudence,[59] he set out to define the 'elusive boundary between legitimate judicial development of the Law on the one hand and impermissible judicial legislation on the other'. The acid test, he suggested, is whether the decision is 'legally motivated', or whether it is

not in truth legally motivated. This will be so if the decision is motivated not by legal but by extraneous considerations, as by the prejudice or predilection of the judge or, worse, by any personal agenda of the judge, whether conservative, liberal, feminist, libertarian or whatever.[60]

No-one could accuse Lord Bingham of that sort of personal agenda. His judgments are always fully reasoned by reference to a wide range of legal materials. They never give the impression that he has decided what he wants the answer to be and then found the reasoning to support it. As a Presider he is adept at moving counsel on with an elongated 'ye-e-e-es'. But he rarely gives an indication of what his decision will be. Indeed, when the Committee give their views immediately after the hearing is over, one by one from the most junior to the most senior, we often do not know what Lord Bingham is going to say. We do not formally discuss the case in advance, as is the custom in the Court of Appeal. We may not have declared our views while the hearing is going on. But what he does say will be hugely influential and may well persuade the others to change their minds. It is not unknown to hear four views going one way, and then to hear Lord Bingham going the other way, after which the four eventually decide to come round to Lord Bingham's point of view. Even when he is in the minority, one often has a sneaking sense that history will prove him right.[61]

---

[57] *Secretary of State for the Home Department v JJ* [2007] UKHL 45, [2008] 1 AC 385.

[58] *Secretary of State for the Home Department v MB, Secretary of State for the Home Department v AF* [2007] UKHL 46, [2008] 1 AC 440; thus using the interpretative obligation in the Human Rights Act 1998, s 3(1), to produce the reverse of what Parliament intended.

[59] 'The Judges: Active or Passive' (2006) 139 *Proceedings of the British Academy* 55; see also Tom Bingham, *The Business of Judging*, (OUP, Oxford, 2000) Part I.

[60] Ibid, p 70.

[61] Whether one is also in the minority, as in *YL v Birmingham City Council* [2007] UKHL 45, [2008] 1 AC 95, or in the contrary majority, as in *Attorney-General for Jersey v Holley* [2005] UKPC 23, [2005] 2 AC 580 or *Kay v Lambeth London Borough Council, Leeds City Council v Price* [2006] UKHL 10, [2006] 2 AC 465.

But although his view is hugely influential, he has never sought to dissuade others from expressing theirs. Under his leadership, there has never been any question of discouraging dissent or encouraging a single majority judgment. But in suitable cases where the decision is unanimous, he has encouraged resort to the device of a single report from the appellate committee[62] rather than a series of separate 'speeches', even if in the usual polite formula.

The reason why his views are so hugely influential with his colleagues is that they are the product of a great intellect with a particular cast of mind: the mind of a scholar who was first trained in history, who has a deep respect for the enduring traditions and fundamental principles of the common law, who understands what international cooperation is all about, and above all, who believes in Parliamentary democracy and the rule of law. Under his leadership, there could be little risk that human rights adjudication would get out of hand, or that a Supreme Court would get above itself. Without him, it might be doubted whether the politicians would ever have taken the risk. That is why we must work to make the Supreme Court a legacy which is worthy of him.

[62] The first was in *R v Forbes* [2001] 1 AC 473.

2

Sweden's Contribution to Governance of the Judiciary*

John Bell

The theme of this chapter is that Sweden has managed to create an approach to the governance of the judiciary which meets the contemporary need to secure accountability of the judiciary whilst respecting judicial independence. In the context of New Public Management, the English judiciary really has yet to develop a coherent view and to relate it in a sensible way to the notion of judicial independence.[1] Andrew Le Sueur[2] has described this as an 'emerging debate' and sees in the 2005 reforms potential lines for development, but the mechanisms are still underdeveloped. By contrast, Sweden already has systems both for the governance and the management of the judiciary which avoid some of the pitfalls of judges doing their own thing or of judges being too dominated by the short-term needs of the executive.

1 Introduction

1.1 Tensions in the governance of the judiciary

A major problem in designing an appropriate governance framework for the judiciary lies in the tension between competing conceptions of justice. There are two prevalent conceptions of justice as delivered by the judiciary. On the one hand, justice can be viewed as a human right. Each individual has a right to access justice and to receive an impartial determination of complaints according to law. These ideas are enshrined in the European Convention on Human Rights. As a

* First published in (2007) 50 Scandinavian Studies in Law 83.
[1] See P Seago, C Walker, and D Wall, 'The Development of the Professional Magistracy in England and Wales' [2000] Crim LR 631, 650–1 and 640; G Drewry, 'Judicial Independence in Britain' in R Blackburn (ed), *Constitutional Studies* (London 1992), 160.
[2] A Le Sueur, 'Developing mechanisms for judicial accountability in the UK' (2004) 24 Legal Studies 73.

right, justice is an entitlement that is owed to all, except in the face of the most imperative public interest requirements.[3] If a person has a right, then it should not be denied. As a public service, justice is only one of the resources that the state makes available for the functioning of social life. It sits alongside services such as education and health, security and sanitation. It competes for the same resources and legislative time. In this context, it makes sense to say that the country will have less justice and more health. These two are competing conceptions. Legal professionals are likely to appeal to the first, rights conception. Concepts such as judicial independence are invoked to justify and support this idea.

These competing conceptions of justice lead to different answers to the key governance questions that need to be asked. The first question is the extent to which government should take an active part in defining and managing the activity. Conceiving justice as one public service among many, the government has the role at least as purchaser of this service on behalf of society at large. It can decide how much it wants and for what it can pay. By contrast, where justice is a right and rights are defined as specially protected interests that may conflict with the interests of the majority, then it is less clear that the government, as representative of the majority, should define the service that is provided. In this context, it is argued that the judiciary, as independent guardians of rights, should play a significant role in determining how the service is run. So the governance questions also involve the extent to which the professionals should have a say in the way the service is designed. The argument would be that the professionals here are more than civil servants; they occupy a guardianship role in securing the social values that justice involves.

Depending on which conception of justice is adopted, then there are consequences for the kind of accountability that is required. If justice is a public service, then those who deliver the public service should be accountable in much the same way as any other person delivering a public service. If, on the other hand, justice has to be protected specially, then a special form of accountability will be appropriate. It seems to me that Sweden has (properly) adopted the public service model of justice and has set in place structures of governance that reflect this. By contrast, England is caught in a tension between the judiciary and legal professions, which adopt a rights-based model, and the government, which adopts a public service model.

1.2 Management issues

Apart from the high level of governance, there is also the question of management. To deliver justice in concrete situations requires organization and planning. People need to be employed to service courts; buildings need to be constructed and so on. Bodies need to be set up and then be given authority and budgets to carry on their task, and they should be required to report on their performance.

---

[3] RM Dworkin, *Taking Rights Seriously* (London 1978), ch 3.

The model that has become popular recently in England and Spain is that there should be two distinct organizations. On the one hand, there is an agency or body responsible for the judges, their appointment, education and training, as well as their careers. On the other hand, there is a service agency that is responsible for buildings, support services and other infrastructure.[4] This dual agency model reflects the tension between justice as a right, dispensed by the judges, and the infrastructure of justice as a public service. In practice, the two are closely linked, but in theory, they can be kept separate. Judicial independence is respected by allowing the judges a significant say in the way in which fellow judges are appointed and their careers are managed. All the same, judicial effectiveness is constrained by the resources placed at their disposal. Cases cannot be resolved if there are too few judges, too few courtrooms, or too few support staff to enable the courts to function. As a result, the role of judges as resource managers can be critical for the character of justice. There is a tension in resource terms between the two and a tension in accountability for the outcome. In Sweden, the two issues are seen as integrally connected through a single agency, Domstolsverket (DV).

1.3 Accountability

Judicial accountability is also a difficult area. For the most part in relation to individual decisions, judges have relied on giving reasons predominantly in a way that is understood within the legal community. This protects the judges in relation to individual outcomes, but is less satisfactory in terms of the way in which justice in general is delivered. Accountability for the pattern of lawmaking that emerges from the higher courts and the effectiveness of routine decisions in the lower courts are both important matters. As justice becomes conceived less as an act of state authority and more as a public service, so the demands for accountability for the system grow. Many higher courts on the continent produce annual reports, justifying and opening to scrutiny their effectiveness and key decisions.[5] In many systems, however, the information is gathered internally by the Ministry of Justice and produced as a set of annual statistics without a serious attempt to produce a publicly available narrative explanation and justification for what has been happening. This is most clearly the case in England. On the whole, systematic public accountability happens most explicitly in Spain and Sweden where an independent agency runs the judiciary. It has to operate within a framework set by a ministry or parliament and respond to it. In a sense, judicial independence is maintained by explicitness on both sides about what is expected and what is being delivered. Without an agency, there is often less explicitness both about expectations and delivery.

---

[4] See further J Bell, *Judiciaries within Europe* (Cambridge 2006).
[5] E.g., the French Cour de cassation and the Conseil d'Etat both produce annual reports to the Minister of Justice, which contain both statistics and syntheses of major judicial decisions, as well as critical reflections on major legal issues.

The freedom of judges to enforce justice as they see it within the mission that they have been given is a relatively recent area of controversy. In part, this is because the judicial system was seen in the past as one of the natural areas of government activity, like lawmaking, policing, and the military, expenditure on which required little justification. As the judicial system has been reconceived as one public service competing with others for a finite pot for public expenditure, this automatic expenditure has come into question. At the same time as justice has come under increasing demand from a variety of groups in society, so the judiciary has perceived the need to be more forceful in arguing for control over what it perceives to be its necessary share of that pot. The legal professionals have increased their demands, but the way of creating responsibility and accountability for expenditure has been more difficult to establish. The creation of agencies which are seen explicitly to be negotiating how resources are allocated is a feature that has become important in Sweden and Spain, but is less transparent in England.

2 Judicial Independence

Judicial independence is a widely cited principle, but in relation to the Government and the management of the judiciary, it needs to be invoked with caution. In particular, the ideas of judicial independence and judicial self-government are often linked in contemporary discussions.[6] For example, Article 6 of the European Judges Charter provides that:

The administration of the judiciary must be carried out by a body that is representative of the Judges and independent of any other authority.

The closest to this idea is the Italian Consiglio Nazionale della Magistratura, which is elected by the judiciary and manages judicial careers.[7] This idea of judicial self-government is gaining ground in countries like Denmark, whose Courts Administration Agency is responsible to Parliament for the whole organization of justice, within the budget given by the Parliament. It is an idea that has been voiced in England by leading judges, not least in the face of attempts by the Lord Chancellor to limit the cost of the provision of the court system.[8] This has culminated in making a judge, the Lord Chief Justice, the person in charge of the judicial system. By contrast, in Sweden, the distinct agency responsible for the judicial system, including the recruitment and management of judges, is composed of

[6] See the German judges union's resolution of 15 November 2002 from its website: <http://www.drb.de/pages/html/texte/beschluss_sv.html>. See also Lord Woolf, 'The Rules of Law and A Change in the Constitution' [2004] CLJ 317, 322–3.
[7] See C Guarnieri, *Magistratura e politica in Italia* (Il Mulino, Bologna 1993).
[8] See N Browne-Wilkinson, 'The Independence of the Judiciary in the 1980s' [1988] PL 44, 53–7.

non-government members, only some of whom are judges. It operates like any executive agency, with the government setting a framework of principles and a budget. But then it can decide how it operates, subject to making an annual report. The agency is also involved in performance appraisal. Whether the agency is a constitutional body as in Spain or an administrative body as in Sweden, the emphasis is on judicial independence from the routine of ordinary politics. But in both cases, the agency responsible for the judiciary has members who are not judges and who are appointed by either Parliament or by the government.

The problem with the appeal to 'judicial independence' is the term used to explain a number of different ideas. The first is freedom from political pressure on individual judges. Judges should be free in coming to their decisions. The idea of freedom from interference is the longest standing idea, but it involves a number of distinct issues. Interference in individual cases must be distinguished from interference in the judicial career, notably appointment and dismissal. In this latter area, political involvement in individual appointments has to be distinguished from political direction of the judicial and courts system as a whole. There are different levels of involvement here. Whilst no one would argue that the judge's decision should be dictated by politicians, and few would argue that a judge should owe his appointment simply to allegiance to a political party, there are fewer misgivings about the idea that the judiciary should be representative of a diversity of political opinions and that, therefore, political opinions should be a relevant factor in determining the composition of the judicial bench as a whole. In order to draw a relevant distinction between these situations, we should distinguish between the independence of individual judges, which should be strongly protected, and the freedom of the judiciary as a whole from political influence. At some level, many systems would accept political direction of the legal system as a whole. The Judges Charter appears to contradict this by asking for the judges to be managed by a body independent of politics.

Of course, the idea of sanctions or rewards given to individual judges in relation to their decisions would be particularly worrying. It leads potentially to a denial of justice where an individual has a concrete entitlement to an outcome, or at least to a due process. For similar reasons, countries are usually more insistent that the dismissal of judges be justified than their appointment. Institutions such as the Latin 'High Council of the Judiciary' started by giving judges and others control over the disciplining of judges, and extended by degrees into involvement in judicial appointments and promotions, to judicial dominance of all these procedures. The term was invented in France to describe the idea of an institution which would protect the independence of the judiciary by dealing with dismissals.[9]

But when it comes to managing the judicial service and setting its budgets, then we are not dealing with potential interference with individual cases, but

    [9] C Guarnieri and P Pederzoli, *The Power of Judges. A Comparative Study of Courts and Democracy* (Oxford 2001), 21–2.

with the setting of priorities between categories of legal activity, and this involves giving a direction to society, which is an inherently political activity. The suggestion that the judiciary should be given untrammelled authority in this area is seriously problematic.

3 Problems with the English Model

3.1 The constitutional changes of 2003–2007

Until 2003, the Lord Chancellor was both a senior judge (presiding judge of the House of Lords) and a government minister responsible for the courts system.[10] The proposals to abolish the office of the Lord Chancellor were sprung on the judiciary (and the wider political community) in June 2003. Judicial criticism of the proposals, including the creation of a supreme court, led to discussions within the Judges' Council and between the Department for Constitutional Affairs (as the Lord Chancellor's Department had become) and senior judges. The result was a 'concordat' between Lord Woolf CJ on behalf of the judges and the Lord Chancellor in which the responsibilities of the judges and ministers were made clear, before the Constitutional Reform Bill was laid before Parliament.[11] The public image was of a deal brokered between a union leader and a minister to enable the latter to secure the safe passage of legislation. Indeed, when a former law lord successfully blocked the legislation by securing that it be referred to a select committee for further scrutiny, Lord Woolf spoke against the delay.[12]

Under the new arrangements of the Constitutional Reform Act 2005, the responsibility for the judiciary has moved from the Lord Chancellor to the Lord Chief Justice. Since April 2006, the Lord Chief Justice inherited some 400 statutory duties from the Lord Chancellor. His principal duties are representing, directing, and managing the judiciary. As a *chief spokesperson*, he represents the views of the judiciary of England and Wales to Parliament and government. Like the heads of the Scottish and Northern Irish judiciaries, he will have the right to make written representations on behalf of the judiciary to Parliament, the Lord Chancellor, and ministers in general. These powers under sections 5 and 7 formalize the practices of recent times, most notably illustrated by the concordat of 2004. As *director of the judiciary service*, he is responsible for the welfare, training, and guidance of the judiciary in England and Wales within resources made available by the Minister of Justice. In this capacity, the Lord Chief Justice discusses with government the provision of resources for the judiciary. The budget comes through what will soon be the Ministry of Justice and

---

[10] At one time the Home Office was responsible for the magistrates' courts, which deal with the majority of criminal cases, but these were transferred to the Lord Chancellor's Department in the 1990s.

[11] See the statement of Lord Falconer, Hansard HL, 26 January 2004, cols 13–17.

[12] *The Times*, 9 March 2004.

it determines the key performance indicators. Judicial salaries are determined by the Ministry of Justice in the light of a report by an independent body on senior salaries. The Lord Chief Justice shares responsibility with the Lord Chancellor for the Office for Judicial Complaints, the body which investigates complaints made against judicial office holders. As a *manager*, he oversees the deployment of judges and allocation of work in courts in England and Wales. The Lord Chief Justice is responsible for personnel management. Connected to him, but outside his control, is the process for appointing judges (which is the province of the Judicial Appointments Commission), nor is he responsible for premises and support (Her Majesty's Court Service). Instead he is responsible for judicial work allocation and judicial training (delivered by another agency, the Judicial Studies Board). In addition to these executive roles, the Lord Chief Justice continues to be a *judge*. He is President of the Courts of England and Wales. He sits in important criminal, civil and family cases. He gives judgments and lays down practice directions in many of the most important appeal cases. He also chairs the Sentencing Guidelines Council, a public body designed to support sentencers in their decision-making, and encourage consistency in sentencing throughout the court system.

The Lord Chief Justice is constituted as a one-person quango (a non-departmental executive body), supported by a body of civil servants located in the Law Courts in the Strand, the Judicial Office. All the powers vest in him and not in an agency as in Spain, Denmark, or Sweden. The Lord Chief Justice has created, on his one initiative and without statutory authority, two advisory bodies, the Judicial Executive Board and the Judges' Council. To quote the description given on his website:

The Lord Chief Justice primarily exercises through the Judicial Executive Board his executive responsibilities for:

a. providing leadership, direction and support to the judiciary of England and Wales;
b. determining the structure roles and responsibilities of the judiciary;
c. developing policy and practice on judicial deployment, authorisations, appointment to non-judicial roles and general appointments policy;
d. putting forward the requirements for new appointments of High Court Judges and Lords Justices of Appeal and holding discussions on specific appointments with the Judicial Appointments Commission and the Lord Chancellor;
e. considering general policy on complaints;
f. directing the judicial communications strategy through the Judicial Communications Office;
g. managing the judiciary's overall relationship with the Executive branch of Government and Parliament, overseas relations and other jurisdictions and bodies, including the legal profession;
h. considering and making recommendations on the spending review priorities, targets and plans as they affect the judiciary and the financing and resources for the court system;

i.   approving the annual budget for the Judicial Offices and approving the agreement with the Permanent Secretary on resources;

j.   setting clear objectives, priorities, and standards for the Judicial Office and monitoring its performance;

k.   overseeing the responsibilities of the Judicial Studies Board for training.[13]

But the members of the Judicial Executive Board are seven senior judges with no outsiders. He chairs the Judges' Council.[14] In the past, this has had a variety of forms. From 1873 until 1981, there was a statutory Judges' Council, set up to review the implementation of the Judicature Act of 1873. From 1988 until 2002, there was an informal Judges' Council covering only senior judges. In 2002, this was dissolved and replaced by a body which included of all the judiciary, now including magistrates and tribunal members. It now includes all the judges, but is dominated by the senior judges. It operates mainly through its executive, which has representatives of all levels of the judiciary. It nominates the judicial members of the Judicial Appointments Commission. The informal Judicial Councils have been convened to discuss matters of general interest, especially at moments of turmoil. Famously, the courts were shut for half a day while the judges debated the reforms proposed in Lord Mackay's Green Papers of 1988.[15] The judges used this mechanism to make formal representations to the 2003 consultation on judicial appointments. In one sense, it operates as a collective voice of the judiciary, but in another it does not operate like a union in the same way that continental judicial unions work.

The problem is that there is no real external governance or accountability built into the model. In terms of governance, there is no independent body that tells the Lord Chief Justice what the policies for the judiciary should be. There is no specific group of people to be involved. The planning for judicial numbers, etc., as part of the Comprehensive Spending Review is conducted by the Ministry of Justice. The contribution of the Lord Chief Justice is significant, but not a matter of public record. The Lord Chief Justice can make representations to the Houses of Parliament, but this is not a very clear process.

In terms of accountability, there is no obvious accountability. As David Feldman has pointed out, the judiciary is accountable for the individual decisions it gives by the reasons that are offered as justifications.[16] Judges have relied on giving reasons predominantly in a way that is understood within the legal community. This protects the judges in relation to individual outcomes, but is less satisfactory in terms of the way in which justice in general is delivered. Accountability for the pattern of lawmaking that emerges from the higher courts

---

[13]   <http://www.judiciary.gov.uk/about_judiciary/governance_judiciary/organisation_judiciary/jeb.htm>

[14]   Lord Justice Thomas, 'The Judges' Council' [2005] PL 608.

[15]   RL Abel, *English Lawyers between Market and State* (London 2003), 57.

[16]   D Feldman, 'Human Rights, Terrorism and the Role of Politicians and Judges' [2006] *Public Law*, p 364.

and the effectiveness of routine decisions in the lower courts are both important matters. As justice becomes conceived less as an act of state authority and more as a public service, so the demands for accountability for the system grow. Many higher courts on the continent produce annual reports, justifying and opening to scrutiny their effectiveness and key decisions. In many systems, however, the information is gathered internally by the Ministry of Justice and produced as a set of annual statistics without a serious attempt to produce a publicly available narrative explanation and justification for what has been happening. This is most clearly the case in France and Germany. On the whole, public accountability happens most explicitly in Spain and Sweden where an independent agency runs the judiciary. It has to operate within a framework set by a ministry or parliament and respond to it. In a sense, judicial independence is maintained by explicitness on both sides about what is expected and what is being delivered. Without an agency, there is often less explicitness both about expectations and delivery. The nearest that we have to this in England is section 54 of the Constitutional Reform Act 2005 requiring an Annual Report of Supreme Court, but the content of this is still to be determined. The idea of a report giving an account in general terms of the way in which the courts have been making decisions would be a significant step in greater openness. Accountability for the use of resources would, I suppose, come through the Public Accounts Committee, but this has to be developed.

3.2 Appointments and dismissals

Compared with the other countries in Europe, English judicial recruitment has traditionally been informal, unstructured, and lacking in transparency. The system was designed for a period when there were 1,000 barristers, 40 senior judges, and 60 county court judges. The Lord Chancellor could become personally involved in appointments, and records could be kept on individuals by his office. In the 1960s, Lord Gardiner LC said that he had interviewed every candidate before appointment to the Bench. This became impossible to sustain as both the numbers of judges and the numbers in the professions increased in the 1970s. But it has taken a very long time for a seriously professional approach to be adopted in relation to judicial recruitment and selection. Until the 1990s, the procedure was more like the election of members to a club than an appointment to a job. The Lord Chancellor's Department published its explanatory document 'Judicial Appointments: The Lord Chancellor's Policies and Procedures' in 1986. Under that procedure, it used to survey the field of qualified applicants and take soundings among senior judges who could be expected to have encountered the individuals at work. The individual was then invited to become a judge. The process of consultation and soundings applied to the top 150 posts, including those in the High Court, until 1997, when advertisements were made inviting applicants to the High Court. Advertisements for posts below the High Court had been introduced in 1994. This informal procedure attracted criticism in two respects. First, it depended on the visibility of individuals to leading judges. Not all suitable individuals would have a practice that brought them sufficiently to the attention of the consultees to enable sufficient comment to be made.[17] Secondly, there has been consistent evidence that those consulted did not always respond in terms of the criteria for appointment set out by the Department. The questions asked were often insufficiently focused on the range of qualities needed for being a judge, as opposed to being an advocate.[18] The creation of job descriptions did not fully achieve focused responses. In part this is because there has been a traditional view that success in the courtroom as an advocate is a good preparation for being a judge, a view that has been criticized.[19]

Progress in creating a formalized appointments process that reflected good public sector practice was hampered by the judges themselves. They clung to soundings and Lord Taylor rejected a Judicial Appointments Commission in 1996. But the procedures adopted in the past did not fit either the Nolan Principles on Appointments to public offices adopted generally in the mid-1990s, nor normal private sector practices, including those used within the legal professions. Many of the proposals of JUSTICE in 1992[20] have found their way into the Constitutional Reform Act 2005. As has been noted, this introduces a Judicial Appointments Commission composed of lay and judicial members, with a lay Chair. Its appointment process is likely to build on the most recent reforms: advertisement, job descriptions, interviews, and formal references, rather than unstructured soundings. The process will resemble the external application routes in other systems, but it marks a significant extension of professionalism in judicial appointments, and a greater recognition of a career.

The most obvious evidence for suitability for appointments to the full-time judicial posts would include performance as part-time judges, e.g., as Recorders or Deputy District Judges. But, until the pilots in 2005, there was no formal system of appraisal of part-time office holders.[21] Indeed, Lord Taylor rejected performance appraisal for judges in general as incompatible with judicial independence.[22] This is an area in which the practices of the English judiciary lag behind continental judiciaries, such as that in Sweden.

In terms of discipline, the powers to remove senior judges remain with Parliament, upon an Address of both Houses. The powers of the Lord Chancellor in relation to other judges are transferred to the Lord Chief Justice. Under section 115 of the Constitutional Reform Act 2005, in consultation with the Lord Chancellor, the Lord Chief Justice may make rules for the procedure to be

---

[17] See *Report on Judicial Appointments and QC Selection, Main Report* (London 1999) (hereafter 'Peach'), 5 and JUSTICE, *The Judiciary in England and Wales* (London 1992) (hereafter 'JUSTICE'), 12.

[18] JUSTICE, 12; Peach, 10; Commission for Judicial Appointments, *Annual Report 2004* (London 2005), § 3.23–24.

[19] See D Pannick, *Judges* (Oxford 1987), 52.   [20] See JUSTICE, n 24.

[21] Peach 16; JUSTICE, 12.   [22] K Malleson, *The New Judiciary* (Aldershot 1999), 64.

followed in disciplinary matters, though the Act does not specify much about the content of such rules. A greater formality will be an essential improvement on the arrangements hitherto, which have lacked the formality expected in other countries.

Overall, the changes introduce a greater formality and professionalism into the processes of appointing, disciplining, and managing judges. As the judiciary has grown in size and complexity, the existing informality of procedures has become inappropriate. The large size of a career judiciary cannot be managed on the procedures for the barristers appointed late in their professional lives.

3.3 Independence and governance

The English conception of judicial independence is complex and it involves as much the status and ways of working of the judiciary as the formal mechanism by which they are appointed and removed.[23] Stevens[24] has suggested that:

Perhaps the most acceptable way of characterising the role of judicial independence in England is to say that, while the independence of the judiciary is casual at best, the English have a strong commitment to the independence of individual judges.

I have argued elsewhere that judicial independence involves characteristics such as impartiality and political neutrality far more centrally than ideas such as irremovability.[25] Shetreet demonstrated that the formal guarantee of judicial irremovability contained in the Act of Settlement 1701 was merely intended to make judges independent of the King, not of Parliament, and certainly not to be a free actor as a third branch of government.[26] Indeed, it is a guarantee that does not apply to judges below the level of the High Court, who form the majority of judges. Judges also cannot be sued for their judicial acts, but this is an immunity that does not apply to magistrates.[27]

The formal position is that judges of the High Court and Court of Appeal cannot be removed from office except by an Address from both Houses of Parliament. The process has never been successfully invoked against an English judge since it was created in 1701 (although it was successfully involved in relation to Irish judges in the early part of the 19th century. More commonly, public criticism of a judge in Parliament and outside may lead to fellow judges putting pressure on him to resign. A good example was Lord Denning who published criticisms of members of a jury which many read as racist in tone. Although he had been a

[23] For a modern judicial restatement of this idea, see T Bingham, *The Business of Judging* (Oxford 2000), 55.

[24] R Stevens, *The Independence of the Judiciary* (Oxford 1997), 5.

[25] J Bell, 'The Judge as Bureaucrat' in J Eekelaar and J Bell, *Oxford Essays in Jurisprudence—Third Series* (Oxford 1987), 51–53.

[26] S Shetreet, *Judges on Trial. A Study of the Appointment and Accountability of the English Judiciary* (Amsterdam 1976), 8.

[27] See generally, AA Olowofoyeku, *Suing Judges: A Study of Judicial Immunity* (Oxford 1993).

very good judge, he was over 80 and he was persuaded to step down. Public criticism of Lord Lane, particularly over his handling of miscarriages of justice, was thought to have contributed to his decision to retire early as Lord Chief Justice in 1992. The ethos of 'doing the decent thing' predominates in the system.

Until the Constitutional Reform Act 2005 created a more formal procedure, all other judges were subject to removal by the Lord Chancellor for misconduct. In practice, the Lord Chancellor would give the person in question a hearing. The process was swift, but rarely involved. An example was when Judge Campbell was found smuggling whisky on his yacht from France to England. In other cases, the Lord Chancellor may issue a reprimand to a judge, sometimes publicly.[28]

The concept of impartiality requires an honest decision, uninfluenced by personal relationships or prejudice, based on general, and not unique considerations, and appealing to standards that are representative, and which the judge would be willing to apply in similar circumstances in the future. The core feature is the appearance of impartiality. In the *Pinochet* case, the House of Lords had to set aside its own decision that had been reached with the participation of Lord Hoffman who was a member of the charitable board of one of the parties to the case. This was a classic common law conception.[29] The European Convention has pushed to a more formalist position, leading to the ending of the role of the Lord Chancellor as a sitting judge and of the participation of the Law Lords in the activity of the legislature. Such a formalist position is derived from a conception of the separation of powers in a more expansive form than the more 'casual' attitude, as Stevens put it,[30] than has prevailed hitherto.

The other connected component of judicial independence is political neutrality. This has been understood in different ways. In one sense, it has been understood as a requirement of disengagement from social activitism.[31] Abel-Smith and Stevens argued that the period from the 1890s up until 1955 or 1960 was marked by limited judicial creativity.[32] The narrower judicial role reflected a greater legislative activity, often from left of centre governments who did not value judicial interference.

A particularly English view of the independence of the judiciary was stressed by the Judges' Council in its response to the consultation papers of 2003 on the

---

[28] For illustrations, see Stevens, *Independence*, 166; Smith, Bailey and Gunn, *On the English Legal Systems* (London 2002), 242.

[29] *R v Bow Street Metropolitan Stipendiary Magistrate, ex p Pinochet Ungarte (No 2)* [2001] 1 AC 119.

[30] Above n 24.

[31] E.g., Sir Henry Slesser, a former Labour minister, wrote: 'When I became a judge, naturally I resigned from all political and semi-political associations, and even in church matters, I felt it right not to take part in any work of a markedly polemical nature, so my retirement from the world really took place in 1929. After that date my only public contacts or utterances were in court.' (*Judgment Reserved* (London 1941), 1).

[32] B Abel-Smith and R Stevens, *Lawyers and the Courts* (London 1967), ch 5.

abolition of the office of the Lord Chancellor. The judges were happy to make a clearer break between themselves and the Lord Chancellor as head of the judiciary, if he was to become increasingly an ordinary minister. This would fit into a model of the separation of powers, even if that model had not been a major feature of the English tradition, compared with that of other jurisdictions. The Judges' Council argued that:

Judicial independence depends, not just on law or resources, but on the tradition of restraint that the stronger arms of the State exercise in their relationship with the judiciary.[33]

In their view, the deployment of judges should be under the judges and adequate resources supplied.

The office of Lord Chancellor was becoming increasingly administrative.[34] Lord Mackay pointed out in 1995 that it had a staff of 11,000 and a budget of £2.3 billion.[35] The need to give directions about the proper administration of the system of justice clashed with the judges' own sense of their right to determine how they conducted cases, especially individual cases. This led to the President of the Employment Appeal Tribunal resigning over a clash with the Lord Chancellor about his courts' failure to use sufficiently certain procedures in order to reduce the backlog of unmeritorious cases.[36]

The debates surrounding the Constitutional Reform Act 2005 threw into relief the issue of the relationship between the role of judges as managers of the judicial process and wider responsibilities for resources in a context of judicial independence. Lord Browne-Wilkinson had already complained of the increasing managerialism of the Lord Chancellor's Department and argued that the judges should have greater control over the disposal of the resources made available for the administration of justice.[37] The Judges' Council pointed to examples in the common law world where judges had been given responsibility for resources as a support for judicial independence, but comments: 'It is recognized, however, that it may not at present be possible to adopt a system of that kind.'[38] But it then went on to press for particular measures to give judges an input into the decisions on resources. With the existence of Her Majesty's Courts Service (from 2005 as a unified administration including the magistrates' courts) dealing as a Next Steps

---

[33] 'Judges' Council Response to the Consultation Papers on Constitutional Reform' (November 2003) § 20.

[34] See Lord Mackay, 'The Lord Chancellor's role within Government' (1995) *New Law Journal* 1650; D Woodhouse, *The Office of Lord Chancellor* (Oxford 2001).

[35] Mackay, Ibid, 1651.

[36] See F Purchas, 'Lord Mackay and the judiciary' (1994) NLJ 527; Smith, Bailey and Gunn, 277–8.

[37] N Browne-Wilkinson, 'The Independence of the Judiciary in the 1980s' [1988] PL 44, 53–7. cf the views of Lord Mackay, *The Administration of Justice* (London 1994), 13–15 and 17–18, who distinguished between judicial decisions and administrative decisions, especially on resources.

[38] 'Judges' Council Response to the Consultation Papers on Constitutional Reform' (November 2003) § 43.

Agency with the operation of court facilities and the treatment of court users, the idea of a Judiciary Agency would be a parallel institution, rather than the odd structure of the Judicial Office and the Lord Chief Justice.

4 The Swedish System of Judicial Governance

4.1 Basic principles of governance

Domstolsverket (DV) is directed by a board (*Domstolsverket styrelsen*) which consists of no more than ten members appointed by the government, including the chief executive. Its membership represents judges, politicians, and legal professions. It is a group which is not composed simply of service providers. Its chief executive appointed in 2005, Thomas Rolén, is a judge who had also worked for some time in an 'advokat' firm and in Stockholm University, before joining the Ministry of Justice as an administrator in 1993.[39] He worked as legal secretary to the privatization commission from 1992 to 1994. He thus epitomizes the mix of administrative and judicial roles which leading judges can undertake.

DV is responsible for the overall management of the courts, its staffing levels, and equipment. The chief judge of a court has only limited budgetary control. There is an annual round of local meetings to discuss the budget for each court. Apart from recurrent expenditure, there is money for special initiatives. The annual report comments on the improving competences of judges and collaboration between courts in order to enhance efficiency of courts.[40] DV is also concerned to improve the competences of judges and more generally the working conditions of all employees, e.g., in the management of stress.[41] DV is charged by the Ministry of Justice not only to distribute the budget, but also to monitor the efficiency of the courts. It produces statistics on the efficiency of courts that look at the numbers of cases resolved, the time to judgment in different types of case, and the throughput of different courts (described in some sections of the report as 'productivity').[42] The Public Administration Act 1985 departed from previous legislation in the field by introducing the idea of the citizen as client of the administration.[43] Many remaining parts of the public sector are governed by objectives set centrally. Rather than ministries directing what is done, agencies or franchisees are expected to perform against agreed targets (*målstyrning*).

This monitoring combined with control of the budget enables DV to play an active role in encouraging improvements in performance. Some of these are

---

[39] Ministry of Justice press release, 25 November 2004.

[40] See *Årsredovisning 2004*, 20–1.

[41] *Årsredovisning 2004*, 28. The report (p 107) sets out plans to create individual training development plans for all chief judges.

[42] See Ibid, ch 2.

[43] See J Pierre, 'Legitimacy, Institutional Change, and the Politics of Public Administration in Sweden' (1993) 14 *International Political Science Review* 387, 393–4, and 397.

proposed by the courts themselves, and some come from working groups that they have set up. These efforts to change practices inevitably give rise to conflicts with the judges themselves who consider that DV is interfering with judicial independence.[44] But DV is not totally autonomous. It is a public sector agency that has to fit within the constraints of the public sector budget. In 1999, there was a particularly severe round of budget cuts that the DV had to administer (over ten per cent) and that obviously clashed with the judiciary's perception of its appropriate role and ways of working.[45] In the end, DV cannot insulate the judiciary from the general financial climate and give it special protection. All it can do is decide how the budget cuts are implemented.

The character of judicial independence is well illustrated by these governance arrangements. The governing organ, DV, is not an institution of judicial self-regulation, much as many judges would now like it to be. On the other hand, DV acts as a buffer between the Ministry of Justice and the judges as managers at court level. Central government seeks to exercise a strong influence over the direction of all branches of government, and this Swedish tradition of integrating judicial activity within social reform perhaps explains an absence of will to translate judicial independence in the application of the law into a strong version of judicial autonomy to decide how it should organize itself as a separate branch of government. Sweden is not unique in this regard, but its way of accommodating the tensions between steering judicial activity as a whole and respecting judicial independence is distinctive. On the whole, the model adopted has been that of other independent agencies of government, of which there are many in Sweden.

4.2 Management

In more recent years, there have been moves to devolve more administration to the courts themselves, with the resultant need to improve the administrative abilities of judges as managers. In this, the Swedish system has a more explicit role for management than the current English system.

The traditional role of the presiding judge of a court was leadership in decision-making and in approach to work. He was to guide the development of the law and the way colleagues came to decisions. He would also recruit and train younger judges (*notarie* and *fiskaler*). He would lead the court in activities such as producing *remisser* (responses) to committee reports. He was often involved in new developments in the courts, but was not responsible for the management of the court, nor for the career development of individuals.

---

[44] See e.g., the article by Judge T Gregow, 'Domstolsverket lägger sig i vårt arbete', *Brännpunkt*, *Svenska Dagbladet*, 4 September 2000.
[45] See the debate between the Minister of Justice and representatives of judges in 'Domstolen i framtiden'(1999) 4 *Tidskrift för Sveriges Domareförbund* 13.

The Swedish court system is now managed in a more specific way. Performance targets are set by the Ministry of Justice for the resolution of different categories of case. The job of the president is to monitor performance and to see how his court can achieve the target. In particular, there are targets for the timescales within which cases are to be decided. The main tool of management is encouragement, rather than orders. Performance is also enhanced by bidding for projects. These are supplements to the budget of the court for activities which the administration approves. Thus the *Svea hovrätt* obtained a rebuilding project and the *Göta hovrätt* obtained some additional posts to undertake an experimental reorganization. The elaboration of such proposals is part of the role of the president. This involves networking to discover the kinds of project likely to be supported.

The other aspect of management is personnel. The presiding judge has a responsibility to develop the careers of judges within his court. He has to produce reports on the progress of judges undergoing training (*notarie* and *fiskaler*). Promotions procedures also require him to provide references on members of his court (which the affected person can see).

DV has been responsible for developing training courses for managers and these are to be developed further under recent proposals.[46] The Hirschfeldt committee suggested that it is necessary to keep together both the management and the leadership aspects of the role of the chief judge in a court.[47] As a manager, the judge is responsible to external authorities, such as DV, for meeting performance targets, and for personnel and financial matters. He is also responsible for achieving developments. Among colleagues, the judge is internally responsible for providing leadership within the court, but as *primus inter pares*. He must, however, respect the independence of judges in coming to their decisions. The manager's concern is to avoid maladministration, but he cannot dictate how decisions should be reached.

4.3 Appointment and discipline

The Swedish selection system is based on a meritocratic competition,[48] which is open and transparent, and which is based on prior experience, predominantly university achievement in law. It is managed by independent bodies. The basic process of initial selection of *notarier* is controlled by DV. But further recruitment is governed by the *Tjänsteförslagsnämnden för domstolsväsendet* (TFN), an

---

[46] See documents produced by working groups of DV: *Praktiska Ledningsfrågor* and *Lederskap och Chefskap* (Jönköping, April 2000).

[47] SOU 2000:99, *Domarutnämningar och domstolsledning—frågor om utnämning av högre domare och domstolschefens roll*, 398.

[48] See generally, DV, *Vägen till domaryrket* (Jönköping, 1999); Ibid, *Det svenska domstolsväsendet—En kort introduction* (Jönköping, 1999), 8; NJ Baas, *Onderzoeksnotities 2000/8: Rekrutering en (permanente) educatie van de rechtsprekende macht in vijf landen* (Ministry of Justice, Netherlands 2000) (hereafter 'Baas'), 102.

independent recruitment body. Particularly since the 1970s, there is scope for individuals to be recruited from outside the career judiciary to more senior posts. The advertising of posts makes this possible. In part this was introduced to have a greater range of experience, but it was also motivated by government concerns that the career judiciary was too conservative and out of tune with current legislation.[49] This open process has been able to deal with the traditional under-representation of women, which is a constant problem in England.[50] At lower levels, the application is examined by TFN, which will make a decision. The candidates are not interviewed. The committee of TFN is made up of senior judges with two employee representatives. As a result, one can say that it constitutes a degree of self-government at this stage. *Senior posts* remain within the control of the Ministry of Justice, as in the past. Traditionally, these have not gone only to career judges.

5 Justice as a Public Service

In modern public sector management, a public service focuses on delivery to the customer. The aim is to meet the legitimate needs of the customer but within both a determined level of service and within an agreed budget. Unlike many private services, the customer is not paying (directly at least) and is not able to define directly the kind of service that is required. The state pays and the state defines the required level of service on behalf of the ultimate users. Now the state does this for a range of services and they are in competition in terms of priority for action and resources. The state is also concerned to monitor performance. The accountability for this performance is provided in a number of ways through New Public Management. There are four elements of the techniques of management in this area. First, the service is typically defined through a public service agreement, a formal document in which the expected level of service is broadly defined. This is particularly necessary where you have the service provided by an agency separate from a ministry. The second aspect will be key performance indicators (KPIs) and a closely connected third aspect is an obligation to report. Typically, there is a fourth element, a devolved administration, rather than in-house provision within a ministry. This ensures that the service delivery body remains focused on its task. Within this framework, there is clarity about what is to be provided, by whom, and with what obligation to report on progress. Regulatory accountability replaces direct political accountability. Her Majesty's Court Service, Business Plan 2006–07, provides an illustration:

[49] KÅ Modéer, *Den svenska domarkulturen—europeiska och nationelle förebilder* (Lund 1994) (hereafter 'Modéer, *Domarkulturen*'), 58.
[50] Thus, 60% of prosecutors under 40 are women, but 73% of those over 55 are men. Among judges, 65% of the *icke ordinarie* judges are women, but 72% of the *ordinarie* judges and 89% of the chief judges (average age 58) are men: DV, *Årsredovisning 2004*, 94.

HMCS adopts a Balanced Scorecard approach to measuring its performance. This reflects the fact that, whilst our P[ublic] S[ervice] A[greement] and financial targets are very important, to build for the future we need to focus on more than just the current performance targets. We need to build our reputation with our customers and the wider community, we need to develop improved ways of working and we need to invest in our staff and their development.[51]

This is perhaps an extreme version of the use of New Public Management language, but it is replicated in the reports in other countries. The structures of New Public Management enable accountability for this kind of activity. It is noticeable that the Court Service has this form of accountability, but not the Judicial Office in England. The link between the two activities within DV enables the Swedish system to offer a more integrated approach in which judges play a part in delivering services and are accountable to DV for that, and DV is then accountable for its performance.

6 Justice as a Human Right

In the focus on human rights, we concentrate on entitlements, which are a strong interest. In a public service model, individuals may have interests or even legitimate expectations based on what the public body has done or promised, but in the area of human rights, then we get a much stronger claim backed by a duty on the public body to deliver. The service required is defined by the objective standards of what the right requires, rather than by the offering proposed by the service provider. The problem is that the content of this right to justice is ill-defined. It is, in French terms, a 'droit-créance', rather than a liberty (such as freedom of association) or an immunity (such as the right not to be tortured). It is a right which is owed, but, rather like 'the right to work', its content is neither obvious nor could it be unlimited. Rather than a defined right, it is a framework right whose content is determined by the state, with the proviso that it must genuinely try to implement the right. As a result, the definition of the right is an important part of its actual content. For that reason, a governance structure for the delivery of the right needs to recognize its inherent indeterminacy and contestability. In such a situation, the judges, even as guardians of justice, need to be put in dialogue with others. Whereas the Swedish governance structure for DV provides a clear forum for this to happen, the governance of the judiciary around the Lord Chief Justice and the Judicial Office is too centred on the role of judges in defining their own agendas and ideas.

Judges tend to see themselves as guardians of access to justice and thus of the rights which protect this. But leaving the definition in the hands of these professionals risks transferring to them the budget, which others have to meet. As a

---

[51] *Her Majestys' Court Service Business Plan 2006/07*, p 8.

result, governance structures are an essential part of the basic structure of justice. Judges can be guardians of justice of established principles, where these have been defined.

Conclusion

The issues of governing and managing the judiciary are issues that have become clearer in England as it has moved from a cosy relationship between the senior judges and the Lord Chancellor to a more distant relationship towards a Ministry of Justice. But the structures have been developed piecemeal and with more thought to achieving a quick resolution of conflicts with the judiciary than with developing a coherent strategy. In this respect, the development of DV in Sweden reflects a more measured and principled approach. It provides a clear response to the issues of how to conceive justice and how to deliver good quality public services. The Swedish model has avoided the excesses of the Italian system which gives too much power to the judiciary to regulate itself. It is by comparing the institutional systems in similar European countries such as Sweden that improvements in the English system can be achieved.

To a great extent, the tradition of a certain form of judicial independence and an important role for the judiciary outside (and to some extent above) politics has fostered a willingness to leave the judges to organize their own affairs in England. (In practice, there was a significant control exercised by the Lord Chancellor's Office over appointments, but the impact of this on judicial independence is often disregarded.)[52] The focus has been on the senior judiciary, and this has failed to recognize the very large increase in numbers of judges at lower levels. The more systematic arrangements in Sweden reflect a willingness to review tradition and to develop an objective-oriented set of arrangements that fulfil policy needs. It has operated in a way which demonstrates that managerialism need not compromise the important values of judicial independence.

[52] Robert Stevens, *The Independence of the Judiciary: The View from the Lord Chancellor's Office* (Oxford 1993).

3

Lord Bingham: a New Zealand Appreciation

Sian Elias*

No legal system of the common law world has been untouched by the life's work and example of Lord Bingham of Cornhill. In New Zealand we certainly have not been immune from the force of his reasoning and the clarity of his expression. They have persuaded New Zealand judges, as they have persuaded judges of many other jurisdictions, to the great benefit of our law. We have benefited, too, from Lord Bingham's judicial leadership in times of constitutional change in the United Kingdom. Such changes have had parallels in New Zealand. They may be particularly unsettling in countries like the United Kingdom and New Zealand where constitutional values are not captured in a written constitutional text. Lord Bingham's patient and scholarly exposition of constitutional principle in the United Kingdom has been reassuring in New Zealand, and at times has provided spine-stiffening example. But these collateral benefits for another jurisdiction of the work of a great English judge should not obscure the first point that must be made in a New Zealand appreciation. Since being appointed a Lord Justice of Appeal, Lord Bingham has been eligible to sit in what was until 2003 the apex court of the New Zealand legal system, the Privy Council. The Chief Justice of New Zealand has been identified in our legislation as head of the judiciary *in* rather than *of* New Zealand, in acknowledgement of the role of the Privy Council. Lord Bingham was Senior Law Lord in the last four years in which the Privy Council remained our final court of appeal. We are proud to claim this special connection and grateful for the important contribution made directly to the law of New Zealand. I am honoured to contribute to this collection as *teina* to an admired *tuakana*.

The Privy Council and New Zealand

This is not the place for an appreciation of the Privy Council and its place in New Zealand legal history. Indeed, as cases continue to limp through the system, it

* The Rt Hon Dame Sian Elias, Chief Justice of New Zealand.

would be bold to imagine that the final line has been drawn under the contribution of the Privy Council. It would, however, be remiss in an acknowledgement of the contribution made directly by Lord Bingham to the New Zealand legal system as a member of the Privy Council not to provide a little context.

The Privy Council served as New Zealand's final appeal court since Crown Colony government was established in 1840. Although it was described by Sir Robert Stout in 1909 as an 'anomaly' in our constitutional arrangements,[1] it proved remarkably durable. The abolition of the right of appeal in 2003 and the establishment of the Supreme Court was adopted by a divided Parliament. The enduring pull of the Privy Council can I think be attributed to a number of factors, not unconnected. Initially, limited judicial resources made local appellate provision unrealistic. There was considerable affection for the ties between our countries and our shared legal heritage. These considerations receded a little after the establishment of a permanent Court of Appeal and in the decades following World War II with shifts in cultural and political focus. But the judicial service provided by the Privy Council continued to be highly valued in New Zealand. And nationalistic stirrings were contained by the very sensible attitude of the Privy Council that the common law of England had developed in different ways in the countries to which it had carried and that divergence was a source of strength.[2] This was the view expressed in extra-judicial writing by Lord Bingham when Lord Chief Justice of England and Wales.[3] It led the Privy Council in *Invercargill City Council v Hamlin*[4] and *Lange v Atkinson*[5] to tolerate different solutions in England and New Zealand in relation to common problems thrown up as to the liability of local authorities for negligence in building inspections and as to the scope of a defence of qualified privilege in defamation.

At times in our history there have been suspicions that the decisions of the Privy Council seemed a little perfunctory compared with those of the House of Lords. Lord Reid, as is well-known, thought that the standing of the decisions of the Privy Council did not compare favourably with those of the House of Lords.[6] He attributed that circumstance to the single opinion formerly delivered by the Privy Council, a verdict with which Lord Bingham has agreed.[7] In later years the inflexibility about single opinions was relaxed, a licence that Lord Bingham took in dissenting in at least two appeals from New Zealand.[8] Whether there is strict

---

[1] 'Appellate Tribunals for the Colonies' (1904) 2 The Commonwealth Law Review 3, 4.

[2] *Australian Consolidated Press Ltd v Uren* (1969) 1 AC 590, *Invercargill City Council v Hamlin* [1996] 1 NZLR 513.

[3] 'The Future of the Common Law' in Tom Bingham, *The Business of Judging, Selected Essays and Speeches* (Oxford 2000).

[4] [1996] 1 NZLR 513.   [5] [2000] 1 NZLR 257.

[6] Lord Reid, 'The Judge as Law-Maker' (1972) 12 Journal of the Society of Public Teachers of Law (NS) 22, 28.

[7] Lord Bingham, 'The Rule of Law' (2007) 66 Cambridge Law Journal 67, 70–71.

[8] *Peterson v Commissioner of Inland Revenue* [2006] 3 NZLR 433; *Haines v Carter* [2003] 3 NZLR 605.

cause and effect here is I think doubtful. It seems to me likely that doubts such as those expressed by Lord Reid may well in themselves have been spur to care. But it is certainly the case that in the discussions in New Zealand that preceded abolition of appeals to the Privy Council, there was no suggestion of dissatisfaction with the legal standing of its decisions in more recent years. Indeed, the tenor of the views expressed was rather the reverse. And if some languor may have crept in from time to time in dealing with pedestrian appeals from a remote territory, there are a number of examples throughout our history when the rigour required by the Privy Council has been salutary indeed and has shaken up comfortable local attitudes.

Maori litigants, who petitioned the Privy Council in a number of cases at the end of the 19th and beginning of the 20th centuries when the lands, forests, and fisheries they had been guaranteed under the Treaty of Waitangi were slipping away, found in the Privy Council a more principled response than was available in the local courts.[9] And claims by Maori continued to be brought to the Privy Council until the right of appeal was abolished.[10] In one of the last of such cases, Lord Bingham, presiding, paid tribute to the retiring Lord Cooke of Thorndon and permitted the Maori litigants to bring the proceedings to a close with a *waiata*. In our culture, that was a fitting way not only to acknowledge a great New Zealand lawyer, but also to acknowledge, in one of the last cases to be brought to London from New Zealand, the beautiful, purpose-built, chamber of the Privy Council through which many New Zealanders and much New Zealand history has passed.

It would be comforting to think that salutary lessons to the New Zealand judges, like that delivered in *Wallis v Attorney-General*,[11] belong to an earlier age. That would, however, be to mistake the nature of the appellate process. It exists to correct error and it reflects the experience that errors occur. Plain error must be corrected plainly. Systemic error must be systematically confronted. And where plain error is made in judicial systems, it has to be faced unflinchingly. In my time, there has been no lesson as salutary as that delivered by the Privy Council in *Taito v R*,[12] with Lord Bingham presiding. The opinion, delivered by Lord Steyn, is direct, as it had to be. It is also undoubtedly correct. While I like to think that the same result would have been achieved had second appeal been available within the local courts, the fact is that it was a correction achieved through our system of appeals by a final court which has served New Zealand well.

The Supreme Court of New Zealand has the benefit of the wider context in which judicial decisions are now taken. One of the principal reasons why the

---

[9] *Nireaha Tamaki v Baker* (1901) NZPCC 371; *Wallis v Attorney-General* [1902–3] NZPCC 23 (PC); *Mana Kapua v Para Haimona* [1913] AC 761.

[10] *New Zealand Maori Council v Attorney-General* [1994] 1 NZLR 513; *Marlborough Aquaculture Ltd v Chief Executive, Ministry of Fisheries* (2005) 12 ELRNZ 1; *Ngati Apa Ki Te Waipounamu Trust v Attorney-General* [2007] 2 NZLR 80; *McGuire v Hastings District Council* [2007] 2 NZLR 80.

[11] [1902–03] NZPCC 23 (PC).   [12] [2003] 3 NZLR 577.

Privy Council remained our final court of appeal for so long was the tug exerted by the great idea of belonging to a wider common law world. When Sir Robert Stout proposed the abolition of appeals to the Privy Council, his preferred solution was not for New Zealand to go it alone, but for the establishment of a new imperial tribunal. (Reluctantly, he thought that an Australasian tribunal based on the newly formed High Court of Australia would not serve.)[13] Even as late as the 1950s there were proponents of a Commonwealth appellate tribunal. It was an idea which foundered on lack of British enthusiasm and was overtaken for the United Kingdom by new European institutions and focus. But the nostalgia for belonging to a greater system, which may be behind both proposals for extra-territorial substitutes and the New Zealand reluctance to relinquish the Privy Council, seems diminished with the increasing interconnectedness of the legal systems of the world, and in particular the common law systems.

Modern communications enable the courts of different countries to keep abreast with current thinking in their counterparts. Comparative legal commentary is enabled by the same improved linkages. The flow of ideas impacts on a world which has shrunk, in which borders are permeable, and in which great tides of people challenge national legal cultures. Legal problems are increasingly common to different jurisdictions and the solutions adopted in one jurisdiction are seized upon in others. Where, as is increasingly the case, domestic legal issues arise out of the implementation of common treaty obligations, close attention to the case law of comparable jurisdictions or to the case law of international tribunals with responsibilities for enforcing treaty compliance, is common sense. In New Zealand, perhaps in part because of our small population, we have long looked to the case law of England, Australia, and Canada for help. Today, with greater accessibility to the case law of other tribunals, we are able to look further afield. It is no longer necessary for participation in the wider world legal community to be achieved through domestic court hierarchies. Such interconnection is achieved rather through the sharing of reasons which convince or which prompt justified divergence. It is Lord Bingham's contribution to this world of ideas, both as a judicial leader and as a judge, that I now turn. But before leaving the Privy Council and Lord Bingham's contribution to it, I make a personal observation.

One of the benefits New Zealand judges have had while we retained appeals to the Privy Council was the ability to sit from time to time with the Board. None of the judges who have had the experience doubts its value to their work. All consider it a very great privilege to have sat with some of the finest judges of the day. All have come away impressed by the care, industry, and learning of the members of the panels on which they have sat. I was fortunate to have two stints on the Privy Council after becoming Chief Justice of New Zealand. Both were after Lord Bingham had become Senior Law Lord. Lord Cooke of Thorndon once named his 'dream team' for an appellate panel. It included, as presiding

---

[13] Stout (n 1 above) 11–12.

judge, Lord Bingham. Lord Cooke described Lord Bingham as 'the most complete chairman of an appellate court under whom I have ever had the privilege of serving'.[14] I count myself similarly privileged to have had the opportunity to observe Lord Bingham in that capacity and to be able to endorse Lord Cooke's choice. Lord Bingham is unfailing in courtesy to colleagues and to counsel, invariably well-prepared, with the marriage of fierce intellect and moral conviction, always tempered with humanity and kindness, that leads him quickly to the answer that more pedestrian judges struggle to reach. Emulation is difficult, but the standard is set.

Judicial Leadership

Few leaders of any judiciary can have lived through times of such upheaval as Lord Bingham. Looking at what has happened from a long way off, as I have been, it has seemed fortunate indeed that the Senior Law Lord was someone of his stature and experience. It should not be thought that what has happened in the United Kingdom is of domestic interest only. In New Zealand we have been grappling with similar issues and against a comparable constitutional background. Our Supreme Court was set up in 2003 in circumstances of some political conflict. A more transparent system for investigating complaints about judges and proposals for reform of judicial appointments have been current issues in the last few years. A sentencing council to constrain judicial discretion in sentencing has been provided under recent legislation. Suspicion of 'activist' judges is voiced periodically. Criminal justice is a consuming political concern, despite the fact that in New Zealand we have one of the most imprisoned populations in the world. The role of judges and courts is not well understood. And constitutional basics are neglected. Judges tend to keep their heads down for fear of seeming 'political'. So, for us, the vibrant debate in the United Kingdom and the judicial involvement in it are matters of practical importance as well as general interest. Lord Bingham's willingness to speak out for individual freedom and the rule of law and to express views which may be controversial in relation to criminal law, provides leadership further afield. It contributes to knowledge about a system broadly comparable to ours and influences our own ideas.

In New Zealand we have had a statutory bill of rights for nearly 20 years.[15] The legal profession has, however, been comparatively slow to realize its potential beyond the criminal law cases that dominated its first ten years of operation. It is perhaps also fair to say that the Act continues to have its detractors, those who think it transfers too much power to 'unelected' judges. Lord Bingham's long support for similar legislation in the United Kingdom through his extra-judicial

---

[14] 'The Law Lords: An Endangered Heritage' (2003) Law Quarterly Review 119, 46, 50.
[15] New Zealand Bill of Rights Act 1990.

writing and speeches has therefore been steadying. In particular, it has been helpful to have so convincing a rebuttal of any suggestion that statements such as
these are a fashion:[16]

> I cannot, however, for my part, accept that these articles represent some transient socio-
> logical mood, some flavour of the month, the decade or the half-century. They encapsu-
> late legal, ethical, social and democratic principles, painfully developed over 2,000 years.
> The risk that they may come to be regarded as modish or passés is one that may safely be
> taken.

Similarly, Lord Bingham's support for the new Supreme Court in the United
Kingdom and his rejection of claims that it would affect the principle of the sovereignty of Parliament has been helpful to cite in answer to similar fears voiced
in New Zealand. The separation of the Supreme Court from the House of Lords
was in order to fit that court better to fulfil its responsibilities under the rule of
law. Lord Bingham's exposition of the rule of law and the role of the courts in
giving content to it, is of direct relevance to New Zealand given recent statutory
recognition of both the rule of law and the sovereignty of Parliament.[17] Lord
Bingham's view that judges are not free to dismiss the rule of law as 'meaningless
verbiage', 'the jurisprudential equivalent of motherhood and apple pie' may yet
prove to be of practical importance in the New Zealand legal system.[18] If so, his
exploration of the content of the rule of law in the sixth David Williams lecture
will be an obvious starting point.[19]

Finally, Lord Bingham's public speeches about the futility of harsh sentences
in deterring serious crime have resonance in New Zealand too. So does the
insight he brought to bear in urging the House of Lords to bear in mind, in considering the mandatory minimum sentences for repeat offenders in the Crime
(Sentences) Bill, 'those of our fellow citizens to whom these provisions will in the
main apply:[20]

> They are mostly young, in their late 'teens' or early twenties and mostly male. They have
> in very many cases endured extreme deprivation; broken homes; truancy and exclu-
> sion from school; unemployment; addiction to alcohol and drugs; and a lack of all those
> beneficial maturing influences which most of us have been able to take for granted. I do
> not insult your Lordships by suggesting that these are innocent victims of determinist
> causes beyond their control. Of course not. But I do suggest that in discharge of our
> duty to our fellow men we should, instead of spending billions on new prisons, double
> and re-double existing efforts to identify and treat delinquents at the very earliest sign
> of delinquency, before—long before—they are sucked into the destructive maw of the
> penal system.... If, as the century and the millennium slide to a close, our penal thinking

---

[16] 'The European Convention on Human Rights: Time to Incorporate' in *Tom Bingham* (n 3)
139.
[17] Supreme Court Act 2003, s 3(2).
[18] 'The Rule of Law' (n 7) 69.   [19] 'The Rule of Law' (n 7).
[20] 'Speech of the Reading of the Crime (Sentences) Bill' in *The Business of Judging* (n 3) 346.

is to be judged by the thinking which animates this Bill, then I, for one, will shrink from the judgment of history.

The Judge

Although I hope I have said enough to indicate that Lord Bingham's direct contribution to New Zealand law as a judge in our hierarchy before 2004 is highly valued in New Zealand, his great influence on the common law world has been through his work as an English judge. I do not believe there can be a sitting judge of any jurisdiction whose judgments are invoked more. There are a number of reasons why these judgments are mined to such profit. I discuss a number that occur to me. Most could be gathered under one of the three traditions which were said by Paul Freund to have been behind the judicial qualities of another great judge, Louis Brandeis:[21]

His power derived from a fusion of three traditions: the biblical tradition, with the moral law of responsibility at the core; the classical tradition, with its stress on the inner check, the law of restraint, proportion, and order, achieved by working against a resisting medium; and not least, the common-law tradition,... teaching that the life of the law is response to human needs, that through knowledge and understanding and immersion in the realities of life law can be made... to work itself pure.

Given the breathtaking scope of Lord Bingham's judicial work my illustrations of his qualities as a judge do not scratch the surface. They are drawn principally from two areas of work in which his contributions are likely to set direction and tone for the future and in which his judgments have been particularly influential in New Zealand. They are negligence, in which his ideas have refreshed stagnating pools, and human rights law, where he has been in at the beginning of a seismic shift.

Of equal, or perhaps more, importance than the solutions reached in the judgments is their demonstration of an approach to judging which touches the ideal. It is that approach, laid out in patient exposition, without condescension or oversimplification, and with great scholarship and scrupulous attention to the limits and the strengths of judicial function that confirms and encourages judges everywhere in their own work.

Lord Bingham has himself said of judging that it is a 'unique function':[22]

That is not to say that it is a better job than anybody else's or a more important job than anybody else's, but it is a different job.

The job of a judge in the common law tradition is not one of mechanical application of rules. The common law, even when substantially overlaid by statute as is

---

[21] Paul Freund, 'Mr Justice Brandeis: A Centennial Memoir' (1957) 70 Harvard Law Review 769, 791–792.
[22] Evidence to the Select Committee on the Constitutional Reform Bill, 22 April 2004.

usual in most jurisdictions today, is not adequately seen as a collection of legal rules. It is rather a method which seeks to meet the twin objectives of law that is stable, but does not stand still.[23] Lord Mansfield made the case for adaptability to meet the needs of society: 'as the usages of society alter, the law must adapt itself to the various situations of mankind'.[24] He thought 'the law of England would be a strange science if indeed it were decided upon precedents only':[25]

Precedents serve to illustrate principles and to give them a fixed certainty. But the law of England which is exclusive of positive law, enacted by statute, depends upon principles, and these principles run through all the cases according as the particular circumstances of each have been found to fall within the one or the other of them.

The method of the common law is the method of judicial application and development of the principles underlying the positive law. It was famously described by Benjamin Cardozo in 1921 as that of the 'working hypothesis'.[26] The description is one Lord Bingham has adopted.[27] Indeed, he once said in an interview that he regarded consistency in a judge 'as a vice'.[28] I do not think he meant to suggest that inconsistency is a virtue, but the method of the working hypothesis is rightly seen as one of change, albeit change that is cautious and modest. Judging in such a system is discipline and obligation. The need to keep in touch with existing precedent means that, as Lord Bingham has said, 'in the law, nothing is the work of one court or one man'.[29] And, standing on the shoulders of those who have gone before, it is only too evident that there are no ultimate truths to be viewed. The judge of today is just another platform for the stargazer of the future. The process is 'ageless':[30]

The work of a judge is in one sense enduring and in another sense ephemeral. What is good in it endures. What is erroneous is pretty sure to perish. The good remains the foundation on which new structures will be built. The bad will be rejected and cast off in the laboratory of the years.... The future takes care of such things.

There is comfort in such view. The individual judge usually does little harm to the overall system, and maybe some good. In the imagery of my country, he is part of a great canoe. In such a system, the work of a judge is often hard to assess. The opportunity to be on the spot at an undoubted turning point, when the law

[23] Benjamin N Cardozo, *The Growth of the Law* (Yale University Press, New Haven 1924) 2, quoting Roscoe Pound, *Interpretations of Legal History* (The Macmillan Company, New York 1923) 1.
[24] *Johnson v Spiller* (1784) 3 Doug 371 at 373.
[25] *Jones v Randall* [1774] Cowp 37.
[26] Benjamin N Cardozo, *The Nature of the Judicial Process* (Yale University Press, New Haven 1921) 23.
[27] Lord Bingham, 'The Common Law: Past, Present and Future' (1999) Commonwealth Law Bulletin 18, 19.
[28] Stephen Moss, 'Cry Freedom' (31 May 2005) <http://www.guardian.co.uk/> accessed 14 July 2008.
[29] 'The Judge as Law Maker' in *The Business of Judging* (n 3).
[30] Cardozo (n 26) 178.

shifts direction by more than the degree or two that is necessary to keep the law fit for modern conditions,[31] does not arise in the lifetime of many judges. And even then, such change is today more often the result of the galvanizing effect of statutory adjustments. But principled response to human needs in individual cases is itself creative and difficult work. Only those who know a great deal of law, drawing both on the decided cases and the body of scholarly writing from which it is criticized,[32] are able to make adaptations which do not rend the fabric of the whole. Identifying the principles and values that stand the test of time and applying them to the controversies of today has rightly been described as 'thinking at its hardest'.[33] And great judges, with mastery of law and who accept the obligation to use it to provide justice to the individual litigant, provide necessary models of thinking and prod the rest of us to similar effort.

The first point to be made in considering Lord Bingham's influence is that he writes beautifully. Not in a flashy, quotable manner, but with great clarity and an unfalteringly apt choice of language and rhythm. He is not beyond a little Latin or the odd literary allusion but only where it distils meaning and does not distract. His style is Augustan. Indeed, might be said of him, as Richard Posner has said of Chief Justice Marshall, that his style is:[34]

Patient, systematic, unadorned, unemotional, unpretentious, it is the calm and confident voice of reason—the quintessential Enlightenment style.

Posner suggests that it must be a matter of doubt whether such a style remains possible in a mature legal system where the modern judge has the 'burden of negotiating a minefield of authoritative precedents'. Lord Bingham, however, leaves no such doubts. His treatment of precedent is masterly. It is always full and scrupulous but is arranged so that it does not interrupt the flow of his own reasons. It may be that such distillation of facts and law in beautiful prose comes easily. But I think it is more likely to be the result of years of effort and experience. What I think needs to be acknowledged is that those who take such trouble save others much labour. An American professor of English once likened writing judgments to writing poetry.[35] While the judge operates within a different discipline and must rehearse facts and law at length, he too, like the poet described by Robert Frost, is 'attempting "a momentary stay against confusion"'. Lord Bingham's 'stays against confusion' are certainly part of his appeal.

The second quality which makes Lord Bingham's judgments the first point of reference for many judges is the care he takes to ground the rule or principle of

---

[31] 'The Rule of Law' (n 7) 71.   [32] Cardozo (n 23) 37.

[33] Roger Traynor, 'Some Open Questions in the Work of State Appellate Courts' 24 U Chi L Rev 211, 218.

[34] *Law and Literature: A Misunderstood Relation* (Harvard University Press, Cambridge Massachusetts 1988) 311.

[35] Walker Gibson, 'Literary Minds and Judicial Style' (1961) 36 NYU Law Review 915, 930.

law he is applying in its legal context. The pedigree of any application in novel circumstances or re-expression of the rule or principle applied is impeccably laid out. Nor is the wider historical or social context in which it was adopted neglected. Only a judge with deep knowledge of law in context can be as assured. So, Cardozo said of Oliver Wendell Holmes:[36]

Historian he is and scholar, a master of the learning of the law and of its traditional technique.

Such connections are essential to legitimate judicial creativity, without which the law cannot respond to human needs in changing societies. Understanding of the context in which legal principles have arisen and how they have been applied in the past is essential in considering how such principles must develop and be applied to emerging needs and to guard against the view that they are immutable. It provides the only sound platform from which a judge can move on. As Bingham LJ said in one such novel case:[37]

It is submitted, I think rightly, that this claim breaks new ground. No analogous claim has ever, to my knowledge, been upheld or even advanced. If, therefore, it were proper to erect a doctrinal boundary stone at the point which the onward march of recorded decisions has so far reached, we should answer the question of principle in the negative and dismiss the plaintiff's action, as the deputy judge did. But I should for my part erect the boundary stone with a strong presentiment that it would not be long before a case would arise so compelling on its facts as to cause the stone to be moved to a new and more distant resting place.

Anchoring a decision to earlier precedents, while critically reviewing the thinking behind them for application in the circumstances of the instant case, is difficult work requiring great craft. It is close attention to such craft that bridges 'doubt to decision'.[38] And although some decisions by Lord Bingham in the Court of Appeal or at first instance may have been held at the time to be a bridge too far, the ideas remain and may yet provide markings for future builders.

The third point to be made about Lord Bingham's judging is his willingness to look to foreign cases. Many examples could be given. I mention a few only. In *Rees v Darlinghurst Memorial Hospital*[39] Lord Bingham derived particular assistance in a wrongful birth case from a decision of the High Court of Australia. In *Banque Bruxelles SA v Eagle Star*,[40] he adopted the view taken by Cooke P in the New Zealand Court of Appeal[41] that:

[36] 'Mr Justice Holmes' in Benjamin N Cardozo, *Selected Writings* (Matthew Border, New York 1947) 77.
[37] *Attia v British Gas Plc* [1988] 1 QB 304, 320.
[38] David H Souter, 'Gerald Gunther' (2002) 55 Stanford L Review 635, 636 (speaking of Learned Hand).
[39] [2004] 1 AC 309.   [40] [1995] QB 375, 406.
[41] In *McElroy Milne v Commercial Electronics Limited* [1993] 1 NZLR 39, 41.

The ultimate question as to compensatory damages is whether the particular damage claimed is sufficiently linked to the breach of particular duty to merit recovery in all the circumstances.

In the Court of Appeal in *Reynolds v Times Newspapers Limited*,[42] dealing with a claim of qualified privilege in defamation, he canvassed decisions from around the Commonwealth and the United States. In the important case of *Locabail (UK) Limited v Bayfield Properties Limited*,[43] concerned with bias in judicial officers, he surveyed the law of other jurisdictions, finding particular assistance in decisions of the Constitutional Court of South Africa and the High Court of Australia.[44] The citation of these decisions indicates the breadth of the review undertaken by a committed and hardworking judge. But, more importantly for those of us from other jurisdictions, the reasons given in such English decisions engage with our own case law in a way that connects us directly to the wider world of legal ideas. And where the case law of a number of jurisdictions is canvassed, the connections expand. Consideration of the reasons given by our courts helps us even when we disagree. Lord Bingham's willingness to ground his decisions on a wider world view is part of the reason why his judgments are cited so frequently in other jurisdictions. It is a reason why his judicial leadership has not been confined to his own country.

The fourth matter is perhaps another aspect of Lord Bingham's contextual approach to judging. It is the pains he takes over constitutional exposition. Much of the thinking is more fully developed in Lord Bingham's extra-judicial writing but it finds expression in a number of significant judgments. In the important case of *A v Secretary of State for the Home Department* Lord Bingham touched upon the relationship between the political and judicial bodies in the constitution:[45]

It is the function of political and not judicial bodies to resolve political questions. Conversely, the greater the legal content of any issue, the greater the potential role of the court, because under our constitution and subject to the sovereign power of Parliament, it is the function of the courts and not of political bodies to resolve legal questions.

In *Millar v Dickson*, he emphasized the fundamental importance of the right to be tried by an independent tribunal:[46]

the right of an accused in criminal proceedings to be tried by an independent and impartial tribunal is one which, unless validly waived by the accused, cannot be compromised or eroded.

Such constitutional understanding is indispensable in much difficult litigation arising out of the Human Rights Act and at a time when the threat of terrorism

---

[42] [1998] 3 WLR 862.
[44] *Cattanach v Melchior* (2003) 215 CLR 1.
[46] [2002] 1 WLR 1615, 1624.

[43] [2000] 1 QB 451.
[45] [2005] 2 WLR 87, 105.

agitates public anxiety. These factors require surer grasp of constitutional principle than some of us have needed in the past.

Writing in 1993, Lord Bingham attributed to Lord Hailsham the observation
that 'Judges are usually illiterate in constitutional matters'.[47] Such illiteracy is
now dangerous in any society that aspires to live under the rule of law. In New
Zealand, as in the United Kingdom, our constitution is unwritten. We, too, operate under an unentrenched enacted statement of rights which leaves parliamentary sovereignty intact as the central principle of the constitution.[48] We need to
work harder to develop a constitutional sense than jurisdictions with more accessible constitutional instruments. In this connection we have benefited greatly
from the focus on the constitution which has been a feature of recent political
and legal consideration in the United Kingdom. Lord Bingham has been a leader
in that consideration both on the bench and off it. His extra-judicial views[49] that
section 1 of the Constitutional Reform Act 2005 may require the courts of the
United Kingdom to give content to the rule of law and as to the likely principles to be taken from it have direct resonance in New Zealand too. They may
well prove highly influential as I have already suggested. In the meantime, Lord
Bingham's judgments bearing on the constitution and in particular the relative
responsibilities and obligations of parliament, the executive, and the judiciary are
of direct relevance and contain in a number of respects more close consideration
than has yet been attempted in New Zealand case law.[50]

We have yet to grapple with some of the more difficult human rights issues that
have troubled the House of Lords in recent years.[51] Its determinations are likely
to be of great assistance to us if similar cases arise in New Zealand. We have yet
to engage closely with the application of the New Zealand Bill of Rights Act to
'public functions', but when we do, Lord Bingham's dissenting judgment in *YL v
Birmingham City Council*[52] is likely to receive much attention. As importantly, the
methodology adopted in relation to human rights in such cases as *R (on the application of Begum v Denbigh High School Governors*[53] is likely to be extremely influential
in New Zealand cases even if, as was the case with the interpretation adopted in *R
Lambert*,[54] we end up taking a different course.[55] What seems difficult to dispute is
the view that where human rights are engaged, the courts must concern themselves
with the 'practical outcome' rather than the decision-making process.[56]

[47] 'The European Convention on Human Rights: Time to Incorporate' in *The Business of
Judging* (n 3).
[48] In a provision which finds partial echo in s 1 of the Constitutional Reform Act (UK), the New
Zealand Supreme Court Act 2003 provides in s 3(2) 'Nothing in this Act affects New Zealand's
continuing commitment to the rule of law and the sovereignty of Parliament'.
[49] 'The Rule of Law' (n 7).
[50] See *R(Jackson) v Attorney-General* [2006] 1 AC 262.
[51] *A* (n 45); *R(Limbuela) v Secretary of State for the Home Department* [2006] 1 AC 396.
[52] [2008] 1 AC 95.   [53] [2007] 1 AC 100.
[54] *R v Lambert* [2002] 2 AC 545.   [55] *R v Hansen* [2007] 3 NZLR 1.
[56] *Denbigh High* (n 53) [29]–[31].

The fifth comment I make about the influence of Lord Bingham is perhaps a major aspect of his judicial craft. It is his willingness to look past the lazy road-blocks that less assured judges see in legal problems to the substance of what is at stake and to acknowledge frankly the legal policies that underlie judicial choice. My illustrations here are largely from Lord Bingham's negligence cases. I think in that field his influence will continue to be felt for some time. Many more examples could be given.

'Floodgates' and 'overkill' arguments are ones Lord Bingham is not prepared to take at face-value without critical examination. In *Attia v British Gas Plc*,[57] a claim for damages where psychiatric harm was said to be a consequence of witnessing the destruction of the plaintiff's home, the only argument for denying liability was one of policy based on the floodgates. Bingham LJ in the Court of Appeal allowed that 'this is not an argument to be automatically discounted', but thought the proof of reasonable foreseeability and psychiatric damage, and 'the good sense of the judge to ensure... that the thing stops at the appropriate point' was better control than 'a necessarily arbitrary rule of law'.[58]

In *M v Newham London Borough Council; X v Befordshire County Council*[59] Bingham LJ, dissenting in the Court of Appeal,[60] was not impressed by the submission that a doctor would be inhibited through fear of potential liability: the doctor would be protected by 'sound performance of his professional duty, and that is how it should be'. If the plaintiff succeeded in the claim of negligence it would be:[61]

... little short of absurd if a child were held to be disentitled to claim damages for injury of the very type which the psychiatrist should have been exercising her skills to try and prevent.

Similar rejection of 'overkill' arguments are to be seen in the judgments of Bingham LJ in *Caparo Industries Plc v Dickman*,[62] and Lord Bingham CJ in the Court of Appeal in *Arthur JS Hall v Simors*.[63]

A restrained and disciplined judge, Lord Bingham believes that 'excessive innovation and adventurism' is precluded by the judicial role.[64] Changes 'by a few degrees' may, however, be foreseeable and predictable.[65] It has to be acknowledged that what some see as changes 'by a few degrees' may seem to others to be revolutionary. And in some of the negligence cases decided by Lord Bingham in the Court of Appeal, where the result was later reversed in the House of Lords, it would be foolish to think the last word has been written on the subject. In New Zealand, our case law has developed along lines more closely resembling the approach taken by Bingham LJ in the Court of Appeal in *Caparo Industries Plc v Dickman* in rejecting the search for a simple litmus test of proximity. We, too, have thought it more important in considering the existence of a duty of care to

---

[57] (n 37).   [58] (n 37) 320–321.   [59] [1995] 2 AC 633.
[60] A dissent vindicated on appeal to the House of Lords in *X*.   [61] *M* (n 59) 664.
[62] [1989] 1 QB 653.   [63] [1999] 3 WLR 873.
[64] 'The Rule of Law' (n 7) 71.   [65] 'The Rule of Law' (n 7) 71.

concentrate on the substance of 'the degree of closeness between the parties'.[66] We, too, have been wary of erecting 'doctrinal boundaries' which will inevitably be overtaken.[67] And we also have seen the determination of questions of liability in novel cases as better addressed by frank acknowledgement of policy considerations, as Lord Denning MR urged in *Dutton v Bognor Regis Urban District Council*,[68] rather than under the conclusionary labels of 'proximity', 'foreseeability', 'neighbourhood' and so on. These are not tests of liability so much as considerations which may be useful in deciding whether imposition of liability is just.

That was the approach Lord Bingham adopted in *Rees v Darlington Memorial Hospital*, in upholding the decision in *McFarlane v Tayside Health Board*[69] that the full financial costs of bringing up a healthy but unwanted child could not be recovered for reasons of legal policy. For reasons of policy too, however (the unfairness of denying the victim of a legal wrong any recompense beyond the immediate costs of birth), Lord Bingham supported a generous 'conventional award' to mark the injury and loss actually suffered to afford 'some measure of recognition of the wrong done' and 'to afford a more ample measure of justice' than the pure *McFarlane* rule.[70]

Similar resort to practical justice is to be seen in the earlier case of *Hunt v Severs*.[71] There, in a decision of the Court of Appeal, Bingham LJ, for reasons of legal policy, thought that practical injustice would result if the plaintiff was unable to recover the costs of nursing care provided to her by the defendant, whom she had married. Lord Bingham considered that 'in human terms' it would be undesirable if recovery were precluded because the husband wished personally to care for his wife.[72] And he was concerned that the law should not give plaintiffs an incentive to rely on paid help rather than the help of someone in the position of the defendant.

In Lord Bingham's view, policies against imposition of liability need to be powerful indeed to outweigh the injustice of leaving a legal wrong without remedy in compensation. In *M v Newham London Borough Council* and *X v Bedfordshire County Council*, Sir Thomas Bingham said:[73]

If [the plaintiff] can make good her complaint (a right or condition which I forbear constantly to repeat), it would require very potent considerations of public policy, which do not in my view exist here, to over-ride the rule of public policy which has first claim on the loyalty of the law: that wrongs should be remedied.

The view that legal policy requires just outcomes leads into the final point I want to make about Lord Bingham's appeal to judges of the common law world. It

---

[66] *Brown v Heathcote County Council* [1987] 1 NZLR 720 (PC); *South Pacific Manufacturing Co v New Zealand Security Investigations Ltd* [1992] 2 NZLR 282; *Couch v Attorney-General* [2008] NZSC 45.

[67] See *Attia* (n 37) 320.   [68] [1972] 1 QB 373, 397.   [69] [2000] 2 AC 59.

[70] *Rees* (n 39) 317.   [71] [1993] QB 815.   [72] *Hunt* (n 71) 831.

[73] *M* (n 59) 663.

is his willingness to express the moral values of the law. This is morality of the muscular, rather than the prosy sort. It seems to me to be based squarely on the justification for law as necessary response to human needs. It is fixed upon living people in today's society. Such necessary focus has been described by Justice David Souter of the United States Supreme Court as 'the judicial paradox':[74]

we have no hope of serving the most exalted without respecting the most concrete. Judicial duty points to Blake's grain of sand.

This is the view that 'details spark the intuition and real judging gets done from the ground up'.[75] Lord Bingham seldom strays from the people caught up in the case. And he is willing to express their needs and explain why the law should respond to them in ways that anyone who believes in law finds hard to resist.

Again, I give a few examples only. In confronting the legal policy argument against compensation in the wrongful birth case of *Rees*, which had earlier been determinative in *McFarlane*, Lord Bingham looked to the realities of the impact upon the living people who had been wronged:[76]

The spectre of well-to-do parents plundering the National Health Service should not blind one to other realities: that of the single mother with young children, struggling to make ends meet and counting the days until her children are of an age to enable her to work more hours and so enable the family to live a less straitened existence; the mother whose burning ambition is to put domestic chores so far as possible behind her and embark on a new career or resume an old one. Examples can be multiplied. To speak of losing the freedom to limit the size of one's family is to mask the real loss suffered in a situation of this kind. This is that a parent, particularly (even today) the mother, has been denied, through the negligence of another, the opportunity to live her life in the way that she wished and planned. I do not think that an award immediately relating to the unwanted pregnancy and birth gives adequate recognition of or does justice to that loss.

In *R v Chief Constable of North Wales Police ex p AB*,[77] Lord Bingham, in holding that the police were justified in releasing information about convicted paedophiles who had served their sentence, expressed the important warning (one I have been grateful to adopt in a case with some similarities in New Zealand) that it is not acceptable that those who have completed their sentences be 'harried from parish to parish like paupers under the old Poor Laws':[78]

It is not only in their interest but in the interest of society as a whole that they should be enabled, and if need be helped, to live normal, lawful lives.

In *Limbuela*, Lord Bingham declined to accept that inhuman treatment under Article 3 of the European Convention on Human Rights is confined to 'your mountainish inhumanity'.[79] It applied to those with no means and no sources of

[74] David H Souter, 'Gerald Gunther' (2002) 55 Stanford Law Review 635, 636.
[75] Souter (n 74) 636.   [76] Rees (n 39) 317.
[77] [1999] QB 396.   [78] *AB* (n 77) 414.
[79] [2006] 1 AC 396, 402 (in citation of Shakespeare and other in *Sir Thomas More*).

support who were 'by the deliberate action of the state, denied shelter, food or the most basic necessities of life'. In *R (on the application of Razgar) v Secretary of State for the Home Department (No 2)*[80] Lord Bingham was prepared to accept that the removal of an asylum seeker to a country where he could not obtain the psychiatric help he had in the United Kingdom and which he needed to 'enjoy a measure of freedom, independence and autonomy' could threaten his right to private life, protected by Article 8:

I think one must understand 'private life' in article 8 as extending to those features which are integral to a person's identity or ability to function socially as a person.

Judges who parrot the thinking of others in different cases, who do not ground their judgment on the justice of the case in hand, or who are blind to the possibilities beyond the actual case for the litigants to come, do not fit the law for living people. Cases such as these demonstrate why Lord Bingham cannot be reproached with lifting his eye from the ball. In a letter to Benjamin Cardozo towards the end of his life, Oliver Wendell Holmes wrote of the satisfaction of judging:[81]

I have always thought that not place or power or popularity makes the success that one desires, but the trembling hope that one has come near to an ideal. The only ground that warrants a man for thinking that he is not living a fool's paradise if he ventures such a hope is the voice of a few masters... I feel it so much that I don't want to talk about it.

In Lord Bingham we hear a master's voice. It gives hope to those who love law that we can come near to the ideal.

---

[80] [2004] 2 AC 368.   [81] 'Mr Justice Holmes' (n 36) 86.

4

The Independence of the Judge

David Keene

Judicial independence has long been seen as the foundation stone of the Rule of Law, and rightly so. In the United Kingdom judges take the oath to do right by all manner of men 'without fear or favour, affection or ill-will', which requires impartiality but also demands freedom from external pressures, whether from other judges or from the executive. The latter has become especially important with the explosive growth of judicial review over the last 30 to 40 years since *Anisminic* [1969] and the modernization of the procedural rules in 1977. No citizen challenging a decision of a government department which affects him wants his case decided by a judge whose tenure or promotion may depend on the goodwill of government, any more than would a civil litigant suing such a body for damages in contract or tort.

The need for a judge's tenure of office to be secure has, of course, been recognized for centuries. Montesquieu himself, observing the British constitution in the 18th century, noted that judicial independence had been declared, basing that conclusion on the inability of the executive to remove a judge of the superior courts from office. The Act of Settlement 1700 had provided that such judges held office during good behaviour and could only be removed 'upon the address of both Houses of Parliament'—a provision now embodied in section 11 of the Supreme Court Act 1981. This was undoubtedly hugely important: it was intended to prevent repetition of such events as the dismissal of Sir Edward Coke as Lord Chief Justice by James I. But patently preventing the dismissal of judges by the executive, vital though it is, cannot suffice to ensure a genuinely independent approach on the part of a judge to cases where the executive is involved. If the executive were able to make partisan appointments to the bench, or even more significantly, if the power to promote existing judges to higher positions is vested in the executive, then there is potential for the executive to exert influence on judicial decision-making.

That is why the effective removal of power from the Lord Chancellor over judicial appointments and promotions is to be welcomed. Though I am aware of no evidence of political influence over judicial appointments in recent decades, that has depended on the personal integrity of the holder of the Lord Chancellor's office, and there could have been no guarantee that that would necessarily have endured. Old political attitudes die hard. It was less than a century ago that there was a recognized practice under which the Attorney-General could not merely move directly to become Lord Chief Justice when that office fell vacant but could assert a *right* to first refusal of the position. Hence Rufus Isaacs in 1913 went from being Attorney-General, with a seat in Mr Asquith's cabinet and a record of nine years as a Liberal MP, to become Lord Chief Justice, attracting little adverse comment—save for his involvement in the Marconi scandal. Sir Gordon Hewart later vigorously advanced his own claims on the same basis and after a certain amount of manoeuvring became Lord Chief Justice in 1922.

This somewhat partisan approach to the appointment of the most senior judges was not new and was not confined to the position of Lord Chief Justice. At the end of the 19th century, when there was a vacancy for the Master of the Rolls, the then Prime Minister, Lord Salisbury, wrote to the Lord Chancellor, referring to the

rule that party claims should always weigh heavily in the disposal of the highest appointments.

It may seem that all this is ancient history, with no contemporary relevance. Two more recent examples suggest otherwise. A former Conservative MP has described to me an occasion when Margaret Thatcher was Prime Minister, and he went to see her to tell her that the then Lord Chief Justice, Lord Lane, was proposing to speak in the House of Lords in opposition to a government proposal which, in his view, would have a damaging effect on access to the courts. Mrs Thatcher's reaction was to exclaim: 'What, *my* Lord Chief Justice?' More recently, when the Constitutional Reform Bill was published, clause 21, dealing with appointments to the new Supreme Court, in its original form proposed that a Judicial Appointments Commission should provide a list of names to the Secretary of State whenever a vacancy occurred, a list with a minimum of two and a maximum of five names, allowing the Secretary of State to choose between them. The only criterion specified in the Bill was that he should choose 'the most suitable' and then that name would go to the Prime Minister and the Queen. Fortunately that proposal did not survive into the final version as enacted.

I recall a conversation around this time with a senior government minister about the proposal that, when a vacancy for Lord Chief Justice arose, the Commission should submit two names, leaving the choice to the Prime Minister. This was defended to me by the minister on the basis that it was necessary that the Lord Chief Justice should be able to work harmoniously with the government. It is true that the Lord Chief Justice or his representatives sit on various boards or committees with government representatives and that a degree of cooperation over administrative problems can be required. But in any event, what that defence overlooked was that governments change, and a Lord Chief Justice chosen because he or she was seen by one government as helpful or understanding may well be seen by the next government, especially if of a different political

persuasion, as quite the reverse. This is a recurrent problem with politically partisan appointments to the bench, as the fate of the 42 'midnight appointees' in
the famous American case of *Marbury v Madison* 5 US 137 (1803), 5 US 137
(Cranch) vividly illustrates. Thus, despite all the safeguards now achieved in the
Constitutional Reform Act, there is a need for continued vigilance to protect the
independence of the judiciary.

That may be thought to be unduly alarmist. Yet there can be little doubt that
the opening years of the present century have seen an unusual degree of tension
between the government and the judiciary. There has for some time been direct
or indirect criticism by government ministers of judicial decisions not to their
liking, particularly in the fields of criminal sentencing and asylum and immigration. But the more recent strains appear to derive from a combination of two factors: the passage of the Human Rights Act 1998 and the increased anxiety about
terrorist atrocities, which has led to legislative inroads into traditional human
rights.

The Human Rights Act, by giving domestic effect to much of the European
Convention on Human Rights, and the new emphasis upon proportionality, has
required the courts to reach judgments on the need for and the reasonableness of
those legislative inroads, judgments for which doctrines of precedent and conventional legal principles often provide little clear guidance. One can see that from
the well-known passage from the Privy Council decision in *de Freitas v Permanent
Secretary of Ministry of Agriculture, Fisheries, Lands and Housing* [1999] 1 AC 69,
80, where it was said that the court must ask itself:

whether (i) the legislative objective is sufficiently important to justify limiting a fundamental right; (ii) the measures designed to meet the legislative objective are rationally
connected to it; and (iii) the means used to impair the right or freedom are no more than
is necessary to accomplish the objective.

All three tests, but perhaps especially the third, necessarily involve a judgment
being applied to the facts of an individual case, and experienced and rational
judges may—and not infrequently do—arrive at different conclusions on the
answers to the questions thus posed. Yet this has been happening at a time when
government takes the view that long-established constraints upon the ability of
the executive to protect the public may need to be put aside. In the words of Mr
Blair when Prime Minister, 'the rules of the game are changing'.

This combination has undoubtedly presented new and complex challenges for
the judiciary, particularly at its highest level in the House of Lords Appellate
Committee. Some of the new anti-terrorist legislation has involved a shift away
from the criminal justice model of punishing those who have committed offences,
and doing so through the ordinary criminal courts, to an approach based upon
pre-emption, that is to say, on an assessment of the *risk* of *future* activity. Thus one
has seen a series of statutes seeking to detain and control individuals who have as
yet committed no crime. They include the Anti-Terrorism, Crime and Security

Act 2001 and the Prevention of Terrorism Act 2005, the former being passed soon after the attacks on New York, Washington DC, and Pennsylvania on 11 September 2001, the latter being enacted some three months after the decision by the House of Lords in *A and Others v Secretary of State for the Home Department* [2004] UKHL 56, which had found section 23 of the 2001 Act (allowing for the detention of foreign nationals suspected of being terrorists) to be incompatible with Articles 5 and 14 of the European Convention on Human Rights (ECHR). Those at whom some of these provisions were and are aimed are people who, as Lord Bingham has pointed out on more than one occasion, are not the subject of any criminal charge nor do they face the prospect of a criminal trial. Inevitably these statutes have given rise to issues which the House of Lords, with Lord Bingham as Senior Law Lord, have been called upon to resolve. Those issues have involved fundamental problems of balancing vital traditional rights to liberty and fair trial with the essential requirement of any society for its own safety. That task has brought the courts into a degree of conflict with the Government.

It is undoubtedly a task which has required, and received, clear judicial leadership to steer a steady and principled course through treacherous waters. A number of themes can be discerned in the judgments given by Lord Bingham in the series of cases dealt with by the House of Lords in this area. The first concerns the respective roles of the courts and the executive.

In the case of *A and Others* (above), it was argued by the Attorney-General that, just as it was for Parliament and the executive to assess the threat facing the nation, so it was for those bodies and not the courts to judge what response was necessary to protect the security of the public, including what restrictions on personal liberty were required for that purpose. Such matters, it was said, fell within the discretionary area of judgment properly belonging to the democratic organs of the state. 'It was not for the courts to usurp authority properly belonging elsewhere.'

With that last proposition no one could argue. But its suggested application to issues involving rights under the ECHR, especially a right as fundamental as that to personal liberty, and the contrast sought to be drawn between democratic institutions on the one hand and the courts on the other, received short shrift in Lord Bingham's judgment. In particular, he rejected the distinction between democratic institutions and the courts, while accepting that Parliament, the executive, and the courts have different functions:

But the function of independent judges charged to interpret and apply the law is universally recognised as a cardinal feature of the modern democratic state, a cornerstone of the rule of law itself. The Attorney General is fully entitled to insist on the proper limits of judicial authority, but he is wrong to stigmatise judicial decision-making as in some way undemocratic. It is particularly inappropriate in a case such as the present in which Parliament has expressly legislated in section 6 of the 1998 Act to render unlawful any act of a public authority, including a court, incompatible with a Convention right, has required courts (in section 2) to take account of relevant Strasbourg jurisprudence, has (in section 3) required courts, so far as possible, to give effect to Convention rights and has conferred a right of appeal on derogation issues. The effect is not, of course, to override the sovereign legislative authority of the Queen in Parliament, since if primary legislation is declared to be incompatible the validity of the legislation is unaffected (section 4(6)) and the remedy lies with the appropriate minister (section 10), who is answerable to Parliament. The 1998 Act gives the courts a very specific, wholly democratic, mandate.

Lord Bingham went on to emphasize (in paragraph 44) that the duty of the courts to protect rights under the ECHR would be emasculated if there were excessive deference to ministerial decisions in matters involving indefinite detention without charge or trial.

None of this can be seen as a reluctance to acknowledge the proper role of Parliament and the executive. As Lord Devlin put it, soon after the *Anisminic* decision:

the British have no more wish to be governed by judges than they have to be judged by administrators.

On issues such as whether a foreign national is a danger to national security, the courts have acknowledged that the Home Secretary is generally better placed to form an opinion: see, for example, *Rehman* [2001] UKHL 47. That approach was followed by Lord Bingham and other Law Lords in *A and Others* on what he identified as the first issue, namely whether or not there existed a 'public emergency threatening the life of the nation' within the meaning of Article 15(1) of the ECHR, thus allowing a state in principle to derogate from its obligations under the Convention. He held that great weight should be given to the judgment of the Home Secretary and Parliament because this was pre-eminently a political judgment. He put the matter in this way:

It is perhaps preferable to approach this question as one of demarcation of functions or what Liberty in its written case called 'relative institutional competence'. The more purely political (in a broad or narrow sense) a question is, the more appropriate it will be for political resolution and the less likely it is to be an appropriate matter for judicial decision. The smaller, therefore, will be the potential role of the court. It is the function of political and not judicial bodies to resolve political questions. Conversely, the greater the legal content of any issue, the greater the potential role of the court, because under our constitution and subject to the sovereign power of Parliament it is the function of the courts and not of political bodies to resolve legal questions. The present question seems to me to be very much at the political end of the spectrum.

However, where fundamental rights were potentially being eroded, Lord Bingham has subjected the justification for the erosion to rigorous and rational scrutiny. It is convenient to remain with the case of *A and Others* for an initial example. During the course of his judgment in that case, Lord Bingham referred to the statement by Lord Hope of Craighead in *Ex p Kebilene* [2000] 2 AC 326, 381, where it had been said that where rights of high constitutional importance were involved, the courts were especially well placed to assess the need for protection. Lord Bingham also cited with approval the words of La Forest J in *RJR-MacDonald Inc v Attorney General of Canada* [1995] 3 SCR 199:

Courts are specialists in the protection of liberty.

That role as the guardian of basic human rights was not one which the courts could relinquish, as the decision in *A and Others* vividly illustrates.

It is sometimes thought that the decision of the House of Lords in *A and Others* to quash the derogation order and to declare section 23 of the 2001 Act incompatible with the ECHR was founded upon the discriminatory nature of those provisions and the consequent conflict with Article 14 of the Convention. It is certainly true that that formed one of the bases for the decision. But the outcome of the case was also based upon a breach of Article 5, the right to liberty and security of person, and that was the first ground upon which Lord Bingham held that the order should be quashed and a declaration of incompatibility made.

His analysis on this identified a fundamental problem with how the government and Parliament had sought to deal with the terrorist threat. Section 23 of the 2001 Act empowered the Home Secretary to detain a 'suspected international terrorist' under, in effect, Schedule 3 of the Immigration Act 1971, even though his removal or departure from the United Kingdom was prevented temporarily or indefinitely by a point of law or a practical consideration. This overcame the well-established limit on the use of Schedule 3, paragraph 2(2), powers, which but for the 2001 Act only enabled the Home Secretary to detain a non-British national pending the making of a deportation order against him and not to do so on a long-term basis or indefinitely. But using powers under the Immigration Act 1971 to detain suspected terrorists produced its own inherent difficulties, since such powers could only be employed in respect of foreign nationals and not British nationals. That was not merely discriminatory, but it undermined the government's whole justification for the interference with the rights of foreign nationals under Article 5 to their personal liberty.

The justification put forward was that these foreign nationals, suspected of involvement in international terrorism, were a threat to the national security of the United Kingdom. Some could be deported, but others could not, because they would face torture, death, or inhuman or degrading treatment in their home countries, and so they had to be detained, perhaps indefinitely, in order to protect this country's security. But in order for that interference with their Article 5 rights, given that they had not been convicted of any criminal offence, to be proportionate, it had to be shown that the interference was *necessary* in order to achieve the objective of safeguarding the security of the United Kingdom.

Yet as Lord Bingham pointed out, the first-instance court, the Special Immigration Appeals Commission, had found that the threat to national security was not confined to foreign nationals but derived also from many British nationals. That latter threat was not addressed by section 23 of the 2001 Act, even though that threat is not said to be qualitatively different from that from foreign nationals (paragraph 33).

It was presumably addressed by other measures not involving the deprivation of liberty, and if that were so, how could it be said that it was necessary to deprive these foreign nationals of their liberty in order to achieve the protection of those living in the United Kingdom? Likewise, if a country could be found willing to receive a foreign national suspected of involvement in international terrorism, he was permitted under the 2001 Act to leave the United Kingdom and to go to

perhaps a country as close as France, there to pursue his criminal designs.

That, said Lord Bingham, was hard to reconcile with a belief in his capacity to inflict serious injury to the people and interests of this country.

In the event, the House of Lords held that the derogation order and section 23 of the 2001 Act were disproportionate. What shines through this analysis which I have sought to summarize is the rigorous intellectual scrutiny being applied to arguments advanced for interfering with a fundamental human right. Given the lack of sympathy in the public at large for those suspected of involvement in international terrorism, this was a powerful upholding of the rights of an unpopular minority.

As is well known, the result of the House of Lords decision in *A and Others* was the introduction of control orders by the Prevention of Terrorism Act 2005, essentially an attempt to constrain suspected terrorists without actually detaining them. Inevitably, such control orders have given rise to complex but important issues involving human rights, particularly those established in Article 5 (the right to liberty) and Article 6 (the right to a fair trial) of the ECHR. Again, the cases have seen the courts having to make difficult judgments on matters involving government and the individual.

In *Secretary of State for the Home Department v JJ* [2007] UKHL 45, the House of Lords was faced with control orders on Iraqi nationals suspected by the Home Secretary of involvement in terrorism and assessed to present a threat to the people of the United Kingdom. The issue was whether the extent of the restrictions imposed on them were so extensive as to amount to a deprivation of their liberty and were thus inconsistent with Article 5. The control orders confined the controlled persons to their residences, in each case a one-bedroom flat, for 18 hours a day, during which time they were only allowed visitors authorized by the Home Office. During the six hours when they were permitted out, between 10am and 4pm, they were confined to restricted areas and were prohibited from meeting anyone by pre-arrangement without Home Office clearance. Other restrictions also applied.

The Strasbourg Court had recognized that the difference between deprivation of liberty, contrary to Article 5, and restriction upon liberty was merely one of degree—in Lord Bingham's words, 'there is no bright line separating the two'. Nonetheless the lower courts had held that these control orders fell into the former category and Lord Bingham could see no error of law in those lower court decisions. But he went further and indicated that he would have reached the same conclusions on the facts, describing the effects of the restrictions as being that the controlled persons

were in practice in solitary confinement for this lengthy period every day for an indefinite duration... Their lives were wholly regulated by the Home Office, as a prisoner's would be, although breaches were much more severely punishable (paragraph 24).

That this was a measured response can be seen from the House of Lords decision delivered on the same day in the case of *Secretary of State for the Home Department v MB* [2007] UKHL 46, where a control order imposing a 14-hour curfew from 6pm to 8am, plus certain other restrictions, was held not to deprive the controlled person of his liberty in breach of Article 5.

However, the *JJ* case is significant for Lord Bingham's identification of the weakness of the procedures prescribed for hearings when the court is reviewing a control order made or to be made by the Home Secretary. Those procedures require (on the face of them) the court not to disclose material contrary to the public interest and the exclusion of the controlled person and his legal representatives from a hearing if that is necessary in the public interest, though provision is made for the appointment of a special advocate to represent the interests of that person. Is this compatible with the right to a fair trial enshrined in Article 6?

Lord Bingham emphasized that the requirements of procedural fairness could not be met where a person was prevented from knowing what was said against him to such an extent that he was not able to challenge or rebut the case against him. While acknowledging that the use of special advocates could assist, he pointed out that the controlled person

... does not know the allegations made against him and cannot therefore give meaningful instructions, and the special advocate, once he knows what the allegations are, cannot tell the controlled person or seek instructions without permission, which in practice (as I understand) is not given. 'Grave disadvantage' is not, I think, an exaggerated description of the controlled person's position where such circumstances obtain.

This led him to conclude that, in cases where the control order could not be justified on the basis of the open material alone and the thrust of the case against the controlled person had not been effectively conveyed to him in some way, then the very essence of the right to a fair hearing had been impaired. He described that right as fundamental and added:

The concept of fairness imports a core, irreducible minimum of procedural protection.

Perhaps the most memorable and indeed passionate statements to have come from Lord Bingham in recent years are to be found in the 'torture case', *A and Others v Secretary of State for the Home Department* [2005] UKHL 71, where the Secretary of State contended that the Special Immigration Appeals Commission (SIAC), when hearing an appeal under the 2001 Act by a detained person, could properly receive evidence which had or might have been procured by torture inflicted by officials of a foreign state without the complicity of the British authorities. A majority of the Court of Appeal had held that it could, albeit that the possibility that it had been so obtained would go to the weight to be attached to such evidence. In a magisterial survey of domestic and international law, Lord Bingham rejected that view.

He noted that from its very earliest days the common law of England had set its face firmly against the use of torture. The argument for the Secretary of State was founded upon the SIAC Procedure Rules 2003, one provision of which stated that SIAC 'may receive evidence that would not be admissible in a court of law': rule 44(3). This, it was said, empowered SIAC to receive evidence obtained overseas by means of torture or which may have been so obtained. Lord Bingham's response was in emphatic terms:

> But the English common law has regarded torture and its fruits with abhorrence for over 500 years, and that abhorrence is now shared by over 140 countries which have acceded to the Torture Convention. I am startled, even a little dismayed, at the suggestion (and the acceptance by the Court of Appeal majority) that this deeply-rooted tradition and an international obligation solemnly and explicitly undertaken can be overridden by a statute and a procedural rule which make no mention of torture at all.
>
> ...
>
> It trivialises the issue before the House to treat it as an argument about the law of evidence. The issue is one of constitutional principle, whether evidence obtained by torturing another human being may lawfully be admitted against a party to proceedings in a British court, irrespective of where, or by whom, or on whose authority the torture was inflicted. To that question I would give a very clear negative answer.'

The concern for human dignity and for the rights of the individual is unmistakeable.

One of the features of this judgment, as with a number of Lord Bingham's judgments, is the extent to which he employs historical research to assist in his analysis. In this 'torture case', one finds not merely references to Coke and to Blackstone, but ones also which go back to the works of Sir John Fortescue 1460–1470, and which are then followed by a discussion of the royal prerogative in the period leading up to and during the English Civil War. This historical perspective is perhaps to be expected of someone who read not law but history at university. Whatever its origins, it is something which has undoubtedly strengthened and illuminated his judgments.

But there is a more significant theme illustrated by the torture case. Once again one can see in Lord Bingham's opinion a deep concern for fair procedures, something already observed in respect of the *MB* case. It is all very well to resolve that evidence which has or may have been obtained overseas by the use of torture should not be admissible, but there then arises the crucial practical problem of proof. Who is required to prove that such is the possible origin of the evidence, and to what degree is that required to be proved? Lord Bingham recognized the difficulties inherent in dealing with evidence obtained by foreign authorities, especially if torture may have been employed. At the same time, it would be 'all but unmanageable' if a generalized and unsubstantiated allegation of torture were to impose a duty on the Secretary of State to prove an absence of torture.

His solution was to require the appellant in such cases to advance some plausible reason why evidence may have been procured by torture, by (for example) showing that it has, or is likely to have, come from a country widely known or believed to practice torture. It would then be for SIAC to

initiate or direct such inquiry as is necessary to enable it to form a fair judgment whether the evidence has, or whether there is a real risk that it may have been, obtained by torture or not.

In formulating such an approach, Lord Bingham was, however, in a minority in the Appellate Committee. The majority took the view that the test should be whether it was established, by means of such diligent enquiries into the sources that it was practicable to carry out, and on a balance of probabilities, that the information relied on was obtained under torture. Lord Bingham was not impressed:

This is a test which, in the real world, can never be satisfied. The foreign torturer does not boast of his trade. The security services, as the Secretary of State has made clear, do not wish to imperil their relations with regimes where torture is practised. The special advocates have no means or resources to investigate. The detainee is in the dark. It is inconsistent with the most rudimentary notions of fairness to blindfold a man and then impose a standard which only the sighted could hope to meet. The result will be that, despite the universal abhorrence expressed for torture and its fruits, evidence procured by torture will be laid before SIAC because its source will now have been 'established'.

Apart from the emphasis on the need for fairness in court procedures, one is struck by the vivid use of the English language. It is not a characteristic to be found universally in judicial pronouncements.

But I return to Lord Bingham's distinguished role in the upholding of fundamental human rights, often in the face of government opposition. These terrorist cases are significant in demonstrating the independence of the judiciary from the executive and also from popular pressures. Many sections of the media failed to understand fully the reasoning in cases such as *A and Others* in December 2004, which produced strident criticism of the Law Lords in some quarters. The decision was presented as having chosen the rights of suspected terrorists over the safety of the British people. But that was not the choice made by the House of Lords. Had it been faced with such a choice, the result would have been likely to have been different. The decision was rather that it had not been shown that it was necessary to interfere with those rights to personal liberty in order to protect the public. The Law Lords did not opt for 'human rights' over public safety, as some newspaper headlines sought to suggest.

Nonetheless, there can be no doubt that these decisions to which I have referred did not go down well with some of the British public. That, of course, is not a rare event: there have in the past been many cases dealing, for example, with those seeking asylum where the decisions have provoked an outcry in the tabloid press. Judges are well aware that their decisions will not always be popular and that, if not moral courage, at least a reasonably thick skin may often be required.

In any event, it is the classic task of the courts in a democracy to protect the rights of the individual, sometimes against the majority. Parliamentary sovereignty alone does not ensure this, as Albert Dicey himself was eventually forced to recognize. When Dicey was asked why Parliament did not command all blue-eyed babies to be killed, an important part of his answer was that MPs were not usually men of outrageous ideas. However, he was an Ulsterman, and in 1913 it became clear that MPs were about to vote in favour of the Home Rule Bill for Ireland. Not long afterwards, Dicey lost his faith in Parliamentary sovereignty and pledged himself to violent resistance by signing the Ulster Covenant. The fact is that a modern liberal democracy is not only about government according to the wishes of the majority. It is also based upon certain fundamental human rights, which do not automatically obtain protection through the rule of the majority. As John Stuart Mill emphasized 150 years ago in his introduction to 'On Liberty', there is a risk of the tyranny of the majority:

The people may desire to oppress a part of their number and precautions are as much needed against this as against any other abuse of power. The limitation therefore of the power of government over individuals loses none of its importance when the holders of power are regularly accountable to the community.

This country has long subscribed to that, which is why the United Kingdom played a major part in drafting the ECHR—so much so that there are some amongst the French judiciary who regard the Convention as an Anglo-Saxon intrusion into the civil law. The role of the courts in protecting the rights of individuals and of minorities, whether they be asylum-seekers, gypsies, prisoners, lesbians or gays, or simply those from a minority ethnic background, is as crucial as ever to our democratic health, and it is a task from which the courts should not shy away. That can be seen, for example, in the problems of Northern Ireland, which were undoubtedly exacerbated by the disregard of the rights of the Catholic minority over a long period of time. The institutions of democratic government can themselves be put in peril if such rights are not respected.

Those who inveigh against 'human rights' need to bear in mind that *their* rights are being protected along with those of obvious minorities. Indefinite detention without charge or trial is a powerful weapon in the hands of any government. History tells us of many groups in various countries against whom it has, in some guise or another, been employed in the past, whether they be Jews in Nazi Germany, middle-class intellectuals in some parts of Communist Europe, or those striving for a multi-racial society in apartheid South Africa. Newspaper editors are not immune from such risks in certain countries if they oppose the Government. The point was well put by Robert Bolt in *A Man for All Seasons*, in a famous passage:

Sir Thomas More: 'What would you do? Cut a great road through the law to get after the devil?'

Roper: 'Yes. I'd cut down every law in England to do that!'

More: 'Oh? And when the last law was down, and the devil turned 'round on you, where would hide, Roper, the laws all being flat? This country is planted thick with laws, from coast to coast, man's laws, not Gods! And if you cut them down (and you're just the man to do it!), do you really think you could stand upright in the winds that would blow then? Yes, I'd give the devil the benefit of law, for my own safety's sake.'

None of this is to deny government its own proper role, as these terrorist cases themselves acknowledge. Our constitution works best when each of our institutions respects the proper province of the others. The courts will loyally apply the law as altered by Parliament from time to time, since it is the law, not the judges, which is supreme. And the courts will recognize the entitlement of the government to govern, so long as the law is observed. One hopes that in turn it can be taken for granted that both Parliament and government will recognize the importance in a free society of a judiciary truly independent, even if the outcome of individual cases is not always to their liking.

That independence has been asserted time and again by Lord Bingham through his decisions made in a long and distinguished judicial career. His legacy may be found not solely in those decisions, however, but also in the model which he has provided for other judges to follow and in the standard he has set for them to strive to attain. His intellect, clarity of expression, and strength of purpose will be greatly missed in the courts of our country.

5

Judicial Independence: A Functional Perspective

Beverley McLachlin

Shortly before his appointment as Lord Chief Justice of England and Wales, Lord Bingham delivered a public lecture at King's College London on the topic of 'The Courts and the Constitution'. Turning to the question of judicial independence, Lord Bingham observed that the constitutional safeguards that protect judicial tenure do not exist to make life easier for judges, to protect them against the consequences of their own mistakes, or to insulate them against legitimate public criticism. Rather, he said, they exist because 'an independent judiciary is recognized as being an essential feature of a free, democratic society, and independence involves not only the doing and saying of things which attract public acclaim but also, on occasion, the doing and saying of things that incur public opprobrium'.[1] Throughout his career, Lord Bingham has been an eloquent and articulate defender of the principle of judicial independence. It thus seems fitting to devote my contribution to this volume in his honour to this topic.

I start from the premise Lord Bingham has articulated: 'An independent judiciary is an essential feature of a free, democratic society'—a premise on which all democracies must concur. Three ideas are subsumed in the phrase, 'an independent judiciary'. The first is that there is a fundamental distinction between the functions of the courts and the functions of the legislature. The second is that in order for both these institutions to effectively discharge their unique and vital functions, each institution must remain independent of the other. The third is that for the judiciary to be independent, certain conditions must be present. Each of these ideas raises difficult issues and merits close consideration. I will argue that the meaning, importance, and pre-conditions of an independent judiciary are best understood by adopting a functional approach focused on the role of judges and how this role intersects with the functions of the legislative and executive branches of governance.

---

[1] Sir Thomas Bingham MR, 'The Courts and the Constitution,' (1996–1997), 7 KCLJ 12 at 13.

1. The Distinctive Roles of the Legislature and the Courts

First, let me turn to the fundamental distinction between the role of the courts and the role of the legislative and executive branches of governance. At first encounter, this distinction is so apparent as to require little explication. Legislatures pass laws, the executive implements them, and courts interpret and pronounce upon their application. Bluntly put, the legislative and executive branches of governance make and implement the law, while the judicial branch interprets and applies it.

Those observations are as sound as they are trite. It is not the role of the legislature or the executive to meddle in how judges apply the laws they have enacted to particular cases. If the legislature is dissatisfied with the courts' application of its legislation, its proper recourse is to amend the law, to make its intention clear. Similarly, it is not the role of the courts to 'make law' by redrafting the law made by the legislatures: if the law is within the constitutional powers of the legislature, the role of the court is confined to applying that law. Judges, outraged by the impact of a law in a particular case, may express their concern; this is in accord with an ancient and noble conception of the judicial function. But there they must stop.

Thus far, all seems clear. The legislature makes the law which is implemented by the executive; the judges interpret and apply it. Yet in practice, two features mar the absolute nature of the distinction between the judicial function and those of the other branches of governance: (1) lawmaking inherent in the judicial function; and (2) the role of the courts in judicial review and legislative invalidation.

The common law tradition of judge-made law needs neither explication nor defence for those who inhabit the considerable part of the legal world that has inherited the English legal system. Legislatures deliberate and enact legislation at a discreet distance from the men, women, and children affected by the laws. Or perhaps, oblivious to the needs of the citizen, they do not act at all. Judges, by contrast, are faced with the reality of how particular laws affect particular individuals. Historically, this reality provoked judges to intervene, and ultimately produced the common law.

This historical development rested on two propositions. First, in the absence of a legislative act precluding a just result, the courts would fill the gap, to do justice 'on the ground'. Secondly, judges faced with similar situations in the future, could use a prior judicial decision as 'precedent', and apply and enlarge on it. In this way, through the courts' exercise of their adjudicative function, the formidable corpus of the common law was built up: criminal law, contract law, tort law, and the law of judicial review of administrative action. Of course, all concerned recognized that the legislature held the upper hand, in that it retained the power to enact laws changing what common law judges had decided.

The civilian tradition proceeded by a different path, but arguably arrived at a not dissimilar result. The Napoleonic code in France provided what purported to be a fully developed legislative statement, covering all situations that might possibly arise. The legislatures of France and of other states that adopted this way of setting out the law effectively purported to occupy the field of legal expostulation. However, the aspiration to set out universal principles applicable to a myriad of human situations resulted in principles stated at a high level of generality. This generality conferred considerable discretion on judges as they applied general principles to particular situations, a discretion enhanced by the absence of a strict doctrine of precedent. Provided the judge could situate a decision within the general rule enunciated in the code as interpreted by academic writers (the jurisprudence), the decision was deemed correct. This was arguably a more elastic standard than that imposed in the common law tradition, where debates could (and did) rage over the minutiae of similarity between the precedential decision and the decision of a judge in a subsequent case.

Case-by-case judge-made law has not traditionally been viewed as an intrusion on the role of the legislature. Nor should it be. It is more accurate to describe the relationship between the two branches as one where each institution maintains its essential role, blurred at the edges owing to the dynamic character of the relationship and the elastic nature of the concept of lawmaking.

The legislature must legislate for the general case, taking into account the broadest considerations of principle, policy, and the wishes of the electorate in choosing how to legislate. In doing so, the legislature chooses its language in such a way as to give courts guidance as to how much scope it intends for judicial interpretation. When seeking to achieve a precise result and constrain judicial innovation, legislatures may spell out legislative injunctions and consequences in precise terms. When it is important to leave flexibility to adapt the law to changing and unforeseen circumstances, legislatures may deliberately use broad, general language—thereby implicitly inviting the courts to determine what effect is to be given to these broad provisions in particular cases.

In both the civilian and common law traditions, judges make law in the course of exercising their adjudicative function, in order to effect 'justice on the ground'. Yet in both traditions, the legislature retains the power to 'correct' the courts by enacting laws displacing the judge-made common law. In both traditions, the fundamental distinction between the role of the legislature and the role of the courts is maintained intact, despite the fact judges sometimes seem to 'make' the law, and legislatures often seem to accept and endorse this judge-made law. The two branches interact dynamically in an intricate constitutional dance, justified in terms of democratic governance and ultimate justice in particular case.

The second development that has blurred the distinction between the role of the legislature and the role of the courts is the adoption of constitutional bills of rights, such as the *Canadian Charter of Rights and Freedoms* and the United

Kingdom Human Rights Act, which have brought to the forefront the role courts play in invalidating and circumscribing legislative acts and the exercise of executive power.[2]

Canada adopted the *Charter of Rights and Freedoms* into the Canadian constitution in 1982. The *Charter* expressly empowered litigants to challenge laws and executive actions on the ground that they were inconsistent with the rights it proclaimed. The courts were required to resolve these challenges. When courts found the law to be inconsistent with the *Charter*, and hence void by section 52 of the Constitution Act, 1982, they attracted criticism that they had usurped the role of the legislature, by effectively nullifying the law it had enacted.

The United Kingdom sought to avoid this result when it adopted the Human Rights Act 1988 (HRA) by limiting the courts' power of remedy in the case of primary legislation to a 'declaration of incompatibility' (HRA, section 4). When it makes such a declaration, a court declares the legislation to be incompatible with a right guaranteed by the European Convention on Human Rights (ECHR) and incorporated into UK law with the HRA. The courts cannot invalidate primary legislation, but must return it to Parliament for reconsideration. Judicial intervention is thus less likely to attract censure. However, the result under the *Charter* and the HRA is arguably not dissimilar.[3]

If a law is declared incompatible with a Convention right, the Parliament in Westminster is faced with a stark choice: to violate its international obligations under the Convention, or to amend the law to conform to what the courts say the HRA requires. Thus far, Parliament has chosen to amend.[4]

The idea that it is the role of courts to rule on disputes over whether the legislature has exceeded its constitutional powers is not novel. Long before the *Charter*, courts in Canada had ruled that legislatures could not enact laws that violated 'implied' constitutional limits, such as freedom of political discourse, or freedom to hold and express minority religious views.[5] In the UK, the principle of judicial independence itself was first stated judicially long before it was enshrined in written constitutional documents, in the 17th century case of *Prohibitions del Roy*.[6]

---

[2] *Canadian Charter of Rights and Freedoms*, Pt I of the Constitution Act, 1982, being Schedule B to the Canada Act 1982 (UK), 1982, c 11; Human Rights Act 1998, 1988, c 42 (HRA).

[3] See Hon Bertha Wilson, 'We Didn't Volunteer,' in *Judicial Power and Canadian Democracy*, ed Paul Howe and Peter H Russell (Montreal and Kingston: McGill-Queens University Press, 2001) 63 at 77–79.

[4] See House of Commons and House of Lords Joint Committee on Human Rights, *Monitoring the Government's Response to Court Judgments Finding Breaches of Human Rights*, Sixteenth Report of Session 2006–07 (London: The Stationery Office, 2007). Of the 24 declarations of incompatibility issued between the Act's coming into force and May 2007, six had been overturned on appeal, one was being appealed, and twelve had been remedied or were in the process of being remedied. In the remaining five cases, the Government was considering how to remedy the incompatibility.

[5] See *Reference re Alberta Statutes* [1938] SCR 100 (press freedom); *Saumur v City of Quebec*, [1953] 2 SCR 299 (religious freedom).

[6] 12 Co Rep 64, 77 ER 1342, [1607] EWHC KB J23. The principle now finds explicit written formulations, most recently in the Constitutional Reform Act 2005, 2005, c 4, s 3.

What is new, is that the adoption of explicit constitutional constraints has made recourse to the courts more frequent and more visible. In the result, courts are more often accused of trammelling the powers of the legislature, while simply doing what they have always been required to do—to interpret and apply the law. The impression of judicial legislation may be exacerbated by the fact that constitutional provisions are typically cast in broad, general terms, leaving considerable scope for judicial definition. When the result is to qualify or set aside a law enacted by the legislature, the view that the courts are making the law cannot be far behind.

Judicial review of executive action on constitutional or administrative law grounds may similarly attract the accusation of judicial over-reaching. Through its remedy provision in section 24(1), the Canadian *Charter* permits judicial review of executive acts for constitutionality, and administrative law principles permit review of their legality. In the UK, the judiciary has long exercised a common law jurisdiction of judicial review of administrative action, and now also exercises powers of judicial review under specific statutes. Section 6(1) of the HRA provides that a public authority cannot 'act in a way which is incompatible with a Convention right' unless it is required to do so by primary legislation, and so now serves as a statutory basis for judicial review of administrative action for compliance with the European Convention on Human Rights.

In summary, a dynamic and functional perspective is required to capture the distinct yet complementary functions of the legislatures, the executive, and the courts. The role of the legislature is to enact legislation, and the role of the executive is to implement it. The role of the courts, by contrast, is to interpret and apply the law in adjudicating particular cases. In fulfilling their essential adjudicative function, courts to some extent inevitably, whether at common law or in the civilian tradition, 'make' law. In interpreting and applying the ultimate law, the constitution, courts may constrain the choices of the legislature, another form of 'making' law. Finally, through constitutional and legal review of executive acts, the courts inevitably constrain the executive power of government. All of this, I would argue, is as it should be. Working independently and in constructive tension, courts and legislatures are both essential to a legal system that is coherent and just in its ultimate application.

2. The Institutional Need for Independence

I have suggested that the legislative, executive, and judicial branches of governance play different but imbricated roles in maintaining the rule of law and day-to-day justice. The distinctiveness of their respective roles require that certain fundamental boundaries be respected by each branch in order to preserve constitutional democracy and the rule of law.

Unlike some other jurisdictions, the constitutional traditions of Canada and the UK do not contain a doctrine of strict separation of powers. In many respects, the relationship between legislative and the executive branches on the one hand, and the judicial branch on the other, is a relationship of interdependence. As discussed, the development of the law and the administration of justice involves all three branches of governance in the common enterprise of maintaining the rule of law, notwithstanding the distinct role each branch plays. The interlock between the judicial branch and the other branches is also replicated in features of how courts are established, staffed, and maintained. Judges are typically appointed by the executive or legislative branches, or some combination thereof. The legislative branch sets judges' salaries and terms of office and votes the money for the operation of the courts, and in most countries, the legislative branch may remove a judge for misconduct. Finally, the judiciary, which must avoid being drawn into debate in the public arena, traditionally relies on the executive, specifically the Minister of Justice, to defend it against misplaced attacks.

Judicial independence does not deny the many ways in which the judicial branch of governance interacts with the executive and legislative branches of governance. What it insists on is that the judiciary be independent in discharging its adjudicative function, that is to say, in deciding the cases brought before the courts. What is required is *functional* independence.

The requirement of functional independence is not unique to the judiciary. We take it for granted, for instance, that elected members of Parliament or the legislature should vote in the way they think best, with a view to the will of the people as expressed through their votes, and unconstrained by the courts. This legislative independence is a basic pre-condition of responsible government, the cornerstone of democracy. As the elected representatives of the people, legislators bring the voice of the people to governance in a way that appointed judges cannot do. Legislators, in casting their vote, may wish to consider how a law will be applied in the courts or whether it will be upheld on a constitutional challenge. But the courts do not tell them how to vote. As a corollary, the courts have a duty to apply duly enacted legislation in the manner intended by the legislature. The courts cannot subvert the rule of law and the principle of responsible government by interpreting legislation capriciously in order to substitute their own policy preferences for those of the legislature.

The power of legislatures to legislate as they see fit is constrained only by the bounds of the constitution. As described in the previous section, it is an essential function of the courts to determine these constitutional limits. In the common law world, this usually arises only after legislation is enacted, in the form of judicial review. In some political systems, as in France, a specialized constitutional court is tasked with advising the legislature on the constitutionality of a law before its final passage. But even in this case, the distinction between the legislative and judicial functions is strictly maintained.[7] In a similar vein, courts in Canada may be asked by a provincial or the federal government for an advisory ruling. Court responses to such requests, or 'references', have precedential value and are regarded as constitutionally binding.[8] But they are binding only in the legitimate judicial sense of enforcing constitutional bounds on legislative power.

The executive branch of governance is closely connected to the legislative branch, and like it, operates independently of interference from the judiciary. Like the legislative branch, the executive branch must operate within the limits set by the constitution. Additionally, the executive is bound by the more general rule of law principle that all exercises of public authority must find their source in law.[9] This principle serves as the constitutional foundation for judicial review for breach of natural justice and rationality. In exercising their administrative law jurisdiction of judicial review, however, the courts are not stepping into the shoes of the executive but rather enforcing the principle that the executive can act only in accordance with the law. Furthermore, in playing their vital role in reviewing the exercise of executive power on these grounds, courts recognize and accord appropriate deference to the exercise of executive power. An independent executive, operating within its proper bounds is, like the legislature, essential to democratic governance.

Like the legislative and executive branches of governance, the judicial branch must exercise its functions independently, with a view to its constitutional function of applying, interpreting, and upholding the law in the adjudication of particular cases. Just as it is essential to the rule of law that the judiciary interpret legislation in accordance with the intention of the legislator, so it is essential that the legislative and executive branches do not attempt to influence judges to apply the law inconsistently or capriciously in particular cases. The litigant is entitled to be judged by a person who decides the facts of every case and applies the relevant law objectively and impartially. This is so whether the dispute be between citizen and citizen, or between citizen and the state. The executive and legislative branches of governance are thus forbidden to interfere, in fact or in appearance, with a judge's exercise of adjudicative function. The executive branch of

---

[7] Art 57 of the Constitution of the Fifth Republic provides that '[t]he office of member of the Constitutional Council shall be incompatible with that of minister or member of Parliament.' See Burt Neuborne, 'Judicial Review and Separation of Powers in France and the United States,' (1982), 57 NYUL Rev 363 at 379–380.

[8] The Supreme Court is given jurisdiction to hear such references by s 53 of the Supreme Court Act, RSC 1985, C S-26. Similar provisions in provincial acts, such as s 8 of the Ontario Courts of Justice Act, RSO, 1990, c C-43, confer jurisdiction on provincial courts of appeal to hear references at the request of provincial governments. The Supreme Court has jurisdiction to hear appeals from provincial references by virtue of s 36 of the Supreme Court Act.

[9] This principle was recently restated by the Supreme of Court of Canada in *Dunsmuir v New Brunswick*, 2008 SCC 8; for its origins see AV Dicey, *Introduction to the Study of the Law of the Constitution*, 10th edn (London: MacMillan, 1959).

governance may make submissions in court, as would any other litigant, but they cannot influence, directly or indirectly, what the judge thereafter decides.

Judicial independence, like legislative independence, is essential to democratic governance. Independent judicial review is the only way yet devised to ensure that legislated laws and executive power do not exceed the bounds set by the constitution. This is true even in the absence of a written constitution, and it is most certainly true where a written constitution delimits the powers of the legislative and executive branches. Judicial independence is also essential to upholding the rule of law and public confidence in the administration of justice, upon which security and prosperity depend.

To summarize, the interlocking yet distinct functions of the legislative, executive, and judicial branches of governance require that these branches discharge their constitutional functions without inappropriate interference from the other branches. In the case of the judiciary in particular, this requirement takes the form of judicial independence in fulfilling its adjudicative functions. In Canada, as in other liberal democracies, it is a basic constitutional requirement that tribunals adjudicating on the rights and responsibilities of citizens be independent of the other branches of governance.[10]

3. The Conditions of Judicial Independence

I have argued that the judiciary plays a unique and vital role in democratic governance and discussed how its functions interact with the functions of the legislative and executive branches of governance, to ensure legitimate constitutional governance and just legal outcomes in accordance with the rule of law. I have further argued that in order to discharge its proper constitutional function, the judiciary, like the other branches of governance, must function independently of the legislative and executive branches of governance in discharging its responsibility of interpreting and applying the law. I now come to the third and final question: what are the necessary conditions of independent judicial functioning?

The answer to this question becomes clear when it is approached from a functional perspective. As already discussed, the judiciary cannot be entirely institutionally independent of the legislative and executive branches of governance, since it depends on them for the appointment and remuneration of judges as well as for the provision of administrative infrastructure and protection against illegitimate attack. Nor can the judiciary claim justice as its exclusive preserve; the legislative, the executive, and judicial branches, each playing their distinct role, all have a part in shaping the legal fabric that structures society. In these

---

[10] This requirement of judicial independence does not extend to administrative tribunals, which are more closely related to the executive branch: *Ocean Port Hotel Ltd v British Columbia (General Manager, Liquor Control and Licensing Branch)*, [2001] 2 SCR 781.

senses, the judiciary is not and cannot be wholly independent. The core of judicial independence lies in a narrower concept—independence in exercising the adjudicative functions of the courts. It follows that the pre-conditions of judicial independence are the conditions that are necessary to enable both judges as individuals and the judiciary as an institution to carry out their adjudicative function in an independent manner.

In the Canadian context, the essential conditions necessary to satisfy the constitutional requirement of judicial independence are set out in *R v Valente*.[11] In *Valente*, the Supreme Court of Canada identified three essential pre-conditions for judicial independence: (1) security of tenure; (2) financial security; and (3) administrative independence. These conditions are relative rather than absolute: what is required is that a standard consistent with effective discharge of the judicial function be met for each of the three conditions. This standard must be satisfied in two senses: it must be met in fact; and it must appear to have been met. To preserve public confidence in the judiciary, it is not enough that the judiciary be independent in fact; it must appear to be independent. A functional approach to judicial independence thus indicates that the standard reflect what is required, in a particular context, to assure that the judiciary is—and is seen to be—capable of exercising its adjudicative function independently and without interference from the other two branches of governance.

Security of tenure

Security of tenure has long been recognized as an essential condition of judicial independence, both in the UK and in Canada. The principle that judges serve during good behaviour was codified in 1701 in the UK in the Act of Settlement,[12] and was incorporated into Canada's founding document, now known as the Constitution Act 1867.[13] Section 99 of that Act guarantees security of tenure for federally appointed superior court judges, providing that judges of these courts are to serve during good behaviour until the age of 75 and are removable only by the Governor General on Address of the Senate and House of Commons.

The standard to be met for security of tenure for the judiciary generally was squarely raised in *Valente*, where the court whose judicial independence had been challenged was the provincially appointed 'inferior' court now known as the Ontario Court of Justice. While commending section 99 of the Constitution Act as offering greater protection for judicial independence than the provisions governing security of tenure in Ontario provincial courts, the Supreme Court (per Le Dain J) held that the essential requirements for security of tenure did not

---

[11] *R v Valente*, [1985] 2 SCR 673.

[12] 12 & 13 Wm 3 c 2: 'That after the said limitation shall take effect as aforesaid, judges commissions be made *quamdiu se bene gesserint*, and their salaries ascertained and established; but upon the address of both Houses of Parliament it may be lawful to remove them.'

[13] Constitution Act 1867 (UK), 30 & 31 Vict, c 3, reprinted in RSC 1985, App II, No 5.

make the section 99 conditions mandatory. He held, however, that security of tenure requires, at a minimum, a tenure that is secure against interference from the executive branch in a discretionary or arbitrary manner. This requires that judges have a defined tenure—whether until a specific age, for a specific term, or for a specific adjudicative task—and that judges can be removed during this tenure only for cause. Effective protection for security of tenure further requires that when cause for removal is alleged, the allegation of cause be subject to independent review and determination by a process at which the judge affected is afforded a full opportunity to be heard.

The *Valente* court clearly understood that the essential requirements of security of tenure are defined by its role in ensuring that judges can appropriately fulfil their adjudicative function. The minimum requirement is not employment for life—or even employment until retirement—but employment on such terms that avoids the appearance of making a judge's continued employment dependent on making decisions with an eye to how others may perceive them. It is essential to the exercise of the judicial function that the judge, in fact and appearance, not be swayed by the possibility of termination as a result of a particular decision. In some contexts, for instance that of the common law courts in the UK and Canada, the mutual career expectations of governments and judges may be such that appointment until a specified retirement age is most appropriate. But in other contexts, the requirements of security of tenure may be met equally well by shorter fixed-term appointments.

The threat to judicial independence posed by the absence of fixed terms of appointment is illustrated by the practice in some jurisdictions of electing judges and requiring them to stand for re-election on periodic basis. The perception that this practice has led to electoral defeats for judges who participated in unpopular decisions, has attracted what one commentator has called an overwhelming sea of academic literature calling for its abolition,[14] as well as official condemnation from the American Bar Association.[15] In a recent concurring opinion expressing concern about the practice, Justice O'Connor of the United States Supreme Court noted that, 'if judges are subject to regular elections they are likely to feel that they have at least some personal stake in the outcome of every publicized case'.[16] Even if judges are able to suppress this feeling or refrain from acting on it, 'the public's confidence in the judiciary could be undermined simply by the possibility that judges would be unable to do so'. Judicial independence requires that judges both have and be seen to have security of tenure.

---

[14] For a recent discussion of the issue in relation to a particular case see Bronson D. Bills, 'A Penny for the Court's Thoughts? The High Price of Judicial Elections,' (2008), 3 NW J L & Soc Pol'y 29.

[15] American Bar Association, *An Independent Judiciary: Report of the ABA Commission on Separation of Powers and Judicial Independence* 96 (1997).

[16] *Republican Party of Minnesota v White*, (2002), 536 US 765 (per O'Connor J concurring).

Financial security

Like security of tenure, financial security has been implicitly recognized as a condition of judicial independence since the Act of Settlement.[17] In Canada, section 100 of the Constitution Act 1867 provides that judicial salaries for federally appointed superior court judges are to be set by Act of Parliament, thereby enacting protection at least against executive arbitrariness.

In a series of decisions after *Valente*, the Supreme Court has expanded on the minimal protections required for financial independence of the judiciary.[18] These requirements, once again, are tied to the conditions required for proper discharge of the judicial function. In order to fulfil their adjudicative functions independently, both individual judges and the courts as institutions must be and be seen to be protected from the possibility of economic manipulation by the other two branches of governance. The relationship between the courts and the other branches of governance must be *depoliticized*: the courts must be seen to be free of political interference in the exercise of their judicial functions through economic manipulation, and must not become entangled in the politics of remuneration from the public purse.

In order to protect the requisite degree of institutional independence, the court has affirmed the requirement of an independent compensation commission to serve as an 'institutional sieve' between the executive and legislative branches and the judiciary. Changes to judicial compensation must be made through a commission process that is *independent*, *effective*, and *objective*. If the government chooses not to accept the recommendations of the independent commission's report, it must give reasons, which are subject to judicial review on a reasonableness standard.[19] Additionally, the commission must meet on a periodic basis to ensure that inflation does not erode judicial salaries to an extent that would threaten judicial independence.

As a consequence of these decisions, salaries for federal judges in Canada continue to be set by statute as required by section 100 of the Constitution Act,[20] but now only after a quadrennial process of consultation through an independent commission known as the Judicial Compensation and Benefits Commission. A similar process exists in each provincial jurisdiction. The UK has also adopted an independent review process for judges' salaries, as part of a wider annual independent review process for the salaries of senior officials.[21]

---

[17] N 12 above.

[18] *Reference re Remuneration of the Judges of the Provincial Court (PEI)* [1997] 3 SCR 3 (*Provincial Judges Reference*); *R v Mackin* [2002] 1 SCR 405; *Provincial Court Judges' Association of New Brunswick v New Brunswick* [2005] 2 SCR 286.

[19] In some provincial jurisdictions, e.g., Ontario, the recommendations of the independent commission are binding: see *Framework Agreement on Judges' Remuneration*, O Reg 407/93, s 2. However, this is not a constitutional requirement.

[20] Specifically, by amending the Judges Act, RSC 1985, c J-1.

[21] This is performed by an independent organization known as the Senior Salaries Review Body. It publishes an annual report, most recently, Review Body on Senior Salaries, *Thirtieth Report on Senior Salaries 2008* (The Stationery Office, 2008).

Administrative independence

In order to discharge their task of rendering judicial decisions fairly and effectively, judges require a basic administrative infrastructure, over which they must exercise at least a measure of independent control.

The justification for minimum conditions of administrative independence is, once again, functional. While the infrastructure of the courts is established by legislation and administered by the executive, the day-to-day functioning of a particular court must be controlled by the judiciary, usually through the Office of the Chief Justice, if the court is to be independent in fact and appearance. Such matters as the scheduling of cases and the assignment of judges to hear cases must remain within the control of the judiciary, if the reality and appearance of judicial impartiality are to be preserved. Moreover, shortage of resources or inadequate facilities may raise concerns that the judiciary may be inclined to 'cooperate' with the government, as the price of securing adequate surroundings and resources to do its work. Like security of tenure and financial security for individual judges, administrative financial security for courts as institutions is an important condition for the independence of the judiciary as an institution.

These concerns are reflected in a report prepared by the Canadian Judicial Council (CJC) in 2006, entitled *Alternative Models of Judicial Administration*.[22] The report considers what measures are necessary to protect administrative independence, in light of the *Provincial Judges Reference*.

The basic premise of *Alternative Models* is that functional institutional independence in the context of judicial administration requires depoliticization of the relationship between the judiciary and the other branches of governance. At present in Canada, the court system is operated by the executive branch as an administrative matter. Although Chief Justices have reached understandings with the executive that provide them with control over aspects of court administration, in principle and in law the executive remains responsible for the operation of the courts.

Alternative Models identifies areas of concern created by this 'executive model' of court administration. In order to work in practice, this model requires a high degree of cooperation between the executive and the judiciary, with the executive in essence delegating much of its administrative authority over the courts to the relevant Chief Justices. Despite this, the potential remains for tension between the executive and judiciary. The courts depend entirely on the executive for their budgets, while at the same time being required to make decisions under the *Charter* (such as the *Provincial Judges Reference*) that have significant budgetary implications for governments generally and their expenditures on the court

---

[22] Canadian Judicial Council, *Alternative Models of Judicial Administration* (Ottawa: Queen's Printer, 2006) (*Alternative Models*).

system in particular. These tensions have the potential to create the appearance that courts may be influenced in their decision-making by the effect of government decisions on their budgets.

Bearing these issues in mind, *Alternative Models* considered six alternatives to the executive model. It identified a 'limited autonomy and commission model' as the model that best supports effective court administration and protects judicial independence, while retaining a place for Parliament and parliamentary responsibility in the overall scheme of courts administration. The basic principle on this model is that responsibility for the administration and strategic direction of the courts lies mainly in the hands of the judiciary and officials who report to it, while governments retain a legitimate influence on specific matters such as the overall budget of the court system. In order to preserve genuine limited autonomy, however, the overall budget of the court system is not left entirely in the hands of the executive. An independent commission would stand between the judiciary and the executive, making decisions about issues likely to be contentious as between the two branches—in particular, the overall budget. Both individually as judges and institutionally as courts, the judiciary would be removed from direct negotiation from the executive in ways that could affect its independence.

Conclusion

I suggested at the outset that the requirement of judicial independence flows from the specific character of the function of the judiciary: to adjudicate disputes between the government and the citizen, or between one citizen and another, in accordance with the law. Constitutional democracy and the rule of law requires a separation between, on the one hand, the legislative and executive branches that make and implement the law, and on the other hand, the judicial branch that interprets and applies the law when disputes arise in particular cases. A dynamic and functional perspective is required to capture the distinct yet complementary functions of the three branches of governance. Each branch must be functionally independent if it is to properly perform its constitutional role. More particularly, an independent judiciary is necessary for the enforcement of constitutional limits imposed on the power of the executive and the legislative branches. If the executive branch is seen as being able to exercise improper influence on the judiciary's exercise of its judicial function, the rule of law is undermined. If the legislative or executive branch is seen as being able to improperly influence the adjudication of constitutional limits on the powers of these branches, the basic structure of constitutional democracy is also undermined.

The necessary pre-conditions for judicial independence are the conditions that remove the apparent or real possibility of inappropriate influence from the other two branches on the judiciary's exercise of its essential adjudicative functions.

Security of tenure and financial security are necessary to remove the possibility that the other branches could influence the judiciary by threatening judges' careers and economic security. Administrative independence is required both as an important intrinsic feature of judicial independence, and also to remove the appearance of inappropriate influence on the courts through executive control of their budgets. The purpose of these conditions is not to create special benefits for judges as individuals, but to enable the judiciary to properly exercise its essential function in the constitutional economy of the modern democratic state.

6

Lord Bowen of Colwood: 1835–94

Aspects of his life, career, and times

John Mummery

I.

Lives

What place is there for aspects of the life of a great 19th century judge in a book on 'The Transformation of the Law' honouring the achievements of a great 20th/21st century judge?

Biography is one of Lord Bingham's interests. He is Patron of the Legal Biography Project launched in 2007 by the Department of Law at the London School of Economics. On 10 October 2007 a large audience saw Professor (now Mr Justice) Cranston interview him about his life, career, and times. Lord Bingham supported the vast enterprise of the Oxford University Press in the publication of a new edition of *The Dictionary of National Biography*. He served a Presidential year (2000) in the Johnson Society. Dr Johnson's *Life* is the greatest biography ever written. He was himself a great biographer and thought that he 'could write the life of a Broomstick'. He believed in the power of example and in the value of 'a judicial and faithful narrative' of a life. 'No species of writing', he said, 'is more worthy of cultivation.'

Lord Bingham's eulogies on the lives of Lord Denning and of Lord Justice Ralph Gibson were fine examples of this difficult art, mixing memories and anecdotes, catching the elusive essence of the person and making a just assessment of a life.

There are common threads in the lives of Lord Bingham and Lord Bowen. Both were brilliant Balliol scholars. Neither read law, though both became active and influential in legal education. Both were attracted by a military career, but, fortunately for the law, opted for practice at the Bar. Bowen became probably the greatest lawyer in England. The judiciary, the legal profession, and the world of legal scholarship, along with recent Masters of Balliol, have the same opinion of Lord Bingham. As great Oxonians, they were both honoured by appointment as

Visitor to their college and by the University with an Honorary DCL. Bowen did not live long enough to achieve the office of High Steward of Oxford University, which has been held by Lord Bingham since 2001. On Jowett's death there was some speculation that Bowen might succeed him as Master of Balliol, but he was appointed a Lord of Appeal in Ordinary in September 1893. His term of office was cut tragically short by death in the following spring.

Fragments

A few fragments and a short sketch of Bowen's life will show that in his time the legal system underwent a transformation.

- 'I simply hate law,' Bowen told the Dean of Wells on a Sunday walk in 1865. After only four years in practice at the Bar Bowen thought of going back to Oxford to teach.

- '*Man on the Clapham omnibus.* In legal parlance, 'the reasonable person.' Possibly the phrase was first used by Sir Charles Bowen, QC (later Lord Bowen) who was junior council (sic) against the claimant in the TICHBORNE CASE (1871–4)': *Brewer's Dictionary of Phrase and Fable (Millennium Edition).*

Bowen did not take Silk. He was appointed direct to the Queen's Bench from the Junior Bar (Treasury Devil). Although 'the man on the Clapham omnibus' is on the top deck of common law clichés, Bowen did not mention him in a reported judgment. In *McQuire v Weston Morning News Co Ltd [1903] 2 KB 100 at 109,* Sir Richard Henn Collins MR said that this description of the ordinary reasonable man was 'as Lord Bowen phrased it', presumably in argument or in conversation. The Clapham bus (No 77A) ran on a route past Westminster Hall, which housed the Common Law Courts before 1882. Given Bowen's evangelical roots and the changing private and public values of his times, it may be the case that 'the Clapham sect gives way to the Clapham omnibus'—Stefan Collini, *English Pasts* (OUP, Oxford 1999) 111.

- 'The Rain it raineth every day,
  Upon the just and unjust fellow,
  But more upon the just, because
  The unjust has the just's umbrella'
  Anon

This Victorian nonsense is anonymous in JM Cohen (ed) *More Comic and Curious Verse* (Penguin Books, London 1956) 288. It is often attributed to Bowen.

- 'Conscious as Your Majesty's judges are of their own infirmities,' began one of the paragraphs in the draft of Lord Chancellor's address to Queen Victoria at the opening of the Law Courts in the Strand on 4 December 1882. The suave voice of Bowen was heard to object, 'may I suggest, Lord Chancellor, that it might be better to say "of one another's infirmities"?': JB Atlay, *The Victorian Chancellors Vol II* (Smith, Elder & Co, 1908) 428.

The opening of the Royal Courts of Justice was the high point of Lord Selborne's professional life. According to Atlay he was the architect of 'the fusion of law and equity, the housing of them both under the same roof, the choice of the Strand for their local habitation'. Passages in his draft address smacking of exaggerated humility were not palatable to all of Her Majesty's Judges.

- 'Let me tell you of two preferments which have given me great pleasure. Mr Barnett's appointment to the Canonry of Bristol [Mr Barnett was married to Octavia Hill, the Victorian social reformer], and the elevation to the Peerage of Lord Justice Bowen, probably the greatest lawyer in England, and now holding the post which is most likely to shew what he is. Does not half the good of the world (like the evils) arise from putting the best men in the best places.'

Benjamin Jowett, Master of Balliol and tutor of Bowen, wrote this to Florence Nightingale (6 September 1893.) Later that month Jowett was taken ill while staying in the Hampshire home of Mr Justice RS Wright, one of his favourite pupils and a friend of Bowen, who called to pay his respects. 'Mine has been a happy life. I bless God for my life,' Jowett said from his sick bed. He died on 1 October 1893.

- 'I have nothing to add to what has already fallen from those of your Lordships who have spoken.'

Bowen's concurring opinion in *James Muirhead v The Forth and North Sea Steamboat Mutual Insurance Association* [1894] AC 72 at 82, dismissing a Scottish appeal on 17 November 1893, is his *only* speech in the Appeal Cases reports. He died in London on 10 April 1894 at the age of 59.

- 'Lord Bowen dead. A heavy loss,' Gladstone wrote in his diary in April 1894. He thought that Bowen was excellent company. Their common interests— the Classics, novels, religion, and politics—cemented a friendship. Mr Justice Holmes (1841–1935) of the Supreme Court of the United States felt the same ('I sincerely regret the loss of Bowen') writing in a letter (26 June 1894) to Sir Frederick Pollock (1845–1937). Pollock, who rated Bowen, Willes, and Macnaghten as the greatest judges that he had known, thought that, of the English judges, Bowen's judicial mind was most like that of Holmes (letter 3 October 1902). Later Laski told Holmes he and Bowen were alike in their 'sense of the environment of the case' (letter 2 April 1926). Unlike Gladstone, Oliver Wendell Holmes found Bowen's conversation wanting. He told Harold J Laski that when he tried to get Bowen 'on serious subjects, he dodged them with an anecdote' (letter 24 June 1926). The quotations of Holmes and Pollock are from De Wolfe Howe (ed), *Holmes-Pollock Letters* (Harvard University

Press 1941), and of Holmes and Laski from De Wolfe Howe (ed), *Holmes-Laski Letters* (OUP 1953).

- 'I did love him with my whole heart, and I thank God for the blessing of his friendship. Jowett might have given us an estimate of him, for no one has done it yet; but he is gone first... How Bowen was loved! How well he deserved it!

> As clouds that rake the mountain summits,
> As waves that own no curbing hand,
> How fast has brother followed brother,
> From sunshine to the sunless land.

This was the reaction of Lord Coleridge (Lord Chief Justice 1880–1894) in a letter written on learning of Bowen's death. Bowen was Coleridge's junior in the greatest civil trial of the century, *Tichborne v Lushington* (more on *Tichborne* later). They were in the same chambers. Coleridge served as a Law Officer, Solicitor-General (1868–71) and Attorney-General (1871–73). He appointed Bowen as his Junior Counsel or Devil in 1872. From that moment Bowen's practice grew and became the busiest at the Bar. It was tactfully noted by Mathew LJ that 'the industry of Bowen supplied what was wanting to the genius of Coleridge', labour being 'altogether foreign to his temperament.' Their shared interests—the Classics, English literature, religion, and Liberal politics—were more important to them than the law. In 1883 they visited the USA in a group invited by the Pacific Railway Company, Coleridge being the first Chief Justice of England to visit the USA. Bowen was a guest at Coleridge's at Heath's Court (The Chandler's House), Ottery St Mary, with its great library, as were major literary figures, like Henry James. Bowen had to put up with his host's criticisms of his translation of the *Aeneid*: 'He shoots over me every morning as if I were a Scotch Moor,' Bowen complained, good-naturedly. Like Bowen, Coleridge was from the Balliol stable. He had also been President of the Oxford Union. Bowen, who wrote poetry and sprinkled his legal writings and correspondence with literary references and quotes, might well have gone to Wordsworth's *Ex tempore effusion on the Death of James Hogg* for a quotation, if he had survived Coleridge, who died only two months after him, on 14 June 1894.

- 'On the whole, as an expositor of law in perfect English, and with unerring accuracy, I should put Bowen as high as, or higher than, any of the judges of my time. But I think he shone more brightly in the House of Lords than as a trial judge.' Sir Arthur Underhill, *Change and Decay: The Recollections and Reflections of an Octogenarian Bencher* (Butterworth & Co 1938) 86.

Sir Arthur got into an octogenarian muddle. Bowen had 11 years of overwork as a Lord Justice of Appeal and suffered some silent months of sickness in the House of Lords before he died. The confusion would have tickled Bowen's sense of humour. Underhill correctly remembered Bowen's ready and charmingly playful wit:

> ... he combined two qualities rarely found in the same person, viz., a most delightful and scholarly wit with a profound knowledge of the law; and a memory such as is possessed by very few indeed. I think, on the whole, that I should consider him the most brilliant man who has sat on the bench in my time.(p 83)

II.

Sketch

> Sit here and watch the hail of occurrence
> Clobber life out to a shape no-one sees.
>
> Philip Larkin: *Send No Money*

A biographer shapes a version of a life from the fragments that he can find, piecing them together to make some sort of sense. Obituary facts—ancestry and education, public appointments and honours, legal cases and anecdotes—are required information, but do not explain what makes a person tick. Bowen had no Boswell and left no autobiography. In his writings there are only brief oblique passages about his life. Facts and events from Bowen's dazzling CV are listed at the end of this chapter, providing a structure that will not obscure the man himself. The chronology is reversed to make the point that it is impossible, looking back from the 21st century over the surviving scraps of someone who lived and died in the 19th century, to re-create the uniqueness of the experience of living that life, forwards into the unknown.

The best that can be done is to select scenes from Bowen's career and to glance at aspects of his life to gain an impression of what he was like, why he was liked, what was his experience of life, and what were his thoughts on what was going on around him.

When Bowen came to the Bar in 1861 he already had the reputation of being the most brilliantly gifted and all-round young man of his time. He had swept the board of academic scholarships and prizes at Rugby and at Oxford. He had distinguished himself on the sports field. His younger brother Edward boasted that Bowen could even jump over a cow standing in a field, though breed and height were not mentioned. A bust of Bowen, presented by Old Rugbeians, has pride of place on the table in the middle of the Temple Reading Room at his old school.

There are surprisingly few published photographs of Bowen. In one of them, taken near the end of his life, he looks extremely ill and utterly exhausted. An earlier photograph of him in the robes of a Lord Justice of Appeal was probably taken on his appointment. In this photo, which is tucked away in a collection in the Benchers' corner of Lincoln's Inn Library, can be seen the hypnotic gaze and the youthful appearance, which impressed his contemporaries. Miss Weldon, a dissatisfied litigant in person, once complained to the Court of Appeal that Vice-Chancellor Bacon was too old to understand her case and that Mr Justice Bowen was, in the words of the court's judgment, 'only a bit of a boy and could not do her justice'.

Bowen was a scholar, shy, subtle, and insightful. He reached the peaks of a competitive and chancy profession without losing friends or making enemies. His success was attributable less to natural advocacy skills or to a focused pursuit of power, office, or wealth than to exceptional intellectual abilities and to an amazing capacity for extremely hard work, superbly well done. His impeccable manners were summed up by a friend in the phrase 'deferential urbanity'. Some suspected affectation, but that was forgiven for his rare charm, famous wit, and total absence of the pernicious pretence of effortless superiority. Behind the glittering prizes the hail of occurrence had clobbered him. His laborious life was dogged by major breakdowns in health, physical and psychoneurotic. He was sent to bed, forbidden to do anything or to see anybody, or went on rest cures in Europe.

At the Bar Bowen's unassertive academic manner and his 'chilling, almost mincing' voice, as an anonymous obituarist described it, did not equip him to be an effective jury advocate in either civil or criminal cases. He succeeded in legal practice by dint of a clear and precise intellect, a remarkable memory, with the ability to recite a whole page after a single reading, and a capacity for taking infinite pains in everything that he did.

After seven years as Treasury Devil (Common Law), which were enough to break a robust constitution, he served for three years as a Queen's Bench judge. His talents were not best suited to trial work. At the age of 47 he was raised to the Court of Appeal, where he quickly made his mark as the pre-eminent reading and writing judge. Many of his judgments are studied and cited over a century on, because he built his judgments to last, like Victorian public architecture: lucid exposition of the foundations of the common law, pithy wisdom gained from wide experience, and memorable phrases turned by a master of the English language.

Bowen was a leading figure in the Victorian intellectual aristocracy. Jowett regarded him as the ablest of all of his many gifted pupils. Yet he spent much of his adult life mastering the mundane details of legal briefs. His absorbing interest was in language and literature and in philosophical, political, and religious questions, but he never allowed his interest in ideas to develop into ideologies that would compel him to leave behind practical common sense and professional detachment. He was a reforming Liberal, who, in his early years, was active in political debates and campaigns and had parliamentary ambitions, yet preferred Virgilian beauty, translating *The Aeneid* and reading novels to practising law or pursuing politics.

He was a Broad Church Anglican, of the faith within reason tradition. His support for the Church of England did not deter him from advocating anti-clerical causes, such as the long overdue abolition of religious tests that had perpetuated clerical domination of the universities, or from seriously considering the case for disestablishment.

He was celebrated for his exquisite wit and gentle irony not all of which can be conveyed on the page. Yet throughout his adult life he was prey to precarious health, disabling stress, and melancholic moods. *Manque*, one of his best poems, is on the 'drifting of Time and I'. It is his meditation on the sadness of life: 'visions full of human wrong', 'doubt and tumult in the brain', 'But hearts grow cold as seasons fly, Life leaves us but the power to sigh', and 'the wild regrets of man, His fever since the world began'. Lytton Stratchey and his group would have mocked such stuff as the sentimental outpourings of a self-deluding Eminent Victorian, but his themes are not that different from those of TS Eliot in the first half of the 20th century and Philip Larkin in the second half.

Biographers

Most of the basic facts of Bowen's life are in a book published shortly after his death (1897). His friend, Sir Henry Stewart Cunningham, wrote *Lord Bowen, A Biographical Sketch with a selection from his Verses* (John Murray, 1897) at the request of his family. Cunningham found it difficult to write, not least because of Bowen's 'impenetrable reserve'. Asquith's impression of Bowen was of an 'elusive personality'. Cunningham's was an affectionate portrait drawing on private correspondence and papers and on personal reminiscences of family, friends, and colleagues. Many of the facts and quotations in this paper are from Cunningham's book.

Sir Henry Cunningham (1832–1920) is worth a moment as one of Bowen's oldest friends. Like Bowen, he was the son of an evangelical Anglican vicar (then Vicar of Harrow). He met Bowen at Oxford, then, as now, a great place for making lasting friendships. They were founding members of an Essay Society. They joined reading parties to Heidelberg and walked in the Hartz Mountains. Cunningham also went to the Bar. After he was called in 1859, he joined the chambers of his brother-in-law, James Fitzjames Stephen (1829–1894), later Mr Justice Stephen. He, Bowen, and Stephen all wrote for *The Saturday Review*.

Cunningham's career suffered a dramatic setback when he decided to leave chambers to go into the tea trade. He lost all his money through a dishonest partner. In 1866 he took up an appointment in Lahore as Government Advocate and Legal Adviser to the Punjab. In 1877 he became a judge of the High Court in Calcutta. He remained in contact with Bowen during his time in India. Besides judgments, he wrote novels about Anglo-Indian Society (*The Dustypur Chronicles*). Bowen told him that Gladstone was 'very excited' about one of his later novels, *The Heriots*.

There are excellent accounts of Bowen in the old and new editions of *The Dictionary of National Biography*. Edmund Heward's life of Bowen is in a quartet of Victorian judges, *Lives of the Judges—Jessel, Cairns, Bowen and Bramwell*, (Barry Rose Law Publishers Ltd, Chichester, 2004). As one would expect of a former Chief Chancery Master, it is specially good on Bowen's involvement in the transformation of the chaotic courts of common law and equity and of the civilian courts and their obscure outdated procedures into a system that is the basis of the modern Civil Justice system. The Civil Procedure Rules are built on solid foundations. The re-structuring of the courts and the reforms of civil procedure in the 19th century may not survive the proposal to abolish the High Court and replace it with a unified civil court.

Bowen's literary interests, his leading cases, his lasting judgments, his family and his friends—these are the aspects of his life for the remainder of this paper.

III.

Reading and writing

In a letter to Mr Justice Holmes in 1924 Harold J Laski wrote:

There has not been a reading judge in England since Lord Bowen.

The reading judge loved style and form, for which his judgments are notable. They have proportion and balance, precision and lucidity, elegance and charm that have been praised by lawyers not noted for handing out compliments—Sir Frederick Pollock, Oliver Wendell Holmes, Lords Esher, Davey, Bryce, Haldane, and Sumner, Lord Justice Scrutton, Sir William Holdsworth, and CHS Fifoot. His was useful writing that enhanced law and literature.

Writing poetry, translating Virgil, and reading novels were more to Bowen than legal practice or political ambition. In his essay on *Progress in the Administration of Justice during the Victorian Period* Bowen quoted, in the same breath as the Judicature Acts, Tennyson (*Ulysses*) and Shakespeare (*Measure for Measure*). Poetry surfaced in letters to his friends, such as Coleridge. In 1877 he published privately a volume of his poetry—*Verses of the Wayside*.

In a hectic professional life he made time to translate and publish Virgil's *Aeneid* (Vols I–VI) and *Eclogues* into English verse. His translations were well reviewed in *The Classical Review* in March 1880 for their fidelity to the original and their literary skill. He planned to translate *The Georgics*. Virgil was a big thing in Bowen's life. He popped up in the most unlikely circumstances. Virgil made an unexpected appearance in the farcical cross examination of the claimant during the civil trial of the *Tichborne* case (of which more later). One of Bowen's contemporaries at Balliol was actually called Aeneas (MacKay). (Lawrence Collins

LJ has an enlarged College group photo of Aeneas with Dicey, Bryce, Swinburne, and other elderly over serious undergraduates, though not Bowen, outside his room in the Royal Court of Justice.)

Bowen spent almost too much of his time on literary activities. In a letter to Florence Nightingale (21 September 1884) about his round of summer holidays (Coniston with Ruskin, Keswick with Professor Caird, Long Niddry with the Earl of Wemyss) Jowett wrote:

… I began my holiday by paying a short visit to my dear friends, the Lord Justice Bowen & his wife at their country place in Sussex [Colwood House, near Cuckfield]. He is, as he always is, a most kind and delightful companion, though I question whether he does not give too much of his extraordinary powers of mind to literature and too little to law. I have rather come to the conclusion that a man of genius had better not go to the Bar. He does not find enough to satisfy him.

As time went on Jowett tried to persuade his able students to take up medicine in order to escape 'the hopeless (often) struggles of the Bar' and 'perplexity of [Holy] orders'.

Bowen's capacious questing mind did not find complete emotional and intellectual satisfaction in legal practice—not enough room for original ideas or creative composition. His lawyer's time was spent disentangling other people's hail of occurrence and trying to make sense of it. He did not find it one of the pleasures of the life. Pleasure was in *Novel Reading*, the title of his address to the Walsall Literary Institute in 1891.

Novels were the pre-eminent cultural form in Victorian England, realistic and detailed narratives with endless possibilities, 'a treasure-house of details' in the words of Henry James. Although Bowen's address was enthusiastic about Georges Sand and George Eliot, Balzac and Dickens, it was not an anthology of passages from favourite authors of the 'Leaves from My Library' sort. Bowen was a serious student of literature as well as law. He developed his ideas on imaginative literature, by which he meant novels 'of lasting literary finish'. They were not scientific truth. Literature was truthful in a different way from scientific truth. Its truth was in the presentation of beauty and knowledge of life by a combination of unity and proportion, form and equilibrium, judgment, and emotion.

Bowen's interest in 'first rate books' did not mean that journalism was beneath him. During his early years at the Bar he wrote regularly for various papers. Members of his Oxford Essay Society were recruited to write for *The Saturday Review*. The paper had been going since 1855 as a weekly review of politics, literature, science, and art for 'educated English opinion'. Many of the contributors, whose articles were published anonymously, were not professional journalists or writers. Trollope contributed, but so did lawyers like AV Dicey, James Fitzjames Stephen, Sir Henry Maine, and RS Wright.

IV.

Work and duty

Every man's work, whether it be literature or music or pictures or architecture or anything else, is always a portrait of himself.

Samuel Butler: The Way of all Flesh

The best portrait of Bowen is his work. The influence of Jowett's work ethic on him and on generations of his pupils entering the public service and the legal profession was enormous. He taught them to *enjoy* public-spirited hard work. Jowett recognized the difference between doing a great deal of work, which he did, and working very hard, which he claimed he did not. He believed in dedication to public service, in the strength that steady work and study give to character and in the sense of power and direction it gave over one's life. His opinion was that the best rest is a change of work.

More than anything else, work done and attitudes to doing it show the sort of life that a person has led and the sort of person that they are. Bowen spent his life doing a great deal of very hard work and being brilliant at it. Like John Ruskin, who was his disturbed, absent, and unsuccessful client in the *Whistler v Ruskin* libel case (more below), Bowen believed that work was a duty to be performed to the very best of his abilities. Ruskin, writing at a time of immense inherited wealth, said that 'God intends no man to live in this world without working', but it was 'no less evident that He intends every man to be happy in his work'. For that three things were necessary: to be fit for the work, not to do too much of it, and to have a sense of success in it.

Bowen was more fitted for work on the Bench than for practice at the Bar, where he had far too much work and ruined his health. As was said at the time, his physical health was unequal to the tasks which his zeal for work imposed on him. He had several psychoneurotic breakdowns from the age of 25 until his premature death at 59, just when he arrived at the point and place most suited to him. It is a miracle that his breakdowns did not stand in the way of his success at the Bar or on the Bench.

We tend to forget the part that being ill and being near to death played in the imaginative lives of the Victorians. Roy Jenkins wrote in his biography of Gladstone that that 'most remarkable specimen of humanity' read 20,000 books, chopped down innumerable trees, walked vast distances in Snowdonia and the Scottish Highlands and lived to nearly 89, yet 'spent a surprising amount of time on a sickbed' from which 'he always bounced back with devastating vigour'. George Eliot's diaries are a daily write up of aches and pains, even recording a visit to her dentist, Mr Mummery, to have her teeth pulled. Dr Arnold was so haunted by forebodings of an early death and an awareness of 'the fragility of human existence' that he explained to one of his ten children why he wrote the commencement date on his sermons, but left a blank for the completion date:

It is one of the most solemn things I do, to write the beginning of that sentence, and think that I may perhaps not live to finish it.

He was only 47 when, in Lytton Stratchey's words, 'he passed from his perplexities for ever'.

Bowen's friends hoped that appointment to the Queen's Bench, which relieved him from the burdens of Treasury Devil, would give him the opportunity for comparative rest, a false hope, even in those days. The breakdowns did not go away, but equally they did not drive him away. He was a realist, who accepted early on that he was stuck with the profession that he had chosen. As he said on his confessional Sunday walk with the Dean of Wells in 1865:

... a man may be a fool to choose a profession, but he must be an idiot to give it up.

Hard work started young. At ten he was sent away with his younger brother to a school in Lille. They worked for ten hours a day and went on ten-mile walks. At Rugby from 1850 to 1854 he won school prizes for a poem on Venice, an essay on theology, and for a Latin Essay, the Queen's Medal for Modern History, and a scholarship to Balliol, *and* he was good at games—cricket, rugby, and athletics. The verdict of his masters was 'delightfully clever'. This did not prevent him from being universally liked then, as he was for the rest of his life. He was modest about his abilities and his achievements. It would never have crossed his mind to think what JS Mill actually had the gall to say: 'My family have no idea how great a man I am!' More typical of Bowen was the anecdote about how, in self-mockery (and a little showing off), Bowen paused in the Porters' Lodge at Balliol to light his pipe with a spill made out of his lecture notes.

The pace did not let up at Oxford. Between 1854 and 1858 he got a First in Greats, was elected to a Fellowship of Balliol while still an undergraduate, won all the scholarships and prizes for Classics and history and was elected President of the Union. He found time, between the swotting spells, to row in the College Eight in Torpids and to make lasting friendships among his contemporaries, many of whom went out to make their mark in the world. Bowen was a member of the Old Mortality Society, which discussed papers and poetry. It was a short-lived Oxford version of the Apostles at Cambridge, to which his brother Edward belonged. Bowen also joined an earnest group of Victorian types, who called themselves The Mutual Improvement Society. Activities in political societies, literary groups, and social clubs continued in London. He became a member of the Century Club, a liberal political grouping. In later life he was elected an honorary member of another group in recognition his contribution to affairs of Church and State.

Bowen's upbringing in an evangelical household and his classical education at Rugby and Balliol had a profound impact on his attitude to the world that he entered on Call to the Bar. The high moral aims of the education received by him alongside many sons of the emerging upper middle class were breadth of vision, clarity of thought, and steadfastness of purpose in the pursuit of the truth. The end-product was to be a governing elite of 'Christian gentlemen of good charac-ter' in public life, motivated by moral earnestness, a strong spirit of public duty, loyalty, courage, and a sense of responsibility. They would exercise sound and disinterested judgment on the competing claims of rival groups in society, with self-discipline and good manners.

As the 19th century progressed, the new idea in the growing professions, in representative government, and in the administration, was that leadership should not be determined by accident of birth, inheritance of wealth, or technical exper-tise, but should come from intelligent men and women of liberal academic educa-tion. Bowen was such a person.

It was a slow start in chambers. He had time for legal writing as well as jour-nalism. His pamphlet on *The Alabama Claim and Arbitration considered from the legal point of view*, urging arbitration, was well received. He was associated with a manifesto by the leaders of young Liberal opinion, who produced *Essays on Reform* in 1867. In recognition for his valuable contribution to success in the *Tichborne* case Sir John Coleridge appointed Bowen to be Treasury Devil in 1872. From then on Bowen's career never looked back.

Reflecting on his time in practice Bowen wrote to a friend in India in 1885:

The worst of these learned professions is that life goes so quick. You begin one morning to read briefs, you go on reading, with short intervals for refreshment, past Christmases, Easters, Long Vacations, just as you pass stations in a first class express. Here you look up, and the time has about come for the guard to take the tickets. There is one thing certain, namely, that professional life is not worth the sacrifices it entails.

Cases and clients

Bowen was briefed as counsel in two of the great cases of his time.

The *Tichborne* case

Bowen was junior counsel in the civil and criminal *Tichborne* trials. He was led in the civil trial by Sir John Coleridge QC and in the criminal trial by Mr Henry Hawkins QC (later Lord Brampton). In his 1936 book on the trials Lord Maugham described them as 'beyond doubt the most celebrated and perhaps the most interesting English trials of the last hundred years'. The claim that gave rise to them was, in the words of another legal commentator, Edgar Lustgarten, 'incredible if it was true, yet more incredible if it was false'.

The claimant brought an action for ejectment against the trustees and a lessee of the Tichborne estates, which produced an annual income of £20,000. The true identity of the claimant is still in dispute. He was probably Arthur Orton, a butcher's son from Wapping, and was engaged in a daring case of identity theft that sent shivers through the landed gentry of England, of which he claimed to be one—Sir Roger Doughty-Tichborne, long lost heir to the Tichborne estates. The claimant was uneducated and practically illiterate. He had never seen Sir Roger and bore no physical resemblance to him. It was thought that Sir Roger had been lost at sea on a voyage from Rio in about 1859, but his grieving mother never accepted that he was dead. When the claimant met her in Paris, she said that he was her son. Quite soon a lot of the people, who knew nothing at all about the case, began to believe him. Other members of the family and their witnesses were sure that he was not the missing heir and disputed his claims.

Bowen was the most junior of the five-man team, which included three Silks and a Chancery junior, appearing for the Tichborne trustees in *Tichborne v Lushington*. After an Examination in Chancery starting in 1867, the trial finally got under way in 1871 in the Court of Common Pleas before Sir William Bovill CJ in Westminster Hall. Though of only ten years standing, Bowen was far and away the ablest lawyer in the defence team. Everyone, especially Coleridge, acknowledged the enormous contribution that Bowen made to the success of the defence. He went on to be a member of the successful prosecution team in the criminal trial of the claimant at Bar in the Queen's Bench Division before Sir Alexander Cockburn CJ and Mellor and Lush JJ on a charge of perjury.

In the civil proceedings Coleridge described Bowen as the 'mainstay of our case all through. He has worked like a horse, and without him I could have done nothing.' It was Bowen's task to keep Coleridge 'stoked and primed'. He knew where every document was, mastered every fact, and knew every date. His over-worked brain made him ill. The case may even have contributed to his early death. Asquith's comment, based on his pupillage with Bowen, was that he 'was one of the hardest workers that I have ever come across. In fact, he worked a great deal too hard. He was so fastidious that he could not avail himself adequately of other people's labours.' He politely binned Asquith's drafts.

Coleridge's opening speech for the defence lasted for 25 days. Although it was too long, it worked and brought the civil case to a successful conclusion. Bowen had produced for Coleridge an index of the sources of information available to the claimant about the career of Sir Roger. It was cross-referenced so that Coleridge could demonstrate from the evidence the state of the claimant's information about Sir Roger at any particular time. He was also able to demonstrate the astonishing ignorance of the claimant about things that he would have known, if he really was Sir Roger. It was on this point that the classical learning of the Coleridge/Bowen team and their love of Virgil came into its own.

Sir Roger was not a classical scholar in the Coleridge or Bowen class, but he had been to Stonyhurst, where the Jesuits taught Latin and Greek. Coleridge cross-examined the claimant about Virgil. The case took a farcical turn. Coleridge showed the claimant a copy of the *Aeneid* and asked him whether it was in Latin or Greek. The claimant, whose stock answer to most of Coleridge's questions was that he had 'no recollection', fancied the latter.

Coleridge asked the claimant: 'Is Virgil Latin or Greek, is he prose or poetry?'

The Chief Justice intervened: 'One question at a time.'

Coleridge was not put off and continued to ask more than one question at a time: 'Virgil. What do you say to Virgil? Is he a general or a statesman?...What is Virgil?'

The claimant replied: 'I told you just now I have no recollection.'

Coleridge also rattled the claimant out with a notorious open question devised by Bowen: 'Would you be surprised to hear that...?' The claimant was bewildered: he did not know whether he should be surprised or not.

The claimant was non-suited, arrested, and charged with and, after another long trial and a summing up by Cockburn CJ lasting from 29 January to 28 February 1874, convicted of, perjury and sentenced to 14 years penal servitude. The claimant outlived Bowen and Coleridge. He died in 1898 and was buried in a coffin bearing the plate 'Sir Roger Doughty-Tichborne'. His widow continued to call herself Lady Tichborne. The whole saga was not so different from the novels that Bowen preferred to briefs. During the course of the trials he was inspired to write poems about the case.

Whistler v Ruskin

Bowen's biographers have overlooked or decided to omit his involvement in the libel case brought by James McNeill Whistler against John Ruskin for writing of a painting of his exhibited in the Grosvenor Gallery.

I have seen, and heard, much of Cockney impudence before now; but never expected to hear a coxcomb ask two hundred guineas for flinging a pot of paint in the public's face.

Bowen appeared for John Ruskin. He advised him that he was unlikely to win. Bowen was led by the Attorney-General, Sir John Holker QC. At that time and down to 1895 the Law Officers combined lucrative private practice with their less-well paid government briefs.

While the case is often called a *cause célèbre* and has been called the most celebrated lawsuit in the history of art, it was, EF Benson thought, more like 'some sheer parody of judicial administration' comparable to *Bardwell v Pickwick*. Like quite a few defamation cases there was an air of *folie à deux* about it. Fortunately for all concerned, the whole case was finished in two days. Although the official transcript was destroyed, Linda Merrill in her excellent book *A Pot of Paint* (Smithsonian Institution Press, Washington and London, 1992) has reconstructed a lot of it from press reports and from legal briefs to provide a corrective to Whistler's own account of it in *The Gentle Art of Making Enemies*.

None of the lawyers, including Bowen, distinguished themselves. Bowen had a thankless task. Ruskin was too unstable to attend the trial. Bowen's leader was not cut out for the case. It was said at the time that Sir John Holker never spoke in court 'without an ear wide open to the voice of his devil'. Even when they were on opposite sides he would often turn to Bowen in a difficulty. Holker had strong points and scored notable victories as a very effective jury advocate, but in this unusual defamation case he missed the legal point by concentrating in his cross examination on trying to persuade the jury that Whistler was not a good artist and getting them to agree with Ruskin, rather than pressing Bowen's point that Ruskin was not liable for expressing an honestly held opinion of Whistler's work. Holker later went, as Law Officers were apt to in those days, direct to the Court of Appeal in 1882, but within four months he was forced by ill health to resign and was replaced by Bowen.

As also sometimes happened in those days, leading counsel left the court after addressing the jury. He went off to do something else. Bowen was left to examine-in-chief the witnesses called for Ruskin's defence. They appeared more out of loyalty to or affection for Ruskin than for their willingness or ability to give relevant evidence to the jury. At least Bowen's examination-in-chief, like his closing speech, was brief. Bowen produced Whistler's painting *Nocturne*, first, to Edward Burne-Jones and then to William Frith RA, who attended under subpoena. He asked Burne-Jones whether it was, in his opinion, a work of art, to which he dutifully replied 'No', adding an unwelcome comment that Whistler 'had very great power as an artist'. Then Bowen asked him whether the picture was worth 200 guineas, to which he replied 'No'. Frith was taken through a similar questioning.

There was a moment of high comedy when Bowen produced a painting by Titian in order to show the jury what was meant by the 'finish' of a work of art. Serjeant Parry, who appeared for Whistler, objected: 'We do not know it is a Titian.' The judge, Baron Huddleston, told Bowen that he would have to prove that it was a Titian, adding that he could only do so by repute. The judge then told the court a story about a recent instance of a fake Titian. Bowen said that he would be able to prove it was a Titian.

Submissions on the meaning of coxcomb did not take the case very far. In his closing speech to the jury Bowen said all that he could say. As Ruskin had no defence to the claim, there was not much that he could say beyond saying that the action was brought to muzzle the famous art critic's honestly held beliefs. All that Ruskin had done, he argued, was to express an opinion on Whistler's picture, an opinion he still held.

Bowen did well for Ruskin. Although the jury, who retired for an hour, found for Whistler, they only awarded him derisory damages of a farthing. Whistler wore the farthing on his watch chain for the rest of his life. The judge made no order for costs. This would have been catastrophic for Ruskin had it not been for well-off friends who rallied round and paid his costs. Ruskin used the outcome as an excuse for resigning from the Slade Professorship at Oxford, saying: 'I cannot hold a chair from which I have no power of expressing judgement without being taxed by British Law.' He was very dissatisfied with a law that assessed at only a farthing the damage inflicted by the opinion of such an eminent art critic as himself. Ruskin made no mention of the litigation case in his autobiography

Praeterita. In it he did offer his opinion that most of the *Aeneid* was nonsense, but there is no evidence that this was a dig at Bowen.

Appeals

Bowen's output in the Court of Appeal was of the highest quality in every department of the law. He was as good on equity, trusts, partnership, company law, copyright, passing off and so on as he was on contract, tort, and constitutional law.

For most of Bowen's 11 years in the court Brett LJ (1815–1899—later Lord Esher MR) presided over the common law appeals on which he sat. Lindley LJ (1828–1921), later Lord Lindley, presided over Chancery appeals. In many cases Bowen sat with Fry LJ (1827–1918). The combination of Lindley, Bowen, and Fry was the greatest constitution in the history of the Court of Appeal, surpassing that of Scrutton, Atkin, and Bankes in the 1920s or anything since. The three of them worked well together. They had great respect for each other and rarely disagreed. Lord Haldane later described both Bowen and Lindley as having 'judicial temperament of the highest order' which is 'a very rare gift'.

The same could not be said of Brett, who sat in the court for 20 years. He had a line in bullying barristers from a privileged position on the Bench. Some of the great Victorians had an unpleasant and menacing manner. Matthew Arnold's look of 'heartbroken forbearance' was extremely insulting. Brett was not the paragon of 'Judicial Politeness', the title for *The Spy* cartoon of a benign Bowen in *Vanity Fair* in 1892. Bowen, who was always patient and courteous to counsel, put up with Brett's abrasiveness during his 11 years in the court without open complaint. His bouts of ill health and the Long Vacations gave him some time away from the court. It was rumoured that, despite Bowen's attempts to persuade him to stay on, Lord Justice Fry resigned in 1892 to get away from Brett. He carried on doing other kinds of legal work elsewhere for many years after.

Fry remembered his time of sitting with Bowen as one of the brightest of his life. What impressed him most of all about Bowen was his intense sense of duty in the discharge of his office, the subordination of personal ambition to it, and his lack of vanity. He was sensitive to anything that appeared to be bad law or anything like the slightest miscarriage of justice. He described the thought and persistent effort that he gave to his brilliant judgments, which were not always appreciated by those who heard them, and the subtlety and 'extreme rapidity of his intellectual operations.' He could hardly recall ever hearing an impatient word from him on the Bench.

Fry said that Bowen was also very jealous of the independence of the individual judge. In times of centralizing tendencies in the judiciary, the increased bureaucracy in judicial administration, internal pressures for single judgments of the court and such like, the constitutional importance of Bowen's views on the need for judges to be independent of one another, as well as of the executive, the media, and other external pressures, should not be underestimated.

Bowen's judgments were discussed in detail in 'The Judicial Characteristics of the Late Lord Bowen', a law review article by Van Vechten Veeder from Chicago (Vol 10 *Harvard Law Review* (1896–7 page 351)). He lavished praise on the rare combination of qualities in Bowen's appellate output. I do not think that any English judge has ever been so highly rated in any academic journal. Veeder listed Bowen's many judicial virtues: unsurpassed learning; literary grace and sense of form; purity, ease, and accuracy of style; cultivated taste; unique knowledge of legal history and mastery in application of the historical method to the evolution of legal doctrine; felicity in expounding legal principles, precision, and clarity of thought; logical faculties; ability to take a broad view *and* to make subtle distinctions; the depth and breadth of insight into what is reasonable and just; a sense of proportion and discrimination; an ability to get to the heart of things; and a practical bent of mind, so that his extraordinary intellectual powers were tempered by good sense. And so it went on. A possible weakness was occasional over-subtlety. Bowen loved distinctions, the finer the better.

Although Veeder laid it on with a trowel, the all-round excellence of Bowen's judgments is beyond question. Writing appellate judgments is not easy, even with practice. Every case is different. *Ex tempore* judgments (and many of Bowen's were delivered on the spot) are demanding, especially at the end of a long day of conflicting arguments. The outcome of the appeal is often the least difficult part. The perennial problems are where to start, when to stop, how much to put in or, most difficult of all, how much to leave out.

Bowen had the knack of hitting on the right way of saying what needed to be said and saying it simply, shortly, and clearly. His judgments were of almost perfect balance and proportion. His writing skills avoided the worst hazards of appellate judgments: unnecessary repetition of the detailed facts of the case; pointless re-statements of law, which has been clearly settled in earlier cases and is not improved by repetition or re-formulation; laboured reviews of all the authorities on the subject; and redundant concurring judgments (in over half of the reported cases Bowen simply agreed with the judgments of a colleague). He rarely and reluctantly dissented.

As a reader of novels, Bowen knew the limits of originality and imagination in fiction. He appreciated that there is much less room for originality and imagination in legal writing. This is not the place for a casebook of Bowen's judgments or for a serious analysis of his judicial method. If limited to one short passage from just one of his many fine judgments to illustrate Bowen's judicial method and vision, I would pick one that is neither well known nor specially significant. It is wise and witty, charming and memorable. It is grounded in the kind of judicial truth that matters most, that learnt from experience. In *Cooke v New River Co* (1888) 38 Ch D 56 at page 71 he said:

...I believe by long experience that judgments come with far more weight and gravity when they come upon points which the Judges are bound to decide, and I believe that *obiter dicta*, like the proverbial chickens of destiny, come home to roost sooner or later in a very uncomfortable way to the Judges who have uttered them, and are a great source of embarrassment in future cases. Therefore I abstain from putting a construction on more than it is necessary to do for this particular case.

Bowen was not saying anything new or anything profound. He was saying something that experience teaches you is true. The same has been said before and since, invariably at greater length and usually with less impact. Bowen's skill and his vision was to say something wise, true, and serious with a light touch, an apt allusion, and a memorable turn of phrase. Who will not think of the 'chickens of destiny' when having to read, or being tempted to write, obese judgments of *obiter* guidance and ill-conceived attempts to impose on future judges unnecessary predictions about the course of the law?

Although Bowen's were not template judgments, he often used the same methods and skills to achieve desired effects. He knew how to achieve them. He would pose a simple, but very precise, question to identify the issue. He would follow this with a clear and firm, but not dogmatic, statement of the relevant legal principles or a summary of the elements of a cause of action or of a defence. He would turn to the appeal of the reason and common sense of the case and to the practical considerations. His respect for the accumulated wisdom of the past led him to cite the relevant authorities, more by way of useful example than to show off his encyclopaedic legal knowledge and as a check that there was nothing in them that would be inconsistent with the principles. Where the contested state of the law required it, he would trace the historical development of the legal principles through the cases, extracting from each authority no more than its essence. In the course of his judgment he would sometimes pause to pose other questions, which would give a change of direction to the argument. He would support his conclusions by examples carefully selected for their aptness and use them in a memorable and amusing way. Finally, and not many pages on from where he had started, he would apply the law to the facts of the case to produce a wholly convincing result. Bowen makes it look and read as if it were easy. It is not.

While respecting the importance of fair procedure, Bowen was impatient with procedural technicalities. For him the cardinal principle of the Judicature Acts was that 'all controversies existing between the parties should be swept away by one litigation'. That was not a feature of the legal system that had evolved down to the reforms of the Judicature Acts and of which he had wide experience at the Bar.

There is no space to quote from or discuss his judgments. A short list is a reminder of the fundamental doctrines discussed in Bowen's judgments: *The Moorcock* (1889) 14 PD 64 (implied terms and the test of business efficacy); *Edgington v Edgington* (1885) 29 Ch D 459 (at page 483 '. . . the state of a man's mind is as much a fact as the state of his digestion . . .'); *Allcard v Skinner* (1887) 36 Ch D 143 (undue influence of religious character disturbing independent judgment); *Quartz Hill Gold Mining Co v Eyre* (1883) 11 QBD 674 (malicious presentation of a winding up petition); *Re Speight* (1883) 22 Ch D 762 (a trustee is only bound to conduct the business of the trust in such a way as an ordinary prudent man of business would conduct his own); *Hutton v West Corke Railway Co* (1883) 23 Ch D 654 at 673 (gifts by a company to its employees—'the law does not say that there are to be no cakes and ale, but there are to be no cakes and ale except such as are required for the benefit of the company'); *Maxim Nordenfelt Guns & Ammunition Co v Nordenfelt* [1893] 1 Ch 630 (covenant in restraint of trade unlimited in time and place on sale of goodwill held reasonable, after review of the development of the restraint of trade doctrine from 17th century); *Ratcliffe v Evans* [1892] 2 QB 524 (damages for loss of business caused by malicious false statements); *The Mogul Steamship Co v McGregor Gow & Co* (1889) 23 QBD 598 (no liability for legitimate and honest exercise of right to trade-attempts by the courts to limit English competition 'would probably be as hopeless an endeavour as the experiment of King Canute'); and, of course, *Carlill Carbolic Smokeball Co v Ball* [1893] 1 QB 256, familiar to all lawyers as one of the first cases on general principles of contract law that law students have to read and remember. It is also, as Professor AWB Simpson's researches show, a fascinating case on Victorian advertising and quack medicine. Bowen's former pupil, Asquith, appeared as counsel at first instance, but not on the appeal heard by Bowen. By that time, Gladstone had appointed Asquith as Home Secretary.

Asquith was, in fact, responsible for Bowen's great final contribution to English law, which was as characteristic of him as anything that can be found anywhere else in his work. In the autumn of 1893 Asquith appointed Bowen to chair a Special Commission to inquire into the disturbances at Ackton Hall Colliery, Featherstone, in the West Riding of Yorkshire. A small number of soldiers, who had been called in to disperse a riot at the colliery, opened fire on a mob of 2,000 people armed with sticks and bludgeons. They threatened to burn down the building in which the soldiers were stationed. The crowd refused to disperse. The soldiers' shots killed two bystanders, who were not taking any active part in the disturbance.

Although Bowen was by now incurably ill, he produced his report promptly after taking evidence in Wakefield. It was described by Dicey in his *The Law of the Constitution* as containing 'an almost judicial statement as to the common law duty of soldiers when called upon to disperse a riot.' Bowen's report stated:

By the law of this country every one is bound to aid in the suppression of riotous assemblages. The degree of force, however, which may lawfully be used in their suppression depends on the nature of each riot, for the force used must always be moderated and proportioned to the circumstances of the case and to the end to be attained.

Human rights lawyers will be struck by the similarity between Bowen's phrasing of the justification principle in a single sentence and the drafting of key justification articles in the European Convention on Human Rights 50 years later.

The report exonerated the soldiers.

V.

Family

They were a vicarage family, and vicarages were the intellectual power houses of nineteenth-century England.

Penelope Fitzgerald: Curriculum Vitae

Bowen was from a vicarage family and his first born son, William, returned to the vicarage after Winchester and Balliol. Bowen himself was the eldest son of the Rev Christopher Bowen (1801–1890), who was Irish and evangelical. He was at Woolaston, near Chepstow, when Bowen was born. He was later Rector of Southwark and of St Thomas, Winchester. He retired to the Isle of Wight and died in 1890.

Bowen's mother, Catherine Emily Steele, was also Irish. Her father was an Irish baronet in the 4th Dragoon Guards. Her mother was the daughter of an Imperial Chamberlain at the Court of Joseph II. Mrs Catherine Bowen died at the age 94, having outlived all her sons. She was a large influence in their lives.

Bowen's younger brother Edward was close in age. There was a third brother, Frank, who went into the army and died young. Edward was born in 1836 and died at the age of 65 while walking in the Cote d'Or. Lord Bryce wrote of the two Bowen brothers:

Like his more famous but perhaps not more remarkable elder brother, Charles Bowen, who became Lord Bowen, and is remembered as one of the most acute and subtle judges as well as one of the most winning personalities of our time, he had a gaiety, wit and versatility which suggested the presence of Celtic blood... He was a great deal more than a teacher, just as his brother Charles was a great deal besides a lawyer. Charles published a verse translation of Virgil's Eclogues and the first 6 books of the *Aeneid*, full of ingenuity and refinement, as well as of fine poetic taste.

Edward went to King's College London, then to Cambridge where he was elected to the Apostles and became a Fellow of Trinity at the age of 23 and a Fellow of King's two years later. He left Cambridge to teach at Harrow and stayed there for the rest of his life, leaving his money to the school. He wrote the Harrow School song *Forty Years On.* Apart from unsuccessfully standing as a Liberal candidate for Hertford against Balfour, he preferred to be a schoolmaster of great gifts leading an uneventful life of unceasing and untiring activity.

Bowen was married in January 1862 to Emily Rendel. She survived him by only three years. They had two sons and a daughter. The elder son William born in November 1862 took Holy Orders and wrote a memoir of Edward Bowen, but not of his father. Another son Maxwell was born in 1865 and went into the army.

Their daughter Ethel was born in 1869. Ethel's story has been told by CV Wedgwood in her biography of her uncle, Josiah Wedgwood MP, later the first Lord Wedgwood. The Wedgwoods were members of the 19th century 'Intellectual Aristocracy' dissected by Lord Annan in his paper on family connections 'as part of the poetry of history'.

Ethel Bowen was 'a handsome, intelligent, extremely serious woman'. She 'treated her family with unvictorian ruthlessness'. She married Josiah Wedgwood in July 1894. Her father gave his consent shortly before his death. The couple were first cousins, Josiah's mother being a Rendel and sister of Lady Bowen. The young couple were Fabians, serious about their radical politics. They had seven children. The marriage, which had never been peaceful, ended in divorce in 1919. Josiah Wedgwood later wrote that it was like 'living in a typhoon'. Ethel left her husband in 1913. She said that she had ceased to love him, to continue to live with him was prostitution, and so she must leave his house. CV Wedgwood thought that this sounded like 'something in Ibsen'.

VI.

All are held together by one of the most complicated and brilliantly worked metaphors anywhere in fiction. It is the metaphor of a web, or tissue…It is both a field of force, a trap like a spider web and a pattern of invisible connecting links between humans meeting each other's eye.

AS Byatt—*On Re-reading Middlemarch*

Friendships

In one sense Bowen was caught in a web, the professional web of unremitting hard work at the Bar and in the Court of Appeal. In another sense he was in a social network invisibly linking him with many others. A pattern emerges of a fuller life outside the law than his work schedule would appear to allow. He did not spend all of his time in his chambers working on endless briefs or writing reserved judgments.

He had a large circle of friends, some of them the most influential people of his time. Some had been at school with him, some at Oxford: AV Dicey (1835–1922) was in chambers with Coleridge and Bowen and went on to become one of the greatest occupants of the Vinerian Chair of English law at Oxford; TH Green (1836–1882), son of a Yorkshire country parson, elected a Fellow of Balliol in 1861, and in his time a great figure in the teaching and writing of moral philosophy, but who also ran the college, engaged in local politics, sat on the City Council, and liked talking to farmers; and Henry Sidgwick (1838–1900), who wrote on ethics, religion, economics, politics, education, and literature, and was one of the great intellectual figures of his time. These friendships, like relationships within a largish Victorian upper-middle class family, seem formal, undemonstrative, and unexpressed, even repressed, but they were no less valuable or valued than the more informal.

Two friends of Bowen are of special interest.

Benjamin Jowett (1817–93)

Jowett, Master of Balliol from 1870 to 1894, was, despite his long silences and devastating remarks, revered by his pupils. He was a major influence on Bowen. AN Wilson's description of Jowett as 'an unclassifiable original' and 'that rather attractive mixture, a person of profound religious feeling and a sceptical cast of mind' catches him well. He thought that there was a place for faith in human life (belief in goodness, prayer, and a Supreme Being), provided that it did not fight against experience. Jowett also had Dr Johnson's gift of incisive speech, putting an argument in a nutshell and confuting an opponent with an epigram.

Bowen was affected by some of the controversies that surrounded Jowett after Bowen went down from Oxford. In 1860 Jowett contributed an essay on 'The Interpretation of Scripture' to a book of theological essays, *Essays and Reviews*. Mark Pattison and Frederick Temple, a future Archbishop of Canterbury and father of a future Archbishop of Canterbury, also contributed. Theologically, Jowett was a liberal in the Church of England, in which he had been ordained in 1845. He argued for a more liberal interpretation of Scripture, making use of reason. Plato, Hegel, and German idealism deeply influenced Jowett's theology, philosophy, and cultural views.

Essays and Reviews was published within months of Darwin's *Origin of Species*. Wilberforce, the Bishop of Oxford, denounced *Essays and Reviews* as an attack on the fundamental truth of Christian scripture. Legal proceedings in the ecclesiastical courts were taken against two other contributors, HB Wilson, who was charged with denying the doctrine of everlasting life or death, and Dr Rowland Williams, who was charged with denying the plenary inspiration of the Holy Scriptures and was defended by James Fitzjames Stephen. The accused lost before Dr Stephen Lushington, the Dean of Arches, but won in the Judicial Committee of the Privy Council by a majority led by the Lord Chancellor, Lord Westbury, the two Archbishops dissenting. Dr Williams acted in person. The judgment of the Privy Council was condemned in both Houses of Convocation.

Although Bowen's name does not appear in reports of the case, he seems to have been there doing something, perhaps as a law reporter for the New Reports on which he worked during early days at the Bar. He may even have been there assisting Coleridge, who appeared for the Bishop of Salisbury. Bowen is the person credited by Atlay with having written on a brief or on something 'He [Lord Westbury] dismissed Hell with costs, and took away from orthodox members of the Church of England Their last hope of everlasting damnation'.

There were proceedings against Jowett in the University Court to block his stipend as Regius Professor of Greek. Although he did not represent Jowett, Bowen remained loyal to him and resigned from *The Saturday Review* in protest against its leader on *Essays and Reviews*. Despite these controversies, Jowett and Bowen remained close friends. In Jowett's opinion Bowen was:

...one of the most gentle and honourable men I have ever known—a man of genius converted, perhaps crushed, into a lawyer, and possibly the greatest English lawyer of his day.

Bowen made plans after Jowett's death for an official biography of him, but they were cut short by his illness and death before any real progress was made.

George Eliot (1819–80)

One valued friendship not mentioned by Bowen's biographers is that of Bowen and his wife with George Eliot. It began in the early 1870s and is recorded in her diaries and journal. The tissue of professional, social, intellectual, and religious links between Bowen, his family, and his friends and contemporaries is as complex and brilliant as anything in *Middlemarch*. The Bowens' friendship with George Eliot extended to her partner, George Lewes, and to her husband-to-be, John Walter Cross (1840–1924 and ex-Rugby), whom she married seven months before her death.

When George Eliot was completing the last part of *Middlemarch* in January 1872, she and George Lewes were guests of the Cross family in Weybridge. Bowen and Jowett were fellow guests. During the 1870s the Bowens were regular visitors to the Priory, George Eliot's home, usually on Sunday evenings. Sometimes there was dinner and a musical evening. There were many other visitors—Frederic Harrison, positivist philosopher, Tennyson, Henry James, and Henry Sidgwick.

The hospitality was not all one way. Bowen got places in court for George Eliot and George Lewes during the *Tichborne* trial. After hearing Sir John Coleridge QC speak for three hours Lewes left court feeling ill, apparently from the bad air. George Eliot's interest in justice, law, and lawsuits is a feature of her novels.

When Jowett invited George Eliot to stay in Oxford the Bowens were invited along. They talked about moral philosophy, Bowen arguing, like the cautious lawyer, that morality was relative and that you had to consider all the circumstances, Jowett arguing for the idealist view, and George Eliot for altruism and for imperatives of duty tempered by fellow feeling. According to her famous declaration in a Cambridge college garden God was inconceivable, immortality was unbelievable, and duty was imperative and absolute. She believed that, in the short span of life, the aim should be to achieve something better within the limits of natural and social forces. Like Bowen, she saw no point in fighting against the future. Change was inevitable, but truth to the past, in her case the peace and harmony of rural life and work, was also important.

They were all very serious people, who enjoyed and were stimulated by each other's company and conversation. When George Eliot died in December 1880 at the age of 61 Bowen joined others in making efforts to have her buried in Westminster Abbey. They were rebuffed. An opponent of the proposal said that the Abbey was a Christian Church, not a Pantheon—an instance of the intolerance that Bowen fought against.

VII.

Example

I return to the beginning and to Dr Johnson's trust in the power and value of a judicial and faithful narrative. Bowen, devoid of all intellectual arrogance and self-importance, would never have thought of his legacy to posterity. Yet his experience of life, his career, and his involvement in the legal, intellectual, and social life of the last half of the 19th century are still relevant to a changed and changing world. His vision for the administration of justice was the transform-ation of a legal system into something less chaotic and more efficient.

Bowen's aim in life, stated privately in a letter to a cousin in 1868, was:

…a sincere wish to learn what is true, however much it may conflict with any of one's cherished ideas, and a resolution, at all costs, to follow what seems to one (after hearing as much of all sides as one can) to be true, is to my mind the one thing to be aimed at in life. I am sure that it is no easy task; it frequently involves pain to others and pain to one's self; often, as in the case of some people whose course I daily am observing, it involves the sacrifice of all social and worldly ambition and success…

This was his aim at the Bar. He achieved success in a subordinate role. He had no natural flair for advocacy. His unassertive and unimpressive court manner and his recurrent bouts of ill health would have been disastrous for a man of lesser abilities. The secrets of his success were not secret at all: exceptional intellectual abilities and an extraordinary capacity for thorough preparation, without which his leaders (usually the Law Officers) could not have won their cases. 'Cases are won at chambers' he told Asquith during his pupillage. This needs to be drummed into pupils today and every day. Bowen gave each case, however small, all of his attention. He revised his drafts continually, but he did not allow his attention to detail to obscure the general legal principles, of which he had a firm grasp, and his overview of the case, which was his sure guide through the detail.

No barrister can expect success unless he works hard. Bowen lived, as barris-ters still live, in neurotic fear of no work. In his first few years of practice Bowen had very little work. He was patient. When he got a practice, his psychoneurotic compulsion was to overwork, leading to the sick bed, seclusion, and long periods of not working at all. He went on extended foreign travels and walking tours to recuperate.

Asquith criticized him for his inability to delegate, which was not a problem for Asquith. Delegation at the Bar and on the Bench is easier said than done. There is in fact little that a busy barrister or a pressured judge can delegate to oth-ers compatibly with the proper personal performance of professional and public duties. Bowen's particular problem was both his strength and his weakness: he was a perfectionist, with the ability to be perfect, but without either the time or the physical constitution to do so without serious harm to his health.

The pursuit of truth was also Bowen's aim as judge and law reformer. His judicial career started young and spanned nearly 15 years. He said of it, with characteristic humour and modesty and more than a grain of truth, that judicial life passed through three stages: in the first stage the judge is always afraid that he is not doing right; in the second stage he is sure that he is always right; and in the third stage he doesn't care whether he is right or not.

Bowen passed through the first stage during his three years as a Queen's Bench Judge. He was not suited to juries and trial work. Fortunately, he found his true home in the Court of Appeal where he was able to make an outstanding contribution to the development of the common law and to the reform of court administration and civil procedure. Bowen realized the need for the law to change and that the task of change is never done because the law works in a world that keeps changing.

In the reforms of the machinery of justice, Bowen put his trust in State institutions. They were essential to progress and a better and just society. He was cautious about the process of reform itself. He knew that it was important to hear as much of all sides as one can and he understood the problem of balancing future gain against past loss. His preference was for the historical method of evolutionary change rather than the imposition of over-ambitious utilitarian solutions. History was a sequence of events and lives and, like many Victorians, he believed that the natural movement was in the direction of progress. While in many ways things were getting better, good things could be lost in the process. New solutions could create a crop of new problems. He wrote:

It would be a mistake to undervalue the merits of the machinery that we have abandoned, or to suppose that the superior machinery which has been substituted is free from its own special elements of weakness.

As he noted, reforms could be so elaborate that they actually increased expense, added to delay, and multiplied litigation. To take a small instance, which is still topical, he appreciated the problems in imposing a requirement of leave to appeal as a means of cutting down the number of appeals. The requirement could have the effect of compelling the court to hear half of the case before deciding whether or not to hear the whole of it and it was difficult to refuse leave on any point of doubt. Thus, in some instances:

... the reforms of the legal system produced or intensified in their turn evils that require to be rectified or to be watched.

He was not against reform. Far from it, he recognized that:

... much is always left to be accomplished. There is and can be no such thing as finality about the administration of the law. It changes, it must change, it ought to change, with the broadening wants and requirements of a growing country, and with the gradual illumination of the public conscience.

On improvements to the machinery of justice, input was required from all those involved in making it work. The court structure, its procedures, and the judiciary underwent an enormous transformation in Bowen's time at the Bar and on the Bench. Bowen understood that, as a constitutional institution operating to serve the people, the judiciary was far greater than any individual judge could be:

The public service is greater than the men who serve it, and no judge, fortunately, is indispensable to the law, any more than a single wave is indispensable to the sea.

He knew where the judges' place was—in the court room. There were already signs of pressure on judges to do too much, and he was concerned about its effects. As for the Court of Appeal, he described 'the incessant labour the fatigue of which few who have not tried it can appreciate'. Nothing has changed.

Bowen wrote:

Judges of the land are not made of cast-iron; the judicial business of the country is performed by men who are no longer young…it requires freshness and mental strength adequately to do justice to a difficult and complicated cause…

Although he sat on committees and Councils and chaired a public inquiry, Bowen belonged in court. He knew how a judge should conduct a court. He was most at home as the detached observer and the trusted umpire of passionate contests. He wrote to a friend whose son was contemplating a career at the Bar:

As for the law, it is of no use following it unless you acquire a passion for it…a passion in the end is necessary if he is to succeed. I don't mean a passion for its archaisms, or for books, or for conveyancing, but a passion for the way business is done, a liking to be in court and watch the contest, a passion to know which side is right, how a point ought to be decided.

He also wrote that 'the success of courts depends on their personnel'. It is still the same. All reforms of the law and the legal system, without sufficient and appropriately qualified and experienced personnel, judicial and support staff, at all levels, are doomed to failure.

VIII.

Legacy

Colleagues hoped that Bowen would go on to be another Mansfield in the Lords. His judicial vision resembled Maitland's on legal history. Bowen would have agreed with Maitland that the law was not just a collection of rules sorted in separate compartments, but was an evolving, principled body of learning. Bowen was never a specialist at the Bar. He did civil and criminal, ejectment and perjury, constitutional and ecclesiastical. With specialization from Day One there is now a greater need than ever for imaginative and intellectual minds to relate the parts to the whole. Maitland wrote:

... law is a body, a living body, every member of which is connected with and depends upon every other member... Science deals with the body as a whole, and with every part of it as related to the whole.

In his approach to the law Bowen was serious without being solemn. His high spirited wit was inseparable from his wisdom. It helped to put everything else into proper perspective.

A child of an evangelical vicarage, a product of Arnold's reformed Rugby and of Jowett's risen Balliol, an adherent of Gladstonian Liberalism, a cultivated scholar, and a public spirited citizen, he engaged in the issues of the day and was close to the centre of them. In his own sphere he helped along the great transformation of law and its institutions, the legal profession and the judiciary, to meet the changing needs of society, which were also served by reforms in the universities and schools, the civil service and armed forces, the electorate and the Church.

Bowen's penetrating mind, gentle manner, and quiet charm stretch across time. Classifying him as an Oxford scholar in the Balliol tradition, an Eminent Victorian, a witty judge or whatever, cannot begin to do him justice. He was beyond classification. The grave in which he and his wife are buried is in one of the loveliest corners of Sussex. It is overgrown and the stone is broken. Bowen's achievements are not overgrown. The power and value of his example is undamaged. His life and work still matter.

Lord Bingham has carried into 21st century English law that great liberal tradition of public service, intellectual integrity, and judicial independence and courtesy. His judgments are as strong as Bowen's on their principles and as stylish in their prose. As other contributors to this volume show, he has transformed the law in ways that will last into and beyond the next century.

Some Facts and Events: 1894–1835

1894	10 April, death age 59: buried in Slaugham Churchyard (inscription—'And I if I be lifted up from the earth will draw all men with myself': St John Ch 12 v. 32).
1893	1 October, death of Jowett.
	25 September, appointed Lord of Appeal in Ordinary: Lord Bowen of Colwood.
	7 September, appointed by Asquith, Home Secretary, to chair Committee to inquire into Featherstone Disturbances at Ackton Hall Colliery. Haldane also a member.
1892	Articles about the 100 resolutions proposed by Council of Judges in *The Times* and *The Law Journal*.
1890	Death of father.
1888	Hon LLD Edinburgh.
1887	Publication of translation of Virgil's Aeneid Books I–VI and The Eclogues into English verse. Contributed chapter on *Progress in the Administration*

of Justice during the Victorian Period in The Reign of Queen Victoria; A Survey of Fifty Years of Progress.

1886	Article on reform of Law Courts in *Law Quarterly Review (Vol 5)*.
1884–93	Appointments: Visitor to Balliol, a Fellow of the Royal Society, and a Trustee of the British Museum.
1883	Visit to the USA with Coleridge and Hannen at invitation of the Pacific Railway Co.
	Hon DCL (Oxon).
1882	May, appointed Lord Justice of Appeal.
1881	Rebuilding of Colwood House, Cuckfield, West Sussex.
1880	Member of Committee to consider the procedure of the Supreme Court. Reported in May 1881. More ill health.
1879	Appointed High Court Judge, QB.
	Bencher of Lincoln's Inn.
1878	Tours Stockholm, St Petersburg, Moscow, Kiev, Constantinople after breakdown in health.
1875	Asquith a pupil.
1873–74	April 1873–February 1874, *Tichborne* criminal trial.
1870	Recorder of Penzance and MA (Oxon).
1871–72	*Tichborne* civil trial led by Sir John Coleridge QC. Ill during the trial.
1872–79	Junior Counsel to the Treasury.
1870	Chairman of Truck Act Commission.
1869	November, birth of daughter Ethel, later Mrs Josiah Wedgwood.
1869	Appointed a Revising Barrister.
1868	Alabama Claims pamphlet.
1866	Move to Coleridge's Chambers at 1 Brick Court, Temple (Western Circuit).
1865–66	A year's holiday in France, Italy, and Switzerland with wife, then in July 1866 with two friends to Norway until October following breakdown in health.
1865	October, birth of son Maxwell.
1863	Chambers at 2 Dr Johnson's Buildings, Temple.
1862	November, birth of son William Edward Bowen, later Rev William Bowen.
1862	January, marriage to Emily Rendel, daughter of James Rendel FRS, a civil engineer.
1861	January, Call to Bar Lincoln's Inn.
1860	Tour of France and Italy from spring to autumn following breakdown
1859–61	Contributor to *The Saturday Review*.
1859	Arnold Historical Prize 'Delphi'.
1858	President of Oxford Union. Read in chambers in Stone Buildings as student of Lincoln's Inn. Hated it.
1857–62	Elected Fellow of Balliol while still an undergraduate.
1858	First in Greats. Ireland Scholarship.
1856	First Class Hon Mods.
1855	Hertford Scholarship.

1854–58	Balliol: pupil of Benjamin Jowett; contemporary of AV Dicey, TH Green, and AC Swinburne. Rowing, cricket, rugby, and racquets.
1850–54	Rugby (School House): Prizes for Theology, Latin, poetry, and Modern History, Cricket XI and Rugby XV.
1846–50	Blackheath Preparatory School.
1845	School in Lille with brother Edward during mother's illness. Learned French and Latin and read the works of Dr Johnson.
1835	1 January, birth at Woolaston, Nr Chepstow, Gloucestershire. Father from Ireland and on the evangelical wing of the Church. Mother of Irish, French, and Austrian extraction.

7

Judging the Administration in France: Changes Ahead?[1]

Jean-Marc Sauvé

In France, the Council of State (*Conseil d'Etat*) is the spinal cord of the whole system aimed at judging the administration. If I had to face the challenge of summing up the Council of State, what it was originally, how it developed, and what it has become today, I think I would use the word 'miracle'. This does not mean at all that I feel that the Council found its origin in the will of divine Providence: this would be more than questionable in a secular state as France is. 'Miracle' is a word which recalls something quite specific in French administrative law theory, thanks to Professor Prosper Weil. Professor Weil is a well-known and respected scholar who refers to 'Le miracle du Conseil d'Etat'.[2] Using this expression, the author wished to capture the complex evolution of this body of law experts. Its original mission was to regulate through law the activity of public authorities from inside the administration; its members did not enjoy the status of judges and enjoyed very limited independence from the Executive branch. However it became, as time went by, an independent protector of the respect of the rule of law by all public entities. The Council achieved this by being both, on the one hand, an independent advisor to the government and, on the other hand, a sovereign court in the field of administrative law whose independence is customary though very strong, building an ambitious body of case law which is legally binding for *every single* public officer, including the President, the prime minister, and members of the Cabinet whenever they act as administrative authorities. At the same time, the Council became the centre of a comprehensive network of administrative courts, which includes now forty-one administrative tribunals and eight administrative courts of appeal.

As you may have noticed, we at once raise an issue which is more than sensitive for us: the very consistent linkage within the Council acting in both of its

---

[1] This is based on the text of the 8th Lord Slynn of Hadley Annual Lecture delivered in London on 27 November 2007.
[2] Prosper WEIL *Le droit administratif*—Paris PUF «Que sais-je» 1994.

capacities, as legal advisor of the government and highest administrative judge. We shall see later on that, if some extra precautions indeed ought to be taken in order to guarantee that this system is in line with the requirements of Article 6.1 ECHR as interpreted by the European Court of Human Rights, the fundamental link between those two capacities are in my eyes essential. I am quite aware that this may seem a bit odd to common law judges and lawyers, but each of our systems has its own specific aspects. As far as we are concerned, we view this fundamental link between our advisory work and our mission as the highest administrative judicial body, not as a threat for our independence but, on the contrary, as the cornerstone of the enforcement of the rule of law by public authorities. It works that way in France because of the central place that the Council of State has taken.

I do not mean that it has always been easy to bring public authorities into compliance with the rule of law. At this stage, also, a major difference can be emphasized between England and France. In the English system the changes have been gradual and the legal system has developed within the framework of a remarkably stable constitutional context. This has not been the case in France and this is also in a sense why Professor Weil's expression is meaningful. Given the complex and often troubled history France went through during the last two centuries, it happened several times that some leaders in the country had in mind simply to abolish the Council but never did so. This is also why, in my mind, being able to chair the Council today as it stands is something of a miracle. It can be said that the Council retained its original name but changed thoroughly from the inside. To that extent, and as paradoxical as it may seem, it can be said that the Council is probably one of the most British-type institutions on the continent.

The Council of State As It Was and As It Is

Historical background and key dates

Under its present form, the Council of State was established by Article 52 of the Constitution adopted on 13 December 1799. This Constitution was issued by Napoleon Bonaparte just a few weeks after he came to power. Article 52 reads as follows: 'A Council of State shall be responsible for drafting the bills and regulations of public administration and for solving difficulties arising in administrative matters.' It can be seen that, from the very beginning, the Council has exercised a double role, both as a legal adviser to the Government and as a judge in charge of settling cases in the field of administrative law. For various historical reasons, litigation taking place between public legal persons, such as the state or local bodies, has always been brought in France to specific jurisdictions. This separation between civil law courts and administrative law courts, quite rare in common law countries, is fairly familiar to most civil law countries.

In fact, the 1799 Constitution did not really create *ex nihilo* the Council; it rather re-established in a modern fashion a body that already existed under the monarchy. As early as the 13th century, the King, who was in charge of delivering justice to his subjects, was being assisted by experienced lawyers forming the King's council, also known as the Council of State. These lawyers had to look into cases submitted to Royal justice, and deliver to the monarch a proposal as to how to settle the case legally and fairly. Soon after the French Revolution started in 1789 and in order to avoid any interference from regular courts into the revolutionary movement, it was decided that decisions made by public bodies would simply not be submitted to courts; the principle of separation of powers was thus set out. However, exonerating public bodies from any form of court authority led to some abuse and therefore Napoleon decided that the Council would renew the old practice, so that ordinary citizens would have access to him through a body of independent and skilful specialists in the field of public law. The Council then acted in first and last instance. Since 1799, certain key dates in the evolution of French administrative courts may be sketched out.

- 1872: the Council was given full authority to issue its own judgments as a sovereign court, 'in the name of the French people' instead of submitting proposals to the Head of State—which he in practice always followed.

- 1873: public legal persons were declared liable for all torts they may commit. From now on, the Council was in charge of granting compensation to all of those who may have suffered damage from any wrongdoing from civil servants and agents acting in such capacity.

- 1953: in most cases authority to determine cases as a first instance court was transferred from the Council to administrative tribunals (now 41 in number). The Council would then be in charge of looking into appeals against judgments issued by tribunals.

- 1987: six (now eight) administrative courts of appeal were established. They have authority to determine appeal cases arising from administrative tribunals, whereas their own judgments may be challenged in front of the Council of State acting as a 'juge de cassation', i.e., in charge of legal review.

- 2001: a new administrative justice code was issued in order to simplify the rules of procedure followed by all administrative courts in the country. It was also aimed at developing urgent and provisional measures to be taken by judges, before the case is determined as a whole.

The Council of State As It Is Now

The Council as the legal adviser to the government

The advisory role of the Council goes back to its very beginning. The drafting of the five Napoleonic codes (the civil code, the penal code, the civil procedure code, the criminal instruction code, and the commercial code) took place within the Council. The 1958 Fifth Republic Constitution now in force does compel the government to submit most of its major legal work for the advice of the Council. The advisory work being done within the Council is carried out by four bodies called 'administrative sections' (the Interior section; the Finance section; the Public works section; the Social section). Each section includes a chairman and approximately 20 members of the Council. There is also a general assembly gathering members of all sections and a standing committee in charge of handling urgent matters.

Each administrative section is in charge of looking into draft bills or decrees having been drafted within governmental departments and agencies. The chairman appoints a rapporteur who has to study the matter in depth before submitting his/her own proposals to collective scrutiny among the section standing in a plenary session, but to which the public does not have access. Based on the work done by the rapporteur, a debate takes place amongst members of the section. When the debate is over, the chairman calls for a vote and the section then decides whether to accept the draft submitted by the government—usually including amendments agreed upon by the section—or to give a negative piece of advice.

Sometimes the Council of State has to reject draft bills or decrees the government has submitted on the ground they are not consistent with constitutional law or principles or with treaty law—including EC law which in the French system prevails over national law, including statute law, but does not prevail over the Constitution itself. When such a negative piece of advice is being issued, the government remains free, in theory, not to follow it but practically always does.

All draft bills and some draft decrees follow a second stage within the Council. After being looked into within a section, such pieces of legislation have to be sent to the general assembly which is the highest advisory body in the Council.

It should be noted also that the government, whenever it wishes to, may request advice from the Council on all matters except on those that involve pending litigation. Some advice is quite technical, but it may relate to social and economic issues. For instance, during the last decade the Council has issued some important advice regarding how to adapt French public utilities to the new competition rules issued by the European Union. Such matters involve thousands of jobs and have a great impact on how huge sectors of the economy are being shaped.

The 'section du rapport et des études' has a particular mission. Unlike the above-mentioned administrative sections, this section is not in charge of dealing with draft bills or decrees that the government is seeking to introduce in domestic law. This section devotes itself to the drafting of the annual report of the Council. Such reports, in addition to yearly statistics and elements relating to the assessment of the work undertaken by the other bodies operating within the Council and all administrative courts in the country, include an in-depth study of a given topic, which changes each year (for instance legal aspects of modern research in the field of biology or genetics, or the updating of French governmental work in the context of EU legal framework). Apart from the annual report and upon request by the prime minister, this section may also set up working groups aimed at issuing draft reports suggesting changes in domestic law or in administrative organization. Such drafts are later debated within the general assembly of the Council, the conclusions which the report included being most usually followed by the government.

The Council as the French administrative supreme court

The Council of State acting as the supreme court in the field of administrative law issues between 10,000 and 11,000 judgments each year. This work is carried out by the Litigation section, which is the largest section in the Council. The Litigation section then serves in different capacities.

- It may serve as first and last instance judge for approximately 20 per cent of the cases determined by the Council each year. In this case all matters, law and/or facts, can be debated before the Council. Most cases are of high importance, such as governmental decrees or ministerial decisions, decisions made by certain public agencies, and individual cases involving certain high-ranking civil servants. All cases arising from decisions made by French public authorities in any place located outside the geographical scope of the authority of administrative tribunals—notably in a foreign country or on the high seas—shall also be submitted directly to the Council.

- It may serve as a 'juge de cassation' for all judgments issued by an administrative court of appeal and also for some judgments of administrative tribunals in certain minor cases which cannot be appealed. The Council then reviews the whole case within all its legal aspects but does not look into the facts which have been debated before the lower court. If the claim is regarded as valid, the Council is then free to determine the case right away—acting either as an appeal or first instance judge—or to send it back to the court whose judgment has been successfully challenged. If the case is sent back, which seldom happens, the court or tribunal has to comply with what has been ruled by the Council.

- It may also serve as an appeal judge, in some cases especially for litigation involving local elections (though national elections to elect the President of the Republic or members of parliament are to be challenged before the Constitutional Council and not the Council of State).

The Litigation section is divided into ten chambers, each one specializing in certain fields of law. A chamber includes a chairman and two senior council members assisting him and approximately ten rapporteurs. It also includes two 'commissaires du gouvernement' who are also members of the Council. Most of the proceedings between the parties are submitted in written form. After a preliminary review has taken place within the chamber, the case is set down for determination in court.

There are different levels of court session, depending on how important the case is, which involve between three and seventeen judges on the bench. During the public hearing the parties are able to make oral submissions, though they seldom do; therefore the most important part of it is the presentation of the case made by the 'commissaire du gouvernement' who sums up the case and the relevant case law and submits its own proposal as for settling the case. It must be noted that the 'commissaire du gouvernement', despite the misleading title, is not responsible for expressing the views of the government on a case; nor is he or she a prosecutor: the role is that of an independent expert.

The most important issue at stake before the Council is whether precedents, if they do exist, should be maintained, adapted, or reversed. A change in international or domestic law is often the reason why a precedent is being reversed. Though a precedent is not legally binding in theory, as it can be in common law systems, administrative courts submitted to the authority of the Council practically always implement it, since their judgments could otherwise be successfully challenged.

The Key Issues and Changes Ahead

It is time to identify the key issues and changes that lie before the French administrative justice system in the years ahead. These are issues and changes that we cannot avoid if we wish to fulfil adequately our role for the benefit of the society as a whole and also to retain what is most essential: our legitimacy and the confidence of the people. Soon after I had the privilege of being appointed as Vice-President of the Council, almost 14 months ago, I decided to launch a process aimed at assessing our situation and building up a collective thinking process as to where we should go. In September 2007 I gathered a meeting of all members of the Council and staff assistants in order to sum up the outcome of this work. I noted that there was a high level of agreement on most options that had been retained. The main issues and answers can be summed up in perhaps four questions:

- What is to be done to address the massive increase in the number of claims?

- How can we reconcile determining an ever increasing number of claims and retaining high quality standards in the manner in which we determine such increasing claims?

- What has to be done to make the Council of State and administrative courts more effective?

- What approach should we follow in order to fulfil our mission in the framework of European law?

What is to be done to address the massive increase in the number of claims?

In France we have to face, if not a tsunami, at least very high waves in terms of increase in litigation. This evolution is all the more significant in France since, at the same time, the number of cases submitted to civil courts, commercial courts, and labour courts has remained pretty stable, if not decreased. In the administrative courts, however, the average growth rate each year since 2002 has been 10.4 per cent. This simply confirms a long-term trend: let us recall that at the level of all administrative jurisdictions 18,000 cases were registered in 1968, 62,000 in 1987, and 173,000 in 2006. The increase in a forty-year period of time is almost ten-fold. This very sharp increase, if one tries to analyze its causes, is due to a combination of factors: the claims administrative courts have to determine in their traditional capacity are expanding by thousands; while in some new fields, litigation is also expanding. There the problem comes not so much from the number of claims *per se* than the crucial importance of what is to be settled for economic growth and social harmony.

The increase rate has remained high in the sectors of public activity which traditionally bring in lots of claims from individual citizens. This is the case for tax, of course, and also civil servants and civil liberties (that is to say, all administrative decisions relating to law and order enforcement). Our administrative tribunals receive thousands of claims each year in relation to foreigners whose application to get a permanent residence permit in France has been rejected by state authorities. The regulations applying to residence permits often change and foreigners use all legal recourses available in order to stay in the country and delay the moment when they can be expelled and sent back to their country. From their individual standpoint, this is quite normal and logical and I not at all wish to criticize them, but managing this flow of claims raises some difficult questions.

In a different field, our tribunals also have to cope with a very time-consuming (and perhaps surprising) type of litigation: driving licences. The authorities are enforcing much more than before the rules on speeding and other driving offences. Depending how serious the offences are, this may involve the loss of a person's driving licence. This is why thousands of angry drivers fill in claims each year to challenge these decisions in the courts. Again this type of claim is essential at the level of the individual; therefore we must be in a position to determine such cases within a reasonable period of time.

At the same time we can notice a sharp increase in other and less traditional fields of litigation. This includes environmental law. Legal rules have developed to a considerable extent in this field, both at the national level and at the level of

EU law. This has many consequences on different types of decisions being made by public authorities, for example authorizing nuclear plants or new industrial or agricultural processes that may cause pollution. Important projects in the field of housing and urban planning are also being challenged to ensure that they comply with environmental rules and regulations. This is also true when you consider the important transfer of power having taken place in France for the past 25 years or so between the central state and local authorities, such as regions, 'departments', and 'communes'. Now such local authorities exercise many powers and levy taxes in order to exercise such powers. This can raise disputes among local authorities, between the central state and these local authorities, or between these authorities and individual citizens or private companies.

Another field which raises a great deal of complicated litigation is the media. We are facing very quick changes in technology and the number of television channels is expanding rapidly. Public authorities ought to keep an eye on the evolution of this sector, in particular in order to have competition rules being implemented and to avoid concentration. The quick development of computer data raises some sensitive issues also. Data sharing becomes technically easier, and protecting civil liberties and the individual citizen can also bring in some extra litigation.

Also in the field of economics, after privatization, in part because of the pressure of EU authorities, it is now crucial to ensure that competition rules are duly respected in order to avoid new monopolies. This issue is particularly important in France in relation to telecoms and energy. Privatizing does not mean doing away with all regulation, and administrative courts must ensure that public authorities take action in order to have the rules of the game respected by all economic actors.

Even if such an evolution may seem uncomfortable, and is indeed very complicated to handle at every stage of administrative justice, the issue is not whether we are going to keep up with this evolution, but what we must do to assume the responsibilities that have been given to us by the Constitution and to do it in a manner that fits with the high expectations of society towards the Council of State and administrative justice as a whole.

How can we reconcile determining an ever increasing number of claims and retaining high quality standards in the manner in which we determine such increasing claims?

A good way to assess the existing quality standards is to consider what percentage of rulings is challenged to the upper court at each level. About 16 per cent of the first instance judgments are challenged in front of the administrative courts; about 12.7 per cent of the rulings of the administrative appeal courts are challenged in front of the Council of State. In my opinion, these figures would not be as low if the claimants were unhappy with the way that the case has been handled.

However, at the same time, one of the most crucial issues for us is to make sure that we will remain in a position to handle this expanding flow of claims to be determined while maintaining such high quality standards in the way we judge. Four points ought to be made at this stage.

First, we wish to *keep an open and fairly easy access to administrative justice.* Private companies, individual citizens, and groups of citizens acting jointly in order to defend interests or causes that they share have an easy access to the courts which enables them to challenge most regulations or individual decisions affecting their rights or liberties. 'Recours pour excès de pouvoir' is the cornerstone of legal review in French administrative law. It is a key element of our legal heritage and we do not wish to limit this easy access to courts.

Secondly, we must *follow with utmost attention the time framework* in which we determine cases. For many years, French administrative courts have been criticized for not determining cases in a timely manner. Some people used to say then that French administrative justice is a good one in spite of being too slow. No one can reasonably say this any more: a court system that would be too slow simply *cannot* be a good one. This comes both from our international obligations under Article 6.1 ECHR and also from the fact that the society has become much more demanding towards the legal system.

The available data shows that things have changed in the right direction but progress remains very fragile as a whole. At the national level, a first instance case being submitted to a tribunal is determined in the average time of one year seven months and five days. An appeal is determined in the average time of one year two months and fifteen days. However the situation varies a lot, depending on the tribunal or court and, in particular, in urban areas where the population is highly concentrated (especially in and around Paris) the average time required by a case is higher, sometimes even more than two years. This is worrying and the average should not exceed one year everywhere. This implies a considerable input of extra means and management efforts.

In the Council itself the situation is reasonably satisfactory; the average being 11 months and 12 days. However, some particularly difficult cases can still require an extended period of time to get through—sometimes up to four years—and this is in no way something we accept as normal. In other words, even within the Council we must increase our efforts aimed at reducing the time we need to settle cases.

Thirdly, we must safeguard all that has been done in order to *maintain the predictability and consistency of the jurisprudence of our administrative law system.* This implies within the Council different systems of reviewing our rulings so as to avoid developing legal solutions that would not be understood elsewhere, or that could be interpreted in diverging ways by the courts and tribunals. The outcome would then be legally insecure and would lead to unfair treatment of claimants, depending on where their case would be looked into.

In that respect, a very interesting system has been developed since 1987. It enables a tribunal or a court, before determining a case, to ask the Litigation section in the Council to deliver within three months the legal answers to what are the core issues being raised by the case. This way, the Council at an early stage can deliver its own 'roadmap' not only to the relevant court or tribunal, but to all of them in the country. This saves a lot of time and helps to avoid a situation in which many courts and tribunals may adopt diverging approaches before the supreme court is in a position to make its own point. This greatly helps to improve, at an early stage, the quality of the rulings being made by the courts and tribunals.

A fourth key issue for maintaining the quality of our rulings is to make sure that judges are fully aware of the responsibility they bear. This is particularly true in relation to ethics on the one hand, and general and even individual liability that should be recognized in case the legal system works in a manner which is not appropriate, on the other hand. I think it is fair to say that a great majority of administrative judges share a high level of *ethical requirements*. We share a customary ethical code which implies, for instance, that a judge should refrain from getting involved in determining a case whenever this person thinks that he or she is not in a position to be fully independent or impartial, for instance when in a position of conflict of interest. Anytime this happens the judge may, and even should, stand down from the panel of judges, even without having to explain why he or she prefers to do so. However, is it still enough to have an informal or customary ethical code? Many people think it is not. Society as a whole probably wants more. It has therefore been decided to draw up written guidelines that all members of the Council and all judges in the tribunals and courts would have to respect. A great deal of attention will be given to conflicts of interest and how to prevent them efficiently and to the fulfilment of all other professional obligations.

At the same time some people think that the administrative legal system should be in a position to *draw all appropriate consequences whenever it has not worked properly*, in particular in terms of extra delay in settling cases. Here also, society is probably not comfortable with a system in which no general or even personal liability can work if a case has not been handled the way it should have been. In other words, all public authorities have to face liability when they unlawfully cause damage to anyone and the court system should be in line with this.

In that sense the Council has reversed its original jurisprudence as to draw all consequences falling from the European Court of Human Rights case law which implies that, when a case has taken too long a time to be determined, compensation should be granted to the person who has suffered damage for this inadequate management of the case, on the ground of Article 6.1 ECHR. This was done in the *Magiera* case in 2002.[3] Now we frequently allow substantial amounts of money to this type of claimant, when the normal time framework has been exceeded.

[3] 28.06.2002 *Magiera* no 239575 p 248.

We now do even more in terms of *personal* liability. A few months ago and for the very first time, an administrative judge was compelled on the order of the Vice-president to reimburse to the Justice ministry's budget part of the compensation awarded to a person who had successfully claimed that the legal system was at fault for not determining the case within a reasonable period of time. In some extreme situations, when it seems clear enough that the reason why the case was not properly handled in due time was not a matter of extreme pressure of work on the court, but simply a matter of gross negligence on the part of the judge in charge of looking into the case, we will be in a position to draw this type of individual consequences. This seems important, both because it is likely to serve as a strong deterrent inside the courts, and because it will serve in a positive manner in order for administrative tribunals to be more credible and legitimate in the eyes of the public.

The Council of State, acting both as a supreme court and as the administrator of the administrative court system, must be a leader when it comes to the evaluation of the quality of its work.

What has to be done to make the Council of State and administrative courts more effective?

An important aspect in this process, which I will simply mention without having much time to elaborate deeply, will be to update the way in which the Council fulfils its task as legal advisor of the government. Very soon, a fifth administrative section will be established, and this section will concentrate on the issue of modernizing public management. France is undertaking a difficult process to modernize administrative processes. We thought it would be important to have within the Council a group of experts able to compare what is being done in the different branches of the Executive, and have each one of them benefit from what has be done elsewhere.

The administrative sections at the general level should be in a position to act at an earlier stage, rather than giving an advice on a draft which has already been done, and which can be difficult to change at the time when the Council deliberates. They could be used also by government agencies as some kind of a 'law firm', able to deliver its expertise and make proposals sooner in the decision-making process. As far as the litigation process is concerned, some key issues ought to be addressed. I will simply highlight four of them.

A first important one is for the administrative judge to *adapt the consequences of some of the decisions he makes*. In French law, as we perform legal review, whenever a decision is declared null and void the court decision has a retroactive effect and the illegal decision is supposed not to have occurred at any time. This can lead to a legal vacuum and can raise some overwhelming difficulties on how to implement the court ruling, or have government agencies be exposed to certain unreasonable financial costs. In the *Association AC!* ruling the Council for the first time stated that in some extreme cases the administrative judge, if the parties ask him to do so, shall define what ought to be the legal effect of its decision.[4] In other words—and this will help to prevent certain very troublesome legal vacuum situations—the court may decide to postpone the implementation of its ruling.

Since the *Tropic Travaux* ruling,[5] the Council of State can choose, whenever we decide to reverse a precedent in our jurisprudence, whether this change in jurisprudence should have a retroactive effect, or if the effects of such change in our jurisprudence should be postponed (for example, if its effect should be limited to cases introduced after the reversal of the precedent).

Along in the same lines, a second issue is *to develop our techniques aimed at ensuring that the court rulings are duly executed by government authorities.* Important reforms have already taken place back in 1980 and 1995. The administrative judge has since then full authority to give orders to public authorities and, if necessary, to impose a fine on them for not executing its ruling within a reasonable period of time. And I want to go further and develop more explicitly the 'roadmap' that should be followed by the relevant public authority in order to meet fully its legal obligations in a given case.

Another issue of crucial importance is to *develop fully our legal possibilities to take all appropriate, urgent, and provisional measures before we determine the case.* Since a very important reform introduced in 2001, the administrative judge is now in a position, much more efficiently than he was before, to order certain provisional measures. The most important one is to suspend all legal effects of a decision made by a public authority, whenever such a decision is legally doubtful and raises some urgent concerns for the claimant. In many cases it may not be acceptable to let an illegal regulation or decision be enforced for months, if not years in the worst case, before declaring it null and void. The claimant rightly wishes the legal system to come to his rescue and, provided that the claimant has some strong legal reasons to ask for this, to block the effects of the regulation or decision until the court issues its final ruling on the case.

A further key issue and reform under way is to *assess all of our court proceedings in order to make sure that they fulfil the requirements of the ECHR*, as interpreted by the case law of the European Court of Human Rights. I wish to draw all possible and reasonable consequences from the legal principles being stated by such decisions; we wish to be realistic enough to consider that carrying on as if these rulings had not occurred would not be satisfactory, and would in the long run undermine the authority and legitimacy of our administrative justice as a whole. In this respect, I am determined to promote substantial reforms.

First, people just cannot understand nor believe that someone called 'commissaire du gouvernement' is truly independent. I am now convinced the official

[4] 11.05.2004 *Association AC!* no 255886 p 197.
[5] 16.07.2007 *Société Tropic Travaux* no 291545.

name of the 'commissaire du gouvernement' has to go. This change of name will have to be associated with a significant procedural change. Today, both the plaintiff and the defendant can only submit written observations after the commissaire has spoken. I want to make it possible for the plaintiff to speak last, after the commissaire.

Secondly, one has to pay attention to the possible conflicts of interest arising from our dual mission: giving legal advice to the government and settling litigation cases. Within the Council, there is a Chinese Wall separating those two missions. The difficulty has been for us to explain and demonstrate the efficiency of it. As early as 1872, any member of the Council was forbidden by statute to deal on the litigation side with a case he had been involved with on the advisory side. That rule, though not forgotten, is not a legally binding rule anymore and I am going to ask the government to reintroduce appropriate legislation for this purpose.[6]

My view is that in this respect we share common concerns. I understand that getting in line with the ECHR as interpreted by the European Court of Human Rights was one of the reasons why British authorities adopted the Constitutional Reform Act in 2005, leading in particular to a deep reform of the institution of the Lord Chancellor, which was over 1,000 years old and very much respected worldwide.

What approach should we follow in order to fulfil adequately our mission in the framework of European law?

This issue is probably one of the most important ones we share on both sides of the Channel. How can we address in general terms the growing challenge of building the rule of law at the level of Europe and, more specifically, what can be done to help the courts in all EU Member States within the framework of the case law issued by both the European Court of Justice (ECJ) and the European Court of Human Rights?

Some decades ago, we had within the Council many debates on the authority that should be given to European law: I am sure that there were and perhaps still are debates within the English courts. This debate can be all the more complex given the fact that basically a national judge gets its legitimacy from its own constitutional order and can be reluctant to give to foreign regulations so big a place that it might undermine the stability of national law.

This issue is particularly sensitive when it comes to applying EU law. The ECJ has developed a jurisprudence that has EU law prevail over practically all domestic

---

[6] From a procedural viewpoint it means that, in a given case dealing with a matter in which the advisory side of the Council was involved, plaintiffs will have access to the names of the members of the Council involved in the delivering of the advice, thus enabling them to make sure that no conflict of interest occurred.

rules, including the member states' constitutions. At the same time, it would be unrealistic on the one hand not to admit the very high level of integration of EU law; and on the other hand, to seem to forget that any person can go to the European Court of Human Rights and challenge any ruling made by a national court.

Since the *Nicolo* case in 1989,[7] the Council has reversed its own traditional jurisprudence and admits that, even though it does not have authority to do the constitutional review of the statutes being voted by Parliament, it may and even should refrain from implementing a piece of legislation that would not be consistent with our treaty obligations, including those that originate in European law.

This issue is of particularly great importance when it comes to implementing EU directives, since in that particular field we must at the same time implement European law, in particular when the directive has not been properly transposed in national law, and respect the Constitution which requires that any citizen benefits from all the rights that it includes.

Things could become really difficult if the terms of this debate were limited to which norm should prevail on the other. It may very quickly lead us into a dead end. Things have become much clearer for us with the help of the Constitutional Council, which has issued a major ruling dealing with this question in June 2004.[8] Now the approach followed to tackle this issue deals with the principle of equivalent protection and no longer with which norm should prevail.

The 1958 Constitution now formally recognizes the existence of a specific European Community legal order to which France takes part. In this respect, both the Constitutional Council and the Council of State now consider transposing EU directives as a constitutional obligation. As far as the Council of State is concerned, an important ruling has been delivered in the *Société ARCELOR* case on 8 February, 2007.[9] This ruling states that reviewing any piece of domestic regulation has to be done in a special manner whenever what is at stake is a directive which issues certain precise and unconditional obligations for France as an EU member state. In this event, if the claimant contends that the domestic regulation violates the Constitution, we first look into EU law, as interpreted by the ECJ, to see if a rule or a principle that can be seen as equivalent to the relevant constitutional rule can be found in this body of law. If that is the case, what we do then is to check whether such rights guaranteed by EU law have been adequately implemented in the directive. This means that we try and find out whether the directive which is at stake does comply with this fundamental rule or principle of EU law. If in our view the answer is clearly that it does comply, we will reject the claim. If the question seems doubtful, we will suspend our proceedings and seek a preliminary ruling from the ECJ under Article 234 EC. We will subsequently determine the case, depending on the answer that the ECJ will have given to us.

---

[7] 20.10.1989 *Nicolo* no 108243 p 190.
[8] 10.06.2004 Décision 2004–496 DC *Loi sur l'économie numérique.*
[9] 8.02.2007 *Société ARCELOR Atlantique et Lorraine* no 287110 p 55.

Another 2007 ruling where the Council of State had to decide what impact decisions of the ECJ were to have on French jurisdictions was known to us as the 'shallot affair'.[10] The Council of State ruled that all interpretations of the Treaty and Community acts issued by the ECJ must be followed by the national court. In *Gardedieu*,[11] the Council of State ruled that the French state was liable for any damage caused by statutory law that did not fully abide by international conventions; this decision gives its full authority to ECJ rulings such as *Francovich*.[12]

This new approach helps us greatly to open the way to a system aimed at *combining* instead of *opposing* European law on the one hand, constitutional rights and liberties on the other hand. This seems consistent with the fact that, when it comes to implementing European law, you simply no longer have the domestic judge on the one hand, the ECJ and the European Court of Human Rights on the other hand. The domestic judge is himself a European judge. When European law questions are raised before him in a given case, the better the answer he will give and the less litigation will later have to be determined by the two above-mentioned courts.

The way we look at EU law has been changed greatly over the past 10 or 20 years. We no longer look at EU law as an *external* source of law; it is simply part of the legal norms that we must implement daily in our courts, some of them being issued by our national authorities, and some being issued by the EU, under a process to which our national authorities take part. Let us keep in mind that the Council of State is required to implement EU law or the ECHR in approximately 40 per cent of the cases it determines.

More generally, my view is that some work should be done in order to develop the institutional cooperation we have with the ECJ, aiming at using Article 234 EC proceedings in a sufficient and efficient way. However, we should go further than that to develop some inventive forms of informal cooperation (such as visits and workshops) not only with the ECJ and the European Court of Human Rights, but also with the high courts of member states which all have to cope with the same difficulties in implementing European law.[13] Certain EU directives, dealing, for instance, with protecting the environment or contracting in the field of public works or public utilities, do raise some germane and very difficult issues; it might then be interesting to share our experiences. As for implementing European law properly at the global level, I strongly advocate developing such new forms of cooperation between us. A common ambition we may share would be to set up a network of European judges. What is at stake is of course not to

---

[10]　11.12.2006 *Société DE GROOT EN SLOT ALLIUM BV* no 234560.

[11]　8.02.2007 *Gardedieu* no 279522 p 78.

[12]　Case C6/90 *Francovich v Italy* [1991] ECR I-5357.

[13]　For instance, on 28 January 2008, the European association of administrative supreme courts will hold a workshop at the European Commission in Brussels, on environmental law. Judges, lawyers, civil servants will attend and share their views on how the implementation of European law in that field has evolved.

determine which model is the best one, to export our domestic legal concepts, nor is it to give away our specific aspects or differences which are part of our legal and even cultural heritage. What we could achieve would be to open our eyes more widely to what is being done across our legal borders, and to improve our proceedings and concepts in the light of other proceedings and concepts already familiar to other systems.

Conclusion

French administrative law now develops in an ever expanding spectrum, which includes protecting civil rights and liberties, in the most noble and traditional sense, implementing market regulations, social and economic regulations, and even more experimental fields such as environmental law, biotechnologies, and the information society. On all of these grounds, the administrative judge is facing very sensitive debates in terms of politics, economics, and society; he must constantly draw a balance between conflicting, though legitimate, rights and preoccupations. He must also keep in mind that he acts in a society which, unlike what happened 50 or 100 years ago, is more and more open to Europe and to the rest of the world.

These issues are such that, now more than ever, the judge is in the heart of the relationship between the different powers and the citizens. When delivering his rulings, when stating what the law is, the judge does more than regulate society, even more than protect the individual against the misuse of public authority. In some cases, he even has to protect the citizen against arbitrary behaviour. The judge is therefore in charge of ensuring day by day that the very heart of the democratic promise is being respected, that is to say the protection of the rights of the citizen.

III

EUROPEAN AND INTERNATIONAL LAW IN NATIONAL COURTS

1

Jurisdiction

Guido Alpa

1. Dedication

The considerations voiced here are the fruit of the reflection on other pages, those read by Lord Bingham at the University of Rome III, on the occasion of the ceremony at which he was conferred the title of *Laurea honoris causa* in jurisprudence. The magisterial lecture, splendidly constructed, was dedicated to the 'Rule of Law'.

In describing the significance, history, and function of the 'Rule of Law', Lord Bingham has made clear that this expression is a general clause which summarizes the very essence of the modern democratic state; for many, it is elusive to define, and can only indeed be understood by means of recourse to an ideological interpretation. Yet he maintained that this expression comprises a constitutional principle, which, notwithstanding that it is extremely wide and elusive, may be enunciated thus:

The core of the existing principle is...that all persons and authorities within the state, whether public or private, should be bound by and entitled to the benefit of laws publicly and prospectively promulgated and publicly administered in the courts.

In order to make it applicable in practice, Lord Bingham has defined eight sub-rules. Of these, the fifth sub-rule reads:

...means must be provided for resolving, without prohibitive cost or inordinate delay, bona fide civil disputes which the parties themselves are unable to resolve. It would seem to be an obvious corollary of the principle that everyone is bound by and entitled to the benefit of the law that people should be able, in the last resort, to go to court to have their rights and liabilities determined. This is not a rule directed against arbitration and more informal means of dispute resolution, all of which, properly resorted to and fairly conducted, have a supremely important contribution to make to the rule of law. Nor is it a rule requiring every claim or defence, however spurious and lacking merit, to be guaranteed full access to the process of the law. What it does is to recognise the right of unimpeded access to a court as a basic right, protected by domestic law,[1] and in my view

---

[1] *Raymond v Honey* [1983] 1 AC 1, 12–13; *R v Secretary of State for the Home Department, ex p Leech* [1994] QB 198, 210; *R v Lord Chancellor, ex p Witham* [1998] QB 575, 585–586.

comprised within the principle of the Rule of Law. If that is accepted, then the question must be faced: how is the poor man or woman to be enabled to assert his or her rights at law? Assuming, as I would certainly wish to do, the existence of a free and independent legal profession, the obtaining of legal advice and representation is bound to have a cost, and since legal services absorb much professional time they are inevitably expensive. It is not enough that justice should be open to all, like the Ritz Hotel. This is a more acute problem in common law countries than in civil law jurisdictions, because the legal process tends to be more lawyer-intensive and therefore, inevitably, more expensive. But the Rule of Law requires that justice should be an affordable commodity, and a party should not have to wait too long for his rights to be finally decided by the courts.

'Rule of Law', which is difficult to translate into Italian, is sometimes associated with that of the 'State of Law'—and thus related to the notion of justice and so to that of the administration of justice, and thus to jurisdiction.

These are assumptions which can also be shared by the civilian lawyer, particularly if the latter, as well as being scholars of private law, are also practitioner advocates.

In my case, by a completely unforeseeable stroke of destiny, I have found myself also fulfilling the role of President of the Italian Bar Council, the public law body that represents Italian lawyers. Thus, I have had to deal myself on numerous occasions not only with the administration of justice and the problems that it presents in this particular moment in our country, but I have also had to preside (a task I still discharge) over the 'disciplinary appeal court', as the Italian Bar Council may be defined, when it administers disciplinary justice in relation to lawyers who have committed an ethical misdemeanour and have suffered a judgment against them by the local Bar Council to which they belong.

There are thus three reasons converging together that have made me choose this theme in order to honour the illustrious jurist. The first relates to the highest and most prestigious appointment that Lord Bingham discharged until very recently, that of Senior Law Lord, and to the distinguished *cursus honorum* which he has pursued in the various courts. It has been a veritable mission; his pronouncements, his dicta, are now part of the heritage of law books and a model for interpretation, studied also by non-English jurists who deal with comparative law. Proof of this was the applause with which the new doctor of Jurisprudence was greeted in the course of the ceremony. The second reason concerns the profession which he chose prior to becoming a judge, that of a brilliant barrister, accustomed to defend rights, to construe defences on statutes, regulations, and case law, to protect the interests of his clients, and to discharge a no less honourable mission by requesting and obtaining justice. The third reason is that, beyond being honoured with his precious friendship, I find that I am his (junior) colleague, since some years ago I was admitted as an honorary bencher to Gray's Inn.

The impression which I have always had, when talking with him and listening to his lectures—those read on the occasion of seminars organized by one of the most prestigious professors in comparative law and, our common friend Sir Basil Markesinis are particularly memorable—is not only the distinction of his grand intelligence, his culture, and capability, but also his sensitivity and humanity, as well as a sense of pragmatism. These are rare virtues, particularly if found in one person, which make his friendship even more precious.

I am thus really grateful to Mads Andenas, a generous friend and most distinguished colleague, for having given me the opportunity to participate both at the seminar of the University of Oxford in honour of Lord Bingham, organized in cooperation with the Oxford Institute of European and Comparative Law directed by Stefan Vogenauer, and to the drafting of the *Festschrift* dedicated to him.

Well then, I asked myself whilst meditating on his words on justice, what is the meaning today of the term *giurisdizione*, which translates literally into English as 'jurisdiction'? The affinity of the words is striking, even if the meanings in the two languages, and thus in the two legal experiences, of Italy and England, are not perfectly in line. We are not indeed dealing with words of little consequence, given that these run right to the heart of the legal system; the exercise of the function of judge, whilst being similar in the two countries, follows rules, traditions, cultures, and practices which are distant from one another. They were distant in the past, but perhaps will not be so forever. At the present, application of European Community law, as a source for the internal legal systems of the member states, and, in the future, the construction of a *Jus Commune Europaeum*, inclusive also of the principles of procedural law, allow one to hope that the distances will become less. Then, if one can consider the constitutionally guaranteed principles which are at the basis of the 'Rule of Law' and of the 'State of Law', we may already say that the two experiences are inspired by mutually shared principles.

2. Jurisdiction: An Evolving Notion

So, why speak of *giurisdizione*, and why speak of jurisdiction on this very day? I believe that reasons, which are different from each other but all converging, impose upon jurists today the requirement to revisit the notion and the function of *giurisdizione*.

For Italy, there are many reasons. The celebration of the 60th anniversary of the Constitutional charter has caused discussion of three real changes, indeed 'revolutions', which we have witnessed in these years.

The first revolution owes its origin to the dissolution of all of the legislative monopoly and the multiplication of all the sources of law. Today, all are agreed in talking of a diffuse power of legislation, including that of a devolution to the Regions of power which is not reserved to the state or of concurrent competence of legislation between state and Regions, as well as the delegated power to independent administrative Authorities. To this, one can add also the recognition of the creative function of the judge and the inclusion of jurisprudence amongst the sources of law.

The second revolution is determined by the so-called *diritto vivente*, or living law—once it was preferred to speak of a 'material constitution'—that is all the transformations in the legal order determined by interpretation of constitutional norms. This has led to the modification of the usual meaning of the term *giurisdizione*, understood as the exercise of a function belonging exclusively to the state, or as the expression of an independent power such as the judiciary is (and must remain), or as the synthesis of judgment and punishment, otherwise as a result of the resolution of conflicts between private persons, between private persons and public administration, and between the various state powers. More recently, beside this have been added new meanings, which enrich the function object and strengthen its role: the duty of the judge to attribute to a law an interpretation in conformity with the Constitution and, in case of doubt, to raise the question of constitutionality before the Constitutional Court.

The third revolution consists of the repeated interventions by the legislature, such as the rules introduced for 'a fair trial', the regulations on procedural mechanisms dictated by the requirement to remedy the crisis in the administration of justice by abbreviating the times for trials and the reform of the system for arbitration, the reform of cassation proceedings and the rules governing the 'nomophilatic' function of the Court of Cassation.

Yet we must also take account of the other changes.

In the European Community context, the notion and function of jurisdiction have changed since a national court—and just as any ordinary court, so any other person who has been empowered to exercise such a function—has the obligation to apply European Community law, to disapply internal rules in conflict with Community law, and, in the event of doubt, to raise the question as a preliminary issue before the European Court of Justice.

In international law, the most alarming problem brought to the attention of jurists has been the Guantánamo affair and the principle of long-arm jurisdiction of the United States' own legal system. In the age of globalization of markets, in which the relationship between *nomos* and *terra* has been dissolved, jurisdiction may seem to have been superseded by consultation, by the new *Lex mercatoria*, which is based on contract more than law, and arbitrators rather than the national courts.

The expression *giurisdizione* appears to us to possess a particular relativism, historical and cultural and also political and social, if it is true that it must be assimilated to (when not identified with) that of justice. In the final analysis, *ius dicere*, but also the interpretation and application of the rules, the punishment of behaviour which is not in compliance with the law, as well as the administration of the law safeguarding the rights and interests of partners together constitute the essential significance of this term, which is highly evocative. It is evocative to the point that, in comparison between legal systems, there are cultural experiences, such as that of England, where the starting point for description of the essential characteristics of the juridical systems is precisely the jurisdiction, the system of courts, and the power and function of the judge.

It is thus not a coincidence that in his magisterial lecture, Lord Bingham has assimilated jurisdiction to the rule of law. One of the hallmarks of the 'Rule of Law' is indeed the function of the judge in the interpretation and application of the law in the public interest, as a safeguard of fundamental rights, and protection for the situations in which the socially deprived live.

From this point of view, all the learned doctrines and complex discussions on the multiple significances of jurisdictions in relation to the powers of the state are far removed and can be consigned to the history of juridical culture. But those debates connected with this function, the problem of unity or otherwise of the jurisdiction, also seem to be distant.

This is perhaps one of the most interesting aspects of the examination of this term. Contrary to what happens in England, in which the jurisdiction is devolved upon the ordinary judge even where it involves the public administration, in Italy, prior to the approval of the Republican Constitution, there was an alternation between the unitary system (from 1865, the year of foundation of the Kingdom, until 1889) and the pluralist system (from 1889 onwards). The change is due to the establishment of a judge who is competent to judge the acts and behaviour of a public administration; thus, not an ordinary, but a special judge. Previously this purpose was served by the institution of an additional section (the fourth) to the sections of the Council of State; to this section were attributed the jurisdictional functions and, given the ample workload which accumulated, over time another two sections were added. Then the Court of Accounts was instituted, which has an accounting jurisdiction over public entities. These two special courts were recognized as such by the Republican Constitution. In the course of the two decades of Fascism, further special tribunals for political crimes were founded. The Constituent Assembly (in the years 1946 and 1947) was intended to lead Italy out of the war and of the struggle with Fascism and Nazism to a new constitution of a republican design, democratic and solid enough to prevent the country from ever being able to return to the tragic trap of dictatorship. It fell to this body to engage in a passionate discussion: Was it necessary to retain, or instead to suppress the special judges? And did that apply also to those pre-existing and not related to the dictatorial regime? In particular, a grand jurist and teacher of civil procedural law, Piero Calamandrei, had defended that notion. His were arguments of a political nature, but also of a formal character. However, learned doctrine ended by entrenching itself behind reasons of a formal nature.

A separate story can be told about the tribunals of commerce, which were eliminated at the end of the 19th century, before in fact the Commercial Code was united into the Civil Code in 1942.

Practical experience as well as the political legislative affairs that have marked the legal system in the 60 years which separate us from the Constituent period, have taught us that one cannot resolve all the questions of the jurisdiction by legal formalism. Also, questions that are apparently technical, such as all those relating to civil procedural law, have their own political value, and a little healthy legal realism suggests not insisting on the *a priori* or dogmatic conceptions too rigidly. Besides, not even the idea, from time to time re-emerging in the studies and proposals of reform for the system, has caught on of abolishing the distinction between special and ordinary judges and, in particular, between the ordinary and administrative judges. Rather, with the exception of the distinction between ordinary courts and those special courts which survived in the Constitution and were not subsequently suppressed (in accordance with the procedure permitted by the Transitional Provision VI)[2], 'specialized' judges have multiplied in the courts, that is, judges belonging to the ordinary magistracy to whom all of the questions belonging to a particular sector have been assigned (Tribunals for minors, sections for the protection of industrial property, and so on). Besides the 'robed' judges, 'honorary' judges have also appeared in the tribunal court, and justices of the peace have been created in order to aspire to the demands required for a more efficient (or less dilapidated) machinery of justice.

There is now general acceptance of the concept of pluralism of the jurisdiction, at the price sometimes of tightrope-walking interpretations, as one sees from the commentaries of the Constitution. Today it is preferred, in order to overcome the possible objections of a logical and dogmatic nature, to start from the functional definition of jurisdiction, rather than from that of the exclusively formal.

3. Jurisdiction and the Crisis in Justice

Reflection on the jurisdiction, that is to say on the jurisdictional function, on the access and administration of justice has become a task which is not only unavoidable for jurists, but also a duty for those who fulfil institutional roles. This is imposed by the crisis, widely proclaimed and apparently irreversible, in which the system of justice finds itself. The daily life of courts is witness to this, as well as the investigations of the Ministry of Justice, the research conducted by the Bank of Italy and by the National Bar Council, and also the documents published by foreign organizations. I refer to the investigations commissioned by the European commission on the economic aspects of legal services, for the purposes of identifying obstacles to competition, to economic development, to the raising of the quality of services, to the reduction of legal costs for enterprises, to the improvement of social conditions for European citizens, and to the expansion of access to justice. To all this should be added the research of the CEPEJ, which

---

[2] VI. Within five years of the Constitution coming into effect, the special jurisdictional bodies still in existence shall be revised, excluding the jurisdiction of the Council of State, the Court of Auditors, and the military tribunals. Within a year of the same date, a law shall provide for the reorganization of the Supreme Military Tribunal according to Article 111.

includes Italy among those countries in which justice is worst administered; the opinions, sometimes also caustic, of the World Bank which places our country amongst the least reliable for investors, given the slowness of the justice machinery, the difficulty of protecting one's rights, and the length of time for recovery of debts; the judgments condemning Italy pronounced by the European Court of Human Rights for the excessive delays in trial.

The crisis reached in the administration of justice is a notorious situation, much debated, and that worries the institutions, the judiciary, the lawyers themselves, as well as, of course, the citizens.

It has been the *leitmotif* that has characterized the inaugural speeches for the judicial year at the Constitutional Court, the Supreme Court of Cassation, the Council of State, and the Court of Accounts, which has been echoed by the Sicilian Administrative Court of Justice, the regional administrative tribunals, and in particular the Lazio Regional Administrative Tribunal. Similar problems have been indicated by the regional sections of the court of accounts, the tax commissions, and even the National Bar Council. The phenomenon is also known elsewhere, and common to many of these, as can be noted from the inaugural speeches of the judicial year of the European Court of Justice itself and of the European Court of Human Rights.

Intermeshed with the debate on the capacity of the current institutions to give an adequate response to the demand for justice of the citizens, the debate on the organization of procedure, whose multiplicity and variety aggravate the current situation, and further the debate on the promotion of alternative dispute resolution mechanisms and on the facilitation of conciliation and arbitral justice, the subject today of legislative initiatives (moreover conflicting between themselves), the debate on the stabilization of 'honorary' justice, together with other aspects of the problem which it is not appropriate here to examine. It is opportune in any event to underline that today the jurisdiction has come to be exercised not any more only by 'robed' judges, recruited by competitive examination and qualified as state employees (according to the Napoleonic tradition transplanted from France), but is carried out by lawyers who perform the functions of 'honorary' judges sitting beside robed judges. The lawyers are judges nominated for a fixed period of time (which had to be limited because the legislative measure introducing the justice of the peace was meant to be provisional and extraordinary, but now they are becoming permanent). They continue, in another sphere, to develop their private practices, provided that they do not enter any conflict of interest.

4. Pluralism of the Jurisdiction as a now Irreversible Condition

Now seen as an expression of an ambiguous constitutional choice (if intended in terms of unique and not a Unitarian state of the jurisdiction, or else unitary of the adjudicating function, or else as unitary of the judiciary, or else as unitary of the guarantees enjoyed by judges), now seen as a fundamental question in the understanding of economic efficiency of the 'machinery of justice', the principal of unity of the jurisdiction has been recently resubmitted for the attention of scholars and practitioners for the uncertainty of interpretation that has arisen from the legislative initiatives on the division of jurisdiction between ordinary and administrative courts.

An ambiguous text of the law, a disputed application of the pronouncements of the Constitutional Court on the subject, still divergent orientations of the plenary sessions of the Council of State, and the United sessions of the Court of Cassation—which the latter court moreover has the functional responsibility to draw the boundary of divisions of jurisdiction—have rendered the situation still more complex. To all of this must be added the ever more perplexing doctrinal positions on the distinction between subjective rights and legitimate interests, the epoch-making pronouncements on compensation for damages for injury of legitimate interests, the impact on the way of exerting the jurisdictional function made by the Community legislation, and some recent positions taken by the European Community judges themselves.

I refer in particular to the European Court of Justice, which, arrogating to itself the discretionary power to decide the application of a Community law by the national judges, has declared the principle on the basis of which, if the Community law is not applied or is not applied correctly, the member state must respond for the damage caused to citizens by the national judges (even where these represent the apex of the national judicial structure).

Recently the Constitutional Court has made a direct reference, under Article 117[3] of the Constitution, to the case law of the European Court of Human Rights, for the protection of fundamental rights in the internal legal system.

---

[3] Legislative powers shall be vested in the state and the Regions in compliance with the Constitution and with the constraints deriving from EU-legislation and international obligations. The state has exclusive legislative powers in the following subject matters: (a) foreign policy and international relations of the state; relations between the state and the European Union; right of asylum and legal status of non-EU citizens; (b) immigration; (c) relations between the Republic and religious denominations; (d) defence and armed forces; state security; armaments, ammunition, and explosives; (e) the currency, savings protection, and financial markets; competition protection; foreign exchange system; state taxation and accounting systems; equalization of financial resources; (f) state bodies and relevant electoral laws; state referenda; elections to the European Parliament; (g) legal and administrative organization of the state and of national public agencies; (h) public order and security, with the exception of local administrative police; (i) citizenship, civil status, and register offices; (l) jurisdiction and procedural law; civil and criminal law; administrative judicial system; (m) determination of the basic level of benefits relating to civil and social entitlements to be guaranteed throughout the national territory; (n) general provisions on education; (o) social security; (p) electoral legislation, governing bodies and fundamental functions of the Municipalities, Provinces, and Metropolitan Cities; (q) customs, protection of national borders, and international prophylaxis; (r) weights and measures; standard time; statistical and computerized coordination of data of state, regional, and local administrations; works of the intellect; (s) protection of the environment, the ecosystem, and cultural heritage. Concurring legislation applies to the following subject matters: international and EU relations of the Regions; foreign trade; job protection and safety; education, subject to the autonomy of educational institutions and

5. Jurisdiction and Legal Formants

From the references just made above, it is obvious that the constitutional model, which entrusted to Articles 102,[4] 103,[5] and 111[6] of the Constitution, in

with the exception of vocational education and training; professions; scientific and technological research and innovation support for productive sectors; health protection; nutrition; sports; disaster relief; land-use planning; civil ports and airports; large transport and navigation networks; communications; national production, transport and distribution of energy; complementary and supplementary social security; harmonization of public accounts and coordination of public finance and the taxation system; enhancement of cultural and environmental assets, including the promotion and organization of cultural activities; savings banks, rural banks, regional credit institutions; regional land and agricultural credit institutions. In the subject matters covered by concurring legislation legislative powers are vested in the Regions, except for the determination of the fundamental principles, which are laid down in state legislation. The Regions have legislative powers in all subject matters that are not expressly covered by state legislation. The Regions and the autonomous provinces of Trent and Bolzano take part in the preparatory decision-making process of EU legislative acts in the areas that fall within their responsibilities. They are also responsible for the implementation of international agreements and EU measures, subject to the rules set out in state law which regulate the exercise of subsidiary powers by the state in the case of non-performance by the Regions and autonomous provinces. Regulatory powers shall be vested in the state with respect to the subject matters of exclusive legislation, subject to any delegations of such powers to the Regions. Regulatory powers shall be vested in the Regions in all other subject matters. Municipalities, provinces, and metropolitan cities have regulatory powers as to the organization and implementation of the functions attributed to them. Regional laws shall remove any hindrances to the full equality of men and women in social, cultural, and economic life and promote equal access to elected offices for men and women. Agreements between a Region and other Regions that aim at improving the performance of regional functions and that may also envisage the establishment of joint bodies shall be ratified by regional law. In the areas falling within their responsibilities, Regions may enter into agreements with foreign states and with local authorities of other states in the cases and according to the forms laid down by state legislation.

[4] Judicial proceedings are exercised by ordinary magistrates empowered and regulated by the provisions concerning the Judiciary. Extraordinary or special judges may not be established. Only specialized sections for specific matters within the ordinary judicial bodies may be established, and these sections may include the participation of qualified citizens who are not members of the Judiciary. The law regulates the cases and forms of the direct participation of the people in the administration of justice.

[5] The Council of State and the other organs of judicial administration have jurisdiction over the protection of legitimate rights before the public administration and, in particular matters laid out by law, also of subjective rights. The Court of Auditors has jurisdiction in matters of public accounts and in other matters laid out by law. Military tribunals in times of war have the jurisdiction established by law. In times of peace they have jurisdiction only for military crimes committed by members of the armed forces.

[6] Jurisdiction is implemented through due process regulated by law. All court trials are conducted with adversary proceedings and the parties are entitled to equal conditions before an impartial judge in third party position. The law provides for the reasonable duration of trials. In criminal law trials, the law provides that the alleged offender shall be promptly informed confidentially of the nature and reasons for the charges that are brought and shall have adequate time and conditions to prepare a defence. The defendant shall have the right to cross-examine or to have cross-examined before a judge the persons making accusations and to summon and examine persons for the defence in the same conditions as the prosecution, as well as the right to produce all other evidence in favour of the defence. The defendant is entitled to the assistance of an interpreter in the case that he or she does not speak or understand the language in which the court proceedings are conducted.

conjunction with Article 24,[7] the role of expressing principles on the subject of the jurisdictional function of the judiciary, has not remained crystallized in time, but in the 60 years which have passed, has composed, or rather recomposed, itself in an articulated manner as a result of certain important factors.

First of all, there is the doctrinal formative influence. The interpretations of the provisions provided by Articles 102 and 103 of the Constitution over the course of time have been numerous, and the meaning is so controversial that, in a recent encyclopaedic work, one can find at least eight different models of explanation. The simplest and most neutral attributes the character of generality only to the ordinary jurisdiction, a constitutional nature within the scope of competence of judges, envisaged by Article 103, but does not involve the constitutionalization of the judges envisaged by this provision. It further assumes the impossibility of resolving the distinction between ordinary and special jurisdiction.

Then, there is the jurisprudential formative influence. This consists, in particular, of the case law of the Constitutional Court, which has legitimized the special jurisdictions existing at the entry into force of the Constitution and not the subject of a revision pursuant to Article VI of the transitional provisions, and also the conservation and institution of specialized sections, the division between ordinary and exclusive jurisdiction, the conservation of the dichotomy between subjective rights and legitimate interests, which moreover could be deduced from the same text of the Constitutional charter.

Finally, there is the formative influence of the legislature, which comes last, not for reasons of priority of the source, but for reasons of shortage of time.

It is thus obvious that when one talks of *giurisdizione*, one is referring not so much to a framework considered together in a static mode, but to a dynamic system, whose frontiers shift from time to time, become clearer, and consolidate according to the operation and the occurrence of the three formative influences.

Yet talking of jurisdiction today—that is of *ius dicere*—also means taking account of the creative function of jurisprudence, now considered a source of law equivalent to the legislative source, and to take account of the pervasiveness of

---

In criminal law proceedings, the formation of evidence is based on the principle of adversary hearings. The guilt of the defendant cannot be established on the basis of statements by persons who, out of their own free choice, have always voluntarily avoided undergoing cross-examination by the defendant or the defence counsel. The law regulates the cases in which the formation of evidence does not occur in an adversary proceeding with the consent of the defendant or owing to reasons of ascertained objective impossibility or proven illicit conduct. All judicial decisions shall include a statement of reasons. Appeals to the Court of Cassation in cases of violations of the law are always allowed against sentences and against measures affecting personal freedom pronounced by ordinary and special courts. This rule can only be waived in cases of sentences by military tribunals in time of war. Appeals to the Court of Cassation against decisions of the Council of State and the Court of Auditors are permitted only for reasons of jurisdiction.

[7] All persons are entitled to take judicial action to protect their individual rights and legitimate interests. The right of defence is inviolable at every stage and level of the proceedings. The indigent are assured, by appropriate measures, the means for legal action and defence in all levels of jurisdiction. The law determines the conditions and the means for the redress of judicial errors.

fundamental rights as such as are recognized and guaranteed by the European Charter of Human Rights to which a juridical and thus binding nature has been explicitly and definitively attributed.

6. Jurisdiction and the Reasonable Duration of Proceedings

In our experience, the Constitutional framework has been enriched by a great novelty, which is to be found in the relationship existing between Articles 102 and 103 of the Constitution. The principle of a 'reasonable duration of proceedings' is provided by Article 111 paragraph 2, as the result of the Constitutional Law of 23 November 1999 No 2.

For criminal proceedings, the principle is strictly linked to the safeguarding of personal freedom, as well as to the damage suffered by the accused for the excessive duration of proceedings to which he has been submitted. For civil proceedings, whether one is dealing with personal rights or with rights of financial substance, the gravity of the effects of the excessive duration cannot be compared to those which affect personal freedom and, in any case, it is of great importance because it impinges directly upon social and economic relationships in which they are involved, of which they are party, and of which individuals are subjects of law, whatever their status.

For civil proceedings, a 'reasonable duration' implies that all legal staff must cooperate so that the trial, taking place before the natural judge, or the competent judge and in the established forms and procedures, and with observance of the right of reply between the parties, in even-handed conditions, before an independent and impartial judge, should not be protracted for an excessive time. Thus, the proceedings should not be transformed into a sort of prison of procedural mechanisms in which the jurisdictional function is confined, hence constricting the right or interest which it is intended to protect. Nor should there be allowed to be uncertainty of the results of the proceedings, thus concluding in a justice denied or delayed, with detriment to the relationship, personal or financial, in which the parties were involved. In an overall vision of the situation, trial proceedings should not lead to damage for the person who seeks justice, to damage to the judicial system, to damage to the economic system, or to damage to the image of the country.

The most serious danger, in a system like that which has gradually come to be created in the Italian experience, is that laws multiply, rights multiply, and judges multiply (ordinary, special, specialized, honorary), and yet that still does not mean there will be a functioning justice in a practical efficient and rapid way, that is, one which ensures the protection of rights and interests.

Beyond the question of the fulfilment of the establishment plan, of financial resources, and of the improvement of organization of the judicial machinery, one has had to turn to the interposition of 'filters' in order to ensure that, whilst maintaining steady and indeed promoting the access to justice, its mechanisms should be simplified.

Unfortunately, the justice administered by the justices of the peace has resulted in a very high level of litigation, which has directly involved the Supreme Court. The appointment of a judge of 'trifling' matters has led firstly to an extension of competence, then into a proposal for consolidation and inclusion in the judicial order, and finally in a perverse mechanism of alteration of the function of control of legitimacy.

The 'illuminist' principle, consecrated by the Constituent Fathers, allowing everybody to act in legal proceedings in order to assert their own rights and interests, Article 24 of the Constitution has been understood in the sense that it is permissible for anybody to accede to the Supreme Court. Nevertheless, Article 111 of the Constitution reserves recourse to the Supreme Court for violation of law only against measures affecting personal freedom; for decisions of the Council of State and Court of Accounts, only on grounds relating to the jurisdiction. One has witnessed instead a strong expansion of the area of jurisdiction, which may be seen in a positive a way, since only the judge can issue all the impartial and concrete practical protection of rules, but also in a negative, way since to guarantee for everybody the possibility of appealing to the Supreme Court for judgment of violation of the law has involved the multiplication of procedures, the multiplication of challenges, and the unbearable increasing burden on a machine of justice, which risks transforming the judge of legitimacy into a judge of the third instance, thus perverting its function.

The situation, close to collapse, requires first aid; amongst other things, the reconsideration, not of the text, but of the interpretation of Article 111 of the Constitution, so that it may be possible to identify filters in the resolution of disputes and the division between degrees of access to the Cassation Court where one is not dealing with measures which restrict personal freedom. Such filters must ensure for everybody the protection of rights and interests obtained through the exercise of the jurisdictional function, seeking to challenge the danger of congestion of the machinery of justice, operating from the bottom and reaching to its very peak.

All this can be done without need to revise the constitutional text, an operation which would require an expenditure of time, resources, and political undertakings which would have implications beyond the substance of the reform.

Taking note of the experiences in other countries, one could consider the reduction of the degrees of jurisdiction according to the types of interest and the value of the dispute. For the resolution of trifling disputes, this could be through forms of alternative dispute resolution, allowing the right of appeal before a judge of the first-degree. One could consider the use of conciliation not only prior to proceedings, but also during the course of the trial, subject to its suspension and referral to the conciliator. One could contemplate a reduced brief reasoning for judicial measures, or the judge's recognition of the admissibility of an application; or the more extensive use of the principle of abuse of process, and other methods which affect the procedure, the means of challenge and the modalities of defence.

Article 113[8] paragraph 2 of the Constitution provides that the jurisdictional protection may not be excluded or limited by particular means of challenge or for determined categories of act. But the interpretation of this provision is open to debate, because it is included within the scope of the rules governing the jurisdictional control of acts of the Public Administration. If one attributes to the provision a restrictive meaning, such principle may be read in a completely different manner, so as to allow limitations to the means of challenge or to the categories of acts.

7. Jurisdiction and Advocacy

From the point of view of the advocacy profession any solution which is compatible with the constitutional principles is very acceptable, and indeed is to be vigorously promoted (proof of this is in the repeated conference occasions in which the advocacy profession has undertaken to cooperate with the institutions for the solution of problems of the crisis of justice). The advocacy profession has even undertaken to improve the system of defence by developing tariffs which are not tied to the times of justice, in order to give the lie to the suspicion of an interest in the protraction of proceedings. The bodies for disciplinary justice have always been involved in championing the observance of ethics of the legal profession, formulated in provisions which have the nature of a primary norm (given the function of a special court performed by the National Bar Council). Amongst the proposals for reform of the legal profession there has even been contemplated the modification of the rules of qualification for the roll of lawyers admitted to the superior jurisdictions, providing an obligatory examination for admission, instead of automatic entry after the accomplishment of the profession of advocate for an adequate period.

The activity of lawyers is the guarantee of the defence of rights within the proceedings. The lawyer's activity 'does not correspond only to the interests of the parties, but also to those of justice, since the arguments by the parties contribute to the correct formation of the judgment'. For the exercise of the jurisdictional function, therefore, there is the 'ministry' of the advocate as a guarantor of rights. Thence the limitations to the powers of the judge in the course of the trial, the cases in which the judge may act *ex officio* without the initiative of a party being rather rare.

---

[8] The judicial safeguarding of rights and legitimate interests before the organs of ordinary or administrative justice is always permitted against acts of the public administration. Such judicial protection may not be excluded or limited to particular kinds of appeal or for particular categories of acts. The law determines which judicial bodies are empowered to annul acts of public administration in the cases and with the consequences provided for by the law itself.

For the lawyer thus called to defend a party, the exercise of the jurisdictional function implies first of all the identification of the appropriate judge, according to whether the question is to be referred to the ordinary judge (civil or criminal) or else to a special court (administrative, accounting, military, tax, or judicial or legal professional disciplinary judge). It is possible to have access to the Constitutional Court only by means of a referral from another judge (ordinary or special), whilst access to the European Community court is direct, for matters which are in the competence of the European Union, and that may occur also through the question of a preliminary reference by the (ordinary or special) Community judge.

In these years, the more serious problems have been produced by the difficult distinction between ordinary and administrative courts in relation to compensation for damages for injury of legitimate interests. This is because it has not yet been established whether the declaration of illegitimacy and the demolition of the administrative act are preliminary questions in relation to the finding and determination and assessment of the damages arising from the injury to the legitimate interest held by the party concerned; or alternatively whether the finding of illegitimacy maybe effected as an ancillary matter by the ordinary judge, or again whether the compensation may be assessed directly by the administrative judge. Further, the boundaries of the areas of exclusive jurisdiction of the administrative judge remain obscure, now that the division of the jurisdiction no longer occurs by the category of person or entity involved but by subject matter. And following initiatives of the legislature, of the Constitutional Court, and of the Court of Cassation, there is still dispute over the question of *traslatio iudicii*, i.e., the transfer from one court to another, avoiding the interruption of the proceeding.

In the context of the ordinary jurisdiction, the advocate must then choose the specialized judge, where this is foreseen. These specialized judges have multiplied over the years, but beyond the praiseworthy intention of better distributing the workload by assigning it to judges who are particularly versed in the subject matter concerned, difficulties have arisen both in the identification of their competence, and in the access to justice, as well as in the practical application of the provisions. I refer in particular to the specialized sections for industrial property, to the (ordinary) sections which dispense justice for the company court procedure, to the tribunal for minors, whose areas of competence in relation to the ordinary tribunal end up—at least for the aspects relating to civil jurisdiction—by fragmenting the subject matter of family relations, which today is in need of a unitary appraisal in the light of constitutional principles concerning the safeguarding of the person, the safeguarding of the family, and the principle of equality. I make allusion also to the 'voluntary' jurisdiction, the exercise of which is overwhelmed by an overcrowding of applications and the lack of personnel and resources, which leads to loss of transparency and compromise of guarantees.

Does one therefore need to favour the tendency to create specialized judges for categories of interests? Should one return to the creation of commercial tribunals, even if their suppression at the end of the 19th century and the unification of the codes which followed were in obedience to the opposite principle aimed at unity of the jurisdiction? Can one contemplate the creation of specialized sections for commerce, that is, for economic activity? Would this subject also catch the relationships between professionals and consumers as well as the relationships between professionals?

A further choice corresponds to the principle of territoriality of the jurisdiction. Thus the lawyer must know whether the competent judge is the Italian court or the foreign court. On this subject, the rules of private international law—whether of substantive or procedural nature—also pose problems of interpretation.

The European Community regulations in relation to this have brought clarity, at least for those subjects covered.

As for ADR, the principle still remains to be overcome, according to which the monopoly of court jurisdiction will not tolerate any interference, whether indirect or substantive, so that obligatory arbitration and conciliation are considered inadmissible. Nevertheless, the recent reform of arbitration has given priority to 'ritual' arbitration as compared with the informal or 'irritual' arbitration. Also, several legislative measures have introduced forms of conciliation to be carried out prior to seizing the ordinary court. In any case, these initiatives always permit recourse to the ordinary courts or to appeal, the principle of redress before the ordinary jurisdiction remaining sacrosanct.

Even this principle, though, taking account of the constitutional importance of the right claimed, could be revised, for a benefit in a reduction of the number of the trials and the workload which derives from that, when the 'unrobed' judge, who operates in the guise of arbitrator, mediator, or conciliator, is impartial, capable, and independent. These are all guarantees which the professional category of lawyers—should they be called upon to perform these functions directly— could readily ensure. Besides, the greatest percentage of justices of the peace is drawn from the legal profession, and the honorary judges, who are recruited to help ordinary judges in their work, replacing them in judging cases, are already lawyers.

2

Aspects of Justiciability in International Law

Lawrence Collins

'Justiciability' is a word of many meanings, and it would, for obvious reasons, not be out of place to begin this contribution with the background to a dissenting judgment of Bingham LJ (he then was), in which he discussed the justiciability of treaties in municipal law, and which was substantially accepted by the House of Lords.

The Arab Monetary Fund (AMF) was an international banking organization established by a treaty in 1976. The parties were 20 Arab states and the Palestine Liberation Organization. The United Kingdom was not a party to the treaty. The AMF had its headquarters in Abu Dhabi, and it claimed that Dr Hashim, its former Director-General, had stolen about US$50 million from it, and that the First National Bank of Chicago and three of its subsidiaries enabled him to launder a substantial part of the money through numbered accounts in Geneva.

The defendants applied to strike out the action on the ground that the fund was not an entity recognized under English law. The application was founded on the principles enunciated in the *International Tin Council* case.[1] The International Tin Council was an international organization established by treaty. It ran out of money trying to support the world price of tin, and it ceased trading, owing creditors large sums of money which the member states refused to pay. Certain creditors obtained an arbitration award against the Council and commenced proceedings in England against the Department of Trade and Industry claiming that each member state was jointly and severally liable to satisfy the award. The House of Lords decided that the English court was not competent to adjudicate on the rights arising from transactions entered into by independent sovereign states on the level of international law. The International Tin Council had no status in English law until it had been created as a legal entity in English law by Order in Council under the International Organisations Act 1968. The Order in Council

---

[1] *JH Rayner (Mincing Lane) Ltd v Department of Trade and Industry* [1990] 2 AC 418.

providing that the International Tin Council was to have legal personality created a separate legal person in English law, and only it was liable on its contracts.

The AMF was recognized as an international organization by Her Majesty's Government, but it had not been given any separate status in English law. As a result, reversing Hoffmann J, and applying the logic of the *International Tin Council* case, a majority of the Court of Appeal decided that the courts could not have regard to the treaty as a source of rights and obligations: *Arab Monetary Fund v Hashim (No 3)*.[2] Lord Donaldson MR said[3] that in the absence of an Order in Council, an international organization was not 'a native' but nor 'is it a visitor from abroad. It comes from the invisible depths of outer space'. The result was that the AMF had no remedy in the English courts against Dr Hashim and the banks.

Bingham LJ dissented. He was plainly sympathetic to the view of Hoffmann J at first instance that, but for the *International Tin Council* decision, legal entities established under international law should be recognized in English law. Bingham LJ questioned whether the decision in the *International Tin Council* case required the court to hold that the AMF treaty should be ignored. He accepted that the House of Lords had very clearly held that issues concerning the meaning and application of treaties were not justiciable in municipal courts. But the decision of the House of Lords did not require the AMF treaty to be ignored altogether. In suing as a juridical person, the AMF did not depend on a status derived from a non-justiciable treaty, but on a status conferred by its recognition by a decree under the law of the United Arab Emirates. That law did not create a domestic corporation but was effective to confer legal personality on it.

On appeal the House of Lords accepted by a majority (Lord Lowry dissenting) the result reached by Hoffmann J at first instance and of Bingham LJ in the Court of Appeal that the English court should recognize the AMF because it had been recognized by the law of the United Arab Emirates. The logic of the *International Tin* Council case led Lord Templeman to describe what was undoubtedly an international organization (and recognized as such by the United Kingdom) as a corporate body created by the laws of the United Arab Emirates. The Federal Decree had conferred legal personality on the AMF and created a corporate body which corresponded roughly to an English company.

This was a highly artificial solution since all that the United Arab Emirates decree did was to confirm and ratify the AMF Agreement and schedule the articles of agreement. But the solution was in line with what Bingham LJ had said[4] was the importance to the City of London as a financial and commercial centre of allowing international organizations involved in finance and commerce to operate effectively.

The theory is, of course, that because the executive can enter into treaties without the consent of or ratification by Parliament, it would be contrary to principle

---

[2] [1991] 2 AC 114.   [3] At 133.   [4] At 142.

for private rights to be affected by treaties unless they have been incorporated into English law. The shorthand version of this principle is that 'treaties form no part of domestic law unless enacted by the legislature'.[5] That was why in two cases, by a bare majority of three to two, the Privy Council held that the Charter of the Organization of American States could give prisoners on death row no rights under the law of the Bahamas, because even though the Bahamas was a member of the Organization, no effect had been given in Bahamas law to the provisions relating to the Inter-American Commission on Human Rights (before which the prisoners' petitions were pending).[6]

A similar issue arose in relation to the effect of the deliberations of the UN Human Rights Committee and the Inter-American Commission on Human Rights, and of an order of the Inter-American Court of Human Rights. By majorities of three to two and four to one, the Privy Council held that the effect of the constitutions of Trinidad and Jamaica was to give condemned men a right not to be executed until the human rights bodies had reported and the authorities in the West Indies had had a chance to consider their reports.[7] But in another decision, by a majority of four to one, the Privy Council decided that an interim order of the Inter-American Court of Human Rights requiring Trinidad to ensure the men were not executed had no effect in Trinidad law.[8]

Those members of the Board who took the view that no account should be taken of the petitions to the human rights bodies emphasized that the international instruments were not part of the law of the country concerned. As Lord Hoffmann said, the right to enter into treaties was one of the surviving prerogative powers of the Crown. The Crown might impose obligations in international law upon the state without any participation on the part of the democratically elected organs of government. The rule that the treaties could not alter the law of the land was one facet of the more general principle that the Crown cannot change the law by the exercise of its powers under the prerogative.[9]

Those who took the view that the condemned men had a right that the reports of the human rights bodies be considered before a final decision on execution were taken did not dissent from the view that unincorporated treaties are not part of the law of the land. But in their view the condemned men had a right under the constitution not to have the outcome of any international process pre-empted by executive action. Lord Millett said[10] that the applicants were not seeking to enforce the terms of an unincorporated treaty, but a provision of the domestic law of Trinidad and Tobago contained in the Constitution. By

[5] *Higgs v Minister of National Security* [2000] 2 AC 228, at 241 (PC, majority opinion delivered by Lord Hoffmann).

[6] *Fisher v Minister of Public Safety and Immigration (No 2)* [2000] 1 AC 434; *Higgs v Minister of National Security* [2000] 2 AC 228.

[7] *Thomas v Baptiste* [2000] 2 AC 1; *Lewis v Attorney General of Jamaica* [2001] 2 AC 50.

[8] *Briggs v Baptiste* [2000] 2 AC 40.

[9] *Higgs v Minister of National Security* [2000] 2 AC 228, at 241 *et seq.*

[10] *Thomas v Baptiste* [2000] 2 AC 1, at 23.

ratifying a treaty which provided for individual access to an international body, the Government made that process for the time being part of the domestic criminal justice system and thereby temporarily at least extended the scope of the due process clause in the Constitution. In the case involving the interim order of the Inter-American Court of Human Rights Lord Millett emphasized that *Thomas v Baptiste* (in which he had delivered the majority opinion) was not intended to overturn the constitutional principle that international conventions do not alter the law of the land except to the extent that they are incorporated by legislation: *Briggs v Baptiste*.[11] But Lord Nicholls, dissenting, said[12] that 'by acceding to the [American Convention on Human Rights] Trinidad intended to confer benefits on its citizens. The benefits were intended to be real, not illusory. The Inter-American system of human rights was not intended to be a hollow sham, or, for those under sentence of death, a cruel charade.'

In *Lewis v Attorney General of Jamaica*,[13] the majority decided that the condemned men had a right not to be executed until the human rights bodies had reported and the governmental authorities in Jamaica had had a chance to consider them. After reference to the general rule that that a ratified but unincorporated treaty does not in the ordinary way create rights for individuals enforceable in domestic courts, Lord Slynn said:[14]

> But even assuming that that applies to international treaties dealing with human rights, that is not the end of the matter... [W]hen Jamaica acceded to the American Convention and to the International Covenant and allowed individual petitions the petitioner became entitled under the protection of the law provision [in the Constitution] to complete the human rights petition procedure and to obtain the reports of the human rights bodies for the Jamaican Privy Council to consider before it dealt with the application for mercy and to the staying of execution until those reports had been received and considered.

The present writer has suggested that this decision may be a sign that one day the courts will come to the view that it will not infringe the constitutional principle to create an estoppel against the Crown in favour of individuals in human rights cases.[15] In *Re McKerr*[16] Lord Steyn referred to this view and said that the rationale of the dualist theory, which underpinned the *International Tin Council* case, was that any inroad on it would risk abuses by the executive to the detriment of citizens. It was, he said, difficult to see what relevance this had to international human rights treaties which created fundamental rights for individuals against the state and its agencies, and a critical re-examination of this branch of the law might become necessary in the future.[17]

---

[11] [2000] 2 AC 40, 54.   [12] At 55.
[13] [2001] 2 AC 50.   [14] At 84–5.
[15] 'Foreign Relations and the Judiciary' (2002) 51 ICLQ 485, 496. See also *R (on the application of Lika) v Secretary of State for the Home Department* [2002] EWCA Civ 1855, at [31].
[16] [2004] UKHL 12, [2004] 1 WLR 807.
[17] At [49] *et seq.* In *Republic of Ecuador v Occidental Exploration and Production Co* [2005] EWCA Civ 1116, [2006] QB 432 the Court of Appeal said (at [29]) that any such re-examination

This is plainly a minority view. In *R v Lyons*[18] the House of Lords rejected the suggestion that the ratification of the European Convention on Human Rights by the United Kingdom could affect the lawfulness of the convictions in the Guinness affair in 1990, ten years before the Convention was incorporated into English law. In particular the fact that in 2000 the European Court of Human Rights had held in the *Saunders* case[19] (and the subsequent cases involving the other accused)[20] that it was contrary to the Convention for evidence obtained under compulsion to be admitted did not affect the result. Lord Hoffmann said[21] that under Article 46 of the Convention the parties agreed to abide by the final judgment of the Strasbourg court in any case to which they were parties. But international treaties did not form part of English law and English courts had no jurisdiction to interpret or apply them. If Parliament had plainly laid down the law, it was the duty of the courts to apply it, whether that would involve the Crown in breach of an international treaty or not. The argument that the courts were an organ of state and therefore obliged to give effect to the state's international obligations was a fallacy. If the proposition were true, it would undermine the principle that the courts apply domestic law and not international treaties. International law did not normally take account of the internal distribution of powers within a state. It was the duty of the state to comply with international law, whatever may be the organs which had the power to do so. In domestic law the position was very different. In domestic law, the courts were obliged to give effect to the law as enacted by Parliament, and this obligation was entirely unaffected by international law.

The treatment by the Privy Council of the order of the Inter-American Court of Human Rights, and of the House of Lords of the decisions of the European Court of Human Rights, may usefully be compared with the treatment by the United States Supreme Court of the orders and decisions of the International Court of Justice. Article 36(1)(b) of the Vienna Convention on Consular Relations (1963) provides that if a foreign national is arrested, on his request the authorities shall without delay inform the consular officers of the state of his nationality, and shall inform the person arrested of his rights to consular access. Article 36(1)(c) gives consular officers the right to visit a national of the sending state who is in custody and to arrange for his legal representation.

Angel Francisco Breard came to the United States in 1986 at the age of 20 from Paraguay. In 1992 he was charged with the attempted rape and capital murder of Ruth Dickie. On his arrest he was not informed of his right of access to the Paraguayan consular personnel. At his trial in 1993 the Commonwealth of

---

was a matter for the House of Lords. For criticism of the suggestion that human rights treaties may provide an exception to the general rule see Sales and Clement (2008) 124 LQR 388, 398–400.

18   [2002] UKHL 44, [2003] 1 AC 976.
19   *Saunders v United Kingdom* (1996) 23 EHRR 313.
20   Lyons, Ronson, and Parnes.
21   At [27], [39] *et seq*. See also Lord Millett at [104]–[106].

Virginia presented overwhelming evidence of his guilt. He was convicted and sentenced to death. Subsequently, he argued for the first time that his conviction and sentence should be overturned because Article 36(1)(b) of the Vienna Convention had been violated when the arresting authorities failed to inform him that, as a foreign national, he had the right to contact the Paraguayan Consulate. The federal courts rejected the claim, concluding that he had defaulted the claim when he failed to raise it in the state court.

On 3 April 1998 Paraguay filed an application against the United States in the International Court of Justice claiming that Breard should have been informed of his rights under the Vienna Convention. It submitted an urgent request for an indication of provisional measures, and on the same day the ICJ gave such an indication, namely that the United States should take all measures at its disposal to ensure that Breard was not executed pending the final decision in the proceedings, and should inform the court of all measures which it had taken in implementation of the order of the ICJ.

Following the order of the International Court, Breard filed a petition for an original writ of habeas corpus and a stay application in the Supreme Court. A stay was denied by the Supreme Court.[22] The Supreme Court said that whilst it should give respectful consideration to the interpretation of an international treaty rendered by an International Court with jurisdiction to interpret it, it had been recognized in international law that, in the absence of a clear and express statement to the contrary, the procedural rules of the forum state governed the implementation of the treaty in that state. It was the rule in the United States that assertions of error in criminal proceedings must first be raised in state court, and the claims not so raised were considered defaulted. Breard failed to exercise his rights under the Vienna Convention in conformity with the laws of the United States and of Virginia. The court noted that on the day before the hearing (14 April 1998) the Secretary of State had sent a letter to the Governor of Virginia requesting that he stay the execution. If the Governor wished to wait for the decision of the International Court, that was his prerogative, but nothing in the case law allowed the Supreme Court to make that choice for him. Justices Stevens, Breyer, and Ginsburg dissented.

Breard was executed by injection the same evening.

Six years later, in the *Case Concerning Avena and Other Mexican Nationals* (*Mexico v United States*),[23] the International Court of Justice held that the United States had violated Article 36(1)(b) of the Vienna Convention by failing to inform 51 Mexican nationals of their rights to consular access and assistance. The ICJ found that the individuals were entitled to review and reconsideration of their US state-court convictions and sentences regardless of their failure to comply with generally applicable state rules governing challenges to criminal

---

[22] *Breard v Greene*, 523 US 371 (1998).
[23] 2004 ICJ Rep 12. For the indication of provisional measures see 2003 ICJ Rep 75.

convictions. In *Sanchez-Llamas v Oregon*,[24] a case involving individuals who were not named in the *Avena* proceedings, the Supreme Court decided, contrary to the ICJ's decision, that the Convention did not preclude the application of state default rules. The President then issued a memorandum stating that the United States would discharge its international obligations under *Avena* by having state courts give effect to the decision.

José Medellín, a Mexican national, confessed to participating in the gang rape and murder of two girls in 1993. He was convicted and sentenced to death, and the Texas Court of Criminal Appeals affirmed his conviction and sentence. Medellín then filed a state habeas corpus action, claiming for the first time that Texas failed to notify him of his right to consular access as required by the Vienna Convention. The state trial court rejected this claim, and the Texas Court of Criminal Appeals summarily affirmed. Relying on *Avena* and the President's memorandum, Medellín filed a second Texas state-court habeas corpus application challenging his conviction and sentence on the ground that he had not been informed of his Vienna Convention rights. The Texas Court of Criminal Appeals dismissed Medellín's application as an abuse of the writ, concluding that neither *Avena* nor the President's memorandum was binding federal law that could displace the state's limitations on filing successive habeas applications.

A majority of the Supreme Court held that neither *Avena* nor the President's memorandum constituted directly enforceable federal law which pre-empted state limitations on the filing of successive habeas petitions.[25] Whilst a treaty might constitute an international commitment, it was not binding domestic law unless Congress had enacted statutes implementing it, or the treaty itself conveyed an intention that it be self-executing and was ratified on that basis. The *Avena* judgment created an international law obligation on the part of the United States, but it was not automatically binding domestic law because none of the relevant treaty sources—the Optional Clause, the UN Charter, or the ICJ Statute—created binding federal law in the absence of implementing legislation, and no such legislation had been enacted. In particular, the UN Charter did not contemplate the automatic enforceability of ICJ decisions in domestic courts. The argument that they were automatically enforceable as domestic law was fatally undermined by the enforcement structure established by Article 94 of the UN Charter. That construction would undermine the ability of the political branches to determine whether and how to comply with an ICJ judgment and 'those sensitive foreign policy decisions would instead be transferred to state and federal courts charged with applying an ICJ judgment directly as domestic law'.[26] The ICJ judgment was not binding on state courts by virtue of the President's memorandum. The Supreme Court said that 'the President has an array of political and diplomatic means available to enforce international obligations, but unilaterally converting a

---

[24] 548 US 331 (2006).   [25] *Medellín v Texas*, 128 S Ct 1346 (2008).
[26] At 1360.

non-self-executing treaty into a self-executing one is not among them'.[27] Nor was the memorandum a valid exercise of the President's foreign affairs authority to resolve claims disputes with foreign nations.

Justice Breyer dissented. In an opinion in which Justices Souter and Ginsburg joined, he expressed the view that the President had correctly determined that Congress need not enact additional legislation. He said:[28]

The upshot is that treaty language says that an ICJ decision is legally binding, but it leaves the implementation of that binding legal obligation to the domestic law of each signatory nation. In this Nation, the Supremacy Clause, as long and consistently interpreted, indicates that ICJ decisions rendered pursuant to provisions for binding adjudication must be domestically legally binding and enforceable in domestic courts at least sometimes.

...

...I would find that the United States' treaty obligation to comply with the ICJ judgment in *Avena* is enforceable in court in this case without further congressional action beyond Senate ratification of the relevant treaties. The majority reaches a different conclusion because it looks for the wrong thing (explicit textual expression about self-execution) using the wrong standard (clarity) in the wrong place (the treaty language). Hunting for what the text cannot contain, it takes a wrong turn. It threatens to deprive individuals, including businesses, property owners, testamentary beneficiaries, consular officials, and others, of the workable dispute resolution procedures that many treaties, including commercially oriented treaties, provide. In a world where commerce, trade, and travel have become ever more international, that is a step in the wrong direction.

The preceding discussion has involved the consequences of the incorporation, or absence of incorporation, of treaty law into national law. What of customary international law? The traditional view has been that customary international law is part of the law of the land.[29] In *R v Jones (Margaret)*[30] the issue was whether it was a defence to a charge of criminal damage to property that the accused were using reasonable force in prevention of crime,[31] namely the waging of an unlawful war. The accused had broken into military bases in order to protest against the war in Iraq which was then expected. Their defence was that they had been attempting to prevent an attack by the United Kingdom in breach of international law. The defence was that a person could use such force as was reasonable to prevent 'crime'. The House of Lords held that although there was under public international law a crime of aggression which was sufficiently certain to be capable of being prosecuted in international tribunals, it was not capable of being a 'crime' within the meaning of the English legislation, since the crime of aggression was not a crime in English domestic law. It would be difficult for the courts, as the judicial branch of government, to hold the state itself, of which the court formed part, had acted unlawfully.

---

[27] At 1368.   [28] At 1384, 1389.
[29] See especially, *Triquet v Bath* (1764) 3 Burr 1478, 1481; *Trendtex Trading Corporation v Central Bank of Nigeria* [1977] QB 529, 554.
[30] [2006] UKHL 16, [2007] 1 AC 136.   [31] Criminal Law Act 1967, s 3.

Lord Bingham did not regard the issue as one of justiciability. But he did say[32] that in considering whether the customary international law crime of aggression had been, or should be, tacitly assimilated into domestic law, it was very relevant not only that Parliament had, so far, refrained from taking this step but also that it would draw the courts into an area which, in the past, they had entered, if at all, with reluctance and the utmost circumspection. In particular, the court was slow to review the exercise of the royal prerogative in relation to the conduct of foreign affairs.[33] As Lord Hoffmann said,[34] the making of war and peace and the disposition of the armed forces had always been regarded as a discretionary power of the Crown into the exercise of which the courts will not inquire. The prerogative origin of the powers did not in itself exclude judicial control. The courts' reluctance to interfere was because of the discretionary nature of the power itself. His view was that the decision to go to war, whether right or wrong, fell squarely within the discretionary powers of the Crown to defend the realm and conduct its foreign affairs.

Similar ideas were expressed in England by the Court of Appeal (and, to a lesser extent, by the House of Lords) when it was held that the British government was not under a legal duty to establish an independent enquiry into the legality of the Iraq war.[35] Such an inquiry would inevitably involve not only questions of international law, but also questions of policy, which were essentially matters for the executive and not the courts. Baroness Hale said that she could not reasonably foresee that the European Court of Human Rights would construct out of the right to life under Article 2 of the European Convention on Human Rights a duty not to send soldiers to fight in an unlawful war. The lawfulness of war is an issue between states, not between individuals or between individuals and the state. To spell such a duty out of Article 2 would require both the domestic courts, and the European Court of Human Rights, to rule upon the legality of the use of force against Iraq in international law. The state that goes to war cannot and should not be the judge of whether or not the war was lawful in international law. That question can only be authoritatively decided by the international institutions which police the international treaties governing the law of war. Nevertheless she thought that if there were such a right, the domestic courts would have to do their best to decide if it had been broken, because the Human Rights Act 1998

---

[32] At [30].

[33] *Chandler v Director of Public Prosecutions* [1964] AC 763, 791, 796; *Council of Civil Service Unions v Minister for the Civil Service* [1985] AC 374, 398; *Lord Advocate's Reference (No 1 of 2000)*, 2001 SC 143, at [60]. On review of the royal prerogative in Canada see *Kamel v Canada (Attorney General)*, 2008 FC 338 (Fed Ct), applying *Operation Dismantle Inc v Canada* [1985] 1 SCR 441, where the Supreme Court of Canada held that cabinet decisions were reviewable under the Canadian Charter of Rights and Freedoms. Wilson J's concurring judgment contains a valuable discussion of justiciability.

[34] At [65].

[35] *R (on the application of Gentle) v Prime Minister* [2006] EWCA Civ 1689, [2007] 2 WLR 195; affd [2008] UKHL 20, [2008] 2 WLR 879.

required the court to decide whether or not a public authority has acted compatibly with the Convention rights. If a Convention right required the court to examine and adjudicate upon matters which were previously regarded as non-justiciable, then adjudicate it must. The subject matter could not preclude that, although it was a factor tending against interpreting a right in such a way as to require the courts to do it.[36]

Reference has been made to Lord Steyn's *obiter* suggestion in *Re McKerr*[37] that the traditional dualist theory should not apply in human rights cases. There are signs of a distinct international trend against using the doctrine of non-justiciability to avoid deciding claims based on fundamental human rights. The justiciability of military operations has arisen often in the Israeli Supreme Court. In the *Targeted Killings* case[38] the State Attorney's Office argued that the Israeli Defence Forces (IDF) combat activities in the occupied territories were not justiciable, because the dominant character of the issue was not legal, and the court should exercise judicial restraint, and not step down into the combat zone. As in many other cases in that court, President Barak rejected this argument on the ground that there was a clear trend in the case law of the Supreme Court, according to which there was no application of what he described as the institutional non-justiciability doctrine (i.e., the question whether a dispute should be decided in a court of law at all) where recognition of it might prevent the examination of impingement upon human rights. The petition before the court was intended to determine the permissible and the forbidden in combat which might harm the most basic right of a human being—the right to life. The doctrine of non-justiciability could not prevent the examination of that question.[39]

In *R v Jones (Margaret)* Lord Bingham supported his conclusion that aggression was not a crime in English law by the point that a charge of aggression, if laid against an individual in a domestic court, would involve determination of his responsibility as a leader, but would also presuppose commission of the crime by his own state or by a foreign state.[40] Such a result would be contrary to the rule that the court would be very slow to adjudicate on rights arising out of transactions entered into by sovereign states on the plane of international law. The authorities in support of this conclusion included, of course, not only the *International Tin Council* case, but *Buttes Gas and Oil Co v Hammer (No 3)*.[41] It is not necessary to restate the extraordinary and colourful facts of that decision.[42] By the time the litigation reached the House of Lords the principal issue was whether Occidental Oil's counterclaim against Buttes Gas for fraudulent conspiracy was precluded by the act of state doctrine because it called into question

---

[36] At [57]–[58].
[37] [2004] UKHL 12, [2004] 1 WLR 807, at [49] *et seq.*
[38] *Public Committee against Torture in Israel v Government of Israel* (2007) 46 Int Leg Mat 375.
[39] cf *Kadic v Karadzic*, 70 F 3d 232 (2d Cir 1995).
[40] At [30].   [41] [1982] AC 888, 933.
[42] See Collins in *Jurists Uprooted*, ed Beatson and Zimmermann, 2004, at 394–396.

the acts of the Rulers of Sharjah and Umm al Qaywayn (originally among the Trucial states under British protection, and subsequently part of the United Arab Emirates) and of the British Government, and also of Iran which had annexed the disputed territory.

In the House of Lords Lord Wilberforce, in the only speech, said that that there was a principle of English law, which was inherent in the very nature of the judicial process, that municipal courts would not adjudicate on the transactions of foreign states; that, accordingly, where such issues were raised in private litigation, the court would exercise judicial restraint and abstain from deciding the issues raised; and that, since the pleadings raised issues involving the court in reviewing transactions in which four sovereign states were concerned and being asked to find at least part of those transactions unlawful under international law, the issues raised were non-justiciable and incapable of being entertained by the Court. In the *Tin Council* case one of the appeals was against the dismissal of a creditor's application for the appointment of a receiver by way of an execution to pursue a claim in the name of the Tin Council for an indemnity against the United Kingdom as a member state. The House of Lords accepted the argument for the British government based on *Buttes Gas*, that issues arising from the treaty were not justiciable because they arose from transactions between sovereign states and so were not issues upon which a municipal court was capable of passing. The creation and regulation by a number of sovereign states of an international organization for their common political and economic purposes was an act *jure imperii*, and an adjudication of the rights and obligations between themselves and that organization or between themselves could be undertaken only on the plane of international law.[43]

In the *Buttes Gas* case, in coming to the conclusion that the issues were not justiciable, Lord Wilberforce relied on the decision of the Court of Appeals for the Fifth Circuit[44] in the American litigation arising out of the same facts, in which the American court had refused to adjudicate on the case. Lord Wilberforce said: 'When the judicial approach to an identical problem between the same parties has been spelt out with articulation in a country...so closely akin to ours in legal approach, the fabric of whose legal doctrine in this area is so closely interwoven with ours...spelt out moreover in convincing language and reasoning, we should be unwise not to take the benefit of it.'[45]

The decision of the Circuit Court of Appeals was based on the 'political question' doctrine. The decision was that determination of the boundary between Sharjah and Umm al Qaywayn was a matter for the US State Department, whose policy as between the contending states was deliberately neutral. The judiciary could not rule on the question without an executive determination. Nor, said the

---

[43] [1990] 2 AC at 519–522.

[44] *Occidental of Umm al Qaywayn v A Certain Cargo of Petroleum*, 577 F 2d 1196 (5th Cir 1978).

[45] [1982] AC at 936–7.

American court, were there judicial or manageable standards for determination of the issue of sovereignty. The views of the executive on the recognition of the boundaries were decisive, and yet the executive had deliberately not expressed a view.

Deference was paid to *Buttes Gas* in the *Kuwait Airways* case[46] by the recognition that there are certain sovereign acts which call for judicial restraint on the part of national courts, particularly where there may be no judicial or manageable standards by which to resolve the dispute, where the court would be in a judicial no-man's land.[47] But the actual decision was that the expropriation of Kuwaiti aircraft by Iraq in gross violation of UN Security Council resolutions condemning the Iraqi invasion of Kuwait was not entitled to recognition in England. It was in breach of international law, it was contrary to English public policy, and did not raise non-justiciable issues. Lord Nicholls recognized that the English court was not disabled from ever taking cognizance of international law or from ever considering whether a violation of international law had occurred. The 'non-justiciable' principle did not mean that the judiciary had to shut its eyes to a plain and acknowledged breach of international law. In such a case the adjudication problems confronting the English court in the *Buttes* case did not arise. The standard being applied by the court was clear and manageable.[48]

It is part of the process of cross-fertilization of English and American law in this area that what Lord Nicholls said about the *Buttes* doctrine not applying in the case of a plain and acknowledged breach of international law has echoes of what the United States Supreme Court said when it revisited the act of state doctrine in 1964 in *Banco Nacional de Cuba v Sabbatino*.[49] The Supreme Court said that the engagement of the judicial branch in challenges to the validity of foreign acts of state might hinder rather than further the policy interests of the United States and of the international community. But it suggested that that would not be so in the case of a treaty or other unambiguous agreement regarding controlling legal principles.[50]

The Supreme Court did not decide whether the act of state doctrine should not be applied if the executive were to express the view that it would not be embarrassed by the court deciding on the validity of expropriation by the foreign country, but in *First National City Bank of New York v Banco Nacional de Cuba*[51] a majority of six to three considered that the application of the doctrine should not depend on the view of the State Department in the particular case. In the *Kuwait Airways* case both the Court of Appeal and the House of Lords relied on the fact that the United Kingdom was fully supportive of the international condemnation of the Iraqi invasion of Kuwait. Consequently, as Lord Hope put it,[52]

---

[46] *Kuwait Airways Corp v Iraqi Airways Co (Nos 4 and 5)* [2002] UKHL 19, [2002] 2 AC 883.
[47] Lord Nicholls at [25] quoting Lord Wilberforce.
[48] At [26].   [49] 376 US 398 (1964).
[50] At 428.   [51] 406 US 759 (1972).
[52] At [147].

'there could be no embarrassment to diplomatic relations' in the court refusing to recognize the Iraqi decree.

In *Baker v Carr*[53] the Supreme Court said that the 'non-justiciability of a political question is primarily a function of the separation of powers'.[54] In determining the presence or absence of a non-justiciable political question, several factors were articulated by the Supreme Court, of which three have had most impact in cases involving foreign relations: those three were (a) a textually demonstrable constitutional commitment of the issue to a coordinate political department; or (b) a lack of judicially discoverable and manageable standards for resolving it; or (c) the impossibility of a court's undertaking independent resolution without expressing lack of the respect due to coordinate branches of government. The political question doctrine came to be of crucial importance in the many cases arising out of the Vietnam war, in which there were numerous challenges to the legality of the war, mainly on the ground that Congress shared in the war-making power and had not authorized the President to widen the war. The overwhelming trend of the decisions was a reluctance by the courts to embroil themselves in that issue.[55] The Supreme Court avoided ruling on the merits by refusing certiorari.

Section 354.6 of the California Code of Civil Procedure gave a right of action in California to Second World War slave labour victims against any entity or successor in interest for whom that labour was performed. It was not to be dismissed for failure to comply with the applicable statute of limitation if it was commenced on or before 31 December 2010. *Mitsubishi Materials Corp v Superior Court of Orange County*[56] was an action by surviving American prisoners of war against a number of Japanese companies for whom they were forced to do slave labour. Most of the plaintiffs were taken prisoner in the spring after the surrender of Bataan in April 1942. There followed the infamous Bataan death march where prisoners, mostly weak and ill, were prodded by bayonets to march in the tropical

---

[53] 369 US 186 (1962). See Barak, *The Judge in a Democracy* (2006), pp 177 *et seq*: the former president of the Israeli Supreme Court says that justiciability is a tool which judges used to fulfil their role in a democracy, that is, judges identify those issues about which they ought not to make a decision, leaving that decision to other branches of the state. He draws a distinction between 'normative justiciability' (which aims to answer the question whether there are legal criteria for determining a given dispute) and 'institutional justiciability' (the question whether the dispute should be adjudicated in a court of law at all). He criticizes *Baker v Carr*, which deals with both aspects. See also Henkin, 'Is there a "Political Question" Doctrine?' 85 Yale LJ 597 (1976).

[54] At 210.

[55] See e.g., *Mora v McNamara*, 387 F 2d 862 (DC Cir 1967), cert den 389 US 934 (1967); *Atlee v Laird*, 347 F Supp 689 (ED Pa 1972), affd (without opinion, Douglas, Brennan, and Stewart JJ dissenting) sub nom *Atlee v Richardson*, 411 US 911 (1973). For the extraordinary case of *Holtzman v Schlesinger*, 414 US 1316 (1973) where the bombing of Cambodia was in effect enjoined for one day, see Collins, n 15 above.

[56] 113 Cal App 4th 55 (2003). *Deutsch v Turner Corp*, 317 F 3d 1005 (9th Cir 2003) was a claim by slave labourers (almost all in relation to Japanese companies) concerning the abuses that German and Japanese corporate interests inflicted both on civilians and on soldiers captured by German and Japanese military forces during the Second World War. The court held 'reluctantly' that s 354.6 was invalid under the United States Constitution and that in its absence the remaining claims were time-barred.

heat for six days and nights with hardly any food and water, and if they failed to keep up they were run through. They were eventually put in 'hell ships' to be taken to Japan, i.e., unmarked POW ships, a number of which were sunk by American submarines. The prisoners were packed like sardines into hatches and sick prisoners could not get air. Once in Japan they were forced into slave labour for private Japanese companies, usually mining, which supplied the Japanese war effort. The use of forced labour was contrary to clearly established international law regarding the use of labour of prisoners of war. There were constant beatings which would increase whenever the United States won an important battle. Over 11,000 of the 27,000 Americans captured and interned by the Japanese military during the Second World War died. Chinese prisoners of war fared even worse. Of the tens of thousands captured, at the end of the war, Japanese authorities acknowledged having only 56 Chinese prisoners. It was held that the Treaty of Peace with Japan superseded any law of the State of California and conflicted with section 354.6. It precluded any claims of American nationals against Japanese nationals arising in the course of the prosecution of the war. The historical context in which the Treaty was negotiated made clear that the intention was to waive all war claims which could have been brought by either side.

Recent examples of the operation of the political question doctrine include *Corrie v Caterpillar, Inc*[57] where the plaintiffs were persons who claimed that their family members were killed or injured when the IDF demolished homes in the occupied territories using bulldozers manufactured by Caterpillar Inc, a United States Corporation. The IDF had ordered the bulldozers directly from Caterpillar, but the United States government paid for them. The action was dismissed because the claims presented non-justiciable political questions which deprived the district court of subject matter jurisdiction. The decisive factor was that Caterpillar's sales to Israel were paid for by the United States. Each claim unavoidably rested on the premise that Caterpillar should not have sold its bulldozers to the IDF. But the sales were financed by the executive branch pursuant to a congressionally enacted programme calling for executive discretion as to what lay in the foreign policy and national security interests of the United States. Allowing the action to proceed would necessarily require the judicial branch to question the political branches' decision to grant extensive military aid to Israel. The court could not find in favour of the plaintiffs without implicitly questioning, and even condemning, United States foreign policy towards Israel. It was not the role of the courts indirectly to indict Israel for violating international law with military equipment the United States government had provided and continued to provide.

When the Republic of the Philippines sued former President Marcos in the United States, alleging widespread and systematic theft of funds and properties which were the property of the Philippine government and its people, Marcos

---

[57] 503 F 3d 974 (9th Cir 2007).

asserted that the claims raised non-justiciable political questions because their determination involved unmanageable standards and because they could potentially cause embarrassment to the executive in its conduct of foreign relations. But the Court of Appeals for the Second Circuit rejected the argument:[58]

...we agree with The Republic that there is nothing more unmanageable about this case than about any other case involving theft, misappropriation, corporate veils, and constructive trusts.

So also the Court of Appeals for the Ninth Circuit said:[59]

Bribetaking, theft, embezzlement, extortion, fraud, and conspiracy to do these things are all acts susceptible of concrete proofs that need not involve political questions.

Language close to the American political question doctrine was used by the High Court of Australia in the *Spycatcher* case, in which the High Court of Australia[60] accepted that there was a principle that the court should not enforce foreign public laws, in the sense that the court would not allow the enforcement outside the territory of the foreign sovereign of claims based on or related to the exercise of foreign governmental power. An injunction to restrain the publication of confidential material by a former member of the British security services was refused on the ground that the court would not enforce a claim arising out of acts of a foreign state in the exercise of such powers in the pursuit of its national security. It was held that there was a rule, founded on international law, whereby a claim to enforce the governmental interests of a foreign state was unenforceable:[61]

It is perhaps tempting to suggest that, because of the close relationship between the United Kingdom and Australia, an exception should be made to enable the United Kingdom to enforce in our courts an obligation of the kind now in question. But what if a less friendly or a hostile State were to resort to our courts for a similar purpose? Our courts are not competent to assess the degree of friendliness or unfriendliness of a foreign State. There are no manageable standards by which courts can resolve such an issue and its determination would inevitably present a risk of embarrassment in Australia's relation with other countries....In any event the principle of law renders unenforceable actions of a particular kind. Those actions are actions to enforce the governmental interests of a foreign State. There is nothing in the statement of the principle, nor in the underlying considerations on which it rests, that could justify the making of an exception or qualification for actions by a friendly State. The friendliness or hostility of the foreign State seeking to enforce its claims in the court of the forum has no relevant connection with the principle.

---

[58] *Republic of Philippines v Marcos*, 806 F 2d 344, 356 (2d Cir 1986).

[59] *Republic of Philippines v Marcos*, 862 F 2d 1355, at 1360 (9th Cir 1988), cert den 490 US 1035 (1988).

[60] *Attorney-General (UK) v Heinemann Publishers Australia Pty Ltd* (1988) 165 CLR 30, 42–43.

[61] At 47. For other cases in Australia on the *Buttes Gas* version of non-justiciability see *Petrotimor Companhia de Petroleos Sarl v Commonwealth of Australia* (2003) 126 FCR 354, 370; *Gamogab v Akiba* [2007] FCAFC 74.

It would be tempting to conclude by elaborating on the question whether this represents English law. But this is a temptation which must be resisted since it is a question which arises or may arise in two currently pending cases, the first of which, at the time of writing, has already been argued (in part) before the House of Lords, with Lord Bingham presiding over a nine-member committee.[62]

Since this piece was submitted for publication the appeal in *Mbasogo v Logo Ltd* has been withdrawn by consent, and the House of Lords has refused leave to appeal in *Government of the Islamic Republic of Iran v Barakat Galleries Ltd*.

---

[62] *Mbasogo v Logo Ltd* [2006] EWCA Civ 1370, [2007] QB 846, at [52] (CA). The other pending litigation is *Government of the Islamic Republic of Iran v Barakat Galleries Ltd* [2007] EWCA Civ 1374, [2008] 1 All ER 1177, at [116]–[124] (CA). See also *Equatorial Guinea v Bank of Scotland International (Guernsey)* [2006] UKPC 7, at [24]–[25]; and generally Collins, 'Revolution and Restitution: Foreign States in National Courts' (2007) 326 Receuil des Cours 13.

3

Le Royaume-Uni, la France et la Convention européenne des droits de l'homme

Jean-Paul Costa and Patrick Titiun

Évoquer la personne de Lord Bingham of Cornhill, c'est, bien sûr, saluer les qualités d'un juriste éminent, d'un juge dans la plus grande tradition britannique. C'est aussi honorer un parcours exceptionnel qui l'a conduit à occuper dans son pays les plus hautes fonctions judiciaires, celles de Master of the Rolls dès 1992 et, bien entendu, de 1996 à 2000, celles de Lord Chief Justice of England and Wales, fonctions qui ont contribué à le faire connaître bien au-delà des frontières de son pays.

Au moment où le Royaume-Uni s'apprête, dans les prochains mois, à se doter d'une Cour suprême, en vertu du *Constitutional Reform Act* de 2005, cet hommage prend un relief particulier quand on sait le rôle que Lord Bingham a joué pour qu'une telle instance voie le jour. Certes, les contraintes du calendrier l'empêcheront de vivre cette réforme de l'intérieur, puisqu'il est appelé à prendre sa retraite, mais elles nous permettent, en revanche, de lui témoigner dès à présent l'estime due à ses grands mérites.

Au titre de la Cour européenne des droits de l'homme, c'est évidemment le rôle joué par Lord Bingham, d'abord pour faire connaître la Convention européenne des droits de l'homme puis, une fois entré en vigueur le *Human Rights Act* de 1998, pour qu'elle soit partie intégrante du droit britannique, qui nous conduisent tout naturellement à participer au présent *Liber amicorum*.

Le thème de cette contribution a trait au Royaume-Uni, à la France et à la Convention européenne des droits de l'homme. Il s'avère lui aussi naturel si on observe le rôle qu'a joué Lord Bingham pour un rapprochement entre le système britannique et les systèmes continentaux, dès la création de la Cour de Strasbourg. Son engagement personnel conduit à rappeler l'attitude de nos pays respectifs à l'égard de la Convention européenne des droits de l'homme.

Cette question exige tout d'abord une évocation du rôle joué par ces deux Etats lors de l'élaboration du texte, puis une présentation de l'applicabilité de la Convention dans les deux pays, enfin, une brève analyse de l'influence de la Convention européenne des droits de l'homme sur le droit interne.

Le Royaume-Uni et la France ont joué un rôle important dans l'élaboration de la Convention européenne des droits de l'homme

Avant même d'évoquer le rôle du Royaume-Uni et de la France dans l'élaboration de la Convention européenne des droits de l'homme, il nous faut rappeler que le Conseil de l'Europe, dans le cadre duquel a été instituée la Cour européenne des droits de l'homme est le fruit de la volonté d'hommes politiques européens qui, dans l'immédiat après-guerre, ont eu à cœur d'éviter qu'un conflit tel que la seconde guerre mondiale ne se reproduise. Parmi eux, la figure de Winston Churchill, lors de ses fameux discours de Zurich ou de Londres. C'est à Londres, précisément, que se tint la Conférence au cours de laquelle un compromis politique fut trouvé qui déboucha sur la création du Conseil de l'Europe et la signature de son Statut, le 5 mai 1949.

Quelques mois plus tard, la question de la création d'une Cour européenne chargée de garantir un certain nombre de libertés et de droits fondamentaux fut envisagée et confiée à une Commission juridique émanant de l'Assemblée Parlementaire nouvellement créée au sein du Conseil de l'Europe. Cette Commission était présidée par un britannique, Sir David Maxwell-Fyfe, tandis que le rapporteur était un Français, Pierre-Henri Teitgen. Les débats furent particulièrement animés et on sait que Français et Britanniques ne furent pas toujours en accord sur le rôle et l'organisation du futur mécanisme de protection juridictionnelle, les Britanniques (et d'autres négociateurs) étant alors en retrait par rapport aux Français. Par exemple, il n'était pas admis par tous les Etats qu'il fallût créer une Cour européenne des droits de l'homme.

Finalement, une solution transactionnelle fut néanmoins trouvée; qui permit d'aboutir, le 4 novembre 1950, à la signature, à Rome, de la Convention de sauvegarde des droits de l'homme et des libertés fondamentales. La France et le Royaume-Uni figureront parmi les signataires, comme les dix autres Etats alors membres du Conseil de l'Europe.

Certes, le texte adopté à Rome était bien éloigné du Protocole n° 11 qui a permis, en 1998, l'établissement de la Cour unique. Il ne donnait pas à l'individu un libre accès à la Cour, la Commission étant l'organe saisi par les requérants, et le Comité des Ministres, organe politique, jouait un rôle essentiel, analogue à celui dévolu à une juridiction. En outre, le droit de recours individuel et la juridiction obligatoire de la Cour étaient subordonnés à des reconnaissances facultatives de la part des Etats signataires de la Convention. Il n'en demeure pas moins que le système élaboré représentait une avancée considérable pour la protection des droits de l'homme et que les Etats parties ont alors consenti un abandon de souveraineté tout à fait inédit. Certes, seuls les Etats de l'Ouest de l'Europe étaient alors concernés, mais on ne peut qu'être frappé en relisant les travaux parlementaires de l'évidente actualité des paroles prononcées alors par Sir David Maxwell-Fyfe, qui déclarait qu'une Convention serait: «un phare pour nos amis qui se trouvent maintenant dans les ténèbres du totalitarisme... une sorte de passeport pour le retour de leurs pays en notre sein». Voilà ce qu'il convient d'appeler des propos visionnaires.

S'agissant de la ratification du traité, indispensable pour permettre son entrée en vigueur, la situation des deux pays sera sensiblement différente. En effet, la France, qui avait joué un rôle moteur dans l'élaboration du texte, notamment grâce à l'intervention de Pierre-Henri Teitgen, va alors adopter une attitude nettement plus timide. A l'inverse, le Royaume-Uni qui avait, au cours des négociations, exprimé un certain nombre de réticences, ratifiera la Convention parmi les premiers et ce, dès le 8 mars 1951.

La France ne figurera même pas parmi les Etats membres du Conseil de l'Europe dont la ratification entraînera l'entrée en vigueur de la Convention (subordonnée au dépôt de dix instruments de ratification). Les raisons de cette attente sont à la fois diverses et connues. Les personnalités alors au pouvoir en France se rangeaient davantage dans la catégorie des souverainistes que dans celles des pro-européens. Plus profondément, on peut imaginer que la réticence à voir un système supranational intervenir pour sanctionner les autorités françaises aura été la cause principale du retard apporté par la France à cette ratification, retard auquel la question longtemps épineuse de l'Algérie n'aura pas été étrangère. Il faudra attendre le 3 mai 1974 pour que la France ratifie enfin la Convention, soit plus de 23 ans après le Royaume-Uni (la ratification ayant été autorisée par la loi du 31 décembre 1973). Quant à la reconnaissance de la compétence obligatoire de la Cour et du droit de recours individuel, elle intervint dès le 14 janvier 1966 pour le Royaume-Uni. C'est par contre seulement avec l'alternance et l'arrivée de la gauche au pouvoir, sous l'impulsion notamment du Garde des Sceaux de François Mitterrand, M. Robert Badinter, que la France procédera, le 2 octobre 1981, à cette double reconnaissance (donc près de seize ans après le Royaume-Uni).

Il y a donc eu un important décalage dans le temps dans la relation des deux pays avec la Convention européenne des droits de l'homme et ce, au bénéfice du Royaume-Uni. Cette avance du Royaume-Uni a certainement eu des conséquences sur la manière dont la Convention européenne des droits de l'homme a été mise en œuvre par la Cour. En effet, les affaires britanniques jugées à Strasbourg ont longtemps précédé les affaires françaises. Un certain nombre d'affaires britanniques figurent d'ailleurs parmi les premières décisions importantes de la Cour. Pour la petite (ou la grande!) histoire, le nom du dédicataire du présent ouvrage apparaît pour la première fois, en tant qu'auteur d'une décision judiciaire britannique, dans une décision de la Commission européenne de 1985, Cheall contre le Royaume-Uni!

En revanche, conformément à un paradoxe juridique, les règles et la chronologie de l'applicabilité de la Convention, dans les deux pays, sont différentes et en quelque sorte inversées.

L'applicabilité de la Convention a obéi dans les deux pays à des règles et à une chronologie bien différente

Si la comparaison de l'application de la Convention européenne des droits de l'homme en France et au Royaume-Uni, telle qu'elle a été décrite ci-dessus, a pu paraître se faire au bénéfice du seul Royaume-Uni, une lecture plus approfondie est sans doute nécessaire pour percevoir les nuances du problème. Elle exige une comparaison des deux systèmes juridiques, le système français et le système en vigueur au Royaume-Uni.

Pour la France, il s'agit, comme on le sait, d'un système moniste, selon lequel un traité international, signé et ratifié, fait immédiatement partie, du droit interne dès sa publication, sans qu'une transposition législative soit nécessaire. Ceci découle directement de l'article 55 de la Constitution française, qui reconnaît la primauté du droit international, notamment du droit européen. Une autre conséquence de cette conception moniste est que la Convention européenne des droits de l'homme, une fois signée et ratifiée, a vocation à être appliquée directement par le juge national au même titre que le droit interne et prévaut même sur celui-ci (à condition toutefois d'être d'effet direct, «*self-executing*», ce qui est bien le cas de la Convention).

S'agissant du système en vigueur au Royaume-Uni, il est radicalement différent et obéit à une conception dualiste: il n'existe pas de Constitution écrite et le droit international ne peut produire d'effets juridiques qu'après avoir été incorporé par un acte du Parlement britannique de Westminster.

Voilà donc le paradoxe: la France a certes mis plus de vingt-quatre ans pour ratifier la Convention européenne des droits de l'homme mais, une fois cette ratification intervenue en 1974, la Convention a eu une autorité supérieure à la loi, conformément à l'article 55 de la Constitution. Elle a pu être invoquée directement par les justiciables devant les tribunaux français, même s'ils n'avaient pas encore la possibilité de porter l'affaire devant la juridiction européenne. Il est toutefois vrai que cette possibilité était rarement utilisée. En outre, si la Cour de cassation a, dès 1975, fait prévaloir la Convention sur les lois même postérieures (affaire dite «*Cafés Jacques Vabre*»[1]), le Conseil d'Etat a attendu jusqu'en 1989, avec l'arrêt *Nicolo*, pour adopter la même solution. Enfin, seule l'acceptation du droit de recours individuel, en 1981, a permis aux citoyens de saisir les organes de la Convention (à l'époque, la Commission européenne des droits de l'homme, puis la Cour). Ceci explique que le premier arrêt de la Cour contre la France n'interviendra que le 18 décembre 1986 avec l'affaire *Bozano*.[2]

---

[1] Cass. Ch. Mixte, 24 mai 1975, Société des Cafés Jacques Vabre, D., 1975, p 497, concl. Touffait.
[2] CE Ass. 20 octobre 1989, Nicolo; Revue française de droit administratif, 1989, p 813 concl. Frydman, note Genevois.

A l'inverse, pendant très longtemps la Convention européenne des droits de l'homme n'a pas fait partie du droit interne du Royaume-Uni. Il semble que l'incorporation de la Convention dans l'ordre juridique interne britannique ait été envisagée dès le début des années 50, mais force est de constater que tel n'a pas alors été le cas. Certes, il est arrivé que les juridictions britanniques prennent en compte la jurisprudence de la Commission et de la Cour européenne des droits de l'homme, mais elles n'y étaient nullement obligées.

Cela étant, l'absence d'incorporation de la Convention n'empêchait nullement les requérants de se tourner vers les organes de la Convention, ce qui explique que le premier arrêt contre le Royaume-Uni, l'arrêt *Golder* c. Royaume-Uni du 21 février 1975,[3] est antérieur de près de 12 ans à l'arrêt *Bozano* c. France. Par ailleurs, un grand nombre d'arrêts britanniques seront rendus par la Cour européenne des droits de l'homme dans les années 70 et 80, de sorte qu'on peut dire que la jurisprudence de la Cour s'est en partie construite grâce à ces grandes affaires contre le Royaume-Uni. Il est clair, également, que le fait pour le Royaume-Uni d'avoir été si tôt partie intégrante du système est à l'origine du nombre relativement important de violations de la Convention par cet Etat constatées par la Cour.

Ceci conduit à faire plusieurs séries d'observations: tout d'abord, le système de la Convention a subi l'influence de différentes traditions nationales. Ainsi, le fait que, assez rapidement, la Cour ait eu à juger des affaires contre le Royaume-Uni a certainement été une des causes de l'influence exercée par la tradition juridique dite de *Common law* sur le mécanisme de la Convention. Un des exemples les plus flagrants est sans doute l'importance prise par la théorie des apparences dans la jurisprudence de la Cour. Il s'agit, comme chacun sait, d'une application de l'adage «*Justice must not only be done; it must be seen to be done*». C'est cette théorie, peu connue du droit français avant qu'il ne soit lui-même influencé par la jurisprudence de Strasbourg, qui a guidé la Cour dans la mise en œuvre de sa jurisprudence en matière d'impartialité objective. D'autres exemples inspirés de la *Common law* peuvent être cités: le caractère accusatoire de la procédure, ou encore le principe d'*Habeas corpus*, qui est reflété dans le corps même de la Convention avec l'article 5 § 4, lequel donne aux personnes privées de leur liberté un certain nombre de garanties directement empruntées au droit en vigueur au Royaume-Uni. Enfin, la jurisprudence concernant le droit à la non-auto-incrimination est également inspirée du droit anglais. On a donc vu la Cour condamner la France (ou d'autres pays) en application de principes directement issus de la *Common law* ce qui peut sembler paradoxal, encore que la jurisprudence s'efforce d'harmoniser les garanties offertes aux citoyens européens.

L'inverse est également vrai. Le droit continental a également influencé la Cour dans sa jurisprudence. Ainsi, le principe de la séparation des pouvoirs dont le caractère français est bien connu depuis Montesquieu (d'ailleurs admirateur

---

[3] Golder c. Royaume-Uni (1979–80) 1 EHRR 524.

de l'Angleterre!) et qui prohibe toute intervention de l'exécutif dans le cours de la justice, a trouvé matière à s'appliquer dans la jurisprudence de la Cour. Autre exemple, la conception française de la laïcité a été reprise par la Cour dans plusieurs affaires, concernant notamment la Turquie.

Il est finalement compréhensible qu'une juridiction internationale telle que la Cour européenne des droits de l'homme, dont la jurisprudence est une œuvre collective, subisse l'influence des juges qui la composent, quand bien même ils sont issus de plusieurs traditions juridiques différentes. Les quarante-sept juges de la Cour arrivent à Strasbourg après avoir suivi une formation juridique, mené un parcours professionnel qui les influencent dans leur pratique et cela ne peut être sans incidence sur la manière dont ils exercent leurs fonctions au sein de la Cour. Certes, leur présence au sein d'un même système les rapproche et la Cour a un rôle harmonisateur, toutefois les juges apportent une contribution qui peut, parfois, relever de l'inconscient et qui trouve sa source dans leur système juridique d'origine.

L'influence de la Convention européenne des droits de l'homme sur le droit interne

Compte tenu de ce qui précède, on ne peut faire l'économie d'une réflexion sur l'influence de la Convention européenne des droits de l'homme sur le droit interne du Royaume-Uni et de la France.

S'agissant du Royaume-Uni, et bien que pendant fort longtemps, la Convention européenne des droits de l'homme n'ait pas fait partie du droit interne, on a pu constater que les juges britanniques ont eu une tendance croissante à considérer que la Convention était une partie de la *Common law,* ou que celle-ci devrait être interprétée à la lumière de celle-là. Une telle attitude était devenue indispensable compte tenu du nombre élevé de condamnations à l'encontre du Royaume-Uni. La situation a été transformée avec l'entrée en vigueur, le 2 octobre 2000, du *Human Rights Act* qui, en incorporant la Convention européenne des droits de l'homme dans le droit interne britannique, a autorisé les juges à déclarer qu'une loi britannique viole la Convention. Le juge du Royaume-Uni est désormais investi d'un pouvoir analogue à celui de la Cour de Strasbourg. Avant même qu'intervienne cette incorporation, on a pu constater l'influence de la Convention lorsqu'à la suite de l'affaire *Sunday Times (n° 1)*[4] a été adoptée la loi de 1981 sur le *Contempt of court*, notion très ancienne que la loi a permis de clarifier.

Il est certain que des évolutions sous l'influence de la Convention européenne des droits de l'homme et de la jurisprudence de la Cour ont eu lieu au Royaume-Uni avant même l'entrée en vigueur du *Human Rights Act.* Ainsi, des législations ou des pratiques condamnées par la Cour ont-elles été abandonnées: c'est le cas

---

[4] *Sunday Times v UK* (1979–80) 2 EHRR 245.

des châtiments corporels à l'école qui ont cessé à la suite des affaires *Campbell et Cosans*[5] du 25 février 1982, de la législation pénale de l'Irlande du Nord interdisant les relations homosexuelles masculines qui a été abandonnée à la suite de la jurisprudence *Dudgeon*[6] du 22 octobre 1981 ou, dans un domaine proche, de l'interdiction faite aux homosexuels de servir dans l'armée qui a disparu après l'arrêt *Lustig-Prean et Beckett*[7] du 27 septembre 1999. Les règles relatives à la correspondance des détenus ont également été modifiées pour être en conformité avec la jurisprudence de la Cour. Ceci est finalement un paradoxe que soulignait Lord Lester of Herne Hill, dans sa contribution en hommage à Rolv Ryssdal: rappelant que la Convention européenne des droits de l'homme ne faisait pas partie du droit interne britannique, il notait que: «*Yet, paradoxically, Convention case-law has had at least as great an influence upon the jurisprudence of United Kingdom and other Commonwealth courts as it has had upon the jurisprudence of the courts in civil law countries*».

La situation française était plus claire du fait de l'existence d'un système moniste. Toutefois, ce n'est pas tant la ratification de 1974 qui a changé l'attitude française par rapport à la Convention que l'acceptation du droit de recours individuel, en 1981. L'apport de la jurisprudence de la Cour, nul avant 1974, faible entre 1974 et 1981 (voir cependant l'arrêt du Conseil d'Etat *Debout* de 1976, avec les conclusions de Daniel Labetoulle), et limité dans les premières années qui ont suivi l'acceptation du droit de recours individuel, connaîtra une montée en puissance à compter du début des années 1990 et l'influence générale de la Convention sur le droit français ne va dès lors cesser de s'amplifier.

C'est d'abord la Cour de cassation, puis le Conseil d'Etat qui ont fait application de la jurisprudence de la Cour de Strasbourg pour s'en inspirer. Au cours des années 90, la situation a considérablement évolué. En effet, les nombreux arrêts rendus contre la France ont eu des incidences sur l'attitude du législateur et sur celles des juridictions internes.

Ainsi, en matière législative, le 10 juillet 1991, à la suite des arrêts *Kruslin et Huvig*[8] du 24 avril 1990, pour la première fois, une loi était adoptée pour mettre le droit français en matière d'écoutes téléphoniques en conformité avec la Convention européenne des droits de l'homme. Dans le domaine du respect de la vie privée et familiale (l'article 8 de la Convention), on a vu également les juridictions et le législateur français prendre en compte la jurisprudence de la Cour en matière de droit des étrangers. Les enfants adultérins faisaient l'objet en droit français d'une discrimination: la France a été condamnée de ce fait par la Cour de Strasbourg, le 1er février 2000, dans l'affaire *Mazurek*.[9] En décembre 2001, le

---

[5] *Campbell and Cosans v United Kingdom* (1982) 4 EHRR 293.
[6] *Dudgeon v UK* (1981) 4 EHRR 149.
[7] *Lustig-Prean and Beckett v United Kingdom* [2000] 29 EHRR 548.
[8] *Kruslin v France* (1990) 12 EHRR 547.
[9] *Mazurek v France* [2000] ECHR 47.

législateur français mettait le droit français en conformité avec la jurisprudence de Strasbourg en modifiant l'article 760 du code civil.

L'applicabilité directe de la Convention européenne des droits de l'homme en France a pour conséquence que les modifications du droit national sont très souvent le fait des juridictions. Un exemple frappant est celui qui a conduit la Cour de cassation, réunie en Assemblée plénière le 11 décembre 1992, à renverser sa jurisprudence en matière de rectification de l'état civil des transsexuels. Se fondant sur des principes considérés alors comme intangibles, à savoir l'indisponibilité et l'immutabilité de l'état civil, les juridictions françaises s'opposaient fermement à la rectification de cet état civil pour les personnes ayant subi une opération de changement de sexe. Il aura fallu et suffi que la Cour de Strasbourg rende, le 25 mars 1992, un arrêt dans l'affaire *B. contre France*[10] pour que cette jurisprudence soit écartée. La situation des transsexuels sous la double influence de la Cour de Strasbourg et de la Cour de cassation aura été modifiée dans un sens favorable.

Il est vrai cependant que, parfois, c'est avec plus de difficulté que les juridictions françaises mettront leur jurisprudence en conformité avec la Convention, comme on a pu le voir avec les réticences de la Cour de cassation à modifier sa jurisprudence relative à la recevabilité du pourvoi formé par une personne en fuite. Il faudra attendre plusieurs années, plusieurs arrêts de la Cour de Strasbourg et, finalement, la loi du 15 juin 2000 pour qu'un terme soit mis à cette jurisprudence nationale.

Cela étant, et sans doute, de ce point de vue, la situation en France a été longtemps plus aisée qu'au Royaume-Uni, l'applicabilité directe de la Convention a permis assez rapidement après l'acceptation du droit de recours individuel, de voir se nouer un dialogue jurisprudentiel entre le juge national et le juge européen. Les juges français ont rapidement pu suivre des formations sur la Convention européenne des droits de l'homme au Conseil de l'Europe ou au sein du système national et pu visiter la Cour de Strasbourg. De leur côté, les juges britanniques ont reçu une sensibilisation un peu différente, notamment depuis le vote du *Human Rights Act*, puis son entrée en vigueur.

Il est sûr en tout cas que certains juges du Royaume-Uni auront été des précurseurs de l'application de la Convention européenne des droits de l'homme dans leur pays. Lord Bingham of Cornhill figure, avec éclat, au nombre de ceux-ci.

La Cour de Strasbourg l'a d'ailleurs reconnu depuis longtemps et cette reconnaissance s'est notamment manifestée à de nombreuses reprises lorsqu'elle a cité Lord Bingham dans ses arrêts. Il serait impossible de mentionner toutes les décisions dans lesquelles son nom figure. Pour ne rappeler que les plus fameuses, l'affaire *Lustig-Prean et Beckett* de 1999 déjà citée,[11] l'affaire *Pretty*[12] de 2002 ou

---

[10] *B. v France*, 25 mars 1992, série A no 232-C, pp 53–54.
[11] *Lustig-Prean and Beckett v United Kingdom* [2000] 29 EHRR 548.
[12] *Pretty v United Kingdom* (2002) 35 EHRR 1.

bien, dans le domaine de la liberté d'expression, les affaires *Observer et Guardian*[13] ou *Sunday Times (n° 2)*[14] de 1991.

Nous souhaitions pour notre part saluer son activité au service de la justice du Royaume-Uni, et des droits de l'homme, par cette contribution qui tend à montrer que, si Strasbourg ne se trouve pas au milieu de la Manche, les deux Etats côtiers ont été et sont, différemment mais profondément, influencés par la Convention et la Cour.

[13] *The Observer and Guardian v United Kingdom*, 14 EHRR 153 (1992).
[14] *The Sunday Times v United Kingdom (No 2)* 14 EHRR 229.

4

The Twisted Road from *Prince Albert* to *Campbell*, and Beyond: Towards a Right of Privacy?

Roger Errera

During the parliamentary debate on the Human Rights Bill in 1998 Lord Bingham said:

Discussion of the new Bill so far would suggest, I think rightly, that one of the most difficult and sensitive areas of judgment will involve reconciliation of the right to privacy guaranteed by Article 8 with the right of free expression guaranteed by Article 10. While the law up to now afforded some protection to privacy (in actions for breach of confidence, trespass, nuisance, the new tort of harassment, defamation, malicious falsehood and under data protection legislation) this protection has been patchy and inadequate. But it seems very likely that difficult questions will arise on where the right to privacy ends and the right to free expression begins. The media are understandably and properly concerned that the conduct of valuable investigative journalism may be hampered or even rendered impossible. It is very difficult, and probably unwise, to offer any opinion in advance about where the line is likely to be drawn.

After commenting on the case of Princess Caroline of Monaco, which had then led in Germany to a judgment of the Supreme Court, Lord Bingham added:

I think it likely that in the years to come we shall see some developments in the law of privacy in actions between private citizens.[1]

A prescient dictum indeed. This was not the first time Lord Bingham addressed the issue of privacy. He had sat in *Kaye v Robertson*.[2] Nor the last one: he discussed the subject in one of the essays included in the book mentioned above.[3] He sat later in *Wainwright*.[4]

---

[1] 'The Way We Live Now. Human Rights in the New Millenium'. The Earl Grey Memorial Lecture, University of Newcastle upon Tyne, 29 January 1998, in *The Business of Judging. Selected Essays*, Oxford University Press, Oxford, 2000.

[2] (1991) FSR 62, CA (Civ Div).

[3] 'Should there be a Law to Protect Rights of Personal Privacy?' in *The Business of Judging*, n1 above.

[4] *Wainwright and Others v Home Office* (2003) UKHL 53.

Anyone studying the problem of privacy and of a right to privacy is bound to be confronted with a number of legal issues which Lord Bingham has met and answered. They may be briefly summed up as follows.

Firstly to discuss privacy leads to discussing several fundamental rights and the balancing between them: The rights of personality, to which privacy belongs, and freedom of expression. Lord Bingham has on many occasions, judicial and extra judicial, expressed his views on fundamental rights. As to the former, several important cases, in which he gave the leading judgment, may be quoted.[5] As to the latter one may cite, again, the Earl Grey Memorial Lecture,[6] where he mentioned his support of the incorporation of the European Convention on Human Rights (ECHR) and other writings.[7]

A second element is the following one: as in many other questions, a reasoned use of comparative law and of other countries' case law is indispensable here. Lord Bingham has been a steady and intensive practitioner of that virtue, and stated clearly where he stood and affirmed his rejection of legal insularism and parochialism. In the foreword to a collection of essays published in 1997 he wrote: 'The book offers no sustenance to the insular and introspective English lawyer whose legal world is bounded by the Tweed to the north, the Channel to the south and the North and Irish seas to east and west. It sends empty away the chauvinist English practitioner who believes we have nothing to learn from sources beyond our shores, and least of all from those bred in the European civil law traditions.'[8] His judgments contain an extensive and illuminating discussion of the case law of foreign jurisdictions.[9]

The third dimension is that of international law. The same attention has been constantly and consistently directed by Lord Bingham to the international obligations of Britain: those stemming from international human rights instruments such as the ECHR, the International Covenant on Civil and Political Rights,[10]

---

[5] *The Queen on the Application of Mrs Dianne Pretty (Appellant) v Director of Public Prosecutions (Respondent) and Secretary of State for the Home Department (Interested Party)* (2001) UKHL 61, § 1–40; *A (FC) and Others (FC) v Secretary of State for the Home Department; X (FC) and Others (FC) v Secretary of State for the Home Department (respondent)* (2004); *A and Others (Appellants) (FC) and others v Secretary of State for the Home Department (Respondent) (Conjoined Appeals)* (2005) UKHL 71, § 1–63; *Secretary of State for the Home Department (Appellant) v JJ and Others (FC) (Respondent)* (2007) UKHL 45,§ 1 ff.

[6] N 1 above.

[7] 'Personal Freedom and the Dilemma of Democracies', (2003) 52 ICLQ 841; 'The Rule of Law', (2007) 66–1 CLJ 67.

[8] *Law Making, Law Finding and Law Shaping: The Diverse Influences. The Clifford Chance Lectures, vol two,* edited and with an Introduction by Basil S Markesinis, Oxford University Press, Oxford, 1997, foreword, V.

[9] See, e.g., *Karina Rees v Darlington Memorial Hospital NHS Trust* (2003) UKHL 52,§ 1–10; *Fairchild v Glenhaven Funeral Services Ltd and another; Matthews v Associated Portland Cement Manufacturers (1978) Ltd and another* (2002) UKHL 22, § 1–35.

[10] *R v Jones* (2002) UKHL 5, § 1–18; *R (on the application of Nicholas Mullen) v Secretary of State for the Home Department* (2004) UKHL 18, § 1–13.

and the 1951 Geneva Convention relating to the status of refugees,[11] or originating in customary international law.[12]

Fourthly, three other elements, apparent in Lord Bingham's judicial pronouncements, are relevant to a proper reflection on privacy: the affirmation of principles;[13] an awareness of the proper limits of the power of the judges;[14] and an ability to ensure fully the interpretation of statutes whenever needed.[15]

Fifthly, and finally, a full consideration of privacy includes a constant reference to the concrete demands of the rule of law, especially in relation to fundamental rights as well as never losing sight of realism, notably in judicial review adjudication. Both are to be found in Lord Bingham's judgments.[16]

In *Prince Albert v Strange* the original bill from Prince Albert used several times the terms 'private' and 'privacy'.[17] During the hearing before the Vice-Chancellor the latter also used the word 'privacy' together with that of 'property': there had been 'the abstraction of one of its most valuable quality, namely privacy'.[18] He added: 'All the cases in which the court has interfered to protect unpublished letters or manuscripts...proceed upon that principle of protecting privacy.'[19] He held that the defendant's conduct had been 'an intrusion—an unbecoming and unseemly intrusion...a sordid spying into the privacy of domestic life'.[20] The final decision was based on breach of trust and breach of confidence.[21]

In 1858 a Paris court had to decide the following case: a famous actress, Mme Rachel, had died. Her sister, who had assisted her, expressly stipulated, upon asking two persons to take a photograph of her face on her deathbed, that the

---

[11] *Secretary of State for the Home Department (Respondent) v K (FC)(Appellant); Fornah (FC) (Appellant) v Secretary of State for the Home Department (Respondent)* (2006) UKHL 46, on the implementation of the Qualification Directive and the notion of 'membership of a particular social group', § 1–33; *Regina v Immigration Officer at Prague Airport and another (Respondents ex p European Roma Rights Centre and others (Appellants)* (2004) UKHL 55, § 1–31.

[12] *Jones v Ministry of Interior Al-Mamluka Al-Arabiya AS Saudiya (The Kingdom of Saudi Arabia) and others*, (2006) UKHL 26, § 1–102.

[13] An appropriate illustration can be found in *R (On the application of) v East London and the City Mental Health NHS Trust and another* (2003) UKHL 58, (2004) 2 AC 280, § 1–13, at 6–7.

[14] See *Sheldrake v Director of Public Prosecutions* (2004) UKHL 13, § 1–54, at 42, quoting with approval Lord Griffith's observation in *R v Hunt (Richard)* (1987) AC 352, 376: 'My Lords, such a fundamental change is, in my view, a matter for Parliament and not a decision of your Lordships' House'. See also his dictum in the *Pretty* case, mentioned at n 4 above: 'The (House of Lords) is not a legislative body. Nor is it entitled or fitted to act as a moral or ethical arbiter', at § 2.

[15] *Turkington and others (practising as McCartan Turkington Breen) v Times Newspapers Ltd (Northern Ireland)* (2000) UKHL 57, § 1–26, at 16 ff; (2001) 2 AC 277; *Quintavalle, R (on the application of) v Secretary of State for Health* (2003) UKHL 13, § 1–19, at 6 ff; *R v Z (On appeal from the Court of Appeal in. Northern Ireland) (Northern Ireland)* (2005) UKHL 35; (2007) EWCA Crim 1473; § 1–24, at 17 ff.

[16] On the former see his article 'The Rule of Law', loc. cit., n 6 above; on the latter see *Begum, R (On the application of) v Denbigh High School* (2006) UKHL 15, § 1–40.

[17] The drawings and etchings were 'principally subjects of private and domestic interest...For greater privacy, they (had been made)' by means of a private press...The impression had been placed in some of the private apartments of Her Majesty...Such etchings were private portraits.

[18] *Prince Albert v Strange* (1849) 1 De G & SM 652, at 670.

[19] At 671.   [20] At 700.   [21] (1849) 1 Mac & G 23.

photographs should remain her own property and that these persons were forbidden to communicate a copy of them to anyone. Some time later a drawing made from such a photograph was on sale. It could have been done only after the print of one of the photographs. The sister brought an action against both the author of the drawing and the photographers. The court ordered the seizure and the destruction of the drawing and the 25 prints of the photograph. It based its decision on the following reasoning:

No one may, without the express consent of the family, copy and publish the face of a person on his deathbed, irrespective of the celebrity of the person and degree of publicity that was attached to the acts of his life. The right to forbid such a reproduction is an absolute one. Its principle lies in the respect owed to the distress of the families. To infringe it will consist in hurting the most intimate and respectable feelings of nature and domestic piety.[22]

Ten years later, in 1868 a French statute created a minor offence consisting in 'the publication in the press of a fact relating to private life'.[23] It does not seem to have been ever enforced and was abrogated in 1881. From the late 1950s on a right to privacy, especially against intrusions by the press, was affirmed first by the case law of the French courts and later on by a 1970 statute introducing into the Civil Code a new Article 9 under which:

Everyone is entitled to respect for his private life.—Courts are empowered, in addition for compensation of damage suffered, to order any measures, such as impounding, seizure or other to prevent or put an end to an interference with the intimacy of private life. Such injunctions may, in cases of urgency, be delivered in interim interlocutory proceedings.

The debate in Britain, which started some 40 years ago and which is not over, on whether to affirm a general right of privacy and on how to protect privacy, is of special interest to an observer of the English legal scene for two reasons. The first one is the importance of the subject itself, privacy. The second reason concerns the way the courts answer a new issue, or give a new answer to a pre-existing one, and, in doing so, make law and the reaction of society at large to what they do, or do not do.

This essay is divided into four parts. Part 1 comments on the first stage of the national debate on privacy, from the early 1960s to the late 1980s. Part 2 relates to the years 1990 to 1993, from the first Calcutt Report to the second one. Part 3 studies the events that took place after the adoption of the Human Rights Act 1998 and focuses on the new case law relating to the protection of privacy. Part 4, 'A view from Western Europe' comments on the present state of English law, then shows how, in two other European countries, France and Germany, the courts have approached the issue of privacy as a right and offers a few remarks on the evolution of English law.

---

[22] *Félix c O'Connell*, D. 1858.3.62.
[23] Statute of 11 May 1868, Art 11.

1. The National Debate on the Right to Privacy: 1961–1989

From the early 1960s on a number of private Bills and public Reports addressed themselves to the question: should a right to privacy be affirmed, and, if so, how? In 1961 Lord Mancroft introduced a Bill relating to a right of privacy. It lapsed after second reading. The reason, according to the *Times*, was '...the difficulties of defining "personal affairs or conduct" and "reasonable public interest"'. On second reading the Lord Chancellor said that if it were possible to ensure by legislation that the press never erred in matters of taste he would be the first to promote it, but he did not believe it could be done.[24] To compound issues of definition with 'matters of taste' was a safe recipe for inaction. In June 1967 a conference organized by the International Commission of Jurists recommended the creation of a law of privacy protecting the right of every person to privacy. It mentioned four elements: the use or publication of information obtained by unlawful intrusion; the exploitation of the name, identity, or likeness of a person without his consent; the publication of words or views falsely ascribed to a person or placing him in a false light; unauthorized disclosure of intimate or embarrassing facts concerning the private life of a person, published when the public interest does not require it.[25] The same year another Bill was introduced by Mr Alexander Lyon, MP.

In 1969 Mr Brian Walden, MP, introduced his own Bill establishing a right of privacy.[26] Public interest was one of the defences. Courts were empowered to award damages or grant injunctions. The Bill attempted to define the meaning of the term 'right of privacy'.[27] The Press Council criticized it immediately.[28] In early 1970 Justice published a Report containing the same recommendations.[29] The consequence was the creation by the then Home Secretary, Mr Callaghan, of a Committee chaired by Mr Kenneth Younger, to consider whether legislation was needed to protect the right of privacy. Mr Walden's Bill was then before the House of Commons for a second reading. 'It would be disappointing', the *Economist* wrote, 'if the Government this time merely shelves the question for further investigation',[30] a prescient description of what was to be the attitude of all governments on the subject.

The Younger Committee Report[31] did not recommend the creation of a new remedy to protect against infringement of privacy. It consisted of a piecemeal approach, recommending that the use of a device for 'surreptitious' surveillance should be made a criminal offence and that it should be actionable at civil law.

---

[24] *The Times*, 16 January 1970. [25] *The Times*, 16 June 1967.
[26] (Bill 25), 26 November 1969. [27] See Art 9.
[28] *The Times*, 16 November 1970.
[29] *Privacy and the Law* (London, Stevens, 1970). For a comment see *TLS*, 22 January 1970.
[30] 17 January 1970, 'Getting the bug out of the rug'.
[31] *Report of the Committee on Privacy* (London, HMSO, 1972, cmnd 5012).

Private detectives should be licensed. There should be a standing Committee to review developments in computer technology. The Report recommended that it should be a civil wrong, actionable at the suit of any person who has suffered damage thereby, to disclose or otherwise use information which he knows, or in all the circumstances ought to have known, was obtained by illegal means. The kind of remedy available would be similar to those appropriate to action for breach of confidence,[32] a statement that perhaps influenced, later on, the case law. The law of confidence needed clarification and the Report suggested that the subject be referred to the Law Commissions. When the Report was discussed in Parliament, the government endorsed its refusal of legislation affirming a right to privacy.[33] In 1974 the Law Commission published its preliminary conclusions.[34] Mentioning what followed the Younger Report it said:

Against this background to our terms of reference, we have not put forward proposals for reform of the law of breach of confidence which would broaden the scope of the law to such an extent as to amount, in effect, to the introduction of a general right of privacy under another name.[35]

Justice regretted that the conclusions of the Law Commission Report[36]did not offer wider protection for privacy. Commenting, also in 1976, on the legal situation the *Economist* aptly wrote: 'the murkiest area is confidentiality'.[37]

The 1980s witnessed a widening of the public debate on all fronts on how to best to protect privacy. In 1981 the Law Commission published its second Report.[38] It recommended the creation of a new statutory tort which would give the courts power to decide whether the disclosure of information is more in the public interest than the protection of confidence in any particular case. It made a distinction between confidence and privacy. In Parliament private Bills on privacy were introduced in the House of Commons by Mr Cash in 1987[39] and Mr Browne in 1988. The debate that took place in the House of Commons on 27 January 1989 is of particular interest.[40] The by now familiar arguments on the pros and cons of an affirmation of a right to privacy were presented. On the pro side Mr Browne quoted the 1970 Justice Report and the link between the protection of privacy and the preservation of the individual's 'sense of identity and the integrity of his personality'. He emphasized the necessity to distinguish between the public interest and the interests of the public and went on to state, '...no

[32] *Report*, at § 632. Two members of the Committee, Mr Alexander Lyon and Mr Donald Ross, were in favour of a statute protecting a right to privacy.
[33] (1973) 859 HC Deb Col 1959. Statement of Mr Robert Carr, Home Secretary.
[34] Law Commission, *Working Paper no 58, Breach of confidence* (London, HMSO, 1974).
[35] Id, § 58, at p 46.
[36] Summed up by Paul Sieghart (1976) *Human Rights Review*.
[37] 31 January 1976: 'Between ourselves', p 14.
[38] Law Commission, *Breach of confidence* (London, HMSO, 1981, cmnd 8388).
[39] (Bill 45), 3 November 1987.
[40] HC Deb Hansard, p 1299–1364.

effective legal protection of personal privacy exists under English law'. The Bill proposed to create a statutory tort of breach of privacy and mentioned several defences: the public interest, including public benefit, and freedom of information. Legal aid was not mentioned.

On the con side the main arguments were the 'unworkable' character of such a Bill, the excessive discretion left to the courts in the absence of the key definitions of privacy and public interest. Mr Browne quoted Lord Alexander who, one week earlier, had written that the law of confidence was indeed 'judge made law',[41] which few would dispute. The Minister of State, Home Office, declared: 'Despite its age the Younger Report is the definitive work on the subject' and mentioned the 'uncertain scope and unpredictable implications of a general right of privacy'. He stressed the danger of legislating for privacy in isolation from other related areas of the civil law, in particular the link between privacy and breach of confidence and privacy and defamation. He seemed to entertain doubts on 'the ability of the courts to construe general concepts' in such a matter.

The media stressed the necessity of a new remedy to protect privacy.[42] Authors writing in legal journals also took sides. Following other articles commenting on the Bills already mentioned,[43] some essays offered general thoughts on the idea of a right to privacy.[44] Most of them were hostile to the very idea of it. Geoffrey. Marshall mentioned a 'general muddle...the conceptual flux...confusion' and concluded:

The terms 'private' and 'privacy' have no succinct or precise legal definition that is universally accepted. The ambiguity which surrounds the notion of 'privacy' confuses any discussion concerning the 'right of privacy'. Legislation purporting to protect an individual's right of privacy would be subject to widely varying interpretation. To be meaningful and effective, reference to a general right of privacy must be avoided: specific rights of privacy must be enumerated and defined.[45]

In an article published a few years later an American jurist, comparing the legal scene in the USA and in Britain in relation to privacy since the publication of the Warren and Brandeis article in 1890, wrote: 'In England, however, legal periodicals did not have this creative effect... Since the failure of the Windfield article[46] English legal writers have looked to Parliament rather than to the courts for the

---

[41] *Daily Telegraph*, 21 January 1989.
[42] See 'Private lives', *The Economist*, 12 December 1987; 'Privacy or the Right to Know', *New Law Journal*, 22 May 1987, 'Ann Diamond and the homosexual QC', Law Magazine, 2 February 1988; 'Indecent assault', *The Economist*, 28 January 1989.
[43] See, e.g., GDS Taylor, 'Privacy and the public' (1971) 34 MLR 288.
[44] Geoffrey Marshall, 'The Right to Privacy. A Sceptical View', (1975)McGill L J 242; Raymond Wacks, 'The Poverty of Privacy' (1980) 96 LQR 73; id, *The Protection of Privacy* (London, Sweet and Maxwell, 1980); Martin Bulmer and Jennifer Bell, 'The Press and personal privacy; Has it gone too far?' (1985) *Political Quarterly* 5.
[45] Marshall, loc.cit., at 242, 243, and 254.
[46] Percy H Windfield, 'Privacy' (1931) 47 LQR 23.

initiative in this field.'[47] This became less true as time passed towards the end of the 1980s.

What followed in 1989 was this: in April the government announced an independent review of the conduct of the press, including the general issue of privacy, as the third reading of Mr Browne's Bill was to take place in the House of Commons. Mr David Calcutt, QC, was appointed to chair the Committee.[48]The national newspaper editors agreed on a common Code of Practice and declared that they would introduce ombudsmen to deal with complaints. Announcing the move the *Times*, in an editorial, affirmed squarely that 'the rights of journalists—to ask, question, state facts, express opinions—are in essence no different from the rights of citizenry at large'.[49] On the same day an editorial in the *Financial Times* stated that 'Statutory regulation, as proposed by several members of Parliament would pose a serious threat to press freedom'.[50] The writing on the wall was clear enough.

2. The National Debate on the Right to Privacy: From Calcutt to Calcutt, 1990–1993

The Calcutt Committee Report[51] was published in June 1990, three months after the judgment of the Court of Appeal in *Kaye v Robertson*[52] ruling out the development of a tort of infringement of privacy. Only Parliament, the Court held, could create such a tort. The Report took sides against such a creation: 'An overwhelming case for introducing a statutory tort of infringement of privacy has not so far been made out.'[53] The Report listed the following arguments: difficulties of definition; the issues of defences—the Committee has serious reservations about a general defence merely labelled 'public interest'; freedom of speech; prior restraint; accessibility; implications outside the press (broadcasting, books, which fell outside its terms of reference).

The Report made a number of recommendations. Physical intrusion should become a criminal offence. Some legal restrictions on press reporting should be introduced (non-identification of minors and of rape victims). 'One final chance' should be given to the press 'to prove that voluntary self-regulation can be made to work', hence the recommendation of the creation of a Press Complaints Committee to replace the Press Council. If this failed, a statutory tribunal,

---

[47] David J Seipp, 'English Judicial Recognition of a Right to Privacy' (1983) OJLS (3) 325, at 327.
[48] 'Reading between the lines', *The Times*, 12 July 1989.
[49] 'Responsible free speech', 28 November 1989.
[50] 'Self-regulation of the press', id.
[51] Report of the Committee on Privacy and Related Matters, cm 1102 (London, HMSO ,1990). I was asked by the Committee to give evidence before it, in writing and orally, which I did.
[52] *Kaye v Robertson* (1991) FSR 62, CA (Civ Div).
[53] Report, § 12–5, p 46.

chaired by a judge and disposing of statutory powers to implement a statutory code of practice should be created. Such an explicit mistrust of courts seems to have been rather common. Commenting on this proposal the *Economist* wrote:

The Calcutt Report...leaves the door ajar to regulation by a body which is not a court but which acts as a court, armed not with law but with a professional rulebook. Anyone watching Britain's judges in recent years can have little faith in their commitment to freedom of the press. To ask them to interpret a journalist's rulebook would be bad in principle and often hair-raising in practice.[54]

The debate went on in 1992. In June Mr Clive Soley, MP, introduced a Freedom and Responsibility of the Press Bill which provided for the creation of a statutory independent Press Authority, a right to a published correction of factual inaccuracy in editorial material, and, in case of refusal to comply with an order of the Authority, a court decision to enforce the order. In July the government asked Sir David Calcutt to assess the effectiveness of the press self-regulation. In October the House of Commons National Heritage Committee began an inquiry on privacy and media intrusion. 1993 was bound to be an interesting year.

Calcutt 2 and after

Sir David Calcutt's Report was published in January 1993. After summing up the previous Report's recommendations and the responses to them, it reviewed the creation of the Press Complaints Commission and duly assessed press self-regulation in 1992. The conclusion was unequivocal:

On an overall assessment, the Press Complaints Commission is not, in my view, an effective regulator of the press...The Commission, as constituted, is, in essence, a body set up by the industry, financed by the industry, dominated by the industry, operating a code of practice devised by the industry and which is over-favourable to the industry.[55]

The Report recommended the introduction of a statutory regime as set out in the previous Report. The new Press Complaints Tribunal 'would have one distinct advantage over the regular courts of law: It would acquire a general expertise which is not generally available to those courts which have to operate over a wider range of human activity'.[56]With the fullest respect one wonders at the logic of such a statement. Distrust of the courts is a rather common attitude, in this domain as well as in others. But to affirm that adjudicating on complaints against the press requires special, indeed specialized skills that courts—which decide every day on much more technical issues—do not possess seems to be a non sequitur.

As to the introduction of a tort of infringement of privacy, the Report held that reconsideration of the case was now necessary. Such a tort would apply to all media

---

[54] 30 June 1990.   [55] At § 5–26, p 41.   [56] At § 7–42, p 57.

and not only to the press, and it recommended that 'the Government should now give further consideration to the introduction of a new tort of infringement of privacy'.[57] The recommendations were, as expected, immediately rejected by the PCC and the press. The government did not adopt the recommendation to create a statutory tribunal. The *Economist* was alone in recommending the introduction of a statutory tort of privacy on the following lines: the serving of the public interest; substance decided by a jury; damages set by a judge; the plaintiff would have to prove that intrusion is unjustified; no injunctions; legal aid would be available.[58]

In March 1993 the House of Commons National Heritage Committee published its Report 'Privacy and Media Intrusion'.[59] It recommended an extension of the right of access to information, i.e., to public documents and the adoption of a protection of privacy Bill in which infringement of privacy would be the main civil offence.[60] Public interest would be a defence. The Report also recommended that further consideration be given to the introduction of legislation on breach of confidence. It suggested the creation of new criminal offences, also with the defence of the public interest.[61] Legal aid would be available. Mentioning Article 9 of the French Civil Code enacted in 1970,[62] the Report said that it 'admirably' expressed 'the Committee's view on privacy'.[63] It rejected the idea of a statutory press complaints tribunal, preferring voluntary regulation, including the payment of compensation and the power to fine.[64] Going further, the Report recommended that 'all journalists should be required to provide proof of identity and a copy of the code (of practice) to those they seek to interview and photograph'.[65] It added, in relation to cheque book journalism, that 'it could be useful if newspapers made it their practice to indicate the stories for which payment for information had been made'.[66] This must count as one of the strangest proposals in the debate on such issues. A statutory Press Ombudsman was to be created and be given authority to order the payment of compensation or of a fine.

---

[57] At § 7–42, p 57.

[58] 19 September 1992 and 16 January 1993.

[59] House of Commons, National Heritage Committee, 4th Report, *Privacy and Media Intrusion*, 2 vols (London, HMSO, 1993).

[60] 'The offence would include obtaining and/or publishing harmful or embarrassing private material or photograph; or obtaining and/or publishing private information (eg medical record) or photographs without the permission of the person concerned or, were that person is not in a position to give permission, by his next of kin; or publishing inaccurate or misleading personal information; or violating the peace of another by intruding upon him, or persistently communicating with him', *Report*, I, xii–xiii, § 48.

[61] Id, I, xiii–xiv, § 52–55.

[62] 'Everyone has the right of respect for his private life', para 1.

[63] *Report*, at § 59, p xv.

[64] Id, at § 75, p xviii.

[65] At § 83, p xix.

[66] At § 88, p xx. What about receipts and tax status of such payments as ' expenses'?

In July the Lord Chancellor's Department published a Consultation Paper on the infringement of privacy.[67] The latter proposed the creation of a civil remedy. A natural person would have a cause of action 'in respect of conduct which constitutes an infringement of his privacy, causing him substantial distress, provided such distress would also have been suffered by a person of ordinary sensibilities in the circumstances of the complainant'. Privacy would include 'matters appertaining to his health, personal communications, and family and personal relationships, and a right to be free from harassment and molestation'. Defences would include consent, lawful authority, absolute or qualified privilege, and public interest.[68]

The Paper is different from the previous Reports in that it stresses, at the outset, the meaning and importance of privacy:[69] 'Privacy is an interest of the human personality. It protects the inviolate personality, the individual's independence, dignity and integrity'.[70] Two main aspects are mentioned: The state of seclusion and personal information. A reference to 20th century, absent from the other reports, was no less welcome: '...privacy is one of the first victims of a totalitarian State'. Hence the following statement: 'Privacy is a political value. It is also a basic human need.'[71] From a legal point of view the Paper stressed that 'there are significant differences between privacy and breach of confidence, which suggests that the latter cannot be relied on as an alternative to introducing a new right in respect of infringement of privacy'.[72]

The government's answer was predictable. In its reply to the Calcutt Report and to the House of Commons National Heritage Select Committee Report, it stated that the creation of a new civil remedy should be left to Parliament.[73] The idea of creating a statutory complaints Tribunal or a Press Ombudsman was also rejected. The PCC was to carry on, in view of further improvements. Industry self-regulation was held to be preferable to the creation of statutory bodies. Professor Eric Barendt, who had consistently held that a right to privacy was a necessity, wrote at the time:

...the Government of Britain is terrified of the press...At the end of last year Lord Wakenham, a former Cabinet Minister, was appointed Chairman of the Press Complaints Commission, with the intention that he would ward off any attempt at legislation. The manoeuvre has succeeded brilliantly...[The White Paper] is an exceptionally feeble document. It fails to address the arguments of principle: Is privacy a fundamental human right, as the European Court of Human Rights and many national Constitutions assert? If so, how should it be protected?[74]

---

[67] Lord Chancellor's Department, *Infringement of privacy*. Consultation Paper (London, Central Office of Information, 1993). I gave evidence before the Department.

[68] At § 11 and 1–2.   [69] See ch 3, p 8 ff.

[70] At § 3–4, p 8. The Paper aptly quotes Edward J Bloustein's seminal article 'Privacy as an Aspect of Human Dignity' (1964) 39 NYU LR 962, at 971.

[71] At § 3–9, p 10.   [72] At § 3–9, p 10.

[73] *Privacy and Media Intrusion*, White Paper (London, HMSO, 1995, cm 2918).

[74] Eric Barendt, 'Britain rejects media privacy law', (1995) *Privacy Law and Policy Reporter*, p 69.

3. New Era or Unfinished Journey?

From the Human Rights Act to *Campbell*

From 2000 on the legal scene changed. The era of Committees' Reports, White Papers, and private Bills was, it seems, over. Two categories of events transformed the public debate on the protection of privacy: a legislative one, the entry into force, in 2000, of the Human Rights Act 1998 (hereafter: the HRA); and a string of judicial decisions, leading to that of the House of Lords in *Campbell* in 2004. The case law of the European Court of Human Rights shall be examined in this context.

The Human Rights Act 1998

The absence of a written Constitution and of a Declaration of Rights led, from the late 1960s on, a number of lawyers to campaign for the incorporation into British law of the ECHR. The first to do so was Anthony Lester, as he then was.[75] He became the architect of such a reform. In several influential essays he criticized the situation of fundamental rights in Britain: 'The principal safeguards against the abuse of power by the government in Parliament are...not legally enforceable.'[76] He mentioned the subordinate position of the judges in relation to the legislative sovereignty of Parliament and regretted 'the narrowness of the judicial function'.[77] In an article published in 1984 he recalled the vehement opposition of the main Cabinet Ministers to the ratification of the ECHR in 1951.[78] Senior judges rallied progressively to the idea of incorporating the Convention.[79] In a book he co-edited with David Pannick,[80] he mentioned how the political scene changed in 1997 when John Smith, leader of the Labour Party, declared that he was in favour of the incorporation, which became part of the programme of the party. In 1994[81] and 1997 Lord Lester introduced two Bills to that effect. In 1997 the Labour Party won the election. One year later the Human Rights Act was enacted.[82]

---

[75] Anthony Lester, *Democracy and Individual Rights*, Fabian Tract no 390 (London, 1968), pp 12–15.

[76] Id, 'Fundamental Rights in the UK: The Law and the British Constitution' (1976) 125 University of Pennsylvania LR 337, 339; 'English judges as law makers' (1983) PL 269.

[77] 'Fundamental rights...', loc. cit., at p 340.

[78] Id, 'Fundamental rights: The UK isolated ?', (1984) P L 46.

[79] Sir Thomas Bingham, MR, 'The European Convention on Human Rights: Time to Incorporate', The Denning Lecture, March 1993.

[80] Anthony Lester and David Pannick (eds), *Human Rights Law and Practice* (London, Butterworths, 1999).

[81] See Lord Lester, 'The Mouse that Roared: HR Bill 1994' (1995) PL 198.

[82] John Wadham and Helen Mountfield, *Blackstone's Guide to the Human Rights Act 1998* (London, Blackstone Press, 1999); Lester and Pannick, op. cit.

During the debate questions were asked, in Parliament and in the press, on the implementation of Article 8 combined with Article 10. Might the former lead to a judicial recognition of a right to privacy and to the use of prior restraint in order to protect it? The answer was two-fold. First a statement by the Lord Chancellor, Lord Irvine, on 24 November 1997, according to which 'The Government did not intend to introduce legislation in relation to privacy but expected that the judges would develop the law appropriately having regard to the requirements of the Convention'.[83] The second answer resided in section 12 of the HRA.[84]

Two years later, in 2000, the HRA entered into force. In a lecture delivered in 2002 in New Zealand[85] Lord Lester mentioned that between 1998 and 2000 an extensive training of judges, lawyers, civil servants, members of the legal profession, and members of non-governmental organizations, led by the Home Office, had been taking place, which was sound policy.[86]

The new case law since 2000: An unfinished journey?

Two main elements seem to have guided or influenced the decisions of the courts in cases relating to the protection of privacy:

- The awareness that such a protection was a 'pressing social need', to use the vocabulary of the European Court of Human Rights and that something was missing in the common law in that respect.

- The consciousness that the HRA was meant to change the legal setting of human rights in Britain and had indeed changed it, and that the incorporation of the ECHR and the obligation to take into account the case law of the Strasbourg court made it somewhat impossible to maintain the status quo illustrated by the dictum of Glidewell, LJ in *Kaye*: 'It is well known that in English law there is no right to privacy and accordingly there is no right of action for a breach of personal privacy.'[87] The extent of the obligations of the UK under the ECHR since the enactment of the HRA was mentioned by Lord Phillips, MR, in the judgment of the court of appeal in *Douglas v Hello!*[88]: Since the decision

---

[83] 583 House of Lords Official Reports (5th Series) col 771. cf Lord Justice Gibran, 'Cinderella's slipper. An overview of British privacy Law', Conference of the Franco-British Lawyers Society, Belfast, 2007.

[84] On s 12 see Lester and Pannick, op. cit., ch 2, at 2–12 ff.

[85] 'The Magnetism of the Human Rights Act' (2002) JR 179.

[86] For comments on the protection of following the HRA see Rabinder Singh, 'Privacy and the Media after the HRA' (1998) EHRLR 712; Richard Clayton and Hugh Tomlinson, *Privacy and Freedom of Expression* (Oxford, OUP, 2001); Hugh Tomlinson (ed), *Privacy and the Media. The Developing Law* (2002); Madeleine Colvin (ed), *Developing Key Privacy Rights* (Oxford and Portland, Justice/Hart, 2002); Michael Tugendhat and Iain Christie, *The Law of Privacy and the Media* (Oxford, OUP, 2002); Lord Phillips of Worth Matravers, 'Private Life and Public Interest' (2003) 56 CLP 156.

[87] *Kaye v Robertson* (1991) FSR 62.   [88] *Douglas v Hello!* (2005) EWCA civ 595.

of the European Court of Human Rights in *Von Hannover v Germany*[89] it had
a positive obligation to provide a remedy against the intrusion of private actors
into private life.

Given the permanent refusal of all governments to propose new legislation in this
domain, it was left to the courts to decide what they would do. Broadly speaking
the choice was between two courses: the first one was to affirm a right to privacy,
together with the appropriate remedies; the second one consisted in using, as far
as possible, the law of confidence.

The refusal to affirm a right to privacy

The first episode of the *Douglas v Hello!* saga[90] provided some answers. This was
not, to say the least, a privacy case. The claimants invoked a breach of confidence.
At the interim injunction case the Court of Appeal overturned the injunction,[91]
after having applied section 12.4 of the HRA. After a full review of the legal
developments of the past 20 years, Brooke LJ weighed 'the competing considerations of freedom of expression on the one hand and privacy on the other'.[92] So
far as privacy is concerned, he added, the case of the claimants was not a particularly strong one. This was 'essentially a commercial dispute between two magazine enterprises which are not adverse to exercising spoiling tactics against each
other'.[93] Sedley LJ affirmed that the couple had 'a legal right to respect for their
privacy which (had) been infringed'.[94] Answering the question 'Is there today a
right of privacy in English law ?' he stressed the limits of the use of the law of confidence by the courts to protect privacy:

They have felt unable to articulate their measure as a discrete principle of law … We have
reached a point at which it can be said with confidence that the law recognizes and will
appropriately protect a right of personal privacy.[95]

The reasons, he explained, were twofold: Such an affirmation was needed to respond
to an increasingly invasive social environment. The HRA required the courts to
give appropriate effect to the right set out in Article 8 ECHR. He concluded:

What a concept of privacy does … is accord recognition to the fact that the law has to protect not only those people whose trust has been abused but those who simply find themselves subjected to an unwanted intrusion into their personal lives. The law no longer

---

[89] *Von Hannover v Germany*, 24 June 2004; (2004) 6 BHRC 545.
[90] *Douglas & Ors v Hello! Ltd & Ors* (2003) EWHC 55 (Ch) (27 January 2003); 95 KB; *Douglas
& Ors v Hello! Ltd & Ors* (2003) EWCA Civ 139 (12 February 2003); 45 KB; *Douglas & Ors v Hello!
& Ors* (2003) EWCA 332 (3 March 2003); 22 KB; *Douglas & Ors v Hello! & Ors* (2003) EWHC
786 (Ch) (11 April 2003); 292 KB; *Douglas & Ors v Hello! & Ors* (2003) EWHC 2629 (Ch) (7
November 2003); 69 KB; *Douglas & Ors v Hello! & Ors* (2004) EWHC 63 (Ch) (23 January 2004);
44 KB; *Douglas & Ors v Hello! & Ors* (2005) EWCA Civ 595 (18 May 2005);257 KB; *Douglas &
Ors v Hello! Ltd & Ors* (2007) UKHL 21 (2 May 2007); 283 KB.
[91] *Douglas & Ors v Hello! & Ors* (2001) QB 967 (CA).
[92] At § 95.   [93] At § 100.   [94] At § 104.   [95] At § 110.

needs to construct an artificial relationship of confidentiality between intruder and victim: it can recognize privacy itself as a legal principle drawn from the fundamental value of personal autonomy.[96]

In his 2003 judgment[97] Lindsay J declined the invitation 'to hold that there is an existing law of privacy' under which the claimants were entitled to relief. He did so for several reasons: Other judgments had taken a view different from that of Sedley's LJ. He quoted that of the Court of Appeal in *Wainwright*.[98] Since the Douglasses were protected, in this case, by the law of confidence, no hole existed in English law. The subject was better left to Parliament. However, the inadequacy of English law had just been shown by the decision of the European Court of Human Rights in *Peck v UK*,[99] which led him to add ominously: 'That inadequacy will have to be made good and if Parliament does not step in the courts will be obliged to.'[100] He also quoted Lord Woolf's CJ guidelines in *A v B*[101] which seemed to put an end to the judicial debate: in most, if not all situations where the protection of privacy is justified, an action for breach of confidence will provide the necessary protection. The judicial reluctance to affirm a right to privacy could be traced back to the dictum of Megarry VC in *Malone*: '... no new right in law fully fledged with all the appropriate safeguards can spring from the head of a judge deciding a case; only Parliament can create such a right.'[102]

Later on the House of Lords gave judgment in *Wainwright*,[103] a case relating to strip search prior to a prison visit. McGonigall J had held that the searches had been an invasion of the claimants' privacy which exceeded what was necessary and proportionate. He found that the law of tort should give a remedy for any kind of distress caused by an infringement of the right of privacy protected by Article 8 ECHR. At the time of the incident the HRA had not yet come into force but the judge considered that he was justified in adapting the common law to the Convention. The court of appeal disagreed.[104] In the House of Lords Lord Hoffmann quoted the famous article by Warren and Brandeis[105] as well as Dean Prosser's writings. Commenting on the case law he said: 'What the courts have so far refused to do is to formulate a general principle of "invasion of privacy"[106] from which the conditions of liability in the particular case can be decided.'[107] He quoted Megarry VC in *Malone*,[108] a decision which led to the judgment of

---

[96] At § 126.   [97] (2003) EWHC 786 (Ch).

[98] *Wainwright v Home Office* (2002) 3 WLR 405 CA.

[99] *Peck v UK* (2003) 36 EHRR 41; 13 BHRC 669.

[100] At § 229.

[101] (2002) EWCA Civ 337; (2003) QB195; (2002) 3 WLR 542,CA (Civ Div), at § 11 ff.

[102] *Malone v Metropolitan Police Commissioner* (1979) 2 All ER 620, at 642.

[103] *Wainwright and another v Home Office* (2003) UKHL 53; (2004) 2 AC 406, HL.

[104] (2001) EWCA Civ 2081, (2003) All ER 943, (2002) QB 1334.

[105] 'The Right to Privacy' (1890) 4 Harvard LR 193.

[106] He used the quotation marks, he explained, 'to signify doubt about what in such a context the expression would mean'.

[107] At § 19.   [108] See n 85 above, at 642–649.

the European Court of Human Rights in 1984 holding the UK government in breach of Article 8 ECHR.[109] The result was, one year later, the Interception of Communication Act 1985.[110] Lord Hoffmann mentioned *Kaye* and the Calcutt Committee Report. Discussing Sedley's LJ dictum in *Douglas* he commented: 'I do not understand Sedley LJ to have been advocating the creation of a high level principle invasion of privacy.'[111] Turning to the jurisprudence of the European Court of Human Rights and especially *Peck*,[112] he added that there was nothing in it suggesting that the adoption of 'some high level principle of privacy' is necessary to comply with Article 8 ECHR. The only obligation is an effective remedy. The appeal was dismissed. Three years later a unanimous European Court of Human Rights held the UK government in breach of Articles 8 and 13 ECHR.[113]

In *Campbell*[114] the House of Lords confirmed the refusal of a judicial affirmation of an independent right to privacy: 'In this country, unlike the USA, there is no overarching cause of action for invasion of privacy.'[115] In 2006, in *McKennitt*, Buxton LJ stated again the state of the law: 'There is no English domestic law tort of invasion of privacy.'[116]

The use of the law of confidence and its limits

What the courts did was to use the law of confidence and stretch it, not without some misgivings.[117] The guidelines affirmed by Lord Woolf, CJ in *A v B* were clear:

It is most unlikely that any purpose will be served by a judge seeking to decide whether there exists a new cause of action in tort which protects privacy. In the great majority of situations, if not all situations, where the protection of privacy is justified, relating to events after the Human Rights Act came into force, an action for breach of confidence now will, where this is appropriate, provide the necessary protection. This means that at first instance it can be readily accepted that it is not necessary to tackle the vexed question of whether there is a separate cause of action based upon a new tort involving the infringement of privacy.[118]

---

[109] *Malone v UK* (1984) 7 EHRR 14.
[110] A similar episode took place in relation with the use by the police of a listening device fixed to the outside of a house. After the House of Lords judgment, *R v Khan* (1996) 3 All ER 289, the UK's government was again found in breach of Art 8 ECHR in *Khan v UK* (2000) 8 BHRC 310. The Police Act 1997 put the use of surveillance devices on a statutory basis.
[111] At § 30.
[112] See n 82 above.
[113] *Wainwright v UK*, 26 September 2006.
[114] *Campbell v MGN Ltd* (2004) UKHL 22.
[115] Lord Nicholls, at § 11.
[116] *Niema Ash and another v Loreena McKennitt and others* (2006) EWCA Civ 1714, at § 8.
[117] 'We cannot pretend that we find it satisfactory to be required to shoe-horn within the cause of action of breach of confidence claims for public unauthorized photographs of a private occasion', Lord Phillips, MR, in *Douglas v Hello!* (2005) EWCA Civ 595, at § 53.
[118] *B and C v A* (2002) EWCA Civ 337, at 11, vi.

The exercise thus consisted in protecting as much as possible some elements of privacy under the umbrella of an existing tort. The very use of the words 'private' and 'privacy' is a semantic illustration. Five years before the coming into force of the HRA Laws J made the following statement:

If someone with a telephoto lens were to take from a distance and with no authority a picture of another engaged in some private act, his subsequent disclosure of the photographs would, in my judgment, as surely amount to a breach of confidence as if he had found or stolen a letter or diary in which the act was recounted and proceeded to publish it. In such a case, the law would protect what might reasonably be called a right of privacy, although the name accorded to the cause of action would be breach of confidence. It is, of course, elementary that, in all such cases, a defence based on the public interest would be available.[119]

This statement has often been quoted in cases before English courts and in Australia.[120]

The method was the progressive dilatation of the three classic components of a successful claim in confidence stated by Megarry J in *Coco*:[121] the information itself must have the necessary quality of confidence about it. It must have been imparted in circumstances imparting an obligation of confidence. There must be an unauthorized use of that information to the detriment of the party communicating it. As early as 1990 the House of Lords held that an obligation of confidence can arise even when the information in question has not been confided by a confider to a confidant.[122] This was illustrated later by the dictum of Laws J in *Hellewell* already quoted.[123] After the coming into force of the HRA this doctrine was applied in *Douglas v Hello!* as well as in *Venables*.[124]

The focus was shifted to the private nature of the information. In *Campbell* the five judges of the House of Lords recognized a right to protection of private information. The majority (Lords Hope and Carswell and Baroness Hale) based it on the law of confidence. Lords Hoffmann and Nicholls recognized 'a shift in the centre of gravity of the action for breach of confidence' which now 'focuses upon

[119] *Hellewell v Chief Constable of Derbyshire* (1995) 1 WLR 804, at 807; (1995) 4 All ER 473, at 476.

[120] E.g., by Gleeson CJ in *Lenah Game Meats v Australian Broadcasting Corporation* (2001) CLR 199, at § 34.

[121] *Coco v AN Clark (Engineers) Ltd* (1969) RPC 41.

[122] '...in the vast majority of cases...the duty of confidence will arise from a transaction or a relationship between the parties—often a contract, in which event the duty may arise by reason of either an express or an implied term of that contract. It is in such cases as these that the expressions "confider" and "confidant" are perhaps most aptly employed. But it is well settled that a duty of confidence may arise in equity independently of such cases...' Lord Goff in *Attorney-General v Guardian Newspapers Ltd (No 2)* (1990) 1 AC 109281.

[123] cf n 119 above.

[124] *Venables v News Group Newspapers Ltd; Thompson v News Group Newspapers Ltd* (2001)Fam 430; (2001) 2 WLR 1038; (2001) 1 All ER 908; (2001) EMLR 10; (2001) 1 FLR 791; (2002) 1 FCR 333; (2001) HRLR 19; (2001) UKHRR 628; 9 BHRC 587; (2001) Fam Law 258; (2001) 98(12) LSG; (2001) 151 NLJ 57; (2001) 145 SJLB 43.

the protection of human autonomy and dignity'.[125] Lord Nicholls went further to affirm that 'the essence of the tort is better encapsulated now as misuse of private information'.[126] As to what is private information, the courts seem to use generally the reasonable expectation (of the person in question) test. As to places it is clear, since *Theakston*[127] and *Campbell*, combined with the two decisions of the European Court of Human Rights in *Peck v UK*[128] and *Von Hannover v Germany*[129] that the mere fact that an incident took place in a public place does not preclude the claimant in a privacy claim.[130]

In 2003 the 5th Report of the House of Commons Culture, Media and Sports Committee was published.[131] It noted that standards of press behaviour and the performance of the PCC had improved over the past decade and urged the government to give the PCC more powers. It endorsed a formal privacy law to protect the public in the following terms:

> On balance we firmly recommend that the Government reconsider its position and bring forward legislative proposals to clarify the protection that individuals can expect from unwarranted intrusion by anyone—not the press alone—into their private lives. This is necessary to satisfy the obligations upon the UK under the ECHR... Privacy is an aspect of human dignity and autonomy.[132]

The Culture Department declared that the Secretary, Mrs Jowell, had already said that there were no plans for a privacy law. The Institute for Public Policy Research, which had published a report on the subject in 2002,[133] stated that a new privacy law was needed to clarify journalists' rights to investigate and individuals' rights to privacy.

The case law since 2001 has attracted many commentaries in legal journals.[134] Most of it is critical. Such criticism seems to be concentrated on three main points. The first one is that stretching the law of confidence in order to be able to offer some protection to some aspects of privacy has major drawbacks. It leads

---

[125] *Campbell v MGN Ltd* (2004) UKHL 22, Lord Hoffmann, at § 51.

[126] Id, at § 14.

[127] *Theakston v MGN* (2002) EMLR 22 QBD; (2002) EWHC 137.

[128] (2003) EMMR 15; (2003) 36 EHRR 41; 13 BHRC 669.

[129] (2004) EMLR 21; (2005) 40 EHRR 1; 16 BHRC 545.

[130] NA Moreham, 'Privacy in public places', (2006) 65 (3) CLJ 606.

[131] House of Commons Select Committee on Culture, Media and Sport, *Privacy and the media Intrusion*, 2003.

[132] At 111.

[133] IPPR, *Ruled by Recluses. Journalism and the Media after the HRA*, Damian Tambini and Claire Heyward, eds, 2002.

[134] Helene Fenwick and Gavin Philipson, 'Breach of Confidence as a Privacy Remedy in the Human Rights Act Era', (2000) 63 MLR 660; Rabinder Singh and James Strachan, 'The Right to Privacy in English Law' (2002) 2 EHRLR 130; (2003) EHRLR special issue: Privacy, including Rabinder Singh and James Strachan, 'Privacy Postponed?' and Gavin Philipson, 'Judicial Reasoning in Breach of Confidence Cases under the Human Rights Act: not taking privacy seriously?'; Basil Markesinis, Colm O'Cinneide, Jörg Fedtke, and Myriam Hunter-Henin, 'Concerns and Ideas About the Developing English Law of Privacy (And How Knowledge of Foreign Law Might Be of Help', (2004) 52 AJCL 133.

not only to a piecemeal development of the law but also to legal uncertainty and inconsistency. The second point is that the courts seems to forget an essential dimension of privacy, i.e., that of a human right, that is something different from a tort. Philipson insists on this in the article quoted above. The third point relates to the timidity and the deference shown by the courts, in judicial review cases, towards self-regulation bodies such as the PCC and the BSC. In their 2002 article Rabinder Singh and James Strachan quote the dictum of Lord Woolf, MR in a case concerning the BBC:

So long as the approach which [the BSC] adopt is one to which, in their statutory context, the words infringement of privacy are capable of applying then the courts should not interfere. It is only if an approach to 'infringement of privacy'…goes beyond the area of tolerance that the courts can intervene. There will be situations which fall within the grey area where it will be very much a matter of judgment whether they fall within [that] ambit or not. In the latter situations having regard to the role the legislation gives [the BSC] the answer to the scope of their remit is that it is something for [the BSC] to determine not the courts. The nature of their work and their membership are important when considering the role of the courts in relation to the adjudications by [the BSC]. What constitutes an infringement of privacy or bad taste or failure to confirm to proper standards of decency is very much a matter of personal judgment. This is not an area on which the courts are well equipped to adjudicate.[135]

They then add: 'The courts have traditionally regarded the protection of privacy as a sensitive task far better suited to experts in the media industry than those who sit on the bench.'[136] Commenting on the dicta of Silber J in another case[137]they rightly ask the following question:

If the court limits its scrutiny of the PCC and BSC on the grounds that it is not best equipped to adjudicate in this area, how is it properly to fulfil its functions under section 12 of the HRA 1998 or, more interestingly, in claims brought in private law under an enhanced concept of breach of confidence or a tort of breach of privacy?[138]

4. A View from the Continent

This part contains four distinct developments. The first one is a general comment on the present state of English law in this domain. The second one shows how, in two countries, France and Germany, a right to privacy has been affirmed and is protected. Part three comments on the use, by French and German law, of the

---

[135] *R v Broadcasting Standards Commision, ex p British Broadcasting Corporation* (2000) EWLR 1327 at 1332.
[136] At p 149.
[137] *R on the application of Anna Ford v PCC* (2001) EWHC Adm 683, 31 July 2001; (2002) EMLR 5.
[138] At p 149.

notion of personality rights. The fourth part contains some observations on the possible developments of the English law of privacy.

On the present state of English law

What is particularly striking to a foreign observer is the combination of the two following elements: the awareness that privacy is a value which ought to be protected because it is an aspect of personality; and the refusal of the courts to affirm an autonomous right to privacy, on the same level as other fundamental rights.

Privacy as an aspect of personality

It is striking to see how early the courts, most reports, and legal commentators have expressed their explicit awareness that privacy was a value which ought to be protected because it was one aspect of personality. The repeated use of the terms 'liberty', 'dignity',[139] and 'autonomy' are an apt illustration. In an article published in 1975[140] commenting on the article by Warren and Brandeis, Walter F Pratt remarked that they used the expression 'inviolate personality'[141] and mentioned 'the right to privacy, as a part of the more general right to one's personality'.[142] In his 1983 article David J Seipp wrote: 'Privacy is a new doctrinal category in the making. In England and elsewhere, it is coming to be perceived as a unified body of rules determining the boundaries we may rely upon to keep out an intrusive world.'[143] He added aptly: 'If tort law was the product of the industrial revolution, privacy is the result of a communications and information revolution.'[144] The dictum of Sedley LJ in *Douglas* was explicit:

What a concept of privacy does, however, is accord recognition to the fact that the law has to protect not only those people whose trust has been abused but those who simply find themselves subject to an unwanted intrusion into their personal lives. The law no longer needs to construct an artificial relationship of confidentiality between intruder and victim: it can recognize privacy itself as a legal principle drawn from the fundamental value of personal autonomy.[145]

In *Wainwright* Lord Hoffmann distinguished between privacy as a value and privacy as a right in the following terms:

There seems to me great difference between identifying privacy as a value which underlies the existence of a rule of law (and may point to the direction in which the law should develop) has privacy as a principle of law in itself. The English common law is familiar

---

[139] On indirect protection of dignity in English law see David Feldman, 'Human Dignity as a Legal Value' II (2000) PL 61, at p 61ff.

[140] Walter F Pratt, 'The Warren and Brandeis argument for a right to privacy' (1975) PL 161.

[141] At p 205.   [142] At p 207.

[143] Seipp, loc. cit., at p 369.

[144] Id, at 370.

[145] *Douglas v Hello!*, Court of Appeal, 21 December 2000, at § 126.

with the notion of underlying values—principles only in the broadest sense—which direct its development.[146]

In their 2004 article Professor Basil Markesinis and the other co-authors, commenting on the case law, added: '... what was really at stake in these cases, despite the convoluted legal routes adopted, was, in essence, the protection of human personality and the private space[147] necessary for it to grow and develop in all its manifestations.'[148]

The refusal to affirm an autonomous right to privacy as a fundamental right

The decisions and dicta mentioned above have repeatedly illustrated such a position. It is explicitly based on three arguments. Two relate to what might be called jurisprudential policy. The first one is summed up by the affirmation that only Parliament, not the courts, may create such a new right. The second one is the conviction that this is not how the common law develops. The third argument is derived from the first two. It is not necessary to affirm a new autonomous right since an alternative means is available: The gradual extension of the scope of the protection offered by an existing remedy, the law of confidence. Hence the use of the words 'misuse of private information'. Since something must obviously be done, especially under the HRA, this is the way to do it. As Gavin Philipson aptly wrote, the overall issue is that of 'the introduction of human rights norms into the common law'.[149]

Privacy as an autonomous right enjoying constitutional protection: (1) France

The French law relating to the right to privacy has developed in several stages.

Stage one: the civil courts (1)

From the mid 1950s on the civil courts, and mainly the Paris ones, began to affirm a right to privacy. In 1955 the Paris Court of Appeal held that 'the remembrances of the private life of each individual belong to his moral patrimony. No one may publish them without an explicit and unequivocal authorization'. The same principle applies to anecdotes and accounts relating to the 'intimacy of private life'. These principles apply to stars.[150]A string of decisions, during the 1960s, affirmed that 'Each individual is entitled to the secrecy of his private life and has

---

[146] At 431.
[147] See Maurice Cranston's seminal article 'A private space', (1975) Social Science information, p 441.
[148] Loc. cit., at p135.
[149] Gavin Philipson, 'Judicial Reasoning in Breach of Confidence Cases under the Human Rights Act: not taking privacy seriously?' (2003) EHRLR, Special issue, p 54, at p 55.
[150] *Marlene Dietrich v Société France-Dimanche*, Paris Court of Appeal, 16 March 1955, D.1955.295.

a right to ask for its protection'.[151] The cases related not only to cinema stars, singers, and celebrities but also to other people. Remedies included not only damages but also, in interlocutory proceedings, injunctions the aim of which was to prevent the imminent violation of such a right, e.g., ordering the seizure of a book or of the whole edition of a newspaper, when this was the only way to limit a blatant and particularly grave intrusion into the privacy of a person.[152]

Three remarks are in order here. The first one is that this new form of liability was distinct from the classic liability affirmed in Article 1382 of the Civil Code which requires the existence of three conditions: a fault, a loss, and a causality link between them. Not so here. The second remark is that the case law mentioned above took place at time when France had not yet ratified the ECHR (it did so in 1973) and when the case law of the Conseil constitutionnel was not what it became later. The third remark is that such power of the courts to order the seizure of the whole edition of a newspaper was totally unknown in French civil law. This led the Cour de cassation, in its first annual Report for the judicial year 1968–1969,[153] to mention the rights of personality, the new case law on the right to privacy, and the nature of the remedies mentioned above, that is prior restraint. Under the 1881 statute on the press a court could order, in libel[154] cases, the seizure of only four copies of a newspaper. The Report called for a new statute. The aim was two-fold: first to clarify the law and conciliate two rights: freedom of the press and the right to privacy; secondly to allow clearly interlocutory proceedings to be used in this matter.

Stage two: the Government and Parliament

The result was a 1970 statute creating a new Article 9 of the Civil Code:

Everyone has the right to respect for his private life (Para 1). Courts are empowered, in addition to compensation for loss suffered, to order any measures, such as impounding, seizure or others to prevent or to put an end to an infringement to the intimacy of private life. Such injunctions may, in case or urgency, be delivered through interlocutory interim proceedings.

What is *not* in this text may be as remarkable as what is in it. It does not contain a definition of privacy, a mention of a publication (it thus applies to all kinds of

---

[151] Paris Court of Appeal, 17 March 1966, D.1966, p 749.

[152] Here is an illustration: the son of the famous actor Gérard Philipe, aged 9, was in a hospital. A weekly planned to publish photographs of him on his bed, plus an article on his illness. His mother, the widow of G Philipe, acting on her own behalf and on that of her son, asked a judge, in interim interlocutory proceedings, to order the seizure of the edition of the weekly, which he did. In appeal the Paris Court of Appeal upheld the judgment, holding that the planned publication of such an unauthorized photograph and of information on the state of the child was 'an intolerable intrusion into the private life of the Philipe family': Paris Court of Appeal, *SARL France Editions et Publications c. Veuve Gérard Philipe*, 15 November 1966, D.1967.181, note P Mimin. For a list of the main cases decided between 1955 and the mid-1960s see D.1966.566, note Cl.F.P.

[153] The annual Report had been created in 1967.

[154] Both a tort and an offence under French press law.

intrusions of privacy not covered by other instruments and to all actors), or a statement of the defences. What it contains is the statement of a right and the confirmation of the jurisdiction of the civil courts, in interlocutory interim proceedings, to order a number of measures. It contains also a distinction between private life and its 'intimacy'. The article may thus be read as a mere codification of the case law.

Stage three: the civil courts (2)

What the civil courts have been doing may be summed as follows. As to the scope of the notion of private life the main areas are health, illness, family, and personal life. Information relating to current events, official and known, is lawful as long as it does not go beyond the aim of information.[155] Defences include the explicit consent of the person, the legitimate information of the public, sometimes the minor character of the intrusion.[156] Remedies may include, in addition to damages, the suppression of a photograph or of parts of a book, or the publication by the newspaper, or by others as well, to be paid by the newspaper, of a statement mentioning the judgment deciding that there has been an intrusion into the privacy of the claimant. Prior restraint is extremely rare. The courts have also been using the notion of human dignity and the protection offered by Article 9 of the Civil Code to private life.[157] The duty of the courts is to balance two rights of equal value, protected by Articles 8 and 10 ECHR and to protect, in each case, the more legitimate interest.[158]

---

[155] See Cass 1re civ, 23 April 2003, D.2003, p 1854; same date, Ibid, note Bigot. The intrusion into private life is independent from the compassionate, friendly, or hostile tone of the publication (id). To publish the photograph of a private residence, with the address and the name of the owner, is an intrusion into privacy: Cass 2ème civ, 5 June 2003, D.2003, p 1461, note Emmanuel Dreyer; RTD civ 2003, p 681, note J Hauser.

[156] See Cass 1re civ, 3 April 2002, D.2002, p 3164, note Chr Bigot.

[157] Claire Geoffroy, 'Le secret dans la vie privée et dans la mort', JCP.1974.I.2604; Roger Nerson and Jacqueline Rubellin-Devichi, note, (1983) 'Revue trimestrielle de droit civil', p 103; Pierre Kayser, *La protection de la vie privée. Protection du secret de la vie privée* (Paris and Aix-en-Provence, Economica and Presses universitaires d'Aix-Marseille, 1984); 7me éd,1995; Jean-Pierre Ancel, 'La protection judiciaire. La voie civile', Gazette du Palais, 1994, p 988; Roger Errera, 'Privacy as a right', in Andras Sajo (ed), *Western Rights? Post-Communist Application* (The Hague, London, Boston, Kluwer Law International, 1996) p 31; Etienne Picard, 'The Right to Privacy in French Law' in B Markesinis (ed), *Protecting Privacy* (Oxford, Clarendon Press, 1999) p 91; Catherine Dupré, 'The Protection of Private Life against Freedom of Expression in French Law' (2000) 6 EHRLR 627; id in Madeleine Colvin (ed), *Developing Key Privacy Rights* (Oxford, Hart, 2002) p 45; Jacques.Ravanas, 'Liberté d'expression et protection des droits de la personnalité', D.2000, no 30, p 459; Jean-Pierre Ancel, 'La protection des droits de la personne dans la jurisprudence récente de la Cour de cassation' in Cour de cassation, *Rapport annuel 2000* (Paris, La Documentation française, 2001, p 55); Jean-Pierre Gridel, 'Le droit à la vie privée et la liberté d 'expression', Bulletin d'information de la Cour de cassation, 15 March 2003, p 11; Alain Lacabarats, 'Les actions en justice pour atteintes à la vie privée', id, p 18; Théo Hassler, 'L'image d'une personne dans un lieu public peut-elle être diffusée sans le consentement du sujet? (Etude critique du droit positif)', Les Petites Affiches, no 99, 15 May 2004, p 15; Jean-Pierre Gridel, 'Liberté de la presse et protection civile des droits modernes de la personnalité en droit positif français', D.2005.391.

[158] See Cass 1ère civ 7 July 2003, *SA Figaro et a. c. C.V.*, JCP 2003, p 1575, note Jacques Ravanas.

Two recent cases might deserve a special comment, the *Gubler* and the *Erignac* ones. Dr Gubler was the personal physician of President Mitterrand. In 1996, a few weeks after the President's death, he published a book describing how, since 1982, the President's cancer had been hidden by him from the public's knowledge, and the President's and his family's behaviour. The late President's widow, his sons and his daughter sued him for breach of privacy, his and their's. In interim interlocutory proceedings the Paris lower court ordered a ban on the distribution on the book. This was upheld by the Court of Appeal, but for one month only. On substance the lower court found that the late President's privacy and that of his family had been infringed and maintained the banning of the book until a number of pages were suppressed. The publisher and the author had to pay damages to the family. The Court of Appeal held that the protection of privacy applies only to living persons, not the dead. The action concerning the President's privacy was thus held inadmissible. As to the banning of the book the Court held that, in the circumstances, it was the only means to suppress the loss created by it as well as the continuation of the criminal offence it constituted (a breach of medical secrecy). This was confirmed in 1999 by the Cour de cassation. The publisher then brought an action before the European Court of Human Rights. The latter's decision[159] can be summed up as follows: immediately after the President's death the outrage caused by such a publication could justify the banning of the book, in order to protect the family's privacy. But the judgment of the Court of Appeal, nine months later, was a different matter. There was then no pressing social need to justify the banning of the book—40,000 copies of which had been already sold. Such a ban, the Court held, was disproportionate with the legitimate aim pursued. In addition the Court affirmed that the public debate on the health of the late President was a legitimate one. France was held in breach of Article 10 ECHR.

The *Erignac* case was different. Mr Erignac, the prefect of Corsica, was killed in Ajaccio by Corsican terrorists. A few days later, two weeklies, *Paris-Match* and *VSD*, published on a double page a photograph, obviously taken immediately after the murder, showing his body, covered by blood, and part of his face, lying on the ground. His widow and his two children asked the court to order the seizure of the copies of the weekly in sale and to ban its distribution. The court refused and ordered, instead, the publication by the two weeklies, to be paid by them, of two statements, of a large size (15cm) and in bold print, mentioning the grave distress caused to Mrs Erignac and her children by the publication of such a photograph. The necessities of information could not justify it. The court's order was based on the respect of the dignity of the body of the assassinated prefect and the elementary protection of the feelings of the claimants at such a moment. The court of appeal upheld the judgment, mentioning Article 10.2 ECHR, affirming that the publication of the photograph had constituted an

---

[159] *Société Plon v France*, 18 May 2004.

intrusion into the privacy of Mrs Erignac and her children and that the court was empowered, under Article 9, second paragraph, of the Civil Code, to order such a step. It ordered the weeklies to publish a statement mentioning its own judgment and that the publication of the photograph, without the permission of the family, was, according to it, an infringement of its privacy. In 2000 the Cour de cassation confirmed the decision of the Court of Appeal: an infringement of the right of the person created an urgent situation justifying the use of interim interlocutory proceedings (Article 809, paragraph 1 NCPC).The image was an attack upon the dignity of the human person and Article 10.2 ECHR allowed the injunction.[160]

A 1983 judgment given in interim interlocutory proceedings may be mentioned here. In 1981 a Japanese madman killed a Dutch tourist in Paris, cut her body into pieces, and ate from it. In November 1983, a monthly photographic magazine, *Photo*, published photographs of the body. The outraged parents brought an action against it. The day after, the president of the Paris court held that this caused them a manifestly illicit distress ('trouble illicite'), given the nature and the circumstances of the crime and their state of shock. The 'information' of the readers had noting to do with it. This was a faulty and intolerable attack upon the feelings of the family, which must be protected. This allowed the court to deliver an injunction: the publisher was ordered to tear off from the copies of the magazine still on sale the supplement containing the photographs and to return all the copies of the edition (243,000) to its premises, under a levy 10 francs (one £) by copy.[161]

This confirmed that the dignity of the body of a dead person could be protected, even if the protection of privacy ceases with the person's death. It is also another illustration of the scope of the notion of human dignity in French civil, criminal, and administrative law.[162] As to the *Erignac* case the European Court of Human Rights rejected the application of the publisher and held that Article 10 ECHR had not been violated. The Court's order was prescribed by law and had a legitimate aim under Article 10.2 ECHR. The Court mentioned the duties and responsibilities of the media, quoted its judgment in *Hannover v Germany*. In

---

[160] Paris tribunal de grande instance, 12 February 1998; Paris Court of Appeal, 24 February 1998, D.1998, p 225, note Beignier; Cass 1ère civ, 20 December 2000, JCP.2001.II.10488, concl Sainte-Rose; D.2001.885; Jean-Pierre Gridel, 'Retour sur l'image du préfet assassiné: dignité de la personne humaine et liberté de l'information d'actualité', D.2001, p 872.

[161] Tribunal de grande instance de Paris, 13 November 1982, D.1984. 110, note RL.

[162] On human dignity in French law see Bertrand Mathieu, 'La dignité de la personne humaine: quel droit? Quel titulaire?', D.1996, p282; Berenard Edelman, 'La dignité de la personne humaine, un concept nouveau', D.1997, p185; Virginie Saint-James, 'Réflexions sur la dignité de l'être humain en tant que concept juridique du droit français', D.1997, p 61; Hugues Moutouh, 'La dignité de l'homme en droit' (1999) revue du droit public p 159; Benoît Jorion,' La dignité de la personne humaine ou la difficile insertion d'une règle morale dans le droit positif, id, p 157; Gridel, loc. cit., n 143 above. For the constitutional case law see Conseil constitutionnel, Decision no 94–343/344, 27 July 1994, p 1000, at § 2, p 101; for the administrative case law Conseil d'Etat, *Commune de Morsang sur Orge*, 27 October 1995, p 372, concl Frydman. I commented on this decision in (1996) Public Law 166.

the circumstances it held that the injunction to publish the statement mentioned above was the minima infringement of freedom of expression.[163]

Stage four: the Conseil d'Etat and the other administrative courts

In a 1980 decision the Conseil d'Etat, France's supreme court for administrative law, held that respect for private life and its intimacy were a fundamental liberty. It quoted Article 9 of the Civil Code.[164] Since then a number of decisions have adjudicated on the legality of administrative acts in cases relating to intrusion into private life. The main domains are, so far, access to public documents[165] and the computerized gathering and processing of personal data.[166]

Stage five: the right to privacy as a constitutional right

The right to privacy is not mentioned in the 1789 Declaration of the Rights of Man and the Citizen, the Preamble of the 1946 Constitution or the 1958 Constitution. It might be relevant to comment on the way by which such a right was eventually affirmed as a constitutionally protected one. From the 1970s on the Conseil constitutionnel had in front of it a triple heritage it could not ignore: that of Article 9 of the Civil Code and of the case law of the civil courts, that of the case law of the Conseil d'Etat, and that of the European Court of Human Rights on Article 8 ECHR. The affirmation of the constitutional standing of the right to privacy came in several stages. In 1977 the Conseil constitutionnel held unconstitutional a statute allowing the police to search cars in streets when the owner or the driver were present, in view of the wide scope of the powers of the police and of the vagueness of the wording of the statute.[167] It held that it constituted a breach 'of the essential principles on which the protection of individual freedom is based'. Some commentators thought that this decision, combined with those which followed[168] could be read as an implicit recognition of the constitutional value of the right to privacy. The second stage was exterior to the Conseil

---

[163] *Hachette Fililipacchi associés v France*, 14 June 2007.

[164] February, 1980, *Confédération syndicale des familles et Fédération nationale Ecole et famille*, p 727.

[165] Under Art 6.II the statute of 17 July 1978, revised in 2001 and in 2005, public documents relating to the confidentiality of private life ('le secret de la vie privée') may be communicated only to person concerned. The same clause applies to medical files. See, for a police file, Conseil d'Etat, 16 March 1998, *Mme Luki*; for the medical files, id, 31 January 1996, *Mme Lepelletier;* Nancy Administrative court of appeal, 30 May 2002, *Centre hospitalier général Maillot*; for a CV, Conseil d'Etat, 30 January 1995, *Ministre de l'éducation nationale c Guigne*; id, 14 June 1995, *M Seidel*; id, 6 December 1993, *Mme Laidin*.

[166] Conseil d'Etat, 30 December 1998, *Syndicat national des personnels de l'éducation surveillée*; id, 12 March 1982, *Confédération générale du travail*, concl Dondoux, AJDA.12982.541; RDP.1982.1967, note Auby.

[167] Conseil constitutionnel, decision no 76–75-DC, 12 January 1977, p33; cf L Favoreu and Loïc Philip, *Les grandes décisions du Conseil constitutionnel* (Paris, Dalloz, 13th edn,2005), p 334.

[168] Decision no 84–172 DC, 26 July 1984, p 58, at p 60; decision no 84–181 DC 10–11 October 1984, p 78, at p 83. For comments see J Rivero in *La Déclaration des droits de l'homme et du citoyen et la jurisprudence. Colloque des 25 et 26 mai 1989 au Conseil constututionnel* (Paris,

constitutionnel. In 1993 an official Report on the revision of the Constitution recommended that the right to respect of privacy and of the dignity of the individual be mentioned in the Constitution.[169] The next stage took place two years later. In a 1995 decision on a statute allowing CCTV the Conseil constitutionnel held, for the first time, that the infringement of the right to respect for private life may constitute a breach of individual freedom.[170] The final stage took place in 1997 and 1999 when the Conseil constitutionnel affirmed clearly that the right to respect for private life was based on Article 2 of the 1789 Declaration on the right to individual freedom.[171] The same method was used by the US Supreme Court in 1965 in *Griswold v Connecticut*.[172]

This case law has been confirmed[173] and has led the Conseil constitutionnel to review strictly statutes relating to personal data.[174]

Privacy as an autonomous right enjoying constitutional protection: (2) Germany

The case of Germany is of particular interest. A strong constitutional affirmation of three rights of equal value led to the judicial affirmation of personality rights and to balancing the right to privacy with that of freedom of expression.[175]

Presses universitaires de France,1989) p 79; Pierre Kayser, 'Le Conseil constitutionnel protecteur du secret de la vie privée à l'égard des lois', *Mélanges Raynaud* (Paris, 1985) p 330.

[169] Comité consultatif pour la révision de la Constitution, *Propositions pour une révision de la Constitution* (Paris, La Documentation française,1993) p 128.

[170] Decision no 94–352 DC, 18 January 1995, p 170, at § 3, pp 171–172.

[171] Decision no 97–389, 22 April 1997, p 45,at § 44, p 55; decision no 99–416, 23 July 1999, p 100, at § 45, p 110. On the case law of the Conseil constitutionnel on privacy see Marthe Fatin-Rouge Stefanini, 'Constitution et secret de la vie privée. France' (2000) XVI Annuaire international de justice constitutionnelle, p 259.

[172] 381 US 479, 85 S Ct 1678.

[173] Decision no 2004–492 DC, 2 March 2004, p 66, at § 75 and 76–81.

[174] Decisions no 98–405 DC, 29 December 1998, p 236; no 99–422 DC, 21 December 1999, p 143, no 99–419, 9 November 1999, p 116; no 2003–467 DC, 13 March 2003, p 211; no 2004–504 DC, 12 August 2004, p 153, at § 5,7 and 8, pp 155–156.

[175] Kurt Sontheimer, ' Principles of Human Dignity in the Federal Republic', in Paul Kirchhof and Donald P Kommers (eds), *Germany and Its Basic Law. Past, Present and Future. A German-American Symposium* (Baden-Baden, Nomos, 1993), p 213; Donald P Kommers, *The Constitutional Jurisprudence of the Federal Republic of Germany*, 2nd edn (Durham and London, Duke University Press, 1997), chs 7 and 8 ; John Craig and Nico Nolte, 'Privacy and Free Speech in Germany and Canada: Lessons for an English Privacy Tort' (1998) 2 EHRLR; Donald P Kommers (ed), *Fifty years of German Basic Law: The New Departure for Germany*, Conference Report, American Institute for contemporary German Studies, The John Hopkins University (1999);Basil Markesinis, 'Privacy, Freedom of Expression and the Horizontal Effect of the Human Rights Bill: lessons from Germany' (1999) 115 LQR 47; Constanze Grewe, 'La protection de la vie privée en droit allemand', (2000) XVI *Annuaire international de justice constitutionnelle* 135; Basil Markesinis et al, loc. cit.; Jackie Jones, 'Common Constitutional Traditions': Can the Meaning of Human Dignity under German Law Guide the European Court of Justice?' (2004) PL 167; Kai Möller, 'On Treating Persons as ends: The German Aviation Security Act and the Federal Constitutional Court' (2007) PL 457.

A strong constitutional affirmation of three rights of equal value

The first one is human dignity. Under Article 1(1) of the Constitution: 'Human dignity shall be inviolable. To respect and protect it shall be the duty of all state authority'. The second right is the right to one's personality. Under Article 2(1): 'Every person shall have the right to the free development of his personality insofar as he does not violate the rights of others or offend the constitutional order or the moral law'. The third right is freedom of expression. Under Article 5:

(1) Every person shall have the right freely to express and disseminate his opinions by speech, writing, and pictures and freely to inform himself from generally accessible sources. Freedom of the press and freedom of reporting by means of broadcasts and films are guaranteed. There shall be no censorship.
(2) These rights find their limits in the provisions of the general laws, the provisions of laws for the protection of young persons and in the right to personal honour.

The judicial affirmation of personality rights

On the basis of Articles 1(1) and 2(1) the German courts have progressively affirmed the scope and meaning of personality rights.[176]In the *Princess Soraya* case[177] the Constitutional Court went to great lengths to explain why the courts could wait for legislative regulation and had to step in in order to protect personality rights, here privacy.

Balancing competing rights and values: personality rights and freedom of expression

German courts have been balancing competing rights and values in carefully reasoned judgments. In *Lebach* it justified the prohibition to broadcast a play relating to a crime that had taken place years ago, using the name of its author, who was going to be released from prison very soon, and his personality. The Court based its decision on the protection of this individual's right of personality as well as his own and society's interest in his rehabilitation.[178]

As to privacy the courts first attempted to define and distinguish several spheres in a person's life and activities: the public sphere, the social one, the private one, the confidential one, and the intimate one, leading to different degrees of protection

---

[176] See the *Schacht case*, BGH 13334, in which the German Supreme Court interpreted civil law (§ 823 of the Civil Code on liability in the context of constitutional values: the right of personality is one of the rights mentioned at Art 823; the *Divorce Records* case 27 BVerfGE 344 (1970), in Kommers, *The Constitutional Jurisprudence...*, op. cit. p 327, according to which the wholesale transmission, by a civil court, of a divorce file to a civil service disciplinary board is a breach or privacy; the 2006 decision of the Constitutional Court invalidating a clause of a statute empowering the Defence Minister to order to shoot down a hijacked plane carrying passengers if it could crash on a city or on nuclear plant (see Möller, loc. cit.).
[177] 34 BVerfGE 269 (1973), in Kommers, *The Constitutional Jurisprudence...*, op. cit. p 124.
[178] *Lebach* BVerfGE 202 (1973).

of privacy.[179] In the same vein and not without some excessive refinement, it tried to distinguish, among public figures ('Personen der Zeitgeschichte'), 'permanent' and 'occasional' ones. They took generally into account a number of factors such as the contribution of the information to a general debate, the way in which it had been obtained, the extent of its dissemination, the circumstances of time and place, and the attitude of the claimant. The Supreme Court held that privacy may, in certain circumstances, be protected in public places.[180] In the *Von Hannover* case the German courts, including the Constitutional Court[181] went a bridge too far in their characterization of some public figures as 'figures of contemporary society par excellence' (Eine 'absolute Person der Zetgeschichte') as to the conditions in which privacy could be protected in public places and on the value of the information published for the public. This led to the unanimous decision of the European Court of Human Rights to hold Germany in breach of Article 8 ECHR, which confirms the firm jurisprudential policy of the Court to take privacy seriously.[182] The decision led the German Constitutional Court to open a debate on the extent of the consequences of such rulings for the German legal order.[183] Such a debate is of direct and lasting relevance for the courts of all State Parties to the ECHR.

Privacy as a personality right

In France as well as in Germany the basis of the constitutional, legislative, and judicial affirmation of a right to privacy was the notion of personality rights, which can be found in the works of such jurists and lawyers as, among many others, Gierke, Gény, and Perreau. In addition, from the mid-20th century on political and social events and trends, such as the experience of the Nazi and communist totalitarian regimes, new issues in bioethics, the development of bioethical issues, new information technologies, etc, have given immediate relevance to this legal category.

Personality rights *are* rights, that is legitimate interests accompanied by a remedy. They have a central purpose. Their affirmation aims at the protection of the

[179] See Markesinis et al, loc. cit., p 188 ff.
[180] BGH 19 December 1995.
[181] BVerfGE 101, 361 (15 December 1999); (1999) 10 BHRC 131.
[182] *Von Hannover v Germany* (2003) EHRR 41; (2004) 16 BHRC 545; see MA Sanderson 'Is *Von Hannover v Germany* a Step Backward for the Substantive Analysis of Speech and Privacy Interests?' (2004) 6 EHRLR 631; Nicolas Nohlen, note, (2006) 100 AJIL 196.
[183] See BVerfGE 111307, 14 October 2004, the Görgülü case; (2004) 25 HRLJ 99; S Beljin, *'Bundesverfassungsgericht on the Status of the European Convention of Human Rights and ECHR Decisions in the German Legal Order. Decision of 14 October 2004'*, (2005) 1 European Constitutional Law Review 553. The dicta of the Court were quickly criticized by the then President of the European Court of Human Rights, Luzius Wildhaber, in an interview published by Der Spiegel on 15 November 2004, p 50. See also the remarks of the President of the German Constitutional Court, Dr Papier, 'Execution and Effects of the European Court of Human Rights From the Perspective of German National Courts' (2006) 27 HRLJ 1.

person as such, of his integrity, identity, autonomy, and dignity.[184] Such rights relate to the individual, but their basis is not a kind of legal individualism. The protection they afford is vital for society itself, and not only for the individuals concerned. There is no complete and closed list of personality rights. They include, for example, the right to personal honour (libel law), the right to privacy, the protection of human dignity, aspects of the law of confidence (in French law the protection of 'secret professionnel'), the presumption of innocence, the right to one's image.

On the possible evolution of the English law of privacy

The English law on privacy has changed, due to the awareness, by the courts, of the necessity to offer protection to some aspects of it, the existence of the HRA,[185] and the case law of the European Court of Human Rights. Will it continue to change and, if so, under which influence and in which directions? I would certainly not presume to be bold enough to answer fully these questions. What follows is an attempt to formulate some tentative and provisional hypotheses.

A preliminary questions arises: does the present state of the law satisfy the prerequisites of the rule of law as analysed recently by Lord Bingham?[186] Is it, to begin with, 'accessible and so far as possible intelligible, clear and predictable'?[187] The case law of the European Court of Human Rights on the meaning of the terms 'prescribed by law' may guide an answer to that question and to future decisions of the Court. In the absence of a new legislation the HRA, combined with the case law of the Court in Strasbourg, will probably be the main exterior influence. According to the DCA's 2006 Report on the implementation of the HRA '...the common law recognises similar rights to those found in the European Convention on Human Rights...The courts have increasingly been prepared to recognise "common law constitutional rights" similar in content to those found in the ECHR'.[188]

What the ECHR requires is that the rights guaranteed by Article 8 be implemented by the law and practice of the State Parties. How this is done belongs to them, as long as the conditions set in the case law are fulfilled as to the 'quality' of the law, whether it is contained in statutes or in the case law. Since *Peck*, *von Hannover*, and *Erignac* the writing is on the wall: privacy, *lato sensu*, is to be

---

[184] David Feldman, 'Human dignity as a legal value' (1999) PL 682; David Kretzmer and Eckhart Klein (eds), *The concept of dignity in human rights discourse*, (The Hague and New York, Kluwer Law International, 2002); Bloustein, loc. cit. n 54.

[185] On the influence of the HRA on human rights in Britain see Department of Constitutional Affairs, *Review of the implementation of the Human Rights Act*, DCA, 38/06.

[186] Lord Bingham, ' The Rule of law' (2007) 66(1) CLJ 69.   [187] Id, at p 69.

[188] *Review of the implementation...*, op. cit., at § 11. The Report quotes *A (no 2) v Home Secretary* (2005) 3 WLR 1249, on the prohibition, for SIAC and courts, to receive evidence based on torture. See also the dictum of Laws LJ 'the common law has come to recognize and endorse the notion of constitutional, or fundamental rights' in *International Transport Roth GmbH v Secretary of State for the Home* Department (2002) EWCA Civ 158; (2003) QB 728, at 71.

protected, irrespective of the identity of the author of the infringement. The recent decision in *Dickson v UK* is an apt illustration of this determination: Dickson had been sentenced to jail for life for murder. He and his wife asked to use artificial insemination in order to have a child, since this was, in the circumstances, the only available means. The Administration refused. He brought an action before the European Court of Human Rights for breach of Articles 8 and 12 ECHR. A first judgment rejected his application: the refusal was neither arbitrary nor unreasonable, in view of the interest of the child, the long absence of the father, and the lack of immediate help available to the mother. The Grand Chamber dissented and held that the refusal was a breach of Article 8 ECHR.[189] In many of the previous cases in which the Court held the UK in breach of Article 8 ECHR the law was changed as a consequence.[190]

Will the courts continue to use the law of confidence in privacy cases or will they, in cases where it cannot manifestly be used, adopt another tool in order to protect privacy rights? If not a right to privacy, which instrument? Will the notion of personality rights, already present in the legal literature, be used in order to create a new remedy?

The ultimate issue is that of law-making by judges, and of the conditions and limits of the exercise of such a power. One critical dimension of it is that of the legal tools or instruments available to the courts. One thing is clear here. On the right to privacy two new instruments exist: a legislative one, the HRA, and, through it, the ECHR and the relevant case law of the European Court of Human Rights. The consequence is that, as in other areas covered by EU law or the ECHR, this change of the legal context is bound to lead, notwithstanding official declarations, to a widening of the powers of the courts and of the scope of their review, irrespective of the nature of the actors or that of the decisions. One essential aspect of it is the affirmation of principles of law, what Hart calls 'some acceptable general principle as a reasoned basis for decision'.[191] In his 1993 article 'English judges as law makers'[192] Anthony Lester, discussing the case law after *Kaye* and *Malone* and quoting the dicta of Megarry, V-C in the former and of Bingham LJ in the latter, suggested that 'this was too narrow a view of the judicial function of developing common law principles in accordance with contemporary and ethical values and social needs... The existing common law principles could be developed to protect personal privacy'.[193] He wrote that in *Kaye* 'the Court of Appeal could have developed a right of privacy, using the line of cases on the right of confidentiality...'.[194]

Will such a new principle emerge one day? Foreign commentators shall continue to observe closely what happens.

---

[189] European Court of Human, Rights, Grand Chamber, 4 December 2007, *Dickson v UK*.

[190] See, in addition to *Malone*, *Dudgeon v UK*, 45 4 EHRR 149 (homosexuality in Ulster); *Lustig-Prean and Beckett v UK* (homosexuals in the army); *Goodwin and I v UK* (2002); and *Grant v UK* (2006), both on homosexuals. See n 94 above.

[191] HLA Hart, *The concept of Law* (1961, Clarendon Press, Oxford) p 200.

[192] N 60 above.   [193] At pp 285–6.   [194] Id at p 284.

5

National Courts and the International Court of Justice*

Rosalyn Higgins

Issues relating to the relationship between national courts and the International Court of Justice (ICJ) arise in two broad sets of circumstances. The first is the use that national courts make of judgments of the ICJ on various points of international law; the second is the position in which a national court may find itself when the ICJ has delivered a judgment directed at the particular state of the national court concerned.

I shall address each of these circumstances in turn.

It is obvious that the use national courts choose to make of judgments of the ICJ on points of international law depends in significant part upon the status of international law in the country concerned. The International Court, being the principal judicial organ[1] of the United Nations, is the first source[2] to which it may be expected that a national court will turn if it is called upon to determine a matter of customary international law. If the ICJ has already pronounced upon the legal issue at hand, a national court is likely to be satisfied that it has available to it the right answer in law, and to look no further. It is not that the judgments of the International Court are specified in Article 38 of its Statute to be hierarchically superior to other sources of international law. Nor is it that national laws specify that customary international law is to be applied by domestic courts by reliance upon the pronouncements of the ICJ. It is rather a reflection of the

---

* While this essay has been prepared for this tribute to Lord Bingham, I have also drawn upon 'Dualism in the Face of a Changing Legal Culture', *Judicial Review in International Perspective, Liber Amicorum in Honour of Lord Slynn of Hadley*, Vol II, (eds Andenas and Fairgrieve) (2000), 9–22; 'The Concept of "The State": Variable Geometry and Dualist Perceptions', *The International Legal System in quest of Equity and Universality, Liber Amicorum Georges Abi-Saab*, (eds L Boisson de Chazournes and V Gowlland-Debbas) (2001), pp 547–561; the chapter on 'International Law' in *The Judicial House of Lords* (eds Blom-Cooper and Drewry) (forthcoming); and the keynote address, 'The Changing Position of Domestic Courts in the International Legal Order', I delivered at the First International Law in Domestic Courts Colloquium, The Hague, 17 March 2008.

[1] Art 92 United Nations Charter.
[2] Art 38 of the Statute of the International Court conveniently gathers the classic sources of international law.

International Court's status as the most senior of the international courts and tribunals, being a main organ of the United Nations[3] and its designated principal judicial organ.

If the International Court has not pronounced upon the point in issue, then the national court will need to grapple with it, assessing (with the assistance of counsel) other relevant sources of international law bearing on the matter.

The extent to which a national court will be prepared to address issues of international law—whether by relying on relevant pronouncements of the International Court or otherwise—will depend on many factors. All legal systems acknowledge customary international law as part of the law of the land. But each state determines, as a matter of national law, the priority which customary international law is to be accorded in the face of conflicting constitutional, or statutory, requirements. So also is the place and status of international treaty law as a matter regulated by the domestic legal system.

It has long been assumed that a particularly pertinent factor will be whether the state concerned adheres to the legal theory of dualism or monism. And indeed, the starting point of the relationship between international law and domestic law lies in the legal theories of dualism, and monism: '*Dualism*...stresses that the rules of the systems of international law and municipal law exist separately and cannot purport to have an effect on, or overrule, the other'.[4] According to this theory, the applicability of international law within the domestic legal system is by courtesy of the state as an act of sovereign decision-making. The dualist approach is obviously the one favoured by legal positivists, for whom the authority of the state is paramount.[5] The *monist* theory, by contrast, insists upon a unitary view of all law, including international law and the other strands of domestic law.[6]

It is thus a truism to say that the monist-dualist dichotomy necessarily influences the way national courts treat issues of international law. But it is also an overstatement. It is an overstatement for two reasons: first, notwithstanding the potential of a monist state for easy receipt of international law into the domestic system, without further domestic enactment being necessary, there still remains the question of how familiar the judges are, even within that monist legal system, with the substance of international law. If counsel and the Bench are not readily conversant with international legal issues, indeed if they do not immediately see whether there *is* an international law issue within an ostensibly domestic case, then the judgment will still be essentially insular. Conversely, although dualism presents certain hurdles to the easy receipt of international law, a great deal can still be achieved if there is the institutional and moral desire to do. And *that* is a matter of legal culture.

---

[3] Art 7, United Nations Charter.

[4] M Shaw, *International Law*, (4th edn, 2003), p 100.

[5] Shaw, Ibid, referring especially to Triepel, *Völkerrecht und Landesrecht* (Berlin, 1899); Anzilotti, *Corso di Diritto Internazionale*, (3rd edn, 1928), pp 43 et seq and R Jennings and A Watts, *Oppenheim International Law* (9th edn, 1992), at p 55.

[6] Shaw, Ibid, pp 101 ff.

It is frequently asserted that common law countries accept the dualist theory while civil law countries are more monist in their approach. That, too, is an oversimplification. Invariably, common law countries accept that general international law is part and parcel of the law of the land, its rules applicable like any others. However, common law countries invariably require something more to be done before international law *treaty* obligations receive a comparable treatment in the domestic courts. Exactly what that 'something more' comprises varies from common law jurisdiction to common law jurisdiction, even if broad parameters of common law practice in the matter are rather well defined.[7] However, not all civil law countries are monist in their approach; often the matter is more complicated and subtle, and reliance on these categories is frequently not helpful. For example, the system in Germany could be described as dualist insofar as treaties are concerned, but is more monist in character when it comes to the status accorded to general international law.[8]

The extent to which national courts will rely on findings of the ICJ may turn not so much on purported monist/dualist, common law/civil law distinctions, but rather on the role that a written constitution plays in the legal life of the country. Thus, it may be the constitution itself which states that general international law is to be applied. Such issues, and any pronouncements the ICJ may have made on them, are thus viewed by courts and litigants alike as being essentially constitutional law matters. Interpretation of general international law will not be engaged in by the lower courts, but is to be reserved to the constitutional court.[9]

The use of the judicial findings of the ICJ, within domestic legal systems, either directly or under the 'authority' of constitutional law, is a contemporary reality. This is so notwithstanding that Article 59 of the Court's Statute provides that: 'The decision of the Court has no binding force except between the parties and in respect of that particular case.' It has long been recognized, however, that while this is a necessary provision (given that the jurisdiction of the court is based on consent), there are other relevant considerations at play. The first is that the court will always seek consistency through time in its own jurisprudence; the

---

[7] For a survey, see Higgins (UK) and Jackson (USA) (being chapters found respectively in F Jacobs and S Roberts (eds), *The Effect of Treaties in Domestic Law* (1987)).

[8] Art 25 of the Basic Law of the Federal Republic of Germany, 1949 (as amended in 2006): 'The general rules of international law shall be an integral part of federal law. They shall take precedence over the laws and directly create rights and duties for the inhabitants of the federal territory.' See also n 9 below.

[9] This is the situation in Germany. Art 100(2) of the Basic Law provides: 'If, in the course of litigation, doubts arise whether a rule of international law is an integral part of federal law and whether it directly creates rights and duties for the individual (Article 25), the court shall obtain a decision from the Federal Constitutional Court.' By contrast, treaties (once incorporated into German law by federal legislation in accordance with Art 59(2) of the Basic Law) may be interpreted by all courts, but may in some circumstances take on the character of a 'constitutional' matter before the Constitutional Court, such as the recent decision of the Constitutional Court in the consolidated cases involving the interpretation of the Vienna Convention on Consular Relations: BVerfG, 2 BvR 2115/01 of 19 September 2006.

second is that if in a case between states C and D an issue identical to that it has pronounced on already in a case between states A and B, the very same judicial answer will be given. That is clearly the way government understands things, and it is taken as a given by national courts when relying on the decisions or *dicta* of the International Court.

All of the above comments relate to customary international law. So far as treaties in domestic courts are concerned, their place and status in the national law concerned is a matter to be regulated by each country. Some countries treat ratified treaties as being part of the law of the land, and indeed may even given them primacy over statutory law and perhaps even a privileged status under constitutional law.[10] For others, some categories of treaties will be 'self executing' under domestic law, though others will require domestic enactment before their terms will be regarded as binding by the natural courts concerned.[11] For yet others, domestic incorporation in one form or another is required before a treaty will be regarded as part of the law of the land.[12]

What use may be made of a treaty that, in a state of this last category, is not domestically incorporated, is itself a matter of domestic law. And perceptions on this topic, too, may change through time. This is strikingly so in the United Kingdom. In 1967 the Court of Appeal in the *Salomon* case (*Salomon v Customs and Excise Commissioners* [1967] 2 QB 116) had revealed divided views on the circumstances in which an unincorporated foreign convention could be looked at. Lord Denning, MR, took a very robust approach, emphasizing the need to make sure the United Kingdom was in conformity with international law:

I am confirmed in my view by looking at the international convention which preceded the Act of 1952...I think we are entitled to look at it, because it is an instrument which is binding in international law: and we ought always to interpret our statutes so as to be in conformity with international law. Our statute does not in terms incorporate the convention, nor refer to it. But that does not matter. We can look at it.

However, Lord Diplock insisted that the sovereign power extends also to breaking treaties, so no such presumption was to be had.

The development in judicial attitudes to the question of what reference may be made to non-incorporated treaties over the last 25 years has occurred largely in relation to the European Convention on Human Rights, before the Human Rights Act of 1998. But the developments in that context have undeniably had

---

[10] The Constitution of the Russian Federation provides in Art 15(4): 'Generally recognized principles and norms of international law as well as international agreements of the Russian Federation shall be a constituent part of its legal system. If an international agreement of the Russian Federation establishes rules which differ from those stipulated by law the rules of the international agreement shall apply.'

[11] This is the situation in the United States. See JH Jackson, 'United States' in F Jacobs and S Roberts (eds), *The Effect of Treaties in Domestic Law* (1987), ch 8, especially pp 147–156.

[12] The United Kingdom is an example of such a system. See R Higgins, 'United Kingdom' in F Jacobs and S Roberts (eds) *The Effect of Treaties in Domestic Law* (1987), ch 7, especially pp 126–130.

their knock-on effect in issues relating to non-incorporation of other sorts of treaties. Looking back, the 1970s may be seen as characterized by inconsistent approaches. Differing views were offered in the *Spycatcher* case (*AG v Guardian Newspapers Ltd (No 2)* [1990] 1 AC 109) and in the *Brind* case (*R v Home Secretary ex p Brind* [1991] 1 AC 696 at 748).

This issue was one of several at the heart of the important International Tin Council litigation. Although the founding treaty—to which the United Kingdom was a party—was not incorporated into English law, other treaty instruments relating to its headquarters and privileges and immunities were the subject of enabling Orders in Council. The extent to which these could be interpreted by reference to the constituting treaty had been a central element in all the very many cases going through different English courts. Lord Templeman, who gave the leading speech in the House of Lords, stated that a non-incorporated treaty was '...outside the purview of the Court not only because it is made in the conduct of foreign relations, which are a prerogative of the Crown, but also because, as a source of rights and obligations, it is irrelevant'.[13] This can be contrasted with the approach of Kerr LJ in the same case in the Court of Appeal.[14] In a powerful analysis and review of the English case law he had insisted that English courts, faced with unincorporated treaties, were not precluded from use of them so long as the line was drawn to ensure that any private rights claimed were not *dependent* upon the treaty concerned.

Today the Law Lords, under the leadership of Lord Bingham, seem to have lost interest in dwelling upon whether treaties, or decisions passed under treaties, were incorporated into English law. In *Kuwait Airways Corporation v Iraqi Airways Company* [2002] 2 AC 883, the Lords simply dealt with the substantive issues rather than dwell upon whether particular Security Council resolutions were or were not part of English law. What mattered was the reality that the United Kingdom was bound by these resolutions by virtue of Article 25 of the Charter.

What must always be recalled is that while the use that may be made by a national court of the substantive content of treaty is a matter of domestic law, the rules relating to interpretation of treaties are, for the most part, a matter of customary international law. The 1969 Vienna Convention on the Law of the Treaties, frequently invoked in international and national courts alike, contains provisions that have been clearly stated by the ICJ to reflect customary international law.[15] And recourse to this convention, for a variety of treaty interpretation issues, has been increasingly had in the English courts.[16]

******

---

[13] *JH Rayner v Dept of Trade* [1990] 2 AC 418, at 500.

[14] [1989] ch 72.   [15] Arts 31 and 32.

[16] The use of *travaux préparatoires*: *Dennis v Johnson* [1979] AC 24, *Fothergill v Monarch Airlines* [1980] 3 WLR 209; object and purpose (autonomous interpretation): *Sidhu v British Airways PLC* [1997] AC 430; *Morris v KLM Royal Dutch Airlines* [2002] AC 6278.

As international law is not foreign law, it is not to be explained to the Bench by experts in foreign law. It is to be deployed by counsel. For this task, in the United Kingdom, the service of barristers who have a particular expertise in international law (perhaps as University Professors in the subject) is often sought. But the great importance for courts, both in discerning that there *is* an international law issue, and in getting that issue right (especially if there has been no clear determination on the point by the ICJ), suggests that international law should be a compulsory element in the courses for admission to the Bar if such a course had not been taken at university.

There is one field, in particular, in which national courts not only look at what the ICJ has said, but themselves contribute to any such determinations.

Domestic courts have long been acknowledged as playing a very particular role in the field of immunities. Typically, when one state believes itself, or a high official, to be immune from the jurisdiction of the courts of another state, it challenges the purported exercise of that jurisdiction in the courts of the forum state. This has created a substantial body of national jurisprudence on this aspect of international law. The 'Oxford Reports on International Law' database, covering the period from 2000 to the present day, contains 59 cases concerning immunities in 20 jurisdictions, ranging from Botswana to Finland to Sierra Leone.[17]

The ICJ rarely sees such immunity cases—but in 2001 the Democratic Republic of the Congo came directly to the ICJ seeking a declaration that the actions of Belgian authorities had violated the customary international law of immunities as regards a senior government official. In spring 2008 the Court was concluding its deliberation on the case Djibouti brought against France, largely concerning mutual criminal assistance questions under treaty law, but also raising interesting points in immunity law.[18]

In the *Arrest Warrant* case (*DRC v Belgium*), at issue was the inviolability of an incumbent Minister of Foreign Affairs from criminal jurisdiction under customary international law. It was put to the Court that international law now clearly precludes immunity for the most grave offences. It was to national courts, and national legislatures, that the International Court turned to illuminate the position in customary international law as it related to immunities in national courts, making extensive use of the state practice that existed at that time. The judgment referred in particular to the judgments rendered by the House of Lords in the UK and by the *Cour de cassation* in France in the *Pinochet* and *Qaddafi* cases respectively. The state practice of the time, including the *Bouterse* case of the Court of Appeal of Amsterdam, the *Pinochet* cases in the House of Lords, the *Nulyarimma* and *Polyukhovich* cases in the Australian High Court, the *Cvjetkovic*

---

[17] <http://ildc.oxfordlawreports.com/>. The database was initiated by the Amsterdam Centre for International Law.

[18] *Certain Questions of Mutual Assistance in Criminal Matters (Djibouti v France)*, Judgment, *ICJ Reports 2008*.

case in the Austrian Supreme Court, the *in re Javor, Munyeshyaka* and *Qaddafi* cases in the French *Cour d'appel*, and US cases brought under the Alien Tort Claims Act, did not suggest that there existed any form of exception in general international law to the rule according immunity from criminal jurisdiction to incumbent Ministers for Foreign Affairs, even where they are suspected of having committed war crimes or crimes against humanity.[19]

In 2008 Spain's *Audiencia Nacional*, referring to the *Arrest Warrant* case and national judgments in Germany and Belgium, concluded that the Spanish courts did not have jurisdiction to prosecute President Kagame of Rwanda for charges of genocide, crimes against humanity, war crimes, and terrorist acts.[20] The Italian Court of Cassation held in a 2004 Judgment that the immunity granted under customary international law to acting heads of state, heads of government, and ministers for foreign affairs did not extend (and could not be applied by analogy) to individuals who held such offices within entities that did not have the status of a sovereign state, such states within a federation (in that case, the immunity of the President of Montenegro was at issue).[21] In two other cases, the Bow Street Magistrate's Court held that a Defence Minister of Israel and the Minister for Commerce and International Trade of China on special mission, were entitled to immunity, and arrest warrants could not be issued against them.[22] The relationship between the ICJ and national courts in the field of immunity law is clearly symbiotic.

The United States Court of Appeals for the Second Circuit has recently had to address the question of whether a detained foreign national who was not informed of his right under the Article 36 of the Vienna Convention to have his consul notified, could succeed in a damages action against the state of New York.[23] The starting point of the leading opinion was that 'respectful consideration' was owed to the ICJ, but only to the extent that its arguments are persuasive. *Skidmore v Swift & Co*, 323 US 134 (1944) and *Christensen v Harris County*, 529 US 576 (2000) were cited to this effect. The Court of Appeals then proceeded to state that 'we do not find the views of the ICJ expressed in *Avena* and *La Grand* to be persuasive in the instant case'.

---

[19] *Arrest Warrant of 11 April 2000 (Democratic Republic of the Congo v Belgium)*, Judgment, *ICJ Reports 2002*, p 24.

[20] Spain, *Audiencia Nactional*, Auto del Juzgado Central de Instruccion No 4, 6 February 2008, pp 151–157. It did, however, confirm the criminal charges against high-ranking military commanders in office, including the incumbent Chief of Staff of the Rwandan Army without raising the question of their immunity: 157–181.

[21] Italy, Court of Cassation (Third Criminal Section), *Public Prosecutor (Tribunal of Naples) v Milo Djukanovic*, No 49666, Judgment of 28 December 2004.

[22] United Kingdom, District Court (Bow Street), *Re General Shaul Mofaz*, Judgment of 12 February 2004, reproduced in ICLQ, Vol 53, 2004, pp 771–773; *Re Bo Xilai*, Judgment of 8 November 2005, ILR Vol 128, pp 713–715 (the fact that the Minister was a member of a special mission was also important in the latter case).

[23] *Mora v People of the State of NY*, Docket No 06–0341-pr, decided 24 April 2008.

It is not clear why the Court should be berated for having held that it was 'clear that rights had been conferred directly upon individuals that can be vindicated in a damages action', when the Court had said no such thing. Indeed the Court of Appeals seems to have understood that what the ICJ did say as to Article 36(1)(b) conferring individual rights was in the context of resolving the very different question of the international law of diplomatic protection. It held that this individual right could be asserted *by the national state* in ICJ, given the 'mixed' character of these clauses of the Convention.

It would have sufficed for the Court of Appeals' Opinion to have noted (as it does in part) that Article 36 creates individual rights that can be asserted by the national state in the ICJ, and that this is not necessarily inconsistent with a finding that such a right cannot be vindicated in a damages action court before the US Court of Appeals.

******

A court that finds itself embroiled in litigation concerning the implementation of an ICJ Judgment directed *at that very state* will undoubtedly find itself in a complex legal situation. Much will depend upon exactly what has been said, in what circumstances by the International Court; and factors relating to the national law, the structures of the state, and the prevailing legal culture, will have their importance, too.

In the Request for an Advisory Opinion transmitted to the International Court from the Economic and Social Council on 5 August 1988, the acts of the Malaysian courts were themselves implicated in the very question of whether Malaysia had or had not acted in conformity with its international legal obligations. The Economic and Social Council adopted a decision,[24] paragraph 1 of which reads as follows:

Requests on a priority basis, pursuant to Article 96, paragraph 2, of the Charter of the United Nations and in accordance with General Assembly resolution 89 (1), an advisory opinion from the International Court of Justice on the legal question of the applicability of Article VI, section 22, of the Convention on the Privileges and Immunities of the United Nations in the case of Dato Param Cumaraswamy as Special Rapporteur of the Commission on Human Rights on the independence of judges and lawyers, taking into account the circumstances set out in paragraphs 1 to 15 of the note by the Secretary-General, and on the legal obligations of Malaysia in this case.

Among the main issues the Court had to consider in the context of the question ('the legal obligations of Malaysia in this case') was the issue of the certification by the Secretary-General as to Mr Cumaraswamy's entitlement to immunity. The Court did not support the contention of the Secretary-General that such a

---

[24] 1998/297.

certification was determinative of the question of immunity for a national court. But it did find that it gave rise to a presumption. The failure of the Malaysian authorities to pass to its courts the certificate of the Secretary-General, and the filing of a certificate by the Minister of Foreign Affairs in terms that the Office of Legal Affairs of the UN had already suggested were incorrect, and without attaching the Secretary-General's certificate, thus constituted a violation of Article 105 of the Charter and of the General Convention on Privileges and Immunities.

This was a case in which the conduct of the legal authorities, the Foreign Secretary, and indeed the courts themselves, were all before the ICJ. The Court advised that:

According to a well-established rule of international law, the conduct of any organ of a State must be regarded as an act of that State. This rule, which is of a customary character, is reflected in Article 6 of the Draft Articles on State Responsibility adopted provisionally by the International Law Commission on first reading, which provides:
     'The conduct of an organ of the State shall be considered as an act of that State under international law, whether that organ belongs to the constituent, legislative, executive, judicial or other power, whether its functions are of an international or an internal character, and whether it holds a superior or a subordinated position in the organization of the State' (*Yearbook of the International Law Commission*, 1973, Vol II, p 193).[25]

This sustained the finding that the action and omissions of the Minister of Foreign Affairs constituted non-compliance by Malaysia with its international obligations.

Even more radically, the principle enunciated above regarding the conduct of state organs also had relevance for the acts of the Malaysian courts. In a novel departure, the Court reminded that 'the conduct of an organ of State—even an organ independent of the executive power—must be regarded as an act of that State'.[26]

It was a generally recognized principle of procedural law that questions of immunity are preliminary issues which must be expeditiously decided in *limine litis*.[27] The failure of the Malaysian courts to rule at the outset on the Special Rapporteur's immunity in effect nullified the absence of the immunity provisions of section 22(*b*) of the Special Convention. That, together with the taxing of costs to Mr Cumaraswamy while the question of immunity was still unresolved,

---

[25] *Difference Relating to Immunity from Legal Process of a Special Rapporteur of the Commission on Human Rights*, Advisory Opinion of 29 April 1999, *ICJ Reports 1999*.

[26] Ibid, para 63. See also the Court's *dictum* in the *Djibouti v France* case where it pointed out that a national court could engage the responsibility of its own state by failing to respect the immunity of an organ of a foreign state: 'The State which seeks to claim immunity for one of its State organs is expected to notify the authorities of the other State concerned. This would allow the court of the forum State to ensure that it does not fail to respect any entitlement to immunity and might thereby engage the responsibility of that State' (para 196).

[27] *Difference Relating to Immunity from Legal Process of a Special Rapporteur of the Commission on Human Rights*, Advisory Opinion of 29 April 1999, *ICJ Reports 1999*, para 2(b) of the *dispositif*.

entailed a failure by Malaysia to act in accordance with its obligations under international law.

In a *dispositif* which broke new ground in going behind 'the unitary veil of the State', the International Court determined, *inter alia*:

2 *(a)* That the Government of Malaysia had the obligation to inform the Malaysian courts of the finding of the Secretary-General that Dato Param Cumaraswamy was entitled to immunity from legal process;
   (b) that the Malaysian courts had the obligation to deal with the question of immunity from legal process as a preliminary issue to be expeditiously decided in *limine litis*.
   ...

4. That the Government of Malaysia has the obligation to communicate this Advisory Opinion to the Malaysian Courts, in order that Malaysia's international obligations be given effect and Dato Param Cumaraswamy's immunity be respected.

It will be seen that the International Court for the first time made determinations directly on the conduct of the courts of a state; and on the obligations of the executive in regard to the passing of information to the state. At the same time, the International Court has recognized that it is for the courts, assisted by the receipt of full information from the executive, to make their own determination on immunity, provided that this was done in *limine litis* and consistently with full consideration being given to the presumption that had already been explained.

As was clear from the speech of the Prime Minister of Malaysia to the General Assembly in September 1999, all this was not without its difficulties. But in due course all elements of the Court's findings were fully acted upon by Malaysia.[28]

The International Court enjoys a very high rate of compliance with its judgments from all kinds of states in all types of cases; a rate that compares favourably with that of any national court. Even in cases that have been bitterly fought and have a volatile history, such as *Qatar v Bahrain*[29] and *Libya/Chad*,[30] there has been an impressive commitment to implement the judgment once it is given.

But difficult compliance questions do occasionally arise and can involve the domestic courts of the state to whom the judgment was directed. In the *Avena* judgment of the ICJ in 2004,[31] the International Court had held that the US had violated the Vienna Convention in most of those cases put before it by Mexico through not informing the Mexican nationals of their right to have their consul notified of their arrest. The International Court in terms refused Mexico's request to set aside the sentences, stating that the remedy under the Convention

---

[28] The Court gave an Advisory Opinion, which while authoritative is technically not binding. At the same time, it was envisaged in the 1946 Convention on the Privileges and Immunities of the United Nations that disputes would be resolved by recourse to the ICJ for an advisory opinion (Art VIII).

[29] *Maritime Delimitation and Territorial Questions between Qatar and Bahrain (Qatar v Bahrain)*, Judgment, *ICJ Reports 2001*, p 40.

[30] *Territorial Dispute (Libyan Arab Jamahiriya/Chad)*, Judgment, *ICJ Reports 1994*, p 6.

[31] *Avena and Other Mexican Nationals (Mexico v United States of America)*, Judgment, *ICJ Reports 2004*, p 12.

was 'review and reconsideration' *by the US courts*, in the light of the ICJ's finding that the Convention had been violated. In any such review and reconsideration, a convicted person might, or might not, have his sentence changed or set aside. But that was a matter for the US courts; what was for the International Court was to determine that the Convention had been violated and to identify the remedy to be provided.

The Court of Criminal Appeals of the state of Oklahoma addressed the *Torres* case of 13 May 2004. Torres was one of the listed persons in the *Avena* case and he based his subsequent application for relief on the Court's judgment in that case. The Oklahoma Court of Criminal Appeals noted that the International Court had found that Torres's rights under the Vienna Convention were violated, 'and ordered the United States to review and reconsider Torres's conviction and sentence in the light of this treaty breach. This Court must determine how to apply that ruling'. As Judge Chapel makes clear, both the United States and Mexico are parties to the Consular Convention, and the United States had both proposed the Optional Protocol whereby disputes relating to it were to be settled by the International Court and 'was instrumental in drafting the Optional Protocol, was the first state to bring a case under its provision, [the *Tehran Hostages* case of 1979], and has consistently looked to the International Court of Justice for binding decisions in international treaty disputes, including those brought under the Vienna Convention'. He went on to observe that, 'the federal government's power to make treaties is independent of and superior to the power of the states'. Further:

Every State or federal court considering the Vienna Convention, for any reason, has agreed that it is binding on all jurisdictions within the United States, individual states, districts, territories... The United States voluntarily and legally entered into a treaty, a contract with over 100 other countries. The United States is bound by the terms of the treaty and the State of Oklahoma is obliged by virtue of the Supremacy Clause to give effect to the treaty... I am not suggesting that the International Court has jurisdiction over this Court—far from it... The issue of whether this Court must abide by that Court's [ICJ] opinion in the *Torres* case is not ours to determine. The United States Senate and the President have made that decision for us.[32]

—that is, by negotiating and ratifying the Vienna Convention.

Accordingly, the Oklahoma Court of Criminal Appeals ordered Mr Torres's execution date to be stayed, and remanded the case to the District Court of Oklahoma County for an evidentiary hearing on the issues of *(a)* whether Torres was prejudiced by the state's violation of his Vienna Convention rights; and *(b)* the inefficient assistance of counsel.

The Supreme Court has seen things differently in the case of *Medellin v Texas*. Mr Medellin had petitioned the Supreme Court for relief when the Texas Criminal Court of Appeals refused to review and reconsider his case. Before the

---

[32] *Oswaldo Torres v Oklahoma*, No PCD-04–442 (Ct Crim App, 13 May 2004).

case could be heard, President Bush ordered the respective state courts to provide the review required by the ICJ. The Supreme Court then dismissed Medellin's case to allow time for this review. The Texas Court again refused to grant such a review, claiming that President Bush did not have the constitutional power to give such an order. Medellin again appealed to the Supreme Court, which granted certiorari on the following questions:

1. Did the President of the United States act within his constitutional and statutory foreign affairs authority when he determined that the states must comply with the United States' treaty obligation to give effect to the *Avena* judgment in the cases of the 51 Mexican nationals named in the judgment?
2. Are state courts bound by the Constitution to honour the undisputed international obligation of the United States, under treaties duly ratified by the President with the advice and consent of the Senate, to give effect to the *Avena* judgment in the cases that the judgment addressed?

In a six–three decision, the majority answered both questions in the negative, saying:

In sum, while the ICJ's Judgment in *Avena* creates an international law obligation on the part of the United States, it does not of its own force constitute binding federal law that pre-empts state restrictions on the filing of successive habeas petitions. As we noted in *Sanchez-Llamas*, a contrary conclusion would be extraordinary, given that basic rights guaranteed by our own Constitution do not have the effect of displacing state procedural rules . . . Nothing in the text, background, negotiating and drafting history, or practice among signatory nations suggests that the President or Senate intended the improbable result of giving the judgments of an international tribunal a higher status than that enjoyed by 'many of our most fundamental constitutional protections'.[33]

The minority stated that:

The majority's two holdings taken together produce practical anomalies. They unnecessarily complicate the President's foreign affairs task insofar as, for example, they increase the likelihood of a Security Council *Avena* enforcement proceedings, of worsening relations with our neighbour Mexico, of precipitating actions by other nations putting at risk American citizens who have the misfortune to be arrested while traveling abroad, or of diminishing our Nation's reputation abroad as a result of our failure to follow the 'rule of law' principles that we preach. The holdings also encumber Congress with a task (postratification legislation) that, in respect to many decisions of international tribunals, it may not want and which it may find difficult to execute . . . [A] strong line of precedent . . . indicates that the treaty provisions before us and the judgment of the International Court of Justice address themselves to the Judicial Branch and consequently are self-executing. In reaching a contrary conclusion, the Court has failed to take proper account of that precedent and, as a result, the Nation may well break its word even though the President seeks to live up to that word and Congress has done nothing to suggest the contrary.[34]

---

[33] 552 US 27 (2008).
[34] 552 US 30–31 (Breyer J dissent) (2008).

On 5 June 2008, Mexico filed with the International Court a Request for interpretation of the *Avena* Judgment citing, *inter alia*, the *Medellin* judgment of the Supreme Court of the United States. It claimed that 'the United States cannot invoke its municipal law as justification for failure to perform its international legal obligation under the *Avena* judgment'. The Request for interpretation was accompanied by an urgent Request for the indication of provisional measures to ensure that Mr Medellin was not executed pending the conclusion of the proceedings in the interpretation case.

The *Medellin* case reveals cross-cutting tensions between the executive and judiciary and between the federal and state governments. Article 34 of the Statute of the Court provides that only states may be parties to cases before the Court, but the reality is that the acts that states perform, that may engage their international responsibility, are in fact performed by a multitude of organs, agencies, and instrumentalities. Among these may be national courts, which in particular circumstances may have a very specific—and difficult—role to perform in the international legal order—that of the implementation of international judgments, while at the same time being answerable to the dictates of applicable domestic law.

******

This volume is a tribute to Tom Bingham upon his 75th birthday. His contribution, both after he assumed the role of Senior Law Lord and before, has been vigorous and profound, as the chapters offered by his friends testify. To an international lawyer, he has been the embodiment of a progressive move away from formal narrow understandings of the place to be accorded to international law in the domestic legal system. Others before him had been of a similar intellectual disposition and had rendered important judgments. Some of them indeed have served, as Tom Bingham does today, as Chairman of the British Institute of International and Comparative Law. The work of treating international law as English law has, in the past decade, been systematically carried forward, in a pleasingly hard-headed and convincing manner. If today we find in the United Kingdom a readiness to tackle, in a fully efficient manner, the various international legal issues of the day, without undue preoccupation with specifically national constraints said to exist in the performance of such a task, much of the thanks is due to Lord Bingham.

6

European Law and the English Judge

Francis Jacobs

I Introduction

'There is a world elsewhere'.[1] In his FA Mann lecture of 1991, Tom Bingham expressed one of his own outstanding qualities: his openness to new ideas from other quarters and other sources.

In this paper, I attempt briefly to assess that quality in the context of two new dimensions of English law which (as foreseen by Leslie Scarman)[2] have in recent years substantially modified, if not wholly transformed, the legal landscape: on the one hand, the European Convention on Human Rights; on the other hand, European Community law. English law has shown itself flexible and receptive to these branches of European law. Lord Bingham has played an important part in this process.

It is especially interesting to consider together the impact of the European Convention on the one hand and EC law on the other. There is much scope for comparison, and for contrast, between the two European systems. In some respects, for example by introducing the principle of proportionality into English law, they have operated jointly. In other respects there is a triangular relationship: an interaction of all three systems. But this is not the place for a full study. This paper will begin with a brief account of the relationship between the English courts and the Convention—a topic which is covered more fully elsewhere in this book. Next the paper will look rather more fully at the relationship with EC law—a topic less widely familiar. Some brief conclusions will be attempted.

---

[1] '"There is a World Elsewhere": The Changing Perspectives of English Law', ICLQ 1992, p 513; reprinted in Tom Bingham, *The Business of Judging: Selected Essays and Speeches* (Oxford 2000), p 87.

[2] Leslie Scarman, *English Law—The New Dimension* (1974 Hamlyn lectures, Sweet & Maxwell).

II Human Rights: the European Convention and the Human Rights Act 1998

Until recently—until the Human Rights Act 1998 took effect—the United Kingdom had no Bill of Rights subsequent to that of 1689, which was designed for a rather specific purpose. In having no general Bill of Rights, the United Kingdom was almost unique among the developed legal systems of the world today. But in 1998 it had already been for nearly half a century a party to the Council of Europe's European Convention on Human Rights; indeed it was the first state to ratify the Convention in 1951. In the United Kingdom ratification of a treaty does not make it part of UK law: specific legislation is necessary for that purpose, and no such legislation was adopted. As a result, the Convention had a limited status in English law: it could be invoked, like other treaties ratified by the United Kingdom, to assist in the interpretation of Acts of Parliament; there could be argument that some of its provisions reflected customary international law; but occasional attempts, by advocates and judges, to give it any special effect proved transitory.[3] However, after the United Kingdom accepted in 1966 the jurisdiction of the European Commission and Court of Human Rights, it became subject to the procedures in Strasbourg on applications brought by individuals—procedures which not infrequently resulted in a finding of a violation of the Convention.

There was, however, for many years strong opposition in legal and judicial circles in the UK to 'incorporating' the Convention into English law. One result was that cases were decided by the European Court of Human Rights in Strasbourg without the English courts having had a proper opportunity to examine the human rights issues.[4]

Tom Bingham was one of the first major figures, as Lord Chief Justice from 1996, to support the incorporation of the Convention.[5] He followed on that point his predecessor, Peter Taylor (Lord Taylor of Gosforth), who had taken a keen interest in the subject of human rights—an interest not apparently shared by many of his predecessors as Lord Chief Justice.[6] Peter Taylor as Lord Chief

---

[3] See Murray Hunt, *Using Human Rights Law in English Courts* (Hart Publishing, Oxford 1997).

[4] In the early years Anthony Lester QC (later Lord Lester of Herne Hill) was a valiant but solitary campaigner for incorporation of the Convention.

[5] He had urged incorporation even before his appointment as LCJ: see T Bingham, 'The European Convention on Human Rights: time to incorporate', Lord Denning Lecture, 2 March 1993: *The Business of Judging* (op. cit. n 1), 131.

[6] Lord Goddard (LCJ 1946–1958) and some other LCJs had a somewhat ferocious reputation: it is difficult to imagine that they would have responded favourably to arguments based on human rights, although the stereotype may be misleading. In any event I still remember a feeling of surprise, when giving the first Paul Sieghart lecture for the British Institute of Human Rights, to see Peter Taylor, then Lord Chief Justice, in the audience.

Justice even devoted his televised Dimbleby lecture[7] to the case for incorporating the Convention. When the Human Rights Bill was introduced in Parliament, Lord Bingham, having succeeded Peter Taylor as Lord Chief Justice, argued elegantly and powerfully in the House of Lords (at a time when senior judges who were members of the upper house of Parliament could still take part in its legislative work) in favour of incorporation. One of his arguments was that English courts would be able to apply the Convention. After most of the Convention rights were enacted into English law, by the Human Rights Act 1998, under the impetus of the new Lord Chancellor, Lord Irvine of Lairg, the English courts played an important part in interpreting the Convention and indeed have had a significant impact on the case law of the European Court of Human Rights.

By a happy historical coincidence, once the Convention rights were enacted into English law, it fell to Lord Bingham to take a leading role in applying them at the highest level of the UK judiciary: the 1998 Act, which effectively incorporates into English law most of the 'Convention rights', as they are termed in the Act, took effect for that purpose in 2000, the year in which Lord Bingham became the Senior Law Lord. Indeed he had a special role in that respect, since the House of Lords has tended in recent years to sit in two divisions of five judges each, the first presided over by Lord Bingham, and that division tended to deal with human rights cases. In the result he has given many leading judgments on the Convention rights.

European human rights and the sovereignty of Parliament

In contrast to the position under European Community law, considered below, the English courts could not under the Human Rights Act give precedence to human rights over Acts of Parliament. The doctrine of Parliamentary sovereignty is preserved.

The Human Rights Act, however, contains two notable innovations. First, the Act requires the courts to make every effort to construe all legislation, whether primary or subordinate, consistently with Convention rights: all such legislation must, by section 3 of the Act, be read and given effect in a way which is compatible with Convention rights 'so far as it is possible to do so'. That requirement appears to go further than the normal requirement to interpret legislation consistently with treaty obligations in order to comply with international law.[8]

Secondly, and more remarkably, the Act provides that where the higher courts (the High Court and above) find a conflict between the Convention rights protected by the Act and another Act of Parliament, while they cannot override the

---

[7] 'The Judiciary in the Nineties', BBC 1, 30 November 1992. The Dimbleby lecture, an annual televised lecture, was founded in memory of the broadcaster Richard Dimbleby.

[8] See generally on the place of treaties in English law the paper by Professor Rosalyn Higgins, 'United Kingdom', in *The Effect of Treaties in Domestic Law* (ed Jacobs and Roberts) (1987), p 123.

other Act they can make a 'declaration of incompatibility'.[9] In that event, the Act found to conflict with the Convention rights can be amended in Parliament by a relatively straightforward procedure in order to remove the defect identified by the court. Under section 10(2) of the Act, if a Minister of the Crown considers that there are compelling reasons for proceeding under those provisions, he or she may by a 'remedial order' make such amendments to the offending Act as he or she considers necessary to remove the incompatibility. Safeguards are added to limit this legislative power of the Executive: in particular, the 'remedial order' must first be laid in draft before Parliament for 60 days and must be approved by resolution of each House. Nevertheless the departure from the normal manifestations of Parliamentary sovereignty, in the interest of effective protection of Convention rights, is a remarkable constitutional innovation.

Interpretation of the Convention rights

In carrying out the task of interpreting Convention rights incorporated into UK law by the Human Rights Act, the English courts have proved receptive to novel principles.

In the first place, they have proved faithful to the case law of the Strasbourg Court.

In *Anderson*[10] the House of Lords ruled that the Home Secretary could not set minimum jail terms for murder. In his judgment, Lord Bingham referred to *R (Alconbury Developments Ltd) v Secretary of State for the Environment, Transport and the Regions*[11] and to a judgment of the European Court of Human Rights and declared that 'the House will not without good reason depart from the principles laid down in a carefully considered judgment of the court sitting as a Grand Chamber'.[12]

More recently, in 2008, Lord Bingham has had occasion to comment on whether judgments of the European Court of Human Rights are binding on the UK. The case challenged the ban on political advertising on radio and TV in the UK, Lord Bingham disagreed with Lord Scott's observations to the effect that domestic courts are not bound by the Strasbourg Court's interpretation of an incorporated article,[13] and reiterated what he had said in *R (Ullah) v Special*

---

[9] Human Rights Act 1998, s 4.

[10] *R v Secretary of State for the Home Department (Respondent) ex p Anderson (FC) (Appellant)* [2002] UKHL 46. For references to English cases on Convention rights, I am indebted to Ndanga Kamau of the British Institute of International and Comparative Law.

[11] [2001] 2 WLR 1389 at 1399.

[12] Ibid at para 26.

[13] 'Section 2 of the 1998 Act requires any domestic court determining a question which has arisen in connection with a Convention right to take into account, inter alia, "any judgment, decision, declaration or advisory opinion of the European Court of Human Rights" (ss (1)(a)). The judgments of the European Court are, therefore, not binding on domestic courts. They constitute material, very important material, that must be taken into account, but domestic courts are

Adjudicator,[14] that 'in the absence of special circumstances our courts should follow any clear and constant jurisprudence of the Strasbourg court, recognising that the Convention is an international instrument, the correct interpretation of which can be authoritatively expounded only by the Strasbourg court'.[15]

Secondly, the English courts have been firm in interpreting the Convention rights to uphold individual liberty as is illustrated by the cases mentioned in this section. Confronted by the broad language of the Convention, unfamiliar in technique compared with the more detailed drafting characteristic of UK legislation, they have applied appropriate methods of interpretation—assisted no doubt by the fact that the Convention itself proclaims the fundamental rights historically protected by the common law.

Thirdly, the courts have not shrunk from making declarations of incompatibility where appropriate. More than 20 such declarations have been made since 2000, and although a few have been overturned on appeal, most have been upheld by the highest courts. Indeed some have been introduced at that level.

In the *Belmarsh*[16] case, the House of Lords ruled that indefinite detention of foreign terror suspects was unlawful. The House had to rule on whether the government's derogation from Convention was lawful and whether the Act of Parliament used to detain suspects was incompatible with the Convention. With a leading judgment by Lord Bingham, the House of Lords quashed the Human Rights Act 1998 (Designated derogation) 2001 and declared section 23 of the Anti-terrorism, Crime and Security Act 2001 incompatible with Articles 5 and 14 of the European Convention because the section was disproportionate and permitted detention of suspected international terrorists in a way that discriminated on the ground of nationality or immigration status.

There are also examples of cases where declarations of incompatibility have been overturned. In *Matthews v Ministry of Defence*[17] a declaration of incompatibility from the Queen's Bench Division was overturned by the Court of Appeal. The House of Lords upheld the decision of the Court of Appeal and dismissed the appeal. Lord Bingham considered the first point at issue, that is, whether in English law the appellant had a 'civil right', according to Article 6 of the European Convention, to claim damages for tort against the Ministry of Defence. He concluded that the appellant had no such right and did not need to consider the second point on incompatibility.

---

nonetheless not bound by the European Court's interpretation of an incorporated article.' *R (on the application of Animal Defenders International (Appellants) v Secretary of State for Culture, Media and Sport* (Respondent)[2008] UKHL 15 at para 44.

[14] *R (Ullah) v Special Adjudicator* [2004] UKHL 26, [2004] at para 20.

[15] *R (ADI) v Secretary of State for Culture, Media and Sport* [2008] UKHL 15 at para 37.

[16] *A (FC) and others (FC) (Appellants) v Secretary of State for the Home Department (Respondent); X (FC) and another (FC) (Appellants) v Secretary of State for the Home Department (Respondent)* [2004] UKHL 56.

[17] [2003] UKHL 4.

In *R (on the Application of MH) v Secretary of State for Health*[18] the House of Lords overturned a declaration of incompatibility made by the Court of Appeal. In this case Lord Bingham did not write the main judgment but agreed with the main judgment written by Baroness Hale of Richmond.

Fourthly, the English courts have shown that there can be a two-way dialogue with the Strasbourg Court. That Court has shown itself to be impressed by and receptive to the decisions of English courts. It has not infrequently cited English judgments, and not least the judgments of Lord Bingham.

Moreover, in what is perhaps the most remarkable tribute, the Strasbourg Court has shown itself prepared, in response to measured and reasoned criticism and questioning from English courts, to modify its own previous case law: it has done so, for example, with regard to the liability of public authorities; with regard to the compatibility of court-martial proceedings with the requirements of a fair trial; and with regard to the system of mandatory life sentences.[19]

Judicial review

In a leading case decided in 2005 about the admissibility of evidence obtained by torture, the House of Lords ruled that evidence that might have been obtained elsewhere by torture cannot be used against terror suspects in the UK.[20] In his judgment, Lord Bingham said that in determining the admissibility of evidence, SIAC, who were the respondents, '...should throughout be guided by recognition of the important obligations laid down in articles 3 and 5(4) of the European Convention and, through them, article 15 of the Torture Convention...'[21]

By a majority of four to three, the House of Lords ruled in favour of a test of admissibility of evidence which Lord Bingham rejected. His speech once again demonstrated his firm stance on human rights, and he said: 'I regret that the House should lend its authority to a test which will undermine the practical efficacy of the Torture Convention and deny detainees the standard of fairness to which they are entitled under article 5(4) or 6(1) of the European Convention.'[22]

In a trio of cases involving control orders, the House of Lords ruled that aspects of the control order regime, including an 18-hour daily curfew, were unlawful.

---

[18] [2005] UKHL 60.

[19] The *Osman* case law: *Osman v United Kingdom* (1998) 29 EHRR 245, modified in *Z v United Kingdom* (2001) 34 EHRR 97; In *Cooper v United Kingdom* [2003] ECHR 48843/99 the Grand Chamber departed from the judgment of a Chamber in *Morris v United Kingdom* [2002] ECHR 38784/97; In *Stafford v United Kingdom* (2002) 35 EHRR 1121, the Court modified its judgment in *Wynne v United Kingdom* (1994) 19 EHRR 333.

[20] *A (FC) and others (FC) (Appellants) v Secretary of State for the Home Department (Respondent) (2004); A and others (Appellants) (FC) and others v Secretary of State for the Home Department (Respondent) (Conjoined Appeals)* [2005] UKHL 71.

[21] Ibid at para 56.

[22] Ibid at para 62.

In the first case,[23] Lord Bingham held that the Secretary of State had no power to make an order that imposed obligations that were incompatible with Article 5. He observed that the court could in special circumstances decline to quash an order but these circumstances did not exist in the case, and '... it would be contrary to principle to decline to quash an order, made without power to make it, which had unlawfully deprived a person of his liberty'.[24]

In the second case,[25] Lord Bingham concurred with the arguments made by three of his fellow Law Lords that the cases should be referred back for consideration by the judge in the light of the committee's conclusions. Here, however, he declined to make a declaration of incompatibility and to rule that the orders be quashed, even though he saw force in the argument for doing so.

More generally, a greater concern for human rights has led to more effective control of the executive and even the legislature. No doubt other influences have been at work, including examples from Commonwealth and European jurisdictions, familiarity with which is facilitated by regular meetings of judges from different systems.

Greater scrutiny of decisions of the public authorities has no doubt been advanced by the use of the principle of proportionality, widely used by both the European Court of Human Rights and the European Court of Justice, and implying a more structured and potentially more incisive review than under the traditional *Wednesbury* test.

III The Impact of European Community Law

Compared with the broad reach of the European Convention on Human Rights, European Community law had initially a limited scope, although its legal effects went further. European Community law became applicable in the UK from 1 January 1973 under the European Communities Act 1972, which gave effect in the UK to the Community Treaties. In appropriate circumstances, the UK courts were required to give 'direct effect' to provisions of EC law; EC law was to prevail over conflicting UK law—including Acts of Parliament; and UK courts were required to follow the case law of the European Court of Justice, which was binding upon national courts. Thus EC law, although largely confined at that time to 'the common market', had an impact on what were perhaps the key features of the English legal system: the sovereignty of Parliament, and judicial precedent.

---

[23] *Secretary of State for the Home Department (Appellant) v JJ and others (FC) (Respondents)* [2007] UKHL 45.

[24] Ibid at para 27.

[25] *Secretary of State for the Home Department (Respondent) v MB (FC) (Appellant); Secretary of State for the Home Department (Respondent) v AF (FC) (Appellant) (Civil Appeal from Her Majesty's High Court of Justice); Secretary of State for the Home Department (Appellant) v AF (FC) (Respondent) (Civil Appeal from Her Majesty's High Court of Justice)* [2007] UKHL 46.

The early years

In the early years of UK membership of the European Community, expertise in Community law was in short supply, but the best lawyers seemed, as always, able to turn their hands, apparently effortlessly, to new fields of law. It is worth recalling that period briefly, not for the sake of anecdote but to give a flavour of the early impact of European Community law in the UK. The main impact in the English courts was in the fields of competition and equal pay. English lawyers were also appearing frequently in a wider variety of cases in the European Court of Justice in Luxembourg.

Tom Bingham, as a leading barrister (whose chambers I had the good fortune to share), was in great demand in that period. I recall an almost unprecedented event from that era: another member state—France—sued the UK before the European Court of Justice. That was exceptional because cases against member states are almost always brought, as the Treaty primarily envisages, by the European Commission rather than by other states. In this case, Tom Bingham was instructed to defend the UK. Whether it was for that reason alone, history does not relate, but the French action was discontinued.

In other cases, I had the privilege of working with Tom Bingham as his 'junior'. One leading case in the European Court of Justice concerned the Columbia trademark for gramophone records, in which, despite powerful opposition, we were successful.[26]

Less successful for us was a huge anti-dumping case, concerning imports into the Community of Japanese ball bearings.[27] The European Community, whose anti-dumping measures were vigorously challenged, was represented by a large team of English, French, and German lawyers. Tom Bingham (and I) acted for the European Commission.[28] Advocate General Warner, in a masterly Opinion, was against us on virtually every issue; for the judgment of the Court, it was sufficient to find against us on a single point—a point on which none of the many applicants had placed much reliance. The case was an exceptional one in many ways: strangely, perhaps, subsequent anti-dumping actions challenging Community measures before the European Court of Justice seemed for many years to fail almost systematically.

---

[26] *EMI Records Ltd v CBS United Kingdom Ltd* [1976] ECR 811. Our team, acting for EMI, was reinforced by Robin Jacob (now Lord Justice Jacob); see his reminiscences in Andenas and Jacobs (eds) *European Community Law in the English Courts* (Oxford, 1998), p 211. CBS was represented by Patrick Neill QC (now Lord Neill of Bladen) and Anthony Watson.

[27] *NTN Toyo Bearing Co Ltd and others v Council of the European Communities* [1979] ECR 1185.

[28] The Council of the European Communities, a joint defendant, was separately represented, by a team including Patrick Neill, Mark Waller (now Lord Justice Waller), and Lawrence Collins (then a solicitor, now Lord Justice Collins). The Japanese applicants' team included Jeremy Lever and David Vaughan. Misguidedly, for my work as his junior in this case, Tom Bingham rewarded me with a red bag, traditionally given by a QC to a junior only once in a junior's career at the Bar, and probably rarely awarded for cases in Luxembourg.

Tom Bingham also had a substantial advisory practice and advised clients, including the Bank of England, on extraordinarily interesting issues of EC law. He was well placed, on appointment as a judge, to take a well-informed view of European law.

The English judge and EC law

Much of EC law is administered and applied by the authorities and courts of the member states. But it has to be applied uniformly. With that in view, the Treaty provides for a system of references from courts and tribunals to the European Court of Justice on questions of EC law. The national court when referring questions suspends its proceedings; the European Court of Justice gives 'preliminary rulings' on the questions; the rulings are binding on the national courts (unless they make a further reference). Under the Treaty (currently Article 234 of the EC Treaty) any national court or tribunal *may* refer; courts against whose decisions there is no appeal *must* refer.

Thus, while final courts of member states are obliged (with narrow exceptions) to refer, lower courts have a discretion whether to refer. It is of great importance that the discretion should be properly exercised.

Tom Bingham's discussion of the issue has been particularly perceptive at all stages of his judicial career. As a High Court judge, he said:

Sitting as a judge in a national court, asked to decide questions of Community law, I am very conscious of the advantages enjoyed by the Court of Justice. It has a panoramic view of the Community and its institutions, a detailed knowledge of the treaties and of much subordinate legislation made under them, and an intimate familiarity with the functioning of the Community market which no national judge denied the collective experience of the Court of Justice could hope to achieve. Where questions of administrative intention and practice arise the Court of Justice can receive submissions from the Community institutions, as also where relations between the Community and non-member states are in issue. Where the interests of member states are affected they can intervene to make their views known. That is a material consideration in this case since there is some slight evidence that the practice of different member states is divergent. Where comparison falls to be made between Community texts in different languages, all texts being equally authentic, the multinational Court of Justice is equipped to carry out the task in a way which no national judge, whatever his linguistic skills, could rival. The interpretation of Community instruments involves very often not the process familiar to common lawyers of laboriously extracting the meaning from words used but the more creative process of supplying flesh to a spare and loosely constructed skeleton. The choice between alternative submissions may turn not on purely legal considerations, but on a broader view of what the orderly development of the Community requires. These are matters which the Court of Justice is very much better placed to assess and determine than a national court.[29]

[29] *Customs & Excise Commissioners v ApS Samex* [1983] 1 All ER 1042.

By implication, he boldly qualified the earlier, more restrictive approach of Lord Denning as Master of the Rolls (president of the Court of Appeal). Despite his great admiration for Lord Denning[30] he described that approach (extra-judicially) as 'disappointingly negative'.[31] Commenting on Lord Denning's remarks in the very early case of *Bulmer v Bollinger*,[32] he added: 'Happily, as I think, a more enlightened approach to references—by which I mean an approach more loyal to the spirit of the Treaty—has now prevailed'.

That more enlightened approach was in no small measure due to Lord Bingham himself.

When he in turn became Master of the Rolls, he said:[33]

I understand the correct approach in principle of a national court (other than a final court of appeal) to be quite clear: if the facts have been found and the Community law issue is critical to the court's final decision, the appropriate course is ordinarily to refer the issue to the Court of Justice unless the national court can with complete confidence resolve the issue itself. In considering whether it can with complete confidence resolve the issue itself the national court must be fully mindful of the differences between national and Community legislation, of the pitfalls which face a national court venturing into what may be an unfamiliar field, of the need for uniform interpretation throughout the Community and of the great advantages enjoyed by the Court of Justice in construing Community instruments. If the national court has any real doubt, it should ordinarily refer.

References on validity

One aspect of the relationship between the English courts and the European Court of Justice merits special attention. The European Court of Justice has been notoriously restrictive in allowing individual access to the Court (now the Court of First Instance, which has jurisdiction in all cases brought by individuals). The requirement in Article 230 of the Treaty that, to be able to challenge a measure not addressed to him, the applicant must show that it is of 'individual concern' to him, has been strictly construed. Measures of any generality, even if they directly affect the individual, cannot be directly challenged. But there is an indirect route available, by way of a reference from the national court, which can refer to the European Court of Justice, at the instance of individuals, the validity of a Community measure. Recently, the European Court of Justice has indicated an express preference for challenges by the indirect route (which incidentally has the effect of by-passing the Court of First Instance).

---

[30] See his remarkable encomium to Lord Denning in *The Business of Judging* (op. cit. n 1), p 409.

[31] T Bingham, '"There is a World Elsewhere": The Changing Perspectives of English Law' FA Mann Lecture, 21 November 1991: *The Business of Judging*, op. cit. n 1, p 87 at p 93–94.

[32] *Bulmer v Bollinger* [1974] 2 All ER 1226.

[33] *R v International Stock Exchange of the United Kingdom and the Republic of Ireland, ex p Else and Others* [1993] 1 All ER 420.

Here the English courts have played a key role. Their approach to standing is generally as broad as that of the European Court of Justice is narrow. They have also been willing to make pre-emptive references on the validity of a measure, before the measure is, or is required to be, implemented in the member states. In consequence, they appear to have become the forum of choice in the EU—at least where costs are of little account—for challenges to EU legislation.

Illustrations can be found in cases such as the challenge to the Tobacco Advertising Directive, where on a reference from the English High Court, coupled with a direct action brought by Germany, the European Court of Justice struck down the Directive on the ground that it was not within the Community's competence.

Another, more recent, example of a challenge to Community legislation of high importance and transnational scope brought in the English High Court is the *Intertanko* case. The European Community acceded to the United Nations Convention on the Law of the Sea (UNCLOS) in 1998. The Community has not (yet) acceded to the Marpol (Maritime pollution) agreement which established rules to combat pollution of the marine environment. The challenge in this case was to EC Directive 2005/35 on ship-source pollution and in particular to the introduction of penalties for infringements. The claimants in this case, a group of organizations within the maritime shipping industry representing substantial proportions of that industry, argued essentially that Articles 4 and 5 of the Directive, which laid down criminal liability for discharge violations, were incompatible with UNCLOS and the Marpol agreement. Here however the challenge failed.

While the active role of the English courts in this arena may be welcomed in some respects, it is perhaps not entirely satisfactory that national courts should exercise this role at all. It seems wholly anomalous that on the one hand the European Court of Justice should close the front door to direct actions, when the restrictions can readily be circumvented by the use of the side door or the back door. This point has frequently been expounded and needs no further mention here.[34]

Additionally, however, many practical difficulties arise from the use of references as the vehicle of challenge to Community legislation. Perhaps its one advantage, if it is an advantage, is that it may sometimes lead to a speedier resolution, as it effectively circumvents the Court of First Instance—although it brings in a different instance, namely the national court—where indeed there may be scope for appeals within the national judicial hierarchy before the reference is made or becomes definitive.

The procedure on a reference is not ideal for debating the validity of a major piece of legislation. On references, as opposed to direct actions, there is under the Statute of the Court, which cannot readily be amended, a single round of written

---

[34] See, e.g., Paul Craig, *EU Administrative Law* (Oxford 2006), pp 331–347.

observations, which in such cases may come from many member states as well as from the Community institutions and the parties to the national proceedings, and to which there is no opportunity to reply in writing: any reply must be made at the very brief oral hearing.

A particular feature of the procedural difficulties arises where validity is challenged. Different grounds of invalidity may be raised, without there being any definitive delimitation of the issues. For example, in the English court, the applicant may argue grounds A, B, C, and D; the judge may refer only on grounds A and C; but the parties, and others taking part in the proceedings, are apparently free to argue grounds which have not been referred (grounds B and D), or indeed wholly new grounds (grounds X, Y, and Z). Such licence would not be available in a direct action, where the grounds relied upon would have to be specified in the originating application to the Court of First Instance, and could not normally be amplified later.

Nonetheless it may be preferable, in the interests of judicial protection and respect for the rule of law, that EU measures can be subject to judicial review, even by an unsatisfactory route, than that they should be wholly immune from review.

The constitutional impact of EC law

In contrast to the European Convention on Human Rights, EC law may of necessity have an impact on the fundamental constitutional principle of the sovereignty of Parliament. Of necessity, EC law must prevail over the national law of the member states. It is the law of the Community as a whole, and it could not be so if it could be overridden by the national law of the member states.

In a lecture delivered in 1994, Tom Bingham recognized as somewhat obvious—but as a striking infringement of Parliamentary sovereignty—the point that a British statute inconsistent with Community law was to that extent unlawful and void.[35] Elsewhere, however, he has suggested that there is no true limit on Parliamentary sovereignty: the courts give precedence to EC law because Parliament has told them to do so: if Parliament were to tell them not to do so, then the courts would comply.[36] The latter hypothesis might well be right, as a prediction for the future. However, as matters stand today it seems plainly arguable that there is a derogation from the traditional orthodoxy of Parliamentary sovereignty, in that the courts will not apply even a *subsequent* Act of Parliament which conflicts with EC law: thus the European Communities Act in effect prevails even over subsequent Acts of Parliament.

---

[35] T Bingham 'Anglo-American reflections', inaugural Pilgrim Fathers' Lecture delivered 29 October 1994: *The Business of Judging* (op. cit. n 1) p 239 at p 248.

[36] Lord Bingham of Cornhill 'The Rule of Law and the Sovereignty of Parliament', *King's Law Journal* Vol 19, 2008, p 223 at p 230.

So the issue of primacy is still debated in the UK. On the one hand it is argued that the courts have given primacy to EC law because Parliament had so prescribed; and that that result was reached not on the heretical basis that Parliament had succeeded in binding its successors, but because it had enacted an interpretation clause, section 2(4) of the Act, which while it remains in force requires all statutes to be interpreted as if they contain a section to the effect that its provisions are without prejudice to directly enforceable Community rights.

On the other hand, it might be claimed that that is no mere rule of interpretation: where the Act conflicts with EC law, it must be disapplied, so that although EC law is given force in the UK by the European Communities Act, the effect of that Act is that it prevails over subsequent Acts of Parliament, contrary to the basic axiom of Parliamentary sovereignty. So, where there is such a conflict, the English courts will simply disapply the later Act, as the House of Lords did in the *Equal Opportunities* case.[37] It would be disguising the legal reality to present that outcome as merely the application of a rule of interpretation.

A rather unusual case of a challenge to an Act of Parliament involved both the European Convention on Human Rights and European Community Law. It was given perhaps more attention by the House of Lords than it merited. The cases were conjoined appeals challenging the Hunting Act 2004, which outlawed, among other things, the traditional English pastime of hunting foxes with hounds.

The House had the task of addressing two types of claims. The first was that the Hunting Act infringed rights under Articles 8, 11, and 14 of the Convention and Article 1 of the First Protocol, as given domestic effect by the Human Rights Act 1998. The second was that the Hunting Act was inconsistent with Articles 28 and 49 of the EC Treaty (free movement of goods and freedom to provide services).

In a carefully argued judgment, Lord Bingham relied heavily on European Court of Human Rights and European Court of Justice case law and concluded in favour of dismissing the appeals under both heads. While he considered that there were issues of possible conflict with the rights and freedoms invoked, he held that interference with those rights and freedoms would in any event be justified, both under the Convention and under the Treaty, in the public interest—Parliament having taken the view that a ban was necessary for the prevention of cruelty to animals. The case, although rather exceptional, presents a clear example of direct challenge to an Act of Parliament, rather than the commoner case of the application of an Act to specific fact-situations.

Judicial review

Decisions by the European Court of Justice in the field of judicial review have highlighted what some have regarded as serious defects in the system of judicial remedies under English law. A good illustration—taking English law to be

---

[37] [1995] 1 AC 1.

closely cognate to the law of Northern Ireland—is provided by the decision of the European Court of Justice in *Johnston v Chief Constable of the Royal Ulster Constabulary.*[38] Here the policy of not allowing policewomen to use guns was at stake. The applicant challenged the Chief Constable's refusal to renew her contract as a member of the RUC full-time Reserve or to allow her to be trained in the handling and use of firearms. Under the Sex Discrimination (Northern Ireland) Order, which gave effect to the EC Equal Treatment Directive (Directive 76/207), none of its provisions prohibiting discrimination were to render unlawful an act done for the purpose of safeguarding national security or of protecting public safety or public order. Moreover a certificate of the Secretary of State certifying that an act was done for one of those purposes was to be conclusive evidence that it was done for that purpose.

Under Article 6 of the Directive, member states were to introduce into their national legal systems 'such measures as are necessary to enable all persons who consider themselves wronged by failure to apply to them the principle of equal treatment... to pursue their claims by judicial process...'[39]

The Court held that the provision for Ministerial certificate having conclusive effect 'allows the competent authority to deprive an individual of the possibility of asserting by judicial process the rights conferred by the directive. Such a provision is therefore contrary to the principle of effective judicial control laid down in Article 6 of the Directive'.

In its judgment the European Court of Justice commented on Article 6 of the Directive as follows:

The requirement of judicial control stipulated by that article reflects a general principle of law which underlies the constitutional traditions common to the member states. That principle is also laid down in Articles 6 and 13 of the European Convention on Human Rights...[40]

The comments of the European Court of Justice on Article 6 of the European Convention proved apposite when a related issue arose subsequently in a case before the European Court of Human Rights. Contractors in Northern Ireland complained that their tender for work on a power station had been unlawfully rejected because they were Roman Catholics. The Secretary of State had issued a statutory certificate that the rejection was on grounds of national security or public safety. The complaint therefore failed in the High Court, because the Act of Parliament provided that such a certificate was 'conclusive evidence' of the purpose stated in it. But the European Court of Human Rights found a violation of Article 6(1) of the Convention, since the right to protection against religious discrimination and the judicial enforcement of that right were disproportionately restricted by Ministerial *fiat.*[41]

[38] [1986] ECR 1651. [39] Para 20.
[40] Para 18. [41] *Tinnelly & Sons Ltd v UK* (1998).

Another lacuna in English law exposed by EC law was the impotence, perhaps self-imposed, of English courts to grant interim relief against the Crown. The issue was exposed in the *Factortame* saga, where UK fishing legislation was challenged as being discriminatory. The applicants sought interim relief to protect their position until final judgment was given. At first instance the Divisional Court, making a reference to the European Court of Justice on the substantive issues, ordered that, by way of interim relief, the application of the national legislation to the applicants should be suspended. That order was set aside by the Court of Appeal, which held that the English courts had no power to suspend, even on an interim basis, the application of Acts of Parliament whose incompatibility with EC law had not been definitively established. The House of Lords upheld that view as a matter of English law, but asked the European Court of Justice whether Community law required or permitted such interim relief to be granted, and if so, under what circumstances.

The Court of Justice held that EC law did require the grant of interim measures where they were needed to protect the full effectiveness of Community law. Its succinct conclusion was that 'a court which...would grant interim relief [to protect Community rights], if it were not for a rule of national law, is obliged to set aside that rule'.[42]

The result was that, in proceedings against the Crown, those asserting rights under Community law enjoyed greater protection than those asserting rights under English law. The House of Lords subsequently remedied the situation by holding that as a matter of English law, also, interim relief must be treated as available against the Crown. Lord Templeman commented that 'the argument that there is no power to enforce the law by injunction...against a minister in his official capacity would, if upheld, establish the proposition that the executive observe the law as a matter of grace and not as a matter of necessity, a proposition which would reverse the result of the Civil War'.[43] Yet English law had apparently maintained that position for many years until it was overturned in response to a ruling of the European Court of Justice.

Various examples could be given of important issues of public law where the English courts have, in the past, proved unable to develop principles as effectively as the European Courts, and where the case law of the European Courts has been held up as a model. As Sir William Wade pointed out in successive editions of his textbook on *Administrative Law*, there was no general requirement in English law that reasons should be given for decisions. Yet, as Wade argued, there is a strong case to be made for the giving of reasons as an essential element of administrative justice. The need for it has been sharply exposed by the expanding law of judicial review, now that so many decisions can be challenged on grounds of improper purpose, irrelevant considerations, or errors of law of various kinds. As Wade

---

[42] [1990] ECR I-2433, para 21.
[43] *M v Home Office* [1994] 1 AC 377.

said, a right to reasons is therefore an indispensable part of a sound system of judicial review. As a report by JUSTICE long ago pointed out: 'No single factor has inhibited the development of English administrative law as seriously as the absence of any general obligation upon public authorities to give reasons for their decisions.'[44]

In an extremely interesting paper in a book of essays in honour of Wade, Sir Patrick Neill (as he then was) contrasted the position in English law with the case law of the European Court of Justice and the European Court of Human Rights. After examining in depth the remarkable case law of the European Court of Justice, in particular, he concluded that the influence of the European Courts might contribute to the development of a general duty in English law to give reasons.[45]

Few would dispute that in the recent past the English courts have exercised a more intensive review of the actions of public authorities than was previously the case. This is indeed central to the development of the rule of law.[46] And many would say that there has been a stricter scrutiny under European law—both under EU law and under the European Convention on Human Rights—than the scrutiny traditionally exercised by the English courts.[47]

It cannot be ascertained how far developments in English law have been attributable to the influence of European law. But three points, at least, seem clear.

First, the standard applied by English courts in the past to review of administrative action—the so-called *Wednesbury* test[48]—was singularly undemanding of the administration. As Lord Bingham put it, under that test the claimant making a challenge has 'a mountain to climb'.[49] The test of proportionality, as applied by both the European Court of Human Rights and the European Court of Justice—perhaps more rigorously by the latter, as is appropriate to a Community court rather than an international court—seems on any view more demanding than the traditional English law test.

Secondly, while the English courts have not shown unreserved enthusiasm for the proportionality principle, they appear to have been influenced by it. By

---

[44] JUSTICE, *Administration Under Law*, p 23.

[45] 'The duty to give reasons: the openness of decision-making', in Forsyth and Hare (eds), *The Golden Metwand and the Crooked Cord* (Oxford 1998), p 161.

[46] Contrary to Lord Bingham's tendency, I would not treat the protection of human rights as part of the rule of law. There are clearly close connections between the two concepts, but they seem to me analytically distinct, and are treated as distinct in much modern usage: see for two fundamental examples out of many, first, the reference to the rule of law in the preamble to the European Convention on Human Rights and second, Article 6(1) of the Treaty on European Union: 'The Union is founded on the principles of liberty, democracy, respect for human rights and fundamental freedoms, and the rule of law, principles which are common to the Member States.'

[47] For further discussion, I take the liberty of referring to my Hamlyn lectures, *The Sovereignty of Law: the European Way* (Cambridge 2007), which discusses the rule of law in the European context.

[48] *Associated Provincial Picture Houses Ltd v Wednesbury Corporation* [1948] 1 KB 223.

[49] *R v Lord Chancellor, ex p Maxwell* [1997] 1 LR 104, 109.

way of example, the policy of the Ministry of Defence of excluding homosexuals from the armed forces was challenged in *Ex p Smith*. Lord Bingham (then Master of the Rolls) succeeded in combining reasonableness and proportionality: he accepted that 'the more substantial the interference with human rights, the more the court will require by way of justification before it is satisfied that the decision is reasonable'.[50] However, when the European Court of Human Rights considered *Smith*, it became clear that the Court of Appeal's review in that case was less intense than the structured proportionality test applied in Strasbourg.

Thirdly, as already mentioned, dialogue has developed between judges of different systems. Dialogue takes different forms, and the outcome cannot be quantified; but mutual influence seems a probable outcome. Senior English judges regularly meet colleagues from the European Courts and from the highest national courts in Europe (and the US). Those who have taken part in these exchanges are aware of their value.

The European Court of Justice and the European Court of Human Rights influence national courts by their case law; indeed English courts are directed by Act of Parliament to follow the case law of the European Court of Justice, and to take account of the case law of the European Court of Human Rights.

But the influence can work in the other direction also: there have been, as already mentioned, several cases where the decisions of the English courts have persuaded the Strasbourg Court to modify its own previous case law.[51]

English courts and the European courts

Contrasts can readily be drawn between English courts and the European courts. The procedures are, in general, very different, with the emphasis in England being on the oral procedure, in the European courts on the written procedure. In the European courts, a single collective judgment; in the highest English courts often one judgment per judge. Contrast, too, in the working of the law itself: there is a stock conception of the civil law being based on codes, the common law on case law.

The reality is of course more complex. The important parts of EC law—what might be called 'the general part', as distinct from the detail, is largely case law—and case law which is hardly less ambitious in scope and reach than the English common law.

In some respects the systems seem to be converging. We have seen some examples in the area of judicial review. Others might be found in the interpretation of legislation, in the use made of materials from other systems, in the regard for the context of the law.

---

[50] *R v Ministry of Defence ex p Smith* [1996] QB 517.
[51] See n 19 above.

A striking example is provided by two newer judicial institutions, the Court of First Instance in the EU judicial system and the Competition Appeal Tribunal in England.

The Court of First Instance was set up in 1989, largely to take over some of the workload of the European Court of Justice, but also and in particular to 'improve the judicial protection of individual interests'. It has an especially great responsibility in reviewing the competition decisions of the European Commission, which are frequently complex and fact-intensive. The Court of First Instance has adapted the procedure of the European Court of Justice accordingly, making appropriate modifications and allowing for relatively long hearings as well as full written exchanges, with often intensive questioning by the Court. Yet the procedure is straightforward and avoids some of the apparent technicality of English procedure. Some observers might regard it as embodying the better elements of both systems. It suffers, however, from lengthy delay and from sometimes excessively long judgments.

The Competition Appeal Tribunal, which was set up some ten years later, in certain respects follows closely the procedure and working methods of the Court of First Instance in competition cases. That is especially appropriate because UK competition law itself is now closely modelled on EC law. The Tribunal's first President, Sir Christopher Bellamy, who was responsible for establishing the Tribunal's procedure and working methods, was previously a judge at the Court of First Instance; his successor, Sir Gerald Barling, is a noted specialist in EC competition law.

The Competition Appeal Tribunal has proved extremely effective and has incidentally demonstrated that English judges and English practitioners can work effectively in a system which might be said to combine some of the best features of English and European practices.

IV Concluding Remarks

The concluding remarks can be brief. English courts, and the senior judges in particular, have been receptive to European law and the case law of the European courts. European law has had a singular and beneficial effect on English law, even if other forces have also been influential and even if it is rarely possible to trace a direct causal nexus.

The European Convention on Human Rights has had a particularly strong impact; moreover there has been a two-way current, to the benefit of both English law and the Convention.

EC law, within a rather narrower, but expanding, field, has had significant effects also. Again there has been, by and large, a positive relationship between the British courts and the European Court of Justice.

The last word can appropriately be left to Lord Bingham. In 2007, at a colloquium held at the Court of Justice to mark the 50th anniversary of the Treaties of Rome, he said this:

The relationship between the Court of Justice and the British courts over the years since 1972 has, I think, been a happy and constructive one. The role of the Court of Justice as the final arbiter on questions of Community law and practice has not been questioned. But the Court has not behaved as if it were an 'Island, entire of itself'. It has interacted with and drawn sustenance from the rich and diverse legal traditions of the Member States. It has been a collaborative enterprise, in which both the Court of Justice and national courts have had important parts to play. And that, surely, was the vision which inspired those who signed the Treaties of Rome fifty years ago.

7

Contrôle de Constitutionnalité, Contrôle de Conventionnalité et Judicial Review: La mise en œuvre de la Convention Européenne des droits de l'homme en France et au Royaume-Uni

Olivier Dutheillet de Lamothe

Le *Human Rights Act* de 1998, qui est entré en vigueur le 2 octobre 2000, à la suite de l'élection en 1997 d'une majorité travailliste, a été décrit comme *«a turning point in the UK's legal and constitutional history»*. La mise en oeuvre de la Convention européenne des droits de l'homme au Royaume-Uni se heurtait, en effet, à une contradiction fondamentale:

- d''une part, la transposition de la Convention par une loi ordinaire ne paraissait pas de nature à offrir aux droits qu'elle protège une protection légale suffisante;
- d'autre part, toute protection légale plus poussée ne paraissait pas compatible avec la Constitution britannique et le dogme de la souveraineté du Parlement.
- La mise en oeuvre de la Convention européenne des droits de l'homme apparaissait a priori plus simple en France:
- d'une part, l'article 55 de la Constitution de 1958 confère aux traités internationaux régulièrement ratifiés et publiés une valeur juridique supérieure à celle des lois;
- d'autre part, la Constitution de 1958 a mis en place, pour la première fois en France, un contrôle de constitutionnalité confié au Conseil constitutionnel.

Depuis une décision du 16 juillet 1971, ce contrôle porte sur le respect par le législateur des droits et des libertés fondamentaux. Depuis une révision constitutionnelle du 29 octobre 1974, ce contrôle peut être exercé à la demande de 60 députés ou 60 sénateurs, faisant ainsi de cette saisine l'une des principales armes de l'opposition.

Pourtant, la mise en oeuvre de la Convention européenne des droits de l'homme a fait l'objet en France d'une histoire chaotique, une histoire qui devrait intéresser les juristes anglais et, je l'espère, Lord Bingham, qui a toujours été très ouvert au droit comparé et qui a joué un rôle décisif dans la préparation et la mise en oeuvre du *Human Rights Act*. Cette histoire conduit, en effet, à s'interroger sur les notions respectives de contrôle de constitutionnalité, de contrôle de conventionnalité et de *judicial review*.

En refusant en 1975 de contrôler la conformité des lois à la Convention Européenne des droits de l'homme, le Conseil constitutionnel a conduit les tribunaux, tant judiciaires qu'administratifs, à développer une nouvelle forme de contrôle des lois: le contrôle de conventionnalité (1).

Ce contrôle de conventionnalité, qui est l'équivalent français de la *judicial review*, s'apparente très largement à un contrôle de constitutionnalité des lois (2).

1. En refusant d'exercer un contrôle de la conformité des lois à la Convention européenne des droits de l'homme dans le cadre du contrôle de constitutionnalité, le Conseil constitutionnel a conduit les juridictions administratives et judiciaires à affirmer et développer une nouvelle compétence: le contrôle de conventionnalité de la loi.

1.1. Au point de départ du processus, on trouve le refus traditionnel et constant des tribunaux français d'exercer un contrôle de la constitutionnalité des lois.

Pour le juge judiciaire, on fait traditionnellement remonter ce refus à l'arrêt rendu par la Cour de cassation dans la célèbre affaire Paulin, selon lequel la loi du 8 octobre 1830 sur les délits de presse *«délibérée et promulguée dans les formes constitutionnelles prescrites par la Charte, fait la règle des tribunaux et ne peut être attaquée devant eux pour cause d'inconstitutionnalité»* (Cass. Crim. 11 mai 1833, S. 1833, 1, p. 357). Plus récemment, la Cour de cassation a réaffirmé que l'exception d'inconstitutionnalité d'une loi *«ne peut être portée devant les tribunaux de l'ordre judiciaire»* (Cass. Civ. 2ème 20 décembre 1956, Bull. civ. n° 714p. 464).

Pour le juge administratif, ce refus a été exprimé par l'arrêt de Section Arrighi selon lequel, *«en l'état actuel du droit public français»*, un moyen tiré de l'inconstitutionnalité d'une loi *«n'est pas de nature à être discuté devant le Conseil d'Etat statuant au contentieux»* (S. 6 novembre 1936, sieur Arrighi, rec p. 966; D. 1938. 3. p. 1, conclusions Latournerie et note Eisenmann). Il a été réaffirmé récemment par une décision d'Assemblée rendue le même jour que l'arrêt Nicolo, selon laquelle *«il n'appartient pas au juge administratif d'apprécier la constitutionnalité de la loi du 7 juillet 1977»* sur les élections européennes (Ass. 20 octobre 1989, Roujansky, J.C.P. 1989, II, n° 21 371).

La décision n° 75–54 DC du 15 janvier 1975 sur la loi relative à l'interruption volontaire de grossesse a déclenché un processus qui a conduit à remettre en cause ce tabou. Avec le recul de trente années, on peut légitimement évoquer à l'égard de cette décision la théorie du battement d'ailes du papillon.

Saisi d'un moyen tiré de la violation par la loi relative à l'interruption volontaire de grossesse de l'article 2 de la Convention européenne des droits de l'homme sur le droit à la vie, le Conseil constitutionnel a jugé qu'il ne lui appartient pas *«lorsqu'il est saisi en application de l'article 61 de la Constitution, d'examiner la conformité d'une loi aux stipulations d'un traité ou d'un accord international»*. Cette décision repose à la fois sur des arguments de droit et des raisons pratiques.

Sur le plan du droit, trois arguments sont invoqués dans la décision. Le premier, à vrai dire déterminant, est tiré d'une interprétation stricte, d'ailleurs traditionnelle, de l'article 61 de la Constitution. Si les dispositions de l'article 55 de la Constitution *«confèrent aux traités, dans les conditions qu'elles définissent, une autorité supérieure à celle des lois, elles ne prescrivent ni n'impliquent que le respect de ce principe doive être assuré dans le cadre du contrôle de la conformité des lois à la Constitution prévu à l'article 61 de celle-ci»*.

Un deuxième argument est tiré de la différence de nature entre le contrôle de constitutionnalité, prévu par l'article 61, qui revêt *«un caractère absolu et définitif»*, et le contrôle de conventionnalité, prévu par l'article 55, qui présente *«un caractère à la fois relatif et contingent»*. Le Conseil constitutionnel a, dans ses décisions ultérieures, abandonné cette formulation qui avait été critiquée par la doctrine.[1] La référence au «caractère relatif et contingent» renvoie, en effet, essentiellement à la condition de réciprocité posée par l'article 55. Or cette condition est sans objet, comme le Conseil a eu l'occasion de le préciser ultérieurement, pour les engagements internationaux relatifs aux droits fondamentaux, comme la Convention européenne des droits de l'homme ou le traité portant statut de la Cour pénale internationale (Décision n° 98–408 DC du 22 janvier 1999, recueil p. 29), et pour les traités communautaires (Décision n° 92–308 DC du 9 avril 1992, recueil p. 55; n° 98–400 DC du 20 mai 1998, recueil p. 251).

Un troisième argument est tiré de ce *«qu'une loi contraire à un traité ne serait pas, pour autant, contraire à la Constitution»*. Cet argument a été également critiqué par la doctrine dans la mesure où la supériorité des traités sur les lois résulte d'une disposition expresse de la Constitution.[2]

Mais la décision IVG repose également sur des raisons pratiques. Selon la Constitution, le Conseil constitutionnel ne dispose que d'un délai d'un mois pour rendre ses décisions. Il serait très difficile d'examiner dans un délai aussi bref la conformité des lois avec les très nombreux engagements internationaux souscrits par la France, évalués à l'époque à plus de 4 000 traités. Dans le cadre du droit communautaire, il serait impossible pour le Conseil constitutionnel de poser, dans ce délai, une question préjudicielle d'interprétation ou d'appréciation de la validité d'un acte communautaire à la Cour de justice des Communautés européennes, conformément à l'ancien article 177 (devenu l'article 234) du Traité instituant la Communauté européenne.

---

[1] Actualité juridique de droit administratif, 1975, p 134, note Jean Rivero sous la Décision du 15 janvier 1975.
[2] Revue française de droit administratif, 1989, p 824, note Genevois sous Ass. 20 octobre 1989 Nicolo.

Cette jurisprudence est absolument constante.[3]

Dès l'origine, le Conseil constitutionnel a estimé que les dispositions de l'article 55 de la Constitution qui confèrent aux traités une autorité supérieure à celle des lois ne devaient pas, pour autant, rester sans sanction. On peut d'ailleurs noter qu'à la date à laquelle le Conseil a pris sa décision, la Cour d'appel de Paris avait déjà, par un arrêt du 7 juillet 1973, Société des Cafés Jacques Vabre, écarté l'application de la taxe intérieure de consommation prévue par l'article 265 du code des douanes du fait de son incompatibilité avec les dispositions de l'article 95 du Traité de Rome au motif que celui-ci, en vertu de l'article 55 de la Constitution, a une autorité supérieure à celle de la loi interne, même postérieure (Paris, 7 juillet 1973, D. 1974. 159, note J. Rideau; Gaz. Pal. 1973.2.661, concl. J. Cabannes).

Le Conseil a, ultérieurement, explicité sa position en jugeant *«qu'il appartient aux divers organes de l'Etat de veiller à l'application de ces conventions internationales dans le cadre de leurs compétences respectives»* (Décision n° 86–216 DC du 3 septembre 1986, ct 6). Comme le notait, dans son commentaire, le Secrétaire Général du Conseil, *«la formulation ainsi adoptée traduit sans aucun doute le souci du Conseil constitutionnel de voir respecter, conformément à la volonté du constituant, la suprématie du traité sur la loi. La référence «aux compétences respectives» des organes de l'Etat manifeste cependant le souci du juge constitutionnel de laisser aux juridictions chargées d'appliquer la règle de droit, le soin de définir elles-mêmes leur sphère de compétence».*[4]

La nature juridique ayant, elle aussi, horreur du vide, les tribunaux allaient s'engager dans la voie ainsi ouverte, selon un rythme très différent pour les juridictions judiciaires et administratives.

1.3. Les juridictions judiciaires se sont immédiatement engouffrées dans la voie ainsi ouverte: quatre mois après la Décision IVG, la Cour de cassation rendait en Chambre mixte un arrêt de principe confirmant l'arrêt de la Cour d'appel de Paris qui avait écarté l'application de l'article 265 du Code des douanes du fait de son incompatibilité avec le Traité de Rome, bien que cet article soit issu d'une loi postérieure au Traité (Cass. Ch. Mixte, 24 mai 1975, Société des Cafés Jacques Vabre, D., 1975, p. 497, concl. Touffait). Cet arrêt est une réponse directe à l'invitation du Conseil constitutionnel, comme le montrent les conclusions du Procureur Général Touffait. Après avoir rappelé le considérant précité de la Décision IVG selon lequel *«si les dispositions de l'article 55 de la Constitution*

---

[3] Décisions n° 77–83 DC du 20 juillet 1977, ct 6; n° 77–92 DC du 18 janvier 1978, ct 3; n° 80 116 DC du 17 juillet 1980, ct 7; n° 86–216 DC du 3 septembre 1986, ct. 6; n° 89–268 DC du 29 décembre 1989, cts 79 et 85; n° 91–293 DC du 23 juillet 1991, ct 5; n° 91–298 DC du 24 juillet 1991, ct 21; n° 91–294 DC du 25 juillet 1991, ct 60; n° 93–321 DC du 20 juillet 1993, ct 37; n° 96–375 DC du 9 avril 1996, ct 9; n° 98–399 DC du 5 mai 1998, ct 11; n° 98–400 DC du 20 mai 1998, ct 4; n° 98–405 DC du 29 décembre 1998, cts 15, 22 et 34; n° 99–416 DC du 23 juillet 1999, ct 16; n° 2006–535 DC du 30 mars 2006, cts 27 et 28.

[4] Revue française de droit administratif, 1987, p 120, note B. Genevois sur la Décision n° 86–216 DC du 3 septembre 1986.

confèrent aux traités une autorité supérieure à celle des lois, elles n'impliquent pas que le respect de ce principe doive être assuré par le Conseil constitutionnel», le Procureur général ajoute: *«On peut donc conclure de cette prise de position du Conseil constitutionnel qu'il doit l'être par les juridictions auxquelles ce problème est posé, et il leur appartient, sous peine de déni de justice, d'y répondre».*

Le Conseil d'Etat a, en revanche, mis quatorze ans pour s'engager dans la voie ouverte par la décision IVG. Ce délai tient à un plus grand respect du juge administratif pour la souveraineté du Parlement. Autant la Cour de cassation, en se faisant juge de la loi, a-t-elle retrouvé, deux siècles plus tard, les accents du Parlement de Paris, autant le Conseil d'Etat a-t-il dû renier tous ses gênes et presque sa raison d'être.

S'il s'est finalement décidé à franchir le pas, c'est pour deux raisons (Ass. 20 octobre 1989, Nicolo; Revue française de droit administratif,, 1989, p. 813 concl. Frydman, note Genevois). D'une part, le Conseil constitutionnel l'y a directement incité en se prononçant, comme juge électoral, sur la conformité de la loi du 11 juillet 1986 relative au mode de scrutin pour l'élection des députés à l'Assemblée Nationale avec le Protocole n° 1 additionnel à la Convention européenne des droits de l'homme (Décision n° 88–1082/1117 du 21 octobre 1988, A.N., Val d'Oise 5ᵉ circ., Revue française de droit administratif,, 1988, p. 908, note Genevois). D'autre part, le Conseil d'Etat ne pouvait rester plus longtemps en retrait du juge judiciaire, sauf à remettre en cause sa place dans l'ensemble de notre système juridictionnel. Les conclusions de M. Frydman sont à cet égard claires: *«On a vu que les juridictions judiciaires savent précisément s'affranchir aujourd'hui, sans le moindre complexe, du respect dû à l'autorité de la norme législative, pour faire prévaloir celle des traités. Et il y a évidemment quelque paradoxe à voir le Conseil d'Etat refuser d'entrer dans une telle logique par humilité face au législateur, alors que de simples tribunaux d'instance contrôlent chaque jour, par ce biais, la validité des lois qu'ils ont à appliquer».*

Pour franchir le pas, le Conseil d'Etat a considéré, comme l'y avait incité la doctrine,[5] que l'article 55 de la Constitution comporte une habilitation donnée implicitement aux juges pour contrôler la conformité des lois aux traités. Implicite dans l'arrêt Nicolo, qui se borne à viser l'article 55, ce fondement a été explicité ultérieurement par un arrêt Deprez et Baillard dans les termes suivants: *«Pour la mise en œuvre du principe de supériorité des traités sur la loi énoncé à l'article 55 de la Constitution, il incombe au juge, pour la détermination du texte dont il doit faire application, de se conformer à la règle de conflit de normes édictée par cet article»* (5 janvier 2005, Mlle Déprez et M. Baillard, Revue française de droit administratif, 2005, p. 56, note Bonnet; Revue trimestrielle de droit européen, 2006, p. 183, note Ondoua).

---

[5] R. Chapus, *Droit du contentieux administratif* (13th edn, Montchrestien, 2008), p 664; B. Genevois, note précitée sous la Décision n° 88–1082/1117 du 21 octobre 1988, A.N., Val d'Oise 5ᵉ circ.

Depuis que le Conseil d'Etat a franchi le Rubicon, le contrôle de conventionnalité a connu un essor considérable. Si l'on s'en tient à la seule Convention
européenne des droits de l'homme qui, par son contenu, rapproche le plus ce
contrôle d'un contrôle de constitutionnalité, il est très intéressant de mesurer la
progression du nombre d'affaires dans lesquelles est invoquée une stipulation de
cette convention: alors qu'en 1989, année de l'arrêt Nicolo, une telle stipulation
n'était invoquée que dans 38 affaires, ce chiffre dépasse les 2000 affaires en 2001,
soit environ 40 % de l'ensemble des affaires jugées par le Conseil d'Etat.

Si l'on retire le contentieux des étrangers, qui est un contentieux à la fois mas-
sif et purement individuel, on peut estimer que dans environ 20 % des affaires,
soit une affaire sur 5, le Conseil d'Etat est amené à se prononcer sur la conformité
d'une norme, législative ou réglementaire, avec la Convention européenne des
droits de l'homme.

Considérable sur le plan quantitatif, ce contrôle de conventionnalité s'apparente
très largement à un contrôle de constitutionnalité.

2. Malgré des différences apparentes, les deux contrôles sont, en effet, de même
nature et ont, en pratique, la même portée et les mêmes effets.

2.1. Les différences paraissent, a priori, considérables compte tenu des conditions d'exercice des deux contrôles.

Le contrôle de constitutionnalité est, dans le système français, un contrôle qui
s'exerce par voie d'action, à l'initiative d'autorités politiques, avant la promulgation de la loi: c'est un contrôle a priori et abstrait.

Le contrôle de conventionnalité est un contrôle qui s'exerce par voie d'exception
à l'initiative d'un justiciable qui conteste devant un juge l'application qui lui est
faite d'une loi en soutenant que celle-ci est incompatible avec une convention
internationale: c'est un contrôle a posteriori et concret.[6]

Il en résulte des effets juridiques très différents.

Les décisions du Conseil constitutionnel bénéficient des effets prévus par
l'article 62 de la Constitution aux termes duquel: *«Elles s'imposent aux pouvoirs
publics et à toutes les autorités administratives et juridictionnelles.»* Si le Conseil
constitutionnel déclare la loi qui lui est déférée contraire à la Constitution, celle-ci
ne peut être promulguée: elle disparaît donc de l'ordre juridique avant même d'y
être entrée. Si le Conseil constitutionnel déclare la loi conforme à la Constitution,
mais sous certaines réserves d'interprétation, ces réserves s'imposent au juge
administratif et judiciaire lorsqu'il fait application de cette loi.[7]

Les décisions du juge judiciaire ou du juge administratif qui écartent dans un
litige l'application d'une loi comme contraire à la Convention Européenne des

---

[6] Ce contrôle peut également s'exercer par voie d'action dans le cadre d'un recours pour excès
de pouvoir.
[7] Pour le Conseil d'Etat, Ass. 20 décembre 1985, S.A. Etablissements Outters, recueil p 382,
D. 1986 p 283, note Favoreu; Ass. 11 mars 1994, S.A. la Cinq, recueil p 117, concl. Frydman.Pour
la Cour de cassation, Ass. Plén. 10 octobre 2001, Breisacher, Revue française de droit constitutionnel, 2002, p 51, concl. De Gouttes.

droits de l'homme n'ont que l'autorité relative de la chose jugée: la loi reste en vigueur et l'autorité de la chose jugée ne peut être invoquée, sur le plan juridique, que si les trois conditions d'identité de parties, d'objet et de cause juridique sont réunies.

Mais, au-delà de ces différences apparentes, les deux contrôles sont, en réalité, de même nature juridique et ont, en pratique, la même portée et les mêmes effets.

Sur le plan juridique, le contrôle de conventionnalité est exactement de même nature qu'un contrôle de constitutionnalité par voie d'exception. Comme l'a souligné le Professeur Denys de Béchillon, *«le mécanisme intellectuel par lequel on parvient à ce résultat ne diffère pas de celui dont use le Conseil constitutionnel: il s'agit bien de juger la loi, de statuer objectivement sur sa conformité à la règle supérieure, de dire sa licéité».*

Il suffit, pour s'en convaincre, de relire l'admirable opinion du Chief Justice Marshall dans l'arrêt Marbury contre Madison qui, deux siècles plus tard, n'a pas pris une ride:

'*It is emphatically the province and duty of the judicial department to say what the law is. Those who apply the rule to particular cases, must of necessity expound and interpret that rule. If two laws conflict with each other, the courts must decide on the operation of each.*

So if a law be in opposition to the constitution; if both the law and the constitution apply to a particular case, so that the court must either decide that case conformably to the law, disregarding the constitution; or conformably to the constitution, disregarding the law; the court must determine which of these conflicting rules governs the case. This is of the very essence of judicial duty.

If then the courts are to regard the constitution; and the constitution is superior to any ordinary act of the legislature; the constitution, and not such ordinary act, must govern the case to which they both apply'.[8]

Le Commissaire du Gouvernement Frydman ne l'avait d'ailleurs pas caché au Conseil d'Etat dans ses conclusions sous l'arrêt Nicolo:

'*Si le juge écarte l'application de la loi, c'est bien, en définitive, et quels que soient les méandres du raisonnement suivi, parce qu'il considère que celle-ci ne saurait trouver application du fait même de sa contrariété au traité. Il est donc à tout le moins difficile de ne pas voir dans une telle démarche un contrôle exercé sur la validité de la loi. Et c'est en vain qu'on objecterait que celle-ci n'aboutirait qu'à déclarer la loi inapplicable à une espèce, et non véritablement à la censurer. On sait, en effet, que c'est précisément par ce biais que s'opère le contrôle de validité des lois dans les pays où, comme aux Etats-Unis, cette fonction relève des tribunaux ordinaires*'.[9]

[8] E. Zoller, *Grands arrêts de la Cour suprême des Etats-Unis*, Presses Universitaires de France, 2000, p 71.
[9] Ass. 20 octobre 1989, Nicolo; Revue française de droit administratif, 1989, p 813 concl. Frydman, note Genevois.

Le Conseil d'Etat l'a, depuis, explicitement admis dans l'arrêt précité *Deprez et Baillard* du 5 janvier 2005 qui, pour la première fois, expose cette théorie de façon complète:

'Considérant que l'article 61 de la Constitution du 4 octobre 1958 a confié au Conseil constitutionnel le soin d'apprécier la conformité d'une loi à la Constitution; que ce contrôle est susceptible de s'exercer après le vote de la loi et avant sa promulgation; qu'il ressort des débats tant du Comité consultatif constitutionnel que du Conseil d'Etat lors de l'élaboration de la Constitution que les modalités ainsi adoptées excluent un contrôle de constitutionnalité de la loi au stade de son application;

Considérant cependant, que pour la mise en œuvre du principe de supériorité des traités sur la loi énoncé à l'article 55 de la Constitution, il incombe au juge, pour la détermination du texte dont il doit faire application, de se conformer à la règle de conflit de normes édictée par cet article'.[10]

Tout est dans le *«cependant»*: le Conseil d'Etat n'exerce pas de contrôle de la constitutionnalité de la loi sauf en ce qui concerne la conformité de celle-ci aux traités internationaux pour laquelle il estime bénéficier d'une habilitation implicite du constituant en vertu de l'article 55. Tout au plus peut-on considérer que ce contrôle de constitutionnalité est indirect.

2.3. Sur le plan pratique, les deux types de contrôle ont une portée identique. En effet, la Convention de sauvegarde des droits de l'homme et des libertés fondamentales signée à Rome le 4 novembre 1950 et complétée par divers protocoles constitue, tant que la Charte communautaire des droits fondamentaux n'a pas de valeur juridique, le catalogue le plus complet des droits et libertés fondamentaux. Elle a été enrichie par une abondante jurisprudence de la Cour européenne des droits de l'homme qui permet de faire évoluer le contenu de ces droits en fonction de l'évolution de la société. Sauf peut-être en matière sociale, la Convention européenne des droits de l'homme englobe et même dépasse le catalogue des droits fondamentaux tel qu'il résulte, en France, de la Constitution de 1958 et de son Préambule, de la Déclaration des droits de l'homme et du citoyen de 1789, du Préambule de la Constitution de 1946 et des principes fondamentaux reconnus par les lois de la République auxquels il renvoie.

Comme l'a souligné le Professeur Denys de Béchillon, *«en ce qui concerne les droits fondamentaux, les normes de références du contrôle de conventionnalité et du contrôle de constitutionnalité des lois au fond sont à peu près les mêmes... L'addition des exigences prescrites par les traités applicables au sein de l'ordre juridique français fournit une liste de droits supérieure ou égale à celle que donne notre bloc de constitutionnalité».*[11]

---

[10] 5 janvier 2005, Mlle Déprez et M. Baillard, Revue française de droit administratif, 2005, p 56, note Bonnet; Revue trimestrielle de droit européen, 2006, p 183, note Ondoua.

[11] Denys de Béchillon, «De quelques incidences du contrôle de la conventionnalité internationale des lois par le juge ordinaire (Malaise dans la Constitution)», *Revue française de droit administratif,* 1998, p 225.

C'est ce qui explique le rôle croissant que joue la jurisprudence de la Cour européenne des droits de l'homme. Le Conseil d'Etat et la Cour de cassation sont tenus de s'y conformer, sous peine de voir leurs décisions désavouées et la France condamnée pour violation de la Convention. Le Conseil constitutionnel, s'il ne l'applique pas directement, s'en inspire étroitement dans la mesure où elle constitue aujourd'hui le principal élément fédérateur des différentes formes de contrôle de constitutionnalité qui s'exercent en France.

2.4. Les deux types de contrôle ont, enfin, les mêmes effets pratiques. Pour le démontrer, je me bornerai à deux exemples.

Le premier est tiré de l'arrêt d'Assemblée du 21 décembre 1990 par lequel le Conseil d'Etat a jugé *«qu'eu égard aux conditions posées par le législateur, les dispositions issues des lois des 17 janvier 1975 et 31 décembre 1979 relatives à l'interruption volontaire de grossesse, prises dans leur ensemble, ne sont pas incompatibles avec les stipulations de l'article 2 de la convention européenne de sauvegarde des droits de l'homme».* (Ass. 21 décembre 1999, Confédération nationale des associations familiales catholiques et autres, rec p. 369; Revue française *de* droit administratif, 1990, p. 1065, concl. Stirn; Actualité juridique de droit administratif, 1991, p. 91, note C.M., F.D. et Y.A.). Cette affaire est symbolique à plus d'un titre. Le moyen sur lequel le Conseil d'Etat s'est prononcé est celui là même sur lequel le Conseil constitutionnel avait refusé de se prononcer dans la décision IVG du 15 janvier 1975. Pour y répondre, le Conseil d'Etat ne pouvait pas ne pas tenir compte de la décision du Conseil constitutionnel. Comme le soulignait, dans ses conclusions, le Commissaire du Gouvernement Stirn:

'*Le Conseil constitutionnel s'est référé «au principe du respect de tout être humain dès le commencement de la vie», rappelé par l'article 1er de la loi soumise à son examen, et aux principes fondamentaux reconnus par les lois de la République pour reconnaître la constitutionnalité des nouvelles dispositions législatives. Les principes auxquels il a ainsi confronté ces dispositions sont les mêmes que ceux qui résultent de l'article 2 de la Convention européenne de sauvegarde des droits de l'homme et des libertés fondamentales*'.

Et si le Conseil d'Etat avait déclaré la loi du 17 janvier 1975 incompatible avec la Convention européenne des droits de l'homme, son arrêt aurait eu pour effet, sous réserve de l'appréciation de la Cour de Cassation en matière pénale, de rendre cette loi inapplicable et aurait donc eu le même effet pratique qu'une censure *ab initio* du Conseil constitutionnel.

Le second exemple est tiré d'un arrêt de la Cour de Cassation du 4 septembre 2001. Renversant une jurisprudence antérieure (Cass. Crim. 14 mai 1996, Bull. Crim. n° 204, p. 577), à laquelle le Conseil d'Etat s'était rallié (S. 2 juin 1999, Meyet, rec. p. 161), la Chambre criminelle de la Cour de cassation a jugé qu'en interdisant la publication, la diffusion et le commentaire de tout sondage pendant la semaine qui précède une élection, les articles 11 et 12 de la loi du 19 juillet 1977 *«instaurent une restriction à la liberté de recevoir et de communiquer des informations qui n'est pas nécessaire à la protection des intérêts légitimes énumérés par l'article*

10.2 de la Convention européenne des droits de l'homme; qu'étant incompatibles avec ces dispositions conventionnelles, ils ne sauraient servir de fondement à une condamnation pénale.»

Intervenant à quelques mois de l'élection présidentielle, cet arrêt, qui privait de toute sanction et donc de tout effet la loi du 19 juillet 1977, laissait toute liberté aux instituts de sondage de publier des sondages y compris le jour de l'élection, risquant ainsi de porter atteinte à la sincérité et à la dignité du scrutin.

Cette situation conduisit le Conseil constitutionnel, en tant que gardien de la régularité de l'élection présidentielle, à intervenir auprès des plus hautes autorités de l'Etat pour les inciter à combler ce vide juridique. Un projet de loi fut déposé le 16 janvier 2002 qui conduisait au vote, de manière consensuelle, de la loi du 19 février 2002 interdisant toute publication de sondage la veille et le jour du scrutin.

Cette affaire montre, de façon éclatante, que les effets d'une décision d'inconventionnalité sont très proches de ceux d'une décision d'inconstitutionnalité. L'expérience des pays qui, comme les Etats-Unis, connaissent un contrôle de constitutionnalité par voie d'exception est là pour confirmer les puissants effets d'un tel contrôle. Et ce contrôle de conventionnalité, on l'a vu, s'exerce dans un beaucoup plus grand nombre de cas que le contrôle de constitutionnalité.

La Décision IVG de 1975 a ainsi déclenché un processus qui, selon la théorie du battement d'ailes du papillon, a conduit à remettre en cause les fondements mêmes du dogme de la souveraineté de la loi en France. Près de deux siècles après Marbury contre Madison, la France a réinventé la *judicial review*. La loi qui, selon l'article 6 de la Déclaration de 1789, *«est l'expression de la volonté générale»*, peut être écartée par tout juge, quelle que soit sa position dans la hiérarchie judiciaire, qui l'estime incompatible avec la Convention européenne des droits de l'homme et la jurisprudence de la Cour de Strasbourg. Jean-Jacques Rousseau doit se retourner dans sa tombe et, avec lui, les constituants de 1789 qui avaient voté la loi des 16–24 août 1790 dont l'article 6 disposait que *«Les tribunaux ne pourront prendre directement ou indirectement aucune part à l'exercice du pouvoir législatif, ni empêcher ou suspendre l'exécution des décrets du corps législatif, sanctionnés par le roi, à peine de forfaiture»*.

La solution du *Human Rights Act* est, elle, beaucoup plus respectueuse de la souveraineté du Parlement. Si, en vertu de l'article 3, les tribunaux doivent dans toute la mesure du possible interpréter la loi en conformité avec les droits de la Convention, ils ne peuvent, si une telle interprétation n'est pas possible, que prononcer, en vertu de l'article 4, une déclaration d'incompatibilité de la loi avec la Convention européenne des droits de l'homme. En vertu de l'article 4 paragraphe 6, aucun tribunal, même s'il a prononcé une telle déclaration d'incompatibilité, n'a le pouvoir d'écarter l'application de la loi qui reste valable et continue à s'appliquer pleinement.

Contrairement aux juges français, le juge britannique ne peut donc écarter l'application d'une loi qu'il juge incompatible avec la Convention européenne des droits de l'homme dans l'affaire dont il est saisi. La satisfaction du requérant, qui a démontré cette incompatibilité, est toute platonique: il lui faudra aller devant la Cour européenne des droits de l'homme, s'il veut obtenir une indemnité pour violation par le Royaume-Uni d'une obligation de la Convention. Le gouvernement britannique a toujours indiqué, tant dans le livre blanc qu'au cours des débats parlementaires, qu'il ne voulait pas accorder aux tribunaux le pouvoir de la *judicial review* compte tenu de l'importance qu'il attachait à la souveraineté du Parlement. L'originalité de la solution du *Human Rights Act* est de séparer les deux fonctions que comportent le pouvoir de la *judicial review*:

- celle de déterminer s'il y a un conflit de normes entre la loi et la Convention;
- celle de paralyser l'effet de la loi si il y a un tel conflit.

Seule la première est accordée aux tribunaux tandis que la seconde reste l'apanage du Parlement. Et le *Human Rights Act* ne crée aucune obligation, autre que morale, pour le Gouvernement et le Parlement de modifier la loi déclarée incompatible par un tribunal, même s'il autorise, par son article 10, le Ministre compétent à la modifier par Ordonnance. Le Parlement reste ainsi seul juge, en dernier ressort, de l'adaptation de la législation à la Convention. Le vieil adage britannique selon lequel *«la Chambre des Communes peut tout faire sauf transformer un homme en femme»* n'a, décidément, rien perdu de sa portée.

8

Rules of International Law in English Courts

*Vaughan Lowe**

This short paper is offered as a mark of my respect and personal and professional esteem for Tom Bingham. He is an active and steadfast champion of international and comparative law, particularly in his capacities as judge and as Chairman and *genius loci* of the British Institute of International and Comparative Law; and all those who scratch around in these fields are greatly in his debt. I am pleased to be able to put forward these arguments within the safe confines of his *Festschrift*: they would be unlikely to withstand the force of his formidable intellect if put forward in a committee room in the House of Lords.

In this paper I will examine the question of the proper relationship between Public International Law and the English courts. To be more precise, I will consider the standing and the role of international law in English courts; and the distinction between the question of standing and the question of role lies at the heart of the main point that I wish to make, which is that rather than focus on the question whether and to what extent international law is a part of English law, one should focus on the question of what the English courts should *do* with rules of international law.

The first of those two questions—whether and to what extent international law is a part of English law—can be answered swiftly. It is usually answered by saying that treaties binding on the United Kingdom do not themselves have the force of law in English courts, but that customary international law[1] is a part, or more properly a source[2] of English law, which may be applied by the English courts.

The last phrase, 'which may be applied by the English courts', is a curious way to describe the position of rules of law in a court. One might think that the court *must* apply the relevant rules whenever they are applicable to the case before it.

---

* QC, Chichele Professor of Public International Law and Fellow of All Souls College, Oxford University.
[1] By which one should probably understand all rules of international law that are not rules of treaty law.
[2] See the discussion of this distinction in Vaughan Lowe, 'Shadows in the cave: the nature of international law when it appears before English courts', in *Festschrift for Colin Warbrick* (2008).

That is, however, to take a view of law and of courts that is perhaps too complex rather than too simplistic. That view supposes that, given the presentation to a court of a set of facts and the identification of an issue in dispute, there will necessarily be a set—and be one set only—of identifiable rules, whose application to the facts will necessarily generate, as in a syllogism, a unique answer to the issue in the dispute, whose job it is the court's to pronounce.

There are many defects in that description of the judicial process. The critical issue is the characterization of the facts, which is frequently a matter of appreciation and judicial discretion rather than of legal prescription or logical necessity; and even when the characterization has been decided upon there is often room for manoeuvre in the application of the rule, and in the interplay between rules, and between rules and principles such as proportionality, reasonableness, and good faith. Again, in any particular case there may be a bundle of different issues and one may effectively eclipse the others, preventing, or releasing the court from the obligation to decide subsequent issues; and the sequence in which such issues are addressed may itself be a matter that remains within the discretion of the court.

For all these, and many other reasons, it is plain that legal rules do not have the complex, sophisticated content and characteristics that would qualify them for 'automaticity'[3] in their application. This radical indeterminacy in the law is, I think, both unavoidable and a wholly desirable phenomenon, injecting human judgment into the process of the application of the law and ensuring a proper role for the judiciary. But it is not the subject of this paper. Rather, I wish to focus upon two other matters. One is the question of the *nature* of the rule of international law that an English court might have to apply; the other, the question of what the court should *do* with the rule.

Let me begin with the question of the nature of the rule. The first point, almost too obvious to need stating, is that it is necessary to determine with some precision what the rule of international law *is*. This is one of the points which lies behind the decision in the *Franconia* case, *R v Keyn*.[4] There the English court refused to say that simply because the rule of international law was that states were entitled to a territorial sea of three miles (as was the rule at that time), it followed that there was a territorial sea of three miles off the English coast in which English law applied.

Chief Justice Cockburn's[5] reasoning in that case merits quotation at some length:

It is obviously one thing to say that the legislature of a nation may, from the common assent of other nations, have acquired the full right to legislate over a part of that which

---

[3] A good nineteenth-century word, whose revival in 2002 was one of the only beneficial aspects of the miserable UN debates which preceded the invasion of Iraq.

[4] (1876) 2 Ex.D.63.

[5] Of whom Lord Bingham wrote: 'as a young man Sir Alexander Cockburn, later Chief Justice of Common Pleas and the Queen's Bench, had on one occasion to escape from bailiffs by climbing out of the window of the robing room at Exeter Castle, and that he fathered two illegitimate

was before high sea, and as such common to all the world, another and very different thing to say that the law of the local state becomes thereby at once, without anything more, applicable to foreigners within such part, or that, independently of legislation, the Courts of the local state can *proprio vigore* so apply it. The one position does not follow from the other; and it is essential to keep the two things, the power of Parliament to legislate, and the authority of our Courts, without such legislation, to apply the criminal law where it could not have been applied before, altogether distinct, which, it is evident, is not always done. It is unnecessary to the defence, and equally so to the decision of the case, to determine whether Parliament has the right to treat the three-mile zone as part of the realm consistently with international law. That is a matter on which it is for Parliament itself to decide. It is enough for us that it has, so far as to be binding upon us, the power to do so. The question is whether, acting judicially, we can treat the power of Parliament to legislate as making up for the absence of actual legislation. I am clearly of opinion that we cannot, and that it is only in the instances in which foreigners on the seas have been made specifically liable to our law by statutory enactment that the law can be applied to them.

Cockburn rests his reasoning on two bases. The first is that the rule of international law is *permissive*. It entitles states to claim a territorial sea. Cockburn did not regard the rule as mandating the maintenance of a territorial sea by each and every coastal state. The relevant rule of international law is, at least arguably, now mandatory. As Judge McNair remarked in his Dissenting Opinion in the *Anglo-Norwegian Fisheries* case, 'International law does not say to a State: You are entitled to claim territorial waters if you want them. No maritime State can refuse them.'[6] How would it have affected the decision in *Keyn* if Cockburn had understood the rule of international law to be mandatory? Certainly, Cockburn could not have argued simply that 'the power of Parliament to legislate' does not automatically entail 'the authority of our courts, without such legislation, to apply the criminal law where it could not have been applied before'. That is an important point; and it indicates the importance of determining precisely what the rule of international law is.

The distinction between permissive and mandatory rules is fundamental. The rule entitling a state to a territorial sea is (or was) permissive: the rule relating to the immunity of a foreign head of state from the jurisdiction of the English courts is mandatory. But that distinction needs further refinement. It is not enough to speak of immunity, for example as a 'mandatory' rule. One must ask what the

---

children. He declined a peerage on appointment as Chief Justice of the Queen's Bench, but was invited to indicate if he changed his mind; when he did so, the peerage was refused by Queen Victoria "upon the ground of the notoriously bad moral character of the Chief Justice". Whereas, in the original *Dictionary* [of National Biography] he was said to have been peculiarly fitted for the Alabama Claims Tribunal of 1871–1872, the new *Dictionary*, more accurately, records that he "formed a low opinion of the competence of the other arbitrators, and allowed his irritation to show through, even to the extent of insulting them"': <http://www.oup.com/oxforddnb/pdf/lives_of_the_law.pdf>. Lord Bingham's own account of the *Alamaba Claims* arbitration is a classic of international legal history, and one of the very few articles in a Law journal that can be read for pleasure: see T Bingham, 'The Alabama Claims Arbitration' (2005) 54 ICLQ pp 1–25.

6 ICJ Reports 1957, p 116, at p 160.

rule actually says. Does it say, 'the United Kingdom must secure the immunity of foreign heads of states from the jurisdiction of its courts' or 'the courts in the UK must accord immunity to foreign heads of state', or 'foreign heads of state have a right to immunity from the jurisdiction of courts in the UK', or 'foreign heads of states are immune from the jurisdiction of UK courts' (to set out but some of the possibilities)? The distinctions are important. If the rule imposes a duty on the United Kingdom as such, the English courts might reasonably adopt the 'Cockburn' approach and say, it is for the United Kingdom as such to secure this immunity, and that is a matter in respect of which the courts should wait upon Parliamentary action, because it is for Parliament (or the Executive) to decide whether the United Kingdom will act in accordance with its duties under international law and exactly how it will do so.

That argument would not be available if the rule specifically directed the English courts to accord immunity to the head of state. Similarly, if the rule gives a right to the head of state, the court would, presumably, consider how far that right is exercisable in the face of any other rules or rights that might conflict with it. If, however, the rule is that the head of state *is* immune, that rule would, if directly applicable in English courts, leave no room for judicial discretion or, indeed, any other approach which defeated the immunity.[7] Hence the need for precision in determining what the rule is.

The points made so far concern what might be called the internal aspect of the rule of international law. Is it permissive or mandatory? Does it create a right or a duty? To whom is it addressed? There is one further distinction to be made before moving on from this consideration of the internal nature of the rule. It concerns what might be called the normative quality or 'normative charge' of the rule.

To take mandatory, prohibitive rules as examples, the question is, what is the nature of the prohibition? In English law there are various reasons why a particular course of conduct might be forbidden. I am bound by the criminal law not to steal; but my duty not to defame another derives not from criminal law but from the law of tort. My duty not to use my home as a shop, in contrast, derives from neither criminal nor tort law, but from the law of contract. Yet all three prohibitions or disqualifications or disabilities[8] are ways of expressing or instantiating the rule, 'x is forbidden' or 'you must not do x'.

The question that I raise here is, when an English court looks at a prohibitive rule of international law, does it ever see anything other than a rule that says 'x is forbidden'? Does the court see a rule that sounds in the equivalent of criminal law, or tort law, or contract? And does it matter?

---

[7] I leave aside here the further complications that flow from the question whether any right or interest deriving from 'the immunity rule' in international law belongs to the head of state or the state, and if the latter, who can act—and who can act definitively—on behalf of the state.

[8] These are not synonyms; but in the present context I do not think that it matters how the prohibition is characterized.

This issue is not wholly unfamiliar to English courts. In the context of private international law and the rule of 'double actionability', derived from the celebrated pronouncement of Willes J in *Phillips v Eyre*,[9] English courts had to consider the question whether a tort committed abroad both (i) was actionable as a tort if committed in England, and (ii) to use the words of Willes J, was 'not... justifiable by the law of the place where it was done'.[10] The requirement that the act be 'not justifiable' under the foreign law was for many years satisfied not only if it involved civil liability under the law of the place where it was done,[11] analogous to tortious liability in English law, but also if the act, while not entailing civil liability, resulted in criminal liability under that foreign law.[12] While that approach, treating criminal liability as rendering an act 'not justifiable', was abandoned in *Boys v Chaplin* in 1971,[13] it remained the case that *any* form of civil liability was sufficient to satisfy the 'not justifiable' requirement, whether that liability was contractual, quasi-contractual, quasi-delictual, proprietary, or *sui generis*.[14]

While it would go too far to suggest that there is any grand theory discernible in *Phillips v Eyre*, one might discern in that decision, and in the cases that followed it, an implicit assumption that there are two levels of prohibition: one, a rule that says 'x is forbidden', and the other, a rule that says 'x is actionable as a tort' or 'x is a crime' or 'x is actionable as a breach of contract', or whatever. It was enough to satisfy the 'foreign law' limb of *Phillips v Eyre* that the primitive 'x is forbidden' rule was in place in the country where the act was committed; but the 'English law' limb was more demanding, and required that the act would be actionable as a tort if committed in England.

As plaintiffs in English courts must base themselves upon some cause of action, and as the rule in *Phillips v Eyre* was set out in the context of actions in tort, the precision required in the 'English law' limb is unsurprising. But its very obviousness may conceal an important underlying principle: that the question of the manner of dealing with wrongful conduct, like questions of remedies generally, is a matter for the *lex fori*. Put crudely, states may agree that particular conduct should not be lawful, but may differ as to the manner in which they choose to proceed against those who engage in that unlawful conduct; and a court should always adopt the approach that has been adopted in the law of the country where it has its seat. In general terms, there is a distinction between the primitive rule and the corresponding 'legal rule' which is located within English law (the law of the 'receiving' state, as it were) in the manner determined solely by English law

[9] (1870) LR 6 QB 1.

[10] The rule in *Phillips v Eyre* was abrogated by the Private International Law (Miscellaneous Provisions) Act 1995.

[11] *Carr v Fracis Times & Co* [1902] AC 176.

[12] *Machado v Fontes* [1987] 2 QB 231 (CA).

[13] [1971] AC 356.

[14] See the discussion in L Collins (ed), *Dicey and Morris on the Conflict of Laws* (11th edn, 1987), Rule 205, pp 1365–1373.

and whose consequences, and the procedures for whose application, are determined solely by English law.[15] The *lex fori* determines the normative charge of the rule.

This distinction between the primitive rule emanating from a legal system outside English law, and its incarnation as a rule—its reception and application as a norm, having normative force—within English law,[16] is one way of understanding the decision of the House of Lords in *R v Jones (Margaret) and Milling*. The question[17] was whether the crime of waging a war of aggression, which the House of Lords accepted was indeed a crime under customary international law[18] counted as a 'crime' for the purposes of section 3 of the Criminal Law Act 1967. That section stipulates that 'a person may use such force as is reasonable in the circumstances in the prevention of crime'; and the appellants had invoked section 3 as a defence to criminal charges brought against them after they had entered on to an airbase in Fairford, Gloucestershire, and sought to prevent aircraft from taking off on missions to bomb Iraq at the beginning of the invasion of that country in 2003. The appellants said that they were acting to prevent *inter alia*, the commission of the crime of aggression. Though many war crimes established by international law had been made crimes in English law by the International Criminal Court Act (and it was accepted that the section 3 defence was available insofar as the appellants were acting to prevent any such crimes), aggression was not among them. The central issue was, therefore, whether the fact that aggression was a crime in international law meant that it was *ipso facto* a crime in English law, prevention of which would in principle fall within the scope of the section 3 defence.

The House of Lords held that aggression was, though a crime in international law, not a crime in English law. The reason was the impeccable constitutional principle that only the legislature can create new crimes in English law.[19] This decision of the House of Lords might be viewed as acknowledging the existence of a primitive 'aggression is forbidden' norm in international law, but treating the characterization of that norm within the framework of English law as a question

[15] This distinction might be useful in considering proposals for the relationship between English law and, e.g., Islamic law, of the kind explored by the Archbishop of Canterbury in his speech in February 2008—a speech rather more thoughtful than was most of the criticism made of it. See <http://www.archbishopofcanterbury.org/1575>.

[16] It will be noted that the foreign law 'non-justifiability' in *Phillips v Eyre* has normative force, because the prohibition of the conduct is critical to the question of liability in the English court, but that its normative force is inchoate or conditional, because such liability also required that it be actionable in English law. This is a good example of the subtlety with which courts may handle the reception of foreign law rules. The superimposition of rules of the *lex fori* on procedure and remedies affords many other examples.

[17] [2006] UKHL 16; [2006] 2 WLR 772. The author appeared as counsel for two of the appellants in this case.

[18] Thus averting the need for an historic apology to whose whom the Allies hanged for that offence after the Nuremberg War Crimes trials.

[19] Though one might ask whether a distinction may not be drawn between the creation of a crime for the purpose of punishing someone under English law, and the acknowledgement of the existence of a crime for the purpose of the defence under section 3 of the Criminal Law Act 1967.

to be answered by reference to English law—and specifically, in this case, by the application of the constitutional principle that the courts cannot create new crimes.[20]

The relationship between rules of international law and English law that I am suggesting here has something (but not a great deal) in common with the relationship between EU Directives and English law. Both indicate the fundamental posture that the national legal system must adopt towards certain legal questions, and both leave it to the national legal system to decide precisely how to implement the directive set out in the Directive. The key difference, of course, is that by a miracle of illogicality and auto-suggestion, the European Court of Justice convinced itself and (most) national courts that EU law is both automatically applicable within national legal orders and superior to the rules of national law.

I have argued that it is for English courts to decide what normative quality to attach to a rule of international law. In *Jones and Milling*, aggression was held not to be a crime under English law; but that decision does not close the door to the possibility that an English court would hold that aggression is unlawful, so that a contract to provide, say, military services to assist an act of aggression might be regarded as unlawful for that reason (quite apart from any other reasons of English law that there might be for reaching that conclusion). That is a question that the English courts are free to decide. They determine the nature of the normative charge that is attached in the context of the English legal system to the primitive rule of international law.

There is a clear link, both linguistic and conceptual, between that argument and my second, and main, argument, which is that it is wrong to focus upon questions of the *status* of international law in English courts. Rather, one should focus upon the question, what may English courts properly *do* with a rule of international law.

A preliminary point, sometimes overlooked, is that not every reference to a rule of law is an application of that rule. One might say that a rule is applied when the content of the rule provides a sufficient reason for deciding a question of law in a particular way. For example, a rule of customary international law might be applied by an English court in order to afford a defendant immunity, as the courts were wont to do in the days before the entry into force of the State Immunity Act 1978.[21] On the other hand, a rule might be referred to by a court not as a rule of decision, but as a fact, to be taken into account in reaching a decision on the basis of other rules of (English) law. That is essentially what happens when courts refer to the provision of treaties in order to construe the terms of an English statute.[22] The legal rule of interpretation is that it is presumed that

---

[20] One might also regard that principle, in this context, as reflecting the allied principle that the *Executive* cannot create new crimes. It is, after all, the Executive that has the primary role in acting for the United Kingdom, and in entering into legal obligations, on the stage of international law.

[21] See, e.g., *Baccus v SRL Servicio Nacional del Trigo* [1957] 1 QB 438 (CA).

[22] See, e.g., *Fothergill v Monarch Airlines* [1981] AC 251.

Parliament did not intend to legislate contrary to the international obligations of the United Kingdom, so that an interpretation of a statute that is consistent with a treaty obligation is to be preferred to an interpretation that is not. That is a rule of English law, not a rule of international law: the international law obligation is referred to as a fact, a datum with which interpretations of the English law rule are to be compared. It is hard to see what possible objections there could be to it.

If, on the other hand, a court were asked to issue an injunction forbidding the Crown to engage in a course of conduct (e.g., bombing Baghdad) on the ground that the conduct would violate British obligations under international law, the position would be very different. As in the case of state immunity under the common law, or the implementation of a treaty, there is a rule of law in the background. If the rule is a rule of customary international law, it is a part or a source of English law. English judges are, in principle, as well equipped to determine the scope and content of that rule as is any other lawyer. It is certainly not 'nonjusticiable' in the sense that there is no clearly discernible rule there at all; and the reason why the courts will not issue such an injunction has nothing to do with the status of international law in English courts. The reason is one that is founded upon the constitutional relationship between the courts and the other branches of government. Just as the courts will not now create new crimes, but leave this function to the legislature, so the courts will not direct the deployment of British armed forces or the conduct of British foreign policy.

There are, of course, few bright line boundaries. In *R (Bancoult) v Secretary of State for Foreign and Commonwealth Affairs (No 2)*[23] two Orders in Council made in 2004 in relation to the British Indian Ocean Territory, which includes the island of Diego Garcia, were struck down by the Court of Appeal because they frustrated the legitimate expectation of the former inhabitants that they would be allowed to return to some of the islands; and the Orders therefore amounted to an abuse of power. That decision plainly affected the conduct of British foreign policy, but in a way that was crucially limited. First, the Court did not tell the government that it must not pursue a particular policy, it simply blocked one way in which the government had sought to achieve it; and secondly, the Court did so on the basis of a rule of English law which secured the constitutional balance between the rights of the individual and the power of the Executive.

What, then, are the limits to what English courts may properly do with rules of international law? The answer to that question is the reason that I cannot answer it. The answer must, on the view that I have advanced here, be a matter for English law, and in the absence of legislation, a matter for the English courts. They must decide the proper constitutional relationship between the courts and the Executive and the legislature, in matters governed by international law. Their

[23] [2007] EWCA Gv 498.

answers need to be based upon a coherent and defensible conception of the constitutional order; but there is no body of *a priori* principles, or even of legal precedents, that maps out what shape that order must necessarily take.

One can point to some markers. The courts should, indeed, not 'create' new crimes by treating crimes under international law as entailing criminal liability in English law without their enactment by the legislature. The courts should not issue orders directing the deployment or non-deployment of British armed forces. They should not issue orders directing the government on the conduct of British foreign policy. None of these things, for reasons that are, at least in broad terms, too obvious to need to be spelled out here, lies within the proper function of the courts.

It is not that the courts *could* not decide on questions of the international legality of government conduct in this field. International law is no more arcane, no more uncertain, and no more difficult to comprehend and to apply, than many other areas of the law routinely applied by the courts. Nor is international law any more overlain by complex political and economic considerations than are many cases before the courts. It is not that these questions are not justiciable: it is that whatever the precise legal position might be it is necessary that in certain areas the government has the right and the freedom to act before, and perhaps in spite of, the completion of legal challenges to its proposed course of action. It simply makes no sense to say that military deployment to retake the Falkland Islands, or to participate in the invasion of Iraq, must be suspended to await the outcome of court challenges and of subsequent appeals.

My central point, however, is that this argument has a limited scope. In particular, it sets up no obstacle to the English courts giving *declaratory* rulings, in which they determine whether or not an action which they have properly left to the Executive is in conformity with international law.

One can see that the courts might consider that they should not give rulings in purely abstract or hypothetical cases, where the facts remain indeterminate. Indeed, this point might be generalized by saying that the courts will only ever give such a ruling in cases where 'it is necessary to do so in order to determine rights and obligations under domestic law'.[24] One can also see that the courts should only give answers to justiciable questions. They cannot properly answer the question, is this action in the best interests of British foreign policy or national security?[25] But the questions of international law are plainly justiciable, and not at all of the same kind as questions of the national interest which must be decided by the exercise of the government's judgment and discretion.

There are also limits to the extent to which English courts can properly rule upon questions which spill over into areas covered by the doctrines of state

[24] *CND v The Prime Minister and Others* [2002] EWHC 2777 (Admin), at para 36.
[25] *Chandler v DPP* [1964] AC 763; *Council of Civil Service Unions v Minister for the Civil Service* (the 'GCHQ case') [1985] 1 AC 374.

immunity and Act of State—although it is by no means clear that this area is as extensive as some commentators might think.

But where the courts are not being asked to make orders that actually interfere directly with the conduct of foreign policy, or matters covered by international law, but simply to declare what the relevant rule of international law is, I can see no good reason why the courts should refuse to do so. Arguments that the courts might embarrass the Executive are unpersuasive. If the Executive is about to violate the United Kingdom's obligations under international law, that is itself an embarrassment to all arms of the government, and to the citizens of this country, which one hopes the Executive would be as keen to avoid or repair as would the courts and others.

9

Towards an International Rule of Law?

Philippe Sands and Blinne Ní Ghrálaigh

The existence of the 'rule of law' as a constitutional principle in English law is recognized by the Constitutional Reform Act 2006,[1] and there is support for the idea that such a principle requires compliance by the state with its obligations under international law.[2] But what of the idea of an 'international rule of law', as a principle or rule of global application, whether of a constitutional or other character? There has been important academic writing on the subject, in particular Phillip Allott's seminal work *Eunomia*, which identifies governments as 'generating an international Rule of Law, whilst still conceiving of themselves as masters of the Rule of Power'.[3] States are willing to evoke 'an international order based on the rule of law', or 'the rule of law at the national and international levels'.[4] Curiously, however, it seems that international courts and tribunals have not yet seen fit to give their imprimatur of approval to the concept of an international rule of law. At the International Court of Justice, for example, that formulation has been invoked in separate or dissenting opinion,[5] but not, it would appear, by the Court itself.

It seems only a matter of time before that changes. The last few years have been marked by a growing debate about the system of international rules that promote humanitarian objectives, human rights, and the notion of international justice. For the first time since the 1940s, the fundamental adequacy of the

---

[1] Constitutional Reform Act 2005, s 1 ('This Act does not adversely affect (a) the existing constitutional principle of the rule of law'); see T Bingham, *The Rule of Law* (6th Sir David Williams lecture), 16 November 2006, available at: <http://www.cpl.law.cam.ac.uk/past_activities/the_rt_hon_lord_bingham_the_rule_of_law.php>.

[2] T Bingham, *The Rule of Law*, n 1 above, at p 29.

[3] P Allott, *Eunomia: New Order for a New World* (1990), s 16.49.

[4] See below, n 37 and accompanying text.

[5] See e.g., Dissenting Opinion of Vice President Weeramantry, case Concerning Legality of Use of Force (*Yugoslavia v Belgium*), Request for Indication of Provisional Measures, 2 June 1999, 38 *ILM* 950 at 1020 ('Whatever the reason for the aerial bombing which is now in progress, and however well-intentioned its origin, it involves certain fundamentals of the international legal order—the peaceful resolution of disputes, the overarching authority of the United Nations Charter and the concept of the international rule of law. It is upon these fundamental principles that the ensuing opinion is based.').

existing concepts and structures has been put in question. The concept of the international rule of law—what it is, how it operates—lies at the heart of that debate.

The events of 11 September 2001—followed by the terrible attacks in London, Madrid, and Bali—have acted as a catalyst, leading to a fundamental rethinking of questions concerning the balance between security and human rights and between political imperatives and the established legal order, although many of the issues were in the ether even before the terrible events of that day. As a reaction to those attacks, key players on the international stage have increasingly sought to pit security and political imperatives *against* human rights and international law in a balancing act which appears to undermine the very notion of an international rule of law. However, does the 'global war on terror' require a rebalancing of human rights and security? Have the rules of the game changed, as British Prime Minister Tony Blair put it after the terror attacks on London in July 2005?[6] Are there circumstances when it may be 'necessary to balance the need to maintain the rule of law against the wider public interest', as then Attorney General Lord Goldsmith told the House of Lords in December 2006?[7] Can aggressive interrogation or even torture ever be justified to obtain information that could protect a population from terrorist attack, as President George W Bush appears to have recently stated in justifying a veto on a Congressional bill that sought to prohibit certain 'interrogation techniques' employed by the CIA?[8] Is it ever lawful to detain people indefinitely without rights at places like Guantanamo and Belmarsh prison? Could Saddam's atrocities have legally justified his overthrow?

These and many other questions have entered public consciousness, informing public discourse on almost every level. At their heart they turn on a central issue, namely whether the system of international rules and norms that was put in place in the 1940s and which had been relied on ever since in dealing with challenges old and new remains adequate and relevant. Have we come to another '1940s moment' when the existing principles of international law, in particular humanitarian and human rights law, and the institutions put in place to uphold them should be totally overhauled? Do the new challenges require allegedly 'obsolete' and 'quaint' rules of international law to be set aside?

It is clear that the international rule of law, such as it is, *has* faced serious challenges in recent times in the form of the rise of international terrorism. But perhaps a greater challenge still has been posed by the rejection or disregard of the established rules of international law by states as a response to those attacks. It is

---

[6] P Wintour, 'Blair vows to root out extremism: Lawyers and Muslim groups alarmed', *The Guardian*, 6 August 2005, p 1.

[7] Lords Hansard, 14 December 2006, column 1715.

[8] President's Radio Address, 8 March 2008 ('The bill Congress sent me would take away one of the most valuable tools in the war on terror—the CIA program to detain and question key terrorist leaders and operatives'): <http://www.whitehouse.gov/news/releases/2008/03/20080308.html>.

a real paradox that gross breaches of the international rule of law have been relied upon by states to justify yet more violations and further disregard for the international rule of law.

In this, the Bush Administration in the United States has made a singular contribution, often assisted by Blair and Brown's Britain. In the conduct of a misconceived 'war on terror', the Administration has jettisoned many rules of international law that the US had done so much to put in place. It has done so in waging an illegal war against Iraq, which was not authorized by the UN Security Council and was not justified—or even claimed to be justified—as self-defence.[9] It has done so in denying rights under the Geneva Conventions to detainees held at Guantanamo, creating a legal black hole which has set people outside the protections of the law for the first time since the Geneva Conventions were agreed. It has done so in a policy of detainee interrogations that rejects the constraints of the 1984 Convention against Torture and Other Cruel, Inhuman or Degrading Treatment or Punishment, which contributed to the chain of events that led to the outrages of Abu Ghraib. And it has done so in pursuing a policy of extraordinary rendition outside the norms of international law.

Other states, spurred on by the flouting of international law and practice by the world's most powerful nation, have used the 'war on terror' to curtail human rights and outlaw political dissent. Thus, security concerns have been used to justify draconian legal and military measures which undermine fundamental rights. Examples include Russia's handling of the Chechen conflict,[10] Iran's efforts to stifle domestic freedoms,[11] and Israel's illegal construction of a wall in the Occupied Palestinian Territory.[12] Other states, including the United Kingdom, are often complicit in those breaches insofar as they provide tacit support for or turn a blind eye to illegal practices, as, for example, in relation to the practice of extraordinary rendition.[13]

All of this signals a return to a world order based on the overt use of force and power to protect and promote self interests, rather than a world order governed by reference to the rule of law and international norms and standards, which is precisely what those norms and standards, and the systems put in place to support them, elaborated and put in place in the 1940s, were designed to guard against. This shift undermines peace, justice, and security. It also challenges the development of a principle of an international rule of law.

---

[9] P Sands, *Lawless World: Making and Breaking Global Rules* (2006), p 174 *et seq* V Lowe, 'The Iraq Crisis: What Now?' 52 *ICLQ* 859 (2003).
[10] See e.g., *Application no 57950/00) Isayeva v Russia*, judgment of 6 July 2005.
[11] Amnesty International Report 2007, p 239 *et seq*, at: <http://thereport.amnesty.org/eng/eng/Homepage>.
[12] *Legal Consequences of the Construction of a Wall in the Occupied Palestinian Territory*, Advisory Opinion of 9 July 2004, *ICJ Reports* 2004, p 136.
[13] P Sands, 'The International Rule of Law: Extraordinary Rendition, Complicity and its Consequences', 2006 *European Human Rights Law Review* 408.

(1) The International Rule of Law: Some Background

In order to understand the nature of current principles and apparatus of international law in force since the end of World War II, it is useful to provide some information as to their background and creation. We begin in August 1941, on a warship off the coast of Newfoundland, at a meeting between US President Franklin Delano Roosevelt and British Prime Minister Winston Churchill. It is a time of great challenge and threat for Britain and the United States, given that the Second World War is still raging. What these two men decide is required is the blueprint for a new international order to prevent another such war occurring in the future. That new rules-based international order would replace the then-existing arrangements that allowed a state do with impunity whatever it wished that was not expressly prohibited by international law. And since not much was prohibited, there was a great deal states could do without constraint of the law. They could wage war without legal restriction. They could commit genocide against their own populations without sanction. They could torture detainees with impunity. That was the world of the 1930s which Churchill and Roosevelt set out to change.

Roosevelt and Churchill drafted a one page document—the Atlantic Charter—by which they intended to make known, as they put it, 'certain common principles in the national policies of their respective countries on which they base their hopes for a better future for the world'.[14] The Atlantic Charter was short but visionary and identified three key pillars to an emerging system of international relations, namely: a general obligation on states to refrain from the use of force, except in self-defence or where expressly authorized to use force by a permanent system of general security;[15] a commitment to human rights, to maintain the 'inherent dignity' and the 'equal and inalienable rights' of all members of the human family; and an undertaking to promote economic liberalization through the adoption of free trade rules and related international obligations in the fields of foreign investment and intellectual property. These three pillars were seen as interdependent, in recognition of the reality that justice and human rights are dependent on meeting social and economic needs, that economic interests cannot trump fundamental rights, and that failing to provide basic human needs leads to violence and the use of force. Overarching them is a commitment—implicit if not plainly articulated—to the international rule of law.

The Atlantic Charter had an immediate and far-reaching impact. Importantly, the international rules it championed were perceived as creating opportunities for peoples and states, not as imposing illegitimate constraints upon them. Writing in his autobiography, Nelson Mandela described the Atlantic Charter as having reaffirmed his faith in human dignity: 'some in the West saw the Charter as

---

[14] 14 August 1941, reproduced in *Lawless World*, n 9 above, p 240.

[15] With the establishment of the UN, this was to become the role of the Security Council.

empty promises', he wrote, 'but not those of us in Africa. Inspired by the Atlantic Charter and the fight of the Allies against tyranny and aggression, the ANC created its own charter...which called for full citizenship for all Africans, the right to buy land and the repeal of all discriminating legislation.'[16]

In a remarkable period between 1941 and 1949, the three pillars on which the Charter was based were recast into international rules and institutions, far-reaching treaties and instruments which together constituted the modern system of international rules which has formed the basis of international law and cooperation for the last 60 years. At their heart are the rules on *human rights* (the UN Charter and the UN Declaration on Human Rights), on *humanitarian law* governing methods and means of warfare (the Geneva Conventions), and on *international criminal justice* (the Nuremburg Statute and Tribunal).

Perhaps the most important achievement of all was the creation in San Francisco in the spring of 1945 of the United Nations, by 51 founding states, crystallizing in law the modern rules governing the use of force and promoting human rights. That was followed by another formidable achievement, namely the UN General Assembly's Universal Declaration of Human Rights which in turn led to the covenants on civil and political rights and on economic and social rights (1966), which in their turn informed subsequent regional and national human rights instruments, like the European Convention on Human Rights and, eventually, the Human Rights Act 1998 in England.

The world's first ever human rights treaty, the Convention on the Prohibition of Genocide was agreed by the UN General Assembly in 1948, the day after the Universal Declaration was adopted. It has been followed over the years by other specialized human rights treaties, such as the 1984 Torture Convention, which obliges state parties to prosecute or extradite torturers (it was this Convention which, some 14 years later in 1998, prevented Senator Pinochet from claiming immunity before the English courts) or the recent 2006 Convention against enforced disappearance.

The US and Britain also led international efforts to negotiate the Geneva Conventions on the law of armed conflict, including the Third Geneva Convention on the treatment of prisoners of war and other detainees. This is the same instrument that was to become the centre of so much attention many years later in relation to events at Guantanamo, in Afghanistan, and Abu Ghraib in Iraq.[17]

The 1945 Statute of the Nuremburg Military Tribunal spurred on the development of international criminal law to deal with individuals committing crimes in the name of the state. This would eventually lead to the Yugoslav and Rwanda tribunals and ultimately to the 1998 Rome Statute of the International Criminal Court, establishing a permanent tribunal to prosecute individuals for genocide, crimes against humanity, war crimes, and—in time—the crime of aggression.

---

[16] Nelson Mandela, *Long Walk to Freedom* (London: Abacus, 1994), p 110.

[17] See Philippe Sands, *Torture Team: Deception, Cruelty and the Compromise of Law* (Penguin, 2008).

Developments in international law were no less far-reaching in the economic field: the Bretton Woods Agreement created the World Bank and the International Monetary Fund, in 1944, and in 1948 agreement was reached on the General Agreement on Tariffs and Trade—the GATT—the world's first global free trade rules and the parent of today's World Trade Organization. These economic rules were recognized to be closely connected to the social rules relating to human well-being.

By *any* standard, these were remarkable achievements in a very short period of time.

Over the past 60 years the principles set forth in the Atlantic Charter have defined the new international order. A great number of international agreements have been adopted, touching on issues that affect each and every person and state very directly. Trade. Investment. Commerce. Air transport. Oceans. Boundaries. Labour standards. Human rights. The great majority of these rules are not controversial and work efficiently and well, establishing the minimum standards necessary for cooperation in an increasingly interdependent world, in which the very nature of globalization poses its own challenges by increasing disparities and tensions. It is no exaggeration to state that the emergence of this great body of rules reflects a silent global revolution.

However, one should not be starry-eyed about international rules. It would be quite erroneous to suggest that global rules can sort out all the wrongs of the world. Plainly they cannot. And certainly the world has changed greatly in the period since the UN was created and the new system of rules emerged. The number of states has grown from approximately 50 to 200, largely as a result of decolonization and the collapse of the Soviet Union. The range of issues requiring international cooperation—and hence international legislation—has also grown, to include issues like the environment, tourism, and consumer safety. New international actors have also emerged: the monopoly of states has diminished and international organizations, NGOs, corporations, and individuals are assuming a role that presents profound challenges for an international legal order constructed on the assumption that the global order is premised upon and revolves around the supremacy of nation states. Failed states, peripatetic travellers, permeable national borders, malign non-governmental actors, and the proliferation of 'weapons of mass destruction' are but some of the issues that pose very real challenges to the established international legal order. However, do those changes really call for and necessitate a radical revision of that legal order and principles and norms behind it?

(2) Recent Challenges

The existing rules are certainly far from perfect. Events over the last 60 years demonstrate how much the international order has failed and continues to fail so many members of the global community. Large scale poverty, atrocities, and abuses have not gone away, and have in some instances grown. The inability of the international community and the UN in particular to prevent, for example, the horrors of Darfur and the systematic violations of fundamental rights in the Israeli/Palestinian conflict stand as stark reminders of the manifest inadequacies of the existing system of rules, which cannot alone deliver justice and human rights.

Furthermore, and fundamentally, the system of international law is inherently precarious in that it is essentially reliant on political will in order for it to be sustained and upheld, and that political will is often lacking. It is clear that, ever since the framing of the Atlantic Charter, international rules and principles have been in the thrall of international politics. Indeed, from the outset, the new rules-based system initiated by the Atlantic Charter reflected a view that international rules would promote Anglo-American interests, serve as a bulwark against the Soviet model, and emphasize select values to be marshalled against Nazi and fascist threats. It was not an exercise in altruism. And over the years, politics has often served to curtail or stifle the effective workings of international systems and the effective implementation of international law. No examples are as marked as the veto held and used all too often by permanent members of the Security Council to protect their interests or those of their allies.

The lack of enforcement mechanisms for international law is one of its main weaknesses and one of the primary criticisms levied against it: international law does not have the system of courts, penalties, and sanctions that are in place under national law and no overarching super entity which could compel the upholding of its standards and the enforcement of its decisions (which makes the domestic application of international rules all the more important). Furthermore, resources, both human and economic, essential to the functioning of the international legal order, are often so profoundly lacking in relation to fundamental needs.[18]

However, these inadequacies or limitations of international law are not new. They have been inherent in the international system throughout the past 60 years, and yet no credible voices were raised before now to suggest that they meant that the international order had failed and should be drastically rethought. Indeed, it was only ten years ago in 1998 that Tony Blair underscored his commitment to the fundamental principles of international human rights law by incorporating them into British national law by way of the Human Rights Act (a singular achievement of his first government). Has the world really changed so much in the short intervening years between then and now so as to render those principles outmoded and irrelevant?

As set out at the beginning of this article, the question of the relevance of international law and its capacity to meet the challenges of the 21st century has been

---

[18] Indeed, although the UN's mandates are global, its staffing and financial resources are less than that of major municipal authorities, leading to its offices being over-committed and over-stretched.

posed with increasing frequency since September 11. The international system of laws has been undermined—implicitly and explicitly—by those who should uphold it. Indeed, it has been accused of and blamed for purportedly *threatening* rather than upholding state security and sovereignty—a position adopted by many in the Bush Administration and their allies.

Even in the months leading up to September 11 it was clear that the Bush Administration was committed to remaking the international legal system, replacing Roosevelt's vision of an international order based on rules by which all would be bound with a new policy of 'à la carte multilateralism' whereby the United States could pick and choose the bits of international law it liked and ignore the rest. The Statute of the new International Criminal Court, the Kyoto Protocol on global warming, and various arms control treaties were the first victims of this new policy. They were not simply jettisoned, but were vilified as instruments that would constrain the United States, undermine its sovereignty, and threaten its national security.

After September 11 little time was lost. Rather than respond to the attack using well-established principles of national and international law, the Bush Administration determined that it would not be constrained by those principles. Security was pitted against the international rule of law in a false dichotomy. Lawyers were charged—without consultation of even the United States' closest of allies—with determining new legal rules which would enable the United States to act unfettered by constraints of the international legal order. An early decision was taken to characterize the response to international terrorism as a 'war'. This had the effect of taking it and, crucially, those suspected of involvement in it, outside the scope of the ordinary criminal law and into the rules of armed conflict, largely governed by the Geneva Conventions. However, even the lesser requirements and guarantees of the Geneva Conventions proved too stringent for those in the White House: acting unilaterally in a manner that was inconsistent with the requirements of international law in times of 'war' or armed conflict, the Administration determined that suspects in its 'war' would be placed outside the constraints of the law. The concept of 'unlawful combatant' was appropriated to deny prisoners of the 'war on terror' any of the protections afforded by the Geneva Conventions. Guantanamo became the location of choice for their detention, following advice from Administration lawyers that its location in Cuba, outside US jurisdiction, would deny them any means of redress under United States constitutional law or international law. Guantanamo was deliberately created as a 'legal black hole', as the English Court of Appeal was later to describe it,[19] where people were purposefully and strategically placed beyond the protections of the law.[20]

---

[19] *R (Abbasi)* v *Secretary of State for Foreign and Commonwealth Affairs* [2002] EWCA Civ 1598, para 66.

[20] It is noteworthy that Israel has long refused to accept the applicability of the Fourth Geneva Convention, concerning the protection of civilian persons in times of war or occupation, in the Occupied Palestinian Territory. Its designation of Gaza as a 'hostile territory', a term coined by

As to the treatment of suspects in this 'war on terror', the US view was based on the belief that international terrorism had created a new paradigm, making 'obsolete' the Geneva Conventions' strict limitations and rendering 'quaint' some of its provisions.[21] The 1984 Convention against Torture, as implemented by US federal law, was reinterpreted to limit the concept of—and therefore the prohibition on—'torture' to only the most extreme acts causing severe pain of a level which is difficult for the victim to endure. Writing in his legal memorandum, Jay Bybee, an Assistant Attorney General (by way of political appointment) explained this new approach: '[w]here the pain is physical it must be of an intensity akin to that which accompanies serious physical injury such as death or organ failure.' Under this new approach, anything less is not deemed to be torture and is therefore allowed. Where the pain is mental, it 'requires suffering not just at the moment of infliction but it also requires lasting psychological harm, such as seen in mental disorders like posttraumatic stress disorder' in order to qualify as torture.[22] Needless to state, there is simply no support in international law for such an interpretation. As candidly admitted by John Yoo, a US Deputy Assistant Attorney General who helped write the Bybee memo, 'What the Administration is trying to do is create a new legal regime'.[23]

The rush to war in Iraq, in the absence of any credible evidence of a threat of attack or even the capacity to make such an attack in the future, was yet a further, painful and terrible example of this abandonment of principles of the international rule of law.

The early years of the 21st century and the associated attempts to create 'a new legal regime' matter fundamentally and importantly because they have significant consequences for international governance. We live in a complex, interdependent world in which social, political, economic, and religious values and interests collide with increasing frequency over an ever greater set of issues. And it is precisely because of that complexity and interdependency that it is dangerous indeed to begin to imagine a system of international governance in which some states—i.e., the large and powerful ones—feel that they can pick and choose the international rules they like and discard those which they do not. Yet that is precisely what the Bush Administration did in its first term, and in so doing it has had considerable support from the British government, by, *inter alia*, its maintaining of an early public silence on the excesses of Guantanamo and buying into a legal argument for war in Iraq which was denuded of international support.

---

the current Administration that has no meaning or standing under international law, is a further attempt to seek to place the inhabitants of Gaza beyond the protections afforded by international humanitarian law.

  [21] *Lawless World*, n 9 above, p 154.
  [22] Ibid, p 213.
  [23] Ibid, p 153. John Yoo was a US Deputy Assistant Attorney General to Attorney General John Ashcroft, charged with advising on the effect of rules such as the Geneva Conventions, the 1984 Convention prohibiting torture, and the ICC Statute.

Such an approach fundamentally undermines and degrades the system of international rules: if you begin to tinker unilaterally with the international rules that do not suit you—on human rights, on the Geneva Conventions, on the use of force—then others will begin to tinker with the rules that do not suit them—on trade, on intellectual property, on the rights of foreign investors. If you send out a message that you consider some rules to be obsolete and incapable of meeting new paradigms, you fundamentally undermine your authority to call to account others who then flout them in their turn. That is a serious problem right now in many areas, such as, for example nuclear proliferation. Imagine how easy it is for those in Teheran to respond to allegations from the US and Britain that they are not complying with the requirements of the Nuclear Non-Proliferation Treaty.

In fact, there is nothing particular to the current challenges that mean that they cannot be resolved within the framework of international law. There is no need for a 'new legal order' to deal with them. The existing international legal framework is not fundamentally flawed. Contrary to the charges levelled by its detractors, international law is not too complex to be workable, nor is it ineffectual or unduly restrictive. Far from it. It is adaptable and able to respond to and deal with challenges of the type with which the world is currently faced. It provides standards and mechanisms to hold to account those who commit the most heinous of crimes or those who threaten national and international security. It protects states from unlawful interference by others and it protects individuals from arbitrary interference with their rights by the state. However, it also allows, within certain clear limits, for the restriction of certain rights where necessary in times of emergency or to protect public order or national security. It sets minimum standards of behaviour for states and those leading them and, aside from bullying tactics or the outright use of force, it is all that there is to provide a framework for confronting challenges both old and new. Without international law we are back to the law of the jungle, the very world which Roosevelt and Churchill committed to change over six decades ago.

(3) The Future: Promoting the Rule of Law

As set out above, the real paradox of the 'war on terror' is that breaches of the international rule of law by acts of international terrorism have been repeatedly relied upon to justify yet further violations and further disregard for the international order. What has become clear is that the main challenge to the international legal order stems not from the *inadequacy* of the existing framework of international law and standards but from the *failure to respect* those norms and standards and the lack of mechanisms to ensure that they are *enforced*.

So where do we go from here?

First of all it is important to acknowledge that, bleak as things may sometimes seem, there is some cause for optimism: the rules of international law which have been the subject of so unremitting an assault in the early years of the 21st century have shown themselves to be remarkably robust. They have not crumbled or been washed away. They have their detractors, but in far larger numbers they have their supporters. In the US, there remains much which is of serious concern. But it is striking that the Bush Administration has not succeeded in killing off Kyoto or the ICC, or rewriting the Geneva Conventions or the Torture Convention, or building any sort of consensus to support its revised approach to the international rules governing the use of force. There are signs that in its second term the Bush Administration has rethought some of its strategies and its policies, dropping its hostile opposition to the ICC, as evidenced in its decision not to veto a Security Council resolution referring the situation in Darfur to the ICC. There is also a broader recognition that peace, justice, and security require cooperation, and that cooperation requires rules.[24]

Further and importantly, although the executive (in the United States and Britain) has played fast and loose with international law, one branch of government in both countries, the judiciary, has continued in important cases to uphold the international rule of law.

The English courts have gone very far in articulating a constitutional principle concerning the rule of law. Recently, in a case that is on appeal to the House of Lords at the time of writing, Lord Justice Moses and Mr Justice Sullivan invoked the rule of law to intervene in a case in which the integrity of the justice system was perceived to have been threatened where the Director of the Serious Fraud Office submitted too readily to an external threat. 'The rule of law is nothing if it fails to constrain overweening power', wrote Lord Justice Moses.[25] The courts in other jurisdictions have also, even in the face of strong political pressures, stood up for the rule of law: as Justice Sandra Day O'Connor put it, 'a state of war is not a blank check for the President when it comes to the rights of the Nation's citizens'.[26] At the international level too, there is an urgent need to reaffirm a commitment to the rule of law. International courts have an important role to play, even if their authority sometimes stands on political ground that is less firm.

In the US one leading decision is that of the US Supreme Court in *Hamdan v Rumsfeld*,[27] which turned on the applicability of common Article 3 of the Geneva Conventions, which President Bush had determined could not be relied upon by detainees at Guantanamo. The Court ruled by a small majority that

---

[24] See, e.g., the Remarks by John Bellinger, Legal Adviser, US State Department, 'The United States and International Law', June 6, 2007, The Hague, The Netherlands, available at: <http://www.state.gov/s/l/rls/86123.htm>.

[25] *The Queen on the Application of Corner House Research and Campaign Against Arms Trade Claimants v The Director of the Serious Fraud Office*, Judgment of 10 April 2008, para 65, available at: <http://www.thecornerhouse.org.uk/pdf/document/JR-Judgment.pdf>.

[26] *Hamdi v Rumsfeld*, 542 US 507 (2004), p 29 (of judgment).

[27] 458 US (2006).

common Article 3, affording basic protections to detainees, had been violated. Importantly, only two of the eight justices—Clarence Thomas—agreed with the Administration's argument that common Article 3 was not applicable at all. The remaining seven ruled that common Article 3 established 'requirements' that the US was bound to follow, prohibiting cruelty, humiliation, and torture. All the Guantanamo detainees could rely upon it as of right. Within a few days the Pentagon adopted a decision giving effect to common Article 3.[28]

In Britain one leading case was that of *Abbasi*,[29] brought in the English courts by some of the British Guantanamo detainees as a challenge to the failure of the British government to take sufficient steps to ensure that the US respected their rights as prisoners under international law. The English Court of Appeal rejected the government's argument that these issues were not justiciable. Although the court was not willing to order the British government to take any particular steps, its invocation of international law and its criticism of the US actions were direct and unambiguous:

What appears to us to be objectionable is that Mr Abbasi should be subject to indefinite detention in territory over which the United States has exclusive control with no opportunity to challenge the legitimacy of his detention before any court or tribunal.[30]

The Court concluded that Mr Abbassi was being detained arbitrarily in a 'legal black hole' in breach of fundamental human rights and basic principles recognized in domestic and international law. The judgment added to political pressure. It reaffirmed the central importance of international law. And it gave a green light to those who considered that the British government should be held to account by reference to the very standards of international law which it had done so much to put in place.

Two years after *Abbasi* in the '*Belmarsh* case'[31] the House of Lords gave judgment on the government's derogation from the European Convention of Human Rights in relation to the right to liberty, made shortly after September 11.[32] In *Belmarsh* the Law Lords relied on a number of principles of international law in ruling that the indefinite detention without charge of non-UK nationals at Belmarsh was discriminatory and unlawful. And the following year, in December 2005, the House of Lords gave a similarly powerful judgment[33] ruling

[28] Yet two years later President Bush still felt able to veto legislation adopted by the US Congress that would have prohibited the use by the CIA of techniques of interrogation that would—if used by the military—violate common Art 3, n 8 above.

[29] *R (Abbasi) v Secretary of State for Foreign and Commonwealth Affairs* [2002] EWCA Civ 1598, para 66.

[30] *Lawless World*, n 1 above, at p 166.

[31] *A & Others v Secretary of State for the Home Department* [2004] UKHL 56.

[32] The UK was the only 1 of 44 Council of Europe members to enter a derogation, a matter for which it has been criticized in some quarters. But at least it did so, unlike the US which simply ignored the requirement of the Inter-American Convention on Human Rights and the ICCPR in relation to Guantanamo and did not bother putting in a derogation.

[33] *A & Others v Secretary of State for the Home Department* [2005] UKHL 71.

that evidence obtained by torture could never be invoked before the English courts, having heard arguments concerning the prohibition on torture under the English common law and international law, including Article 15 of the Torture Convention. The case sent a clear message that the use of torture is universally prohibited in all circumstances and that states have a positive obligation to give effect to that prohibition.

These cases signalled the courts' commitment to ensure that the US and Britain respected their international obligations. The judicial decisions represent an endorsement of the international rule of law. They also represent a rejection by the courts of the view that the existing legal standards are incapable of dealing with the new challenges posed by international terrorism in a post-September 11 world.

However, whilst recognizing the optimistic signs, it is clear that the 'war on terror' has had a profound and detrimental effect on the international legal framework and on long accepted norms and standards. In the face of this onslaught, the international rule of law needs to be reasserted and the key challenge of enforceability has to be addressed.

In this regard, four principles to set the framework for the way forward might be identified. They recognize that the effectiveness of international law depends to a degree on the existence of political will by the world's most powerful nations. Where such political will is absent—where there is a departure from the values that are reflected in a 'rule of law approach'—the challenges will become even greater. It is therefore a necessary but regrettable reality that there is a need to return to—and restate—some fundamentals.

(1) **The international rule of law must be promoted and faith restored in the strength and relevance of norms and frameworks of international law.**
The 'war on terror' cannot be allowed to undermine the international legal framework of norms created for the protection of all people. There must be a renewed commitment to international law on a national and international level. Its fundamental importance must be reasserted and its reputation restored. In that the Berlin Declaration of the International Committee of Jurists[34] should serve as a guiding principle in redressing the balance between human rights and national security. It was described by Mary Robinson in a lecture given in London as 'the rule of law charter to counter the imbalances of what has been called today's "new normal"',[35] calling as it does on all states to 'adhere strictly to the rule of law' and reasserting that 'there is no conflict between the duty of states to protect the rights of persons

---

[34] The Declaration on Upholding Human Rights and the Rule of Law in Combating Terrorism, adopted on the occasion of the International Commission of Jurists' biennial conference in Berlin in August 2004.
[35] Justice *International Rule of Law Lecture 2006*: 'Five Years on from 9/11—Time to Reassert the International Rule of Law' (20 March 2006).

threatened by terrorism and their responsibility to ensure that protecting security does not undermine other rights': rather 'safeguarding persons from terrorist attacks and respecting human rights form part of a seamless web of protection incumbent upon the state'.

(2) **The universality of international law must be underscored and effectively enforced.** International law loses credibility if it is not applied to, and seen as applying to, *all* states, at *all* times, whether in peace or crisis, for the protection of *all* people under that state's authority. The international community must hold to account—and must be seen to hold to account—the powerful as well as the weak. If the adherence to international law becomes merely a stick with which to beat poorer, less powerful states, then international law loses all credibility. Indeed, the willingness and ability of the international community to hold to account states and individuals who violate fundamental international principles in the name of counterterrorism as well as through terrorism will be a crucial factor in reasserting and strengthening the international rule of law.

(3) **Where necessary, changes must be made to ensure that international law keeps abreast of the needs and requirements of the world in the 21st century.** As previously stated, the international rules and framework are far from perfect and changes are needed within the framework of the UN to ensure it meets the challenges faced, as underscored by Kofi Annan, then Secretary General of the United Nations, in his Millennium Report. In particular, the UN must look to the problem posed by breaches of international law by non-state actors, and ways of preventing or punishing such abuses. The international system has shown itself to be adaptable to change, as indicated by the recent establishment of the Human Rights Council to replace the discredited Commission for Human Rights: although this change may have been limited, what it has done is to elevate the institutional standing of the body dealing with human rights to a subsidiary body of the General Assembly, thereby underscoring and reasserting the fundamental importance of human rights.[36]

(4) **National and international courts have an important role to play in protecting the international rule of law.** The recent judgments discussed above stand as testimony to the important role that the judiciary has to play in ensuring that states respond to the challenges with which they are faced within the boundaries of the law, including fundamental norms of international law outlawing torture and indefinite detention. The Pinochet case exemplified the crucial role that universal jurisdiction can play in doing away with impunity and applying international norms in national courts. International courts and tribunals, such as the newly operational International Criminal

---

[36] A number of measures were also introduced to improve the functioning of the body. It is imperative that in making those changes the protections afforded by international law are strengthened and not watered down.

Court, have an increasingly important role to play. However, in order to be effective, they must be granted greater support by states, including in their investigations and the implementation of their decisions.

These principles develop themes that were picked up by heads of state and government when they met at the United Nations in New York in September 2005. In the Outcome Document, adopted by consensus at the end of the session,[37] heads of state and government:

- reaffirmed 'the vital importance of an effective multilateral system, in accordance with international law' to better address the challenges and threats confronting our world and to achieve progress in the areas of peace and security, development and human rights (paragraph 6);
- acknowledged that 'good governance and the rule of law at the national and international levels are essential for sustained economic growth, sustainable development and the eradication of poverty and hunger' (paragraph 11);
- recognized that 'international cooperation to fight terrorism must be conducted in conformity with international law', and that states 'must ensure that any measures taken to combat terrorism comply with their obligations under international law, in particular human rights law, refugee law and international humanitarian law' (paragraph 85);
- recommitted themselves to 'actively protecting and promoting all human rights, the rule of law and democracy and recognize that they are interlinked and mutually reinforcing and that they belong to the universal and indivisible core values' (paragraph 119);
- reaffirmed the solemn commitment of their states to 'fulfil their obligations to promote universal respect for and the observance and protection of all human rights and fundamental freedoms for all in accordance with the Charter, the Universal Declaration of Human Rights and other instruments relating to human rights and international law', the universal nature of which is 'beyond question' (paragraph 120);
- recognized the need for 'universal adherence to and implementation of the rule of law at both the national and international levels' and reaffirmed their commitment to 'an international order based on the rule of law and international law' (paragraph 134(a)).

These commitments could amount to no more than empty words; but this need not be the case.

In 1947, George Kennan, the great American diplomat, implored the Administration of President Truman to have the 'courage and self-confidence to cling to our own methods and conceptions of human society', warning that

---

[37] See 2005 World Summit Outcome Document, UN General Assembly resolution 60/1, 24 October 2005, UN Doc, A/Res/60/1.

the greatest danger that might befall the United States in coping with Soviet communism was that 'we shall allow ourselves to become like those with whom we are coping'. In the 21st century, that stark warning must be heeded and the international rule of law be reasserted and reaffirmed as a constitutional principle lying at the heart of an international order which we all must have the courage and self-confidence to uphold.[38]

[38] This article was submitted for publication on 1 December 2008.

10

The Movement Towards Transparency in Decision Taking[1]

Konrad Schiemann

When Lord Bingham came to the Bar it was common practice for judges and magistrates in England, particularly the latter, to give rulings without giving the reasons which had prompted them. Judgments consisting of 'Bail refused', 'We find the case proved', 'This is not a case for an injunction', 'Costs to the Claimant', and 'Leave to appeal refused' were commonplace. There was no question of transparency. Many an advocate was left wondering why he had lost.[2]

In England administrative authorities for their part, whether acting in a legislative capacity or handing down decisions concerning an individual, also regularly refrained from giving reasons. Inevitably, at times it was genuinely difficult for an outsider to know what the motivation was for a particular regulation, byelaw, or decision.

By way of contrast let me cite two general legislative provisions which in substance have been in force in the Communities since the 1950s. Article 36 of the Statute of the European Court of Justice provides that:

Judgments shall state the reasons on which they are based.

Article 253 of the EC Treaty provides:

Regulations, directives and decisions adopted jointly by the European Parliament and the Council, and such acts adopted by the Council or the Commission, shall state the reasons on which they are based...

---

[1] The views expressed in this chapter are those of the author and may not be attributed to the court.

[2] In order to discover whether I should advise an appeal I once asked magistrates to tell me at the end of a case whether I had lost because they did not believe my client or because, although they believed my client, they rejected my legal submissions. A smiling chairman of the Bench countered with 'No. We are far too wise to give reasons.' As a result time, energy, and money were spent drafting a case stated on the optimistic basis that they had believed my client but had wrongly rejected my legal submissions. In due course the magistrates settled a short case saying they had disbelieved my client.

I know of no parallel statutory provision of such generality and apparent simplicity in England.

However, since the United Kingdom joined the European Communities in 1973 there has inevitably been much interaction in both directions between the UK and the developing law of the Communities. During the same period somewhat similar interactions can be observed between the UK and the case law of the European Court of Human Rights. Legislation and practice in the Communities have pointed in the direction of greater transparency in decision taking. The UK has gradually followed suit—in part as a matter of legal obligation and in part because parallel thought processes and valuation judgements have taken place. This is a development for which we can be grateful. I propose to examine the stages in which this has come about in the different contexts of decisions by judges, legislators, and administrators.

The Giving of Reasons by Judges

The refusal in some circumstances of the English courts to give reasons was exemplified in the House of Lords where in *Anataios Compania SA v Salen AB*[3] as late as 1985 Lord Diplock said 'A judge ought not normally to give reasons for a grant or refusal under section 1(3)(b) [of the Arbitration Act 1979] of leave to appeal to the High Court from an arbitral award'.

In a lecture given two years later, 'Reasons and Reasons for Reasons: Differences Between a Court Judgment and an Arbitration Award',[4] Tom Bingham said he personally regretted that commercial judges (to whom all applications for leave to appeal to the High Court are initially assigned) should have been enjoined against giving reasons in this way. Here he was in tune with both the Strasbourg and the Luxembourg case law and underlying legislation.

The European Convention on Human Rights in Article 6—which is headed 'Right to a fair trial'—provides that:

In the determination of his civil rights and obligations or of any criminal charge against him, everyone is entitled to a fair and public hearing within a reasonable time by an independent and impartial tribunal established by law. Judgment shall be pronounced publicly...

The Strasbourg Court regularly states that Article 6(1) of the Convention, although it does not do so in terms, requires courts and tribunals adequately to state the reasons upon which their judgments are based. As a unanimous Court put it in *Garcia Ruiz v Spain*:[5]

The Court reiterates that, according to its established case-law reflecting a principle linked to the proper administration of justice, judgments of courts and tribunals should

---

[3] [1985] 1 AC 191, at 205.   [4] (1988) 4 Arb Int 141.
[5] (2001) 31 EHRR 22, para 26.

adequately state the reasons on which they are based. The extent to which this duty to give reasons applies may vary according to the nature of the decision and must be determined in the light of the circumstances of the case...Although Article 6 § 1 obliges courts to give reasons for their decisions, it cannot be understood as requiring a detailed answer to every argument.... Thus, in dismissing an appeal, an appellate court may, in principle, simply endorse the reasons for the lower court's decision...

Following this case and as a result of the incorporation of the European Convention into English law, the Court of Appeal in *North Range Shipping Ltd v Seatrans Shipping Corpn*[6] ruled that the guidance given by Lord Diplock in *Anataios* was no longer good law. Reasons had to be given, albeit that they need not necessarily be long or detailed. What was required depended on the facts of the case.

The same approach was adopted by a differently constituted Court of Appeal in the following month in a judgment given in three cases concerned with the question whether reasons need to be given and if so with what degree of detail.[7] The rationales behind requirements that judges give reasons for their judgments are well expressed in the unanimous judgment. Lord Phillips CJ, approving a judgment delivered in 1999,[8] stated:

6. In giving the judgment of the Court, Henry LJ remarked...that it was clear that today's professional Judge owed a general duty to give reasons for his decision...He made the following comments...:

(1) The duty is a function of due process, and therefore of justice. Its rationale has two principal aspects. The first is that fairness surely requires that the parties especially the losing party should be left in no doubt why they have won or lost. This is especially so since without reasons the losing party will not know...whether the court has misdirected itself, and thus whether he may have an available appeal on the substance of the case. The second is that a requirement to give reasons concentrates the mind; if it is fulfilled, the resulting decision is much more likely to be soundly based on the evidence than if it is not.

(2) The first of these aspects implies that want of reasons may be a good self-standing ground of appeal. Where because no reasons are given it is impossible to tell whether the judge has gone wrong on the law or the facts, the losing party would be altogether deprived of his chance of an appeal unless the court entertains an appeal based on the lack of reasons itself.

(3) The extent of the duty, or rather the reach of what is required to fulfil it, depends on the subject matter. Where there is a straightforward factual dispute whose resolution depends simply on which witness is telling the truth about events which he claims to recall, it is likely to be enough for the judge (having, no doubt, summarized the evidence) to indicate simply that he believes X rather than Y; indeed there may be nothing else to say. But where the dispute involves something in the nature of an intellectual exchange, with reasons and analysis advanced on either side, the judge must enter into the issues canvassed before him and explain why he prefers one case

---

[6] [2002] 1 WLR 2397. [7] *English v Reimbold and Strick* [2002] 1 WLR 2409.
[8] *Flannery and Another v Halifax Estate Agencies Ltd* [2000] 1 WLR 377.

over the other. This is likely to apply particularly in litigation where as here there is disputed expert evidence, but it is not necessarily limited to such cases.

(4) This is not to suggest that there is one rule for cases concerning the witnesses' truthfulness or recall of events, and another for cases where the issue depends on reasoning or analysis (with experts or otherwise). The rule is the same; the judge must explain why he has reached his decision. The question is always, what is required of the judge to do so; and that will differ from case to case. Transparency should be the watchword.

...

7....It is clearly established by the Strasbourg jurisprudence that the right to a fair trial guaranteed by Article 6 of the Convention, which includes the requirement that judgment shall be pronounced publicly, normally carries with it an obligation that the judgment should be a reasoned judgment. *In response to this requirement*[9] Magistrates Courts now give reasons for their decisions.

During Lord Bingham's professional life, and in part as a result of his influence, judges in England have in general become more open in their judgments and find it more natural to give full and genuine reasons. They are less inclined to pose impotently as mere mouthpieces of the law in the manner suggested by Montesquieu.[10] As Lord Bingham pointed out:

The declaratory approach is radically inconsistent with the subjective experience of Judges, particularly appellate Judges, of the role which they fulfil day by day. They know from experience that the cases which come before them do not in the main turn on sections of statutes which are clear and unambiguous in their meaning. They know from experience also that the cases they have to decide involve points which are not the subject of previous decisions, or are the subject of conflicting decisions, or raise questions of statutory interpretation which apparently involve genuine lacunae or ambiguities. They know, and the higher the Court the more right they are, that decisions involve issues of policy.[11]

He continues: 'If, as is accepted, it is generally incumbent on a judge to give reasons for his decision, then it must surely follow that such reasons should be full and genuine.'[12] He supports the position enunciated by Lord Cooke of Thorndon: 'I am against hidden policy factors. Major premises should not be inarticulate, although they do not need constant restatement. A just decision is surely more likely if the judge recognizes a responsibility to be frank.'[13]

But it is not without interest that Lord Bingham, after a career spent observing how judges operate, opines on the same page that, even in England:

one can not resist the suspicion that on occasion a duty of care is denied because the Court apprehends that, if a duty were held to exist, insurance would be impossible or

---

[9] The italics are mine.
[10] *De l'esprit des lois*, Book XI ch 6 'Les juges...ne sont...que la bouche qui prononce les paroles de la loi; des êtres inanimés qui n'en peuvent modérer ni la force ni la rigueur.'
[11] Tom Bingham, *The Business of Judging* (Oxford, 2000), p 28.
[12] Ibid, 30.   [13] Robin Cooke, 'Fairness' (1989) 19 VUWLR 421.

prohibitively expensive to obtain in the future. But such a reason is rarely explicitly stated, probably because the Court has no evidence before it of what the insurance position might be if a duty of care were held to exist.

Such a practice, however, meets with his disapproval. As he says, 'It is, surely, an abnegation of the judicial role if a judge allows himself to be influenced in his decision by considerations to which he does not allude'.

This must particularly be the case when there is a possibility of an appeal against the judgment since the litigant may not know of a motivating factor in the judgment which an appellate court might consider erroneous. However, even in a court from which there is no appeal and in respect of which such reasoning would not apply, I still think that transparency is a virtue worth pursuing for itself, and not only because the loser in the litigation is entitled to know why he lost. Formulating a judgment concentrates the mind and a judge who is open and frank about his reasons is less likely to make mistakes in logic or indeed to act improperly than one who has got into the habit of concealing from the public and perhaps himself his real motivation and thought processes. Where the court from which there is no appeal is, as will usually be the case, a collegiate court it seems to me, moreover, that the other judges are entitled to know what in fact is motivating the judge who drafted the judgment in question. They can then more easily test his reasoning.

It was for long the tradition in England[14] that each judge express his own judgment in his own words and that the litigant and the public are entitled to know the thought processes of each judge. This makes it easy to give full and genuine reasons and has the advantage that it fixes the judge with the personal responsibility in his own eyes, in the eyes of his peers, and at the bar of public opinion with what appears as his judgment. Although I have drawn attention to the fact that magistrates in substantive hearings and judges in relation to less important matters often did not give reasons, it is only fair to our forebears to point out that this did not in general apply to the higher judiciary when dealing with matters of substance.

The delivery of several frank and fully reasoned judgments has, however, the recognized disadvantage that the totality of judgments can run to many scores of pages and that, by reason of differing reasoning processes, the legal proposition established by the case can be difficult to discern. In future cases these difficulties tend to be reflected in delay and expense. Recognition of those factors, coupled with an increased work load, led, in the course of Lord Bingham's working life, a number of presiders in the Court of Appeal to try and persuade those sitting with them, or at least those who agreed with the result, to combine in one judgment. Some Lords Justices were more amenable to such pressures than others who took the view that clarity of exposition of a

---

[14] Except, oddly enough, in cases decided by the Court of Appeal (Criminal Division).

particular viewpoint would solve the case in hand and was better for the development of the law in the future than some form of compromise wording, and that the price in terms of delay and uncertainty was worth paying. I rather suspect that in the European Court of Human Rights (ECtHR)—where individual opinions are also permitted to be expressed—the same sort of tensions can be found. It is certainly true in my experience that where judges cannot deliver dissenting opinions, or indeed concurring ones, there is a greater willingness to work towards a satisfactory compromise than I sometimes observed in the Court of Appeal. As one would expect, in the most significant cases there are frequently initial differences of opinion amongst the 13 judges sitting in the Grand Chamber. Often these can be resolved in discussion, and the ultimate judgment is, by common consent, better than the draft which was first prepared by the reporting judge.

On the other hand, the injunction to the European Court of Justice (ECJ), found in the Court's Statute, to state the reasons upon which its judgments are based is not in practice all that easy to obey in a system which only allows for the delivery of one judgment by the Court. As a result of successive enlargements of the Union, the number of judges in the ECJ has grown. As a consequence, the experiences of its members have been more diverse and the expression of different viewpoints has increased. Sometimes the differences of opinion persist even after discussion. In such cases one is conscious not only of the differences amongst those sitting but also of the possibility that any majority in the Grand Chamber would not inevitably be echoed if all 27 of us were sitting. Even if we have no formal system of *stare decisis*, in practice the Court is very loath to depart from one of its earlier formulations of the law. This imbues us with caution and encourages a formulation of the judgment which minimizes the enunciation of legal propositions with which some are—and others are likely to be—in profound disaccord. This can be inimical to the formulation of the broad principles for which the preliminary reference procedure was established—namely, to declare the law of the Communities in terms which will help the court which made the reference but also all the other actors in the Communities. Ideally the answer should be of such clarity that similar questions do not need to be asked in the future. In practice, for the reasons which I have indicated, although this often happens it is not invariably the case.

The English system of individual judgments at times makes patent that there can be several routes to a single decision and that the advocate of each of these routes is convinced that the advocates of each of the other routes are mistaken. While there may in principle be no formal objection to an ECJ judgment which makes plain that the Court was divided as to the reasoning but unanimous in its conclusion, I do not know of an example where this has been done. There are undoubtedly those who would simply not be at ease with that degree of openness and find it unsatisfactory that a court should expose to the world that no majority could be found for any single course of reasoning.

The Giving of Reasons by Decision-Makers

Neither in the Union nor in the UK is there an obligation to give the reasons which led to the enactment of the Treaties or Statutes. In the UK, although the practice of setting out a long preamble to an Act of Parliament used to be widespread, it has now been more or less abandoned. By way of contrast, the primary legislation of the Union frequently includes preambles. It is well known that the ECJ gives some weight to those Preambles in its construction of a Treaty.[15] Thus that part of the preamble to the 1957 Treaty of Rome, which is still to be found in the current consolidated version and which reads 'determined to lay the foundations of an ever closer union among the peoples of Europe' has not been regarded by the Court as vacuous political rhetoric but as indicating the general direction in which the Member States wish the Union to move.[16]

When it comes to secondary legislation and decisions, the rest of Europe has been somewhat in advance of developments in England. Already in the Treaty establishing the European Coal and Steel Community which came into force in 1952 one finds not only that Article 5 provides that 'The Community shall publish the reasons for its actions' but also that Article 15 provides that 'Decisions, Recommendations and Opinions of the High Authority shall state the reasons on which they are based...'. This has been part of the law of the Communities ever since and is now found in Article 253 EC quoted at the beginning of this chapter.

The philosophy behind this provision has been the subject of a number of decisions of the Court. Thus in Case 24/62 *Germany v Commission* the Court said:

In imposing upon the Commission the obligation to state reasons for its decisions, article [253] is not taking mere formal considerations into account but seeks to give an opportunity to the parties of defending their rights, to the court of exercising its supervisory functions and to member states and to all interested nationals of ascertaining the circumstances in which the Commission has applied the treaty. To attain these objectives, it is sufficient for the decision to set out, in a concise but clear and relevant manner, the principal issues of law and of fact upon which it is based and which are necessary in order that the reasoning which has led the Commission to its decision may be understood.

In 1987 the Court decided Case 222/86 *Heylens*, a case in which the defendant was not a Community institution and thus Article 253 EC was not in play. The

---

[15] Thus the Court in the leading Case 26/62 *Van Gend en Loos* stated: 'The objective of the EEC Treaty, which is to establish a Common Market, the functioning of which is of direct concern to interested parties in the Community, implies that this treaty is more than an agreement which merely creates mutual obligations between the contracting states. This view is confirmed by the Preamble to the Treaty which refers not only to governments but to peoples.'

[16] It is noticeable that in the ill-fated Constitutional Treaty the cited preamble was not reproduced. However it has been retained in the Treaty of Lisbon.

Court was nonetheless concerned to apply a principle of transparency to national decisions in the field of Community law. The Court pointed out:

15. Effective judicial review, which must be able to cover the legality of the reasons for the contested decision, presupposes in general that the court to which the matter is referred may require the competent authority to notify its reasons. But where, as in this case, it is more particularly a question of securing the effective protection of a fundamental right conferred by the treaty on community workers, the latter must also be able to defend that right under the best possible conditions and have the possibility of deciding, with a full knowledge of the relevant facts, whether there is any point in their applying to the courts. Consequently, in such circumstances the competent national authority is under a duty to inform them of the reasons on which its refusal is based, either in the decision itself or in a subsequent communication made at their request.

It should be borne in mind when reading the foregoing that it is extremely difficult to apply some of the tests—proportionality is the most obvious example—which are close to the centre of judicial control of a measure in a Community context unless the reasoning in the mind of the decision taker is exposed. Both the decision taker and the person affected benefit from an exposé of such reasoning—the former because a decision which might appear disproportionate and unreasonable may turn out to have perfectly sustainable reasons; the latter because either flaws in the reasoning are exposed or because it becomes manifest that there are none such.

What is of interest in the present context is the similarity of the reasoning in these cases with that pronounced by the Court of Appeal some 37 years later in *Flannery*[17] but only in the context of the giving of reasons by judges.

In Case 266/05 *Sison v Council* the Court stated:

80. As is clear from settled case-law, the statement of reasons required by Article 253 EC must be appropriate to the act at issue and must disclose in a clear and unequivocal fashion the reasoning followed by the institution which adopted the measure in question in such a way as to enable the persons concerned to ascertain the reasons for the measure and to enable the competent Community Court to exercise its power of review. The requirements to be satisfied by the statement of reasons depend on the circumstances of each case, in particular the content of the measure in question, the nature of the reasons given and the interest which the addressees of the measure, or other parties to whom it is of direct and individual concern, may have in obtaining explanations. It is not necessary for the reasoning to go into all the relevant facts and points of law, since the question whether the statement of reasons meets the requirements of Article 253 EC must be assessed with regard not only to its wording but also to its context and to all the legal rules governing the matter in question (see, in particular, *Interporc v Commission*,[18] paragraph 55 and the case-law there cited).

So far as access to reasons behind the taking of administrative decisions is concerned, the consensus of European opinion as it stood already in 1977 is contained

---

[17] Cited at n 8 above.   [18] Case C-41/00 P.

in Resolution (77) 31 of the Committee of Ministers of the Council of Europe which recommended governments of member states be guided by the principles annexed. Among these were the following:

II—Access to information
At his request, the person concerned is informed, before an administrative act is taken, by appropriate means, of all available factors relevant to the taking of that act.

VI—Statement of reasons
Where an administrative act is of such nature as adversely to affect his rights, liberties or interests, the person concerned is informed of the reasons on which it is based. This is done either by stating the reasons in the act, or by communicating them, at his request, to the person concerned in writing within a reasonable time.

English law, by way of contrast, started from the position that the administrator was not required to give reasons for his decisions. Again there has been a noticeable change in Lord Bingham's lifetime. The gradual change which has been taking place in English law in the direction of giving reasons was well described by Lord Clyde delivering the advice of the Privy Council in *Stefan v General Medical Council*[19] before the Human Rights Act 1998 was wholly in force:

The trend of the law has been towards an increased recognition of the duty upon decision-makers of many kinds to give reasons. This trend is consistent with current developments towards an increased openness in matters of government and administration. But the trend is proceeding on a case by case basis (*Reg v Royal Borough of Kensington and Chelsea, Ex parte Grillo* (1996) 28 HLR 94), and has not lost sight of the established position of the common law that there is no general duty, universally imposed on all decision-makers. It was reaffirmed in *Reg v Secretary of State for the Home Department, Ex parte Doody* [1994] 1 AC 531, 564, that the law does not at present recognize a general duty to give reasons for administrative decisions. But it is well established that there are exceptions where the giving of reasons will be required as a matter of fairness and openness. These may occur through the particular circumstances of a particular case. Or, as was recognized in *Reg v Higher Education Funding Council, Ex parte Institute of Dental Surgery* [1994] 1 WLR 242, 263, there may be classes of cases where the duty to give reasons may exist in all cases of that class. Those classes may be defined by factors relating to the particular character or quality of the decisions, as where they appear aberrant, or to factors relating to the particular character or particular jurisdiction of a decision-making body, as where it is concerned with matters of special importance, such as personal liberty. *There is certainly a strong argument for the view that what were once seen as exceptions to a rule may now be becoming examples of the norm, and the cases where reasons are not required may be taking on the appearance of exceptions.*[20] But the general rule has not been departed from and their Lordships do not consider that the present case provides an appropriate opportunity to explore the possibility of such a departure. They are conscious of the possible reappraisal of the whole position which the passing of the Human Rights Act 1998 may bring about. The provisions of Article 6(1) of the Convention on Human Rights, which are now about

---

[19] [1999] 1 WLR 1293.   [20] Italics supplied.

to become directly accessible in national courts, will require closer attention to be paid to the duty to give reasons, at least in relation to those cases where a person's civil rights and obligations are being determined. But it is in the context of the application of that Act that any wide-reaching review of the position at common law should take place.

It will be noted that, once more, the potential influence of the European Convention was referred to and the position following the incorporation of that Convention into English law was left open.

However the trend in English law towards requiring a greater clarity in the giving of reasons does not extend to secondary legislation. In contrast, the requirements of Article 253 EC do extend to such legislation when enacted by the Community. As is well known, the Treaties set up various institutions and mechanisms for creating secondary law, and the vast bulk of Community law making is achieved by secondary legislation. In consequence the provisions of Article 253 are of daily importance both in the formulation of Community law and when its validity is tested in court. There tends to be a much greater and more regular reference to the reasons behind any particular piece of secondary legislation than is customary in England.

Access to Documents Outside a Litigation Context

Although in Sweden 200 years ago documents prepared in the course of drafting legislation were already publicly available this liberality was the exception. Both on the Continent and in England 50 years ago the general position was that documents in the hands of the administration were not accessible by the public. However the desirability of increased openness by the administration and the legislator has been gradually recognized, first by the European Community and then by the UK even in fields not covered by Community law.

In the Community context the attachment to transparency in the decision-making process was first expressed formally in Declaration No 17 Relating to the Right of Access to Information annexed to the Final Act of the Treaty on European Union, signed in Maastricht on 7 February 1992, which recommends the adoption of measures designed to improve public access to information held by the institutions.

In the absence of general Community rules laying down the scope of that right of access, it was the institutions who took the initiative of breaking with the traditional principle of administrative secrecy. Following the adoption by common agreement, on 6 December 1993, of a code of conduct concerning public access to documents held by them, the Council, and the Commission, on the basis of their power of internal organization, each took a decision formally adopting a code which implemented the principle of transparency.

The Treaty of Amsterdam in 1997, in the words of Article 1, marked:

a new stage in the in the process of creating an ever closer union among the peoples of Europe in which decisions are taken as openly as possible and as closely as possible to the citizen.

That Treaty contained provisions which are now found as Article 255 EC:

1. Any citizen of the Union, and any natural or legal person residing or having its registered office in a Member State, shall have a right of access to European Parliament, Council and Commission documents, subject to the principles and the conditions to be defined in accordance with paragraphs 2 and 3.
2. General principles and limits on grounds of public or private interest governing this right of access to documents shall be determined by the Council...

The Council in due course made Regulation (EC) 1049/2001 regarding public access to European Parliament, Council, and Commission documents. Recitals 2 and 4 read as follows:

(2) Openness enables citizens to participate more closely in the decision-making process and guarantees that the administration enjoys greater legitimacy and is more effective and more accountable to the citizen in a democratic system. Openness contributes to strengthening the principles of democracy and respect for fundamental rights as laid down in Article 6 of the EU Treaty and in the Charter of Fundamental Rights of the European Union.

    ...

(4) The purpose of this Regulation is to give the fullest possible effect to the right of public access to documents and to lay down the general principles and limits on such access in accordance with Article 255(2) of the EC Treaty.

Article 2(1) of that regulation provides, under the heading 'Beneficiaries and scope':

Any citizen of the Union, and any natural or legal person residing or having its registered office in a Member State, has a right of access to documents of the institutions, subject to the principles, conditions and limits defined in this Regulation.

Article 4 (1) of the Regulation provides that:

The institutions shall refuse access to a document where disclosure would undermine the protection of:

(a) The public interest as regards:
    • public security
    • defence and military matters
    • international relations
    • the financial, monetary or economic policy of the Community or a Member State.

Various other interests are listed later.

The *Sison* case cited above was concerned with the freezing by the Community of funds belonging to Mr Sison. The Council had adopted Decision 2002/848/EC implementing Article 2(3) of Regulation (EC) No 2580/2001 on specific restrictive measures directed against certain persons and entities with a view to combating terrorism. Mr Sison wished to challenge his inclusion on a list of such persons and wished to have access to various documents.

The position was summarized by the ECJ in its judgment as follows:

61. As is clear from Article 1 of Regulation No 1049/2001, read, in particular, in the light of the fourth recital in the preamble, the purpose of the regulation is to give the fullest possible effect to the right of public access to documents held by the institutions.

62. However, it also follows from that regulation, particularly from the 11th recital in its preamble and from Article 4, which provides for a scheme of exceptions in that regard, that the right of access to documents is nonetheless subject to certain limitations based on grounds of public or private interest.

63. As they derogate from the principle of the widest possible public access to documents, such exceptions must ... be interpreted and applied strictly ...

64. In that regard, however, it must be pointed out that such a principle of strict construction does not, in respect of the public-interest exceptions provided for in Article 4(1)(a) of Regulation No 1049/2001, preclude the Council from enjoying a wide discretion for the purpose of determining whether disclosure of a document to the public would undermine the interests protected by that provision. For the reasons stated by the Court in its examination of the first ground of appeal, the review by the Court of First Instance of the legality of a Council decision refusing access to a document on the basis of one of those exceptions is limited to verifying whether the procedural rules and the duty to state reasons have been complied with, whether the facts have been accurately stated and whether there has been a manifest error of assessment or a misuse of powers.

In case C-39/05 *Sweden and Turco v Council* the question arose whether the legal opinion obtained by the institutions prior to legislating as to the legality of the proposed legislation were disclosable. The relevant Article was Article 4(2) which provides:

2. The institutions shall refuse access to a document where disclosure would undermine the protection of:
    − ...
    − court proceedings and legal advice,
    − ...
    unless there is an overriding public interest in disclosure.

The Court said this:

59. As regards, first, the fear expressed by the Council that disclosure of an opinion of its legal service relating to a legislative proposal could lead to doubts as to the lawfulness of the legislative act concerned, it is precisely openness in this regard that contributes to conferring greater legitimacy on the institutions in the eyes of European citizens and increasing their confidence in them by allowing divergences between

various points of view to be openly debated. It is in fact rather a lack of information and debate which is capable of giving rise to doubts in the minds of citizens, not only as regards the lawfulness of an isolated act, but also as regards the legitimacy of the decision-making process as a whole.

60. Furthermore, the risk that doubts might be engendered in the minds of European citizens as regards the lawfulness of an act adopted by the Community legislature because the Council's legal service had given an unfavourable opinion would more often than not fail to arise if the statement of reasons for that act was reinforced, so as to make it apparent why that unfavourable opinion was not followed.

61. Consequently, to submit, in a general and abstract way, that there is a risk that disclosure of legal advice relating to legislative processes may give rise to doubts regarding the lawfulness of legislative acts does not suffice to establish that the protection of legal advice will be undermined for the purposes of the second indent of Article 4(2) of Regulation No 1049/2001 and cannot, accordingly, provide a basis for a refusal to disclose such advice.

62. As regards, secondly, the Council's argument that the independence of its legal service would be compromised by possible disclosure of legal opinions issued in the course of legislative procedures, it must be pointed out that that fear lies at the very heart of the interests protected by the exception provided for in the second indent of Article 4(2) of Regulation No 1049/2001. As is apparent from paragraph 42 of this judgment, that exception seeks specifically to protect an institution's interest in seeking legal advice and receiving frank, objective and comprehensive advice.

63. However, in that regard, the Council relied before both the Court of First Instance and the Court on mere assertions, which were in no way substantiated by detailed arguments. In view of the considerations which follow, there would appear to be no real risk that is reasonably foreseeable and not purely hypothetical of that interest being undermined.

64. As regards the possibility of pressure being applied for the purpose of influencing the content of opinions issued by the Council's legal service, it need merely be pointed out that even if the members of that legal service were subjected to improper pressure to that end, it would be that pressure, and not the possibility of the disclosure of legal opinions, which would compromise that institution's interest in receiving frank, objective and comprehensive advice and it would clearly be incumbent on the Council to take the necessary measures to put a stop to it.

65. As regards the Commission's argument that it could be difficult for an institution's legal service which had initially expressed a negative opinion regarding a legislative act in the process of being adopted subsequently to defend the lawfulness of that act if its opinion had been published, it must be stated that such a general argument cannot justify an exception to the openness provided for by Regulation No 1049/2001.

66. In view of those considerations, there appears to be no real risk that is reasonably foreseeable and not purely hypothetical that disclosure of opinions of the Council's legal service issued in the course of legislative procedures might undermine the protection of legal advice within the meaning of the second indent of Article 4(2) of Regulation No 1049/2001.

67. In any event, in so far as the interest in protecting the independence of the Council's legal service could be undermined by that disclosure, that risk would have to be weighed up against the overriding public interests which underlie Regulation

No 1049/2001. As was pointed out in paragraphs 45 to 47 of this judgment, such an overriding public interest is constituted by the fact that disclosure of documents containing the advice of an institution's legal service on legal questions arising when legislative initiatives are being debated increases the transparency and openness of the legislative process and strengthens the democratic right of European citizens to scrutinize the information which has formed the basis of a legislative act, as referred to, in particular, in recitals 2 and 6 of the preamble to Regulation No 1049/2001.

68. It follows from the above considerations that Regulation No 1049/2001 imposes, in principle, an obligation to disclose the opinions of the Council's legal service relating to a legislative process.

69. That finding does not preclude a refusal, on account of the protection of legal advice, to disclose a specific legal opinion, given in the context of a legislative process, but being of a particularly sensitive nature or having a particularly wide scope that goes beyond the context of the legislative process in question. In such a case, it is incumbent on the institution concerned to give a detailed statement of reasons for such a refusal.

In a litigation context, the requirements of disclosure in English procedural law, while notoriously broad insofar as concerns actions between individuals, were traditionally very narrow so far as the administration was concerned. Since the 1978 judicial review reforms, however, the courts have become increasingly prepared to order disclosure against administrative bodies.[21]

Outside the context of litigation, in a series of legislative measures at the turn of the century, employing techniques broadly similar to those used in Regulation 1049/2001, the UK has set out various rights to information while qualifying those rights by a series of exemptions.[22] Once more we are moving in the same direction.

Conclusion

Government over the centuries has largely been a secret thing. Decisions have been taken by those in power. Reasons for those decisions have often not been given at all and at times false or misleading reasons have been given. There has in general been a reluctance to be honest and truthful. The motives for this reluctance have no doubt sometimes, but not always, been dishonourable: if a nation is expecting attack it will appear sensible to spread misleading stories about the strength and location of its armed forces. If a devaluation of the currency is envisaged openness may not be the best policy. If a prime minister thinks it in the interests of his party—which he tends, perhaps in all honesty, to equate with the interests of his country—he may well be less than honest about the date when he plans to hold the next election or as to the changes which he hopes to introduce

---

[21] De Smith, *Judicial Review* (6th edn) 7–057, 16–065–068.
[22] The Data Protection Act 1998, The Freedom of Information Act 2000.

if elected. If a nation is seeking to secure a trading advantage for reasons and by means forbidden to it by international agreement, it may well claim that an action is motivated by reason A when in truth it is motivated by reason B.

One of the interesting developments during the last half century both on the Continent of Europe and in the UK has been the growth in the legal requirement of transparency in decision-making—a requirement of the giving of reasons for decisions and a requirement of disclosure of documents which have a bearing on such reasons. This has been played out in the field of decisions made by the legislator, by the administration, by the judiciary, and in the field of decisions made by other decision takers, such as employers and investors. What has happened is this. It has remained the case that some things and documents must be revealed but that not all things must be revealed. However, whereas the default position used to be that there was no disclosure save where there was a good reason for disclosure, now the default position has tended to become that there is disclosure unless there is a good reason for non-disclosure. The motives behind this increasing insistence on transparency have been manifold.

One has been the feeling that democratic life rests in part on the involvement of the people in decision-making and that this should go beyond mere influence on the choice of the people who make the decisions; a feeling that the choice in the final decision or at any rate the choice in the people who make the final decision should be made after an open discussion based on all possibly relevant material upon which such decisions could be based.

Another is that peace in the world, whether between nations or between employers and employees, is more easily secured if people play with their cards on the table. This was a major motivation behind the creation of the European Coal and Steel Community.

A third is the hope that the quality of the ultimate decision will be improved if the factual bases upon which it is based are open for discussion and refutation prior to the decision being made so that factual errors in the input should as far as possible be avoided and so that potentially useful material should be exposed to the decision-maker.

A fourth is the conviction that if a decision-maker is required to give not merely a decision but also to expose his reasons for making that decision then he will be more likely to make a good decision; a conviction that if required to expose his reasons, he would himself realize that his instinctive unreasoned impulse was pointing him in a wrong direction.

A fifth is the hope that if things are done openly and reasons are given for decisions, even those whose position may not in the event have prevailed will nonetheless perceive the strength of the position on the other side and why their own position has not prevailed.

A sixth is the increase in the conviction that the legality of decisions should be capable of being tested and that this often cannot be done effectively if no reasons are exposed.

Governments and administrators, and even judges at times, have not been completely open in their dealings. Those in a position of power are inevitably exposed to a number of temptations running from misusing power for their own ends, through laziness, to an unshakable conviction that they know best. It would, of course, be going too far to say that the invariable explanation for reluctance by judges, legislators, administrators to disclose is that given by St John—'Men loved darkness rather than light because their deeds were evil'.[23] However, openness undoubtedly can help avoid evil. It can lead to better decision-making by the decision-maker. It can lead to a greater understanding by the public of the difficulties which face the legislator, administrator, and judge. There must be limits to disclosure, but the move which has been led by the European institutions during the last half century towards greater transparency has been a move in the right direction. I have little doubt that it has the support of Lord Bingham.

---

[23] St John, ch 3, verse 19.

11

The Principle of Procedural Autonomy and the Duty of Loyal Cooperation of National Judges under Article 10 EC

Vassilios Skouris

I. Introduction

The principle of national procedural autonomy and the duty of loyal cooperation under Article 10 EC from a judicial perspective are issues that are at the very heart of the cooperation between the European Court of Justice (ECJ) and national courts. The preliminary reference procedure is essentially a mechanism of dialogue between the ECJ and national courts. Nevertheless, it has also proven to be an effective mechanism of judicial enforcement and therefore the task of balancing the duty of loyal cooperation of national judges under Article 10 EC with the so-called national procedural autonomy is always a very delicate one and was recently the source of some very interesting developments in the case law of the ECJ. The reasons that led us to the choice of this topic for a contribution to the *Liber Amicorum* published in honour of Lord Bingham are apparent. The title of this collection of essays, *Tom Bingham and the Transformation of the Law*, refers, among others, to the osmosis between EC law and national law and the effects of this osmosis during the constantly evolving process of European integration. Therefore, some reflections on the principle of national procedural autonomy and the limits imposed on this principle by the duty of loyal cooperation, particularly in view of the Court's recent case law, is a fitting offering to a distinguished colleague who, through his excellence on the bench, has acquired international recognition and renown.

The basic notion underlying the legal issues that will be addressed in this paper is that of the division of labour between the ECJ and national courts established by the Treaty in order to ensure the judicial enforcement of EC law. In somewhat simplified form, the Court's case law is governed by the idea that the substantive definition of rights conferred upon individuals by the EC treaty or secondary legislation is a matter of Community law, while the remedies for the enforcement of those rights are, in the absence of relevant EC rules, to be provided by national law. This institutional and procedural autonomy[1] is somehow a specific expression of Article 5 EC and the fundamental principle of subsidiarity pursuant to which each specific competence must be exercised at the most appropriate level.

One of the main consequences of this division of labour is the fact that national judges are entrusted with the primary judicial enforcement of EC law. But such a privileged position carries with it certain obligations. As the Court stated in *Van Gend & Loos*, the status of Community law in the national legal systems is a matter of Community law itself.[2] In fact, as is well-known, this national 'institutional and procedural autonomy' in the enforcement of EC rights is restricted in order to ensure the so-called *effet utile* of EC law and its uniform implementation. The precise boundary limiting national procedural autonomy is established by the treaties in Article 10 EC. Over time, the Court of Justice has gradually specified more precisely the requirements which Article 10 EC imposes on member states with a view to securing the 'full effectiveness' of EC law rights in the national legal order.

In this paper, we shall first provide a general overview of the principle of national procedural autonomy and the duty of loyal cooperation separately in an attempt to define their respective content and implications. We will then outline the specific duties and obligations of national judges in the application of EC law as they result from the ECJ's classic case law. In the main part, we will examine some recent judgments in which the balancing exercise between the duty of loyal cooperation and national procedural autonomy has proven to be quite delicate and has attracted much praise but also criticism from academics, lawyers, and judges. The concluding remarks will be aimed at placing this recent case law in its proper perspective.

II. The Duty of Loyal Cooperation

Regarding first of all Article 10 EC and the duty of loyal cooperation, it is well known that, where a provision of EC law contains a specific obligation for member states, a finding that there has been a failure to fulfil the obligation may unquestionably be made.[3] Where, in contrast, there is no such specific obligation, a member state's conduct may nonetheless constitute a breach of the duty to cooperate in good faith.[4]

---

[1] Regarding the term procedural autonomy, see, among others, ECJ, Case C-212/04 *Adeneler and Others* [2006] ECR I-6057, para 95; ECJ, Case C-53/04 *Marrosu and Sardino* [2006] ECR I-7213, para 52; ECJ, Case C-180/04 *Vassallo* [2006] ECR I-7251, para 37; ECJ, Case C-307/05 *Del Cerro Alonso* [2007] ECR I-0000, para 25; ECJ, Case C-201/02 *Wells* [2004] ECR I-723, para 67; Case C-1/06 *Bonn Fleisch* [2007] ECR I-0000, para 41.

[2] ECJ, Case 26/62 *Van Gend & Loos*, ECR 1963, 1, paras 10–12.

[3] See e.g., ECJ, Case C-48/89 *Commission v Italy*, ECR 1990, I-2425.

[4] In fact where a piece of Community legislation makes no specific provision, its implementation is a matter in the first place for the member states, see ECJ, Case C-476/93 P *Nutral v Commission*, ECR 1995, I-4125, para 14.

Article 10 EC requires member states to 'take all appropriate measures, whether general or particular, to ensure fulfilment of the obligations arising out of this Treaty or resulting from action taken by the institutions of the Community', while at the same time they must 'abstain from any measure which could jeopardize the attainment of the objectives of this Treaty'.

Therefore the duty of loyal cooperation includes both a positive and a negative obligation. Article 10 EC puts member states under a duty to implement provisions of Community law so as to ensure fulfilment of the obligations contained therein. The Court considers this as an expression of Community solidarity.[5] This provision is binding on 'all the authorities of the member states',[6] including decentralized authorities,[7] and, most notably, national judges.[8] But it must be underlined that EU Institutions are also under a duty to collaborate with member states' judicial authorities. As far as the ECJ is concerned, that cooperation takes the form of the preliminary reference procedure provided for in Article 234 EC.

It is true that Article 10 EC does not confer enforceable rights upon individuals. However, it can be used as an additional argument where the member state in question is alleged to have breached an unconditional and sufficiently precise obligation. As far as transposition of EC legislation into the national legal order is concerned, Article 10 EC constitutes an additional legal basis establishing the duty of member states to repeal national provisions incompatible with a Community regulation[9] and the direct effect of non-implemented directives which are unconditional and sufficiently precise.[10]

III. The Principle of National Procedural Autonomy

The Court has consistently held that, in the absence of Community rules governing the matter, it is for the domestic legal system of each member state to designate the courts and tribunals having jurisdiction and to lay down the detailed procedural rules governing actions for safeguarding rights which individuals derive from Community law.[11] However, it follows from the duty of loyal cooperation (Article 10 EC) that the member states—including the domestic courts—are, in

---

[5] ECJ, joined cases 6 and 11/69 *Commission v France*, ECR 1969, 523, para 16.

[6] ECJ, Case 80/86 *Kolpinghuis Nijmegen*, ECR 1987, 3969, para 12.

[7] ECJ, Case 85/85 *Commission v Belgium*, ECR 1985, 1149, paras 22–23.

[8] ECJ, Case 14/83 *Von Colson and Kamann*, ECR 1984, 1891, para 26; and ECJ, Case 80/86 *Kolpinghuis Nijmegen*, ECR 1987, 3969, para 12.

[9] ECJ, Case 74/86 *Commission v Germany*, ECR 1988, 2139, paras 10–12.

[10] ECJ, Case 190/87 *Oberkreisdirektor des Kreises Borken*, ECR 1988, 4689, paras 22–24.

[11] ECJ, Case 13/68 *Salgoil* [1968] ECR 453, at p 463; ECJ, Case 33/76 *Rewe-Zentralfinanz* [1976] ECR 1989, para 5; ECJ, Case 179/84 *Bozzetti* [1985] ECR 2301, para 17; ECJ, Case C-312/93 *Peterbroeck* [1995] ECR I-4599, para 12; ECJ, Case C-453/99 *Courage and Crehan* [2001] ECR I-6297, para 29; ECJ, Case C-224/01 *Köbler* [2003] ECR I-10239, para 46; ECJ, Case C-432/05 *Unibet* [2007] ECR I-2271, para 39; and ECJ, Joined Cases C-222/05 to C-225/05 *Van der Weerd and Others* [2007] ECR I-0000, para 28.

terms of their procedural autonomy, required to ensure judicial protection of an individual's rights under Community law.[12] It is for the member states to *ensure in each case* that those rights are effectively protected.[13] This reflects the principle of effective judicial protection which, according to settled case law, is a general principle of Community law and forms part of the fundamental principles protected by the Community legal order,[14] which must therefore also be observed by the member states when applying Community law.[15]

Furthermore, the Court has defined two principles that national procedures must respect in order to be consistent with the requirements of the Treaty. First, it must not be more difficult to enforce EC rights than similar domestic rights (principle of equivalence). Secondly, the relevant rules must not render it virtually impossible or exceedingly difficult to exercise these Community rights (principle of effectiveness).

A problem may arise because of the fact that the implementation of EC law relies on domestic organization: this is evident for directives (Article 249 EC, third paragraph), but also for regulations that require more specific measures to be taken or that have to be applied in individual cases in order to be effective.[16] member states implement EC law in accordance with their particular constitutional traditions. However, since *Costa v Enel*, the Court holds that Community law can not be overridden by 'domestic legal provisions, however framed'.[17]

The separation of powers within a member state does not preclude a breach of the duty to implement Community legislation from being invariably imputed to the state itself at community level 'whatever the agency of the state whose action or inaction is the cause of the failure to fulfil its obligations, even in the case of a constitutionally independent institution'.[18] This principle is applicable whether it concerns the federal structure of the member state,[19] or the domestic procedures.[20]

---

[12] ECJ, Case C-432/05 *Unibet* [2007] ECR I-2271, paras 38–39.

[13] ECJ, Case 179/84 *Bozzetti* [1985] ECR 2301, para 17; Case C-446/93 *SEIM* [1996] ECR I-73, para 32; Case C-54/96 *Dorsch Consult* [1997] ECR I–4961, para 40; Case C-462/99 *Connect Austria* [2003] ECR I-5197, para 35; and ECJ, Case C-224/01 *Köbler* [2003] ECR I–10239, para 47.

[14] See, e.g., ECJ, Case 222/84 *Johnston* [1986] ECR 1651, paras 18 and 19; ECJ, Case C-50/00 P *Unión de Pequeños Agricultores v Council* [2002] ECR I-6677, para 39; and ECJ, Case C-432/05 *Unibet* [2007] ECR I-2271, para 39.

[15] See, to that effect, by way of example, ECJ, Case C-81/05 *Cordero Alonso* [2006] ECR I-7569, para 35; similarly, in relation to European Union law, ECJ, Case C-303/05 *Advocaten voor de Wereld* [2007] ECR I-3633, para 45; and Art 51(1) of the Charter of fundamental rights of the European Union.

[16] E.g., see ECJ, Case 30/70 *Scheer*, ECR 1970, 1197, para 10.

[17] ECJ, Case 6/64 *Costa v ENEL*, ECR 1964, 585, at 594.

[18] ECJ, Case 77/69 *Commission v Belgium*, ECR 1970, 237, para 15.

[19] ECJ, Case C-423/00 *Commission v Belgium*, ECR 2002, I-593 (the requirement of a cooperation agreement between the federal authority and part states before implementation of EC law, does not justify the breach of the delay provided for by EC law).

[20] ECJ, Case 8/70 *Commission v Italy*, ECR 1970, 961, para 11 (a member state must take account in its domestic legal system of the consequences of its adherence to the Community and, if need be, adapt its budgetary procedures accordingly).

To sum up, member states implement community law in accordance with the procedural and substantive rules of their own national law. In so doing, however, they must always pay due regard to the requirements of the uniform application of Community law.

IV. Resulting Obligations for National Judges

The first duty of the member state is to take all measures necessary to implement provisions of EC law. They must guarantee the full scope and effect of Community law. They must lay down the necessary sanctions in so far as Community provisions do not provide for any,[21] and have a general duty of dealing with any irregularities as quickly as possible.[22] The conduct of other member states or the apprehension of internal difficulties cannot justify a failure to apply Community law correctly.[23]

In accordance with the principle of loyal cooperation, national courts are entrusted with securing the legal protection which citizens derive from the direct effect of provisions of EC law as already stated by the Court in 1976.[24] To satisfy that aim, national judges must be able to effectively ensure the correct application of EC law in their member state. In so doing, they have certain very specific duties.

(i) Setting aside conflicting national rules

First of all, national courts have to refrain from applying conflicting provisions of domestic law, so long as these provisions have not been amended by the national legislator.[25] Member states must allow measures preventing Community rules from having full effect to be set aside: a national court which has to apply Community law must therefore have jurisdiction to do everything necessary to set aside provisions of law which might prevent Community rules from having full force.[26]

As early as in 1978 and the *Simmenthal* judgment, the ECJ held that 'every national court must, in a case within its jurisdiction, apply Community law in its entirety and protect rights which the latter confers on individuals and must accordingly set aside any provision of national law which may conflict with it,

---

[21] ECJ, Case 68/88 *Commission v Greece*, ECR 1989, 2965, para 24; ECJ, Case C-326/88 *Hansen*, ECR 1990, I-2911, para 17.

[22] ECJ, Case C-34/89 *Italy v Commission*, ECR 1990, I-3603, para 12; ECJ, Case C-277/98 *France v Commission*, ECR 2001, I-8453, para 40.

[23] ECJ, Case C-265/95 *Commission v France*, ECR 1997, I-6959, paras 55 and 63.

[24] ECJ, Case 33/76 *Rewe*, ECR 1976, 1989, para 5; ECJ, Case 45/76 *Comet*, ECR 1976, 2043, para 12.

[25] ECJ, Case 106/77 *Simmenthal*, ECR 1978, 629, para 24.

[26] ECJ, Case C-213/89 *Factortame* (I), ECR 1990, I-2433, para 20.

whether prior or subsequent to the Community rule'.[27] In addition, national courts must refuse to apply any conflicting provision of national law of its own motion and does not have to await a ruling of its Constitutional Court as required by its national legal system on the constitutionality of the domestic provision.[28] The ECJ made no mention of Article 10 EC in that ruling.

However, national courts are not required to raise of their own motion an issue concerning the breach of provisions of Community law where examination of that issue would oblige them to breach the passive role assigned to them by the contradictory national judicial system, in which the ambit of the dispute is exclusively defined by the parties (as opposed to an inquisitorial system).[29]

Nevertheless, where a national court can raise of its own motion pleas in law based on a binding national rule which was not put forward by the parties, it must examine of its own motion whether national legislative or administrative authorities implementing a directive remained within the limits of their discretion.[30]

In general terms, national courts can apply any directly effective Community measure and therefore must be able to set aside any conflicting national rule.

(ii) Consistent interpretation of national law with EC law

Article 10 EC puts all national authorities, including courts, under a duty to interpret national law in the light of the wording and purpose of Community law.[31] More generally, the national courts must, as far as is at all possible, interpret national law in a way which accords with the requirements of Community law.[32] National judicial authorities must therefore consider whether national law, legislation, and case law[33] can be interpreted or applied in such a way that there is no conflict with EU law.[34]

The requirement for national law to be interpreted in conformity with Community law is inherent in the system of the Treaty, since it allows national courts, for the matters within their jurisdiction, to ensure the full effectiveness of Community law in disputes pending before them.[35] Although this principle concerns chiefly domestic provisions enacted in order to implement EC law, it does not entail an interpretation merely of those provisions but requires the national

---

[27] ECJ, Case 106/77 *Simmenthal*, ECR 1978, 629, para 21.
[28] ECJ, Case 106/77 *Simmenthal*, ECR 1978, 629, para 22.
[29] ECJ, Joined Cases C-430/93 and C-431/93 *Van Schijndel and Van Veen*, ECR 1995, I-4705, paras 19–22.
[30] ECJ, Case C-72/95 *Kraaijeveld*, ECR 1996, I-5403, para 60; ECJ, Case C-126/97 *Eco Swiss China Time*, ECR 1999, I-3055, paras 31–34.
[31] ECJ, Case 14/83 *Von Colson and Kamann*, ECR 1984, 1891, para 26; ECJ, Case C-106/89 *Marleasing*, ECR 1990, I-4135, para 8.
[32] ECJ, Case C-262/97 *Engelbrecht*, ECR 2000, I-7321, para 39; ECJ, C-60/02 *Criminal proceedings against X*, paras 59–60.
[33] ECJ, Case C-456/98 *Centrosteel*, ECR 1998, I-6007, paras 16–17.
[34] ECJ, Joined Cases C-397/01 to C-403/01 *Pfeiffer and Others* [2004] ECR I-0000, para 115.
[35] Case C-160/01 *Mau* [2003] ECR I-4791, para 34.

court to consider national law as a whole in order to assess to what extent it may be applied so as not to produce a result contrary to that sought by EC law, as stated in the recent *Pfeiffer* judgement.[36] In that context, if the application of interpretative methods recognized by national law enables, in certain circumstances, a provision of domestic law to be construed in such a way as to avoid conflict with another rule of domestic law or the scope of that provision to be restricted to that end by applying it only insofar as it is compatible with the rule concerned, the national court is bound to use those methods in order to achieve the result sought by the directive.[37]

However, this duty of consistent interpretation is limited by general principles of Community law, such as the principle of legal certainty, the principle of legality, and the prohibition of retroactivity.[38] Moreover, the relevant provision of national law must be amenable to such interpretation,[39] meaning that the national court cannot be obliged to make an interpretation *contra legem*.

(iii) The possibility of bringing a damages claim in the national courts on account of a member state's breach of EC law

As already stated above, under Article 10 EC, national courts are under a duty to secure the effective application of Community law. In a Community governed by the Rule of Law, any unlawful consequence of a breach of law must be nullified.[40] Since the 1991 judgement in *Francovich*, an individual may claim damages from a member state whose breach of Community law causes them to suffer loss or damage.[41] For the sake of the uniform application of EC law, this holds good irrespective as to whether the breach committed within the national legal order is attributable to the legislature,[42] the executive, or the judiciary. As to the conditions to be satisfied for a member state to be required to make reparation for loss and damage caused to individuals as a result of breaches of Community law for which the state is responsible, the Court has held that these are threefold: the rule of law infringed must be intended to confer rights on individuals; the breach must be sufficiently serious; and there must be a direct causal link between the breach of the obligation incumbent on the state and the loss or damage sustained by the injured parties.

---

[36] See, to that effect, ECJ, Case C-131/97 *Carbonari and Others* [1999] ECR I-1103, paras 49 and 50.

[37] ECJ, Joined Cases C-397/01 to C-403/01 *Pfeiffer and Others* [2004] ECR I-0000, paras 113–116.

[38] ECJ, C-60/02 *Criminal proceedings against X*, paras 59–60; ECJ, Case 80/86 *Kolpinghuis Nijmegen*, ECR 1987, 3969, para 13; also see Joined Cases C-387/02, C-391/02, and C-403/02 *Criminal proceedings against Silvio Berlusconi* ECR, 2005 I-03565.

[39] ECJ, Case C-334/92 *Wagner Miret*, ECR 1993, I-6911, para 22.

[40] ECJ, Joined Cases C-6/90 and C-9/90 *Francovich*, ECR 1991, I-5357, para 36.

[41] ECJ, Joined Cases C-6/90 and C-9/90 *Francovich*, ECR 1991, I-5357, para 33.

[42] ECJ, Joined Cases C-46/93 and C-48/93 *Brasserie du Pêcheur and Factortame* (IV), ECR 1996, I-1029, paras 34–36.

The legal basis of the principle of state liability lies especially in Article 10 EC.[43] This duty of loyal cooperation between the institutions and member states is the reason why the Court established, in *Factortame IV*, a clear parallel between the conditions governing the liability of the Community and the liability of the member states for violations of EC law.[44]

V. Striking a Balance between the Duty of Loyal Cooperation and National Procedural Autonomy: The Recent ECJ Case Law

The duties of national judges analyzed above stem from a case law which can be considered well established even though it is in constant evolution. However, in a number of recent cases the Court had to engage in a particularly delicate balancing exercise regarding the duty of loyal cooperation and national procedural autonomy.

(i) The *Köbler* judgment: the principle of state liability extended to violations of EC law by national courts

Although the principle of state liability for breaches of Community law had been firmly established in the Court's case law, there had been no judgment on the question whether that principle is applicable in cases of violations of EC law committed by national courts. The *Köbler* case gave the Court the opportunity to clarify that point.[45]

The regional civil court of Vienna requested an interpretation of the Court's case law on state liability, to make clear if a loss or damage caused by a decision of a national court adjudicating at last instance that breached EC law should be repaired under this doctrine. The *Verwaltungsgerichtshof*, one of Austria's supreme courts, withdrew a request for a preliminary ruling from the ECJ and proceeded by applying the existing case law of the ECJ in an allegedly wrongful manner.[46] Mr Köbler filed a claim for the damages he suffered as a result of the *Verwaltungsgerichtshof's* alleged wrongful interpretation of EC law.

The ECJ held that the essential role played by the judiciary in the protection of individual rights derived from Community law would be weakened if

---

[43] ECJ, Joined Cases C-6/90 and C-9/90 *Francovich*, ECR 1991, I-5357, paras 35–36.

[44] ECJ, Joined Cases C-46/93 and C-48/93 *Brasserie du Pêcheur and Factortame (IV)*, ECR 1996, I-1029, paras 40–42. Also see ECJ, Case C-352/98P *Laboratoires pharmaceutiques Bergaderm and Goupil*, ECR 2000, I-5921, paras 38–44. These three conditions apply to legislative acts of the Community since ECJ, Case 5/71 *Zuckerfabrik Schöppenstedt v Council*, ECR 1971, 975, para 11.

[45] ECJ, Case C-224/01 *Köbler*, paras 51–53.

[46] ECJ, Case C-15/96 *Schöning-Kougebetopoulou* [1998] ECR I-47.

individuals were not able to obtain reparation for damage caused by an infringement of Community law attributable to a member state court adjudicating at last
instance. Applying the three conditions for state liability, the Court considered
that when determining whether the infringement is sufficiently serious the specific nature of the judicial function has to be taken into account. State liability can be incurred only in the exceptional case where the national court has
manifestly infringed the applicable Community law or the Court's case law in
the area.

Moreover the ECJ underlined the specific role of the national courts and considered that in assessing the existence of liability one must take account of the
clarity and precision of the rule infringed, whether the infringement and the damage caused was intentional or involuntary, whether any error of law was excusable
or inexcusable, and the fact that the position taken by a Community institution
may have contributed towards the adoption or maintenance of national measures
or practices contrary to EC law.[47]

As far as liability for judicial decisions is concerned, the approach of the ECJ
in *Köbler* tries to strike the appropriate balance between the national procedural
autonomy and the obligation of loyal cooperation of Article 10 EC. While the
Court accepts that national courts can in principle incur liability for breaches
of EC law, it nonetheless sets a series of very strict conditions in order to establish the existence of a sufficiently serious breach that could justify such liability. And in applying those conditions, the ECJ found that the failure of the
Verwaltungsgerichtshof to maintain its preliminary reference before the ECJ cannot be regarded as a breach being manifest in nature.

(ii) The *Kühne & Heitz* and *Kempter* judgments: the duty to amend administrative decisions that have become final

The *Kühne & Heitz* case law has been the subject of an important doctrinal discussion. Although the principle of legal certainty precludes an administrative
authority from going back on a decision which has become final, an administrative body may be obliged to review it, when it subsequently becomes clear
that it is based on a wrong interpretation of Community law, in order to take
account of the interpretation of the relevant provision given in the meantime by
the Court.[48] In fact, the duty of loyal cooperation obliges all national authorities
to remedy any unlawful consequences of an infringement of EC law.

In this case, a Dutch firm exporting poultry meat parts to non-member countries
had been ordered to reimburse paid export refunds according to Dutch law pursuant a reclassification of its products. During those proceedings, Kühne & Heitz

---

[47] ECJ, Case C-224/01 *Köbler*, paras 55; also see ECJ, Case C-118/00 *Larsy*, ECR 2001, I-5063,
para 39.
[48] ECJ, Case C-453/00 *Kühne & Heitz*, [2004] ECR I-837, paras 20–28.

did not request that a question be referred to the Court for a preliminary ruling. Subsequently, the ECJ, in its judgment in case *Voogd Vleesimport en-export*,[49]
modified the tariff classification of the chicken's 'piece of back that remains
attached and must therefore be described as a leg'. Kuhne & Heitz asked for a
reassessment of the decision ordering reimbursement, which was refused, and
then brought an action against that latter decision before the Administrative
Court for Trade and Industry, which referred to the ECJ the following preliminary question: does EC law require judgments of the ECJ to be take into consideration even for cases which have been subject to a definitive administrative
decision?

The ECJ's reasoning has as a starting point the principle that the interpretation which the Court gives to a rule of Community law clarifies and defines,
where necessary, the meaning and scope of that rule as it must be or ought to
have been understood and applied from the time of its coming into force. It follows that a rule of Community law interpreted in this way must be applied by an
administrative body within the sphere of its competence even to legal relationships which arose or were formed before the Court gave its ruling on the question
on interpretation.

Nevertheless the Court acknowledged that the principle of legal certainty
must also be taken into account in that context because the finality of an administrative decision, which is acquired upon expiry of the reasonable time-limits
for legal remedies or by exhaustion of those remedies, contributes to such legal
certainty. Therefore the Court considered that Community law does not require
that administrative bodies be placed under an obligation, in principle, to reopen
an administrative decision which has become final in that way.

However, when examining the particular facts of the case the Court concluded
that the principle of loyal cooperation arising from Article 10 EC imposes on
an administrative body an obligation to review a final administrative decision,
where an application for such review is made to it, in order to take account of
the interpretation of the relevant provision given in the meantime by the Court
where four very specific conditions are met: (1) under national law, the administrative body must have the power to reopen that decision; (2) the administrative
decision in question has become final as a result of a judgment of a national court
ruling at final instance; (3) that judgment is, in the light of a decision given by the
Court subsequent to it, based on a misinterpretation of Community law which
was adopted without a question being referred to the Court for a preliminary
ruling under the third paragraph of Article 234 EC; and, finally (4), the person
concerned complained to the administrative body immediately after becoming
aware of that decision of the Court.

It was probably clear from the outset that these four conditions would be
subject to further interpretation by the Court. In a judgment rendered on the

---

[49] C-151/93 *Voogd Vleesimport en-export* [1994] ECR I-4915.

12 February 2008 the ECJ already interpreted further the principle of loyal cooperation construed in the light of the judgment in *Kühne & Heitz*. In *Kempter*,[50] the referring German court essentially asked whether the *Kühne & Heitz* case law requires an administrative decision that has become final by virtue of a judgment of a court of final instance, to be reviewed and amended only if the claimant relied on Community law in the legal action under domestic law which he brought against that decision. The Court answered that question in the negative. After restating the principles it had already set out in *Kühne & Heitz* the Court further explained that the system established by Article 234 EC instituted direct cooperation between the Court of Justice and the national courts by means of a procedure which is completely independent of any initiative by the parties.[51] Moreover, it underlined that Community law does not require national courts to raise of their own motion a plea alleging infringement of Community provisions where examination of that plea would oblige them to go beyond the ambit of the dispute as defined by the parties. Nonetheless, they are obliged to raise of their own motion points of law based on binding Community rules where, under national law, they must or may do so in relation to a binding rule of national law.[52]

The second question referred by the German court in *Kempter* concerned whether Community law, as interpreted in *Kühne & Heitz*, imposes a limit in time for making an application for review of an administrative decision that has become final. In fact, in *Kuhne & Heitz*, the claimant had introduced its application for review of the administrative decision within a period of less than three months after becoming aware of the judgment in case *Voogd Vleesimport en-export*[53] pursuant to which the administrative decision was deemed to be unlawful. The Court restated its classic case law on the procedural autonomy of member states and the principles of equivalence and effectiveness[54] that pose limits to this autonomy and concluded that it is compatible with Community law to lay down reasonable national time-limits for bringing proceedings in the interest of legal certainty.[55]

---

[50] ECJ, C-2/06 *Willy Kempter*, not yet published.

[51] See, to this effect, ECJ, Joined Cases 28/62, 29/62 and 30/62 *Da Costa and Others* [1963] ECR 31, at 38; ECJ, Case 62/72 *Bollmann* [1973] ECR 269, para 4; and ECJ, Case C-261/95 *Palmisani* [1997] ECR I-4025, para 31.

[52] ECJ, Joined Cases C-430/93 and C-431/93 *van Schijndel and van Veen* [1995] ECR I-4705, paras 13, 14, and 22; ECJ, Case C-72/95 *Kraaijeveld and Others* [1996] ECR I-5403, paras 57, 58, and 60.

[53] ECJ, Case C-151/93 *Voogd Vleesimport en-export* [1994] ECR I-4915.

[54] See, in particular, ECJ, Case C-432/05 *Unibet* [2007] ECR I-2271, para 43; ECJ, Joined Cases C-222/05 to C-225/05 *vander Weerd and Others* [2007] ECR I-4233, para 28; *Peterbroeck*, para 12; *Courage and Crehan*, para 29.

[55] ECJ, Case 33/76 *Rewe-Zentralfinanz and Rewe-Zentral* [1976] ECR 1989, para 5; ECJ, Case 45/76 *Comet* [1976] ECR 2043, paras 17 and 18; ECJ, *Denkavit italiana*, para 23; ECJ, Case C-208/90 *Emmott* [1991] ECR I-4269, para 16; ECJ, *Palmisani*, para 28; ECJ, Case C-90/94 *Haahr Petroleum* [1997] ECR I-4085, para 48; and ECJ, Case C-255/00 *Grundig Italiana* [2002] ECR I-8003, para 34.

(iii) *Unibet* and *Impact*: the duty to ensure effective judicial protection of EC law rights

The recent *Unibet* judgment explicitly dealt with the more specific issue of the appropriate balance between national procedural autonomy and the necessity to ensure effective judicial protection of EC law derived rights.[56]

The facts of *Unibet* are rather complex and for the purpose of this paper we will present them in a simplified manner. Unibet had purchased advertising space in a number of different Swedish media with a view to promoting its gaming services on the internet. In accordance with the national Law on Lotteries, the Swedish State took a number of measures, including obtaining injunctions and commencing criminal proceedings, against those media which had agreed to provide Unibet with advertising space. Unibet tried to introduce an action for a *declaration* that certain national substantive provisions were in conflict with Article 49 EC, a claim for damages and an application for interim relief. The case was brought twice before the Court of Appeal. The preliminary reference of the Court of Appeal essentially raised three issues:

(1) whether the principle of effective judicial protection of an individual's rights under Community law must be interpreted as requiring it to be possible in the legal order of a member state to bring an action seeking the simple declaration of the incompatibility of a national provision with EC law if other legal remedies permit the question of compatibility to be determined only as a preliminary issue;

(2) whether the principle of effective judicial protection of an individual's rights under Community law *requires* it to be possible in the legal order of a member state to obtain interim relief suspending the application of national measures until the competent court has given a ruling on whether those measures are compatible with Community law; and

(3) whether the grant of interim relief in such cases is governed by the criteria laid down by the national law applicable before the competent court or by Community criteria.

On the first issue, the Court based its reasoning on its well-established case law on procedural autonomy and the principles of effectiveness and equivalence. Community law does require member states to provide for (free-standing) declaratory actions on the compatibility of national law with EC law, if such an action is also not available for claims based on national law and if the other legal remedies available are likely to guarantee effective judicial protection. The ECJ analysed in detail the remedies available under Swedish law and came to the conclusion that such remedies provide adequate judicial protection.

---

[56] ECJ, Case C-432/05 *Unibet* [2007] ECR I-2271, para 43.

It is important to clarify that this right to an effective judicial protection is not an 'invention' of the ECJ. In fact, the principle of effective judicial protection is a general principle of Community law stemming from the constitutional traditions common to the member states, which has been enshrined in Articles 6 and 13 of the European Convention for the Protection of Human Rights and Fundamental Freedoms[57] and which has also been reaffirmed by Article 47 of the Charter of Fundamental Rights of the European Union, proclaimed on 7 December 2000 in Nice.[58] Under the principle of loyal cooperation laid down in Article 10 EC, it is for the member states to ensure judicial protection of an individual's rights under Community law.[59] But this important principle aiming for uniform protection under EC law does not impose uniform procedural rules. As the Court concluded in *Unibet*, insofar as there is an effective legal remedy allowing the verification of whether a national measure violated EC law, member states do not have to provide a new type of legal action.

Concerning the two preliminary questions regarding interim relief the Court applied its *Factortame* case law and ruled that effective judicial protection of an individual's rights under Community law requires it to be possible in the legal order of a member state for interim relief to be granted, where the grant of such relief is necessary to ensure the full effectiveness of the judgment to be given on the existence of such rights.[60] Furthermore, the Court considered that the conditions for granting interim relief in such a case are governed by the criteria laid down by the national law applicable before that court, provided that those criteria are no less favourable than those applying to similar domestic actions and do not render practically impossible or excessively difficult the interim judicial protection of those rights.

A few months after the ruling in *Unibet*, the ECJ was faced once again with issues related to judicial protection at the national level in the *Impact*[61] case. The reference was on the interpretation of Directive 1999/70/EC of 28 June 1999 concerning the framework agreement on fixed-term work concluded by ETUC, UNICE, and CEEP. The directive had to be transposed into national law by the member states by 2001 but it was transposed into Irish law by the Protection of Employees (Fixed-Term Work) Act of 2003. Jurisdiction was granted to the Labour Court to hear claims based on this Act. Nevertheless, the work contracts in the *Impact* case all started before the entry into force of the Protection

---

[57] ECJ, Case 222/84 *Johnston* [1986] ECR 1651, paras 18–19; ECJ, Case 222/86 *Heylens and Others* [1987] ECR 4097, para 14; ECJ, Case C-424/99 *Commission v Austria* [2001] ECR I-9285, para 45; ECJ, Case C-50/00 P *Unión de Pequeños Agricultores v Council* [2002] ECR I-6677, para 39; and ECJ, Case C-467/01 *Eribrand* [2003] ECR I-6471, para 61.

[58] OJ 2000 C 364, p 1.

[59] ECJ, Case 33/76 *Rewe*, [1976] ECR 1989, para 5; ECJ, Case 45/76 *Comet* [1976] ECR 2043, para 12; ECJ, Case 106/77 *Simmenthal* [1978] ECR 629, paras 21–22; ECJ, Case C-213/89 *Factortame* [1990] ECR I-2433, para 19; and ECJ, Case C-312/93 *Peterbroeck* [1995] ECR I-4599, para 12.

[60] ECJ, Case C-213/89 *Factortame* [1990] ECR I-2433, para 21, and ECJ, Case C-226/99 *Siples* [2001] ECR I-277, para 19.

[61] ECJ, Case C-268/06 *Impact* (judgment of 15 April 2008, not yet published in the Reports).

of Employees Act, and thus the relevant claims are partly based on the directly applicable provisions of the directive itself. Such claims could have been introduced before other Irish courts but on less favourable terms. The question therefore arose whether a national court is required to apply directly effective provisions of Community law if, notwithstanding the fact that it has not been given express jurisdiction to do so under domestic law, it does have jurisdiction to apply the national transposing legislation enacted in relation to those provisions and those provisions could otherwise be directly relied upon by individuals only before other domestic courts and on less favourable terms.

After restating its classic case law on procedural autonomy and the principle of effectiveness, the ECJ held that that, in those circumstances, it would be contrary to this principle to require individuals in the situation of the complainants to bring two separate actions, one before ordinary courts for the period before the transposition of the directive and one before the specialized courts for the period after the transposition of the directive, if that requirement would result in procedural disadvantages such as rendering excessively difficult the exercise of rights deriving from that directive.

Furthermore, in response to Ireland's argument that it was possible, under national law, for the complainants to bring both actions before the ordinary courts since the jurisdiction of the Labour Courts for such disputes was optional, the Court considered that, even if that was so, in cases where individuals relied on the optional jurisdiction of the Labour courts, the principle of effectiveness still requires that they should also be able to seek before the same courts the protection of the rights which they can derive directly from the directive itself, if it should emerge from the checks undertaken by the referring court that the obligation to divide their action into two separate claims and to bring the claim based directly on the directive before an ordinary court leads to procedural complications liable to render excessively difficult the exercise of those rights conferred on the parties by Community law.

The court further added that it was up to the national judge to proceed to the necessary checks in order to find whether such an infringement of the principle of effectiveness took place. In so doing the national court would have to interpret the domestic jurisdictional rules in such a way that, wherever possible, they contribute to the attainment of the objective of ensuring effective judicial protection of an individual's rights under Community law.[62]

VI. Concluding Remarks

The purpose of this paper was twofold. First, the objective was to establish that the, now classic, case law of the ECJ on Article 10 EC and the obligations of national judges under this article can best be explained by the necessity to ensure

---

[62] To that effect the Court cited para 44 of the *Unibet* judgment.

that national judges do have all the necessary powers to satisfy their role as judges responsible for the primary enforcement of Community law.

Secondly, it was considered necessary to present in detail the Court's recent case law in order to place it in the appropriate context. In fact, this case law has often been interpreted as disproportionately affecting national procedural autonomy. Nevertheless, it was our intention to suggest an alternative to this one-sided approach in the sense that this case law is better understood when analysed precisely as an attempt to strike a balance between the duty of loyal cooperation and the principle of national procedural autonomy.

In the context of this approach, *Köbler, Kühne & Heitz, Unibet,* and *Impact* should not be interpreted as evidence of 'judicial activism' or a 'pre-established hidden agenda' on the part of the ECJ. In the absence of uniform Community rules, it is for the member states to provide *remedies* and *procedures* for the protection of Community *rights*. Nevertheless, in order to ensure effective and uniform judicial protection, all over the European Union, the ECJ has to verify if the national procedures implementing EC law are appropriate to ensure its *effet utile*. Procedure cannot be considered as having an overriding importance over the substantive objectives of an EC law provision. An extensive interpretation either of the principle of national procedural autonomy or of the duty of loyal cooperation under Article 10 EC would lead to inefficient and undesirable results. The treaties aim to guarantee national procedural autonomy as long as it is loyally exercised towards EC law.

Thus in *Köbler*, while the ECJ extended the principle of state liability for breach of EC law to cover actions of national courts, it did not apply that principle in this particular case because it adopted a rather restrictive interpretation of what constitutes a serious breach. Similarly, in *Kühne & Heitz*, the ECJ established four very strict cumulative conditions to be met in order to proceed to the re-examination of an administrative act which has become final. In *Unibet* the court considered that as long as there is an effective and equivalent national legal remedy that makes it possible to verify if EC law had been complied with, Community law will not impose the establishment of a specific national procedure for the protection of rights derived from EC law. Finally, in *Impact*, the Court's ruling could be viewed as rather measured given, first, that the potentially disadvantageous procedural position of the complainants resulted for the delay in the transposition of the directive and, second, that the ECJ left it up to the national court to decide whether this disadvantageous position was an established fact.

It is apparent, in our view, that such a careful balancing exercise cannot be considered as judicial activism. After all, one must not overlook the fact that the body of case law related to the issues examined in this paper was established over several decades and, almost in its entirety, through preliminary rulings. Therefore, the genesis of this case law came about not at the initiative of the ECJ, which as it is well known does not have any control over its docket, but through cooperation between national courts and the ECJ. To ensure the continuation of this cooperation, the Court fully relies on the competences of national judges and believes in their fundamental role for the efficient functioning of the EU legal order.

12

Lord Bingham: Of Swallows and International Law

*Gillian Triggs**

Shortly after the decision of the House of Lords in the *Belmarsh* decisions in 2005, Lord Bingham gave an interview that was reported as follows:

Last December, [Lord Bingham] and seven of his fellow law lords delivered a landmark ruling against the government in the case of nine men being held at Belmarsh prison on suspicion of having links with terrorists. They ruled that their indefinite detention without trial contravened the European Convention on Human Rights... Bingham, who as senior law lord gave the lead judgment, became an instant hero to liberals. One Guardian columnist called him 'the radical who is leading a new English revolution'. Does that description please him? 'I didn't dislike it,' he says with a nice sense of understatement that draws a laugh from the audience. 'But I didn't think it was at all apt.'[1]

'Radical' and 'revolutionary' are not words that spring to mind when considering Lord Bingham's distinguished contribution to international legal jurisprudence. Rather, his defining characteristic as a jurist has been a restrained approach to the exercise of judicial power, seeking evidence of rights through the traditional means of judicial reasoning, statutory interpretation, and compelling evidence. Lord Bingham's decisions in international law attest to an unwavering commitment to protect human rights and a willingness to rely on human rights standards and the authority of international courts and institutions. He is equally unwavering in upholding parliamentary sovereignty, respecting the doctrine of non-justiciability and requiring evidence of asserted rules.

At the heart of Lord Bingham's legal methodology lies a process of weighing legal authorities to identify the applicable rule. He sets out the legal issues, reviews the arguments of counsel, and considers the relevant domestic and international authorities. Only once this examination is complete does Lord Bingham draw his legal conclusions; determinations that seem to emerge, almost inevitably, and

* The author is grateful for the legal research and analytical ideas suggested by Ms Laura Crommeli.
[1] Moss, Stephen, 'Cry Freedom' (an interview with Lord Bingham), 31 May 2005, *The Guardian*, available at <http://www.theguardian.co.uk>.

unsurprisingly from the process itself. Indeed, his logic and economy of style leave the reader feeling more than usually intelligent. Such a methodology seems obvious as a sound foundation for any legal opinion, though not always one adopted by scholars or judges.

Lord Bingham's judicial technique is illustrated by *Jones v Saudi Arabia* where, on examination of the slight evidence of an asserted right to deny immunity in civil claims, he observed that 'one swallow does not make a rule of international law'.[2] Tempting though it might have been to extend the *Pinochet (No 3)*[3] ratio in respect of criminal prosecutions to civil claims for damages, Lord Bingham remained true to the need to identify the rule of law by rigorous examination of the legal instruments and precedents. Judicial activism in international law has not been for him. Rather, he has adopted an approach that might be described as a 'rights-based traditionalism'.[4]

This paper seeks to explore the contribution Lord Bingham has made to the jurisprudence of international law. It is notable that while he is a judge within a national judiciary, rather than an international court or tribunal, he has had an influence on the substance of international law that is wider than within the United Kingdom alone. Lord Bingham has been a leader in recognizing the role of international law in domestic law and in referring to and employing international legal materials. He has provided judgments on sovereign immunity, the extraterritorial application of national human rights legislation, treaty interpretation, the validity of derogations from international obligations, and the admission of evidence obtained by torture. These topics are briefly examined to gain some insight into the unique contribution, as a national jurist, that Lord Bingham has made to the application and articulation of international law.

Alabama Claims Arbitration

Before considering some examples of Lord Bingham's international jurisprudence, it might be observed that his juristic skills are informed by his scholarship in international law, by an intellectual curiosity for its historical origins, and by a talent for pithy, lucid writing. In 2005, Lord Bingham wrote a lecture, later published in the International and Comparative Law Quarterly, on 'The Alabama Claims Arbitration'.[5] The influence of this paper is illustrated in modern parlance by the fact that the website of the British Institute of International and Comparative Law, on which the text can be found, has been the subject of more 'hits' than any other scholarly paper.[6] The opening paragraph tells the reader

---

[2] [2006] UKHL 26, para 22.   [3] [2000] 1 AC 147.
[4] Lord Bingham, with Lord Steyn, has been consistent in favouring a rights-based solution to the cases at hand; Bingham, *The Business of Judging: Selected Essays and Speeches* (Oxford: OUP, 2000, Part IV).
[5] 54 *ICLQ* 1–25 (2005).   [6] BIICL website <http://www.biicl.org/>.

they are in for an entertaining journey through the diplomatic negotiations that finally settled the claims arising from the American Civil War in 1849:

A lecturer on the Alabama claims and the Geneva Tribunal of 1871–2, like a director of Hamlet, has to accept one inescapable fact; that everyone knows, broadly at least, how the story ends. There can be no reliance on suspense to sustain interest in the narrative. So I shall begin at the end.[7]

And so begins a fascinating, and brilliantly written, historical analysis of an international dispute, the roots of which lay in slavery, preservation of the Union, and English antipathy for the North of the United States.[8] There were profound differences between the British and Americans over the applicable principles of international law, particularly the laws of neutrality during war. 'Quiet diplomacy' found what was to become a very modern solution to international legal disputes. 'Amidst the greatest good humour and jollity',[9] the United States and Britain agreed to submit their disparate views to international arbitration by five arbitrators to be named by Italy, Brazil, the Swiss Confederation, Britain, and the United States. Lord Bingham's research unearthed some less than flattering pen portraits of the arbitrators, providing an amusing insight into the personalities that lie behind all arbitral proceedings. As he points out, the *Alabama Claims Arbitration* provided a stimulant for the agreement by the Tsar and President Theodor Roosevelt to seek ways of making international arbitration more effective. These efforts laid the foundations for the Permanent Court of Arbitration, the Permanent Court of International Justice (PCIJ) and the International Court of Justice (ICJ), demonstrating, Lord Bingham observes:

... one of the few instances in history when the world's leading nation, in the plenitude of its power, agreed to submit an issue of great national moment to the decision of a body in which it could be, and it was, heavily outvoted.[10]

The detailed research that informed Lord Bingham's lecture on the *Alabama Claims Arbitration* is typical of the forensic methodology he has adopted when considering the international legal issues that have arisen for his determination. As the following examples show, his respect for the rule of law applies equally to the international rule of law.

Relationship between International Law and Domestic Law

One of the vital challenges for international law in the 21st century is its interaction and harmonization with domestic laws. International law, said Lord Chancellor Talbot, is in its fullest extent 'part of the law of England'.[11] This

---

[7] Ibid, at 1.   [8] 54 *ICLQ*1, at 2.
[9] Ibid, at 14.   [10] Ibid, at 24.
[11] *Buvot v Barbuit* (1737) Cases Talbot 281.

deceptively simple notion is oft-cited but inconsistently applied. It has stimulated much analysis of the effect that an international rule might have in domestic law. As a rule of common law, international custom must defer to any legislation and to the constitution.[12] Moreover, the English courts are not competent to create new criminal offences, or to recognize new crimes that are developed at international law.

Lord Bingham appreciated the impediments to applying international custom without the consent of Parliament and proposed in *R v Jones and Ors* that international law might better be understood as a 'source' of English law upon which the courts could draw.[13] His decision in this case illustrates Lord Bingham's approach to the relationship between international law and domestic law. The appeal to the Lords concerned 20 Iraqi war protesters who had been arrested for trespass and criminal damage at the Royal Air Force base at Fairford in Gloustershire. By way of legal justification, the appellants argued that they were entitled to impede the commission of the crime of waging aggressive war. Vital to the success of their defence was that 'the crime of aggression, if established in customary international law, is a crime recognized by or forming part of the domestic law of England and Wales'.[14] Lord Bingham put the issue as follows:

The immense, perhaps unprecedented, suffering of many people in many countries during the twentieth century had at least one positive result: that it promoted a strong international determination to prevent and prohibit the waging of aggressive war. This determination found expression in the international legal order, and understandably so, since it is states which wage wars and states that must suppress them. At issue in these appeals is the extent to which, if at all, this international determination is transposed into the domestic legal order of England and Wales.[15]

The Court of Appeal had earlier posed the question for consideration by the House of Lords in the following terms:

Is the crime against peace and/or crime of aggression capable of being a 'crime' within the meaning of section 3 of the Criminal law Act 1967 and, if so, is the issue justiciable in a criminal trial?

As might be expected, the appellants relied upon the maxim that the law of nations in its full extent is part of the law of England. Lord Bingham considered that he could not 'accept this proposition in quite the unqualified terms in which it has often been stated'.[16] He preferred instead to consider international law as a legitimate 'source' of domestic law. It is not clear what this means. Lord Bingham's subsequent analysis in *R v Jones* suggests that, in this case, it amounted to very little.

---

[12] James Crawford, *International Law in the House of Lords and the High Court of Australia 1996–2008: a comparison*, in 'The first of the Michael Kirby lectures', ANZSIL, Canberra, 27 June 2008.

[13] *R v Jones (Margaret)* [2006] 2 All ER 741, 751, para 11.

[14] Ibid, para 2.   [15] Ibid, para 1.   [16] Ibid, para 11.

Demonstrating a familiarity with the evidences of custom, Lord Bingham traced the evolution of the prohibition on aggressive war as an international crime. He examined the principles adopted by the League of Nations, the 'Kellogg-Briand Pact', the Charter of the United Nations, General Assembly resolutions, the Draft Code of offences of the International Law Commission of 1996, the Rome Statute for an International Criminal Court, and jurisprudence of the International Court of Justice. Rejecting the argument that the crime of aggression lacked legal certainty, he found that the 'core elements of the crime of aggression have been understood, at least since 1945, with sufficient clarity to permit the lawful trial...of those accused of this most serious crime'.[17] This is a powerful finding and one that will doubtless be persuasive for other national courts and international tribunals in dispelling any lingering doubts about the nature of this crime that have been fostered by the failure to agree upon its 'elements' for the purposes of the Rome Statute.[18]

Having met the need to determine the status of aggression at custom, an often insurmountable obstacle for those asserting an international rule, Lord Bingham determined that a crime recognized at customary law 'may be assimilated into the domestic law of this country' despite the absence of implementing legislation. Of particular influence in reaching this conclusion was the Royal Warrant of 1945 that had been issued under a royal prerogative to provide for trials of those charged with 'violations of the laws and usages of war'.[19] At this point, Lord Bingham arrested his progress. Assimilation was not, in his view, automatic. Citing English, Australian, and United States authorities, Lord Bingham confirmed the traditional view that the power to create new crimes lay with parliament. A review of the Criminal Law Act 1967 indicated that the 'focus of the Act is entirely domestic'.[20] Applying the usual principles of statutory interpretation, he concluded that there was nothing in the Act to suggest that the term crime meant anything more than an offence against a statute or the common law.

Confirming his view that the Act does not include international crimes was Lord Bingham's observation that the practice of the United Kingdom has been to legislate to implement international obligations in domestic law; as is typical of most states. The Rome Statute was, for example, given domestic effect in the United Kingdom by the International Criminal Court Act 2001. Lord Bingham argued that it would be 'anomalous if the crime of aggression, excluded (obviously deliberately) from the 2001 Act, were to be treated as a domestic crime, since it would not be subject to the constraints...applicable to the crimes which were included.'[21] As a matter of logic, this must be correct. Lord Bingham thus

---

[17] Ibid, para 19.

[18] The crime of aggression is listed in Art 5 of the Rome Statute, but the Court has jurisdiction over this crime only once the parties have agreed to adopt a definition through amendment of the Statute itself; see ILC Draft Code of Crimes Against Peace and Security of Mankind of 1996, art 16.

[19] Ibid, para 22.   [20] Ibid, para 26.   [21] Ibid, para 28.

exposed the weakness in the appellants' argument that custom is automatically incorporated in English law. While custom may, as Lord Bingham recognized, be assimilated into United Kingdom law, as a matter of interpretation, the Act had not done so. Logically, if the international prohibition on waging aggressive war is not an offence under English criminal laws, acts to prevent the crime of aggression could not, therefore, provide a justification for breaches of those laws.

In practice, if assimilation of customary law into national law is strictly for Parliament, and if a cautious approach to statutory interpretation is adopted, it is hard to see when, if ever, 'assimilation' can take place. The strength of Lord Bingham's adherence to the primacy of Parliament is illustrated in the following passage:

> ... it is for those representing the people of the country in Parliament, not the executive and not the judges, to decide what conduct should be treated as lying so far outside the bounds of what is acceptable in our society as to attract criminal penalties.[22]

For Lord Bingham, there were no compelling reasons to depart from this principle.

Lord Bingham was quick to realize that the justification claimed by the appellants would, unless the aggression had been sanctioned by the UN Security Council, have called for a decision as to the culpability of the British government in going to war. While such a finding was presumably what the appellants hoped to achieve, Lord Bingham chose not to embark upon these dangerous waters. He favoured the principles of justiciability and 'act of state', observing that the:

> courts will be very slow to review the prerogative powers in relation to the conduct of foreign affairs and the deployment of the armed forces, and very slow to adjudicate upon rights arising out of transactions entered into between sovereign states on the plane of international law.

Lord Bingham also identified yet another anomaly that underscores the wisdom of avoiding such international questions. Where a person seeks to avoid liability for impeding government preparations to wage illegal aggression, his acts might equally be construed as sedition or within the Treason Act 1351. As it has never been a defence that the state is engaged in an unlawful war, it would, Lord Bingham found, 'be strange if the same conduct could be both a crime and a defence'.[23] His judgment in *R v Jones* is thus an illustration of Lord Bingham's emphasis on the principles of constitutional supremacy of Parliament, non-justiciability, and statutory interpretation. These foundational principles of judicial reasoning in national law provided a solution to the question of whether international custom might have been assimilated into domestic law without legislative implementation.

---

[22] Ibid, para 29.   [23] Ibid, para 31.

Unincorporated Treaties in Domestic Law

While the assimilation of customary law remains a possibility, national courts have been firmly resistant to the implementation of unincorporated treaties in domestic law.[24] Some judges have, however, flirted with the idea that there might be a legitimate expectation that states will act in accordance with the treaties to which they have become a party. Such an implication is not entirely unreasonable in light of the international obligation that is created by ratification of a treaty and the political expectations that this excites.

In *R v Asfaw* Lord Bingham considered the appellant's claim that he had a 'legitimate expectation' that the United Kingdom would honour its obligations under the 1951 Refugee Convention even though the relevant legislation, the Immigration and Asylum Act 1999, was to the contrary.[25] As the United Kingdom is a dualist common law country that does not apply unincorporated treaties in domestic law, the question in *R v Asfaw* amounted to an invitation to abrogate the traditional rule.[26] The background to appellants' argument is that some judges have, for some years, been attracted—moth-like to the flame—to recognize a legitimate expectation that officials will act in accordance with treaties to which the state has become a party, but which have not yet been implemented by legislation. The high water mark of the doctrine of legitimate expectation arose in the decision of the Australian High Court in *Minister for Immigration and Ethnic Affairs v Teoh* (1995) where the majority found that:

> ... ratification of a Convention is a positive statement by the executive government of this country to the world and to the Australian people that the executive government and its agencies will act in accordance with the Convention. That positive statement is an adequate foundation for a legitimate expectation, absent statutory or executive indications to the contrary, that administrative decision-makers will act in conformity with the Convention...[27]

While initially recognized by English courts, there has been a retreat from the *Teoh* approach in Australian and English jurisprudence. In *R v Asfaw* the House of Lords considered the protection afforded by Article 31 of the Refugee Convention where the defendant had been charged with an offence that had not been specific in section 31(3) of the Immigration and Asylum Act 1999. Lord Bingham, in the leading judgment, considered that:

> ... the Convention as a whole has never been formally incorporated or given effect in domestic law. While, therefore, one would expect any government intending to legislate inconsistently with an obligation binding on the UK to make its intention very clear,

---

[24] See generally, G Triggs, *International Law: Contemporary Principles and Practices*, Butterworths, 2006, Ch 3.

[25] [2008] All ER (D) 274 (May).   [26] Crawford, op. cit., n 12.

[27] (1995) 183 CLR 273, at 291.

there can on well known authority be no ground in domestic law for failing to give effect to an enactment in terms unambiguously inconsistent with such an obligation.

The Appellant sought to assert that she had a legitimate expectation that the UK would honour its obligation under article 31 of the Convention. But she cannot, at the relevant time, have had any legitimate expectation of being treated otherwise than in accordance with the 1999 Act.[28]

As the domestic law was clearly inconsistent with the international obligation, Lord Bingham unsurprisingly considered the Lords to be bound by the Act, regardless of any potential breach of the Convention. The door thus remains open, in less obvious cases of inconsistency, for the usual presumption of statutory interpretation to apply that the legislature intends to abide by its international obligations. It is encouraging that Lord Bingham did not deny the possibility of a legitimate expectation. By confining his analysis to construction of the legislation, he was able to reach the simpler conclusion that the unequivocal language prevented any contrary expectation. Lord Bingham, true to form, employed principles of statutory interpretation to determine only so much as he was required to do in order to dispose of the matter before him. In this way, he preserved the potential to assess whether the evidence might, on another day, be sufficient to raise a legitimate expectation. Such judicial economy has become a reliable feature of Lord Bingham's judgments, leaving scope for other judges to identify the law in other contexts.

Validity of Derogations from Treaty Obligations

Human rights treaties typically allow state parties to derogate from their obligations in time of war or other public emergency threatening the life of the nation.[29] Lord Bingham, in the lead judgment in *A (and others) v Secretary of State for the Home Department (Belmarsh* cases),[30] provides a valuable guide to judicial reasoning when assessing the validity of derogation by a state from a treaty-based obligation. In this case the question arose in respect of nine suspected terrorists, (each of them a non-national), who were held in indefinite detention by the United Kingdom government. The question for determination was the weight to be given to the derogation by the government from Article 5 of the European Convention on Human Rights which prohibits the deprivation of individual liberty. The derogation was made under Article 15 which allows a state to take measures 'in time of war or other public emergency threatening the life of the nation' so long as these measures are 'strictly required by the exigencies of the situation'.

---

[28] [2008] All ER (D) 274 (May) paras 29–30.
[29] See, e.g., Art 4, ICCPR.
[30] [2004] UKHL 56. See also, *X and another v Sec of State for the Home Department*, [2004] UKHL 56; for a commentary see, Sangeeta Shah, 'The UK's anti-terror legislation and the House of Lords: the first skirmish', 5 *Human Rights Law Review* 403.

The Attorney General had submitted that it was for Parliament and the executive to assess the threat facing the nation and that this was a question for the democratic organs of the state not the judiciary. Lord Bingham accepted that derogation is a predominantly political rather than judicial judgment that warrants according significant weight to the government's derogation decision.[31] In a robust speech, Lord Bingham, nonetheless, challenged the implicit notion that the courts are not democratic. He declared that:

> I do not accept the full breadth of the Attorney General's submissions. I do not in particular accept the distinction which he drew between democratic institutions and the courts. It is of course true that the judges of this country are not elected and are not answerable to parliament. It is also of course true... that Parliament, the executive and the courts have different functions. But the function of independent judges charged to interpret and apply the law is universally recognised as a cardinal feature of the modern democratic state, a cornerstone of the rule of law itself. The Attorney General is fully entitled to insist on the proper limits of judicial authority, but he is wrong to stigmatise judicial decision-making as in some way undemocratic. It is particularly inappropriate in a case such as the present in which Parliament has expressly legislated in section 6 of the 1998 Act to render unlawful any act of a public authority... incompatible with a Convention right, has required courts... to take account of relevant Strasbourg jurisprudence, has... required courts, so far as possible, to give effect to Convention rights and has conferred a right of appeal on derogation issues.[32]

Lord Bingham thus rejected any notion that the courts are not democratic and stressed that the functions of the judiciary in respect of the Human Rights Act had been specifically granted to it by Parliament. Rather than deferring to the views of the Home Secretary, Lord Bingham adopted the notion of 'relative institutional competence' to determine whether the decision lay at the political or legal ends of the spectrum.[33] The question whether the threat of terrorism in the period post-September 11 justified derogation from Article 5 thus depended upon whether the executive decision was within the competence of the Home Secretary. Lord Bingham agreed that derogation might be justified in light of contemporary concerns about terrorism. In this respect, the appellants were not able to show sufficiently strong grounds to displace the decision of the Secretary of State on the threshold question as to the essentially political nature of his judgment.

Despite his view that the derogation was not subject to judicial review, Lord Bingham went on to conclude that the indefinite detention went beyond measures that were 'strictly required' as 'the choice of an immigration measure to address a security problem had the inevitable result of failing adequately to address that problem'.[34] This was because indefinite detention applicable only to one subgroup of suspected terrorist allowed other suspected terrorists either to leave the

---

[31] Ibid, para 37.　　[32] [2004] UKHL 56, para 42.

[33] Ibid, para 29.　　[34] Ibid, para 43.

country or, in the case of United Kingdom citizens, to remain at large.[35] Lord Bingham found it 'irresistible' that the Detention Order and section 23 were, in Convention terms, disproportionate. The derogation was consequently quashed as it was incompatible with the Human Rights Act.

The *Belmarsh* cases illustrate how the Human Rights Act has liberated British judges from the traditional practice of deferring, almost without question, to government decisions founded in perceptions of national security. The Human Rights Act now requires that the validity of a government measure be assessed proportionately against the rights of the individual. There is moreover some irony in that Lord Bingham was able to take a more restrictive view of the compatibility of the measure with the Human Rights Act than was likely to have been taken by the European Court of Human Rights (ECtHR) itself.[36] This is because the ECtHR allows a certain margin of appreciation when assessing the proportionality of government decisions; a constraint that did not apply to Lord Bingham.

The derogation order was also thought by Lord Bingham to be discriminatory under the Article 14 of the ECHR on the grounds of nationality or immigration status.[37] As Article 15 of the ECHR requires the United Kingdom to act in accordance with its other international obligations, the measure was also in breach of Article 26 of the International Covenant on Civil and Political Rights (ICCPR).[38]

These aspects of Lord Bingham's speech make a valuable contribution to the scholarship of discrimination under international law, and demonstrate his readiness to employ international jurisprudence to determine the very contemporary issues of indefinite detention. He recognized that while the 'materials I have cited are not legally binding on the United Kingdom . . . the Council of Europe is the body to which the states parties to the European Convention belong'.[39] Lord Bingham made ample use of these authorities to conclude, with his fellow members of the Lords, that the detentions under the Anti-Terrorism, Crime and Security Act 2001 were incompatible with Articles 5 and 14 of the European Convention. While Lord Bingham's speech is memorable for this reason alone, his spirited defence of the judiciary within a democracy is also likely to inform our understanding of the courts and of individual rights for many years to come.

Security Council Resolutions and Treaty Obligations

Lord Bingham in early 2008 revisited the compatibility of an indefinite executive detention with the Human Rights Act in the leading speech in *R (Al Jedda) v Secretary of State for Defence.*[40] The case raised the impact of UN Security Council

---

[35] Ibid.
[37] [2004] UKHL 56, paras 45–70.
[39] Ibid, para 63.

[36] Shah, op. cit., n 30 at 416.
[38] Ibid, para 68.
[40] [2008] 2 WLR 31.

resolutions under Chapter VII on human rights treaties and the scope of Article 103 of the UN Charter. The claimant, a dual national of the United Kingdom and Iraq, had been interned for reasons of security by Britain in an Iraqi detention facility since 2004 without any prospect of being charged or tried. The Lords unanimously dismissed the appeal on two grounds. The first was that UNSCR 1546 gives the multilateral force the authority 'to take all necessary measures to contribute to the maintenance of security and stability in Iraq'. The second is that Article 103 of the UN Charter overrides Article 5(1) of the ECHR. While recognizing the effect of both a UN Security Council resolution and the pre-eminence of the Charter over competing obligations, Lord Bingham, found that Article 103 does not exclude due process rights. He concluded that the Human Rights Act remained in effect except to the extent that the Security Council resolution expressly provided otherwise, saying that:

... there is a clash between on the one hand a power or duty to detain exercisable on the express authority of the Security Council and, on the other, a fundamental human right which the UK has undertaken to secure to those (like the appellant) within its jurisdiction. How are these to be reconciled? There is in my opinion only one way in which they can be reconciled: by ruling that the UK may lawfully, where it is necessary for imperative reasons of security, exercise the power to detain authorised by UNSCR 1546 and successive resolution, but must ensure that the detainee's rights under article 5 are not infringed to any greater extent than is inherent in such detention.[41]

Lord Bingham thus applied Article 103 of the Charter so that the Security Council Resolution prevailed over the fundamental human right. He did so with economy, however, by confining the detention to the degree necessary in the circumstances.

Admission of Evidence Obtained by Torture

Lord Bingham's strong sense of fairness and belief in the rule of law is illustrated in his approach to the admission of evidence that might have been obtained by torture in a case following the *Belmarsh* decisions, *A v Secretary for Home Department* in 2004.[42] Lord Bingham joined the unanimous decision of the House of Lords denying the admission of evidence that has, or may have been, obtained by torture by officials of a foreign state. A critical aspect of the case concerned the burden of proof. Lord Bingham, with Lords Nicholls and Hoffman, placed the burden on the Special Immigration Appeals Commission

---

[41] Ibid, para 38; as Crawford points out, op. cit. n 12, despite the failure of the claimants appeal to the Lords, the executive released Mr Al-Jedda in Baghdad, depriving him of British nationality; 'Imperative reasons of national security seem to have evaporated—asserted one week, ignored the next'.
[42] *A (FC) and Others (FC) v Sec of State for the Home Department* [2005] UKHL 71.

(SIAC).[43] While part of the minority on this point, they argued that, if there is a plausible reason to suspect that torture has been employed, the SIAC has the burden of proving the contrary. On this view, evidence must therefore be excluded if the SIAC is unable to demonstrate that there was no real possibility that it was obtained by torture.

By contrast, the majority, per Lord Hope, required the SIAC to exclude the evidence only:

...if it concludes on a balance of probabilities that it was obtained by torture. In other words, if SIAC is left in doubt as to whether the evidence was obtained in this way, it should admit it...[44]

The minority approach reflects the revulsion felt by the international community towards the use of torture, justifying rejection of the conventional rules allocating the burden of proof. While discussing the common law rule, Lord Bingham set out the inherent, moral foundations of the principle, viz, that evidence obtained by torture is cruel, produces unreliable evidence, and degrades all those associated with the practice. These ideas apply equally to our understanding of the international rule and their articulation provides a domestic law source for application of the rule in international legal practice. Lord Bingham was also concerned that the SIAC procedures restrict both the rights of the appellant to know the charges and his access to legal advice.

Characteristically, Lord Bingham employed a memorable analogy in response to Lord Hope's analysis:

Lord Hope proposes...the following test: is it established, by means of such diligent enquiries in to the sources that it is practicable to carry out and on the balance of probabilities, that the information relied on by the Secretary of State was obtained by torture? This is a test which, in the real world, can never be satisfied. The foreign torturer does not boast of his trade. The security forces...do not wish to imperil their relations with regimes where torture is practiced. The detainee is in the dark. It is inconsistent with the most rudimentary notions of fairness to blindfold a man and then impose a standard which only the sighted could hope to meet.[45]

The decision was courageous in light of public concerns that the government should be free to respond to the undeniable reality of terrorism without interference from the courts applying international human rights standards. Although Lord Bingham might, in common with other Law Lords, have reached his conclusions on the basis of common law principles that also reject evidence obtained by torture, he insisted that the SIAC 'should throughout be guided by recognition of the important obligations laid down in articles 3 and 5 (4) of the European Convention, and through them, article 15 of the Torture Convention'.[46] In doing so, Lord Bingham, uniquely among his fellow judges, cited the international law

---

[43] Ibid, paras 54–62.   [44] Ibid, para 118.
[45] Ibid, para 59.   [46] Ibid, para 56.

arguments relied upon by the appellants. He also set out the international treaties and jurisprudence proclaiming torture to be a breach of a peremptory norm of international law. The depth of research underlying Lord Bingham's judgment provides a valuable source of legal materials for future scholars.

While reaching out to international legal principles, fundamental British constitutional law lay at the heart of his decision. He observed that:

> ... the English common law has regarded torture and its fruits with abhorrence for over 500 years, and that abhorrence is now shared by over 140 countries which have acceded to the Torture Convention. I am startled, even a little dismayed, at the suggestion (and the acceptance by the Court of Appeal majority) that this deeply rooted tradition and an international obligation solemnly and explicitly undertaken can be overridden by a statute and a procedural rule which make no mention of torture at all.[47]

Lord Bingham's emphasis upon the historical record and established legal precedents underlying the exclusion of evidence obtained by torture is consistent with his approach to identifying the legal principles. Lord Bingham's search for evidence of the law contrasts, for example, with the approach taken by Lord Carswell. While recognizing the historical development of the common law rule, Lord Carswell was additionally willing to extend the common law if necessary as he was 'of the clear opinion that the principle can be accommodated'.[48] It may be doubted that Lord Bingham would have been willing to so extend the rule in the absence of precedent. Indeed, he would not go so far as to exclude evidence obtained through the use inhumane and degrading treatment, arguing that 'special rules have always been thought to apply to torture, and for the present at least must continue to do so'.[49] While crystal clear in his application of the law founded in precedent, Lord Bingham was not prepared to develop the recognized principle into less well charted territory.

Influence of the European Court of Human Rights on United Kingdom Law

Lord Bingham's reluctance unilaterally to evolve a rule beyond its well recognized parameters was relaxed somewhat in *R v Special Adjudicator ex p Ullah*.[50] In this case, he found that there was nothing in European or British law that would deny advancing an argument that a person could not be deported if his removal was to a state that did not respect the rights to freedom of thought, conscience, and religion. In a purposive interpretation, Lord Bingham argued that '... it would seem inconsistent with the humanitarian principles underpinning the Convention to accept that, if the facts were strong enough, a claim would be rejected even if it

---

47 Ibid, at para 51.   48 Ibid, para 152.
49 Ibid, para 53.   50 2204] UKHL 26.

were based on Article 4 alone'.[51] Adopting an expansive approach, Lord Bingham argues:

It is of course open to member states to provide for rights more generous than those guaranteed by the Convention, but such provision should not be the product of interpretation of the Convention by national courts, since the meaning of the Convention should be uniform throughout the states parties to it. The duty of the national court is to keep pace with the Strasbourg jurisprudence as it evolves over time: no more, but certainly no less.

I find it hard to think that a person could successfully resist expulsion in reliance on article 9 without being entitled either to asylum on the ground of a well-founded fear of persecution for reasons of religion or personal opinion or to resist expulsion in reliance on article 3. But I would not rule out such a possibility in principle unless the Strasbourg court has clearly done so, and I am not sure that it has.[52]

Too much should not be built upon these shifts in language. It suffices to observe that Lord Bingham considers himself bound to apply evolving jurisprudence of the Strasbourg court and will do so by reference to the humanitarian principles that underlie the European Convention. His decision in *ex p Ullah* leaves the door open for other jurists to develop domestic law both in conformity with the Convention and by adopting a progressive approach to interpretation.

Sovereign Immunity from the Jurisdiction

Lord Bingham has been steadfast in his view that it is not the proper role of judges to override the established principles of international law. He was a member of the Court of Appeal when it considered the application by Spain for the extradition of Senator Augusto Pinochet Ugarte on a range of charges including conspiracy to commit murder and detention of hostages in *R v Evans and others ex p Ugarte*.[53] Senator Pinochet opposed the extradition order *inter alia* on the ground that, as the head of state at the time the offences were alleged to have occurred, he was immune from prosecution.

Despite seeing 'some attraction' in the view that immunity under the State Immunity Act cannot extend to acts as morally repugnant as genocide, torture, and the taking of hostages, Lord Bingham held that Head of State immunity would apply to the applicant as a former President of Chile.[54] Lord Bingham was concerned that to allow inroads into the traditional principle of sovereign immunity might render it difficult to know where to draw the line between acts that attract a right to immunity and those that do not. As a matter of legislative

---

[51] Ibid, para 16.

[52] Ibid, para 20; compare Lord Brown's view in *Al–Skeini*, op. cit. para 106, that he preferred an approach that is 'no less, but certainly no more'.

[53] Unreported, UK Court of Appeal, Lord Bingham CJ, Collins and Richards JJ, 28 October 1998, (High Court proceedings); The Times, 3 November 1998.

[54] Ibid.

interpretation, it was clear to Lord Bingham that the United Kingdom statutes implicitly relied on for the requested extradition did not refer to an intention to override the State Immunity Act in respect of heads of state, even when charged with genocide.[55] Lord Bingham also observed that the Statutes and Charters establishing the International Tribunals at Nuremberg, Rwanda, and the Former Republic of Yugoslavia explicitly stated that the tribunals would have jurisdiction over foreign sovereigns. This, he concluded, indicated that jurisdiction over foreign sovereigns in other contexts might not automatically have been asserted.

Citing the decision of the English Court of appeal (Civil Division) in *Al-Adsani v Government of Kuwait*, Lord Bingham observed that the plaintiff's argument, that immunity from a civil claim was available only if the government had been acting in accordance with the Law of Nations, had been rejected. Interpretation of the State Immunity Act supported the findings of the Court of Appeal that the draftsmen of the 1978 Act had not intended conformity with international law to be an overriding qualification. While *Al-Adsani* raised no issue of official functions, Lord Bingham concluded that:

> ...if the Government there could claim sovereign immunity in relation to alleged acts of torture, it would not seem surprising if the same immunity could be claimed by a defendant who had at the relevant times been the ruler of that country.[56]

Lord Bingham's decision in *R v Evans* shows a consistency of approach to statutory interpretation and a strong preference to uphold international law, particularly its classical doctrines. The decision was, nonetheless, significantly at odds with contemporary concerns to protect human rights and to ensure that those who sanction torture do not avoid responsibility. The subsequent decision of the House of Lords in *Pinochet (No 3)* gave voice to these ideas. The majority of the Lords determined that immunity from prosecution for torture would not be afforded to a former head of state because acts of torture could not be classified as 'official' for the purposes of the State Immunity Act.[57] Lord Bingham's cautious approach to assimilating international rules as part of domestic law, and to interpretation of United Kingdom legislation, militated against adopting the novel, unprecedented view that 'official' acts could not include torture.

Application of the Doctrine of Immunity in Civil Claims

Just as Lord Bingham has not been an activist, declining to discover law where no precedent exists, he has been firm in his belief that, even when the law is in a state of flux, it is not the role of the judiciary to 'develop' the law. Rather he has

[55] E.g., see Art 4 of the Genocide Convention.
[56] *R v Evans, ex p Ugarte*, op. cit., n 53.
[57] [2000] 1 AC 147.

preferred to take account of the jurisprudence of other international lawmaking bodies and to assess the weight to be given to evolving principles. In *Jones v Saudi Arabia*,[58] for example, where the victims of torture in Saudi Arabia brought civil claims for damages against the Kingdom of Saudi Arabia and its officers, Lord Bingham made a thorough examination of international authorities in reaching his decision to grant immunity to the Saudi Kingdom. The claimants argued that upholding the Kingdom's claim for immunity would be incompatible with the right of access to a court implied by Article 6 of the European Convention on Human Rights.[59] The House of Lords therefore was asked to find that section 3 of the Human Rights Act 1998 (UK), required that the State Immunity Act 1978 (UK) should be interpreted so as to deny immunity in respect of civil claims arising out of torture. This interpretation, the claimants argued, was necessary to ensure the State Immunity Act is not incompatible with their rights under Article 6 of the European Convention.

Lord Bingham considered that the first issue to be resolved was whether Article 6 of the Convention is engaged by the grant of immunity to the Kingdom and that, in his view, it was not. He applied the principle, *par in parem non habet imperium*, to the effect that the rule is not that a state should not exercise over another state a jurisdiction that it has, but rather that a state has no jurisdiction over another state. Lord Bingham found it difficult to understand 'how a state can be said to deny access to its court if it has no access to give'.[60] With respect, Lord Bingham understands the international principle that, at long established custom, the foreign sovereign is quite simply not within the jurisdiction of the courts of another sovereign and equal state. To recognize that the state has no jurisdiction over another state should not, at the same time, breach the international obligation to ensure a right of access to the domestic courts. It is notable that, despite his view of the doctrine of sovereign immunity, Lord Bingham deferred to the decision of the European Court in *Al-Adsani v United Kingdom* where it found Article 6 had been engaged by a grant of immunity on the facts of that case.[61]

Having resolved the question of jurisdiction, Lord Bingham identified the second issue, being whether a grant of immunity would deny the claimants access to an English court inconsistently with their right of access to a court. As it plainly would do so, Lord Bingham moved to the third issue; whether the claimants could show that the restriction was not directed to a legitimate object and was disproportionate. The claimants argued that as torture is prohibited as a peremptory norm of international law, it cannot be a governmental act or exercise of state authority entitled to the protection of state immunity *rationae materiae*. If so, a grant of immunity would not be directed to a legitimate object and must be disproportionate.

---

[58] [2006] UKHL 26.   [59] Ibid, para 13.
[60] Ibid, para 14.   [61] (2001) 34 EHRR 273.

Lord Bingham reviewed the international precedents, including decisions of the Grand Chamber of the European Court of Human Rights, House of Lords, United States, Supreme Court, the International Criminal Tribunal for the Former Yugoslavia, and the Italian Court of Cassations and recommendations of the United Nations Committee Against Torture. While recognizing that these provided valuable authorities, he concluded that 'on examination they give the claimants less support than at first appears'.[62] In short, Lord Bingham distinguished these earlier international and British authorities, finding that *Pinochet (No 3)* concerned criminal, not civil proceedings, and that only criminal acts fell within the universal jurisdiction mandated by the Torture Convention.[63]

Lord Bingham exposed an apparent contradiction in the claimant's argument that acts of torture cannot be official acts:

It is, I think, difficult to accept that torture cannot be a governmental or official act, since under article 1 of the Torture Convention torture must, to qualify as such, be inflicted by or with the connivance of a public official or other person acting in an official capacity. The claimant's argument encounters the difficulty that it is founded on the Torture Convention; but to bring themselves within the Torture Convention they must show that the torture was (to paraphrase the definition) official; yet they argue that the conduct was not official in order to defeat the claim to immunity.[64]

To the contrary, it might be that the word 'official' means different things, depending upon the context. It is one thing for the definition of torture to require that an act be 'official', in the sense that it is performed by someone exercising governmental authority. It is quite another to define the term 'official' for the purposes of the limits of the doctrine of sovereign immunity so as to exclude acts that are contrary to fundamental human rights and breach a peremptory norm of international law. The failure by Lord Bingham to give greater weight to the *Pinochet (No 3)* findings (albeit in a criminal case), that those responsible for torture cannot seek immunity, has been subject to comment. Steinerte *et al* argue that this aspect of his decision is a backward step where:

...broadly considered, current jurisprudence, taken in conjunction with developments on impunity, the right to reparation, and state responsibility under international law, indicates a move away from the availability of state immunity in criminal and civil proceedings involving jus cogens norms.[65]

Lord Bingham sought instead stronger, unequivocal evidence of a right to deny immunity in civil cases. He noted that the international authorities 'are for present purposes important only to the extent that they express principles widely shared

[62] [2006] UKHL 26, para 17.
[63] Ibid, para 19.
[64] Ibid.
[65] Steinerte, Elina and Wallace, Rebecca, 'Jones v Ministry of Interior of the Kingdom of Saudi Arabia. Case No [2006] UKHL 26' (2006) 100 *American Journal of International Law* 901 at 908.

and observed among other nations. As yet, they do not.'[66] On examination of the decision of the Italian Court de cassation, for example, which had recognized a civil claim based on war crimes, Lord Bingham doubted that it was an accurate view of international law. As has been observed above, Lord Bingham quipped, in any event, 'one swallow does not make a rule of international law'.[67] In so deciding, he relied on the joint separate opinion of Judges Higgins, Kooijmans, and Buergenthal in *Democratic Republic of the Congo v Belgium* in which they had questioned the unilateral exercise of jurisdiction by the United States over civil actions under the Alien Tort Claims Act, concluding that, while it had been 'much commented upon, it has not attracted the approbation of States generally'.[68]

After a careful examination of the international authorities, Lord Bingham adopted the reasoning of the majority of the European Court in *Al-Adsani* to the effect that it had not found 'any firm basis for concluding that, as a matter of international law, a state no longer enjoyed immunity from civil suit in the courts of another state where acts of torture were alleged'.[69] Accordingly, he found that no international law had been established that requires states to exercise universal jurisdiction for all *jus cogens* breaches, 'nor is there any consensus of judicial and learned opinion that they should'.[70]

Lord Bingham's analysis and methodology in the *Jones* case indicate that he is entirely open to consideration of international authorities as evidences of the international rule. He will not, however, adopt a purported rule unless it is supported by a preponderance of international judicial opinion and state practice. Isolated national and international decisions lack legitimacy, he considers, until they are confirmed by broader international judicial opinion. Commenting upon the contrary view of the Court of Appeal, Lord Bingham considered that it had:

> ... asserted what was in effect a universal tort jurisdiction in cases of official torture ... for which there was no adequate foundation in any international convention, state practice or scholarly consensus, and apparently by reference to a consideration (the absence of a remedy in the foreign state: para 86 of the judgment) which is, I think, novel. Despite the sympathy that one must of course feel for the claimants if their complaints are true, international law, representing the law binding on other nations and not just our own, cannot be established in this way.[71]

In these respects, Lord Bingham's methodology for identifying an international rule echoes that adopted in the International Court of Justice by Judges Higgins, Kooijmans, and Buergenthal in *Congo v Belgium*. These international judges also have been meticulous in their search for clear evidence of the asserted rule, most particularly a consensus of state practice.

---

[66] [2006] UKHL 26, para 20.
[67] Ibid, para 22.
[68] [2002]ICJ Rep 3, para 48.
[69] [2006] UKHL 26, para 18.
[70] Ibid, para 27.
[71] Ibid, para, 34.

Extraterritorial Application of National Human Rights Legislation

The question whether national legislation can have an extraterritorial effect has been determined by domestic courts as a matter of statutory interpretation, the default position being that legislation, especially as it relates to criminal offences, is presumed to be confined to the territorial limits of the state. It is a reflection of the globalization of law that attempts are now increasingly being made to apply legislation beyond the territorial mandate of the state, wherever it has a measure of effective control.[72] Lord Bingham considered the extraterritorial jurisdictional reach of the Human Rights Act in *Al-Skeini and ors v Secretary of State for Defence*,[73] and differed, unusually, from his fellow members of the Lords. He adopted the traditional principles of statutory interpretation to conclude that, in the absence of a contrary intention, the law presumes the Human Rights Act does not apply outside the United Kingdom.

Al–Skeini concerned a claim by the families of six Iraqi nationals killed by British troops during their occupation of Basra, Iraq, for a governmental review of the deaths. Section 6 of the Human Rights Act renders it unlawful for a public authority of the United Kingdom to act in a manner incompatible with certain articles of the ECHR, including Article 3 (which has been held to impose an obligation to fully investigate a violent death caused, or allegedly caused, by state agents).[74] The primary question was whether the Human Rights Act applies to the acts of authorities which take place outside British territory. While recognizing as 'very relevant' that the Human Rights Act is intended to protect human rights, Lord Bingham gave little weight to arguments suggesting that the purpose of the statute or the context of the complaints might demand a more flexible response than the legal presumption in favour of territorial scope.[75]

A secondary matter for determination was whether the acts of the British troops fall within one of the exceptions to the general rule that the European Convention does not apply to the extraterritorial acts of a member state. As Lord Bingham found nothing to override the usual presumption in the text of the Human Rights Act he did not need to consider the extraterritorial application of the Convention.[76] He, nonetheless, examined the international authorities that have considered the extraterritorial scope of the Convention. The Grand Chamber of the Strasbourg Court, for example, considered the scope of Article 1 in *Bankovic v Belgium and Others*[77] and concluded that it 'must be considered to reflect this ordinary and essentially territorial notion of jurisdiction, other bases

---

[72] The ICJ in the *Israeli Wall* case relied on the asserted effective control over the occupied Palestinian Territories to reject justification of the security wall on the grounds of self defence.

[73] [2007] UKHL 26.   [74] Ibid, para 5.

[75] Ibid, para, 9.   [76] Ibid, para, 27.

[77] (2001) 11 BHRC 435, p 449, para 61.

of jurisdiction being exceptional...'.[78] The Chamber recognized an 'exceptional' basis of jurisdiction in cases when 'as a consequence of military action (lawful or unlawful) [a contracting state] exercised effective control of an area outside its national territory'. Lord Bingham distinguished the jurisdictional base in *Bankovic* on the ground that it concerned the occupation by Turkey of the territory of Cyprus, an exception that was, in his view, 'problematical' in the context of British troops in Iraq. No explanation for making such a distinction is offered.

In taking a restrictive view of the application of the Human Rights Act, Lord Bingham appears to have been influenced by the 'real practical difficulties' of mounting such an inquiry and by his understanding that many other options at both international and United Kingdom law are available directly or indirectly to the claimants:

> This does not mean that members of the British armed forces serving abroad are free to murder, rape and pillage with impunity. They are triable and punishable for any crimes they commit under the three service discipline Acts..., no matter where the crime is committed or who the victim may be. They are triable for genocide, crimes against humanity and war crimes under the International Criminal Court Act 2001. The United Kingdom itself is bound, in a situation such as prevailed in Iraq, to comply with the Hague Convention of 1907 and the Regulations made under it...An action in tort may, in appropriate facts, be brought in this country against the Secretary of State...[79]

While it is probable that justice for the Iraqi families of those killed at Basra can be achieved through other means, the options listed by Lord Bingham do not provide a complete or satisfactory answer to the vital question as to the scope of the Human Rights Act.

Lord Bingham's adoption of the presumption against extraterritorial effect stands in stark contrast to the approach by his fellow members of the Lords who preferred to give effect to the purposes of the Human Rights Act. Lord Roger argued that it would be to:

> offend against the most elementary cannons of statutory construction which indicate that, in case of doubt, the Act should be read so as to promote, not so as to defeat or impair, its central purpose. If anything, this approach is even more desirable in interpreting human rights legislation.[80]

In addition to adopting a purposive approach to legislative interpretation, Lord Roger was also influenced by the reasoning of the European Court in *Bankovic* that where a state has effective control of an area beyond its territory, it should secure to all within its jurisdiction the rights and freedoms in section 1 of the Convention. Lord Roger would not, however, accept the extensions to extraterritorial jurisdiction adopted by the European Court in *Issa v Turkey*,[81] where

---

[78] Ibid, para 61.   [79] Ibid, para 26.   [80] Ibid, para 57.
[81] (2004) 41 EHRR 567, para 73.

shepherds were said to have been killed by Turkish troops operating in Northern Iraq. The European Court found that:

...a state may also be held accountable for violation of the Convention rights and freedoms of persons who are in the territory of another state but who are found under the former state's authority and control through its agents operating—whether lawfully or unlawfully in the latter states...Accountability in such situations stems from the fact that article 1 of the Convention cannot be interpreted so as to allow a state party to per-petuate violations of the Convention on the territory of another state, which it could not perpetrate on its own territory.[82]

In this statement, Lord Roger went further than the court's own jurisprudence and was not fully reasoned. Lord Brown agreed with Lord Bingham's assessment of the lack of guidance provided by the textual indications as to the scope of the Human Rights Act. He differed, however, in arguing that it was inappropriate to treat the Human Rights Act as 'just another domestic statute'.[83] He chose instead to take into account 'the object, subject-matter and history of this Act'.[84] Lord Carswell and Baroness Hale similarly chose to adopt the purposive approaches of Lords Brown and Roger.[85] Lord Carswell quoted Lord Bingham in *R (Ullah) v Special Adjudicator* that it is the 'duty of national courts to keep pace with the Strasbourg jurisprudence as it evolves over time: no more, but certainly no less'.[86] It is all the more notable that Lord Bingham's earlier view that national courts should 'not without strong reason dilute or weaken the effect of the Strasbourg case law' was outweighed, in his view, by the principle that legislation is pre-sumed to apply territorially.

Refugee Status and 'Membership of a Particular Social Group'

While Lord Bingham has generally adopted a strict and textual, rather than pur-posive, approach to treaty interpretation, this can lead to surprisingly progressive outcomes. In two cases, *Secretary of Home Department v K* and *Fornah v Secretary of Home Department*[87] the House of Lords was asked to consider the meaning of the phrase 'membership of a particular social group' under Article 1A(2) of the 1951 Refugee Convention.

In the *Fornah* case, the appellant had fled Sierra Leone to avoid being subjected to female genital mutilation. Lord Bingham found that 'the starting point of the construction exercise must be the text of the Refugee Convention itself, because it expresses what the parties to it have agreed'.[88] Lord Bingham's approach is methodical, analysing a broad selection of authority to determine whether such

---

[82] Ibid, para 71.
[84] Ibid, para 138.
[86] Ibid, para 105.
[88] Ibid, para 10.
[83] [2007] UKHL 26, para 138.
[85] Ibid, paras 57, 98, and 88.
[87] [2006] UKHL 46.

mutilation constitutes treatment amounting to persecution within the meaning of the Refugee Convention. His review includes references to international authorities, including decisions of the UNHCR, views of the European Parliament, various national guidelines, each of which concludes that female genital mutilation is a form of 'persecution'. Lord Bingham notes that his methodology is 'wholly consistent with the humanitarian objectives of the Convention'.[89] Even though it had been agreed by the parties that the language of the Convention was not controversial, Lord Bingham construed the treaty by reference to existing authority. Adopting a strict evidence-based approach Lord Bingham notes, consistently with his views in *Al–Skeini*, that 'this is a submission to be appraised in the context of Sierra Leonean society as revealed by the undisputed evidence, and without resort to extraneous generalization'.[90] He concluded that:

... Female genital mutilation is an extreme expression of the discrimination to which all women in Sierra Leone are subject, as much those who have already undergone the process as those who have not. I find no difficulty in recognising women in Sierra Leone as a particular social group for the purposes of article 1A(2).[91]

While Lord Bingham did not intend to push new boundaries, relying upon the evidence and existing jurisprudence, he adopted a broad definition of a 'particular social group' which includes all Sierra Leonean women. Ironically, his strict constructionist approach produced an outcome that may prove to be more 'progressive' than that of the majority.

Lord Bingham's evidence-based methodology might be contrasted with that of Baroness Hale who found that these cases were 'blindingly obvious' and that it was 'a mystery to some as to why either of them had to reach this House'.[92] She refers explicitly to the policy purpose underlying her concurring judgment saying:

I would like to add a few words only because each case, in its different way, raises issues of gender-related and gender-specific persecution.[93]

Baroness Hale found that the Refugee Convention does not include sex as a reason for persecution so as automatically to give rise to refugee status.[94] Rather, she employs the category of 'membership of a particular social group' so as to 'push the boundaries of refugee law into gender-related areas'.[95] Lord Bingham is not opposed to reaching such progressive outcomes—he is not an ideological conservative—but he will do so on established principles of treaty interpretation to reach the same result.

---

[89] Ibid, para 26.   [90] Ibid, para 31.
[91] Ibid.   [92] Ibid, para 83.
[93] Ibid, para 83.   [94] Ibid, para 84.
[95] Ibid, para 97.

Conclusions

A review of Lord Bingham's decisions concerning international law shows him to be a man of humanity and sound legal scholarship. He is quick to recognize injustice when he finds it and to see the dangers in automatic deference to executive decisions. His defence of the judicial function against the charge that only Parliament is democratic is likely to inform international and domestic courts for decades to come. Many of Lord Bingham's international legal decisions have contributed to some of the most difficult jurisprudential questions of our times; how to balance a response to international terrorism with fundamental human rights; where to place the burden of proving evidence has been obtained by torture; when to assume jurisdiction over a foreign sovereign charged with international crimes; how to define discrimination at international law. Unusually for a senior judge within a national judiciary, his judgments in international law not only provide a scholarly survey of relevant comparative and international sources of the law—a boon to legal scholars—but also highly persuasive national precedents for international courts and tribunals.

Lord Bingham has adopted a rigorous, evidence-based approach to identifying the international rule of law, resisting the temptation to develop the law as he thinks fit. He is no judicial activist. Rather, he has respected parliamentary sovereignty and been faithful to the principles of treaty and statutory interpretation. He has done so with judicial economy and reasoned logic, invariably with memorable wit and compassion.

13

Who Calls the Shots? Defence, Foreign Affairs, International Law, and the Governance of Britain

Colin Warbrick

1. Introduction

This paper is based on my inaugural lecture as Barber Professor of Jurisprudence in the University of Birmingham, which was given on 28 February 2008. There have been significant developments since the lecture was delivered and I have incorporated some of these but the general thrust and style of the paper follows that of the original lecture.

'The Governance of Britain' is the title of a Green Paper,[1] the publication of which was practically the first act of the Brown government. The Prime Minister and the Secretary of State for Justice said then:

We want to forge a new relationship between government and citizen and begin a journey towards a new constitutional settlement—a settlement which entrusts Parliament and the people with more power.[2]

The document ends by looking forward to:

...a concordat between the executive and Parliament or a written constitution.[3]

For myself, I should look forward to the written constitution, not least because, as we shall see, the promises of government can be fragile things. It will be a long haul—according to the Green Paper, we shall not get either concordat or constitution:

...except over an extended period of time

which, the Minister of Justice says, means 20 years.

---

[1] 'The Governance of Britain' Cm 7170; C Warbrick, 'The Governance of Britain' (2008) 55 *International and Comparative Law Quarterly* 209.
[2] Id, p 5.   [3] Id, para 212, p 62.

But this journey has to start somewhere—and it started with another Green Paper instituting a consultation process on two, on the face of it, unrelated topics—the power to deploy troops abroad and the power to make treaties.[4] The consultation period ended in early January and the publication of the results was published on 25 March 2008,[5] the same day on which the next step, the Constitutional Renewal Bill,[6] was made public. What connects the two consultation subjects is that they are examples of the prerogative powers of the Crown, a means of exercising public power subject to not much political or legal scrutiny. Other powers are mentioned in the first Green Paper. Most of them are, in one way or another, to do with foreign affairs, that is, an area of public conduct which, among other things, falls under the constraints of international law. Because of the increasing impact which acts of foreign affairs have within the UK (or, put another way, because of the increasing scope of what now falls within the rubric 'foreign affairs'), the relationship between international law and UK law is a central element in the legal aspect of the questions put out for consultation. What is the effect of international law on the constitutional powers of government, in particular, what role in applying international law falls to domestic courts? As far as foreign affairs as a whole goes, the orthodox answers have been that foreign affairs is essentially a matter for the executive, which is the 'one voice' with which the state must speak in the international sphere and to the expertise and authority of which the other organs of state should defer.[7] The claim represents both the old aristocratic tradition of the right to conduct foreign affairs and a rather more modern assertion that only the expertly elect have the knowledge and skill effectively to protect and further the state's interests in the international field.[8] One of the most weighty powers within the ambit of foreign affairs is the power to use armed force or, as constitutionalists would say, the power to deploy troops overseas.

2. Defence—the Power to Deploy the Troops

It was a great surprise to me when I was asked in the summer of 2005 to be the adviser to the House of Lords Committee on the Constitution about what

---

[4] 'The Governance of Britain—War Powers and Treaties: Limiting Executive Powers' Cm 7239.

[5] 'Governance of Britain—Analysis of Consultations' Cm 7342-III.

[6] 'Draft Constitutional Renewal Bill' Cm 7324–II. A Joint Select Committee has been established to provide pre-legislative scrutiny, <http://www.parliament.uk/parliamentary_committees/jcdcrb.cfm>.

[7] FA Mann, *Foreign Affairs in English Courts* (OUP, Oxford, 1986); JG Collier, 'Foreign Relations Law', *Halsbury's Laws of England* (4th edn reissue, Butterworths, London, 2000, ed Lord Mackay of Clashfern) paras 606–612.

[8] A Ponsonby, *Democracy and Diplomacy: A Plea for Popular Control of Foreign Policy* (Methuen, London, 1915) pp 22–23, 60–70, 102–114. For concern about elite bureaucratic capture of international law, M Koskenniemi, 'The Fate of Public International Law: Between Technique and Politics' (2007) 70 Modern Law Review 1.

it called 'The War Power'. I should say that anything I write now should not be taken in the slightest to represent the views of the Committee and, further, that what I do write relies on documents of theirs which are in the public domain. I have, though, retrieved one item from the Committee's wastepaper basket—the title of this paper—'Who calls the shots?' is taken from a putative title of the Constitution Committee's Report, which was rejected in favour of the more prosaic 'Waging War...'.[9] The only reason I could guess why I had been asked to advise the Committee was that the subject seemed as though it might have something to do with international law, for it has nothing much to do with domestic law. We began in October 2005 with the Committee expecting its job would be done by the end of the year. That it was not was because the question the Committee was seeking to pursue was a somewhat different one from that which it had anticipated: it was not about declaring war but about deploying troops overseas.[10] It was surprised to learn that the UK had not declared war on anyone since 1941[11] and was unlikely ever to do so again. The formal legal condition of war has been replaced by fact-based categories of international and internal armed conflicts, to which international humanitarian law, in one form or another, applies.[12] The decision to use of force may be unlawful and even criminal in international law, but its legality or otherwise will have only limited impact on the application of humanitarian law: states are required to fight according to the rules of the law of armed conflict whether they see themselves as defenders or aggressors.[13]

What the Committee was really interested in was the power to deploy troops overseas. (I shall use 'troops' to mean those of all the services and the weapons at their disposal, except where I say otherwise.) The Committee's proceedings were by no means the first Parliamentary consideration of this question in recent times. Indeed, even earlier, there was an attempt to put this power on a statutory footing in 1886, a reaction to Gladstonian adventures and the debates then had much of the flavour of contemporary deliberations on this matter.[14] Generally or specifically, there have been several attempts by private members in the Commons and individual members of the House of Lords to introduce legislation to regulate the deployment power and other Parliamentary committees had had a look at it

---

[9] Waging war: Parliament's role and responsibility, HL 236-I (2005–2006), Report.

[10] 'Overseas' here is used to mean outside the UK (and the British Islands) but it includes areas of jurisdiction at sea and dependent territories—for instance, no discussions leave out the Falklands campaign in 1982.

[11] The UK declared war against Rumania in 1941and Siam declared war on the UK in 1942. *R v Bottrill ex p Kuechenmenister* [1946] 1 All ER 635 (Foreign Secretary's certificate conclusive as to a state of war), cf *Amin v Brown* [2005] EWHC 1670 (Ch)—no enemy aliens in 2003 conflict with Iraq because no state of war, per Lawrence Collins J. See C Greenwood, 'The concept of war in modern international law', (1987)36 International and Comparative Law Quarterly 283–306.

[12] United Nations Charter 1945, Art 2(4); Geneva Conventions on the Law of Armed Conflict 1949, Arts 2 and 3.

[13] *United Kingdom Manual of Military Law* (OUP, Oxford, 2006), para 1.7.

[14] Hansard (Commons), 3rd series, Vol 303, cols 1386–1423. See PG Richards, *Parliament and Foreign Affairs* (George Allen & Unwin, London, 1967), pp 20–21.

too.[15] The most recent instance had been the introduction of a private members Bill by Clare Short, following her success in the ballot.[16] I thought it was a pretty sound piece of work and that it might enjoy some success but it was opposed by the government and did not receive enough support in the Commons to continue its progress. Some of these initiatives had preceded the invasion of Iraq in 2003 but, of course, the decision to send forces to Iraq loomed over all the subsequent deliberations about the deployment power.[17] Like the decision to declare war (and the making of treaties), the decision to deploy troops is taken under the Royal Prerogative. The prerogative is the residue of powers of the mediaeval monarchs which has survived legislative abolition or replacement and is available to the executive government for the conduct of its affairs.[18] Until relatively recently, the exercise of all prerogative powers was beyond judicial supervision but, since the *GCHQ* case[19] in 1984, the courts have asserted piecemeal authority over certain prerogative powers as falling within the scope of judicial review, while making it clear that certain powers, including the deployment power, remain beyond their jurisdiction. Apart from those powers the exercise of which the courts will look at, control over the prerogative is a political matter, Parliament (more exactly the House of Commons) having the power to call the government to account, as it may, of course, about any government decisions. In the UK's system of government, with the executive generally exercising actual power over the House of Commons, the consequence is that the prerogative remains, as it has sometimes been described, an 'arbitrary' power, quite in keeping with its origins and a kind of authority quite welcome to some governments. There is no need for the House of Commons to approve any decision; indeed, it has no right even to be informed about what a government is contemplating, even if practice is generally for government to make ministerial statements to Parliament about its intentions.[20]

In the early 19th century, the leading treatise about the prerogative described its virtues in managing foreign affairs thus:

One of the chief excellencies of the constitution consists in the harmony with which it combines all that strength and dispatch in the executive department of the State, which might expected only from a despotic government; with every liberty and right of interference on the part of the subject which is not inconsistent with the public welfare.

---

[15] Public Administration Committee, *Taming the Prerogative: Strengthening Ministerial Accountability to Parliament* HC422 (2004).

[16] Armed Forces (Parliamentary Approval for Participation in Armed Conflict) Bill 2005. The second reading was on 21 October 2005, HC Hansard Vol 437, cols 1085–1162.

[17] There have been suggestions that Iraq has cast too great a shadow over consideration of the deployment power and that more modest reform in the light of a broader consideration of the practice is all that is required, see evidence of Professor Steven Harmes to the Joint Committee on the Constitutional Renewal Bill, 13 May 2008 (to be published as HC551-I (2008)).

[18] See D Feldman (ed), *English Public Law* (OUP, Oxford, 2007).

[19] *Council of Civil Service Unions v Minister for the Civil Service* [1983] UKHL 6.

[20] N White, in C Ku and H Jacobson (eds), *Democratic Accountability and the Use of Force in International Law* (Cambridge University Press, Cambridge, 2003).

That such strength and dispatch are politically necessary throughout the whole of government, and more especially in that part which relates to foreign transactions, cannot be doubted: and experience has shown that the rapidity and secrecy which are generally necessary to the due execution of public measures, will never be found in large assemblies of the people.

Wavering with doubts, and distracted by the jealousies and the animosities of party, such assemblies would be discussing the propriety of the step after the opportunity and occasion for its adoption had transpired. It is only by assigning and executing State measures to one individual that they can be effectually and properly transacted.

When the rights in question are concentrated in one department of the State and the power of the realm is wielded by one hand, the execution of public measures will inspire the people with confidence, and strike into the enemies of the people of the country that awe, that dread of its activity and power, which it is the constant endeavour of good policy to bring about.

For these reasons, the constitution has made the King the representative of the people with regard to foreign affairs; and has invested His Majesty with the supreme, exclusive power of managing them.[21]

Not much time for democratic legitimacy there. If we were to substitute 'Prime Minister' for 'King' and to acknowledge the rather more elegant quality of Chitty's style, we have here more or less the way in which the Blair government defended the existing dispensation to those Parliamentary Committees which had suggested that there might be room for change in the deployment power. Lord Falconer told the Constitution Committee:

The Government's position is that the current arrangements on the power to deploy UK troops abroad in conflict should continue as it is at the moment. The power to deploy troops is an Executive power. Such decisions are by their nature most suitable for the Executive to take. They are often made in difficult, uncertain, fast-moving circumstances and operational effectiveness must be paramount. The Executive necessarily will have access to full information, or fuller information than Parliament... [any change] would both blur the essential distribution or responsibility and unwisely hamper the proper prosecution of intervention and the process of accountability.[22]

He said that the possibility of the government deploying troops without Parliamentary support was 'more theoretical than real'.[23] He later wrote to the Committee than encumbering the deployment power might prejudice a government's capacity to take swift action necessary to defend national security. The necessity for the most efficacious use of the power trumped any enhancement of the means for its accountability.[24]

---

[21] J Chitty, *A Treatise on the Law of the Prerogatives of the Crown: and the relative Duties and Rights of the Subject* (Butterworth, London, 1820, Gregg, 2nd reprint 1970) pp 39–40.

[22] Waging war: Parliament's role and responsibility, HL 236-II (2005–2006), Evidence, p 123.

[23] Id, Memorandum by the Rt Hon Lord Falconer of Thornton, Secretary of State and Lord Chancellor, p 120.

[24] Id, p 121.

Practice was confirming the government's position. The Lord Chancellor's statements were made at the same time as the government was *not* consulting Parliament about substantial increases in the deployment of UK troops to Afghanistan, with a much more ambitious mandate than that of the forces already there.[25] Later, the decision to put a battalion on stand-by for Kosovo was made without any Parliamentary consultation.[26]

Chitty's language supports the ambition of some politicians of both major parties that the UK should 'punch above its weight',[27] at a time when others have their doubts whether it should be doing much punching at all. Mr Blair's millenarian ambitions expressed in his famous Chicago speech in 1999—to hold the threat of force over those governments which did not share his democratic or humanitarian inclinations and to make the general threat effective by actually engaging in trying to secure regime change by using military force from time to time[28]—required some such repository of power in his own hands, when more sceptical voices might have meant that securing political support for these operations would not have been easy. And he had it. Force for non-defensive purposes had been used in Sierra Leone, in the Federal Republic of Yugoslavia (to do with events in Kosovo),[29] and against Iraq—goodness knows for what real purpose in the last case[30]—though it has later been justified on the basis that an evil despot had been overthrown (a cause for which the Prime Minister must have known that he would not have had sufficient political support to launch the mission). The decision to attack Iraq followed a process which appears formally and substantively to have ignored most of the checks and constraints of the system of cabinet government, that is to say, that although the government described the power as an 'executive' one, it was a power which could be effectively exercised by the Prime Minister.[31] 'Ah, but'—the government said—'the participation of the Commons was enlisted in reaching the decision to attack Iraq: though not bound to by law, we did put the expedition to the Commons on a substantive motion and we won the vote before the bombing started.' Furthermore, the vote was not won solely on the basis of party affiliation; to the contrary, the government needed opposition votes to see it through. This, it argued, showed that it was the Commons which had the final word, not the government. The reiteration of the Blair programme, even subject to certain caveats and directed in a slightly different direction, by Foreign Minister Miliband in February 2008 shows that use of force for democratic and humanitarian purposes is a prospect

---

[25] See below, n 39.

[26] HC Hansard, 29 April 2008, Vol 475, col 3WS.

[27] The phrase was Foreign Secretary Douglas Hurd's in a lecture at Chatham House in 1993.

[28] 24 April 1999.

[29] Foreign Affairs Committee, Fourth Report 1999–2000, Kosovo.

[30] For instance, Prime Minister Brown's answer, HC Hansard 19 March 2008, Vol 473 col 916.

[31] Review of Intelligence on Weapons of Mass Destruction, Report of a Committee of Privy Counsellors (Chairman: The Rt Hon The Lord Butler of Brockwell KG GCB CVO) HC 898 (2004), chs 5 and 6 and pp 146–148.

which has not been removed from the political prospectus.[32] The same military posture may be struck again. The question is, then, 'How should such decisions be taken?'

The decision to go to the Commons for a vote to support action before the attack against Iraq was an almost unprecedented step. Lord Rowlands told the House of Lords recently that the power of Parliament over supply, once thought to be the most formidable constraint on executive war-making, is now a very weak reed (and has been for a long time).[33] That being so, the government usually decides what it will tell Parliament and when it will tell it, confident that it will not be asked for anything more and sure, too, that the money will be there to pay for the operations. Government has seldom allowed its own time for debate, relying on Ministerial statements or, at most, replying to adjournment debates. Parliament is frequently told only after the operations have started. Almost all assessments of operations that there have been are ex post facto—Franks on the Falklands;[34] Hutton[35] and Butler[36] on Iraq; the Select Committees on Kosovo;[37] and various 'lessons learned' inquiries, some published, most not. And governments have made much of their free hand, comparing their own speedy and flexible responses to the halting, conditional commitments of some of their allies, especially so when the planned operations are within NATO or some ad hoc coalition.[38]

Anyway, as I have said, the government maintained that it was now 'inconceivable' that troops would be deployed abroad on any major mission without support for the decision by the House of Commons. As I have said, these soothing words were repeated as the Government prepared to send more troops to fight a quite different campaign in Afghanistan from the one on which they had originally embarked (itself, of course, started without any Parliamentary consultation), with no more than the occasional ministerial statement about what was going to happen.[39] At the same time, in some of the UK's allies, such as Canada[40]

---

[32] 'The Democracy Imperative', 12 Feb 2008, <http://www.fco.gov.uk/resources/en/speech/2008/02/fco_hp_nsp_milibanddemoc120208>.

[33] HL Hansard, 31 January 2008, Vol 698, col 781.

[34] Franks et al, *Falkland Islands Review, Report of a Committee of Privy Counsellors*. HMSO, January 1983, Cmnd 8787.

[35] Report of the Inquiry into the Circumstances Surrounding the Death of Dr David Kelly CMG, HC 207 (2004), <http://www.the-hutton-inquiry.org.uk/content/report/>.

[36] Above n 31.

[37] Foreign Affairs Committee, Seventh Report 1998–1999, Fourth Report 1999–2000, above n 29.

[38] Adam Ingram, Evidence to Constitution Committee, above n 22, Vol II, p 131, Q.304.

[39] For instance, statement of the Defence Secretary (John Reid), HC Hansard 26 January 2006, Vol 441, cols 1529–1533 (Afghanistan). For criticism of the ministerial statement device, see Constitution Committee, Vol II Evidence, above n 22, p 69, Q.121 (Lord Garden).

[40] The Canadian House of Commons voted 149–145 on 17 May 2006 to continue Canada's commitments in Afghanistan, fulfilling an electoral commitment of the new government to put 'international treaties and military engagements' to a vote. An extension of the mission was approved following another vote on 13 March 2008, Hansard 066.

and the Netherlands,[41] the participation of the legislatures was solicited and votes held before troops were committed and the terms of their deployments were established. Everyone remembers Defence Secretary Reid's optimistic prognosis for the Afghan mission—that the forces going to Afghanistan might not hear a shot fired in anger. That miscalculation could hardly have been more grievous. Whether it was an attempt to mislead or an expectation based on defective intelligence, it points to the reason why the Iraq decision was so contested and why better decision-making might result from more transparent processes. The complaint about Iraq was not just that the decision was wrong but that it was based on wrong or insufficient or untimely information—and that if correct and adequate information had been provided in a timely manner, the process would have been better (and, of course, might have resulted in a different decision).[42] Decisions reached by better procedures would enjoy greater legitimacy—in the political sphere and with those who would be called upon to do the fighting. What is more, military leaders are now aware of their own potential legal liability, as well as that of their men. Admiral Boyce's particular concerns about legal accountability for the decision to use force might have been misplaced (as I shall say later, the chances of the legal accountability of anyone for the decision to go to war are remote) but his sensitivity to the impact that international law might have had on the operation was acute.[43]

The Committee rejected the government's commitment to the status quo and accepted most of this reasoning about the defects in the process as well as its location. It rejected a legislative solution, that the power should be put on a statutory footing, fearing that the legal problems which might arise from a domestically unlawful conflict (i.e., where a deployment was made in breach of the legislation) were not amenable to satisfactory solution—in particular, the Committee was concerned about the legal position of individual troops who fought in such a conflict and about the prospect of those troops who objected to the decision to send them to fight might be able to raise the matter in the courts.[44] The risk of the involvement of the courts has been a feature of the concerns of individual ministers. The Attorney-General's first opinion on the international legality of the Iraq war expressed his worries that any decision might be challenged in some court,[45] somewhere, and the then Leader of the House, Geoff Hoon, raised the

[41] There were prolonged debates in the Netherlands Parliament before the Government obtained support for the deployment of Dutch units to Afghanistan in February 2006.
[42] See generally Constitution Committee, Vol II Evidence, above n 22, pp 2–16. On the capacity of a government to manage the supply of information appropriate to the decision to use force, see A Blick, *How to Go to War: a Handbook for Democratic Leaders* (Politico's, London, 2005), ch 3.
[43] A detailed account of the context in which the Attorney-General's opinion on the legality of the attack on Iraq was formulated is attached as Annex Six to Information Commissioner's Office, Enforcement Notice 22 May 2006. See paras 19, 20, and 21 (civil service).
[44] Constitution Committee Report, Vol I, above n 9, paras 79–84, 104.
[45] See Attorney-General's opinion, 7 March 2003, paras 32–35, in [2006] UKMIL, (2006) 77 British Yearbook of International Law 828–829.

threat of legal proceedings as one of his main objections to Clare Short's Bill.[46] I should be more confident in the fertility of the draftsman's imagination to meet the detailed difficulties if it were decided to introduce legislation, but the Committee recognized the political context—the technical problems presented by a statutory solution were simply another argument used by those who wished to keep the deployment power away from the courts. A recent debate in the House of Lords has shown that the Committee's calculation was exactly right.[47] It had proposed instead a 'constitutional convention', created by a governmental statement of how the deployment power would be exercised in future—the statement would set out, *inter alia*, the operations to which it applied, the parliamentary process which was to be followed, and the information which was to be given to Parliament.[48] The model, though not an exact precedent, was the 'Ponsonby Rule' which covers the presentation of treaties to Parliament before their ratification and which established a procedure which has been capable of modification by practice as time as gone on.[49] I think that it would be a fair conclusion that the extensive debates in each House of Parliament have revealed that the preponderant opinion is in favour of change but there are substantial divisions still about that[50] and there is far from agreement about what is the right way to proceed.

Whether by legislation or by some Parliamentary device, I should not expect too much from any change of procedure, however radical. Writing about the United States, Professor Michael Glennon made the following observation about the War Powers Act:

The most a statute can do . . . is to facilitate the efforts of individual members of Congress to carry out their responsibilities under the Constitution. To do that requires understanding, and it also requires courage . . . For a Congress composed of such members, no War Powers resolution would be necessary; for a Congress without them, no War Powers resolution would be sufficient.[51]

The question of the deployment of troops will always have substantial political connotations and a government contemplating action will usually be able to get its way. In its Consultation Paper on the Deployment Power, the government expressed a certain scepticism about any lessons which might be drawn from other countries with different processes, maintaining that the constitutional context of any arrangement was crucial.[52] I agree. There are those who say that some apparent constraints on executive action are chimeras—when it comes to it, the

---

[46] HC Hansard, 21 October 2005, Vol 437, col 1152.

[47] HL Hansard, 31 January 2008, Vol 698, cols 747–796.

[48] Constitution Committee Report, Vol I, above n 9, 85–93, 108–110.

[49] See <http://www.fco.gov.uk/Files/kfile/ponsonbyrule.0.pdf>.

[50] See, for instance, the very different views of three previous Chiefs of the Defence Staff, Lords Boyce, Bramhall, and Craig, Evidence to the Joint Committee on the Constitutional Renewal Bill, 14 May 2008 (to be published as HC551-i, (2008)).

[51] M Glennon, *Constitutional Diplomacy* (Princeton, Princeton University Press, 1991), p 122.

[52] Consultation Document, above n 4, para 32.

government gets its way.[53] There are, however, examples the other way, that is to say, where the legal constraints on action have been applied against the plans of the government, either completely or on matters such as timing or details of commitment, and it is probably this prospect which fuels the government's suspicion of foreign models and feeds its opposition to anything like them being introduced here. One imagines, for instance, that any reference to the German model of a 'Parliamentary Army' would not find much resonance in Whitehall, precisely because, in this case, there is evidence that the legislature makes its voice count and the courts can have their say.[54] Of course, any change in procedure can only lead to a reduction of the number of occasions on which troops are sent to fight abroad—no one suggests an enhanced power for Parliament to order men into battle in defiance of governmental reluctance to do so. The hope, indeed the expectation, is that future decision-making would accord more closely with democratic principle and that greater accountability would lead to more considered judgment about when it was right to fight. A significant factor in changing perceptions about deployment decisions has been the recognition that a far greater proportion of them now involve 'wars of choice'—UN-authorized operations, peace-keeping,[55] humanitarian interventions—which have political preconditions to them as well as the military aspects which would predominate in cases of immediate defence of national territory or facilities.[56]

3. The Deployment Power—the Consultation Paper[57]

The Consultation on the deployment power put a series of options, including legislation, for reform. I cannot go through all the questions which arose, though I shall mention some of the main ones. Anyway, the government has now indicated where it stands in the White Paper on Constitutional Renewal (see below) but some of the observations I have to make apply to its position as well.

---

[53] D Jenkins, Constitutional Reform goes to War: Some Lessons from the US, (2007) Public Law 258–279. See also, RF Grimmett, War Powers Resolution: Presidential Compliance, Congressional Research Service, IB81050, 5 April 2006.

[54] KS Ziegler, 'Executive Powers in Foreign Policy: the Decision to Dispatch the Military', in KS Ziegler, D Baranger, and A W Bradley (eds), *Constitutionalism and the Role of Parliament* (Hart, Oxford and Portland, Oregon, 2007), pp 141–166.

[55] Although there is not a template for the construction of Security Council authorizations, there are a number of common features of Council practice which might be useful guides to what should be done domestically, notably the writing of a clear mandate, the imposition time-limits, and reporting obligations on a regular basis to the Council. See D Sarooshi, *The United Nations and the Development of Collective Security* (Oxford, Oxford University Press, 1999) pp 142–246.

[56] One substantial disadvantage of constitutional reform on a piecemeal basis is that some sensible proposals depend on other changes, such as the completion of reform of the House of Lords, the conferring of real independence on Select Committees, or revision of the role and powers of the Attorney-General, see Public Affairs Committee, above n 6, para 95.

[57] 'The Governance of Britain—War powers and treaties: limiting executive powers', above n 4.

In that document, the government sets out a model 'War Powers Resolution' ('the Resolution') for the House of Commons to consider. I am assuming that, in the absence of reform of the House of Lords, any approval necessary as a precondition for action will be restricted to the House of Commons.

The first question is to determine which deployments would fall within the new regime. The Consultation Paper used the terms from the Geneva Conventions and their Protocols (principally 'international' and 'internal' 'armed conflicts').[58] I should have preferred the threshold to be 'armed conflicts to which international humanitarian law applies'—this would include actions under Security Council authorization and any commitments of forces to 'robust' UN peace-keeping operations, such a UNPROFOR in Yugoslavia. I have been astonished to learn informally that it is not the regular practice of the Ministry of Defence to make a specific determination as to whether or not international humanitarian law would apply in anticipation of committing troops abroad. It seems to me a necessary condition that troops should know under what rules they fight, not least because of their personal, criminal liability if they commit serious breaches of the law of armed conflict. If this necessary step became standard (and published) practice, the threshold condition would be a matter of record. The Resolution uses the term 'a use of force... [which] would be regulated by the law of armed conflict', which reinforces the need for a public declaration of the Government's assessment of the applicability of international humanitarian law[59] (and which, though using slightly different language, is the test I think best).

Further, I see the requirement to use the new procedure arising when a deployment is actively contemplated in which it is foreseeable that the troops would participate in a conflict to which humanitarian law would apply. The definition I propose (as the one suggested in the Consultation Paper) would exclude deployments for training purposes and policing operations undertaken by the armed forces, principally naval interdictions of one kind and another, like those aimed at drug traffickers—but a naval deployment to enforce an embargo, such as the Adriatic operation against the former Yugoslavia would require authorization. There is a practical problem that military operations do not always go to plan and that the purposes of an operation or the units which are necessary to implement them become subject to revisions. There is probably no bright line to be drawn between anticipated redeployment or reinforcement and 'mandate drift' where the nature of the operation changes. However, there are some clear cases, of which the extension of the British commitment in Afghanistan in 2006 is an example—more troops, with a different mission in essentially a different theatre[60]—to which the new dispensation should apply. The Resolution contains no provision to deal with the expansion of deployments, nor for any periodic

---

[58] Id, p 44 (s 1(6)).
[59] Constitutional Renewal Bill, above n 6, s 1(2)(b).
[60] Above, n 39.

reviews, but practice does show that the changes in mandate are a significant proportion of 'new' deployments and the House of Commons should be alive to the need to keep operations under review. I suggest that there be at least an annual reporting requirement about deployments, the dangers of incremental increase in commitment over a period should be taken care of at the presentation of the Report.

Nobody opposes the inclusion of an emergency power to deploy troops in response to an immediate threat of an attack against the state and the Resolution does contain one, though in very wide terms, which might be hard to control if the Resolution lacks a legal basis.[61] Further, once troops are deployed, their right to respond to changing circumstances which give rise to a need for the use of defensive force would simply be an aspect of their own rules of engagement. What should be required is a report to Parliament in short order about what has happened, with, I should say, a right of Parliament to disapprove the deployment, which would create an obligation of safe withdrawal. The Resolution gives a Prime Minister considerable leeway to determine that a deployment falls within the emergency exception and when, if at all, he will report to Parliament about such dispositions. It seems to me that too much would be conceded by the 'security condition' which the Resolution proposes as the test which moves power back to the Prime Minister from the Commons.[62]

The Consultation questionnaire asked, 'What information should be provided to Parliament?' In the various solutions the government canvassed, there was a common provision about the information to be provided to Parliament:

The Prime Minister [starts the process] by laying before the House a Report setting out...

(b) the information about objectives, locations and legal matters that the Prime Minister thinks appropriate.[63]

Those emphasized words suggest to me that the government's heart might not really be in the process it has started, a conclusion confirmed by the reiteration of clause (b) in the Resolution. It was the inadequacy of the information which accompanied the proceedings before the attack on Iraq and the explanation for that is usually laid at the Prime Minister's door. If future Prime Ministers are to remain the gatekeepers of information, then it does not look as though we have gone on from the situation which caused so much controversy in 2003 and since.

I want to address further only one of the informational questions and that is the legal justification for any overseas deployment. Because of the absence of domestic legal constraints on the deployment power, the legal question here referred to means legality under international law. As in all legal advice to the government as a whole, giving an opinion on the international legality of troop deployments is the responsibility of the Attorney-General, who has to provide independent

---

[61] Resolution, cl 3 (which also allows a 'security' exception).
[62] Id, cl 3(5).   [63] Consultation Paper, above n 4, s 2 (3)(b).

instruction to the government of which he is a member. Revelations after the invasion of Iraq cast something of a cloud over the substance of the Attorney-General's published opinion and over the circumstances surrounding its evolution.[64] What was publicly known at the time was that immediately before the first operations against Iraq the Attorney-General had given a short written answer to a question in the House of Lords, saying why he thought the actions were lawful under international law[65] and the Foreign and Commonwealth Office (FCO) wrote a rather longer memo to the Foreign Affairs Committee (FAC), setting out its view of the legal position,[66] which, of course, had to be compatible with the Attorney's opinion. It was a matter on which the Constitution Committee heard a good deal of evidence, including some from Lord Goldsmith who had provided the advice about Iraq and was still Attorney-General when he met the Committee. He made much of the need for confidentiality, based on the principle of professional privilege and the now, surely discredited, claim that advice given in the knowledge that it might one day be revealed would not be as frank as it would be if its secrecy were guaranteed.[67] This was the excuse trotted out for years and years about advice to government in general and it has largely been jettisoned for the unworthy explanation that it is. I should have thought that considerations of professional integrity would have reinforced the obligation of the government's senior law officer not to be deflected from his task by possibilities that he might later have to account for his advice in public. Lord Goldsmith quite rightly rejected the homely notion that the Attorney-General stood in relation to government like the family solicitor did to his established private clients.[68] The in-house lawyer's job of facilitator can be done by departmental lawyers, on matters of international law, by the FCO legal advisers.[69] I think that it is time that future Attorneys adopted a more quasi-judicial role, certainly on questions of war and peace, and sought the best answer, not simply one which best fitted with a transient policy. However, as things stand, the Attorney is protected by the Ministerial Code, which prohibits revelation, even of the fact that he has been asked for his opinion.[70] The Constitutional Affairs Select Committee has conducted a substantial inquiry into the role of the Attorney-General in which it made reference to the international legal advice about Iraq but made no specific

---

[64] P Sands, *Lawless World: America and the Making and Breaking of Global Rules* (Penguin, London, 2005), disentangling the various titles given to the different 'advices' proffered to the Government before the attack against Iraq.

[65] House of Lords Hansard, 17 March 2003, Vol 646, col WA3.

[66] Letter from Foreign Secretary to the Chairman, Foreign Affairs Committee, 17 March 2003, in UKMIL [2003], (2003) 74 British Yearbook of International Law 793–796.

[67] Constitution Committee Report, Vol II Evidence, above n 22, p 116, Q.242.

[68] Id, p 115, Q.238.

[69] The Attorney-General's view was that the policy Department (in this case, the FCO), should inform Parliament of the 'legal justification' for the proposed deployment. One problem with this is that such information as the FCO has provided has not always been very helpful, e.g., Baroness Symons, HL Hansard 17 February 1998, vol 586, col 148.

[70] Ministerial Code, Cabinet Office (2005), pp 23–24.

recommendations about advice on international law distinct from any other legal advice provided by the Attorney.[71] The government's responses equally have not singled out advice on matters of international law. Following the Consultation on the Role of the Attorney-General, the Constitutional Renewal White Paper rejects any change in the practice on the (non-) publication of the Attorney-General's legal advice, although it does not rely on the danger to the frankness of opinions as a reason for doing so. What the government does say is:

> The government should, and does, explain the legal basis for key decisions to Parliament and the public. Any such explanation must of course be *consistent* with the legal advice received . . . and must not dishonestly represent that advice [it seems extraordinary that such a caveat needed to be made]. But generally this process will not entail disclosing the legal advice itself.[72]

Exceptionally, the government may deem it proper to disclose the Attorney's advice—'waive privilege', it says, apparently claiming its privilege, rather than the Attorney's, ordinarily to refuse disclosure.[73] The revelation of Lord Goldsmith's opinion about the assault on Iraq followed a leak of his opinion and was not an exceptional decision on transparency by the government.

Particularly after what became known about the processes which attended the final formulation of Lord Goldsmith's opinion on Iraq and, since the government does not envisage any greater distance between the Attorney and his political colleagues as part of its reforms, we should expect more. I go with Lord Bingham that the Attorney is not in a position comparable to either family solicitors or in-house counsel. He is a very special kind of public servant whose opinions in general should be available to the public.[74] In my view, this applies with particular strength to his opinions about the international legality of deployments. The courts have from time to time said that the rule of law requires executive compliance with the state's international obligations.[75] The then Lord Chancellor, Lord Falconer, underlined to the Constitution Committee his responsibilities for securing obedience to the international rule of law as part of his statutory duties.[76] If legitimacy of decision-making is one of the objectives of the government's reforms, that the deployment power be exercised only in accordance with the best opinion of its international legality seems to me to be the minimum condition for securing legitimacy.[77] I shall not labour the point here but I do not think that the

---

[71] Constitutional Affairs Select Committee (now Justice Select Committee), The Constitutional Role of the Attorney-General, Fifth Report, HC306 (2007), paras 47–50.

[72] Constitutional Renewal White Paper, above n 4, para 68.

[73] Id, para 69.

[74] Lord Bingham, 'The Rule of Law' (2007) 66 Cambridge Law Journal 67, 83–84.

[75] See below, n 103.

[76] Constitution Committee Report, Vol II Evidence, above n 22, p 122, Q.266.

[77] Public Administration Committee, above n 15, para 78, citing evidence to the Committee arguing that advice about the use of armed force was at the very centre of the principle and not an exception to it.

attack on and occupation of Iraq in 2003 was in accordance with the best view of international law[78]—mere plausibility of legal justification should not have been enough.

The reservation of the Prime Minister's powers over the provision of information to Parliament is the greatest defect in the Resolution put forward in the Renewal White Paper. It is such a fundamental weakness that there seems to me to be very little point in going any further with the present proposals to condition the exercise of the war power. It may be possible for a government which has obtained the endorsement of the House of Commons for its military initiatives to claim that the formal demands of democratic decision-making have been satisfied, but it will be no better off in asserting the substantive legitimacy of its actions than it is at present. The Constitution Committee caught a rising political tide with its report. There are, though, other voices still calling for legislation. They are not likely to be appeased by the dilution of the less demanding alternative proposed by the Constitution Committee. There may be a further reason for going the legislative route, to which I shall shortly turn.

There is something of a shadow hanging over the deployment power project. It is the developing initiatives of the European Union in the defence field. I do not want to be misunderstood about what I say next. I have been involved with European Community law since before the UK was a member of the Communities and I remain convinced about the worth of the European project. However, as the EU asserts its competence in matters of defence it is committing troops to a force in Chad (EUFOR Chad/RCA)[79] and will supply a body of technocrats to Kosovo (EULEX), there is a risk that some states will take advantage of the relative lack of accountability which applies to activities within the Foreign and Security Policy of the Union as a means of avoiding any national procedures which would apply to purely unilateral decisions about the use of force. I should make it clear, then, that I regard it as important that any new procedures apply to deployments under the auspices or authority of international organizations, such the UN Security Council or NATO. The same goes for the EU as its projects become more ambitious.[80] It is important now to pre-empt arguments that commitments made by the Government in the European Council to contribute British forces to its operations will be 'binding' in the same way as European law in general. The UK should make it clear that the participation of British troops in this kind of operation will be subject to whatever new dispensation is adopted as in any other case.

---

[78] C Gray, *International Law on the Use of Force* (Oxford, OUP, 2nd edn 2007); S Murphy, 'Assessing the Legality of Invading Iraq' (2004) 92 Georgetown Law Journal 173. For a different perspective, arguing that the project to subject the use of force by states to legal restraint has failed, see M Glennon, 'Why the Security Council Failed' (2003) Foreign Affairs 16.

[79] <http://www.consilium.europa.eu/cms3_fo/showPage.asp?id=1366&lang=en>.

[80] 'European HQ heads Sarkozy plan for greater military integration', 9 June 2008, <http://www.guardian.co.uk/world/2008/jun/07/eu.france>.

4. International Law and Foreign Affairs

I have emphasized the international law question. It is not the only one and, arguably, not the most important one but its salience is part of the increasing impact
that matters of international law have for transactions within the UK's national
legal order. (I shall talk in what follows about 'English' law. British law would be
incorrect for there are differences, sometimes of more than detail, between English
and Scots law in this area of law.) The courts have frequently said that 'the subject
has unquestionably left the Crown or the executive a free hand in the conduct of
foreign affairs'.[81] The instrument for the conduct of foreign affairs is the prerogative.[82] Many of the powers identified in the original Governance of Britain Green
paper were foreign affairs powers.[83] The Constitutional Renewal Bill contains
provisions which will put the Ponsonby Rule on procedure preceding the ratification of treaties on a statutory footing but has left most of the other powers as they
are.[84] Indeed, the government has specifically said that it intends no change in the
way the prerogative is used for the administration of the Dependent Territories,[85]
a particularly troublesome conclusion in the light of the way the power has sometimes been used in the past, a prominent example of which we have not heard
the last, being the treatment of the Chagos Islanders and the arrangements with
the US for its occupation of Diego Garcia.[86] Recently, we have seen the recognition of Kosovo by government decision, simply announced to Parliament, despite
the legal complications and political features which surround it.[87] Quite apart
from the macro-political aspects of recognition decisions, they can have effects in
domestic law of great importance to individuals. It is clear that no sea-change is
proposed here, so that decisions of this kind will continue to be taken on the back
of unpublished legal advice under the 'arbitrary' prerogative power.[88]

While the creation and development of international obligations is something
which falls within the executive's foreign affairs power, the impact of many of
these activities is felt in domestic law. The reason is that whole swathes of the
law of international cooperation are ultimately directed at the conduct of non-
governmental persons and institutions—conduct is made criminal, financial
institutions must be regulated, laws must be made for commercial transactions,
transnational communication must be established, and mechanisms must be put
in place to secure the enjoyment of human rights in order that the state might

---

[81] *Attorney-General v Nissan* [1970] AC 179, per Lord Wilberforce.
[82] FA Mann, above n 7, ch 1.   [83] Above n 1.
[84] Constitutional Renewal Bill, ss 21–24.
[85] Governance of Britain, above n 1, para 49, n 13.
[86] See *Foreign Secretary v R (Bancoult)* [2007] EWCA 498 and S Allen, 'Looking beyond the
Bancoult cases...' (2007) 7 Human Rights Law Review 441.
[87] HC Hansard, 19 February 2008, Vol 472 col WS21–22.
[88] L Collins, 'Foreign Affairs and the Judiciary' (2002) 51 International and Comparative Law
Quarterly 485, 487–493.

discharge its international obligations: the executive may undertake these duties at the international level but their implementation requires enlisting the whole extent of government power.[89] For the UK, there is a democratic consideration which impinges here—while the government may make international treaties (in which the bulk of the law of cooperation is to be found), those agreements have no domestic legal effect in the absence of implementing legislation—so that the great principle that government may not make law be preserved.[90] The courts, then, will ordinarily not be confronted with the treaty but will be faced with legislation which transforms the treaty obligations into national law. The interpretation of that legislation, increasingly, both on their own initiative and because of legislative instruction, the courts try to effect in accordance with the international law meaning of the treaty the statutes are designed to implement.[91] Speaking about 'Convention rights' under the Human Rights Act, Lord Bingham said in *Ullah* that the courts' task was 'to keep pace with the Strasbourg jurisprudence as it evolves over time: no more, but certainly no less',[92] a duty which Lord Brown later wryly recharacterized as a duty to do this, 'no less, but no more'.[93] The ECHR presents a special (but not unique) example of a treaty as 'living instrument', where the international obligations of the parties may develop over time and where effective cooperation requires the organs of states to take this into account. A receptive view to implementing legislation is desirable so that the cooperative objective which underpins the treaties is given best effect and Lord Bingham, particularly in Convention cases, has shown a notable commitment to following the technique of the European Court of Human Rights to establish the content of 'Convention rights' under the Human Rights Act. Lord Bingham gave extensive attention to the proper approach to matters of international law in his judgment in *European Roma Rights Centre R (on the application of) v Immigration Officer at Prague Airport*.[94]

However, this still means that treaties which are binding on the UK but which have not been implemented by legislation may not be a source of rights or obligations in national law[95]—and this includes treaties with obvious possibilities of utility to litigants like the International Covenant on Civil and Political Rights and others of high political importance, such as the UN Charter.[96] The treaty

---

[89] This is the technical 'how?' question and is both an inevitable and indisputable element in securing international cooperation. I do not address here the 'why?' question—why is international cooperation a necessary good.

[90] Accordingly, the executive works on the principle that it will not ratify treaties which require legislation for their implementation until that legislation has been enacted by Parliament.

[91] See R Gardiner, *International Law* (Longman, London, 2003), ch 4.

[92] *R v Special Adjudicator ex p Ullah* (FC) (Appellant) [2004] UKHL 26, para 20.

[93] *Al-Skeini and others v Secretary of State for Defence* [2007] UKHL 26, para 106.

[94] [2004] UKHL 55, paras 11–30.

[95] E.g., *J H Rayners v Department of Trade* [1988] 3 All ER 257, per Lord Templeman.

[96] The United Nations Act 1946 does not implement the UN Charter as a whole but provides some narrow powers to the Government to act by Order to implement binding obligations under ch VII.

rule applies in principle as well to decisions of international organizations, which themselves will have been created by treaty which is why the United Nations Act takes the form that it does. Like practically all the rules which apply to international law, the treaty rule is a general principle, subject to exceptions difficult to conceptualize. The most important, to which I shall return, is that courts may take international law into account when it is indirectly necessary to do so to resolve a dispute properly before them. For instance, the claim that, exceptionally, a foreign law ought not to be recognized by the English court because it would be contrary to 'public policy' to do so may sometimes involve an investigation into whether or not the disputed foreign law is contrary to international law.[97] In the other direction, individual judges have alluded to the possibility that certain non-implemented treaties may have some weight in English law, a claim made about human rights treaties, especially, a matter to which it will be necessary to return.[98]

The other important source of international obligations is customary international law—the general practice of states in their relations with each other, undertaken by them conscious of the legal dimensions of what they are doing. The bulk of state practice does consist of executive activity—sometimes arresting foreign ships but never arresting foreign diplomats, protecting nationals but not being concerned about aliens and so on—though there are important roles for legislatures—establishing the reach of criminal jurisdiction and laying down the limits of immunities under international law—and for courts—interpreting treaties, for instance and, perhaps, holding the executive government to account, relying on international law. Determining that there is the concordant and generalized practice necessary to generate a customary rule can be an involved and extensive process, as the proceedings before international courts frequently demonstrate—but it is a judicial one and one which does lie within the competence of English courts, even if they may not always choose to exercise it. The reason why courts look at customary international law is that there is a long-established, if still controversial, rule that 'the law of nations is part of the common law of England'. This is a single rule which enables the English court to have direct access to all the rules of customary international law and to take account of changes in custom brought about by changes in international practice—it is international law as it is for the time being on which the courts rely.[99] This means that it is the holder of the international law right that may rely on customary international law and the bearer of the international law duties that can be called to account. These will

---

[97] The 'foreign act of State'—for the exception, *Kuwait Airlines Corporation v Iraqi Airways Company* [2002] HL 19.

[98] Lord Steyn in *Re McKerr* [2004] UKHL 12, paras 50–52, suggesting that human rights treaties might be treated differently.

[99] The original statement comes from Blackstone who based himself on some 18th-century decisions (mainly but not exclusively to do with immunities). The modern understanding comes in *Trendex Trading v Central Bank of Nigeria* [1977] 1 All ER 881 (CA) (another immunity case).

usually be states (though we should not ignore the development of rights and duties for individuals under customary international law). Nonetheless, cases do arise when reference to customary international law is required indirectly, just as oblique reference may have to be made to unimplemented treaties. In either case, there is a further consideration—the English courts have referred to the 'justiciability' of questions of international law, otherwise properly before them.[100] There are various strands to the justiciability jurisprudence, but prominent among them is where a court takes the view that it is not the best forum to decide the question.[101]

Foreign states as defendants in domestic courts will often be protected by one kind of immunity or another from proceedings directly against them. There is further protection for foreign states under the 'foreign act of State doctrine', which says that UK courts will not ordinarily examine the acts of foreign states within their own jurisdictions against the standards of international law, so that the indirect implication of the acts of other states as incidental matters in private litigation is also a limited prospect.

This leaves the possibility that it is the application of international law to the acts of the British government which is the significant jurisdiction of the English courts. If it were, it would be an acknowledgement (as there should be) that it is the United Kingdom as a whole which is bound by international law and that all the organs of state should play their parts in securing the fulfilment of the state's international obligations, to the extent that they each have the constitutional power to do so. This would not necessarily presage the wholesale embracing of international law by the courts: where attempts have been made to use the courts to fetter the foreign affairs powers of government, litigants have frequently been met by the answer that what they are seeking is beyond the power of the courts to provide.[102] Nonetheless, from time to time British judges have recognized that there is an international dimension to the rule of law and that they have a responsibility to provide protection against excesses of public power, regardless of the origin of the constraint on government.[103] Another forthright assertion of the courts' responsibility to protect the rule of law has come in *R (on the application of Corner House Research etc v Director of the SFO etc.*[104] Here, the international dimension to the case was of a different character—the defendant was seeking support for his decision from an

---

[100] The courts have been willing to take on difficult questions of customary international law, sometimes satisfactorily (e.g., *Maclaine Watson v Department of Trade* [1988] 3 WLR 1033 (CA)), sometimes less so (e.g., *Ex p Pinochet (No 3)* [2000] AC 151).

[101] *Buttes Gas and Oil Company v Hammer* [1982] AC 888, per Lord Wilberforce.

[102] See n 114.

[103] *R v Horseferry Road Magistrates ex p Bennett* [1993] UKHL 10, per Lord Griffiths at para 8, using the abuse of process doctrine to supply a remedy where agents of the state had obtained custody of a defendant without relying on extradition procedures, a remedy Lord Bingham described as 'salutary' in *R v Home Secretary ex p Mullen* [2004] UKHL 18, para 8.

[104] [2008] EWHC 714 (Admin).

unimplemented treaty provision but the court would not be deflected from what it saw as its duty by such an argument.[105] In his 'Rule of Law' lecture, Lord Bingham put forward as one of his 'sub-rules' 'the existing principle of the rule of law requires compliance by the state with its obligations in international law...'[106] One has to be careful about precise formulations here—what I understand to be meant is the domestic version of the rule of law. Other considerations might well apply to the rule of law in the international system, where its institutional limitations suggest at least that any particular national concept of the rule of law might not translate exactly to the different environment.[107] The idea which I am canvassing here is that the courts should do what is in their constitutional and practical powers to keep the state (which means the state's officials) within its international obligations.[108] The courts should seek to harmonize[109] the rules of domestic and international law and seek avenues by which the duties imposed under international law might be given best effect. I want to examine now how the courts have done this with respect to the power to deploy the troops, given that there are well-established rules of international law which regulate the use of force by states.

5. International Law, English Law, and the Deployment Power

If I may plagiarize again, I should have liked this next section to have been a law report, the report of the case of *Regina v Anthony Charles Linton Blair* at the Old Bailey, determining a charge of planning, preparing, and waging a war of aggression, that is, the attack on Iraq in March 2003. So far, we have had to make do with Nicholas Kent's and Richard Norton-Taylor's revealing little play, 'Called to Account'.[110] The mere fact that the action against Iraq was unlawful under international law does not necessarily require that a criminal prosecution should follow or that it would succeed, and my report would not necessarily been

---

[105] OECD Convention on Combating Bribery of Foreign Public Officials in International Business Transactions 1997. See Addenda.

[106] Above, n 74, pp 81–82.

[107] Sir Arthur Watts, The International Rule of Law, *German Yearbook of International Law* 5. As I was finishing this paper, I learned that Lord Bingham will give the Grotius Lecture for 2008 under the rubric, 'The Rule of Law in the International Order'. The lecture was delivered on 18 November 2008, see <http://www.biicl.org>. For an example of how differences arise, see *Tadic (Jurisdiction)*, ICTY Appellate Chamber decision, IT-94–1, especially para 43.

[108] The two fields of operation of the rule of law are not totally distinct—there is an increasing recognition of the effective protection the rule of law in national legal systems contributes to international stability; see Attorney-General's Speech to Launch the Justice Assistance Network <http://www.attorneygeneral.gov.uk/sub_international_projects.htm>.

[109] D P O'Connell, International Law, Volume 1 (London, Stevens 2ed 1970).

[110] R Norton-Taylor and N Kent, 'Called to Account: The indictment of Anthony Charles Lynton Blair for the crime of aggression against Iraq—a Hearing' (Oberon Books, London, 2007).

of a conviction but it would have been a report of a trial. I do not align myself with the normally fastidious Alan Watkins, who calls the ex-Prime Minister, 'the young War Criminal', but there is a case to answer. There is no international court where a prosecution presently could be instituted. Of course, none has been started here. The question, then, is why not? Indeed, why have there been no legal proceedings reaching the merits of the international legality of the operation in any English court? With the decision in *Gentle*[111] (see below), national judicial channels are probably exhausted. It is possible to imagine an inquiry into the decision to attack Iraq but, as Lord Falconer might say, 'it is more theoretical than real' to imagine any inquiry being authorized to take on the international legality of the decision.

The questions which would need to be addressed are fairly easy to isolate—was the action lawful or not and, if it were unlawful was any senior British politician or military leader engaged in the unlawful act responsible for the international law crime of planning etc a war of aggression? The first question would require an examination of the UN Charter and decisions of the Security Council. The second would need reference to international customary law about the Nuremburg crime of aggression. Both, then, raise questions of international law and it is necessary to establish the circumstances in which an English court may have recourse to these rules of international law.

In late 2002, CND sought a declaration from the courts on the true meaning of SC Resolution 1441, particularly whether or not it authorized the use of military force against Iraq.[112] CND argued that recourse to force without further and specific authorization would be a breach of customary international law (the applicants could not rely on the Charter itself because the relevant provision, Article 2(4) has not been made part of UK law by legislation) and, since the government had committed itself not to act contrary to international law, it would be obliged not to use force in the absence of further resolution providing a specific basis for doing so. CND maintained that this was a pure question of law which fell within the Court's compass and capacity to determine. It received pretty short shrift. Courts could look at unimplemented international instruments only where it were necessary to do so to determine rights and duties in domestic law. English courts, therefore, had no power to interpret SC resolutions—indeed, Simon Brown LJ said:

Why should the English courts presume to give an authoritative meaning [to a SC resolution]? Plainly such a ruling would not bind other States. How could our assumption of jurisdiction here be regarded around the world as anything other than an exorbitant arrogation of adjudicative power?[113]

---

[111] *R (Gentle) v Prime Minister* [2008] UKHL 20; see below n 125.
[112] *Campaign for Nuclear Disarmament v Prime Minister* [2002] EWHC 2777 (Admin).
[113] Id, para 37. This, it should be remembered, is after *Iraqi Airlines*, above n 97.

Simon Brown LJ went on to say that the environment in which international law took effect was not the same as a domestic one. He didn't quite say, 'It's a tough old world out there', but he did defer to the government's view that it might endanger national security if the government were obliged to comply with any finding by a domestic court which it, the government, thought inhibited it from acting in the high national interest.[114] What we have here is the reverse of the rationale of *GCHQ*, where there the court said that it was not the source of a power (whether statutory or prerogative) which determined whether its exercise could be reviewed but the nature of the power (whether or not it were susceptible to legal control). In *CND*, the court was saying that even if there were a question of (international) law to be examined, the nature of the power sought to be reviewed against the international legal standard sometimes meant that a court should decline to do so. Most emphatically of all, Simon Brown LJ said:

> CND must inevitably recognize that any future decision to take military action would plainly be beyond the court's purview...
>
> Nor, in any event, could there be any question here of declaring illegal whatever decision or action may hereafter be taken in the light of the United Kingdom's understanding of its position in international law.[115]

So this seems to make the direct issue of the international legality of any use of force something that the courts will not examine.

Another strategy was relied on in a series of cases involving direct action against coalition military objectives in the UK—for instance, a group of protestors broke into Fairford air base, used by the USAF for missions against Iraq, and tried to disable some of the planes.[116] These cases potentially raised the criminality, as well as the illegality, of the Iraq war. I simplify the legal arguments; in particular, I do not go on to consider whether or not, even if the applicants had been able to establish the international criminality of the attack against Iraq, that they would have been able to make out the defence of reasonable force. The demonstrators were charged with various offences and sought to raise as one of their defences that their actions were the exercise of reasonable force for the prevention of crime, a defence provided by section 3 of the Criminal Law Act 1967. The crime which they claimed to be trying to thwart was the crime of planning etc a war of aggression—the Nuremburg crime, a crime under customary international law. The House of Lords was prepared to accept that there had been such a crime for many years, following the endorsement by states of the Nuremburg Principles in the aftermath of the Second World War.[117] Further, the crime was of a sufficient specificity to satisfy the principle of legality: anyone contemplating waging an aggressive war would have adequate notice of what conduct constituted the offence. As we have seen, there is a long-established rule which says that

---

[114] Id, para 45.   [115] Id, para 47.
[116] *R v Jones etc* [2006] UKHL 16.
[117] Id, per Lord Bingham at para 19—'at least since 1945'.

customary international law is part of the common law. It would have appeared then that there was a crime of aggression in English law to which the defence in section 3 might be appropriate. But no. Lord Bingham said that national courts could only do what they may do—and the House of Lords had decided in a series of judgments from the 1960s that it had no power to introduce new common law crimes. By then, if Lord Bingham's analysis of customary international law were correct, the crime already existed in customary international law and so it could be said that it was already part of English law—the later doctrine of judicial restraint should have had no purchase against it. Taking notice of it now was not different from (and in no way precluded) any common law crime established before those 1960s cases. In this, Lord Bingham follows the House of Lords in *Pinochet (No 3)*, where the contention that there had long been a crime of torture in customary international law and, accordingly, such a crime in English law, found favour with only a single member of the panel which decided the case. For Lord Bingham, statutory incorporation would always be necessary to make an international crime a crime in English law—he gave the International Criminal Court Act 2001 as an example. His position was supported by the rest of the panel, though with varying degrees of enthusiasm, and it has been endorsed by commentators.[118]

Lord Hoffmann agreed with Lord Bingham but he gave another reason why the courts should not, absent legislation, recognize the crime of aggression. He said to do so:

...would be inconsistent with a fundamental principle of our constitution.

Among the constitutional infirmities he identified was:

...the practical difficulty that the making of war and peace and the disposition of the armed forces has always been a discretionary power of the Crown in to the exercise of which the courts will not enquire...It is because of the discretionary nature of the power itself...

It is of course open to the court to say that the act in question falls wholly outside the ambit of the discretionary power. But that is not the case here. The decision to go to war, whether one thinks it was right or wrong, fell squarely within the discretionary powers of the Crown to defend the realm and conduct its foreign affairs.[119]

Lord Hoffmann's analysis would seem to keep the courts away from ever deciding that the deployment of troops were contrary to international law—and would

---

[118] See R O'Keefe [2006] 77 British Yearbook of International Law 472–480, accepting that there is no distinction in practice between the original recognition of a crime under customary law and the creation of a new crime by a domestic court; P Capps, 'The Court as Gatekeeper: Customary Law in English Courts' (2007) 70 Modern Law Review 458–471, regarding the 'acceptance' of a crime under customary international law as an act of transformation and the courts should defer to legislative authority where the 'acceptance' would have serious constitutional implications—as the 'acceptance' crime of planning, preparing etc undoubtedly would.
[119] *Jones*, above n 116, paras 63, 65–66.

seem to render the protestations about securing compliance with the international rule of law matters of mere rhetoric—or, perhaps, considerations to be taken seriously only by squaddies and policemen, who might face national prosecutions for their conduct in the fighting.[120]

Of course, *Jones* was not a prosecution for the crime of aggression and no criminal liability for the Iraq war would have followed from the conclusion that there was a crime of aggression as part of the common law. What the judgment does, though, is clearly rule out any possibility of such a prosecution. Only Parliament can change this. It might do. The states parties to the ICC Statute are working on a definition of a crime of aggression to be included in the Court's statute. If they reach a conclusion, Parliament will have to decide whether or not it wants to add this crime of aggression to the existing offences, made crimes in English law by the ICC Act.[121] The new crime would not have retrospective effect so there is no prospect of their ever being a prosecution in England for invading Iraq, but the enactment of a crime of aggression would be in keeping with the UK's so far positive support for the ICC.[122] To do so would be an affirmation of the UK's commitment to securing that the international rule of law would be augmented by its own law. It would be a logical next step to reform of the deployment power. And because the offence would have been introduced by legislation, any questions of justiciability would have to be resolved by the courts. The judgments in *Jones* suggest that the judges think the courts are up to managing the questions which would arise.

Apart from the direct creation of a crime of aggression in domestic law by legislation, accountability before the courts might have arisen in an indirect way where the necessary determination of a question domestic law required the resolution of the legality of recourse to military force.[123] *Jones* was an example, where the legality of the resort to force was raised as a defence and a similar possibility would be where the same question was raised by a serviceperson as a reason for not obeying an order.[124] Another example is the argument raised in *Gentle*.[125] The case was heard before a nine-member panel in the House of Lords, a quite

---

[120] A British soldier, Corporal Donald Payne, pleaded guilty before a court martial to war crimes committed in Iraq in 2003, <http://www.guardian.co.uk/uk/2006/sep/20/iraq.military>.

[121] International Criminal Court Act 2001, ss 50, 51.

[122] There are complications with the 'crime of aggression' project which go beyond the definition of the offence and relate to the relationship between the ICC and the Security Council, see N Blokker, 'The Crime of Aggression and the United Nations Security Council' (2007) Leiden Journal of International Law 867.

[123] The practice is now strong, that where the courts discern the necessity of deciding a point of international law as the result of some legislative initiative, they will not be put off from deciding by claims of non-justiciability, see *Ecuador v Occidental Exploration & Production Co* [2007] EWCA Civ 656.

[124] An attempt to raise the question of the legality of the attack against Iraq in this way failed, not least because the serviceman was not deployed after the passing of SC resolution 1546 which authorized the future presence of coalition forces in Iraq, <http://www.ukwatch.net/article/the_kendall-smith_case>.

[125] *R (Gentle, on the application of) v Prime Minister* [2008] UKHL 20.

exceptional arrangement and indicative of the constitutional importance of what was at stake. The applicants, parents of soldiers killed in action in Iraq, maintained that they had a right under the Human Rights Act that an independent inquiry be held into all the circumstances in which forces were committed to the conflict in Iraq, including the question of whether the government had obtained timely and accurate advice about the legality of any deployment. The argument was that Article 2 of the ECHR imposes an implied obligation on a state to take reasonable steps to ensure that its deployments overseas are lawful according to international law where there is a risk to the lives of its troops. The European Court has incrementally expanded the duties in Article 2, including requiring independent inquiries into the facts of cases in which persons have been killed by the state in circumstances which raise arguable claims that they were killed in breach of Article 2.[126] The claim in *Gentle* takes this a step further. If they had been right, the parents would have had a 'Convention right' under the Human Rights Act. The courts have decided that the domestic 'Convention right' is to be understood as it would be by the Strasbourg Court. That Court has said that the ECHR is to be interpreted in its international legal context.[127] It is an international court and will hear arguments about international law. The ramifications of the claim, had it succeeded, would have been substantial, hence the large bench of Law Lords called to decide it. It would have reinforced the suggestions I made earlier about a government's responsibility to make known the legal basis on which it intends to send men to fight outside the UK. The argument had received peremptory rejection by the Court of Appeal.[128] The House of Lords, too, was unanimously of the view that it should fail, though some of their Lordships were more receptive to the view that ECHR case law might be developed in a way which would have been helpful to the applicants. The applications failed, though, because the judges could not discern any primary obligation under Article 2 on to which the procedural duties could fix—Article 2 does not impose duties on States not to commit soldiers to life-threatening conflicts, whether the conflict be lawful or not. This is faithful to the Strasbourg case law and it recognizes that not every exercise of public power will have an impact on the enjoyment of human rights such that the procedural obligations to test the legality of government decision-making will always have a part to play in securing the accountability for the exercise of power. In the UK, it is for Parliament to speak clearly to that effect. It seems that there is no incapacity in the courts to address and decide relevant questions of international law if Parliament were to take the initiative.

After *Gentle*, then we return to where I began—if the courts cannot or will not take on the international legality of proposed military operations abroad, then the case for Parliament doing so is strong. After all, it is the State which is bound

---

[126] Importantly, the investigatory duty has been held to apply to deaths in (internal) conflicts, e.g., *Incal v Turkey* No 22678/93, ECtHRs (2000).
[127] *Al–Adsani v UK* ECtHRs No 35763/97 (2001), paras 55 and 56.
[128] [2006] EWCA Civ 1689.

by international law—only the government can beach the international law on the use of force; elementary constitutional considerations suggest that it ought not to have the last word on whether or not it is behaving properly, even though the established practice allows the government to be the ultimate judge of the legality, as well as the propriety of its war-making. Indeed, I should go further and argue that the combination of the timid reform proposals in the Renewal Bill and the present unwillingness of the courts to examine the question of the international legality of a deployment of force overseas combine to require that the device of seeking accountability solely through a House of Commons resolution ought not be abandoned and the statutory route adopted. Government would be required to act and the courts would then have a legislative peg on which to hang their obligation to inquire into the adequacy of the arguments about the international lawfulness of the expedition.

6. Conclusion

The matters about which I have been talking are 'constitutional'—clearly not in the sense that they can be found in some single, formal document, 'The Constitution of the United Kingdom', but in the sense that they are questions of fundamental importance as to how a society sees itself and part of that mysterious process of interaction between 'the Constitution' and society. One of the foundational principles is commitment to the rule of law. We can ask a lot of questions about the rule of law but one of them is 'rule of *what* law?': in the present context, does it include international law? While the answer is not unqualified, the UK legal system has been increasingly receptive to dealing with matters of international law. The concern is that the judgments in *CND* and that of Lord Hoffmann in *Jones* suggest that there may be limits on how far the writ of international law will run against the British Government and its high officials on decisions about the use of military force, a barrier not built on the capacity of the courts to manage such questions, but because of concern to preserve the power of the executive to take unhindered action to deploy its forces. It can hardly be anticipated that if the government is free from national limits on its powers, it would submit easily to the judicial application of the constraints of international law. This takes us back to Chitty and his encomium for the prerogative:

When the right...in question [is] concentrated in one department of State...the execution of public measures will inspire the people with confidence and strike into the enemies of the country that awe, that dread of its activity and power, which it is the constant endeavour of good policy to create.[129]

---

[129] Above n 21.

This is the language of 'shock and awe'—the strategy adopted for the bombing of Iraq. One might think that that were enough to say that a constitutional arrangement which fostered such an attitude ought not to be preserved—but that might take us into operational aspects of the deployment decision. However, even if the means ought not to be subject to review, the ends of conflict should be. If it be the case that most deployments not for self-defence of the state will have some element of choice surrounding them—and the mere invocation of a limitless notion of national security should not be confused with an armed attack against the state on which the right of self-defence is predicated[130]—then it is right that people should know why the troops are being sent so that in good time, other opinions than those of government may have an influence on the political choice which must be made—and I should say as an international lawyer, that it can be established according to the best argument in international law, any choice which is made lies within the rules of international law. If the courts will not take responsibility to scrutinize government decision-making here, then that enhances the argument that Parliament must do it and make the best assessment it can of the case the government puts forward. It should take the opportunity to make it clear that it intends to do so as a central element in its reform of the power to deploy the troops. It should assert its own voice in 'Calling the Shots'. And in doing so, it would reject Chitty's justification for continuing with the prerogative regime—that it helps the state 'to punch above its weight'.

---

[130] See Lord Goldsmith, HL Hansard 21 April 2004, Vol 660, cols 369–372, in [2004] UKMIL, (2004) 75 British Yearbook of International Law 822.

IV

COMMERCIAL LAW AND GLOBALIZATION

1

'... With a view to despatch and the saving of expense'.[1] How the Commercial Court has attempted to meet the demands of the business community for efficient and cost-effective litigation procedures.[2]

Richard Aikens

It is a great honour to have been asked to contribute to this *Liber Amicorum* for Tom Bingham. I have had the good fortune to know him since he led me (in about 1977) in an application for an injunction to restrain a shipowner from acting contrary to the terms of a charterparty.[3] After his appointment to the High Court Bench in 1980, Tom Bingham sat frequently in the Commercial Court until his elevation to the Court of Appeal in 1986. During that time I often appeared before him in his usual court, Court 1, St Dunstan's House. He quickly became renowned for his courtesy to counsel and solicitors, the speed with which he despatched business, and his unerring ability to spot the key point in a case and the flaw in counsel's argument.

During the time that Bingham J sat in the Commercial Court, the work of the court expanded very quickly, not only in the total number of cases heard but also in the type of cases that came before the court. By 1986 the court's traditional diet of shipping and commodity cases was supplemented by an increasing number of complex insurance and particularly re-insurance disputes. During this time also, the court developed its rules of procedure for dealing with what were then known as *Mareva* injunctions. Quite apart from his later massive contributions to the law, as a Commercial judge Tom Bingham contributed much to the development of many aspects of commercial law, but particularly the law concerning charterparties, bills of lading, marine insurance, arbitration, and conflicts of laws.

---

[1] The phrase is used in para 3 of the Notice issued by the Queen's Bench Division judges in February 1895, establishing a separate list for Commercial Causes—the 'Commercial List'.

[2] An earlier version of this paper was given as the KPMG Annual Law Lecture 2008.

[3] Our instructing solicitor was Mr MA Brown, a senior partner of Norton Rose, Botterell & Roche. He used to wear a bowler hat, although not during the consultation itself.

Because the work of the Commercial Court was expanding so rapidly during the period 1980 to 1986, there were suggestions for reforms. These will be considered later in this article. But Tom Bingham was always ready to consider ways of improving the Commercial Court's procedure in order to meet the requirements of its business customers. They, in turn, had the utmost respect not only for his deep knowledge of commercial law, but also his understanding of the ways of the commercial community, particularly those in the City of London.

Disputes between merchants have existed as long as men have been producing and trading goods. There are records of tribunals hearing cases between merchants in England during the Middle Ages. These were the so-called courts of *pie-poudre*,[4] which were set up in towns where there were merchants' fairs and at courts in maritime towns. They were not the King's Courts, but were a kind of commercial tribunal, which had to give quick decisions because the merchants moved on to the next fair or the vessel set sail with the next tide. To resolve disputes, they did not apply the common law but the customs of merchants, which were found as fact by the judge.[5]

It was only in the 18th century that the 'custom of merchants' was systematized as 'the law merchant' and became a part of the common law of England. This systemization was largely the work of Lord Mansfield, Chief Justice of the King's Bench from 1756–1788.[6] Mansfield had studied widely and was well acquainted with the classical philosophers, Roman Law, and international law as well as Scots and French law. Buller J, in giving his judgment in one of the most significant cases in mercantile law in the 18th century, *Lickbarrow v Mason*,[7] described Lord Mansfield as 'the founder of the commercial law of this country'.

The High Court of Admiralty had, of course, existed since at least the 14th century. However, because of the jealousy of the Common Law Courts, that Court had been heavily restricted in the type of commercial case that it could determine. Even after the scope of its work had been widened by the Admiralty Court Acts of 1840 and 1861, its jurisdiction remained strictly limited.[8]

As the 19th century progressed, however, the English courts were bound to be affected by the huge expansion in trade, industry, and commerce that took place following the end of the Napoleonic Wars in 1815. Nelson's victory at Trafalgar had secured the supremacy of the oceans for Britain. Her triumph in naval warfare

---

[4] Because the decisions were given while the dust fell from the feet of the merchants in dispute.

[5] Referred to in a lecture given by Scrutton LJ to the Cambridge Law Society in November 1920, printed in (1923) 1 CLJ p 6: see pp 10–11.

[6] Commercial preoccupations were increasing in England in the 18th century. In Dr Johnson's phrase 'there never was a time in which trade so much engaged the attention of mankind, or commercial gain was sought with such general emulation': see his Preface to Rolt's *New Dictionary of Trade and Commerce (1756)*, quoted in CHS Fifoot, *Lord Mansfield* (Oxford 1936, reprinted by Scientia Verlag Aalen in 1977) at p 4. Mansfield was a friend of Dr Johnson, who described him as '... not a mere lawyer: he drank champagne with the wits': Ibid p 30.

[7] 2 TR 63.

[8] See: *A Treatise on the Jurisdiction and Practice of the English Courts in Admiralty Actions and Appeals. Being a Third Edition of Williams' and Bruce's Admiralty Practice* (1902) ch 1, particularly at p 9.

has been described as marking the end of '...Britain's apprenticeship for commercial and industrial supremacy...which alone made long-term investment and economic growth possible'.[9] Industrialization and the ever-increasing urban population of Britain in the first four decades of the 19th century meant Britain could no longer be self-sufficient in foodstuffs. The repeal of the Corn Laws in 1846, which ushered in a period of free-trade, was largely led by the business classes, who had become convinced that cheap imported food and raw materials were the key to international competitive success against rivals in Europe and the USA.[10]

Industrialization, population growth, and technological innovations in transportation led to a massive increase in the volume of world trade between 1800 and 1914.[11] A huge global railway network of 675,000 miles had been created by 1920, giving vast tracts of hinterland and their products access to the sea.[12] During the second half of the 19th century, Britain's imports of both primary goods and manufactured goods increased enormously. Chief amongst these was the import of grains, cotton, timber, wool, and meat.[13] Although Britain's share of world trade had declined from 23 per cent in 1876 to 19 per cent in 1885, and her production of iron and steel was surpassed by that of Germany and the USA in the 1890s,[14] the fact remained that Britain's international trade grew in absolute terms throughout the latter half of the 19th century.[15] This vast seaborne trade was conducted by British shipping enterprises. Steam tonnage grew in the second half of the 19th century so that from the early 1880s tonnage of steam vessels had surpassed that of vessels under sail. By 1895 over ten million tons of steamships were registered in the United Kingdom. This figure doubled by 1914 and at that time over 50 per cent of the world's merchant marine was trading under the Red Ensign.[16] As the volume of tonnage rose, so shipping rates fell, although this had happened even before vessels of steam and iron or steel replaced those of wood and sail.

It has been said that the City of London was at the heart of this huge expansion in international trade.[17] It provided credit for the world's trading through the

---

[9] NAM Rodger, *The Command of the Ocean* (Penguin Books, 2005) p 582.

[10] See: 'Economics and the Empire' by PJ Cain in *The Oxford History of the British Empire* (Oxford, 1999), Vol III, ed AN Porter, *The Nineteenth Century* at ch 2 p 40 and nn 45 and 46.

[11] Between 1800 and 1850 world trade grew two and a half times; between 1850 and 1914 it multiplied by ten. See AH Imlah, *Economic Elements in Pax Britannica* (Ithaca NY, 1958) p 189, Table 27, referred to in PJ Cain, Ibid at p 42.

[12] See PJ Cain, Ibid at p 32 and n 55.

[13] PJ Cain, Ibid, pp 46–7.

[14] Ronald Hyam, *Britain's Imperial Century 1815–1914* (3rd edn, 2002) at p 198.

[15] In PF Clarke, *Hope and Glory: Britain 1900–1990* (Allen Lane, 1996), at pp 10–11, Professor Peter Clarke points out that exports of cotton piece goods, Britain's most important export, increased from 1,000 million yards in 1846 to 6,000 million in 1905. The domestic market was 1 million yards only!

[16] Clarke, Ibid pp 9–10. By 1903 a greater number of steam vessels than sailing ships were registered in the United Kingdom. In contrast, France maintained its sailing fleet, as a result of state subsidies to protect against the competition from steam. France had the largest sailing fleet in the world in 1900. See Robert and Isabelle Tombs, *That Sweet Enemy* (William Heinemann, 2006) at p 326.

[17] David Kynaston, *The City of London* Vol 1, *A World of its Own* (Pimlico Press, 1994), ch 11, p 167.

guarantee of bills of exchange by the City's acceptance houses. In the 1870s these houses guaranteed trade bills which amounted to £55 million at any one time.[18] By the 1860s it was the world's leading international capital market.[19] The Baltic Exchange was firmly established before 1850 as the centre for chartering ships as well as dealing in tallow, timber, and grain.[20] Lloyd's still predominated in the marine insurance market, although it had lost its monopoly (shared with the Royal Exchange and London Assurance companies) in 1824.[21]

There were, of course, various centres of business in Britain in the 19th century. Liverpool was pre-eminent in trade. In 1860, the Lancashire cotton industry was the largest processing industry in the world. Until the American Civil War it had depended largely on imports from the Southern States. Those imports dwindled to nothing when Union forces imposed the naval blockade on the secessionist states and they were largely replaced by imports from the Indian Empire from 1865. This trade was controlled by the Cotton Brokers' Association of Liverpool, which had been formed in April 1841.[22] In 1863 the association drew up rules for the conduct of transactions, based on existing trade practices. Other trades in Liverpool followed, such as the Liverpool Corn Trade Association. Each association introduced standard forms of contract and in each there was invariably a reference to arbitration, 'probably developed at much greater length than other terms or rules'.[23] Although there were not usually proper law clauses in these standard forms, it was tacitly assumed that the contracts would be governed by English law. By the third quarter of the 19th century there can be no doubt that English law was the predominant law of commerce.

Standard forms of charterparties and bills of lading had existed at least since the beginning of the 19th century,[24] but the growth in the reliance on arbitration by commercial men in order to resolve their disputes was new. It was the result of frustration with the court system at the time. By 1867 it was clear that the operation of the King's Courts, which had grown up and operated more or less autonomously since the Middle Ages, was inefficient and badly needed reform. In 1867 a Royal Commission[25] was appointed to consider the operation of all the courts. The Royal Commission produced two interim reports. Then in 1872 the scope of the Commission's work was further enlarged to 'inquire whether it would be for

---

[18] Ibid, at ch 17, p 309.   [19] Ibid, ch 12, p 167.

[20] Ibid, ch 5, p 53, referring to Hugh Barty-King, *The Baltic Exchange* (1977) pp 62–66.

[21] Ibid, ch 5, p 62.

[22] See AW Brian Simpson, *Leading Cases in the Common Law* (Oxford, Clarendon Press, 1995) Ch 6 (on *Raffles v Wichelhaus and Busch* (1864) 2 H&C 906) at p 145.

[23] See 'The Rise and Rise of Standard Form Contracts: International Commodity Sales 1800–1970' by Professor Ross Cranston (now Cranston J) in 'Commercial Law Challenges in the 21ˢᵗ Century' in memory of Jan Hellner, Lustus Forlag 2007.

[24] Ibid, at p 13.

[25] Its membership initially included Lord Cairns, who became Lord Chancellor, Lord Hatherley, Cairns' successor on the Woolsack, Sir Robert Phillimore, the Admiralty Judge, Bramwell B and Sir Robert Collier A-G and Sir John Coleridge S-G. Further illustrious names were added as the Commission continued its work until 1874.

the public advantage to establish Tribunals of Commerce for the cognizance of disputes relating to commercial transactions...and if so in what manner and with what jurisdiction such Tribunals ought to be constituted, and in what relations, if any, they ought to stand to the Courts of ordinary Civil Jurisdiction, if any'.[26]

The Commission prepared a questionnaire, which it sent to Chambers of Commerce in England and Wales. It also took evidence from those centres in France, Prussia and other German States, Italy, the Austro-Hungarian Empire, and Belgium where there were Tribunals of Commerce. Written and oral evidence was taken from many witnesses, both businessmen and lawyers. The Commission also considered two reports of Select Committees of the House of Commons on Tribunals of Commerce[27] and two Parliamentary Bills that had been introduced in the House of Commons in 1872–3.

Three things are clear from the evidence to the Royal Commission. First, there was general dissatisfaction with the way the English court system dealt with business disputes. It was said that this was why businessmen resorted to arbitration. The London Chamber of Commerce's reply to the question asking whether a Tribunal of Commerce should be created was, yes, because the present system was 'unjust and demoralizing; because the Attorney, the Barrister and the Common Law Judge constitute a trinity to favour quirk and quibble, which often override equity through some technicality of the law'.[28] This dissatisfaction was the principal reason given for proposing a system of Tribunals of Commerce in which the members of the tribunal would have knowledge of and understand the trades concerned. Secondly, the evidence demonstrated that there were many different types of Commercial Tribunal in other countries. Thirdly, it was clear that there was no consensus, either amongst businessmen or judges and lawyers, as to which system might be best suited for England and Wales.

Therefore, when the Commissioners reported on 21 January 1874,[29] it found that although it was agreed that there should be '...some provision...for more summary proceedings in many commercial cases', there was no agreement on the character of the tribunals that might be introduced. There was also no agreement on what sort of judges should sit in the tribunals, what their powers should be, what types of case the tribunals should deal with, or whether they should be bound by the principles of law set down in the existing courts. The Commissioners' view was that recognized rules of law and precedent should be applied to all areas of commercial law and that '...only Judges who have been trained in the principle and practice of law can be expected to be so Guided'.

---

[26] This was part of the terms of the Second Supplemental Commission, 'given' by Queen Victoria on 25 November 1872.

[27] Those of 12 July 1858 and 3 August 1871. Each of those Select Committees had itself taken evidence from witnesses.

[28] P 16 of the evidence attached to the Third Report.

[29] *Royal Commission to inquire into the Operation and Constitution of the Courts*; Parl Papers 1874, XXIV, C957.

However, the report accepted that there was 'ground for complaint that cases are sometimes tried at Nisi Prius before a Judge and jury who have not the practical knowledge of the trade or business which is necessary for their proper determination'. The Commissioners suggested that the answer might be to have a court which was '... presided over by a legal Judge, assisted by two skilled assessors, who could advise the Judge as to any technical or practical matters arising in the course of the inquiry and who by their mere presence would frequently deter skilled witnesses from giving such professional evidence as is often a scandal to the administration of justice'.[30]

The consequence of these rather diffident suggestions was that when the Judicature Acts of 1873 and 1875 were passed, no specialist court and procedure for mercantile disputes was created. Instead, the Acts were '... the handiwork of the great Chancery lawyers who undertook the duty of fusing into one harmonious whole the antagonistic systems of common law and equity, but they were not designed to promote the economy and speed which the City wanted'.[31]

In fact the Judicature Acts arguably made matters worse. That was because the slow and expensive procedures of the former Court of Chancery, including such processes as interrogatories and discovery, were now available to all litigants in all courts. They were frequently used but, as Mathew commented, 'often with little result, save substantially to increase the costs and delay of the trial'.[32]

The disquiet of the City grew. In 1892 the Judges' Council[33] proposed numerous reforms in the High Court. One was the creation of a new Commercial Court, which would deal with a separate Cause List called 'the Commercial List'. Then in August 1892 a High Court Judge (unidentified) wrote a two-part article on 'The Judges' Reforms' for *The Times*. In the second part of this article,[34] the judge described, in trenchant terms, the problems of delays and cost in commercial litigation. The judge regarded the system as slow and unpredictable.[35] He said that two considerations were of importance to men of business when contemplating the possibility of litigation: '... the first is money—how much will it cost? The second is time—how soon at the latest will the thing be over?' Businessmen wanted to write off their losses and know how to deal with similar situations if they arose in future trades. The judge stated that the dissatisfaction of the commercial community with the courts meant that businessmen '... prefer

[30] P 8 of the Report. The notion that 'professional witnesses' were disingenuous or worse survived after the introduction of the Commercial List in 1895. In his lecture to Cambridge law students on 'The Work of the Commercial Courts' given in 1920, Scrutton LJ referred to expert witnesses as '... that particular class of relatives of Ananias...': (1923) 1 CLJ p 10.
[31] *Mathew's Practice of the Commercial Court* (2nd edn 1967 by AD Colman (subsequently Colman J)) Oxford, at p 5.
[32] Ibid. [33] This had been created by The Judicature Acts 1873, s 74.
[34] Published in *The Times* on 10 August 1892. The first part of the article had been published on 9 August 1892.
[35] In those days a losing party was given one year in which to appeal to the Court of Appeal and a further year in which to Petition the House of Lords.

even the hazardous and mysterious chances of arbitration, in which some arbitrator, who knows about as much of law as he does of theology, by the application of a rough and ready moral consciousness, or upon the affable principle of dividing the victory equally between both sides, decides intricate questions of law and fact with equal ease'.

Bowen LJ and Mathew J were behind the attempts to persuade the Lord Chief Justice, Lord Coleridge, to create these two separate lists for cases entered for trial in the Queens Bench Division. Indeed, a resolution of the Queen's Bench judges on 17 June 1892, that there should be a 'Commercial Court for London cases' arising out of the ordinary transactions of merchant and traders in the City of London, had been passed by a vote of 20 to 5. But the Lord Chief Justice was against this idea, believing that all judges of the Queen's Bench should be able to determine all types of case.[36] However, the campaign for a separate Commercial List, to be tried by judges who had specific experience of commercial cases, was given considerable impetus by the notorious case of *Rose v Bank of Australasia*. It concerned a claim by shipowners for a General Average contribution from cargo owners. The matter came before Lawrance J,[37] who had no experience of commercial law and who, in the words of MacKinnon LJ '...was a very stupid man, a very ill-equipped lawyer and a bad judge [who] knew as much about the principles of general average as a Hindoo about figure-skating'.[38] The trial went on for 22 days in May 1891.[39] The judge reserved judgment and only gave it, after much prompting, some nine months later. It was clear he had understood nothing of the issues involved. Lawrance's judgment was overturned by the Court of Appeal but restored, on different grounds, by the House of Lords.[40] The City was

[36] See 'Mr Justice Lawrance: the 'true begetter' of the English Commercial Court' by V V Veeder QC: (1994) 110 LQR 292, n 1. The Prime Minister, Lord Salisbury, had a low opinion of Coleridge's legal abilities, stating that he could boast only 'a very slender garment of legal knowledge to keep him warm'. Quoted in *Salisbury: Victorian Titan* by Andrew Roberts (Weidenfeld & Nicholson 1999) at p 684.

[37] In his lecture to the Cambridge law students in 1920, Scrutton LJ ascribed the elevation of 'Long Lawrance' to the High Court Bench as being '...not wholly unconnected with his devoted services to his party...': (1923) 1 CLJ 6 at p 15. Certainly neither Lord Halsbury LC, nor Lord Salisbury, when Prime Minister, were averse to making appointments to the High Court Bench on the basis of party service. When Halsbury baulked at the appointment of one of Salisbury's suggestions to the post of Master of the Rolls, Salisbury rebuked him, writing: '...there is no clearer statute in [the unwritten law of our party system] than the rule that party claims should always weigh heavily in the disposal of legal appointments...Some day no doubt the Master of the Rolls will be appointed by a competitive examination in Law Reports. But it is our system for the present: and we shall give our party arrangements a wrench if we throw it aside': quoted in *Salisbury* (above), at p 684.

[38] MacKinnon LJ expressed these forthright views in a note entitled 'The Origin of the Commercial Court' published in (1944) 60 LQR p 324. Mackinnon had been the pupil of TE Scrutton in 1896–7 and Scrutton had apparently then described Lawrance J as the 'Only Begetter' of the Commercial Court.

[39] A vivid description of the trial was given by Scrutton LJ, who was one of the juniors in the case (the other being Scrutton's great rival JA Hamilton) in Scrutton's lecture to the Cambridge Law students in 1920: (1923) 1 CLJ 6 at p 14.

[40] [1894] AC 687.

fed up with delays and unsatisfactory judges. It instigated a Court of Arbitration in 1892.

Mathew J persevered. In June 1894 Lord Coleridge died and his successor, Lord Russell of Killowen, was much more sympathetic to the idea of a Commercial List. The judges of the Queens Bench met in the autumn of 1894 and appointed a committee from amongst themselves to consider the creation of a special list for commercial causes. This was all to be done within the scope of the existing orders and rules of the Supreme Court then in force.

In February 1895 this committee produced a draft 'Notice concerning Commercial Causes' which was agreed to by all the judges of the Queens Bench. In 12 succinct paragraphs the Notice defined commercial causes, set out how pre-trial and trial procedures should be adopted for commercial cases, and identified Mathew J as the first Commercial Judge. Paragraph 3 of that Notice, from which the quotation in the title of this article comes, identified what was to become the key difference between the procedure for commercial cases and others tried in the Queen's Bench Division. It provided:

With respect to town commercial causes it is considered desirable, with a view to dispatch and the saving of expense, that all applications shall be made direct to the judge charged with commercial business and with respect to country commercial causes, applications may, by consent of the parties, be made to him in like manner.

In January 1897 the periodical *The Edinburgh Review* commented that '. . . for the first time in the history of English law, the commercial section of the people has a court solely for the purpose of settling the disputes which arise in the course of business.[41] A new series of reports of Commercial Cases was started by *The Times*. The editor was Mr Theobold Mathew. He wrote an introduction to the first volume of the reports, which explained the procedure adopted in interlocutory stages and at the trial of commercial cases. He made two particular points about the aim of the new procedure. The first was that if the legal advisers of the parties were willing to assist the court, then commercial disputes could be settled as promptly by a judge as by an arbitrator. Secondly, for this to be done it was necessary that the judge should be able to get a grip of the nature of the dispute between the parties at the earliest possible stage of the proceedings. If that could be achieved, then in many cases disputes could be settled. Mr Mathew commented: 'The grasp which the judge obtains of the case in chambers and the power which he consequently acquires to prevent the taking of steps which will not assist the court at the trial, have been found to be of extreme value in securing expedition.'

The 'Commercial List' was thus established. It became popularly known as the 'Commercial Court' although that title only became official when the Administration of Justice Act 1970 was passed. The new court was immediately

---

[41] Quoted in *Mathew's Practice of the Commercial Court* (2nd edn) at p 12.

successful. In the early years most of the cases involved shipping and marine insurance disputes, but a look at the Times Reports of Commercial Cases reveals that the court took commodities cases, banking disputes, intra-company disputes, and appeals from arbitrations. The procedures were quick and informal. Pleadings were often dispensed with altogether; and evidence was dealt with much more informally than in other courts. The barristers appearing in commercial cases in the years to 1914 included such giants of commercial law as TE Scrutton, JA Hamilton, FD MacKinnon, JR Atkin, and RA Wright.[42]

The similarity between the position in the late 19th century and the position in the early 21st century concerning commercial litigants is striking. The importance of having an efficient means of settling commercial disputes, the concerns about cost and delay in litigation, the anxiety for simplicity of procedure, and the need for a judge who would understand commercial practices and have a grip on the case from the outset were all present then. Today these all remain the key concerns and requirements of the commercial community for efficient dispute resolution.

The Commercial List was popular with the commercial community and it remained able to act swiftly and efficiently. In 1920 the average time from a summons to transfer a case to the Commercial List to trial was two months.[43] This popularity continued until the early 1950s. But by then the Commercial List seemed to have lost its impetus. In one case Devlin J remarked that the business of the list occupied so little time of the judge assigned to take the Commercial List that perhaps it was no longer useful.[44] In 1960 this apparent decline led Viscount Kilmuir, the Lord Chancellor, to set up a Commercial Court Users' Conference, to report on the views of the business community upon '...the decline in recent years of the business of the Commercial Court, and upon any reforms of the constitution, practice and procedure of the Court which might improve the service which it has long given to that community'.[45] The chairman was Mr Cyril Miller[46] and 21 industries and trade organizations were represented at the Conference.[47]

[42] The latter three had been Scrutton's pupils. See the Note on TE Scrutton in the 17th edn of *Scrutton on Charterparties* (1964), edited by Sir W McNair, Sir AA Mocatta, and MJ Mustill. The first two must have appeared before Scrutton LJ before he died in office, just short of his 78th birthday, in August 1934.

[43] This was the figure given by Scrutton LJ to the law undergraduates of Cambridge University in his address in November 1920, having sought the information from Bailhache J (then in charge of the Commercial List): (1923) I CLJ at p 17. At that time the Commercial List was very busy dealing with a spate of 'scuttling' cases after the collapse of the freight market following a boom in the immediate aftermath of the First World War. In those days a 'long' scuttling case was a week!

[44] *Peter Cassidy Seed Co Ltd v Osuustukkukauppa IL* [1957] 1 WLR 273 at 280.

[45] *Commercial Court Users' Conference Report,* Cmnd 1616 (February 1962) para 1.

[46] A partner in Thos R Miller & Son, managers of the UK Protection and Indemnity Association, then, as now, a leading P&I Club. He was a leading figure for many years in shipowners' protection and indemnity insurance and London arbitration.

[47] The legal profession was not specifically represented but Pearson LJ (as he then was) was chairman of a Legal Sub-Committee.

The Report of the Conference, which was published in February 1962, stated that its unanimous opinion was that '...the commercial community earnestly desires that the Commercial Court shall continue to be available for the adjudication of commercial disputes'.[48] The Conference did not think it would be justified in predicting expansion of the court's work, but it recommended reforms be adopted to arrest the decline in the court's use. The Report noted various trends which it thought might diminish commercial litigation in the future. These included, first, the growth of non-UK parties to litigation in the court, who, it was thought, preferred arbitration to litigation; secondly, the fact that there was already a large body of case law that had settled many areas of dispute, particularly in shipping law; thirdly, the commercial community's dislike of a public system of dispute resolution; and fourthly, '...and this is a very potent factor, the increasing cost and delays of litigation discourage business men from resorting to it'.[49]

The Report identified two particular defects in the procedure of commercial cases which are relevant to this article. The first was '...the casual treatment of the Summons to Transfer' a case from the ordinary Queen's Bench Division list to the Commercial List. The Report noted the lapse in the practice which was universal in the early days of the Commercial List. In those days counsel for the parties would attend the Commercial judge in chambers and explain to him in detail the nature of the case and the issues, so that the judge could give comprehensive directions (often dispensing with pleadings) '...to secure a trial at the earliest convenient date'. The Report noted that, nowadays, frequently only solicitors' clerks attended and the judge made pro-forma orders for pleadings and directions. The Report recommended that in future all Summons for Transfer should be attended by junior counsel, who should be in a position to tell the judge what the main issues were, thereby saving much time and expense.[50]

The second main defect noted by the Report was '...the prolixity of modern pleadings and the time which is consumed in their delivery'. The Report regretted the fact that the original conception of short 'Points of Claim' and 'Points of Defence' had been forgotten. It recommended that, except in cases of fraud and misrepresentation, pleadings should be '...avoided in the Commercial Court whenever possible and that far more use should be made than at present of trial on agreed statements of fact'.[51]

Following the report of the conference, the judge then in charge of the Commercial List, Megaw J, issued a Practice Direction in October 1962.[52] In it he stressed the need for brevity in Commercial Court pleadings. He directed that '...When pleadings are required...their object is to define the real issues and avoid surprise. If this object is kept in mind—and the court will have it in

---

[48] Para 7.   [49] Para 9.   [50] Paras 13 and 14.
[51] Para 17. This echoed the Report of the Legal Sub-Committee: see s C of its report at p 18 of Cmnd 1616.
[52] [1960] 1 WLR 1216.

mind—it ought to be possible to shorten and simplify the pleadings in many commercial cases, with a saving of time and cost'. The direction also stressed the need to treat the Summons to Transfer seriously, at which a full order for directions leading to the trial should be made.

In 1964 a new Rule of the Supreme Court was introduced which specifically governed commercial actions.[53] The new Rule permitted parties to start cases in the Commercial List; there was no need to seek leave to transfer them into the List. This had two consequences. First, there was an enormous expansion in the number of cases being handled by what became the Commercial Court from 1970.[54] This meant the number of judges nominated to hear Commercial cases had to increase and the number of Commercial judges sitting at one time increased from one to four by 1981.[55] Those sitting has subsequently increased to eight or, occasionally, nine. The second consequence was that it became impossible for the Commercial judge to have the same degree of control over individual cases as had formerly occurred. This may have been the seed of the problems which the most recent proposals for reform have attempted to tackle—which are essentially problems of success.

In the 1980s there was a huge increase in interlocutory hearings and trials which led to increasing delays, with consequent disquiet amongst the users of the Court. In 1985, a working party, under the chairmanship of Mr NA Phillips QC, (as he then was) was formed to consider possible improvements to the procedure of the Court, with the aim of reducing time spent at hearings and, thus, waiting times. It recommended important changes which have now become key elements of the Court's procedures. The first was that written arguments and summaries of issues should be more widely used. The second was a recommendation to change the Rules of Court to permit the exchange of statements of evidence of witnesses of fact before a trial, so as to cut down on the time spent in examination in chief. The third was to amend the Rules of Court so that a judge could order expert witnesses to meet before a trial to identify the relevant issues in dispute and to record them. The fourth affected the way trials were to be conducted by counsel.

---

[53] In 1964 a completely new set of Rules of the Supreme Court (RSC) was promulgated. The new rule that governed Commercial actions was Rule 72.

[54] The growth in business was also affected by two other developments. The first was the invention of the so-called *Mareva* injunction in 1975—see *Mareva Compania Naviera SA v Intenational Bulkcarriers SA* [1975] 2 Lloyd's Rep 509. The second was the growth in insurance and re-insurance litigation in the 1970s and 1980s. The latter culminated in the outburst of 'Lloyd's litigation' with which the Commercial Court had to cope following the dramatic collapse of many syndicates after a series of natural and man-made disasters in the late 1980s and early 1990s.

[55] In 1980, when Bingham J was appointed, the Queen's Bench judges nominated by the Lord Chancellor to sit in the Commercial Court (pursuant to s 3 of the Administration of Justice Act 1970, now s 6(2) of the Supreme Court Act 1981) were Mocatta, Kerr, Goff, Slynn, Parker, Lloyd, Mustill, Neill, Webster, and Bingham JJ. Sheen J was the Admiralty judge. Five of them (Goff, Slynn, Lloyd, Mustill, and Bingham JJ) subsequently became Law Lords. When not sitting in the Commercial Court, the judges would try criminal cases, sit in the Court of Appeal Criminal Division, in the Queen's Bench Division, or the Divisional Court. The same pattern continues today.

Opening speeches by a claimant's counsel would be replaced by short 'uncontentious' outlines by both parties, moving swiftly on to the evidence. Detailed argument would only take place after the conclusion of the evidence. Lastly, the Phillips Working Party recommended the production of a 'Commercial Court Guide' to help practitioners with the new procedures. This *'Guide'*, now called the 'Admiralty and Commercial Court Guide', is in its 7th edition, published in 2006. It has remained the 'Bible' of Commercial Court procedure.

The 'Phillips' Working Party recommendations settled the procedural framework for both interlocutory hearings and trials until the Long Trials Working Party reported in 2007. In the late 1990s the Civil Justice Reforms, spearheaded by Lord Woolf, proposed a totally new procedural code for civil cases in the High and County Court. This became the Common Procedure Rules, or 'CPR'. In some instances the current practices of the commercial court were adopted for use in civil cases generally. But the Commercial Court retained its own distinct approach, based upon the 'Phillips' reforms and as developed subsequently in the *Guide*.

And so to 2005. That year saw the dramatic collapse of two pieces of large-scale litigation in the Commercial Court. The first case was that of *Three Rivers District Council v Governor and Company of the Bank of England*—the so called *'BCCI'* case. The action had been brought against the Bank of England by the Liquidators of the collapsed Bank of Credit and Commerce International. Proceedings were issued in the Commercial Court in 1993, claiming £850 million for alleged 'misfeasance in public office' by senior bank officials and also for alleged breaches of European Community law.

The second piece of litigation consisted of a series of claims by the Equitable Life Assurance Company. Those arose as a result of the ruling of the House of Lords in 2000, in which it held that Equitable Life was obliged to meet 'Guaranteed Annuity Rates' in various personal pension contracts. The company did not have the resources to meet these requirements and it had had to take dramatic steps to survive. Following a report by Lord Penrose, which held that the company was the author of its own misfortune, Equitable Life launched claims against 15 ex-directors, alleging negligence in performing their duties. It claimed damages of £2 billion from them. The company also sued its former auditors, Ernst & Young, alleging that they had signed off its accounts without giving the company warnings of the problems that led to its subsequent financial crisis.

In the *BCCI* case, the Commercial judge struck out the whole claim.[56] The House of Lords subsequently held that the claim was arguable,[57] although on grounds which were not subsequently at the forefront of the liquidators' case.[58] In the *Equitable Life* case the Commercial judge[59] had struck out large parts of the case against the auditors, but the Court of Appeal had permitted the vast

---

[56] [1997] 3 All ER 558. The Commercial judge was Clarke J, now Clarke MR.
[57] [2003] 2 AC 1.   [58] See n 60 below.   [59] Langley J.

majority of the claim to be reinstated. The *BCCI* trial started in 2004. After 256 days of trial before Tomlinson J and a total of 13 years of litigation, the liquidators suddenly dropped their claim entirely, without withdrawing their allegations of dishonesty against the Governor of the day or senior Bank officials. Nor did the liquidates proffer any apology.[60] Tomlinson J had recognized during the trial itself that it had become a farce and that the litigation could damage the reputation of the English legal system. He decided that he was unable to stop the liquidators from carrying on.[61]

The trial of the Equitable Life's claims had started in April 2005. The company abandoned all its claims against its auditors in September 2005 and the cases against the ex-directors were subsequently quickly settled. Both those cases were very different and also most unusual. The particular factual circumstances that produced the claims are most unlikely ever to be repeated. But the dramatic collapse of both cases produced comments in the press which suggested that there was some fundamental flaw in the procedure or methods of the Commercial Court, and asking why it had permitted apparently 'hopeless' cases to be pursued for so long and at such cost.

In his Mansion House speech on 21 June 2006, the Governor of the Bank of England, Professor Mervyn King, made highly critical remarks about a legal system which he described as '. . . powerless to prevent a case so hopelessly misconceived [from] continuing for thirteen years' and leading to costs of over £100 million. He urged an examination of the whole system, including the adversarial nature of litigation.

These criticisms led the Judge in Charge of the Commercial Court at the time, David Steel J, to organize a symposium on Long Trials in the Commercial Court. Barristers, solicitors, users of the Commercial Court, judges, arbitrators, mediators, and academics were all invited to attend. Interested parties were urged to prepare papers in advance of the symposium, in which they could make any reasoned criticism and offer any suggestions they wished regarding the court's procedures for heavy and complex trials. Twenty-six papers were received before the symposium, which was held on 30 October 2006.[62] At the symposium itself five oral addresses were given and a wide ranging discussion took place.

---

[60] See the judgment of Tomlinson J on the question of costs: [2006] 5 Costs LR 714 at para 11. At para 23 of the same judgment, Tomlinson J remarked that the case presented to him by the liquidators had been markedly different from that which the House of Lords had permitted them to pursue.

[61] Ibid. Tomlinson J had decided to discuss the matter with the Lord Chief Justice, Lord Woolf, but he took full responsibility for the decision that he could not and would not intervene to try and persuade the liquidators to stop the 'farce'.

[62] It was attended by the Lord Chief Justice, Master of the Rolls, the Chancellor of the High Court, the President of the Queen's Bench Division, Lords Justices and judges of the Commercial Court, Technology and Construction Court, Chancery Division, and many barristers, solicitors, arbitrators, academics, and users of the Court, including a representative of the Governor of the Bank of England.

These press criticisms of the Commercial Court and the trenchant remarks of the Governor need to be put into the current economic context of the City of London and the UK generally. The general profile of the UK economy has changed beyond all recognition since the late 19th century, but commerce and financial services remain of vital importance. Financial services accounted for 10.1 per cent of UK GDP in 2007. The UK banking sector is the largest in Europe and the second largest in the world, with deposits of US$ 4.6 trillion at the end of 2005. The UK is the world's largest centre for cross-border banking and bank lending. London has offices, branches, or headquarters of almost every major international bank and financial institution in the world. London is by far the world's largest foreign exchange market with a daily turnover of 32 per cent of the global total. In April 2007 the daily turnover in London in the traditional foreign exchange market was US$3.2 trillion. London is the world's most important market place for over the counter derivatives, with 43 per cent of global trades. It had a 46 per cent share of global foreign equity trading in 2007. London is a leading centre for trading international bonds, particularly Euro-bonds.

The UK is also the world's leading market for international insurance, with UK worldwide premium income totalling £166.7 billion in 2005. The UK has the largest single share of marine insurance by premium income, with a 24 per cent share of the world total. It is the world leader in supplying services to the maritime community. Fifty per cent of the world tanker trading and between thirty and forty per cent of the dry cargo trading is brokered in London. Fifty per cent of the sale and purchase of the world's new second hand tonnage is arranged through London. It is the most important world centre for protection and indemnity insurance for shipowners and charterers. Lloyd's Register of Shipping is the second largest ships' classification society in the world, covering 19 per cent of the world's fleet. Financial services produced a trade surplus of £33.2 billion in 2007.[63]

It is not surprising therefore that the City is regarded as being one of the two top financial centres in the world, alongside New York. In 2003 the Lord Mayor stated, in his Mansion House speech, that the Bank of England held the view that the single most important factor contributing to London's position as a financial centre was the high standing of the country's judicial and legal system. There are no statistics to indicate what percentage of the vast quantity of financial and other commercial transactions carried out in London are stated to be governed by English law. But it must be likely that a great proportion of them are.

It is not surprising therefore that the UK professional services sector, which includes accountancy, legal services, and management consultancy, has become so important. In 2006/7 London had four of the six largest legal companies in the world (by fee income). At present over 200 foreign law firms have offices in

---

[63] All the figures in these paras are taken from a report of the International Financial Services London's report on International Financial Markets in the UK dated 12 May 2008. See: <http://www.IFSL.ORG.UK/RESEARCH>.

London. Legal services alone contributed £14.9 billion to the UK's GDP in 2004. International law firms based in London account for nearly 50 per cent of the UK law firms' gross fees. These figures suggest strongly that the UK, and London in particular, remains not only one of the two top financial centres of the world, but is also arguably the top legal marketplace in the world.

London has no automatic right to be a top financial centre of the world; and neither do English commercial law or the English court system have any right to continue to be pre-eminent as arbiters of commercial disputes. Business litigants can choose any law and any forum to resolve their disputes. There is active competition. New York has always been a competitor, but there are others. The Chief Justice of Delaware noted, in a speech given in 2002 in London, that the Superior Court of Delaware had in recent years become a popular national forum for the resolution of '. . . billions of dollars of claims in major insurance coverage disputes [which] . . . bring to the Superior Court . . . insurers from across the United States and Europe, including some . . . in London'. At the end of December 2004, after China acceded to the World Trade Organization (WTO), the Supreme Peoples Court of China introduced a range of measures to enhance the capacity of courts throughout China to try foreign-related commercial cases. The aim of the measures was to prevent '. . . the loss of foreign related commercial cases . . . and ceaselessly upgrading capabilities in trying foreign related commercial cases'.[64] A quick check on the internet demonstrates how many 'Commercial Courts' have been set up throughout the world, all anxious to become centres of business dispute resolution. The recently established commercial courts in Dubai and Qatar and the Caribbean are only the most notable examples. Bermuda has had a commercial court for some time. Paris, Frankfurt, Bombay, Singapore, and the new, dedicated, commercial centre at Wuhan in China are all competitors for commercial litigation. Each will say that its procedure is quicker, cheaper and more reliable than others. London therefore cannot be complacent.

That is the commercial background to the discussion at the symposium on 30 October 2006. The general view of the meeting, despite the comments of the Governor, was that the adversarial method of conducting commercial litigation should be retained. But many participants stated that there should be major modifications in the way the adversarial method was used for commercial litigation, both during the pre-trial period and the trial itself. Many also sounded a note of caution about rushing into 'reforms', doubtless recalling Burke's dictum that '. . . to innovate is not to reform'.[65] There was scepticism that it would be possible to make noticeable reductions in the costs of commercial litigation.

Following the Symposium, David Steel J decided to set up a Working Party under the auspices of the Commercial Court Users' Committee. He asked the

---

[64] Notice No 265 of 2004 of The Supreme People's Court of China, effective 29 December 2004.
[65] Letter to a Noble Lord, 1798.

present writer to chair it. This group became known as the 'Commercial Court Long Trials Working Party'. It had nine members: another Commercial Court judge, Gloster J; three barristers, one of whom acted as secretary to the Working Party;[66] litigation partners from the City solicitors firms of Clifford Chance and Lovells;[67] and representatives of two companies[68] who had been users of the Commercial Court and who had recently been involved in heavy litigation in the court. The Working Party met between January and October 2007. It reported to the Commercial Court Users Committee in November 2007. Its report was published in December 2007.[69] The recommendations put forward by the Working Party are being put into practice by the Commercial Court for a trial period from February 2008 until the end of November 2008. There will then be a further review to see whether those procedures should be adopted in full, modified or rejected.

The first task of the Working Party was to set itself terms of reference within which it could operate. Initially it anticipated confining its work to heavy and complex cases and the terms of reference were framed accordingly.[70] In fact its recommendations apply to almost all cases heard in the Commercial Court. The Working Party then considered some basic premises on which Commercial Court procedure had always been based. First, was the Governor right to question whether the adversarial method of conducting litigation in the Commercial Court was suitable for heavy and complex cases? The group decided that it would be too revolutionary to change the system, but it worked properly in heavy cases only if kept under strict control. Secondly, were there any irremediable problems in conducting trials of heavy and complex cases in the Commercial Court? The answer was 'no', although heroic surgery might be needed in various areas of procedure. Thirdly, were the basic elements of preparation of a case for trial, that is stating a case in writing; the disclosure of relevant documents (whether electronic or in hard copy); the exchange of witness statements; and the exchange of experts' reports, the right framework for long and complex cases? The Working Party concluded that this framework should remain. Lastly, was any attempt at 'reform' doomed to failure? The Working Party was conscious of the fact that approximately 70 per cent of all cases in the Commercial Court settle before the start of a trial. Some commentators had said that the Woolf civil justice reforms

---

[66] Robin Knowles QC, CBE, the immediate past Chairman of the Commercial Bar Association, Alec Heydon and Alison Padfield, who acted as secretary.

[67] Respectively, Simon Davis, the President of the London Solicitors Litigation Association; and Graham Huntley, the immediate past President of the same association.

[68] Victoria Cochrane, a director of Ernst & Young; and Stephen Pearson, Head of Litigation at the Royal Bank of Scotland Group.

[69] *Report and Recommendations of the Commercial Court Long Trials Working Party*, December 2007.

[70] 'The Commercial Court Long Trials Working Party will consider all aspects concerning the management of heavy and complex cases in the Commercial Court and report and make recommendations to the Commercial Court Users' Committee, including, if necessary, recommendations for changes in practice and/or to the Admiralty and Commercial Courts Guide (7th Edition, 2006)'.

led to increased costs at the interlocutory stages of a case, producing so-called 'front loading' of costs. The Working Party appreciated that it must try to avoid making changes in procedures which might look attractive but could have the unintended consequence of an even greater 'front loading' of costs.

With these considerations in mind, the Working Party developed a number of essential principles to guide its recommendations for changes in procedure that we might make.[71] They were aimed specifically at heavy and complex cases although they must apply to all types of litigation in the commercial court. They are:

(i) the existing rule that a commercial court Judge is in charge of all preparatory procedures must remain. Furthermore the judge must be able to keep firm control over all the procedure before trial and during the trial itself;

(ii) the procedure must be kept as simple as a heavy and complex case will allow;

(iii) clients, whose litigation it is, must be kept informed and given responsibility for the litigation being conducted in their names;

(iv) costs have to be kept under control;

(v) as far as possible, bad claims or defences must be recognized as such as early as possible and rejected;

(vi) parties must always be encouraged to compromise their disputes, using alternative dispute resolution (ADR) or other means, including the court's assistance;

(vii) technology should be used as much as possible to facilitate procedures before and at the trial, whilst keeping costs of using at as low as practicable;

(viii) where possible and appropriate, the appellate stages in the litigation (especially those concerned with preliminary issues or procedural points), must be kept consistent with the aim of the efficient conduct of the litigation as a whole.

The Working Party also considered it imperative that any recommendations it made must be capable of being implemented without the need for either primary legislation or any changes to the existing Civil Procedure Rules (CPR). If legislation or rule changes of any kind were needed, it would involve delay and, possibly, opposition from others outside the Commercial Court. It was therefore resolved that, if at all possible, any recommendations for change must be within the existing structure of legislation and Court Rules. In this regard the Working Party was following the precedent set by the Queen's Bench judges in 1894.

The Working Party reminded itself that the CPR[72] already gives judges wide powers with regard to case management and these can be used for heavy and complex trials. The Admiralty & Commercial Court Guide also often provides

---

[71] S B.2, para 28, pp 15–16. [72] In particular CPR Pt 1.4(2) and Pt 3.1.

solutions to problems that arise in such cases. But it concluded, sadly, that in some cases either the parties or the judge involved or both were not enforcing provisions of the CPR or the *Guide* with sufficient rigour. The Working Party suggested that there would have to be a re-education programme for both practitioners and the Commercial Court judges to remind them of the procedures and powers that were already in place as well as introducing them to any recommendations it made.

The Working Party decided that the dangers of high costs, delay, and obfuscation of issues were present in all stages of the litigation process. Inevitably, therefore, it considered recommendations concerning the stages of setting out the parties' cases; discovery; the production of witness statements; experts' reports; and lastly, the management of the case to the trial of the dispute if it had not been settled beforehand.

On the first of these, as the Working Party Report states, 'the length and complexity of statements of case in even "average" cases in the Commercial Court, let alone heavy and complex cases, has increased, is increasing and ought to be diminished. The prolixity of Statements of Case means that they become virtually unreadable.'[73] One reason for the present inordinately long pleadings is undoubtedly the wording of the current CPR, Part 16.4(1)(a), which provides that 'Particulars of Claim *must include* a concise statement of the facts on which the claimant relies'. There is no longer a positive statement in the CPR that evidence should not be pleaded, in contrast to the injunction in the old Rules of the Supreme Court, Order 18 Rule 7(1).[74] Although the *Guide* urges conciseness,[75] there is bound to be a difference in attitude by the pleader who formerly had to draft 'Points of Claim' and who now has to provide the more expansive sounding 'Particulars of Claim', which invites elaboration.

The Working Party's solution was to recommend a general limit of 25 pages for all pleadings, subject to permission being granted if a judge was convinced that a longer pleading was essential.[76] The present requirement in the *Guide*[77] that there should be a short summary for all pleadings over 25 pages should be enforced rigorously.

The next recommendation is at the heart of the Working Party's proposals. It is the creation of a new style, judicially settled, 'List of Issues'. The view of the

[73] S D.1, para 44 of the Report. This is not a new phenomenon. As already noted, court users complained in the 1890s and so did the Commercial Court Users' Conference in 1960–2. In a case in the early 1990s, Mr Peregrine Simon QC, now Simon J, told a Commercial judge that the pleadings in the case, when laid end to end, were longer than all the novels of Sir Walter Scott—and considerably less interesting.

[74] That stipulated that 'every pleading must contain, and contain only, a statement in a summary form of the material facts o which the party pleading relies for his claim or defence, as the case may be, but not the evidence by which those facts are to be proved, and the statement must be as brief as the nature of the case admits'.

[75] Para C1.1(a): 'Particulars of Claim, the defence and any reply must be…as brief and concise as possible'.

[76] Report, S D.2, para 50.   [77] Para C1.4.

Working Party was that this document should become the keystone to the proper management of all Commercial Court cases, but especially of heavy and complex cases. The present Commercial Court Guide[78] provides that the parties should produce a List of Issues prior to the first Case Management Conference. In the view of the Working Party most examples of the present List are not much use to the judge, being either too short or far too detailed. The Working Party proposed that the parties produce a draft List of Issues, but is settled by the court at the first Case Management Conference, with the active participation of the judge. It should, in general, be no more than ten pages long. Once it has been produced it will be a court document, which can be amended, with the judge's approval, as the case progresses.[79] It will be used to define the scope of disclosure, to identify the topics that can be covered in statements of factual witness, and to define the areas to be covered in experts' reports.

The Working Party contemplated that once the List of Issues has been produced, the pleadings will retain only secondary importance. They should only be referred to if there is a doubt about the accuracy of the List of Issues or in order to confirm a party's position with respect to a particular issue. Attempts by parties to take 'pleading points' at a trial must be actively discouraged. A party should only be refused permission to raise a point at a trial if its opponent can demonstrate that it is genuinely prejudiced by the lack of reference in the List of Issues to the point concerned.

Participants in the symposium frequently identified disclosure as being one of the most expensive and time consuming aspects of heavy litigation. The burden of disclosure has grown hugely now that tape recordings of telephone conversations, email, and electronic storage of information are almost universally used in all forms of commerce. The Working Party's view was that all too frequently large numbers of files are disclosed, produced at the trial, and then ignored. This is wasteful, costly, and should be impermissible. The Working Party considered whether the common law tradition of 'disclosure' of relevant documents should be retained but decided it must. It is a hallmark of the common law's procedure. However, it also concluded that the present discovery procedure is a blunt instrument; a more surgical approach was needed. This applies to all types of case.

The Working Party therefore recommended that the present powers contained in the CPR[80] to make appropriate special orders as to the scope of disclosure should be used more often by the court, doing so by reference to the List of Issues. It is proposed that the claimant will state succinctly those issues in the List of Issues for which it contends that either 'standard' or another level of disclosure is needed and why. The defendant will respond to this. If there are disputes about the scope of discovery, then the judge must deal with it in court. However, the approach should be always that discovery, even standard discovery, must be justified.

---

[78] Para D.6.1.   [79] Report, S D.4, para 54.   [80] Pts 31.5 and 31.12.

The Working Party then turned its attention to witness statements. Production of them is labour-intensive and thus very expensive. Because these documents are almost invariably drafted by lawyers, they read more like pleadings or a written argument. Frequently they include long recitations from documents that a party wishes to have in evidence. The collective experience of the Working Party was that witness statements, particularly in heavy cases, frequently fail to concentrate solely on the evidence that the witness concerned can give and they show blatant disregard for the guidance given in the CPR and the *Guide*.[81] Rarely do they confine themselves to a witness's statement of what he did, or saw, or read or understood from a document with which he was personally concerned.

The Working Party therefore sought to give additional emphasis to the existing framework and guidance of the CPR and the *Guide* and so recommended that its proposals should apply to all Commercial Court cases. It proposed that witness statements must identify, by reference to the List of Issues, the particular topics on which that witness would give evidence. If necessary the court should give directions that witness statements will be kept within a certain length.[82] Where possible, references to documents should be hyperlinked.[83]

The Working Party also concentrated on expert evidence, which was another area identified in the symposium as being particularly expensive and time-consuming. The Working Party concluded that there was often an insufficiently clear identification of the precise areas that should be covered by the experts. Frequently, particularly if the expert reports were served simultaneously, they did not cover the same ground, but, in order to guard against an accusation of missing something, the reports ventured way beyond the key expert areas in dispute. The Working Party's proposed solution was to use the List of Issues as the tool for defining, at a Case Management Conference, the precise areas that should be covered by the experts. These will have to be approved by the judge. Prolixity could be curbed by setting limits to the length of the reports.

Often the subject matter of experts' reports is recondite—so that not even a Commercial judge knows much about it. In the past counsel opening a case has had to try and educate a judge on such exotic subjects as metallurgy, naval architecture, actuarial techniques, or foreign bond markets. But it is not the best method of instruction for counsel, who is rarely an expert on such topics, to attempt to teach expert areas to the judge by way of submission. A more efficient method, adopted recently by the House of Lords in a patent case and used in a recent Commercial Court trial concerning methods of financial modelling for the purposes of a securitization, is to have a pre-hearing 'teach in' on the relevant areas of expertise. In the Commercial Court trial this was given by the experts

---

[81] In particular, CPR Pts 32.4, 32.5, 32.8 and the Practice Direction, para 18. See also the *Guide*, particularly para H.1.1.

[82] A court already has this power under the CPR, in furtherance of the 'overriding objective': CPR 3.1(2)(m).

[83] Recommendations at S F.2, para 75 of the Report.

themselves. Counsel had to sit silently whilst the experts explained matters to the judge and answered his questions. It was generally agreed that this was a much more effective and economical way of introducing technical subjects to the judge.[84]

Whilst all these new proposals should assist in cutting costs and making litigation more efficient, they will not get anywhere unless the judges retain a firm grip on the issues of a case during the interlocutory stages. As was recognized by our Victorian predecessors, (although they would have been appalled at the expression), 'Case Management' is even more important than ever. The Working Party emphasized in particular that the judges must be prepared to use case management to weed out the hopeless cases or defences—or any part of them. It thought there was much to recommend the approach of the late Lord Hobhouse of Woodborough in his dissenting speech in the House of Lords in the Bank of England's application to strike out the liquidators' case in the *BCCI* action. In characteristically firm terms he noted that it is particularly the cases where there would be a long and complex trial that most strongly cry out for the exclusion of anything that is unnecessary for the achievement of a just outcome for the parties.[85]

The Working Party was urged by some to recommend a change in the test for summary judgment on a claim or for striking out claims or defences in heavy and complex cases.[86] Another point made was that appellate courts seemed too ready to interfere with the Commercial judge's view on applications for summary judgment or to strike out a claim or defence. It was observed that interlocutory appeals on summary judgment or striking out applications had to wait many months before they could be heard by the Court of Appeal and in the meantime the case was put in limbo.

The Working Party decided that it could not make any recommendation that might involve a change in the substantive or procedural law in this area. But it was anxious that Commercial Court judges should be as robust and flexible as the present law would allow. Therefore it recommended three ways to deal with these issues. First, the Commercial judge should be more active in identifying particular issues which might be suitable for summary judgment or strike out applications, using the new List of Issues to do so. Secondly, a more flexible approach on costs could be taken. Under the present CPR costs regime, if a striking out application is unsuccessful, the costs of the exercise will generally be awarded to the party that has staved off the strike out. The Working Party recommended that the court should be more flexible in dealing with costs on this type

---

[84] The case subsequently settled just before final oral submissions were to be made.

[85] *Three Rivers District Council v The Governor and Company of the Bank of England (No 3)* [2003] 2 AC1, at para 156.

[86] At present the CPR are clear. The claim or defence must have no reasonable prospect of success. See CPR Pt 24.2 and 24 PD for summary judgment and CPR 3.4(2) for striking out. It is now clearly established in the ECtHR that striking out a claim is not a breach of Art 6(1) of the ECHR if an essential element of the cause of action for a claim under domestic law is missing from the statement of case: *Z v United Kingdom* [2003] 24 EHRR 3.

of application. In the pre-CPR days if an application for summary judgment was unsuccessful, the order for costs was usually 'costs in case', particularly if it were shown that parts of a defence were bad or the defence as a whole barely sustainable. Why should that more flexible approach not be adopted again?[87]

Lastly, it was recommended that the judge in charge of the Commercial Court should liaise with the Lord Justice who oversees the progress of Commercial appeals. The hope is that heavy and complex cases that are likely to produce interlocutory appeals can be identified early. Then, if possible, a Lord Justice with Commercial Court experience can be identified to keep continuity in the appellate team hearing appeals in that case and also ensure some expedition of hearings.[88]

There are three further areas of the recommendations of the Working Party that are worth emphasizing in this chapter. The first is the issue of management of the trial itself. The Working Party concluded that if its proposals on the pre-trial stages were dealt with robustly by the Commercial judges, then trials ought to be shorter and less expensive. But it also made positive recommendations about the trial process. The first proposal was that there should be strict limits on the length of trials, which should be no more than 13 weeks, save in exceptional cases.[89] Secondly, the judge and the parties should be ready to be flexible about sitting times. Thirdly, the Working Party also proposed that there should be much more use of the electronic presentation of evidence in court, because experience has shown that this saves time (and so money) in trials.[90] It also recommended the imposition of limits on opening written and oral submissions and time limits for the cross examination of witnesses in appropriate cases.[91] Lastly, it recommended that judges should make full use of their powers to decide the order in which issues are taken and to decide certain issues before moving on to others.[92]

The second topic is that of costs. The costs of large scale litigation is enormous, although hopefully none will ever approach the £100 million costs figure mentioned by the Governor of the Bank of England in relation to the *BCCI* case. The conclusion of the Working Party was that the present costs regime is generally successful in discouraging vexatious litigation or the prosecution of doubtful claims or defences in commercial cases.[93] It considered whether a more general

---

[87] Working Party recommendations H.3 para 98.

[88] Ibid.   [89] Recommendations at K.18 para 159 (b).

[90] In two recent trials all the pleadings, witness statements, trial bundles, and transcripts were prepared in electronic form. They were kept on one external hard drive which enabled the judge to work on documents without bundles in his room or even at home! Evidence was presented on screen in court.

[91] The court has power to do this under the 'case management powers' set out at CPR Pt 3.1(2) (m), which provides that the court may '…take any other step or make any other order for the purposes of managing the case and furthering the overriding objective'. In the *BCCI* case itself, Tomlinson J imposed a time limit on the cross examination of the Bank's witnesses, which was upheld by the Court of Appeal: *Thee Rivers DC v Bank of England (Restriction on Cross Examination)* [2005] EWCA 889.

[92] See CPR Pt 3.1(2)(i), (j), (k), and (l).

[93] See Report, S J.1, para 112.

use of the power to cap costs could be used to control costs in heavy commercial cases.[94] Cost capping is most useful where one party has much greater funds available to spend on litigation than the other and engages in expensive procedures and incurs large costs as a means of forcing the other party into submission. But in commercial litigation, where usually the parties have reasonably similar funds available, any attempt to use cost capping procedures would be likely to produce 'satellite' litigation, which would only increase costs. However, the Working Party did make two recommendations on costs. First, Commercial judges should use more generally the power to demand that the parties provide it with cost estimates.[95] Secondly, Commercial judges should make greater use of their powers to assess costs summarily for all hearings other than trials. For many users of the court, speed and certainty in ascertaining the amount of costs to be received by the winning party is almost as important as the amount of costs awarded, within reason.[96]

The last topic of the Working Party's report worth emphasizing is what the Working Party called 'Client Accountability and Responsibility for Litigation'.[97] The Working Party, in particular the members who have been recent users of the court, concluded that a major danger of heavy and complex litigation is that it can run out of the control of the senior management of one or more of the parties to it. Hard pressed and busy senior management may be tempted to leave complicated legal disputes to in-house legal teams or the independent lawyers hired for the case. For example, procedural documents, such as Statements of Case, are often so long, complex, and expressed in stylized, if not rebarbative, language so as to make them impenetrable for non-lawyers. It is difficult to explain the intricacies of interlocutory procedures easily to the layman. In the lawyers' zeal for the chase, the senior management may not have been asked to consider ADR or other means of dispute resolution. All this makes it more difficult for senior management to be accountable for the litigation that is being carried on in its name and for which it is in turn responsible to shareholders and employees.

The Working Party made two recommendations. First, lawyers must ensure that senior management is able to follow what is going on in cases so it can effectively exercise its ultimate responsibility to control the litigation. The emphasis on shorter pleadings and the introduction of the concise List of Issues should help re-engage senior management's attention on the essential points in dispute. The Working Party also recommended that representatives of the parties should have to sign fresh statements of truth shortly before a trial verifying the statements

---

[94] The courts' power to impose 'cost capping orders' derives from CPR Pt 3.1(2)(m). 'Cost capping' orders, although they might seem admirable in theory, present great practical problems, as Buxton LJ observed in *Willis v Nicholson* [2007] EWCA Civ 199, para 10.

[95] See CPR Pt 3.1(2)(ll) and para 6.3 of the Costs Practice Direction, supplementing CPR Pts 43 and 44.

[96] Report: Costs recommendations: S J.7, para 124.

[97] See S L of the Report, paras 160–162.

of case. It proposed further steps to ensure senior management has actively considered ADR. Lastly, it emphasized that the court has the power to require senior representatives of parties to be present in court, or in contact by video link.[98] This power should be used if there are to be discussions between the judge and parties on the conduct of the case, or, in appropriate cases, its merits.[99]

What will be the consequences of these proposals? The most obvious, which the Working Party recognized, is that it will involve the judges in more work, because of their more active participation in case management. Some participants in the symposium suggested that Commercial judges be confined to hearing commercial cases so that a 'docket system' could be developed by the Court. The Working Party did not recommend that course. The Commercial judges believe, rightly or wrongly, that it is better for the Court and the system generally if they continue to deal with cases in other areas of the law, particularly criminal law. The Working Party concluded that the needs of heavy and complex cases can be met by the existing procedures of appointing a 'two-judge team' if the arrangements are carefully handled. It emphasized, however, that sufficient judicial resources must be provided to enable the judges to deal efficiently with cases in the Commercial Court. If the resources are not provided it will lead to further criticism of the Court[100] and it would undermine the reputation of the City of London to the extent that it could no longer rely on the backing of a specialist judiciary to deal with commercial litigation.

At the end of the report of the Working Party there is a Postscript by its Chairman. It notes that the Report takes counsel, solicitors, and experts to task, complaining that pleadings, witness statements, experts reports, and written submissions are all too long and insisting that they should be made shorter. In return it had been pointed out that judgments have got longer and perhaps they too should be shorter. No one could dissent from that view. Often, like Pascal's famous letter, the reason the judgment is longer is because the judge has not had enough time to write a shorter one. Perhaps the judges could learn from their French colleagues, who are masters of the short judgment. However, one hopes that judges whose judgments are regarded as too long by the parties (or the Court of Appeal) do not suffer a 21st century version of the fate of a litigant in 1595, as reported in *Mylward v Weldon*.[101] The unfortunate man produced a pleading of 120 pages, which The Lord Keeper deemed could have been 'well contrived' in 16 pages. The miscreant was fined and led around the courts at Westminster Hall with the offending pleading hung around his neck like the proverbial albatross,

---

[98] CPR Pt 3.1(2)(c).

[99] Client Accountability and Responsibility: Recommendations: L.2, para 162.

[100] In the early 1990s, when the Commercial Court was inundated with litigation arising from problems at Lloyd's, there was widespread criticism because of insufficient judges and the delays in trials that this caused.

[101] (1596) Tothill's Reports p 102.

so that he could be exhibited, as an example, to the members of the Bar appearing before the courts.

The Commercial Court was founded in 1895 because the British business community, particularly that of the City of London, demanded a specialist court to decide its commercial disputes as quickly and cheaply as possible. The City of London was predominant then and English law was unquestionably the predominant law of commerce across the world. The resurgence of London as a world financial centre, particularly since the 'Big Bang' in 1986 and the continued widespread use of English law internationally for commercial transactions[102] underline the fact that London still needs a Commercial Court to decide disputes that arise out of '. . . the ordinary transactions of merchants and traders'.[103]

The Commercial Court has always recognized that its procedure must attempt to meet the needs of commercial litigants. Since 1895 the Court has tried to fashion its procedure accordingly. The Long Trials Working Party's recommendations were made in the hope that the aims of the Court's founders that commercial disputes be handled '. . . with a view to dispatch and the saving of expense . . .' can continue to be met in the face of the new challenges of the 21st century. The proposals will not succeed unless the judges, lawyers, and experts are prepared for a cultural change. The judges must lead. The reputation of the Commercial Court and therefore the position of London as a world centre for commercial dispute resolution is at stake.

---

[102] The Commercial Court statistics have consistently shown for about ten years that in 80% of its cases, at least one of the parties is a non-UK entity. In 50% of its cases all the parties are non-UK entities.

[103] This was part of the original definition of a 'commercial cause' as set out in the Notice of the Queen's Bench Division issued in February 1895.

2

Lord Bingham and Three Continuing Remedial Controversies

Andrew Burrows

1. Introduction

Lord Bingham indisputably ranks as one of the greatest judges of modern times. This is not merely because he has held the positions of Master of the Rolls, Lord Chief Justice, and Senior Law Lord. It is rather that, throughout his judicial career, he has produced numerous outstanding judgments across a vast array of different areas. These have ranged from commercial law (his first love) through criminal law and procedure to interpretation of the Human Rights Act 1998 in which he has spearheaded the approach of the House of Lords to what, by any standards, is a novel and challenging piece of legislation. Principled common sense shines through his many judgments as does their clarity and their succinct, and yet comprehensive, analysis of past decisions. This makes them a pleasure to read. One can only wonder at the workload required to produce such a steady flow of high quality reasoning.

Within the area of contract and commercial law, and wearing my hat as a teacher of these subjects, one thinks immediately of his judgments in the Court of Appeal in the following cases: *Blackpool and Fylde Aero Club Ltd v Blackpool Borough Council*[1] on offer and acceptance; *Watts v Morrow*[2] on mental distress damages in contract; *Lauritzen AS v Wijsmuller BV, The Super Servant Two*[3] on self-induced frustration; and, most famously, *Interfoto Picture Library Ltd v Stiletto Visual Programs Ltd*[4] on the non-incorporation of an onerous contract term. Then in the House of Lords we have had *Director General of Fair Trading v First National Bank plc*[5] on the Unfair Terms in Consumer Contracts Regulations; and *Homburg Houtimport BV v Agrosin Private Ltd, The Starsin*[6] on construction of a contract in the context of a contract for the carriage of goods by

---

[1] [1990] 1 WLR 1195.
[2] [1991] 1 WLR 1421.
[3] [1990] 1 Lloyd's Rep 1.
[4] [1989] QB 433.
[5] [2001] UKHL 52, [2002] 1 AC 481.
[6] [2003] UKHL 12, [2004] 1 AC 715.

sea, the 'identity of carrier' problem, and the applicability to a third party actual performing carrier of the Hague rules.

With all those decisions and many more, I agree fully with what Lord Bingham said and decided. For legal academics, however, it is the controversial aspects of judicial reasoning that tend to provoke the greatest interest and trigger the inspiration to publish one's own views. In this chapter, and by way of tribute to a great judge, I therefore wish to focus on three continuing controversies in our law on remedies which are neatly reflected in three much-discussed judgments of Lord Bingham, one at first instance, one in the Court of Appeal, and one in the House of Lords.

The three controversies are, first, when does the law create a trust to reverse an unjust enrichment?; secondly, what is the basis of '*Wrotham Park* damages'?; and, thirdly, what is the date for assessing damages for breach of contract? Central to these three questions are, respectively, Bingham J's judgment in *Neste Oy v Lloyds Bank plc*;[7] Sir Thomas Bingham MR's judgment in *Jaggard v Sawyer*;[8] and Lord Bingham of Cornhill's dissenting speech in *Golden Strait Corporation v Nippon Yusen Kubishika Kaisha, The Golden Victory*.[9]

2. Trusts to Reverse Unjust Enrichment: *Neste Oy v Lloyds Bank plc*

In this case, the claimants were shipowners. From time to time the claimants employed Peckston Shipping Ltd (PSL) as their agent to discharge their liabilities in respect of jetty, pilotage, berth fees and the like when their ships entered a UK port. PSL was also paid an agency fee. In January and February 1980, the claimants paid money in advance into PSL's bank account at Lloyd's for liabilities that they anticipated PSL would discharge on their behalf. But PSL was in financial difficulty and, on the appointment of a receiver by Lloyd's Bank, that bank sought to set off PSL's debts owed to it against the accounts in credit.

The claimants argued that the unspent monies it had paid in advance to PSL could not be used in the set-off by the bank because they were held on trust for the claimants by PSL. Of the six payments made some had been used to discharge liabilities. However, there was an overall balance of £58,872. Moreover no part of the sixth and last payment had been used to pay off the claimants' liabilities and that last payment had been made after PSL's resolution to cease trading.

Bingham J held that, looking at the claimants' and PSL's intentions, there was no express or *Quistclose* trust[10] in relation to any of the payments. They were not to be kept separate from the agent's other funds; and that no trust was intended

[7] [1983] 2 Lloyd's Rep 658.   [8] [1995] 1 WLR 269.
[9] [2007] UKHL 12, [2007] 2 WLR 691.
[10] Named after *Barclays Bank Ltd v Quistclose Investments Ltd* [1970] AC 567.

was further supported by the fact that often the agent would be reimbursed from those funds having already discharged the claimants' liabilities. A debtor-creditor relationship was what was intended, therefore, and not the creation of a trust.

However, as regards the sixth payment there was held to be a *constructive* trust. This was essentially because that payment was received by PSL after PSL's resolution to cease trading. It was therefore received at a time when there was bound to be a total failure of consideration as PSL well knew. In Bingham J's words, 'It would have seemed little short of sharp practice for PSR to take any benefit from the payment, and it would have seemed contrary to any ordinary notion of fairness that the general body of creditors should profit from the accident of a payment made at a time when there was bound to be a total failure of consideration.... [A]t the time of its receipt PSL could not in good conscience retain this payment and...accordingly a constructive trust is to be inferred.'[11]

The importance of this decision in the broader picture of the law (and it is, of course, the job of the academic to provide that perspective) is, it is submitted, that it provides a relatively rare example of a constructive trust being imposed to reverse an unjust enrichment. The trust here was not based on the parties' intentions. Nor was it imposed because PSL had committed a tort or breach of contract or other civil wrong. Rather it was imposed to prevent PSL (and hence its general body of creditors) being enriched at the claimants' expense in a situation where that enrichment was unjust; and the injustice in play was that, unknown to the claimants, but known to PSL, there would inevitably be a total failure of consideration in respect of the payment.

Huge strides forward in understanding the recently discovered law of unjust enrichment (or law of restitution) have been made in the 25 years since Bingham J's judgment. However, proprietary restitution remains a topic shrouded in difficulty. Normally, of course, the cause of action of unjust enrichment triggers *personal* rights and remedies only. So on the facts of this case it is indisputable that, as regards the sixth payment, the claimants had a personal right to restitution enforceable in an action for money paid for a consideration that had totally failed. They had paid the money for services to be rendered by PSL which, in the event, PSL did not render. Similarly, it is indisputable that the claimants had an action for damages against PSL for breach of contract in failing to perform the requested services. However, neither a personal restitutionary remedy nor a claim for contractual damages would have afforded the claimants any worthwhile remedy given PSL's insolvency. Those claims would simply have ranked alongside all other claims by unsecured creditors. What the claimants wanted and needed was the recognition of a proprietary right that would enable them to withdraw 'their' assets from the pool of PSL's assets available for distribution among PSL's creditors. Hence their argument, accepted by Bingham J as regards the sixth payment, that that payment was held by PSL on constructive trust for the claimants.

---

[11] [1983] 2 Lloyd's Rep 658, 666.

This was a controversial decision at the time it was given and has remained so ever since. Even today we cannot be sure of its exact status. In general, the decision has tended to be distinguished in subsequent cases.[12] Yet the decision has not been overruled and, for at least three reasons—in addition to the stature of the judge—its long-term fate is unlikely to lie in being overruled.

First, *Neste Oy* lines up alongside the crucially important earlier case of *Chase Manhattan Bank NA v Israel-British Bank (London) Ltd*[13] in which a constructive trust was imposed in respect of a mistaken payment. There the claimant bank by a clerical error mistakenly made two payments of some £2 million, instead of one, to the defendant. Goulding J held that the defendant, now insolvent, held the second payment on constructive trust for the claimant. Although the status of this decision too is not free from doubt, the major criticism of it—in controversial *obiter dicta* of Lord Browne-Wilkinson in *Westdeutsche Landesbank Girozentrale v Islington London BC*[14]—suggests that, had the defendant known of the mistake, the finding of a constructive trust would probably have been unimpeachable. Given Bingham J's emphasis on the defendant's knowledge, one can argue that *Neste Oy* is strengthened rather than diminished by Lord Browne-Wilkinson's *obiter dicta*.[15]

Secondly, *Neste Oy* has recently been directly applied in *Re Farepak Food and Gifts Ltd*.[16] A company, subsequently in administration, had been operating a Christmas savings scheme. Under this, customers paid money month by month to the company's agents so that by November/December enough would have been accumulated to buy Christmas gifts. In October 2006 the directors decided to cease trading and instructed their agents to stop collecting payments. Some money kept coming in after that date and the question was whether that money was held by the company on trust for the customers. It was held by Mann J that there was no *Quistclose* trust because the agents and the company had never been obliged to keep the monies collected separate from other funds. Rather the parties' intentions were that these were contractual payments. Nevertheless it was held that, in principle, a constructive trust should be imposed applying *Neste Oy* because the monies had been received after Farepak had decided to cease trading so that the contracts could not be fulfilled. However, before there could be a

---

[12] See, e.g., *Re Goldcorp Exchange Ltd* [1995] 1 AC 74, PC (not inevitably a failure of consideration, and not known by the payee that that would be so, at the time of payment); *Box v Barclays Bank plc* [1998] Lloyd's Rep Bank 185 and *Shalson v Russo* [2003] EWHC 1637 (Ch), [2005] Ch 281 (in both a *Neste Oy* constructive trust was refused in a situation where a fraudulently induced contract first had to be rescinded); *Triffit Nurseries v Salads Etcetera Ltd* [2000] 1 All ER (Comm) 737 (no failure of consideration as between payor and insolvent payee: payor simply paying for goods already received).

[13] [1981] Ch 105.   [14] [1996] AC 669, 709, 714–5.

[15] One distinction between *Chase Manhattan* and *Westdeutsche*, on the one hand, and *Neste Oy* on the other is that, in the former two cases there was no valid contract to pay the money. But there is an analogy because in *Neste Oy*, the valid contract had been terminated by the claimants for the defendants' repudiatory breach, constituted by its inability because of insolvency to perform.

[16] [2006] EWHC 3272; [2007] 2 BCLC 1.

direction to the administrators to treat monies as held on trust, there needed to be clearer evidence as to whether particular monies had, or had not, been paid after the date of the resolution to cease trading.

Thirdly, in terms of principle and policy, *Neste Oy* has much to commend it. In terms of principle, the late Professor Peter Birks[17] and Professor Robert Chambers[18] have powerfully argued that, in general, if any unjust enrichment would trigger a personal right to restitution, it should also trigger a proprietary right to restitution provided the enrichment is surviving in an asset to which the proprietary right can directly attach. An exception is where there is a subsequent failure of consideration because then the defendant will have had full beneficial entitlement to the asset in question and this should not be disrupted. For them, *Chase Manhattan* as a case of mistake, and *Neste Oy* as a case of inevitable failure of consideration—it was inevitable at the time of payment that the consideration would fail—both fall on the side of the line where proprietary restitution is justified. Indeed Lord Bingham may be pleased to know that, in his later writings, Peter Birks[19] elevated the status of *Neste Oy* by referring to the '*Neste Oy* doctrine.' Turning to policy it is helpful to focus on the extent to which proprietary restitution would unacceptably undermine our law of insolvency. If a subsequent failure of consideration were generally to trigger a trust to reverse an unjust enrichment, all unsecured creditors would be turned into beneficiaries under a trust where the enrichment survives. That would plainly be unacceptable. However, there was no such threat in recognizing a constructive trust on the facts of *Chase Manhattan*. Such a mistaken payor, while an unsecured creditor, had not taken the risk of the payee's insolvency because it did not truly intend to make the second payment at all. The situation in *Neste Oy* is similar to that in *Chase Manhattan*. An unsecured creditor can be said to have taken the risk that the payee will not perform but not in a situation where the payee already knows at the time of receipt that there is no possibility of its performance. Indeed the distinction between that failure of consideration and a fraudulently-induced mistake (which clearly triggers a proprietary right)[20] is paper-thin.

Alongside *Neste Oy* and *Chase Manhattan* there are other examples of proprietary rights being recognized that, on the best analysis, reverse an unjust enrichment. So, although not everyone would agree, failed resulting trusts, the power to rescind with proprietary consequences (for misrepresentation, duress, or undue influence), non-contractual subrogation to secured rights, and liens and trusts imposed after tracing in 'unauthorized substitution' cases are, it is submitted,

[17] E.g., *Unjust Enrichment* (2nd edn, 2005) ch 8.
[18] E.g., *Resulting Trusts* (1997).
[19] *English Private Law* (1st edn, 2000), paras 15.192–15.198, co-written with Charles Mitchell. See also 2nd edn, 2007 paras 18.183–18.191.
[20] The proprietary right triggered in the fraud context normally takes the form of a power to rescind: i.e., the power to revest legal title that has been transferred to the defendant. It is unclear why the relevant proprietary right reversing an unjust enrichment is sometimes a trust and sometimes a power to rescind: see for discussion, Birks, *Unjust Enrichment* (2nd edn, 2005) ch 8.

best viewed as examples of proprietary rights reversing unjust enrichment.[21] It is in the light of that bigger picture that the temptation to cast aside *Neste Oy*—or to distinguish it as a one-off decision reacting to very specific facts—is a flawed and ill-informed strategy.

Finally, however, it should be emphasized that *Neste Oy* should not be taken as indicating that a trust should *only* be imposed where the defendant knows of the relevant 'unjust factor'. Throughout the law of unjust enrichment, there is an underlying tension between a model of strict liability plus change of position and a model of fault-based receipt. In the realm of personal rights, the strict liability approach has largely won the day (albeit not yet in the realm of so-called 'knowing receipt'.)[22] The battle is still being fought out in the context of proprietary rights. *Chase Manhattan* indicates that the knowledge of the recipient is irrelevant when the payor is mistaken. The same can be said, for example, of *Re Diplock*,[23] where the recipient charities did not know of the executors' mistake and yet were still held liable to the *in rem* (and *in personam*) claims. Lord Browne-Wilkinson's *obiter dicta* in the *Westdeutsche* case indicate a preference for a fault-based approach to proprietary rights but, in principle, provided a change of position defence is applied, the strict liability approach is to be preferred precisely because defendants may otherwise be left with an unjust (because unintended) enrichment. It is submitted, therefore, that the inevitability of a failure of consideration at the time of payment is sufficient to trigger a proprietary right in respect of that payment whether or not the payee knows of that inevitable failure.

3. The Basis of 'Wrotham Park Damages': Jaggard v Sawyer

A much-discussed issue, both in the courts and especially in legal academia, is the basis of so-called 'Wrotham Park damages.' In *Wrotham Park Estate Co v Parkside Homes Ltd*,[24] 14 houses and a road had been built by the defendants in breach of a restrictive covenant with the claimant. The claimant accepted that it had suffered no loss in the sense that the value of its own land had not been diminished by the development. Brightman J refused the claimant's action for a mandatory injunction to knock down the houses but he awarded £2,500 damages under Lord Cairns' Act on the basis that this was a reasonable price for the claimant to have accepted for releasing the defendants from their covenant. In fixing a reasonable price under the posited hypothetical release bargain, Brightman J thought it relevant to consider the defendants' actual profit from the development.

'Wrotham Park damages'—that is, damages based on such a hypothetical release bargain—have since been awarded in a range of tort and contract cases

---

[21] Burrows, *The Law of Restitution* (2nd edn, 2002) 66.
[22] Burrows, *The Law of Restitution* (2nd edn, 2002) ch 4.
[23] [1948] Ch 465.   [24] [1974] 1 WLR 798.

where the duty in question has been concerned to protect real or personal property or interests analogous to property. So, for example, they have been awarded for breach of a restrictive covenant over land as in *Wrotham Park* itself;[25] for breach of a collateral contract restricting the development of land;[26] for tortious trespass to land;[27] for the tort of nuisance by infringement of the right to light;[28] and for breach of negative contractual obligations concerned to restrict the defendants' use of master tapes.[29]

The puzzle is in understanding the precise justification of these '*Wrotham Park* damages.' Are they simply compensating for loss so as to fit within our traditional understanding of damages as compensatory? Or does the methodology of looking to the defendant's profits indicate that, analogously to an account of profits, the damages are really restitutionary designed to remove at least some of the defendant's gains made from the wrong? Or, is there some other explanation that justifies the damages on the basis that they are neither compensatory nor restitutionary?

Of great importance to this ongoing debate is the leading judgment of Sir Thomas Bingham MR in *Jaggard v Sawyer*. Here the claimant and the defendants owned houses on a small residential estate of ten houses served by a private road. The defendants bought a plot of land adjoining their own and built a house on it. The only access to the new house was along the private road. Use of that road as a means of access to the new house constituted a breach of the defendants' restrictive covenant with the claimant (and with the other owners of houses on the estate) and a trespass over the claimant's part of the road. The claimant had threatened to bring proceedings for an injunction before the defendants had begun building the new house but had only actually brought proceedings when the building of the house was at an advanced stage. The claimant was refused an injunction to prevent the continuing trespass and breach of restrictive covenant but the Court of Appeal upheld an award of '*Wrotham Park* damages', in lieu of the injunction, of £694.44.

Sir Thomas Bingham MR (with whom Kennedy LJ agreed) emphasized that *Wrotham Park* damages are, in his view, compensatory and not restitutionary. After referring to Steyn LJ's *obiter dicta* in *Surrey CC v Bredero Homes Ltd*[30] that *Wrotham Park* damages were only defensible as restitutionary and that justifying them on the basis of a loss of bargaining opportunity was a fiction, Sir Thomas Bingham MR said the following:

---

[25] *Amec Developments Ltd v Jury's Hotel Management (UK) Ltd* (2000) 82 P & CR 286.

[26] *Lane v O'Brien Homes Ltd* [2004] EWHC 303.

[27] *Bracewell v Appleby* [1975] Ch 408; *Severn Trent Water Ltd v Barnes* [2004] EWCA Civ 570.

[28] *Carr-Saunders v Dick McNeil Associates Ltd* [1986] 2 All ER 888; *Tamares (Vincent Square) Ltd v Fairpoint* [2007] EWHC 212.

[29] *Experience Hendrix LLC v PPX Enterprises Inc* [2003] EWCA Civ 323; [2003] 1 All ER (Comm) 830.

[30] [1993] 1 WLR 1361, 1369.

I cannot...accept that Brightman J's assessment of damages in *Wrotham Park* was based on other than compensatory principles. The defendants had committed a breach of covenant, the effects of which continued. The judge was not willing to order the defendants to undo the continuing effects of that breach. He had therefore to assess the damages necessary to compensate the plaintiffs for this continuing invasion of their right. He paid attention to the profits earned by the defendants, as it seems to me, not in order to strip the defendants of their unjust gains, but because of the obvious relationship between the profits earned by the defendants and the sum which the defendants would reasonably have been willing to pay to secure release from the covenant...I can see no reason why a judge should not assess damages on the *Wrotham Park* basis when he declines to prevent commission of a future wrong...The only argument pressed on damages was that the only damages properly awardable on compensatory principles would have been nominal and that therefore an injunction should have been granted. As already indicated, I think that the *Wrotham Park* approach was appropriate even on pure compensatory principles and the judge followed it correctly.[31]

The difficulty with this reasoning is to understand the precise loss that 'Wrotham Park damages' are meant to be compensating. On the facts of *Jaggard v Sawyer* it is conceivable that there was a true non-pecuniary 'loss of amenity'—the increased noise and inconvenience of more people using the private road—but that was not how the damages were explained. Rather, applying the methodology of a hypothetical bargain, it appears that the damages were treated as compensating the claimant for its financial loss in not being paid a reasonable price for releasing the defendant from its covenant and for granting a right of way. Treating the damages as compensating for such a 'loss of opportunity to bargain' may have been realistic on the facts of *Jaggard v Sawyer*. The claimant might have been willing to 'sell' its right at that price. But it is clear—and this underpins Steyn LJ's description of this analysis as a fiction—that in *Wrotham Park* itself, and in several other cases in which it has been applied, the claimant would not have been willing to bargain away its right at any price and certainly not at the reasonable price fixed by the court.

It is for this reason that many academics, and some highly respected judges, have sought to explain 'Wrotham Park damages' as restitutionary rather than compensatory.[32] That is, the damages are explained as stripping away at least some of the gain made by the commission of the wrong. 'Wrotham Park damages' on this view, share an affinity with an account of profits. The latter is a remedy standardly awarded to strip away profits made by a wrongdoer in committing an intellectual property tort or an equitable wrong, such as breach of fiduciary duty or breach of confidence, and was for the first time held to be a possible remedy for a breach of contract in *Attorney-General v Blake*.[33] Admittedly, 'Wrotham Park

---

[31] [1995] 1 WLR 269, 281–3.
[32] Burrows, 'Are "Damages on the *Wrotham Park* Basis" Compensatory, Restitutionary or Neither?' in Cunnington and Saidov, *Contract Damages: Domestic and International Perspectives* (2008) ch 7.
[33] [2001] 1 AC 268.

damages' never aim, as an account of profits may do, to remove *all* the profits causally acquired by a defendant from the commission of a wrong. However, even with an account of profits, some apportionment of profits is possible through the mechanism of allowing the wrongdoer an allowance for skill and effort. The quantum of restitution awarded by means of these two different remedies may therefore be very similar.

This is not to suggest that there are no difficulties with a restitutionary analysis. Even if one accepts that restitution for a wrong has a place in the civil law, it plainly can only apply where the wrongdoer has made a gain from the wrong. In other words, just as compensation runs out where the claimant has suffered no loss, restitution runs out where the wrongdoer has made no gain (whether 'expense saved' or 'profit'). There is also a tricky question as to the relationship between compensation and restitution. Should the latter only be available where the former is inadequate (as suggested by *Attorney-General v Blake* in the context of breach of contract) or is it simply a matter of election for the claimant subject to the need to avoid double recovery (as suggested by the law on the intellectual property torts).

Sir Thomas Bingham MR was not, of course, suggesting that there is no place in the law for restitution as a response to a wrong. And he was no doubt correct to seek initially to explain '*Wrotham Park* damages' on the firmer sands of compensation than on the shifting sands of restitution. Moreover, in *Jaggard v Sawyer* itself, a compensatory analysis, as we have seen above, may well have been realistic. However, '*Wrotham Park* damages' are very often only realistically analysed as concerned to remove a gain from a wrong and, where I part company from Sir Thomas Bingham MR is that, in my view, the *Wrotham Park* case itself was one where there was no realistic compensatory analysis.

Two more recent contributions to this on-going debate are worthy of mention. The first is the disappointing *obiter dicta* of Chadwick LJ in *World Wide Fund for Nature v World Wide Wrestling Federation*.[34] While commendably seeing a close link between an account of profits and '*Wrotham Park* damages', Chadwick LJ bafflingly linked them as both being compensatory rather than 'gains-based'. Yet surely to regard an account of profits as compensatory is either to distort the meaning of compensation so that it loses any explanatory force or to reveal a serious misunderstanding about that remedy.

Secondly, Professor Robert Stevens in his brilliant and controversial book *Torts and Rights*[35] has argued that '*Wrotham Park* damages' are neither compensatory nor restitutionary. They are instead concerned to value the right infringed. Their purpose is to be a substitute for, and vindication of, the right infringed. It may be that Sir Thomas Bingham MR would have found this analysis attractive for at one point in *Jaggard v Sawyer* he did expressly talk of *Wrotham Park* damages being concerned to 'value the right'.[36] However, such an approach would

---

[34] [2007] EWCA Civ 286 at [59].   [35] (2007) ch 4.
[36] [1995] 1 WLR 269, 282.

radically change our traditional understanding of damages and would relegate compensation (and restitution) to being merely consequential add-ons to a basic non-compensatory measure. There are also significant difficulties in understanding how the three measures would fit together. It seems to me, therefore, that where the infringement of a right has neither resulted in loss to the claimant nor in gain to the defendant, the relevant monetary remedy is merely concerned to declare that the right of the claimant has been infringed. Arguably, nothing more than nominal damages is therefore justified. If it is felt that some more substantial incentive to a claimant is needed, so as not to discourage the vindication of one's rights, the way forward would be to increase the sums presently awarded as nominal damages rather than to recast what have traditionally been regarded as compensatory damages as being merely concerned to value the infringed right.

4. The Date for Assessing Damages for Breach of Contract: *The Golden Victory*

It is usually taken to be a trite statement of law that, in general, the date for the assessment of contractual compensatory damages is the date of the breach of contract. Yet this is a surprisingly ambiguous and ultimately misleading proposition for at least two reasons.

First, a court is clearly bound to take into account consequential losses or consequential gains, provided they are not ruled out by limiting principles such as remoteness and causation, even though these have occurred after the date of breach. So, for example, if as a consequence of a carrier's delay in delivering a broken crank-shaft to manufacturers for a replacement, the claimant's mill is kept at a standstill for several days longer than it otherwise would have been, the number of days of standstill—and hence loss of profits during those days—is relevant in assessing damages for the breach of the carriage contracts. It does not matter that those days of standstill occurred after the date of breach.

Secondly, even if one confines the proposition to being concerned with the assessment of the claimant's basic, as opposed to consequential, loss, it is riddled with exceptions. Say, for example, the contract in question was one for the sale of goods and that the vendor has broken the contract by failing to supply the goods. One's starting point for assessing the purchaser's damages may very well be the market value of the goods at the date of the breach. But where the market value has fluctuated, whether by reason of ordinary market movements or changes in the internal or external value of money, a court will take those fluctuations into account subject to the important limiting principles of the duty to mitigate and actual mitigation. The so-called date of breach rule, even when confined to the assessment of basic loss, turns out on close inspection merely to reflect the starting point that a claimant's duty to mitigate is triggered as soon as a breach occurs. Assessment by the market values at the date of breach is accurate only insofar as it is reasonable for a purchaser to mitigate its loss by straightaway going into the market to buy substitute goods. As sometimes a claimant acts reasonably by not immediately going into the market for a replacement, so sometimes a later valuation date is appropriate. It is for this reason that, while one might state the general rule in line with the traditional convention, as being that basic loss is assessed at the date of breach subject to exceptions where the claimant has acted reasonably in delaying the acquisition of a replacement,[37] the more accurate proposition is that damages are assessed at the date of hearing unless the claimant ought reasonably have mitigated its loss at an earlier date. This was precisely Oliver J's formulation in *Radford v De Froberville.*[38] The defendant in breach of contract had failed to build a wall. In assessing the claimant's damages one issue was the date at which the cost of (the claimant) building the wall should be assessed. Although that date was not decided on because of insufficient evidence, Oliver J said the following:

> …The proper approach is to assess the damages at the date of the hearing unless it can be said that the plaintiff ought reasonably to have mitigated by seeking an alternative performance at an earlier date.[39]

With that surprisingly turbulent background in mind, let us now turn to *Golden Strait Corporation v Nippon Yusen Kubishika Kaisha, The Golden Victory.* This concerned a seven-year charterparty made in 1998. After three years in December 2001 there was a repudiation by the charterers who redelivered the vessel. This repudiation was accepted a few days later by the owners. Some 15 months later (after arbitration proceedings and failed negotiations between the parties for another charter of the vessel) the second Iraq war broke out which, under a war clause in the charterparty, would have entitled the charterers to terminate the contract in any event and it was assumed that they would have done so. The question was whether damages for the charterers' breach of contract should be assessed as at the date of breach (which was the date of the owners' acceptance of the repudiation) on the basis of the value of a four-year remaining charterparty ignoring the outbreak of war; or as at the date of trial, taking into account the known outbreak of war and hence on the basis of a 15-month remaining charterparty. The House of Lords by a three to two majority (Lords Scott, Carswell, and Brown; Lords Bingham and Walker dissenting) held that it should be the latter: damages should be assessed taking into account the known outbreak of war and therefore on the basis of a 15-month remaining charterparty.

With great respect to Lord Bingham, my own view is that the majority was here correct for the following reasons.[40]

---

[37] See, e.g., *Johnson v Agnew* [1980] AC 367.

[38] [1977] 1 WLR 1262.

[39] [1977] 1 WLR 1262 at 1286.

[40] The majority's view is also favoured by Liu, 'The Date for Assessing Damages for Loss of Prospective Performance under a Contract' [2007] LMCLQ 273.

First, as has been explained above, it is misleading to regard the starting point as being that damages are assessed at the date of breach. In line with Oliver J's formulation, the correct proposition is that damages are assessed at the date of trial unless the claimant could reasonably have mitigated its loss by going into the market to make a substitute contract at an earlier date. The great merit of Oliver J's formulation is that it gives full effect to the compensatory principle: that is, the claimant is entitled, subject to mitigation, to be fully compensated for its actual loss. Moreover, on these facts, the duty to mitigate was essentially irrelevant. It was events outside the parties' control (the outbreak of war) that had meant that the owners' actual loss on the contract had been reduced (from loss of a four-year remaining charterparty to loss of a 15-month remaining charterparty); and substitute contracts would themselves have contained equivalent war clauses. Had the owners gone out into the market and reasonably made substitute contracts, those substitute contracts would have formed the basis of the assessment. But that is not what had happened. The owners had not gone out into the market and made substitute charters; and their delay—while arbitration and negotiations were pursued—had the consequence that their actual loss was reduced from the loss of a four-year contract to the loss of a 15-month contract.

Secondly, applying standard principles of certainty,[41] a court assessing damages at the date of breach would be bound to take into account the significant possibility of war breaking out and triggering the war clause. Without the benefit of hindsight, such an assessment of possibilities would inevitably be inaccurate. The majority's approach removes the need for that inaccuracy precisely because one has the benefit of hindsight. As it was expressed in *Bwllfa & Merthyr Dare Steam Collieries (1891) Ltd v Pontypridd Waterworks Co*,[42] a court should not speculate when it has the evidence about the true facts. That principle is no less applicable in commercial than non-commercial cases.

Thirdly, as Lord Brown pointed out, the logic of assessing damages at the date of breach would appear to produce very odd consequences if one varied the facts of this case. Say, for example, the second Iraq war had broken out only a few weeks or months after the repudiation and before there was any reasonable prospect of concluding a substitute charterparty with a third party. Surely then a court would be bound to take the war's outbreak into account. So why should it be ignored (assuming no failure to mitigate) when it occurred later than that? Then switch the whole facts round more dramatically. Say there was a probability of war breaking out in December 2001 but by the time of trial that possibility had disappeared. It surely could not then be correct to award *lower* damages to the shipowner to take into account the risk which never in fact eventuated.

---

[41] See, e.g., *Chaplin v Hicks* [1911] 2 KB 786; *The Mihalis Angelos* [1971] 1 QB 164.
[42] [1903] AC 426.

This is not to suggest that the arguments are all one way. Lord Bingham's central concern was to ensure certainty, predictability, and finality in commercial law. In his words:

[T]he decision [of the majority] undermines the quality of certainty which is a traditional strength and major selling point of English commercial law, and involves an unfortunate departure from principle.

Such concerns have also been voiced against the majority's approach by Edwin Peel[43] and Guenter Treitel[44] and more generally as regards the date for assessment by Stephen Waddams.[45] However, it is hard to see why Oliver J's formulation is any less certain or predictable or final than a general rule of assessment at the date of breach which is then qualified by exceptions. The correct message, which is a clear and certain one, is that, provided claimants act reasonably to minimize loss, they are entitled to their full non-remote loss taking into account all facts known at trial. Even if their reasonable efforts, viewed in retrospect, augment rather than reduce their loss, it is recoverable.[46] Furthermore, courts are not going to be astute to hold that innocent parties have acted unreasonably;[47] and the burden of proof in relation to a failure to mitigate is firmly on the defendant.[48]

In the latest edition of *Treitel, The Law of Contract*, Edwin Peel[49] suggests that the majority's approach has the drawback of potentially encouraging repudiating parties to delay the assessment of damages to see if a suspensory condition might come into operation. With respect, this seems a spurious concern. This is because a delay might equally well lead to an increase of damages payable by the repudiating party. So, for example, had the prospect of the second Iraq war disappeared altogether 15 months after breach, the need to reduce the owners' damages to reflect the possibility of the outbreak of war would have been removed.

5. Conclusion

The three cases I have focused on give much food for thought on the remedial issues raised; and disagreement with some of Lord Bingham's reasoning in no way diminishes my deep admiration for his judgments and approach.

---

[43] *Treitel, The Law of Contract* (12th edn, 2007) para 20–071.

[44] 'Assessment of Damages for Wrongful Repudiation' (2005) 121 LQR 9. See also Coote, 'Breach, Anticipatory Breach or the Breach Anticipated' (2007) 123 LQR 503, 510.

[45] 'The Date for the Assessment of Damages' (1981) 97 LQR 445. For criticism of Waddams' position, see Burrows, *Remedies for Torts and Breach of Contract* (3rd edn, 2004) 192, 197–198.

[46] *Esso Petroleum Co Ltd v Mardon* [1976] QB 801; *Hoffberger v Ascot International Bloodstock Bureau Ltd* (1976) 120 Sol Jo 130.

[47] *Banco de Portugal v Waterlow & Sons Ltd* [1932] AC 452, 506; *London and South of England Building Society v Stone* [1983] 3 All ER 105, 121.

[48] *Roper v Johnson* (1873) LR 8 CP 167; *LE Jones (Insurance Brokers) Ltd v Portsmouth City Council* [2002] EWCA Civ 1723, [2003] 1 WLR 427, at [26].

[49] At para 20–071.

To finish on a personal note, I have had the great privilege of working with Tom Bingham in his role as Chair of the Trustees of the Oxford Law Foundation. He has been a huge supporter of Oxford Law over many years and has been generous to a fault with the time he has been willing to expend on our behalf. Whatever formal retirement has in store for him, we look forward to a continuing close relationship with one of Oxford's greatest alumni.

3

Economic Reasoning and Judicial Review*

Stephen Breyer

This chapter will focus upon the use of economics in the law, and in particular, at the United States Supreme Court.

Edmund Burke pointed out that such matters do not stir the soul. He said that 'the age of chivalry is dead;' 'that of sophists and calculators,' i.e., lawyers and economists, 'is upon us'. And 'the glory of Europe is extinguished forever'. But there is no need for such pessimism. Men and women in our modern society seek prosperity; prosperity requires an economy that works well; that economy depends upon well-functioning governing rules of law; and to produce that law, at least sometimes, lawyers and economists must work together. In my view, their partnership is essential to a well-ordered democratic, mixed economy.

My object today is to illustrate how that partnership functions at the Supreme Court of the United States. I shall consider cases arising in legal fields where the law—if it is to work well—must draw upon insights provided by economists, for example, the law of economic regulation, the law of antitrust, and the law of intellectual property. I have deliberately chosen cases where, dissenting, I disagreed with the majority as to whether or how the law should take account of those economic insights. By doing so, I hope to illustrate some of the relevant institutional issues, highlighting some that make cooperation between our disciplines difficult. My object is to encourage both economists and lawyers to look for ways to overcome them.

I

Let me begin with a brief description of the Supreme Court. We are nine judges, appointed for life by the President and confirmed by the Senate. Each of us,

* This is the text of a lecture delivered at the British Institute of International and Comparative Law 12 September 2007. Portions of the lecture are based upon a lecture delivered in December 2003 at a meeting of the AEI-Brookings Joint Center for Regulatory Studies, available online at the website of the American Enterprise Institute.

before appointment, was a federal court of appeals judge. Before that, three of us were academics, three have come from private practice, and three were lawyers practising in the public sector.

Our Court decides only questions of federal law (the lion's share of American law is state law, not federal law). Like the Law Committee of the House of Lords, we have the last word as to the interpretation of statutes. Unlike the Law Lords, we also have a federal constitutional responsibility. We definitively interpret the Constitution of the United States. Our jurisdiction is discretionary; and we take cases primarily to resolve differences of legal interpretation arising among the lower courts.

You should be aware of several special features of our institution that make it difficult to take account of economic considerations—even when one of its members (namely me) was previously a law professor who specialized in antitrust and economic regulation.

First, unlike many European high courts, we do not divide decision-making authority among ourselves. We do not ask one Justice to specialize in respect to a particular case or to prepare a report on a case for use by the others. We do not try to develop different areas of expertise over time. We are generalists. We recognize that some of our members may have developed greater knowledge of a particular field; but we also recognize that such knowledge can bring with it a perspective that, as generalists, we might find skewed. Thus any deference we may show to our other colleague's expert knowledge is limited. We each participate fully in each judicial decision. We believe we are appointed to exercise our own judgment. And each of us takes full responsibility for his or her decision in each case. All this means that one Justice's expertise in a particular field, while not totally irrelevant, will rarely prove determinative.

Secondly, time is limited. At the Supreme Court, we review about 8,500 petitions each year. We grant about 80, each of which raises a legal question that different lower courts have answered differently. The difficulty of the case, the size of the petition docket, the need to decide, all create pressure to move on. And that pressure militates against a Justice, once having reached a decision, changing his or her mind. We are not obstinate, but we recognize that, were we to change our minds too often, the work of the Supreme Court would not get done. Until a dissenting view in a technical case—involving, say, complex economic analysis—is reduced to a draft in writing, its persuasive power is limited. It takes time to produce that writing. By the time the dissent circulates, a majority may have reached a contrary conclusion. And, because of the time pressures I mentioned, that consensus can prove resistant to change.

Thirdly, cases involving economics are often cases in which the law instructs courts to defer to other governmental decision-makers. They may, for example, arise where agencies have created economically-based public policy. And courts must decide, not whether that policy is wise, but whether it is so wrong as to be 'arbitrary,' 'capricious', or an 'abuse of discretion.' It is particularly difficult to show that an agency decision, or a congressional decision, is *that* wrong. And

courts are consequently tempted not to engage in economic reasoning themselves, or to examine the agency's economic reasoning that closely, but simply to
approve an agency's efforts to take account of economics as reasonable ones.

These factors explain why, institutionally, appellate courts sometimes seem
inhospitable to economic reasoning. And with this institutional backdrop in
mind, I would like to turn to three examples that illustrate more directly some of
the difficulties involved in trying to maintain a productive law/economics relationship. The first concerns a cast of mind. Economists are happy with quanti-
tative, and particularly marginal, analyses; lawyers are happier with rules. The
second concerns precision. One can describe the relationship as one in which
economics *informs* the law; but just what does this mean? The third concerns the
law's distrust of novelty. That fact often requires new approaches, such as economic approaches, slowly to win acceptance in other institutions before a court
will introduce them into the law. Three cases, in which I filed separate opinions,
will help explain these three considerations.

II

An economist might think that the first case, *Whitman v American Trucking
Association*,[1] helps to explain why Justice Louis Brandeis once said, 'A lawyer
who has not studied economics ... is likely to become a public enemy'.[2] The case
involved the Clean Air Act. The relevant statutory language instructed the US
Environmental Protection Agency (EPA) to set ambient air standards 'the attainment and maintenance of which ... are requisite to protect the public health' with
'an adequate margin of safety'.[3] The Court held that this language does not permit the EPA to consider economic costs. The majority reasoned as follows: First,
the language says nothing about costs. Secondly, in other similar parts of the statute the language does mention economic costs. Thirdly, absence of the language
here, along with its presence there, means that here Congress intended to leave
economic costs out. Fourthly, the Court reached a similar conclusion in other
similar cases, where it said that Congress did not want the EPA to consider economic costs unless there is a 'clear ... textual commitment' to such consideration.
Fifthly, there is no such 'clear commitment' here.

I wrote separately to set forth different reasons for reaching a similar conclusion.[4]
From a purely linguistic perspective, I thought that the EPA might find that a standard that imposes huge costs but secures little, if any, added safety is not a standard
that is 'requisite to the public health' with 'an adequate margin of safety'. But I

---

[1] 531 US 457(2001).

[2] Brandeis, *The Living Law in The Curse of Bigness*, 316, 325 (Osmond K Frankel ed 1935) (quoting Professor Charles Henderson).

[3] 42 USC § 7409(b)(1).

[4] 531 US at 490–96 (Breyer, J, concurring).

nonetheless thought that the statute's legislative history made clear that Congress intended to force industry to create new, cheaper, more effective pollution control technologies. Congress also thought that any agency effort to weigh costs along with benefits would ordinarily prove too time-consuming. Thus, I agreed with the majority that the statute *ordinarily* forbids taking account of economic costs. And in the particular case before us nothing justified departing from that presumption.

The point of my writing, however, was to say that the statute did not forbid consideration of costs in *unusual* cases. Its language, read in light of the history, is sufficiently flexible to permit the EPA to take account of costs where necessary to avoid counter-productive results. A world filled with standards 'requisite to the public health' is not a world without *any* risk. The safest possible football pads and helmets do not prevent every injury; and a degree of risk that falls well within any football injury 'margin of safety' may seem unreasonably dangerous in the context of safe drinking water. Hence, the EPA must have authority to decide, within limits, what counts as 'adequately safe' or what counts as 'requisite to the public health'. It must have authority to decide related matters, such as whether an anti-pollution standard poses greater health risks than it eliminates: for example, in setting ozone standards, the EPA can account for countervailing health benefits such as a reduction in the number of skin cancers.

And if so, the EPA must also have similar authority to determine whether, because of unusually high costs, and unusually small benefits, a proposed standard will prove counter-productive—at least in unusual cases. Let me explain why: it may be that a regulation intended to address 90 per cent of a given environmental risk may impose reasonable costs, but a regulation intended to address 100 per cent of the same risk would impose truly prohibitive costs. If there were a blanket prohibition on the consideration of costs, the EPA might feel statutorily obligated to adopt the latter, more stringent regulation in the name of public health. But doing so could force companies to divert resources that would otherwise be used to address *other* environmental risks. And since resources available to combat environmental hazards are not limitless, addressing the 'last 10 per cent' of one risk may, because of resource diversion, have the unintended and undesirable consequence of exposing the public to other more serious risks.[5]

I thought that Congress would never have countenanced a scenario in which a regulatory action, because of its costs, would bring about more harm than good. Accordingly, I thought that, in respect to consideration of costs, the Clean Air Act could not possibly mean 'never.' And I thought it important to say so.

---

[5] See S Breyer, Breaking the Vicious Circle: Towards Effective Risk Regulation (Cambridge, Massachusetts: Harvard University Press 1993) and Breyer J in *Barry Wright Corp v ITT Grinnell Corp*, 724 F. 2d 227 (1st Cir. 1983):

[u]nlike economics, law is an administrative system the effects of which depends upon the content of rules and precedents only as they are applied by judges and juries in courts and by lawyers advising their clients. Rules that seek to embody every economic complexity and qualification may well, through the vagaries of administration, prove counter-productive. See, P Areeda, *Antitrust Law* (1st edn 1989).

Now you can see the real difference of opinion in this case. If the majority means, 'never take costs into account', its interpretation risks counter-productive results—results that Congress could not have intended. Of course, my own view that 'sometimes an agency may take costs into account' is also open to objection. It invites the question, 'well, just when?' The argument, which on its face concerned the need for, and value of, considering economic costs in pollution cases has become an argument about the need for, and value of, bright-line rules in the law.

This fact explains some of the difficulty of judges' use of economic reasoning. Economic reasoning does not automatically welcome the use of bright-line rules. Economics often concerns gradations with consequences that flow from a little more or a little less. But the law, at least in a final appeals court, often seeks clear administrable distinctions of kind, not degree. This is understandable. Bright-line rules sometimes reduce the transactions costs of judging, as such rules are easier and simpler to administer. Additionally, bright-line rules can have the benefit of providing greater clarity to the public at large, thereby reducing compliance costs and even, perhaps, litigation costs, as well.

Anti-trust law reveals this tension between economics' preference for flexible standards and law's preference for bright-line rules. A *per se* rule against price fixing, for example, does not embody a judgment that price fixing is *never* economically justified. Rather the rule reflects a judgment that economic justifications for price fixing are so few, arise so infrequently, and are so difficult to prove, while the enforcement advantages of a clear rule are so great, that a more complex, more economically sophisticated legal rule is not worth the effort required to develop and to enforce it. Indeed, the difficulty the courts may have in applying a more sophisticated rule may create mistakes that outweigh the rule's benefits.

Could similar reasoning justify a *per se* Clean Air Act rule forbidding consideration of costs? I thought not because I believe that such a rule would sometimes bring about serious, counter-productive harm. And the statute's language and purposes permit more open-ended interpretation. The upshot: such vague legal words as 'ordinarily' and 'unusual' would have to provide sufficient administrative guidance.

I am less interested in the merits of the particular conclusion, however, than in pointing out how the difference between my view and that of the majority in this case raises larger legal issues: How often is a bright-line justified? When will more open, less definite interpretations of statute prove workable? To what extent will a statute's language, including its statutory context, provide a definitive answer to a difficult interpretive question? Given Congress's purpose in enacting this statute, which would a reasonable Member of Congress be likely to have preferred: the harms flowing from an absolute rule forbidding administrators and judges to take account of costs, or the uncertainties that accompany a vague standard implicit in a work like 'ordinarily'? The answer, the degree of 'brightness', 'absoluteness', or scope of a legal rule set forth in an opinion, should itself reflect a judicial weighing of relevant considerations—of legal costs and benefits.

Making such a judgment is easier said than done. In general I believe that Congress would rarely intend a bright-line legal interpretation that would bring about seriously counter-productive results. And I consequently tend to disfavour absolute legal lines, believing instead that life is normally too complex for absolute rules. Moreover, the more open, less definite approach to interpretation is likely to prove more compatible with the law's incorporation of knowledge drawn from other disciplines, particularly disciplines that themselves reason by way of 'a little more, a little less', such as economics.

III

Professor Areeda in his treatise on anti-trust law says that law is not economics and economics is not law; but sometimes economics must *inform* the law.[6] The second case, *Leegin Creative Leather Products, Inc v PSKS, Inc*[7] well illustrates what that means.

The case involved resale price maintenance. Ever since the Court had decided *Dr Miles Medical Co v John D Park & Sons Co* in 1911, the Court applied a rule of *per se* unlawfulness to agreements fixing resale prices. The rule required that courts, without examining justifications for a particular agreement, assume that such agreements are always (or almost always) anti-competitive and consequently unlawful under the Sherman Act, a statute that forbids anti-competitive agreements among competitors.

In *Leegin* the Court overruled its earlier cases. It held instead that courts must apply a 'rule of reason,' not a rule of *per se* unlawfulness, to resale price-fixing agreements. Such a 'rule of reason' permits defendants to produce evidence showing that an individual resale price maintenance agreement is justified, on the ground that the agreement's economic benefits outweigh anti-competitive harms. Four judges, including me, dissented. We thought that the proponents of a 'rule of reason' had not shown sufficient justification for overturning well-established existing law.

The case shows how American anti-trust law blends both economic and administrative considerations. It required us to consider: (1) potential anti-competitive effects; (2) potential economic justifications; and (3) concerns related to the ability of the courts to administer the resulting rule of law. The three sets of considerations pointed in different directions. Economists helped considerably in respect of the first two sets of considerations. I should also ask whether they might not have shed more light on the third set, those concerning administration, as well.

---

[6] See S Breyer, Breaking the Vicious Circle: Towards Effective Risk Regulation (Cambridge, Massachusetts: Harvard University Press 1993) and Breyer J in *Barry Wright Corp v ITT Grinnell Corp*, 724 F. 2d 227, 234 (1st Cir 1983):

[u]nlike economics, law is an administrative system the effects of which depend upon the content of rules and precedents only as they are applied by judges and juries in courts and by lawyers advising their clients. Rules that seek to embody every economic complexity and qualification may well, through the vagaries of administration, prove counter-productive, undercutting the very economic ends they seek to serve.

[7] 551 US ___, 127 S. Ct. 2705 (2007).

We judges had no difficulty in learning what economists thought. The parties and supporting groups set out their views in briefs filed with the Court, and those briefs also referred to economic books and journal articles on the subject. The economists basically agreed that resale price maintenance agreements could have serious anti-competitive consequences. *In respect to dealers*, resale price maintenance agreements, rather like horizontal price agreements, can diminish or eliminate price competition among dealers of a single brand or (if practised generally by manufacturers) among multi-brand dealers. In doing so, they can prevent dealers from offering customers the lower prices that many customers prefer; they can prevent dealers from responding to changes in demand, say falling demand, by cutting prices; they can encourage dealers to substitute service, for price, competition, thereby threatening wastefully to attract too many resources into that portion of the industry; they can inhibit expansion by more efficient dealers whose lower prices might otherwise attract more customers, stifling the development of new, more efficient modes of retailing; and so forth.

In respect to producers, resale price maintenance agreements can help to reinforce the competition-inhibiting behaviour of firms in concentrated industries. In such industries firms may tacitly collude, i.e., observe each other's pricing behaviour, each understanding that price cutting by one firm is likely to trigger price competition by all. Where that is so, resale price maintenance can make it easier for each producer to identify (by observing retail markets) when a competitor has begun to cut prices. And a producer who cuts wholesale prices *without* lowering the minimum resale price will stand to gain little, if anything, in increased profits, because the dealer will be unable to stimulate increased consumer demand by passing along the producer's price cut to consumers. In either case, resale price maintenance agreements will tend to prevent price competition from 'breaking out'; and they will thereby tend to stabilize producer prices.

There was also empirical evidence suggesting that, were resale price maintenance lawful, these anti-competitive consequences would prove important. In 1975 Congress repealed the Miller-Tydings Fair Trade Act and the McGuire Act. Those Acts had permitted (but not required) individual states to enact 'fair trade' laws authorizing minimum resale price maintenance. At the time of repeal minimum resale price maintenance was lawful in 36 states; it was unlawful in 14 states. Empirical studies compared prices in the former States with prices in the latter states. The Department of Justice argued its empirical study of the matter showed that minimum resale price maintenance had raised prices by 19 to 27 per cent.

After repeal, minimum resale price maintenance agreements were unlawful *per se* in every state. The Federal Trade Commission staff, after studying numerous price surveys, wrote that collectively the surveys 'indicate[d] that [resale price maintenance] in most cases increased the prices of products sold with [resale price maintenance]'. Most economists today agree that, in the words of a prominent anti-trust treatise, 'resale price maintenance tends to produce higher consumer prices than would otherwise be the case'.

At the same time the economists agreed that *sometimes* resale price mainten-ance agreements could prove justified, for *sometimes* they might provide import-ant consumer benefits. For example, resale price maintenance agreements can facilitate new entry. A newly entering producer wishing to build a product name might be able to convince dealers to help it do so—if, but only if, the producer can assure those dealers that they will later recoup their investment. Without resale price maintenance, late-entering dealers might take advantage of the earl-ier investment and, through price competition, drive prices down to the point where the early dealers cannot recover what they spent. By assuring the initial dealers that such later price competition will not occur, resale price maintenance can encourage them to carry the new product, thereby helping the new produ-cer succeed. The result might be increased competition at the producer level, i.e., greater *inter*-brand competition, that brings with it net consumer benefits.

Moreover, in the absence of resale price maintenance a producer might find its efforts to sell a product undermined by what resale price maintenance advocates call 'free riding'. Suppose a producer concludes that it can succeed only if dealers provide certain services, say, product demonstrations, high quality shops, adver-tising that creates a certain product image, and so forth. Without resale price maintenance, some dealers might take a 'free ride' on the investment that others make in providing those services. Such a dealer would save money by not paying for those services and could consequently cut its own price and increase its own sales. Under these circumstances, dealers might prove unwilling to invest in the provision of necessary services.

Finally, the economists agreed that, where a producer and not a group of deal-ers seeks a resale price maintenance agreement, there is a special reason to believe some such benefits exist. That is because, other things being equal, producers should want to encourage price competition among their dealers. By doing so they will often increase profits by selling more of their product. And that is so, even if the producer possesses sufficient market power to earn a super-normal profit. That is to say, other things being equal, the producer will benefit by charg-ing his dealers a competitive (or even a higher-than-competitive) wholesale price while encouraging price competition among them. Hence, if the producer is the moving force, the producer must have some special reason for wanting resale price maintenance; and in the absence of, say, concentrated producer markets (where that special reason might consist of a desire to stabilize wholesale prices), that special reason may well reflect the special circumstances just described: new entry, 'free riding', or variations on those themes.

A problem arises, however, because these economic answers, helpful though they are, by themselves cannot provide an answer to our legal question, namely whether to overturn a near century-old line of cases setting forth a *per se* rule and substitute a 'rule of reason' instead. That is because law, unlike economics, is an administra-tive system the effects of which depend upon the content of rules and precedents only as they are applied by judges and juries in courts and by lawyers advising their clients. These circumstances mean that courts sometimes should apply rules of *per se* unlawfulness to business practices even when those practices sometimes produce economic benefits. And, as a judge, I must know whether resale price maintenance is such an instance. To help decide, I should like to know how often the various harms and benefits are likely to occur. I should like to know how easy it is for courts to separate the anti-competitive goats from the beneficial sheep.

On these crucial questions, however, many (not all) of the economists fell silent. We were left with economic analyses and some empirical studies indicating that resale price maintenance can cause harm, certainly when dealers are the driving force. We were left with some analyses (though little empirical evidence) indicating that *sometimes* resale price maintenance can produce benefits. But how often are those benefits likely to occur in practice? How easy is it for courts to identify their presence in individual cases? I could find no economic consensus on these points.

There is a consensus that 'free riding' takes place. But 'free riding' often takes place in the economy without any legal effort to stop it. Many visitors to California take free rides on the Pacific Coast Highway. We all benefit freely from ideas, such as that of creating the first supermarket. Dealers often take a 'free ride' on investments that others have made in building a product's name and reputation. But how often is the 'free riding' problem serious enough significantly to deter dealer investment? One can easily *imagine* a dealer who refuses to provide important presale services, say a detailed explanation of how a product works (or who fails to provide a proper atmosphere in which to sell expensive perfume or alligator billfolds), lest customers use that 'free' service (or enjoy the psychological benefit arising when a high-priced retailer stocks a particular brand of billfold or handbag) and then buy from another dealer at a lower price. But are there really many such dealers? We do, after all, live in an economy where firms, despite *Dr Miles'* *per se* rule, still sell complex technical equipment (as well as expensive perfume and alligator billfolds) to consumers.

How easy is it for courts to identify instances in which the benefits are likely to outweigh potential harms? The agreement is not likely to be justified where the dealers, not the producer, are the 'moving force'. But suppose several large multi-brand retailers all sell resale-price-maintained products. Suppose further that small producers set retail prices because they fear that, otherwise, the large retailers will favour (say, by allocating better shelf-space) the goods of other producers who practice resale price maintenance. Who 'initiated' this practice, the retailers hoping for considerable insulation from retail competition, or the producers, who simply seek to deal best with the circumstances they find?

These questions are important because a shift from a bright-line rule to a 'rule of reason' itself has costs. A shift here upsets the settled expectations of those who have relied upon the prior rule, for example, investors in retail firms that engage in discounting, their customers, the mall operators, or the computer service firms that have offered them financial support. And as the courts develop the contours of a 'rule of reason', the resulting legal confusion generates costs. So does the presence of mistakes as courts or juries wrongly apply a more complicated rule. Indeed, without a bright-line rule, it is often unfair, and consequently impractical, for enforcement officials to bring criminal proceedings. And since enforcement resources are limited, that may tempt some producers or dealers to enter into agreements that are, on balance, anti-competitive, even where such agreements would not pass legal muster were they actually to be litigated.

Without much help from economists on these administrative matters, the Members of our Court split five to four in favour of changing the relevant legal rule from a rule of *per se* unlawfulness to a 'rule of reason'. The dissenters thought their administrative concerns made the issue a close one. They also asked what had changed since Congress 30 years ago repealed federal statutes authorizing resale price maintenance and effectively applied a rule of *per se* unlawfulness to those agreements. They noted that the arguments had not changed since, even, earlier, the British scholar Sir Basil Yamey had listed those arguments in his book about resale price maintenance. We concluded that, for legal reasons, having to do with the law's reluctance to overrule earlier case law upon which the public would probably have relied. In the absence of new information providing new reasons for change, we believed that the law in this area should not change.

I find both positions reasonable. But I want to ask whether the many economic experts participating in the case could not have given us more help. Could the economists who favoured a 'rule of reason', as most did, not have provided us with more information and analysis about the practical administrative concerns which, along with economics, must inform this area of the law?

The information should exist. For example, unlike the European Union, which categorically bans resale price maintenance, the United Kingdom employs something of a 'rule of reason': while the British Competition Act 1998 generally prohibits vertical price-fixing agreements, companies can nonetheless apply to the Office of Fair Trading (OFT) for exemptions from the general ban where resale price maintenance would not thwart economic competition and would either improve production or distribution or promote technical or economic progress. Has OFT found many instances of justified resale price maintenance or only a few? No one told us. For example, while the European Union and the United Kingdom regard resale price maintenance as a practice which has the object of restricting competition and therefore prohibited under Article 81 EC and section 2 of the Competition Act 1998, there was the possibility, until 2004, of applying for an exemption from this prohibition.[8] Companies could have applied to the European Commission or the OFT for exemptions from the general ban where resale price maintenance would not thwart economic competition and would either improve production or distribution or promote technical or economic progress while allowing consumers a fair share of the resulting benefit and this approach has something of the flavour of a 'rule of reason'. Had the European Commission or the OFT found many instances of justified resale

---

[8] Post-2004 companies must, in general, make their own assessment as to whether or not their agreements fall foul of the prohibition or may benefit from the exemption.

price maintenance or only a few?[9] No one told us. Regardless, is it not possible to design a questionnaire or study that would shed light on, say, *the extent* to which 'free riding' is a problem in various consumer goods industries?

Hence, my questions: Why did no one examine *quantities*? Could the courts themselves have made better use of economic experts? Could they have asked economic experts directly to examine the relevant administrative questions? It is not easy for our Court to do so because we receive expert views primarily in the form of arguments contained in legal briefs written by the parties' lawyers. But lower courts might retain their own experts—who could focus on questions to which the court, as well as the parties, seeks an answer.

I note that British courts have recently adopted rules that would encourage courts to appoint neutral experts.[10] Under the revised British Civil Procedure Rules, a trial court can appoint a single expert when parties wish to submit expert evidence on the same issue.[11] Evaluative reports from the Lord Chancellor's Department have praised the increased use of single joint experts as creating a less adversarial culture and reducing both time and cost.[12] Britain based its experiments on practices that are fairly common in civil law countries, where a judge will select an expert from lists provided by scientific or technical institutions or maintained by the courts themselves. In France, for example, the courts maintain a 'regional' and a 'national' list of experts who meet certain criteria. The court appoints the expert (often, though not exclusively, from these lists) and sets the issues to be investigated. Upon completion of the assignment, the expert is required to file a written report with the court.[13]

I read with interest a recent French case, *La Ligue Contre Le Racisme Et L'Antisemitsme v Yahoo!, Inc*,[14] in which a French court forbade Yahoo.com from providing French internet users access to a service selling Nazi memorabilia as well as to other pro-Nazi websites. The key question concerned the practical ability of Yahoo to segregate search requests from users in France from those in other countries. In response, the judge commissioned a report from a panel of experts, while permitting Yahoo to criticize or object to portions of that report. The result was speed and agreement—not about the result—but about many of the technical facts that underlay it.

[9] For OFT decisions on retail price maintenance see: *Price-fixing of Replica Football Kit*, 1 August 2003, *Agreements between Hasbro U.K. Ltd, Argos Ltd and Littlewoods Ltd fixing the price of Hasbro toys and games*, 21 November 2003.
[10] See Lord Woolf, *Final Report: Access to Justice*, Ch 13 (26 July 1996).
[11] UK Dept for Constitutional Affairs, Civil Procedure Rules 35.7, 35.8 (2003).
[12] See The Lord Chancellor's Dept, Civil Justice Reform Evaluation, *Emerging Findings: An Early Evaluation of the Civil Justice Reforms* (March 2001); The Lord Chancellor's Dept, Civil Justice Reform Evaluation, *Further Findings: A Continuing Evaluation of the Civil Justice Reforms* (August 2002).
[13] See, e.g., M Neil Browne et al, 'The Perspectival Nature of Expert Testimony in the United States, England, Korea, and France', 18 Conn J Int'l L 55, 96–100 (2002).
[14] High Court of Paris, 22 May 2000, Interim Court Order No 00105308 (cited in *Yahoo!, Inc v La Ligue Contre Le Racisme Et L'Antisemitsme*, 169 F Supp2d 1181 (ND Cal 2001)).

But here I drift away from my subject. In discussing the resale price mainte-nance case, I mean to illustrate how American courts have relied upon economic expertise while noting that experts might further help the courts were they to focus upon certain legal or administrative factors relevant to the ultimate legal conclusion. I leave you with a question: How can courts encourage those experts to do so?

IV

The third case, *Eldred v Ashcroft*,[15] concerns a statute that extends the copy-right term by 20 years for both future and existing copyrights. For some works it extends the term from 50 to 70 years after the author's death; for others, from 75 years to 95 years. The question was whether the Constitution's Copyright Clause granted Congress the power to enact this extension. That Clause grants Congress the power to 'promote the progress of science' i.e., learning and knowledge, 'by securing for limited times to authors…the exclusive right to their respective writings'.[16] The Court held that this language covers the extension.

I dissented because I thought that the statute extending the term for 20 years fell outside the scope of the Clause.[17] It seemed to me that the extension amounted to an unjustified effort to create, not a limited, but a virtually perpetual, copy-right term. As I understand the Clause, it requires copyright statutes to serve cer-tain public, not private, ends, namely to 'promote the progress' of knowledge and learning by providing incentives for authors to create works and by removing the related restrictions on a work's dissemination after a 'limited' time.

The 20-year extension would serve private ends. It would transfer billions of dollars of income from consumers of existing works, e.g., readers or movie-goers, to the heirs of the long-dead producers of those works (or connected corpora-tions). But from the public's standpoint, it would bring about considerable harm: it would unnecessarily block dissemination of works that, with a shorter term, would sooner fall into the public domain. The extension, for example, would require those who wish to use century-old, often commercially valueless, works to find, and to obtain permission from, difficult-to-locate current holders of those copyrights.

Consider the teachers who wish their students to see albums of Depression Era photographs, to read the recorded words of those who actually lived under slavery, or to contrast, say, Gary Cooper's heroic portrayal of Sergeant York with filmed reality from the battlefield of Verdun. Consider the historian, writer, art-ist, database operator, film preservationist, researchers of all kinds, who wish to make the past accessible for their own use or for that of others. Requiring them

---

[15] 123 S Ct 769 (2003).   [16] US Constitution, Art I, § 8, cl 8.
[17] 123 S Ct at 801–814 (Breyer, J, dissenting).

to obtain a copyright holder's permission for an additional 20 years—starting 75 years after the work was created—would often fatally impede their efforts.

I could find no justification for the extension that might offset this harm. No one could reasonably conclude that copyright's traditional justification—providing an incentive to create—could apply to this extension. Past works, say Mickey Mouse films, by definition need no incentive, for they already exist. And any added incentive to create works in the future is insignificant.

To understand why that is so requires reference to undisputed data that interested groups submitted to the Court; and it requires reference to the economic analysis that other groups provided (including Nobel Prize winning economists). They made clear that no potential author could reasonably believe that he or she has more than a tiny chance of writing a classic that will survive long enough for a copyright extension (of 20 years beginning 75 years in the future) to matter. Indeed fewer than 2 per cent of all copyrighted works retain any commercial value after 75 years. And any remaining monetary incentive is diminished radically by the fact that the relevant royalties will not arrive until 75 years or more into the future, when, not the author, but distant heirs, or shareholders in a successor corporation, will receive them. A 1 per cent likelihood of earning $100 annually for 20 years, starting 75 years into the future, is worth less than 7 cents today.

What potential Shakespeare, Wharton, or Hemingway would be moved by such a sum? Regardless, that added present value does not significantly differ from the present value added by a perpetual copyright. Indeed, the 20-year extension produces a copyright term that generates more than 98 per cent of the value of perpetual protection.

Neither could I find other copyright-related justifications for the extension. It did not produce significant international uniformity. It had no other significant copyright-related international commercial effect. It did benefit several publishers, shareholders, and various entertainment companies, including Walt Disney and AOL Time Warner (the current holder of the copyright on the 'Happy Birthday to You' melody, first published in 1893 and copyrighted after litigation in 1935). But this kind of private commercial benefit, in my view, falls outside the Copyright Clause. My conclusion was that the copyright extension was unconstitutional.

For present purposes, I want to focus, not upon the substance of my copyright conclusion, but upon the fact that seven of my colleagues disagreed with it and with the empirical and logical arguments that supported it. Putting aside the possibility that the disagreement just means I was wrong on the merits, and knowing, as I do, that my colleagues are not in any sense benighted, I would ask why my arguments were unconvincing. There may be an interesting answer to this question.

In saying this I am not referring to the technical, specialized, and complex subject-matter, to the need for time to write the dissent, or to the legal fact that we courts must defer heavily in this area to the judgment of Congress. I point to another factor that I believe is more important. That factor consists of the novelty of the approach I accepted, an approach that depends heavily upon an economic-type weighing of costs and benefits. The approach is not completely novel. It finds support in the literature and in prior case law. But, in its heavy reliance upon economic and commercial factors, it departs from the style, if not the substance, of most previous copyright opinions. Justice Holmes once said that: 'For the rational study of the law, the black letter man may be the man of the present, but the man of the future is the man of statistics and the master of economics.'[18] That 'future' apparently is still a way off.

The law, of course, is a conservative institution. Courts must protect those who have relied upon prior law and prior approaches. Thus, courts ordinarily will rightly hesitate to adopt a new approach to an important body of law—at least until the relevant members of the public, acting through other institutions, themselves seem to have found the new approach acceptable. Here those groups and other institutions include Congress, the copyright bar, publishers, authors, schools, libraries, research institutions, and many others beside. A critical mass has not embraced the approach that my dissenting opinion reflects. But I add, for I do not despair: at least not yet.

I do not mean to say that courts, in applying or developing copyright law or any other branch of law, follow public opinion. But I do mean to point out that the shaping of law in America is a highly democratic process. New law is less often decreed from on high by a court or a legislature than it 'bubbles up' from below. Often the law-making process resembles a kind of conversation among many interested groups, including experts, specialists, commercial enterprises, labour unions, various interest groups, and ordinary citizens. That conversation takes place in journals, at seminars, in newspapers, at hearings, and in court proceedings. The decision of one institution is taken as a datum by another. It may be embodied in administrative rules, statutes, even constitutional interpretations; but none of these is permanent; all are subject to change or gradual evolution.

Michael Oakeshott, in describing liberal education, better explained what I have in mind. 'The pursuit of learning', he said,

is not a race in which the competitors jockey for the best place, it is not even an argument or a symposium; it is a conversation... [E]ach study appear[s] as a voice whose tone is neither tyrannous nor plangent, but humble and conversable... Its integration is not superimposed but springs from the quality of the voices which speak, and its value lies in the relics it leaves behind in the mind of those who participate.[19]

Similarly, the development of legal methods and analysis is a collaborative, evolving process. The law is continuously renewed. To steal a philosophical metaphor, we renew it plank by plank while, like a ship, it floats upon the sea.

So viewed, a dissent continues to play a role in an ongoing policy debate. Even though it is not the law, others may find its arguments or approaches persuasive;

---

[18] Holmes, The Path of the Law, 10 Harv L Rev 457, 469 (1897).
[19] Michael Oakeshott, *The Voice of Liberal Learning* (1989), 109–110.

they may adapt or adopt them for use in different forums; and if there is sufficiently widespread acceptance, even judicial approaches may change. So seen, a dissent will be judged in terms of its persuasive force, which, despite the majority to the contrary, is not irretrievably lost. With this larger process in mind, I have hope that my lonely dissent invoking economic reasoning will not be so lonely in the future.

V

I have used the three dissenting opinions to illustrate three features of the law, features relevant to its use of economic policy. The first concerns the law's need to interpret statutes with, what I might call, an open-textured approach—an approach that finds greater value in the consideration of underlying human purposes than in the proliferation of strict legal categories. Bright-line rules, while sometimes useful, are not always a preferred alternative, particularly when such a rule brings about results that, in terms of a statute's basic purpose, prove counterproductive.

The second concerns the need to provide economic information and insight in a form that incorporates basic legal considerations that are likely to be of interest to the judge—in particular considerations of the administrability of a legal rule. I intend it to illustrate the need for experts to understand the role that administrative considerations, such as the need for rules, play in the law.

The third concerns the need, given the law's reluctance to rely upon novel approaches, for institutions outside the judiciary to debate and eventually to adopt approaches that will permit judicial intellectual property decisions to incorporate economic considerations.

Overall, I hope to have encouraged those interested in economics and law not to take legal decisions as a given. They must understand the importance of institutional factors, including the need for rules that judges and lawyers can administer. But they cannot assume that only judges or lawyers are experts on questions of administration. The shape of a legal rule, the extent to which it ought to be a 'bright-line' rule, is itself open to study. And those who are intellectually comfortable with concepts of equilibrium, who see virtues in considering a little more, a little less, might have something to contribute in this area as well.

Clearly I favour participation in the judicial process by those with economic or regulatory policy-making expertise. The more you are aware of judicial decision-making and willing to undertake informed criticism, the better. Whether serving as experts in individual cases, or more generally as informed court watchers and critics, you can make more accessible to lawyers and judges the tools of economic analysis and encourage their use.

That kind of participation is consistent with my own view of the legal process—that it is too important to be left simply to the legal specialists, to the lawyers, or even to the judges.

4

What Could the Selection by the Parties of English Law in a Civil Law Contract in Commerce and Finance Truly Mean?

*Jan Dalhuisen**

The central question in this contribution is what the choice of English law as the applicable law may mean in a contract drawn up in the civil law tradition between parties from civil law countries.

Here I assume first that both parties are professionals mainly operating in commerce or finance and have no need for special protection as there may be in consumer or employment contracts. I shall not propose a precise definition of professionals except to say that in professional dealings one may expect both parties to make it their business to enter into this particular type of contract, regularly do so, and are knowledgeable in the field,[1] although not necessarily in

---

* Professor of Law King's College London, Visiting Professor of Law UC Berkeley, Corresponding Member Royal Netherlands Academy of Arts and Sciences, Member NY Bar, FCI Arb.
[1] Traditionally the French Commercial Code refers here to acts of commerce and the German one to merchants, but neither are precisely defined and in any event also non-commercial acts or non-merchants may sometimes be covered by the respective commercial codes, notably where cheques are drawn, see Dalhuisen *on Transnational and Comparative Commercial, Financial and Trade Law*, 3rd edn (2007), 25ff.

Internationally, the issue arises e.g., when it must be established whether arbitrations are commercial (and international), see Redfern and Hunter, *Law and Practice of International Commercial Arbitration*, 4th edn (2004), 20. Also in that context there is no clear definition. The Uncitral Model Law does notably not define the term, but in a fn to Art 1(1) gives it a wide interpretation and uses a list approach but only by way of example. The UNIDROIT Contract Principles although, according to its Preamble, only applying to 'international commercial contracts' do not define them either.

Commerciality and internationality are increasingly closely connected and it may be argued that, in their structure, all professional business dealings are commercial and now ever more internationalized even if parties on occasion hail from the same country. That may not then make a difference so that in fact all such dealings start forming a different class of locally detached business arrangements then operating, it is posited, in the international commercial and financial legal order under a trans-national law (the modern law merchant or *lex mercatoria*), well to be distinguished therefore from consumer dealings which remain in essence localized and subject to domestic laws, see Dalhuisen *op.cit. supra*, 33 and JH Dalhuisen, 'Legal Orders and their Manifestation:

the law chosen. Not seldom the clause is little or poorly considered and enters at the end of long negotiations when few have the heart or stomach to continue the discussions. A similar fate may await the jurisdiction or arbitration clause. Businessmen will often see them as mere boiler plate (until problems arise) and may not want learned argument at that late stage of the negations when the signing date has often been set.

However the clause may have come about, its meaning will have to be determined and the more one thinks about it, the more wondrous a clause of this nature, here in favour of English law, may become. The idea will often be that in this manner a *neutral* law is chosen, with a language (though probably not the legal terminology) known to the parties and their (Continental) lawyers, and of a country advanced in commerce (even though not necessarily in all of its commercial law). In fact, it is unlikely that Continental lawyers can truly judge the meaning and impact of the clause. The obvious suggestion and prudent thing to do is then to consult English lawyers, assuming there is time. But even if English lawyers were consulted, it is likely that they would have little understanding of what would concern the civil law lawyers and they may not spot what could become a grave issue for them later, e.g., that amendments may require new consideration, that certain documentation may be required for them to be valid, that a parole evidence rule would operate in interpretation, that there are entirely different rules of invalidity and illegality or rescission, that there is also a rule that *ex dolo malo non oritur actio*, not to forget the entirely different attitude (in principle) to specific performance or even *force majeure*.

This would all go without saying for the English lawyer but could be puzzling to the Continental one and lead to a risk distribution with which he would be unfamiliar and which would therefore not have been discounted in the transaction. In fact, proper legal advice requires here a specialist in *both* the English legal system and that of the legal system of the parties (or of both of them) to give proper warning and such lawyers remain rare till this day,[2] even where there is now no shortage of e.g., combined English and German law firms. It does not necessarily solve this problem of perception and understanding of the relevant differences.

The Continental lawyers may at least vaguely realize that the whole concept of good faith finds a different expression in common law, but how? They might think it does not truly operate in England—their clients may prefer it—although in truth it is there differently packaged and is cast rather in terms of (a) the nature of the relationship between the parties to which common law is traditionally

---

The Operation of the International Commercial and Financial Legal Order and its *Lex Mercatoria*', (2006) 24 Berkeley Journal of International Law, 129.

[2] It has become an important feature of the legal education of King's College in London to educate students in two legal systems and give them the professional degree in both, for French law together with Paris I (Sorbonne) and for German law together with the Humboldt University in Berlin.

much more sensitive than civil law and easily accepts, for example, different law in consumer and professional sales.[3] Especially in situations of dependency, English law further relies heavily on (b) fiduciary duties which are much better developed than in civil law. The Continental good faith notion may also be cast as (c) implied term or condition, as (d) natural justice (sometimes), or may figure (e) through the notion of reliance.[4]

On the other hand, would Continental lawyers realize that where many on the Continent now hold that good faith notions are always mandatory, see the EUROPEAN and UNIDROIT Contract Principles and now also the 2008 Draft Common Frame of Reference (DCFR),[5] at least the UCC, which is not averse to the notion of good faith, makes it very clear that professional parties may still set standards amongst themselves and are encouraged to do so, unless manifestly unreasonable (section 1–302). These standards are not assumed therefore and there is no censorious or correcting attitude innate in professional private law except in extreme circumstances when fundamental principle (which could be cast in good faith terms) may adjust the relationship. It is an important clarification and facility which at least in professional dealing would seem the better approach and may also obtain in England.[6] It might indeed be a sound reason to prefer the English law, but is the Continental lawyer sufficiently aware of this? It also raises the question, discussed below, whether through a choice of law clause of this nature otherwise applicable mandatory law can be left behind.

What else should concern the Continental lawyer whilst choosing English law? It is an old problem but the question of public policy continues to bedevil the notion of the contractual choice of law. This is a more general issue and strictly

---

[3] See Bingham LJ in *Interfoto Picture Library Ltd v Stiletto Visual Programmes Ltd* [1989] 1 QB 433, 439, in which it was held that particularly onerous or unusual conditions had to be brought to the special attention of the counter-party, that the conventional analysis of offer and acceptance was not followed in that case, and that the English authorities looked instead at the nature of the transaction and the character of the parties to it to consider what was necessary to conclude to a binding contract.

[4] See Dalhuisen n 1 above at 293.

[5] Art 1.201(2) European Principles and Art 1.7 (2) Unidroit Principles and Art III-1: 103 DCFR.

[6] Another question is whether it is sufficiently realized by Continental lawyers that even in civil law the notion of good faith might restrict as well as expand protection. Often I find that they do not properly understand this, which for them may be a reason to 'flee' to another law. Especially in professional dealings, good faith itself may require that contracts designed as roadmaps are literally interpreted, that pre-contractual duties, post-contractual renegotiation rights, and hardship notions, even notions of mistake, duress, and *force majeure*, may have to be interpreted in a limited fashion and in any event do *not* receive their cue from consumer law.

Good faith could thus extend but also limit the protection of parties, especially professional ones. That is a key insight, although it must be admitted that civil law lawyers often still think that good faith is always extra protection. This is consumer law thinking and for professionals it may not be so. It shows the unfortunate influx of consumer law notions and thinking in all of civil law, an important confusion, reflected in both the EUROPEAN and even UNIDROIT Principles of Contract Law, although the latter only apply to international commercial contracts, therefore to professional dealings, and hence also in the DCFR. Here the choice of English law may prove a clarification of what in civil law should no less obtain.

speaking not particular for choosing the law of a common law country, but what does the choice here mean? What does it cover or not? Especially in regulation or antitrust matters, and most obviously in matters of taxation, nobody assumes that by choosing the law of another country parties can opt out of the otherwise applicable regime. But this is no less so in many other areas, like public health, security, environment, financial regulation, and the like. Again the Americans lead the way in Sections 402/403 of the Restatement (Third) Foreign Relations Law of the United States of 1987[7] and the English may well follow. It is the issue of which country has in these cases the proper power to regulate or to prescribe which may foremost depend on the question in which territory there is most conduct and effect in respect of the transaction in question.

Awareness of the problem, though hardly guidance, we find in Europe in Article 7(1) of the Rome Convention on the Law Applicable to Contractual Obligations, never accepted by the UK and Germany now replaced by Article 9(1) of the EU regulation of 2008 in this area (Rome I). An example may clarify the point: if the contract had been about the sale of mineral water from France into Germany and, assuming that France, Germany, and England all had strict quality requirements that were nevertheless different, the German ones would most likely prevail as those of the country mostly concerned, although EU law might still have to say something about it if the German requirements unduly prevented the free movement of goods, but at least the choice of English law by

---

[7] The text is as follows:

Par. 402. Bases of Jurisdiction to Prescribe: Subject to Par. 403, a state has jurisdiction to prescribe law with respect to (1) (a) conduct that, wholly or in substantial part takes place within its territory, (b) the status of persons, or interests in things, present within its territory; (c) conduct outside its territory that has or is intended to have substantial effect within its territory; (2) the activities, interests, status, or relations of its nationals outside or within its territory;...

Par. 403. Limitations on Jurisdiction to Prescribe: (1) Even when one of the bases for jurisdiction under Par. 402 is present, a state may not exercise jurisdiction to prescribe law with respect to a person or activity having connections with another state when the exercise of such jurisdiction is unreasonable. (2) Whether exercise of jurisdiction over a person or activity is reasonable is determined by evaluating all relevant factors, including where appropriate (a) the link of the activity to the territory of the regulating state, i.e., the extent to which the activity takes place within the territory or has substantial, direct, and foreseeable effect upon or in the territory; (b) the connection such as nationality, residence or economic activity, between the regulating state and the person principally responsible for the activity to be regulated, or between that state and those whom the regulation is designed to protect; (c) the character of the activity to be regulated, the importance of regulation to the regulating state, the extent to which other states regulate such activities, and the degree to which the desirability of such regulation is generally accepted; (d) the existence of justified expectations that might be protected or hurt by the regulation; (e) the importance of the regulation to the international political, legal or economic system; (f) the extent to which the regulation is consistent with the traditions of the international system; (g) the extent to which another state may have an interest in regulating the activity; and (h) the likelihood of conflict with regulation by another state.

Par. 403 (2) (c), (e) and (f) might even suggest the introduction of general minimum standards.

See for case law in the US most famously *Timberlane Lumber Co v Bank of America*, 549 F2 597 (1976) and more recently the US Supreme Court in *Hartford Fire Insurance Co v California*, 509 US 764 (1993).

the parties would here be entirely irrelevant and English regulation would not come into it even though its laws were chosen as applicable by the parties.

The disturbing factor remains, however, that courts may well react differently depending on whether the case was brought in Germany, France, or England, as they may consider themselves bound by their *leges fori* in the matter, a problem less likely to surface in international arbitrations where there is no *lex fori* proper, reasons why in these matters arbitration may be preferred. Indeed, these issues are now entirely arbitrable and since the American *Mitsubishi* case and the EU *Eco Suisse* case, international arbitrators must decide them.[8]

Decisions in these matters are of necessity very *factual*. The balancing that may here result between conflicting policies that may all lay claim to being applied is in truth a matter of international public order. Thus in the US, comity language is here often used even though mostly still considered a domestic concept. It may eventually be superseded by resort to internationally accepted minimum regulatory standards, here in terms of quality. Bilateral investment treaties (BITs) might start showing the way, at least in labour and environmental protections and also in matters of financial stability.

In fact, in choosing a law, parties only have a choice in matters at their free disposition, no more. That excludes public policy like tax, competition, and other regulatory law, but this problem of what parties can opt into or opt out of is not confined to public policy issues. In mandatory private law, similar issues arise. Can parties, for example, really choose the law that determines the validity and legality of their own contract? Quite apart from whether the contract needs to find a base in a domestic or transnational law, also an international or transnational contract needs more *objective* law to support it and that may not be the law of the parties' choice.

Above, it was noted that good faith notions are often considered mandatory in civil law, therefore an expression of some profound public imperative. If that were really true, there could also be a problem in opting out of them and their standards or in setting others if that was the idea behind a contractual choice of law clause. Also, is it possible to choose the law applicable in proprietary matters, e.g., in terms of title transfer and their modalities in international sales (although parties may still set or vary the time of the transfer)? Obviously, in respect of land, parties cannot usefully choose the mortgage law of a country other than the *situs*. But even in respect of movable property it is hardly possible for parties to create a floating charge or conditional (finance) sale under English law in respect of assets located, for example, in France. Similarly it would seem a common law trust can hardly be created by parties in respect of assets situated in Germany.

---

[8] As is well known, the US Supreme Court first showed the way in *Mitsubishi Motors Corp v Soler Chrysler-Plymouth, Inc* 473 US 614 (1985). Sometimes, as in competition issues, arbitrators may or must even raise them *ex officio*, see *Eco Swiss v Benetton* case, ECJ Case C–126/97 [1998] ECR I–3055.

In respect of movable assets that travel between countries it is not different even if the *situs* is less clear and it may become a matter of recognition in the country of destination of rights properly acquired in the country of origin, although for receivables case law may be more accommodating, connected as this is with the controversy on the proprietary nature of this type of asset and the uncertainties that remained here even under Article 12 of the Rome Convention on the Law Applicable to Contractual Obligations now replaced by Article 13 of Rome I (2008).[9]

[9] In more recent Dutch case law, even in the proprietary aspects of assignments, sometimes the law of the underlying claim and in other cases the law of the assignment have been upheld as applicable following Art 12(1) and (2) of the 1980 Rome Convention on the Law Applicable to Contractual Obligations rather than on the law of the debtor or that of the assignor. The important point to make here is that this allows for party autonomy and a contractual choice of law in proprietary matters.

There are in the Netherlands three Supreme Court cases in this connection the last two of which have elicited considerable international interest: see HR, 17 Apr 1964 [1965] NJ 23, HR, 11 June 1993 [1993] NJ 776, and HR, 16 May 1997 [1997] RvdW 126. See for a discussion of the first two cases, JH Dalhuisen, 'The Assignment of Claims in Dutch Private International Law', in *Festschrift Kokkini-Iatridou, Comparability and Evaluation* (Asser Institute, 1994) 183 and for the last one THD Struycken, 'The Proprietary Aspects of International Assignment of Debts and the Rome Convention, Article 12' [1998] *LMCLQ* 345.

Usually, though, the issue is who has the collection right, therefore to whom should the debtor pay, and this is in truth a proprietary issue, according to many authors not covered therefore by the Rome Convention. Not so, or no longer so, in the opinion of the Dutch Supreme Court, which applied Art 12(1) in proprietary matters, probably by way of analogy. Whether these proprietary issues are put under Art 12(1) as a question of validity of the assignment (as the HR did in 1997) or under Art 12(2) as a matter of assignability (as it did in 1993), both solutions seem to allow for *party autonomy* in the proprietary aspects of an assignment, either as a matter of party choice of law under the assignment agreement (Art 12(1)) or under the contract producing the assigned claim (assuming it was contractual).

Dutch case law seems here to follow German law, which has always had difficulty in distinguishing between the proprietary and contractual side of assignments because it does not qualify claims as proper assets. Neither does modern Dutch law, although, German law looks to the law of the underlying contract rather than to the law of the assignment in this connection; there is also some support for the law of the assignment, see EM Kieninger, 'Das Statut der Forderungsabtretung in Verhaeltnis zu Dritten', 62 *RabelsZ*, 678 (1998). The law covering the assignment agreement is then thought controlling.

On the other hand, the applicability of the law of the underlying claim is defended in the proprietary aspects in a more recent Dutch dissertation: see LFA Steffens, *Overgang van Vorderingen en Schulden in het Nederlandse Internationaal Privaatrecht* [Transfer of Claims and Liabilities in Dutch Private International Law] (1997). Earlier in the Netherlands, RIVF Bertrams and HLE Verhagen preferred the law of the assignment: *Goederenrechtelijke Aspecten van de Internationale Cessie en Verpanding van Vorderingen op Naam* (1993), WPNR 6088, 261. THD Struycken, above, prefers the law of the residence of assignor. Dalhuisen, n 1 above, 719 defends the applicability of the law of the residence of the debtor, see also R Goode, *Commercial Law* (3rd edn, 2004), 1140.

See more recently in England in support of the law of the assigned underlying claim, and also for the validity of the assignment (in respect of an insurance policy), *Raffeisen Zentralbank Osterreich AG v Five Star General Trading LLC*, [2001] 3 All ER, 257.

See, for a defence of party autonomy in these matters and therefore the acceptance of the use of private international law as a route to open up the *numerus clausus* system of proprietary rights in civil law (without much emphasis on the equivalency test), A Flessner and H Verhagen, *Assignment in European Private International Law, Claims as property and the European Commission's Rome 1 proposal* (2006). Some degree of party autonomy in proprietary matters with the attendant inroads into the notion of the *numerus clausus* of proprietary rights might be acceptable but only if there

Again, party autonomy, although a favoured concept in matters of choice of law, clearly has its limits and it must in each instance be determined how far it goes.

There is here yet another facet that needs discussion. If parties choose English law to achieve a result that they could not possibly have intended or even considered, could that result still prevail, for example if it led to the invalidity of a contract that was clearly wanted? Professor Lando early identified this problem in connection with the consideration requirement.[10] What if there was no consideration in the English sense? Would the choice of English law invalidate the contract even though parties clearly wanted it?

I like to highlight here a broader issue. Is the operation of a domestic law in an international contract, whether chosen by the parties or not, really the same as the operation of the same law in a domestic contract? Again this is not a question typical for a contractual choice of English law, but if it is chosen (or results as applicable under other rules of private international law), the question is whether English law operates in the same manner in an international business transaction as it does in a local one. It is posited that this is *not* necessarily the case (unless the parties indeed have made it clear that they wanted to be treated as in a local transaction, a clause I have never seen).

The fact that there may be a difference here may in the above example save the Continental lawyers from the consequences of their ignorance of the notion of consideration and its operation by choosing English law, at least to some extent. For example, if it is true that internationally the consideration requirement has lapsed, see the Vienna Convention on the International Sale of Goods, the earlier Hague Conventions (ratified by the UK), and the EUROPEAN and UNIDROIT Contract Principles and the DCFR which do not maintain it,[11] it might be said that in international transactions there is now a consensus that the consideration requirement has no longer a meaning, therefore that there is some transnational general principle or even custom to the effect that will save such a contract without consideration even if governed by English law.

Thus it may well be that upon a proper interpretation of the choice of law clause in favour of English law, parties might *not* be found truly to have intended its rules of validity and consideration to operate so as to annul their deal whilst

---

is an adequate protection for *bona fide* purchasers or collectors of the underlying asset, which is mostly not available as a matter of domestic law except in respect of equitable proprietary interests in common law countries. This may indeed facilitate the acceptance of party autonomy in international assignments in common law countries subject to the conversion of the resulting interests into equitable proprietary rights as nearest equivalents, cut short in such cases by the protection of *bona fide* purchasers or collectors, but this is notably missing in the above continental proposals suggesting a greater degree of party autonomy.

[10] Ole Lando, 'The Lex Mercatoria in International Commercial Arbitration' (1985) 34 ICLQ 747, 748.
[11] Even domestically there have been proposals in England to abolish it. The UCC in Art 2 maintains it but mitigates its effects, e.g., in offers not being binding for lack of consideration.

transnational custom,[12] general principle, or even treaty law may support this. Perhaps on a more elevated note, the rule *pacta sunt servanda* prevails here as fundamental transnational legal principle, therefore the will to conclude the contract over more esoteric or atavistic local sub-rules that may distract from it.

At least in international commercial or financial dealings, we thus may see a number of additional rules starting to impact on or explain the parties' choice of law and the expression of their autonomy in this regard: it is not only local regulatory law and local domestic property or other mandatory law, like that which may affect the contracts' validity and legality, that may impact on the freedom to choose domestic law or more likely on its effect especially when meant to be displaced, but there may now also be limitation, clarification or amplification derived from transnational law—in terms of fundamental principle, custom, treaty law, general principle, or innate public order limitations when mandatory. Such mandatory transnational law we see upon a proper analysis indeed in the laws concerning bills of lading[13] and negotiable instruments, especially eurobond and euromarket practices including clearing and settlement,[14] in international assignments,[15] and in set-off and

---

[12] The notion of custom is important and by no means uncontested. Its meaning and content may well give rise to interesting discussions but it will not here be analysed any further, see JH Dalhuisen, 'Custom and its Revival in Transnational Private Law', forthcoming in Duke JICL (2008).

[13] See Haak, 'Internationalism above Freedom of Contract' in *Essays on International and Comparative Law in Honour of Judge Erades* (1983), 69. It is sometimes also suggested that international mandatory customary law overrides the jurisdiction of the *forum actoris* (of the plaintiff therefore), see Verheul, 'The Forum Actoris and International Law' in the same *Essays in Honour of Judge Erades*, 196.

[14] It is often said that the negotiability of eurobonds derives from the force of market custom: see the older English cases on international bonds law *Goodwin v Roberts* [1876] 1 AC 476 and *Picker v London and County Banking Co* (1887) 18 QBD 512 (CA), which relate to Russian and Prussian bonds and emphasized that the financial community treated these instruments as negotiable regardless of domestic laws, see further P Wood, *Law and Practice of International Finance* (London, 1980), 184. See also *Bechuanaland Exploration Co v London Trading Bank* [1898] 2 QBD 658, in which it was accepted in connection with the negotiability of bearer bonds that 'the existence of usage has so often been proved and its convenience is so obvious that it might be taken now to be part of the law'.

Modern case law does not, however, exist confirming the point but in England these cases are still considered good law. See, for the explicit reference in this connection to the custom of the mercantile world which may expressly be of recent origin, *Dicey, Morris and Collins on the Conflict of Laws* (14th edn, 2006), Rule 222, 1800.

The transnational status of eurobonds is probably not affected, even now that in most cases they have become mere book-entry entitlements in a paperless environment, see Dalhuisen, n 1 above at 806. It affects also the way these instruments are repo-ed or given in security, cleared, and settled, see Dalhuisen at 230.

[15] Here important issues of notification and documentation arise especially in respect of the use of receivables in modern financing where local law impediments in this regard to bulk assignments are increasingly removed and a reasonable description and immediate transfer upon the conclusion of the assignment agreement is becoming normative. Future (replacement) receivables are increasingly likely to be able to be included so that questions of identification and sufficient disposition rights do no longer arise either. Exceptions derived form the underlying agreements out of which these receivables arise are increasingly ignored, especially any third party effect of contrac-

netting,[16] which may all be considered transnational custom, supported by general principles wherever necessary which are then also of a mandatory (mostly proprietary) nature. It truly concerns here the infrastructure of the international markets. On the other hand, in letters of credit (UCP) and trade terms (Incoterms),[17] we see examples of transnational law that is merely directory (or default rule).

tual assignment restriction, whilst others are limited to situations in which the assignment gives rise to unreasonable burdens, see also S 2–210 and 9–404 UCC and for a comparative summary Dalhuisen, n 1 above at 968 ff.

The promissory note as negotiable instrument with its independence from the underlying transaction out of which it arises becomes here the better transnational analogy, perhaps aided by the UNCITRAL 2001 Convention on the Assignment of Receivables in International Trade, although it has not received any ratifications and is certainly not as clear and advanced as it could have been, see Dalhuisen n 1 above at 970 and 1014.

[16] In this connection, in the swap and repo markets, the ISDA Swap Master Agreements and the PSA/ISMA Global Master Repurchase Agreement may also acquire the status of custom in the areas they cover, at least in the London and the New York markets where they operate. This may be particularly relevant for their close-out and netting provisions in an event of default. The status of contractual bilateral netting with its enhancements of the set-off principle and its inclusion of all swaps or repos between the same parties, leading to a netting out of all positions in the case of default at the option of the non-defaulting party and *ipso facto* in the case of bankruptcy, could otherwise still remain in doubt under local laws.

In the 1996 Amendments to the 1988 Basel Accord on Capital Adequacy, the netting principle was internationally accepted, see also Dalhuisen, n 1 above at 1265. It concerns here so-called soft law but nevertheless a most important international acknowledgement of the concept of netting, although still subject to the condition that the law of the country of the residence of the counterparty (or his place of incorporation) and of the branch through which the bank acted as well as the law applicable to the swap must accept the netting concept (which had required changes or clarifications in domestic law of several countries).

[17] The idea of the UCP being transnational customary law is associated with the views of the Austrian Frederic Eisemann, Director of the Legal Department of the ICC at the time, and was first proposed by him at a 1962 King's College London Colloquium, see *Le Credit Documentaire dans le Droit et dans la Pratique* (Paris 1963), 4. This approach was followed in England by Clive Schmitthoff, although in his views always in the context of some national law.

See for France, Y Loussouarn and JD Bredin, *Droit du Commerce International*, 48 (1969). In France, their status as international custom is now well established, see also J Puech, *Modes de paiement*, in Lamy, Transport Tome II, No 324 (2000); see also Berthold Goldman, *Lex Mercatoria*, in Forum Internationale, No 3 (Nov 1983); *Trib De Commerce de Paris*, 8 March 1976; 28 Le Droit Maritime Francais 558 (1976) (Fr); *Cour de Cass, 14 Oct 1981*, Semaine Juridique II 19815 (1982), note Gavalda & Stoufflet; *Cour de Cass, 5 Nov 1991*, Bull Civ, IV, no 328 (1992) (Fr).

In Belgium their status as international custom was accepted by the *Tribunal de Commerce of Brussels*, 16 Nov 1978, *reprinted in* 44 Rev de la Banque, 249 (1980). In Germany, see Norbert Horn, *Die Entwicklung des internationalen Wirtschaftrechts durch Verhaltungsrichtlinie*, 44 Rabels Zeitschrift 423 (1980), but the German doctrine remains uncertain, especially because of the written nature of the UCP and its regular adjustments which is seen there as contrary to the notion of custom, see CW Canaris, *Bankvertragsrecht*, Part I, 926 (3rd edn, 1988).

In the Netherlands, the Supreme Court has not so far fully accepted the UCP as objective law. See *Hoge Raad, 22 May 1984*, NJ 607 (1985). The lower courts are divided. So are the writers with PL Wery, *De Autonomie van het Eenvormige Privaatrecht*, 11 (1971) and this author in favour, see Jan Dalhuisen, *Bank Guarantees in International Trade*, 6033 WPNR 52 (1992).

English law does not require any incorporation in the documentation. See *Harlow and Jones Ltd v American Express Ban Ltd & Creditanstalt-Bankverein*, [1990] 2 Lloyd's Rep 343 (concerning the applicability of the ICC Uniform Rules for Collection (URC) which are less well known, but

As in public international law,[18] also in transnational (private) law a number of sources of law thus start to operate side by side. This may suggest a *hierarchy*,[19] in which party autonomy also plays a role and is itself one of the sources of law.

I have always considered this the essence of the modern *lex mercatoria* or law merchant which therefore constitutes for practitioners a law-finding process of a particular nature. This hierarchy descends from fundamental legal principle,[20]

nevertheless subscribed to by all banks in England); *Power Curber Int'l Ltd v Nat'l Bank of Kuwait SAK*, [1981] 2 Lloyd's Rep 394 (per Denning, L considering the UCP as such, also with reference to the fact that all or practically all banks in the world subscribe to them, which seems the true criterion in England).

For the US, see *Oriental Pac (USA) Inc v Toronto Dominion Bank*, 357 NYS2d 957 (NY 1974), in which the force of law of the UCP was accepted 'to effect orderly and efficient banking procedures and the international commerce amongst nations.' *Id* at 959. In the US the Incoterms and UCP are matched by similar rules in Arts 2 and 5 UCC, which may leave open the question of them operating as international custom in the US but they would likely have that status in international cases and then supersede any conflicts of law rules in this area.

[18] Well known from Art 31 Statute International Court of Justice.

[19] Although important authors like Lando, see n 10 above and P Fouchard, see *Fouchard Gaillard Goldman on International Commercial Arbitration*, Part Five (1999), consider the new law merchant indeed also as a forward moving process of law-finding in which different sources of law are to be considered, they do not identify the hierarchy nor the residual role of domestic law in this transnationalized sense.

[20] See Dalhuisen, n 1 above 213, where the most important fundamental principles are (without limitation) identified as follows (and may in contract often be cast in terms of good faith):

(a) *pacta sunt servanda* as the essence of contract law and party autonomy;
(b) the recognition, transferability and substantial protection of ownership as the essence of all property to be respected by all;
(c) the liability for own action, especially
    (i) if wrongful (certainly if the wrong is of a major nature) as the essence of tort law,
    (ii) if leading to detrimental reliance on such action by others as another fundamental source of contract law,
    (iii) if creating the appearance of authority in others as an essential of the law of (indirect) agency, or
    (iv) if resulting in owners creating an appearance of ownership in others as an additional fundamental principal in the law of property and at the heart of the protection of the *bona fide* purchaser (setting aside the more traditional *nemo dat* principle).

There are other fundamental principles in terms of:

(d) fiduciary notions in situations of dependency, e.g., in contract and in agency leading on the one hand to special protections of counterparties (or principals against agents, or companies against directors), especially if weaker (including consumers against wholesalers, workers against employers, individuals against the state, smaller investors against brokers), and leading on the other hand to duties of disclosure and faithful implementation of one's contractual and other obligations;
(e) notions of unjust enrichment;
(f) respect for acquired or similar rights, traditionally particularly relevant to outlaw retroactive government intervention, but also used to support owners of proprietary rights in assets that move to other countries;
(g) the possibility to create limited proprietary rights that rank according to the time in which they were created *(prior tempore, potior iure)*.
(h) equality of treatment between creditors and shareholders within the same class and of other classes of interested parties with similar rights unless they have postponed themselves.

Then there are:

mandatory custom,[21] mandatory treaty law,[22] mandatory general principle,[23] party autonomy, directory custom, directory treaty law, and directory general principle. In this hierarchy, domestic law found through the traditional conflicts of law principles is also a source of law and retains as such a place as the *residual* rule (either of a mandatory or directory nature) and is applicable if there are no rules found in preceding sources of law. This residual rule of domestic law makes at the same time for a full system of law—its alleged absence (by those who believe in legal systems) being therefore an incorrect (but often heard) criticism of the modern *lex mercatoria*—but there is an important caveat in the sense that when domestic law applies in this way, it still operates as transnational law within the new law merchant and must make sense in that context. This may suggest an extra measure of judicial discretion or special interpretation facility. Again, it confirms that English law in domestic cases is not necessarily the same as in international

(i) fundamental procedural protections in terms of impartiality, proper jurisdiction, proper hearings and the possibility to mount an adequate defense, now often related to the more recent (and also internationalized) standards of human rights and basic protections (see Art 6 of the 1950 ECHR);

(j) fundamental protections against fraud, abuse, sharp practices, excessive power, cartels, bribery, and insider dealings or other forms of manipulation in market-related assets (also in their civil and commercial aspects) and against money laundering;

(k) finally, there are also fundamental principles of environmental protection developing.

As the latter are public order or even human rights related, they are as such no less mandatory.

In recent times, the impact of human rights on private law formation has been noted and is now often referred to as the *constitutionalization* of private law. In commerce and finance, these rights or principles are not many and must then always be seen in a typically private law context, especially in commerce and finance. The term 'constitutionalization' may not therefore be well chosen. See for this concept in Germany CW Canaris, *Grundrechte und Privatrecht, eine Zwischenbilanz* (Berlin, 1998) and in England, D Friedmann and D Barak-Erez (eds), *Human Rights in Private Law* (2001) and Hugh Collins, 'Utility and Rights in Common Law Reasoning: Rebalancing Private Law through Constitutionalization', LSE Law Dept. Law and Society Working Paper Series, 2nd issue Sept 2007.

[21] As mentioned before true mandatory custom is most likely to emerge in non-contractual matters, therefore in proprietary matters or in contractual aspects that, like issues of validity, cannot be freely determined or changed by the parties. It was already said that transnational rules of set-off and netting may also be in this category. It is for expert witnesses to demonstrate their existence and for international arbitrators and the courts when asked to rule on them, to acknowledge international customs and practices in these areas.

[22] So far uniform treaty law is rare, but cf Art 12 of the Vienna Convention as an example. It allows Contracting States to demand written international sales agreements.

If the 2001 UNCITRAL Convention on the Assignment of Receivables in International Trade were to be widely adopted, there would be a great deal more of these mandatory provisions in Contracting States particularly in the formalities and proprietary aspects of international bulk assignments of receivables. There are also some in the 2001 UNIDROIT Mobile Equipment Convention.

If EU Directives or Regulations were also taken into account in this category, there could be many more viz. the Collateral and Settlement Finality Directives.

[23] Mandatory general principle could develop e.g., in the area of set-off and netting but may then soon figure in the higher category of mandatory custom. In sales, minimum quality requirements may also be deduced from the mandatory rules or practices in modern countries. These mandatory general principles may fill in the detail of mandatory fundamental principle, custom, and treaty law.

cases. It should be noted also that the end result is not necessarily uniform law as custom and domestic law may still vary per business and territory.

The key is therefore multiple sources of law and the ranking between them and it confirms that English law in English cases need not be the same as English law in international cases, whether or not selected by the parties. It is likely increasingly to be affected by the operation of competing sources of law whilst it is itself transnationalized when operating in international transactions.

This idea is not as provocative as one may think. Indeed, the Vienna Convention on the International Sale of Goods in its Article 7 contains the idea of multiple sources of law with domestic law functioning as the residual rule but it expresses it unclearly and only in the context of supplementation or gap filling of the Convention itself.[24] It does not enter into the subject of the sources of law in any more fundamental manner (although it is concerned with it in Article 4) and deals with custom and practices also very perfunctorily (in Articles 8 and 9), only as a matter of contract interpretation.[25] Yet it has some list in Article 7 but it is a hotchpotch of all kind of ideas and the clause was never properly thought out.[26] It also

[24] The relevant language is as follows:

(1) In the interpretation of this Convention, regard is to be had to its international character and to the need to promote uniformity in its application and the observance of good faith in international trade.

(2) Questions concerning matters governed by this Convention which are not expressly settled in it are to be settled in conformity with the general principles on which it is based or, in the absence of such principles, in conformity with the law applicable by virtue of the rules or private international law.

The Vienna Convention thus goes into the interpretation and supplementation of its own text. It may be argued that that is less usual or even inconvenient and in any event not absolutely dispositive. Also, the separation of interpretation and supplementation itself may be subject to serious criticism. In a more normative or teleological approach this would not seem to be necessary or even proper. Applying greatly differing criteria is in any event puzzling without some further explanation which has not been forthcoming.

[25] Here the text is as follows:

Article 8

(1) For the purposes of the Convention statements made by and other conduct of a party are to be interpreted according to his intent where the other party knew or could not have been unaware what that intent was.

(2) If the preceding paragraph is not applicable, statements made by and other conduct of a party are to be interpreted according to the understanding that a reasonable person of the same kind as the other party would have had in the same circumstances.

(3) In determining the intent of a party or the understanding a reasonable person would have had, due consideration is to be given to all relevant circumstances of the case including the negotiations, any practices which the parties have established between themselves, usages and any subsequent conduct of the parties.

Article 9

(1) The parties are bound by any usage to which they have agreed and by any practices which they have established between themselves.

(2) The parties are considered, unless otherwise agreed, to have impliedly made applicable to their contract or its formation a usage of which the parties knew or ought to have known and which in international trade is widely known to, and regularly observed by, parties to contracts of the type involved in the particular trade concerned.

[26] See Dalhuisen, n 1 above, 411ff.

leaves the matter of contract interpretations and supplementation, as distinguished from the interpretation and supplementation of the Convention, substantially in the air.[27] It is unfortunately often repeated, as in the EUROPEAN Contract Principles[28] (but in different ways in the UNIDROIT Contract principles)[29] and conventions that deal with *proprietary* matters like the UNCITRAL 2001 Convention on the Assignment of Receivables in International Trade, and the UNIDROIT Mobile Equipment or Cape Town Convention of the same year (as in the 1988 UNIDROIT Leasing and Factoring Conventions of 1988) where especially the reference to good faith in interpretation is wholly inappropriate in the proprietary issues covered in these conventions.

Any impact of the fundamental or more general principles of the *lex mercatoria* is not excluded, however, by a Convention of this nature. Their effect depends on the applicability of other sources of the law which the Vienna Convention cannot regulate. This is recognized at least in respect of custom and usages in Article 4.

In fact, it is submitted that the uniform sales laws and their general principles (to which Article 7(2) refers) only acquire their proper place and meaning within

---

[27] Remedied to some extent in the UNIDROIT (Chapter 5) and European Contract Principles (Chapter 4), see for a discussion Dalhuisen, n 1 above, 350ff.

[28] The text is as follows:

Article 1.106 Interpretation and Supplementation

(1) These Principles should be interpreted and developed in accordance with their purposes. In particular regard should be had to the need to promote good faith and fair dealing, certainty in contractual relationships and uniformity of application.

(2) Issues within the scope of these Principles but not expressly settled by them are so far as possible to be settled in accordance with the ideas underlying the Principles. Failing this, the legal system, applicable by virtue of the rules of private international law is to be applied.

[29] The following is the relevant text:

Article 1.6 Interpretation and supplementation of the Principles:

(1) In the interpretation of these Principles, regard is to be had to their international character and to their purposes including the need to promote uniformity in their application.

(2) Issues within the scope of these Principles but not expressly settled by them are as far as possible to be settled in accordance with their underlying principles.

Especially the reference to private international law as the last resort is here absent. It also was absent from the earlier Hague Sales Conventions, cf Art 2 of the Hague Sales Convention, which only accepted conflict references in specific cases, Arts 16, 38(4), and 89. The Hague Conventions did also not distinguish between interpretation and supplementation and Art 17 of the Sales Convention required all matters in principle covered by the Convention to be generally decided in conformity with the general principles on which it was based, thus the first part of the Vienna formula for both supplementation and interpretation.

This is in accordance with the general civil law approach to codification which assumes completeness in the areas of the law it covers. Gap filling or supplementation then becomes a matter of interpretation. In the area of uniform law, there is the added argument that this approach allows for a liberal interpretation of that law and of its scope. This approach is therefore in essence uniform law friendly and internationalist.

But if accompanied by a reference to private international law it spells danger if, as in Art 7(2) of the Vienna Convention, the general principles on which the Convention is based are unknown and no other general principles may be invoked. The reference to domestic law as the residual rule then undermines the reference to general principles. There was here an important shift in the nature of the argument and even definitional problems may now have to be resolved with reference to a national law. It greatly undermines the advance of uniform law through this type of instruments.

the hierarchy of norms of the *lex mercatoria*, in which therefore the Vienna Convention itself must also find its place whilst other sources like fundamental principle and custom may be higher. In this hierarchy, even party autonomy figures above the Convention to the extent the latter is only directory (default) law, as it generally is (Article 6). Even the reference in Article 7(2) of the Vienna Convention to private international law and therefore to domestic law to supplement the Convention can therefore only be properly understood in the context of the hierarchy of norms within the new law merchant or *lex mercatoria* concerning international sales, where it has only residual rank and the domestic law so found must be adjusted to play its transnational role, as already suggested above, even though the Convention itself appears not to be aware of it.[30] The DCFR in Article I-1:102 does not advance here a great deal. The distinction between interpretation and supplementation is abandoned. There is no reference to local laws (they are indeed meant to be supersceded). A special reference is made to human rights but not to other fundamental principles. In particular, general principle and custom are not mentioned. Other sources of law like party autonomy and usage or practices operate by legislative *fiat* only and have no autonomy, see Articles II-1:102 and 104. This is the typical civil law codification approach. Uniformity of application, notions of certainty and fair dealings and of good faith are a guide to application of the text, no more.

Coming back to a choice of English law in international agreements between civil law parties and the meaning of such a clause, the foregoing means that such a contractual choice of law clause must be put in its proper place in the modern law merchant.

---

[30] When it comes to supplementation or gap filling, in the internationalist *lex mercatoria* approach, transnationalized notions of good faith may also play a role in the supplementation of the Convention as a matter of general or even fundamental principle notwithstanding the fact that the Convention only mentions it in Art 7(1) in connection with its interpretation (as distinguished from supplementation). In a *lex mercatoria* approach based on a hierarchy of norms from different legal sources, this would be clear.

In respect of the Convention more narrowly, the reference to good faith may have a more distinct meaning and may refer to teleological or normative interpretation of the text. Thus the literal approach to statutes, treaties, and contractual terms, normally adopted by the UK and towards which there may also be a bias in the Vienna Convention (certainly more so than in the earlier Hague Sales Conventions that preceded it), may be somewhat relaxed, also it would then appear for supplementation;

It follows that the appropriate reference for supplementation and interpretation of the Convention, if it needs to be covered, should have been to the text of the Convention itself, its international character, its general principles, and to the need for uniformity in its application. At the same time, it should have been made clear that other sources of law remain unimpeded so that fundamental principle, customs as they develop, as well as other general principles remain unaffected. Private international law would only come in if no objective legal regime could otherwise be found in the hierarchy of norms here presented and domestic law so becoming applicable will still become part of the transnational law and be interpreted or adjusted accordingly. Again, the issue of public policy under state law and its prevalence in international transactions is another matter altogether and a question of competition between the international commercial and financial legal order and domestic legal orders or a question of the jurisdiction to prescribe, see n 7 above and accompanying text.

It follows that parties choosing a national law move the application of domestic law higher up to the level of party autonomy, although no more. It means that such a selection remains conditioned by any mandatory rules that may respectively derive from fundamental legal principle, custom, treaty law, and general principle. It is itself followed by directory custom, treaty law, and general principle which still figure in that order in the interpretation and supplementation. Again, the result is transnational law with the consequence that English law so applied in international cases may well be quite different from what it is in domestic cases, but conceivably not as much as if no such contractual choice of law had been made and English law had come up only as the residual rule. In that case, directory custom, treaty law, and general principles would have preceded its application, *not merely* have supplemented it. That is, I believe, the difference.

It leaves two further questions to be discussed. First whether the modern *lex mercatoria* itself can be chosen as the applicable law. It would appear that the question is improperly put. Parties in international professional dealings cannot avoid the *lex mercatoria*. It is the law of the legal order in which they operate.[31] They can vary it only to the extent the resulting law is directory and they cannot exclude it altogether.

The other question is what a contractual reference to general principles may mean.[32] Here again it is submitted that such a reference must be seen in the context of the hierarchy of the *lex mercatoria* and cannot pre-empt the whole field.

---

[31] JH Dalhuisen, 'Legal Orders and their Manifestation', n 1 above.

[32] The reference to general principles became common in international law in connection with concession agreements in oil and gas. Lord Asquith of Bishopstone appears to have been the first one (in 1951) to refer in this connection to 'the application of principles rooted in the good sense and common practice of the generality of civilised nations—a sort of "modern law of nature"', see *Award in the Matter of an Arbitration between Petroleum Development (Trucial Coast) Ltd and the Sheikh of Abu Dab*i, reported in 1 *Int'l & Comp* (1952) *LQ* 247 and 18 (1951) ILR 144 9.

Subsequently, in oil concessions references to the law of all civilized nations became common, although now probably considered offensive to the oil producing country in question, see the Iranian Petroleum Agreement of 1954 referring to 'principles of law common to Iran and to the various countries to which the other parties belong and, failing that, by principles of law generally recognized by civilized nations, including such principles applied by international tribunals'. Under *ad hoc* exploration agreements with Libya, the arbitrations that eventually also decided on the nationalization issues were to be governed by the 'principles of the law of Libya common to the principles of international law and in the absence of such common principles then by and in accordance with the general principles of law, including such of these principles as may have been applied by international tribunals' *Texaco Overseas Petroleum Co & Cal Asiatic Oil Co v The Gov't of the Lybian Arab Republic*, 4 YB COM (1979) ARB 177, 181.

There were many similar clauses. Thus the Aminoil Concession Agreement of 1979 made reference to the law of the Parties 'determined by the Tribunal, having regard to the quality of the parties, the transnational character of their relations and the principles of law and practice prevailing in the modern world' *Kuwait v Aminoil, reprinted in* 21 ILM 976, 980 (1982). Where such a choice of law is made, one must assume the fuller set of *lex mercatoria* norms and their hierarchy to apply, but also that the Applicability of public law may not be affected.

It was never clear, however, in how far such a clause deprived host governments from their freedom as sovereigns to act in the public interest and supersede the concessions, although it became

This is in a nutshell the picture international adjudicators are likely to bear in mind (even though often only aware of vaguer notions of general principle) and the method which upon a proper analysis they will use in adjudicating international cases and in dealing with choice of law clauses. Transaction lawyers should very much bear this in mind too whilst legally structuring international transactions or whilst giving advice in matters of performance. It results in a substantive transnational private law, not unlike the way public international law is found under Article 38(1) Statute of the International Court of Justice, as already noted. Indeed, there is here significant convergence in method, if not in result.[33]

accepted that if they nationalized them in the public interest, damages would still be payable on the basis of such general principle but rather as breach of contract and not of international law, see the *Aminoil* case referred to above.

In similar vein but more in a private law context, the construction contract of the Channel Tunnel provided that it was to be governed by 'the principles common to both English law and French law, and in the absence of such common principles by such general principles of international trade law as have been applied by national and international tribunals' *Channel Tunnel Group v Balfour Beatty Constr Ltd,* [1995] AC 334, 347. In the international commercial and financial legal order as a newly emerging order, one would expect, however, an attitude to problem solving that is less encumbered by the past even where concepts are borrowed from domestic law in a comparative law search for better solutions.

It follows that the chosen law could itself point in the direction of the *lex mercatoria*, although it always leaves the question of whether otherwise applicable mandatory law and regulatory law can be so affected.

[33] See also Roy Goode on this divergence in attitude between public and (civil law) private law in the acceptance of different sources of law, in 'Usage and its Reception in Transnational Commercial Law' (1997) *ICLQ* 1 and JH Dalhuisen, 'International Law Aspects of Modern Financial Products', (1998) *European Business Law Review,* 281. The difference in attitude to the operation of various sources of law in international public and private law has always been hard to explain.

5

Lord Bingham, Anti-Suit Injunctions and Arbitration

Steven Gee

In *Ashville Investments v Elmer Contractors*[1] the Court of Appeal decided that a wide arbitration clause covered disputes about mistake giving rise to rectification and claims for misrepresentation. In his judgment Bingham LJ first approached the matter looking at the words of the arbitration clause and whether the disputes fitted within them. He then looked at the previous authorities seeing whether they required a different view. Arbitration is an area of the law where policy seldom stands still, and older cases can be the product of different times. Then he said:

I would be very slow to attribute to reasonable parties an intention that there should in any foreseeable eventuality be two sets of proceedings.

It was a sentence which set the theme for the later case law on the scope of arbitration clauses, blazing a trail to the decision of the House of Lords in *Premium Nafta Products v Fili Shipping*,[2] where claims of bribery said to avoid the underlying contract were held to fall within an 'under the contract' arbitration clause, and which encouraged the development of the principle that nothing short of a direct attack on the validity of the arbitration clause itself could impeach it. It cast literalism and formalism on one side. It contained a concise thought, with a strong appeal for lawyer and layman alike.

Lord Denning MR considered that his greatest achievement was the birth of the *Mareva* injunction. He was grateful that it survived the decision of the House of Lords in *the Siskina*, to be placed on a statutory basis by section 37 of the Supreme Court Act 1981. Injunctions can be viewed as a remedy derived from the Old High Court of Chancery. But that is only part of the picture. The *Mareva* injunction has evolved into a free standing process available on its own.

An injunction is a measure which can be granted by the court not confined to traditional relief in respect of a substantive cause of action such as patent infringement or threatened breach of contract. It is a powerful remedy granted as a means to an end. It can be a measure to protect the court's own process, or which can be

[1] [1989] QB 488.   [2] [2008] 1 Ll Rep 254.

granted under its inherent jurisdiction to allow the court to function properly as a court. On this there has been a major debate in the context of anti-suit injunctions. Arbitrators cannot grant injunctions as such. Under section 48 of the Arbitration Act 1996 they can make a final award which is prohibitory; but its effect is only contractual (under the implied obligation to perform an award), unless and until an injunction is granted by the court in enforcement proceedings. A procedural order which is prohibitory likewise only has contractual effect (based on the contract to arbitrate). Under the Arbitration Act 1996 the arbitrators are the gatekeepers for the granting of interim relief by the court in support of the arbitral process.

Another important use of the injunction, and the interim receiver, is to facilitate eventual enforcement of judgments or awards. This is not governed by the restriction that execution can only be had where an asset is located. There are also jurisdictions conferred on the court by statute other than the Supreme Court Act 1981, jurisdictions which speak of the power to grant an injunction and build on and modify the pre-existing jurisdiction.

The word injunction is not a term of art. Conceptually one starts from a clearly formulated court order the breach of which can result in proceedings for contempt of court. The power to grant an injunction in aid of proceedings anywhere in the world under section 25 of the Civil Jurisdiction and Judgments Act 1982 is an example of a further statutory jurisdiction. Another is the power to grant an injunction in support of arbitral proceedings wherever they may be under section 44 of the Arbitration Act 1996. Other statutory categories are to protect people from harassment and to restrain breach of planning control. In these cases what order can be granted, and in what circumstances, is shaped by the statute. In modern times the court, whilst retaining its former jurisdiction bequeathed by High Court of Chancery, has been developed through statute.

The idea of one-stop adjudication in arbitration if it is to be realized means that the courts have to be able to give support by injunction to the arbitral process at every stage, from the moment the arbitration agreement has been concluded, up until final successful enforcement of the award.

The Anti-Suit Injunction and Arbitration

(i) The nature of the anti-suit jurisdiction

An important part of the role of the Commercial Court has been the granting of an injunction to enforce an arbitration agreement—and particularly those contemplating arbitration in London. The theory is an injunction granted to restrain a threatened breach of contract in submitting a dispute for resolution on its merits to a court or tribunal other than the agreed arbitral tribunal. In *West Tankers v Ras Riunione*[3] Lord Hoffmann described the jurisdiction:

---

[3] [2007] 1 Ll Rep 391, in which the House of Lords referred to the European Court of Justice whether in a case concerning proceedings before the courts of a member state the Brussels Lugano

21 The Courts of the United Kingdom have for many years exercised the jurisdiction to restrain foreign court proceedings as Colman J did in this case: see Pena Copper Mines Ltd v Rio Tinto Co Ltd (1911) 105 LT 846. It is generally regarded as an important and valuable weapon in the hands of a court exercising supervisory jurisdiction over the arbitration. It promotes legal certainty and reduces the possibility of conflict between the arbitration award and the judgment of a national court. As Professor Schlosser also observes, it saves a party to an arbitration agreement from having to keep a watchful eye upon parallel court proceedings in another jurisdiction, trying to steer a course between so much involvement as will amount to a submission to the jurisdiction (which was what eventually happened to the buyers in The Atlantic Emperor: see [1992] 1 Lloyd's Rep 624) and so little as to lead to a default judgment. That is just the kind of thing that the parties meant to avoid by having an arbitration agreement.

It arises from the moment the arbitration agreement has been made. It applies not only to the contracting party, but also to a person who invokes rights which are themselves subject to an agreement to arbitrate, even though he is not a party to the arbitration agreement. Thus it applies to assignees of the underlying contract or the claims, subrogated insurers and to those who rely upon a statutory provision enabling them to enforce the underlying contract to which the arbitration agreement applies.[4] The English doctrines of privity of contract and consideration do not prevent enforcement of the arbitration agreement because the rights on the underlying contract are themselves subject to the arbitration agreement which modifies them, setting out a condition governing their enforcement.

The anti-suit jurisdiction may also be exercised against a person independently of there being any relevant arbitration or jurisdiction clause. An example is where proceedings are brought abroad which are vexatious or oppressive. Another is where the foreign proceedings risk interfering with pending proceedings before the English courts or their integrity or effectiveness, or with the recognition or enforcement of an English judgment or order.[5] An injunction may also be granted against a person in order to prevent that person committing a threatened contempt of court, or in order to make fully effective an injunction granted against another. An illustration of the latter is where an injunction is granted against a company restraining it from dealing with assets held by it which may be assets belonging to a person who is subject to a *Mareva* injunction. The injunction against the company is not restricted to assets belonging to the individual. Such a formulation is unclear whilst the question of beneficial ownership remains

---

regime precluded this jurisdiction being exercised, or whether this was within the exclusion of arbitration from that regime.

⁴ *West Tankers v Ras Riunione* [2005] 2 Ll Rep. 257 following *Schiffahrtsgesellschaft Detlev von Appen GmbH v Voest Alpine Intertrading GmbH (The Jay Bola)* (CA) [1997] 2 Lloyd's Rep 27 and distinguishing *Through Transport Mutual Insurance Association (Eurasia) Ltd v New India Assurance Association Co Ltd* (CA) [2005] 1 Lloyd's Rep 67 in which the Jay Bola had not been cited, and which would probably have been decided differently if it had been.

⁵ *Masri v Consolidated Contractors International* [2008] 2 Ll Rep 301, anti-suit injunction granted to prevent proceedings in Yemen threatening to re-litigate the claim , and interfering with the enforcement of an English money judgment.

unresolved. The injunction identifies what particular assets the company cannot deal with except in accordance with the court order.

(ii) Supreme Court Act 1981, section 50 and damages for breach of the arbitration agreement

A consequence of this width of the injunction jurisdiction is that damages can be awarded against such a person who acts inconsistently with the arbitration agreement, even though that person is not a party to the arbitration agreement. This is because of the jurisdiction to award damages under section 50 of the Supreme Court Act 1981 which reads:

50. Where the Court of Appeal or the High Court has jurisdiction to entertain an application for an injunction or specific performance, it may award damages in addition to, or in substitution for, an injunction or specific performance.

This is a provision which contains words based on Lord Cairns's Act. That Act was passed to enable the old High Court of Chancery to award damages in proceedings for specific performance or an injunction where otherwise it might not have been able to give full relief in the action. Before the Act the Court of Chancery had been able in a specific performance action to assess compensation where the land to be conveyed was not in accordance with the contract and allow that as an abatement from the price when ordering specific performance.[6] A purpose of the 1858 Act was to enable the High Court of Chancery to grant full and complete financial relief in the action and so avoid the plaintiff from having to seek damages in a common law court. The underlying policy was to enable one-stop adjudication—the thought expressed by Bingham LJ in *Ashville*.

The context in which section 50 was enacted was different. The High Court can grant both an injunction and damages. It has the powers of the old High Court of Chancery and those of the common law courts. The facts which made the one-stop adjudication purpose of Lord Cairns's Act such a pressing need in 1858 were not present in 1981. Section 50 is an ancillary jurisdiction to the injunction jurisdiction of the court, allowing damages to be awarded whenever the court has jurisdiction to entertain an application for an injunction. For example the court may act to protect its own orders by granting an injunction to restrain a threatened contempt of court. This injunction may be granted against a non-party against whom there is no substantive cause of action. Damages may be awarded under section 50 to a claimant who suffers loss through a contempt, against a contemnor who might have been restrained by injunction granted in the proceedings before he committed the contempt of court. Likewise an injunction may be granted against a defendant seeking to litigate abroad an issue over which the English court is already seized or has already determined on the merits.[7]

---

[6] *Grant v Dawkins* [1973] 1 WLR 1406.
[7] *Masri v Consolidated Contractors International* [2008] 2 Ll Rep 301.

Damages can be awarded under section 50 for loss caused by the foreign proceedings to the English claimant.

The jurisdiction is discretionary. It is not necessary that an injunction is granted in the proceedings as a pre-condition to its exercise. Nor is it necessary that to grant the injunction would have been wise.

It permits damages to be awarded for threatened future breaches of contract which have not yet occurred—just as the 1858 Act permitted. It applies to losses incurred during the relevant proceedings, which could have been avoided had the injunction sought (or which could have been sought) been granted when the proceedings were commenced. There could be a question whether it could apply to losses already incurred prior to the bringing of proceedings had the injunction sought in the proceedings been sought and granted earlier. An example might be costs of foreign proceedings already wasted by the time the injunction proceedings were commenced in England. It would seem fair and reasonable that all the wasted costs arising from impugned foreign proceedings should be dealt with together in one proceeding by the English court, rather than splitting them up according to the date the English proceedings were commenced. It is not hard to envisage circumstances where the claimant has unsuccessfully sought undertakings from the defendant to discontinue the foreign proceedings before commencing the injunction proceedings in England and in the meantime incurred some costs.

Would those earlier costs be outside section 50? The jurisdiction of the court depends upon there having been during the proceedings jurisdiction for the court to entertain an application for an injunction. The court formulates what injunction it had jurisdiction to entertain an application for, and then considers what damages to award to cover losses caused by that injunction not having been granted at all or not having been granted earlier, by the court. It is suggested that because in the period prior to the issue of the claim form the court still had jurisdiction to entertain an application for *that* injunction, therefore under the section it can award damages to compensate the claimant for losses sustained which would have been avoided had *that* injunction been granted at any stage when the court could have entertained an application to grant it.

In practice the court normally can be expected to leave damages to be decided only by the arbitral tribunal exercising its jurisdiction to award damages for breach of the arbitration clause. This is because where the claims for damages are coextensive, there is only one decision to be made. That should be left to the arbitrators as the chosen tribunal. Once decided, the matter has been adjudicated upon and there will be nothing left to be resolved by the court[8] under section 50. Under the contractual claim for breach of the arbitration clause it is well established that the wasted costs incurred in defending the proceedings brought in breach of the

---

[8] Under the wording of s 50 the jurisdiction to award damages is vested in the court.

arbitration agreement are recoverable as damages for breach of contract.[9] One would expect the court to be prepared to award these damages in its discretion under section 50. There is nothing too remote about them. Even if the foreign court could not award such costs, or would not as a matter of its practice, this would not prevent recovery of damages in an equivalent amount in England.

The court will usually award costs of the anti-suit proceedings before it, caused by breach of the arbitration agreement, on an indemnity basis.[10] This is because whatever may be decided by the court on costs will prevent the same question being re-litigated as a claim for damages. The question is to be answered once and once only. Furthermore there is a policy underlying the costs jurisdiction of the courts that the award or withholding of costs enables the court properly to manage the litigation before it. That policy can best be achieved through restricting any award of costs of the proceedings to one made under the discretionary costs jurisdiction of the court, and not permitting any decision to be reopened under a claim for damages. An award of costs on the standard basis allows questions of proportionality to arise, whilst costs on an indemnity basis reflects what might have been recovered by way of costs for breach of contract. The principle is that where costs are incurred as a direct result of breach of the arbitration clause, fairness requires the contract breaker to provide an indemnity against those costs to the other party.

What happens if foreign court proceedings are brought in breach of an arbitration clause and the foreign court allows them to continue and renders a money judgment in them against the defendant? Can the defendant to the foreign proceedings obtain damages in England for the loss it has been caused by the granting of the foreign judgment because that judgment is inconsistent with the result reached or which would have been reached in arbitration?

In the context of purely English domestic court proceedings the defendant could have applied for a stay under section 9 of the Arbitration Act 1996, and it was the omission to ask for the mandatory stay, and not the breach of the arbitration clause, which has led to the court judgment. This would negative causation. Furthermore it is difficult to conceive that an English court or an arbitral tribunal sitting in England could properly award damages based on the contention that an English court judgment, which has not been set aside, or successfully appealed, has caused loss through being wrongly decided. The remedy, if any, is to apply to set aside the judgment or to appeal. If that is barred then the judgment in England is conclusive. This appears to be the reasoning behind the dictum of Fletcher Moulton LJ in *Dolemann v Ossett* [1912] 3 KB 257 at 267–268:

If in breach of [an arbitration] clause one of the parties brought an action, the other could sue him in contract for the breach, and recover such damages as a jury might award. It

   [9] *Dolemann v Ossett* [1912] 3 KB 257 at 267–268; *Mantovani v Carapelli SpA* [1980] 1 Ll Rep 375; *Union Discount v Zoller* [2002] 1 WLR 1517; *National Westminster Bank Plc v Rabobank Nederland (No 3)* [2008] 1 Ll Rep 16.
   [10] *National Westminster Bank Plc v Rabobank Nederland (No 3)* [2008] 1 Ll Rep 16.

will be evident, however, that the remedy in damages must be an ineffective remedy in cases where the arbitration had not been actually entered into, for it would then seem difficult to prove any damages other than nominal.

What about where the judgment on the merits is a foreign judgment? The argument here would start from the proposition that the foreign court proceedings were brought in breach of the arbitration clause and the foreign judgment was a product of that breach. It would then be said that the foreign judgment was for more than what was properly due (if anything) and that had the case been resolved in arbitration only the proper sum due (if anything) would have been awarded. In practice there could be problems of issue estoppel, *res judicata*, or judgment recognition which might preclude the claimant from even getting such a case off the ground in England. This could be because the foreign money judgment is conclusive on the merits in England or because there has been a foreign judgment which precludes assertion that there is a valid arbitration agreement. One also has to have regard to questions of causation and remoteness of loss. For example, if the cause of the foreign judgment was a witness being believed in a civil law jurisdiction where he could not be cross-examined, one would question whether that impediment was sufficiently connected with the breach of the arbitration clause to have been caused by it, or whether this type of loss was too remote to be fairly recoverable for breach of the clause. On the other hand, one can envisage a case where the foreign court granted judgment because a defence which would have been conclusive in London arbitration was simply not available in the foreign court. Here selection of the forum would have been crucial.

The anti-suit jurisdiction for an injunction arises under section 37(1) of the Supreme Court Act 1981. There is also a separate jurisdiction under section 44(1)(e) of the Arbitration Act 1996. These are parallel jurisdictions. The jurisdiction under section 44 is confined to making orders as between parties to the arbitration and does not extend to non-parties.[11] This could be important because of the need to obtain territorial jurisdiction through service out of the jurisdiction on a foreigner who is to be restrained. The court when exercising its jurisdiction under section 37(1) will take into account the policies underlying the constraints of the statutory regime under section 44.[12]

One of the features of the 1996 Act was to protect the *Kompetenz-Kompetenz* jurisdiction of an arbitral tribunal. The tribunal cannot decide finally its own jurisdiction but it has the power to pronounce upon it. Under section 32 of the Act there is a provision preventing a respondent, except for one 'who takes no part' in the arbitral proceedings,[13] or the claimant, from going straight to the

---

[11] *Vale do Rio Doce Navagaçao SA v Shanghai BAO Steel Ocean Shipping Co Ltd* [2000] 2 Lloyd's Rep 1; *Starlight Shipping Co v Tai Ping* [2008] 1 Ll Rep 230.
[12] E.g., the requirements of urgency in s 44(4) and the need for permission of the arbitrators once there is a tribunal appointed: see *Elektrim SA v Vivendi Universal SA (No 2)* [2007] 2 Lloyd's Rep 8 and *Starlight Shipping Co v Tai Ping* [2008] 1 Ll Rep 230.
[13] S 72(1).

court on the question of jurisdiction.[14] *Kompetenz-Kompetenz* is an idea which finds expression through particular rules in each jurisdiction. It promotes a policy that arbitration should so far as possible be a one-stop jurisdiction. It also respects the point that a person who has not agreed to arbitrate cannot have his legal rights affected by a decision of the tribunal. Under English law, section 72 confers a right of immediate access to the courts of a person who claims not to be bound by an arbitration agreement, but once he takes some part in the arbitral proceedings then under English law he must wait until the tribunal has pronounced on its own jurisdiction. Unless he has entered into an ad hoc agreement to confer jurisdiction on the tribunal to decide its own jurisdiction, and after the Arbitration Act 1996 these are not found simply through a respondent taking steps in the arbitration, he can then go to the court under section 67 and have a rehearing. This is one of the few areas in which English law allows re-litigation of the same issue between the same parties, and one can question whether it might not be much better to provide that if the respondent chose to take part in challenging jurisdiction before the arbitrators then he would be bound by their decision.

One can often have a case in which a foreigner is threatening to pursue foreign proceedings in breach of an arbitration clause where it is urgent for the claimant to seek an anti-suit injunction. In the foreign proceedings the claimant has to walk a delicate line to avoid these going in default against him, and submitting to the jurisdiction. In such circumstances section 32[15] should not bar the claimant from seeking immediate anti-suit relief, and in due course final relief. The exigency outweighs the desirability of the arbitral tribunal being left to pronounce on its jurisdiction.

What is the position when the threatened arbitral proceedings are abroad? In such circumstances the claimant may still be able to obtain territorial jurisdiction over the defendant (e.g., by service in England), and if so the court may grant an injunction, or may leave the position to be dealt with by the arbitral tribunal abroad leaving challenges to be brought in the court having jurisdiction at the seat of the arbitration.

What is the position when the threatened arbitral proceedings are abroad and the claimant has brought proceedings on the underlying merits before the English court? In this case a question can arise about preserving the integrity of the English proceedings. The same question of whether there is a relevant arbitration agreement may be raised both before the court in the form of a stay application, and the foreign arbitral tribunal. Who should decide it? The answer is that it depends on the circumstances. These may point towards the English court not

---

[14] *Vale do Rio Doce Navagaçao SA v Shanghai BAO Steel Ocean Shipping Co Ltd* [2000] 2 Lloyd's Rep 1.
[15] S 32 bars the asking of a question whether there is jurisdiction but does not apply when there is a need for an injunction.

intervening at all and allowing the foreign arbitral tribunal to proceed.[16] In one case the claimant in proceedings on the merits in England was confronted with an agreement including an arbitration clause which he said had been forged.[17] The issue was about complete nullity of the alleged arbitration agreement, and there was some evidence of forgery. In those circumstances the claimant was able successfully to invoke the jurisdiction of the English court to protect the integrity of its own proceedings concerning the merits by granting an injunction preventing the foreign arbitral proceedings going forward, and asserting its own jurisdiction to decide the forgery issue.

(iii) *West Tankers v RAS Riunione Adriatica di Sicurta SpA (The Front Comor)*

In *West Tankers*,[18] a ship had collided with the charterers' jetty. The insurers of the charterers brought an action in Syracuse against the shipowners for negligence. The ship owners succeeded in anti-suit proceedings in England based on the arbitration clause in the charterparty, because under English law the analysis was that the insurers were invoking the charterers' rights under the charterparty (available to the insurers by subrogation) and had to respect the arbitration clause which qualified those rights. In Italy the insurers had a direct cause of action in their own right for economic loss and had not agreed to go to arbitration. One can see that on the facts there was no direct contract to arbitrate between the insurers and the shipowners, and that the common law and civil systems had logically defensible analyses which led inexorably to diametrically different results.

The Advocate General concluded that no injunction could be granted restraining the Italian proceedings because of the Brussels/Lugano regime. Such an injunction would interfere with the Italian court's decision on whether it had jurisdiction under the Judgments Regulation over the substantive claim. The Italian court was the court first seized which had to decide on its jurisdiction under the regime—which in turn depended on whether there was an arbitration agreement. The Brussels/Lugano regime bars an anti-suit injunction interfering with proceedings before the courts of another member state which are being dealt with under that regime.[19] The ECJ may adopt the same view. The contrary argument is that the New York Convention 1958 was not intended to be affected by Brussels/Lugano, and that the court can act under the protective umbrella of the arbitration exception. However, Article II of the New York Convention does not specify any particular court which is to decide whether there is an arbitration agreement. Therefore leaving the decision to the court

---

[16] *Weissfisch v Julius* [2006] 1 Ll Rep 716.
[17] *Albon v Naza Motor Trading* [2008] 1 Ll Rep 1.
[18] [2007] UKHL 4 and Case C-185/07.
[19] *Turner v Grovit* Case C-159/02 [2004] ECR I-3565.

first seized under Brussels/Lugano, and not giving priority to the courts of the seat of the arbitration, is not inconsistent with the New York Convention.[20]

What the facts in *West Tankers* illustrate is potential conflict between the two systems and the possibility that there will be a judgment of the courts of a European member state, which might be inconsistent with an arbitration award dealing with the same claim. The fact that there might be a problem with conflicting judgments between the English courts and those of other member states on issues about whether there was a binding arbitration agreement was referred to by the Court of Appeal in *Through Transport v New India Assurance* [2005] 1 Ll Rep 67 at para 51:

51. The fact that arbitration is excluded from the Convention means that from time to time there are likely to be conflicting judgments in different member states and it is therefore possible that questions of recognition and enforcement of conflicting judgments may arise in the future in a case like this.

A decision to ban anti-suit injunctions in respect of proceedings before the courts of a member state does not solve this, because then both the arbitral proceedings and the member state proceedings can go on simultaneously. One then enters into questions of which decisions have binding effect on whether there is an arbitration agreement, and on the underlying merits. The Advocate General in *West Tankers* recognized this, suggesting that the Brussels/Lugano regime should be made to prevail:

73. Instead of a solution by way of such coercive measures, a solution by way of law is called for. In that respect only the inclusion of arbitration in the scheme of Regulation No 44/2001 could remedy the situation. Until then, if necessary, divergent decisions must be accepted. However it should once more be pointed out that these cases are exceptions. If an arbitration clause is clearly formulated and not open to any doubt as to its validity, the national courts have no reason not to refer the parties to the arbitral body appointed in accordance with the New York Convention.

The courts of the other member state could be expected to apply their own decisions. What would be the position in England after *West Tankers* is decided by the European Court of Justice (ECJ)?

If the member state decision holding that the arbitration clause did not apply and there was jurisdiction to entertain the merits, came before any English decision on the issue, there could then be an argument about whether the decision on the arbitration issue would be the subject of an issue estoppel in England. The first question would be what has to be recognized under the Regulation; the second is whether recognition is affected by the arbitration

---

[20] A decision at the courts of the seat setting aside an award is a ground for another court refusing enforcement of a New York Convention award; but this provision does not require a decision of the courts at the seat, on whether there is an arbitration agreement, to be recognized and given effect to by all other courts.

exclusion; and the third is whether the decision on the underlying issue would be binding and could not be reopened on the ground of issue estoppel. On the first question a decision which decides that there is jurisdiction over the merits means that the relevant court had jurisdiction to entertain the underlying merits. On the second question there are English decisions[21] giving the arbitration exclusion a wide meaning enabling English courts when deciding arbitration issues to regard their proceedings as being within the exception and to decide that they are not bound in those proceedings by the strictures of the Brussels/Lugano regime. In *West Tankers* Lord Hoffmann said at paragraph 15:

It is settled by the decision of the Court of Justice in Marc Rich & Co AG v Società Italiana Impianti PA (The Atlantic Emperor) [1992] 1 Lloyd's Rep 342 that the exclusion applies not only to arbitration proceedings as such but also to court proceedings in which the subject-matter is arbitration. In Van Uden Maritime BV v Deco-Line [1998] ECR I-7091 the court decided that the subject-matter is arbitration if the proceedings serve to protect the right to have the dispute determined by arbitration.

The decision of the House of Lords in *West Tankers* was that because the English court was acting under the supervisory jurisdiction over arbitrations this placed the court proceedings in England within the umbrella of the arbitration exception.

In *Through Transport* there had been a decision of the Finnish court that it had jurisdiction over the merits, and the Court of Appeal said at paragraph 50:

'... there was some debate on the question whether the judgment of the District court of Kotka is entitled to recognition under art. 33. However, we do not think that this question arises for decision at present. As we understand it, the judgment obtained to date is simply to the effect that that court has jurisdiction to entertain a claim by New India under the Finnish Act. That was essentially a matter for that court in proceedings which seem to us to be within the Regulation. Whether that judgment is entitled to recognition or not does not seem to us to be relevant to the question whether the Judge was correct to grant the declarations or injunction which he did.

This was because of the protective umbrella analysis which enabled there to be anti-suit proceedings outside of the Brussels/Lugano regime. But once the ECJ has decided *West Tankers* the analysis may have to be different. The Advocate General[22] considered that the analysis went wrong with the initial question:

32. The House of Lords, West Tankers and the United Kingdom Government lay emphasis on the proceedings pending in England for the issue of an anti-suit injunction.

---

[21] See *Through Transport v New India Assurance* [2005] 1 Ll Rep 67 at paras 32–49; approving *Navigation Maritime Bulgare v Rustal Trading Ltd (The Ivan Zagubanski)* [2002] 1 Lloyd's Rep 107.
[22] Opinion of Advocate General Kokott delivered on 4 September 2008 Case C-185/07 *Allianz SpA (formerly Riunione Adriatica Di Sicurta SpA) and Others v West Tankers Inc.*

They assume that those proceedings cannot be contrary to the regulation since they fall within the arbitration exception. On the other hand, the national court appears to regard as irrelevant the effect of the anti-suit injunction on the proceedings before the court in Syracuse.

33. That view is surprising, since in Turner the Court found that the effect of an anti-suit injunction on the foreign proceedings infringed the Brussels Convention, even if it were assumed that the anti-suit injunction, as a measure of a procedural nature, was a matter of national law alone. Accordingly, the decisive question is not whether the application for an anti-suit injunction—in this case, the proceedings before the English courts—falls within the scope of application of the Regulation, but whether the proceedings against which the anti-suit injunction is directed—the proceedings before the court in Syracuse—do so.

Thus the starting question may have to be whether a decision of the courts of a member state that there was jurisdiction over the merits notwithstanding the alleged arbitration agreement is within the exception? A decision that there was jurisdiction would not be within the arbitration exception, because what controls the exception is not the characterization of the underlying issue(s), but the subject matter of the actual decision.[23] In such a case the subject-matter of the foreign judgment is to decide jurisdiction under the Regulation. Therefore the arbitration exclusion does not apply to that decision. Therefore that decision has to be recognized in England and is conclusive that the other court has jurisdiction to decide the underlying substantive merits of the dispute under the Brussels/Lugano regime.

On the third question there can be an issue estoppel arising from the decision of the courts of the other member state, and one would have thought that the decision of the courts of the other member state first seized on a jurisdiction dispute, if it has to be recognized, would have to be regarded in England as a decision of a court of competent jurisdiction for the purposes of issue estoppel. A decision on whether there is a binding arbitration agreement would be a decision 'on the merits'. There might also be no difficulty in showing that the decision was final and conclusive. Therefore the elements required for an issue estoppel under English law might be proved.

If the European decision on the merits of the underlying dispute came out before any arbitration award in England this would be final and conclusive in England on those merits.

But timing might be otherwise—there might be an English court declaration that there is an arbitration agreement binding on the insurers.[24] There might be an arbitration award on the merits which has been enforced by the English court.

---

[23] Such an argument could be advanced by reference to *Rich (Marc) & Co AG v Società Italiana Impianti PA* (Case C-190/89) [1991] ECR I-3855, ECJ where the fact that there was a preliminary issue on whether there was an arbitration agreement did not affect the conclusion that an application to appoint an arbitrator was within the arbitration exception.

[24] Perhaps under s 32(2)(b) of the Arbitration Act 1996.

These would be decisions within the arbitration exception, and would not have to be recognized by the courts of other member states. The member state judgment on jurisdiction might come later. If so, the English court under article 34 might refuse to recognize the later judgment of a court of a member state on the ground that it was inconsistent with the earlier English judgment.

If there are conflicting systems there is the possibility of arbitral awards of damages in respect of loss caused through the respondent bringing proceedings in the courts of a member state in breach of the arbitration clause. Those awards could include the costs wasted and potentially even damages because the claimant had been exposed to liability abroad through breach of the arbitration clause. *West Tankers* could be such a case because in Italy with the direct action the insurers would say that the Hague Rules defence, of negligent navigation available under the charterparty, would not be available in the direct action brought by insurers in their own right.

The Brussels/Lugano regime, when providing for arbitration and therefore the New York Convention to be outside of it, has left unresolved which regime is to prevail. A decision that anti-suit injunctions are not available abolishes one procedure which in practice helpfully reduced the potential for conflict between the two systems, and leaves unanswered how the two regimes are to be operated consistently.

In 2009 the European Commission will implement improvements to Brussels I. A preliminary report known as the Heidelberg Report[25] has proposed deletion of the arbitration exception and the possibility of more specific rules, for example a rule conferring an exclusive jurisdiction on the courts at the place of the seat of the arbitration (if any). The Report stated[26] '...the present situation is not satisfactory and the interfaces between the Judgment Regulation and arbitration should be addressed in a more sophisticated way than by the all embracing exclusion of arbitration in Article I (2) (d) JR.'

Addendum of the Judgment Regulation to resolve the conflict is needed, because it offends against the principle that the same issue between the same parties should be decided only once, it leaves open the possibility of inconsistent judgments and awards being enforced, and it does not give effect to the expectations of commercial men. In short it falls short of the words of Bingham LJ in *Ashville*.

---

[25] Study JLS/C4/2005/03 see especially paras 106-136 (http://ec.europa.eu/justice_home/doc_centre/civil/studies/doc/study_application_brussels_1_en.pdf).

[26] Para 131.

6

Earth, Air, and Space: the Cape Town Convention and Protocols and their Contribution to International Commercial Law

Roy Goode

I first met Tom Bingham in 1981 in Michael Kerr's room at the Law Courts, when at Michael's suggestion I invited him to take over as Chairman of the Committee of Management of the newly established Centre for Commercial Law Studies at Queen Mary College following Michael's elevation to the Court of Appeal. Mr Justice Bingham, as he then was, gladly accepted and, like Michael, proved a wonderful Chairman. Whenever I needed his advice about a knotty problem concerning the Centre a detailed reply would come back within 48 hours, replete with wisdom and common sense. We in the Centre basked in reflected glory as he went on to become successively the Master of the Rolls, the Lord Chief Justice, and the Senior Law Lord. This paper is a modest tribute to an outstanding judge and a brilliant commercial lawyer whose commitment to the rule of law and enthusiasm for the strengthening of links between the academic world and the legal profession have endeared him to scholars and practising lawyers alike.

I Introduction

Disputes involving points of contact with different jurisdictions have traditionally been resolved by reference to private international law, and, since each jurisdiction has its own conflict of laws rules, the applicable law, and possibly the outcome of the dispute, will depend on where proceedings are brought. There is thus wide scope for forum shopping. In the field of commercial law, and particularly the law governing cross-border transactions, there have been concerted efforts to reduce dependence on the conflict of laws by means of international uniform law. Two international conventions have been particularly successful: in substantive law, the 1980 UN Convention on Contracts for the International Sale of Goods (CISG); and in the recognition and enforcement of arbitral awards, the 1958 New York Convention. A few model laws, such as UNCITRAL's 1997 Model Law on Cross-border Insolvency, have also been influential. But such successes are rare. It is hard enough to secure consensus on a text to go before a Diplomatic Conference, but—a point often overlooked—conclusion of an international convention is only halfway to success; it is then necessary to secure a sufficient number of ratifications to make the convention a useful tool of international lawmaking.

If, say, 20 years ago anyone had ventured to suggest the creation of an international regime for security and title-retention interests in mobile equipment, such as aircraft objects, railway rolling stock, and space assets, backed by an international registry to record such interests and secure priority for them, the suggestion would almost certainly have been met with derision. One can imagine a typical comment:

Everyone knows that property rights are particular to individual jurisdictions and do not lend themselves to harmonization. Such a thing has never been done. Even CISG, with its 101 Articles, avoids dealing with property issues in contracts of sale. Can you seriously imagine that States will agree on a set of uniform registration and priority rules? Do you really think that a single international registry to record interests in a particular category of equipment on a world-wide basis is remotely feasible? And do you not realize that it would be impossible to secure acceptance of rules giving protection against national insolvency law?

Such a view, if expressed in the late 1980s, would certainly have been widely shared. Yet scarcely more than a decade later its proponents would have been confounded. The 2001 Convention on International Interests in Mobile Equipment and its associated Aircraft Protocol were concluded on 16 November 2001 under the joint auspices of the International Institute for the Unification of Private Law (UNIDROIT), which initiated and oversaw the project, and the International Civil Aviation Organization (ICAO).[1] It is a testimony to the keen interest they aroused that no fewer than 20 States, including the United Kingdom, signed both instruments on the final day of the Diplomatic Conference. They both came into force on 1 March 2006[2] and provide precisely the international legal regime that

---

[1] UNIDROIT is an international, intergovernmental organization established in 1926 to promote the progressive harmonization of private law. Though originally set up under the auspices of the League of Nations it was re-established as an independent body in 1940. It has 61 member States drawn from five continents and is based in Rome. ICAO is an international, intergovernmental organization set up in 1944 by 52 nations with the aim of assuring the safety, security, and efficiency of international air transport. Based in Montreal, ICAO is a specialized agency of the United Nations. Most countries of the world are ICAO Contracting States.

[2] Apart from some final clauses and other provisions of the Convention which became operative upon its conclusion on 16 November 2001. There is a curious quirk in the provisions of the Convention relating to entry into force. According to Art 49 the Convention enters into force on the first day of the month following the expiration of three months after the date of deposit of the

would once have been dismissed as wildly unrealistic. What is more, in a mere seven years—a very short time in international lawmaking—the Convention has already secured 26 ratifications and the Protocol 24, and this not counting any member states of the European Union, other than Ireland and Luxembourg, progress in the EU being blocked for some years because of diplomatic difficulties between the UK and Spain which have now been resolved, so that a proposal for signature is shortly to come before the Council. Moreover, a little over a year ago a second Protocol, the Luxembourg Protocol, was concluded relating to railway rolling stock, and a third is in preparation covering space assets.

It is not merely the content of these instruments that is instructive but also the mechanism by which these impressive results were reached and I shall have a few comments about this in the last part of the paper.

II A Bird's-Eye View of the Convention[3]

Ambit of the Convention

The Cape Town Convention is concerned with security, title reservation, and leasing agreements[4] relating to mobile equipment of high unit value, notably aircraft objects,[5] railway rolling stock, and space assets. The characteristic of the first two of these categories of object is that they regularly move across national borders, with the result that from the perspective of the creditor the legal regime is uncertain. A security interest validly created in one jurisdiction and conferring effective remedies for the creditor against default by the debtor and priority against competing claimants may at the relevant time be located in another jurisdiction which provides inadequate default remedies and is more hostile to non-possessory security interests. In the case of assets in outer

third instrument of ratification (i.e., on 1 April 2004) but only, as regards a category of object to which a Protocol applies, as from the time of entry into force of that Protocol, which in the case of the Aircraft Protocol was 1 March 2006. But the only provisions not applicable to an aircraft object are those governed by Art 24(4) of the 1969 Vienna Convention on the Law of Treaties and entering into force on 16 November 2001. So despite Art 49(1) the date of deposit of the third instrument of ratification is irrelevant.

[3] Only the briefest outline can be given here. For a comprehensive analysis, see the writer's *Official Commentary on the Convention on International Interests in Mobile Equipment and the Protocol thereto on Matters Specific to Aircraft Equipment: Revised Edition* (2008), and *Official Commentary on the Convention on International Interests in Mobile Equipment and the Luxembourg Protocol on Matters Specific to Railway Rolling Stock* (2008).

[4] For brevity these agreements will be referred to as security agreements and the interests they protect as security interests. It should, however, be borne in mind that in the United States, Canada, and New Zealand conditional sale agreements and certain types of leasing agreement are considered to create security interests.

[5] Namely airframes, aircraft engines, and helicopters. Aircraft engines are not infrequently financed separately from airframes and are therefore dealt with separately. It is not possible to register an international interest in an aircraft as a whole. The position is otherwise with helicopters.

space the problem is different in that they are not within any jurisdiction at all. Ownership of objects launched into outer space, including landed or constructed on a celestial body, is not affected by their presence in outer space or on a celestial body or by their return to Earth.[6] However, there are no rules governing the disposition of objects in outer space and thus no means of protecting such dispositions.

Approach of the Convention and Protocols

The Convention and its associated Protocols seek to address these problems by:

(1) establishing a set of simple rules for the creation of an international interest in mobile equipment, the interest being derived from the Convention itself, not from national law;

(2) prescribing basic default remedies, coupled with the availability of speedy judicial relief pending final determination of a claim where the creditor adduces evidence of default;

(3) establishing an international registry for each category of object in which security interests can be registered electronically, registration securing priority over subsequently registered interests and over unregistered interests even if of a kind not capable of registration;

(4) providing for the protection of registered interests on the debtor's insolvency, subject to insolvency rules as to avoidance of transactions in fraud of creditors or as preferences;

(5) providing for the assignment of associated rights to payment or other performance under security agreements, and for the registration and priority of such assignments.

The Convention and Protocols are designed to provide a secure foundation for creditors' rights and to improve the predictability and speed of legal outcomes, thereby facilitating the release of funds for the acquisition or leasing of mobile equipment (particularly to developing countries) which might not otherwise have been available and reducing borrowing costs and credit support exposure fees. These benefits were predicted in a study carried out under the auspices of INSEAD and the New York University Salomon Center,[7] a prediction which proved well founded in that the US Export-Import Bank has for some years offered a reduction of one-third in its exposure fees for credit insurance for foreign buyers of large aircraft in countries ratifying the Convention and Aircraft

---

[6] Outer Space Treaty 1967, Art VIII.

[7] Anthony Saunders and Ingo Walter, *Proposed Unidroit Convention on International Interests in Mobile Equipment as Applicable to Aircraft Equipment Through the Aircraft Equipment Protocol: Economic Impact Assessment*, September 1998.

Protocol with specified declarations,[8] while more recently the OECD has issued guidelines providing for a 'Cape Town discount' in the fixing of exposure fees in similar conditions.[9]

The two-instrument approach

It is quite common for a Convention to be amended, extended, or supplemented by a Protocol. What is unusual about the Cape Town Convention is the dominant role assigned to Protocols by the Convention itself. The Convention prescribes a separate Protocol for each of the three categories of equipment.[10] The equipment in question must be designated in and uniquely identified in conformity with the Protocol,[11] the establishment of the Supervisory Authority for the oversight of the International Registry and the criteria for registration, including identification of the equipment, are left to the Protocol,[12] and so too is the immunity of the Supervisory Authority from legal or administrative action.[13] Still more striking is the fact that the provisions of the Convention relating to an object can come into force only when the relevant Protocol comes into force and subject to the terms of that Protocol and as between states Parties to the Convention and Protocol.[14] In other words, the Protocol can not only supplement but override the Convention. Thus the Aircraft Protocol provides certain additional default remedies, contains elaborate provisions as to the creditor's rights on the debtor's insolvency, and extends the registration and priority rules to outright sales of aircraft objects. Similarly the Luxembourg Protocol modifies the Convention in various respects as regards railway rolling stock.

The two-instrument approach was seen as possessing several advantages. It secured a uniformity of provisions; it allowed different industry sectors to proceed at different speeds; it enabled the Convention to be modified to take account of the particular needs of each sector; and it avoided cluttering the Convention with technical provisions relating to a particular type of equipment, so that its provisions are equipment-neutral. Even so, the approach proved controversial. There were several who favoured having a separate stand-alone Convention for each category of equipment, despite the fact that this risked divergences resulting from the drafting of different Conventions by different hands, thus weakening the uniformity of provisions that were not equipment-specific. Only on the first day of the Diplomatic Conference was the controversy resolved in favour of the two-instrument approach.

---

[8] In particular, the selection of Alternative A (the 'hard' option) of Art XI of the Aircraft Protocol dealing with creditors' rights on insolvency.

[9] OECD *Sector Understanding on Export Credits for Civil Aircraft* (27 July 2007), App III, S 2 and Annex I.

[10] Art 1(aa).   [11] Arts 2(2), 7(c).   [12] Arts 17(1), 18(1).

[13] Art 27(2).   [14] Art 49(1).

Definitions

The Convention has an unusually large number of defined terms—some 40 in all, with further sets of definitions being added by the Protocols. These need to be constantly borne in mind, because there are several terms which are given a special meaning, such as 'agreement', 'creditor', 'debtor', and 'writing'.

Constitution of the international interest

For an interest to qualify as an international interest five conditions must be observed. The interest must take the form of a security interest or the interest of a conditional seller or lessor under a security, title reservation, or leasing agreement;[15] the agreement must relate to an object falling within one of the three Convention categories, namely an aircraft object, railway rolling stock, or a space asset; the object must be uniquely identifiable in accordance with the relevant Protocol; it must also conform to the formal requirements laid down in Article 7 of the Convention; and the debtor must be situated in a contracting state at the time of conclusion of the agreement. Many, if not most, security and title-retention interests arising under national law will qualify as international interests, but the international interest is the creature of the Convention, not of national law, and if the conditions of the Convention are fulfilled the fact that the resulting interest is not of a kind recognized by the national law of a particular contracting state is irrelevant.

Default remedies

Chapter III of the Convention contains a set of basic default remedies—possession, sale, and the like—which the parties can limit or expand, subject to observance of certain mandatory rules. The creditor is also provided with the right to speedy relief pending final determination of its claim on adducing evidence of default. This relief could take the form of an order for preservation of the object or its value, possession, control, or custody of the object, immobilization of the object, or lease or management of the object.[16]

Registration

The Convention and Protocol provide for the establishment of an International Registry for each category of equipment, to be operated by a Registrar under

---

[15] The Convention definitions of these forms of agreement must be applied in the first instance to determine whether the agreement falls within the scope of the Convention. If it does, then the agreement falls to be characterized or recharacterized in accordance with the applicable law (Art 2(4)).
[16] Art 13(1).

the general superintendence of the Supervisory Authority. Registration is against the object, not the debtor, hence the requirement that the object be uniquely identifiable[17]—in the case of aircraft objects, by manfacturer's name, model, and serial number. The registration system is purely electronic, so that registrations, searches, and the issue of search certificates are made and dealt with electronically without human intervention at the Registry end. Registration is not confined to international interests. A variety of other forms of interest may be registered, including assignments, subordinations, and categories of non-consensual right or interest which under a declaration by a contracting state are to be registrable as if the right or interest were an international interest. Moreover, it is possible to register a prospective international interest or a prospective assignment which, on the interest or assignment being complete, will take effect as from the time of such registration without the need for any new registration.[18]

That the aviation industry has come to rely heavily on the International Registry for aircraft objects is demonstrated by the fact that in the 15 months since the Registry first became operative there have been almost 100,000 registrations. It is a tribute to the technological sophistication of the Registry that, despite the inevitable teething troubles, it has been able to handle this volume of traffic and can look forward with confidence to a much greater volume of registrations as ratifications increase.

Priorities

The priority rules governing competing interests are remarkably simple and are gathered together in a single Article which eschews the complexities of priority rules under national legal systems. A registered interest has priority over a subsequently registered interest and over an unregistered interest,[19] whether or not the holder knows of a prior interest.[20] An exception is made in favour of an outright buyer, who lacks the ability to register[21] and who is therefore given priority over an interest if acquiring the object before the interest has been registered.[22] A conditional buyer or lessee is protected against the interest of a third party, such as a person granted a security interest by the conditional seller or lessor, if

---

[17] However, at the Luxembourg Diplomatic Conference it was pointed out that unique identifiability was essential only for registration, not for the constitution of the agreement, so that in contrast to the Aircraft Protocol the Luxembourg Protocol, in prescribing the requirements for the constitution of an international interest in railway rolling stock, allows any method by which it can be seen that the object falls within the scope of the agreement, whether uniquely identifiable or not.

[18] Art 18(3). As a corollary, the search certificate must be neutral as to whether the international interest has been acquired or is intended to be acquired (Art 22(3)).

[19] Art 29(1).   [20] Art 29(2).

[21] Except in the case of aircraft objects, as regards which Art III of the Aircraft Protocol extends the registration and priority provisions to outright sales, so that no special provision is needed.

[22] Art 29(3).

the interest of the conditional seller or lessor was registered first.[23] The holders of competing interests are free to vary the priority rules as between themselves.[24] In addition a contracting state may at any time make a declaration as to categories of non-consensual right or interest which under that state's law have priority over an interest equivalent to an international interest and are to have priority over a registered international interest. There are a few other rules which do not require attention here.

Protection from insolvency

An international interest registered prior to the commencement of insolvency proceedings against the debtor is effective in those proceedings.[25]

Associated rights

Finally, there are elaborate provisions governing a creditor's assignment of 'associated rights', that is, rights to payment or other performance by a debtor under an agreement which are secured by or associated with the object.[26] Such assignments, if properly constituted, are registrable and registration carries a limited priority.[27]

The declaration system

The Convention and Protocol contain an elaborate system of declarations by which certain provisions that contracting state might find unacceptable as contrary to their basic legal philosophy are dependent on an opt-in or alternatively can be disapplied by an opt-out. For example, a contracting state may make a declaration that would allow certain types of non-consensual interest to be registered in the International Registry as if they were international interests,[28] and in the Aircraft Protocol the remedies given to a creditor on the debtor's insolvency are dependent on an opt-in,[29] while contracting states whose laws do not permit self-help may by declaration require a court order for the exercise of what would otherwise be a self-help remedy.[30] It is, of course, true that the availability of opt-ins and opt-outs to some extent weakens the uniformity which the Convention and Protocol are designed to achieve, but that is a price which was considered worth paying to secure agreement, given the great advantages of the remaining provisions of the two instruments.

---

[23] Art 29(4).   [24] Art 29(5).

[25] Art 30(1), which is without prejudice to any other ground of effectiveness under national law (Art 30(2)). 'Effective' means that the property rights of the creditor must be respected, subject, however, to rules of law of the insolvency jurisdiction as to avoidance of a transaction as a preference or a transfer in fraud of creditors and to rules of procedure relating to the enforcement of rights to property which is under the control or supervision of the insolvency administrator (Art 30(3)).

[26] See ch IX of the Convention.   [27] Arts 35, 36.

[28] Art 40.   [29] Protocol, Arts XI and XXX(3).   [30] Art 55.

III The Aircraft Protocol

The Aircraft Protocol modifies the Convention in various ways so as to accommodate the particular needs of the aviation industry, while respecting the principle that only changes required for that purpose should be made. It adds 16 definitions to the 40 defined terms in the Convention. Of particular importance are those which define airframes, aircraft engines, and helicopters. It took several months for industry experts to hammer these out and even then they did not get it quite right the first time round! It was necessary not only to give the meaning of these terms but to define them in such a way as to exclude airframes and aircraft engines used in light aircraft. In order to allow financiers and lessors of aircraft objects the benefits of the registration system and its associated priority rules, the Protocol extends to outright sales the provisions of the Convention relating to registration and priorities. This enables the special provision for the protection of the outright buyer previously mentioned to be dispensed with, for the buyer can protect its interest by registration, which cannot be done under the Convention itself.

The Aircraft Protocol adds two default remedies to the set of remedies provided by the Convention, namely de-registration of the relevant aircraft from its nationality register and export to another country where it can be re-registered. The Protocol also contains significant provisions governing creditors' rights in the event of the debtor's insolvency. These provisions, which apply only where the contracting state that is the primary insolvency jurisdiction makes a declaration to that effect, come in two alternative versions. In the first, the insolvency administrator is given a limited time within which to cure defaults and undertake future performance of the security agreement, failing which the creditor is entitled to possession, with no power in the court to intervene. In the second, repossession is dependent on an order of the court. Alternatively a contracting state may make no declaration and continue to apply its domestic insolvency law. The Protocol also contains provisions the effect of which is that, together with the Convention, it overrides the 1933 Rome Convention on the precautionary attachment of aircraft, the 1948 Geneva Convention on the international recognition of rights in aircraft, and the 1988 UNIDROIT Convention on international financial leasing. These provisions demonstrate the power of Protocols to tailor the Convention provisions to the needs of the particular industry affected.

IV The Luxembourg Protocol

This Protocol relates to railway rolling stock, which frequently crosses national borders. It might be asked why this should be of interest to Britain, which is an island. But quite apart from the Channel tunnel, UK lenders, conditional sellers, and lessors frequently engage in cross-border transactions, so that it is important to them to have in place a Convention and Protocol safeguarding their interests. The Luxembourg Protocol, while not extending the scope of the Convention to outright sales of railway rolling stock, closely follows the Aircraft Protocol, though with some modifications to reflect the particular needs of the rail industry and to avoid a drafting error in the Aircraft Protocol as well as clarifying the Convention's rather opaque transitional provisions. The Protocol adds a further option as regards creditors' remedies on insolvency of the debtor. At the Diplomatic Conference there was a particular concern about the prospect of a creditor enforcing its rights in such a way as to disrupt the provision of rail services of public importance, and the result of the deliberations of a public service exemption working group a balance was eventually struck between the needs of states to be able to maintain rules of law securing the continuity of public services and the of creditors to safeguard their assets.[31]

V The Draft Space Protocol

The need for the Protocol

Many years of work went into the preparation of the Cape Town Convention and Aircraft Protocol because of the complexities of the subject, attested by the fact that the two instruments together occupy no fewer than 99 Articles. Further years elapsed before the conclusion of the Luxembourg Protocol relating to railway rolling stock. A similar Protocol for space assets—satellites, transponders, space stations, and the like—is still in course of completion. This was held up in part because of uncertainty over the project in consequence of the relatively limited number of satellite transactions, in part because of the practical difficulties of repossessing a satellite and the inability to change its orbit or use its reduced value as collateral, leaving a heavy dependence on satellite receivables, so that transactions partook more of the nature of project finance than asset finance. However, the situation has changed over the past few years. There is a growing recognition that the potential for the development of the market is huge. Satellites fulfil a variety of functions that have become essential to modern living and commerce, including media and communications, weather forecasting, disaster relief, detection and management of climate change, astronomical observations and the study of the Universe, navigation, and military surveillance. It has been estimated that in the next 12 years the global market in space systems and satellite-enabled applications will have grown from £62.5 billion to £543 billion, nearly a tenfold increase.[32] Moreover, technological advances mean that it is now

---

[31] See below p 661.
[32] *UK Civil Space Strategy: 2008–2112 and Beyond* (British National Space Centre, 2008), p 10.

possible to change the orbit and use of a satellite, paving the way for the transfer of control of a satellite by the creditor from the defaulting debtor to a third party for a different purpose. So the show is back on the road and if all goes well there will be a Diplomatic Conference in 2010 to conclude the Protocol.

If there was a need for an international legal regime for aircraft objects and railway rolling stock in order to displace the need to resort to conflict of laws rules to determine the applicable, there is an even greater need for such a regime as regards dealings with assets in outer space, for which there is no clearly applicable law beyond the very general provision of Article VIII of the Outer Space Treaty reserving jurisdiction and control over objects launched into outer space to the state Party on whose registry the object is carried and preserving ownership rights of objects launched into outer space.

Sphere of application

(1) 'Space assets'

Earlier drafts of the Protocol defined 'space assets' in very wide terms, and the text as revised by the first meeting of the Committee of governmental experts covers any identifiable asset in or assembled or manufactured in space or intended to be launched into space, as well as any identifiable launch vehicle and any separately identifiable components of any such assets.[33] It is generally accepted that satellites, transponders, and the like should be covered by the Protocol before as well as after launch, if only because there would be nothing to prevent a creditor from registering a prospective international interest in them which, after their launch, would become an international interest and trump any interest created under national law. Moreover, the bulk of the financing provided for space assets is incurred prior to launch and repayment has to be secured against the risk that the launch will be unsuccessful.

The real problem concerns components. In the other Protocols components are not in themselves capable of being subject to an international interest; they simply form part of the relevant aircraft object or railway rolling stock. To allow registration of international interests in a potentially huge number of components with differing identifiers would cause great complications, and all to little purpose, because while components are on the ground they can be subject to national law and once they are incorporated they are lost to the creditor anyway. Moreover, it may not always be easy to establish prior to incorporation which

---

[33] Preliminary draft Protocol on Matters Specific to Space Assets, UNIDROIT 2004, Study LXXIIJ—Doc 13 rev), Art 1(2)(g), as revised by the UNIDROIT Committee of governmental experts during its first session in Rome, 15 to 19 December 2003. This remains the only official preliminary draft text, but further examination has revealed numerous problems requiring attention, and under the aegis of a Steering Committee set up in Berlin in May 2008 a revised text is being taken as the basis for a new draft which it is hoped to present to the Committee of governmental experts in 2009.

components are destined for space assets and which for other uses. So there is much support for the idea that components should not be a separate category of space asset but should form part of the asset in which they are incorporated.

(2) 'Debtor's rights'; 'related rights'

Reference has already been made to the fact that hitherto satellites as such have had a limited value as collateral, and attention has focused on income derived from the satellites. The Convention itself, as we have seen, provides for the assignment to the creditor of associated rights, that is, rights to payment or other performance due from the debtor to the creditor. But space financiers and lessors want to go further and have the facility of taking an assignment of 'debtor's rights', that is, payments and other rights due *to* the debtor from third parties—for example, rentals payable to the debtor by lessees of satellites—and of 'related rights', namely government and other licences and permits authorizing the manufacture, launch, control, use, or operation of the satellite or the use of orbits positions, and the like. It had been proposed that a creditor should be able to register an international interest in debtor's rights and related rights, but this was rightly opposed on the ground that the Convention is concerned with uniquely identifiable tangible assets, not with intangible claims, and to extend the concept of an international interest to such intangibles would disturb the central thrust of the Convention and risk taking its application into general receivables financing, for which there is already a UN Convention in being.[34] So what is now proposed is that assignments of debtor's rights and related rights should not be the subject of independent registration but should be recordable in the registration of the international interest in the satellite to which they relate and should remain within the Convention only while that registration persists. A separate ground of objection is that many government licences are not transferable, but this is dealt with by a provision leaving the question of transferability to the applicable law, so that any assignment concerns only the relations between assignor and assignee.

Of course, one cannot simply stop at a provision for registration of an assignment of debtor's rights and related rights. It is also necessary to deal with re-assignments, priorities, duties of the grantor of the rights to the assignee, default remedies, and the like. The provisions of the draft under consideration address all these questions. It remains to be seen whether they will be accepted.

Default remedies in relation to linked space assets

A rather more difficult problem is posed by the possibility that a creditor's exercise of default remedies against a space asset functionally linked to another space asset in which a different creditor has an interest could adversely affect the latter

---

[34] The 2001 UN Convention on the assignment of receivables in international trade.

interest, for example by changing the location of the linked asset. A sub-committee has been established to address this particular issue.

Public service exemption

The second knotty problem concerns the exercise of default remedies against a space asset used to provide a service of public importance, for example, broadcasting or navigation. States clearly have an interest in maintaining the continuity of such a service, as well as in preserving national security, and to that end it is necessary to impose restrictions on the exercise of creditors' remedies. On the other hand, creditors cannot be expected to advance substantial funds without payment for the use of assets they have financed. Article XXV of the Luxembourg Protocol addresses this problem in relation to railway rolling stock (1) by allowing a contracting state whose law provides for the suspension of creditors' remedies in such cases to continue to apply that law, and (2) by providing that a person who under the rules of law of the contracting state exercises a power to take or procure possession, use, or control of any public service railway rolling stock is to maintain it until possession has been given back to the creditor and meanwhile to pay the creditor the greater of any amount prescribed by the law and the market lease rental of the railway rolling stock. A separate sub-committee has been established to examine the question in relation to space assets. Informal groups are also being set up to examine the insolvency options and the protection of interests of salvage insurers who pay out a claim on the basis of a total loss or total constructive loss but currently have no ability to effect a registration so as to ensure a priority in relation to the space asset taken over (which may still have value) and the receivables flowing from it.

Which Protocol is applicable?

In order for a space object to reach outer space it must first pass through airspace. Does this mean that during the airspace phase it is capable of being governed by the Aircraft Protocol? To have the same asset governed first by one Protocol and then by another would cause the utmost confusion; hence a provision in the revised draft now under consideration is that the Aircraft Protocol would not apply to a space asset whether it is on earth, in air, or space.

Conclusions on the draft Space Protocol

Much work has still to be done to produce a text suitable for consideration at a Diplomatic Conference. But with energy and goodwill on the part of all the participants there is no reason why this important project should not be completed in time for a Diplomatic Conference in 2010, a Conference which Russia has already offered to host if the text is ready.

VI Regional Economic Integration Organizations

The Convention and Protocols contain provisions enabling a Regional Economic Integration Organization (REIO) constituted by sovereign states and having competence over certain matters governed by the Convention to sign, accept, approve, or accede to the Convention, and in that event the REIO has the rights and obligations of a contracting state as regards the matters in question. The most important such organization is, of course, the European Community, whose representatives played an active role at the Diplomatic Conference. In subsequent negotiations the Commission asserted competence over two aspects of the Convention and Aircraft Protocol, namely the provisions governing jurisdiction and the remedies given by the Aircraft Protocol to the creditor on the debtor's insolvency. As to the latter, the Commission's position was that it did not care which of the alternatives were adopted by member states so long as they all adopted the same alternative. It was clear that the European Community had competence over jurisdictional questions but far from clear that this applied to the insolvency provisions. The Commission's argument was that the provisions could affect the EC Insolvency Regulation, but it is hard to see how this could be, given that the Regulation is essentially a conflict of laws regulation which does not itself lay down rules of substantive insolvency law, whereas the insolvency provisions are entirely substantive law provisions. In the end, member states that had protested the Community's competence over the insolvency provisions agreed not to pursue their objections, while the Commission in turn agreed that this concession would not be taken as a precedent and that each member state would be free to select the insolvency option it wished.

What is interesting is that while the matters falling within the external competence of the European Community related to no more than a handful of provisions out of a total of 99 Articles, the result has been to preclude member states from proceeding to ratification without close cooperation with the Community and, in practice at any rate, an affirmative decision of the Council on the basis of proposals submitted by the Commission.[35]

VII Some Thoughts on Process

There is still a widespread belief that all that is required for the success of an international instrument is the quality of the product. Nothing could be further from

---

[35] As a matter of international law it is not open to a State to ratify part only of a Convention unless the Convention itself so provides. The Cape Town Convention and Protocols do not permit reservations, only certain types of declaration. So a member state of the European Union could not ratify only those provisions (albeit the vast majority) falling outside the external competence of the European Community.

the truth. As in the case of a proposal for domestic legislation, legislative time must be found, and faced with relentless pressure on the parliamentary timetable governments are reluctant to ratify an international convention or protocol unless either it has a popular appeal or there is pressure from finance or industry to proceed to ratification. Many conventions which in themselves may be of high quality have been doomed to oblivion because of the failure of their proponents to recognize the importance of post-convention political pressure.

One of the reasons for the success of the Cape Town Convention and Aircraft Protocol was the recognition by the aviation industry that it had to commit to the project, by way of policy and technical input into the content of these instruments, participation in negotiations before and during the Diplomatic Conference, and intensive activity thereafter to secure acceptance by governments. Acting through the Aviation Working Group, consisting of major aviation manufacturers, leasing companies, and financial institutions, the industry devoted an immense amount of time and effort to driving the project forward, securing texts that were not only conceptually sound but practical and responsive to the needs of the various interest groups, including both developing and developed countries, and engaging in follow-up activity to ensure that governments understood the importance of ratification. Of course, the industry did not obtain all it wanted. Governments, in particular, had to be satisfied that there was a fair balance of competing interests. But there can be little doubt that the high quality of the Convention and Aircraft Protocol and their relatively rapid adoption by many states were the result of this expenditure of time and effort. Another key factor was the working method. Traditionally, international organizations engaged in the preparation of uniform law have felt constrained to hold plenary sessions no more frequently than once a year, if that, and to engage in little, if any, activity between sessions. Experience with the Cape Town Convention, as later with the Hague Convention in intermediated securities, showed the importance of intersessional work to drive the project forward and to draft proposals for revision without waiting for the next plenary meeting.

VIII Final Reflections

What conclusions can we draw from the success of the Cape Town instruments? First, fields of law traditionally regarded as no-go areas for harmonization have ceased to be sacrosanct. The imperatives of international commerce and finance mean that property law and even aspects of insolvency law need no longer be regarded as outside the purview of international uniform law. Secondly, the focus has to be on best solutions to common problems, not on vain attempts to combine what may be widely different conceptual approaches. The most revolutionary feature of the Cape Town Convention is its creation of an autonomous international interest which is not dependent on national law either for its creation or its perfection. It is the Convention itself which determines the essential elements of this new interest and it is the Convention which establishes the machinery for its protection through the International Registry and its priority status. Thirdly, the active involvement of industry experts at all stages is essential to the success of a uniform law project, in order to ensure that the rules are sound and are responsive to commercial needs. Finally, there needs to be a sustained effort to raise the level of awareness of the project and to build up industry support for pressure on governments to implement the resulting international instrument. Only through these measures is success likely to be achieved.

7

Lord Bingham's Contributions to Commercial Law

Bernard Rix

Tom Bingham was appointed to the bench of the Queen's Bench Division in 1980 and thereupon became one of the judges of the commercial court. He was appointed to the Court of Appeal in 1986 and presided there over its civil division as Master of the Rolls from 1992 until 1996 when he was appointed Lord Chief Justice. In 2000 he went to the House of Lords as Senior Law Lord. He has therefore been a judge for over a quarter of a century, and for much of that time has been deciding commercial cases, even if during his periods as Lord Chief Justice and Senior Law Lord the demands of the criminal law and, especially in recent years, of public and human rights law, have been dominating his output.

In this chapter I will address his judicial contribution to commercial law, a little diffidently perhaps, since I have spent my professional life either listening to his submissions, or making submissions to him on the bench, or submitting my judgments to his appellate review. Moreover, I lack the academic's analysis and professorial insight. Nevertheless, I propose to set about my task, as best I can, by selecting a number of cases from the three main stages of Lord Bingham's judicial career—commercial court, Court of Appeal, and House of Lords—to see what emerges.

Commercial Court (1980–1986)

The Lloyd's Reports are full of Mr Justice Bingham's judgments. I have looked at about 70 of them. The subject matter of those years is rather different from today's: predominately shipping and little in the way of insurance or financial services. The judgments are taut, easy to read and understand, introduce their issues early and plainly, and, after an elegant consideration of fact, principle, and authority, come to straightforward and well-defined conclusions.

Tor Line AB v Alltrans Group of Canada Ltd (The TFL Prosperity) [1982] 1 Lloyd's Rep 617 came from arbitration. Numerous issues arose for which the losing shipowners sought leave to appeal, but *The Nema* [1982] AC 724, only recently decided in the House of Lords, meant that only one of those issues, which concerned the standard Baltime exceptions clause, clause 13, managed to win leave to appeal. The resultant appeal was innovatively and efficiently, despite opposition, heard immediately as part of the same hearing which had led to the grant of leave to appeal. The issue was whether the vessel's failure to meet its contractual description in terms of the height of its main deck was, in the absence of 'personal act or omission or default of the Owners' (who had merely passed on the measurements which had been given to them), exempted from liability. Bingham J, who under the *Nema* guidelines needed to be persuaded in the first place, in order to grant leave to appeal, that a strong *prima facie* case had been made out that the arbitration award was wrong, frankly stated that further consideration after the conclusion of argument had persuaded him otherwise. Despite previous authority on clause 13 giving it wide effect, he concluded that its terms could not have been intended to render the owners immune from breaches of description so far as structural statistics were concerned. It proved to be a House of Lords point.

The Court of Appeal thought otherwise, and reversed judgment and award: [1983] 2 Lloyd's Rep 18. However, the House of Lords restored them: [1984] 1 WLR 48, even if it took Lord Roskill to acknowledge his judicial error in *The Charalambos N Pateras* [1972] 1 Lloyd's 1. That was a fine early success for the intuitive judgment of Bingham J.

Tradax Export SA v Dorada Compania Naviera SA (The Lutetian) [1982] 2 Lloyd's Rep 140 concerned a disputed withdrawal for late payment of hire under a time charter. There was a seven-day trial which led to ten separate issues and a lengthy judgment. Those were the days when withdrawal disputes came frequently before the courts, with many proceeding to the House of Lords. Perhaps in the anticipation that this case would go there as well, Bingham J answered all ten questions fully, even though the first one, namely whether monthly hire was due at a time when the vessel was off-hire, was itself decisive in favour of the charterers. That was a novel issue.

Also decisive in the charterers' favour was a most interesting point of estoppel (issue 7, at 156/8). Charterers had in good faith deducted four days' hire for anticipated off-hire: it was on this ground that the owners ultimately withdrew, following an anti-technicality notice procedure required by the contract. However, the owners did not make their objection to the charterers' calculation plain. Founding himself on Baron Parke's dictum in *Freeman v Cooke* (1848) 2 Ex 654 at 663 about 'a duty cast upon a person, by usage of trade or otherwise, to disclose the truth' and upon what Lord Wilberforce had said, *obiter* and in a dissenting judgment, in *Moorgate Mercantile Co Ltd v Twitchings* [1977] AC 890 at 903 which Bingham J reformulated, but making use of much of Lord Wilberforce's language, to the effect that:

the duty necessary to found an estoppel by silence or acquiescence can arise where a reasonable man would expect the person against whom the estoppel is raised, acting honestly and responsibly to bring the true facts to the attention of the other party known to him to be under a mistake as to their respective rights and obligations (at 157),

he concluded thus:

The relationship of owner and charterer is not one of the utmost good faith. One must be careful not to impute unrealistically onerous obligations to those who may choose to conduct their relations in a tough and uncompromising way. There is nonetheless a duty not to conduct oneself in such a way as to mislead. I have no doubt that the owners knew that the charterers believed that they had paid the right amount. It was their duty, acting honestly and responsibly, to disclose their own view to the charterers. They did not do so and indeed thwarted the charterers' attempts to discover their views. Their omission to disclose their own calculation led the charterers to think, until a very late stage, that no objection was being taken to the calculation. It would in my view be unjust in the circumstances if the owners could rely on the incorrectness of a deduction which they had every opportunity to point out at an earlier stage and which their failure to point out caused the charterers to overlook. I answer this question in favour of the charterers (at 158).

On this issue too, this was cutting-edge law. However, for all that Bingham J may have anticipated a journey to the House of Lords in *The Lutetian*, it was not to be. The parties rested content with his decision.

In *La Banque Financière de la Cité SA (Banque Keyser Ullmann en Suisse SA) v Westgate Insurance Co Ltd (formerly named Hodge General & Mercantile Insurance Co Ltd)* [1990] 1 QB 665 [1988] 2 Lloyd's Rep 513 at 554 and 565, Slade LJ approved this decision in *The Lutetian* on its facts as an instance of estoppel founded on conduct amounting to a positive representation. However, he expressed disquiet (at 565) about the use to which in *The Good Luck* [1988] 1 Lloyd's Rep 514 at 548 Hobhouse J had put Lord Wilberforce's dictum and Bingham J's reformulation of it to support a duty to speak founding a claim for damages, in the absence of a positive misrepresentation. Slade LJ concluded (at 566):

Like the Judge we deplore the fact that we live in a world in which commercial dishonesty...is rampant. Like him we wish it could be eliminated, particularly from the insurance markets of the world, and not least the London insurance market. But we cannot regard our decision in the present case as an appropriate instrument for seeking to achieve that purpose.

In the House of Lords (*Banque Keyser Ullmann SA v Skandia (UK) Insurance Co Ltd* [1991] 2 AC 249) their Lordships were able, on a point of construction and an issue of causation, to avoid many of the difficulties with which the lower courts had struggled, so that these issues of a duty to speak went unvisited. Similarly, in *The Good Luck* [1992] 1 AC 233, the House of Lords was able to restore Hobhouse J's decision without entering upon these issues. In that case, the commercial judge, Hobhouse J, had separately used *The Lutetian* to support a duty to speak founding a claim in damages. The Court of Appeal, however, had disagreed with Hobhouse J in this respect, [1990] 1 QB 818. In sum, Bingham J's use of the notion of commercial honesty in order to create a duty to speak has survived and been approved in the realm of estoppel (to prevent owners unfairly withdrawing their vessel) but not for the purpose of creating a right of action in damages.

In *Industrie Chimiche Italia Centrale SpA v Nea Ninemia Shipping SA (The Emmanuel C)* [1983] 1 Lloyd's Rep 310 Bingham J had to decide the familiar, but often difficult, question of whether an exclusion or indemnity clause covers negligence, a pure issue of construction. He held that 'errors of navigation' did not include negligent errors, despite characterizing the argument to the contrary as 'extremely formidable' (at 313), as indeed it was. The judgment is a model of concision, scope, and clarity. The authorities, running from *Price & Co v Union Lighterage Co* [1904] 1 KB 412 via the well-known *Canada Steamship Lines Ltd v The King* [1952] AC 1952 to *The Raphael* [1982] 2 Lloyd's Rep 42, are succinctly analysed in four paragraphs of 'general conclusions'. The losing submissions are fully set out, and the reasoning towards the judge's conclusions is comprehensive and persuasive. Much later in his judicial career, Lord Bingham had occasion to revisit Lord Morton's *Canada Steamship* formulation in *HIH Casualty & General Insurance Ltd v Chase Manhattan Bank* [2003] UKHL 6, [2003] 1 All ER (Comm) 349 at 357, where he concluded that the clause in question, although not mentioning negligence in terms, did exclude liability for negligent misrepresentation. He was surely right to warn against the idea that the *Canada Steamship* formulation is a code or litmus test which yields a certain and predictable result: 'The courts' task of ascertaining what the particular parties intended, in their particular commercial context, remains.'

It may be rare, but there has been one famous occasion when Bingham J's judgment was reviewed on appeal and reversed. *The Popi M* [1983] 2 Lloyd's Rep 235 concerned a vessel which sank in calm seas and whose loss led to a claim on hull underwriters. What caused the initial entry of seawater? The only explanation put up by the underwriters was wear and tear. The only explanation put up by the owners which survived examination was collision with a submarine. Bingham J concluded that, despite its inherent improbability and his initial disbelief, such a collision was on the balance of probabilities the cause, and so the owners succeeded in proving a loss by perils of the sea. The Court of Appeal upheld that judgment, [1984] 2 Lloyd's Rep 555. However, the House of Lords decided otherwise: [1985] 2 Lloyd's Rep 1. The judge should have taken the third way, of simply finding the owners' case not proved. It was a great compliment to Bingham J, however, that Lord Roskill said (at 7):

...I am driven, reluctantly but inescapably, to the conclusion that on this occasion even Homer nodded.

The Court of Appeal (1986–2000)

Interfoto Picture Library Ltd v Stiletto Visual Programmes Ltd [1989] QB 433 has been an influential case on basic principles of contract law. It was decided by a two-judge Court of Appeal consisting of Dillon and Bingham LJJ. They agreed in the result but did not speak with a single voice. Interfoto ran a photographic transparency lending library. A telephone inquiry from Stiletto led to the delivery to them by Interfoto of 47 transparencies together with a delivery note which stipulated that the transparencies had to be returned within 14 days after which a holding fee of £5 per transparency per day would be charged. Stiletto did not read the delivery note, had not used Interfoto before, returned the transparencies only after 28 days, and were charged £3,783.50. Interfoto had to sue to recover this charge. The judge in the Lambeth county court gave judgment for Interfoto, but Stiletto's appeal was allowed on the basis that the 14-day charging clause was ineffective: instead Interfoto could only obtain a *quantum meruit*. The judge had decided in the alternative that a *quantum meruit* would have been £3.50 per transparency per week after a reasonable time of 14 days had elapsed for their return.

Dillon LJ held that the contract in question was only made after receipt of the transparencies and the delivery note and that the question was whether the holding fee clause, which he described as very onerous and exorbitant, had ever become part of the contract. He regarded the delivery note as a 'notice' of conditions. He referred to Lord Denning's famous dictum from *J Spurling v Bradshaw* [1956] 1 WLR 461 at 466 that: 'Some clauses which I have seen would need to be printed in red ink on the face of the document with a red hand pointing to it before the notice could be held to be sufficient.' He said that nothing whatever was done by Interfoto to draw Stiletto's attention in particular to the relevant clause 2 and that it had never become part of the contract.

Bingham LJ adopted a broader and deeper analysis, regarding the early 'notice' authorities as speaking not only to the question of incorporation of terms into a contract but also to 'a somewhat different question, whether it would in all the circumstances be fair (or reasonable) to hold a party bound by any conditions or by a particular condition of an unusual or stringent nature' (at 439). In particular he cited Bramwell LJ from the leading case of *Parker v South Eastern Railway Co* (1877) 2 CPD 416 at 427/8, where he dealt in broad vein with questions of fairness on both sides of the transaction, that is to say as they affect both the party who says 'But I never read the conditions' and the party who seeks to hold the other to unreasonable terms: e.g., 'I think there is an implied understanding that there is no condition unreasonable to the knowledge of the party tendering the document and not insisting on its being read'. Bingham LJ commented: 'This is not a simple contractual analysis whether an offer has been made or accepted' (at 442). He described Lord Denning's dictum as making explicit what Bramwell LJ had perhaps foreshadowed, 'that what would be good notice of one condition would not be notice of another'. Passing to *McCutcheon v David MacBrayne Ltd* [1964] 1 WLR 125, he found there dicta which he took to refer 'to a concept of fair dealing that has very little to do with a conventional analysis of offer and acceptance' (at 443). Finally he referred to *Thornton v Shoe Lane Parking Ltd* [1971] 2 QB 163 for its doctrine of whether a particular condition had been sufficiently brought to a party's notice. He concluded as follows (at 445):

The crucial question in this case is whether the plaintiffs can be said fairly and reasonably to have brought condition 2 to the notice of the defendants…In my opinion the plaintiffs did not do so…The result would be that a venial period of delay, as here, would lead to an inordinate liability. The defendants are not to be relieved of that liability because they did not read the condition, although doubtless they did not; but in my judgment they are to be relieved because the plaintiffs did not do what was necessary to draw this unreasonable and extortionate clause fairly to their attention.

This is intriguing language. On the one hand, Bingham LJ says that the crucial question is whether the term was fairly and reasonably brought to the customer's notice, which appears to be adopting Dillon LJ's incorporation analysis. However, Bingham LJ says 'fairly and reasonably' and not just 'sufficiently'. Moreover, he concludes not, as Dillon LJ had done, by saying that the clause had never become part of the contract, but by saying that Stiletto was to be 'relieved of liability' because the extortionate clause had not been brought fairly to the customer's attention. This is more the language in which statute might speak of a term being unenforceable because it failed the requirement of unreasonableness (see the Unfair Contract Terms Act 1977) or of a penalty being unenforceable (see Bingham LJ's final reservation of an argument that condition 2 was challengeable as a disguised penalty, at 445/6).

What then is Bingham LJ signifying here? We are concerned with one of the most basic questions of contract law, the extent to which consumers in particular (not that Stiletto was a consumer, as distinct from a small business) or those who contract on another's standard terms, whether a consumer or not, are to be bound by anything in an agreement. If a contract is made with the aid of a notice, then the doctrine of limited incorporation may assist. That, however, will not work where the contract has been plainly assented to, in the most typical case where it has been signed, see *L'Estrange v Graucob Ltd* [1934] 2 KB 394 (and some contracts contain a representation that the contract has been read, typically in the kind of contract which is the least likely to have been read!). It seems to me that in *Interfoto* Bingham LJ is reaching for a wider doctrine than that of incorporation of terms, a more general 'concept of fair dealing'.

That this is so is strongly suggested by the more general passages in Bingham LJ's judgment, such as those with which he started (at 439):

In many civil law systems, and perhaps in most legal systems outside the common law world, the law of obligations recognises and enforces an overriding principle that in making and carrying out contracts parties should act in good faith. This does not simply mean that they should not deceive each other, a principle which any legal system must recognise; its effect is perhaps most aptly conveyed by such metaphorical colloquialisms as 'playing fair,' 'coming clean' or 'putting one's cards face upwards on the table.' It is in essence a principle of fair and open dealing…

English law has, characteristically, committed itself to no such overriding principle but has developed piecemeal solutions in response to demonstrated problems of unfairness. Many examples could be given. Thus equity has intervened to strike down unconscionable bargains. Parliament has stepped in to regulate the imposition of exception clauses and the form of certain hire-purchase agreements. The common law has also made its contribution, by holding that certain classes of contract require the utmost good faith, by treating as irrecoverable what purport to be agreed estimates of damage but are in truth a disguised penalty for breach, and in many other ways.

The well known cases on sufficiency of notice are in my view properly to be read in this context. At one level they are concerned with a question of pure contractual analysis, whether one party has done enough to give the other party notice of the incorporation of a term in the contract. At another level they are concerned with a somewhat different question, whether it would in all the circumstances be fair (or reasonable) to hold a party bound by any conditions or by a particular condition of an unusual or stringent nature.

After considering the authorities, Bingham LJ returned to the point of his departure, saying (at 445):

The tendency of the English authorities has, I think, been to look at the nature of the transaction in question and the character of the parties to it; to consider what notice the party alleged to be bound was given of the particular condition said to bind him; and to resolve whether in all the circumstances it is fair to hold him bound by the condition in question. This may yield a result not very different from the civil law principle of good faith, at any rate so far as the formation of the contract is concerned.

In these passages, I feel I can detect the same aspiration as Bingham J showed in *The Lutetian* (see above) in the context of estoppel and the duty to speak, towards a general concept of fair dealing. Whether the authorities he relied on in *Interfoto* do in themselves take one past the doctrine of limited incorporation, I would myself beg leave to doubt. But I would equally ask leave to applaud his developing analysis.

Ashville Investments Ltd v Elmer Contractors Ltd [1989] QB 488 concerns the scope of arbitration clauses. Bingham LJ was the junior lord justice and gave his judgment third, but his analysis is penetrating and has foreshadowed the more recent decision in the House of Lords in *Fiona Trust and Holding Corporation v Primalov* [2007] UKHL 40, [2007] Bus LR 1719. The issue was whether an arbitration clause could give jurisdiction to arbitrators to arbitrate questions of misrepresentation or mistake in the formation of the contract. The Court of Appeal held that it could, and that the arbitration clause in that case, which required the parties to refer to arbitration any disputes which arose 'in connection with' the contract covered issues of misrepresentation and mistake and therefore issues of rectification too. That conclusion required some reassessment of earlier authority, but, as Bingham LJ said (at 510):

the leading cases were decided at a time when both the general attitude towards arbitration and the judicial approach towards arbitration clauses were very different from what they are today.

In reaching his conclusion, Bingham LJ was motivated in part by practical wisdom and his confidence in the institution of arbitration. Thus he said:

Looking at the matter more broadly, I find nothing surprising or unattractive about these conclusions. In any case at all similar to this, there are virtually bound to be claims which an arbitrator will have to resolve because only he has the power to do so. As I have tried to show, his task is likely to be one of considerable difficulty, calling for great skill and judgment in its effective discharge. I find it hard to suppose that any informed and detached observer, untouched by the acrimony of this case, would not think it sensible for Elmer's disputed claims to be resolved by the same responsible arbitrator who was to investigate and decide the rest of the case (at 509);

and

I would be very slow to attribute to reasonable parties an intention that there should in any foreseeable eventuality be two sets of proceedings. Rectification, misrepresentation and negligent mis-statement are unlikely to raise questions more difficult than those an arbitrator under this form of contract must already resolve. The privacy of an arbitral tribunal is likely to be more, not less, welcome than the publicity of proceedings in court. I see no reason why the employer (or architect) or the contractor should flinch from the decision of these questions by an experienced professional man duly agreed or appointed (at 517).

Ashville Investments has set the modern tone of confidence in arbitration which is increasingly the home of commercial disputes: see *Overseas Union Insurance Ltd v AA Mutual Insurance Co Ltd* [1988] 2 Lloyd's Rep 63; *Ethiopian Oilseeds & Pulses Export Corporation v Rio del Mar Foods Inc* [1990] 1 Lloyd's Rep 86; *Harbour Assurance Co (UK) Ltd v Kansa General International Insurance Co Ltd* [1993] 1 Lloyd's Rep 455; *Continental Bank NA v Aeakos Compania Naviera SA* [1994] 1 Lloyd's Rep 505; *The Angelic Grace* [1995] 1 Lloyd's Rep 87; and now *Fiona Trust v Privalov*.

Dresser UK Ltd v Falcongate Freight Management Ltd [1992] QB 502 concerned the Brussels Convention on Jurisdiction and the Enforcement of Judgments in Civil and Commercial Matters, enacted into English law by the Civil Jurisdiction and Judgments Act 1982, one of the relatively few points at which English commercial law is affected by the law of the European Union. The particular issue was as to the moment when the English court became 'first seised' or the proceedings before it 'definitively' pending for the purposes of the *lis pendens* rules of the Convention: was it on issue of the writ (which might never be served and of which the defendant would be ignorant) or on its service? The former had been the rule of English law, for instance for the purpose of limitation. The issue however raised new problems in its international setting. In many European countries the rule was that service marked the moment when courts regarded themselves as seised of proceedings. Bingham LJ concluded the matter in this powerful paragraph (at 523):

...it is in my judgment artificial, far-fetched and wrong to hold that the English court is seised of proceedings, or that proceedings are decisively, conclusively, finally or definitively pending before it, upon mere issue of proceedings, when at that stage (1) the court's involvement has been confined to a ministerial act by a relatively junior administrative officer; (2) the plaintiff has an unfettered choice whether to pursue the action and serve the proceedings or not, being in breach of no rule or obligation if he chooses to let the writ expire unserved; (3) the plaintiff's claim may be framed in terms of the utmost generality; (4) the defendant is usually unaware of the issue of proceedings and, if unaware, is unable to call on the plaintiff to serve the writ or discontinue the action and unable to rely on the commencement of the action as a lis alibi pendens if proceedings are begun elsewhere; (5) the defendant is not obliged to respond to the plaintiff's claim in any way, and not entitled to do so save by calling on the plaintiff to serve or discontinue; (6) the court cannot exercise any powers which, on appropriate facts, it could not have exercised before issue; (7) the defendant has not become subject to the jurisdiction of the court.'

It is therefore ironic that in the revision of the Brussels Convention which became the Judgments Regulation (Council Regulation (EC) No 44/2001) new Article 30 defines seisure as the time of issue ('at the time when the document instituting the proceedings or an equivalent document is lodged with the court, provided that the plaintiff has not subsequently failed to take the steps he was required to take to have service effected on the defendant'). That, however, is because it proved defective in practice to have a rule (a) which varied from member state to state (see preamble 15 to the Judgments Regulation) and (b) which turned the dominant rule of priority in time which informs the *lis pendens* provisions of the Convention into the serendipity of first service.

Tempora mutantur et nos mutamur in illis. The question of seisin is a microcosm of the difficulty of formulating a principled rule that does justice to the interests involved, to the exceptional case which tests the rule, and to the context, here not merely the issue of when one country, such as the UK, holds that its courts have seisin for its own purposes, but the issue when its courts do so for the purposes of an international convention relating to *lis pendens* which is formulated on the rule of temporal priority. The issue was very recently revisited in the House of Lords in *Phillips v Nussberger* [2008] UKHL 1, [2008] 1 WLR 180. Although decided some years after the change wrought by the Judgments Regulation, it concerned a case under the Lugano Convention under the old rule of Article 21 (itself due to change with a revision of the Lugano Convention). Moreover, the other competing jurisdiction was Switzerland, which adopts a seisin rule at the time of issue, not service. The House of Lords was asked, in the light of the exceptional facts of that case, to rule that the *Dresser* rule of seisin at the time of service was wrong, or at any rate should admit of exceptions, as contemplated by Bingham LJ in *Dresser*, such as where a court gains seisin even before issue at the time when it grants a *Mareva* injunction or an *Anton Pillar* order (see *Dresser* at 523).

Lord Brown gave the leading speech, with which the others (who included Lord Bingham) agreed, holding that even under the *Dresser* rule the courts of England established seisin first, at latest at the time of service, even though service was defective. A majority of their Lordships did not question the *Dresser* rule. Lord

Mance, however, with the support of Baroness Hale, went further, so as to propose that the *Dresser* rule of seisin at the time of service, especially as tightened in *The Sargasso* [1994] 2 Lloyd's Rep 6 (CA), was mistaken. However, Lord Mance's reasoning depends in part on the development of jurisprudence in *Canada Trust Co v Stolzenberg (No 2)* [2002] 1 AC 1 (on the question of when a party's domicile should be tested, namely at the time of issue) and in part on the changes brought about by the Civil Procedure Rules (CPR). I cannot help feeling that, however anomalously and silently, the fundamental change introduced by the Judgments Regulation, and the practical experience which had led to that change, contributed to Lord Mance's observations. Just as the *Dresser* rule was influenced by the learning of the civil law, so an alternative domestic rule of seisin at the time of issue can be influenced by the development of the modern European conventional rule. One sees here a fascinating case study of legal history (albeit within a short time frame) and of pragmatic rule-making.

In *First Sport Ltd v Barclays Bank plc* [1993] 1 WLR 1229 the issue before the Court of Appeal was whether Barclays was bound, under its terms then applicable to the use of its cheque guarantee cards, to meet its guaranteed liability to pay a supplier who provided goods or services in reliance on such a card even when its use was fraudulent. The sum in issue was £49. But there could hardly be an issue with more impact on the everyday commercial life of the nation. Evans LJ gave the leading judgment to the effect that Barclays was bound, Kennedy LJ dissented, and Sir Thomas Bingham MR gave his own short judgment for holding Barclays liable. It is, if I may say so, a model of that kind of short, incisive judgment so clearly delineating issue and solution which Lord Bingham came to write in the House of Lords in cases where he presided as Senior Law Lord and therefore gave the first speech but where the task of writing the main speech had been assigned to another of their Lordships. The judgment is also remarkable for its practical wisdom. I illustrate with the following citations (at 1240D/1241B):

It is clear that the dishonest buyer lacked actual authority to bind the bank. By its opening statement on the back of the card (that the card could be used only by the authorised signatory) the bank made that clear...

It is of course elementary that a finding of ostensible authority cannot be based on the false assertion of the purported agent that he has authority which in truth he lacks. Such a finding must be based on a holding out by the alleged principal of the alleged agent as having his authority to act on his behalf in the relevant respect, which authority (after reliance upon it by the third party) the alleged principal is not permitted to deny. The simple justice underlying the rule is obvious: if A induces B to treat C as A's agent with authority to bind him, it would be quite unfair if A were afterwards free to disavow the transaction on the basis that C was never his agent at all, even though in truth he never was...

After considerable hesitation, born of the able arguments on each side and strengthened by Evans and Kennedy LJJ's disagreement I am persuaded that First Sport is right. My reasons are as much practical as legal. If the bank had made clear that it would in no circumstances accept any liability at all on any cheque not signed by the authorised signatory of the card, then the shop assistants and garage attendants to whom such cards are usually presented would have been put on notice, and it may be that evidence of a buyer's true identity would have been demanded as a matter of routine. But read as a whole the bank's offer (including the conditions) did not make that clear: instead, it encouraged the belief that if the written terms of the offer and the conditions were met the bank would accept liability to the extent specified. Thereby, as it seems to me, it held out anyone able to fulfil all those conditions as having authority to bind it.

My next citation, of *Phillips Electronique Grand Public SA v British Sky Broadcasting Limited* [1995] EMLR 472, is for the pleasure of finding in this out-of-the-way series of reports Sir Thomas Bingham MR's remarkable synopsis and restatement of the law of implied terms and of the rationale of making or declining to make the alleged implication. I will not set out the passage in full (at 480/2), but I unhesitatingly recommend it to anyone interested in this vital issue of contract and commercial law. I will merely confine myself here to this extract dealing with the rationale of the subject:

The courts' usual role in contractual interpretation is, by resolving ambiguities or reconciling inconsistencies, to attribute the true meaning to the language in which the parties themselves have expressed their contract. The implication of contract terms involves a different and altogether more ambitious undertaking: the interpolation of terms to deal with matters for which, ex hypothesi, the parties themselves have made no provision. It is because the implication of terms is potentially so intrusive that the law imposes strict constraints on the exercise of this extraordinary power.

There are of course contracts into which terms are routinely and unquestionably implied. If a surgeon undertakes to operate on a patient a term will be implied into the contract that he exercise reasonable care and skill in doing so...Again, quite apart from statute, the courts would not ordinarily hesitate to imply into a contract for unseen goods that they should be of merchantable quality and answer to their description and conform with sample...

But the difficulties increase the further one moves away from these paradigm examples. In the first case [that of the surgeon], it is probably unlikely that any terms will have been expressly agreed, except perhaps the nature of the operation, and the time and place of operation. In the second case [that of sale of goods], the need for implication usually arises where the contract terms have not been spelled out in detail or by reference to written conditions. It is much more difficult to infer with confidence what the parties must have intended when they have entered into a lengthy and carefully-drafted contract, but have omitted to make provision for the matter in issue. Given the rules which restrict evidence of the parties' intention when negotiating a contract, it may well be doubtful whether the omission was the result of the parties' oversight or of their deliberate decision; if the parties appreciate that they are unlikely to agree on what is to happen in a certain not impossible eventuality, they may well choose to leave the matter uncovered in their contract in the hope that the eventuality will not occur.'

There are many other decisions in the Court of Appeal which could well be visited here. They would include *The Super Servant Two* [1990] 1 Lloyd's Rep 1 (on frustration); *Hyundai Merchant Marine Co Ltd v Gesuri Chartering Co Ltd*

(The Peonia) [1991] 1 Lloyd's Rep 100 (on late redelivery of a time chartered vessel); *Everglade Maritime Inc v Schiffahrtsgesellschaft Detlef von Appen mbH* [1993] QB 780 (where Bingham LJ, unusually, found himself dissenting, in a case about sealed offers in arbitration); *L'Office Cherifien des Phosphates v Yamashita-Shinnihon Steamship Co Ltd (The Boucraa)* [1994] 1 AC 486 (where, equally unusually, he was to find the House of Lords disagreeing with him, on the subject of the retrospectivity of section 13A of the Arbitration Act 1950); and *Reichhold Norway ASA v Goldman Sachs International* [2000] 1 WLR 173 (where he upheld the commercial judge in staying English court proceedings pending arbitration in Norway).

House of Lords (2000–2008)

With the coming into force on 2 October 2000 of the Human Rights Act 1998, Lord Bingham's time in the House of Lords, which he entered as senior law lord, was much occupied with human rights, public and constitutional law issues. However, he continued to be involved in commercial cases. Among those well worthy of comment are *HIH Casualty & General Insurance Co Ltd v Chase Manhattan Bank* [2003] UKHL 6, [2003] 1 All ER (Comm) 349 (where exclusion clauses against fraud and negligence were considered); *Homburg Houtimport BV v Agrosin Private Ltd (The Starsin)* [2003] UKHL 12, [2004] 1 AC 715 (an important case on many issues, including the construction of standard form commercial contracts, the identity of carriers under a bill of lading, and the Himalaya Clause); and *JI MacMillan Co Inc v Mediterranean Shipping Co SA* [2005] UKHL 11, [2005] 2 AC 423 (whether a straight bill of lading is a bill of lading within the Hague Rules and/or a document of title). However, I will refer in particular to four others below.

Among the earliest cases on which Lord Bingham sat in the House of Lords was *Whistler International Limited v Kawasaki Kisen Kaisha Limited* [2001] 1 AC 638. It was a classic commercial dispute between an owner and charterer of a time-chartered vessel. Was the charterer's order for the vessel to sail by the most direct and thus the shortest and quickest ('great circle') route an order as to 'employment' within the charterer's rights to direct the vessel's employment, and thus within the owner's obligation to prosecute its voyages with the utmost despatch? Or was this a matter of 'navigation', responsibility for which under the charter had been retained and liability for errors of which had been excluded by the owner under the charter? The master had preferred to take the longer 'rhumb line' route because of bad weather. The appeal arose from arbitration. The arbitrators, but only by a majority, considered the master's decision to be unjustifiable, and found for the charterer, and also held that the planning of the voyage was a matter of employment not navigation. The vessel was well equipped to withstand the heavy weather. The commercial judge disagreed, and reversed the arbitrators on appeal. The Court of Appeal upheld the commercial court judge. The House of Lords restored the majority award of the arbitrators.

It had obviously been a finely balanced dispute. However, one would not think so from reading Lord Bingham's elegant speech. It begins with an incisive overview of the 'complex commercial bargain' which a time charter strikes between its parties. Three brief paragraphs suffice for the exposition of these complexities (at 641). Lord Bingham then reached into the tangled skein of argument and immediately pulled out the critical piece of wool, which he described as the 'starting point', namely the obligation on the master to prosecute his voyages with the utmost despatch (at 641H). He then, as briefly, got to the heart of the majority arbitrators' factual analysis, pointing out that the effect of their findings was that the great circle route was not only the shortest and quickest route but also the usual route. It followed that it was the route which the master was obliged to take, unless he had good navigational or other reasons for not doing so (at 642F). So he came to the submission that the choice of route at any rate for reasons of weather was a matter of 'navigation' not 'employment'. On that question he considered previous authority, and found in it useful guidance (at 643H/646E). He also cited and clearly took appreciative note of articles written about the case itself by Mr Brian Davenport QC (who had recently died and to whom Lord Bingham paid a characteristically generous tribute) and by Mr Donald Davis ('the doyen of London maritime arbitrators'); and also of a recent decision on indistinguishable facts by New York arbitrators (at 643E/F). In the result, he was able to encapsulate the relevant difference between employment and navigation in these succinct remarks (at 646F/647C):

The charterer's right to use the vessel must be given full and fair effect; but it cannot encroach on matters falling within the specialised professional maritime experience of the master, particularly where the safety or security of the vessel, her crew and her cargo are involved ... The responsibility for making good, so far as practicable, whatever course is chosen of course remains with the master and crew, as does that for navigating the vessel safely into and out of port, and responding to maritime problems encountered in the open sea. But subject to safety considerations and the specific terms of the charter, the charterers may not only order a vessel to sail from A to B but may also direct the route to be followed between the two.

Following hard on the heels of the speeches in *Whistler International v KKK* (although heard earlier) came *Johnson v Gore Wood & Co* [2002] 2 AC 1, a case of professional negligence against solicitors but concerned primarily with an issue of general application, that of abuse of process. Mr Johnson's property development company sued Gore Wood & Co and settled its claim in the middle of trial. Mr Johnson alleged that the firm owed a personal duty to him as well which it had broken. He gave notice of that claim to the firm, but he did not proceed with it at the time when his company sued the firm, partly because he lacked legal aid to do so, and partly because it would have delayed the proceedings and possibly led to the collapse of the company before trial, as well as for other reasons. The compromise of the company's claim acknowledged the possibility of Mr Johnson's personal claim by containing a clause capping it at £250,000. Following the compromise, Mr Johnson brought his own proceedings. Over four years later, well on the way towards a second trial, the firm applied to strike out Mr Johnson's claim as an abuse of process. At first instance, Pumfrey J held that the firm was estopped by convention from contending that Mr Johnson's personal action was an abuse and that it would be unconscionable for the firm to argue such a point. The Court of Appeal disagreed: there was no estoppel, and there was an abuse of process on the part of Mr Johnson: he could and should have brought his own claim at the time of commencing his company's proceedings.

Lord Bingham reviewed in detail but also with great analytical skill the whole history of the doctrine of *Henderson v Henderson* (1843) 3 Hare 100. Building on the insight of Somervell LJ in *Greenhalgh v Mallard* [1947] 2 All ER 255 at 257, he showed that the doctrine, which had at one time been thought of as a species of *res judicata*, was better regarded as a form of abuse of process. Along the way, he cited (at 27F, with anonymous modesty) the Court of Appeal's judgment (which had been written by him) in *Barrow v Bankside Agency Ltd* [1996] 1 WLR 257 at 260 as follows:

The rule is not based on the doctrine of res judicata in the narrow sense, nor even on any strict doctrine of issue or cause of action estoppel. It is a rule of public policy based on the desirability, in the general interest as well as that of the parties themselves, that litigation should not drag on for ever and that a defendant should not be oppressed by successive suits when one would do. That is the abuse at which the rule is directed.

In what has become a famous and much cited passage, Lord Bingham then reformulated the doctrine in these words (at 31A/D):

The underlying public interest is the same: that there should be finality in litigation and that a party should not be twice vexed in the same matter. This public interest is reinforced by the current emphasis on efficiency and economy in the conduct of litigation, in the interests of the parties and the public as a whole. The bringing of a claim or the raising of a defence in later proceedings may, without more, amount to abuse if the court is satisfied (the onus being on the party alleging abuse) that the claim or defence should have been raised in the earlier proceedings if it was to be raised at all. I would not accept that it is necessary, before abuse may be found, to identify any additional element such as a collateral attack on a previous decision or some dishonesty, but where those elements are present the later proceedings will be much more obviously abusive, and there will rarely be a finding of abuse unless the later proceeding involves what the court regards as unjust harassment of a party. It is, however, wrong to hold that because a matter could have been raised in earlier proceedings it should have been, so as to render the raising of it in later proceedings necessarily abusive. That is to adopt too dogmatic an approach to what should in my opinion be a broad, merits-based judgment which takes account of the public and private interests involved and also takes account of all the facts of the case, focusing attention on the crucial question whether, in all the circumstances, a party is misusing or abusing the process of the court by seeking to raise before it the issue which could have been raised before.

The influence of this passage has been considerable: see *Carnoustie Universal SA v International Transport Workers' Federation* [2002] 2 All ER (Comm) 657; *Giles v Rhind* [2003] Ch 618; *Chaudhary v Royal College of Surgeons* [2003] ICR 1510; *Hussmann (Europe) Ltd v Pharaon* [2003] 1 All ER (Comm) 879; *Motorola Credit Corporation v Uzan (No 2)* [2004] 1 WLR 113; *R (Foster) v Eastbourne Borough Council* [2004] ICR 1149; *Lincoln National Life Insurance v Sun Life Insurance Co of Canada* [2005] 1 Lloyd's Rep 606; *WWF—World Wide Fund for Nature v World Wrestling Federation Entertainment Inc* [2007] Bus LR 1252; *Special Effects Ltd v L'Oréal SA* [2007] Bus LR 759.

Donahue v Armco Inc [2001] UKHL 64, [2002] 1 All ER (Comm) 97 is one of a series of important decisions which the House of Lords has had to consider in the last three decades concerning anti-suit injunctions. This common law doctrine, developed to police and protect parties' autonomous agreements as to where and how they would wish, if necessary, to conduct their disputes, has recently come under strong attack from the European Court of Justice (see *Erich Gasser GmbH v MISAT Srl* (Case-C 116/02) [2005] QB 1). In *Donahue v Armco*, however, the House of Lords had to consider both the validity of the traditional approach taken to the upholding of exclusive jurisdiction clauses and at the same time the complex difficulties of international disputes where it may be impossible to channel all aspects of such disputes into a single forum. In a broad ranging but concise speech, Lord Bingham considered and rationalized the jurisprudence as a whole, but nevertheless differed from the solution of the Court of Appeal (which had granted an injunction) because he identified as a crucial aspect of the complicated litigation the fact that it would not all be resolved in the English forum but nevertheless might be in New York (at paragraphs 36 and 38). The danger of a New York forum, however, was that Mr Donahue, who had the benefit of the exclusive jurisdiction clause for an English forum, might there be exposed to multiple or punitive damages, for instance under the US federal RICO statute. That difficulty, however, was resolved by an undertaking from the Armco appellants not to enforce any such award. Lord Bingham's speech is characteristic in its lucid balance: principles and facts are carefully analysed so as to expose the critical issue; the underlying rationale is developed and applied; all in pursuit of a fair result which does justice to jurisprudence and the public and private interests involved.

Golden Strait Corporation v Nippon Yusen Kubishka Kaisha (The Golden Victory) [2007] UKHL 12, [2007] 2 AC 353 is perhaps the last of Lord Bingham's speeches in a commercial case in the House of Lords. Unusually, he was in a minority (together with Lord Walker of Gestingthorpe). The majority was made up of Lord Scott of Foscote, Lord Carswell, and Lord Brown of Eaton-under-Heywood. There are signs that Lord Bingham was unhappy with the result. He said (at paragraph 1):

I give my reasons for doing so, unauthoritative though they must be, since in my respectful opinion the existing decision [of the Court of Appeal] undermines the quality of certainty which is a traditional strength and major selling point of English commercial law, and involves an unfortunate departure from principle.

The facts are interesting and carefully poised to maximize dispute. A seven-year time charter made in 1998 was repudiated by the charterer in December 2001. The hire arrangement reflected something of a partnership: there was a minimum guaranteed base hire rate, increasing over the period of the charter, but subject to a specified reduction if market rates should fall to a certain level; moreover, the owners were also to receive a share of operating profits earned by the charterer. The charter contained a war clause under which both parties had the right to cancel if war or hostilities were to break out between any two or more of a number of countries including the US, the UK, and Iraq. In March 2003 the outbreak of the Second Gulf War would have permitted the charterer to cancel under the war clause had not the charter already terminated. By then the owner had already obtained an interim arbitration award in September 2002 under which the arbitrator resolved preliminary issues to the effect that the charterer had repudiated, the owner had accepted the repudiation, and the earliest date for contractual redelivery would have been 6 December 2005. In the immediate run-up to the outbreak of war the parties were in negotiation for the reinstate-ment of the charter on the same terms as before together with damages for the intervening period from acceptance of the repudiation to delivery under the rein-stated charter. However, the owner declined this offer on receiving advice that the charterer would have been able to cancel the reinstated charter under the war clause if the impending war broke out.

In a further interim award made in October 2004 the arbitrator declared that the owner had not failed to mitigate by refusing the charterer's offer of reinstate-ment and, reluctantly, that damages under the repudiated charter were limited by the outbreak of war. He found that at the time when the charter had terminated the outbreak of war was no more than a mere possibility. He would have liked to have decided that in such circumstances the damages were to be calculated as of the time when the charter had terminated, irrespective of the fact that, as he also found, the charterer would have cancelled under the war clause if the charter had still been in existence. He felt obliged, however, to decide in the charterer's favour by reason of previous authority in *BS&N Ltd (BVI) v Micado Shipping Ltd (Malta) (The Seaflower)* [2000] 2 Lloyd's Rep 37. As Lord Bingham would dem-onstrate (at paragraph 19), the arbitrator probably misunderstood *The Seaflower*, but for which he would have decided the award in the owner's favour.

In the commercial court Langley J had upheld the award [2005] 1 All ER (Comm) 467, and the court of appeal (Auld and Tuckey LJJ and Lord Mance) also did so [2006] 1 All ER (Comm) 235.

In the House of Lords, Lord Bingham explained (at paragraphs 10/12) that the issue was whether damages were to be assessed, according to the traditional prin-ciple in cases, such as here, where there was an available market, as at the date of breach, or whether it was an exceptional case where 'the *Bwllfa* principle' applied (*Bwllfa and Methyr Dare Steam Collieries (1891) Limited v Pontypridd Waterworks Company* [1903] AC 426), viz the principle whereby the court need not speculate when it knows (or 'you need not gaze into the crystal ball when you can read the book'). However, as Lord Bingham observed, while 'it is clear that in some contexts the court may properly take account of later events, none of these cases involved repudiation of a commercial contract where there was an available market' (at paragraph 12). This Lord Bingham proceeded to demonstrate by his review of the relevant authorities (at paragraphs 12/20). He accepted that a calculation of the profit share aspect of the owner's remuneration would be difficult to calculate prospectively as of the date of breach, but observed that this point had not been raised at the arbitration or in the commercial court, and would in any event be insufficient to displace the general rule (at paragraph 21).

In concluding, Lord Bingham expanded on the importance of the date of breach rule both as a fair guide to a commercially just result and as a rule which supported the certainty, consistency, and coherence of English commercial law. In rebutting the counter-argument that the owner would be over-compensated by the application of the date of breach rule, he observed:

... The first is that contracts are made to be performed, not broken. It may prove disadvantageous to break a contract instead of performing it. The second is that, if on their repudiation being accepted, the charterers had promptly honoured their secondary obligation to pay damages, the transaction would have been settled well before the Second Gulf War became a reality. The third is that the owners were, as the arbitrator held ... entitled to be compensated for the value of what they had lost on the date it was lost, and it could not be doubted that what the owners lost at that date was a charterparty with slightly less than four years to run. This was a clear and, in my opinion, crucial finding ... On the arbitrator's finding, it was marketable on that basis ... By describing the prospect of war in December 2001 as 'merely a possibility', the expression twice used by the arbitrator ... the arbitrator can only have meant that it was seen as an outside chance, not affecting the marketable value of the charter at that time.

There is, however, a further answer which I, in common with the arbitrator, consider to be of great importance. He acknowledged the force of arguments advanced by the owners based on certainty ('generally important in commercial affairs'), finality ('the alternative being a running assessment of the state of play so far as the likelihood of some interruption to the contract is concerned'), consistency ('the idea that a party's accrued rights can be changed by subsequent events is objectionable in principle') and coherence ('the date of repudiation is the date on which rights and damages are assessed') ... The importance of certainty and predictability in commercial transactions has been a constant theme of English commercial law at any rate since the judgment of Lord Mansfield in *Vallejo v Wheeler* (1774) 1 Cowp 143, 153) ...

This is a powerful speech, but their Lordships as a whole were on their mettle, for there are powerful speeches as well from the others. Lord Walker, in his brief speech concurring with Lord Bingham, made the telling point that 'cases concerned with the assessment of damages for tort for personal injuries are in a quite different category' (at paragraph 41). Lord Scott, on the other hand, observed that *Bwllfa* itself was concerned with statutory compensation for loss of working of a colliery (at paragraph 65), and distinguished the time charter market, which was predominately a market for hiring services over a period, from a market for the buying and selling of goods. The owner's rights 'would not, in practice, have been marketable for a capital sum' (at paragraph 37). Even a long term sales contract for supply stretching into the future 'cannot escape the uncertainties of the future' (at paragraph 36). As for 'the so-called principle of certainty', there was 'no such principle': it was merely a (very important) desideratum, but 'must give way to principle', in this case the compensatory principle (at paragraph 38). The owners were seeking compensation 'exceeding the value of the contractual benefits of which they were deprived' (at paragraph 38). Lord Carswell agreed that considerations of certainty and finality had 'to yield to the greater importance of achieving an accurate assessment of the damages based on the loss actually incurred' (at paragraph 63). Lord Brown made powerful points on the facts or possible facts of the case: a war which had started before a new fixture could have been arranged could not be ignored; the profit-sharing element would require an arbitrator to take account of actual events over the charter period; a substitute charterer could similarly be assumed to wish to cancel the new charter on the outbreak of war (at paragraphs 81/82); and finally (at paragraph 84): 'When market movements can be eliminated from the assessment of damages (as here with regard to the charterparty rate) it should be (by the breach date rule). But not history; the Court need not shut its mind to that.'

Recent decisions have indicated that in the field of remedies, which include damages, the courts have been demonstrating an increasing willingness to escape from rigid limitations, to seek the flexibility to do justice: see, for instance the new-found but old-based caution about the single statutory remedy of avoidance for non-disclosure in insurance law (*per* Lord Lloyd in *Pan Atlantic Insurance Co Ltd v Pine Top Insurance Co Ltd* [1995] 1 AC 501 at 555; *per* Lord Hobhouse of Woodborough in *Manifest Shipping Co Ltd v Uni-Polaris Insurance Co Ltd* [2001] UKHL 1, [2003] 1 AC 469); or the difficult question of damages for negligent misstatement (*SAAMCO v York Management Ltd* [1997] AC 191); or the subject of damages for conversion (*Kuwait Airways Corporation v Iraqi Airways Co (Nos 4 and 5)* [2002] UKHL 19, [2002] 2 AC 883). However, in *The Golden Victory* much appears to have ultimately depended on whether a time chartered vessel should be regarded as an item whose value essentially depended on current markets. Markets, of course, wait for no man, nor history. Articles in support of Lord Bingham's classical market-based solution have appeared from distinguished authors: see Lord Mustill 'The Golden Victory - Some Reflections' at (2008) LQR 569 and Francis Reynolds, 'The Golden Victory - A Misguided Decision' at (2008) HKLJ 333.

Lord Bingham's concern for the right result, on the right principles, appears, unusually for him, to have produced a speech with all but naked advocacy in it. It is almost as though, in his taking leave of the commercial law in his judicial role, he was anxious to see that it fared no less well in the future than in the times when Lord Mansfield had set the path for its growth several centuries ago.

He should have no fear of that. Like Lord Mansfield he has been prepared to listen hard to the experience of commercial men, and to find assistance in the civil as well as in the common law. His judgments in commercial court, Court of Appeal, and House of Lords have, with consummate skill, elegance, and clarity, but also almost imperceptibly, wrought change with stability. There is a remarkable sense of balance in his treatment of facts and law alike. Jurisprudence is reinterpreted, but principle is respected. Concise analysis brings out what often lies hidden or obscured by detail. Restatement of the law is a series of balanced propositions, within which the reader can find the answer to the case in hand and other cases. But the protection of principle is not at the cost of justice, and when there is room for a doctrine which ultimately requires to be applied with flexibility, on all the circumstances of the case, there is no insistence on a bright line test for the sake of undue simplicity. Moreover, when there is room for a doctrine which recognizes and reflects the importance of fairness and good faith in business dealings, Lord Bingham has not been afraid to state it. His contributions to English commercial law, as to so many other areas of the law, have been considerable, and will long be appreciated, bearing their fruit into years still to come.

V

COMPARATIVE LAW IN THE COURTS

1

The Road Ahead for the Common Law[1]

Robin Cooke

Purpose

Dr Cranston extended the invitation; Dr Andenas prescribed the subject. The Director of the Institute has requisitioned from me a lecture expressing views on recent developments in English public law. Among the suggestions for a title made by him was 'I told you so'. This was because he thinks that the English developments now show a trend towards ideas or approaches, once regarded as unsound or heretical, which over many years I have pursued in judgments and extra-judicial writings, mainly in New Zealand but also to some extent in other jurisdictions, including the House of Lords and the Privy Council.

I do not intend to adopt that suggested theme. To do so would be embarrassingly smug. It would also be, in part, to claim some credit for nothing other than a degree of longevity. For a sobering truth, from which no satisfaction is to be derived, is that no currently sitting English judge is as old. If I have reached some tenets earlier than English judges, it has to be remembered that I have had longer to think about them. Furthermore, the confluence of thinking, though happy as far it goes, is not altogether complete. If writing a school report today on the work of the English courts, I would say 'Pleasing progress in some areas, but could do better'. The purpose of this lecture, then, is to illustrate both parts of that possible verdict by identifying some current lines of development and some that can lie ahead.

The Diminishing Englishness of the Common Law

In the 1996 Hamlyn Lectures, under the title *Turning Points of the Common Law*, I examined four great cases where the House of Lords set the law of England, and

---

[1] Lord Cooke wished to contribute to this Liber Amicorum but died while it was still only a proposal. This is a lecture he delivered at the British Institute on International and Comparative Law and a version of which is published in (2004) 53 International and Comparative Law Quarterly 273.

consequently the law of most of the English-speaking world, on a new course by reversing decisions of the courts below. They were *Salomon v Salomon & Co Ltd*[2] (insistence on separate identities of company and controlling shareholder); *Woolmington v Director of Public Prosecutions*[3] (discovery of a golden thread about onus of proof in English criminal law); *Hedley Byrne & Co Ltd v Heller*[4] (qualified acceptance of duty of care in tort to safeguard against economic damage); and *Anisminic Ltd v Foreign Compensation Commission*[5] (affirmation that material errors of law by administrative bodies are always redressable by courts).

Although one of my points in 1996 was that Commonwealth case law was beginning to have some impact in the shaping of English common law, there was nothing unnatural in 1996 in speaking of the House of Lords changing the course of the law of most of the English-speaking world. Certainly the day had passed in independent Commonwealth countries when decisions of the House were treated as binding or almost automatically followed. Yet an aura and a degree of leadership still attached to the Lords. In the ensuing seven years the picture has changed, subtly but nonetheless significantly. There has been a widespread movement towards a common law of the world in the fields of human rights and commercial law (e.g., Uncitral) in which the English judiciary has been but one player, and far from the leading one. With the domestic force given to the European Convention on Human Rights and Fundamental Freedoms by the Human Rights Act 1998, including the adjuration to take into account decisions of the European Court of Human Rights and other European bodies, the United Kingdom has gone further in submitting to European influences—a process most clearly begun by the direct enforceability of some rules of Community law under the European Communities Act 1972 and the *Factortame* cases extending from 1990 to 1999.[6] It will go even further if the proposed European Constitution is adopted. As David Heathcoat-Amory MP puts it,[7] 'The European Court of Justice (ECJ) will essentially become the supreme court of all citizens of the new Union'. Courts in (for instance) Canada, Australia, and New Zealand avowedly, if respectfully, now abjure British primacy in any sense. And to the extent that there remains any instinctive deferment and affection for the House of Lords, reflecting the ties of history, it will hardly transfer should the House be shorn of its judicial functions. A new Supreme Court of the United Kingdom will be one national supreme court among many—and indeed not even supreme if Heathcoat-Amory is right and the deeper plunge into Europe taken.

In other words, the common law of England is becoming gradually less English. International influences—from Europe, the Commonwealth, and even

---

[2] [1897] AC 22.   [3] [1935] AC 462.
[4] [1964] 2 AC 465.   [5] [1969] 2 AC 147.
[6] See *R v Secretary of State for Transport, ex p Factortame Ltd (No 5)* [2000] 1 AC 524.
[7] *The European Constitution and what it means for Britain*, Centre for Policy Studies, June 2003, 6. The author has served for 15 months and more on the Convention on the Future of Europe, representing the House of Commons.

the United States, sometimes themselves pulling in different directions—are gradually acquiring more and more strength. This is the first line of development that I think I see. And in turn it influences the other lines.

The Fallacy of Omnicompetence

The classic theory of English 'public law' (a term popularized by Lord Diplock) is that Parliament (the Queen, the Lords, and the Commons acting together) is sovereign, supreme, omnicompetent. It cannot bind its successors. Acceptance by the courts that it has done so, as by the European Communities Act, is acquiescence in a revolution. Judicial checks upon the operation of statutes can only be based ultimately on the doctrine of ultra vires, however strained. The pervading fiction must be that Parliament cannot have intended the impugned result. Implication and presumption prevail. As the now classic administrative law textbook, Wade and Forsyth, says[8] of the powers of the courts to invalidate 'improper' action, 'Somehow they must be forced into the mould of the ultra vires doctrine, for unless that can be done the court will be powerless'. But some cautious notes are sounded in that work, while the other leading English administrative law textbook, Craig, is noticeably less wedded to ultra vires.[9]

Up to a point it is a question of labels. Ultra vires can be used as a compendious term to characterize decisions which the courts hold to be invalid on any ground: whether for straying outside a permitted area ('excess of jurisdiction') or error in law or unreasonableness or disproportionality or breach of fundamental rights. A vigorous academic debate is nevertheless being waged about this issue. And it is not merely semantic.

The latest shot that I have seen in the exchange of fire is a paper by Professor Philip Joseph of the University of Canterbury in New Zealand, delivered in Oxford at a conference of the Society of Legal Scholars in September 2003. The title, 'Parliament, The Courts and The Collaborative Enterprise', conveys the pith of his case. Invoking the historical fact that what is now called judicial review long preceded democracy and the company law concept of ultra vires, he sees the political and judicial branches as equally committed to the business of government. Neither branch is sovereign. Tensions may arise between them. Neither should seek to supplant the other. The values safeguarded by the judicial branch

---

[8] (8th edn 2000) 37.

[9] (4th edn 1999) ch 1, passim. Professor Paul Craig has contributed many other significant writings to the general field. In the present lecture I can make no attempt at comprehensiveness in citing relevant discourse. For a recent helpful survey of the field, conveying a more-or-less standard current judicial view in England, one may cite a lecture by Sir Roger Toulson, chairman of the Law Commission, 'Democratic Values and the Judicial Process', published in Issue 4 of Amicus Curiae, Journal of the Society for Advanced Legal Studies, July/Aug 2003, 3–14.

are constitutional; and constitutional review is his favoured term.[10] But there is a vast legislative area into which the courts do not intrude.

In another recent paper Philip Joseph has dug out a proposition that I offered in 1988[11] that the English and New Zealand legal systems derive from 'two complementary and legally unalterable principles: the operation of a democratic legislature and the operation of independent courts'. *Anisminic* may be seen as confirming as much. Questions of law are always ultimately for independent courts. If the courts were to submit to an Act replacing them by a hierarchy of tribunals holding office at government pleasure, they would be parties to a revolution. It is gratifying to note that Wade and Forsyth, based as their work is on the superb analytical power of Sir William Wade, seem implicitly to accept that proposition, even though speaking prominently of the sovereignty of Parliament and even though the co-editor is in other writings an ultra virist. For instance, we read early in the textbook:

The British constitution is founded on the rule of law, and administrative law is the area where this principle is to be seen in its most active operation... The affected person may always resort to the courts of law, and if the legal pedigree is not found to be perfectly in order the court will invalidate the act, which he can safely disregard.[12]

Again: 'Even under the British system of undiluted sovereignty, the last word on any question of law rests with the courts.'[13]

Wade and Forsyth also give prominence[14] to the suggested dismissal by Lord Irvine of Lairg QC of those of us who believe that there are legal limits upon the power of Parliament as indulging in 'extra judicial romanticism'.[15] But a close reading of the context in which Lord Irvine used that expression shows that it was not unqualified.[16] And if consideration be directed, for theory, to the textbook formulation just quoted and, for practice, to some of the recent decisions about to be discussed, it may be thought that realism is a better description than romanticism. Moreover, although the Human Rights Act 1998, which will be the constitutional monument of Lord Irvine QC, nominally preserves the 'sovereignty' of

[10] Among other leading proponents of this concept is Professor Jeffrey Jowell QC. See for instance 'Beyond the Rule of Law: Towards Constitutional Judicial Review' [2000] PL 671.
[11] 'Fundamentals' [1988] New Zealand Law Journal 158, 164, cited by Joseph in 'The Demise of Ultra Vires—A Reply to Christopher Forsyth and Linda Whittle' (2002) 8 Canterbury Law Review 463, 472.
[12] (8th edn 2000) 20.
[13] Ibid, 29.
[14] Ibid, 28, nn 38, 40.
[15] 'Judges and Decision-Makers: The Theory and Practice of Wednesbury Review' [1996] PL 59, 77. Lord Irvine acknowledged the assistance of Jason Coppel in the preparation of this lecture.
[16] For instance, as to any assault by Parliament on the basic tenets of democracy, 'Certainly, if such a tide in our affairs were ever to come, it would be for the judges of that time, and not of today, to decide how they should properly respond. The South African experience does show that the judges may have a role [citing *Harris v Ministry of the Interior* [1952] 2 SA 428]; and I am ready to suppose that the judges of tomorrow might gain some comfort in their endeavours from the extra-judicial writings of distinguished judges of today.'

Parliament, the experience of creating that legislation may conceivably have led to some change of mind.

The Depth of Common Law Rights

It has become settled law that the rights and freedoms guaranteed under the European Convention, to which further effect has been given domestically by the Human Rights Act, are not the only human rights that the English courts enforce. In *Daly*[17] Lord Bingham of Cornhill listed some common law rights, pertaining unromantically to prisoners, which he said 'may be curtailed only by clear and express words, and then only to the extent reasonably necessary to meet the ends which justify the curtailment'. The Senior Law Lord's list is the right of access to a court; the right of access to legal advice; and the right to communicate confidentially with a legal adviser under the seal of legal professional privilege.

In his Brian Dickson Memorial Lecture 2003, delivered in Ottawa only seven days ago,[18] Lord Steyn in effect added to the list. He said that the courts protect as constitutional, quite apart from the Human Rights Act, the right of participation in the democratic process, equality of treatment, freedom of expression, religious freedom, and the right of unimpeded access to the courts. Also the right to a fair trial. How deep do such common law rights go? In carefully measured terms and without suggesting that the various rights are absolute, Lord Steyn explains the significance of classifying a right as constitutional as follows:

It is a powerful indication that added value is attached to the protection of the right. It strengthens the normative force of such rights. It virtually rules out arguments that such rights can be impliedly repealed by subsequent legislation. Generally, only an express repeal will suffice. The constitutionality of a right is also important in regard to remedies. The duty of the court is to vindicate the breach of a constitutional right, depending on its nature, by an appropriate remedy.

Judges are inching towards ever stronger expressions when treating some common law rights as constitutional. A passage often cited is in the speech of Lord Hoffmann in *Simms*,[19] where a blanket ban on interviews by journalists of prisoners was held unlawful. Speaking of the sovereignty of Parliament, he said that in the absence of express language or necessary implication to the contrary, the courts presume that even the most general words were intended to be subject to the basic rights of the individual. 'Fundamental rights cannot be overridden by general or ambiguous words.' In speaking, as he did, of 'fundamental principles of human rights' Lord Hoffmann used language which comes naturally today

---

[17] *R (Daly) v Home Secretary* [2001] 2 AC 532, 537–538.
[18] The lecture is entitled 'Dynamic Interpretation Amidst an Orgy of Statutes'.
[19] *R v Home Secretary, ex p Simms* [2002] 2 AC 115, 131.

but would probably have seemed heretical to some leading English judges even as recently as the 1980s.

And in June this year in *Anufrijeva*[20] Lord Steyn has gone a step further, in reasoning with which Lord Hoffmann and Lord Scott of Foscote expressly agreed and which powerfully influenced Lord Millett. The issue was whether an asylum seeker's income-support benefit terminated when the Home Secretary's rejection of her claim to asylum was 'recorded', as the statutory regulation provided, or whether her entitlement continued until notice of that rejection was sent to her some months later. By a majority of four to one the House of Lords held for continuation, applying the constitutional principle of elementary fairness that a decision takes effect only upon communication. The strength attributed by the majority to the principle is perfectly brought out by the dissenting opinion to which Lord Bingham of Cornhill was driven. In the context of the regulations as a whole, he held that 'recorded' was not in any way ambiguous. He said that it is 'a cardinal principle of the rule of law, not inconsistent with the principle of legality, that subject to exceptions not material in this case effect should be given to a clear and unambiguous legislative provision'.

With respect, Lord Bingham's reasoning, just summarized only briefly, will surely be utterly convincing to lawyers undertaking what he calls 'a conventional exercise of construction'. But the common law has now reached the point where, to quote from Lord Steyn's speech in the same case, in the context of a determination of a fundamental right as to status, the principle of communication is not displaced unless Parliament has so legislated 'in specific and unmistakable terms'. The provision considered in *Anufrijeva* was of course subordinate legislation, but the issue was treated at least primarily as one of interpretation of the regulations. The meaning of the regulations was, it may be thought, specific and unmistakable, though the empowering legislation was more general, simply authorizing regulations to exclude asylum claimants from income support. A principle capable of transforming statutory regulations in this way seems so potent that the depth of common law constitutional rights is virtually measureless.

A technique sometimes resorted to by critics of judges who believe in fundamental common law rights is to label us[21] 'judicial supremacists'. Even Lord Irvine made some use of the label in the article already quoted.[22] It is a label as misleading as romanticism. As Lord Steyn says in his Ottawa lecture, '. . . statute law is the dominant source of law of our time. . . The truth is that the common law has an important but nevertheless residual role to play.' The number of decisions in which judges of the criticized school of thought have recognized that

---

[20]   *R (Anufrijeva) v Home Secretary* [2003] 3 WLR 252.

[21]   Other suspects include Lord Woolf and Lords Justices Laws and Sedley: Wade & Forsyth, op. cit. 28, n 38. And only this week a copy has reached me of an article by the Chief Justice of New Zealand, Dame Sian Elias, which confirms that she is a notable recruit: 'Sovereignty in the 21st century: another spin on the merry-go-round' 14 Public Law Review (Sept 2003) 148. A judicial prelude is her judgment (with Tipping J) in *R v Pora* [2001] 2 NZLR 37. For some of Laws LJ's views judicially expressed, see *Thoburn v Sunderland City Council* [2003] QB 151.

[22]   Above n 14.

actual legislative or administrative intent should prevail is untold and huge.[23] All that we assert, as I see it, is that in a liberal democracy there must be a bottom line of minority rights, certainly sometimes difficult to define, which cannot be crossed without a legal revolution. The legislative and judicial functions are complementary; the supremacism of either has no place.

Vindicating Fundamental Common Law Rights

Accepting that there are such rights, how are they to be safeguarded by the courts? Sometimes traditional remedies, such as damages for classified torts, may be appropriate. But this may not always apply. Tort law is the product of ages before the Universal Declaration of Human Rights 1948. Its origins in the need to redress physical violations of person or property, or fraud, may make it inadequate for a more complex and fairer society. Statutory restrictions with older ancestry on actions against the state, for instance, may not have been enacted with the importance of human rights in mind.[24]

In the United Kingdom the Human Rights Act 1998, section 8, recognizes this by including damages in the remedies available against public authorities for acts incompatible with Convention rights; the principles applied by the European Court of Human Rights are to be taken into account. So too in New Zealand it was judicially recognized that public law compensation may be awarded against the state for breach of a right declared in the New Zealand Bill of Rights Act 1990.[25] That Act contains no remedies clause, but to treat the solemn enactment of Parliament as window-dressing was seen as unattractively cynical. As my colleague Sir Michael Hardie Boys J (later Governor-General) said in his judgment in the Court of Appeal:

The New Zealand Bill of Rights Act, unless it is to be no more than an empty statement, is a commitment by the Crown that those who in the three branches of the government

[23] In personal self-defence there may be given, merely as two examples of many decisions generous to administrators to which I have been party, *R v Chief Constable of Sussex, ex p International Trader's Ferry Ltd* [1999] 2 AC 418 and *New Zealand Fishing Industry Association Inc v Minister of Agriculture and Fisheries* [1988] 1 NZLR 544.

[24] These considerations seem to be given insufficient weight by those who approach the common law along traditional paths, such as the authors of the excellent textbook *The Law of Torts in New Zealand* by Professor Stephen Todd and others, (3rd edn 2001) 20–21, 978–987. As Lord Diplock said in *Maharaj v Attorney-General of Trinidad and Tobago (No 2)* [1979] AC 385, 399, constitutional redress against the state by way of compensation 'is not a liability in tort at all; it is a liability in the public law of the state...' If the authors of works on tort do not like it, their remedy is to leave it out of their books.

[25] *Simpson v Attorney-General [Baigent Case]* [1994] 3 NZLR 667. This case was decided on a strike-out application before trial and was subsequently settled before trial. The plaintiffs alleged that police officers had insisted on searching a home, rifling through drawers etc, in execution of a search warrant for drugs, although they had been advised that the warrant specified a wrong address. An officer was alleged to have said: 'We often get it wrong, but while we are here we will have a look round anyway.' Statute may have excluded tort liability, but the later Bill of Rights Act gave everyone the right to be secure against unreasonable search.

exercise its functions, powers and duties will observe the rights that the Bill affirms. It is I consider implicit in that commitment, indeed essential to its worth, that the Courts are not only to observe the Bill in the discharge of their own duties but are able to grant appropriate and effective remedies where rights have been infringed. I see no reason to think that this should depend on the terms of a written constitution. Enjoyment of the basic human rights is the entitlement of every citizen, and their protection the obligation of every civilised state. They are inherent in and essential to the structure of society. They do not depend on the legal or constitutional form in which they are declared. The reasoning that has led the Privy Council and the Courts and the Courts of Ireland and India to the conclusions reached in the cases to which I have referred (and they are but a sample) is in my opinion equally valid to the New Zealand Bill of Rights Act if it is to have life and meaning.

By parity of reasoning the same approach should be applicable to breaches of human rights recognized to be fundamental by common law. For this view there is now something close to the authority of the House of Lords, in the Northern Ireland case of *Cullen*.[26] The appellant had been arrested and taken into custody on a charge connected with terrorism. He was entitled to consult a solicitor privately, but statutory provisions empowered a senior police officer to defer consultation for reasons to be given to the prisoner. In this case there were valid reasons but they were not given to him. Pleading guilty to the offence, he was sentenced to community service. Subsequently he claimed damages, but there was no evidence that he had suffered harm of any kind, not even distress or injured feelings. A majority of the House of Lords—Lords Hutton, Millett, and Rodger of Earlsferry—held against the claim. They were influenced in part by the sparing awards of damages made by the Strasbourg court. In a (possibly unique) joint speech or opinion, Lord Bingham and Lord Steyn dissented. They would have awarded £500 for breach of a right actionable per se.

The case is important on at least two levels. First, the minority Law Lords expressly said that at common law, apart from the statute, there was a general right in an accused person to communicate and consult privately with his solicitor outside the interview room. And of the majority Lord Millett described the right as quasi-constitutional. On the other hand Lord Hutton rejected a constitutional rights approach, on the ground that the case related to a provision in an ordinary statute, while Lord Rodger was primarily influenced by the fact that detainees have no right to consult a solicitor in Scotland. On balance, though, the case supports, in English common law, at least something of a constitutional right. It is consistent with *Simms* and *Daly*; a potent and expanding corpus is emerging.

Secondly and just as importantly, Lord Hutton, with whom Lords Millett and Rodger concurred, accepted that the harm for which compensation may be granted extends beyond injury to person or property and economic loss. It includes damages for substantial inconvenience, distress, or other disadvantage.[27]

---

[26] *Cullen v Chief Constable of the Royal Ulster Constabulary* [2003] 1 WLR 1763.
[27] See [2003] 1 WLR at 1779–1780.

This represents, in my view, an improvement on previous English case law.[28] In *Baigent's* case[29] the New Zealand Court of Appeal thought that, in addition to physical damage, intangible harm such as distress and injured feelings could be compensated for; the gravity of the breach and the need to emphasize the importance of the affirmed rights and to deter breaches were also proper considerations; but extravagant awards were to be avoided. We did not need to focus on such an unusual situation as apparently rose in *Cullen* of no kind of suffering whatever beyond the bare infringement of a right. Whether in such a case a nominal or a near-nominal award should be made to emphasize the importance of the right, or whether a declaration of illegality would suffice, is not an issue that should excite strong controversy. Both the majority and the minority in *Cullen* have advanced the law of human rights.

Duties of Care in the Public Field

Another field of advance, with some affinity to the constitutional one, is that of the negligence liability of public authorities. Welcome decisions of the House of Lords have included *Barrett v Enfield London Borough Council*[30] (common law duty to protect and promote welfare of children in care; undesirability of strike-out determinations before facts investigated at trial) and *Phelps v Hillingdon London Borough Council*[31] (failure to provide appropriate educational services to handicapped pupils). *Phelps* is a mine of dicta, among which particular interest attaches to the distinction drawn between the direct and vicarious liabilities of a public authority. Matters of policy and resource allocation, wherein the courts are inevitably slower to interfere, belong more to the direct liability issue. Operational

---

[28] See *Johnson v Gore Wood & Co* [2002] 2 AC 1 and *P v Liverpool Daily Post and Echo Newspapers plc* [1991] 2 AC 370, 420 per Lord Bridge of Harwich. In the latter case damages for breach of statutory duty were said to be only for personal injury, injury to property, or economic loss. In *Cullen* Lord Hutton has expressly widened this, at least in relation to the kind of duty there considered. Indeed what he has said appears to have an even wider application, to actionable breaches of statutory duties generally.

[29] Above n 23. See [1944] 3 NZLR at 678, 692, and 703.

[30] [2001] 2 AC 550. On the occasion of this lecture it is appropriate to mention the value placed by Lord Slynn of Hadley at 570 on the work of Andenas and Fairgrieve in support of the proposition that while the courts should restrain within reasonable bounds claims against public authorities exercising statutory powers in a social welfare context, it is equally important to set reasonable bounds to their immunity. This might seem a platitude, but is a corrective to the familiar type of observations that emphasize a need for judicial restraint as paramount over everything else. Consider *Rowling v Takaro Properties Ltd* [1988] AC 473, 501–503, on the question of duties of care falling on Ministers of the Crown. Dr Andenas has indeed suggested that English law is now catching up with the New Zealand approach overruled in that case. It would not be fitting for me to comment on that suggestion. I merely note that the Privy Council acted on a view as to the Minister's state of mind apparently contrary to the trial judge's finding of fact and to the understanding of counsel on both sides: see [1988] AC 473, at 483 B–C and 489 B and compare 510 A–C and 511 B–E. The case seems to belong to a bygone era and must be of limited help as a precedent.

[31] [2001] 2 AC 619, a unanimous decision of seven Law Lords.

negligence by employees is different. Here one is tempted to ask the noble and learned Lord in the chair a question about *Stovin v Wise*[32] (omission to remove earth bank making road junction dangerous). By a majority of three to two the House, stressing public funds and budgetary considerations, decided against a duty of care. There can be no harm this evening in saying that the dissenting opinion of Lord Nicholls of Birkenhead seems preferable. What I continue to find puzzling is that the case was not seen as turning on vicarious liability. The Council had decided to do the necessary remedial work and the money, less than £1,000, was available. But the Council's staff let the project go to sleep. Why was this not a straightforward instance of the responsibility of an employer for an employee's negligence in the course of employment?

Progressive as are *Barrett* and *Phelps*, it has to be added that some of the speeches are sprinkled with rather dubious expressions. Thus, while it is not asserted in the speeches that judicial review and negligence liability are always governed by the same principles, there are some suggestions that, even in negligence cases concerning direct liability, it may be material to ask the question, partly tautologous and partly misleading, whether the impugned action was 'so unreasonable that no reasonable authority' would have decided on it. The plain and robust 'reasonable' was enough for Atkin J[33] 88 years ago. It should be enough for us today, always remembering that the intensity of curial scrutiny varies with the subject matter.[34]

By the same token, to speak of some areas of administrative discretion as 'nonjusticiable' is unhappy. For example, if a high level governmental decision is found to have been genuinely based on security grounds, the courts are most unlikely to interfere. But this is because, performing their constitutional function, they adjudge that such were in truth the grounds and that the assessment was fairly within the function of political government. As Lord Steyn observes in his Ottawa lecture,[35] 'in point of principle there are not any no-go areas'. In the light shed on governmental workings by the Hutton Inquiry, this is healthy doctrine.

Hansard

I have already cited Lord Steyn on a range of matters, including the modern prevalence of statute law. Usually I am an admiring supporter of his views. But, as to statutes, I must now come to a rare disagreement.

When trying to ascertain the intention of Parliament, it is occasionally helpful to consider what has been said in Parliament. One might have expected this to

---

[32] [1996] AC 923.

[33] *Theatre De Luxe (Halifax) Ltd v Gledhill* [1915] 2 KB 49, 59–60.

[34] See *Daly*, above n 16.

[35] Citing Jowell, 'Judicial Deference and Human Rights: a Question of Competence' in *Essays in Law and Administration in Europe*, ed by Craig and Rawlings (2003).

be an understatement. On the contrary it is heresy—according to an approach which has some impressive support. English courts came later than many other English-speaking courts in relaxing the rule against reference to Hansard; but eventually in *Pepper v Hart*[36] six out of seven Law Lords accepted that clear ministerial statements in Parliament could be used as an aid to the construction of ambiguous legislation. That was the unambiguous essence of the decision. The speeches were addressed essentially to reference to Hansard to help resolve an ambiguity (or to overcome an absurdity). The very question was the meaning of the statutory words 'the cost of a benefit'. But for some lawyers of the old school this meat is too strong. Some traditionalists react as if to be seen openly to read Hansard is akin to being caught with pornography. And this reluctance has been not without effect on judges who are usually much more realistic. The whole subject was much debated in the *Spath Holme* case.[37] The issue was whether a statutory power to restrict rent increases could be exercised only for counter-inflationary purposes (as had been the case under the legislation replaced) or whether alleviating hardship to a class of tenants was a permitted purpose. The Hansard point produced a spectacular range of answers. The Court of Appeal held that the words of the Act were sufficiently ambiguous to let Hansard in, and that the ministerial statements were clear and unambiguous in support of the more limited construction. Of the Lords, some thought that the Act was unambiguous to the opposite effect, so Hansard could have no influence; others that there was enough doubt to permit consideration of the statements but that they were unambiguously against the Court of Appeal's understanding of them. One thing nonetheless is tolerably certain. All eight judges had read Hansard before reaching their various positions.

Also, most lawyers would probably agree with Lord Nicholls that there can be no difference between looking at parliamentary proceedings to help with the interpretation of a particular word or phrase and doing so when deciding, as a matter of interpretation, what was the purpose for which the power was conferred.[38]

While *Spath Holme* re-emphasized that resort to Hansard is rare or exceptional, all the speeches left intact the authority of *Pepper v Hart* and the conditions there laid down. But *Wilson's*[39] case in the Lords this year raised an issue different from the clarification of an ambiguity or the avoidance of an absurdity. The new issue was whether a domestic statute was compatible with European Convention rights. The Court of Appeal, in searching for the justification for the statute, described the parliamentary debates as tending to confuse rather than

---

[36] [1993] AC 593. For developments in other jurisdictions, see the argument reported at 601–603.

[37] *R v Secretary of State for the Environment, ex p Spath Holme Ltd* [2001] 2 AC 349.

[38] See [2002] 2 AC at 398. Contra, however, Lord Hope of Craighead at 407–408 and Lord Hutton at 473–414.

[39] *Wilson v First County Trust Ltd (No 2)* [2003] 3 WLR 568.

illuminate. Possibly nervous about such comments, the senior officers of the two Houses intervened in the argument. On their behalf Jonathan Sumption QC argued that there are no circumstances in which it is appropriate for a court to refer to the record of parliamentary debates in order to decide whether an enactment is compatible with the Convention.

Not surprisingly that extreme submission did not prevail, but in varying ways the speeches of the Law Lords limit the use of Hansard in compatibility issues. Lord Nicholls put it[40] that on such issues clear and unambiguous ministerial statements in Parliament are no more than part of the background: they cannot control the meaning of an Act; there are constitutional difficulties in treating the intentions of the government as reflecting the will of Parliament. He mentioned an influential article by Lord Steyn[41] re-examining *Pepper v Hart*. I can only be highly selective in citing from this leading speech. Taken as a whole the relevant passages in it are far from destructive of *Pepper v Hart*, nor do they by any means rule out some reference to Hansard even on Convention issues.

Now in his Ottawa lecture Lord Steyn has returned to the field. He accepts some uses of Hansard as sensible; for instance, to identify the mischief which Parliament tried to correct or to found an estoppel. But:

What I regard as constitutionally wrong in the English system is to treat the intentions of the government as revealed in debates as the will of Parliament. That is how the dicta in *Pepper v Hart* had until recently been interpreted. Slowly these distinctions and clarification of *Pepper v Hart* are gaining ground in England.

For the latter proposition Lord Steyn cites Lord Nicholls in *Wilson*.

With due deference I have to suggest that *Pepper v Hart* needs no clarification. The speeches seem clear enough to the ordinary reader. Whether one likes them is another matter. On the whole I do. It is not apparent that anyone has confused the intentions of the government as revealed in debates with the will of Parliament. What is thought is that, if Parliament's will is obscurely expressed, one aid to interpreting it is to look at what Parliament was told by the government promoting the Bill. This will not often be helpful. Often the questions on which the courts have to focus are more precise than the broad ones addressed by government spokesmen.

There is an analogy with the references made by three of the Law Lords in *Cullen* to the Report of the Royal Commission on Criminal Procedure.[42] Regret was expressed that it had not been drawn to attention by counsel.

Never can parliamentary speeches override the plain meaning of an enactment. That is elementary. But not all enactments do have plain meanings, a truism which accounts for a large proportion of large incomes at the bar. Concern at the costs of research lies behind hostility to *Pepper v Hart* in some quarters. But

[40] Ibid, 584–588.
[41] (2001) 21 OJLS 59.
[42] See [2003] 1 WLR at 1768–1769; 1771; 1779–80.

the level of some professional fees should not be allowed to dictate the substantive law of England. The realistic road ahead is not to shut eyes to Hansard when truly solid help is to be found there.

The Reach of the Judicial Arm

To end on an upbeat, in a foreword to the second edition (2001) of Philip Joseph's book *Constitutional and Administrative Law in New Zealand*, I was able to write, regarding judicial review, of:

> ...a refreshing and healthy move away by New Zealand courts from the more formalistic constraints once orthodox. The judges are accepting that they have a responsibility to do practical justice in administrative law as in other fields. Ample room for respect for administrative discretion remains.

A comparable move appears to be occurring in England under the leadership of some of the judges whom I have named this evening. *Anisminic* provided a breakthrough impulse. Latterly the European doctrine of proportionality has contributed an exemplary influence not confined to a European context. In the metaphor of Nicholas Green QC,[43] judges are rolling their sleeves further up the judicial arm.

An excellent illustration is a judgment of the Privy Council delivered at the end of June last in a New Zealand appeal, *Waikato Regional Airport Ltd v Attorney General*.[44] As customary with New Zealand appeals, the hearing was by a Board of five. As entirely uncustomary, although there was no dissent the judgment is shown as delivered by two of their Lordships, Lord Nicholls of Birkenhead and Lord Walker of Gestingthorpe. Thus the presiding Law Lord specifically lent his cachet. An educated guess might be that the labour of quite a complex composition was not all borne by him.

The Privy Council reversed a unanimous judgment of a Court of Appeal of five[45] and restored the first instance judgment of Wild J.[46] The subject was charges for government-provided biosecurity services (pest detection and the like) at international airports. The Act authorized the Director-General of Agriculture to recover costs 'by such methods as he believes on reasonable grounds to be the most suitable and equitable in the circumstances...' Some monies, however, were appropriated towards the cost by Parliament. When certain provincial airports began taking international flights, the Director-General continued to apply the appropriated monies entirely to the longer-established metropolitan airports, leaving the newcomers without any share and alone bearing charges. The Court

---

[43] Evelyn Ellis (ed), *The Principle of Proportionality in the Laws of Europe* (1999) 164.
[44] Privy Council Appeal No 77 of 2002.
[45] [2002] 3 NZLR 433.
[46] [2001] 2 NZLR 670.

of Appeal held that this was within the Act. The Privy Council, after an in-depth sifting of the facts, held that there had been a failure to impose an equitable system. The Director-General's reasoning simply did not prove any justification for the stark disparity: '... this differential charging scheme may have been convenient and economical, but it was not equitable.' The decision was 'flawed by being based on erroneous or irrelevant considerations'. Note 'erroneous'.

That judgment did not turn on any speciality of New Zealand administrative law. Refreshingly the judgment cites no authorities on the scope of judicial review.[47] In that respect the law is taken to be settled beyond the need for citation. Here is a case which may be said to capture to the full its current probing but judicious character. By and large administrative law is on the right road, as is shown by the fact that until now, the very end, this lecture has required not a single utterance of the word 'Wednesbury'.

---

[47] There are a few citations on other issues, including money extracted *colore officii*.

2

Recent Reforms in Australia to the Law of Negligence with Particular Reference to the Liability of Public Authorities

David Ipp

In 2001 there was an insurance crisis in Australia. The cause of the crisis was and remains a matter of dispute. Some said that it had to do with the poor state, at the time, of the global insurance market, the fact that a large Australian insurance company had become bankrupt, and incompetence and greed on the part of insurers themselves. Others argued that a major contributing factor was the state of the law of negligence. They said that plaintiffs succeeded far too easily and the damages awarded were far too high.

Whatever the causes, the fact is that several insurers had left the country. Some of those who remained refused to insure certain kinds of risks and most were only prepared to provide cover at very high premiums. This adversely affected many aspects of community life.

Some country hospitals, which could not obtain insurance at affordable rates, closed down completely. Other hospitals, including city hospitals, experienced difficulties in providing important facilities. The premium paid by neurosurgeons, obstetricians, and gynaecologists for liability cover usually exceeded AUD100,000 a year (a sum regarded as oppressively high, particularly for practitioners commencing these specialities). Young and some older obstetricians and gynaecologists, and neurosurgeons as well, gave up their practices and turned to other, less risky areas, of medicine. Small local authorities, particularly in rural areas, were unable to obtain public liability insurance and accordingly closed roads for the maintenance of which they were responsible. This required the making of long and burdensome detours. Many volunteers stopped providing their services to the elderly and others. Some schools and kindergartens had to close and others were not able to offer the facilities they would wish. All manner of community gatherings and events could no longer take place. The basic fabric of society was being harmed. This was not something that government could ignore.

There was no conclusive evidence that the state of the law of negligence bore any responsibility for this situation. But insurance companies took the position that they were not prepared to provide the necessary insurance, or were only prepared to provide it at unaffordable rates, because of the unpredictability of the law, the ease with which plaintiffs succeeded and the generosity of courts in awarding damages. They referred to a survey that asserted that Sydney was the second most litigious city in the world, second only to Los Angeles.

The Commonwealth and state governments (which are notoriously unco-operative) appointed a panel of four to recommend legislative reforms of the common law 'with the objective of limiting liability and quantum of damages arising from personal injury and death'. The Panel was told, in its Terms of Reference, that '[t]he award of damages has become unaffordable and unsustainable as the principal source of compensation for those injured through the fault of another'. The Panel's recommendations, when they were made, were severely criticized by plaintiffs' lawyers and many academics as being too severe on plaintiffs, but its brief, its mandate, was to attempt to achieve the object stated in the Terms of Reference.

The composition of the Panel reflected government's main concerns. It consisted of a judge as chairman (myself), a leading tort academic (Prof Peter Cane), the president of the college of procedural medicine, and the mayor of a large country town. Plainly, the surgeon was there to watch out for the interests of medical practitioners, and the mayor was there to protect the interests of public authorities.

The Panel was given two months within which to report. It was told that it was addressing what was in effect a national emergency. It concluded that there was a widely held view in the Australian community that there were problems with the law of negligence stemming from a perception that in recent times it had become too easy for plaintiffs to establish liability, and that damages awards were frequently too high. For example, in those few jurisdictions where the parties still could have jury trials for negligence claims, defendants preferred juries and plaintiffs sought judges. Not only were many judges notorious for awarding vast sums of damages, there was a perception that judges would stretch the law, and even the facts, in favour of plaintiffs. The pendulum had swung markedly in favour of plaintiffs since the 1970s. Before then, it was difficult for plaintiffs to succeed against establishment defendants. Now, things had gone to the opposite extreme.

The Panel heard evidence for one month and drafted for one month. It reported in time. This was a major complaint by those who objected to the reforms that followed. They said that reforms of this kind needed years of investigation, not two months. Australian legislatures, however, reacted with like celerity. Within months of the Panel reporting, a plethora of reforming legislation issued from every legislature throughout the country. This concerted reaction by the various Australian governments was virtually unprecedented.

The first and strongest recommendation of the Panel was that there should be uniform legislation throughout the country. This was not accepted. So there is now a crazy patchwork of legislation, not only between states but within states. Unfairness and complexity abound because of these differences. Damages caps differ depending on the state in which one is injured, and differ within each state depending on the particular legislation that governs the claim. One gets less for a motor vehicle accident than some other negligence claim, and, in one jurisdiction, least of all if one sues one's employer.

This situation has led to thickets of complexity as well as arbitrary and inexplicable inconsistencies in the law of negligence. Assume, for example, that the combined negligent acts of a motor car driver, a construction company, and a road authority cause a motor vehicle to drive over a bridge into a river, thereby injuring a passenger in the vehicle, a worker employed by the construction company, and a swimmer in the river below. In these circumstances, the liability of the driver, the construction company, and the road authority will be governed by different tests for negligence. Further, if the passenger in the car, the worker, and the swimmer are all successful in their claims, the damages of each will be governed by different caps and thresholds, so each may be awarded a significantly different sum than the other two, even if their injuries are more or less the same.

The complexity of the situation has led to the publication of at least one large loose-leaf textbook that covers only the different civil liability statutes in each state and territory. It is constantly being updated. Other expansive works deal with claims by workers and yet others with road accident claims. Different causes of action in negligence attract a multitude of different rules.

In this great intricate web of differing legislation, Lord Atkin's notion of the law of negligence being based on a moral imperative has disappeared. Those who think that the law of negligence should be based on considerations of risk distribution and economic rationalism will look in vain for consistent principle amongst the mass of differing threads. The web is akin to that of the virulent Australian redback spider; large, untidy, messy, asymmetrical with indeterminate borders and spreading single strands, and with deadly dangers lurking underneath.

This mishmash seems irreparable now. Nevertheless, many of the Panel's recommendations were implemented in a reasonably uniform fashion, and what has been described as 'quasi-consistency' in regard to major issues of principle has occurred in the various jurisdictions. The states, generally, have followed the recommendation that the reforms should apply to all claims that are in substance based on negligence, irrespective of whether they are pleaded in breach of statutory duty, contract, some other tort, or even equity.

Far-reaching changes were made. The more important included making the test of foreseeability more stringent, limiting liability for dangerous recreational activities and giving increased importance to obvious risks and risk warnings. A modified *Bolam* test was introduced that now applies to all professions, not only doctors. The laws relating to limitation of actions relating to negligent personal injury claims were transformed. The critical date for limitation purposes is now the date when plaintiffs first learn that they have been harmed and that some other person was responsible. Subject to certain safeguards, time runs against children and mentally incapacitated persons. In this way gynaecologists and obstetricians are given much greater protection.

Significant changes were made to the assessment of damages in personal injury cases. Throughout the country, there are now various legislative provisions relating to thresholds and caps. Many of these thresholds and caps are arbitrary, but there is no way, based on recognized legal principle, that could inform the selection of thresholds and caps. Limits have been imposed on claims for future economic loss, gratuitous care, and claims for pure mental harm. No claim for any kind of mental harm lies unless the harm is a recognized mental illness. Exemplary, punitive, and aggravated damages have been abolished.

One of the main purposes of the caps and thresholds was to weed out small claims. In 2002, small claims and their administrative and legal costs formed almost half of amounts paid by defendants and this, legislatures thought, was out of proportion to the overall benefit to the community. The view was taken that it was more important to provide compensation for those who were more seriously injured and to keep premiums at a reasonable level. The reforming legislation contains several provisions designed to discourage small claims. These provisions appear to have served their purpose. Many injured persons, for whom it is now not economically worthwhile to sue, strenuously object to these laws but, at this stage, the impetus to remove them is not strong.

A reform that has been particularly effective is that concerning costs. Following the Panel's recommendation, most states now have legislation providing that no legal costs are recoverable where the award of damages is less than a stipulated sum. Costs are capped when the award does not exceed another stipulated sum.

The reforms have clearly succeeded in reducing drastically the number of claims brought, and insurance premiums have fallen sharply. There has been a renewed emphasis on individuals taking responsibility for their own actions. This has made establishing liability more difficult. For example, the busiest court in the country, the New South Wales District Court, has seen its civil caseload drop from over 23,000 in 2001 to just under 8,000 by the end of 2005, and it has continued to drop significantly each year since then. Average compulsory third party premiums have been reduced by more than 25 per cent and are decreasing. Workers compensation premiums have been reduced by 20 per cent. Permanent impairment benefits for injured workers have *increased* by 10 per cent. In 2006, in New South Wales, workers compensation (which is financed by the State) produced a surplus of AUD85 million compared with a deficit of AUD3.2 billion in 2002. The average public liability premium has decreased by about 30 per cent. The annual premium for new obstetricians and neurosurgeons has fallen to about

AUD60,000. The number of public liability policies issued has increased markedly. Public liability insurance has suddenly become very profitable. Many insurers have returned to Australia and several new ones have arrived. To the concern of the public, they are now making a lot of money.

While insurance cover is more accessible and affordable, this has come at plaintiffs' expense. From a plaintiff's perspective the reforms have reduced the circumstances in which they can bring claims and the causes of action upon which such claims may be based. Some people with serious injuries are no longer able to receive any, or any adequate, compensation from negligence claims. Damages, generally, have been substantially reduced. Negligence practitioners have seen their practices severely affected.

The situation illustrates Isaiah Berlin's aphorism that 'total liberty for wolves is death to the lambs'. He was pointing out that most of the cardinal values to which human beings aspire are not compatible with each other. So, justice may clash with mercy and compassion; unrestrained liberty may have to make way for forms of social welfare; the pursuit of truth does not justify torture. The fact is that more money for the plaintiff lambs means less for the rest of society. Less for plaintiffs means too much to insurance wolves. The key is to find the correct balance.

In determining the correct balance, due regard must be had to the purpose of the tort of negligence. This remains the subject of controversy. It is difficult to argue that the tort has any significant corrective or penal function. A negligent individual hardly ever pays damages (the source of payment ordinarily being an insurer) or even the insurance premiums (which are ordinarily paid by employer corporations of various kinds). Furthermore, only a very small percentage of injured persons receive tort damages. Most receive assistance solely through social welfare. Nevertheless, almost all, especially those who are concerned with their professional or business reputations, have a great dislike of being found to be negligent, or even involved as a party to a negligence cause of action. In the course of the tort reform process, I became convinced, for example, that the fear of being sued and found to have been negligent was causing those involved in medical practice, particularly hospital managers, to focus very carefully on their procedures and standards. This fear is an important deterrent against negligent conduct in all spheres of life. Additionally, and significantly, the existence of the tort, and the open court adversarial process, satisfies a deep need of society, namely, the public exposure of negligent conduct, irrespective of the political power or economic or social standing of the defendant. The common law of negligence applies equally to all, irrespective of the identity, race, religion, politics, and occupation of the parties. In this way, it is an essential aspect of democratic society and the rule of law.

A major area of criticism of the reforms concerns the additional protection given to public authorities. There are many instances in Australia where public authorities have been held liable where their negligence in exercising their regulatory powers has led to persons being injured.[1] Generally speaking, a public authority under no statutory obligation to exercise a power comes under no common law duty of care to do so. Nevertheless, it 'may by its conduct place itself in such a position that it attracts a duty of care which calls for exercise of the power'.[2] It may do this, for example, by placing itself in such a position that others rely on it to take care for their safety. Additionally, the powers vested by statute in a public authority may give to it such a 'significant and special measure of control' over the safety of the person or property of the plaintiff as to oblige it to exercise its powers to avert danger or to bring the danger to the knowledge of the plaintiff.[3]

The Terms of Reference required the Panel to make recommendations limiting the liability of public authorities. At all levels of government there was concern as to the frequency and nature of claims in negligence against public authorities. The Panel received evidence that negligence claims made up a major proportion of the budgets of public authorities, and substantially affected their capacity to provide services to the public. Two types of case caused particular problems.

The first involved claims based on a failure to take care to make a place, over which the authority had control, reasonably safe for users. The authority would have a limited budget available and would make decisions in good faith about the allocation of funds. There was a widespread view that decisions, made in good faith about the allocation of scarce resources, should not result in liability. The second type of case involved decisions made by public authorities, based on political, social, or environmental policies. The Panel responded by recommending that a policy decision by a public authority should not be subject to challenge, unless it was so unreasonable that no reasonable public authority could have made it. This, of course, is the *Wednesbury* test.[4] This mixing of public or administrative law with private law (as occurred in *Stovin v Wise*)[5] caused an outcry from the purists, and also plaintiffs' lawyers.

But the governments went much further than the Panel recommended. The New South Wales Civil Liability Act 2002, for example, applies the *Wednesbury* test to *all* actions where a plaintiff alleges that a public authority has breached a statutory duty in exercising, or failing to exercise, one of its functions. In other words, the Act applies the *Wednesbury* test to *all* actions for breach of a statutory duty, not merely decisions based substantially on financial, political, or social

---

[1] See, e.g., *Pyrenees Shire Council v Day* (1998) 192 CLR 330; *Crimmins v Stevedoring Industry Finance Committee* (1999) 200 CLR 1; *Brodie v Singleton Shire Council; Ghantous v Hawkesbury City Council* (2001) 206 CLR 512; *Graham Barclay Oysters Pty Ltd v Ryan* (2002) 211 CLR 540.

[2] *Sutherland Shire Council v Heyman* (1985) 157 CLR 424 per Mason J at 460.

[3] *Crimmins v Stevedoring Industry Financing Committee* per Gummow J at 61, [166]; see also *Graham Barclay Oysters Pty Ltd v Ryan* per Gummow and Hayne JJ at 598, [151].

[4] *Associated Provincial Picture Houses Limited v Wednesbury Corporation* [1948] 1 KB 223.

[5] [1996] AC 923.

factors, as the Panel recommended. Thus, the Act limits significantly the potential liability of the Crown. Government is not treated by the law in the same way as an ordinary citizen.

Curiously, the Act's breadth of application is its Achilles heel. There is of course a distinction between a cause of action based on a common law duty of care and one based on breach of a statutory duty. It is well recognized that circumstances may impose a common law duty of care on a public authority requiring the exercise of statutory powers. In such a case, the basic claim is that the public authority was negligent because it failed to exercise statutory powers and the action, itself, is a common law action for breach of duty of care; not an action for breach of a statutory duty. Thus, in cases of this kind, the statutory protection against causes of action based on breaches of statutory duty does not apply. Whether this is what was intended by the statute is a matter of conjecture.

The Civil Liability Act also creates a resources defence. It provides that the authority's general allocation of the financial and other resources that are reasonably available to it for the purposes of exercising its functions is not open to challenge. That is, the general allocation of financial and other resources by an authority is not justiciable. The Act also provides that the functions the authority is required to exercise are to be determined by reference to the broad range of its activities and not merely by reference to the issues to which the proceedings relate.

Resources, of course, affect private entities as well as public bodies. Sometimes, private defendants make decisions about the allocation of scarce resources, or decisions about the allocation of risks as between different groups, just as public bodies do. General Motors, for example, has at times decided to build heavier cars to protect their occupants at the expense of pedestrians, and at other times has decided to design lighter cars to save petrol at the cost of extra risk for their occupants. The Civil Liability Act, however, gives only public authorities the benefit of the resources defence. This, of course, is the traditional approach. Nevertheless, it is curious that the notion that public authorities, but not private entities, should have some sort of resources defence has met with general acceptance and has never been queried. A policy decision of a public authority involving resources may involve politics and decisions by elected or at least public bodies, and not be justiciable on that ground. But a policy decision of a private entity involving resources may involve business management decisions that courts, also, have often considered not to be justiciable.

The resources defence has, so far, not proved to be very successful. It has seldom been upheld. There are two principal reasons for this. The first is that the courts have held that, where a defence involving availability of resources and conflicting priorities is raised, there is an evidentiary onus on the defendant to prove why these matters reasonably justify its conduct in not taking the particular measures for which the plaintiff contends. The second is that defendants, generally speaking, do not call witnesses who are in a position to support the reliance by the authority on an absence of resources. The authorities have tended to rely simply on the production of their financial accounts or the explanatory evidence by a relatively low level official and this has been held to be insufficient. The fact is that bosses are reluctant to come to court to justify their decisions.

Road authorities have long enjoyed a particular immunity in Australian law. Until 2001, road authorities were governed by the common law highway immunity rule. Simply put, by the highway rule a road authority was liable only for misfeasance and not for non-feasance. The rule, however, gave rise to difficulties. The line between non-feasance and misfeasance was difficult to draw. The non-feasance rule applied only to the actual roadway itself and artificial structures that could fairly be considered part of the road. It was often difficult to determine whether a particular structure was part of the road or not. Awkward distinctions between policy and operational decisions arose.

In 2001, in a case called *Ghantous v Hawkesbury City Council*,[6] the High Court overturned the highway rule. *Ghantous* caused considerable concern to government and local authorities; they feared an avalanche of claims that previously could not have been brought. The impetus for tort reform allowed government to introduce legislation that to a degree reversed *Ghantous*. The Civil Liability Act, for example, provides that a road authority is not liable for harm arising from a failure to carry out roadwork unless the authority has actual knowledge of the risk that materializes. The question of what actual knowledge means is uncertain. Does it mean the knowledge of those making resources decisions? Or does it mean the knowledge of the authorities employees in general? It has been observed that, if it means only those who make decisions, road authorities would be discouraged from setting up effective risk reporting systems. The more incompetent the street sweeper in reporting holes in the roads, the better the position of the Council.

This kind of provision has been tried elsewhere without success. The city of New York adopted a law to the effect that the city could not be sued for a defect in a road or sidewalk unless it had had 15 days' notice of the specific defect. The New York trial lawyers established the BAPSPC. This acronym stands for the Big Apple Pothole and Sidewalk Protection Committee. The function of this committee was to employ persons to tour the streets and footpaths of New York continually and to note each and every blemish. The committee members would then, forthwith, give the city of New York precise details of each defect. Regular reports cataloguing the notices that had been given to the City were available for sale to trial lawyers. At any one time the total cost of curing the defects of which the City had been given notice was several billions of dollars. In 2004 the Mayor of New York complained that in the calendar year of 2002 alone, the City received 5,200 maps from BAPSPC spotters that identified some 700,000

---

[6] (2001) 206 CLR 512 (reported together with as *Brodie v Singleton Shire Council*, both having the same citation).

blemishes. Needless to say, the City has never successfully defended a case under the 15 days' notice law.[7]

Leaving aside the legislation that now protects public authorities, reference should be made to a recent decision of the High Court explaining *Ghantous*, namely, *RTA v Dederer*.[8] In *Ghantous*, a critical part of the decision was a statement by the majority that the duty of care is to be formulated 'in terms which require that a road be safe not in all circumstances but for users exercising reasonable care for their own safety'.[9]

The meaning of this statement led to a difference of opinion in the New South Wales Court of Appeal. Did *Ghantous* mean that the road authority owed no duty of care to road users who failed to exercise reasonable care for their own safety? Or was the reference to 'users exercising reasonable care for their own safety' intended only to emphasize that contributory negligence by the road user would lead to a high degree of apportionment of damage? This is a critical question as, if no duty of care is owed, apportionment of damage does not arise. Many judges found it difficult to believe that the majority in *Ghantous* intended to affect the law relating to contributory negligence and apportionment of damage.

Dederer, to some extent, clarifies these questions. The case concerned a 14-year-old boy who dived off a bridge, for which the RTA was responsible, into the waters of an inlet below and became paraplegic. The boy's argument was that the bridge, to the knowledge of the RTA, had been constructed in such a way (by the RTA's predecessor, for which it was responsible) that it constituted an allurement. Gummow J (with whom Callinan and Heydon JJ agreed) said:[10]

The RTA's duty of care was owed to all users of the bridge, whether or not they took ordinary care for their own safety; the RTA did not cease to owe Mr Dederer a duty of care merely because of his own voluntary and obviously dangerous conduct in diving from the bridge. However, the extent of the obligation owed by the RTA was that of a road authority exercising reasonable care to see that the road is safe for users exercising reasonable care for their own safety. The essential point is that the RTA did not owe a more stringent obligation towards careless road users as compared with careful ones. In each case, the same obligation of reasonable care was owed, and the extent of that obligation was to be measured against a duty whose scope took into account the exercise of reasonable care by road users themselves.

This statement affirms that a road authority owes a duty of care to all users of the road, whether they are negligent or not. That, of course, has long been the law.

---

[7] The Hon JJ Spigelman AC, 'Tort Law Reform: an Overview' (2006) 14 Tort Law Review 5 at 15.

[8] [2007] HCA 42 (I was part of the majority of the Court of Appeal overturned by that decision, see *Great Lakes Shire Council v Dederer & Anor; Roads & Traffic Authority of NSW v Dederer & Anor* (2007) 234 CCR 330).

[9] *Ghantous v Hawkesbury City Council* (2001) 206 CLR 512 per Gaudron, McHugh and Gummow JJ at [163].

[10] *RTA v Dederer* [2007] HCA 42 per Gummow J at [47].

What is noteworthy, however, is the statement that the scope of the duty must be 'measured against' the exercise of reasonable care by road users themselves. This concept of 'scope of duty' has been growing in importance in Australia. Its precise connotations have yet to be clearly defined. Whatever they may be, the statement that the scope of the authority's duty is to be measured by taking into account the exercise of reasonable care by road users themselves is of great importance.

This means, I think, that the scope of the duty is limited to exercising reasonable care for those who take reasonable care for their own safety when they use the road. This duty, so limited in scope, is owed to all road users, whether they are negligent or not. The plaintiff in *Dederer* was not a pedestrian. It follows that the expression of principle applies to all road users, not only pedestrians.

At first blush, the concept of limiting the scope of the duty to exercising reasonable care for those who take reasonable care for their own safety might be thought to be inconsistent with the concept that a road authority owes a duty of care to all users of the road, whether they be negligent or not.

Circumstances may arise, however, where a road authority might still be liable to road users who do not exercise reasonable care. Take the case where there is a concealed trap in a road, which might not be avoided by users taking reasonable care. In this scenario, the scope of the duty owed by the authority would be wide enough to require it to take reasonable steps to protect *all* users of the road (whether they do or do not take reasonable care for their own safety) from injury from the trap. The trap may cause injury to a road user who does not take reasonable care for their own safety. The user's absence of reasonable care, however, would not be causative as the accident would have happened even had reasonable care been exercised. In these circumstances, *Dederer* does not prevent the user from succeeding against the road authority.

There are, perhaps, other circumstances, according to the *Dederer* rule, under which road users, who do not take reasonable care for their own safety, could recover damages in negligence from road authorities. The argument involves some mental gymnastics.

Assume that it is foreseeable that drivers travelling at a speed limit of 50 mph— and taking reasonable care for themselves—*might* not be able to negotiate a bend in the road. That is to say, most drivers exercising reasonable care by driving at that speed *would* be able to pass safely through the bend, but the occasional reasonable driver *might not*. Assume that, for that reason, reasonable care required the authority to erect a warning sign, but it did not do so. Take the case where a driver negligently travelling at 80 mph goes off the road and is injured. Plainly, the driver's contributory negligence in driving so fast materially contributed to the accident. But reasonable care (even to drivers exercising reasonable care for their own safety and driving at 50 mph) required the authority to put up a warning sign. Assume that, had there been a warning sign, the injured driver who drove at 80 mph would have not driven so fast. In these circumstances, does the driver's contributory negligence in driving at 80 mph mean that the claim fails?

I do not think so. The road authority has breached its duty of care, the plaintiff is therefore entitled to recover, but apportionment of damage will apply.

Nevertheless, in many cases, plaintiffs who do not take ordinary care for their own safety will have no claim against a road authority. *Dederer*, itself, is an example. Other examples are easy to postulate. For instance, there are often cases where a road authority, working on a road, negligently leaves machinery or other equipment in the path of oncoming vehicles. Motorists who take reasonable care for their own safety should often be able to see and avoid these obstacles. In such circumstances, a motorist who does not keep a proper lookout and collides with an unattended earthmover will have no claim against the road authority. Thus, in many situations, the effect of *Dederer* is to remove the effect of the apportionment of damages legislation insofar as it applies to road authorities. In many cases, contributory negligence will be a complete defence. The notion that road authorities are to be afforded protection to this extent from the apportionment of damages legislation is a change to the law.

In *Edson v Roads and Traffic Authority*,[11] it was proved that, to the knowledge of the road authority, about 25,000 people each year (many of whom were children) crossed the four lanes of a freeway in an area that was not controlled by traffic signs or other means. The attractions of the area on one side of the freeway (shops, cinemas, pubs, etc) to those living on the other (which was purely a residential area) outweighed the dangers of vehicles travelling at speeds of 110 kph and more. The footsteps of the vast numbers who had passed over the fields bordering this area of the freeway had created paths (like transhumant pastoralists in ancient times) through the grass. The situation was extraordinarily dangerous and over the years it had caused several serious accidents, including fatalities. An inspector from the authority had seen mothers pushing children in prams dodging the speeding vehicles. The facts demonstrated that the road authority knew that pedestrians in the area were not exercising reasonable care for their own safety. The Court of Appeal believed that the *Ghantous* proposition (that a road authority was duty bound only to require the road to be safe, not in all circumstances, but only for pedestrians exercising reasonable care for their own safety) had to be underpinned by the facts. It held that, in *Edson*, the factual underpinning was absent. Thus, the authority had breached the duty of care it owed the pedestrians. According to the *Dederer* majority, however, this reasoning was erroneous 'as the expectation of reasonable care was not merely a "factual underpinning", but rather a legal aspect of the scope of the duty owed by the RTA'.[12] Thus, the limitation on the liability of road authorities, as held by *Dederer*, is an absolute rule of law; it does not depend on the facts of the case.

Whether the *Dederer* principle applies to public authorities other than road authorities is not clear, but there seems to be no apparent reason why it should not.

---

[11] (2006) 65 NSWLR 453 (a case in which I delivered the lead judgment).
[12] *RTA v Dederer* (2007) 234 CLR 330 per Gummow J at [48].

Once the scope of the duty of care owed by a road authority is limited to taking reasonable steps to make roads safe for users exercising reasonable care for their own safety, it follows that the more obvious the hazard (and, hence, the more careless the road authority is likely to have been) the less likely it is that the scope of the authority's duty of care will be engaged. There may be cases where the bigger and deeper the hole in the road, the more likely it is that the road authority will escape liability for it.

The density and complexity of the law of negligence that one now finds in Australia is not an unusual phenomenon in the common law world. The detailed work, *The Negligence Liability of Public Authorities* by Booth and Squires,[13] discusses this subject alone in nearly 900 closely reasoned pages. This is to be contrasted with the civil law. Mr Tony Weir has written:

The law of delict in the French code civil consists of a mere five short articles and one very long one. The German civil code (BGB) is less general and therefore more extensive, but even so it deals with the law of unlawful acts in 31 brief sections.[14]

According to Lord Atkin, in order that the debris of the old cases should not stand in the way of development consonant with both common sense and social needs, a framework had to be worked out within which the law of negligence could grow, unconstrained by logical or nice distinctions.[15] The last edition of Beven's *Negligence in the Law* was published in 1928. By then it had grown to 1,570 pages of text, much of which was devoted to the treatment of duty-situations based on the old-established categories of negligence. *Donoghue v Stevenson*[16] was initially thought to have destroyed these categories. The first edition of Beven's work was published in 1889. It was not reissued after 1928. Presumably it was thought that there was no longer any need for it. Many thought that a generalized conception of the law of negligence had finally been established.[17]

The law, however, has developed, and continues to develop, new categories, with different rules, involving different values. The old stultifying categories such as occupiers, trespassers and invitees, innkeepers and the like, may have been eradicated, but they are being replaced with new categories more subtly defined, often with amorphous boundaries which are equally problematic, create complexity, uncertainty, and litigation. The hope that fine distinctions would be removed, and the barren exercise of different formulae eradicated, has been disappointed, not least in the area of public authorities.

---

[13] 2006.

[14] *A Casebook on Tort*, (10th edn 2004).

[15] G Lewis, *Lord Atkin*, (1983) at 62.

[16] [1932] AC 580.

[17] DJ Ibbetson, 'The Tort of Negligence in the Common Law in the Nineteenth and Twentieth Centuries' in Eljo J H Schrage (ed), *Negligence: The Comparative Legal History of the Law of Torts* (2001).

3

The Lords, Tom Bingham, and Australia

Michael Kirby

A Continuing Conversation

Recently the High Court of Australia, far away in Canberra, was about to deliver its decision in the South Australian appeal in *Ayles v The Queen*.[1]

The appeal concerned the conduct of a District Court judge who, of her own motion, amended the criminal charges faced by the appellant without application from the Crown Prosecutor. The need for amendment had arisen when the effect of supervening legislation was belatedly discovered during the trial. The High Court of Australia was divided over the consequences of the judge's taking her own initiative in this way.

A majority of the judges affirmed the decision in the intermediate court, concluding that, although the prosecutor ought to have made a formal application for amendment in open court, the statutory provisions relied upon had been made clear enough during the trial, so that there was no miscarriage of justice. In dissenting reasons, Justice Gummow and I insisted on the importance of adherence to strict procedures in the formulation of criminal accusations. We demanded a clear delineation between the responsibilities of prosecutors to formulate charges and of judges to try them.

In the way of these things, as we were about to publish our reasons, the House of Lords, on the opposite side of the world, delivered its opinion in *R v Clarke*,[2] an appeal from the Criminal Division of the English Court of Appeal. That case too concerned the technicalities of pleadings in criminal cases. There the defect was that the bills of indictment found against the accused had not been signed by the authorized officer. Unanimously, the House of Lords insisted that such signature was an integral and essential element in the correct presentment of the document that initiated the criminal trial of the accused. It was the foundation for the entire procedure. The defect was fatal to its validity.

[1] [2008] HCA 6.
[2] (2008) 82 ALJR 502.

As so often happens, the participating Law Lords agreed in the analysis and conclusions of the senior Law Lord, Lord Bingham of Cornhill.[3] Moreover, in a succinct statement of principle, Lord Bingham encapsulated the issue of legal policy that was at stake and the reason why a seemingly technical rule should be observed in an age and legal culture that otherwise gives so much prominence to substance over form. He said:[4]

Technicality is always distasteful when [such a rule] appears to contradict the merits of a case. But the duty of a court is to apply the law, which is sometimes technical, and it may be thought that if the state exercises its coercive power to put a citizen on trial for a serious crime a certain degree of formality is not out of place.

Naturally, Justice Gummow and I pounced upon this affirmation of the approach that we thought proper to the Australian case in respect of which it bore certain similarities.[5] The reminder by Lord Bingham of the fundamental policy of the law and his exposition of decisional authority dating back to the early 19th century[6] represented a *tour de force* of judicial reasoning. It was typical of this great judge. Dissenting judges far away were glad to call on his reasons to explain, and strengthen, their own efforts of persuasion. They were not cited because of his Imperial sway. Now they were embraced for reasons of logic and analogy.

Tom Bingham is honoured in Australia as a man, a judge, and a much respected legal scholar. He has been saluted as a visitor and he has welcomed us to London as judicial friends. In this essay, I will use the occasion to recount the debt to the judicial work of the House of Lords that Australian law owes to Lord Bingham and his distinguished colleagues and predecessors. I will also mention his enormous contribution to the ongoing conversation that takes place, especially between the highest courts of countries in the Commonwealth of Nations and specifically with the judicial members of the House of Lords.

Until quite recently, the transnational judicial conversation was substantially a one-way affair. The House of Lords, the Privy Council and the English Court of Appeal spoke and we listened. They rarely cited from Commonwealth, specifically Australian,[7] judicial authority. A significant contribution of Lord Bingham to Commonwealth-wide jurisprudence in the past 20 years has been his interest in, and use of, judicial reasoning from other English-speaking countries of the common law tradition. I will illustrate this point with a number of references

---

[3] [2008] UKHL 8 at [24], [25], [37], [43].

[4] [2008] UKHL 8 at [17].

[5] *Ayles* (2008) 82 ALJR 502 at [11], [28]–[30]; cf at [85] per Kiefel J; [2008] HCA 6. Thus in *Clarke*, the indictment was signed by the proper officer during the trial at what Lord Bingham described as 'the eleventh hour' after the evidence had ended. This was held not to 'throw a blanket of legality over the invalid proceedings already conducted'.

[6] *Jane Denton's Case* (1823) 1 Lewin 53; 168 ER 956; *Guiseppe Sidoli's Case* (1833) 1 Lewin 55; 168 ER 957.

[7] The statistics of citations of decision in the *Commonwealth Law Reports* in the Appeal Cases is 1910–0; 1920–0; 1930–0; 1940–1; 1950–1; 1960–4; 1970–15; 1980–8; 1990–5; 2000–12; 2007–14.

to his judicial opinions citing reasons of my own court. I will point out that his compliment has been repaid many times.

As Lord Bingham's retirement from judicial office heralds the approaching end of the House of Lords era and the beginning of the new Supreme Court of the United Kingdom, it is timely for an Australian lawyer and judge to pause and reflect upon the impact of the House of Lords' judicial authority on the law of Australia and the debt that we owe to their Lordships and specifically to Tom Bingham.

An Unusual Arrangement

The House of Lords was never part of the Australian judicial hierarchy. No appeal ever lay from an Australian court to the judicial members of the House of Lords. Instead, from colonial times, appeals lay to the Judicial Committee of the Privy Council, whose personnel were largely (but not entirely) the same as the Law Lords. Appeals continued to be taken to the Privy Council from Australia until 1986, by which time successive Australian legislation[8] finally had the effect of terminating such appeals for the future.

As chance would have it, in the New South Wales Court of Appeal, I presided in the last Australian appeal that went to the Privy Council.[9] Happily, our orders were affirmed. The story of the impact of the Privy Council upon the law in Australia is another but different and interesting story.[10]

Given the lack of formal links between Australian courts and the House of Lords, it is at first blush surprising that the decisions of their Lordships were followed so closely by Australian courts, well into the 20th century, virtually as a matter of course. In Australia, it was said that the Lords 'had sometimes been mistaken for a part of the Australian doctrine of precedent'.[11] Lionel Murphy, one-time Australian Attorney-General and Justice of the High Court, put this tendency of obedience down to an attitude 'eminently suitable for a nation overwhelmingly populated by sheep'.[12]

---

[8] Appeals to the Privy Council from Australian Courts were abolished in stages: first in federal matters (*Privy Council (Limitation of Appeals) Act* 1968 (Cth)), secondly, appeals from the High Court (*Privy Council (Appeals from the High Court) Act* 1975 (Cth)) and finally, appeals from State Supreme Courts (*Australia Act* 1986 (Cth) and (UK)). In *Viro v The Queen* (1978) 141 CLR 88 the High Court held that it was no longer bound to follow decisions of the Privy Council, with minor possible exceptions.

[9] *Austin v Keele* (1987) 10 NSWLR 283 (PC).

[10] AM Gleeson, 'The Influence of the Privy Council on Australia' (2007) 29 Australian Bar Review 123.

[11] AR Blackshield, 'The High Court: Change and Decay' (1980) 5 Legal Service Bulletin 107, 107.

[12] LK Murphy, 'The Responsibility of Judges' Opening Address for the First National Conference of Labor Lawyers, 29 June 1979 in G Evans (ed) *Law, Politics and the Labor Movement* (Melbourne: Legal Service Bulletin, 1980) p 5.

There were, however, at least three other reasons why Australian judges paid so much attention to the judicial opinions of the House of Lords. First, there was the realistic appreciation that the same personalities substantially constituted both their Lordships' House and the Privy Council, so that a very high coincidence of judicial approach and conclusion was to be expected from each tribunal. Secondly, the habits of Empire inculcated in Australian lawyers a high measure of respect for just about everything that came from the Imperial capital. Not least in the pronouncements of law which was the glue that helped to bind the Empire together. Thirdly, traditions long observed and utility derived from linkage to one of the great legal systems of the world as well as the high standards of reasoning typical of the House of Lords, helped maintain the impact of its influence long after the Imperial tide had receded.

When Australia and other lands became British colonies, the colonists inherited so much of English statute and decisional law as was applicable to 'their own situation and the condition of the infant colony'.[13] The inheritance of English law was regarded as a precious birthright of the settlers. It was generally embraced as part of the shared Imperial tradition, not only by lawyers but by the general population when they thought about such matters. Well into the 20th century, there was a reluctance to diminish the unity of the worldwide common law. As Justice Gibbs, later Chief Justice of Australia, explained:[14]

The presumption, at least, is that the entire fabric of common law, not shreds and patches of it, was carried with them by the colonists to the newly occupied territory.

Whilst the common law, so adopted, was not forever frozen in the form in which it was originally received,[15] there was a common reluctance amongst Australian judges to vary and adapt even the most unsuitable of rules on the ground that they were inappropriate to the conditions of the new land.[16] This judicial and professional attitude therefore made it quite natural for Australian judges, virtually from the beginning, to look to the decisions and reasons of the House of Lords as expressing the last word on the state of the common law throughout the Empire and the meaning of British statutes, many of which applied, or were copied, in far away countries such as Australia.[17]

To these conditions of *Realpolitik*, pride and practical utility, the Privy Council in *Robbins v National Trust Company*[18] added its own authoritative instruction

---

[13] There was statutory recognition of this principle in s 24 of the *Australian Courts Act* 1828 (Imp) (9 Geo IV c 83). In New Zealand, the principle was reflected in the *English Laws Act* 1858 (Imp), which likewise adopted the laws of England.

[14] *State Government Insurance Commission v Trigwell* (1979) 142 CLR 617 at 626 per Gibbs J.

[15] *Trigwell* (1979) 142 CLR 617 at 625.

[16] *Trigwell* (1979) 142 CLR 617 at 626.

[17] J Chen, 'Use of Comparative Law by Australian Courts' in A E-S Tay and C Leung (eds), *Australian Law and Legal Thinking in the 1990s: A collection of 32 Australian reports to the XIVth International Congress of Comparative Law presented in Athens on 31 July–6 August 1994* (Sydney: Faculty of Law, University of Sydney, 1994) 61.

[18] [1927] AC 515 at 519 (PC) per Viscount Dunedin.

on how dominion and colonial judges should take into account decisions of the House of Lords:

... [W]hen an appellate Court in a colony which is regulated by English law differs from an appellate Court in England, it is not right to assume that the Colonial Court is wrong. It is otherwise if the authority in England is that of the House of Lords. That is the supreme tribunal to settle English law, and that being settled, the Colonial Court, which is bound by English law, is bound to follow it. Equally, of course, the point of difference may be settled so far as the Colonial Court is concerned by a judgment of this Board.

However discordant this instruction was for the formal hierarchy of courts, and the line of appeal to London, colonial, and dominion judges read and understood what they were supposed to do. So did the local legal profession that closely followed not only the decisions of the Privy Council but also those of the House of Lords. Right up to recent times it has been usual for the libraries of judges and advocates throughout Australia to contain the English casebooks. They were presented in pride of place with the *Commonwealth Law Reports* and the local *State Reports* as the regular source books of basic legal principle and authority. The general view prevailed that, so long as a right of appeal to the Privy Council remained in Australia, the policy of following House of Lords decisions was a 'practical necessity'.[19]

It is ironic that one of the strongest opponents to the separate development of the common law, as late as 1948, was Justice Owen Dixon, later Chief Justice of Australia.[20] Writing in *Wright v Wright*,[21] Dixon declared that: '[d]iversity in the development of the common law...seems to me to be an evil'. This would have been a common, certainly a majority, attitude in Australia well into the 1970s. It helps to explain the largely unquestioning reference to House of Lords authority until (and even beyond) that time.

When the Australian Constitution was drafted and negotiated with the Imperial authorities, a sticking point (only resolved at the last minute) was the access given to appellants from Australian courts to the Privy Council. Qualified access was eventually granted in the Constitution.[22] Yet, in the earliest days of the High Court of Australia, the utility of having available the body of principle and learning emanating from the House of Lords was recognized by the new Court itself. In 1909, in *Brown v Holloway*,[23] Justice O'Connor observed:

In matters not relating to the Constitution this Court is, no doubt, bound in judicial courtesy by the decision of the House of Lords, the tribunal of the highest authority in the British Empire.

---

[19] P Brett, 'High Court—Conflict with Decisions of Court of Appeal' (1955) 29 Australian Law Journal 121, 122; see also BJ Cameron, 'Law Reform in New Zealand' (1956) 32 New Zealand Law Journal 72, p 74; *A-G for Hong Kong v Reid* [1992] 2 NZLR 385 at 392; A Mason, 'Future Directions in Australian Law' (1987) 13 *Monash University Law Review* 149, p 150.

[20] J Spigelman, Foreword, in P Ayers, *Owen Dixon* (Melbourne: The Miegunyah Press, 2nd edn, 2007) vii.

[21] (1948) 77 CLR 191 at 210.   [22] Australian Constitution, s 74.

[23] (1909) 10 CLR 82 at 102.

The same point was acknowledged as late as 1943 in *Piro v W Foster and Co Ltd*.[24] Whilst accepting that House of Lords decisions were not 'technically' binding on Australian courts, Chief Justice Latham declared:[25]

[I]t should now be formally decided that it will be a wise general rule of practice that in cases of clear conflict between a decision of the House of Lords and of the High Court, this Court and other courts in Australia, should follow a decision of the House of Lords upon matters of general legal principle.

Given that this *dictum* was written in the midst of wartime dangers, when the very survival of an independent Australian nation was under threat, it seems astonishing, in retrospect, that such an extra-hierarchical view should be taken towards a court, unmentioned in the Australian Constitution and having no formal links to the Australian judicature.

It did not take long for criticisms of this viewpoint to arise. Chief Justice Barwick in 1970 declared that Latham's attitude amounted to an abdication by the High Court 'of its own responsibility as a Court of Appeal within each State system'.[26] Yet, the Latham declaration and longstanding practice proved quite difficult to eradicate from traditional legal thinking, including amongst Australian judges who should have known better because of the text of the Constitution and the pain involved in settling its final provisions in respect of appeals beyond Australian shores.

I said that it was ironical that Justice Dixon should have emerged as such a strong proponent of the unity of the common law because it was his decision in *Parker v The Queen*[27] in 1963 that amounted to a declaration of judicial independence towards the status of English precedent in Australian courts. There, the High Court of Australia declined to follow the decision of the House of Lords in *DPP v Smith*.[28] In time, the Privy Council would substantially follow the approach of the High Court of Australia, returning to the more orthodox doctrine of English law concerning the subjective test for intent for murder.[29] And in 1967, the British Parliament effectively disapproved of *Smith* by enacting section 8 of the Criminal Justice Act 1967 (UK). In private correspondence with Justice Felix Frankfurter of the Supreme Court of the United States, Dixon conceded that his leanings 'towards purity in the common law have been counterpoised by too much British sentiment'.[30]

[24] (1943) 68 CLR 313.
[25] 1943) 68 CLR 313 at 320. See also 325–6 per Rich J; 326–7 per Starke J; 336 per McTiernan J; and 341 per Williams J.
[26] G Barwick, 'Precedent in the Southern Hemisphere' (1970) 5 *Israel Law Review* 1, p 28–9; Z Cowen, 'The Binding Effect of English Decisions Upon Australian Courts' (1944) 60 LQR 378, 381.
[27] (1963) 111 CLR 610.
[28] [1961] AC 290.
[29] *Frankland v The Queen* [1987] AC 576 at 594.
[30] Sir Owen Dixon to Felix Frankfurter, 20 December 1960, in Correspondence 1960–1973, Owen Dixon, Personal Papers. See P Ayers, *Owen Dixon*, above, 276–277.

After the decision in *Parker* several cases in the High Court of Australia gave the Justices the opportunity to prefer their own approach to particular common law rules expressed in House of Lords reasoning.[31] Often, it has to be said, these rebellions reflected a view that Australian law was perhaps more orthodox and more purely English than the House of Lords was becoming over time. Perhaps this was the highest tribute that could be paid to the great English judges of the 19th and early 20th centuries. To this day, there remain Australian judges who adhere to similar sentiments.[32]

A little belatedly, the Privy Council acknowledged the entitlement of the High Court of Australia to express its own opinions where they conflicted with a House of Lords precedent.[33] Yet despite this, to this day, cases arise where distinguished Australian judges still reach unquestioningly and almost automatically for House of Lords authority and apply it as if it were still binding as a statement of the law applicable in the Australian Commonwealth.[34] It is not and, as a matter of law as distinct from practical reality, it never was so.

With the emergence of the High Court as the final appellate court for Australia, the need for a clear new rule was ultimately recognized. Eventually, it was stated by the High Court of Australia in *Cooke v Cooke*:[35]

The history of this country and of the common law makes it inevitable and desirable that the courts of this country will continue to obtain assistance and guidance from the learning and reasoning of United Kingdom courts just as Australian courts benefit from the learning and reasoning of other great common law courts. Subject, perhaps, to the special position of decisions of the House of Lords given in the period in which appeals lay from this country to the Privy Council, the precedents of other legal systems are not binding and are useful only to the degree of the persuasiveness of their reasoning.

In my view even the postulate of a pre-1986 exception can no longer be admitted as a matter of constitutional principle. In a country that is wholly independent in law and politics and in all of its branches of government from the authorities of any other country, self-respecting legal principle obliges a single, simple, rule.

Thus, Australian courts may use House of Lords authority, like any other judicial reasoning, as and when it helps them in their reasoning and analogical deliberations. However, such decisions have no binding force whatsoever unless an Australian judge, with the constitutional power and legitimacy, decides to adopt the decision or the reasoning in it and to declare that it represents a correct

---

[31] A good example was *Skelton v Collins* (1966) 115 CLR 94 where the court declined to follow *H West and Sons Ltd v Shephard* [1964] AC 326.

[32] *Coventry v Charter Pacific Corporation Ltd* (2006) 227 CLR 234 at 249–253 [35]–[51] per Gleeson CJ, Gummow, Hayne, and Callinan JJ; cf at 267 [110]–[113] of my own reasons.

[33] *Australian Consolidated Press Ltd v Uren* [1969] 1 AC 590; *Geelong Harbour Trust Commissioners v Gibbs, Bright and Co* (1974) 129 CLR 576.

[34] See e.g., *International Air Transport Association v Ansett Australia Holdings Limited* (2008) 82 ALJR 419; [2008] HCA 3 at [154].

[35] (1986) 162 CLR 376 at 390.

statement of the law of Australia. Thus we refer to House of Lords opinions for the power and force of their reasoning and persuasiveness of their logic. Nothing more. The relationship is therefore now one of rational respect, not Imperial or other power. The greatest tribute to the House of Lords can be found in the fact that, despite this change in the precedential authority of its decisions, they continue to be cited in so many fields of contested principle involving the common law, the rules of equity, and the approach to statute law.[36]

In a landscape that discloses countless instances where the reasoning of the House of Lords has been considered and adopted as still expressing the law of Australia, the exceptions, where that authority has been departed from, are the more notable. Some of the areas where Australian law, as expressed in the High Court, has taken a different direction include in cases on the law of nervous shock;[37] the law on the liability of local authorities;[38] the law of judicial disqualification for financial interest;[39] the law of resulting trusts;[40] the liability of advocates for negligence;[41] and the law on exemplary damages in tort.[42]

It is an indication of my own particular regard for the principles stated by the House of Lords that in two of the foregoing instances (judicial disqualification and advocates immunity) I preferred the approach favoured by the Law Lords to that embraced by my colleagues. Yet I gave effect to them not because of their source but because I considered that they should be accepted and declared to state the applicable law of Australia.

A New Dialogue

During the time of Imperial power, suggestions were occasionally made for institutional arrangements that would ensure a more equal participation of judges

---

[36] A good recent illustration is found in *Koompahtoo Local Aboriginal Land Council v Sanpine Pty Ltd* (2007) 82 ALJR 345. In that case a majority of the High Court (Gleeson CJ, Gummow, Heydon, and Crennan JJ) applied the reasoning of Lord Diplock, as Diplock LJ, in *Hong Kong Fir Shipping Co v Kawasaki Kisen Kaisha Ltd* [1962] 2 QB 26 recognizing the 'intermediate term' category for termination of contracts. My own preference (Ibid, [107]–[108]) was to adopt an alternative Australian taxonomy. The case is an instance of the ongoing influence of English judicial pronouncements upon Australian legal doctrine.

[37] *Alcock v Chief Constable of South Yorkshire Police* [1992] 2 AC 310; cf *Annetts v Australian Stations Pty Ltd* (2003) 211 CLR 317.

[38] *Anns v Merton London Borough Council* [1978] AC 728; cf *Sutherland Shire Council v Heyman* (1985) 157 CLR 424, later followed in *Murphy v Brentwood DCC* [1991] 1 AC 398.

[39] *Dimes v Proprietors, Grand Junction Canal* (1852) 3 HCL 759 (HL); 10 ER 301; cf *Ebner v Official Trustee in Bankruptcy* (2000) 205 CLR 337. The writer followed and applied the stricter House of Lords principle.

[40] *Tinsley v Milligan* [1994] 1 AC 340; cf *Nelson v Nelson* (1995) 184 CLR 538.

[41] *Arthur JS Hall v Simons* [2002] 1 AC 615; cf *D'Orta-Ekenaike v Victoria Legal Aid* (2005) 223 CLR 1. The writer preferred the House of Lords opinion.

[42] *Rookes v Barnard* [1964] AC 1129; *Broome v Cassell and Co Ltd* [1972] AC 1027; cf *Uren v John Fairfax and Sons Ltd* (1966) 117 CLR 118.

from the dominions, such as Australia, in the Imperial courts whose authority beyond England was so remarkable and enduring.

The most obvious way that this could have been done would have been the reconstitution of the Judicial Committee of the Privy Council to include more than an occasional visiting judge from the British dominions. Alternatively, it might have been possible in the 1950s and 1960s to constitute a Privy Council for Pacific countries of the Commonwealth (including Australia, New Zealand, Papua New Guinea, Fiji, Solomon Islands, Tonga, Nauru, Samoa, etc) substantially comprising judges of high authority from that part of the world. The fact is that there was never much interest in Britain in any of these ideas. This proves that it is not only Australian lawyers who suffer from an occasional inflexibility of mind.

The historical moment for institutional creativity passed. The possibility of building a true Commonwealth-wide court of final appeal (if that ever was feasible) was lost. For the most part, the countries of the Commonwealth of Nations went their own way. Thus Australia finally did in 1986 and New Zealand in 2003.[43] Viewed from the other side of the world, one is left with an impression that, in the earlier decades of the 20th century, the British interest in judicial thought and reasoning in the British dominions and colonies was never a fraction of that moving in the opposite direction. Considering this reality, we can lament lost institutional opportunities. However, they make all the more important the recent contributions that Lord Bingham has made to rebuilding a new judicial relationship across borders on a foundation of mutual respect and interactive utility.

In fact, one of the most significant contributions that Lord Bingham has made to English law and British judicial practice in recent decades has been his consistent attention to the decisions of Commonwealth and American courts (and also European courts) on questions of basic general principle. In this respect, he has led the way in the transnational judicial dialogue which is such a feature of the current age.[44] He has done so, in part, by example and, in part, by insisting that counsel appearing to argue cases involving questions of basic legal principle before the House of Lords (and the Privy Council) must be armed with any

---

[43] *Supreme Court Act* 2003 (NZ).

[44] See e.g., A-M Slaughter, 'Transnational Conversation'; A-M Slaughter, 'A Typology of Transjudicial Communication' 20 *University of Richmond Law Review* 99 (1994); Vicki C Jackson, 'Constitutional Comparisons: Convergence, Resistance, Engagement' 119 *Harvard Law Review* 109 (2005) (describing Philippines litigation); Vicki C Jackson, 'Transnational Challenges to Constitutional Law' (2007) 35 *Federal Law Review* (Aust) 161 (describing Australian constitutional developments); Sujit Chowdhry, 'Globalization in Search of Justification: Toward a Theory of Comparative Constitutional Interpretation' 74 *Indiana Law Journal* 819 (1999); Kim L Schaeppele, 'Aspirational and Aversive Constitutionalism: The Case for Studying Cross-Constitutional Influence Through Negative Models' (2003) 1 *International Journal of Constitutional Law* 296; Michael D Kirby, 'Transnational Judicial Dialogue, Internationalisation of Law and Australian Judges' (2008) 9 Melbourne Journal of International Law 171.

analogous decisions made by judges in other lands that may throw light on the resolution of the problem before the highest courts in Britain.

Lord Bingham's leadership in this respect has consequences far from London. By showing what can be done, particularly within the English-speaking judiciary, to utilize the reasoning of other courts, he has enhanced the realization that all wisdom is not home-grown; that there is no necessity to reinvent judicial wheels; and that common questions of principle can be better decided with the aid of comparative legal materials. The age of Imperial deference has passed. A new age of transnational dialogue has opened. Lord Bingham has been a leader in the new age.

Take, first, a number of cases where, in the House of Lords (and earlier in the English Court of Appeal), Lord Bingham has utilized Australian and other foreign judicial authority. The case of *R v Clarke*,[45] mentioned at the outset of this essay, is a classic case in point. Not only did Lord Bingham's opinion in that appeal refer to a mass of English authority on the legal question in issue. It also drew on Australian authority, including that of the Court of Criminal Appeal of New South Wales in *R v Janceski*.[46] There too the Australian court had adopted a strict approach to the requirement of a valid indictment at the outset of the trial. Tellingly, that case was repeatedly cited to their Lordships by counsel. The Internet citations of the cited foreign decisions are given. There is no doubt that the Internet with its search engines has made more accessible foreign authority that would earlier have been undiscoverable but now may readily be discovered and bear on a point in contention.

There have been many other instances. Some, doubtless, are the product of the researches of counsel. Some are probably the product of the researches of Lord Bingham and his colleagues themselves. Sometimes acquaintance with recent Commonwealth decisions comes from the invaluable references to worldwide authority contained in law reviews of which the *Law Quarterly Review* is a most precious example. Sometimes there is nothing more than personal conversation and friendly personal contact.[47]

One area where final courts are constantly looking to colleagues in other countries concerns treaty law such as the law on the *Refugees Convention* and *Protocol*. In many leading cases touching this subject, Lord Bingham has referred to, and applied, overseas authority on the meaning of that Convention.[48]

---

[45] (2008) UKHL 8.

[46] (2005) 64 NSWLR 10; [2005] NSWCCA 281 at *Clarke* [2008] UKHL at [12].

[47] This was the source of the writer's citation of Indian Supreme Court authority in *Osmond v Public Service Board of NSW* [1984] 3 NSWLR 447 at 461 (CA). The Indian decisions in *Siemens Engineering Mfg Co of India v Union of India Air* 1976 SC 1785 and *Maneka Gandhi v Union of India Air* 1978 SC 597 were cited following a visit of Bhagwati J to Australia. The reaction of the High Court of Australia at the time was unfavourable and somewhat dismissive. See *Public Service Board of NSW v Osmond* (1986) 159 CLR 656 at 668 per Gibbs CJ. It would be different today.

[48] See e.g., *R v Secretary for Home Department; Fornah v Secretary of State for the Home Department* [2007] 1 AC 412 at 430 [13], 431 [14] citing *Applicant A v Minister* (1997) 190 CLR

The law of torts, and the troublesome issue of tortious liability in negligence for pure financial loss has been a rich field for transnational borrowing.[49]

Another field where, as *Clarke* shows, similarities between English and Australian law make examination of common issues specially fruitful, is criminal law. Thus, in *R v Coutts*,[50] Lord Bingham followed the 'strong statements' of Justices McHugh and Hayne in *Gilbert v The Queen*.[51] He pointed to the fact that their approach reflected, even if unconsciously, the principle generally applied in the United States in *Stephenson v United States*[52] and later cases.[53]

Sometimes, a dissenting opinion in the Australian court is preferred to that of the majority. So it was in the closely divided decision of the High Court of Australia in *Chappel v Hart*[54] on the issue of causation in cases of medical negligence. When like questions arose for decision in *Chester v Afshar*,[55] Lord Bingham adopted the dissenting approach of Justice McHugh. In another case of medical negligence, *Reece v Darlington Memorial Hospital NHS Trust*,[56] Lord Bingham again drew on the closely divided opinions in the Australian courts declaring that he had found them 'of particular value since, although most of the arguments deployed are not novel ... the division of opinion amongst the members of the Court gives the competing arguments a notable sharpness and clarity'.[57] In a world of many common legal problems, a number of them presented by shared technology, often arising at the same time, there is value and assistance to be gained in looking at the reasons of those who have gone before.

Occasionally it may be thought that those who have gone before, whilst deserving of respect, have taken too bold a course.[58] But often the treatment of basic issues in the common law will be helpful. Occasionally an Australian exposition of the common law may succinctly express the conclusions reached elsewhere. In considering issues of causation in *Fairchild v Glen Haven Funeral Services Ltd*,[59] it was natural that Lord Bingham would find utility in Chief

225, 263, 234. See also *Sepet v Secretary of State for the Home Department* [2003] 1 WLR 856 at 872 [22] applying *Minister for Immigration v Ibrahim* (2000) 204 CLR 1 at 33 [102].

[49] *Customs and Excise Commissioners v Barclays Bank Plc* [2007] 1 AC 181 at 189–190 [4] where reference was made to my own reasons in *Perre v Apand Pty Ltd* (1999) 198 CLR 180 at 275 [259] and of Brennan J in *Heyman v Sutherland Shire Council* (1985) 157 CLR 424 at 481.

[50] [2006] 1 WLR 2154 (HL).

[51] (2000) 201 CLR 414.

[52] 162 US 313 at 323 (1896).

[53] *Berra v United States* 351 US 131 at 134 (1956); *Keeble v United States* 412 US 205 at 212–3 (1973) per Brennan J cited Ibid 2166–2167 [21].

[54] (1998) 195 CLR 232.

[55] [2005] 1 AC 134 (HL) at 141–142 [9].

[56] [2004] 1 AC 309 (HL).

[57] [2004] 1 AC 309 at 314 [2]. See also at 314 [3], 315 [5], 316 [6], 317 [9].

[58] *Transco Plc v Stockport MBC* [2004] 2 AC 1 (HL) at 8 [4]–[6] concerning the Australian absorption of *Rylands v Fletcher* in general negligence law in *Burnie Ports Authority v General Jones Pty Ltd* (1994) 179 CLR 520.

[59] [2003] 1 AC 32 (HL) at 44 [10].

Justice Mason's Australian decision in *March v E & M H Stramare Pty Ltd*,[60] as so many Australian courts have also done. Especially when considering an advance on previously stated common law principles, being armed with the decisions of judges in other countries can help to steer the way ahead.

When great issues arise, or where it is suggested that old common law rules are ripe for reconsideration, it is natural and helpful in every country to look to other lands, specifically with similar legal systems, both as a stimulus to change and as a precaution against excessive ardour. This, Lord Bingham has done on many occasions, as in his restatement of the law on advocate's immunity[61] and of privileged discussions on matters of political opinion and argument.[62] In the last-mentioned case, Lord Bingham reached not only for developments that had occurred in Australian courts but also to decisions from Canada,[63] India,[64] and South Africa.[65] By the end of the 20th century there was no disparagement for taking this course. It was natural and perfectly accepted.

This utilization of foreign, but analogous, judicial authority is one of the great legacies of the British Empire. Now it is sometimes working in a reverse direction. Even before his appointment to the House of Lords, Lord Bingham adopted this course. Thus, in the English Court of Appeal, in striking the correct balance in the often contentious issue of judicial disqualification for apparent bias,[66] he drew repeatedly on judicial remarks in several Australian cases.[67] Similarly, he embraced the reasoning of Chief Justice Mason and Justice Deane in *Teoh's Case*[68] in accepting that, sometimes, a court can discern from a statute a legitimate expectation of proper and timely governmental conduct.[69]

Where, as quite often occurs, the search for foreign authority detects reasoning that runs counter to his own judgment, Lord Bingham has been forthright in identifying the authority, noting that a different rule prevails, sharpening his own opinion and explaining why he prefers a different rule.[70] In such cases, access to the foreign reasoning, in legal systems sharing so much in common in matters of basic doctrine, can be helpful even when the reasoning is not followed.

---

[60] (1991) 171 CLR 506 at 508.

[61] *Arthur JS Hall and Co v Simons* [2002] 1 AC 615 at 635 [29], where *Giannarelli v Wraith* (1988) 165 CLR 543 was cited.

[62] *Reynolds v Times Newspaper Ltd* [2001] 2 AC 127 at 175–176 noting *Lange v ABC* (1997) 189 CLR 520.

[63] *Stopforth v Goyer* (1979) 97 DLR (3d) 369; *Loos v Robbins* (1987) 37 DLR (4th) 418.

[64] *Rajogopal (R) v State of Tamil Nadu* (1994) 6 SCC 632.

[65] *National Media Ltd v Bogoshi* (1998) 4 SA 1196.

[66] *Locabail (UK) Ltd v Bayfield Properties Ltd* [2000] QB 451 at 479–480 [22]–[25], 496–496 [86]–[87].

[67] Especially *In re JRL; ex p CJL* (1986) 161 CLR 342, 352; *Vakauta v Kelly* (1989) 167 CLR 568 at 570–571.

[68] *Minister for Immigration v Teoh* (1995) 183 CLR 273 at 291.

[69] *R v DPP; ex p Kebilene* [2000] 2 AC 326 at 337–339.

[70] See e.g., *Banque Bruxelles SA v Eagle Star Co Ltd* [1995] QB 375 at 417, 422 (CA).

Ongoing Borrowings

The cases which I have cited are just a handful of those in which Lord Bingham's reasons have drawn upon Australian authority and that of other common law countries. Even more frequent has been the citation of his opinions in Australian courts.

In the recent defamation decision in *Channel Seven Adelaide Pty Ltd v Manock*,[71] several members of the High Court of Australia drew on what Lord Bingham had said in the English Court of Appeal in *Brent Walker Group Plc v Time Out Ltd*.[72] If he has cited our decisions in a number of refugee cases, he has often been for us a source of elucidation on the meaning of the *Refugees Convention*.[73]

Whereas in matters of treaty law it is natural for every country, facing similar problems, to look to approaches of other countries, it is when the law is concerned with the rules of private obligations that the use of overseas authority is the more striking. Yet, there are countless instances where Lord Bingham's reasoning has been invoked in such cases. Thus, it has happened in consideration of the substantive law of defamation[74] where I found great assistance from his opinion in *Grobbelaar v News Groups Newspapers Ltd*;[75] in the law of limitations of actions;[76] in the law of recklessness in criminal cases;[77] in the law of privity of contracts;[78] in the law of contribution between tortfeasors[79] and on the general approach to striking out pleadings involving novel causes of action.[80]

Sometimes, Australian judges, searching for an apt phase[81] or explanation of a basic legal principle[82] will discover an extra-judicial contribution that Lord

---

[71] 82 ALJR 303 at [5], [12], [35].

[72] [1991] 2 QB 33. See also *Pervan v North Queensland Newspaper Co Ltd* (1993) 178 CLR 309 at 321–322.

[73] See e.g., *SZAT v Minister* (2007) 81 ALJR 1659 at 1663–4 [19]–[22] per Gleeson CJ; [25] per Gummow, Hayne, and Crennan JJ, 1669 [53]–[59]–[71] of my own reasons all referring to *Januzi v Secretary of State for the Home Department* [2006] 2 AC 426 (HL). See also *NAIS v Minister* (2005) 228 CLR 470 at 478 [20], 495 [81]–[82] citing *Dwyer v Watson* [2004] 1 AC 379.

[74] *John Fairfax Publishers Pty Ltd v Gacic* (2007) 81 ALJR 1218; see also *John Fairfax Pty Ltd v Rivkin* (2003) 77 ALJR 1657 citing *Grobbelaar*.

[75] [2003] 1 WLR 3024.

[76] *Singel v Clarke* (2006) 226 CLR 442 at 452–453 [11] citing *Stubbings v Webb* [1992] QB 197 (CA).

[77] *Banditt v The Queen* (2005) 224 CLR 262 at 267 [7] citing *R v G* [2004] 1 AC 1034.

[78] *Toll (FGCT) Pty Ltd v Alphapharm Pty Ltd* (2004) 219 CLR 165 citing *Homburg Hautimport BV v Agrosin Ltd* [2004] 1 AC 715. See also *Royal Botanic Gardens and Domain Trust v South Sydney Council* (2002) 76 ALJR 436 at 445 [39] citing *Bank of Credit and Commerce International SA v Ali* [2001] 2 WLR 735.

[79] *Alexander v Perpetual Trustees WA Ltd* (2004) 216 CLR 109 applying *Royal Brompton Hospital NHS Trust v Hamond* [2002] 1 WLR 1397.

[80] *ABC v Lenah Game Meats Pty Ltd* (2001) 208 CLR 199 at 268 [161] citing *Johnson v Gore Wood and Co* [2002] 2 AC 1. See also Ibid 224 [95], 319–320 [308].

[81] *Dow Jones and Co Inc v Gutnick* (2002) 210 CLR 575 at 612 [66].

[82] *Ebner v Official Trustee in Bankruptcy* (2006) 205 CLR 337 at 357 [56].

Bingham has made to supplement the case books. Yet in the case books, there are plenty of comments over his long years of judicial service that show the sharpest intellect applied to common questions coming before appellate courts everywhere. These include the changing context of judging witness credibility on courtroom appearances;[83] the capacity of equity, like the common law, in appropriate circumstances, to fill perceived 'gaps' in the coherent system of law;[84] and the developing law on the dissemination of confidential information.[85]

The foregoing is just a sample of the very many cases in which Australian judges, toiling away far from the Strand and Westminster, have reached for Lord Bingham's words where they did not have to and where they were not bound by them. They have done so for the wisdom, experience, and sharpness of thought that have helped them to arrive at their own conclusions about where justice according to law should take the busy Australian judge.

A Very Modern Legacy

Like all judges of the common law, Tom Bingham walks in a journey begun by famous forebears. When those forebears include the great judges of the House of Lords, it is inevitable that his works will be compared with the great judges of the past—Hailsham, the Halsburys, Atkin, Reid, Diplock, Scarman, Wilberforce, and yes, the occasional Tom Denning. In such company it is difficult to shine. But shine Tom Bingham has.

None of us can say how words we have written may be used in the future. They are reified and have taken on their own lives independent of the minds that conceived them. In the global economy of ideas and values represented by the common law, it is the intellectual market that makes the decision according to perceived usefulness. By that criterion, Tom Bingham's stocks, as he leaves the judgment seat, are extremely high.

It is natural that he should be praised in his own country to which he has given much sterling service. But that he is so admired and valued in independent countries throughout the world, linked now only by the power of persuasion, is a most significant accolade. Tom Bingham inherited the mantle of respect won by the House of Lords in colonial and post-colonial times when judges elsewhere followed their reasoning because of the actuality and habit of Imperial obedience.

---

[83] *State Rail Authority of NSW v Earthline Constructions Pty Ltd (In Liq)* (1999) 73 ALJR 306 at 327 [87] citing *R v Ministry of Defence; ex p Smith* [1996] QB 517 at 554 per Sir Thomas Bingham, MR.

[84] *Hill v Van Erp* (1997) 188 CLR 159 at 231, 234 where Gummow J cited *Al-Kandari v J R Brown and Co* [1988] QB 665 (CA).

[85] *Johns v Australian Securities Commission* (1993) 178 CLR 408 at 429 per Brennan J citing Bingham LJ in *Attorney-General v Guardian Newspapers [No 2]* [1990] 1 AC 109 at 214.

When the duty of obedience fell away, only the power of reason could explain the continued citations and perceived usefulness.

By showing himself a child of the modern age, by insisting on outreach at home and by utilizing the technology of the Internet, Tom Bingham has extended the contribution of the English law in an environment where extension was by no means assured. This is a unique, special, and precious achievement because it points to the future. It sets a challenge for his successors. It gives an example to judges far away to reject parochialism. To search for principle. To be concerned with basic legal doctrine for it matters.[86] To embrace conceptual thinking. To consider legal principle and legal policy. And to do all this, where appropriate, with the aid of colleagues of the same and other judicial traditions.

At a watershed moment for the judicial institutions of the United Kingdom, it is proper for us to honour Tom Bingham's service and leadership.

---

[86] *Koompahtoo* (2007) 82 ALJR 345 at [78].

4

Goethe, Bingham, and the Gift of an Open Mind

Weltliteratur and Global Law
Lessons from Goethe

Basil Markesinis

Preliminary Remarks

The genius of Goethe has been the subject of a huge multilingual literature, not only because of the breadth of his interests—on this ground, he scores over Shakespeare and Dante, with whom he has invariably been ranked—but also for the richness of his poetic talent. To me, as a jurist who has dedicated his professional life to understanding and comparing different systems, the aspect of Goethe's work that has particular significance—beyond his love for action rather than words—is his ability to achieve a synthesis between Northern and Mediterranean, Romantic and Classic, Eastern and Western.

No lawyer should jump and put forward the objection that this endeavour is radically different from what comparative lawyers try to do for the gaps that had to be breached by these Goethian efforts were huge. He also had to do it at a time when the public opinion called for a German culture, literature, theatre, opera, poetry, and law—all after the *Volksgeist* of the *German* people had been discovered and understood. Goethe's success was partly because his restless and open mind allowed him to approach sympathetically the 'other' culture, and also because his literary gifts enabled him to imitate the foreign style and sensibilities in a manner that earned him the admiration of the experts of that 'other' culture. His collection of poems under the general title *West-östlicher Divan* is an example, but not the only one supporting this point.

This bridging of cultures, though evident in early works, became Goethe's major preoccupation during the last ten years of his life when he fought for the creation of what he called a *Weltliteratur*—a world literature. Modern English legal academics tend, in accordance with the impoverishing demands of our

times, to be specialists or 'technicians', as gifted (of course) as they are indus-
trious, but often dismissive of the advantages that wider culture can confer. Yet
comparative law is a discipline that requires something more than the ability to
use Socratic reasoning in the handling of legal rules. The wisdom of this observation, however, has escaped the attention of gifted but inexpert (in matters of
foreign law) lawyers and allowed them to express their views about how—indeed,
whether—comparative law should be studied.[1] The impulse to express a view is
understandable, since lawyers often speak confidently about many matters; yet
the results of such sorties into *terra incognita* can be poor. After all, two and a half
thousand years ago, it was Thucydides who had argued in his Funeral Oration
that 'ignorance provokes rashness while knowledge nourishes restraint'.

Let us, however, return to Goethe, since his thoughts deserve attention even
from lawyers.

First, Goethe's thoughts, unlike those Frederick the Great expressed in a prima
facie parallel but earlier attempt, were close to what some modern lawyers believe
comparative law does. For Fredrick, in his *De la literature allemande*[2] envisaged a
grand programme of translations from French and the classical languages *to help
shape German culture* while ignoring its own autochthonous stirrings. Frederick's
mistake was one often made by those who deal (or dabble) in contemporary comparative law, who somehow suppose that the aim of studying foreign law is to
find precedents for a quick and easy transplantation. This can never can be so;
at best, the foreign solution can have only some persuasive force, especially if the
purpose of invoking it is to show whether the result it produced worked in the
other system and thus to make one wonder whether it might also work in one's
own. The foreign idea, solution, or institution may, on the other hand, offer the
national lawyer a starting point for reflection about his own law, especially where
it is unclear, dated, or contradictory; but it rarely provides more than that.

Secondly, unlike Frederick's aim, Goethe's was not to use foreign models for
the purposes of shaping the ideas and practices of his own country, but to study
them for the sake of enhancing comprehension, mutual understanding, and
inspiration. In the words of a distinguished Germanist:[3]

For [Goethe] *Weltliteratur* was neither the sum of all national literatures nor the ever
increasing canon of world masterpieces, rather he conceived of it as a dynamic process of
rapprochement among European nations—above all Britain, France and Germany *with
the goal of breaking down the walls of national prejudices* that hampered peaceful coexist-
ence in the wake of Napoleonic Wars. To realize this social function of literature, Goethe
called upon contemporary authors *to serve along with himself as mediators and facilitators
across the frontiers* in periodicals, translations and memoirs. *He hoped this common market*

---

[1] 'Benefits of Comparative Tort Reasoning—Lost in Translation', ch 7, below (henceforth
referred to simply as Stapleton).
[2] Published in 1790 in French.
[3] Gerhart Hoffmeister, 'Reception in Germany and Abroad' in Lesley Sharpe (ed), *The
Cambridge Companion to Goethe* (2002), 232.

of ideas would eventually manifest itself in a greater sense of understanding and tolerance, first among the intellectuals and thereafter also among the peoples.

Thus, Goethe never saw the exercise of stripping the person seeking inspiration from a foreign source of his own natural or cultural characteristics. The desire to understand, correspond, and learn from and assist as diverse a group of authors as Lord Byron, Shelley, Carlyle, George Eliot, and Alessandro Manzoni—to mention just a handful of important and self-confident individuals—led him to advocate over and over again the value of 'mutual enrichment', 'the develop-ment of one's powers through contact with others', but also the need to preserve 'the individuality of each national literature'. And on the dangers of translations, which obviously worry Professor Stapleton sufficiently to make her borrow as a subheading of her article the title of a Hollywood film, Goethe gives the matter a twist that anyone who has worked across (legal) cultures will appreciate deeply. For he wrote to Thomas Carlyle:[4]

... the translator works not only for his own country but also for the country from whose language he has taken the work. For it happens more often than one imagines that a nation sucks the sap and strength from a work, and absorbs it into its own inner life, in such a way as to be able to derive no further pleasure, and draw no further nourishment, from it. This applies especially to the Germans, who assimilate all too quickly everything that is offered them and, in the course of transforming it by sundry repetitions, in a sense destroy it. *Therefore it is of great benefit to them to see something of their own re-appear endowed with new life through the means of a successful translation.*

Thirdly, though Goethe (like many of his contemporaries) sought to discover the *Volksgeist* of his nation in order to build on it a German culture, theatre, and poetry, and thus did not see German literature growing out of foreign (e.g., French or classic) literature, he never saw in culture—conceived in general terms—an obstacle to mutual borrowing and inspiration. His own work shows this inspiration from other cultures, whether we look at his *Strum und Drang* phase (replete with English borrowings), his classic dramas (such as *Iphigenie in Tauris*, involving a brilliant adaptation of a classic Greek theme to fit his idea of 'ethical action' and 'universal humanism') or, later, his *Römischen Elegien* or his *West-östlicher Divan*. In *Römischen Elegien* and *West-östlicher Divan*, Italian and Persian (respectively) motifs *and style* are skilfully re-represented or recreated through the medium of the German language, which most people, until his time (and, perhaps, even now), would have thought simply impossible.

Time and space do not allow us a great elaboration of these ideas, but enough has been said to plant the seed that Goethe's cultural crusade to bring different languages and literatures together presents transplantable features to law, where, in addition to the unifying element that modern globalization provides, we have

---

[4] Quoted by Richard Friedenthal, *Goethe. His Life and Times*, (1965, 1989 paperback edition), 513 (italics supplied).

the very practical need (and not just the pursuit of a poetical ideal) to harmonize or even synthesize different legal solutions. Before one rushes to differentiate law, one should read what Schiller had to say about the way his friend 'fused his German personality to a Mediterranean one'. In brief, the task can be accomplished if one is willing to undertake it.

Do our lawyers see things in this way? More importantly, can they be persuaded to open their eyes and (merely) consider the possibility that 'There is a World Elsewhere,'[5] which is not only as old (if not even older) than theirs, but also potentially useful to those, at least, who wish to keep the City of London as one of the centres of the (commercial) universe and are not wholly absorbed by the monastic environment of academic cloisters? The work of Lord Bingham clearly falls within the category of imaginary, pioneering, and open-minded work, which, one suspects, would have appealed to Goethe—and indeed, resembles greatly his own outlook—hence the unusual title of this essay. Pioneers and original minds, however, are never in the majority of any society; conservative traditionalists always are. This should not surprise us, for following accepted practice is always safer and easier, though it does not mean that those who favour 'preservation' cannot themselves also be exceptionally gifted. All it means is that history suggests that they are eventually forgotten.

Being specific is always more instructive than being general and bland, even if the *unintended* consequence may be to make the disagreement *appear* personal rather than scientific. Still, I feel one has to run the risk, unintended though it is in my case, since I have repeatedly tried to launch a debate about the importance of judicial mentality[6] and outlook in explaining the final judgments handed down by judges all over the world. In other words, you cannot understand a judge's work without knowing his character and personality.

What applies to judges also applies to academics; and I see Professor Stapleton's recent article in the same light, even though a good one-third struck me as a persistent attack on my views in a way that might give the impression that she was attacking me personally and not just disagreeing with my view of tort law in general, or how to teach comparative law in particular.

In what follows, I would thus like to use the work of two jurists whose talents and learning I respect greatly but with whose approach and views I have the misfortune to disagree strongly. They are Lord Hoffmann and Professor Stapleton. I repeat, focusing on the work of two individuals could—*but should not*—be seen as an attack on persons; but it is a disagreement on mentality, outlook, philosophy,

---

[5] "'There is a World Elsewhere'—The Changing Perspectives of English Law" FA Mann lecture given on 21 November 1991, published in 41 ICLQ (1992) 513–29 and reprinted in his *The Business of Judging. Selected Essays and Speeches* (2000), pp 87 ff. Baroness Hale in her recent but as yet unpublished Maccabaean lecture 'Minority Opinion?' at the British Academy seems to me to have argued along similar lines.

[6] 'Judicial Mentality: Mental Disposition or Outlook as a Factor Impeding Recourse to Foreign Law', (2006) 80 Tulane Law Rev, pp 1325 ff.

and methodology, and it has to be concretized so that the reader can see for himself exactly where the intellectual disagreement lies. If this way of contrasting opinions is taken in a personal way I will be the first to regret it *deeply*; for what I am fighting for is a method which, in my view, may help my subject not only survive in a cluttered curriculum but also prove its worth in that of legal practice.

Two Ways of Closing Ones' Eyes to the 'Other' World

The judicial

Lord Hoffmann has, thus far, opted for what one might call a 'laconic', 'above the fray', or 'silent' approach towards the subject of foreign law. For someone who began life as an academic and, of course, a South African (and one assumes, in part at least, influenced by that country's double legal culture), his reticence is both surprising and disappointing. Lord Hoffmann has also been the President of the Anglo-German Legal Association for many years so, though this does not mean that one should expect him to advocate (or criticize) German law, it could have justified occasional intrusions into foreign law based on his enhanced experience thus acquired with (foreign) lawyers and their ideas. In his 'pronouncements', however, judicial *and extra-judicial*, references to the utility of foreign law have, as stated, been 'aphoristic and dismissive', or he has simply remained 'silent', even when others on the Bench gave him the cue to follow.

An example of his 'summary' or 'dismissive' style can be found in a Foreword recently contributed to an interesting academic monograph.[7] There, he tells us that 'Comparative Law does not help'. This categorically phrased view was justified by the statement that 'Continental lawyers have the same problems; *but their answers are hidden by obscurity or absence of reasoning*'.

I would not be surprised if many on the Continent of Europe felt offended by the italicized part of the statement. For why has a British judge of impeccable learning expressed himself in such an absolute manner? For, had he, for instance, limited the italicized part of his sentence to the decisions of the Cour de cassation (but not lower French courts) he would have been right. Had he directed his attack against the decisions of the German constitutional courts, one would have felt sympathy for his difficulty in following their complexity and, one might add, their prolixity. But phrasing his thoughts as widely as he did, to encompass European legal thought in general, is little short of unacceptably wrong. For who has ever even insinuated that the there is 'absence of reasoning' in the German legal culture on matters of private or public law? One does not expect a modern judge to have studied German law as closely as William Maitland did (and then described it as one of the finest creations of human mind); but one would have

---

7 Robert Steven, *Torts and Rights* (2007), at p vi.

thought that at least in his capacity as Chairman of the Anglo-German Lawyers' Association he would have had ample opportunity to see in practice and admire the German pursuit of detailed and logical reasoning.

The most plausible explanation for such brevity must thus be that one could not be expected to be too detailed in a Foreword. Moreover, one could also try to escape the meaning I ascribe to his words by arguing that he meant that the German reasoning was, in (all or some?) English cases, neither relevant nor transplantable. Alas, this attempt to escape the wide dictum he created cannot work either; and this is proved by the case he uses a few lines above the cited extract, in which he suggests the decision that (presumably) prompted him to make this comment. For there, he refers to House of Lords opinion in *Anns*, the implication being that the German reasoning, opaque and non-discoverable (if existent at all), was not transplantable and would not have helped the English courts.

Yet in *Anns*, Counsel—at Mr Tony Weir's prompting—submitted to their Lordships two German decisions,[8] translated and produced by Mr Weir, dealing with a key issue in that case: what was the plaintiff's hurt, physical material damage (as Lord Denning had suggested in *Dutton*[9] and approved in *Anns*[10]) or pure economic loss? German law, in its cases and doctrine, has agonized much over this issue and the question whether damage *to* the property is similar to damage caused *by* the property and thus actionable in tort or only in contract. In the end, in the case of immovables, Germans gave the right answer: the harm was pure economic loss—a result which, after ten years of tergiversation following *Anns* (which refused even to consider the German reasoning), the House of Lords came to accept as right in *Murphy v Brentwood*.[11]

Now no one is suggesting that German law is here used or should be used as a precedent; but we have here an answer to Professor Stapleton's quite remarkable question 'Why should a citizen of country A be interested in the law of country B'? Well, quite apart from the fact that he may be doing business there, living there, taxed there, or dying there, he may, if he is also a judge, be interested to see how others solve similar problems so that he can think out his own solution more clearly when the problem he is facing is new, uncovered by authority, international in nature, etc.[12] Had the correct characterization of the plaintiff's loss in *Murphy* been accepted ten years earlier in *Anns*, it could have saved litigants much cost

---

[8] BGH 27 May 1963, BGHZ 39, 358, English version in Basil S Markesinis and Hannes Unberath, *The German Law of Torts. A Comparative Treatise* (4th edn 2002), 615 at 617.

[9] *Dutton v Bognor Regis Urban District Council* [1972] 1 QB 373.

[10] *Anns v Merton London Borough Council* [1978] AC 728.

[11] *Murphy v Brentwood District Council* [1991] 1 AC 398.

[12] This is precisely what Professor James Gordley did most recently in 'When Is the Use of Foreign Law Possible? A Hard Case: The Protection of Privacy in Europe and the United States', in 67 *Louisiana Law Review* (2007) pp 1073 ff, and explained in a detailed manner how American courts could learn by studying French and German cases. I return to the issue of privacy later on in this contribution but here am content to state that if such learning is possible even by a system that is on this topic structurally very different from the European systems then this learning process must surely work even better for our own developing case law.

and academics much ink in arguing a point their German colleagues had correctly addressed before them. German theorizing therefore does exist; and, much as it can be very English to mock it or caricature it, it is sound and often better than ours.

'Ignoring' the value of foreign law by means of silence is another way favoured by Lord Hoffmann. Two examples can be given because they offer one the opportunity to compare his style to Lord Bingham's. The first is the *Fairchild*[13] case and the second is the *East Berkshire*[14] case.

In the first case, two learned Law Lords—Lords Bingham and Rodger of Earlsferry—spent much space and, obviously, even more thought on foreign law. They felt, one suspects rightly, that English law could have gone either way on the question before them. Faced with this clear lack of guidance, they thought it was legitimate, *inter alia*, to look at what other systems had done in comparable situations and—this is important—how had they coped with the issue of principle. Lord Hoffmann felt no such need to look at foreign law.

The silence of Lord Hoffmann (and, it must be added, the remaining Law Lords) could, I suppose, be explained on any of the following grounds:

(a) that as Law Lord, he is obliged to resolve disputes according to English law and has no duty to consider or refer to foreign law;

(b) that speculating about foreign law is dangerous, difficult, wastes time, adds to the expense of the trial—all points addressed by others in the past;

(c) that citing foreign law in such cases is a form of 'show off', a practice he disapproves of;

(d) that if the court can give a judgment using English cases or reasoning, it has no place in becoming a forum for discussing foreign possibilities, and

(e) that his colleagues undertook this task, and he saw no reason to repeat it, or, more interestingly (surprisingly?), had no arguments or information to contradict their use of foreign law.

I would venture the thought that among the above, we can find the reason for his silence. Yet I also accept that this is speculation; and like all speculation, it may be entirely unfounded. Yet if the reasons I offered may be wrong, the reason for speculating is legitimate. For when one sees two learned Law Lords enter this domain and a third one—academically and culturally just as learned—choose to remain silent, one has to ask why he is doing this. Is this *really* an endeavour that has no place in national judgments, or are there other reasons for such silence?

Professor Stapleton comes close to taking the first view, at any rate where systems expressed in a different language are concerned. Yet this dialogue between top judges representing different cultures—which she dislikes (or, at the very least, sees as replete with dangers)—*is* happening the world over; and though one

13 *Fairchild v Glenhaven Funeral Services Ltd* [2003] 1 AC 32.
14 *D v East Berkshire Community Health NHS Trust and Others* [2005] 2 AC 373.

may not like it, as American neo-conservatives (and Lord Hoffmann) do not, it is neither forbidden nor useless. After all, other senior British judges have done this as well—Lords or Lord Justices Denning, Scarman, Woolf, Steyn, Hope, Clyde, Slynn, Sedley, and Schiemann among them. Professor Stapleton may not approve, but some of our most senior judges across the world have thought otherwise. To avoid endless lists, let us simply mention the names of Chief Justice MacLoughlin (Canada), former President Barak (Israel), Justices Breyer, O'Connor, and Ginsburg (USA), and former Chief Justice Chaskalsson (South Africa). Professor Stapleton is silent on all of the above. Why, may we ask, *given that they have taken a very practical or forensic view about comparative law very similar to the one I have been developing for over 40 years*, are they not also included in her sights?

Silence protects. Silence also gives the impression that no justification is needed for 'ignoring' foreign law. It seems to suggest that this is 'evident'; and one needs no citation for evident truths.

The Hoffmann silence, however, needs further probing. Why was foreign law worth considering in *Fairchild* but not in *East Berkshire*? Here, no amount of speculation will ever provide us a definitive reply. If it were a question of expense, we should have been given a hint. If it were a question of not being relevant, Lord Bingham would not have raised it (or is this an indirect accusation that he is raising frivolous points simply because he has a mind as alive to intellectual disputes as that of Lord Hoffmann?). If—and this is particularly relevant to a constant theme of Lord Hoffmann's in this type of case—the non-liability rule was a question of unbearable state expense, Counsel should have 'urged' their Lordships to re-think this for reasons that I, among others, have raised before and since that decision was delivered. This question of 'cost' is not as evident as those who invoke it wish it to appear, quite apart from the fact that I do not think it is legitimate for a judge to base his judgement on the grounds that he is trying to save money for the state.

Professor Stapleton defends Lord Hoffmann by not only dismissing the reliability of the empirical evidence adduced but also saying that Lord Hoffmann's decision in *Stovin v Wise*[15] (which contains one of the lengthiest expositions of his reluctance to impose tort liability on local authorities for breach of statutory duty) was not based on empirical evidence, nor could it ever become dependent on such kind of work, since such surveys are incomplete, expensive, not likely to be carried out in the future, or non-existent in many countries. The Hoffmann judgment was thus largely based on his assessment of the *risks* that a liability rule might involve.

Deciding about *risks based on judicial hunches* is not, I feel, the best way of resolving disputes, especially if reputable 'law professors' dispute how real these risks are and the Senior Law Lord takes the same doubting stance. And when I am referring to 'reputable law professors', I am, naturally, *not* referring to comparatists

---

[15] [1996] WLR 388.

like myself but to Professor Paul Craig, Professor of *English Law* at the University of Oxford, and Dr Duncan Fairgrieve, a widely admired (younger) Oxford jurist. For writing together, they have argued that a switch from 'duty' to 'breach' would *not* lead to a lasting economic chaos that lies at the basis of Lord Hoffmann's hesitations. We are thus back to the starting point: Lord Hoffmann's approach is no more convincing, necessary, or desirable than that taken by others—to quote Goethe—'in everything his equal'. The difference thus seems to boil down simply to mentality, outlook, disposition, tradition, habit, conservatism, and the list goes on forever. Which terms apply to Lord Hoffmann is not for us even to try and guess.

If that is the case, an advocate should thus be free, indeed encouraged, to adduce evidence from wherever he could find it, to give the (English) court some assistance as to how sound (or imaginary) its fears may be. At the end of the day, it would equally be for the court to tell us why it remained unconvinced about the evidence put before it; but we would need reason for this for, to cite Lord Hoffmann words (uttered in another but not unrelated context), 'opaque or non existent reasons' will not do. Much as one tries to evaluate them, one finds it difficult to judge the validity of his 'hunches'.

The academic

Professor Stapleton, an Australian tort lawyer with a deep knowledge of English and American law, recently launched forth in the domain of comparative law and methodology. After describing the subject as 'a noble' subject—and I confess I (and others to whom I showed her text) remain unsure what this means—she then offers a series of arguments why the use of foreign law is not only not useful but may also be dangerous. Clearly, we cannot unpick all of her arguments in this short essay; this may have to wait for another article. Here it will suffice to focus on one or two observations in order to suggest that she misunderstands my work, which strikes me as being the main target of her article. The reasons which lead her to this critical position are, of course, legitimate; but it does not follow that they are objectively correct.

First is what she calls the problem of the monoglots and their inability to access foreign sources. She concretizes her complaint as follows:[16]

[none] of the six or so most authoritative and extensive commentaries on the German Civil Code and extra-code law of obligations...has been translated into English. This means that English speakers do not have these texts available so as to provide the necessary foils for one extensive text on German tort law that has been written in English [reference to the 4th edition of my own *The German Law of Torts A Comparative Treatise*.][17]

This statement is best answered by splitting it into two parts.

---

[16] Op. cit. at p 34.   [17] (2000), 969 pp long.

First her complaint that none of the German *Kommentare* has been translated into English is aimed to show that we do not have enough information about what Germans think German law is. In one sense, she is right; but, in my view, she is entirely wrong to suggest that if these great (and grand) books had been 'translated' she would have had a foil—I suppose this is a polite way of saying a correctant—to what I say in my own book.

The reason why she is utterly wrong in thinking that a mere translation would solve her problem is simply because the kind of books she is referring to are written in extremely difficult German, which, in some cases—Palandt for instance—even German lawyers would find difficult to follow. Whoever informed Professor Stapleton of the existence of these 'great' German books should have also told her that they are virtually unusable by English lawyers. What is instead needed is what I have endeavoured to do over 40 years—no doubt sometimes less successfully than others—and that is to 'package' German law to make it usable by Common lawyers. To be sure, some academics have argued that in this way I may have 'betrayed' the true nature and flavour of German law; but far too many German jurists and judges of great repute, who have advised me in the writing of this book, reviewed it, or contributed forewords to its various editions, have taken the opposite view in a way that does not even merit giving references. My own conscience is thus untroubled on this score.

The second part of her statement refers more specifically to my book. Though she does not comment on it or its details, she does, quite rightly, ask for supplementary information as to what the law is; and she suggests that there is little or none available to the monoglot readers. On this point, as well, she is wrong again on two counts.

First she is wrong as to the lack of further evidence of German tort law in English. Professor Christian von Bar's *The Common European Law of Torts*[18] is replete with references to German tort law. So is Professor Walter Van Gerven's casebook on *Tort Law*.[19] James Gordley and Arthur von Mehren's *An Introduction to the Comparative Study of Private Study of Private Law, Readings, Cases and Materials*[20] also devotes a reasonable section of their casebook to German tort law. Last but by no means least, in a website established and maintained at the University of Texas—where both Professor Stapleton and I spend a fair amount of our teaching duties—the website of translated French and German cases devoted to contract and tort are close to 900, many not included in any of the above-mentioned books.

The way Professor Stapleton treats these books can be used to judge the validity of her argument that 'we need a foil' to test the veracity of the Markesinis material before we can use it. For von Bar gets only a passing reference in a note;

[18] Vol 1 (1998); vol 2 (2000), amounting to a total 1,268 pp.
[19] (2000), 969 pp long.
[20] (2006) 580 pp long.

Van Gerven is cited only through mentioning a critical (if not defamatory) review of his book; Gordley is ignored, as indeed is the website. Given that English law students get nowhere near as many cases to study during the year they read torts at law school, and given the abundance of material that does exist (but is under-played by Professor Stapleton), her argument that 'there are no other texts that deal in detail with tort law in other foreign jurisdictions' does not seem very strong. This may be true as far as, say, systems such as the Spanish are concerned; I cannot answer for that system, as I never claimed an expertise in it, but I can refute her claims as far as the system in which I have cultivated a personal interest is concerned.

There is a second reason why Professor Stapleton is wrong in suggesting—which I believe she is—that even with the material I am referring to our knowledge of German law is inadequate. Stated simply this way, the argument has some force; the knowledge we have of a foreign system can never be adequate, given the ever-growing volume of statutory and decisional law experienced by all major modern systems.

Yet, it depends on how you intend to use this corpus of law. If you wish to have detailed advice on a very specific point of foreign law, you must turn to a native expert for it; no comparative lawyer has, to my knowledge, denied that. But if you wish to treat foreign law as a source of ideas, especially where your own law is under-developed, contradictory, or needs to be harmonized with the laws of other countries, then the amount of information needed for such exercise is there to be used. What is missing is the mentality, i.e., the individual outlook, which may be closed to foreign ideas, suspicious of them because they are foreign, uncomfortable with them because they come from cultures that are alien (or seem alien) to the potential borrower, or unable to comprehend these ideas because of the individual's linguistic limitations. I cannot enumerate all the psychological obstacles that *may* account for the reticence of colleagues (and I am here speaking in general terms) to use foreign material; but I have tried elsewhere[21] to refute in a more detailed manner why I think the more usually invoked arguments about cost, delays, lack of expertise, and different social backgrounds are less convincing as reasons for inactivity. So let me instead invoke a specific example taken from Professor Stapleton's text that suggests, to me at least, that for a variety of reasons it may be difficult to budge her from her views. The topic she chooses to discuss this idea is *Fairchild* and, later in her text, the troublesome topic of civil liability for breach of statutory duties imposed on local authorities.

---

[21] Sir Basil Markesinis and Jörg Fedtke, *Judicial Recourse to Foreign Law, A New Source of Inspiration?* (2006), including essays by Justice Laurie Ackermann (South African Constitutional Court), President Barak (Israeli Supreme Court), Otto Brun-Bryde (German Constitutional Court), Guy Canivet (French Supreme Court), Sir Sydney Kentridge QC, Christos Rozakis (Court of Human Rights, Strasbourg), and Konrad Schiemann (Court of the European Communities).

First she seems—to me at least—to pay inordinate attention to Tony Weir's statement that:

> The tour d'horizon attempted by the House of Lords was admittedly superficial. Omitted is the salient fact that in almost none of the jurisdiction glanced at would the claimants in Fairchild have succeed; in most places an employee simply cannot sue his employer in tort, since workmen's compensation or social security takes its place.

Professor Stapleton complained earlier on about inadequate information to act as a foil to a particular opinion put to a common lawyer. Yet Professor Fedtke (a German and comparative jurist) and I had provided much more detailed information than that given by Mr Weir in his somewhat aphoristical phrased statement.

Paraphrasing what we said elsewhere, we stressed that the House of Lords used the foreign material in the context of possible multiple tortfeasors, enquiring as to the ability of the 'but for' test to produce a just result. This was the main conceptual point that had to be decided; and this was also the point that attracts most of Mr Weir's attention. We submitted that the useful and detailed information their Lordships supplied on this point on foreign law is impeccable. Indeed, the House of Lords made history by citing a famous German practitioners' book—Palandt—and even the 'Motive' of the BGB both in German and English. The BGB is, of course, one of the major German textbooks, which Professor Stapleton regrets that it has never been adduced as evidence of what German law was. Well, in *Fairchild* it was; and remarkably, it was cited both in German and in English!

Criticizing their Lordships for not looking *at other aspects of foreign law as well* is another matter, and it should have been carefully distinguished from the criticism that the Court's look at foreign law was nothing more than a 'glance' or 'superficial'. Mr Weir's phrase that in 'almost none of the jurisdictions glanced at would the claimants in *Fairchild* have succeeded' is such a *further point*, which the House of Lords did not choose to investigate. Perhaps they should have. But if they had, they would have discovered a situation that differs from Mr Weir's.

That is the second reason why his throwaway statement is worrying. More precisely, it is worrying because, in the view of some of us, it is misleading. A more careful study suggests that in some systems, including Spain, Italy, the Czech Republic, Hungary, and Turkey, the possibility of a tort action is or has become available in the *Fairchild* scenario. Employers' liability thus ended in the Netherlands in 1967 when the traditional workers' compensation insurance was integrated into the general health and pension insurance systems, which allows asbestos victims to be compensated under tort law. Similarly, since 1997, asbestos cases are subject not only to social law but also to tort law in France following decisions of the Cour d'Appel of Dijon of 18 December 1997 (involving the company Eternit) and the social law division of the Cour de cassation of 28 February

2002[22] (ruling for the first time on the question of asbestos, a case again involving Eternit and various other companies linked to asbestos multinationals).

Until the late 1990s, liability of French employers under the general rules of tort law (supplementing the standard coverage by workers' compensation) was limited to narrowly defined exceptions ('faute inexcusable'), which covered less that 0.05 per cent of all occupational accidents and diseases. Both cases radically expanded the concept of 'faute inexcusable' and established a form of safety guarantee of employers, reversing the old rule/exception relationship between (limited) social law liability and (unlimited) tort liability. Employers, so runs the argument of the courts, could simply not have been unaware of the dangers of asbestos (a point fully corroborated by the American history on asbestos litigation). Liability insurers today thus view employers' liability as the biggest subclass of general liability in France (in terms of both premium volume and claims potential).[23]

Thirdly, careful observers of the German system would have discovered that in this system, the replacement of tort law by the workers' compensation scheme (*Gesetzliche Unfallversicherung*) is suspended whenever the employer is guilty of intent, recklessness, or gross negligence—*the latter in German case law often being found in cases which we would call 'negligence' in the absence of the notion of 'gross' negligence.*

Fourthly, one could argue that in the United States, state law often allows employers to stay outside workers' compensation schemes and, where this happens, tort law remains applicable. Students of the American system should also take into account the bad side effects that the workers' compensation schemes have had in practice, namely to drive plaintiffs' lawyers to find new additional defendants. Products liability litigation was thus often fed by and grew as a result of the difficulties that workers' compensation schemes caused to plaintiffs.

Finally, did Mr Weir look at the *levels* of compensation provided under the schemes in the various European legal systems? His statement in the CLJ is so short, one cannot tell. Such a study, however, shows how *distinctly* inferior they are to what can be obtained through general tort law. This is true for both Germany and France (where a finding of 'faute inexcusable' can more than double the amount of compensation awarded to asbestos victims by the workers' compensation scheme).[24]

All these important points are 'lost' (not in translation but) in abbreviated statements; and that 'loss' is neither mitigated nor, in this case, excused by Mr Weir's

---

[22] Société Eternit industries contre M-L X et CPAM de Valenciennes, *Les Petites Affiches*, no 62, 27 mars 2002, pp 15–19.

[23] On this, see Munich Re Group, *2nd, 6th and 7th International Liability Forum* (1999, 2002, and 2003 respectively) a typical thorough Germanic survey—unmatched, as far as we know, in this country.

[24] For a comparative survey of the relationship between general tort liability and social security systems (including workers' compensation), see U Magnus (ed), *The Impact of Social Security Law on Tort Law* (2003).

carefully qualifying words 'in almost none'. Worse still, they feed the insular attitudes of national lawyers and make them distrust the undoubted benefits that the study of foreign ideas can bring in its wake. We thus believe most strongly that condensed statements of this kind may produce a rhetorical effect, but that they rarely lead to an adequate understanding of foreign law.

This repetition of arguments made elsewhere (and known to Professor Stapleton) has one aim only. I wish to question Professor Stapleton's search for 'foils' or details before she makes up her mind on how important foreign law can be. If our statement was set aside because it is *wrong*, she should say this in detail. American judges—Justice Scalia for instance—have argued that comparative law allows a judge to cherry pick the statements which most suit his or her aim. Could it be that (subconsciously) she has chosen to pay much attention to the Weir statement because, philosophically, it is closer to the non-liability rule? Naturally, she is perfectly entitled to choose the policy view she thinks is right as well as the author who best serves her aims or is compatible with her frame of mind; but all that does not make her argument stronger; it merely makes it different.

The philosophical 'suspicion' Professor Stapleton nourishes towards foreign (i.e., non-Common law) systems surfaces in another part of her article where she gives the following reason why citing foreign law is an *unnecessary luxury*. Referring to the well-known cases of frustrated beneficiaries suing an attorney for negligently drafting wills, she writes:

Were the Supreme Court of California and the High Court of Australia in some sense wrong or at least unwise not to refer to the German concept of contract with protective benefit for a third party when they found that a claim lay in the tort of negligence when due to a lawyer's carelessness the intended beneficiary of a will failed to inherit?

As a comparative lawyer, I am anxious to encourage non-comparatists to show an interest in foreign law; but when they do show such an interest and criticize the possible use of foreign law, I wonder whether either I have not expressed myself sufficiently clearly *or* they have not read my entire text? Professor Stapleton is a meticulous scholar; yet she seems to me to have paid inadequate attention to the fact I stressed there that American and English law had the luxury of using tort law to solve this problem (but, because of the doctrine of consideration, did not have the same ease in using contract law) whereas our German colleagues were faced with the reverse difficulty: a rigid tort law but an expandable contract law. So, citing German law here was not—*prima facie*—necessary. She is right, but only partially right.

For *Lucas v Hamm*,[25] cited by Professor Stapleton as a tort case, also accepted, as a number of American jurisdictions have done,[26] that a contractual action was

---

[25] 56 Cal 2d 583, 364 P 2d 685 (1961).

[26] For further details, see my 'Understanding American Law by Looking at it Through Foreign Eyes: Towards a Wider Theory for the Study and use of Foreign Law', (2006) 81 Tulane Law Rev pp 123 ff.

also possible in that case. Professor Stapleton's article makes no mention of this though, of course, no one would deny that she is aware of this double option (available to American but not English law). No doubt she is also aware that the possibility of an additional contractual approach was first proposed by no less a judge than Benjamin Cardozo and was echoed in *Lucas*. If we stop here—and we will not—we have already made our student or general reader aware of the fact that the German contractual approach, so summarily dismissed by Professor Stapleton's above-cited statement, is possible in the United States as well. The question then arises, 'is it also preferable?' That is where comparison with German law can come into the picture and (a) make lawyers think, and (b) even provide solutions that are not open to the American tort approach. Professor Stapleton does not even reach this point of enquiry because she does not exploit the difference offered by German law in order to question the advantages of a rot-inspired solution. The first is essential to any teacher who believes that his duty in the classroom is to make his students think, reflect, and decide which rules of his law are necessary and which are the products of accidents of history. Professor Sir Otto Kahn-Freund built a whole and famous lecture[27] around them; and the contract/tort possibilities, available in American but not English law, emerge clearly from such a discussion of the laws of the two countries if done in logical juxtaposition.

Secondly and more importantly, the contractual approach has the potential advantage of designating the range of plaintiffs more accurately through the search of who was the intended beneficiary or, in Cardozo's better terms, who was the 'end and aim of the transaction'. Unlike the multiple, contradictory, and arguably repetitive multi-criteria test expounded first in the *Binkanja*,[28] the contract approach keeps things under control. Also relevant and unanswered in tort is the question whether the defendant-attorney can assert against the plaintiff-beneficiary any defences or limiting clauses he may have had in his contract with his client. If a pure tort approach is adopted, the answer must be 'no' because these clauses are *res inter alios acta*; if a contract approach is adopted, the answer is clearly 'yes'. Given that this issue is relevant not only in attorney malpractice cases but also in triangular building cases, the theoretical examination whether these actions should sound in contract or in tort becomes even more important.

The common-law way of avoiding this dilemma, by saying that this is an action shaped by the underlying contract, is fudging the issue; but if people wish to do things that way, I will accept it because in this context, this so-called tort way is exactly what the Germans have done through their 'contract with protective effects towards third party'. And there is, finally, a postscript in this diversion: the German *sui generis* type of contractual action is not, as the American would

---

[27] 'On Uses and Misuses of Comparative Law' (1974) 37 MLR pp 1 ff.
[28] 49 Cal 2d 647, 320 P 2d 16 (1958). This, does Professor Stapleton ask her students whether the six criteria are different or repetitive? Do they have to be applied cumulatively or selectively? And, finally, if one is enough which is the most important? The contractual approach, though not perfect, strikes me as much more focused.

call it, a contract in favour of third parties because it does not give the frustrated beneficiary plaintiff the right to sue the attorney and demand that he write the will properly and expeditiously. In short, once again, Professor Stapleton has conflated too many issues under one sentence which thus leaves the reader unsatisfied. Because it is short, it does just that; but what she says strikes me as superficial (if not wrong), though it may not be picked up easily by anyone reading her text who is not well versed in German law.

How to Teach Comparative Law

My disagreement with Professor Stapleton starts from her opening statement:

> In this article I argue that the noble cause of comparative law as an intellectual activity is undermined by those who focus on its forensic utility.

If that means treating the subject as an 'also ran' to Roman law, wherever it is still taught (which essentially excludes the USA and most Commonwealth countries), or in conjunction with subjects such as anthropology, then, in my view, it will sound the death knell of the subject. Those who write or teach in that way have seen class attendance and citation to their work diminish. This must be an indication, along with others, that if you really think the subject is a 'noble' one, you have to find a way to make it sound relevant to our times and keep it alive. I shall not return to details I have stressed elsewhere, not least because a new book of mine will soon appear entitled *Engaging with Foreign Law*, which will deal *in extenso* with the views put forward by Professor Stapleton's article. I note, however, three things coming, this time from France.

First, I note that those who have not seen the debates between Justice Breyer and (former) First President Guy Canivet about the need for comparative studies, the need for legal cooperation, and the observation by both justices that their systems are converging, will not be able to notice how unrepresentative Professor Stapleton's statement is of the views of certain important, senior, judges. Academics, especially those who live in cloisters, can discard these developments or downplay them; but politicians and practitioners must note them with care, not least because they would have been unthinkable five years ago.

Secondly, I note with pride (because I played an active part in the establishment of both) that the Cornell Law School has established a centre for Documentation of American Law *housed in the French Supreme Court*. The generous donation that made this possible was accepted because both Lord Phillips, at the time President of the EU Association of Chief Justices, and President Lamada stressed the perceived need for judges to study and understand each other's law. It goes without saying that the study they envisaged was not theoretical or academic but forensic and practical. In the same context, I note the most recent development of the establishment of a position of a 'law clerk' based at the French Constitutional

Court. This development was undertaken, once again, by Cornell, with the warm welcome of the President of that Court, M Jean-Louis Debré. Debré, in a joint press release with the Cornell Law School, stressed the need for such studies at a time of enhanced need for cooperation, understanding, and borrowing.

If one combines these moves with a score of others—some mentioned by Professor Stapleton in her article—one wonders who are the ones looking ahead? Surely, the answer is the pragmatists and not the theoreticians. For that, however, one must be be prepared to face the emerging new world with courage and not be terrified by language barriers.

Professor Stapleton seems to reserve this courage for those (advanced) common-law cultures that operate in the same language. She thus seems to me to place extraordinary (negative) importance on the relevance of the same language, forgetting, for instance, how the House of Lords misunderstood the importance of the *East River Steamship v Transamerica Delaval Inc*[29] case of the US Supreme Court as a case expressing American law; of course, it did not, but only resolved a dispute between two differing circuits. Lord Cook's subsequent poignant attack[30] on his brethren shows how language is not a bar from error, even at the level of the House of Lords, which (to borrow a well-known phrase) is infallible because it is final and not final because it is infallible.[31]

Of course, one could immediately counter-argue (and do so with some force) that if such errors can happen when the same language is involved, one shudders to think how much more can go wrong when non-English languages are brought into play. As a general proposition, that must be a valid one. Yet Professor Stapleton seems to underestimate how much globalization is bringing us closer to each other, and that will inevitably mean that a host of rules will have to be interpreted in a more or less harmonized way. This is not only the case where international conventions or treaties are adopted or formally ratified by many countries; it will also occur in the areas of human rights, where the view is gaining ground that at least some basic human rights are cut from the same cloth.

Again, I can foresee her reply (and that of Lord Hoffmann) invoking the difference accorded to speech rights in the USA, England, and the EU; and, no doubt, Lord Hoffmann will choose to express this difference (and preference) by invoking the historical pedigree of the Common law, which he would (implicitly, one might argue), also treat as superior to that of, say, Continental Europe or Strasbourg. That is all very good, at any rate for those who like judgments couched in terms of patriotism—another difference, by the way, between Goethe's promotion of German culture and his willingness to learn from others—but it ignores present realities. And the present realities in England are that we allow the police to detain people without charging them for 28 days; we are about to raise this to

---

[29] 476 US 858 (1986).
[30] Sir Robin Cooke 'An Impossible Distinction' (1991) 107 LQR 46 ff.
[31] *Brown v Allen* 344 US 443, 540 (1953) (per Mr Justice Jackson).

50 or so; we are about to exceed almost all the maxima allowed by other—'lesser' (?)—systems. And all this says nothing of the 'related' Anglo-American law which has tolerated Guantanamo, Abu Graib, rendition, and torture practices that the civilian systems do not sanction now, whatever they may have done three centuries ago. Thus, in my opinion, Lord Hoffmann's patriotic proclamation of the antiquity of the Common law sits uncomfortably with the poor record the UK has had at the Court of Strasbourg for violating the Convention it helped draft. To put it differently, though it is satisfying to claim that 'we were there first', it also matters and, perhaps, matters more, if we are still ahead. Some of us would argue that we are not.

Yet there is one more point that should be added here because it is close to Lord Hoffmann's and Professor Stapleton's way of thought, and this concerns the slowly emerging right of privacy in English law.

Is this not an area of the law where German law was ahead of English law (ahead in the sense that we are moving closer to them and away from the USA than they are moving closer to us)? Is this not an area where German law, casuistic and judge-made, is transplantable? And if the remaining objection is one of differing principle—Americans prefer speech to privacy—well, is that not a matter of preference, historical and personal, but not immutable once judges and litigants are made aware of the fact that there are alternatives? How best to make one thus aware of alternatives than to give them German cases, show them that they have not numbed free speech, and also show them that they have not opened the floodgates of litigation. If in the process of doing the above, jurists such as myself err on matters of methodology or detail, the likes of Professor Stapleton will help us correct our errors and refine our methods. But that is very different from the wider position she seems to be favouring, which is that anything beyond England, Australia, and maybe New Zealand is out of bounds because it is hardly likely to be useful and perhaps even likely to be dangerous. If that is the case, Professor Stapleton is not just condemning my writings; she is condemning the practice of the South African Constitutional Court, the Israeli Supreme Court, the Canadian Constitutional Court, and, to the extent that she is interested in it or aware of its activities, the German Constitutional Court, which has performed wonders in the area of human rights law comparable to the much more publicized German economic miracle of the 1950s.

Postscript: Back to Goethe

I began this chapter by citing some of Goethe's views about *Weltliteratur* and suggesting that they contained useful ideas for those interested in comparative methodology as well as managing the legal side of globalization. I now wish to end by looking at this same scholarship in an attempt to sketch an answer to two other questions. First, does the Goethian literature give any clues as to why some people remove, without thought or hesitation, foreign experiences from the bank of ideas available to them merely because they come from another culture or are expressed in another language? Secondly, how did the Goethian *œuvre* survive the 'deforming' effect of translation? Can this experience tell us anything about the 'dangers' of translation?

To answer the first question, attention must be paid to the time when the assessment was made. Literature scholars, like legal scholars commenting on German law, have varied in their reactions to Goethe from enthusiasm to derision and rejection but not at the same chronological time. Thus, a confident middle and late-Victorian England was enthusiastic about Goethe, as were its lawyers about their German counterparts; and in both cases, we are talking of some very great names. It is only as German industrial, political, and, finally, military power began to be seen as a menace that interest in things German waned, hitting a deep low from the First World War onwards.

Something not that different may be happening today as England tries to come to terms with the fact that it can only rival Germany if it is seen as an appendage of the USA whose size, might, and prestige it can try to appropriate by exploiting the highly misleading shibboleth of 'the special relationship' in order to enhance its *current* stature. Take that away, and all that the British—or, more accurately, the English—can do is invoke their values and perfection of days gone by in order to conceal the fact that in areas outside commercial law, they can no longer credibly claim primacy in doctrinal thinking (if indeed they ever did). Indeed, even in the area of commercial law, the claim does not stand up to scrutiny unless we talk of the Common law (in all its contemporary diversity) and not just English commercial or company law. How painfully true this is can only be realized once we absorb the fact that the precedential value of our highest court's decisions, though respected in the Commonwealth (but largely ignored in America), has diminished in recent years. This includes the area of human rights, where not only Strasbourg but also newer courts such as the Constitutional Courts of Germany and South Africa and the Supreme Courts of Israel and Canada are coming up with ideas that often reveal a foreign and not English ancestry. I confess some of Lord Hoffmann's 'patriotic' outbursts[32] to the effect that that 'we were there first' (and thus need no lessons from others) strike me as meaningless given that at present others have overtaken us. It must thus be galling to admit that, in the domain of human rights— privacy, death sentence, extradition, sexual identity, and equality—the German Constitutional Court has achieved for its citizens a human rights protection that rivals (by American admission) the protection given by US courts to its citizens, and exceeds ours.

---

[32] 'Freedom from arbitrary arrest and detention is a quintessentially British liberty, enjoyed by the inhabitants of this country when most of the population of Europe could be thrown into prison as the whim of their rulers.' *A & Ors v Secretary of State for the Home Dept*, [2004] UKHL 56, § 88.

Though much of what I said above is believed by many, it is, admittedly, controversial to proclaim it openly and boldly. But what is the benefit of boasting about our past if the primacy of yesterday is not acknowledged to continue today? Such comfort talk may be psychologically reassuring; but it is no more real than believing that Britannia (still) rules the waves. All this then boils down to mentality and individual psychology, which enables judicial and academic outlooks to remain in denial about the understanding that knowledge of other major and relevant cultures can bring.

Is this a caricature? If it is, it is only to a point. For those who condemn foreign law—German law, both private and public—on such spurious grounds that we do not have enough of it in the English language to use it even as a source of further thinking are avoiding it simply because they ignore it completely. Instead of curing their ignorance, they attempt to deny what exists or to describe it as useless.

That is precisely what happened to the Goethain *œuvre* when times made people suspicious towards Germany. The general climate affected the evaluation process of great artists, even when personally free of jingoism. Joyce thus condemned Goethe as 'a boring civil servant'[33] while the author of *Lady Chatterley's Lover* decried the total immorality of *Wilhelm Meister*. Why, then, should we be surprised if contemporary lawyers, less equipped in broadly European culture than Joyce or Lawrence, dismiss the German world as irrelevant, even at a time when we know (and so should they) that we are culturally no more self-sufficient than we are politically and economically?

On the second question, namely the dangers of being instructed (wrongly) by foreign writings accessed via translations, Goethe's work is, again, able to teach us much. For it has given rise to considerable *general* discussion as to whether poetry can ever be adequately rendered in another language. General but also very specific because Goethe's use of stress patterns, metrical constructions, and rhymes is so extremely rich—indeed he uses every metrical and strophic form imaginable in *Faust*, which, for this reason, has been aptly described as a 'metrical pandemonium'—that he poses enormous problems for his translators. As if all this were not enough, the text is extremely rich in philosophical meaning. On the Stapleton principle, why bother to translate it? After all, we have Shakespeare! Yet a quick search suggests that there exist something in the region of one hundred English translations of *Faust*, some, according to the experts, quite outstanding.

Lawyers, good at argument (and sophistry) may rush to make a distinction between translation of poetry and legal texts. In the light of the previous paragraph, the distinction should not be pursued without at the very least having studied the difficulties encountered in the Goethian translations and recalling that his translators were not only faced with complex metric and rhyming issues but also with complex ideas.

---

[33] Richard Ellmann, *James Joyce* (1959), 406.

In an excellent collection of essays published to celebrate Goethe's 250th birthday anniversary, Professor John R Williams has analyzed[34] eight famous lines from Faust (501–09), which contain a deep Goethian thought and a metaphor that has given rise to endless difficulties to critics and literary critics. For this text, he reproduces six well-known English translations and discusses their strong and weak points. He mentions what is lost in translation and what was gained by different approaches in tackling the text. The difficulties encountered are very similar to those my translators and I had to face when writing my books and building up my website of translated decisions. Anyone who reads these texts carefully can draw conclusions about different kinds of translation and what they aim to achieve. Professor John R Williams' conclusions are richer still because he adds a further dimension to the art of translating. He thus states:[35]

Translations can be illuminating, not only to readers without German, *but also to the student of German literature*, provided that they are used intelligently in conjunction with the original, not as mere cribs.

I venture to suggest that the same benefits can be derived by lawyers using available legal translations in the same manner and, when doing this, we shall discover the dangers of homonyms, the pitfalls of dictionary translations of legal concepts, and the need to replace them with their functional equivalents. In any event, given that in comparative law we are not looking for precedents but *stimuli* for further thought and, ideally, flashes of originality, the difficulty becomes a welcome intellectual challenge and the successful discovery of the right 'equivalent' a possible source for enrichment. Expressing one's single cultural background through the title of a Hollywood film looks like an easy opt-out from doing something that our times badly need.

---

[34] 'What Gets Lost? A Look at Some Recent English Translations of Goethe', in *Goethe and the English-Speaking World*. Essays from the Cambridge Symposium for His 250th Anniversary (N Boyle and J Guthrie eds, 2002) at pp 213 ff.

[35] 'What gets Lost? A Look at Some Recent English Translations of Goethe', in *Goethe and the English-Speaking World* (N Boyle and J Guthrie eds, 2002), 213, 225 (my emphasis).

5

On the Waning Magic of Territoriality in the Conflict of Laws

Horatia Muir Watt

Territory is increasingly losing significance in the contemporary understanding of state sovereignty, which is now perceived by international public lawyers as essentially decisional or 'functional'. In other words it is now linked to political and economic influence rather than to the ability to assert exclusive coercive power within geographical boundaries.[1] However, in the field of the conflict of laws, the reach of national laws, and of the power of the courts, largely perceived as coextensive with sovereignty, is still measured in terms of territory; extraterritoriality continues to be suspect in academic and judicial discourse, or at least exceptional and requiring specific justification as potentially overstepping the authorized reach of prescriptive sovereignty. This position is clearly difficult to correlate to the loss of relevance of territory in a global economy and certainly requires rethinking.[2] Indeed, the very shape of conflicts of laws today seems to indicate that territory is an increasingly insignificant factor in their occurrence, while territoriality loses ground as a guiding principle.[3] If the time has come, therefore, to revisit anew some of the traditional foundations of the conflict of laws,[4] there can hardly be a more appropriate place to start than this homage to

---

[1] Anne-Marie Slaughter, 'Sovereignty and Power in a Networked World Order', 40 Stanford Journ Internat'l Law (2004) 283.

[2] There have been notable attempts to rethink issues of private international law in a global, de-territorialized environment. See Paul Schiff Bermann, 'The Globalization of Jurisdiction', 151 U Pa L; Rev 311 (2002); Robert Wai, 'Transnational Liftoff and Juridical Touchdown: The Regulatory Function of Private International Law in a Global Age', 40 (2002) Columbia J Transnat'l L 209.

[3] Thus, conflicts of laws are now increasingly framed within the new problematic of inter-systemic competition. And whereas such competition was once based on physical cross-border mobility (territory), it has now been superseded by purely metaphorical exit from a given legal system, given the extraordinary leeway given to party autonomy, commercial arbitration, or choice of forum clauses, and the increasingly liberal regime under which foreign judgments and arbitral awards circulate internationally. See Horatia Muir Watt, 'Aspects économiques du droit international privé', RCADI t 307 (2004) (*Aspects économiques*), no 93 *et seq.*

[4] For far more ambitious attempts, see FA Mann, 'The doctrine of jurisdiction in international law', RCADI vol 111, 1964, then, 'The Doctrine of International Jurisdiction Revisited after Twenty Years', RCADI vol 186, 1984.

Lord Bingham of Cornhill, who authored the leading opinion in *Société Eram Shipping Co Ltd v Cie Internationale de navigation* (2004) 1 AC 260, at the centre of which was the issue of 'extraterritorial jurisdiction'.[5]

Société Eram raised the issue of the power of the English court to make a final third party debt order (formerly a garnishee order absolute) in respect of debts situate abroad (in this instance, in Hong Kong). Here, the judgment creditor was a Romanian shipping company and the debtors, a French company, and an individual resident of Hong Kong. The creditor obtained a judgment from the Commercial court of Brest with which the debtors refused to comply. Having registered the French judgment with a view to recognition and enforcement in England under the Civil Jurisdiction and Judgments Act 1982, the creditor applied to the High Court and obtained an interim third party order in respect of the debt owed to the judgment debtors by a third party (garnishee), a Hong Kong bank with a branch in London. Called upon to decide whether the interim order should be made absolute, the Commercial Court declined to do so and set it aside on the grounds, firstly, that under the conflict of laws principles in force in Hong Kong, the English order would not extinguish the debt of the third party, which was thereby exposed to the risk of having to pay twice if the judgment debtors subsequently brought suit against it in Hong Kong. Secondly, the court was reluctant to make an order affecting the conduct of foreigners outside its territorial jurisdiction. On appeal, however, the judgment was reversed; the risk of double payment could be discounted since a restitutionary remedy was available to the third party in Hong Kong. But the House of Lords held in turn that the English court had no power to make a final third party debt order in respect of debts situate abroad.

This conclusion is supported by at least three different strands of reasoning, which converge to inhibit the court's power to make such an order over assets (that is, the monies standing to the judgment debtors' credit in an account in the Hong Kong bank) situated abroad. The first is that the order represents an enforcement procedure which cannot take effect in a foreign territory. Thus, Lord Bingham analysed the third party debt order as a proprietary remedy which operates by way of attachment *in rem*; as such, it could not take effect on assets situated beyond the court's territorial jurisdiction to enforce. This is of course a traditional and apparently simple sovereignty argument generally attributed to public international law.[6] The reality is more complex however. If, as Lord Hoffman observes,[7] the rationale for the prohibition is that one sovereign state should not trespass on the authority of another by attempting to seize assets there, then it would seem that any form of judicial interference with foreign assets—or alternatively, foreign enforcement procedures—should be proscribed. However,

[5] § 22 et seq.
[6] See *The Lotus*, PCIJ 7 September 1927 series A no 10.
[7] §54.

as is very clear from the practice of worldwide freezing orders, it is the fact that, technically, the order operates directly on the assets by way of attachment that makes it unwarranted, and not the perception of such interference by the foreign sovereign; thus, nothing is thought to preclude English courts from granting *Mareva*-type injunctions against defendants extending to assets outside the jurisdiction.[8]

Secondly, Lord Bingham stated, in addition, that it is not open to the English court to make the order when the third party's debt is not discharged under the applicable law. This distinct line of argument is concerned with the risk of double payment to which the third party is exposed wherever, under the applicable law, it would still be liable to pay the judgment debtor despite having paid the sum owed into the hands of the judgment creditor. Grounded in private interest, the objective of avoiding contradictory obligations or injunctions (or double jeopardy) is a central and familiar consideration in contemporary private international law theory.[9] However, Lord Millett casts doubt on its relevance, at least in the context of the line of authority which, on the basis of sovereignty considerations, prevents the English court from ordering attachment of foreign assets.

> The reasoning in those cases does not support the gloss which has been put upon them. The judgments were directed to the territorial reach of the court's jurisdiction, and were founded on the rule of international law that a debt can be discharged only by the law of the place where it is recoverable. There was no attempt to evaluate the risk that the third party might be compelled to pay twice. It was enough that the English court could not itself protect the third party and discharge the debt by the force of its own order.[10]

Thirdly, under the heading 'extraterritorial jurisdiction', Lord Bingham discussed yet another line of authority relating to the exercise by the English court of powers affecting the conduct of foreigners outside its jurisdiction. Disconnected from any consideration of the nature of the powers the court is exercising, particularly in respect of whether its order operates *in rem* or *in personam*, this argument is best described as expressing 'positive' or 'prescriptive' comity,[11] insofar as it requires the English court to refrain from intruding on foreign interests abroad. Here, as the argument goes, it would be unseemly for the English court to regulate the actions of a Hong Kong bank in Hong Kong. The positive comity strand

[8] *Babanaft International Co SA v Bassatne* [1990] ch 13 per Kerr LJ 32.
[9] It frequently appears as the very justification for choice of law rules or at least their international unification (which is designed to enhance 'international harmony' by ensuring that one law—the one with the foreseeably closest connection to the legal relationship—will apply). Today, it legitimates the 'new unilateral method of recognition' which is beginning to emerge under the pressure of fundamental rights and which requires the recognizing state not to interfere with the continuity of a personal relationship protected by the European Convention on Human Rights, even if the conflicts rule of the forum dictates otherwise (see e.g., in the field of recognition of foreign adoptions, ECHR 28 June 2007, *Wagner*, invoking Arts 8 and 14).
[10] § 107.
[11] The expression appears in recent cases of the US Supreme Court: on its genesis, see *Aspects économiques*, no 270 *et seq.*

was developed in *Mackinnon v Donaldson, Lufkin and Jenrette Securities Corpn* (1986) Ch 482, in which the issue arose as to the power of the court to order the inspection of accounts or the production of books held by a bank in an office abroad. Here, Hoffman J held that:

> the court should not, save in exceptional circumstances, impose such a requirement upon a foreigner and, in particular a foreign bank. The principle is that a state should refrain from demanding obedience to its sovereign authority by foreigners in respect of their conduct outside the jurisdiction.

Interestingly, all three of the reasons thus put forward—sovereignty as an absolute limit to jurisdiction, private interest as fairness, or positive comity as noninterference—in order to justify the English court's duty of self-restraint, seem to be framed in some way or another in terms of territory—or, to put it another way, whatever the argument invoked, the fact that the assets were situate abroad appears to have been decisive. This is of course quite obvious in respect of territorial sovereignty, perceived as coextensive with the power to enforce (here by ordering a proprietary remedy over assets). Similarly, the issue of judicial regulation of foreign conduct abroad lies at the heart of the distinction between territoriality and extraterritoriality. But even the private interest argument, indifferent at first glance to geography or territorial sovereignty, is no exception, since the risk that the third party's debt might not be discharged despite payment in the hands of the judgment creditor only arises when the *lex sitae* is foreign, in other words, when the assets to be attached are physically located in a foreign jurisdiction. Thrice invoked in defining the reach of the powers of the English court, the relevance of the territorial principle appears hard to challenge, federating as it appears to do here both public and private interests.

A comparative perspective reveals, however, that this foundational distinction between territoriality and extraterritoriality in the conflict of laws is of far lesser significance outside the common law tradition. There is little reference to territory in civilian legal discourse. The explanation for this is historical. Civilian private international law is the legacy of the medieval statutists, whose reflection on the reach of various local laws in respect of persons, things, and obligations was unaffected by inhibiting considerations of territorial sovereignty because conflicts of laws emerged, prior to the concept of state, as among the 'community of laws' which coexisted within the sway of the Catholic Church. The authority of the Church was personal, irrespective of geographical location; local statutes were thus unashamedly exterritorial.[12] Unsurprisingly, it was only when the newly independent Dutch provinces sought to protect themselves from the influence of Spain and the Spanish Church, that personalism was dethroned by the idea that each local law was enclosed within the limits of the territory in which it was in force, so that no statute could have an extraterritorial reach other than through

---

[12] See Joel Paul, 'Comity in International Law', (1991) 32 Harv Int'l Law Rev 1.

the recognition of the 'fact' of rights acquired elsewhere under the appropriate territorial law. The doctrine of the Dutch School then crossed the Atlantic where it served the similar political ambitions of the newly independent American states, and then later returned to England, in the form of Dicey's vested rights. Today, at least until recently, English courts subscribed to a presumption of territoriality of English statutes in international conflicts,[13] and, still tending to consider the jurisdictional factor far more than the reach of the applicable law, continue largely to adhere to the idea that territory delimits the remedial powers of the court.

Territoriality equally weighs heavily still upon the conflict of laws in the United States. In federal cases, the international reach of regulatory or constitutional law has been similarly framed in terms of a presumption against extraterritoriality. International regulatory conflicts are, however, increasingly affranchised from the sway of territory by virtue of the functional 'effects' test,[14] the new limit to international subject-matter jurisdiction residing rather in the considerations of positive or prescriptive comity.[15] In interstate cases, the prevalence of territoriality in Beale's First Restatement of the Conflict of Laws was ultimately the main factor of the rise of functionalism, which sought to re-inject into an excessively mechanical methodology those policy considerations which were covered in continental Europe by Savigny's analysis of the nature of legal relationships.[16] But while governmental interests analysis has largely done away with territoriality in respect of interstate conflicts of laws in the field of tort and contract,[17] curiously, the Commerce Clause seems to limit the reach of regulatory statutes in terms of territoriality, without the respective scope between the two areas and methods being entirely clear. Thus for example, Commerce Clause issues involving regulation of activities over the internet, or pertaining to corporate takeover statutes, show that the courts have a distinct tendency to curb extraterritorial application of regulatory law.[18]

The significance thus given to territoriality as a guiding principle stands in stark contrast to the position within the civilian tradition, which has other foundational axes. Civilian conflict of laws is structured by categories which may in turn be of very little import, at least in this context, in common law systems. These are the private/public law distinction; the separation between the applicable law and the issue of jurisdiction; the difference between the court's jurisdictional

---

[13] Territoriality appears now rather a matter of construction: see *Office of Fair Trading v Lloyds TSB Bank plc* (2007) UKHL 48.

[14] On the progress of reasonableness, from *American Banana* 1909 to *Empagram* 2004, see *Aspects économiques*, no 266 *et seq*.

[15] The issue of the extraterritorial reach of constitutional law is not settled, however: see TB Wolff, 'The Thirteenth Amendment and Slavery in the Global Economy', 102 Colum LR 973.

[16] B Audit, 'Le caractère fonctionnel de la règle de conflit (Sur la crise des conflits de lois)', RCADI 1984, t186, 219 *et seq*.

[17] Not without resistance, however: see D Laycock, 'Equal Citizens of Equal and Territorial States: The Constitutional Foundations of the Conflict of Laws', 92 (1992) Colum LR 249.

[18] See *Aspects économiques*, no 193 *et seq*.

function and its powers of *imperium*. As long as the conflict is deemed to arise in a field labelled 'private law', then the reach of a statute can perfectly well be extra-territorial, as can be the judgment of the court, as long as it is exercising a purely jurisdictional function and not its powers to coerce or enforce. Indeed the term 'extraterritorial' is actually absent from both academic and judicial discourse in both contexts. For example, the 'lois de police' governed by Article 7 of the Rome Convention (now Article 9 Regulation), a permanent source of inter-cultural misunderstanding,[19] must apply whenever their policy so requires in functional terms, to the extent that they are 'private law'.[20] Extraterritoriality, in the sense of including foreign acts within the reach of the law of the forum, is no more an obstacle here than it is, say, in the field of tort, where foreign conduct is assessed according to rules of the forum and the defendant, a foreigner living abroad, is ordered to pay compensation. Article 4 of the Rome II Regulation on the law applicable to extra-contractual obligations allows just this. The reasons for the remarkable insignificance of territoriality in civilian conflict of laws reasoning today is threefold, a reverse mirror image of the various strands of reasoning to be found in Lord Bingham's opinion in *Société Eram*.

First, the reach of civil judgments, as long as they do not involve enforcement, raise no specific issues as far as territoriality is concerned. Of course, the remedial powers of the court are far weaker in the civilian tradition, so this difference is perhaps unsurprising. But, in respect of enforcement, the civilian position is, as a matter of principle, no different from the limit formulated by Lord Bingham in *Société Eram*. Both systems are confronted with the real theoretical difficulty of circumscribing enforcement or the court's *imperium*, which triggers the territorial principle. While attachment of assets such as moneys in a bank account abroad is clearly perceived as being beyond the powers of the English court, the position is less clear-cut in civilian systems, where ideas and judicial practice seems to have evolved considerably in recent years to allow courts to make various orders relating to assets abroad. In France, a recent decision of the Cour de cassation has been heralded as 'reversing the principle of territoriality of enforcement procedures'[21] by allowing the French court to seize assets in an account opened in the foreign branch of a French bank. Although of course this situation might be seen to be distinguishable from that in which the same court might order similar seizure of assets in a foreign bank with a home branch (as in *Société Eram*), this difference can only be relevant under the comity argument (since the degree of intrusion in foreign affairs is no doubt lesser, politically, when the account is held in the foreign

---

[19] To the extent that the terminology itself is uncertain. They are now called 'overriding manda-tory provisions' in Art 9 of the English text of the Rome I Regulation.

[20] However, the new public-law-orientation of Art 9 of the Rome I Regulation may actually eliminate this possibility altogether for the future, confining derogatory private laws within the scope of Arts 6 (protection of consumers) and 8 (protection of workers).

[21] Cass civ 2e, 14th February 2008, no 05.16.167, *Lamy Droit de l'exécution forcée*, May 2008, no 27, note Gilles Cuniberti.

branch of a domestic bank), but not under the enforcement argument, where the mere fact of the assets being situated abroad should suffice to justify a prohibition to attach them, regardless of the status of the bank account. Moreover, perhaps less spectacularly, when the court's function is merely to authorize the seizure of assets, without actually piloting acts of public officers on a foreign soil, it is considered as not having crossed the line.[22] Furthermore, provisional and protective measures may have extraterritorial effect even when they purport to freeze assets abroad temporarily—as the case law of the European Court of Justice relating to Article 24 of the Brussels Convention/31 of the Regulation clearly suggests.[23]

Secondly, when private interests are involved, territory has no particular incidence on determining the applicable law or the jurisdiction of the court—other than accidentally, when the connecting factor takes account of physical location. Often, in areas such as immovable property, considerations of physical location in the connecting factor were the expression of perceived requirements of sovereignty. However, contemporary understanding of conflicts in that area tends to lend little or no weight to sovereignty type arguments.[24] In fact, state power and its links with territory are now practically eliminated from private international legal discourse whenever private law is involved. This is an epistemological issue. Private law, deemed 'neutral' and as such uncontaminated by governmental interests and policies, is thereby presumed to be potentially universal, and will apply according to purely functional criteria (of which the 'principle of proximity' constitutes the most contemporary expression), indifferent to territory. By contrast, giving extraterritorial effect to foreign public law is far more problematic because its content is deemed to be political, and can therefore only take place incidentally. These principles are equally applicable to the reach of civil judgments rendered on the basis of the applicable law.

Finally, as far as regulating foreign conduct is concerned, the key of the difference may lie in the fact that, in civilian systems, there is no difference between personal and subject-matter jurisdiction. The latter distinction, which separates the determination of who can be brought before the court (personal jurisdiction) and the extent to which the court can claim to regulate the conduct of those persons (subject-matter jurisdiction) was imported to England from the Unites States by Hoffmann J in *Mackinnon v Donaldson Lufkin & Jenrette* 1986 Ch 482. Here, a US bank was subject to the English court's personal jurisdiction, but that court had no jurisdiction to regulate the conduct of that bank. From a civilian standpoint, by contrast, once personal jurisdiction (*compétence*) is established, on the basis of various connections with the parties or the situation (domicile, but also the place of the tort, the performance of the contract, etc), the court may

---

[22] See Cass Civ 1re, 22 June 1999, *Rev crit DIP* 2000.42, note Cuniberti, D.Aff, 2000.211, note D. Ammar.

[23] See ECJ *De Cavel* C-120/90; Denilauler C-125/79.

[24] For an excellent demonstration in the field of immovable property, see L d'Avout, 'Sur les solutions du conflit de lois en droit des biens, Economica' 2006, preface by H Synvet.

decide or indeed order without concern for territory. Personal jurisdiction will suffice to legitimate the court's regulatory powers, including in respect of foreigners abroad.[25]

While of course none of these differences mean that there is a right way or a wrong way of defining jurisdiction or the reach of the applicable law, they certainly draw attention to the fact that a principle such as territoriality must be envisaged with a certain degree of circumspection, since its weight may be entirely relative according to culture and historical context. Various strong indications of the relative explanatory power of territoriality emerge from the comparison above. Thus, from the perspective of comity, extraterritorial injunctive relief can be just as intrusive as the direct seizure of foreign assets. It is irrelevant from this standpoint whether a given measure purports technically to act *in rem* rather than *in personam*. The only possible significance that this distinction can and does have is to allow the courts to ignore the territoriality principle for enforcement purposes. However, this particular slight of the hand may in fact be becoming increasingly pointless, since the territoriality of enforcement is slowly eroding in its own right. Indeed, whereas enforcement is generally accepted as being confined to territory, there is very little agreement on what enforcement actually covers. In the Cour de cassation's 2008 decision cited above, the proprietary effects of the attachment (its 'effet attributif') apparently no longer comes within that category, and so may take effect extraterritorially. Another example of such uncertainty can be found in the neighbouring field of obtaining evidence abroad, where a foreign court's injunction for the production of documents in home territory may or may not be considered as a violation of local sovereignty in respect of enforcement according to the domestic conception of process (this will in turn depend on whether or not obtaining evidence for trial is a judicial monopoly).[26]

When, on the other hand, the real reasons for judicial self-restraint are examined, two in particular do indeed emerge, but neither are grounded on the territorial principle. Thus, first of all, if in certain cases, a court should refrain from regulating foreign conduct, it is not because such conduct takes place abroad but because self-restraint is warranted in cases in which there are close or closer connections to other states whose policies may be more directly affected: the American *Empagran* case[27] illustrates this consideration, in which the federal Supreme Court decided that the exercise of federal subject-matter jurisdiction (and application of the Sherman Act) to foreign claimants who had suffered, outside the Unites States, adverse effects of antitrust activities conducted in violation of the Sherman Act. Here, the positive comity argument resided not in the fact that the court should not regulate foreign conduct abroad—territory did

[25] This stops short, however, of allowing the court to regulate either through implementing public law or through recourse to enforcement procedures.
[26] On this issue, see L Collins, 'The Hague Evidence Convention and Discovery: A Serious Misunderstanding?', *Essays in International Litigation and the Conflict of Laws* (Oxford 1993), 289.
[27] *F Hoffman-La Roche Ltd v Empagran SA*, 124 S Ct 2359 L Ed 2d 226.

not come into it—but that the policies of various states such as Germany which were more closely concerned by the cartel would be frustrated by application of American law.[28]

Although unconnected to territory, the second most convincing reason for judicial self-restraint lies in the risk of double jeopardy. It is probably in fact the flip side of the previous non-interference argument, but formulated in terms of private interest. Courts are concerned to mitigate the risks of contradiction and incoherence affecting the regulation of private interests in a complex world. To do so, it may be necessary to refrain from making an order that could lead to double payment, or indeed limping personal relationships etc. Such restraint is of course only justified when the defendant (or the relationship) is clearly integrated in a foreign community, whose courts might therefore (if they have not done so already) legitimately claim to regulate. Deference to more closely connected regulators doubles over as a concern to avoid incoherence for the private actors involved. There is nothing particularly new in this conclusion as it stands, since this double public-private dimension has probably always been present, since their medieval beginnings, in all conflict of law theories, whose main source of variation has been to emphasize, alternately, one or the other. It merely emphasizes that territoriality is just one way of formulating whatever limits and values are considered essential in defining the reach of jurisdiction or statue in the conflict of laws. A rapidly evolving global context will no doubt gradually do away with the territorial nomenclature altogether, to leave room for other, more contemporary but equally value-laden categories, such as private or fundamental rights, or indeed positive comity and governmental interests.

---

[28] Particularly to the extent that American federal legislation would allow for (potentially ruinous) punitive damages under the Clayton Act, whereas Germany, although pursuing a similar anti-cartel policy, has a radically different clemency strategy.

6

Shielding the Rule of Law

Anne-Marie Slaughter

All persons and authorities within the state, whether public or private, should be bound by and entitled to the benefit of laws publicly and prospectively promulgated and publicly administered in the courts.

That is how Lord Bingham has defined the rule of law, with the addition of eight very valuable sub-rules elaborating on this basic precept.[1] In the same speech he recognized the tendency of the 'rule of law' to become a synonym for any legal system that works, or indeed for any political system that works.[2] That tendency is certainly true in international development and democracy promotion circles, where 'rule of law' becomes a mantra to achieve everything a country might need at a given moment: clean government, contract enforcement, or political liberty.

I do not choose to engage that debate in this essay. Let us instead accept Lord Bingham's definition of the rule of law and accept that it is an essential component of good governance and liberal democracy, even if we are still far from sure how to get from one to the other. My proposition is that for all the emphasis on building the rule of law in countries around the globe, far less attention is paid to the human dimension of building a legal community—the lawyers who argue cases and the judges who decide them. Those lawyers and judges create a working legal system through a willingness to bring cases and to decide them in a neutral, independent manner according to the law. That system then creates opportunities and shelter for many more lawyers advising corporate clients and making deals.

The role of lawyers and judges in building and defending the rule of law has come to the fore recently in what I have called Pakistan's 'black revolution,' the protests against Musharraf led by lawyers demanding the release of Chief Justice Chaudhry and the reinstatement of the Supreme Court and the higher judiciary.[3] They took to the streets in their black court suits, exchanging their briefcases

---

[1] Speech delivered by The Rt Hon Lord Bingham of Cornhill KG, House of Lords, 16 November 2006. Available at <http://www.cpl.law.cam.ac.uk/past_activities/the_rule_of_law_text_transcript.php> and published as T Bingham 'The Rule of Law' [2007] CLJ 67.

[2] Ibid.

[3] See Anne-Marie Slaughter, 'Pakistan's Black Revolution,' *The Guardian*, 25 April 2008.

for signs and occasionally stones. Looking on, many American lawyers recalled the brave judges and lawyers who helped lead the US civil rights movement. Alongside the lunch counter sit-ins and freedom marches were lawyers like the great Thurgood Marshall, chief legal strategist for the National Association for the Advancement of Colored People and the nation's first black Supreme Court justice. They brought case after case, gradually widening not only the ambit but also the enforcement of voting rights, educational access, and equal employment opportunities for African Americans.

These images present both lawyers and judges in their most heroic, idealistic light. It should take nothing away from that heroism and idealism to note that these ideals cloak an equally important set of interests. The Pakistani lawyers were safeguarding their livelihoods as much as their principles. Lawyers cannot practice without judges to hear their cases. And clients will not bring those cases unless they believe that the judges are independent enough to decide cases on the merits, rather than on the basis of bribes or political considerations. Once such a legal community has developed, lawyers, judges, and litigants all have a significant incentive to defend it. That community may have emerged around purely commercial cases, or land use cases, or environmental cases. But once it exists, it makes its living from the law. A government effort to destroy judicial independence, in this context, puts livelihoods as well as lives and liberties at stake.

A brief exploration of the role of lawyers in Kenya in the early 1990s and in China over the past decade, as well as the Pakistani experience, highlights the intertwining of material and moral factors in building communities of law. Their experiences are usefully contrasted with the experience of the European Court of Justice in building the EU legal system, which required showing many distinguished domestic lawyers in EU member countries that they and their clients could benefit by appealing to the ECJ to review questions of European law.[4] That example, in turn, brings us to the importance of having international institutions to help strengthen the domestic foundations of a rule of law system, of helping to create 'islands of legality' where judges and lawyers can both profit from their practice as a way of building bulwarks against more widespread attacks on the rule of law.[5]

Here too, Lord Bingham was predictably prescient. His eighth sub-rule of law states plainly: 'the existing principle of the rule of law requires compliance by the state with its obligations in international law.'[6] The task for international lawyers

---

[4] See Anne-Marie Burley and Walter Mattli, 'Europe before the Court: A Political Theory of Legal Integration,' *International Organization* 47 (Winter 1993), pp 41–76.

[5] An example from the Andean Community is discussed in Laurence R Helfer, Karen J Alter, and M Florencia Guerzovich, 'Islands of Effective International Adjudication: Constructing an Intellectual Property Rule of Law in the Andean Community,' forthcoming.

[6] Speech delivered by The Rt Hon Lord Bingham of Cornhill KG, House of Lords, 16 November 2006. Available at <http://www.cpl.law.cam.ac.uk/past_activities/the_rule_of_law_text_transcript.php>.

who would see the rule of law prevail in both the international and domestic spheres is to design international rules and institutions that look not only to relations between states, but also to relations between judges, lawyers, and litigants within them.

Pakistan

The lawyers marched, sang, danced, and exchanged their briefcases for signs and, occasionally, eggs and stones. As one Pakistani blogger wrote, 'They danced in black coats and they danced in black ties. Their black coats their Kalashnikovs and their black ties their bullets.' In a world of colour revolutions—the Orange Revolution in Ukraine, the Rose Revolution in Georgia—Pakistan's was clothed in the sober hues of the law.

The movement began in the spring of 2007 when General Perez Musharraf deposed the Chief Justice of the Pakistani Supreme Court, Justice Iftikhar Muhammad Chaudhry. But Chaudhry, whose defiant independence on the bench had made him a nuisance to the regime, proved even more of a problem off it. Touring the country and speaking to lawyers, Chaudhry soon became the focus of large-scale protest from the legal profession. Organizing through long-established channels, many of Pakistan's 80,000 lawyers began regular protests. When the Supreme Court went against the president and reinstated Chaudhry in July, credit rested as much with the advocates in the street as those in the courtroom.

In November, however, Musharraf effectively declared war on both the bar and the judiciary, dismissing all judges who refused to recognize his declaration of a state of emergency, purportedly aimed at protecting the nation from terrorists. The seven-member Supreme Court, still headed by Justice Chaudhry, countered by issuing an order barring the government from proclaiming emergency rule.

Musharraf dissolved the Supreme Court and the four High Courts, put Chaudhry and his entire family under house arrest, sealed the Supreme Court premises under army guard, and proceeded to arrest and detain all judges who refused to swear allegiance to the Provisional Constitutional Order upholding the state of emergency. The result was the detention of most of the senior judiciary, as well as bar association presidents across the country and all leading lawyers and human rights activists seeking to defend judicial independence.

But the protest movement could not be disposed of so easily. In the ensuing protests, lawyers were routinely beaten, gassed, brutalized, and humiliated. They stood with and for their judges, making it virtually impossible for judges willing to take Musharraf's oath of allegiance to operate. The lawyer's movement, it seems, drove a historic wedge between the judiciary and the executive. Their motivations were a powerful mix of high aspirations and self-interest; as one protest leader put it, 'How do you function as a lawyer when the law is what the general says it is?'[7]

Lawyers formed the vanguard of the diverse social movement that forced President Musharraf to accept a new coalition government in the March 2008 elections, a major blow to the General's authoritarian rule. However, at the time of writing the deeply divided coalition government has yet to meet the lawyers' demand to reinstate the judges banned by Musharraf—something it had promised to do upon taking power. After giving the government an ultimatum, the lawyers are again protesting in the streets, insisting that any government—military or civilian, authoritarian or elected—uphold the rule of law.

Kenya

Lawyers in Kenya have periodically played an active role in opposition to government corruption and human rights violations. During the colonial period Africans were largely denied access to legal education. Even following independence, African lawyers did not form a majority of the legal profession until the 1970s.[8] They gradually developed their own practice and took over the Law Society, the nation's premier professional association.

When Daniel arap Moi succeeded Jomo Kenyatta as President in 1978 he brought fresh hope that the country would leave behind the system of political patronage and corruption that had come to mar its first decades of independence. Indeed, amongst Moi's first acts was the release of political prisoners. For several years in the 1980s Kenya enjoyed a reputation of respect for the rule of law that set it apart from many of its neighbours.

However, as Moi's power began to be challenged by various social forces (including an attempted *coup d'etat* in 1982), he too resorted to anti-democratic and extra-legal tactics. In 1982 the government banned, *de facto*, all political parties except the ruling Kenya African National Union. It used violence, arbitrary arrest, and torture to silence political opposition throughout the 1980s, including the manipulation of all political cases to ensure that they were assigned to judges who favoured the government's position.[9] Individual Kenyan lawyers fought to protect civil liberties in various ways. However, according to one scholar and close observer of Kenyan politics, 'the profession itself only took a firm stand when the Law Society of Kenya opposed the 1986 constitutional amendments which gave the President more power over civil servants, and which destroyed judicial

---

[7] Babar Sattar, quoted by Amitabh Pal, 'Pakistan Lawyers' Movement Shows Global Reach of Nonviolence', *The Progressive*, 9 November 2007.

[8] Stanley D Ross, 'The Rule of Law and Lawyers in Kenya' *The Journal of Modern African Studies*, Vol 30, No 3 (Sept, 1992), pp 421–442.

[9] Ibid.

tenure'.[10] In 1988 the government took a step further and gave Moi additional authority over the selection of judges.

Once the profession as a whole was mobilized, the lawyers had an impact. In 1991 the Nairobi Law Monthly published a list of Moi's kinsmen who were, it alleged, involved in corruption of the highest level. Gitobu Imanyara, the journal's editor, was promptly arrested on sedition charges, a move that led to similar protests from the legal profession. The Law Society itself became such an important source of opposition that the government attempted to rig its elections on several occasions, sending armed police to bar troublesome members from meeting. One president of the Society, Paul Muite, was subject to extensive harassment and intimidation, including attempts to run his car off the road. Muite was a senior partner in Nairobi's oldest law firm run by Africans, and was described by the *New York Times* as 'a high-profile lawyer who combines a busy commercial practice with human rights work'.[11]

These efforts and international pressure eventually forced Moi to relinquish his hold on power and lead the country to multiparty elections in the 1990s. Since then, lawyers concerned with human rights and the rule of law have remained busy. During the most recent round of elections in December 2007, tribal violence re-emerged as a debilitating force in Kenyan politics. Groups like the Kenyan branch of the International Commission of Jurists have been active in documenting the human rights abuses that followed the elections and proposing electoral reforms that seek to prevent similar breakdowns in the future. The wider legal profession, however, as represented by institutions like the Law Society, has not been nearly as evident as they were when judicial independence was on the line.

This account is but a sketch of the complexities of Kenyan politics and the role of lawyers as opposition forces. Even a brief examination, however, suggests the rise of independent African lawyers able to earn their living from and take pride in a legal system with a judiciary that included some number of good, independent judges. When the integrity of the entire system was challenged, the lawyers mobilized. Their protests as a profession appear to have had more effect than the activism of individual civil rights lawyers, as heroic as they have been.

China

The profile of the legal system has increased steadily in the People's Republic of China since the initiation of reforms in the late 1970s. Indeed, one of the first post-Mao reforms was the reinstitution, in 1979, of the Ministry of Justice, which

---

[10] Ibid, p 435.
[11] Jane Perlez, 'In Kenya, the Lawyers Lead the Call for Freedom', *The New York Times*, 10 March 1991.

had been abolished in 1959. At that time there were only 200 law firms and 2,000 lawyers in the entirety of China. In 2001 this number grew to 8,300 firms and over 110,000 lawyers in the country.[12]

Much of the turn to law has been driven by rapid economic development and liberalization. As the Chinese economy grows ever more market-oriented, complex, and globalized, it requires a sophisticated legal architecture. The central government has invested significant resources in developing a modern commercial legal system conducive to rapid development.

However, these changes do not necessarily translate into increased legal protections for individual rights. Randall Peerenboom speaks of a 'two track model of legal reforms, with rapid development of commercial law combined with tight restrictions on the exercise of civil and political rights when it was deemed to threaten socio-political stability'.[13] While the central government has actively embraced the rule of law (*fazhi*) in its rhetoric, with Jiang Zemin calling for a socialist rule of law state (*shehui zhuyi fazhiguo*), some observers have suggested the government is moving more toward a 'rule *by* law' (*yifaweizhi*) system, where the government acts through law but is not ultimately bound by legal principles.[14]

For present purposes, however, what is most striking is the rapid growth of a commercial bar, in the sense both of a bar bringing commercial cases and a profession of lawyers making a living from litigation. According to Professor Jingwen Zhu, commercial practice has seen a steady expansion in litigation at the expense of mediation, while arbitration has remained stable.[15] Randall Peerenboom documents that of these cases, contract disputes are by far 'the major cause of litigation'. Further, and perhaps not surprisingly, he notes 'a strong correlation between litigation per capita and lawyers per capita'.[16]

Against this backdrop of steadily growing commercial practice, some of China's burgeoning legal professionals are pushing the rule of law far beyond the commercial realm. The environmental area has been particularly active. Civil society groups have used environmental laws to challenge large infrastructure projects the government believes are central to China's economic growth,

[12] Randall Peerenboom, 'Globalization, Path Dependency and the Limits of Law: Administrative Law Reform and the Rule of Law in the People's Republic of China', *Berkeley Journal of International Law*, Vol 19, 2001, p 191.

[13] Randall Peerenboom, 'Economic Development and the Development of the Legal Profession in China,' forthcoming. See also Peerenboom, Randall and Weitseng Chen 'Development of Rule of Law,' in L Diamond and B Gilley (eds), *Political Change in China and the Taiwan Experience* (Boulder, Co: Lynne Reinner, 2008).

[14] Randall Peerenboom, *China's Long March to the Rule of Law* (Cambridge: Cambridge University Press, 2002) asserts that the country is moving toward rule of law, a view that is questioned by other observers, e.g., Matthew C Stephenson, 'A Trojan Horse behind Chinese Walls? Problems and Prospects of U.S.-Sponsored "Rule of Law" Reform Projects in the People's Republic of China', UCLA Pacific Basin Law Journal, Vol 18, 2000.

[15] Zhu, Jingwen (ed), *Zhongguo falü fazhan baogao (1979–2004)* China Legal Development Report (1979–2004) (Beijing: People's University Press, 2007).

[16] Randall Peerenboom, 'Searching for political liberalism in all the wrong places: the legal profession in China as the leading edge of political reform,' forthcoming, pp 3–4.

perhaps most notably a plan to build a massive dam on the Nu River in Yunnan Province. Fearing the project would be forced through, like the Three Gorges Dam in neighbouring Sichuan, a coalition of local communities, environmental activists, and international groups demanded the government hold hearings and conduct impact studies as a recently enacted Chinese law requires. The government, to the surprise of many, has delayed the project in order that it be 'carefully discussed and decided on scientifically'.[17]

One group at the forefront of these efforts is the Beijing-based Centre for Legal Assistance to Victims of Pollution (CLAPV). While China's environmental laws are increasingly stringent, enforcement is difficult because the local officials charged with implementing pollution controls are also under enormous pressure to generate economic growth. CLAPV and organizations like it fill this enforcement gap by helping ordinary Chinese bring suit against lawbreakers. They have even won cases against the government, successfully suing the Beijing police department for non-enforcement of a noise-pollution complaint—not a major environmental victory, but an important precedent in a country where the government rarely loses in court. By selecting cases strategically, working closely with sympathetic governmental regulators, and training lawyers and judges, CLAPV has shown that civil society groups can use the law to effect change in ways the government may not have imagined.

Perhaps even more significant than the environmental work is the rural phenomenon Kevin O'Brien and Lianjiang Li term 'rightful resistance'.[18] Despite rapid urbanization, the majority of Chinese continue to live in small villages that have not shared in the growth and reform that has transformed China's cities. Corruption is a major problem in village, township, and county level governments, with local officials and developers often colluding for personal enrichment. Peasants have increasingly invoked the law in struggles against such official malfeasance, relying on 'barefoot lawyers' to bring suit in provincial courts. The central government, mindful of how local corruption can undermine its rule and lead to instability, has generally supported these cases. No one is certain how extensive the phenomenon of rightful resistance is, but anecdotal evidence suggests these types of cases have increased dramatically in recent years.

Last, some Chinese legal activists have engaged directly in human rights protection, though such work can be quite dangerous. One exceptional case is the blind lawyer Chen Guangcheng. When local officials in Chen's native Shandong province used extra-legal means such as forced abortions, violence, and compulsory sterilization to enforce population laws, Chen brought suit against them on behalf of local women. The government responded by putting Chen and his wife under de facto house arrest, 'disappearing' him for three months, and eventually

---

[17] Jim Yardley, 'Seeking a Public Voice on China's "Angry" River', *New York Times*, 26 December 2006.
[18] Kevin J O'Brien and Lianjiang Li, *Rightful Resistance in Rural China* (Cambridge: Cambridge University Press, 2006).

imprisoning him on trumped up charges of damaging property and disturbing traffic. While Chen did not win in court, his efforts earned him significant international attention—including a profile in *Time* and, in 2007, the prestigious Ramon Magsaysay Award—which in turn increased pressure on the central government to reign in local-level violators of human rights.

Scholars of the legal profession debate the extent to which 'cause lawyering' in China is actually bringing about significant political change.[19] I suggest, however, that the larger significance of a rising commercial bar is as a bulwark against future efforts by the Chinese government to restrict the independence of the judiciary. As political cases begin to succeed through the decisions of individual judges who dare to push the boundaries of 'acceptable decisions', a natural response is to try to clamp down on the judiciary and/or to alter judicial selection procedures, just as we saw in Pakistan. Yet the numbers above suggest that the space for the government to take such moves is narrowing as the numbers of lawyers with a direct stake in a competent independent judiciary rises. For now, the balance is maintained by a relatively clear line between 'commercial' and 'political' cases. Anti-corruption cases, however, as in Pakistan and to some extent in Kenya, are often the cases that blur that line, and unite the commercial and the cause lawyers in one body. Those are the conditions for a pinstripe revolution.

Europe

Scholars of the European Court of Justice (ECJ), including Walter Mattli and myself, argued throughout the 1990s that one of the principal ways that the Court built the EU legal system was by creating incentives for individual lawyers and their litigants to ask national courts to send questions of European law up to the ECJ for review. ECJ judges also actively courted national judges, through seminars and trips to Luxembourg to learn how the ECJ worked and to assess the quality of its judges.[20] As Karen Alter later demonstrated, various lower national

---

[19] Fu and Cullen distinguish three degrees of 'cause lawyers:' moderate, critical, and radical. While the first protect individual rights, they do so within the confines of the political system. The second category attempt to change the system but do not call for the end of one-party rule. The last group actively challenged the rule of the Chinese Communist party. Fu Hualing and Richard Cullen, '*Weiquan* (Rights Protection) Lawyering in an Authoritarian State: Toward Critical Lawyering,' 15 January 2008. Available from the Social Sciences Research Network at <http://papers.ssrn.com/sol3/papers.cfm?abstract_id=1083925>. See also Randall Peerenboom, 'Searching for political liberalism in all the wrong places: the legal profession in China as the leading edge of political reform?'

[20] See Anne-Marie Burley and Walter Mattli, 'Europe before the Court: A Political Theory of Legal Integration', *International Organization* 47 (Winter 1993), pp 41–76; JHH Weiler, 'A Quiet Revolution: The European Court of Justice and its Interlocutors', Comparative Political Studies, Vol 26, No 4, 510–534 (1994); Federico Mancini, 'The Making of a Constitution for Europe', Common Market Law Review 26 (Winter 1989).

courts found particular reasons to send cases to the ECJ to get a different and preferred answer than they might get from higher national courts.[21]

In 1997 Laurence Helfer and I published an article attempting to set forth a set of conditions for effective supranational adjudication.[22] We included a section on the European Court of Human Rights as well as the ECJ, and argued that the ability of individuals to bring cases to both courts as part of their supranational jurisdiction was a key ingredient of their success. 'Such jurisdiction,' we later wrote, 'allows individuals and other private actors to petition the tribunals directly. Tribunals with these wider access rules can penetrate the surface of the state and thereby influence, and be influenced by, domestic politics.'[23] We noted further, building on the European experience, that the most successful international tribunals are supported by larger professional communities of judges and also deliberately target domestic constituencies in their rulings who are likely to press for the enforcement of both national and international judicial decisions.[24]

The relevance of the European experience for lawyers and judges around the world concerns the ways in which supranational tribunals can help strengthen domestic 'communities of law' in specific practice areas (European law, human rights law) or more generally (backing domestic judges who are trying to maintain their independence and rule of law values). The history of the ECJ, in particular, demonstrates that a strong legal constituency can be built around what was originally a trade court, created to monitor trade liberalization among the states party to the original Treaty of Rome. Time will tell, but the adoption of the *acquis communautaire* by new EU member states with its hundreds of thousands of pages of legal rules creates countless new opportunities for the growth of the legal profession and the strengthening of the legal system in those new members, all of whom would be likely to be among the first to protest efforts to roll back the rule of law were their governments so inclined. As it happens, many of those European countries had already been through their own traumas regarding the abolition or perversion of liberal democratic government.

Latin America

As Laurence R Helfer, Karen J Alter, and M Florencia Guerzovich have noted, courts, including supranational ones, can help promote the rule of law by joining the higher purpose of respect for law with the interests of particular groups.[25] The

---

21 Karen Alter, *Establishing the Supremacy of European Law: The Making of an International Rule of Law in Europe* (Oxford: Oxford University Press, 2001).
22 Anne-Marie Slaughter and Laurence Helfer, 'Why States Create International Tribunals: A Response to Professors Posner and Yoo,' 93 California Law Review 899 (2005).
23 Ibid, p 10.   24 Ibid, pp 10–11.
25 Laurence R Helfer, Karen J Alter, and M Florencia Guerzovich, 'Islands of Effective International Adjudication: Constructing an Intellectual Property Rule of Law in the Andean Community', forthcoming.

case they cite is the Andean Tribunal of Justice's (ATJ) intellectual property jurisprudence. The AJT is not usually celebrated as a model of effective supranational adjudication; though highly active, it has generally found little scope or will to influence the policies of the nations under its jurisdiction. In the realm of intellectual property, however, it has created what the authors call a 'rule of law island' in a sea of weak judicial systems.[26] In this area the court's decisions effectively guide the jurisprudence of national courts, and demonstrate that supranational courts can serve to strengthen the rule of law even under adverse circumstances.

Helfer et al attribute this success to the way the ATJ has connected its intellectual property cases to the interests of other groups. First, intellectual property is often a valuable commodity for private parties, which take an interest in upholding the ATJ's decisions. Secondly, the ATJ has earned the support of domestic administrative agencies in Andean countries, who share a legal-rational view that makes them natural allies of the court. Thirdly, the ATJ has promoted Andean interpretations of intellectual property law that, typically less expansive than those promoted by foreign corporations, have proven useful to regional interests.[27]

Conclusion

The rule of law is a universal ideal, even if it means many different things to different people. Building the rule of law, however, requires more than idealism. Lawyers are likely to take to the media, to meeting rooms, and even to the streets to defend the rule of law if their livelihoods depend on a fair and independent judiciary. In such circumstances they may revere their judges, but they also need them.

It follows, if this insight holds, that building a strong legal profession around commercial litigation practice makes an important contribution to the rule of law. Human rights lawyers and constitutional litigators willing to try to hold the government directly to account for not living up to its word are the swords of a rule of law campaign, willing to risk their livelihoods and even their lives for the cause. A strong commercial bar, by contrast, is more likely to function as a shield, blocking government efforts to weaken or politicize an existing legal system.

International institutions can help create and strengthen that shield. International tribunals can decide the cases before them in ways that ensure not only that the law as they find and interpret it is upheld, but that also create incentives for individual litigants and their lawyers to use the courts to enforce their rights under the treaty or international instrument in question. This approach creates compliance constituencies for that treaty, but also creates broader

---

[26] Ibid, p 2.   [27] Ibid, p 3.

constituencies for regulating affairs through legal interpretation rather than political influence.

In the lecture referenced at the beginning of this essay, Lord Bingham concludes with a description of the rule of law as a fundamental bargain between 'the individual and the state', the 'governed and the governor', in which both accept constraints for the sake of the common interest and the common good.[28] Monitoring and enforcing this bargain, he reflects, makes judges and lawyers more than 'mere custodians of a body of arid prescriptive rules'. They are, 'with others, the guardians of an all but sacred flame which animates and enlightens the society in which we live'.[29] No lawyer could fail to feel a thrill at his words. But the fuel for that sacred flame is the crooked timber of human interest as well as the oxygen of human ideals.

[28] Speech delivered by The Rt Hon Lord Bingham of Cornhill KG, House of Lords, 16 November 2006. Available at <http://www.cpl.law.cam.ac.uk/past_activities/the_rule_of_law_text_transcript.php>.

[29] Ibid.

7

Benefits of Comparative Tort Reasoning: Lost in Translation

*Jane Stapleton**

Few Americans, even clever and ambitious ones feel a need to inform themselves about abroad.[1]

In this article I argue that the noble cause of comparative law as an intellectual activity is undermined by those who focus on its forensic utility. Specifically, I examine the practical value to practitioners and judges in the court of final appeal in an English-speaking jurisdiction of paying attention to how tort issues are analysed in a different jurisdiction when the subject-matter of the domestic case at hand does not positively require it. Part I argues that the benefits of resorting to 'comparative tort reasoning' vary greatly according to the focus of the legal analysis in issue: outcomes, arguments, principle, or conceptual arrangement; and that by far the greatest potential for enrichment is in the context of comparative tort argumentation. Part II addresses the study of law across not just jurisdictional but language barriers: 'comparative foreign-language law'. My argument here is that the practitioner and judge in an English-speaking jurisdiction should exercise extreme caution in using comparative materials from foreign language systems. Part III considers 'coordinated' tort materials: materials that seek to expound tort law across multiple intra-national tort jurisdictions, such as restatements of law by the American Law Institute, or across multiple national tort jurisdictions such as Helmut Koziol's 'Principles of European Tort Law' published in 2005.

* Thanks to Leslie Zines, John Blackie, Martin Hogg, Jens Scherpe, Reinhard Zimmermann, John Keeler, Peter Handford, Ronen Perry, Harold Luntz, Mads Andenas, and Peter Cane. This work was supported by a Discovery Grant from the Australian Research Council. This article first appeared in Vol 1 (Issue 3) of the on-line Journal of Tort Law in 2007.
[1] Max Hastings, Comment & Debate, Guardian (London), 4 May 2006, at 32.

Introduction

Every year I shuttle between three continents: perhaps this is why I have been asked to reflect on the value of 'comparative tort law'.[2] This is a huge and enriching field. A decade ago when I was writing about good faith in private law Reinhard Zimmermann kindly alerted me to how in the 1920s German courts had used the general provisions of the German Civil Code to engage in 'far-ranging juridical interventionism',[3] and how, starting in 1933, German courts exploited this technique to imbue the traditional German legal order with Nazi ideology. It was obvious that; unless I took a greater interest in comparative law and comparative legal history, I would not address critical issues nor face some of the most important dilemmas presented to a legal system; and that it is a poor legal education that does not expose students to the intellectual riches to be found in a contemplation of how other legal systems work across all levels—doctrinal, procedural, social, historical, and so on. Comparative tort law stretches from theoretical issues such as the possible relationship of a tort system's vitality and prominence with the relative paralysis of its legislature,[4] to procedural matters such as how facts are discovered and dealt with, to empirical issues such as how the judicial use of comparative tort reasoning has varied over time and between jurisdictions.[5] So I must be extremely selective.

The argument I will make in this paper is that the noble cause of comparative law as an intellectual activity is undermined by those who focus on its forensic utility. Specifically, I will examine the practical value to practitioners and judges in the court of final appeal in an English-speaking jurisdiction of paying attention to how tort issues are analyzed in a different jurisdiction when the subject matter of the domestic case at hand does not positively *require* it. Why would a tort lawyer in Kansas be interested in how tort law operates in England? Of what value might an appreciation of the tort case law of the Tasmanian Supreme Court be to a lawyer in New Zealand? What dangers lurk for the Canadian judge tempted to dip into the Scots law of delict?

---

[2] In this article, 'tort law' covers both judge-made common tort law as well as statutes in fields that were traditionally governed by the common law of torts (e.g., defamation statutes). By 'tort law,' I also mean 'the law of delict'.

[3] Reinhard Zimmermann, '"Was Heimat hieb, nun heibt es Holle" The Emigration of Lawyers from Hitler's Germany: Political Background, Legal Framework and Cultural Context', in *Jurists Uprooted: German-Speaking Émigré Lawyers in Twentieth-Century Britain* 1, 58 (Jack Beatson and Reinhard Zimmerman, eds, 2004).

[4] For a fine starting point containing more theoretical perspectives with an American focus see David Nelkin, 'Beyond Compare? Criticizing "The American Way of Law"', 28 Law & Soc Inquiry 799 (2003).

[5] For an outstanding short account in a much-to-be-recommended collection on this topic see H Patrick Glenn, 'Comparative Legal Reasoning and the Courts: A View from the Americas', in *Comparative Law before the Courts*, 217 (Guy Cavinet, Mads Andenas, and Duncan Fairgrieve eds, 2004), as well the outstanding essays in *The Oxford Handbook of Comparative Law* (Mathias Reimann and Reinhard Zimmerman, eds, 2006).

The paper is divided into three Parts. Part I looks at possible benefits that a practitioner or judge in an English-speaking jurisdiction might find in considering tort materials from other English-speaking jurisdictions. I will argue that the benefits of resorting to 'comparative tort reasoning' vary greatly according to the focus of the legal analysis in issue: outcomes; arguments; principle; or conceptual arrangement. For example, an awareness of the outcomes of similar fact situations in other jurisdictions has pragmatic value in relation to forum shopping. When the focus is on legal argument, a grasp of comparative materials yields its richest intellectual rewards for the practitioner and judge because 'it is arguments that influence decisions'.[6] What about where the focus is on principle, that is where the balance of competing arguments has crystallized into legal principle? Because that balance is contingent on cultural context, the value in considering which legal principles have been accepted in other jurisdictions is also contingent: for example, in the US it seems to be a principle that a defendant in the tort of deceit cannot be liable for coincidental consequences; but that principle is rejected in England. Finally, where the focus is on conceptual arrangements, that is on how principles are organized, there is typically very little utility in considering the structures of other systems.

In short, I argue that tort materials from other English-language jurisdictions may be of value in the work of the domestic practitioner and judge but that by far the potential for enrichment is greatest in the context of comparative tort *argumentation*. Moreover, when a comparativist asserts that 'comparative law and methodology . . . should be used by all [legal academics] when teaching their own topics of national law',[7] we need not be dismayed. In all English-speaking jurisdictions tort practitioners and judges routinely *do* use comparative materials, that is material from outside their domestic jurisdiction,[8] most notably the fundamental concerns and arguments that courts in other English-speaking jurisdictions have thought of legitimate weight. California cites concerns and arguments from New Jersey judgments, Australia cites Canada, England cites New Zealand, and we all cite Scottish law on a daily basis![9] Indeed, cross-jurisdictional comparison is central to legal training in the US where the typical torts teacher uses far more out-of-state material concerning legal arguments than in-state. Among English-speaking jurisdictions the real question, therefore, is simply whether the future resort to even more comparative material would be worth the candle.

But in Part II, I address a very strange phenomenon about which we must not be coy: when many people refer to 'comparative law' they mean the study of law across, not just jurisdictional but language barriers. I will call this 'comparative foreign-language law'. There are a number of reasons why comparative law has been seen as a cross-language study. One has been the popularity in

---

6 *White v Jones*, [1993] WLR (AC) (Civ Div) (UK) per Steyn LJ.
7 Basil S Markesinis, *Foreign Law and Comparative Methodology: A Subject and a Thesis* (1997) 2.
8 E.g., see the immense influence of the great comparative torts text John G Fleming, *The Law of Torts* (9th edn 1998).
9 Namely, *Donoghue v Stevenson* [1932] AC 562 (HL) (appeal taken from Scot)(UK).

recent decades of the search for the 'common core of legal solutions throughout the world... [wherein] the focus has been on the similarity of practical results'.[10] This, of course, required comparison across language barriers. There has been a lot of abstract writing on the 'methodology' of comparative foreign-language law which I will not address since much of it seems tediously to state the obvious: the most effective comparative method is to compare the legal treatment of factually equivalent situations; always read foreign law in its full social, legal, cultural, political, and economic context; beware assuming that the law in the books coincides with the law in action and so on. My argument here is that the practitioner and judge in an English-speaking jurisdiction should, for a variety of reasons, exercise extreme caution in using comparative materials from foreign-language systems.

Finally, in Part III, I turn to a body of material I call 'coordinated' tort materials: materials that seek to expound tort law across multiple intra-national tort jurisdictions, such as restatements of law by the American Law Institute, or across multiple national tort jurisdictions such as Helmut Koziol's 'Principles of European Tort Law' published in 2005.

I. Benefits of Comparative Tort Materials from English-Language Jurisdictions

A. Basic contributions

So what can a comparison between the tort systems of English-speaking jurisdictions bring us? There is no doubt that tort tourism can be an entertaining end in itself. It can simply be very amusing to appreciate the quaint doings of foreigners.[11]

---

[10] Erik Jayme, *Multicultural Society and Private Law German Experiences* (1999) 9–10. Jayme notes reasons for this such as 'the needs for collaboration in international commerce, the idea of an international community and the anthropological view of human beings as having equal needs'.

[11] We can learn, e.g.: that in some cultures a clan has standing to sue for damages but not in Scotland; that New Zealanders cannot sue each other in tort for accidental personal injuries; that Australia no longer has a *Rylands v Fletcher* rule; that Canadians no longer have a tort of breach of statutory duty; that breach of fiduciary duty is a tort in the US; that in the Scots law of defamation no distinction is made between written and oral communication, nor does the defamatory statement have to be communicated to a third party; that in the US there are native American legal systems and courts such as the Navajo Supreme Court which resolve cases on principles that include specifically Navajo norms; that there is at least one English court in technical existence that is, arguably, a civil law court and can proceed only in accord with that law (from 1737 the High Court of Chivalry lay dormant until reconvened in 1954 for *Manchester Corp v Manchester Palace of Varieties Ltd* [1955] 1 All ER 387 (C Chiv) (UK)); that in Scotland, Shetland and Orkney still retain Udal law derived from the Norse law brought by the Vikings in about 800AD (for a modern acknowledgement of Udal law see definition of 'owner' in § 2(1) of the Housing Benefit Regulations 2006 No 213 (United Kingdom); major differences between Udal and Scots law include shore ownership rights, important for pipelines and cables); that most US employees cannot sue their employer in tort for negligently inflicted injuries; that judgments of the Judicial Committee of the House of Lords are never joint because, technically, they are speeches to the House of Lords Chamber of the Westminster Parliament; and that until the 1960s there was only one judgment issued by the Judicial Committee of the Privy Council because, technically, it is the 'advice' of the Privy Councillors to the Queen (on the members' experience of their unanimity rule see Alan Paterson, *The Law Lords* (1982) 98–99.

Beyond mere intellectual curiosity, we should ask in what general ways might an appreciation of the tort systems of other English-speaking jurisdictions illuminate the work done by domestic lawyers? The diversity of experience suggests a number of ways. First, it is often the case that fact situations have been the subject of tort litigation and given rise to the testing of doctrine in other jurisdictions but not yet locally. A knowledge of such phenomena arms domestic lawyers with some very effective tools with which to examine their domestic tort doctrine and may lead to the conclusion that there is a gap, ambiguity, or incoherence in such doctrine.

For example,[12] the Canadian case of *London Drugs Ltd v Kuehne and Nagle International Ltd*[13] highlighted the fact that no common law system has yet formulated a general approach to the question of where, when, and why a defendant to a tort claim can rely on a contractual term, such as an exclusion clause, in a contract which is not between the plaintiff and that defendant. Another example is recovery in negligence for pure economic loss. While this is a backwater in US tort law, it has generated a vast case law in non-US common law systems. An appreciation of the factual scenarios of these cases and how courts dealt with them would definitely enhance the perspective of US tort lawyers. As Justice Posner notes, 'just as our states are laboratories for social experiments from which other states and the federal government can learn, so are foreign nations laboratories from whose legal experiments we can learn'.[14]

Of the other general ways in which comparative tort law might assist domestic lawyers, perhaps the most important is that it helps remind domestic lawyers and courts that the local results of cases, the arguments used to support them, and the conceptual arrangements of principles are not some unique and universal order ordained by inexorable 'logic' or legal 'science'. They are culturally and temporally contingent and therefore may be open to forensic re-evaluation.

Now, if we look in detail at how comparative tort law might illuminate the work of domestic lawyers, and so obtain an idea of what future research might be interesting, it is helpful to deal separately with the different types of focus such lawyers may adopt.

---

[12] Yet another example involves the issue of a pharmaceutical manufacturer's tort liability for unforeseeable side effects of prescription drugs, which the Thalidomide disaster squarely presented to the tort systems of a number of English-speaking jurisdictions, notably the UK and Australia in the 1960s. Had US products liability lawyers been sufficiently sensitive to this issue, they may have more quickly realized that in tort claims against drug manufacturers for unforeseeable risks, despite deploying the rhetoric of 'strict' liability found in § 402A of the Second Restatement of Torts, US courts were scarcely ever prepared to impose such tort liability: a situation that became patent after the hostile furore that followed the extraordinary imposition of such strict liability in *Beshada v Johns-Manville Products Corp*, 447 A2d 539 (1982). Conversely, tort lawyers in English-speaking jurisdictions that have enacted the 1985 European Directive on product liability (namely, England, Scotland, and Eire) or clones of it (such as Australia) would today do well to test their interpretation of that Directive with the type of claim known as the 'classic' US products liability case: a crashworthiness claim involving the adequacy of the strength of a car's side panels, truck axle, chair, and so on.

[13] *London Drugs Ltd v Kuehne and Nagle Int'l Ltd* [1992] 97 DLR 261 (Can).

[14] Richard Posner, 'No Thanks, We Already Have Our Own Laws', Leg Aff, July–Aug 2004, <http://www.legalaffairs.org/issues/July-August-2004/feature_posner_julaug04.msp>.

B. A focus on outcomes

There is no doubt that parties attempt forum-shopping.[15] It is important to note why this can happen even within a federal system such as Australia where there is only one final court of appeal on matters of judge-made 'common law': it is because the states have legislative capacity in areas in which the common law of torts has been active. For example, until 2006 Australian states had divergent statutes with respect to liability in defamation. So while Australia has a unified 'common law', its 'tort law' may diverge on a particular issue:[16] hence forum shopping can be attractive.[17]

Forum shopping arises where more favourable outcomes may be produced because of differences in doctrine,[18] procedural rules,[19] or other aspects of the

---

[15] See e.g., *BHP Billiton Limited v Schultz* (2004) CLR 61 (Austl) (South Australian asbestosis plaintiff seeking to sue employer and asbestos suppliers in New South Wales for, inter alia, negligence and breach of statutory duty).

[16] See Leslie Zines, 'The Common Law in Australia: Its Nature and Constitutional Significance', 32 Fed Law Rev 337; Francis Trindade and Peter Cane, *The Law of Torts in Australia* (4th edn 2006) ch 7.

[17] Conversely, in the US, the 'common law' element of tort law is a state matter but certain aspects of 'tort law' may be unified by constitutional principles laid down by the Supreme Court and federal legislation, either by direct action or pre-emption. See Samuel Issacharoff and Catherine Sharkey, 'Backdoor Federalism: Grappling with the "Risk to the Rest of the Country"', 53 UCLA L Rev 6 (2006). Compare § 23 of the Marriage Amendment Act (Comm of Austl No 209, 1976) abolishing the action for breach of promise.

[18] E.g., the unique trust law of the Cayman Islands provides tight asset protection that in combination with strict bank secrecy and lack of local income taxes has made this jurisdiction one of the most popular for offshore trusts. Recent examples of forum-shopping in the field of defamation include *Dow Jones and Co Inc v Gutnick* (2002) 210 CLR 575 which held that words published on the Internet overseas, that are accessible in Australia, can amount to a defamation committed in Australia; and *Berezovsky v Michaels* [2000] 1 WLR 1004 (HL) (UK) where the plaintiff, a Russian, brought a libel action in England in respect to an article in the magazine Forbes 98.9% of the issue in question was sold in the USA, Canada, or to US forces, while the English circulation was only about 2,000 copies. Lord Hoffmann noted:

'... the notion that Mr Berezovsky, a man of enormous wealth, wants to sue in England in order to secure the most precise determination of the damages appropriate to compensate him for being lowered in the esteem of persons in this country who have heard of him is something which would be taken seriously only by a lawyer. An English award of damages would probably not even be enforceable against the defendants in the United States... The common sense of the matter is that he wants the verdict of an English court that he has been acquitted of the allegations in the article, for use wherever in the world his business may take him. He does not want to sue in the United States because he considers that *New York Times v Sullivan*, 376 US 254 (1964) makes it too likely that he will lose. He does not want to sue in Russia for the unusual reason that other people might think it was too likely that he would win. He says that success in the Russian courts would not be adequate to vindicate his reputation because it might be attributed to his corrupt influence over the Russian judiciary... The plaintiffs are forum shoppers in the most literal sense. They have weighed up the advantages to them of the various jurisdictions that might be available and decided that England is the best place in which to vindicate their international reputations. They want English law, English judicial integrity and the international publicity which would attend success in an English libel action.' (1023–24)

[19] On the importance of the distinction for forum-shoppers see *Harding v Wealands* [2006] UKHL 32 (UK).

legal environment. Other factors may be the attraction of a more specialized judiciary,[20] more compassionate juries and trial judges, or better access to the courts and so on. The greater a lawyer's awareness of the pattern of outcomes in other jurisdictions and the reasons for them, the better will be his advice to his client and the arguments on forum that he can put to the relevant court. Thus, for example, lawyers for a group of more than 3,000 South African asbestos victims, most black and of modest means, overcame a claim of *forum non conveniens* before the House of Lords by, *inter alia*, bringing extensive evidence of the unavailability of funding for their claims in South Africa and the absence, as yet, of developed procedures for handling group actions there.[21] Similarly, settlements and bankruptcy reorganization plans that seek to cover plaintiffs from different jurisdictions depend on knowledge about the varying domestic doctrinal and process environments as they actually play out.[22]

Another potential role for an appreciation of outcomes in tort cases in other jurisdictions is as a 'good example or terrible warning'. For example, based on cogent analysis the Australian High Court has held that the builder of a dwelling may owe a duty of care in the tort of negligence to a remote purchaser.[23] This result contrasts starkly with the earlier refusal of such a duty by the House of Lords[24] and may usefully remind litigants in Britain that the exposition of this refusal by the Lords was extremely weakly reasoned. My argument here is not that the mere fact of the Australian decision provides a reason to doubt the Lords decision: we should reject justice by head-count. My point is that it might remind us that the reasoning of the Lords does not withstand scrutiny and that their refusal to recognize a duty *may* therefore be vulnerable to attack.

Outcomes in other jurisdictions may also serve as terrible warnings. For example, 'no one can pretend that the existing law [on recovery in negligence for nervous shock] . . . is founded upon principle'.[25] In Britain, for example, the development of the 'bright-line' rules in this field arrived at the bizarre point where they would prevent recovery by a mother who suffers psychiatric injury after finding her child's mangled body in a mortuary on the grotesque basis that

---

[20] As we can see in the case of US corporate bankruptcy law, e.g., Marcus Cole, '"Delaware is not a State": Are We Witnessing Jurisdictional Competition in Bankruptcy?' 55 Vand L Rev 1845, 1863–64 (2002).

[21] *Lubbe v Cape Plc* [2000] UKHL 41; [2000] 1 WLR 1545 (UK).

[22] See H Luntz, 'Heart Valves, Class Actions and Remedies: Lessons for Australia?', in *Torts in the Nineties* (N Mullany ed, 1997) 72, and Hans W Baade, 'Foreign Oil Disaster Litigation Prospects in the United States and the "Mid-Atlantic Settlement Formula", 7 J Energy and Nat Res L 125 (1989).

[23] *Bryan v Maloney* (1995) 182 CLR 609 (Austl). But see *Woolcock Street Investments Pty Ltd v CDG Pty Ltd* (2004) HCA 16, 205 ALR 522 (Austl).

[24] *D and F Estates v Church Commissioners* (1989) AC 177 (Austl) on which see Jane Stapleton, 'Duty of Care Factors: a Selection from the Judicial Menus', in *The Law of Obligations: Essays in Honour of John Fleming* (Peter Cane and Jane Stapleton eds, 1998) 58, 65.

[25] *White v Chief Constable of South Yorkshire* [1998] UKHL 45, [1999] 2 AC 455, 511 (per Lord Hoffmann)(UK).

'her child's blood [was] too dry to found an action'.[26] Once one jurisdiction has held 'thus far and no further',[27] as the House of Lords has done in this area, this might remind other jurisdictions that it is both legitimate and sensible to abandon hope that the common law could ever lay down coherent and respectable boundaries to such liability, or confirm a jurisdiction in its refusal to allow any such claim.[28]

On the other hand, it seems clear, at least to me, that the *mere* fact that a domestic lawyer can show that a party in a comparable suit prevailed in another jurisdiction provides no weight for his client's claim: again, law should not turn on head counts (see below).

C. A focus on doctrine

1. Outline

In standard judicial analysis in tort a consideration of various 'legal concerns',[29] often in tension, and the arguments based on them lead to the formulation of 'principles' which are then arranged in a 'conceptual framework'. For example, most common law jurisdictions have crystallized a principle that a person is not liable for failing to rescue a stranger: here the legal concern with the victim's interest in his person is judged to be outweighed by other legal concerns such as the libertarian concern that individuals should be free to do whatever they wish with their person or property, as long as they do not infringe the same liberty of others.[30] In most common law jurisdictions this principle is lodged within the conceptual device known as 'duty': there is no duty in the tort of negligence to rescue a stranger. At each of these three levels of doctrinal focus—arguments, principles, and conceptual arrangement—an appreciation of comparative tort may be illuminating.

2. Concerns and arguments

Let me first take concerns and the arguments based on them. Mainstream domestic legal analysis seeks to excavate the legal concerns embedded in, perhaps masked by, the legal reasoning published by courts. As Justice Posner has

---

[26] Jane Stapleton, 'In Restraint of Tort', in *The Frontiers of Liability* (P Birks ed, 1994), Vol 2, 83, 84.

[27] *White v Chief Constable* [1999] 2 AC 455, 500 (per Lord Steyn).

[28] US jurisdictions that have taken a hard line on such claims include Arkansas, Georgia, Kentucky, and Oregon: see Nicholas Mullany, Peter Handford and Philip Mitchell, *Tort Liability for Psychiatric Damage* (2nd edn 2006), ¶¶ 1.250–1.280, ch 1, n 143; and DJ Gilsinger, 89 ALR 5th 255.

[29] The term 'policy' is too limiting: see Jane Stapleton, 'Legal Cause: Cause-in-Fact and the Scope of Liability for Consequences', 54 Vand L Rev 941, 985–86 (2001).

[30] There are also economic concerns that support the rule: see Alon Harel and Assaf Jacob, 'An Economic Rationale for the Legal Treatment of Omissions in Tort Law: The Principle of Salience', in Vol 3, *Theoretical Inquiries in Law* (Online Edition): No 2, Art 4 (2002).

acknowledged,[31] the form and substance of legal concerns and arguments excavated from judgments and tort discourse in other jurisdictions can also be valuable to the domestic lawyer by widening his palette of ideas. This can be true even where those judgments originate from a tort system with different general principles arranged within a different conceptual superstructure. It may be that a very specific legal concern is raised in a foreign case but has a parallel application domestically: a particularly important example here being the concern that tort rules should not tend positively to encourage abortion.[32]

A more general example[33] of an emerging dual-concern for many of our systems is whether the tort law of our domestic communities should respond as those communities become increasingly multi-cultural, and if so what form that response should take.[34] As Erik Jayme asserts, 'difference as such has emerged as a value in itself',[35] and this concern with multiculturalism presents many diverse challenges to tort law. The statement that X was seen drinking beer would not be shameful or 'defamatory' in most Anglo-Saxon Christian circles; but how is

---

[31] Posner, n 14 above, for the proposition that it is entirely appropriate for a US court 'to cite a decision by a foreign or international court not as a precedent but merely because it contains persuasive reasoning (a source or informational citation), just as one might cite a treatise or a law review article because it was persuasive, not because it was considered to have any force as precedent or any authority.'

[32] See the decisions of the Court of Appeal of England and Wales in *Emeh v Kensington AHA*, [1985] QB 1012, 1021 (UK) (where the concern weighed in favour of the recognition of a duty of care in the context of a birth following a negligent sterilization) *and* of the Supreme Court of Canada in *Winnipeg Child and Family Services (Northwest Area) v G (DF)* [1997] 152 DLR 4th 193, ¶ 44 (where the concern weighed against recognizing the right of a foetus to an order detaining its pregnant mother whose addiction to glue sniffing threatened to damage its developing nervous system) both cited by the High Court of Australia in *Harriton v Stephens* (2006) HCA 15, ¶¶ 73, 133, and 248.

[33] Legal concerns also arise in relation to how legal reasoning should be presented. Take the unanimous House of Lords decision in *Fairchild v Glenhaven Funeral Services Limited* [2003] 1 AC 32 (UK), on which see Jane Stapleton, 'Lords a'leaping Evidentiary Gaps', 10 Torts Law J 276 (2002). This allowed claimants, who had contracted mesothelioma after several parties had wrongly exposed them to asbestos, to recover from each even though it was not possible to prove that the exposure of any particular defendant was a factual cause of the cancer because of medical ignorance of the aetiology of that disease. All but one of the Law Lords were concerned to avoid using legal fictions when presenting the new rule being created. They explicitly refused to present this new rule in terms of the legal fiction that 'on the evidence' factual causation was sufficiently established. An awareness of these *Fairchild* judgments should galvanize American tort lawyers to appreciate that, although it has gone virtually unremarked, most US asbestos cases have so far proceeded on the basis of legal fictions. See Jane Stapleton, 'Two Causal Fictions at the Heart of US Asbestos Doctrine', 122 Law Q Rev 189 (2006). Similarly, Australian courts which have so far sanguinely allowed such mesothelioma claims must now accept that in doing so they have resorted to the very legal fiction wisely deprecated by the Lords.

[34] For a useful introduction to many general issues, see Alison Dundes Rentelin, *The Cultural Defense* (2005).

[35] Jayme, n 10 above, at 4. See also 'a new order based on differences which are accepted and are no longer levelled down by resort to national public policy . . . is the very essence of private law in a multicultural society' (at 25). And the equally splendid analysis by Guido Calabresi, *Ideals, Beliefs, Attitudes and the Law: Private Law Perspectives on a Public Law Problem* (1985). Published by The Berkeley Electronic Press, 2006, 9.

such an issue to be treated in Muslim sub-communities such as those of Leicester (where one-third of the population is Asian) and Bradford (where 22 per cent of the population are from ethnic minority groups, particularly from Pakistan)? What is not reasonably foreseeable behaviour in one sub-community may be reasonably foreseeable in another.[36] What is an acceptable lifestyle choice in one sub-community (loud music, scanty or otherwise revealing attire, religious calls to prayer,[37] cooking odours, or slaughter of cows) is a gross nuisance in another. If a reasonable Christian would wear a crash helmet, is it unreasonable conduct (contributory or comparative fault) when a Sikh does not? When tort law requires a warning to be given, say on a product, what languages should be used?[38] When parties seek to resolve such conflicts within the bilateral form of tort law, bald notions of 'accommodation', 'mutual respect', and 'tolerance' may well be useless platitudes. Courts will need to isolate and enunciate the specific legal concerns at play in such cultural-clash cases, a task in which the experience of the tort systems of other multi-cultural societies would be especially valuable.[39]

Next we might ask whether material from another jurisdiction can be legitimately deployed to *attack* a legal concern enunciated by a domestic judge. Suppose in his reasons for judgment a domestic judge in the court of final appeal cites the alleged socio-economic consequences of a certain legal principle: perhaps he has refused to impose negligence liability on, say, a medical provider or public authority on the basis, *inter alia*, of his concern with the possibility of 'defensive medicine' or the 'distortion' of public budgets. Might a comparativist legitimately attack such economic intuitions on the basis that they are undermined by the absence of these effects in other jurisdictions?[40] There are three reasons to think such an attack is not legitimate.

First, the possibility that empirical evidence about the social effects of a specific law in a foreign jurisdiction exists in an adequately rigorous and refined

---

[36] See e.g., *Kavanagh v Akhtar* (1998) NSWCA 779 (Austl). See also *Mustapha v Culligan of Canada Ltd* [2005] 138 ACWS 3d 767, where the Ontario Superior Court of Justice at ¶ 211 noted 'the background of Mr. Mustapha in the Middle East, where the devotion to and concern for the family is at a higher level than is found in North America…predisposed Mr. Mustapha for the reaction that occurred', namely psychological injury from observing a fly in an unused bottle of commercially supplied water.

[37] Church bells; Muslim call to prayer broadcast over loudspeakers; etc.

[38] See e.g., Julian Fulbrook, 'Cycle Helmets and Contributory Negligence', 3 J Pers Inj Law 2004, 171–91 (2004).

[39] Of course some nations do not embrace their multi-culturalism in the same way. In a highly perceptive comparative analysis, Chief Justice McLachlin of the Supreme Court of Canada noted that 'the American ethic is basically one people, one language, one culture. Canada, by contrast, is not a melting pot but a mosaic'. *The American Law Institute, Remarks and Addresses at the 78th Annual Meeting, 14–17 May 2001.*

[40] E.g., see the attack on Lord Hoffmann by Basil Markesinis and Jörg Fedtke, 'Authority or reason? The Economic Consequences of Liability for Breach of statutory Duty in a Comparative Perspective', EBLR 5 (2007). Also see Basil Markesinis, 'Judicial Style and Judicial Reasoning', CLJ 294, 304 (2000).

form is vanishingly small:[41] and it is highly unlikely that sufficient funds will be allocated in the future to designing and carrying out the research required to collect and appropriately analyze statistically significant data. Even in the US, where a great effort has been put into empirical analysis of the tort system, we find that the most reliable results are merely impressionistic and do not address the sort of fine-tuned issues at stake in individual cases.[42] Secondly, even if such empirical evidence of another tort regime were available, there may be social, economic, or cultural reasons why that experience cannot be translated to the domestic context.

Thirdly, while it is a valid objection to the domestic judge in the court of final appeal merely asserting 'unconfirmed' economic intuitions, he can easily cure the problem and put his reasoning on a sound basis by expressing his concern in terms of the *risk* that these socio-economic consequences *might* flow from a finding of liability.[43] Such a concern is legitimate and it is up to such a judge to place a value on the concerns he legitimately identifies, including a preference for any doctrinal shifts that occur within the law to be incremental if possible. If the judge thinks there is even a mere chance that doctors or public authorities might indulge in wasteful defensive measures he might well assess that risk as one that weighs very heavily against the imposition of liability. The same is true of the mere risk that imposition or failure to impose liability might positively encourage abortion. As an individual we might not agree with the judge's assessment of the relevant risk but it is not incoherent. We must acknowledge that judges' valuations may have deep cultural roots that are not the same as those of other

[41] See Don Dewees, David Duff and Michael Trebilcock, *Exploring the Domain of Accident Law: Taking the Facts Seriously* (1996) 414: 'The great disappointment is that the deterrent effect of tort is limited and uneven and cannot be established by existing studies…'; Carol Harlow, *State Liability—Tort Law and Beyond* (2004) 28: 'Studies of the effect of tort law on public decision-making are uncommon, inconclusive and sometimes unreliable, and such information as we do possess is fragmentary'; Basil S Markesinis et al, *Tortious Liability of Statutory Bodies: A Comparative and Economic Analysis of Five English Cases* (1999) 117: 'the testing of hypotheses using empirical research techniques…is expensive and rarely done'; Stephen J Carroll, Asbestos Litigation: Costs and Compensation (2005); and Peter Cane, 'Consequences in Judicial Reasoning', in *Oxford Essays in Jurisprudence* (Jeremy Horder ed, 4th edn 2000) 41.

[42] Ironically, the best recent illustration of the inadequacy of empirical data from foreign systems is provided in Basil Markesinis and Jörg Fedtke, 'Authority or Reason? The Economic Consequences of Liability for Breach of Statutory Duty in a Comparative Perspective', EBLR 5 at 59–60 and 72 (2007). The authors seek to persuade British courts to expand the liability of public authorities into new fields such as exercising a statutory power to order the removal of an object obstructing vision at an intersection, see *Stovin v Wise* [1996] 3 WLR 388. In support, these authors cite somewhat dated surveys which investigated the financial burden of liability on German public authorities between 1974–7 and 1993–5. Yet, as the authors themselves concede, not only did these surveys not provide a 'price-tag' for the administration of these liabilities, but the surveys did not even differentiate the new fields in issue such as that in *Stovin's* case (e.g., the surveys merely state that 73.4% of payments were made in relation to 'traffic accidents').

[43] As Lord Hoffmann put it in 'Human Rights and the House of Lords', 62 Mod L Rev 159 at 162 (1999): 'the payment of compensation *might* in fact be detrimental to good policing, because it *might* make the police defensively unwilling to take risks' (emphasis added). Published by The Berkeley Electronic Press, 2006, 11.

jurisdictions,[44] producing different judicial responses even if the risks could be assessed as identical. In short, it is not incoherent for a domestic court to ignore 'evidence' of how a legal principle operates elsewhere.

Finally, even though it is in the area of legal concerns and basic argument (for example about abortion,[45] indeterminacy of liability, self-help, or encouragement of rescue, etc[46]) that comparative tort reasoning offers its richest rewards, a domestic court must be selective in its use of tort material from other English-speaking jurisdictions. The human mind has 'bounded rationality': gathering and processing information is costly so not all material can be addressed. Given there must be limits on what the domestic court can look at, it needs some sort of rule of thumb by which to select the sources which may be of most value. For example, within the group of nations consisting of the UK and the 'Old Commonwealth'[47] (Canada, Australia, and New Zealand) the *de facto* rule of thumb seems to be that, while much may be of value in one another's jurisprudence, explorations of comparative materials from farther afield is probably not cost efficient.[48]

This is not a surprising approach: the legal concerns, principles and conceptual arrangements of tort law are closely related to the cultural values and legal structures of a society;[49] and there is little doubt that lawyers and judges within this group of nations tend to think there is a greater affinity with each other in all these respects than with other, even English-speaking, jurisdictions. This is, at least, a more palatable explanation for their Western neglect of comparative English-language legal materials from outside this 'white Commonwealth'.[50] It

---

[44] E.g., in France extensive liability is imposed on public authorities and the justification given is that since the collective benefits from the activities of these bodies the burden of those activities should be shared, while in stark contrast, in England such liability is much narrower, and this is explained by a philosophical emphasis on the collective benefit that flows from having the individual yield to the wider public interest: Duncan Fairgrieve, *State Liability in Tort: A Comparative Law Study* (2003) 265–66.

[45] Posner, n 14 above: 'Suppose a judge happened to read a decision of the German Constitutional Court concerning the right to an abortion and found in it an argument against abortion (or perhaps facts about the motives for or procedures of abortion) that he hadn't seen before and that he found persuasive... All these are examples of unexceptional citation to foreign decisions.'

[46] Dozens of such concerns are identified and evaluated in Jane Stapleton, 'Duty of Care Factors: A Selection from the Judicial Menus', in *The Law of Obligations: Essays in Honour of John Fleming* (Peter Cane and Jane Stapleton eds, 1998) 59.

[47] This informal term describes that subset of the (British) Commonwealth of Nations comprising the pre-1945 Dominions. The less diplomatic term is the 'white commonwealth'.

[48] Within the UK-Old Commonwealth group there exists a vigorous email discussion group: the Obligations Discussion Group run by Jason Neyers of the University of Western Ontario. To be added to the list send a message to obligations-request@uwo.ca. .

[49] Even among those who accept that tort law is conditioned by cultural context, there is disagreement about the nature and extent of that influence. See Nikolas Roos, 'NICE Dreams and Realities of European Private Law', in *Epistemology and Methodology of Comparative Law* (Mark Van Hoecke ed, 2004) 197, 202–13, comparing the 'culturalist' approaches of Reinhard Zimmermann and Pierre Legrand.

[50] E.g., legal materials from the world's largest democracy, India, are available at <http://www.commonlii.org> but are rarely referred to in the West. But see Michael Kirby, 'The Supreme Court

is also an explanation why courts in this group of nations rarely venture into US tort law in any fully engaged manner.[51]

Moreover, within this group of nations, we often see domestic courts being even more selective on the basis of the relative intellectual utility[52] of the materials from other jurisdictions. Not unexpectedly a domestic court finds greater illumination in material from other jurisdictions which: attempts to provide general guidance rather than to decide a case on the narrowest possible grounds; provides succinct reasoning about the case in hand rather than an exhaustive survey of previous case law or an academic discourse on the general area of law; and above all contains lucid reasoning raising sound and persuasive legal concerns, crystallized where possible into general principles that are presented in a simple transparent conceptual arrangement. When one or more of these qualities is lacking the domestic court is unlikely to gain much from the material from another jurisdiction.[53]

3. Principles

At the level of the crystallization of tort principles there is some potential for fruitful cross-fertilization. There are, of course, classic examples of this from the past. When in *MacPherson v Buick* (1916)[54] a US court re-analyzed the balance of legal concerns in the tort of negligence, it swept away the privity fallacy and ushered in the modern era of that dominant and voracious tort. Sixteen years later the House of Lords also swept the fallacy aside, expressly drawing support from the principle found in *MacPherson*, with Lord Atkin famously formulating it as the 'neighbour principle'. This principle of law recognized in *Donoghue v Stevenson*,[55] formally an appeal on the Scots law of delict, went on to be adopted throughout the rest of the common law world. While on Scots law, we might note

---

of India and Australian Law', in *Supreme but not Infallible: Essays in Honour of the Supreme Court of India* (BN Kirpal et al, ed, 2000).

[51] It is more common for such a court selectively to cite only those US cases that accord with the result the British or Commonwealth court intends to adopt locally.

[52] And therefore prestige. These characteristics are not static but wax and wane. There was a time when John Fleming, the 'doyen' of Commonwealth torts scholars (according to Lord Cooke of Thorndon in *Hunter v Canary Wharf Ltd* [1997] AC 655, 717 (UK)), vividly contrasted the intellectual power of the Supreme Court of Canada and the House of Lords (John Fleming, 'Employee's Tort in a Contractual Matrix: New Approaches in Canada', 13 Oxford J Legal Studies 430, 439 (1993); see also John Fleming, 'Economic Loss in Canada', 1 Tort L Rev 68 (1993)) concluding that the former clearly eclipsed the latter. Today I am sure John would say the current House of Lords had more than made up the lost ground.

[53] See, alas, the prolixity of some recent decisions of High Court of Australia such as: *Cattanach v Melchior* (2003) 199 ALR 131 with 69,493 words supported by 606 fns; *Perre v Apand* (1999) 164 ALR 606 (68,900 words, 539 fns); and *Brodie v Singleton Shire Council* (2001) 180 ALR 145 (61,918 words, 599 fns). The barriers such length presents to courts in other jurisdictions is reflected in how rarely these landmark Australia decisions have been cited by British courts: *Cattanach* twice; *Perre* three times; and *Brodie* only twice. Published by The Berkeley Electronic Press, 2006, 13.

[54] *MacPherson v Buick Motor Co*, 217 NY 382, 111 NE 1050 (1916).

[55] *Donoghue* [1932] AC 562.

that, being an English-speaking 'mixed system'[56] of law, the influence of its civil law heritage can be studied free of the distortion of translation. For example, we can see that in Scots law precedents tend often to be used more to illustrate principle and 'rights' than to provide a close factual analogy.[57] By an appeal to principle, specifically to the general principle of reparation for loss wrongfully caused, *damnum injuria datum*, it may therefore be possible to create new entitlements in delict more freely than in England and Wales where the focus is on (the availability of) remedies under specific 'nominate' wrongs or 'torts'. Since the highest court of appeal for delict claims from Scotland, the House of Lords, is the same body as the highest court of appeal for tort claims from England and Wales, the development of principle in Scotland has the potential to influence the tort law of the latter jurisdiction in significant ways.[58] A future example here might be personality rights.[59]

A final lesson from Scots law of delict is that the value of comparative law to the domestic lawyer is in inverse proportion to the density of local case law. If, as in Scotland, that density is low there will be more perceived need and enthusiasm to search for ideas from other systems. And if, as in Scotland, the local system is a mixed one this comparative law strategy has a double potential to be fruitful.

But we should not ignore the fact that, though there has long been considerable comparative communication and cross-inspiration between English-speaking common law systems, their *principles of tort law now diverge in many ways*.[60] The cultures, legal cultures[61] and legislative environments within which tort law operates are not equivalent and such differences, though not necessarily apparent,

---

[56] Other mixed systems include: Quebec, Louisiana, Puerto Rico, The Philippines, Sri Lanka, and Israel. South Africa and Scotland are particularly interesting examples for English-speaking lawyers: see e.g., *Southern Cross: Civil Law and Common Law in South Africa* (R Zimmermann and D Visser eds, 1996); Reinhard Zimmermann, Kenneth Reid and DA Visser, *Mixed Legal Systems in Comparative Perspective Property and Obligations in Scotland and South Africa* (2005).

[57] Martin Hogg, *Obligations* (2003) 73; see also Joe Thomson, *Delictual Liability* (3rd edn 2004). Indeed in Scotland certain law texts, written principally in the 17th, 18th, and 19th centuries, are regarded as a source of law. Alan Rodger, 'Savigny in the Strand', 28–30 The Irish Jurist 1, 14 (1995) argues that 'any generalisations ventured by the Scottish judges themselves tend to be drawn from the convenient quarries of the institutional writers'.

[58] Nonetheless, this strong informal tendency to 'coordination' and convergence between the two jurisdictions in tort/delict operates formally on an opt-in basis.

[59] On which, see 'Privacy, Property, Personality,' a project of the Arts and Humanities Research Council Research Centre for Studies in Intellectual Property and Technology Law based in the School of Law at the University of Edinburgh. E.g., at a highly stimulating conference on rights of personality rights at the Law School, University of Strathclyde in May 2006 I was delighted to witness a debate on whether dwarf tossing might be a tort and, if so, owed by whom to whom and under what circumstances!

[60] A dynamic fuelled by the gradual abolition of appeals to the Privy Council.

[61] See generally Jeremy Webber, 'Culture, Legal Culture and Legal Reasoning', 29 Austl J Leg Phil 27 (2004); *Adapting Legal Cultures* (David Nelken and Johannes Feest, eds, 2001); Maria Rosaria Ferrarese, 'An Entrepreneurial Conception of the Law? The American Model through Italian Eyes', in Comparing Legal Cultures 157 (David Nelken, ed, 1996); and John Bell, *French Legal Cultures* (2001).

may profoundly influence how tort principles are shaped, applied, and perceived: the concerns of tort law are culturally and historically[62] contingent. As Justice Windeyer of the High Court of Australia noted, 'too much store can be put upon uniformity of law when it operates in conditions that are not uniform'.[63]

For example, determination of important tort issues such as duty, standard of care, vicarious liability, and immunities are influenced by domestic cultural attitudes, for example to medical practitioners[64] and patients' rights, insurance, commercial product suppliers such as bars, the profit motive in general, employers, the home and family,[65] lawyers, the press, organized religion,[66] and public authorities.[67] There are even differences between English-speaking jurisdictions in relation to which torts are actionable *per se*, and this may signal quite significant variations in how the respective cultures value the underlying interest at stake.[68] Judicial perceptions of such 'instincts and traditions of the people' and 'common law rights'[69] are sometimes asserted in proud terms. For example, in one case Lord Goff of Chievely stated:

[W]e may pride ourselves on the fact that freedom of speech has existed in this country perhaps as long as, if not longer than, it has existed in any other country in the world... we in this country (where everybody is free to do anything, subject only to the provisions of the law) proceed... upon an assumption of freedom of speech...[70]

Even bolder were the comments of Lord Hoffmann in a recent case:

Freedom from arbitrary arrest and detention is a quintessentially British liberty, enjoyed by the inhabitants of this country when most of the population of Europe could be thrown into prison at the whim of their rulers.[71]

---

[62] The modern Western concern with privacy is an example here. In medieval times European travellers shared their hostelry bed with strangers, often with up to ten strangers, and the practice of sleeping several to a bed, usually naked, was not considered demeaning. Norbert Ohler, *The Medieval Traveller* (Caroline Hillier trans, 1989) 93.

[63] *Skelton v Collins* (1966) 115 CLR 94, 136 (Austl).

[64] Contrast *Arndt v Smith* [1997] SCR 539 (Can) with *Hollis v Birch* [1995] SCR 634 (Can). See Jane Stapleton, 'Legal Cause: Cause-in-Fact and the Scope of Liability for Consequences', 54 Vand L Rev 941, 964 n 57 (2001).

[65] Lord Cooke of Thorndon in *Hunter v Canary Wharf Ltd* [1997] AC 655: 'The reason why I prefer the alternative... is that it gives better effect to widespread conceptions concerning the home and family.'

[66] Is circumcision a battery?

[67] See Duncan Fairgrieve, *State Liability in Tort: A Comparative Law Study* (2003). Published by The Berkeley Electronic Press, 2006, 15.

[68] See e.g., S Balganesh, 'Property Along the Tort Spectrum: Trespass to Chattels and the Anglo-American Doctrinal Divergence', 35 Common Law World Review 135 (2006).

[69] On which see e.g. Robin Cooke, 'The Road Ahead for the Common Law', 53 ICLQ 273 (2004).

[70] *Attorney-General v Guardian Newspapers (No 2)* [1990] 1 AC 109, 283 (UK). See also *Derbyshire County Council v Times Newspapers Ltd* [1993] AC 534 (UK).

[71] In *A & Ors v Secretary of State for the Home Dept* [2004] UKHL 56, ¶ 88. See also: '...a power to detain people indefinitely without charge or trial... Nothing could be more antithetical to the instincts and traditions of the people of the United Kingdom.'(¶ 86); '...such a power in any form

More generally Lord Hoffmann has emphasized 'the real differences...in the history, cultures, and political structures of' the United States, Germany, and the United Kingdom, and concluded that in the latter:

...confident democracy...we have our own hierarchy of moral values, our own cultural-ly-determined sense of what is fair and unfair, and I think it would be wrong to submerge this under a pan-European jurisprudence of human rights.[72]

Examples of divergences abound.[73] For example, the judge-made law of torts in England and Wales: did not develop analogues of the tort set out in §402A of the Second Restatement or the US tort of retaliation against an employee in violation of public policy; and, despite its abolition in another part of the common law world, has retained the tort of breach of statutory duty. Perhaps the most promi-nent recent example of divergence from within the Commonwealth is when the Privy Council acknowledged that the common law of New Zealand appropri-ately embraced a principle of negligence liability[74] which the House of Lords, drawn from the same pool of Law Lords, has refused to admit to the common law of England and Wales.[75] Lord Lloyd of Berwick, speaking for the Privy Council, noted 'whether circumstances are in fact so very different in England and New Zealand may not matter greatly. What matters is the perception.'[76] Similarly, though Australia and New Zealand are extremely close in many socio-economic and cultural ways, aspects of their tort systems could not be in starker contrast.

is not compatible with our constitution. The real threat to the life of the nation, in the sense of a people living in accordance with its traditional laws and political values, comes not from terrorism but from laws such as these.' (¶ 97). Similarly strident were His Lordship's comments in *A & Ors v Secretary of State for the Home Dept* [2005] UKHL 71, ¶ 82: 'When judicial torture was routine all over Europe, its rejection by the common law was a source of national pride and the admiration of enlightened foreign writers such as Voltaire and Beccaria. In our own century, many people in the United States, heirs to that common law tradition, have felt their country dishonoured by its use of torture outside the jurisdiction and its practice of extra-legal "rendition" of suspects to countries where they would be tortured. See Jeremy Waldron, "Torture and Positive Law: Jurisprudence for the White House", 105 Colum L Rev 1681, 1681–1750 (2005).'

[72] Lord Hoffmann, 'Human Rights and the House of Lords', 62 Mod L Rev 159, 160, 165 (1999).
[73] As an Australian my favourite illustration of this has to do with bush hospitality: since 1914 the Australian High Court has rejected the special *ignis suus* rule (which makes the landowner vic-ariously liable for such escapes caused by the negligence of mere licensees) on the explicit basis that 'contemporary conditions in this country have no real similarity to urban conditions in medieval England where the escape of domestic fire rivalled plague and war as a cause of general catastrophe' and that such a liability rule would have been an intolerable restriction on 'the tradition of hospital-ity in the bush and would have been a disincentive to pastoralists to allow Aboriginal communities to camp on their holdings'. *Burnie Port Authority v General Jones Pty Ltd* (1992)179 CLR 520, 534, 566. See also *Whinfield v Lands Purchase and Management Board* (1914) 18 CLR 606, 616 (per Griffiths CJ).
[74] That a local government inspector owed a duty of care to avoid economic loss to the plain-tiff when he inspected the foundations of a building. *Invercargill City Council v Hamlin* [1996] 1 NZLR 513 (PC); [1996] AC 624.
[75] *Murphy v Brentwood District Council* [1991] 1 AC 398 (UK).
[76] *Invercargill City Council v Hamlin* [1996] UKPC 56, 56 ¶ 31 (Appeal taken from New Zealand).

Finally we have seen that even when a federal system such as Australia has a unified 'common law', the 'law of torts' will diverge where the states have legislative capacity in the field traditionally addressed by common law of torts.[77]

We might speculate about the causes of this divergence of principles within the common law world. What is clear, however, is that modern Commonwealth tort lawyers do not regard this phenomenon as objectionable *per se*. Indeed, most would probably argue that it is the inevitable and healthy manifestation of the adaptability of the common law to local circumstance and its ability to fashion appropriate principles. As Lord Cooke has remarked:

[I]t has become widely appreciated that there may be more ways than one in which national common law systems, starting from the same roots, may justifiably go. Different chains of reasoning and weightings of values may be reasonably open... national ethos is allowed its own weight.[78]

In short, while legal argument is easily transferred across jurisdictional boundaries because the concerns on which argument rest are foundational and simply expressed, the same cannot be said for principles crystallized by a local evaluation of legal concerns.

Finally, we must acknowledge that the role of the court of final appeal is to 'judge', not provide some intellectual survey of world law. Suppose a court of final appeal in one jurisdiction is reliably informed that another English-language jurisdiction resolved the exact tort issue in dispute in favour of the plaintiff on the basis of principle X. Suppose further that both jurisdictions are extremely similar in all cultural parameters and share the same range of legal concerns and conceptual arrangements. Besides prompting extra care in the evaluation of the issues, even 'anxious review',[79] does the existence of principle X in the other jurisdiction have any legitimate role in the resolution of the case? I do not think so. In my view it is not an incoherent or necessarily objectionable situation that: a barrister's immunity from suit in negligence is wider in Australia than in New Zealand, Canada, and the UK; British local authority building inspectors do not owe the duty of care to building owners that New Zealand ones do; US lawyers who carelessly fail to lodge a client's private law claim within the limitation period are not liable to the client if that claim had a less than even chance of success while in a parallel situation the British lawyer would be liable; and so on.

Accepting Lord Steyn's view that 'tort is not underpinned by a single overarching rationale... it is a mosaic of interwoven principles of corrective and distributive justice',[80] I argue that the tort principles embraced by courts staffed by reasonable people may legitimately be different, and therefore produce different results

---

[77] See n 16 above.

[78] Robin Cooke, 'The Dream of an International Common Law', in *Courts of Final Jurisdiction: The Mason Court in Australia* (Cheryl Saunders ed, 1996) 138, 143.

[79] *Fairchild* [2003] 1 AC 32, ¶ 32 (per Lord Bingham).

[80] Lord Steyn, 'Perspectives of Corrective and Distributive Justice in Tort Law: the John Maurice Kelly Memorial Lecture' (2002) 7–8.

between jurisdictions. The reason the courts of final appeal diverge may not even be based on different circumstances but merely on 'an intellectual preference for one outcome over another'.[81] It is, therefore, dangerous to argue that a determination of tort entitlements in another jurisdiction '*must* also have some bearing in giving concrete effect to the vague notions of "fair" and "reasonable"'.[82] I see no reason for such an extraordinary conclusion. But what if a considerable number of other jurisdictions have adopted the same principle X? Even here I believe there is a slippery slope from the argument that material describing the position in other legal systems 'provides a check . . . that the problem identified in these appeals [by the Appellants] is genuine'[83] to the separate assertion that it 'is one that *requires* to be remedied'[84] in the appellants' favour. A 'head-count of decisions and codes adopted in other countries around the world, often against a background of different rules and traditions'[85] should be irrelevant. What is critical is the judge's '*basic sense of justice*'.[86]

4. Conceptual

Arrangement of Principles Two systems of tort law might embrace identical principles and produce identical results, but these may not be arranged in the same conceptual architecture. Even more rarely than in the case of principles of tort law will a comparison with the different conceptual arrangement in another jurisdiction be fruitful for the local practitioner or judge. For example, unusually in the common law world, breach of fiduciary duty is a tort in the US, yet it is hard to see how an awareness of this arrangement would in itself be of assistance to a non-US judge or practitioner.[87]

---

[81] Anthony Mason, 'Old and New–Commonwealth Final Courts of Appeal and Their Perspectives on the Common Law' (13th Commonwealth Law Conference, Melbourne 16 April 2003), 18. My favourite example of this concerns two US cases involving the same defendant and the same allegedly defective intra-uterine device: the first court, a federal appellate court applying Arkansas law, found for the plaintiff; two days later the second court, the Delaware Supreme Court, reached the opposite conclusion. Juries were not involved at any stage of either case. Marianne Corr, 'Problems with the EC Approach to Harmonization of Product Liability Law', 22 Case W Res J Int'l L 235, 242 (1990). The cases are: *Hill v Searle Labs* 884 F2d 1064, 1070 (8th Cir 1989) and *Lacy v GD Searle & Co*, 567 A2d 398 (Del 1989).

[82] Basil S Markesinis, *Foreign Law and Comparative Methodology: A Subject and a Thesis* (1997) 352, emphasis added.

[83] *Fairchild* [2003] 1 AC 32, ¶ 165 (UK) (per Lord Rodger).

[84] Id (emphasis added). Also see *Macfarlane v Tayside Health Board* [1999] UKHL 50; [2000] 2 AC 59 at 81 (per Lord Steyn): 'the discipline of comparative law does not aim at a poll of the solutions adopted in different countries. It has the different and inestimable value of sharpening our focus on the weight of competing considerations. And it reminds us that the law is part of the world of competing ideas markedly influenced by cultural differences.'

[85] *Fairchild* [2003] 1 AC 32, ¶ 32 (per Lord Bingham).

[86] Id (emphasis added).

[87] See also the structural line between contract and tort: in Scotland consideration is not a requirement for contract; English courts are well aware of this structural difference but see no advantage in adopting the Scottish position. Needless to say, the feeling is mutual. Published by The Berkeley Electronic Press, 2006 19.

But there may be occasions when a domestic court of final appeal might fruitfully be prompted to reconsider the structural form of local tort law on the basis that it is less intellectually 'convenient' for some reason than that in another system. Take the area of causation in the law. Historically many common law jurisdictions have used causal language to capture two quite distinct legal questions: was the tortious conduct of the defendant historically involved in any way with the injury of which complaint is made? And if so, is that consequence of the tortious conduct judged to be within the (normatively) appropriate scope of liability for the particular cause of action? Thus in some US jurisdictions we have the twin labels of 'factual cause' and 'proximate cause'; in others 'legal cause' is used for the former enquiry; while in yet others it is used for the latter. To make the situation even more fractured the First and Second Restatements used the term 'legal cause' to refer to the amalgam of both enquiries! Meanwhile, in the past some Commonwealth courts have tried to distinguish the enquiries by saying that they are concerned respectively with the search for 'a cause' and 'the cause'. Others have referred to the latter enquiry as a determination of whether the damage was 'too remote', a bizarre term given that it does not refer in any was to physical or spatial proximity!

Many of us have argued that this is an obfuscatory state of affairs. Now the American Law Institute's *Draft Restatement (Third)* has adopted a much more transparent conceptual arrangement:[88] causal language is to be restricted to the first enquiry which is termed 'factual causation' and the second enquiry is to be labelled 'scope of liability.' Henceforth the factual nature of the former enquiry and the normative nature of the second will be patent. Old terms such as 'proximate cause' and vacuous 'fudges' such as 'substantial factor' are to be abandoned, and the relevance of a factor intervening between tortious conduct and injury, such as lightning or a criminal act by a third party, will be seen for

---

[88] The Draft Restatement arrangement also allows us to identify issues more accurately. Take coincidences. A coincidental consequence of a course of conduct is a consequence the risk of which is *not generally* increased by the occurrence of that type of conduct. For example: D carelessly speeds along a road and this happens to bring the vehicle to a position where a tree falls on the vehicle injuring a passenger. It is well settled that speeding is careless and it is foreseeable that trees sometimes fall onto vehicles passing along a road. But, although in this freakish event the speeding was historically involved in the injury to the passenger (because but for the speeding, the tree would have missed the passenger), in general speeding does not increase the risk of trees falling on vehicles. The fact that speeding resulted in such an outcome on this particular occasion is a coincidence. The current assumption in the US seems to be that a tortfeasor is never held legally responsible for a coincidence, but this is not the case in other common law jurisdictions (see e.g., *Smith New Court Securities Ltd v Scrimgeour Vickers Ltd* [1997] AC 254 (UK)). It is therefore misleading to mask the coincidence issue as one of whether there is, what Justice Calabresi calls, a 'causal linkage' between tortious conduct and injury (Guido Calabresi, 'Concerning Cause and the Law of Torts: An Essay for Harry Kalven, Jr', 43 U Chi L Rev 69, 71–72 (1975); *Liriano v Hobart Corp* 170 F3d 264, 271–72 (2d Cir 1999)). Far more convenient, because it allows more future flexibility in the development of the common law, is to identify this issue as a straightforwardly normative one. The Draft Restatement does this by treating coincidences as raising an issue going to the scope-of-liability. Other common law jurisdictions would greatly benefit from this conceptual arrangement because coincidental consequences are a common problem in tort cases.

what it is: relevant, not to the factual issue of whether the tortious conduct was involved in the history leading to the injury of which complaint is made, but relevant to the normative issue of whether the tortfeasor should be liable for this particular consequence of his tortious conduct. Lawyers in non-US common law systems would benefit from examining this new conceptual arrangement. For example, the current jurisprudence of the Supreme Court of Canada continues to deploy 'substantial factor' in just the sort of incoherent and indefensible ways that are rightly condemned in the Draft Restatement. Similarly, important decisions of the House of Lords and High Court of Australia would have been much clarified and simplified had such a conceptual arrangement as that of the Draft Restatement been used.[89]

Finally, we must note that, while in jury-free tort systems the debate about which conceptual arrangements are preferable is not skewed by institutional competition between judge and jury decision-making, this has a profound influence in the US. There is a deep fracture in US tort law that divides the loud rhetoric of the importance, almost sanctity, of jury decision-making[90] and the typically covert manoeuvres made by US courts and advocated by tort academics to prevent issues from reaching the jury.[91] Fundamental structures of US tort doctrine reflect this fracture, which is most nakedly exposed in cases where courts seek to restrain liability in negligence. The polarization between two crystallized duty *rules of law* with which the judge governs access to the jury (namely: a duty-owed-to-the-whole-world; and no duty to rescue a stranger) is unique to US tort law and a fine illustration of this schizophrenic attitude to jury decision-making. The most astute US tort lawyers are prepared candidly to concede that 'whether we are better served by giving juries or judges more or less normative work to do…is largely a political judgment, not a legal one';[92] but it is clear that any analysis of the conceptual arrangements adopted in US tort law would be incomplete without reference to this normative context.

D. A digression on theory

Though my focus in this paper is on the utility of comparative tort law for practitioners and judges, I want to digress at this point to say something about theory.

---

[89] See Jane Stapleton, 'Occam's Razor Reveals an Orthodox Basis for *Chester v Afshar*', 122 LQ REV 426 (2006).

[90] A conceptual arrangement that allocates the decision on an issue to the jury has important consequences: the decision will be unelaborated; it will be heavily protected from appellate review; and it will not provide any precedent in the future.

[91] Jane Stapleton, 'Controlling the Future of the Common Law by Restatement', in *Exploring Tort Law* (M. Stuart Madden, ed, 2005) 262. Contrast the 'subterfuge' of allocating to the jury, which 'can give results without reasons of explanations', tragic choices that we wish to 'paper over'. Guido Calabresi, *Ideals, Beliefs, Attitudes and the Law: Private Law Perspectives on a Public Law Problem* (1985) 88.

[92] William Powers, Jr, 'Judge and Jury in the Texas Supreme Court', 75 Tex L Rev 1699, 1715 (1997). Published by The Berkeley Electronic Press, 2006, 21.

US tort scholars now embrace 'high theory' with an enthusiasm their peers in other English-speaking jurisdictions do not. Indeed, it has been asserted that today 'tort scholarship in the United States veers from one universal solvent to another...',[93] while Posner, in noting the anti-theoretical tradition of the common law, observes that 'suspicion of theory is a bright thread in the tapestry of English thought'.[94] It was not always thus in the US. In 1907, James Coolidge Carter wrote:

In nothing is human vanity more largely displayed than in the love of a theory. The simple and beautiful forms in which consequences develop themselves when a sufficient cause is assumed... furnish a pleasure which the mind desires to hold in its grasp, and it recoils from any scrutiny into facts from a secret fear that the possession will be endangered, and turns back to revel in the delights of the theory.[95]

Later, in 1930, Karl Llewellyn also did not see great merit in constructing a general theory of law:

[T]he difficulty... is that there are so many things to be included, and the things to be included are so unbelievably different from each other. Perhaps it is possible to get them all under one verbal roof. But I do not see what you have accomplished if you do.[96]

There is, no doubt, an intriguing cultural history behind why, in the closing decades of the 20th century, there was this 'flight from doctrine'[97] to theory in US legal academia. Certainly it has its critics, one of whom noted:

[T]he obsession of United States torts theorists with superficially attractive simplifying arguments, which, after being denounced by the partisans of some other simplifying argument, seem inevitably to end up more complex than the material they set out to simplify. If, as I believe, there is an irreducible complexity in most important problems, then a strategy which accepts complexity from the start is more likely to avoid disaster than one which starts with impossible simplifications. But the cost of such a strategy is the inevitable disappointment for those who seek 'breakthroughs'.[98]

There seem to me to be structural as well as cultural reasons for the popularity of tort theory in the US. Within the one nation of the United States there is a multiplicity of tort-law jurisdictions and therefore a diverse range of persuasive

[93] David Howarth, 'O Madness of Discourse, That Cause Sets Up with and Against Itself!', 96 Yale LJ 1389, 1423 (1987).

[94] Posner, n 14 above at 418. See also Allan C Hutchinson, *Evolution and the Common Law* (2005) for the argument that no grand theory will satisfactorily explain the dynamic interactions of change and stability in the common law.

[95] James Coolidge Carter, *Law: Its Origin Growth and Function* (GP Putnam's Sons 1907) 217.

[96] Karl N Llewellyn, 'A Realistic Jurisprudence—The Next Step', 30 Colum L Rev 431 (1930).

[97] Comment to the author made by Geoffrey Hazard (Thomas E Miller Distinguished Professor of Law at the University of California, Hastings School of Law), at the Council Meeting of the American Law Institute in New York City, October 2006.

[98] Howarth, n 90 above at 1423. See also Christopher J Robinette, 'Can There be a Unified Theory of Torts? A Pluralist Suggestion from History and Doctrine', 43 Brandeis LJ 369 (2005); and Allan C Hutchinson, *Evolution and the Common Law* (2005) who argues that no grand theory will satisfactorily explain the dynamic interactions of change and stability in the common law.

precedents by which a court may be influenced. Added to the resultant phenomenon of doctrinal fragmentation, there is the fact that within any one US jurisdiction lower courts are subjected to weak control by appellate courts, thanks in great part to the reverence paid to that institutional buffer or 'black-box', the jury. This means that courts enjoy greater freedom from the shackles of precedent, and therefore greater freedom to make law than that enjoyed by courts in non-US common law systems.[99] A 'theory' of 'US tort law' must, like a 'restatement' of it, seek some abstract, common denominator account and thereby may falsely suggest some convergence dynamic. In addition, the career profile of US tort scholars requires an output that addresses more than the tort materials of their state jurisdiction. In such an environment theory can be expected to flourish.

But if we contrast the common law systems of the England and Wales, Canada, Australia, and New Zealand we find that doctrinal development of the judge-made common law of torts is formally unified: nationally there is only one final court of appeal on such issues. So while in the US there may be dozens of final pronouncements on a point of common law torts, in non-US common law jurisdictions there will only be one and, unlike Continental courts labouring under the formal supremacy of a private law Code, these pivotal judgments of the final court of appeal in non-US common law jurisdictions can be and are noticeably more candid in their reasoning. Yet the reasoning in these final courts of appeal is, for theorists claiming descriptive legitimacy, embarrassingly pluralistic and uninfluenced by legal philosophers.[100] Tort law is revealed to be generated by a melange of legal concerns, some moral, some economic, some symbolic, some distributive:[101] quite impossible to capture by rarefied mono-theory.

There are other reasons besides descriptive failure why I think lawyers in non-US common law jurisdictions eschew tort theory. In England and Wales, Canada, Australia, and New Zealand the common law of torts is not only unified, as it is in say Germany and France, but it consists of the pronouncements of one final court of appeal, the judges of which enjoy pre-eminence and great prestige within the national legal system. Legal academics in these jurisdictions

---

[99] Robert S Summers and PS Atiyah, *Form and Substance in Anglo-American Law* (1987). Published by The Berkeley Electronic Press, 2006, 23.

[100] 'There is little overt sign…that the work of legal philosophers has yet greatly shaped the opinions of our judges.' Alan Rodger, 'Savigny in the Strand', 28–30 The Irish Jurist 1, 8 (1995). Note also Lord Rodger's view that 'precisely because the law has evolved in thousands of cases, there may be no completely satisfying principles to be discovered' in the common law, just as 'the texts of Roman Law which have come down to us do not on the whole contain statements of general legal principles' (14–15).

[101] Johan Steyn, 'Perspectives of Corrective and Distributive Justice in Tort Law: the John Maurice Kelly Memorial Lecture' (Faculty of Law University College Dublin, 2002) 7–8. Such a corrective justice lens also ignores what the most eminent judges tell us: that in cases determined by the court of final appeal reasons of distributive justice may well be 'decisive' and that more generally 'tort is not underpinned by a single overarching rationale. It is a mosaic of interwoven principles of corrective and distributive justice'. In short, when we look to restate the actual lawmaking performed by courts, theory is of little use in identifying sufficiently clear standards let alone the appropriate overarching architecture.

therefore have a realistic hope of affecting, quite directly and quite soon, the development of the common law of torts: their work is not a source of law but many seek as their audience the few judges sitting on that final court of appeal and the intermediate courts that feed that court. In such an environment theory tends to be a less attractive career strategy than providing this audience with a compelling, doctrinally thorough and precise, critique of a quite small body of relevant precedent, not least when these appellate judges openly tell academics that 'we are...helping each other to make law'.[102]

In this connection I should report that at the Conference at which this paper was delivered in the Fall of 2006, a number of participants offered another reason why theory was popular in the US legal academy and not in the rest of the Western world. The argument, as one person expressed it, is 'that theoretical research may present a higher level of thinking, and that perhaps American scholars are simply ahead of their counterparts in Europe and other places'. Moreover, it was pointed out that tort theory has recently become popular in a few non-US elite institutions such as Toronto and in Israel. Unsurprisingly, I prefer not to conclude that tort scholars in the US, Toronto, and Israel are somehow simply intellectually 'ahead' of those elsewhere. Rather, my experience suggests to me that, for non-academic reasons, Israelis and some Canadians tend to seek respect, success, and even jobs in US legal academia. In contrast, Britons and Australasians tend not to do so. They confine their ambition to directly influencing the creation of tort law in their jurisdictions, and anywhere else courts are open to doctrinal analysis with a high level of precision.

Once we understand why a certain theoretical account of tort law has influence in one jurisdiction and not in another, we might then ask what value might comparative law be to theorists? One obvious advantage is that it provides yet wider landscapes against which to test descriptive theories. An acknowledgement of the significant divergences between superficially comparable English language jurisdictions would push economic theorists to accept the weight given by courts to socially contingent values incommensurable with money; and press certain corrective justice theorists to acknowledge the cultural and temporal relativity of 'rights'. Normative theories might also find the comparative perspective chastening to the extent that a comparative sensibility carries with it a norm of respect for cultural difference and an acknowledgment of socially validated legal change; and it can challenge the myopia of a theory with its implicit assumptions and static bias. For example, the corrective justice standard of justification of private law might itself be revealed as no more than a Western cultural artefact, the norms of which ignore the phenomenon of societies elsewhere that happily base core socio-legal relations on group standing and group responsibility.

---

[102] Lord Hope, 'Opening Remarks, at Conference on Rights of Personality in Scots Law' (The Law School, University of Strathclyde, 5 May 2006). Published by The Berkeley Electronic Press, 2006.

E. The special case of the United States

1. Non-US English-speaking lawyers looking at US tort doctrine

It is worth addressing the United States specifically at this point not least because there is a marked, if unreciprocated, enthusiasm by many non-US tort lawyers to delve into US tort doctrine. For academics attraction lies, understandably, in the domestic and international prestige of acquiring an understanding of the diverse legal environment in the world's current superpower, and getting published in one of its law reviews! This appreciation can also sometimes advantage non-US practitioners, for example when a reference to the US phenomenon of market-share liability prompts the domestic court to create a similar liability or draw support for a finding of proportionate liability for an indivisible injury.[103] But, as in all comparative 'borrowings,' such reference to US tort law is impressionistic, merely illustrative, and scarcely qualifies for the description of 'legal transplant'. Tort law cannot simply be 'exported' because there will always be structural and cultural features which cannot be ignored and which have no equivalent in the potentially 'importing' system. Not least of these in the US system is the 'consti-tutionalization' of tort law by the Supreme Court.

So we should ask, of what perils should a non-US lawyer looking to US tort materials be aware? US tort law is certainly the outrider within the English-language jurisdictions for reasons that may not be easily adjusted for by non-US practitioners and judges.[104] For example, though tort law is overwhelmingly a state matter, state legislatures are relatively paralyzed when it comes to enacting comprehensive private law reform and this has effects that the non-US tort lawyer may not appreciate. For example, she may be shocked to discover that contributory negligence was a complete defence to US tort claims until relatively recently, and that in many jurisdictions the abandonment of this bar was only achieved by judicial decision. Without this comparative insight the non-US lawyer would fail to understand the crucial subtext of many US tort cases dating from before this change.

Indeed, the non-US lawyer must be alert to the general fact that in the US it is culturally accepted that courts can be considerably more adventurous with doctrine and the boundaries between causes of action than non-US common law courts can.[105] For example, the new tort recorded in § 402A *Restatement (Second) of Torts (1965)* arguably had its origins in a 1913 case[106] where a single

---

[103] Compare the House of Lords decision in *Barker v Corus UK Ltd* [2006] UKHL 20, 2 AC 572 (UK) with the decision of the Hoge Raad of 9 October 1992 on which see Ewoud Hondius, 'A Dutch DES Case—Pharmaceutical Producers Jointly and Severally Liable', 2 Eur Rev Priv L 409 (1994).

[104] See Jane Stapleton, 'Bugs in Anglo-American Products Liability', 53 SC L Rev 1225, 1256–57 (2002).

[105] Summers, n 94 above.

[106] *Mazetti v Armour & Co*, 135 P 633 (Wash 1913).

trial judge simply abandoned the doctrine of privity and decided that a commercial buyer of food should be able to sue the distant seller in warranty. Today, just as the various state enactments of the Uniform Commercial Code have made the US law on warranty quite complex, so too the state common law versions of the rule in § 402A are riddled with variables that are daunting for the non-US lawyer.[107]

But there is also a trap for the unwary non-US lawyer who believes that US judges say what they mean in authentic 'legal realist' style. For example, the emergence of § 402A was uniformly accompanied by ringing pro-consumer judicial rhetoric of 'strict liability' for defective products.[108] But in fact, when push came to shove and courts were faced with cases in which the relevant product danger was unforeseeable at the time of supply, US courts refused to impose strict liability in design and warning cases: they refused to require manufacturers to conform to impossible standards. For example, out of the thousands of design defect cases brought against product manufacturers over the past few decades there seem to be, at most, only three[109] where a US court was prepared to follow the logic of its strict liability rhetoric and impose that liability. Not one involved a pharmaceutical! Had Europeans been more sensitive to this it may have alerted them to the fundamental political and doctrinal dilemmas of imposing strict tort liability on manufacturers for unforeseeable risks, and they may have balked at agreeing to the ambiguous 'all-things-to-all-parties' wording of the notorious 1985 Directive on Products Liability.[110]

Process and procedure are also culturally contingent in ways that may not be obvious. The non-US lawyer might not appreciate fundamental features of US tort doctrine, for example, that most US employees injured at work are unable to sue their employer because workers' compensation is their 'sole' remedy. The non-US lawyer will, therefore, fail to understand why the emergence of the common law rule in § 402A of the *Restatement (Second) of Torts (1965)* had such an impact on US tort law: it provided employees with a route to tort-level damages if they could identify some product with which they worked and successfully allege that its 'defective' condition caused their injury. Though rarely remarked on in the US, the results can seem bizarre to the non-US lawyer. For example, where an employer buys an unguarded cutting machine and later his employee

---

[107] And, of course, results can diverge even where the law is identical: see the two US cases, n 78 above.

[108] See n 12 above.

[109] David G Owen, *Products Liability Law* (2005) 700, n 167. Owen states 'the two pillars of modern products liability law in America' are 'that manufacturers must guard against risks only if they are *foreseeable*, and that manufacturers must guard against those risks only by precautions that are *reasonable*' (38).

[110] How can a product be defective for failing to warn of something no one could have known about? Why is the state of the art of substitutes relevant but not the state of the art of discovering the need for a substitute? See also Jane Stapleton, 'Liability for Drugs in the US and EU: Rhetoric and Reality, 26 Rev Litigation 991 (2007).

is severely injured by the blade, the employer escapes any tort sanction. The loss either remains on the victim[111] or is shifted to a, perhaps entirely innocent, non-manufacturing party in the chain of supply of the machine such as a wholesaler or retailer.[112]

Also, as I noted earlier, a tort lawyer from outside the US may not appreciate that a covert concern with jury decision-making in the US generates a pronounced tendency to crystallize rules of law with which the trial judge can govern access to the jury. Conversely, in the United States access to a jury trial is so much taken for granted as a right, that it evokes scant comment. Yet in other jurisdictions there is far more ambivalence: for example in the recent Scottish case of *Heasman v JM Taylor & Partners*[113] a person suffered personal injuries in a car accident and sued the defender in delict; thereupon the defender challenged the use of a jury on the basis that it would contravene his right to a fair hearing under Article 6 of the Convention for the Protection of Human Rights and Fundamental Freedoms! Indeed, it is a striking feature of the US tort system that lawyers seem to find little if anything to object to in two juries reaching opposite outcomes in cases of identical facts. In non-US systems the ideal of like cases being treated alike is much more in evidence.

Similarly, the nature and degree of concern over rates of litigation is culturally contingent. For example, to establish that American resort to tort litigation is far greater than in economically comparable countries does not establish that its litigation system is in need of reform.[114] There is no doubt, for example, that the role of tort law in the US is not the same as in New Zealand where for decades tort claims for personal injury by accident have been excluded in favour of a state-run comprehensive accident compensation scheme. Clearly, empirical findings may also be highly location-dependent. For example, the landmark work of Lloyd-Bostock,[115] that suggested individuals' attribution of responsibility for accidents in England was influenced by what they knew of the law's attribution, may well be specific and not generalizable to the US which was outside her empirical frame of reference.

---

[111] This is the result in jurisdictions that evaluate design defect using consumer expectations. See Owen, n 104 above, at 296 and 490.

[112] This is typically the result in jurisdictions that evaluate design defect using risk-utility: on the basis that the removability of the guard meant the machine's risks outweighed its utility. See Owen, n 104 above, at 302 and 315. Published by The Berkeley Electronic Press, 2006.

[113] 2002 SC 326, [2002] ScotCS 63 (Inner House, Court of Session).

[114] See David Nelkin, 'Beyond Compare? Criticizing "The American Way of Law"', 28 Law & Soc Inquiry 799 (2003).

[115] See Sally M Lloyd-Bostock, 'Common Sense Morality and Accident Compensation', in *Psychology, Law, and Legal Processes* (David P Farrington et al, eds, 1979) 93, 101 (noting that accident victims may first determine a right to compensation and then attribute fault to justify compensation); and Sally Lloyd-Bostock, 'Fault and Liability for Accidents: The Accident Victim's Perspective', in *Compensation and Support for Illness and Injury* 139, 150–51 (Donald Harris et al, eds, 1984) 139, 150–51.

2. *US lawyers looking at tort materials from other English-speaking jurisdictions*

Bounded rationality explains and partially justifies the indifference of US legal practitioners and judges to otherwise-relevant non-US English-language materials. In US tort law the palette of domestic tort ideas and arguments is probably sufficiently rich not to require or justify looking farther afield unless, of course, the case has some overt foreign element such as a *forum non conveniens* claim. Moreover, there will be important aspects of US tort law that have no close parallels elsewhere, such as the specific constitutional constraints on it recognized by the US Supreme Court. So, each year as I teach US products liability in Texas,[116] I do not find much need to trawl non-US case law for ideas additional to those available within US material: not least because the comparative palette of tort ideas presented to US law students is drawn from across the country, not merely the state of tuition.

There is, however, one area in which US lawyers would benefit from a comparative perspective on tort law. An awareness of the issues presented to courts of final appeal in other English-speaking jurisdictions can fruitfully expose them to types of claim, and thereby to legal issues, that have either not yet been litigated in a US jurisdiction[117] or have been 'fudged' in local jurisprudence. As we noted early on, this appreciation can challenge, illuminate, and enrich a lawyer's grasp on his or her own system of tort law. Though an individual US lawyer may not have the resources to engage in such research, the Restatement projects of the American Law Institute, of which the torts restatements have by far been the most used and influential, provide one valuable avenue by which notice of useful non-US English-language developments can be given to domestic lawyers. Restatements are, however, only reconsidered after long interludes. Other avenues

---

[116] Remember I am only concerned in this chapter with the value of comparative tort law to practitioners and judges. Those engaged in academic projects such as legal history and theoretical comparative studies must address the wider world where the international circulation of ideas can be a fascinating phenomenon: how Roman law affected legal systems down the ages (Reinhard Zimmermann, *The Law of Obligations: Roman Foundations of the Civilian Tradition* (1996); Peter Stein, *Roman Law in European History* (1999); how from Mediterranean mercantile customs the law merchant spread to English law, thereafter to the United States and then into treaty law (see Theodore Plucknett, *A Concise History of the Common Law* (5th edn 2001) 663, and R Coquillette, 'Legal Ideology and Incorporation II: Sir Thomas Ridley, Charles Molloy, and the Literary Battle for the Law Merchant, 1607–76', 61 BUL Rev 315 (1981)); how the special tort liability for commercial suppliers of defective products spread from the US to the EU and thereupon to other nations; and how non-Western legal systems deal with the issues we call tort or delict (see e.g., the alternative to the 'winner takes all' litigation rule of the Tiv tribe of Northern Nigeria discussed in Ewoud Hondius, 'The Supremacy of Western Law', in *Viva Vox Iuris Romani: Essays in Honour of Johannes Emil Spruit* (L De Ligt et al, eds, 2002) 337, 340: arguing that the idea of the supremacy of Western law is basically flawed. In general see H Patrick Glenn, *Legal Traditions of the World: Sustainable Diversity in Law* (2nd edn 2004)).

[117] See e.g., the pure economic loss claim in *Perre v Apand* [1999] HCA 36 (Austl). In general see Jane Stapleton, 'Comparative Economic Loss: Gary Schwartz and Case Law Focussed "Middle Theory"', 50 UCLA Law Review 531 (2002).

need development: perhaps the ALI might consider some electronic technique for notifying highly relevant tort cases from other English-speaking jurisdictions?

II. Benefits of Comparative Tort Materials from Foreign-Language Jurisdictions

A. For US, Canada, Australia, and New Zealand

Next we need to consider whether in their work a legal practitioner or judge in an English-speaking jurisdiction outside the European Union would be assisted by a consideration of the tort law of a foreign language jurisdiction? Apart from the general advantages of perhaps being alerted to novel types of factual dispute and formulations of legal argument, is it likely, for example, that a Supreme Court judge in a New Zealand tort case would find significant further illumination by seeking to understand the relevant Spanish law on the contentious issues? Were the Supreme Court of California[118] and the High Court of Australia[119] in some sense wrong or at least unwise not to refer to the German concept of contract with protective benefit for a third party when they found that a claim lay in the tort of negligence when due to a lawyer's carelessness the intended beneficiary of a will failed to inherit? Certainly the case law suggests that courts in the US, Canada, Australia, and New Zealand do not find any advantage in a regular consideration of the tort law of foreign-language jurisdictions. Why might this be?

1. *The multi-linguist's problems*

Assume our common law judge or practitioner is perfectly multi-lingual: she would still face a number of problems handling foreign-language *law*. First, consider concepts and conceptual arrangements: once we leave the common law world, as we do when we enter foreign-language jurisdictions, we find highly sophisticated legal environments within which we will search in vain to find direct parallels of certain distinctive legal categories that common lawyers use such as trustee, consideration, and estoppel. Conversely, we will find concepts with no direct parallel in the common law, and though these can be of use in English-speaking jurisdictions with a mixed heritage such as Louisiana[120] and Scotland,

---

[118] *Biakanja v Irving*, 49 Cal 2d 647, 650 (1958) held that a notary public who negligently failed to direct proper attestation of a will became liable in tort to an intended beneficiary damaged because of the invalidity of the instrument. See also *Lucas v Hamm*, 56 Cal 2d 583 (1961) which extended the *Biakanja* rationale to the attorney-client relationship and held that an attorney who negligently drafted a will could be held liable to a person named in the will who suffered deprivation of benefits as a result of the negligence.

[119] *Hill v Van Erp* (1997) 188 CLR 159 (Austl).

[120] There are 'many cases where common law judges employ the concepts of the civil law in order to assist them in their interpretation of the common law'. WJ Zwalve, '*Ryall v Rolle* and the Commune, Canon Law, and Common Law in England' 66 Tul L Rev 1745, 1755 (1992). On mixed systems see n 54 above. *Civilian Tradition*, 56 LA. L. REV 437, 439 (1995). See also Charles Donahue, Jr., *Ius*.

their transplantation into simple common law systems is perilous. Again take the German concept of a contract with protective benefit for a third party, a construct that Germans exploit to deal with the perceived inadequacies of tort law as codified in the German Civil Code: why on earth would California or Australia want to address this foreign phenomenon when local tort law suffers from no such inadequacy?

There may also be many structural features of a foreign jurisdiction that need to be understood: thus a recent decision of the House of Lords has been attacked for its referring to German tort law while apparently neglecting the allegedly relevant fact that, like most US employees, German workers cannot sue their employer in negligence.[121]

More generally, there are broad contrasts in legal style between Old and New World jurisdictions. For example, reference to common Roman law origins can help deflate trivial or artificial differences between jurisdictions within the Old World.[122] In contrast, amongst judges and practitioners in the New World jurisdictions of North America and Australasia there is a pronounced indifference to Roman law,[123] perhaps based not merely on their common law rather than civilian heritage (Quebec and Louisiana excepted) but also on an embarrassment about Roman law's tolerance of slavery and a repulsion for a legal system that had been accessible only to a Latin-comprehending Christian elite.[124]

Another vital contrast relates to the status and form of judicial reasoning. Though it is widely known in the common law world that the status of case law is different in Code systems, it is not widely known what that status is for individual foreign-language jurisdictions and how, for example, it might vary between areas of tort law and over time.[125] Moreover, not all tort doctrine is derived from the Code and later statutes: there is a great deal of judge-made tort law, some of which exhibits a spirit that is antithetical to that originally associated with the

---

[121] Tony Weir, 'Making it More Likely v Making it Happen', Cambridge LJ 519, 521 (2002): 'The *tour d'horizon* was admittedly superficial. Omitted is the salient fact that in almost none of the jurisdictions glanced at would the claimants in *Fairchild* have succeeded: in most places an employee simply cannot sue his employer in tort, since workmen's compensation or social security takes its place.'

[122] But see n 164, below.

[123] Even in US academe, there may be open hostility. E.g., John G Fleming, who had escaped the holocaust as a schoolboy, noted Roman law has a 'curious, almost neurotic, fascination for British scholars' and that 'the whole retention [in a modern comparative law text] of this Roman law relic [of the Lex Aquilia] surely owes more to nostalgia than to functional justification'. 'Comparative Law of Torts', 4 Oxf J Leg Studs 235 (1984).

[124] The exclusion of Jews from the Western legal world slowly eroded during the 19th century. See Reinhard Zimmermann, '"Was Heimat hieb, nun heibt es Holle" The Emigration of Lawyers from Hitler's Germany: Political Background, Legal Framework, and Cultural Context', in *Jurists Uprooted: German-Speaking Émigré Lawyers in Twentieth-Century Britain* (Jack Beatson and Reinhard Zimmermann, eds, 2004) 1, 16–17.

[125] Ewoud Hondius, 'Precedent in East and West', 23 Penn St Int'l L Rev 521. An interesting question is whether the recent development of electronic resources, making case law more accessible across the Continent may lead judicial analysis to converge as judges cite and engage with a wide pool of cases.

Code.[126] Indeed the great John Fleming noted that 'the modern law of torts in all of the principle civil law countries is today judge-made, a vast gloss overlaying a few exiguous Code articles'.[127]

Yet how intellectually accessible is that case law to the common lawyer? In the New World legal realism urges courts to provide reasoning that is not only coherent and rigorous, but also candid and transparent in identifying and evaluating the underlying values in tension. While it is true that, within the subtle and rich jurisprudence surrounding a Civil Code, civilian courts sometimes treat Code text as an impassable obstacle, narrow tram-tracks that allow only a very limited amount of manoeuvre and adaptation to new challenges, often such courts covertly manipulate the Code's provisions. Typically adopting the direction pointed to by some eminent jurist, these courts are willing to be highly 'creative' in their manipulation to reach the desired result,[128] far more creative than (at least non-US) common law courts tend to be in their respectful approach to statutory interpretation. Such nuances are not a simple matter for the practitioner or judge in an English-speaking jurisdiction to grasp.

The importance of this for our purposes is that a common lawyer looking for inspiration from the legal values in play in Continental judgments will often be disappointed because the latter can be 'absorbed with ways to outflank the Code without taking us into their confidence why these manoeuvres are thought desirable. German, no less than French, courts are articulate about means but not ends'.[129] Furthermore, even where the court in a foreign-language jurisdiction does enunciate values, the weight put on them is culturally contingent in ways that are complex and hard for the outsider to appreciate. For example,[130] in one society there may be a long tradition of expecting young adults to assume responsibility and care for the elderly which is supported by an expectation that people will be supported in their old age.[131]

---

[126] Such as the right of personality and privacy in German law. See Huw Beverley-Smith, Ansgar Ohly and Agnès Lucas-Schloetter, *Privacy, Property and Personality—Civil Law Perspectives on Commercial Appropriation* (2005) ch 4, 10. On this 'decodification' dynamic see John G Fleming, 'Comparative Law of Torts', 4 Oxf J Leg Studs 235, 238–39 (1984).

[127] Fleming, Ibid, at 241.

[128] Using 'surreptitious techniques… [and] covertly through subtle manipulation' of the Code text. *Pure Economic Loss in Europe* (Mauro Bussani and Vernon Palmer, eds, 2003) 124. See also Koziol's paper for this conference.

[129] Fleming, n 126 above, at 242. Consider also the 'inscrutable language in which the [European Court of Justice] traditionally clothes its judgments': Alan Rodger, 'Savigny in the Strand', 28–30 The Irish Jurist 1, 10 (1995). For an enlightening general study of the contrasting approaches to judicial discourse and accountability between the US Supreme Court, the French Cour de cassation, and the European Court of Justice, see Mitchel De S-O-L'É Lasser, *Judicial Deliberations: A Comparative Analysis of Transparency and Legitimacy* (2004).

[130] Another example is the absolute protection to human dignity enshrined in Art 1 of the 1949 post-Nazi Constitution (Basic Law, Grundgesetz) of Germany.

[131] Contrast the social functions of adoption in the US with those in Turkey where adopters must be over 35, adoptees are mostly over 30, and usually remain part of their natural family. David Nelken, 'Book Review of *The Enigma of Comparative Law: Variations on a Theme for the 21st Century* by Esin Orucu, 26 Legal Stud 129, 134 (2006).

In short, the general indifference of North American and Australasian courts and practitioners to the tort law of foreign-language jurisdictions seems a wise response to inescapable phenomena. For them there is no more to be *reliably* derived from foreign-language jurisdictions than from English-speaking ones, namely notice of novel types of factual dispute and formulations of legal argument: moreover, there are added perils of misinterpretation. The common law world seems, at least to me, to be rich enough for most needs of tort practitioners and judges in English-speaking jurisdictions, and claims that they should also address foreign-language legal materials, let alone that they should routinely do so, are not supported by compelling argument. Indeed we should be mightily relieved that our North American and Australasian judges are not tempted to acquiesce to the pressure of such claims.

2. *The Mono-Linguist's Problems*

But of course the perils involved when tort practitioners and judges in English-speaking jurisdictions resort to foreign-language legal materials are even graver because most common law judges and practitioners are fully fluent only in English: access to foreign-language legal materials will be second hand. For that reason, the legal and linguistic capacity of the translator is crucial, but so too is availability and quality of the translated materials. As we all know from experience of our domestic tort system, some judges, legal commentators, and empiricists are more gifted than others; and even between gifted lawyers there are large disagreements about the law. I have no doubt that the percentage of gifted lawyers in foreign-language jurisdictions is at least as high as that in English-language ones. But how confident can a domestic practitioner or judge be that it is the output of these foreign lawyers that are put up for translation into English?

This problem is especially acute in Code systems where certain academic commentaries on tort law both within and outside the Civil Code have influence and authority far beyond any academic materials in English-speaking jurisdictions,[132] except for the US Restatements. The fact that, whereas the English legal tradition treats judges as the senior partners in lawmaking, the Continental tradition recognizes legal academics in this role, partly explains why some Continental jurists make statements that such and such is the 'correct' 'solution'[133] to a legal issue. Such language can shock lawyers in common law jurisdictions where it is customary to couch normative arguments with greater reserve, unless they appreciate that these Continental lawyers seek to have their academic commentaries

---

[132] Indeed, Continental jurists are sometimes mandated reading for common law judges! See Civil Jurisdiction and Judgments Act 1982 (United Kingdom, ch 27), § 3(3) as amended.

[133] Another reason is the limits of language. English has words that convey the 'resolution', 'remedy', or 'resolution' of a problem without the implication that this is the only 'solution' that may be possible. Languages other than English may not have this diversity of expression so that a translation into the term 'solution' may mislead the English reader into thinking the writer means something more normatively loaded than merely 'a resolution'.

accepted as law. The legal cultural reasons for this difference in the role of jurists are fascinating in their own right, especially in comparison to US and other common law systems.[134] But the point I want to make here is that of the six or so most authoritative and extensive commentaries on the German Civil Code and extra-code law of obligations, none has been translated into English. This means that English speakers do not have these texts available so as to provide the necessary foils for the one extensive text on German tort law that has been written in English.[135] Moreover, to my knowledge there are no other texts, written in English or in translation, that deal in detail[136] with tort law in other foreign-language jurisdictions.

This raises a further problem, that of appropriate selection. Faced with the practical limits of adjudication and bounded rationality, even the most enthusiastic advocate of the use of foreign-language legal materials in common law courts could not support a comprehensive survey of all such materials from all foreign-language jurisdictions: no sane Taxing Master would approve the costs a party would have to expend to marshal the necessary experts in such material. Nor could such an advocate defend a selection that was random. But there seems to be little debate about possible methodologies of selection.[137]

It is true that Basil Markesinis and Jörg Fedtke have recently asserted that when, in following their direction to address the law of foreign jurisdictions, we make our selection:

[A] single one can be enough, provided it is an advanced system, with a roughly comparable socio-economic environment and offers reasonable accessibility to its sources and experience.[138]

Accordingly, in their campaign to persuade British courts to expand the liability of public authorities into new fields, they select Germany as their favoured foreign jurisdiction. This is not simply because they believe that the German legal system deserves lavish praise: 'structure, system, and internal consistency are attributes highly valued by German lawyers; and their Civil Code...has adopted them to perfection'.[139] They select Germany on the basis of their belief that 'Germans

---

[134] On the comparative role of the academic, judge, and practitioner in a legal system see: William Twining, Ward Farnsworth, Stefan Vogenauer and Fernando Téson, 'The Role of Academics in the Legal System', in *The Oxford Handbook of Legal Studies* (Peter Cane and Mark Tushnet, eds, 2003) 920; Alan Rodger, 'Savigny in the Strand', 28–30 The Irish Jurist 1 (1995). Few common lawyers seem to appreciate the extent of the role of the civilian judge in discovering the relevant law, rather than relying on the submissions of counsel.

[135] Basil Markesinis and Hannes Unberath, *The German Law of Torts: A Comparative Treatise* (4th edn 2002).

[136] Contrast e.g., John Bell, Sophie Boyron and Simon Whittaker, *Principles of French Law* (1998).

[137] Jack Beatson, 'Book Review', 120 Law Q Rev 175, 178 (2004).

[138] Basil Markesinis and Jörg Fedtke, 'Authority or reason? The Economic Consequences of Liability for Breach of statutory Duty in a Comparative Perspective', EBLR 5 at 66–7 (2007).

[139] Ibid at 9.

have masses of'[140] the kind of raw empirical data relevant to the liability of public authorities. The flaw in their approach is that these data are in no way adequate to the purpose Markesinis and Fedtke seek to put them: they are simply too crude. Moreover, it is extremely unlikely that the research and analysis needed to produce compelling socio-legal data in the future from any jurisdiction will receive the necessary funding.

So we are left without an obvious criterion of selection. This is problematic since there would seem to be a number of different possible criteria. For example, the United States has more citizens of German descent than of French; New Zealand has more citizens of Scottish descent than Spanish; Australia has more citizens of Greek descent than of German. Should this affect the selection? What about language pools within the domestic jurisdiction? In which case US courts should presumably prioritize materials from Spanish-speaking jurisdictions.[141] What about a traditional comparativists' device, the 'legal family'? In which case England should look to Singapore rather than Germany.[142] What about the relationship between 'parent' systems and 'colonies' or 'derivatives'?[143] In which case India and many African nations should look to England rather than culturally closer jurisdictions. What about major trade partners? In which case Australian courts should address Japanese law[144] and US courts will need to look at Chinese law.[145] What about military partners? Should US courts give particular emphasis to the law of those countries that contain most of the overseas US Defense Department installations: Germany (302), Japan (111), and South Korea (106)?[146]

B. For Eire, Scotland, England, and Wales

These three Old World English-speaking jurisdictions share membership of the European Union with a large number of foreign-language jurisdictions and, for some judges in this trio of jurisdictions, this provides a reason to pay attention to foreign-language materials from the individual member states even where the case at hand involves a purely domestic legal issue of tort law. For example, having specifically asked counsel for material describing the position in European

---

[140] Ibid at 67. See n 41 and accompanying text.

[141] Spanish is the second most common language in the US after English. According to the 2000 United States Census, Spanish is spoken most frequently at home by about 28.1 million people aged five or over.

[142] Materials from the Commonwealth are available on the net at <http://www.commonlii. org>.

[143] Basil S Markesinis and Jörg Fedtke, 'The Judge as Comparativist', 80 Tul L Rev 11, 68 (2005). See also 34, 97.

[144] On which, see Hiroshi Oda, *Japanese Law* (2001).

[145] On which, see e.g., George W Conk, 'People's Republic of China Civil Code: Tort Liability Law', 5 Private Law Rev 77 (2005).

[146] Department of Defense, Base Structure Report, Fiscal Year 2005 Baseline, at 2.

legal systems[147] in a landmark mesothelioma case, *Fairchild*, creating a special rule of proof of causation, Lord Bingham stated that:

In a shrinking world (in which the employees of asbestos companies may work for those companies in any one or more of several countries) there must be some virtue in uniformity of outcome whatever the diversity of approach in reaching that outcome.[148]

Must there be? One by one, jurisdictions will confront an issue. When are there enough resolutions so that a sufficient 'uniformity' of outcome can be detected and exercise this normative pull on the undecided? What if the early consensus offends a court's sense of justice? What if the source of the foreign-language material or its translator is not reliable? What if, as alleged by Tony Weir in relation to this same decision, the foreign-language material was superficially 'glanced' at without reference to a highly relevant contextual fact?[149]

Significantly, in this same case the Lords also looked at English-language materials to which they wisely paid very much greater attention. In the decision of the Supreme Court of California of *Rutherford v Owens-Illinois Inc*[150] the Lords found a range of pertinent arguments in a familiar common law conceptual framework and in their own language the subtle nuances of which presented no barrier to understanding.[151] Again in the subsequent case addressing the issue of whether liability under *Fairchild* should be *in solidum* or proportionate, no member of the House of Lords referred to the material concerning foreign-language jurisdictions that had been proffered by counsel, but three members[152] used arguments found in a variety of materials from the US.[153] In short, the practice of the judges in English-language jurisdictions, even those in the EU, to look to foreign-language materials on tort cautiously and only intermittently is both legitimate and wise. Indeed, were we to accept the extraordinary argument of Basil Markesinis that, once a judge does refer to foreign material in one case, he must explain why he is not using it in each and every case thereafter,[154] a new judge would have a real incentive not to refer to that material in any case—ever!

---

[147] See Jane Stapleton, 'Lords a'leaping Evidentiary Gaps', 10 Torts Law J 276, 302 (2002).

[148] *Fairchild* [2003] 1 AC 32, ¶ 32 (UK) (per Lord Bingham).

[149] See n 116 above.

[150] 67 Cal Rptr 2d 16 (1997).

[151] Lord Rodger has noted that 'our judges can read the cases [from other English-language jurisdictions] for themselves and can assess how their reasoning could be fitted into the existing scheme' which is crucial because 'to be really helpful...the [foreign] authority would have to be investigated in detail and would have to be capable in some way of application within the framework of our own system', Alan Rodger, 'Savigny in the Strand', 28–30 The Irish Jurist 1, 19 (1995).

[152] See *Barker v Corus (UK) Plc* [2006] UKHL 20, per Lord Hoffmann, per Lord Walker of Gestingthorpe at ¶ 111 and Baroness Hale of Richmond at ¶ 122.

[153] Such as *Prosser and Keeton On Torts* (5th edn 1984); the Supreme Court of California decision in *Brown v Superior Court*, 751 P 2d 470 (1988); and the Court of Appeals of New York in *Hymowitz v Eli Lilly and Co*, 539 NE 2d 1069 (1988).

[154] Basil Markesinis, 'Judicial Mentality: Mental Disposition or Outlook as a Factor Impeding Recourse to Foreign Law', 80 Tul L Rev 1325, 1361–62 (2006): 'If that same judge had, on an earlier occasion, himself resorted to foreign law, one would expect him to tell his audience why in

III. Benefits of 'Coordinated' Tort Materials: Restatements, EU 'Principles'

A. Intra-national coordination by restatement of tort law

A final possible source of comparative tort materials for the practitioner and judge in an English-speaking jurisdiction are what I will call 'coordinated' materials: those that seek to capture or review tort law across more than one formal judicial or legislative jurisdiction. American lawyers are completely familiar with ALI restatements.[155] Restatements exist for and are funded by US practitioners, judges, and other users: they are in this sense 'bottom-up' projects. The general motive for these intra-national projects is apolitical, in the sense that there is no explicit or covert aim to rearrange formal lawmaking power.[156] Rather the aim is to provide a fulcrum for the dissemination of information about divergences and convergences among the dozens of jurisdictions that operate within one nation and one national market place. That such divergences have grown up after a relatively short time since they developed from a common source in England (Louisiana excepted) is testament to the centrifugal tendencies of the common law method, it not being tied to any Code text.[157] In addition, US tort law is further fragmented by local state legislative reforms, perhaps most notoriously in the area of joint and several liability.[158] As noted earlier, this doctrinal fragmentation is, I suspect, one reason why tort theory is much more popular in the US than in

---

this newer case the foreign experience was of no relevance.' (Markesinis also asserts that where one judge mentions foreign law 'would it not be reasonable, constructive and courteous to expect [his colleagues in the same decision] to try and counter in a specific manner this material rather than pass it by in silence?' (at 1371).) Justice Scalia asserts a similar point to attack *any* citation of foreign law: 'to invoke alien law when it agrees with one's thinking, and ignore it otherwise, is not reasoned decision-making, but sophistry.' *Roper v Simmons*, 543 US 551, 627 (2005) (Scalia J, dissenting).

[155] See e.g., *The Restatement (Third) of Torts: Liability for Physical Harm* (Proposed Final Draft No 1, 2005).

[156] There are however debates about the degree to which the ALI processes are or can be politically neutral. See e.g., Frank J Vandall, 'Constructing a Roof Before the Foundation is Prepared: The Restatement (Third) of Torts: Products Liability Section 2 (b) Design Defect', 30 U Mich JL Reform 261, 279 (1997), 'the ALI's mission is no longer to restate the law, but rather to issue pro-manufacturer political documents'; Richard A Posner, 'Address to the American Law Institute', 18 May 1995, 'who would have imagined that the special interests would place the Institute under siege, as if it were a real legislature... the increasing political character of American law [means] ... it is more and more difficult for the Institute to engage with important questions... without crossing the line that separates technical law from politics.'

[157] Legal history can illuminate the socio-politico-economic reasons for broader centrifugal fashions such as the rise of post-revolutionary French interest in reflecting national identity and culture in their law, and a comparable concern in other Continental countries after the collapse of Napoleonic empire. See Franz Wieacker, Reinhard Zimmermann and Tony Weir, *A History of Private Law in Europe with Particular Reference to Germany* (1996); and n 163 below. Contrast the 'top-down' politically motivated centripetal projects in the EU today, see below.

[158] The resultant state of disarray, set out in *Restatement (Third) of Torts: Apportionment of Liability* (2000) 153–59, has been described by Tony Weir as 'such a trackless morass, Dismal

other English-speaking jurisdictions: it allows academics to write for a national audience which activity is attractive both intellectually and because it enhances career prospects. In contrast, academics in English-speaking jurisdictions with unified tort law need only deal with a relatively small set of appellate cases before their doctrinal analysis can be attractive to a national academic, practitioner, and judicial audience. Moreover it can directly influence the judicial development of a tort law that is national.[159]

Three features of US tort restatements are important in comparative perspective, especially in light of the moves to unification in the European Union. First, the Reporter's Notes of the recent third round of torts restatements have a much increased citation of non-US cases and secondary materials, virtually all of which refer to the law in other English-speaking jurisdictions. Secondly, non-US tort lawyers should appreciate that the black-letter format of restatements provides an institutionalized way of crystallizing potential rules of law with which the judge can govern access to the jury.[160] This crystallization is not required in jury-free systems.

Thirdly, non-US tort lawyers should understand how a restatement might seem to encourage convergence. A restatement consists of three types of text: the black-letter section, comments on the black-letter, and Reporter's Notes. In virtually all restatements the black-letter does not record divergences between jurisdictions:[161] this is discussed in the comments and actual cases are only recorded in the Reporter's Notes. By elevating an approach which has only so far been taken by a few jurisdictions to the status of a black-letter 'rule', a Reporter can promote that approach across the nation: this is the story of the rule in §402A of the Second Restatement which was, subsequent to its publication, adopted by US courts in virtually all jurisdictions.

Conversely, by including within the black-letter a requirement the Reporter believes is imposed by a majority of jurisdictions, he can encourage the minority of states to follow suit: an example is the requirement of a reasonable alternative design in §2(b) of the Third Restatement on Products Liability.[162] However, this appearance that restatements promote convergence is highly deceptive: as US practitioners know only too well. State courts have, for example, interpreted the

---

Swamp, and Desolation of Smaug that surely a very wrong turning must have been taken in order to reach them.' Tony Weir, 'All or Nothing?', 78 Tul L Rev 511, 524. n.63 (2004).

[159] Or in the case of England and Wales, and Scotland, can be if the decision on an appeal from one jurisdiction is stated to apply to or is later accepted in the other.

[160] See text at nn 87–89, above.

[161] A notable exception is *The Restatement (Third) of Torts: Apportionment of Liability* (2000).

[162] *Restatement (Third) of Torts: Products Liability* (1998). S 2(b) reads: 'A product is defective when, at the time of sale or distribution, it contains a manufacturing defect, is defective in design, or is defective because of inadequate instructions or warnings. A product: (b) is defective in design when the foreseeable risks of harm posed by the product could have been reduced or avoided by the adoption of a reasonable alternative design by the seller or other distributor, or a predecessor in the commercial chain of distribution, and the omission of the alternative design renders the product not reasonably safe.'

special tort liability in §402A differently and so today state regimes of products liability manifest considerable variations. This confirms that US tort law, even when it stems from a common text such as §402A, will diverge because there is no single court of ultimate appeal on tort matters.

B. International coordination by harmonization/codification of tort law

The European Union began to issue uniform laws relating to private law with the 1985 product liability Directive which, albeit described as a harmonization measure, bizarrely introduced an *additional* layer of potential liability on product suppliers across all member states.[163] Since then there has been increasing interest in comparing private law regimes within the Union. For example, the projects of the Trento Group[164] seek to identify divergences as well as the convergent 'common core' of European private law: these projects have no political goal. The Group has produced a number of works in English such as a volume on economic loss in which Mauro Bussani and Vernon Palmer provide profound insights into the divergences and convergences of the law in this field across jurisdictions.[165] A similar political agnosticism is manifest in recent comparative studies on public authority liability[166] and in the monograph on European tort law by Cees van Dam[167] who doubts, rightly in my view,[168] that pro-active harmonization of tort law across the Union is authorized by the Treaty of Rome. The EU has no direct power as such to enforce harmonization, let alone codification, across tort law.[169] There is simply no evidence that the real differences across tort systems appreciably distort trade or competition, which according to the European Court of Justice is a Treaty pre-requisite for any EU legislative initiative to harmonize tort law. Moreover, such a move arguably offends the EU's alleged commitment to 'preserving diversity and ensuring that decisions are taken as close as possible to the citizens'.[170] Indeed there are profound philosophical arguments in

---

[163] For a list of the relevant measures see *Fundamental Texts on European Private Law* (Oliver Radley-Gardner, Hugh Beale, Reinhard Zimmermann and Reiner Schulze, eds, 2003) Sub I.

[164] On which, see Mauro Bussani, 'Current trends in European Comparative Law: The Common Core Approach', 21 Hastings Int'l & Comp L Rev 785 (1998).

[165] *Pure Economic Loss in Europe* (Mauro Bussani and Vernon Palmer, eds, 2003).

[166] See *Tort Liability of Public Authorities in Comparative Perspective* (Duncan Fairgrieve, Mads Andenas and John Bell, eds, 2002); and Duncan Fairgrieve, *State Liability in Tort: A Comparative Law Study* (2003) which is a French-English law comparison. Contrast Basil S Markesinis et al, *Tortious Liability of Statutory Bodies: A Comparative and Economic Analysis of Five English Cases* (1999).

[167] Cees Van Dam, *European Tort Law* (2006) 133–35.

[168] Jane Stapleton, *Product Liability* (1994) 53–58.

[169] Jonathan Mance, 'Is Europe Aiming to Civilise the Common Law?', 7 Eur Bus Law Rev (2006) (forthcoming).

[170] See <http://europa.eu/abc/panorama/index_en.htm>. On the 'difficulty in a budding federal system of setting pragmatic limits to centralizing idealism and giving real meaning to "subsidiarity"', and Mance, n 161 above.

favour of diversity of law as a source of enrichment of a community's identity.[171] Nonetheless, there has been quite an embarrassing amount of work published that asserts, not merely that there is much harmony already between the tort law of European systems, but also that they are rapidly converging. Where 'convergence' authors do not declare their political motivations,[172] such work must be treated as deeply suspect. But there is also much recent material in English on European tort law that is more or less candid in its politically-motivated enthusiasm for pro-active harmonization[173] across existing jurisdictions, a dynamic that can be assisted, albeit superficially,[174] by appeal to the 'common heritage' of civilian systems in Roman Law, the Corpus Juris Civilis, and the European Ius Commune.[175] Though we can expect 'distortion as the price of uniformity,'[176] support for full codification is also now fashionable among many academics.[177] For example, Christian von Bar has published large volumes on the 'common European law of torts'[178] and heads the 'Study Group on a European Civil Code'[179] which is drafting common European principles for the most important

---

[171] 'At the end of the eighteenth century, in reaction against the rationalism of the Enlightenment, it was recognized that nations and peoples also had an individuality of their own, which found expression in, among other things, their laws, and that these national individualities were valuable, and ought to be cherished. Scots law is different from English law. Not only may it be none the worse for that…but it is a positive merit, contributing a further thread to the web of Scottish identity. Although there are advantages in a uniform Code Napoleon or Whitehall-drafted Statute Law, these are usually purchased at too high a price of impersonality and alienation. The diversity of peoples ought to be reflected in a diversity of laws, in order that we may all feel at home in our own laws; the anomalies of devolution are a small price to pay for our all being able collectively to do our own thing.' JR Lucas, 'The Nature of Law', 23 Philosophica 37, 43 (1979).

[172] Contrast the admirably explicit declaration of political motivation in his emphasis of similarities among EU jurisdictions by Basil Markesinis, *Foreign Law and Comparative Methodology: A Subject and a Thesis* (1997) 6.

[173] See *The Harmonization of European Private Law* (Mark Van Hoecke and Francois Ost, eds, 2000); *The Institutional Framework of European Private Law* (Fabrizio Cafaggi, ed, 2006); Gert Bruggemeier, *Common Principles of Tort Law: A Pre-Statement of Law* (2004).

[174] See e.g., Fleming, n 126 above, 'True it certainly is that many of the still recalcitrant problems were already identified by the Roman jurists (omissions, economic loss, etc.), but the modern law of torts in Europe bears few discernible traces of that heritage.'

[175] See e.g., Klaus Luig, 'The History of Roman Private Law and the Unification of European Law', 5 ZEUP 405 (1997). Roman law, as it was systematized in the Corpus Juris Civilis (the collection of laws initiated by the Emperor Justinian I around 530), was rediscovered, interpreted, and reshaped by medieval jurists with elements of canon law and of Germanic custom, especially feudal law. Some argue that by the middle of the 16th century, there had resulted a European Ius Commune that was common to all continental Europe (and Scotland). This era of apparent unity of legal system ended when national codifications were adopted beginning with the French Civil Code in 1804. For a strident critic of the notion of a 'ius commune which previously existed', see Pierre Legrand, 'Book Review of Torts Ed by Walter van Gerven', Camb LJ 439, 440 (1999). A more nuanced account is H Patrick Glenn, *On Common Laws* (2005) 16–20.

[176] HLA Hart, *The Concept of Law* (2nd edn 1994) 38.

[177] *Towards a European Civil Code* (Arthur Hartkamp et al, eds, 3rd edn 2004); *The Politics of a European Civil Code* (Martijn W Hesselink, ed, 2006).

[178] Christian Von Bar, *The Common European Law of Torts*, Vol 1 (1998); Christian Von Bar, *The Common European Law of Torts*, Vol 2 (2000).

[179] The first volumes of this project began to appear in 2006.

aspects of the law of obligations and certain aspects of the law of property in movables. So far, however, only Helmut Koziol's group, the European Group on Tort Law,[180] has published in hard copy its model tort rules, the 2005 'Principles of European Tort Law' (PETL).

Such principles may lead to a future EU Code and so they may be of some current value to the practitioner or judge in Eire, Scotland, England and Wales: so long as they clearly understand the political motivation and compromise nature of the Principles and take account of the large variation between member states in how a common text will be perceived and applied.[181] But are such principles of value for the non-EU practitioner or judge in, for example, the US, Canada, Australia, and New Zealand? There are a number of reasons to suggest not. First, there are all the reasons why such lawyers would be wise to avoid a consideration of the law of individual foreign-language jurisdictions.[182] Secondly, at least in relation to the 2005 PETL, the format of the text follows, understandably given the vast majority of EU members with civilian legal systems, the layout of civilian Codes and does not map easily onto the common law landscape. Thirdly, the future standing of the black-letter articles is problematic. Even were an EU Code of tort principles to be adopted, it is unlikely to be accompanied by mechanisms sufficiently thorough to prevent the divergences of interpretations and development we see in common law systems.[183] The reality seems to be that the European Court of Justice could never exercise the control of tort doctrines that is currently

---

[180] European Group on Tort Law, *Principles of European Tort Law: Text and Commentary* (2005). The home page of the Study Group on a European Civil Code, <http://www.sgecc.net>, has the text of its articles on tort law in the version dated December 2005.

[181] For legal-cultural reasons it might be, e.g., that French courts will read a common text as merely a broad guideline (requiring only 'soft convergence') within which they can exercise considerable discretion (using devices such as the opaque French approach to causation. See n 123 above), but English courts will read such a text in terms of hard convergence requiring a rigorous attempt to accommodate other member states' applications of the text. More generally there is a school of thought, prominently represented by Pierre Legrand, that argues that harmonization is impossible because people from different legal cultures may understand the same legal text in quite different ways. See Pierre Legrand, 'The Same and the Different', in *Comparative Legal Studies: Traditions and Transitions* (Pierre Legrand and Roderick Munday, eds, 2003); Pierre Legrand, 'European Legal Systems Are Not Converging', 45 Int Comp LQ 52 (1996); Pierre Legrand, 'Against a European Civil Code', 60 Mod L Rev 44 (1997). Thus 'even if there are identical legal rules, the legal cultures will still be different, a fact which may ultimately lead to different practical results.' Erik Jayme, *Multicultural Society and Private Law German Experiences* 10 (1999). See also Stephen Weatherill, 'Why Object to the Harmonization of Private Law by the EC?', 12 Eur Rev Priv Law 633 (2004); Stephen Weatherill, 'Harmonisation: How Much, How Little?' [2005] EBLR 533; G Teubner, 'Legal Irritants: Good Faith in British Law or How Unifying Law ends up in New Divergences', 61 MLR 11 (1998); and the Manifesto or Study Group on Social Justice in European Private Law (see Study Group on Social Justice in European Private Law, 'Social Justice in European Contract Law: A Manifesto, 10 Eur L J 653 (2004)) which produces material that seeks to highlight the political dimensions of the effort to Europeanize private law and the cultural embeddedness of law which can produce divergences in the application of an identical legal rule.

[182] Compounded when, as here, the legal materials rely on translations from *many* languages.

[183] There is an important parallel here with the divergences that past empires and monarchies had to tolerate. See H Patrick Glenn, *On Common Laws* (2005).

possible in domestic systems with tight adherence to precedent and a single court of final appeal on matters of judge-made common law such as Australia, Canada, and, subject to reciprocal acceptance of House of Lords' decisions, the United Kingdom.

Finally, there is still some doubt about how stable the EU will prove in the long term as a political, as opposed to economic, union. Before its dissolution into 15 nations in 1991 the population of the USSR was 293 million; today the EU has 27 member states and 490 million people and it uses 23 official languages.[184] If tort law does manifest features that are culturally specific, how much might the social fabric of local jurisdictions be damaged by elimination of such features in a unifying 'code'? For example, unlike French parents, British parents are not vicariously liable for their underage offspring who live with them: were a future EU Civil Code to impose such liability, would there be an outcry in Britain? Would this and similar frustrations contribute to a future collapse of the political union? It is a shame that we do not seem to know or care whether frustrations in the private law area played any part in the agitation that produced the collapse of the USSR, let alone the extent to which the private law systems of the resultant separate nations have diverged since that collapse.

But, whatever the fate of the EU, there is of course one use to which materials such as the 2005 PETL might fruitfully be put: namely, as yet another source of plausible arguments and legal concerns. The admirable commentaries on the Principles adopt a 'flexible system'[185] which allows a variety of differing concerns and arguments to be spelt out. Thus, in the unlikely event that a practitioner and judge in an English-speaking jurisdiction is in need of yet further inspiration beyond that available in the pool of English-language jurisdictions, these commentaries would be a valuable additional resource.

Conclusion

Comparative law is a vast field. I believe it is one that provides a crucial enrichment of the lawyer's perspective and understanding. It invites a deep respect for difference even across shared values.

In this paper I have only focused on one dimension of comparative tort law: its utility for courts of final appeal and practitioners in cases where the subject-matter does not positively *require* knowledge of a foreign system (as it would require, for example, when EU law or the judgments of the European Court of Human Rights are in issue). My conclusion is that comparative tort law can enrich the palette of ideas, concerns, perceptions—in short, arguments—that a

---

[184] *New York Times*, 1 January 2007. The United Nations has only six official languages.
[185] *European Group On Tort Law, Principles of European Tort Law: Text and Commentary* (2005) 15.

judge brings to bear on the matters in dispute, since 'it is arguments that influence decisions'.[186] Moreover comparative law provides the insight that there is nothing inevitable about current domestic conceptual arrangements, and so can ease the path of the tort lawyer who is inviting a domestic court to alter those arrangements because it can show that others are at least intellectually viable. This is well-appreciated in English-speaking jurisdictions where, except in the United States, tort practitioners and courts have always regarded each other's national systems as an important source of readily accessible and intelligible ideas. In the US it is arguable that, in a nation as large and litigious as it is, there may be sufficient diversity of arguments to oust a role for comparative non-US English-language law given the practical constraints when practitioners advise and courts decide cases. Even so, the experience of other English-speaking jurisdictions is not identical to the US and as Justice Posner notes: US lawyers can learn from the social laboratories of other nations.[187]

In contrast, foreign-language comparative tort law is fraught with dangers: how to select resources, their degree of reliability and so on. It is rightly unpopular with courts and practitioners in English-speaking jurisdictions, which typically have sufficiently rich resources from within their own language pool.[188]

Finally, comparative tort law can give a court of final appeal no guidance on the justice of a case—how the law should be applied to the facts. In English-speaking common law jurisdictions it makes no sense for a legal academic baldly to attack a decision of the final court of appeal as 'wrong' on the mere basis that it is not the same as that of another jurisdiction or set of jurisdictions. To do so misunderstands the core role of such courts: to determine the weight of arguments in a case and reach a reasoned decision. Legal reasoning can be incoherent, inconsistent, or facile, and rightly attacked on those grounds. But even if an academic could identify all the relevant coherent, consistent, and perceptive concerns in a case, she cannot claim that, by virtue of some objective 'legal science,' she has deduced the correct 'conclusions about the proper policy for the law to adopt',[189] or more generally the 'best answer to [tort] problems,'[190] let alone that the foreign idea is 'superior'.[191] Such claims seem more common among Continental comparativists than among common lawyers who accept that 'in the nature of things, there

---

186 *White* [1993] 3 WLR 730 (UK) 'it is arguments that influence decisions rather than the reading of pages upon pages from judgments' per Lord Steyn LJ.

187 Posner, n 14 above.

188 The same is probably true of the pool of Spanish-speaking jurisdictions and that of the Chinese.

189 K Zweigert and H Kotz, *An Introduction to Comparative Law* (Tony Weir trans, 3rd edn 1998) 6.

190 Basil S Markesinis et al, *Tortious Liability of Statutory Bodies: A Comparative and Economic Analysis of Five English Cases* (1999) 105.

191 Basil S Markesinis and Jörg Fedtke, 'The Judge as Comparativist', 80 Tul L Rev 11, 54 (2005).

is no "right" answer'.[192] In short, while the normative rhetoric of the 'correct' or 'best' or 'superior' solution fits the accepted role of the Code commentator, the perceptive comparativist should, from his sensitivity to comparison and context, see that it is simply inappropriate usage in a common law system, unless he clearly acknowledges that it merely signifies his personal subjective preference.

---

[192] Alan Rodger, 'What are Appeal Courts For?' 10 Otago L Rev 517, 535 (2004). 'Whatever the decision and whatever the reasons, critics will always be able to question them if only because, in the nature of things, there is no "right" answer. The court has simply got to choose and, when it does so, it puts forward the best set of reasons it can devise. Those reasons may not be compelling but that does not mean that the decision itself is incorrect.'

8

Le Conseil d'Etat, so British?

Bernard Stirn

La question aurait surpris et peut-être même indigné Dicey, qui écrivait en 1885 que «la soumission de tous aux mêmes juridictions, sans privilèges pour l'administration est l'expression même de l'Etat de droit».

Il est vrai qu'elle peut sembler relever du paradoxe. Que pourrait avoir de britannique une institution dont les fondements ont été posés par Napoléon, qui incarne une dualité de juridiction, entre l'ordre administratif et l'ordre judiciaire, parfaitement inconnue outre-Manche, qui délivre des avis au gouvernement en même temps qu'elle rend des décisions de justice, selon une dualité de fonctions parfois difficile à comprendre même pour les meilleurs esprits du Royaume-Uni, qui a construit un droit dont les piliers, le service public et la puissance publique, sont des termes difficiles à traduire en anglais?

La question n'est pourtant pas un «joke». Les liens mêmes que Lord Bingham a tissés avec le Conseil d'Etat conduisent à la prendre au sérieux: le grand avocat, le juriste éminent, le Senior Law Lord a porté sur le droit administratif français le regard attentif d'un ami et noué avec de nombreux membres du Conseil d'Etat de cordiales relations d'échange. Le voyage dans les couloirs et les salles du Palais Royal n'était sans doute pas un dépaysement exotique pour l'un des plus fins connaisseurs du droit britannique. Aussi est-il agréable de pouvoir écrire, dans ce livre d'hommage, que, si le Conseil d'Etat, est en apparence la moins britannique des institutions françaises, il est sans doute, en réalité, dans les profondeurs, la plus britannique d'entre elles.

Par son histoire, par ses missions, par le statut de ses membres, le Conseil d'Etat peut sembler «typically french».

Son histoire est intimement liée à celle de la France.

Si certains font remonter ses origines les plus lointaines au Conseil des empereurs romains, il apparaît véritablement au XIII ème siècle, sous la forme du Conseil du Roi, lorsque la monarchie devient organisée et administrative. A partir de Philippe le Bel, qui règne de 1285 à 1314, le Conseil, où siègent déjà des maîtres des requêtes et des conseillers d'Etat, devient un rouage permanent et structuré, qui éclaire le souverain en matière d'administration et de justice. Appelé parfois Conseil d'Etat du Roi, il évolue dans ses structures mais conserve et développe son rôle dans ces deux domaines, en donnant des avis sur l'administration et en préparant le règlement contentieux des affaires d'intérêt public évoquées par la justice royale.

Aussi Bonaparte s'inspire-t-il de l'héritage de la longue histoire lorsque la constitution consulaire du 22 frimaire an VIII donne sa forme moderne au Conseil d'Etat, «chargé de rédiger les projets de lois et de règlements d'administration publique et de résoudre les difficultés qui s'élèvent en matière administrative». Les titres de maîtres des requêtes et de conseillers d'Etat sont repris. Par ce génie de la synthèse qui inspirait le Premier Consul, l'idéal révolutionnaire est aussi reconnu, au travers du nouveau grade qui apparaît , celui d'auditeur. Conformément aux exigences de l'article 6 de la Déclaration des droits de l'homme et du citoyen du 26 août 1789, selon lequel tous les citoyens sont également admissibles à toutes dignités, places et emplois publics, sans autre distinction que elle de leurs vertus et de leurs talents», les auditeurs sont en effet recrutés par un concours, créé par un arrêté des consuls du 9 avril 1803. Des conseils de préfecture, ancêtres des tribunaux administratifs, sont parallèlement placés auprès des préfets.

Sous le Consulat comme sous l'Empire, le Conseil d'Etat joue un rôle déterminant dans l'administration intérieure du pays. Il élabore les grands codes napoléoniens, en commençant par le code civil de 1804. Mais l'institution survit à l'Empire. La Restauration le maintient, la Monarchie de Juillet renforce son indépendance contentieuse en instaurant en 1831 la publicité des audiences de jugement et en créant le commissaire du gouvernement. La II ème République poursuit dans cette voie et adopte des textes qui seront repris par la III ème République. Après avoir retrouvé, sous le second Empire tout le lustre qui avait été le sien durant le premier, le Conseil d'Etat est en effet définitivement adopté par la République, sous l'impulsion notamment de Gambetta. La loi du 24 mai 1872 lui confie la «justice déléguée». Désormais en matière contentieuse, il ne conseille plus, comme au temps de la «justice retenue», le chef de l'Etat mais statue lui-même «au nom du peuple français». Le Tribunal des Conflits, composé de manière paritaire de conseillers d'Etat et de conseillers à la Cour de cassation, qui avait fait une première apparition sous la II ème République, est définitivement mis en place pour trancher les difficultés de compétence entre les deux ordres de juridiction.

Les constitutions de la IV ème République (1946) et de la V ème (1958) mentionnent le Conseil d'Etat et le confirment dans le rôle qu'au travers de la succession des régimes, la Monarchie, l'Empire, la République lui ont successivement attribué. Reflet d'une histoire constitutionnelle mouvementée, marquée par des révolutions et des changements de constitution, le Conseil d'Etat paraît bien loin du processus progressif qui caractérise l'instauration de la monarchie parlementaire en Grande-Bretagne. Ses missions n'ont pas davantage d'équivalent au Royaume-Uni.

A partir du Conseil du Roi s'affirment l'existence d'une juridiction particulière pour connaître des litiges dans lesquels l'autorité publique est impliquée, qui assure en même temps une mission de conseiller du gouvernement. La Révolution conforte la dualité de juridiction dans la crainte que les tribunaux d'Ancien Régime, dont les cours souveraines s'appelaient «parlements», restent attachés aux privilèges du passé. L'Assemblée constituante adopte la loi des 16 et 24 août 1790 qui dispose: «Les fonctions judiciaires sont distinctes et demeureront toujours séparées des fonctions administratives. Les juges ne pourront, à peine de forfaiture, troubler de quelque manière que ce soit les opérations des corps administratifs, ni citer devant eux les administrateurs pour raison de leurs fonctions». Repris par un décret de la Convention du 16 fructidor an III, selon lequel «défenses itératives sont faites aux tribunaux de connaître des actes d'administration, de quelque espèce qu'ils soient, aux peines de droit», ces principes conduisent, à partir de la mise en place en l'an VIII du Conseil d'Etat et des conseils de préfecture, à l'affirmation d'une juridiction administrative qui, tout au long du XIX ème siècle, renforce le contrôle juridictionnel de l'administration et développe un droit original, qui assure l'équilibre entre les prérogatives de la puissance publique et les droits des citoyens. En même temps qu'il exerce ce rôle contentieux, le Conseil d'Etat éclaire le gouvernement de ses avis. Selon une décision du Conseil constitutionnel du 23 janvier 1987, la compétence de la juridiction administrative pour connaître des actes pris en vertu de prérogatives de puissance publique traduit «la conception française de la séparation des pouvoirs». La formule montre à la fois l'originalité et la force d'une construction qui, reposant sur un principe fondamental reconnu par les lois de la République, reçoit valeur constitutionnelle.

Même s'ils exercent des fonctions juridictionnelles, les membres du Conseil d'Etat ont la qualité de fonctionnaires. Pour le recrutement des auditeurs, l'Ecole nationale d'administration succède en 1945 au concours institué sous le Consulat. Les auditeurs poursuivent ensuite leur carrière, en accédant aux grades de maître des requêtes puis de conseiller d'Etat. Ils sont appelés à exercer des fonctions tantôt à l'intérieur du Conseil d'Etat, tantôt à l'extérieur: sur les trois cent membres du corps au total, un tiers environ sont détachés dans d'autres administrations. Un maître des requêtes sur quatre, un conseiller d'Etat sur trois est, en outre, nommé au «tour de l'extérieur», par un choix du gouvernement. Des personnalités qui sont issues de l'administration ou d'autres secteurs de la vie nationale enrichissent ainsi le Conseil d'expériences variées. Les équilibres entre recrutement par concours ou par décision du gouvernement, entre carrière à l'intérieur du corps et fonctions exercées à l'extérieur, reflètent une conception de la fonction publique qui repose sur des notions largement propres à la France.

En dépit du fort ancrage national qui le caractérise, le Conseil d'Etat présente aussi des traits qui ne sont pas sans rappeler ceux des institutions britanniques, avec lesquelles il entretient ainsi des rapports de parenté. Son indépendance et son autorité forgées par l'histoire, son droit largement jurisprudentiel, sa place originale dans les institutions, aux confins des trois pouvoirs, évoquent ainsi des figures que l'on pourrait croire, sur ces points essentiels, venues d'outre-Manche.

Dès le Conseil du Roi, l'indépendance en matière de justice commence à être reconnue. Si l'on en croit Saint-Simon, Louis XIV ne se serait écarté des avis de son Conseil en matière de justice que six fois au cours de son long règne. Au temps encore de la justice retenue, Napoléon lui-même suivra toujours les avis contentieux du Conseil d'Etat. Il en manifeste parfois de l'humeur: «On me fait signer aveuglément des décisions délibérées dans le Conseil d'Etat sur des mat-ières contentieuses: je suis pour cela qu'une griffe» écrit-il. Mais il n'envisage pas de juger autre chose que ce qui lui est proposé. Renforcée par le passage, en 1872, à la justice déléguée, l'indépendance du Conseil d'Etat est un acquis de l'histoire. Sa force vient de l'ancienneté, de la tradition, de la permanence au travers des régimes successifs.

De l'institution, l'indépendance s'étend à ses membres. Sans qu'ils soient pro-tégés par un statut particulier, ils bénéficient d'une inamovibilité qu'aucun texte ne prévoit. D'auditeur à maître des requêtes puis de maître des requêtes à conseiller d'Etat, les avancements de grade se font, par coutume bien établie, à l'ancienneté. De manière plus importante encore, l'attribution des différentes fonctions au sein du Conseil d'Etat est décidée par les seules autorités de l'institution. Des institu-tions que les textes ne consacrent pas jouent un grand rôle dans la vie du Conseil d'Etat. Son administration relève du «bureau», qui réunit, sous la présidence du vice-président, les présidents de section et le secrétaire général. Au contentieux, le président et les présidents adjoints de la section se retrouvent chaque mardi en «troïka» pour veiller à la cohérence des délibérés. La présidence de l'assemblée géné-rale consultative par le Premier ministre est de caractère purement honorifique et protocolaire. Le Conseil d'Etat est effectivement présidé par son vice-président.

L'indépendance et l'autorité du Conseil d'Etat se trouvent ainsi consacrées d'une manière toute britannique. Elles sont le fruit de la longue histoire. Elles sont d'autant plus fortes qu'elles s'appuient non pas sur des textes mais sur des traditions plus solides en réalité que les écrits. La pratique qui les consacre s'écarte parfois de la lettre des textes, moins protecteurs, mais, par le respect que sa per-manence inspire, elle a plus de portée qu'eux.

Par son caractère principalement jurisprudentiel, le droit administratif, tel que le Conseil d'Etat l'a créé, a aussi un parfum britannique.

Il n'y pas, en droit public, de textes généraux, comparables au code civil, au code pénal ou au code de commerce. Certes le législateur a eu, ces dernières années, tendance à intervenir davantage sur les questions administratives, décen-tralisation et organisation des collectivités territoriales, création des autorités administratives indépendantes, protection des droits des citoyens, recrutement, carrière, droits et obligations des fonctionnaires et même procédure administra-tive contentieuse, avec les astreintes, les injonctions, le référé. Il n'en demeure pas moins vrai que le droit administratif est plus un droit jurisprudentiel qu'un droit écrit, qui s'apprend au travers des «grands arrêts» du Conseil d'Etat.

Le Conseil d'Etat a créé et défini le recours pour excès de pouvoir, ouvert même sans texte pour contester la légalité de toute décision administrative. Il a construit le régime de responsabilité de la puissance publique, pour faute et même sans faute. Les grands modes d'action de l'administration, le pouvoir de police, les contrats publics, le service public, s'exercent dans un cadre tracé par ses décisions. Avec les principes généraux du droit, il a conféré une place supérieure aux règles non écrites, que le juge dégage à partir des différents éléments de la conscience collective à un moment donné.

Cette œuvre jurisprudentielle se poursuit. La place croissante du droit international et du droit européen conduit à redéfinir la hiérarchie des normes et à préciser les articulations entre les normes constitutionnelles, le droit international ou européen et la loi nationale. Les impératifs de sécurité juridique s'imposent avec une autorité accrue. De grandes questions de société appellent de nouveau arbitrages du juge, sur la laïcité, le séjour et l'intégration des étrangers, la bioéthique, la préservation de l'environnement.

Année après année, les décisions se succèdent pour construire un édifice où, comme en doit britannique, l'autorité du précédent revêt une grande importance. Si elle peut certes évoluer, la jurisprudence est d'abord stable et cohérente. Les règles de droit découlent du rapprochement de points jugés sur des questions semblables. Plus qu'au droit romain, le droit administratif emprunte au case law et au common law en dégageant peu à peu ses règles à partir des cas d'espèce tranchés par le juge.

La dernière originalité du Conseil d'Etat, qui évoque l'univers britannique, tient à sa place dans les institutions.

Il est, en effet, difficile situer le Conseil d'Etat au regard de la théorie classique des trois pouvoirs, législatif, exécutif et judiciaire.

Conseiller du gouvernement, le Conseil d'Etat est un rouage important du processus de décision de l'exécutif. Les fonctions exercées en détachement par ses membres auprès des autorités gouvernementales renforcent cette association au pouvoir exécutif. Le secrétaire général du gouvernement est ainsi, par tradition, un membre du Conseil d'Etat. Cette proximité avec l'exécutif symbolisée, du temps de l'uniforme, par le fait que ses membres portaient, jusqu'à la fin du Second Empire, l'épée et non la robe, n'empêche en rien le Conseil d'Etat d'exercer en toute indépendance ses fonctions juridictionnelles. Au travers du contentieux, qui représente environ la moitié de son activité, il assure avec exigence le respect du droit par l'ensemble des autorités administratives, à commencer par le gouvernement. Juge suprême des tribunaux administratifs, des cours administratives d'appel et des juridictions administratives spécialisées, il a sans conteste le rôle de cour suprême de l'ordre juridictionnel administratif. Il a en outre la responsabilité de l'administration des tribunaux administratifs et des cours administratives d'appel ainsi que de la Cour nationale du droit d'asile. Par les avis qu'il donne sur tous les projets de loi, le Conseil d'Etat n'est pas non plus dépourvu de liens avec le Parlement. Ces liens se trouvent au demeurant renforcés par la révision constitutionnelle du 23 juillet 2008, qui prévoit que le président de l'Assemblée Nationale et le président du Sénat peuvent demander au Conseil d'Etat son avis avant l'inscription à l'ordre du jour d'une proposition de loi déposée par un parlementaire. Comme juge, le Conseil d'Etat apprécie la responsabilité de l'Etat du fait des lois, y compris lorsque la loi méconnaît les engagements européens et internationaux de la France. Il connaît du contentieux de la fonction publique parlementaire et de la responsabilité contractuelle ou quasi-délictuelle des assemblées.

Ce n'est donc pas à partir d'une vision théorique inspirée de la raison de Descartes ou des principes de Montesquieu qu'il faut chercher à comprendre le Conseil d'Etat. La place originale que l'histoire lui a donnée à l'intersection des pouvoirs rappelle plutôt celle qui revient, jusqu'à la mise en place de la Cour suprême du Royaume-Uni, au comité judiciaire de la Chambre des Lords, commission ancrée dans la chambre haute du Parlement britannique, qui rend souverainement la justice et auquel participait jusqu'en 2006 le Lord chancelier, membre du cabinet.

Une autorité qui découle de l'histoire plus que des textes, un droit forgé par la jurisprudence, une place singulière dans les institutions publiques: on comprend que, sur les points essentiels, Lord Bingham ait pu se sentir «at home» au Conseil d'Etat.

Ces parentés profondes expliquent aussi les liens privilégiés qui se sont développés entre les Law Lords et le Conseil d'Etat depuis la première réunion commune de travail, en 1987, à Londres. Plus nombreux que jamais sont les sujets d'échange. Par sa jurisprudence, la Chambre des Lords a développé le contrôle juridictionnel de l'administration britannique. Veiller à ce qu'une décision administrative ne soit pas «unreasonable» n'est pas sans évoquer le contrôle de l'erreur manifeste d'appréciation. Des juridictions compétentes sur les questions administratives se mettent en place au Royaume-Uni, avec en particulier l'Administrative court créée au sein de la High Court de Londres en 2000. Les réflexions magistrales de Lord Woolf sur les enjeux et l'efficacité de la justice dépassent les frontières du Royaume-Uni et trouvent en France des échos particuliers. Des deux côtés de la Manche, les juges ont à prendre position sur les mêmes grandes questions, identité nationale et intégration des étrangers, liberté individuelle et lutte contre le terrorisme, adaptation de l'action publique à l'économie mondialisée. Le cadre juridique est de plus en plus commun, avec la double application du droit communautaire et, notamment depuis l'entrée en vigueur, en 2000, du Human Rights Act, de la convention européenne des droits de l'homme.

Des adaptations de procédure découlent certes des exigences européennes. En France, le commissaire du gouvernement devient le rapporteur public, au Royaume-Uni, le Lord Chancelier ne participe plus aux délibérations juridictionnelles et la Cour suprême succédera en 2009 au comité judiciaire de la Chambre des Lords. Derrière ces évolutions qui, si elles sont nécessaires, touchent aux apparences plus qu'aux réalités profondes, le dialogue entre les cours suprêmes des pays européens est plus que jamais nécessaire. Le rôle joué par Lord Bingham pour le consolider entre Londres et Paris n'en mérite que davantage de reconnaissance.

«On peut continuer de rêver, de part et d'autre de la Manche, à ce qu'eût été l'Europe si la fortune des Plantagenêts avait été durable» a écrit l'historien français Jean Favier. Dans l'Europe telle qu'elle se construit aujourd'hui, il continue d'exister plus de parentés profondes qu'il n'y paraît parfois entre la Grande-Bretagne et la France. Qu'il soit permis, en terminant, de dire à Lord Bingham que son action et sa pensée ont contribué à les mettre en évidence et qu'au Palais Royal, si différent et pourtant si proche du Palais de Westminster, l'honneur de le compter comme ami se conjugue avec la richesse, passée et future, des réflexions et des travaux communs.

9

The Bingham Court*

Vincenzo Zeno–Zencovich

For eight years Lord Bingham has presided over the Judicial Committee of the House of Lords. These have been years of intense legal change, not only in England but also in the Western world. These changes are reflected in the House of Lords' jurisprudence.

My reflections start from a simple question: is it possible to speak of what our American colleagues would call 'the Bingham Court'?

This is clearly an over-simplified label which cannot cover striking differences. One does not need to be a full-time comparatist to be aware of how much the Judicial Committee of the House of Lords is different from the US Supreme Court (even now that its name will soon been changed to 'Supreme Court'); how different the procedures of appointment to the two Courts; the role of Senior Law Lord in respect of that of Chief Justice; and how implausible it would be to call their Lordships 'brethren'.

However, once we have made all the necessary caveats and measured the distance between the Houses of Parliament and Capitol Hill, a comparatist cannot avoid noticing significant changes in the jurisprudence of the House of Lords since Lord Bingham has been at its summit.

Elegance and discretion forbid even to suggest the idea of a Judicial Committee moulded by the personality of its highest representative. But a comparatist—especially if he is a hard-to-die legal-realist—has the task of pointing out how legal ideas and models circulate, whether within a legal system or between different ones. And how this circulation happens, beyond—and even against—subjective intentions, and self-perception.

What one notices, strikingly, in the last eight years, which coincide with Lord Bingham's role as Senior Law Lord, is that the decisions it has taken not only indicate new directions in English law, but especially suggest different approaches

---

* This paper expands the *laudatio* that was read on March 14th 2008 in occasion of the bestowal of the honorary doctoral degree in law to Lord Bingham of Cornhill by the University of Roma Tre. The *Lectio Magistralis* delivered by Lord Bingham was, quite properly, on the subject on which he is a master, '*The Rule of Law*' (published in the proceedings of the ceremony by University of Roma Tre Press, 2008, p 34ff).

to legal reasoning and deciding and pave the way, in many fields, towards a European *ius commune*.

The analysis has been conducted on the nearly 500 (475) decisions handed down by the House of Lords between mid-2000 and 2007.

Let us first look at the numbers: in nearly 250 decisions the issue is that of the interpretation and enforcement of some transnational or international piece of law, or foreign, transnational, or international law are used to solve problems of domestic law.

The largest share (over 100 decisions) is taken by the European Convention on Human Rights (ECHR), understandably an element of necessary reference after the enactment of the Human Rights Act in 2000.

One can explain the fact considering that for 50 years the UK contrary to many continental European countries—has refused to apply the ECHR directly in its courts considering it an international treaty which bound only the state towards other states, but did not create enforceable rights for British citizens or established obligations upon the government. Now that the floodgates have been opened there is an urgent need to direct the lower courts, enabling them to make consistent decisions. However, in the last years taken into consideration, the number is steadily growing: in practically two decisions out of three there is a more or less extended reference to the ECHR and to Strasbourg jurisprudence.

The second group—in order of number (over 50 decisions)—is that in which the House of Lords has to tackle EU law. Here we find not only direct interpretation of Regulations, but also several cases of referral to the ECJ under Article 234 of the Rome Treaty,[1] or of decisions following referral.[2]

If one looks at the areas of the law which are mostly affected, the foremost is that of individual freedom in its many facets: investigation,[3] fair trial,[4] sentencing,[5] prisoner's treatment,[6] asylum seekers and refugees,[7] procedures concerning deportation of immigrants,[8] extradition.[9] An important area is also that

---

[1] *Ex multis* see *CPP, Sinclair Collins, Consorzio Prosciutto di Parma, Optident, Scandecor, Celtec* I, *ex p Barker, Stringer, Marks&Spencer.*

[2] *Ex multis* see *Wolverhampton Healthcare* I & II, *R v Minister of Agriculture, Celtec* II, *Inntrepreneur.*

[3] E.g., *R v Sargent, Clingham, R v Commissioner of Police for Metropolis, ex p Amin, Attorney General Ref no 5/2002, In re McKerr, ex p LS, ex p Middleton, ex p Green, In re O, Laposte, In re Officer L.*

[4] E.g., *R v A* [2001], *Loosely, R v Jones, Lyons, Attorney General Ref no 2/2001, Laval, R v H* [2003], *Sheldrake, Davidson, Connor, R v H* [2004], *A v Home Dept* [2004], *Scotcher, MH v Dept Health, Camberwell Green Youth Court, Mushtaq, R v Parole Board (ex p Smith), ex p Hasan, Coutts.*

[5] E.g., *Lichniak, ex p Anderson, Drew, ex p Giles, ex p Uttley, In re Hammond, Roberts, ex p Dudson, R v Home Dept (ex p Smith), Clift.*

[6] E.g., *R v Governor HM Prison Brockhill, ex p Daly, Wainwright.*

[7] The number of cases in this field is impressive. See *ex multis ex p Saadi, ex p Zeqiri, ex p Thangarasa, ex p Anufrijeva, ex p Sivakumar, Sepet, ex p Razgar, ex p Hoxha, ex p Adam, Januzi, Home Dept v K* [2006].

[8] E.g., *Rehman, Immigration Office at Prague Airport, ex p Ullah, N v Home Dept, ex p Bagdanavicius, Huang.*

[9] *In re Guisto, R v Commissioner of Police for Metropolis, Montila, Armas, Dabas.*

of civil rights, ranging from sex discrimination[10] to freedom of expression,[11] privacy rights,[12] protection of property,[13] family relations.[14]

Obviously the decisions do not all have the same intensity, however the sheer number is impressive.

If one made a similar survey on other courts—whether 'Supreme' or 'Constitutional'—it would not be easy to find equivalents.

This does not mean that the decisions in themselves are to be approved. Rather it indicates that the 'Bingham Court' is everything except 'insular'. Nor does it mean that the use of EU, transnational, and foreign law and cases is, alone, a guarantee of judicial wisdom. A comparatist is not looking for that, but for the common way of reasoning, the willingness for the judge to be influenced by legal materials different from those which come from his own tradition.

If one tries to find a *fil rouge* that runs through the decisions that have been selected, a comparatist cannot help noticing the following features:

(a) The House of Lords is in constant dialogue with the European Court of Human Rights. Its decisions, and not only those in which the United Kingdom is part, are scrutinized, commented, distinguished.[15] To my knowledge no other 'Supreme' or 'Constitutional' Court of great European countries does so consistently use the ECHR jurisprudence not as *obiter dicta* or, worse, as a topping, but as *ratio decidendi*. It would surely be profitable for all if this dialogue were two-sided and that at least occasionally Strasbourg looked at London.[16]

(b) The House of Lords is constantly construing EU law.[17] It is a line indicated by the European Court of Justice to whom the House of Lords refers questions

---

[10] See *Wolverhampton Healthcare* I & II, *Macdonald, Relaxation Group, A v Chief Constable of West Yorkshire Police* [2004], *Ghaidan, Percy, ex p Wilkinson, ex p Hooper, Secretary of State for Work and Pensions v M* [2006].

[11] See *Turkington, Punch, Shayler, ex p ProLife Alliance, ex p Rusbridger, Cream Holdings, In re S* [2004], *Campbell* II, *Polanski, Jameel, Miss Behavin*.

[12] See *Ashworth Security Hospital, R v Commissioner of Police for Metropolis, ex p Morgan Grenfell, Qazi, Campbell* I.

[13] See *Benjafield, Marcic, Parish of Aston Cantlow, ex p Quark Fishing*.

[14] See *In re B* [2001], *Bellinger, Rees, In re D* [2005], *In re J* [2005], *Down Lisburn Health and Social Services Trust, In re G* [2006], *In re M* [2007].

[15] The issue is well worth a thorough analysis: one can start with the statement of Lord Bingham in *Qazi* according to whom 'Strasbourg authority is of course the primary source of guidance on the interpretation and application of the Convention' and compare it with the various opinions in *Al-Skeini*. In particular Lord Bingham's when he states that national courts 'must be slow to rule on the scope of an international treaty where its ruling, if correct, would apply to contracting states other than itself'. And again Lord Bingham's opinion in *Kay*: to the question 'whether a court which would ordinarily be bound to follow the decision of another court higher in the domestic curial hierarchy is, or should be, no longer bound to follow that decision if it appears to be inconsistent with a later ruling of the Court in Strasbourg' his reply is that 'degree of certainty is best achieved by adhering, even in the Convention context, to our rules of precedent'.

[16] Quite correctly Lord Rodger, in *Al-Skeini*, points out that 'the judgments and decisions of the European Court do not speak with one voice'; and that 'some of them [differences] appear much more serious and so present considerable difficulties for national courts which have to try to follow the jurisprudence of the European Court'.

[17] *Ex multis* see *Berkeley, Imperial Tobacco, Cantabrica Coach, Consorzio Prosciutto di Parma, Optident, Scandecor, White v Motor Insurers Bureau, Celtec* (I & II), *ASDA, Macdonald, Junttan*

which are not trivial and greatly contribute towards the clarification of often obscure and contradictory Brussels legislation.[18] A European judge that does so on a regular basis shows that he is perfectly acquainted with one of the main sources of legislative law, but at the same time knows that it must fit in national traditions.[19] And this is one of the most engaging tasks of today's judges.

(c)   The House of Lords does not look at European law and jurisprudence only:[20] countless are the quotations of US cases from the Supreme and Federal Courts, together with decisions from other Commonwealth jurisdictions (especially Canadian). And if one is familiar with the north-American style one knows that its intellectual vivacity is difficult to resist.[21] Solutions may not coincide but a substantive—rather than procedural or formal—way of reasoning inevitably seeps into their Lordships' opinions.[22]

(d)   Many decisions—and not only those that are already on the international hit charts (*Fairchild*, *Three Rivers*, *Diane Pretty*)—are in themselves a stimulus to comparative enquiry: accountability and rule of law (*Alconbury*); what is an 'insurance transaction' (*CPP*); good faith (*First National Bank*)[23]; undue

Oy, Johnstone, Borough of Bromley (I & II), *Relaxation Group, Hoechst, A v Chief Constable of West Yorkshire Police, Archibald, Montila, Armas, Percy, Szoma, Stringer, Inntrepreneur, Majroski, Preston, Serco.*

[18]   EC VAT and taxation directives are under constant scrutiny: see *CPP, Liverpool Institute for Performing Arts, Sinclair Collins, Plantiflor, Smith Glaziers, Lex Service, Royal Sun Alliance, Beynow, Autologic, College of Estate Management, Grenalls, Marks & Spencer* (I & II), *Deutsche Morgan Grenfell, Pirelli Cable Holding, Boak Allen.*

[19]   As Lord Hoffmann, in *R v Lyons*, points out 'In domestic law, the courts are obliged to give effect to the law as enacted by Parliament. This obligation is entirely unaffected by international law'.

[20]   And for the joy of the lovers of Roman Law one finds an ample quotation of the Digest in *Mark v Mark* (*per* Lord Hope) on the distinction between '*domicilium*' and 'home'. Remarkable how Lord Rodger in *R v Bentham* disposes of the case simply by quoting Ulpian: '*Dominus membrorum suorum nemo videtur*'.

[21]   For some examples see: *Darker* (*per* Lord Cooke), *Loosely* (*per* Lord Nicholls), *Fairchild* (*per* Lord Bingham), *Cullen* (*per* Lord Bingham, dissenting), *A v Home Dept* (*per* Lord Bingham), *Deep Vein Thrombosis* (*per* Lord Scott), *Gregg v Scott* (*per* Lords Nicholls and Hoffmann), *Lesotho Highlands* (*per* Lord Steyn), *National Westminster Bank* (*per* Lord Nicholls), *Mushtaq* (*per* Lord Hutton), *Coutts* (*per* Lord Bingham), *Jones* (*per* Lord Hoffmann).

[22]   For some examples see Lord Bingham's opposition in *Dabas*, to 'reintroducing an element of technicality which the Framework Decision [on arrest warrant] is intended to banish and by frustrating the intention that a warrant in common form should be uniformly acceptable in all member states'. Or Baroness Hale's opinion in *In re M*—a child abduction case—where after having described the appalling conditions of life in Zimbabwe, the balance is that 'against all this…the policy of the [1980 Hague] Convention can carry little weight'. But for a less substantial approach towards humanitarian reasons see *N v Secretary of State for Home Dept* (*per* Lord Nicholls): 'An AIDS sufferer's need for medical treatment does not, as a matter of Convention right, entitle him to enter a contracting state and remain there in order to obtain the treatment he or she so desperately needs.'

[23]   'Good faith in this context is not an artificial or technical concept; nor, since Lord Mansfield was its champion, is it a concept wholly unfamiliar to British lawyers. It looks to good standards of commercial morality and practice' (*per* Lord Bingham); and for the opposite, more traditional, view 'Any purely procedural or even predominantly procedural interpretation of the requirement of good faith must be rejected' (*per* Lord Steyn).

The Bingham Court 827

influence in financial practice (*RBS*); interpretation of contracts (*Amoco*)[24];
the balance between fair trial and dignity of the victim (*RvA*); when is a proceeding or a penalty civil or criminal (*Clingham, Benjafield*); what is a 'bodily
injury' (*Bristow Helicopters*)[25]; rights of the accused and court-martials or trial
in absentia (*Boyd*,[26] *Jones*); mandatory life sentences (*Lichniak*); the privilege
against self-incrimination (*Lyons, Mushtaq*); official secrets versus freedom
of the press (*Shayler*); reasonable time in criminal charges (*Attorney General
no 1/01*); the problems related to trans-sexualism (*Bellinger, Chief Constable
of North Yorkshire*) and homosexual relations (*MacDonald, Ghaidan, In re
D, In re G, Secretary of State for Work and Pensions v M*); liability of public
bodies (*Matthews, Transco*); unwanted children (*Rees*); sale of goods *a non
domino* (*Shogun Finance*); the privacy of famous people (*Campbell*)[27]; evidence procured by torture (*A v Home Dept* [2005]); loss of a chance (*Gregg v
Scott*); prospective overruling (*National Westminster Bank*); limitation period
and knowledge of negligence (*Haward*); negligent misrepresentation in contractual negotiations (*Hamilton*); Islamic veil at school (*Begum*). These are
questions with which judges, lawyers, scholars, legislators around the world
are confronted every day. A comparatist finds in the House of Lords reports a
bonanza for his classes and case-books.

(e) It would be short-sighted not to see that on certain aspects the House of Lords
continues to be the strenuous defender of views that have long outlived their
time. In the field of the law of torts—if one sets aside the white-elephant decisions in *Lister v Hesley Hall, Fairchild v Glenhaven Funeral Services*, and *Chester
v Afshar*—liability, especially of public bodies,[28] is denied on very formalistic
and contortionist arguments that would be—and generally are—disregarded
in any other jurisdiction, whether of common law or of civil law (*McGrath*,

[24] One should 'construe the agreement in a way that is consistent with its commercial purpose
and the context in which it was entered into' (*per* Lord Hope); and see also Lord Hoffmann's reference to 'performative utterances'.
[25] The interpretation of the Warsaw Convention 'should, if possible, be consistent with the
mainstream views expressed in leading overseas authorities' (*per* Lord Nicholls); and in the same
sense see Lord Mackay's opinion: 'The Warsaw Convention should have a common construction
in all the jurisdictions of the countries that have adopted the Convention,[therefore] I attach crucial importance to the decisions of the United States Supreme Court in *Eastern Airlines Inc v Floyd*
(1991) 499 US 530 and *El Al Israel Airlines v Tseng*, particularly as the United States is such a large
participant in carriage by air.' Lord Steyn devotes a whole paragraph of his opinion to an analysis
of comparative case law.
[26] 'A man does not by becoming a soldier cease to be a citizen' (*per* Lord Bingham).
[27] 'The time has come to recognize that the values enshrined in articles 8 and 10 [of the ECHR]
are now part of the cause of action for breach of confidence' (*per* Lord Nicholls).
[28] And not only in tort cases: see *ex p Wilkinson* (a tax case) 'In any claim against a public authority for financial compensation in respect of past discrimination, it must be remembered that the
general public (often the general body of taxpayers) will be footing the bill' (*per* Lord Brown). There
has not been time or space to examine the decisions delivered by the House of Lords in the last seven
months of Lord Bingham's appointment as Senior Law Lord. Therefore his vigorous dissent in *Smith
v Chief Constable of Sussex Police* remains outside this review. The majority's restrictive position on
the liability of police forces, however, confirms the critical comment presented in this paragraph.

Marcic, Rees, Matthews,[29] *Thomson, Tomlinson, Transco,*[30] *Adams, Gorringe, Brooks, Scott v Gore*). And in the field of the law of contract the door is closed on suggestions to update it in the light of European harmonization (*Shogun Finance*)[31]. From this point of view a comparatist notices that the huge opening made by the Human Rights Act does not bring significant changes to the core subjects of private law which are still governed by tradition.

(f) The 'Bingham Court' has had to face one of the main dilemmas of modern democracies after the 2001 tragedies: are anti-terrorist laws, regulations, and administrative and police decisions compatible with the standards of human rights and civil liberties that are guaranteed in Western societies?[32] To what extent is the 'war on terrorism' an entirely political and military issue, exempt from judicial scrutiny?[33] One can easily understand that this is an extremely delicate field, where balancing requires both an extremely attentive analysis of the facts and a very broad and clear view of the general interests at stake. In the many cases in which, directly or indirectly, the House of Lords is confronted with these problems, Lord Bingham's opinions generally take the lead and set the general principles which are, generally, followed by the rest of the court. But it is easy to notice that practically all the Law Lords feel it necessary to give their contribution to the development of the law in these difficult circumstances. It is sufficient to quote the conclusion of Lord Nicholls' opinion in *A v Home Dept* [2004]: 'The real threat to the life of the nation, in the sense of a people living in accordance with its traditional laws and political values, comes not from terrorism but from laws such as these. That is the true measure of what terrorism may achieve. It is for Parliament to decide whether to give the terrorists such a victory.' A comparatist immediately is brought to examine the parallel case law of the House of Lords and of the US Supreme Court, which has rendered, in these same years, several decisions on the rights of the Guantanamo detainees.[34]

---

[29] 'I think it is well arguable that human rights include the right to a minimum standard of living, without which many of the other rights would be a mockery. But they certainly do not include the right to a fair distribution of resources or fair treatment in economic terms—in other words, distributive justice. Of course distributive justice is a good thing. But it is not a fundamental human right.' (*per* Lord Hoffmann).

[30] Although Lord Bingham acknowledges that a 'fault-based rule would increase disparity between English law and laws of France and Germany' he prefers that activities under a strict liability rule be selected by Parliament.

[31] 'To attempt to use this appeal to advocate, on the basis of continental legal systems which are open to cogent criticism, the abandonment of the soundly based *nemo dat quod non habet* rule (statutorily adopted) would be not only improper but even more damaging.' (*per* Lord Hobhouse). Lord Millett's dissent is to no avail: 'Our inability to admit such an exception compels us to adopt a different analysis, but it would be unfortunate if our conclusion proved to be different. Quite apart from anything else, it would make the contemplated harmonization of the general principles of European contract law very difficult to achieve.'

[32] See *A v Home Dept* [2004], *A v Home Dept* [2005], *Dabas*.

[33] See e.g., *Rehman, Jones v Minister of Interior of Saudi Arabia, R v Jones, Al-Skeini*.

[34] For the latest decision, which recalls all the precedents, see *Boumediene v Bush*, 558 US (2008). The outcome of the challenges to the Patriot Act of 2001 has, however, been different: see *Doe v Gonzales*, 546 US 1301 (2005).

(g) The Rule of Law is a constant and guiding principle in a great number of deci-
     sions, and not only in Lord Bingham's opinions in e.g., *Anderson, Davidson,
     A v Home Dept* [2005]. For a few examples one needs only to peruse the deci-
     sions in *Alconbury* (*per* Lords Hoffmann[35] and Nolan[36]), *R v Loosely* (*per* Lord
     Nicholls), *Clingham* (*per* Lord Steyn)[37], *Matthews* (*per* Lord Hoffmann)[38],
     Anufrijeva (*per* Lord Steyn)[39], *A v Home Dept* [2004] (*per* Lord Nicholls). A
     comparatist—and even more so a legal-realist—even if he may harbour the
     impression that the Rule of Law is a portmanteau expression, must under-
     stand how the concept is in practice used and the result it brings forth. It
     would be easy to write a handbook on the subject looking only at the House
     of Lords' jurisprudence.

This last feature points at a further element that should be stressed. It would be
at best *naïf* to present the 'Bingham Court' as the result of some kind of judicial
superhero. It is instead very clear—if one goes through the various decisions—
that there is a widespread agreement between their Lordships in tackling the
problems in a broader (i.e., transnational, EU, comparative) perspective.[40]

Lord Bingham is surrounded by Lord Nicholls, Lord Hoffmann, Lord Steyn,
Lord Hope, Baroness Hale, and other Law Lords, who share—albeit with variable intensity[41]—the same approach. Dissents are rare and do not, generally, illuminate the aspect that we are here considering. There is nothing even vaguely
similar to the vigorous and even scorching dissent against the use of comparative
law of Justices O'Connor and Scalia in the US Supreme Court case of *Roper v
Simmons*.[42]

[35] 'The principles of judicial review give effect to the rule of law'.

[36] 'Electoral accountability alone is, of course, plainly insufficient to satisfy the rule of law'.

[37] According to whom there is a risk of 'prejudice of liberal democracies to maintain the rule of
law by the use of civil injunctions'.

[38] 'Article 6 [of the ECHR] is concerned with standards of justice, the separation of powers and
the rule of law. It would seem to have little to do with whether or not one should have an action in
tort.'

[39] 'In our system of law surprise is regarded as the enemy of justice'; and Lord Bingham, dissenting: 'It is however a cardinal principle of the rule of law, not inconsistent with the principle of
legality, that…effect should be given to a clear and unambiguous legislative provision.'

[40] It is therefore surprising to note that in two bioethics cases (*ex p Quintavalle* I & II) there is no
reference nor to the Oviedo 1999 Convention on Human Rights and Biomedicine, nor to the Nice
Charter on Fundamental Rights.

[41] It would be incorrect to state that Lord Bingham plays the role of the ECHR hard-liner: see
e.g., the differences of opinions between him and Lord Hope in *Attorney General Ref no 2/2001*, in
which the former provides a broad notion of the 'reasonable time' rule in Article 6 of the ECHR,
and the latter dissents from a conclusion that 'empties the reasonable time guarantee almost entirely
of content'.

[42] 543 US 551 (2005). One can compare the US judicial style with the following statements:
'I regard the idea of a conventional award in the present case as contrary to principle. It is a novel
procedure for judges to create such a remedy. There are limits to permissible creativity for judges.
In my view the majority have strayed into forbidden territory. It is also a backdoor evasion of the
legal policy enunciated in *McFarlane*. If such a rule is to be created it must be done by Parliament.
The fact is, however, that it would be a hugely controversial legislative measure…I cannot support the proposal for creating such a new rule.'(*Rees, per* Lord Steyn). 'The lack of any consistent or
coherent ratio in support of the proposition in the speeches of the majority is disturbing.' (*Rees, per*

Here again the results are uneven, but what is interesting is the overall direction the House of Lords is taking.

One could explain the present state of things and make the simple observation that what is happening is not surprising. After all, in the year 2000 the Human Rights Act of 1998 came into force and it was inevitable that it influence also the House of Lords.

But the objection appears to be formalistic. On the one hand one must not forget that Lord Bingham has been one of the most respected advocates of the Human Rights Act and therefore he is now harvesting what he sowed. And on the other hand that—not only in the Common law tradition—general and high-flying principles need to find a judge that puts them into practice. And that judge happens to be not in some local jurisdiction or the judge of first instance, but the House of Lords in its full representation.

This brings us to the core of the argument: the 'Bingham Court' is profoundly different from the House of Lords we have known and admired through the last—shall we say—two and a half centuries and to whose decisions we look at as the pillars of the common law.

In its role of adjudicator of fundamental rights it is moving towards models scholars have studied comparing the US Supreme Court with the Constitutional Courts of Germany and Italy. Something similar has already happened with the Canadian Supreme Court since the enactment of the Canadian Charter of Rights and Freedoms in 1982.

An Act—or even a written Constitution—however, is not in itself sufficient to change a legal system. Ideas walk on the legs of women and men. And so, at the end of day, it is of them we must speak.

In this light, and observing the role that the House of Lords has and will have in the British constitutional system, the initial proposition—the envisaging of a 'Bingham Court'—may not appear far-fetched, especially if seen in a historical perspective when it will be necessary to compare the first decade of application of the Human Rights Act and its impact on British institutions, with what will happen in future times and in the novel Supreme Court for the United Kingdom which will be inaugurated in 2009.

Lord Hope). The highest level of internal criticism seems to be reached in Lord Bingham's opinion in *ex p Anderson*, where, he states that following the argument that the Home Secretary should be excluded from the parole procedure 'would not be judicial interpretation, but judicial vandalism'.

10

'There is A World Elsewhere'—Lord Bingham and Comparative Law

Mads Andenas and Duncan Fairgrieve

I. Introduction

Courts make use of comparative law. Some form of comparative law has always been part of the judicial process, and its use has been on the increase over the last two decades. Lord Bingham has been a pioneer in developing comparative law in modern court practice.[1]

In jurisdictions where the form of judgments allows it, judges make open reference to comparative law sources, and in particular to judgments by foreign courts.[2] Where the form of judgments does not open for citation of foreign law sources, there may be an advocate-general or *rapporteur* who makes direct references, or the use of comparative law sources may be acknowledged in less formal ways.

The breakdown of the closed and hierarchical national system of legal authority[3] goes some way in explaining why comparative law is increasing in importance. The role of comparative law, and method of comparative law, however, remains

[1] Sir Thomas Bingham, '"There is A World Elsewhere": The Changing Perspectives of English Law' (1992) 41 ICLQ 513, reprinted in T Bingham, *The Business of Judging* (OUP Oxford 2000) 87. He says that 'in showing a new receptiveness to the experience and learning of others, the English courts are not, I think, establishing a new tradition, but reverting to an old and better one', at 527.

[2] B Markesinis and J Fedtke *Engaging in Foreign Law* (Hart Publishing, Oxford 2009) is the new leading treatise on comparative law method, and deals extensively with comparative law in the courts. We have otherwise made use of the different complementary perspectives and material from many fields and jurisdictions in G Canivet, M Andenas and D Fairgrieve (eds), *Comparative Law before the Courts* (BIICL London 2004). The book accounts for the reasons for the new and important role of comparative law, and how comparative law sources are received and recognized in different jurisdictions, sometimes in different ways within a single national jurisdiction. See also generally M Reimann and R Zimmermann, *The Oxford Handbook of Comparative Law* (OUP Oxford 2006), especially the ch by S Vogenauer, 'Sources of Law and Legal Method in Comparative Law' at 869–898.

[3] Contemporary written constitutions offer one example where comparative law is expressly received as a formal source of law. In the South African Constitution of 1996, Art 39 (c) states that when interpreting the Bill of Rights, a court, tribunal or forum may consider foreign law. Also

controversial. There are discussions of the policy and method of comparative law among judges, among lawmakers and among scholars, and sometimes between the legal professions. Enthusiasm is increasingly in evidence, as in Justice Breyer's address to the 2003 annual meeting of the American Society of International Law: nothing could be 'more exciting for an academic, practitioner or judge than the global legal enterprise that is now upon us'.[4] There is an emerging body of scholarship providing support for the use of comparative or foreign law, and also critical perspectives.[5]

In this chapter, we will use Lord Bingham's judgments to approach some of the problems, and also in developing a typology of some current applications of comparative law in the courts.

We look at the dialogues between different national and international courts. An international market place for judgments is emerging, where also the form and style of judgments may be influenced by the increased use of comparative law.

Comparative law plays a role in resolving fundamental issues such as the relationship between national and international law, in implementing international and European human rights law, in developing constitutional review, in review of administrative action, and in developing effective remedies. Comparative law also plays a role in developing the substantive law in different areas, including in finding normative solutions to questions of a more technical kind. One can hardly expect always to find the ideal solutions to problems of globalisation within one's own jurisdiction. Nonetheless, there is still disagreement on when comparative law can be invoked, where it is convenient to do so, and how it should be done.

Similar questions are posed to courts in jurisdictions across the world, but there is much variation in the solutions found. For instance, some courts still find that the autonomy of their legal system prevents them from expressly acknowledging the use of foreign judgments. This is one of the issues where there has been a rapid development in the practice of courts, including the French courts,[6] the Italian *Corte di cassazione*, the International Court of Justice and the European Court of

---

several of the new constitutions in the former communist countries provide other and interesting examples in this respect.

[4] S Breyer, 'Keynote Address' (2003) 97 *ASIL Proceedings* 265.

[5] B Markesinis, 'Goethe, Bingham and the Gift of an Open Mind', above p 729, and J Stapleton, 'Benefits of Comparative Tort Reasoning: Lost in Translation', above p 773, cover the ground well here in the course of setting out their different views. The titles of their articles indicate their respective positions. B Markesinis, 'Judicial Mentality: Mental Disposition or Outlook as a Factor Impeding Recourse to Foreign Law', 80 TUL. L.REV. 1325, 1361–62 (2006) also argues in favour of a more consequent use of comparative law. If one judge uses foreign law in support of an outcome, it may not be satisfactory for another judge, arguing for another outcome, to pass it by in silence. See S Vogenauer, 'Sources of Law and Legal Method in Comparative Law', M Reimann and R Zimmermann, *The Oxford Handbook of Comparative Law* (OUP Oxford 2006) 869.

[6] See G Canivet, 'Variations sur la politique jurisprudentielle : les juges ont-ils une âme?', p 17 above, and B Stirn, 'Le Conseil d'Etat, so British', p 815 above.

Justice, which in different ways have relaxed the restrictions on citing judgments by courts from other jurisdictions.

Our discussion of the cases and typology of current applications of comparative law will illustrate the methodological problems of the use of comparative law in the courts. There are cases which reflect a general recognition of comparative law as a persuasive authority or source of law, which apply normative models from other jurisdictions where national law is undetermined, and which use comparative law in reviewing factual assumptions about the consequences of legal rules, or assumptions about the universal applicability of rules or principles.

Comparative law has been seen to provide courts with persuasive and non-binding arguments. At the current stage, there is an argument about the consequences of a call for more consistency. One question is if courts are ever bound to make use of comparative law sources, for instance in certain situations when an authority is based on comparative law sources.

Comparative law is becoming a practical academic discipline. The role of academic scholarship, and its response to the developments in practice, is another issue we return to towards the end.

We will commence this chapter by pointing to some of Lord Bingham's achievements in the field of comparative law.

II. Lord Bingham's contribution

Lord Bingham's contribution to comparative law is on several levels. One is as a comparative law source on matters of substantive law, as a persuasive authority outside his own jurisdiction. Lord Bingham has been a pioneer in developing the judicial dialogues that attracts the interest of comparative lawyers and international relations scholars.[7] The Law Lords have gradually lost their previous position, as the court followed in many common law jurisdictions around the world, sitting as the Appellate Committee of the House of Lords or the Judicial Committee of the Privy Council (which also has lost its formal position as final court of appeal for many of the Commonwealth jurisdictions).[8] When the Law Lords today are cited and followed in other countries, it is in most instances not as formal or binding authority but when their 'speeches' or 'advice' persuade.[9]

---

[7] See, e.g., A-M Slaughter, *A New World Order* (Princeton University Press Princeton 2004) and 'Comparative Law in the Lords and in the US Supreme Court', above p 761, N Krisch 'The Open Architecture of European Human Rights Law' (2008) 71 Modern Law Review 183, and B Stirn, 'Le Conseil d'Etat, so British?', above p 815.

[8] See R Cooke, 'Future of the Common Law', above p 687.

[9] See S Elias, 'Courts and Human Rights in the UK and NZ', above p 241, A Gleeson, 'The value of clarity' , above p 107, M Kirby, 'The Lords, Tom Bingham and Australia', above p 713, B McLachlin, 'Judicial Independence: A Functional Perspective', above p 713, D Ipp, 'Recent Reforms in Australia to the Law of Negligence with Particular Reference to the Liability of Public Authorities', above p 701.

Lord Rodger has made this point before and has drawn attention to some consequences for the form of judgments. Whereas the House of Lords and the Privy
Council 'once could command assent merely by their position...in a world,
where courts may pick and choose among a variety of authorities...the form
in which the judges have expressed their view may well play a significant role in
determining which of those views ultimately win acceptance'.[10] Lord Bingham's
judgments on personal liberty and anti-terror measures have left his imprint on
the constitutional law of many countries, and also beyond the commonwealth
and common law world. His decisions on tort law, including those on public
authority liability, have left a further legacy. Where other judges are cited for their
literary allusions or striking paradoxes and statements, Lord Bingham persuades
through his reasoning.[11] More than the authority of the positions he has held,
his influence depends on the clarity and convincing force of his judgments, often
supported by his academic scholarship.

The reasons given in judgments, and also the form and style of supreme court
judgments, have taken on a new importance in Europe with the new roles of
national constitutional courts in many countries, and the importance of the EU
Court of Justice and the European Court of Human Rights.[12] Reasons that convince the courts in what is effectively the next instance, can safeguard against
what is in effect an overturning. Lord Bingham's judgment in *Boyd*[13] provides an
instructive example of this.[14]

In *Findlay* the European Court of Human Rights held that the United
Kingdom was in violation of Article 6 § 1 of the European Convention on
Human Rights.[15] A soldier successfully challenged the court-martial procedure on grounds of lack of independence and impartiality. The UK court-martial
procedure was subsequently, in 1996, reformed in new legislation. In 2002, in
Morris,[16] the European Court of Human Rights held that the new legislation still
violated the independence and impartiality requirements.

Another case, *Boyd*,[17] reached the House of Lords in 2002, before new legislation could be introduced in response to *Morris*. Lord Bingham analyzes the case

[10] Lord Rodger 'The Form and Language of Judicial Opinion' (2002) 118 LQR 226, 247.
[11] See B Markesinis and J Fedtke, 'Authority or reason? The Economic Consequences of
Liability for Breach of Statutory Duty in a Comparative Perspective', (2007) EBLR 5 at 66–7,
which compares Lord Bingham's style of argument to that of Lord Hoffmann, and also M Andenas
in (2007) EBLR 1 at 2–3.
[12] See the discussion of different instances of dialogues between the European and the national
judicial level in N Krisch, 'The Open Architecture of European Human Rights Law' (2008) 71
Modern Law Review 183.
[13] *Boyd, Hastie and Spear Saunby and Others* [2002] UKHL 31.
[14] See the discussion of the reception of Lord Bingham's judgment in L Garlicki 'Cooperation
of courts: The role of supranational jurisdictions in Europe', (2008) 6 International Journal of
Constitutional Law 509.
[15] *Findlay v United Kingdom* (1997) 24 EHRR 221.
[16] *Morris v United Kingdom* (2002) 34 EHRR 1253.
[17] *Boyd, Hastie and Spear Saunby and Others* [2002] UKHL 31. <http://www.publications.
parliament.uk/pa/ld200102/ldjudgmt/jd020718/boyd-1.htm>

law of the European Human Rights Court, and the UK 1996 legislation. He makes clear that it is for UK courts to accept the decisions of the European Human Rights Court. However, he finds that the legislation satisfies the requirements of independence and impartiality as developed in the case law of the European Human Rights Court. Then, in *Cooper*,[18] a unanimous Grand Chamber of the European Court of Human Rights overturns the previous ruling in *Morris*, making extensive use of Lord Bingham's analysis, including express references in its own discussion of the law, and agreeing with his conclusions.

Lord Bingham's contribution to comparative law is also to the method of the discipline. Lord Bingham is a pioneer in the use of comparative law as a judge,[19] and he has made important scholarly contributions also in this field.[20] In English courts, Lord Denning and Lord Goff are examples of judges making use of comparative law, and inviting counsel and other judges to do the same. Lord Bingham has built on their contributions, gone further in making use of comparative law, and has also provided criteria for when comparative law sources are relevant. In *Fairchild*,[21] he states his basic conviction that 'in a shrinking world (in which the employees of asbestos companies may work for those companies in any one or more of several countries) there must be some virtue in uniformity of outcome whatever the diversity of approach in reaching that outcome.'[22] In the same paragraph of the judgment, he also sets out his view on the use of comparative law in the development of the common law:

Development of the law in this country cannot of course depend on a head-count of decisions and codes adopted in other countries around the world, often against a background of different rules and traditions. The law must be developed coherently, in accordance with principle, so as to serve, even-handedly, the ends of justice. If, however, a decision is given in this country which offends one's basic sense of justice, and if consideration of international sources suggests that a different and more acceptable decision would be given in most other jurisdictions, whatever their legal tradition, this must prompt anxious review of the decision in question.

In the Supreme Court of the United States, Justice Kennedy addressed similar issues in *Roper and Simmons*.[23] The case concerned a very different matter and area of law. But the criteria were not that different. Justice Kennedy states that international and comparative law provides 'respected and significant confirmation' for the majority's view while not controlling the outcome:

---

[18] *Cooper v the United Kingdom*, (2004) 39 EHRR 8.

[19] See, H Muir Watt, 'Comparative law and the decision in Fairchild', above p 751, and A-M Slaughter, 'Comparative Law in the Lords and in the US Supreme Court', above p 761.

[20] See in particular, Sir Thomas Bingham '"There is A World Elsewhere": The Changing Perspectives of English Law' (1992) 41 ICLQ 513, reprinted in T Bingham *The Business of Judging* (OUP Oxford 2000) 87.

[21] *Fairchild v Glenhaven Funeral Services Ltd*, [2002] UKHL 22.

[22] At para 31.

[23] *Roper v Simmons* 543 US 551 (2005).

It is proper that we acknowledge the overwhelming weight of international opinion against the juvenile death penalty, resting in large part on the understanding that the instability and emotional imbalance of young people may often be a factor in the crime. See Brief for Human Rights Committee of the Bar of England and Wales et al. as Amici Curiae 10–11. The opinion of the world community, while not controlling our outcome, does provide respected and significant confirmation for our own conclusions. It does not lessen our fidelity to the Constitution or our pride in its origins to acknowledge that the express affirmation of certain fundamental rights by other nations and peoples simply underscores the centrality of those same rights within our own heritage of freedom.

In both cases, the courts considered overturning a previous decision. Both courts had good reasons of legal principle and policy for doing so. In *Roper*, Justice Kennedy finds that comparative law provides 'confirmation for our own conclusions.' Lord Bingham reasons along the same lines in *Fairchild*. 'Anxious review' is called for when (1) a national decision offends one's basic sense of justice, and (2) there is a more acceptable decision in most other jurisdictions.

Both courts decided to overturn the previous decision. *Fairchild* was a unanimous decision, whereas the US Supreme Court had only a narrow majority for setting aside its previous decision. The *Roper* minority provided arguments against the use of comparative law in US courts in general (with one justice strengthening the argument for comparative law in general but disagreeing with the majority's conclusions in the particular case). The other view in the House of Lords was first expressed in the subsequent decision of *Barker*[24] where an activist panel invented a new concept of 'proportionate liability' to limit the effect of *Fairchild*. These cases will be discussed further below, but what is of particular interest in the introduction to this chapter is the parallel approach that Lord Bingham and Justice Kennedy took in *Fairchild* and *Roper*. In spite of the many differences between the cases, the method used was similar.

Lord Bingham and Justice Kennedy also address the question of whether the use of comparative law is disloyal to the national legal system. Both answer no to this, and provide both a principled and practical argument. In *Fairchild*, the issues appear legal and technical although the outcome would have social implications. Lord Justice Bingham stated in the early 1990s that '(p)rocedural idiosyncracy is (like national costume or regional cuisine) to be nurtured for its own sake'.[25] In *Fairchild*, Lord Bingham sets out the social and economic issues. Comparative law is both of assistance in dealing with the social and economic issues but even more so when it comes to the more technical legal solutions. In *Roper*, the question was whether it was unconstitutional to impose capital punishment for crimes committed while under the age of 18. The case went to the core of the question of the extension of constitutional rights protection. On another level, both cases concerned the arguments a court can take into account when it

---

[24] *Barker v Corus (UK) plc* [2006] UKHL 20.
[25] *Dresser UK Ltd v Falcongate Ltd* [1992] QB 502, 522.

considers to set aside the authority of a previous decision. The question in *Roper* and *Fairchild* is about how comparative law fits into the system of sources of law as the closed and hierarchical national system of legal authority associated with Kelsian (or Hartian) positivist traditions is breaking down. We will return to this question below, and also revisit the use of comparative law in the most closed and hierarchical national systems.

We will argue that Lord Bingham's use of comparative law provides tools for courts in dealing with the opening up of the national legal system and its sources. At the same time, his arguments in favour of, and method for the use of, comparative law remain valid within a closed national legal system in a positivist tradition.

An equally important aspect of Lord Bingham's use of sources which do not derive from domestic law, is his willingness to make use of European human rights law to develop the common law. In his judgments, the case law of the European Human Rights Court or the European Union Court of Justice is not seen as belonging to separate systems of law. When it can be used in the development of the common law, a strong case for doing so is recognized.

In *Van Colle and Smith*,[26] Lord Bingham sets out the case for developing the common law action for negligence in the light of the case law of the European Human Rights Court. In paragraph 58 of the judgment, he develops the general argument for doing so:

Considerable argument was devoted to exploration of the relationship between rights arising under the Convention (in particular, the article 2 right relied on in *Van Colle*) and rights and duties arising at common law. Should these two regimes remain entirely separate, or should the common law be developed to absorb Convention rights? I do not think that there is a simple, universally applicable answer. It seems to me clear, on the one hand, that the existence of a Convention right cannot call for instant manufacture of a corresponding common law right where none exists: see *Wainwright v Home Office* [2003] UKHL 53, [2004] 2 AC 406. On the other hand, one would ordinarily be surprised if conduct which violated a fundamental right or freedom of the individual did not find a reflection in a body of law ordinarily as sensitive to human needs as the common law, and it is demonstrable that the common law in some areas has evolved in a direction signalled by the Convention: see the judgment of the Court of Appeal in *D v East Berkshire Community NHS Trust*, [2003] EWCA Civ 1151, [2004] QB 558, paras 55–88. There are likely to be persisting differences between the two regimes, in relation (for example) to limitation periods and, probably, compensation. But I agree with Pill LJ in the present case (para 53) that "there is a strong case for developing the common law action for negligence in the light of Convention rights" and also with Rimer LJ (para 45) that "where a common law duty covers the same ground as a Convention right, it should, so far as practicable, develop in harmony with it".

[26] *Chief Constable of the Hertfordshire Police (Original Appellant) and Cross-respondent) v Van Colle (administrator of the estate of GC (deceased)) and another (Original Respondents and Cross-appellants) and Smith (FC) (Respondent) v Chief Constable of Sussex Police (Appellant)* [2008] UKHL 50.

This is another expression of the role of comparative law in a national system, following his views developed in extra-judicial writing,[27] in his dicta on the 'virtue in uniformity of outcome' in *Fairchild*,[28] and that '(p)rocedural idiosyncracy is not (like national costume or regional cuisine) to be nurtured for its own sake' in *Dresser*.[29] The issue is more pressing in *Van Colle*, as the outcome otherwise could establish in the common law a restrictive rule which would likely to be contrary to the case law of the European Court of Human Rights.

Parallel issues come up again in *JD v East Berkshire*.[30] In paragraph 50 Lord Bingham states that:

(T)he question does arise whether the law of tort should evolve, analogically and incrementally, so as to fashion appropriate remedies to contemporary problems or whether it should remain essentially static, making only such changes as are forced upon it, leaving difficult and, in human terms, very important problems to be swept up by the Convention. I prefer evolution.

A final aspect of Lord Bingham's contribution to comparative law as a judge, is in the application of foreign law as the law of the case. This covers two main categories of situations: one is where Private International Law requires the application of foreign law, and the other is in appeals from civil law jurisdictions.

We first turn to Private International Law. National law recognizes party autonomy in commercial contracts, so that parties can choose the national law that shall govern the contract. Tort claims or insurance cases are other cases where foreign law may apply, and in tort cases and many insurance cases there is no contractual provision for which jurisdiction should apply. The Commercial Court, where Lord Bingham started his judicial career, has one foreign party to most of its cases, and only foreign parties to half of them.[31] The choice of English law is usual but parties choose the jurisdiction of the Commercial Court also for contracts where they agree to apply the laws of another country.[32] Cases may involve extensive evidence on foreign law, and method and legal context place great demands on the judge.

Lord Bingham has heard many appeals from civil law jurisdictions.[33] Here it is not the civil law features of Scottish law we have in mind, although that too may require comparative law skills. In the Privy Council, Lord Bingham has for

---

[27] T Bingham in B Markesinis, *The Coming Together of the Common Law and the Civil Law*, (Hart Oxford 2000) 27 at 34.

[28] *Fairchild v Glenhaven Funeral Services Ltd*, [2002] UKHL 22.

[29] *Dresser UK Ltd v Falcongate Ltd* [1992] QB 502, 522.

[30] *JD (FC) (Appellant) v East Berkshire Community Health NHS Trust and others (Respondents) and two other actions (FC)*, [2005] UKHL 23.

[31] See R Aikens, 'Reforming Commercial Court Procedures', above p 563.

[32] See the discussion in L Collins, 'Tom Bingham and the Choice of Law', above p 347.

[33] Also other European supreme courts hear cases of a similar character, e.g., from jurisdictions within the country which apply the law of other countries or traditions, and the US Supreme Court is the federal supreme court of states with laws deriving from non common law traditions.

instance heard a number of appeals where *Code Napoleon* inspired statutes have been the decisive source of law.

Gujadhur v Gujadhur from the Court of Appeal of Mauritius[34] illustrates the challenges. Both procedural and substantive questions depended on Mauritian legislation based on French models (and limitation rules adopted from the Code of Quebec). The case concerned the beneficial ownership of shares, and the law on 'caducité' could determine the outcome. This is a technical expression of French law which refers in general terms to a juridical act which has ceased to have effect by reason of some subsequent event. There is no single English equivalent. The question was whether the *contre-lettre* establishing the beneficiary ownership ('contrary' to the registered ownership) had become *caduque*. In addition to dealing with Mauritian legislation and case law, Lord Bingham referred to article 1321 of the French Code Civile, applied French case law (a decision by the Cour d'appel de Paris) and sought assistance in French doctrine.

We have here looked at Lord Bingham's contribution to comparative law at several levels. Summing up, it is not surprising that his judgments are comparative law sources, as persuasive authority, all over the world. Lord Bingham has strengthened the judicial dialogues that have become a feature of our legal systems. We have just pointed to some experiences of a Law Lord that can explain, legitimate and provide experience in the use of foreign law. We have shown how Lord Bingham's judicial work required the application of foreign law in many cases. We pointed to the private international law cases of the Commercial Court, and the Privy Council cases from civil law jurisdictions, which require the use of 'foreign' law, and with it, its methods and wider legal contexts. There is no approach or technique that can save the judge from this. The use of European Union law and European human rights law is similar. It requires that the judge moves beyond the national tradition, and its method, in which he is trained. There is considerable variation between judges, and one of Lord Bingham's contributions here is in his clear and convincing analysis of the sources from other legal orders. He looks at the different legal orders with respect and from the inside. It is not a matter of distinguishing or limiting the case law of other legal orders so that they have little no effect on the common law. This is also a matter of reciprocity, and gaining respect and confidence can be important. Lord Bingham's judgment in *Boyd*,[35] as discussed above, provides an instructive example. He combined his analysis of the case law of the Human Rights Court on independence and impartiality, and of the new UK legislation, convincing a unanimous Grand Chamber European Human Rights Court in *Cooper*[36] to overturn its previous *Morris* ruling. Even more important is Lord Bingham's willingness to make use of European human

---

[34] *Ghaneshwar Gujadhur, Lajpati Gujadhur, Rajkumar Gujadhur, Sheoshankar Gujadhur and Dimeshwar Gujadhur (Appellants) v Gunness Gujadhur and Sewpearee Singh* (Respondents) [2007] UKPC 54.

[35] *Boyd, Hastie and Spear Saunby and Others* [2002] UKHL 31.

[36] *Cooper v the United Kingdom*, (2004) 39 EHRR 8.

rights law to develop the common law concepts. As the case law of the European Human Rights Court or the European Union Court of Justice does not belong to a separate system of law but is part of English law, there is in Lord Bingham's view a strong case for using it in the development of the common law. Under certain circumstances that can apply beyond European human rights law and European Union law, and to foreign law as developed in other national jurisdiction and by their national courts. We have pointed to Lord Bingham's pioneer judgments here, and will now turn to a more general discussion of comparative law in the courts which will assist in a fuller appreciation of Lord Bingham's contribution.

III. Comparative law and dialogues between courts

Courts make use of comparative law, and make open reference to it, to an unprecedented extent. This *Liber Amicorum* provides many different complementary perspectives, in particular on this topic, and much material from many areas. There are different reasons for the new and important role of comparative law. We will enquire into some of them. The conclusions of our enquiry concern the consequences this development has had for the system of sources of law and for legal argument. They also point to the role that courts are playing in a legal system no longer adhering to 20th century positivist and national paradigms, and not restricted in the same way as before by traditional national doctrines of statutory interpretation or precedent. In the new more open legal systems, it is left to courts to weigh and balance ever more complex sources of law. The courts will also have competing claims to legitimacy. The sources of law may still to most lawyers be supported on a unitary, nationally based, rule of recognition. But the way in which courts deal with the more complex issues of validity of norms and their hierarchy, has one outcome: that is an opening up of the legal system, mainly through the recognition of sources of law from outside the traditionally closed national system.

Comparative law has become a source of law. Comparative law also offers assistance with many of the new issues of method that courts have to resolve in the more open legal systems. The first issue is: how does one deal with comparative law? When is it relevant, what weight should it have, how does one sort out the many practical problems that arise? Comparative law can also assist courts in dealing with other fundamental issues such as international law, European law, their relationship with national law, or for that matter, the relationship of courts with the legislatures as parliamentary supremacy (in the sense of the national legislature's supremacy) is eroded.

Comparative law is itself one of several new types of challenge that courts have to deal with. A situation with sources of law with competing claims to legitimacy, leaves a whole set of issues to be determined by the courts.[37] The traditional

---

[37] What Hart termed the 'secondary rules', representing the constitutional arrangements of any particular society, are undergoing fundamental change. The 'primary rules' are also changing in a

form of a unitary rule of recognition (if it ever applied fully anywhere)[38] kept the picture simple. The possible recourse to a clear hierarchy, resolving conflicts between norms, seemed to leave the major issues for determination by the legislature. The present, more complex constitutional systems of validity of norms and their hierarchy, leave courts to resolve a number of fundamental issues. There are certain constitutional issues that traditionally have been left to practice. On the macro level, this applies to the relationship between legal orders. On the micro level, it applies to remedies protecting private parties against the state. These are issues that have come to the fore in most jurisdictions, with courts rapidly developing the law. The macro level developments include for instance the role of international and European law in national law, or the role of the case law of one international court before another international court. At the micro level, examples are the intensity of judicial review of administrative action and of legislation, tort liability of administrative authorities, and injunctive remedies against the state.

This opens up for the use of and increases the utility of comparative law. It is not surprising that courts are to an increasing degree involved in dialogues with one another across the traditional jurisdictional divides. A horizontal exchange between national courts is becoming active, both on an informal level with meetings and systems for the provision of information. At another horizontal level, international courts and tribunals, including the International Court of Justice, the European Human Rights Court and the European Court of Justice, are involved in dialogues with one another.[39] At a vertical level, the dialogues between the international and national courts are developing and are also formally recognized in a way they were not a few years ago. One may talk about an international market place for judgments,[40] where the form of judgments may be influenced by the accessibility and increased use of comparative law.[41]

---

way that reflects the change of the secondary rules, developing rights of individuals, harmonizing the laws of European countries over a very wide field etc. See H L A Hart, *Concept of Law* (OUP Oxford 1961) 151 about 'secondary rules'.

[38] See the brief setting out of the case against a universal rule of recognition, or Austin's illimitable and indivisible sovereign, or traditional statehood concepts, in M Andenas and J Gardner, 'Introduction: Can Europe have a Constitution' in (2000) 11 KCLJ 1.

[39] There is an increasing literature taking account of this dialogue, and Anne-Marie Slaughter has been a pioneer in studying its role and placing it in a broader context, in particular as seen from a US perspective, see A-M Slaughter, 'A Typology of Transjudicial Communication' 20 *University of Richmond Law Review* 99 (1994) and A-M Slaughter, *New International Order* (2005). Judicial dialogue is a main theme of the introduction and several of the articles in G Canivet, M Andenas and D Fairgrieve (eds), *Comparative Law before the Courts* (BIICL London 2004).

[40] See Lord Rodger, 'The Form and Language of Judicial Opinion' (2002) 118 LQR 226, 247 and Lord Goff of Chieveley, 'The Future of the Common Law (1997) 46 ICLQ 745, 756–7 on the accessible form of common law judgments. M Adams, J Bomhoff and N Huls (eds), *The Legitimacy of Highest Courts' Rulings* (The Hague: Asser Press, 2008) provide important contributions to this analysis.

[41] There is an increasing access to foreign court judgments and other legal sources in the citations made by courts and in legal scholarship. The court web sites that provide translations of important judgments are increasing in number and quality.

The constitutional role of the courts has developed in practically all jurisdictions. Judicial review of administrative action is more intense, and practically no field is exempt where previously there would have been many formal or functional immunities.[42] Court review of parliamentary legislation is also becoming more intensive, whether it is based on domestic law, 'constitutionnalité', or European or international law, 'conventionnalité'. The increased constitutional role of courts is a universal feature. The dynamic way in which comparative law is used, is only one of several developments, providing tools for, and legitimacy to, the development.

IV. The use of foreign judgments in supreme courts

English courts have long been open to consider how legal problems are solved in other jurisdictions. Lord Cooke of Thorndon has stated that 'the common law of England is becoming gradually less English. International influences— from Europe, the Commonwealth and even the United States, sometimes themselves pulling in different directions—are gradually acquiring more and more strength.'[43]

Since the 1960s, English courts have paid more and more respect to decisions by courts from other common law jurisdictions. For some 30 years many important English cases include detailed discussions of the case law of a number of the most influential common law jurisdictions, in particular of Australia and New Zealand.[44]

During the 1990s, Lord Goff of Chieveley, the Senior Law Lord, made extensive use of European materials, in particular German case law.[45] In extra judicial writings, Lord Goff, and other leading English judges, committed themselves to the use of comparative law in their judicial work.[46] Lord Woolf, while he was Master of the Rolls, said that 'there was a time when English lawyers, if they were

---

[42] Formal legal immunities have different standing in different traditions. Head of state or government and parliamentary immunities are still controversial and play a role in some jurisdictions. But otherwise areas of state activity, or 'vital' state interests, do not any longer merit immunities of the formal or the functional kind. In the common law, one cannot easily assert that an issue is 'not justiciable'.

[43] Lord Cooke of Thorndon 'The Road Ahead for the Common Law' see below, p 687.

[44] Some parallel may be found in the German speaking courts use of one another's decisions.

[45] In the case of *White v Jones* [1995] 2 AC 207, Lord Goff, recognizing the challenges posed by comparative law, opined that 'in the present case, thanks to material published in our language by distinguished comparatists, German as well as English, we have direct access to publications which should sufficiently dispel our ignorance of German law and so by comparison illuminate our understanding of our own.' (263).

[46] Lord Goff of Chieveley, 'The Future of the Common Law' (1997) 46 ICLQ 745. Lord Goff has also been a pioneer in establishing regular meetings between senior judiciaries in different jurisdictions to discuss developments in the law of mutual interest. M Guy Canivet has in his term as the President of the French Supreme Court made an unprecedented contribution to the development of informal cooperation between courts and judges, also more formalized through

prepared to seek help from another jurisdiction, would only look to other common law jurisdictions. This is now changing. The House of Lords and the judiciary in general now recognise that civil jurisdictions have much to offer... there is, I believe, a real process of harmonisation between the civil and common law legal systems'.[47] Lord Bingham, while he was Lord Chief Justice, said that judges in English courts were developing the practice to 'use case law from other European countries in much the same way as we use Commonwealth authorities'.[48] This was supported by numerous other judges of the highest courts.[49] Lord Bingham also observed that 'in showing a new receptiveness to the experience and learning of others, the English courts are not, I think, establishing a new tradition but reverting to an old and preferable one'.[50]

In the case law, an important breakthrough came in *Fairchild v Glenhaven Funeral Services Ltd.*[51] Lord Bingham, by then the Senior Law Lord (president of the highest United Kingdom court), conducted a comparative law survey on a point of causation which we have cited above.[52]

Lord Bingham has continued to make use of comparative materials in later cases. Comparative law assisted in determining the effect of continuing the incremental development of the common law on tort liability of public authorities in *JD v East Berkshire*.[53] The experience from other countries showed that floodgates were not about to open in the way that had sometimes been asserted. Lord Bingham surveyed the experiences from other countries:

It would seem clear that the appellants' claim would not be summarily dismissed in France, where recovery depends on showing gross fault: see Markesinis, Auby, Coester-Waltjen and Deakin, *Tortious Liability of Statutory Bodies* (1999), pp 15–20; Fairgrieve, "Child Welfare and State Liability in France", in *Child Abuse Tort Claims against Public Bodies: A Comparative Law View*, ed Fairgrieve and Green (2004), pp 179–197, Fairgrieve,

associations of judges. The French Conseil d'Etat has similarly developed such exchanges over a number of years.

[47] Foreword to Steiner and Ditner, *French for Lawyers* (London 1997).

[48] Introductory speech at the launch of W V Gerven *Tort Law: Scope of Protection* (Hart Oxford 1998) in Gray's Inn, May 1998.

[49] Sir Jonathan Mance, 'Comparative Law', University of Texas Journal of International Law, forewords in Sir Basil Markesinis' books by Sir Stephen Sedley, Lord Phillips, and the book review in the ICLQ by Sir Konrad Schiemann of one of Sir Basil's books.

[50] Sir Thomas Bingham, ' "There is A World Elsewhere": The Changing Perspectives of English Law' (1992) 41 ICLQ 513. Reprinted in T Bingham *The Business of Judging* (OUP Oxford 2000) 87.

[51] *Fairchild v Glenhaven Funeral Services Ltd* [2002] UKHL 22, [2003] 1 AC 32.

[52] [2002] UKHL 22, [2003] 1 AC 32, para 32. Lord Rodger also observed that '[t]he Commonwealth cases were supplemented, at your Lordships' suggestion, by a certain amount of material describing the position in European legal systems... The material provides a check, from outside the common law world, that the problem identified in these appeals is genuine and is one that requires to be remedied' (para 165).

[53] *JD (FC) (Appellant) v East Berkshire Community Health NHS Trust and others (Respondents) and two other actions (FC)*, [2005] UKHL 23.

"Beyond Illegality: Liability for Fault in English and French Law", in *State Liability in Tort* (2003), chap 4.

The survey also allowed Lord Bingham to consider a precedent which was in the process of being gradually overturned. Central policy considerations of that judgment had been considered and rejected in another jurisdiction:

Nor would they be summarily dismissed in Germany where, it is said, some of the policy considerations which influenced the House in *X v Bedfordshire* were considered by those who framed §839 of the BGB and were rejected many years ago: see Markesinis *et al., op. cit.*, 58–71.

The conclusion on the empirical analysis was clear: 'Yet in neither of those countries have the courts been flooded with claims'.

It seems obvious that this kind of empirical and comparative analysis is much to be preferred over the bold assertions of negative consequences which have on occasion been resorted to when courts have wished to reject extensions of tort liability or of duties on public authorities.

There have been parallel developments in many other national jurisdictions.

During his tenure as Premier Président of the French Cour de Cassation (French Supreme Court in civil and criminal matters), Guy Canivet, stated:

Citizens and judges of States which share more or less similar cultures and enjoy an identical level of economic development are less and less prone to accept that situations which raise the same issues of fact will yield different results because of the difference in the rules of law to be applied. This is true in the field of bioethics, in that of economic law and liability. In all these cases, there is a trend, one might even say a strong demand, that compatible solutions are reached, regardless of the differences in the underlying applicable rules of law.[54]

In French administrative law, foreign law sources are becoming an increasing reference point for judicial decision-making. In doctrinal terms it remains a somewhat overlooked factor.[55] In the case of *Kechichian*,[56] which concerned administrative liability for failure to supervise banks and was heard by the Plenary Chamber of the *Conseil d'Etat*, Commissaire du Gouvernement Alain Seban started his detailed and impressive *conclusions*,[57] with a survey of comparative

---

[54] In an address at the British Institute in November 2001 under the chairmanship of Lord Bingham. He has developed the analysis in 'The Use of Comparative Law Before the French Private Law Courts' in G Canivet, M Andenas and D Fairgrieve (eds), *Comparative Law before the Courts* (BIICL London 2004) 181.

[55] One could expect doctrine to provide this kind of comparative material that courts find useful in their decision-making. In fact, it is the courts that lead the way. It is for doctrine to follow in the countries that we have studied.

[56] See further discussion of this case in D Fairgrieve, *State Liability in Tort* (OUP Oxford 2003) ch 4, s 3.2.1.2. See also M Andenas and D Fairgrieve, 'Misfeasance in Public Office, Governmental Liability and European Influences' (2002) 51 ICLQ 757.

[57] The court subsequently adopted the solution which *CG* Seban proposed in his *conclusions*.

law, covering Germany, the United States and England,[58] concluding with the remark that 'despite the different legal and administrative traditions, the same features may be found [in the three systems].' Noting the English courts' tendency to broaden the tort of misfeasance in public office, the Commissaire du Gouvernement concluded that the comparative law survey highlighted the 'liberalism of French administrative law.'

Similarly, in two decisions concerning wrongful life actions[59] brought independently before the *Conseil d'Etat* and *Cour de Cassation*, both courts were referred to comparative law solutions respectively in the *conclusions* of Commissaire du Gouvernement Pécresse,[60] and Avocat Général Sainte-Rose.[61]

The *Conseil d'Etat* has had the first occasion for this court to expressly cite a foreign judgment of a national court in its own decision. In the case of *Techna SA*,[62] the *Conseil d'Etat* made reference to a decision by the English High Court concerning labelling requirement under EU law, and held that the relevant European directive should be suspended in France. It explicitly cited the English case as support in giving the reasons underpinning the need to suspend the directive.[63]

Several other European jurisdictions provide parallels. The German *Bundesgerichtshof* makes use of decisions by other national and international courts, and cites them expressly, often making use of the academic literature. That also applies to the German *Bundesverfassungsgericht*. Foreign law is sometimes recognized in the interpretation of provisions of Dutch law in the opinion of Advocates General, but rarely in the judgment itself.[64] Express references to foreign law do not occur in the general Spanish courts, and some judges accredit this to Spanish fascism and isolationism and prescribe the use of foreign law as a remedy against this experience.[65] Judges of Italian courts would informally acknowledge their use of comparative law but previously not expressly refer to foreign law or court judgments.[66] In a 2007 judgment on the termination of life

---

[58] Including an analysis of the most recent House of Lords decision in *Three Rivers DC v Bank of England* [2001] UKHL 16.

[59] Parallel cases came before supreme, administrative and constitutional courts in many countries. Courts were aware of the decisions of courts in other jurisdictions, and made use of them, even in the courts where there is no tradition of acknowledging such use.

[60] CE 14 February 1997, *Epoux Quarez*, RFDA 1997.375, 379–380.

[61] Cass Ass Plen 17 November 2000, *Perruche, Gazette du Palais*, 24–25 Jan 2001; D 2001 *Jurisprudence* 316.

[62] N° 260768 *Techna SA* 29 Oct 2003.

[63] R Errera, 'The Use of Comparative Law Before the French Administrative Law Courts' in G Canivet, M Andenas and D Fairgrieve (eds), *Comparative Law before the Courts* (BIICL London 2004) 153.

[64] A S Hartkamp, 'Comparative Law Before the Dutch Courts' in G Canivet, M Andenas and D Fairgrieve (eds), *Comparative Law before the Courts* (BIICL London 2004) 229 at 231–2.

[65] J M Canivell, 'Comparative Law Before the Spanish Courts' in G Canivet, M Andenas and D Fairgrieve (eds), *Comparative Law before the Courts* (BIICL London 2004) 209 at 216.

[66] A Sandulli, 'Comparative Law Before the Italian Public Law Courts' in G Canivet, M Andenas and D Fairgrieve (eds), *Comparative Law before the Courts* (BIICL London 2004) 165. Sandulli explains that it this the autonomy of national law and constitution which will bar the

of individuals in a vegetative state, the Italian *Corte di cassazione* cites the draft EU Constitutional Treaty, the case law of the European Court of Human Rights, the House of Lords, the *Bundesgerichtshof,* and the Supreme Court of the United States and several state supreme courts.[67] The only individual judge referred to is Lord Goff in the *Bland* case:[68] because the argument was 'particolarmente articolata nel parere di Lord Goff of Chieveley'. In the subsequent decision of the *Corte costituzionale,* reference is made to the international conventions and the case law of the European Court of Human Rights, also cited by the *Corte di cassazione.* There is however no reference made to the different national supreme court decisions cited by the *Corte di cassazione.*

The tradition of transnational jurisprudence is growing in strength and in the controversy it attracts in the United States. We have already cited Justice Breyer's address to the 2003 annual meeting of the American Society of International Law as marking this important development.[69] He said there that 'comparative analysis emphatically is relevant to the task of interpreting constitutions and human rights'. He continued that nothing could be 'more exciting for an academic, practitioner or judge than the global legal enterprise that is now upon us'.[70]

Justice Breyer has indeed made use of comparative law and commented upon it in several judgments. In *Knight v Florida* he stated that the 'Court has long considered as relevant and informative the way in which foreign courts have applied standards roughly comparable to our own constitutional standards in roughly comparable circumstances'.[71] In *Printz v United States* he went into some further detail:

Of course, we are interpreting our own Constitution, not those of other nations, and there may be relevant political and structural differences between their systems and our own...But their experience may nevertheless cast an empirical light on the consequences of different solutions to a common legal problem— in this case the problems of reconciling central authority with the need to preserve the liberty-enhancing autonomy of a smaller constituent governmental entity.[72]

In *Lawrence et al v Texas*[73] the use of foreign law makes a notable breakthrough. In this case the majority overruled an earlier Supreme Court decision in *Bowers v Hardwick*[74] which had upheld Georgia's sodomy law as constitutional. For the

---

Italian courts, and the Corte costituzionale in particular, from citing judgments from foreign courts.

[67] Sentenza n. 21748 del 16 ottobre 2007 (Sezione Prima Civile, Presidente M. G. Luccioli, Relatore A. Giusti).

[68] *Airedale NHS Trust v Bland* [1993] AC 789.

[69] S Breyer, 'Keynote Address' (2003) 97 *ASIL Proceedings* 265.

[70] See also S Breyer, 'Economic Reasoning and Judicial Review', above in this *Liber Amicorum.*

[71] 528 US 990, 997 (1999).

[72] 521 US 898, 921 (1997).

[73] 539 US 558 (2003).

[74] 478 US 186 (1986).

first time the court (as individual justices such as Kennedy himself had previously done) relied on international human rights law and practice. Justice Kennedy observed:

When homosexual conduct is made criminal by the law of the State, that declaration in and of itself is an invitation to subject homosexual persons to discrimination both in the public and private spheres. The central holding of *Bowers* has been brought into question by this case, and it should be addressed. Its continuance as precedent demeans the lives of homosexual persons.

'The sweeping references' in the majority opinion by Chief Justice Burger in *Bowers*, to the history of Western civilization and to Judeo-Christian moral and ethical standards, provided a particular justification to take account of other authorities pointing in an opposite direction. Justice Kennedy refers to the United Kingdom *Wolfenden Report* (1963) and the subsequent law reform, decriminalizing homosexuality.[75]

Justice Kennedy then refers to the case law of the European Court of Human Rights:

Of even more importance, almost five years before *Bowers* was decided the European Court of Human Rights considered a case with parallels to *Bowers* and to today's case. An adult male resident in Northern Ireland alleged he was a practicing homosexual who desired to engage in consensual homosexual conduct. The laws of Northern Ireland forbade him that right. He alleged that he had been questioned, his home had been searched, and he feared criminal prosecution. The court held that the laws proscribing the conduct were invalid under the European Convention on Human Rights. *Dudgeon v United Kingdom*, 45 Eur. Ct. H. R. (1981). Authoritative in all countries that are members of the Council of Europe (21 nations then, 45 nations now), the decision is at odds with the premise in *Bowers* that the claim put forward was insubstantial in our Western civilization.

Justice Kennedy completes his use of comparative law by investigating how *Bowers* had been received in other jurisdictions:

To the extent *Bowers* relied on values we share with a wider civilization, it should be noted that the reasoning and holding in *Bowers* have been rejected elsewhere. The European Court of Human Rights has followed not *Bowers* but its own decision in *Dudgeon v United Kingdom*. See *P. G. & J. H. v United Kingdom*, App. No. 00044787/98, (Eur. Ct. H. R., Sept. 25, 2001); *Modinos v Cyprus*, 259 Eur. Ct. H. R. (1993); *Norris v Ireland*, 142 Eur. Ct. H. R. (1988). Other nations, too, have taken action consistent with an affirmation of the protected right of homosexual adults to engage in intimate, consensual conduct. See Brief for Mary Robinson et al. as Amici Curiae 11–12. The right the petitioners seek in this case has been accepted as an integral part of human freedom in many other countries. There has been no showing that in this country the governmental interest in circumscribing personal choice is somehow more legitimate or urgent.

---

[75] *The Wolfenden Report: Report of the Committee on Homosexual Offences and Prostitution* (HMSO London 1963) and the Sexual Offences Act 1967, §1.

In *Lawrence*, also Justice Scalia found occasion to express his views on foreign law. Justice Scalia, in the minority with Chief Justice Rehnquist[76] and Justice Thomas, said that the majority had signed up to what he called the homosexual agenda. He observed:

The court's discussion of these foreign views (ignoring, of course, the many countries that have retained criminal prohibitions on sodomy) is...meaningless dicta. Dangerous dicta, however, since this court...should not impose foreign moods, fads, or fashions on Americans.

However, it has been pointed out by Harold Koh that 'Justice Scalia himself has been far from consistent in insisting upon the irrelevance of foreign and international law.'[77] Justice Scalia too has looked to other jurisdictions when they offered support, in Scalia's case for limiting constitutional rights.[78]

In his minority opinion in *Roper*, Justice Scalia continues his attack on the use of foreign law: 'to invoke alien law when it agrees with one's thinking, and ignore it otherwise, is not reasoned decision-making, but sophistry.'[79] Consistency is often a problem, as Harold Koh makes clear. It is not surprising that both those in favour and those against the use of comparative law in the courts will require consistency. It can serve as an argument for *less use* of comparative law (Scalia J), but also as an argument for *more extensive use* of comparative law.

Sir Basil Markesinis has used the consistency argument in support of further use of comparative law. Sir Basil argues that a judge using comparative law in one case, should not in a similar case disregard it without telling his audience why in this newer case the foreign experience was of no relevance. And where one judge mentions foreign law, other judges who come to another result than that the first judge supported on comparative law, should try and counter in a specific manner this material rather than pass it by in silence.[80] The form of giving reasons in judgments, may allow judges making use of the same authorities or sources of law, and legal and factual arguments, and then reaching different conclusions. In many cases this will be done without making clear why, for instance the appellate court disagrees with the first instance court, or one judge with another in the same court. Judgments may also include or exclude sources or arguments, and the discretion may be perceived to be particularly wide when one is dealing with merely persuasive and non-binding authorities or arguments. This may lead

[76] Chief Justice Rehnquist has also expressed different views. In a 1989 speech he stated that 'Now that constitutional law is solidly grounded in so many countries, it is time that the United States Courts begin looking to the decisions of other constitutional courts to aid in their own deliberative process.' W H Rehnquist, 'Constitutional Court – Comparative Remarks' (1989), reprinted in P Kirchhof and D P Kommers (eds) *Germany and Its Basic Law: Past, Present and Future* (1993).

[77] H H Koh 'International Law as Part of Our Law' AJIL 43, 47 (2004). See also H H Koh 'Foreword: On American Exceptionalism' Stanford Law Review 55 (2003).

[78] See *McIntyre v Ohio Election Commission* 514 US 334, 381 (1995).

[79] *Roper v Simmons*, 543 US 551, 627 (2005) (Scalia J, dissenting).

[80] B Markesinis, 'Judicial Mentality: Mental Disposition or Outlook as a Factor Impeding Recourse to Foreign Law', 80 TUL LREV 1325 (2006) at 1361–62 and at 1371.

to inconsistencies which are unsatisfactory in many instances. At a stage where comparative law provide mostly persuasive and non-binding authorities or arguments, this will often mean that the courts or judges who do not find support in comparative law for their preferred outcome, will disregard comparative law arguments in their reasons. It is difficult to disagree with Sir Basil's call for more consistency. In particular, the call for consistency is powerful in cases where one judge mentions foreign law. Reasonable consistency requires that other judges who come to a different result from that the first judge supported on comparative law, address and counter in a specific manner also the first judge's arguments based on comparative law.

We have above discussed Justice Kennedy's majority opinion in *Roper*.[81] Justice Kennedy states that international and comparative law provides 'respected and significant confirmation' while not controlling the outcome. It does not lessen the 'fidelity to the Constitution or our pride in its origins to acknowledge that the express affirmation of certain fundamental rights by other nations and peoples simply underscores the centrality of those same rights within our own heritage of freedom.' This builds on Justice Breyer's opinions in *Knight* and *Printz*. It is a cautious continuation of the line of comparative judgments. However, *Roper*, and Justice Scalia's minority opinion there, highlights the problems of making use of comparative law as a supernumerary argument.

Roper is interesting also for the middle position of Justice O'Connor. She disagreed with the majority but still recognized the relevance of foreign law (even if it did not determine the outcome in her view), satisfying the requirements of Sir Basil Markesinis. When Justice O'Connor turns to the discussion of foreign and international law, she recognized that there, 'without question', has been a global trend toward abolishing capital punishment for under-18 offenders: 'very few, if any, countries other than the United States now permit this practice in law or in fact'. She then turns to how the majority find confirmation for its own conclusions in foreign law. As she disagrees on these conclusions, she 'can assign no such confirmatory role to the international consensus'.

Justice O'Connor then provides us with a clear dictum on the role of comparative law:

Nevertheless, I disagree with Justice Scalia's contention, post, at 15–22 (dissenting opinion), that foreign and international law have no place in our Eighth Amendment jurisprudence. Over the course of nearly half a century, the Court has consistently referred to foreign and international law as relevant to its assessment of evolving standards of decency. See Atkins, 536 U.S., at 317, n. 21; Thompson, 487 U.S., at 830–831, and n. 31 (plurality opinion); Enmund, 458 U.S., at 796–797, n. 22; Coker, 433 U.S., at 596, n. 10 (plurality opinion); Trop, 356 U.S., at 102–103 (plurality opinion). This inquiry reflects the special character of the Eighth Amendment, which, as the Court has long held, draws its meaning directly from the maturing values of civilized society. Obviously, American law is

---

[81] *Roper v Simmons* 543 U S 551 (2005).

distinctive in many respects, not least where the specific provisions of our Constitution and the history of its exposition so dictate. Cf. post, at 18–19 (Scalia, J., dissenting) (discussing distinctively American rules of law related to the Fourth Amendment and the Establishment Clause). But this Nation's evolving understanding of human dignity certainly is neither wholly isolated from, nor inherently at odds with, the values prevailing in other countries. On the contrary, we should not be surprised to find congruence between domestic and international values, especially where the international community has reached clear agreement—expressed in international law or in the domestic laws of individual countries—that a particular form of punishment is inconsistent with fundamental human rights. At least, the existence of an international consensus of this nature can serve to confirm the reasonableness of a consonant and genuine American consensus. The instant case presents no such domestic consensus, however, and the recent emergence of an otherwise global consensus does not alter that basic fact.

International and foreign law has been a recurring theme at the confirmation hearings of US Supreme Court justices. Chief Justice Roberts stated at his 2005 Senate confirmation hearings that 'If we are relying on a decision from a German judge about what our constitution means, no president accountable to the people appointed that judge and no senate accountable to the people confirmed that judge. And yet he's playing a role in shaping the law that binds the people in this country'.[82] Justice Alito said at his 2006 confirmation hearings that 'I think the framers would be stunned by the idea that the Bill of Rights is to be interpreted by taking a poll of the countries of the world.'[83]

The Supreme Court of the United States is much cited internationally. It has had a notable impact on the constitutional law of most jurisdictions, in particular through its due process and freedom of press jurisprudence. Guido Calabresi, sitting as a judge of the Second Circuit of the US Court of Appeals in *US v Manuel Then*, cited the German and Italian constitutional courts and added that 'these countries are our "constitutional offspring", and how they have dealt with problems analogous to ours can be very useful to us when we face difficult constitutional issues. Wise parents do not hesitate to learn from their children.'[84]

Justice Sandra Day O'Connor has also extra-judicially restated her support for the use of comparative law. She has stated that 'I suspect that with time we will rely increasingly on international and foreign law in resolving what now appear to be domestic issues. Doing so may not only enrich our own country's decisions; it will create that all-important good impression. When U.S. courts are seen to

[82] Committee on the Judiciary US Senate. *Confirmation hearing on the nomination of John G. Roberts, Jr. to be chief justice of the United States.* In: S.Hrg.109–158. 109th Cong. 1st Sess. (2005) Washington, DC: U.S. Government Printing Office.
[83] Committee on the Judiciary US Senate. *Confirmation hearing on the nomination of Samuel A. Alito, Jr. to be an associate justice of the United States.* In: S. Hrg. 109–277. 109th Cong. 2nd Sess. (2006) Washington, DC: U.S. Government Printing Office. S G Calabresi ' "A Shining City on a Hill": American Exceptionalism and the Supreme Court's Practice of Relying on Foreign Law' 86 BOSTON U L REV 1335 (2006) sets out the case against using foreign law in the Federalist Society tradition that these two judges belong to.
[84] *US v Manuel Then*, 2nd Circuit, 56 F.3d 464 (1995).

be cognizant of other judicial systems, our ability to act as a rule-of-law model for other nations will be enhanced.'[85]

Aharon Barak, then the Chief Justice of the Supreme Court of Israel, criticized in 2002 the position of US Supreme Court justices who did not cite foreign judgments: 'They fail to make use of an important source of inspiration, one that enriches legal thinking, makes law more creative, and strengthens the democratic ties and foundations of different legal systems.' Partly as a consequence, the United States Supreme Court 'is losing the central role it once had among courts in modern democracies'.[86]

V. Foreign Law

We have discussed Lord Bingham's contribution to comparative law in the application of foreign law as the law of the case. Supreme courts hear cases where Private International Law requires the application of foreign law. Just as the Law Lords hear appeals from civil law jurisdictions, several other European supreme courts hear cases from jurisdictions within the country which apply the law of other countries or traditions, and the US Supreme Court will hear cases as the federal supreme court of states with laws deriving from non-common law traditions.

This has long traditions. Before the 19th century nation state, courts would in most countries regularly apply another law than the local law. In the British Empire, the Privy Council, as a centralized court of last instance, applied the laws of a much larger number of jurisdictions than it does today.

Private International Law has a new importance in a globalized economy where the transnational contract is no longer an extraordinary occurrence. The courts will as a consequence be ever more strongly exposed to foreign law. The application of judgments from other jurisdictions is also for this reason becoming more usual. There are similarities in the use of law from European or international law jurisdictions, as we turn to below in the next subsection about indirect entry points for judgments of other jurisdictions. Each time a court deals with European Union law, European human rights law, World Trade Law, international human rights law or the law of any other treaty regime, that court has to apply the legal method of the other jurisdiction, and consider the legal questions in their correct context, which could be of a wider legal order or of a more narrow and self-contained treaty regime.

One may draw certain conclusions about courts' ability to deal with comparative law from this. The hermeneutical and epistemological challenges to the legal

[85] Remarks by Sandra Day O'Connor Southern Center for International Studies, Atlanta, Georgia, October 28, 2003, at< http://southerncenter.org/OConnor_transcript.pdf>.

[86] A Barak, 'Foreword: A Judge on Judging: The Role of a Supreme Court in a Democracy' 116 Harvard L. Rev. (2002) 16, at 158.

method are considerable where foreign law has to be applied as the law of the case, and not less so than in the other instances where courts use comparative law to develop the law of their jurisdiction.

VI. Some indirect entry points for judgments from other jurisdictions

We can complement the analysis with the several new indirect entry points for judgments of other jurisdictions. Some of these are new or have increased in importance in recent years. The emergence of international human rights standards, the European Convention of Human Rights and the European Union are important such entry points. Already in *Bulmer v Bullinger*,[87] Lord Denning cites judgments of German and Dutch courts on the application of Article 234 EC on references from national courts to the European Court of Justice.[88] This, as we discuss elsewhere in this chapter, is not something the European Court of Justice would have done, not recognizing the practice of national courts as a source of European Union law.

In our own work on tort liability of public authorities we have analyzed how the application of the law of the European Convention of Human Rights and the European Union provide indirect entry points for judgments from other jurisdictions.[89] We have noted the influence of European Community law, which has both focused attention upon the illegality-fault relationship in English law,[90] and provided an example of alternative ingredients for determining state liability, most notably with the 'sufficient seriousness' test.[91] It is interesting to note that not only have the courts adopted the Community law test for state liability with equanimity, avoiding the protectionist language that has often marked the domestic law, but the application of Community law has also led certain judges to go through remarkable metamorphoses. This is illustrated by Lord Hoffmann's views on state liability. In the well-known case of *Stovin v Wise*,[92] Lord Hoffmann was in a restrictive frame of mind regarding the conditions of public authority liability. This case concerned an allegedly negligent failure of a local authority

---

[87] [1974] ch 401.

[88] See also Lord Goff of Chieveley 'The Future of the Common Law (1997) 46 ICLQ 745, 757 on the use of a French judgment to determine whether a question was *acte claire* under the Art 234 EC procedure.

[89] M Andenas and D Fairgrieve, 'Misfeasance in Public Office, Governmental Liability and European Influences' (2002) 51 ICLQ 757.

[90] See D Fairgrieve, *State Liability in Tort* (OUP Oxford 2003) ch 3, s 3.3.1.

[91] P Craig, 'The Domestic Liability of Public Authorities in Damages: Lessons from the European Community?' in J Beatson and T Tridimas, *New Directions in European Public Law* (Oxford, 1998). See ch 4, s 2.2.3. See generally W V Gerven, J Lever and P Larouche *Tort Law* (Oxford 2000) ch 9.

[92] [1996] AC 923.

to exercise a statutory power to direct a private landowner to remove an obstruction from his land in order to improve visibility at a dangerous road junction. In rejecting the claim, Lord Hoffmann held that 'the trend of authorities has been to discourage the assumption that anyone who suffers loss is prima facie entitled to compensation from a person (preferably insured or a public authority) whose act or omission can be said to have caused it. The default position is that he is not.'[93] He later described *Stovin* as one of an established line of cases denying financial compensation for claimants who had failed to receive a benefit from public services.[94]

In a different case, looking again at the topic of state liability but this time through the lenses of Community law, Lord Hoffmann was in more liberal mode. When the *Factortame* litigation returned to the House of Lords on the issue of liability for damages, he upheld the lower court's decision that the enactment of the Merchant Shipping Act 1988 constituted a sufficiently serious breach of Community law.[95] In a crucial part of his judgment, Lord Hoffmann declared that 'I do not think that the United Kingdom . . . can say that the losses caused by the legislation should lie where they fell. Justice requires that the wrong should be made good.'[96]

In the United Kingdom,[97] another avenue for the introduction of comparative law influences, and perhaps even the changing of mindsets, is the Human Rights Act 1998. The jurisprudence of the European Human Rights Court has clearly been influenced by civil law systems. This can be seen in various fields, including the articulation of the rules concerning just satisfaction. In terms of loss the European Human Rights Court has, in contrast with English law, made monetary awards for a wide variety of non-pecuniary loss, as well as taking a broad approach to the recovery of pure economic loss, and lost chances.[98] In its apparently open attitude to the heads of loss for which compensation can be awarded, the European Human Rights Court is probably closer to the French law tradition[99] than the common law. In formulating the rules governing damages under the HRA, the English courts must take account of this more liberal attitude.[100] In turn, this might well prompt a more general re-evaluation of the present stance of the courts in respect of pure economic loss and moral damage in light of practice under the HRA, through the first-hand application of concepts shaped by

[93] Ibid, 949.

[94] 'Human Rights and the House of Lords' (1999) 62 MLR 159, 163.

[95] *R v Secretary of State for Transport ex p Factortame Ltd (No 5)* [2000] 1 AC 524.

[96] At 548.

[97] An interesting study of the French experience is in O Dutheillet da Lamothe, 'European Law and the French Constitutional Council' in G Canivet, M Andenas and D Fairgrieve (eds), *Comparative Law before the Courts* (BIICL London 2004) 91.

[98] See e.g., *Allenet de Ribemont v France* (1995) 20 EHRR 557 (compensation inter alia for loss of business opportunities); *Pine Valley Developments Ltd v Ireland* (1993) 16 EHRR 379 (loss of value in land).

[99] J Bell, S Boyron and S Whittaker *Principles of French Law* (Oxford 2008) 393.

[100] S 8(4) HRA.

foreign law influences. In a broader sense, it has been argued that the HRA is challenging orthodox common law philosophy of state liability, with the introduction of a rights-based approach, rather than the traditional focus on defining tortious wrongs by reference to duties,[101] and not rights.[102]

VII. European and international courts

Comparative law has also been given formal recognition in the case law of the European Court of Justice and the European Court of Human Rights. The approach is generally that 'autonomous' concepts are developed but they are building on national law.

Article 288 EC Treaty on tort liability of European Community institutions supports this approach. It states that 'in the case of non-contractual liability, the Community shall, in accordance with the general principles common to the laws of the Member States, make good any damage caused by its institutions or by its servants in the performance of their duties'. In many instances the Court of Justice will refer to the 'legal traditions', the 'constitutional traditions',[103] the 'legal orders', the 'legal notions' or the 'legal principles' common to 'all' Member States or, at least, to 'several' Member States. The Court may be supported by comparative surveys and analysis in the opinions for the Advocate General and in submissions by the Commission or other parties.[104] When the rule of EU law is established, the link back to the national jurisdictions is broken. The Court of Justice from then on relies on EU legal sources only. In general, there is very rarely any material about the national courts' application of Community law. The interest is limited to their practice on national law. The Court rarely cites doctrine, and internal court guidelines attempts to restrict this also in the opinions of advocates-general.[105]

There are developments also in the European Court of Justice. In 2006, Advocate General Maduro in his Opinion in *Fenin*[106] makes use of the practice of several national courts on matters of EU competition law.

---

[101] See e.g., N McBride and R. Bagshaw *Tort Law* (London 2001) ch 1.

[102] See T Hickman 'Tort Law, Public Authorities and the Human Rights Act 1998' in D Fairgrieve, M Andenas and J Bell, *Tort Liability of Public Authorities in Comparative Perspective* (BIICL London 2002).

[103] Which is used in the EU Charter of Human Rights and in the texts of the Treaty on the EU Constitution and the Lisbon Treaty.

[104] K Lenaerts 'Interlocking Legal Orders in the European Union and Comparative Law' in G Canivet, M Andenas and D Fairgrieve (eds), *Comparative Law before the Courts* (BIICL London 2004). See also W V Gerven, 'The Emergence of A Common European Law in the Area of Tort Law: The EU Contribution' in D Fairgrieve, M Andenas and J Bell, *Tort Liability of Public Authorities* (British Institute of International and Comparative Law London 2002) 125. The Court will also regularly be supported by surveys undertaken by its own research and documentation service.

[105] This is justified by resource reasons: it affects the length of the texts that are to be translated into ever more languages.

[106] Case C-205/03 P *Fenin* [2006] ECR I-06295.

The relationship between the European Court of Justice and the European Court of Human Rights is another issue. The Court of Justice initially followed its general line and did not cite decisions by the European Court of Human Rights. Several Advocates General referred to decisions by the European Court of Human Rights before the Court of Justice itself in *Familiapress*[107] expressly followed the conclusions of the Court of Human Rights in *Lentia*[108] and in *Criminal Proceeding v X*[109] where the Court of Justice mentioned the interpretation of the Court of Human Rights in *Kokkinakis v Greece*.[110]

The European Court of Human Rights goes further, and it cites national case law on the European Human Rights Convention.[111] It cites decisions from international courts and tribunals (including the European Court of Justice[112]), and of other international bodies and committees. The United Nations Human Rights Committee has a special position in the UN human rights system, and the European Human Rights Courts has in a number of cases cited and taken due account of the Human Rights Committee's decisions.[113] There are interesting examples of dialogues with national courts in the Human Rights Court's

---

[107] Case C/368/95 *Familiapress* [1997] ECR I-3689, para 26.

[108] *Lentia* ECHR (1994) 17 EHRR 93.

[109] Case C-129/95 *Criminal Proceedings v X* [1996] ECR I-6609.

[110] *Kokkinakis v Greece* (1994) 17 EHRR 297.

[111] The ECtHR also makes use of comparative law in determining the national margin of appreciation, and in some recent judgments undertakes broader surveys under the heading 'Comparative Law', see eg *TV Vest AS & Rogaland Pensjonistpart v Norway* (Application no. 21132/05) Judgment 11 December 2008, where it recognizes that the absence of a European consensus is relevant when considering the national margin of appreciation. This case also provides an interesting instance of a national judge arguing in a way which finds favour with the ECtHR, and his proportionality discussion lending support to the finding of a violation by the ECtHR. Many of the important judgments of the ECtHR have been decided with the assistance of surveys of national law, eg. *Lingens* (1986) 8 EHRR 407, but previously the references to such surveys were not made as expressly or at least not so extensively as they are today.

[112] In *Bosphorus Hava Yollari Turizm Ve Ticaret Anonim Sirketi v Ireland* (2006) 42 EHRR 1, the ECtHR discusses the case law of the ECJ in detail. It held that, in principle, the protection offered within the EC legal system meets a requirement of equivalency and gives rise to a 'presumption of conventionality.' In combination, the guarantees offered on the domestic level and by the ECJ, would in most cases obviate any need for Strasbourg to intervene in the process of applying EU law.

[113] See for instance, *Kurt v Turkey* (1999) 27 EHRR 373, *Frette v France* (2002) 38 EHRR 438, *Py v France* [2005] ECHR 7, *Issa v Turkey* (2005) 41 EHRR, *Mamatkulov and Askarov v Turkey* (2005) 41 EHRR 494, *Öcalan v Turkey* (2005) 41 EHRR 985, *Riener v Bulgaria* [2006] ECHR 553, *Folgerø v Norway* (2008) 46 EHRR 47 and *Saadi v UK* (Application no. 13229/03) judgment 29 January 2008. J Sætrum has in a dissertation (not yet published, Oslo, 2009) found some 30 references to the UNHRCtte in the case law of the ECtHR. This is in fact a limited number of cases if one takes into account the many decisions of the UNHRCtee that have a direct bearing on the issues discussed by the ECtHR.

The UN Human Rights Committee cites the ECtHR much more often. This may have something to do with the recognition that the ECtHR has a long established court. The relative reticence of the ECtHR in citing the UNHRCtee may in some part be due to the committee's lack of status as a 'court'.

recent practice.[114] Above, we have discussed *Cooper*,[115] where a unanimous Grand Chamber European Human Rights Court overturned a previous ruling in *Morris*, making extensive use of Lord Bingham's analysis in a House of Lords decision, and agreeing with his conclusions.[116]

Public International Law recognizes state practice as a primary source of law. This entails close study of court decisions as an expression of state practice. However, the International Court of Justice (ICJ) does not cite national court decisions or their application of public international law.[117] Neither has the ICJ traditionally cited decisions by other international tribunals. However, in *Bosnia and Herzegovina v Serbia and Montenegro* (2007), the ICJ refers to both the Trial Chamber of the International Criminal Tribunal for the former Yugoslavia (ICTY) and the International Criminal Tribunal for Rwanda (ICTR).[118] Here the ICJ cites and relies on the ICTY on the intent required for the crime of genocide.[119] It also cites the ICTY and the ICTR on the requirement of 'substantiality' in establishing intent.[120]

VIII. A short typology

Courts function within a system of sources of legal authority. The domestic law paradigm remains strong, and the methodological problems in the use of comparative law add to the challenge. The role of comparative law remains open and controversial. It may be interesting to analyze some of the cases with a view to

---

[114] See the studies of N Krisch, 'The Open Architecture of European Human Rights Law' (2008) 71 Modern Law Review 183, and L Garlicki, 'Cooperation of courts: The role of supranational jurisdictions in Europe', (2008) 6 International Journal of Constitutional Law 509.

[115] *Cooper v the United Kingdom*, (2004) 39 EHRR 8.

[116] *Eriksen v Norway* (1997) 29 EHRR 328 is one of several other examples where the ECtHR makes use of a national supreme court's ruling on the compliance of national law with the ECHR. Here the ECtHR cites the discussion in the Norwegian Supreme Court's ruling in Rt.1996.93, in support for rejection of the application against Norway. The form of the national judgment and the style of the argument, and also how it makes use of the ECtHR case law, and how directly it addresses the questions that are relevant for the ECtHR, are (not unsurprisingly) important for the impact it has on the ECtHR.

[117] National court decisions are often referred to in submissions to or in argument before the court, and may be cited in the ICJ's references to parties' submissions. They are not referred to in the ICJ's own discussion of the law in the judgments. However, judges of the ICJ often refer to the importance that national court judgments have in the deliberations of the court. In the judgments, there are no references to academic literature (but often in the individual dissenting or concurring opinions).

[118] *Application of the Convention on the Prevention and Punishment of the Crime of Genocide (Bosnia and Herzegovina v Serbia and Montenegro)* Judgment of 26 February 2007, para. 88 and 198. The ICJ also refers to the European Court of Human Rights in the context of accounting for the parties' submissions but does not rely on or make any further use of these references.

[119] *Kupreškić et al.* (IT-95-16-T, Judgment, 14 January 2000, para 636).

[120] *Krstić*, IT-98-33-A, Appeals Chamber Judgment, 19 April 2004, paras 8–11 and the cases of *Kayishema*, *Byilishema*, and *Semanza* there referred to.

formulating a typology of the use of comparative law by courts. There are some clear situations that stand out in the recent case law, and many of them can be linked to important judgments by Lord Bingham.

The tentative typology is grouped into seven categories. Comparative law can provide or be used to: (1) support for a rule or an outcome, (2) normative models in comparative law where national law is undetermined, (3) review factual assumptions about the consequences of legal rules, (4) review assumptions about the universal applicability of a particular rule, (5) overturn authority in domestic law, (6) develop principles of domestic law, (7) resolve problems of the application of European and international law, including European Human Rights law.

(1) Support for a rule or an outcome

The existence of a solution in other jurisdictions may under certain circumstances provide persuasive arguments for that solution in one's own jurisdiction if one agrees with Lord Bingham's views on the 'virtue in uniformity of outcome' in *Fairchild*,[121] and that '(p)rocedural idiosyncracy is not (like national costume or regional cuisine) to be nurtured for its own sake' in *Dresser*.[122] See also his statement that 'it should be no easier to succeed here than in France or Germany', in *JD v East Berkshire*.[123] But where domestic sources support another rule or outcome, this kind of argument does not seem to have much weight. In practice, comparative law arguments will not often be used where domestic law is clear. There are certain particular situations such as those discussed below where comparative law carries more weight.

The discussion in the United States Supreme Court has brought out into the open a disagreement about the validity of a general assumption about the virtue of uniformity of outcome. The majority in the line of cases we have discussed above, have based their argument on there being some current connexion between US law and international and foreign law. We have above also discussed Justice Scalia's arguments about 'foreign moods, fads or fashions'. The 'US exceptionalism' has counterparts in all countries where some judges and academics will more or less openly base resistance to comparative law on assumptions about the superiority of their own system. Justice Scalia has counterparts arguing for English, French, German, Norwegian, Icelandic or Lichtenstein superiority or exceptionalism. Empirically, claims to national superiority are difficult to assess, as are other claims to autonomy or 'separateness' of legal systems.

---

[121] *Fairchild v Glenhaven Funeral Services Ltd,* [2002] UKHL 22.
[122] *Dresser UK Ltd v Falcongate Ltd* [1992] QB 502, 522.
[123] *JD (FC) (Appellant) v East Berkshire Community Health NHS Trust and others (Respondents) and two other actions (FC),* [2005] UKHL 23.

(2) Normative models in comparative law where national law is undetermined

The least complicated situation could be the one where national law does not determine any particular outcome. The judge may be looking for ways of resolving a problem, and finding no solution based on the traditional sources of law, she seeks solutions in rules or normative arguments from other jurisdictions. Here the use of comparative law takes place in a process of developing or interpreting the law without any conflict with domestic law sources. The judge is operating in a field of open discretion or 'policy'.[124] A variation is found where national law leaves more than one solution, and foreign law may assist in choosing between them.

Assistance in finding normative solutions to situations where one's own system has none, may be found to be useful and is not often controversial. There should not be any strong, or any at all, limitations in the national legal system where it does not prescribe any solution.

(3) Comparative law to review factual assumptions about the consequences of legal rules

In the development of the law in different fields, one encounters the 'floodgates' argument. A new rule is considered, for instance giving access to information held by the administration, requiring that some authority has to give reasons for their decisions, giving procedural rights or standing to groups, or giving rights to compensation for breach of rights. The financial, administrative or behavioural consequences are considered. Some courts will reject the new rule with an assertion that the rule will open the floodgates for claims, with disproportionate consequences of different kinds. The assertions are often made in a seemingly authoritative way. However, judgments in such cases often contain speculations about risks without much foundation.[125] There is practically always a state financial or other interest on the one side, and a particularly weak individual (dyslexic pupil, victim of sexual abuse as a minor) or public interest (environment, human rights) on the other. The acceptance of risks and the different related assertions

---

[124] See the parallel here in *Application of the Convention on the Prevention and Punishment of the Crime of Genocide (Bosnia and Herzegovina v Serbia and Montenegro)* Judgment of 26 February 2007, where the ECJ cites the ICTY and the ICTR on the requirement of 'substantiality' in establishing intent, and also to the European Court of Human Rights in the context of accounting for the parties' submissions (but does not rely on or make any further use of the ECtHR references).

[125] Jane Stapleton, 'Benefits of Comparative Tort Reasoning: Lost in Translation', see above, argues that there can be reasons for basing conclusions on risk assessments, and for not requiring too much for establishing them. She also points out that the possibility for misunderstandings when courts and scholars are dealing with judgments from other common law jurisdictions is considerable. When the other jurisdiction belongs to the civil law and judgments are in another language, her view on comparative law is that it is a rather hopeless enterprise, and in particular for courts.

are more based on values, and giving more weight to the interests of the state in balancing with other interests, than openly admitted to.

Sir Basil Markesinis has compared the argument of Lord Bingham and Lord Hoffmann, as two of the most active comparativists in the House of Lords, in a number of cases.[126] Lord Hoffmann has in a number of cases asserted that granting rights or remedies to disadvantaged groups will lead to the opening up of the floodgates and also have unwanted consequences of other kinds.

Lord Bingham has long rejected this kind of broad assertion. In *JD v East Berkshire*,[127] he sought recourse to comparative law in dealing with similar assertions. If a rule has been applied in another jurisdiction, and has not opened the floodgates there, the court cannot base its conclusions on assertions to the contrary.

(4) Review assumptions about the universal applicability of a particular rule

In *Lawrence*,[128] the use of foreign law in part refuted the claims to universality in *Bowers*[129] (which the *Lawrence* majority used in support of overturning *Bowers*). In *Bowers*, Chief Justice Burger made 'sweeping references' to the history of Western civilization and to Judeo-Christian moral and ethical standards. He did not take account of sources pointing in another direction. Legal developments in other countries could then be used to undermine the claims in *Bowers* and to overturn it.

Claims to universality may be challenged by variations in a temporal dimension (for instance in interpreting an old constitutional text), or in a jurisdictional dimension (the case law of another country or international tribunal contradicts the claim). Comparative law may have a role to play in different ways in this context, and may provide powerful arguments against the universality claims made in an authority.

Another feature of *Lawrence* is the way in which Justice Kennedy makes use of the judgment of the European Court of Human Rights in *Dudgeon v United Kingdom*.[130] Justice Kennedy points out how the European Court of Human Rights followed not *Bowers* but its own previous decision in *Dudgeon* in a number of cases after *Bowers*, and that this applies to other countries. This has

---

[126] See in particular B Markesinis and J Fedtke, 'Authority or reason? The Economic Consequences of Liability for Breach of Statutory Duty in a Comparative Perspective', (2007) EBLR 5 at 66–7, and also M Andenas (2007) EBLR 1 at 2.

[127] *JD (FC) (Appellant) v East Berkshire Community Health NHS Trust and others (Respondents) and two other actions (FC)*, [2005] UKHL 23. Lord Bingham deals with the matter in para 49. This passage is interesting also in the extensive way that academic scholarship is used and relied upon.

[128] 539 US 558 (2003).

[129] 478 US 186 (1986).

[130] (1983) 5 EHRR.

consequences for the value of the fundamental freedom involved, and for the possible governmental interests in its limitation.

(5) Additional support to overturn authority in domestic law

Fairchild[131] and *Roper*[132] may be instances of this category. Both cases are based on there being 'some virtue in uniformity of outcome whatever the diversity of approach in reaching that outcome.'[133] They may express a general principle that 'if consideration of international sources suggests that a different and more acceptable decision would be given in most other jurisdictions, whatever their legal tradition, this must prompt anxious review of the decision in question'.[134]

However, in *Fairchild*, the anxious review was also prompted by the fact that the existing authority offended 'one's basic sense of justice'. In *Roper and Simmons*, Justice Kennedy makes very clear that he had sufficient support in US constitutional law for overturning the previous authority. The dissenting judges disagree between themselves on the use of international and comparative law, but Justice Scalia is highly critical of this way of claiming support for a result which the majority says is also fully supported in domestic law. We have discussed the use of this argument above.

The other view in the House of Lords, as expressed in the subsequent decision of *Barker*,[135] is interesting in that the panel's invention of a new concept of 'proportionate liability' to limit the effect of *Fairchild*, did not make use of comparative law. It was clearly policy based, in spite of the references to authority and legal principle. It protected a strong economic interest, industrial employers, over traditionally weaker applicants, dead or sick workers and their families. *Barker* was overturned by legislation. *Barker* was an 'activist' decision in the sense that it had an outcome based on the kind of reasoning and solution that judicatures typically will concede to legislatures. *Barker* satisfied many of the criteria that English courts have developed for limiting judicial decision-making, in that it concerned allocative and financial matters, social priorities and a balancing with typical political factors. In the event, it was not unsurprising that it was regarded as an exercise of political discretion that the legislature overturned. Sir Basil Markesinis' criticism that comparative law arguments here deserved consideration, particularly in light of the role that comparative law arguments had played in *Fairchild*, which *Barker* limited, seems well supported.

---

[131] *Fairchild v Glenhaven Funeral Services Ltd*, [2002] UKHL 22.
[132] *Roper and Simmons* 543 US 551 (2005).
[133] *Fairchild*, at para 31.
[134] Ibid.
[135] *Barker v Corus (UK) plc* [2006] UKHL 20.

As mentioned, in *Lawrence*,[136] the use of foreign law in part refuted the claims to universality in *Bowers*[137] which the majority overturned. Comparative law may provide powerful arguments against universality claims of an authority, and support for the overturning of the authority.

The *Lawrence* and *Roper* line of cases has seen the use of comparative law providing support for overturning precedents to strengthen the protection of individual rights. *Fairchild* appears as a technical causation case but has a more complicated background against case law favouring employers over employees by limiting liability in different ways, and creating a clear tension with fairness and effective remedies. It is not surprising that the disagreement about the role of precedent and comparative law, and the discussion about an American exceptionalism, have to some extent been coloured by the views on the outcome of the cases.

(6) Develop principles of domestic law

Comparative law can support the development of principles of domestic law. The minority opinion in *JD v East Berkshire*,[138] as discussed above, falls into this category. In this case, Lord Bingham argues for evolution of tort law, 'analogically and incrementally, so as to fashion appropriate remedies to contemporary problems'. The European Human Rights Convention, as incorporated by the Human Rights Act 1999, provides the assistance in doing so here. The alternative outcome is to leave tort law 'essentially static, making only such changes as are forced upon it, leaving difficult and, in human terms, very important problems to be swept up by the Convention.'[139]

We discuss *de Freitas v Permanent Secretary of Ministry of Agriculture, Fisheries, Lands and Housing*[140] under the next heading. This judgment also fits in under the present heading in that the Privy Council here used South African, Canadian, United States, Zimbabwean and German authority to develop the constitutional principles of freedom of expression and proportionality, in the constitutional law of Antigua and Barbuda.

(7) Resolve problems of applying European and international law, including European Human Rights law

In *de Freitas*, the Privy Council, drawing on South African, Canadian and Zimbabwean authority, defined the questions generally to be asked in deciding

---

[136] 539 US 558 (2003).

[137] 478 US 186 (1986).

[138] *JD (FC) (Appellant) v East Berkshire Community Health NHS Trust and others (Respondents) and two other actions (FC)*, [2005] UKHL 23. See the quotation of para 49 from this judgments above.

[139] Unfortunately, the majority, not following Lord Bingham, did fall into an error which it will take a decade to work English law out of.

[140] *de Freitas v Permanent Secretary of Ministry of Agriculture, Fisheries, Lands and Housing* [1999] 1 AC 69.

whether a measure is proportionate.[141] This formulation was built on by the parties in *Huang v Secretary of State for the Home Department*,[142] and the applicants argued in favour of an overriding requirement which featured in a judgment of the Supreme Court of Canada. Dickson CJ in *R v Oakes* had included the need to balance the interests of society with those of individuals and groups.[143] In *Huang*, the House of Lords accepts the argument,[144] and refers to having recognized as much in its previous decision of *R (Razgar) v Secretary of State for the Home Department* (in Lord Bingham's speech).[145]

This is one of a long line of decisions where the House of Lords have made use of Commonwealth authorities in the application of European Human Rights law. In particular Canada offers a relevant experience of applying constitutional protection of individual rights in a common law tradition. This may surprise in other European jurisdictions but both counsel and judges have felt comfortable with these judgments. Decisions from other European national courts have been less easily applied.

We also have another opportunity to refer to *Bulmer v Bullinger*,[146] where Lord Denning cites judgments of German and Dutch courts on the application of Article 234 EC on references from national courts to the European Court of Justice.[147]

Yet another example is provided by *Techna SA*.[148] As discussed above, the French *Conseil d'Etat* made reference to a decision by the English High Court concerning labelling requirements under EU law, explicitly citing an English case in support of suspending a directive.[149]

---

[141] *de Freitas v Permanent Secretary of Ministry of Agriculture, Fisheries, Lands and Housing* [1999] 1 AC 69, at 80. They asked whether: (i) the legislative objective is sufficiently important to justify limiting a fundamental right; (ii) the measures designed to meet the legislative objective are rationally connected to it; and (iii) the means used to impair the right or freedom are no more than is necessary to accomplish the objective.

[142] *Huang (FC) (Respondent) v Secretary of State for the Home Department (Appellant) and Kashmiri (FC) (Appellant) v Secretary of State for the Home Department (Respondent) (Conjoined Appeals)* [2007] UKHL 11.

[143] *R v Oakes* [1986] 1 SCR 103, at p 139.

[144] In para 19, where it also refers to *de Freitas*. The judgment had the form of an 'Opinion of the Committee', and was not reported as individual 'speeches', as is the tradition. This form, and the general form and content of the opinion clearly owes much to Lord Bingham.

[145] *R (Razgar) v Secretary of State for the Home Department* [2004] UKHL 27, [2004] 2 AC 368, paras 17–20, 26, 27, 60, 77.

[146] [1974] ch 401.

[147] See also Lord Goff of Chieveley, 'The Future of the Common Law' (1997) 46 ICLQ 745, 757 on the use of a French judgment to determine whether a question was *acte claire* under the Arte 234 EC procedure.

[148] N° 260768 *Techna SA* 29 Oct 2003.

[149] R Errera, 'The Use of Comparative Law Before the French Administrative Law Courts' in G Canivet, M Andenas and D Fairgrieve (eds), *Comparative Law before the Courts* (BIICL London 2004) 153.

a. Some conclusions

We have looked at some situations where courts make use of comparative law. They illustrate how comparative law is used in a context where domestic law paradigms remain strong. The cases and the typology illustrate some of the many methodological problems in the use of comparative law in the courts. There are cases which reflect a general recognition of comparative law as a persuasive authority or source of law. There are more and perhaps clearer cases of applying normative models from comparative law where national law is undetermined. There are clear cases where comparative law has been given weight reviewing factual assumptions about the consequences of legal rules, or assumptions about universal applicability of rules or principles. Arguments based in this kind of analysis have been used to overturn authority in domestic law in a number of cases. Comparative law has also had a further role in developing principles of domestic law. It has a particular role in applying European and international law, including European Human Rights law.

We find support for the proposition that the use and acknowledgement of comparative law sources is on the increase. The use in some of the cases has been criticized as opportunistic. This argument can be turned against the use of comparative law in general, or in favour of the development of a method for the use of comparative law. We have above discussed the positions of Justice Scalia[150] and Sir Basil Markesinis who have used the consistency arguments in these different ways.[151] We pointed out the more general feature that judges make use of the same authorities or sources of law, and legal and factual arguments, and then reach different conclusions. In many cases this will be done without making clear why, for instance the appellate court disagrees with the first instance court, or one judge with another in the same court. Judgments may also include or exclude sources or arguments, and this discretion may be perceived to be particularly wide when one is dealing with merely persuasive and non-binding authorities or arguments. This may lead to inconsistencies which are unsatisfactory in many instances. At a stage where comparative law provide mostly persuasive and non-binding authorities or arguments, this has often meant that the courts or judges who do not find support for their preferred outcome in comparative law, will disregard comparative law arguments in the reasons they give. We find it difficult to disagree with Sir Basil's call for more consistency here. In particular, the call for consistency is powerful in cases where one judge mentions foreign law. We agree with Sir Basil that reasonable consistency requires that other judges who come to a different result from that the first judge supported on comparative law, addresses and counter in a specific manner also the first judge's arguments based on comparative law.

---

[150] For instance, in *Roper v Simmons* 543 US 551 (2005).

[151] B Markesinis, ' Judicial Mentality: Mental Disposition or Outlook as a Factor Impeding Recourse to Foreign Law', 80 TUL LREV 1325 (2006) at 1361–62 and at 1371.

IX. Consequences for scholarship

Comparative law is no longer an impractical academic discipline. We have discussed how comparative law is more actively used, and its use more openly acknowledged, by courts, and this is also the case in teaching, scholarship and in statute law reform. This new awakening puts the academic discipline under some pressure. One response is in the growing scholarship on the purposes and methods of comparative law.

A generation ago, there were some disagreements about the purpose and method in academic comparative law. Looking back, the prevailing impression is nonetheless of an established academic discipline with a high degree of cohesion. There were parallel discourses across jurisdictions, often dominated by private lawyers, but with important contributions made by public and criminal lawyers.[152]

Comparative law has lost whatever common language it had as an academic discipline. This is one consequence of the expansion of the discipline: it does not have the coherence of the academic discipline of a generation ago. It is a current and rather pressing challenge to engage comparative law scholars in a discourse on what can be agreed upon as the core issues. The growing scholarship on the purposes and methods of comparative law is a good beginning,[153] although the present phase demonstrates the wide range of views, some rather fundamentally opposed to one another,[154] many of which are represented in this *Liber Amicorum*.

---

[152] Sir Thomas Bingham ' "There is A World Elsewhere": The Changing Perspectives of English Law' (1992) 41 ICLQ 513, 527, reprinted in T Bingham *The Business of Judging* (OUP Oxford 2000) 87, sets out how the academic comparative law discipline and the courts have interacted in the English tradition, in particular after the Second World War.

[153] Two magisterial volumes from 2006 provide extensive overviews of the rapidly expanding scholarship, see M Reimann and R Zimmermann (eds), *The Oxford Handbook of Comparative Law* (OUP Oxford 2006) and J M Smits (ed), *Elgar Encyclopedia of Comparative Law* (Edward Elgar Cheltenham 2006). See also W Twining, W Farnsworth, S Vogenauer and F Téson, 'The Role of Academics in the Legal System', in P Cane and M Tushnet (eds), *The Oxford Handbook of Legal Studies* (OUP Oxford 2003) 920.

[154] See the following authors representing some of the divergence in the current comparative private law scholarship: P Legrand, 'European Systems are not Converging' (1996) 45 ICLQ 52; M Bussani and U Mattei, 'The Common Core Approach to European Private Law' (1997/98) 3 Columbia Journal of Comparative Law 339; W V Gerven, J Lever and P Larouche, *Tort Law* (Oxford, 2000); B Markesinis, *Foreign Law and Comparative Methodology: a subject and a thesis* (Hart Oxford 1997); B Markesinis, *Always on the Same Path: Essays on Foreign Law and Comparative Methodology* (Hart Oxford 2001); B Markesinis, *Comparative Law in the Courtroom and Classroom* (Hart Oxford 2003); B Markesinis and J Fedtke, 'Authority or reason? The Economic Consequences of Liability for Breach of Statutory Duty in a Comparative Perspective', (2007) EBLR 5, B Markesinis, Judicial Mentality: Mental Disposition or Outlook as a Factor Impeding Recourse to Foreign Law, (2006) 80 TUL. L.REV. 1325, 1361–62; A Peters and H Schwenke, 'Comparative Law beyond Post-Modernism' (2000) 49 ICLQ 800; H Muir Watt, 'La Fonction Subversive du Droit Comparé' RIDC 2000.503; 3; A Rodger, Savigny in the Strand, 28–30 The Irish Jurist 1 (1995); R Sacco, 'Legal Formants, A Dynamic Approach to Comparative Law (I)' (1991) 39 American Journal of Comparative Law 1; (II) (1991) 39 American Journal of Comparative Law 343; A Watson, *Legal*

There is much left before the academic discipline can emerge from this phase with the degree of agreement on what are the fundamental issues as required for a critical academic discourse to be meaningful. The active comparative law discourse needs to rediscover the core of a common language.[155] It requires this common language for scholarship and comparative law to have full impact on legal scholarship, lawmaking and legal practice. It needs a mainstream academic discipline to emerge.

The relationship between the traditional disciplines of law is more than ever in need of exploration. International law, European law and national legal orders are now perhaps best understood as open systems coexisting without any clear hierarchy. Beyond that, their relationship remains unresolved at the most fundamental levels. The relationship between disciplines within the different legal orders or systems is of increasing importance, and distinctions, such as those between private and public law, become difficult to maintain. There is a clear need to see this in context, and to provide an institutional framework and support for academic research and legal practice dealing with the many issues that arise.

There is another problem common to all countries. The well-established legal approaches, limited by narrow definition of disciplines and by national traditions, do not meet the present needs. In comparative law the encyclopaedic collection and organization of materials is still useful but not sufficient. The traditional teaching and scholarship in public international law, and indeed in the still relatively young disciplines of European law, are equally inadequate. The focus on one's own national approaches (for instance to public international law, human rights law and to EU law), which while practically important, needs to give way to a broader perspective. Fundamental assumptions about the nation state based on nineteenth-century thinking still rule most of us. The way that international, European and domestic legal systems open up and recognize one another, requires critical analysis of the foundations and will continue to provide a fertile ground for research and policy discussion.

The Society of Comparative Legislation, when it was founded in 1894 (marking the beginning of the British Institute of International and Comparative Law over which Lord Bingham presides), was part of a European movement of

---

Transplants; an Approach to Comparative Law (London 1993); R Zimmerman, 'Savigny's Legacy: Legal History, Comparative Law, and the Emergence of a European Legal Science' (1996) 112 LQR 576; K Zweigert and H Kotz, *An Introduction to Comparative Law* (3rd edn Oxford 1998); G Alpa and V Zeno-Zencovich, *Italian Private Law* (Taylor and Francis (Routledge-Cavendish) London 2007); G Alpa, MJ Bonell, D Corapi, L Moccia, V Zeno-Zencovich, A Zoppini, *Diritto privato comparato. Istituti e problemi,* (Laterza, 2004); G Alpa and M Andenas, *Fondamenti del diritto privato europeo* (Guiffré Milano 2005); M Andenas, S Diaz Alabart, and B Markesinis, *Liber Amicorum Guido Alpa: Private Law Beyond the National Systems* (BIICL London 2007); *Tort Liability of Public Authorities in Comparative Perspective* (BIICL London 2002); D Fairgrieve, H Muir Watt, *Common law et tradition civiliste* (Presses Universitaires de France Paris 2006).

155 B Markesinis and J Fedtke *Engaging in Foreign Law* (Hart Publishing, Oxford 2009) makes an important contribution in this respect.

comparative law. The aims and reception of comparative law has changed much through the years. John Austin wrote in 1834 about 'general or comparative jurisprudence' as the process of ascertaining the 'principles common to maturer systems,' in order to establish a system of universal principles of positive law.[156] Sir Frederick Pollock, in 1905, attacked the 'high priests of a moribund utilitarian orthodoxy' for their rejection of comparative law. For 'comparative research within the last twenty or thirty years... have revolutionised our legal history and largely transformed our current text-books'. He continued that 'the work of the present generation in the field of comparative jurisprudence is mostly work of detail... But there is no rest for knowledge,... and there will again be a time of large adventure'.[157]

Comparative law has again reached such a time of large adventure. Comparative research is on the threshold of once again revolutionizing legal history and transforming textbooks. Pollock's enthusiasm of some hundred years ago is parallel to that of Justice Breyer's 2003 address cited at the outset of this chapter. He says that nothing could be 'more exciting for an academic, practitioner or judge than the global legal enterprise that is now upon us'.[158] In his 1992 article,[159] Lord Bingham says 'we should not expect too much too quickly' but warns that judges may seek more foreign adventures. There is still room for adventure.

---

[156] *Austin on Jurisprudence* (London 1869) ii, 1107.

[157] F Pollock 'The History of Comparative Jurisprudence' [1903] Journal of the Society of Comparative Legislation 74.

[158] S Breyer 'Keynote Address' (2003) 97 *ASIL Proceedings* 265.

[159] Sir Thomas Bingham '"There is A World Elsewhere": The Changing Perspectives of English Law' (1992) 41 ICLQ 513, reprinted in T Bingham *The Business of Judging* (OUP Oxford 2000) 87.

Index